COMPUTER

Applications with Microsoft® Office 2013

Denise Seguin
Fanshawe College, London, Ontario

St. Paul

Director of Editorial: Christine Hurney
Developmental Editor: Spencer Cotkin
Production Editor: Lori Michelle Ryan
Cover and Text Designer: Leslie Anderson
Senior Design and Production Specialist: Jack Ross
Copy Editor: Susan Capecchi
Indexer: Schroeder Indexing Services

ISBN 978-0-76385-186-6 (Text + Disc)
ISBN 978-0-76385-182-8 (Text)

875 Montreal Way
St. Paul, MN 55102
Email: educate@emcp.com
Website: www.emcp.com

Printed in the United States of America

22 21 20 19 18 17 16 15 14 13 1 2 3 4 5 6 7 8 9 10

Brief Contents

Preface ix

Chapter 1
Using Windows 8 and Managing Files 3

Chapter 2
Navigating and Searching the Web 43

Chapter 3
Exploring Microsoft Office 2013 Essentials 71

Chapter 4
Organizing and Managing Class Notes Using OneNote 105

Chapter 5
Communicating and Scheduling Using Outlook 127

Chapter 6
Creating, Editing, and Formatting Documents Using Word 157

Chapter 7
Enhancing a Document with Special Features 187

Chapter 8
Creating, Editing, and Formatting Worksheets Using Excel 223

Chapter 9
Working with Functions, Charts, Tables, and Page Layout Options in Excel 257

Chapter 10
Creating, Editing, and Formatting a Presentation Using PowerPoint 289

Chapter 11
Enhancing a Presentation with Pictures, Sound, Video, and Animation Effects 321

Chapter 12
Using and Querying an Access Database 353

Chapter 13
Creating a Table, Form, and Report in Access 389

Chapter 14
Integrating Word, Excel, PowerPoint, and Access Components 419

Chapter 15
Using Windows Live SkyDrive and Other Cloud Computing Technologies 441

Glossary 467

Index 477

Contents

Preface ix

Chapter 1
Using Windows 8 and Managing Files..... 3

- Topic 1.1 Using Touch, Mouse, and Keyboard Input to Navigate Windows 8 4
- Topic 1.2 Starting Windows 8 and Exploring Apps 8
- Topic 1.3 Revealing the Charms Bar, Searching for an App, and Closing Apps 12
- Topic 1.4 Locking the Screen, Signing Out, and Shutting Down Windows 8 14
- Topic 1.5 Customizing the Start Screen...... 16
- Topic 1.6 Personalizing the Start and Lock Screens 18
- Topic 1.7 Using the Desktop 20
- Topic 1.8 Browsing Files with File Explorer 22
- Topic 1.9 Creating Folders and Copying Files and Folders 24
- Topic 1.10 Moving, Renaming, and Deleting Files and Folders, and Ejecting a USB Flash Drive 28
- Topic 1.11 Finding Help in Windows........... 32
- Chapter 1 Review...................................... 34
- Chapter 1 Projects 40

Chapter 2
Navigating and Searching the Web........ 43

- Topic 2.1 Introduction to the Internet and the World Wide Web 44
- Topic 2.2 Navigating the Web Using Internet Explorer 10................... 46
- Topic 2.3 Navigating the Web Using Google Chrome 50
- Topic 2.4 Navigating the Web Using Mozilla Firefox 54
- Topic 2.5 Searching for Information and Printing Web Pages 58
- Topic 2.6 Downloading Content from a Web Page 62
- Chapter 2 Review...................................... 64
- Chapter 2 Projects 68

Chapter 3
Exploring Microsoft Office 2013 Essentials.. 71

- Topic 3.1 Starting and Switching Programs, Starting a New Presentation, and Exploring the Ribbon Interface 72
- Topic 3.2 Using the Backstage View to Manage Documents 76
- Topic 3.3 Customizing and Using the Quick Access Toolbar 80
- Topic 3.4 Selecting Text or Objects, Using the Ribbon and Mini Toolbar, and Selecting Options in Dialog Boxes 82
- Topic 3.5 Using the Office Clipboard......... 86
- Topic 3.6 Finding Help in an Office Program 90
- Topic 3.7 Using SkyDrive for Storage, Scrolling in Documents, and Using Undo 92
- Topic 3.8 Changing Display Options.......... 96
- Chapter 3 Review...................................... 98
- Chapter 3 Projects 102

Chapter 4
Organizing and Managing Class Notes Using OneNote 105

Topic 4.1 Opening a Notebook and Adding Notes, Sections, and Pages 106
Topic 4.2 Inserting Web Content into a Notebook 110
Topic 4.3 Inserting files into a Notebook 112
Topic 4.4 Tagging Notes, Viewing Tags, and Jumping to a Tagged Note 114
Topic 4.5 Searching Notes and Closing a Notebook 116
Topic 4.6 Creating a New Notebook and Sharing a Notebook 118
Chapter 4 Review 120
Chapter 4 Projects 123

Chapter 5
Communicating and Scheduling Using Outlook 127

Topic 5.1 Using Outlook to Send Email ... 128
Topic 5.2 Attaching a File to a Message and Deleting Messages 132
Topic 5.3 Previewing File Attachments and Using File Attachment Tools 134
Topic 5.4 Scheduling Appointments and Events in Calendar 136
Topic 5.5 Scheduling a Recurring Appointment and Editing an Appointment 138
Topic 5.6 Scheduling a Meeting 140
Topic 5.7 Adding and Editing Contacts 142
Topic 5.8 Adding and Editing Tasks 144
Topic 5.9 Searching Outlook Items 146
Chapter 5 Review 148
Chapter 5 Projects 153

Chapter 6
Creating, Editing, and Formatting Documents Using Word 157

Topic 6.1 Creating and Editing a New Document 158
Topic 6.2 Inserting Symbols and Completing a Spelling and Grammar Check 162
Topic 6.3 Finding and Replacing Text 164
Topic 6.4 Moving Text and Inserting Bullets and Numbering 166
Topic 6.5 Formatting Text with Font and Paragraph Alignment Options ... 168
Topic 6.6 Indenting Text and Changing Line and Paragraph Spacing 170
Topic 6.7 Formatting Using Styles 172
Topic 6.8 Creating a New Document from a Template 174
Chapter 6 Review 176
Chapter 6 Projects 181

Chapter 7
Enhancing a Document with Special Features 187

Topic 7.1 Inserting, Editing, and Labeling Images in a Document 188
Topic 7.2 Adding Borders and Shading and Inserting a Text Box 192
Topic 7.3 Inserting a Table 194
Topic 7.4 Formatting and Modifying a Table 196
Topic 7.5 Changing Page Layout Options 200
Topic 7.6 Formatting a Research Paper with a Header and Page Numbers 202
Topic 7.7 Inserting and Editing Citations ... 204
Topic 7.8 Creating a Works Cited Page and Using Word Views 206
Topic 7.9 Inserting and Replying to Comments 208
Topic 7.10 Creating a Resume and Cover Letter from Templates 210
Chapter 7 Review 212
Chapter 7 Projects 217

Chapter 8
Creating, Editing, and Formatting Worksheets Using Excel 223

Topic 8.1 Creating and Editing a New Worksheet 224
Topic 8.2 Formatting Cells 228
Topic 8.3 Adjusting Column Width and Row Height, and Changing Alignment 232
Topic 8.4 Entering or Copying Data with the Fill Command and Using AutoSum 234
Topic 8.5 Inserting and Deleting Rows and Columns 238
Topic 8.6 Sorting and Applying Cell Styles 240
Topic 8.7 Changing Orientation and Scaling and Displaying Cell Formulas 242
Topic 8.8 Inserting and Renaming a Worksheet, Copying Cells, and Indenting Cells 244
Topic 8.9 Using Go To, Freezing Panes, and Shading, Wrapping, and Rotating Cell Entries 246
Chapter 8 Review 248
Chapter 8 Projects 253

Chapter 9
Working with Functions, Charts, Tables, and Page Layout Options in Excel........ 257

Topic 9.1 Using Absolute Addressing and Range Names in Formulas........ 258
Topic 9.2 Entering Formulas Using Statistical Functions 260
Topic 9.3 Entering, Formatting, and Calculating Dates 262
Topic 9.4 Using the IF Function 264
Topic 9.5 Using the PMT Function 266
Topic 9.6 Creating and Modifying a Pie Chart 268
Topic 9.7 Creating and Modifying a Column Chart 270
Topic 9.8 Creating and Modifying a Line Chart 272
Topic 9.9 Using Page Layout View, Adding a Header, and Changing Margins 274
Topic 9.10 Creating and Modifying Sparklines and Inserting Comments 276
Topic 9.11 Working with Tables 278
Chapter 9 Review 280
Chapter 9 Projects 285

Chapter 10
Creating, Editing, and Formatting a Presentation Using PowerPoint........... 289

Topic 10.1 Creating a New Presentation and Inserting Slides 290
Topic 10.2 Changing the Theme and Inserting and Modifying a Table 294
Topic 10.3 Formatting Text with Font and Paragraph Options 296
Topic 10.4 Selecting, Resizing, Aligning, and Moving Placeholders.......... 298
Topic 10.5 Using Slide Sorter View and Moving, Duplicating, and Deleting Slides 300
Topic 10.6 Modifying the Slide Master....... 302
Topic 10.7 Adding Notes and Comments... 304
Topic 10.8 Displaying a Slide Show 306
Topic 10.9 Preparing Audience Handouts and Speaker Notes 308
Chapter 10 Review 310
Chapter 10 Projects 315

Chapter 11
Enhancing a Presentation with Pictures, Sound, Video, and Animation Effects... 321

Topic 11.1 Inserting Graphics from Clip Art and Picture Collections....... 322
Topic 11.2 Inserting a SmartArt Graphic 324
Topic 11.3 Converting Text to SmartArt and Inserting WordArt............. 326
Topic 11.4 Creating a Chart on a Slide 328
Topic 11.5 Drawing Shapes and Adding Text Boxes.............................. 330

Topic 11.6 Adding Video to a Presentation 332
Topic 11.7 Adding Sound to a Presentation 334
Topic 11.8 Adding Transitions and Animation Effects to a Slide Show 336
Topic 11.9 Set Up a Self-Running Presentation 340
Chapter 11 Review.................................. 342
Chapter 11 Projects 347

Chapter 12
Using and Querying an Access Database 353

Topic 12.1 Understanding Database Objects and Terminology 354
Topic 12.2 Adding Records Using a Datasheet 358
Topic 12.3 Editing and Deleting Records in a Datasheet.......................... 360
Topic 12.4 Adding, Editing, and Deleting Records in a Form 362
Topic 12.5 Finding and Replacing Data and Adjusting Column Widths... 364
Topic 12.6 Sorting and Filtering Records... 366
Topic 12.7 Creating a Query Using the Simple Query Wizard............... 368
Topic 12.8 Creating a Query Using Design View 370
Topic 12.9 Entering Criteria to Select Records in a Query................. 372
Topic 12.10 Entering Multiple Criteria to Select Records and Sorting a Query 374
Topic 12.11 Creating a Calculated Field in a Query and Previewing a Datasheet 376
Chapter 12 Review.................................. 378
Chapter 12 Projects 384

Chapter 13
Creating a Table, Form, and Report in Access................................ 389

Topic 13.1 Creating a New Database File and Understanding Table Design Guidelines 390
Topic 13.2 Creating a New Table............... 392
Topic 13.3 Creating a New Table in Design View and Assigning a Primary Key 394
Topic 13.4 Adding Fields to an Existing Table 396
Topic 13.5 Modifying Field Properties in Design View 398
Topic 13.6 Creating a Lookup List............ 400
Topic 13.7 Displaying and Editing a Relationship 402
Topic 13.8 Creating and Editing a Form..... 404
Topic 13.9 Creating, Editing, and Viewing a Report.................................. 406
Topic 13.10 Compacting, Repairing, and Backing Up a Database 408
Chapter 13 Review.................................. 410
Chapter 13 Projects 415

Chapter 14
Integrating Word, Excel, PowerPoint, and Access Components..................... 419

Topic 14.1 Importing Excel Worksheet Data into Access....................... 420
Topic 14.2 Exporting an Access Query to Excel.................................. 424
Topic 14.3 Embedding an Excel Chart into a Word Document............ 426
Topic 14.4 Embedding Excel Data into and Editing the Data in a PowerPoint Presentation 428
Topic 14.5 Linking an Excel Chart with a Presentation and Updating Links 430
Chapter 14 Review.................................. 434
Chapter 14 Projects 437

Chapter 15
Using Windows Live SkyDrive and Other Cloud Computing Technologies............ 441

Topic 15.1 Creating a Document Using Microsoft Word Web App 442
Topic 15.2 Creating a Worksheet Using Microsoft Excel Web App 446
Topic 15.3 Creating a Presentation Using Microsoft PowerPoint Web App 448
Topic 15.4 Editing a Presentation in Microsoft PowerPoint Web App 450
Topic 15.5 Downloading and Uploading Files from and to SkyDrive....... 452
Topic 15.6 Sharing a File on SkyDrive....... 454
Topic 15.7 Creating a Document Using Google Docs............................ 456

Chapter 15 Review.................................... 460

Chapter 15 Projects 463

Glossary 467

Index 477

Preface

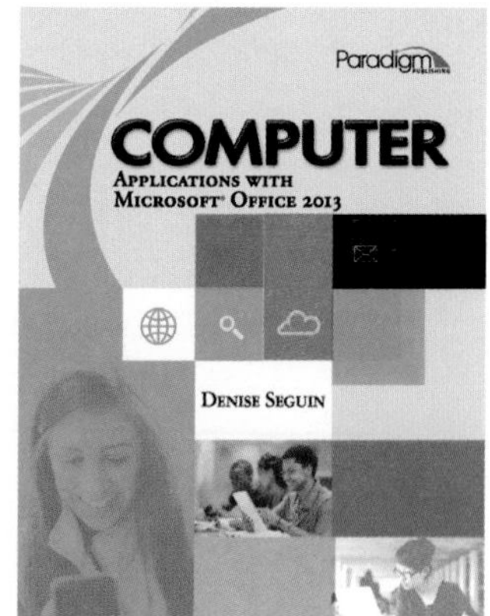

Today's students arrive in the classroom with more confidence in using technology than any generation before them. Students have grown up with technology as a part of their lives and the Internet as a source of information, entertainment, and communication. Chances are students have used a word processor and a presentation program for several years to prepare materials for school projects.

Many students have learned their way around a computer application by trial and error. However, to be efficient and successful, students need to learn how to use software applications in a way that saves them time and makes the best use of the available feature set. To that end, students are looking for a textbook that provides them with the tools they need to succeed immediately in their academic and personal lives as well as prepare them for success in their future careers. In this book, students will learn skills they can apply immediately to accomplishing projects and assignments for school and to organizing, scheduling, recording, planning, and budgeting for their personal needs. Students will find the work done in this course to be relevant and useful with the content presented in a straightforward approach.

According to Forbes.com, 90 to 95 percent of the office productivity suite market and 70 to 75 percent of the operating system market is held by Microsoft products. Therefore, to be successful in one's career, competence with the Microsoft Windows operating system, Internet Explorer web browser, and applications within the Office suite is essential. In this book, students will learn to navigate and operate these software programs at a standard expected of an entry-level employee.

Overview of Course and Textbook

Computer Applications with Microsoft Office 2013 offers instruction in the use of the Microsoft Windows operating system, Internet Explorer web browser, and applications within Microsoft Office. The instructional text is designed as two- and four-page topics. Many screen shots illustrate software features so that students can check their work. Reading time is minimized; students will learn just what they need to know to succeed within these programs. Students will practice features with step-by-step instruction interspersed with text that explains why a feature is used or how the feature can be beneficial to them. Students should work through each chapter at a PC or with their tablet or other mobile device so that they can complete the steps as they learn.

At the end of each chapter, students will have a chance to review a summary of the presented features, to complete several objective summary tasks, and then to apply the skills in projects that will reinforce and expand the knowledge they have gained. Instructors should assign projects based on their goals for the course and the skill level of their students. A variety of projects that include recall, application, synthesis, research, and composition are included.

Although well-designed textbook pedagogy is important, students learn technology skills through practice and problem solving. Technology provides opportunities for interactive learning as well as excellent ways to quickly and accurately assess student performance. To this end, this textbook is supported with SNAP, Paradigm Publishing's web-based training and assessment learning management system. Details about SNAP as well as additional student and instructor resources appear on pages xiv–xv.

Which Applications Are Included?

Computer Applications with Microsoft Office 2013 provides instruction in achieving entry-level competence with the latest editions of Microsoft Windows, web browsers, and the Microsoft Office productivity suite, including OneNote, Outlook, Word, Excel, PowerPoint, and Access. Students will also be introduced to cloud computing alternatives to the traditional desktop suite. No prior experience with these software programs is required. Even those with some technological savvy can benefit from completing the course by learning new ways to complete tasks or skills. After completing a course that uses this textbook, students will be able to:

- Navigate the Windows operating system and manage files and folders.
- Use web browsers such as Internet Explorer, Google Chrome, or Mozilla Firefox to navigate and search the Web, as well as download content to a PC or mobile device.
- Use navigation, file management, and commands within the Microsoft Office suite that are standard across all applications.
- Organize and manage class notes in OneNote.
- Communicate and schedule items in Outlook.
- Create, edit, format, and enhance documents in Word.
- Create, edit, analyze, format, and enhance workbooks in Excel.
- Create, edit, format, and enhance slides and set up a slideshow in PowerPoint.
- Create and edit tables, forms, queries, and reports in Access.
- Integrate information among the applications within the Microsoft Office suite.
- Use cloud computing technologies to create, edit, store, and share documents.

Are You Using Microsoft Office 2013 with Windows 7?

A version of Chapter 1, written for Windows 7 users, is available for purchase. Students who use a computer with the Windows 7 operating system can use this supplement in place of Chapter 1. In Chapters 2 through 15, instructions for Windows 7 users are included for those steps in which Windows 7 and Windows 8 procedures differ. Therefore, students using Microsoft Office 2013 with a Windows 7 computer can learn with confidence using this textbook.

What Makes this Textbook Different from Others?

Many textbooks that teach computer applications were designed and organized for software that was in effect one or two decades ago. As software evolves and becomes more flexible and streamlined, so too should software textbooks. With this mandate, this textbook has been designed and organized with a fresh look at the skills a student should know to be successful in today's world. The freedom to create a new book from scratch allowed the author to choose and place in a logical sequence those skills that are considered essential for today's student. Consider this book a "software survival kit for school and life." Nothing more, nothing less!

Many of the student data files in this textbook are based on files created by students for projects or assignments in courses similar to those students may be enrolled in now. Students will open and manipulate real work completed by someone just like them. Other files include practical examples of documents that students can readily relate to their school and personal experiences.

Because more students are acquiring and using tablets for school work, this textbook was written with touch gestures included. Tablet users can learn with confidence knowing that the book has been written and tested with them in mind!

Chapter Features

This textbook is divided into 15 chapters that are best completed in sequence; however, after completing the essential skills learned in Chapters 1 through 5, instructors may opt to complete Word, Excel, PowerPoint, Access, integration, and cloud computing technologies in the order of their choice.

Each chapter begins with a brief introduction to the chapter content along with a list of chapter objectives. Following each chapter opener, chapter topics are presented in two or four pages. A variety of marginal notes and other features expand or clarify the content. Students will gain experience with topic features by working through hands-on exercises, which consist of step-by-step instructions and illustrative screen shots. Finally, the end-of-chapter materials include a summary, objective assessments, and projects. These features are described below.

SKILLS
Lists of skills that will be learned by completing the steps.
App Tip
Useful tips that extend or add to your knowledge about a feature.
Quick Steps
Brief summaries of steps to complete major tasks. Use for quick reference or review.
Screen captures with step numbers provide visual confirmation.
Beyond Basics
Provide additional information about the feature that extends the skills described in the topic.
Locking the Screen, Signing Out, and Shutting Down Windows 8
Signing Out of a Windows Session
Shutting Down the PC or Mobile Device
Other Power Options

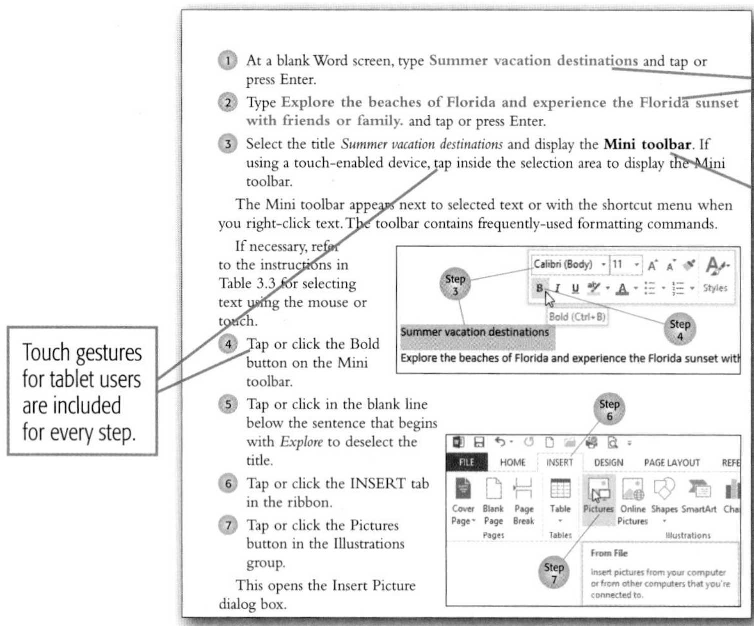

1. At a blank Word screen, type **Summer vacation destinations** and tap or press Enter.
2. Type **Explore the beaches of Florida and experience the Florida sunset with friends or family.** and tap or press Enter.
3. Select the title *Summer vacation destinations* and display the **Mini toolbar**. If using a touch-enabled device, tap inside the selection area to display the Mini toolbar.

The Mini toolbar appears next to selected text or with the shortcut menu when you right-click text. The toolbar contains frequently-used formatting commands.

If necessary, refer to the instructions in Table 3.3 for selecting text using the mouse or touch.

4. Tap or click the Bold button on the Mini toolbar.
5. Tap or click in the blank line below the sentence that begins with *Explore* to deselect the title.
6. Tap or click the INSERT tab in the ribbon.
7. Tap or click the Pictures button in the Illustrations group.

This opens the Insert Picture dialog box.

Text to be typed stands out from the instructional text.

Key words included in the glossary are in bold.

Touch gestures for tablet users are included for every step.

Instructions for completing exercises are presented in simple, easy-to-follow steps.

All instructions include steps for touch-enabled devices. Students with a tablet or other mobile device learn with touch gestures, which are the first instruction for each task.

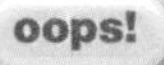

Start screen is miniaturized? If you drag a tile to the bottom of the screen, the Start screen zooms out to show all of the tiles as miniatures. Release the tile and the Start screen will return to normal size.

oops! margin hints anticipate common challenges and provide solutions so that students succeed with the topic.

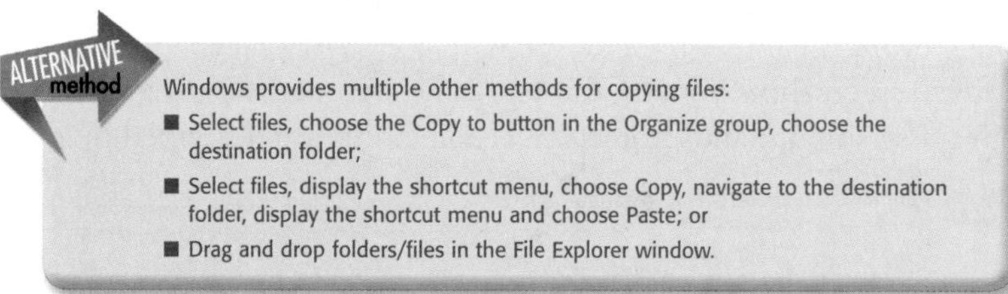

Windows provides multiple other methods for copying files:

- Select files, choose the Copy to button in the Organize group, choose the destination folder;
- Select files, display the shortcut menu, choose Copy, navigate to the destination folder, display the shortcut menu and choose Paste; or
- Drag and drop folders/files in the File Explorer window.

Whenever possible, an Alternative Method feature box provides different ways to accomplish the task learned in the topic.

Check This Out
google.com/chrome
Go here to download and install Google Chrome on your PC or mobile device.

Related websites that students can explore or that include useful downloads are provided where appropriate.

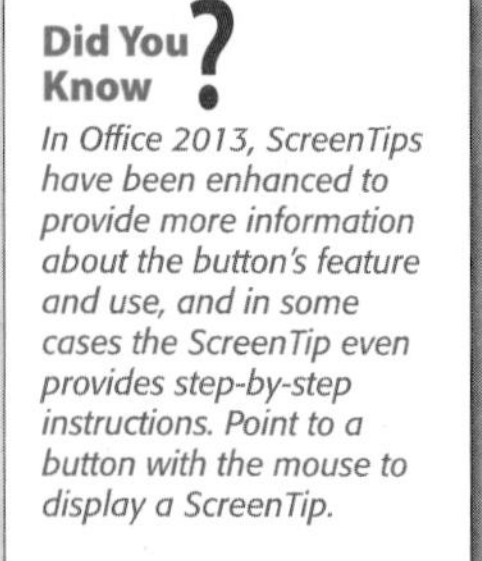

Did You Know?
In Office 2013, ScreenTips have been enhanced to provide more information about the button's feature and use, and in some cases the ScreenTip even provides step-by-step instructions. Point to a button with the mouse to display a ScreenTip.

Did You Know? features provide facts or trivia of interest about the topic.

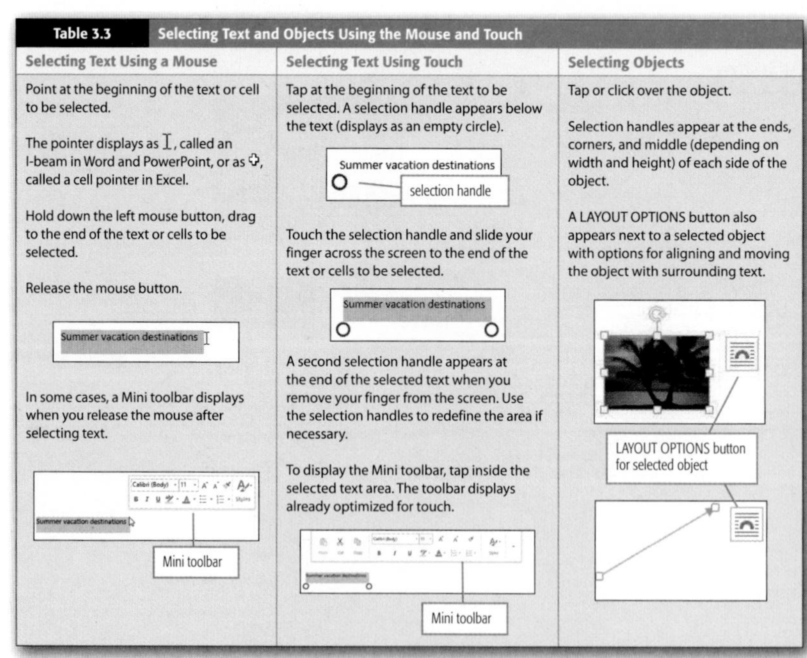

Table 3.3 Selecting Text and Objects Using the Mouse and Touch

Selecting Text Using a Mouse	Selecting Text Using Touch	Selecting Objects
Point at the beginning of the text or cell to be selected. The pointer displays as I, called an I-beam in Word and PowerPoint, or as ✥, called a cell pointer in Excel. Hold down the left mouse button, drag to the end of the text or cells to be selected. Release the mouse button. [Summer vacation destinations] In some cases, a Mini toolbar displays when you release the mouse after selecting text. [Mini toolbar]	Tap at the beginning of the text to be selected. A selection handle appears below the text (displays as an empty circle). [Summer vacation destinations / selection handle] Touch the selection handle and slide your finger across the screen to the end of the text or cells to be selected. [Summer vacation destinations] A second selection handle appears at the end of the selected text when you remove your finger from the screen. Use the selection handles to redefine the area if necessary. To display the Mini toolbar, tap inside the selected text area. The toolbar displays already optimized for touch. [Mini toolbar]	Tap or click over the object. Selection handles appear at the ends, corners, and middle (depending on width and height) of each side of the object. A LAYOUT OPTIONS button also appears next to a selected object with options for aligning and moving the object with surrounding text. [LAYOUT OPTIONS button for selected object]

Information that can be presented in a table format is included whenever possible to minimize reading load.

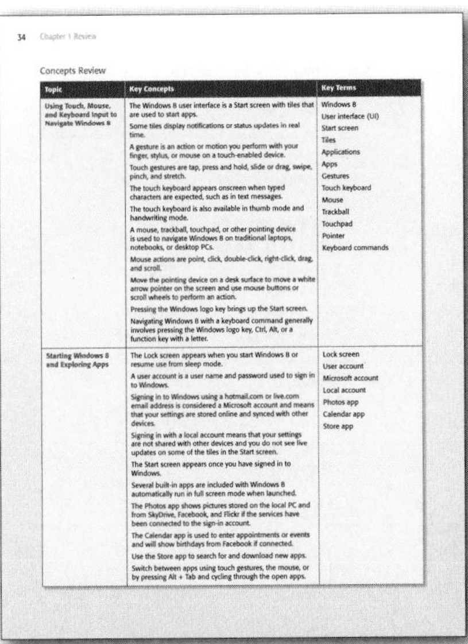

34 Chapter 1 Review

Concepts Review

Topic	Key Concepts	Key Terms
Using Touch, Mouse, and Keyboard Input to Navigate Windows 8	The Windows 8 user interface is a Start screen with tiles that are used to start apps. Some tiles display notifications or status updates in real time. A gesture is an action or motion you perform with your finger, stylus, or mouse on a touch-enabled device. Touch gestures are tap, press and hold, slide or drag, swipe, pinch, and stretch. The touch keyboard appears onscreen when typed characters are expected, such as in text messages. The touch keyboard is also available in thumb mode and handwriting mode. A mouse, trackball, touchpad, or other pointing device is used to navigate Windows 8 on traditional laptops, notebooks, or desktop PCs. Mouse actions are point, click, double-click, right-click, drag, and scroll. Move the pointing device on a desk surface to move a white arrow pointer on the screen and use mouse buttons or scroll wheels to perform an action. Pressing the Windows logo key brings up the Start screen. Navigating Windows 8 with a keyboard command generally involves pressing the Windows logo key, Ctrl, Alt, or a function key with a letter.	Windows 8 User interface (UI) Start screen Tiles Applications Apps Gestures Touch keyboard Mouse Trackball Touchpad Pointer Keyboard commands
Starting Windows 8 and Exploring Apps	The Lock screen appears when you start Windows 8 or resume use from sleep mode. A user account is a user name and password used to sign in to Windows. Signing in to Windows using a hotmail.com or live.com email address is considered a Microsoft account and means that your settings are stored online and synced with other devices. Signing in with a local account means that your settings are not shared with other devices and you do not see live updates on some of the tiles in the Start screen. The Start screen appears once you have signed in to Windows. Several built-in apps are included with Windows 8 automatically run in full screen mode when launched. The Photos app shows pictures stored on the local PC and from SkyDrive, Facebook, and Flickr if the services have been connected to the sign-in account. The Calendar app is used to enter appointments or events and will show birthdays from Facebook if connected. Use the Store app to search for and download new apps. Switch between apps using touch gestures, the mouse, or by pressing Alt + Tab and cycling through the open apps.	Lock screen User account Microsoft account Local account Photos app Calendar app Store app

A chapter summary provides a review of the main chapter content and key words in table format, allowing students to easily return to the content if more review is necessary.

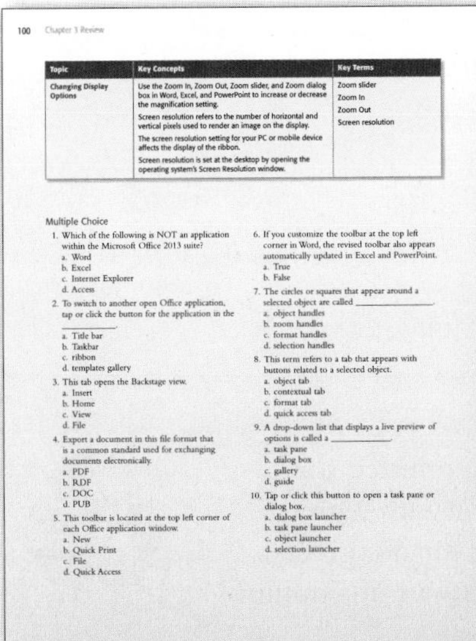

100 Chapter 3 Review

Topic	Key Concepts	Key Terms
Changing Display Options	Use the Zoom In, Zoom Out, Zoom slider, and Zoom dialog box in Word, Excel, and PowerPoint to increase or decrease the magnification setting. Screen resolution refers to the number of horizontal and vertical pixels used to render an image on the display. The screen resolution setting for your PC or mobile device affects the display of the ribbon. Screen resolution is set at the desktop by opening the operating system's Screen Resolution window.	Zoom slider Zoom In Zoom Out Screen resolution

Multiple Choice

1. Which of the following is NOT an application within the Microsoft Office 2013 suite?
   a. Word
   b. Excel
   c. Internet Explorer
   d. Access
2. To switch to another open Office application, tap or click the button for the application in the ___________.
   a. Title bar
   b. Taskbar
   c. ribbon
   d. templates gallery
3. This tab opens the Backstage view.
   a. Insert
   b. Home
   c. View
   d. File
4. Export a document in this file format that is a common standard used for exchanging documents electronically.
   a. PDF
   b. RDF
   c. DOC
   d. PUB
5. This toolbar is located at the top left corner of each Office application window.
   a. New
   b. Quick Print
   c. File
   d. Quick Access
6. If you customize the toolbar at the top left corner in Word, the revised toolbar also appears automatically updated in Excel and PowerPoint.
   a. True
   b. False
7. The circles or squares that appear around a selected object are called ___________.
   a. object handles
   b. zoom handles
   c. format handles
   d. selection handles
8. This term refers to a tab that appears with buttons related to a selected object.
   a. object tab
   b. contextual tab
   c. format tab
   d. quick access tab
9. A drop-down list that displays a live preview of options is called a ___________.
   a. task pane
   b. dialog box
   c. gallery
   d. guide
10. Tap or click this button to open a task pane or dialog box.
    a. dialog box launcher
    b. task pane launcher
    c. object launcher
    d. selection launcher

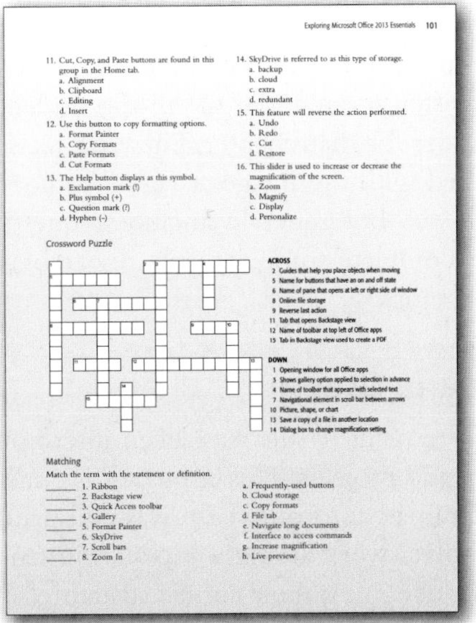

Exploring Microsoft Office 2013 Essentials 101

11. Cut, Copy, and Paste buttons are found in this group in the Home tab.
    a. Alignment
    b. Clipboard
    c. Editing
    d. Insert
12. Use this button to copy formatting options.
    a. Format Painter
    b. Copy Formats
    c. Paste Formats
    d. Cut Formats
13. The Help button displays as this symbol.
    a. Exclamation mark (!)
    b. Plus symbol (+)
    c. Question mark (?)
    d. Hyphen (-)
14. SkyDrive is referred to as this type of storage.
    a. backup
    b. cloud
    c. extra
    d. redundant
15. This feature will reverse the action performed.
    a. Undo
    b. Redo
    c. Cut
    d. Restore
16. This slider is used to increase or decrease the magnification of the screen.
    a. Zoom
    b. Magnify
    c. Display
    d. Personalize

Crossword Puzzle

ACROSS
2 Guides that help you place objects when moving
5 Name for buttons that have an on and off state
6 Name of pane that opens at left or right side of window
8 Online file storage
9 Reverse last action
11 Tab that opens Backstage view
12 Name of toolbar at top left of Office apps
15 Tab in Backstage view used to create a PDF

DOWN
1 Opening window for all Office apps
3 Shows gallery option applied to selection in advance
4 Name of toolbar that appears with selected text
7 Navigational element in scroll bar between arrows
10 Picture, shape, or chart
13 Save a copy of a file in another location
14 Dialog box to change magnification setting

Matching

Match the term with the statement or definition.

_______ 1. Ribbon
_______ 2. Backstage view
_______ 3. Quick Access toolbar
_______ 4. Gallery
_______ 5. Format Painter
_______ 6. SkyDrive
_______ 7. Scroll bars
_______ 8. Zoom In

a. Frequently-used buttons
b. Cloud storage
c. Copy formats
d. File tab
e. Navigate long documents
f. Interface to access commands
g. Increase magnification
h. Live preview

Multiple-choice questions, a crossword puzzle, and a matching exercise provide an opportunity to practice and review understanding of the concepts.

40 Chapter 1 Projects

Project 1 Exploring Windows 8 Apps

Individual

Deliverable: Screen capture of Start screen with Switch list

1. Start Windows 8 and sign in.
2. Reveal the Charms bar and choose the Search charm. From the Apps list, launch the Travel app. Browse the list of featured destinations and tap or click a destination of your choice. Slide or scroll the destination information, reading the Overview, browsing photos, panoramas, list of attractions, and so on.
3. Display the Start screen and launch the News app. Slide or scroll the top news stories and tap or click a story that interests you.
4. Display the Start screen and launch the Store app. Slide or scroll to the Education category and tap or click the tile to the Top free Education apps.
5. Display the Start screen and reveal the Switch list in the left pane.
6. Press the Print Screen key on the keyboard to capture an image of your screen with the Switch list displayed. The key may be labeled Prt Sc, PrtScrn, or PrtSc and is generally located in the top row of keys at the right near the last function key. On some PCs or devices you may need to press Shift + Print Screen or a function key with Print Screen. If you are using a tablet without a keyboard, check with your instructor for instructions on how to submit projects with screen capture deliverables.
7. Use the Search charm to search for and launch the Paint app. Paint is a desktop app and will open in the Windows 8 desktop.
8. Tap or click the Paste button in the Home tab of the Paint ribbon.
9. Tap or click the Save button on the Quick Access toolbar. At the Save As dialog box, navigate to your USB flash drive, select the current file name in the File name text box, type C1-Project1-AppsSwitchList-Your Name, and tap or click the Save button. ***Note: You will move this file to another location in Project 4.***
10. Close the Paint window and close the desktop app.
11. Switch to and close each of the three apps you launched in this project.
12. Submit the project to your instructor in the manner she or he has requested.

Project 2 Customizing the Start Screen

Individual

Deliverable: Screen capture with customized Start screen

Note: Skip steps in this project that ask you to customize a tile if the tile is already at the instructed setting.

1. At the Windows Start screen, select the Calendar tile and resize the tile smaller.
2. Select the News tile and resize the app smaller.
3. Select the Store tile and resize the app larger.
4. Select the People tile and turn the live tile off.
5. Select the Photos tile and turn the live tile off.
6. Rearrange the tiles that you have customized in this project within the first group of tiles in a manner that suits you.
7. Capture an image of your customized Start screen and paste it into a new Paint document. See Project 1, Steps 6 to 8 if you need help.
8. Save the image in Paint on your USB flash drive as **C1-Project2-CustomizedStartScreen-Your Name**.
9. Close the Paint window and close the desktop app.
10. Submit the project to your instructor in the manner she or he has requested.
11. Restore the Calendar, News, Store, People, and Photos tiles to their original settings and rearrange the tiles back to their original locations.

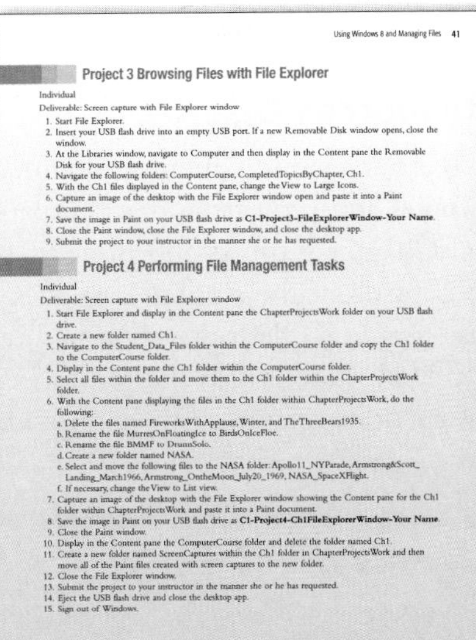

Using Windows 8 and Managing Files 41

Project 3 Browsing Files with File Explorer

Individual

Deliverable: Screen capture with File Explorer window

1. Start File Explorer.
2. Insert your USB flash drive into an empty USB port. If a new Removable Disk window opens, close the window.
3. At the Libraries window, navigate to Computer and then display in the Content pane the Removable Disk for your USB flash drive.
4. Navigate the following folders: ComputerCourse, CompletedTopicsByChapter, Ch1.
5. With the Ch1 files displayed in the Content pane, change the View to Large Icons.
6. Capture an image of the desktop with the File Explorer window open and paste it into a Paint document.
7. Save the image in Paint on your USB flash drive as **C1-Project3-FileExplorerWindow-Your Name**.
8. Close the Paint window, close the File Explorer window, and close the desktop app.
9. Submit the project to your instructor in the manner she or he has requested.

Project 4 Performing File Management Tasks

Individual

Deliverable: Screen capture with File Explorer window

1. Start File Explorer and display in the Content pane the ChapterProjectsWork folder on your USB flash drive.
2. Create a new folder named Ch1.
3. Navigate to the Student_Data_Files folder within the ComputerCourse folder and copy the Ch1 folder to the ComputerCourse folder.
4. Display in the Content pane the Ch1 folder within the ComputerCourse folder.
5. Select all files within the folder and move them to the Ch1 folder within the ChapterProjectsWork folder.
6. With the Content pane displaying the files in the Ch1 folder within ChapterProjectsWork, do the following:
   a. Delete the files named FireworksWithApplause, Winter, and TheThreeBears1935.
   b. Rename the file MurresOnFloatingIce to BirdsOnIceFloe.
   c. Rename the file BMMF to DrumSolo.
   d. Create a new folder named NASA.
   e. Select and move the following files to the NASA folder: Apollo11_NYParade, Armstrong&Scott_Landing_March1966, Armstrong_OntheMoon_July20_1969, NASA_SpaceXFlight.
   f. If necessary, change the View to List view.
7. Capture an image of the desktop with the File Explorer window showing the Content pane for the Ch1 folder within ChapterProjectsWork and paste it into a Paint document.
8. Save the image in Paint on your USB flash drive as **C1-Project4-Ch1FileExplorerWindow-Your Name**.
9. Close the Paint window.
10. Display in the Content pane the ComputerCourse folder and delete the folder named Ch1.
11. Create a new folder named ScreenCaptures within the Ch1 folder in ChapterProjectsWork and then move all of the Paint files created with screen captures to the new folder.
12. Close the File Explorer window.
13. Submit the project to your instructor in the manner she or he has requested.
14. Eject the USB flash drive and close the desktop app.
15. Sign out of Windows.

Three to seven projects at the end of each chapter allow students to apply and demonstrate comprehension of the major skills learned in the chapter. In general, projects increase in complexity from the first to the last. Most projects are intended to be completed individually; however, instructors may opt to assign some to pairs or teams of students.

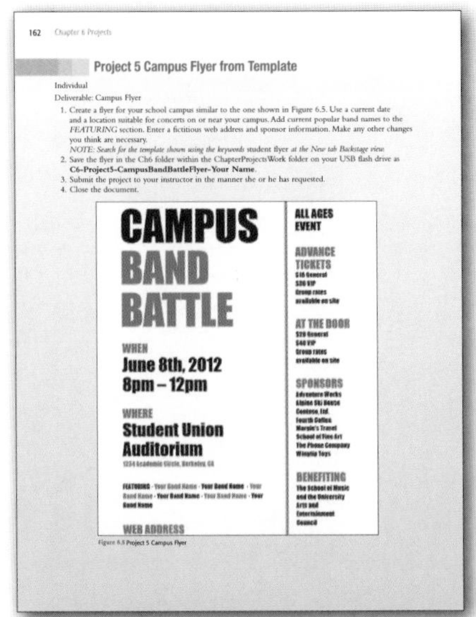
162 Chapter 6 Projects

Project 5 Campus Flyer from Template

Individual

Deliverable: Campus Flyer

1. Create a flyer for your school campus similar to the one shown in Figure 6.5. Use a current date and a location suitable for concerts on or near your campus. Add current popular band names to the *FEATURING* section. Enter a fictitious web address and sponsor information. Make any other changes you think are necessary.
   NOTE: Search for the template shown using the keywords student flyer *at the New tab Backstage view.*
2. Save the flyer in the Ch6 folder within the ChapterProjectsWork folder on your USB flash drive as **C6-Project5-CampusBandBattleFlyer-Your Name**.
3. Submit the project to your instructor in the manner she or he has requested.
4. Close the document.

Beginning with Chapter 3, most chapters include a project—indicated with a green banner—that presents a culminating visual project in which the student is to create a document similar to the examples shown. The visual project requires that the student notice details and problem solve to create a deliverable with less direction. In some cases, students will be required to do some Internet research and composition to complete the visual project.

Starting in Chapter 4, the last project in each chapter instructs students to send output to a OneNote notebook. The OneNote notebook is a repository for all student work. Instructors may opt to have the student share his or her OneNote notebook with the instructor in a SkyDrive folder. Instructors then have the option to check all work in one place.

Starting in Chapter 6, some projects instruct students to listen to an audio file in the student data files folder for that chapter. These projects are designated with the image at right. Audio instructions vary but generally include requesting the student complete some Internet research and compose a report.

This Book Is Green!

Instructions to print results have been intentionally omitted for all exercises and projects. This approach is consistent with a green computing initiative to minimize wasteful printing for nongraded topics or project work and also provides instructors with maximum flexibility in designing their course structure.

Student and Instructor Resources

Student Resources Disc

The Student Resources disc contains documents and files needed to complete topics and projects and accompanies the textbook. By completing all Chapter 1 topics and projects, students set up a folder structure and copy all of the student data files from the Student Resources disc to a USB flash drive. As an alternative, instructors may choose to load student data files on a network, in which case alternative instructions may need to be provided.

SNAP Web-Based Training and Assessment

Available at snap2013.emcp.com, SNAP is a web-based program that offers an interactive venue for learning Microsoft Office 2013, Windows 8, and Internet Explorer 10. Along with a web-based learning management system, SNAP provides multimedia tutorials, performance skill items, matching activities, Grade It projects, comprehensive performance evaluations, a concepts test bank, an online grade book, and a set of course planning tools.

Instructor Resources Disc

Instructor support is available on the Instructor Resources disc and includes syllabus and course planning suggestions, chapter teaching hints, model answers, PowerPoint® presentations for student study or classroom instruction for each chapter, and the ExamView® Assessment Suite and test banks.

Internet Resource Center

All content on the Student Resources disc and most content on the Instructor Resources disc are also available at the book-specific Internet Resource Center at www.paradigmcollege.net/computerapplications2013. Instructor materials, such as model answers, are password-protected.

Blackboard Course Files

Blackboard files provide course content, self quizzes, and study aids, and facilitate communication among students and instructors via email and e-discussion.

eBook

For students who prefer studying with an eBook, *Computer Applications with Microsoft Office 2013* is available in an electronic form. The web-based, password-protected eBook features dynamic navigation tools, including bookmarking, a linked table of contents, and the ability to jump to a specific page. The eBook format also supports helpful study tools, such as highlighting and note taking.

Acknowledgments

The author and editors would like to thank the following for developing supplements for this project: Janet Blum, Fanshawe College, London, Ontario; Jeff Johnson, Minneapolis, Minnesota; Judy Peterson, Two Harbors, Minnesota; and Janine Violini, Calgary, Alberta. The following students are thanked for their contributions to and feedback on preliminary versions of the textbook: Patti Ann Reynolds, Toni McBride, and Nicole Oke, Fanshawe College; and Michael Seguin, University of Windsor, Windsor, Ontario.

About the Author

Denise Seguin has served on the Faculty of Business at Fanshawe College of Applied Arts and Technology in London, Ontario, since 1986. She has developed curriculum and taught a variety of office technology, software applications, and accounting courses to students in postsecondary Information Technology diploma programs and Continuing Education courses. Seguin has served as Program Coordinator for Computer Systems Technician, Computer Systems Technology, Office Administration, and Law Clerk programs and was acting Chair of the School of Information Technology in 2001. Along with authoring *Computer Concepts* and *Computer Applications with Microsoft Office 2013*, she has also authored Paradigm Publishing's *Microsoft Outlook* 2000 to 2013 editions and co-authored *Our Digital World* first and second editions, *Benchmark Series Microsoft Excel* 2007, 2010, and 2013, *Benchmark Series Microsoft Access* 2007, 2010, and 2013, *Marquee Series Microsoft Office* 2000 to 2013, and *Using Computers in the Medical Office* 2003 to 2010 editions.

Applications with Microsoft® Office 2013

Chapter 1

Using Windows 8 and Managing Files

After successfully completing this chapter, you will be able to:

- Navigate Windows 8 using touch, a mouse, or a keyboard
- Start Windows 8 and sign in
- Launch an app, switch between apps, and close apps
- Reveal the Charms bar and use the Search charm
- Lock the screen, sign out, and shut down Windows 8
- Customize the Start screen and Lock screen
- Launch and close Desktop apps
- Browse files with File Explorer
- Create new folders and copy, move, rename, and delete files and folders
- Eject a USB flash drive
- Use Windows Help

Windows 8 is the operating system (OS) software published by Microsoft Corporation. An OS provides the user interface that allows you to work with the computer or mobile device. The OS also manages all of the hardware resources, routes data between devices and applications, and provides the tools for managing files and application programs. Every computing device requires an OS; without one your computer would not function. Think of the OS as the data and device manager that ensures data flows to and from each device and application. When you touch the screen, click the mouse, or type words on a keyboard, the OS recognizes the input and sends the data to the application or device that needs it. If a piece of hardware is not working, the OS senses the problem and displays a message to you. For example, if a printer is not turned on, the OS communicates that the printer is offline. When you power on a computer or mobile device, the OS loads automatically into memory and displays the user interface when the computer is ready.

Computers and mobile devices have an OS preloaded and ready to use. Some tasks you perform require that you interact with the OS directly such as when you launch applications (called "*apps*" in Windows 8), switch windows, and manage your files and folders. In this chapter you will learn to navigate in Windows 8 and work with files.

Note: You will need a removable storage medium (USB flash drive) with enough space to copy the student data files for this textbook.

Windows 7 Users?

A version of Chapter 1 written for Windows 7 users is available. For instructors who ordered the supplement, this version of Chapter 1 is packaged with the textbook. Windows 7 users should read and complete the topics in the Windows 7 supplement rather than those in the textbook chapter.

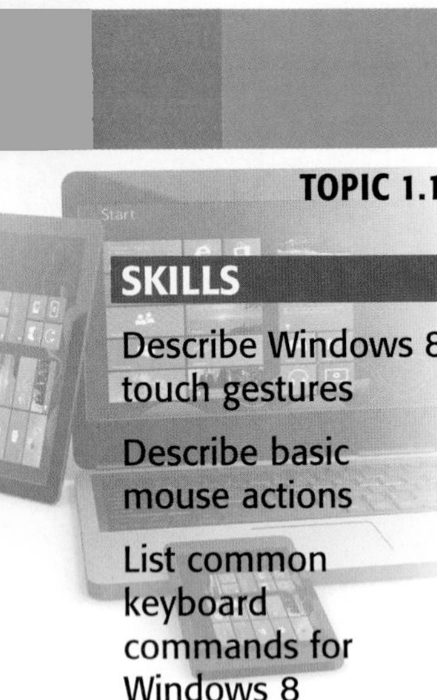

TOPIC 1.1

SKILLS

Describe Windows 8 touch gestures

Describe basic mouse actions

List common keyboard commands for Windows 8

Using Touch, Mouse, and Keyboard Input to Navigate Windows 8

Windows 8, released in October 2012, is the latest edition of Microsoft's popular OS for PCs and mobile devices. The Windows 8 **user interface (UI)** has been totally redesigned with a new **Start screen**. The Start Screen contains **tiles** that are used to start **applications**, called **apps**. Some tiles display updates in real time so that you are immediately informed when a new message arrives, a news story is released, the weather updates, or a friend posts a new status in Facebook. Tiles let you see all of your programs in one place as opposed to using the Start button and navigating menus to find a program, as was the case in earlier Windows versions.

Windows 8 is designed to work with devices capable of touch screen input, mouse input, and keyboard input. Before starting Windows 8, becoming familiar with input actions using touch, the mouse, and the keyboard will assist with navigating the user interface.

Using Touch to Navigate Windows 8

You can adjust settings for some touch actions in the Pen and Touch dialog box accessed from the Control Panel.

On touch-enabled PCs or tablets designed for Windows 8, you perform actions using **gestures**. A gesture is an action or motion you perform with your finger(s), thumb, stylus, or mouse. In some cases, users with a touch-enabled device will still use a mouse or keyboard for some purposes. Windows 8 accommodates all three input methods easily. Table 1.1 explains the gestures used to interact with the Windows 8 interface on a touch-enabled PC or mobile device.

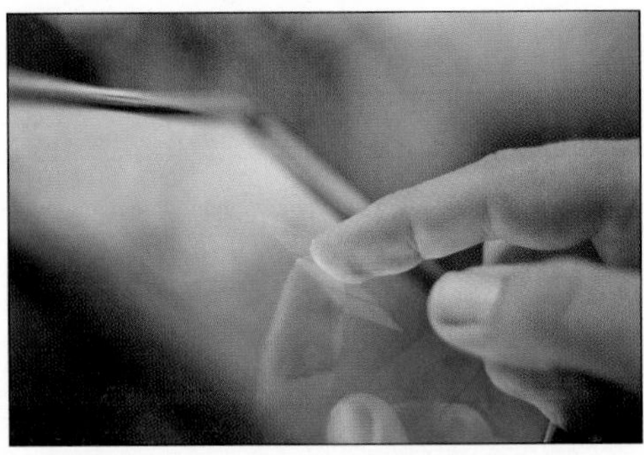

In Windows 8, touch actions are called *gestures*.

You can perform the gestures with one or two fingers or by using a stylus. For tasks that require typed characters such as email addresses, message text, or web addresses, the **touch keyboard** shown in Figure 1.1 is used. Tapping in an area of the screen that requires typed input generally causes the touch keyboard to appear. The touch keyboard is also available in thumb keyboard mode (Figure 1.2) and in handwriting mode (Figure 1.3).

At times, you will use a mouse and traditional keyboard with a touch-enabled device. For example, typing an essay for a school project would be easier using a traditional keyboard, or doing precise graphics editing may be easier with a mouse. Connect a USB or wireless mouse and/or keyboard for intensive work where touch input is not as productive.

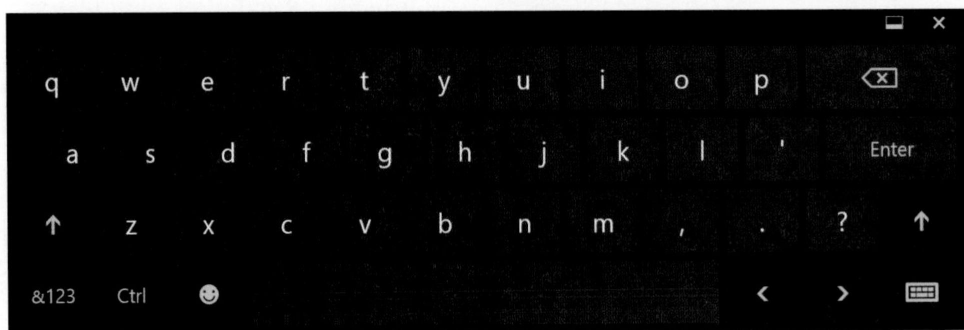

Figure 1.1 The full touch keyboard in Windows 8 appears whenever typed characters are expected. You can also launch the touch keyboard from the Touch Keyboard icon in the Taskbar of the Desktop app.

Table 1.1 Windows 8 Touch Gestures

Gesture	Description and Mouse Equivalent	What It Does	What It Looks Like
Tap or Double-tap	One finger touches the screen and immediately lifts off the screen once or twice in succession. **Mouse:** Click or double-click left mouse button.	Launches an app Follows a link Performs a command or selection from a button or icon	
Press and hold	One finger touches the screen and stays in place for a few seconds. **Mouse:** Point or right-click.	Shows a context menu Shows pop-up information or details	
Slide	Move one or two fingers in the same direction. **Mouse:** Drag (may need to drag or scroll using scroll bars).	Used to drag, pan, or scroll through lists or pages	
Swipe	Move one finger in from the left or right, up from the bottom, or down from the top a short distance. **Mouse:** Point to upper right corner or lower right corner to reveal Charms bar.	In from the right reveals the Charms bar with system commands	
	Mouse: Point at upper left corner and click.	In from the left switches between open apps	
	Mouse: Point at upper left corner and slide down along left edge to view list of open apps.	In and back out quickly from the left shows a list of open apps	
	Mouse: Right-click.	Up from the bottom or down from the top shows app commands	
Pinch	Two fingers touch the screen apart from each other and move closer together. **Mouse:** Ctrl + scroll mouse wheel toward you.	Shrinks the size of text, an item, or tiles on the screen	
Stretch	Two fingers touch the screen together and move farther apart. **Mouse:** Ctrl + mouse scroll wheel away from you.	Expands the size of text, an item, or tiles on the screen	

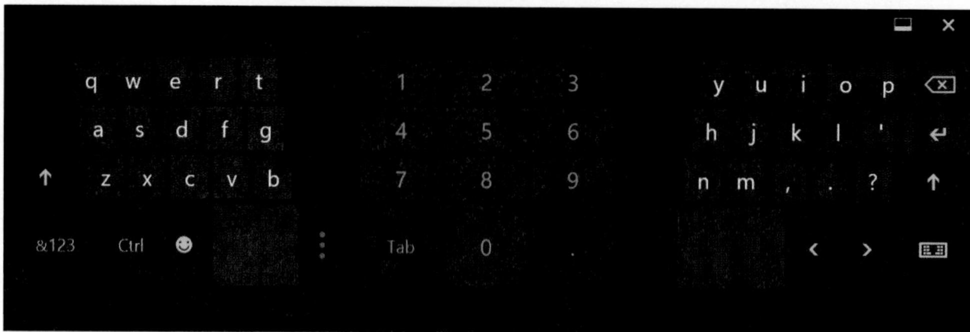

Figure 1.2 The Windows 8 touch keyboard in thumb mode with the keys split on either side of the screen for comfortable typing while using the device for text messaging or similar application.

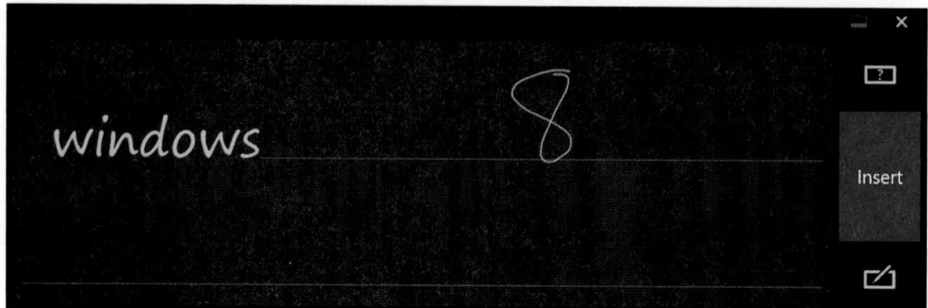

Figure 1.3 The Windows 8 touch keyboard in handwriting mode. Text can be inserted into an application by writing in the keyboard area using a stylus or your finger. When you stop writing, Windows converts the handwriting to text.

Using a Mouse to Navigate Windows 8

For traditional desktops, laptops, or notebook PCs, navigating the Windows 8 user interface requires the use of a **mouse**, **trackball**, **touchpad**, or other pointing device. These devices are used to move and manipulate a **pointer** (displayed as) on the screen; however, the white arrow pointer can change appearance depending on the action being performed.

If you run out of desk surface, lift the mouse up off the desk, place it back down, and then continue moving in the same direction to extend the mouse movement further.

To operate the mouse, move the device up, down, right, or left on the desk surface to move the pointer on the screen in the corresponding direction. A scroll wheel on the top of the mouse can be used to scroll up or down. Newer mice include the ability to push on the left or right side of the scroll wheel to scroll right or left. Left and right buttons on the top of the mouse are used to perform actions when the pointer is resting on an item. Table 1.2 provides a list and description of mouse actions.

To use a touchpad, move your finger across the surface of the touchpad in the direction required. Tap the touchpad or a button below the touchpad to perform an action.

A mouse, trackball, or touchpad can be used as a pointing device to navigate Windows 8.

Using a Keyboard to Navigate Windows 8

Most actions in Windows 8 are easier to perform using touch gestures or a mouse; however, some **keyboard commands** are fast and easy to use. The Windows logo key is positioned at the bottom left of a keyboard between the Ctrl or Function key (labeled Fn) and the Alt key. Many keyboard shortcuts use the Windows logo key. For example, press the Windows logo key in any app to bring up the Start Screen. Pressing the Windows logo

Press the Windows logo key with a letter to perform an action.

key toggles between the Start Screen and the most recently opened app. The Menu button at the right side of the keyboard (between Alt and Ctrl) brings up context menus (similar to right-clicking with the mouse). Useful keyboard shortcuts are described in Table 1.3.

If you prefer using keyboard shortcuts, use the Help system (see Topic 1.11) to search for other keyboard navigational commands.

Note: Instructions in this textbook are written with touch and mouse gestures. If necessary, check with your instructor for the equivalent touchpad or other pointing device action.

Table 1.2	Mouse Movements and Actions
Term or Action	**Description**
Point	Move the mouse in the direction required to rest the white arrow pointer on a button, icon, option, tab, link, or other screen item.
Click	Quickly tap the left mouse button once while the pointer is resting on a button, icon, option, tab, link, or other screen item.
Double-click	Quickly tap the left mouse button twice. On the desktop, a program is launched by double-clicking the program's icon.
Right-click	Quickly tap the right mouse button. A right-click in Windows 8 or Windows 8 apps reveals app controls or options. Within a software application such as Microsoft Word or Microsoft Excel, a right-click causes a shortcut menu to appear. Shortcut menus in software applications are context-sensitive, meaning that the menu that appears varies depending on the item the pointer is resting upon when the right-click occurs.
Drag	Hold down the left mouse button, move the mouse up, down, left, or right, and then release the mouse button. Dragging is an action often used to move or resize an object.
Scroll	Use the scroll wheel on the mouse to scroll in a window. If the pointing device you are using does not include a scroll wheel, click the scroll arrows on a horizontal or vertical scroll bar at the right or bottom of a window, or drag the scroll box in the middle of the scroll bar up, down, left, or right.

When navigating Windows 8 with a mouse, point to the corners of the screen (referred to as *hot corners*) to access Start and system commands and to switch apps.

Table 1.3	Keyboard Commands or Shortcuts
Keyboard Shortcut	**What It Does**
Windows logo key	Displays Start screen. Pressing the Windows logo key also toggles between the Start screen and the most recently used app.
Windows logo key + c	Reveals the Charms bar along the right side of the screen
Windows logo key + d	Goes to the desktop (similar window as the desktop in Windows 7 and earlier)
Windows logo key + e	Displays a Computer window on the desktop
Windows logo key + f	Searches Files
Windows logo key + l	Locks the screen
Windows logo key + q	Searches Apps
Alt + F4	Closes an app
Menu button	Reveals app controls and options (similar to a right-click)
Esc	Removes app controls, pane, or backs out of a menu or option
Up, Down, Left, or Right Arrow keys	Moves pointer to select a tile or charm; press the Enter key to launch the app or charm options.

To use a keyboard command, hold down the Windows logo key or Alt, press and release the letter or function key, and then release the Windows logo key or Alt.

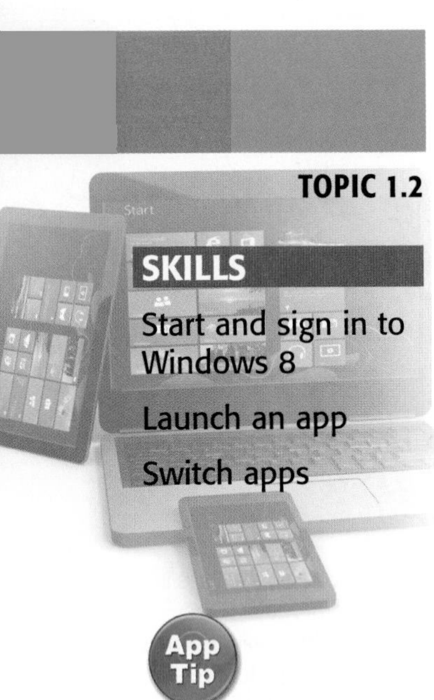

TOPIC 1.2
SKILLS
Start and sign in to Windows 8
Launch an app
Switch apps

Starting Windows 8 and Exploring Apps

Windows 8 starts up faster than earlier versions of Windows. If you are turning on your PC from a no power state, the **Lock screen** shown in Figure 1.4 appears in approximately 10 to 20 seconds. The Lock screen also appears if you resume computer use after the system has gone into sleep mode. Depending on your PC or mobile device, turning on or resuming system use from sleep mode involves pressing the Power button or moving a mouse.

Each person who uses a PC or mobile device will have his or her own **user account**. A user account includes a user name and a password. Windows stores program and settings information for each user's account so that each person can customize options without conflicting with the setttings for other people who use the computer. In Windows 8, Microsoft provides for two types of user accounts at sign-in: a Microsoft account or a local account.

App Tip

Signing in with a Microsoft account is considered connecting to the cloud. Your apps, games, music, photos, files, and settings are stored online and can be used or viewed from any other Windows 8 device.

Signing In with a Microsoft Account

A user account that has been set up as a **Microsoft account** means that you sign in to Windows 8 using an email address from hotmail.com or live.com (referred to as a Windows Live ID). A Microsoft account means you can download new apps from the Windows store, see live updates from messaging and social media services in tiles, and sync your Windows and browser settings online so that you see the same settings when you sign in on a different device.

Signing In with a Local Account

A user account that has been set up as a **local account** means that Windows and browser settings on the PC or mobile device cannot be shared with other devices and that automatic connections to messaging and social media services do not work.

Note: The screens shown throughout this textbook show Windows 8 signed in with a Microsoft account.

1 Turn on the computer or mobile device, or resume system use from sleep mode.

You can customize the image that appears on the Lock screen.

Status and notifications appear here from Mail, Messaging, and Calendar by default. You can add other apps to your Lock screen notifications area.

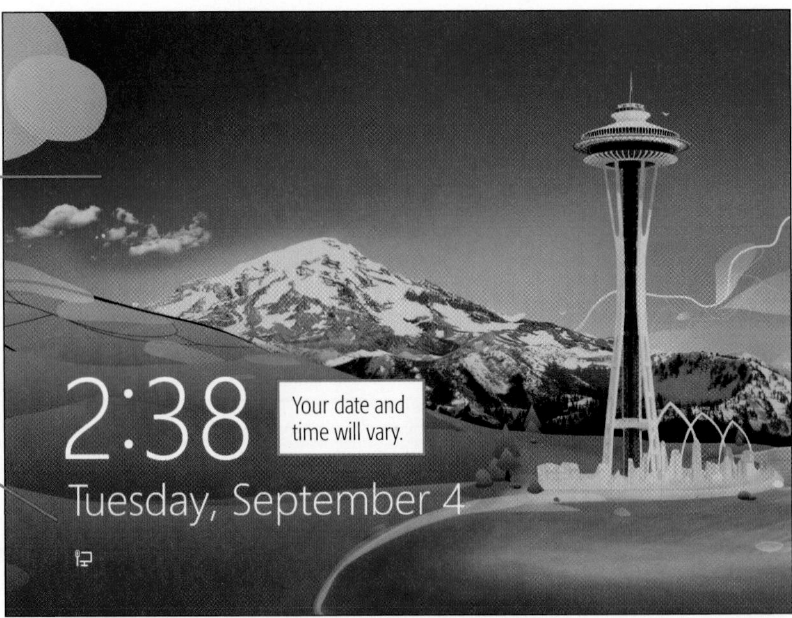

Your date and time will vary.
Tuesday, September 4

Figure 1.4 The Windows 8 lock screen appears after you start up the computer from a no power state or when resuming use from sleep mode.

2 At the Lock screen shown in Figure 1.4 on the previous page, swipe up from the bottom edge of the screen, click anywhere on the screen, or press any key on the keyboard to reveal the sign-in screen.

3 Depending on the system, the next step will vary. Complete the sign-in by following the steps in 3a, 3b, or 3c that match the configuration of your PC or mobile device:

a. Type your password in the *Password* text box below your Microsoft account name and email address and tap or press Enter, or tap or click the Submit button (displays as a right-pointing arrow).

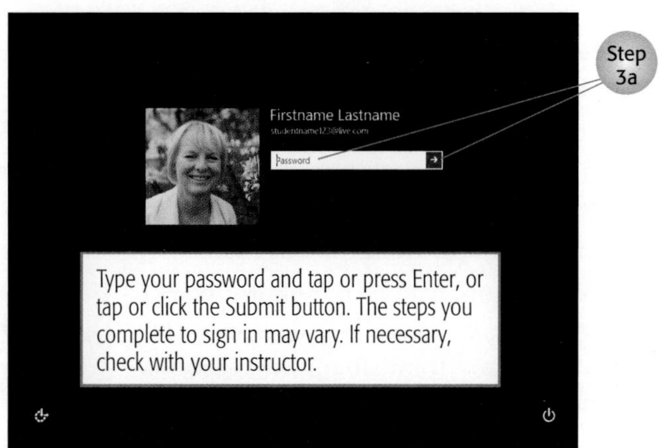
Step 3a
Firstname Lastname
Password
Type your password and tap or press Enter, or tap or click the Submit button. The steps you complete to sign in may vary. If necessary, check with your instructor.

oops!

Your account is not shown on the sign-in screen? Tap or click Switch user (left-pointing arrow inside circle) next to the existing account name to see a list of accounts set up for the device. If necessary, check with your instructor for sign-in instructions.

b. Perform the touch gestures over your account's picture password.

c. If more than one user account is shown on the sign-in screen, tap or click the account picture or icon you want to use. Type your password in the *Password* text box and tap or press Enter, or tap or click the Submit button (displays as a right-pointing arrow).

The Start Screen

Once signed in, the Start screen, similar to the one shown in Figure 1.5, appears. The Start screen displays a series of tiles that are used to launch apps. A tile is a square or rectangle with an icon and name for an app.

App Tip

Slide left and right or scroll to view more tiles. Pinch the Start screen or click the button at the bottom right corner that displays like a minus symbol to zoom out and see all tiles as miniatures. Stretch the Start screen or click anywhere on the screen to return tiles to normal size.

Start
Your Start screen tiles, placement, and groupings may vary.
Firstname
Live tiles show real time updates.
Tiles for installed programs appear in this group and are called Desktop apps.
14
NASDAQ

Figure 1.5 The Windows 8 Start screen. Apps are accessed from tiles, some of which display live updates.

Some tiles display status updates or notifications such as the number of new email messages, a weather update, a breaking news headline, or a status update from a Facebook friend. The Start screen and tiles are customizable. You will learn about customization in a later topic.

In the next steps, you will explore the Windows 8 environment by launching apps and switching between apps.

Launching an App

Built-in apps for Windows 8 include Microsoft Mail, Calendar, Internet Explorer, Store, People, Photos, Maps, SkyDrive, Desktop, Messaging, Weather, News, Bing, Travel, Finance, Sports, Games, Camera, Music, and Video. Apps in Windows 8 automatically run in full-screen mode.

To launch an app, tap or click the app's tile from the Start screen. You can return to the Start screen using a touch gesture or mouse action, or by pressing the Windows logo key on the keyboard.

4 Tap or click the **Photos app** from the Start screen.

Step 4

Photos

Your Photos tile may vary, showing images if the tile is live.

The Photos app shows thumbnails of the photos stored in the Pictures library on the PC or mobile device, in the Pictures folder in SkyDrive, and from albums in Facebook and Flickr if the services have been connected.

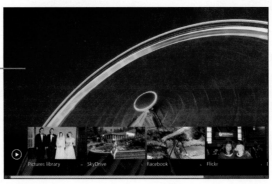

Your Photos app will vary. SkyDrive, Facebook, and Flickr will not show images if the services have not been connected to your Microsoft account or you are signed in with a local account.

Pictures library SkyDrive Facebook Flickr

oops!

Calendar does not appear? If you are signed in with a local account, the Calendar does not show. Tap or click Cancel, press the Windows logo key, and launch the News app instead. Substitute News app for Calendar in the rest of this topic.

5 Swipe in from the right edge of the screen and tap Start, or press the Windows logo key on the keyboard.

6 Tap or click the **Calendar app** from the Start screen.

The Calendar for the current month loads. Those connected to Facebook see birthday reminders in their calendars.

Your Calendar tile will vary, showing reminders from your connected services.

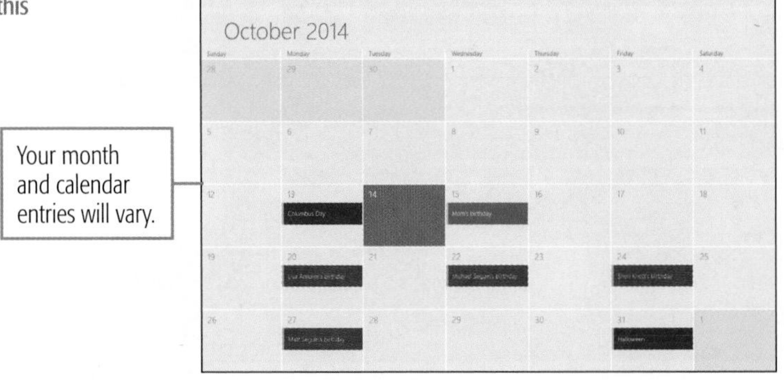

Your month and calendar entries will vary.

7 Swipe in from the right edge of the screen and tap Start, or move the pointer to the lower left corner of the screen until a thumbnail of the Start screen appears and then click the left mouse button.

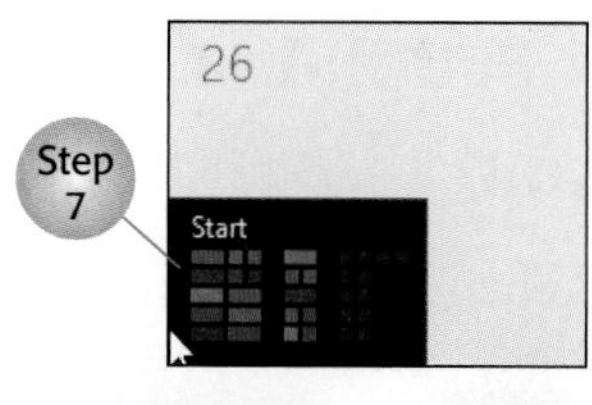

8 Tap or click the **Store app** from the Start screen.

In the Store app you can search for and download new apps for your PC or mobile device.

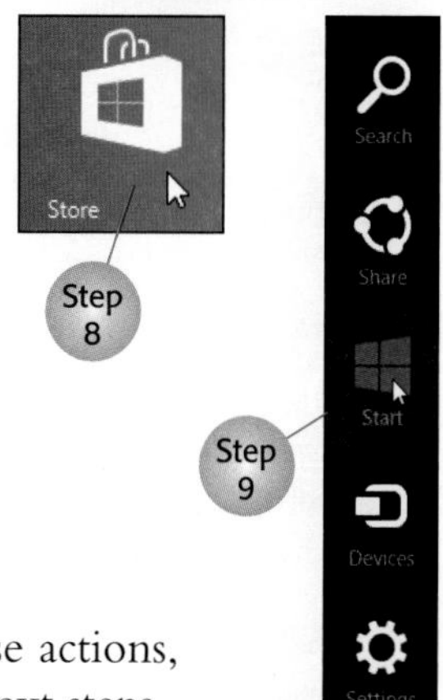

9 Swipe in from the right edge of the screen and tap Start, or move the pointer to the top right or bottom right corner, slide the pointer down or up along the right edge when you see the five icons (called charms) appear in a column, and then click the Start charm (third from the top).

Switching between Apps

You can switch to an open app using touch gestures or mouse actions, or by pressing Alt plus the Tab key on the keyboard. In the next steps you will switch between the Photos, Calendar, and Store apps.

10 Swipe in from the left edge of the screen a short distance and immediately swipe back to the left edge, or move the pointer to the top left corner of the screen until a thumbnail of the Store app appears and then move the pointer down along the left edge to see thumbnails of all open apps.

11 Tap or click the Photos app.

12 Hold down the Alt key on the keyboard and press the Tab key repeatedly to cycle through the open app windows one at a time. Notice the selected app displays with a border around it in the middle of the screen where the open apps are listed. Release the Alt key when the Calendar app is selected. Skip this step if you are using a tablet with no keyboard.

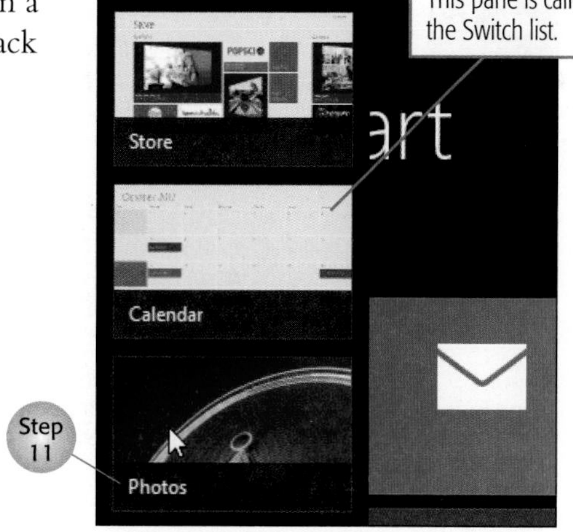

13 Press the Windows logo key on the keyboard to return to the Start screen.

Quick STEPS

Start Windows 8 and Sign In
1. Turn on power or resume system from sleep mode.
2. Swipe up or click to remove Lock screen.
3. Type password and tap or press Enter, or tap or click Submit button.

Launch an App
Tap or click tile for app in Start screen.

Switch between Apps
1. Swipe in from left edge and immediately swipe back, or point to top left corner and move down until vertical list of open apps appears.
2. Tap or click desired app.

App Tip

With a touch-enabled device, you can switch between open apps by swiping in (also called thumbing in) from the left edge of the screen. As you swipe inward, the last open app comes into view and fills the screen as you continue moving your finger or thumb inward. Repeat the motion until you return to the desired app.

View All Apps at Start Screen

See a list of all apps on your PC or mobile device at the Start screen by swiping up from the bottom or right-clicking, and tapping or clicking All Apps. At the time of publication, early reports on Windows 8.1 (due to be available in the fall of 2013) indicate the All Apps button will appear at the bottom left of the Start screen.

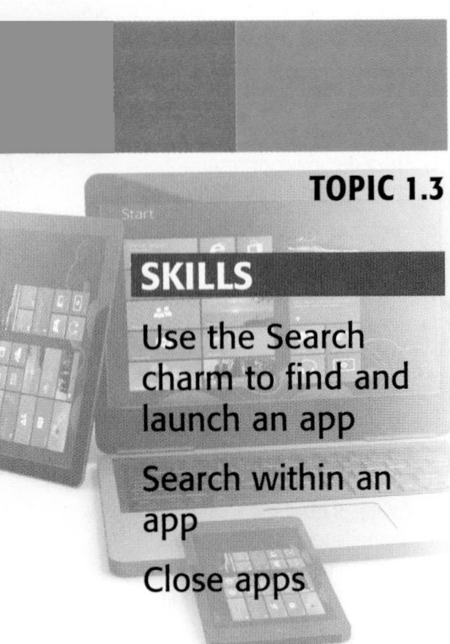

TOPIC 1.3
SKILLS
Use the Search charm to find and launch an app
Search within an app
Close apps

Revealing the Charms Bar, Searching for an App, and Closing Apps

When you swipe in from the right edge of the screen or move the pointer to the top right corner or bottom right corner, the **Charms bar** shown in Figure 1.6 appears.

Charms are used to access system resources and commands. As you saw in the previous topic, the Start charm is used to return to the Start screen. The Search charm is used to search for something in apps, settings, files, or the Web. You can use Search to find a program, a document or other type of file, a setting in an application or the control panel, or search for a word or phrase within an app. Search can be used to quickly find and launch a program rather than scrolling through the Start screen, or find a program that does not have a tile on the Start screen.

In Windows 8 you do not need to close apps. When you switch to another app, the app you switched from remains running in the background and will eventually close if not used. However, you can close an app if you are done with it by swiping from the top edge of the screen down to the bottom, or by dragging the pointer when it changes to a hand at the top edge of the screen down to the bottom edge of the screen.

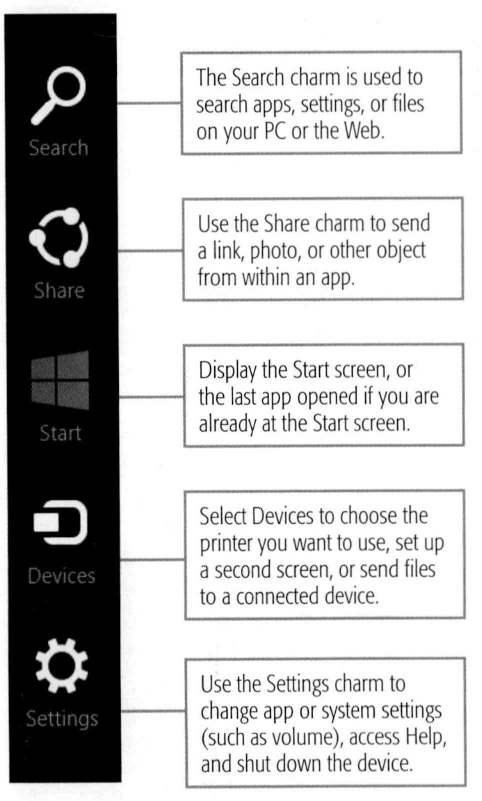

Search
Your Apps list will vary.
Share
Start
Devices
Settings
The Search charm is used to search apps, settings, or files on your PC or the Web.
Use the Share charm to send a link, photo, or other object from within an app.
Display the Start screen, or the last app opened if you are already at the Start screen.
Select Devices to choose the printer you want to use, set up a second screen, or send files to a connected device.
Use the Settings charm to change app or system settings (such as volume), access Help, and shut down the device.

Figure 1.6 The Charms bar displays when you swipe in from the right edge of the screen or point at the top right corner or bottom right corner.

1. At the Start screen, display the Charms bar by swiping in from the right edge of the screen or by moving the pointer to the top right or bottom right corner and sliding up or down the edge of the screen.
2. Tap or click the Search charm.

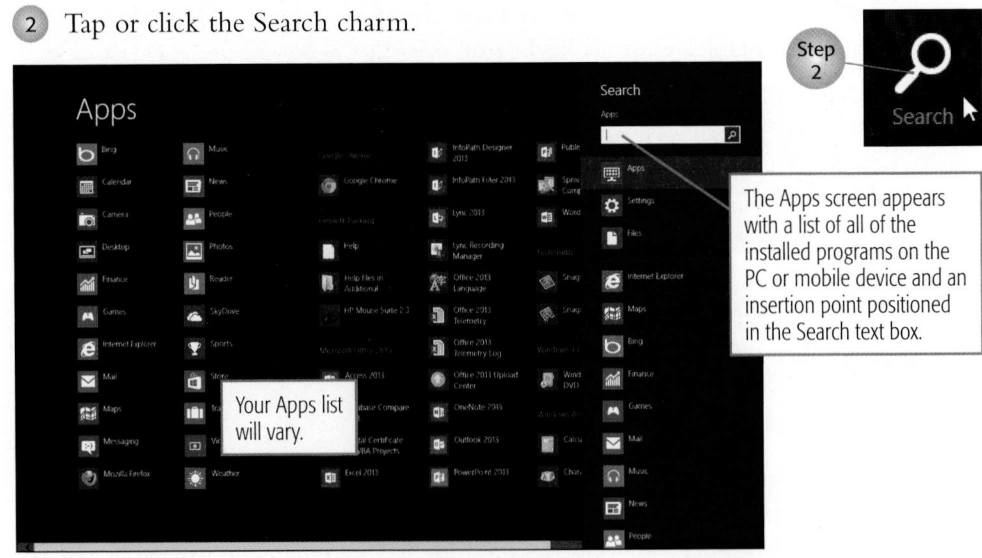

The Search charm changes focus depending on the app that is open. For example, in the Photos app, the search defaults to searching the Pictures library.

3 Type **ma**. (If necessary, tap inside the text box to bring up the touch keyboard.)

As soon as you start typing, Windows returns a list of programs that match the text in real time. Each letter typed narrows the search results.

4 Tap or click *Maps* in the search results list to launch the Maps app. If prompted, tap or click Allow to use your location and turn on location services.

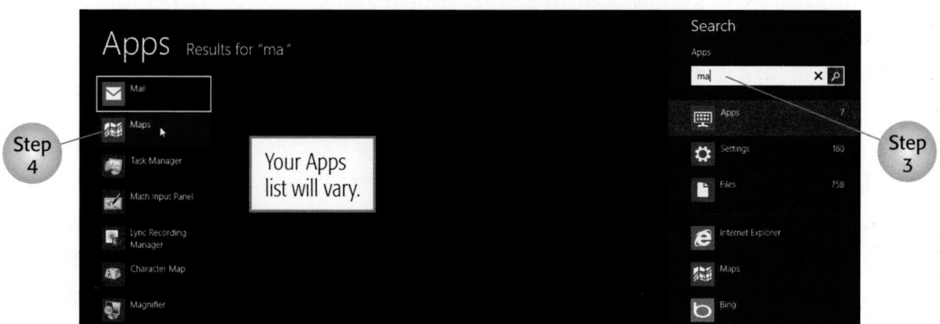

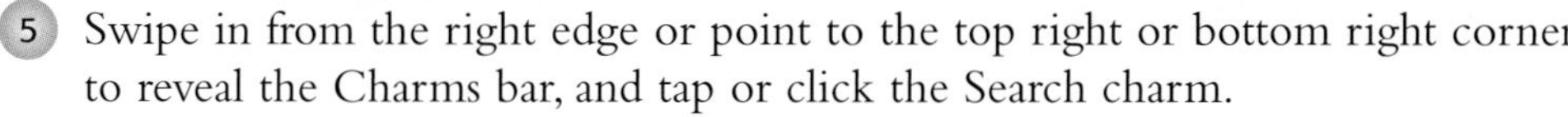

5 Swipe in from the right edge or point to the top right or bottom right corner to reveal the Charms bar, and tap or click the Search charm.

Notice the Search text box reads *Search for a location or business* and Maps is selected in the Apps list because the Search charm was launched inside Maps.

6 Type **McDonald's Restaurants** and press Enter or tap or click the Search button (displays as a magnifying glass).

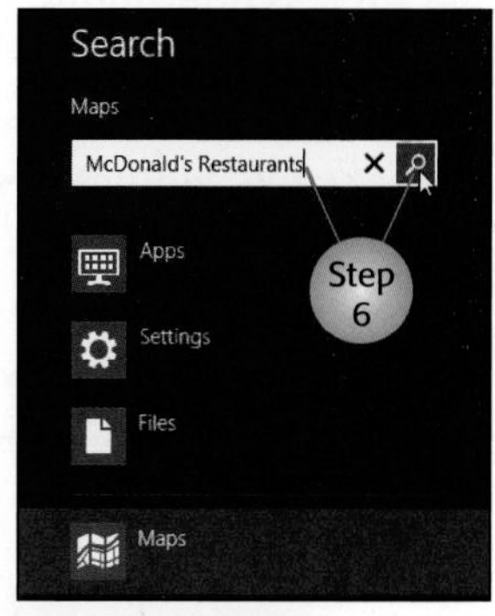

The locations of McDonald's Restaurants in your area are highlighted on the map with the corresponding addresses along the top of the screen.

7 Swipe from the top edge of the screen all the way to the bottom, or point to the top edge of the screen until the pointer changes to a hand and drag down to the bottom of the screen to close the Maps app.

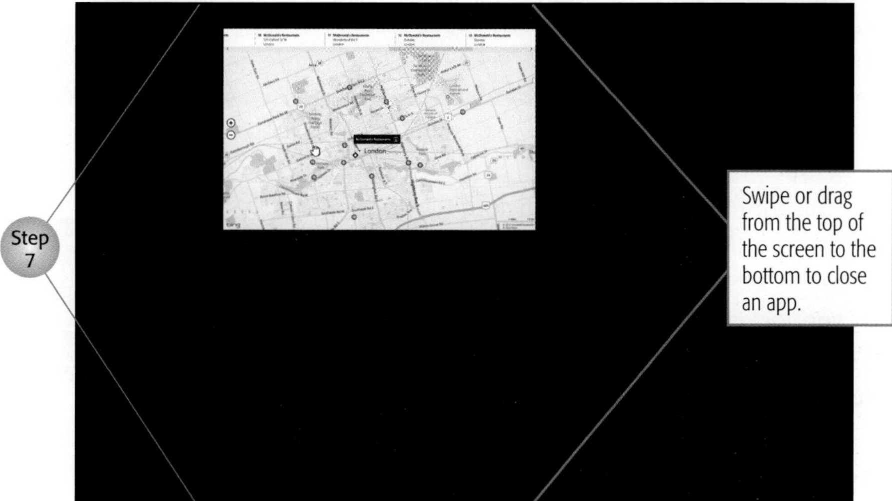

8 Switch to the Calendar app and swipe or drag from the top of the screen down to the bottom of the screen to close the app.

9 Repeat Step 8 to close the Photos app and the Store app.

Reveal the Charms Bar
Swipe in from right edge of screen, or point at top right corner or bottom right corner.

Search for an App
1. Reveal Charms bar.
2. Tap or click Search.
3. Type name of app you want to find.

Close an App
Swipe or drag from top edge of screen to bottom edge of screen.

oops!

No results for McDonald's Restaurants in your area? Change the search text to the name of a restaurant you know exists in your area, or tap or click the Close button in the message box that says no results were found.

The keyboard command Alt + F4 closes an app.

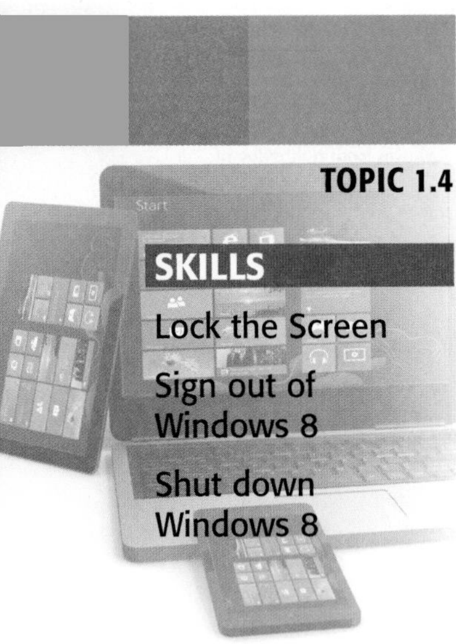

Locking the Screen, Signing Out, and Shutting Down Windows 8

If you need to leave your PC or mobile device for a short period of time and do not want to close all of your apps and documents, you can lock the device. Locking the system causes the lock screen image to appear full screen so that someone else cannot see your work. All of your apps and documents are left open in the background so that you can resume work right away once you enter your account password.

1. At the Start screen, tap or click the Photos tile to launch the Photos app.
2. Press the Windows logo key on the keyboard, or swipe in from the right and tap Start to return to the Start screen.
3. Tap or click your account name at the top right corner of the screen.
4. Tap or click *Lock* at the drop-down list.

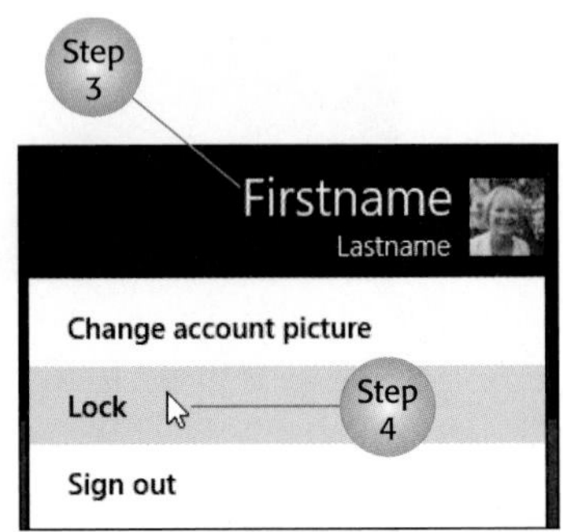

The Windows lock screen appears with the current date and time. Notifications appear below the date to show network connectivity status, power status, and updates from apps such as mail.

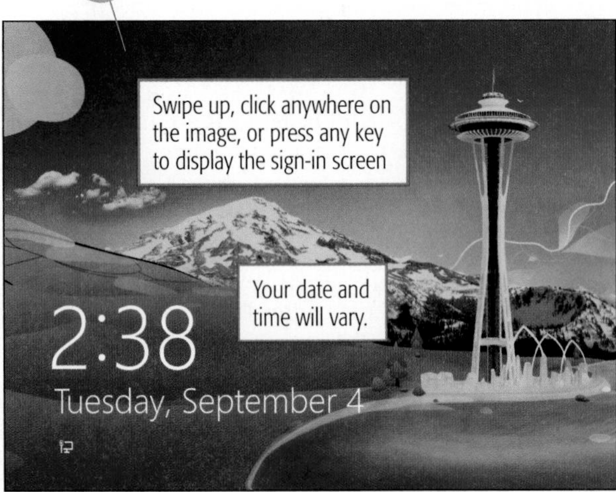

5. Swipe up, click anywhere on the lock screen, or press any key on the keyboard to display the sign-in screen.
6. Type your password in the *Password* text box and tap or press Enter, or tap or click the Submit button to return to the Start screen.
7. Swipe in from the left edge or click at the top left corner of the screen when the Photos app thumbnail appears to return to the Photos app.

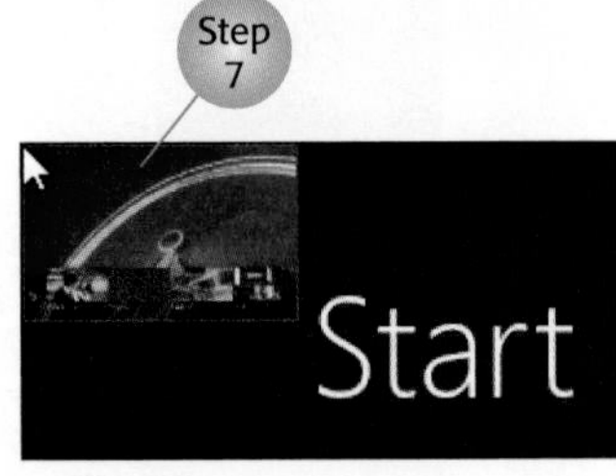

When you locked the screen, the Photos app stayed open in the background.

8. Display the Start screen.

If you have documents open, Windows prompts you to save changes before proceeding with the sign-out process.

Signing Out of a Windows Session

When you are finished with a Windows session, you should **sign out** of the PC or mobile device. Signing out is also referred to as **logging off**. Signing out closes all apps and files. If a computer or mobile device is shared with other people, signing out is expected so that the next user can sign in to his or her account. Signing out and locking also provide security for your device because someone would need to know your password to access programs or files.

9 At the Start screen, tap or click your account name and tap or click *Sign out* at the drop-down list.

The Windows lock screen appears; however, this time Windows closes the Photos app automatically.

10 Display the sign-in screen, type your password and tap or press Enter, or tap or click the Submit button.

11 Swipe in from the left edge or point to the top left corner. Notice that nothing happens because no apps were left open when you signed out.

Shutting Down the PC or Mobile Device

If you want to turn off the power to your computer or mobile device, perform a **shut down**. Shutting down the system ensures that all Windows files are properly closed. The power will turn off automatically when shut down is complete.

12 Swipe in from the right edge, or point to the top right corner or bottom right corner to reveal the Charms bar, and tap or click the Settings charm.

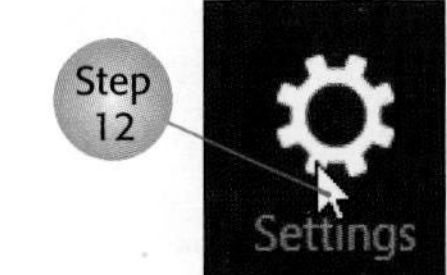

13 Tap or click Power at the bottom of the Settings pane.

Note: Check with your instructor before proceeding to Step 14 because some schools do not allow students to shut down computers. If necessary, tap or click two times in an unused area of the Start screen to remove the Power pop-up list and Settings pane and proceed to the next topic.

14 Tap or click *Shut down* at the pop-up list.

The system will perform the shut down operation, and in a few seconds the power will turn off.

15 Wait a moment or two and then press the Power button to turn the PC or mobile device back on.

16 When the lock screen appears, display the sign-in screen and sign back in to Windows.

Quick STEPS

Lock PC or Mobile Device
1. Tap or click account name at top right corner of screen.
2. Tap or click *Lock*.

Sign Out of Windows
1. Tap or click account name at top right corner of screen.
2. Tap or click *Sign out*.

Shut Down PC or Mobile Device
1. Reveal Charms bar.
2. Tap or click Settings charm.
3. Tap or click Power.
4. Tap or click *Shut down*.

In the *Balanced* power plan (the default power option), the system will automatically go into sleep mode after 15 minutes (battery power) or 30 minutes (plugged in).

Other Power Options

Use the *Sleep* option from the Power pop-up list if you are leaving the computer for a while and want to leave all programs and documents open but use less power. Choose *Restart* to shut down Windows and immediately start it up again without turning off the power. A restart may be needed if the system is not performing correctly, hangs, or is otherwise not responding.

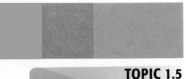

TOPIC 1.5

SKILLS

- Pin/Unpin tiles to/from the Start screen
- Move tiles
- Resize tiles
- Turn on and off live updates

Customizing the Start Screen

You can personalize the Start screen to suit your preferences by adding or removing tiles, rearranging tiles, resizing a tile larger or smaller, and by turning a live tile off to stop notifications and updates from appearing in the tile.

Note: In some school computer labs, the ability to change Windows settings is disabled. If necessary, complete this topic and the next topic on your PC or mobile device at home.

Selecting a Tile

Select a tile using a touch gesture by pulling the tile down a short distance until you see a check mark appear and then releasing the tile. Select a tile using the mouse by right-clicking the tile. Once selected, a tile displays a check mark in the upper right corner of the tile, and app commands appear along the bottom of the screen, as shown in Figure 1.7.

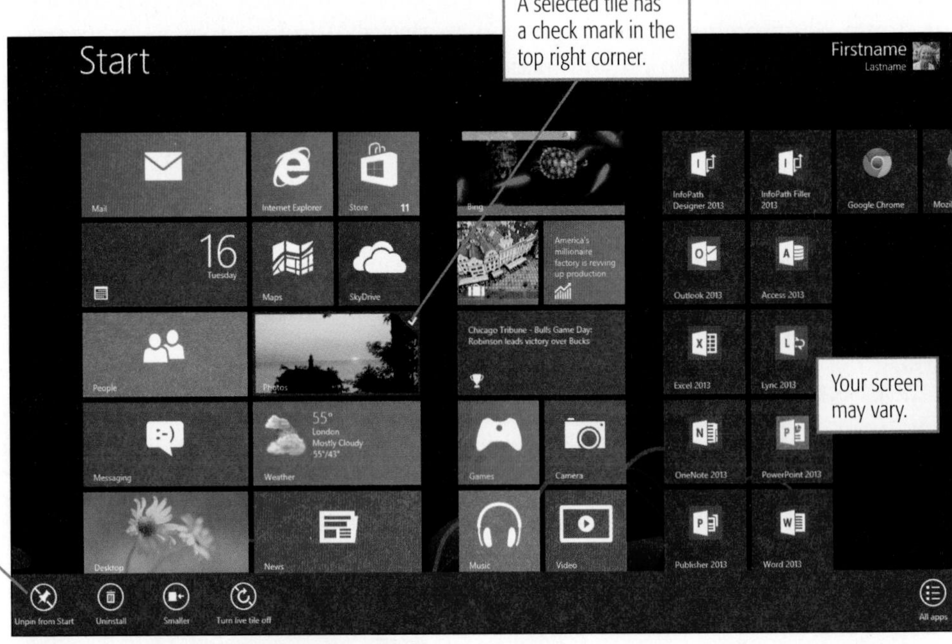

Figure 1.7 Selecting a tile on the Start screen displays tile options along the bottom of the screen to unpin the tile, uninstall the app, resize the tile, or turn off live updates (if the tile is live).

Pinning and Unpinning Tiles to and from the Start Screen

Select a tile to reveal the commands along the bottom of the screen and choose **Unpin from Start** to remove the tile from the Start screen. A tile can be added to the Start screen by selecting the tile in the Apps list and choosing **Pin to Start**.

oops!

No Weather tile on the Start screen? Select any other tile to remove. You will repin the tile to Start after you practice removing it.

1. Select the Weather tile by pulling the tile down a short distance and releasing it or by right-clicking the tile.
2. Tap or click Unpin from Start to remove the tile from the Start screen.

3 Swipe up from the bottom edge of the screen or right-click in an unused area of the Start screen.

4 Tap or click All Apps.

5 Select the Weather tile and tap or click Pin to Start.

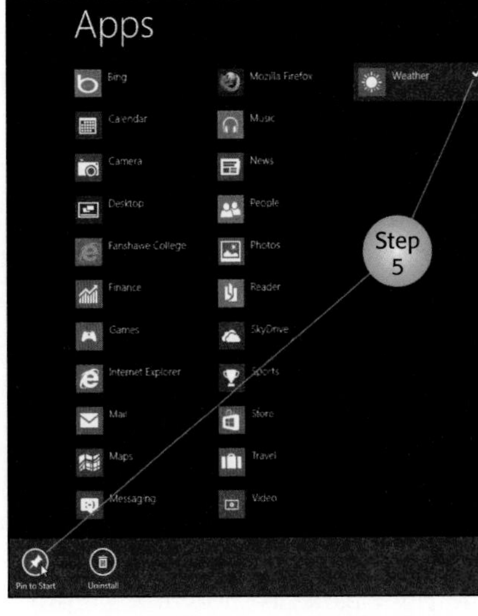

The Weather tile is added back to the Start screen.

6 Display the Start screen and slide or scroll right if necessary to see the Weather tile.

Notice the Weather tile is added to the right end of the Start screen tiles.

Rearranging Tiles

Tiles can be moved to a new location on the Start screen by sliding the tile using touch or by dragging the tile using the mouse to the desired location.

7 Move the Weather tile back to its original location in the Start screen by sliding the tile down and across, or by dragging the tile using the mouse.

As you move the tile down and across the Start screen, the tile is dimmed and you will notice other tiles shifting around to make room for the tile.

Resizing a Tile and Turning Off Live Updates

Built-in app tiles are either square or rectangular in shape. Some of the square-shaped tiles can be made larger and the rectangular-shaped tiles can be made smaller. Select the tile and choose Larger or Smaller in the App commands.

Some tiles display live updates by default. For example, the Finance and Sports tiles display headlines from financial and sports news throughout the day, and the Mail tile displays the number of new messages received along with a few lines of each new message. Live updates can be turned off by selecting the tile and choosing **Turn live tile off** in the app commands.

8 Select the Finance tile and tap or click Larger or Smaller depending on the current setting.

9 Select the Finance tile and tap or click Turn live tile off.

The Finance tile displays an image of a chart with an upward trending arrow when live updates are off.

10 Select the Finance tile and tap or click Larger or Smaller to resize the tile back to its original size.

11 Select the Finance tile and tap or click Turn live tile on.

Select a Tile
Pull down short distance and release, or right-click desired tile.

Remove a Tile from the Start Screen
1. Select tile.
2. Tap or click Unpin from Start.

Add a Tile to the Start Screen
1. Swipe up from bottom or right-click.
2. Tap or click All Apps.
3. Select tile.
4. Tap or click Pin to Start.

Rearrange Tiles
Slide or drag tile to desired location.

Resize a Tile
1. Select tile.
2. Tap or click Larger or Smaller.

Turn Off/On Live Updates
1. Select tile.
2. Tap or click Turn live tile off or Turn live tile on.

Start screen is miniaturized? If you drag a tile to the bottom of the screen, the Start screen zooms out to show all of the tiles as miniatures. Release the tile and the Start screen will return to normal size.

oops!

No Finance tile? Select any other live tile to customize. In Steps 10 and 11 you restore the tile's original settings.

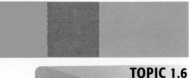

TOPIC 1.6

SKILLS

Change the Lock screen background image

Add an app to the Lock screen notifications

Change the Start screen design and color scheme

Personalizing the Start and Lock Screens

Most people like to put a personal stamp on their PC or mobile device. In Windows 8, you can personalize the Lock screen by changing the picture that displays and the apps that provide notifications when the screen locks. The Start screen can be personalized to a different color scheme and design behind the tiles.

Display the Charms bar, tap or click the Settings charm, and tap or click **Change PC settings** at the bottom right of the Settings pane to change the Lock and Start screen settings at the PC settings window, as shown in Figure 1.8.

1. At the Start screen, swipe in from the right edge, or point to the top right corner or bottom right corner to reveal the Charms bar, and tap or click the Settings charm.
2. Tap or click Change PC settings at the bottom right of the Settings pane.

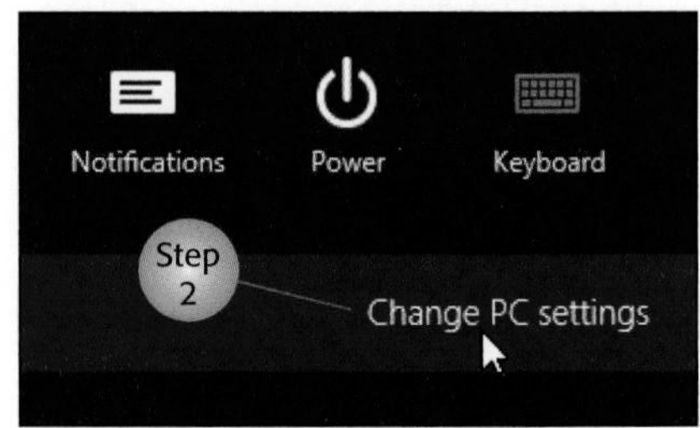

By default, the *Personalize* category with *Lock screen* options are active. The current Lock screen image is shown above five thumbnails for other background pictures in the right pane, as shown in Figure 1.8. Tap or click a different picture to preview the image or tap or click the Browse button to choose a picture on your PC or mobile device to use as the Lock screen image.

Did You Know?

At the time of publication, early reports on Windows 8.1 (due to be available in the fall of 2013) suggest that Personalize *will be accessed directly from the Settings charm.*

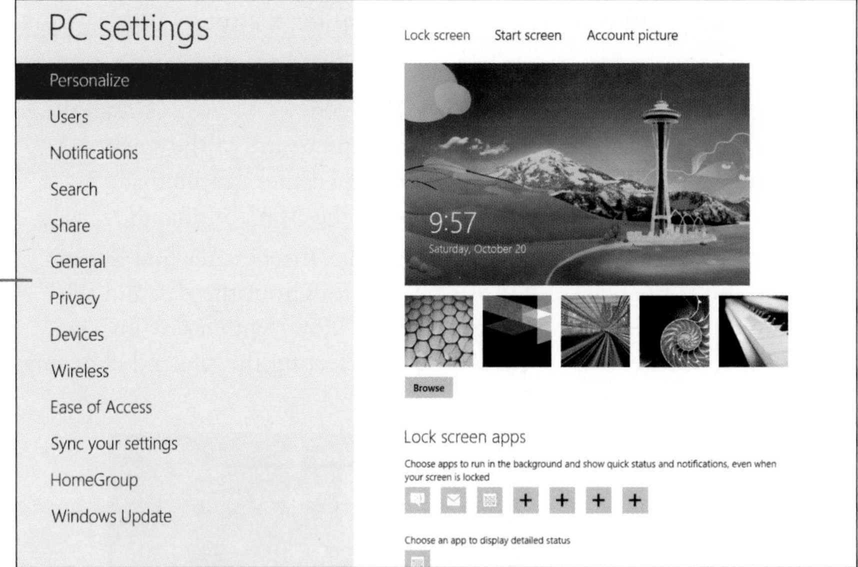

Figure 1.8 In the PC settings window, *Personalize* and *Lock screen* are selected by default. From PC settings you can make changes to your system by choosing a category in the left pane and changing options for the category in the right pane.

3. Tap or click one of the five background thumbnails below the current Lock screen image. You determine the background image you want to view.

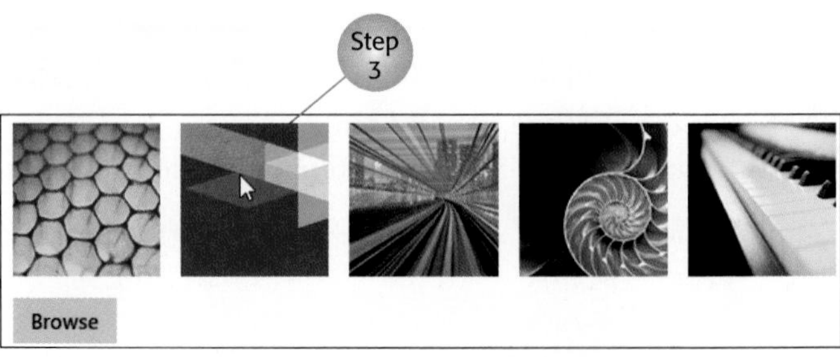

oops!

Lock screen options not shown? Tap or click Lock screen at the top of the PC settings window to display the options.

By default, the Messaging, Mail, and Calendar apps provide quick status and notifications on the Lock screen.

4 Tap or click the first button with a plus symbol in the Lock screen apps section and tap or click *Weather* at the pop-up *Choose an app* list.

The Weather app will now provide notifications when the screen is locked.

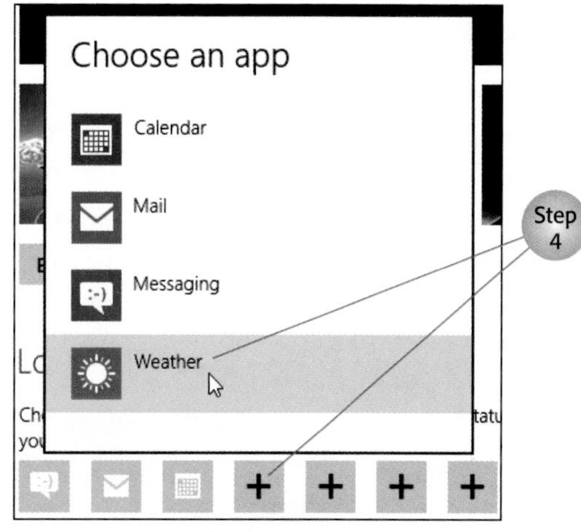

5 Tap or click Start screen at the top of the PC settings window.

6 Tap or click one of the 20 designs below the image of the current Start screen background. You determine the design you want to view.

7 Slide or drag the color slider to change the color of the Start screen background and designs. You determine the color you want to view.

8 Display the Start screen to view the new design and color scheme.

9 Tap or click your account name at the top right of the Start screen and tap or click *Lock* to view the new background.

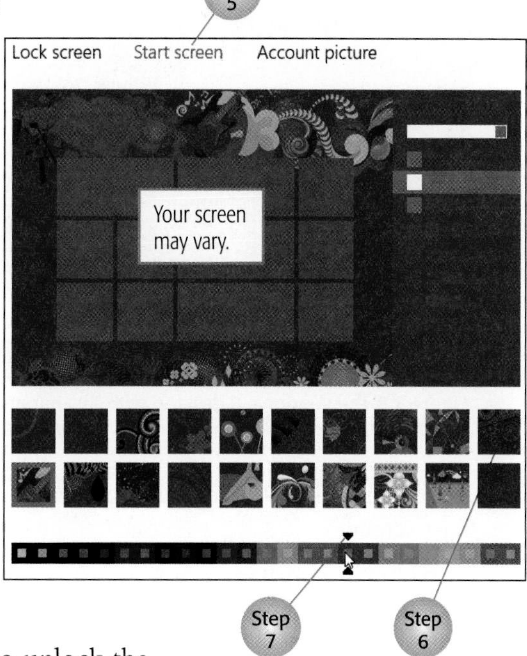

10 Sign back in with your password to unlock the system.

Note: Check with your instructor if you are completing this topic in a school computer lab to see if he or she wants you to restore the Lock and Start screen to the original settings by redoing Steps 1 through 8 and choosing the default Lock screen and Start screen options. Remove the Weather app from the Lock screen notifications by tapping or clicking the Weather button and tapping or clicking* Don't show quick status here *at the top of the Choose an app list.

Change the Lock Screen Background

1. Reveal Charms bar.
2. Tap or click Settings.
3. Tap or click Change PC settings.
4. Tap or click desired background picture.
5. Display Start screen.

Add an App to the Lock Screen

1. Reveal Charms bar.
2. Tap or click Settings.
3. Tap or click Change PC settings.
4. Tap or click first plus symbol button in Lock screen apps section.
5. Tap or click desired app.
6. Display Start screen.

Change Start Screen Design or Color Scheme

1. Reveal Charms bar.
2. Tap or click Settings.
3. Tap or click Change PC settings.
4. Tap or click Start screen.
5. Tap or click desired design.
6. Slide or drag color scheme slider to desired color.
7. Display Start screen.

When you are signed in with a Microsoft account, your Lock and Start screen settings are saved online. Sign in from another PC or mobile device and your new background, design, and color scheme will appear on the other device.

Adding a Picture for your Account

Tap or click Account picture at the top of the PC settings window to add a picture to your account name on the Start screen. Tap or click the Browse button and navigate to the image file you want to use at the Files window. You can also use the Camera button to take a new picture of yourself using your PC or mobile device webcam.

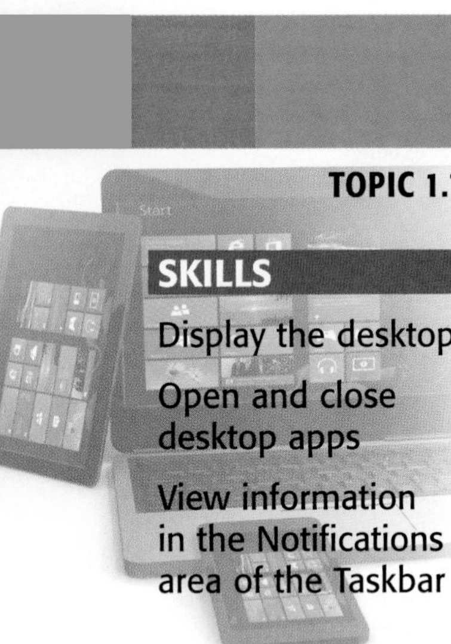

TOPIC 1.7
SKILLS
Display the desktop
Open and close desktop apps
View information in the Notifications area of the Taskbar

Did You Know?

At the time of publication, early reports on Windows 8.1 (due to be available in the fall of 2013) indicate that Microsoft is considering an option to start Windows directly in Desktop mode and to bring back the Start button.

Some apps such as Internet Explorer offer both an app and a desktop version. Desktop apps offer the traditional user interface from Windows 7 and earlier and include more features.

Using the Desktop

For people who have used Windows 7 or earlier, the desktop is a familiar place. The **Desktop** tile on the Start screen opens a window with the Windows 8 desktop, as shown in Figure 1.9. With the exception of the Start button being removed, the Windows 8 desktop functions the same as the desktop in Windows 7.

You will use the desktop in Windows 8 for applications that are considered desktop apps such as Microsoft Word or Microsoft Excel. Even Windows 8 accessory programs such as Notepad or Calculator open on the desktop.

Figure 1.9 The Windows 8 desktop with Taskbar and desktop icons is used for working in desktop apps such as File Explorer, in which you perform tasks such as copying or moving files.

1. Tap or click the Desktop tile from the Start screen.

The **Recycle Bin** icon is at the top left corner. Icons for other desktop programs that are installed on your computer may also appear on your desktop. The **Taskbar** along the bottom of the window contains an icon to launch Internet Explorer and **File Explorer**. Other program icons may also be pinned to the Taskbar. The **Notification area** at the right end of the Taskbar shows the current date and time, speaker icon, network status indicator, and Action Center flag. A power status indicator and other icons may also appear in your Notification area depending on the desktop programs installed on your PC or mobile device.

2. Double-tap or double-click the Recycle Bin icon on the desktop.

Double-tapping or double-clicking launches programs from an icon on the desktop. Desktop apps window features are described in Figure 1.10 on the next page. You will learn more about desktop windows in the next topic.

3. Tap or click the **Close button** (red button with white ×) at the top right corner of the Recycle Bin window.

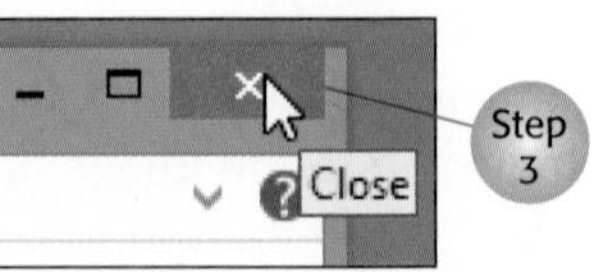

Show the Desktop
Tap or click Desktop tile.

Launch a Desktop App
Double-tap or double-click icon on desktop OR tap or click icon in Taskbar.

4 Tap or click the File Explorer icon on the Taskbar.

File Explorer
Step 4

Programs with icons pinned to the Taskbar are opened with a single tap or click. You will learn more about File Explorer in the next three topics.

5 Tap or click the Close button at the top right corner of the Libraries window.

6 Tap or click the current date and time at the right end of the Taskbar.

Monday, October 20, 2014
October 2014
Your date/calendar and time will vary.
Change date and time settings...
Step 6

The current month's calendar appears above the date and time. You can change the date or time if necessary by tapping or clicking the Change date and time settings hyperlink to open a Date and Time dialog box.

7 Tap or click in an unused area of the desktop to remove the pop-up calendar.

8 Tap or click the Speakers icon at the right end of the Taskbar to open the Volume control slider.

Mixer
Step 8

You can drag the slider up or down to raise or lower the volume.

9 Tap or click in an unused area of the desktop to remove the volume slider.

10 Swipe in from the right edge or point to the top right corner or bottom right corner to reveal the Charms bar, and tap or click Start.

The Settings charm on the desktop provides options to personalize the desktop window and access the Control Panel from which you can control more system features.

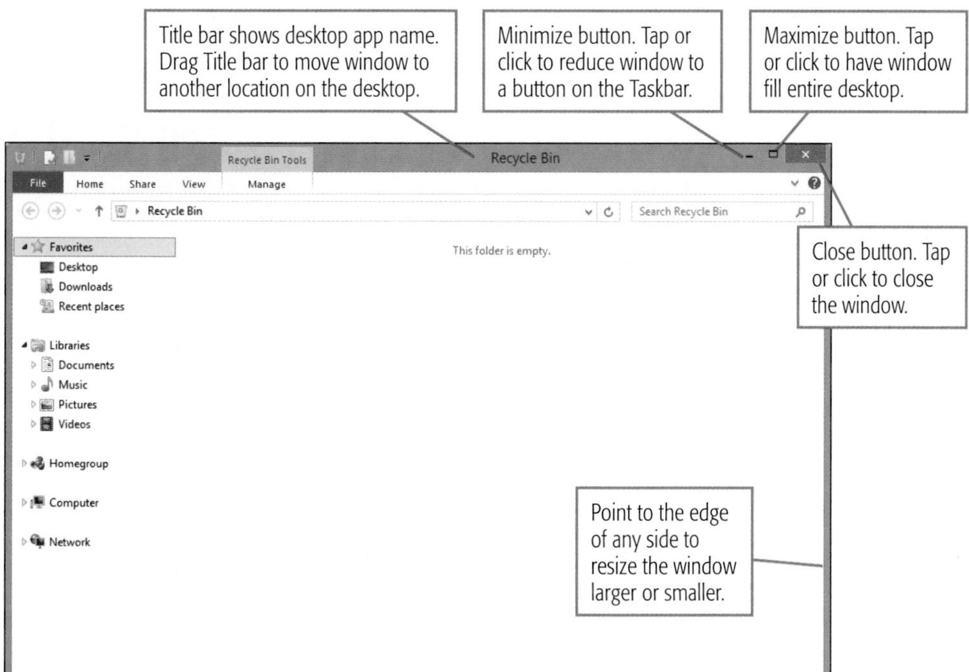
Title bar shows desktop app name. Drag Title bar to move window to another location on the desktop.
Minimize button. Tap or click to reduce window to a button on the Taskbar.
Maximize button. Tap or click to have window fill entire desktop.
Close button. Tap or click to close the window.
Point to the edge of any side to resize the window larger or smaller.
Recycle Bin
This folder is empty.

Figure 1.10 The Recycle Bin window. Desktop app windows contain standard features for moving, resizing, and closing windows.

The desktop is also opened automatically if you launch a desktop app from a Start screen tile or from the Search apps screen.

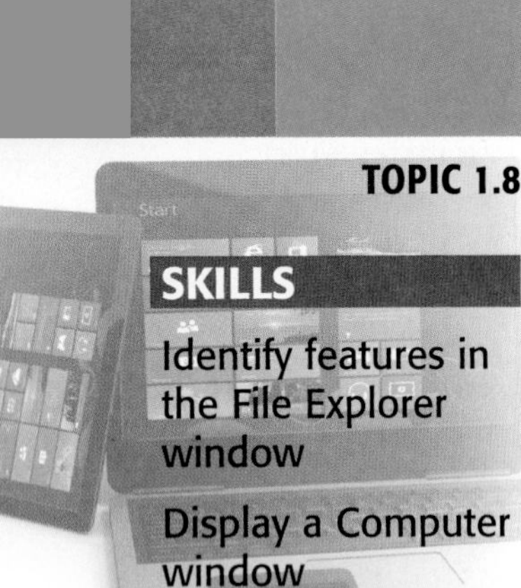

SKILLS

Identify features in the File Explorer window

Display a Computer window

Browse content of devices using File Explorer

Browsing Files with File Explorer

As you work on a PC or mobile device you are creating and modifying files. A **file** is a document, spreadsheet, presentation, picture, or any other text and/or image that you have saved as digital data. Files are also videos and songs that you play on your PC or mobile device. Each file has a unique **file name**, which is a series of characters you assign to the file when you save it that allows you to identify and retrieve the file later. File Explorer is the utility used to browse the contents of various storage devices and perform file management routines.

Note: You will need the student CD that came with this textbook and a USB flash drive to complete the steps in this topic and the next two topics.

1. Tap or click the Desktop tile from the Start screen.
2. Tap or click the File Explorer icon in the Taskbar.

A **Libraries window** opens. The features of the Libraries window are identified in Figure 1.11. Windows creates four libraries by default: Documents, Music, Pictures, and Videos. A **library** is a name associated with a group of related files.

A library can display files from multiple locations in one window. For example, the Pictures library could display images saved on the local hard disk drive, an external disk, and a network storage device.

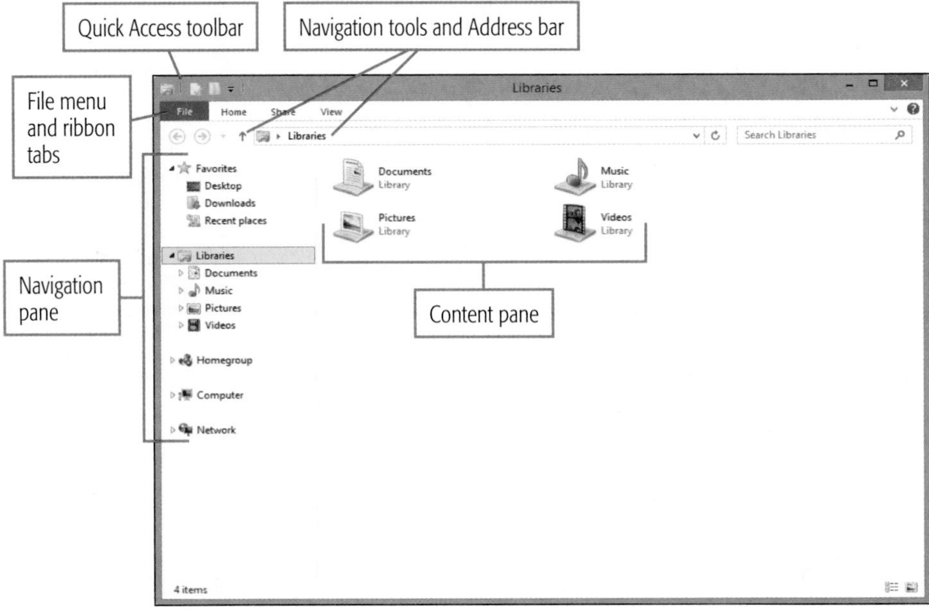

Figure 1.11 The Libraries window is divided into two panes. The Navigation pane at the left displays the list of places associated with the PC or mobile device. The right pane, called the Content pane, displays the files and folders stored in the selected item.

3. Tap or click Computer in the Navigation pane.

A **Computer window** displays all of the available storage options.

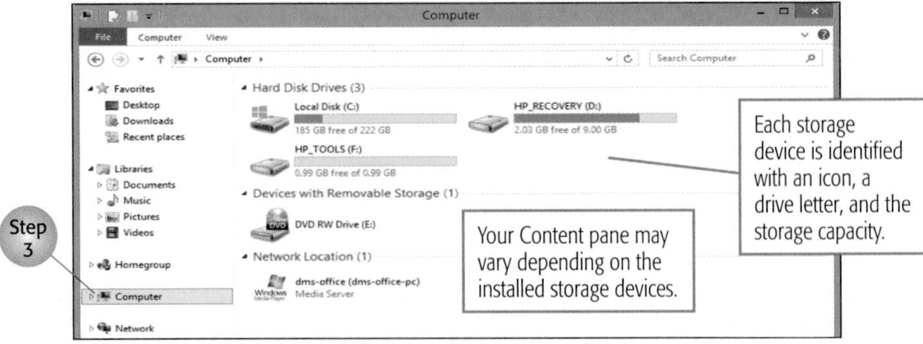

A Computer window contains all of the same features as a Libraries window.

4 Insert the student resources CD that came with this textbook into the DVD drive. If a new window opens for the DVD drive, tap or click the Close button to close the window.

5 Insert your USB flash drive into an empty USB port. If a new Removable Disk window opens, tap or click the Close button to close the window.

6 Double-tap or double-click the DVD drive in the *Devices with Removable Storage* section to view the contents of the student resources CD.

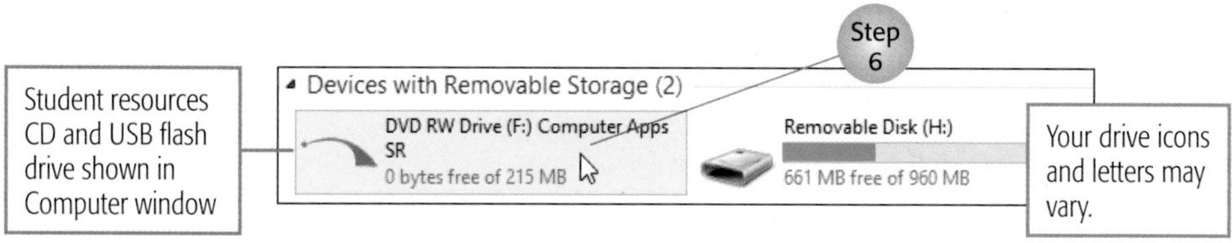

The Content pane shows the names of the folders on the student resources CD. A **folder** is a name assigned to a placeholder or container in which you store a group of related files. Think of a folder on the computer in the same way you consider a paper file folder in a desk drawer in your home. You might have one file folder for your household bills and another file folder for your school documents. Separating documents into different file folders makes storage and retrieval quicker and easier. Similarly, electronic files on a storage medium are organized into folders.

Folders

Step 7

7 Double-tap or double-click the folder named *Student_Data_Files*.

A list of folders stored within the Student_Data_Files folder appears. A folder within another folder is sometimes referred to as a **subfolder**.

Step 8

8 Double-tap or double-click the folder named *Ch1*.

A list of files stored in the Ch1 subfolder appears in the Content pane.

9 Tap or click Libraries in the Navigation pane.

You can browse content by tapping or clicking names in the Navigation pane or by double-tapping or double-clicking names in the Content pane.

10 Tap or click the Close button in the Libraries window Title bar.

11 Display the Start screen.

Note: Leave the Student Resources CD and your USB flash drive in the PC or mobile device for the next topics.

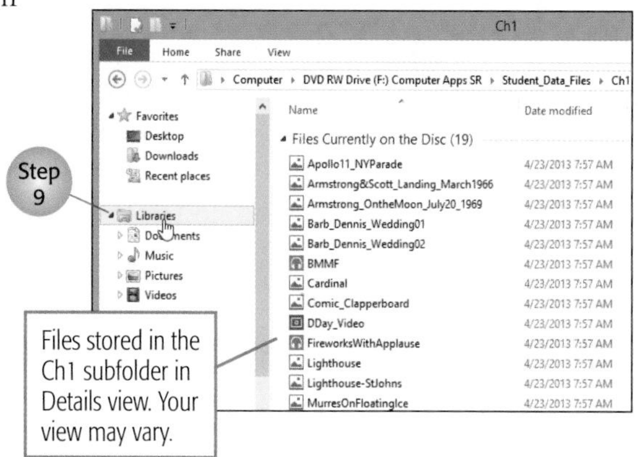

Browse Files in File Explorer

1. Display the desktop.
2. Tap or click File Explorer in the Taskbar.
3. If necessary, insert a removable storage medium such as a DVD or USB flash drive.
4. Tap or click desired location or device in Navigation pane OR tap twice or double-click a folder or device name in Content pane.

oops!

Using a tablet or other device with no DVD drive? Check with your instructor for information on where you will look for the student data files. You may be directed to a website or network location. If necessary, practice the remaining steps using folder names on your local disk drive.

Tapping twice or double-clicking a file name opens the program associated with the file and automatically opens/plays the document, image, video, or sound.

Tap or click the View tab to change the way the Content pane displays the file list. You can choose to display the files with different sized icons as well as a Preview pane or Details pane.

Creating Folders and Copying Files and Folders

As you work with software applications such as Microsoft Word or Microsoft Excel you will create many files that are documents or spreadsheets. You may also download files from a digital camera or a website and receive other files from emails or text messages. Storing the files in an organized manner with easily recognizable names will mean you can easily locate the document or picture later. Creating folders in advance of creating files will mean you have an organizational structure already in place. From time to time you also need to rename, copy, move, or delete files and folders to maintain a storage medium in good order.

Creating a Folder

Creating a folder on a computer is like placing a sticky label on the outside of an empty paper file folder and writing a title on it. The title provides a brief description of the type of documents that will be stored inside the file folder. On the computer, in File Explorer, you tap or click a **New folder** button and then type a name for the folder to set up the electronic equivalent of a paper filing system.

1 Tap or click the Desktop tile from the Start screen and then tap or click the File Explorer icon in the Taskbar.

2 Tap or click Computer in the Navigation pane of the Libraries window.

3 Double-tap or double-click the Removable Disk representing your USB flash drive in the *Devices with Removable Storage* section.

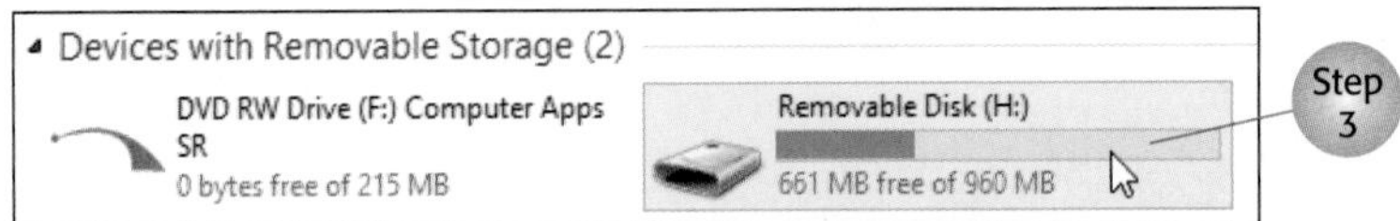

Tabs and/or buttons in the ribbon change and become available or unavailable depending on what is selected in the window.

4 If necessary, tap or click the Home tab at the top of the Removable Disk window to display the ribbon interface.

The **ribbon** provides the buttons you need to perform file management tasks. Buttons are organized into tabs such as Home, Share, View, and Manage. Within each tab, buttons are further organized into groups such as Clipboard, Organize, New, Open, and Select (on the Home tab).

5 Tap or click the New Folder button in the New group.

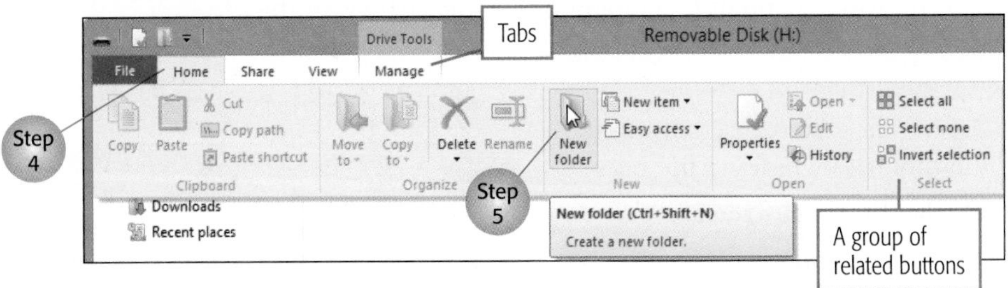

In the folder structure you are creating, no spaces between words are used. Windows allows the use of spaces; however, common practice is to avoid spaces in folder names.

6 Type **ComputerCourse** and tap or press Enter.

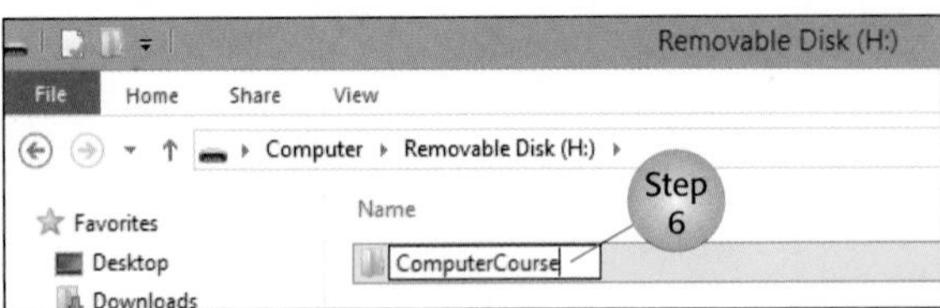

7 Tap or click the View tab and tap or click the List button in the Layout group.

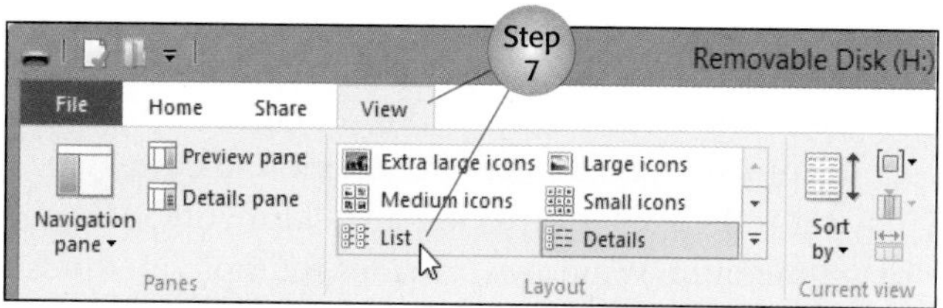

List view displays names with small icons representing each file or folder and without details such as the date or time the file or folder was created or modified, the file type, and the file size. Each folder can have a different view.

8 If necessary, tap or click the Home tab and tap or click the push pin icon at the right end of the ribbon below the Close button. This displays the ribbon permanently in the window.

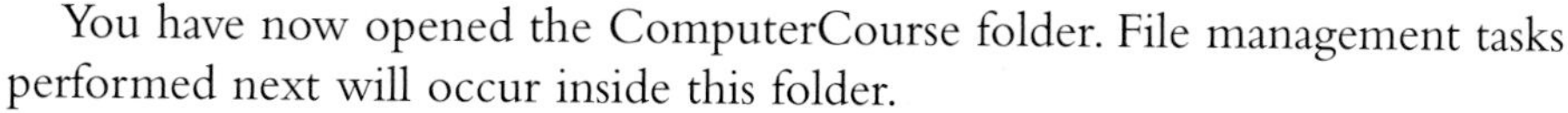

9 Double-tap or double-click the *ComputerCourse* folder name in the Content pane.

You have now opened the ComputerCourse folder. File management tasks performed next will occur inside this folder.

10 With the Home tab active, tap or click the New Folder button, type **ChapterTopicsWork**, and then tap or press Enter.

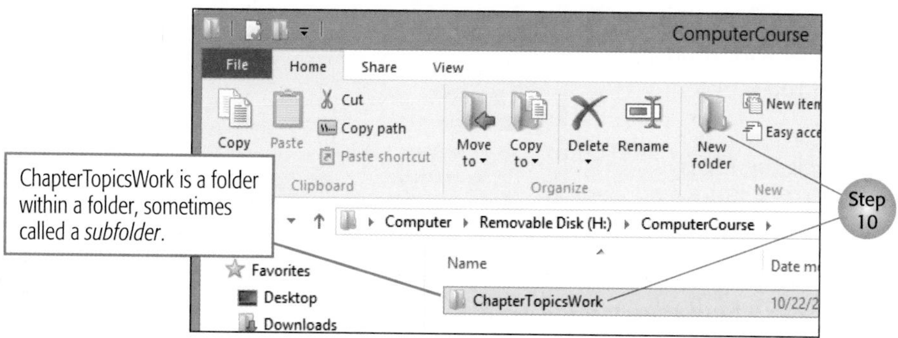

11 Tap or click the New Folder button, type **ChapterProjectsWork**, and tap or press Enter.

You now have two subfolders within the ComputerCourse folder.

12 Tap or click the Up arrow button at the left of the Address bar.

Notice you now see the ComputerCourse folder name only. The two folders created in Steps 10 and 11 are no longer visible because they are *inside* the ComputerCourse folder.

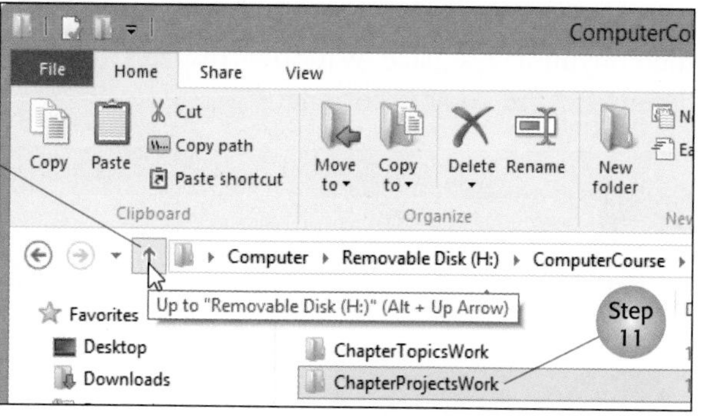

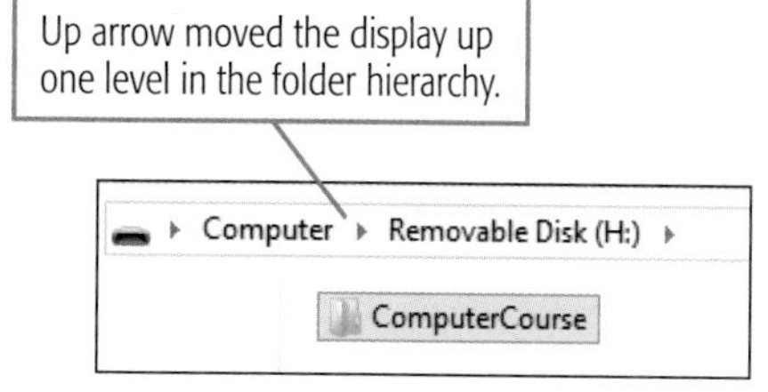

Up arrow moved the display up one level in the folder hierarchy.

Create a Folder
1. Display desktop.
2. Tap or click File Explorer.
3. Navigate to desired storage medium and/or folder.
4. If necessary, tap or click Home tab.
5. Tap or click New folder button.
6. Type folder name.
7. Tap or press Enter.

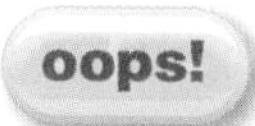

No push pin icon below the Close button? Then your ribbon is already pinned in the window. Skip Step 8.

The terms *folder* and *subfolder* are used interchangeably when a subfolder exists. Windows does not distinguish a subfolder from a folder; however, some people prefer to use *subfolder* to differentiate a folder within the hierarchy on a disk.

The Back button (left-pointing arrow) returns the display to the previous folder list.

Copying Files and Folders

Copying a file or folder from one storage medium to another makes an exact copy of a document, spreadsheet, presentation, picture, video, music file, or other object. Copying is one way of making a backup copy of an important file on another storage medium. Windows provides multiple methods for copying files or folders.

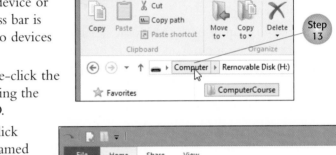

13 Tap or click Computer in the Address bar.

Tapping or clicking a device or folder name in the Address bar is another way to navigate to devices or folders.

14 Double-tap or double-click the DVD drive representing the student resources CD.

15 Tap once or single-click to select the folder named *Student_Data_Files*.

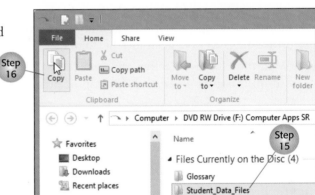

Before you can copy, you must first select a file or folder. A selected file or folder displays with a blue background in the Content pane.

16 Tap or click the **Copy** button in the Clipboard group.

Ctrl + C is the universal keyboard shortcut to Copy.

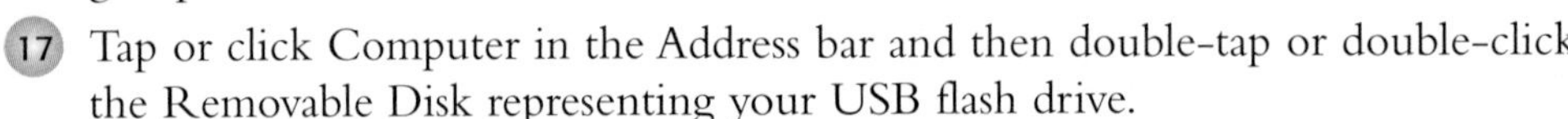

17 Tap or click Computer in the Address bar and then double-tap or double-click the Removable Disk representing your USB flash drive.

18 Double-tap or double-click the folder named *ComputerCourse* in the Content pane.

19 Tap or click the **Paste** button in the Clipboard group.

This step is copying all of the student data files you will need for your course onto your USB flash drive and placing them in the ComputerCourse folder. As the copying takes place, Windows displays a progress message. When the message disappears, the copy is complete.

Ctrl + V is the universal keyboard shortcut to Paste.

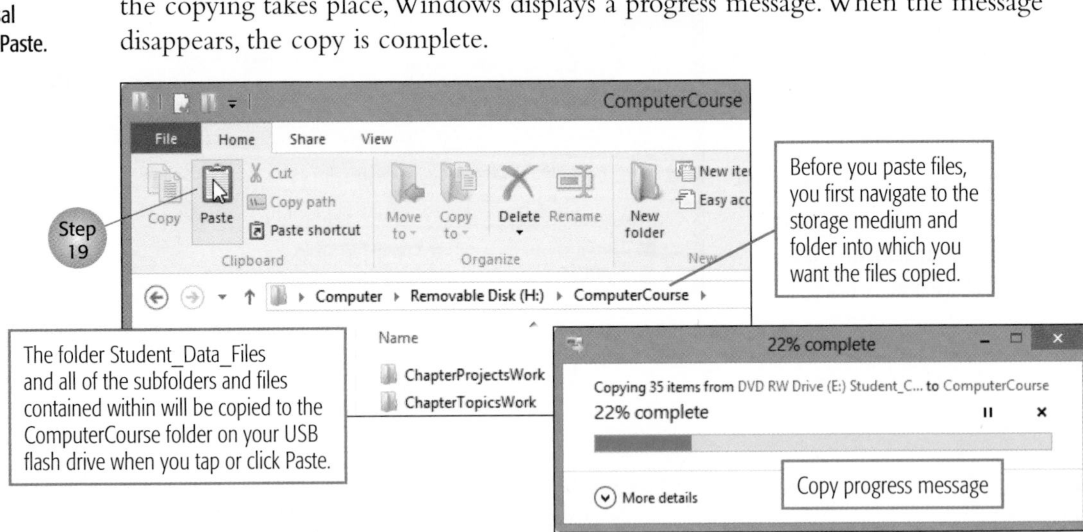

20 Double-tap or double-click the *Student_Data_Files* folder name.

21 Double-tap or double-click the *Ch1* folder name.

In the next steps you will copy individual files to a folder on the same storage medium.

22 If necessary, tap or click the View tab and tap or click List to show only the file names in the Ch1 folder.

23 Swipe your finger from the bottom of the list up over the file names starting at **Winter** and ending at **Lighthouse**; or single-click ***Lighthouse***, hold down the Shift key, and single-click ***Winter***.

This selects all of the files starting with **Lighthouse** and ending with **Winter**.

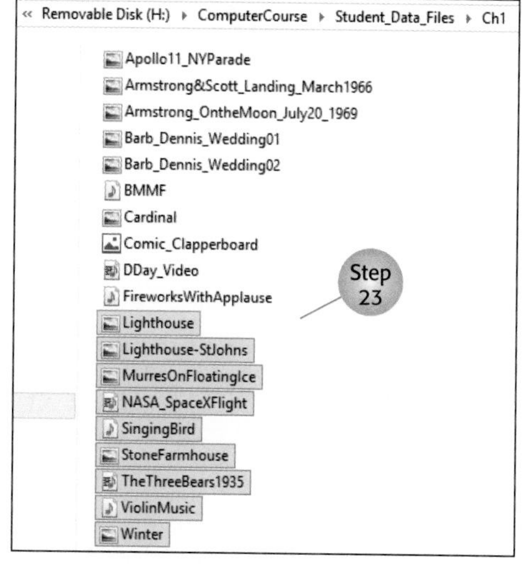

24 If necessary, tap or click the Home tab.

25 Tap or click the Copy button.

26 Tap or click *ComputerCourse* in the Address bar and tap twice or double-click *ChapterTopicsWork* in the Content pane.

27 Tap or click the Paste button.

The selected files are copied into the ChapterTopicsWork folder.

28 Tap or click the Close button to close the ChapterTopicsWork window and return to the desktop.

29 Display the Start screen.

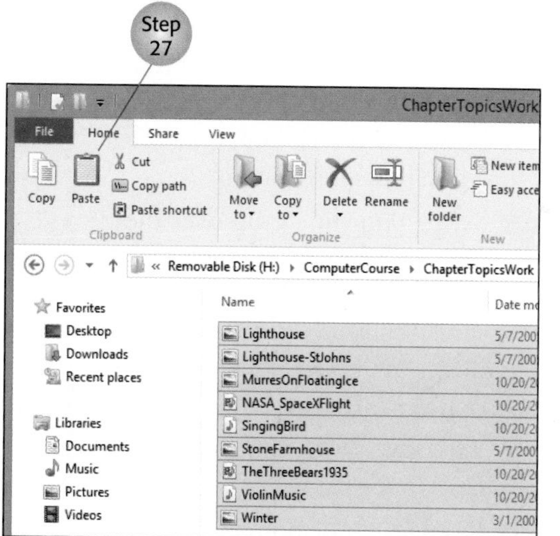

Copy Files or Folders

1. Display desktop.
2. Tap or click File Explorer.
3. Navigate to source data storage medium and/or folder.
4. Select files or folder to be copied.
5. If necessary, tap or click Home tab.
6. Tap or click Copy button.
7. Navigate to destination storage medium and/or folder.
8. Tap or click Paste button.

Select multiple adjacent files using Shift + click. Use Ctrl + click to select multiple files that are not next to each other in the list.

Touch-enabled devices display a check mark next to each selected file.

Windows provides multiple other methods for copying files:

- Select files, choose the Copy to button in the Organize group, choose the destination folder;
- Select files, display the shortcut menu, choose Copy, navigate to the destination folder, display the shortcut menu and choose Paste; or
- Drag and drop folders/files in the File Explorer window.

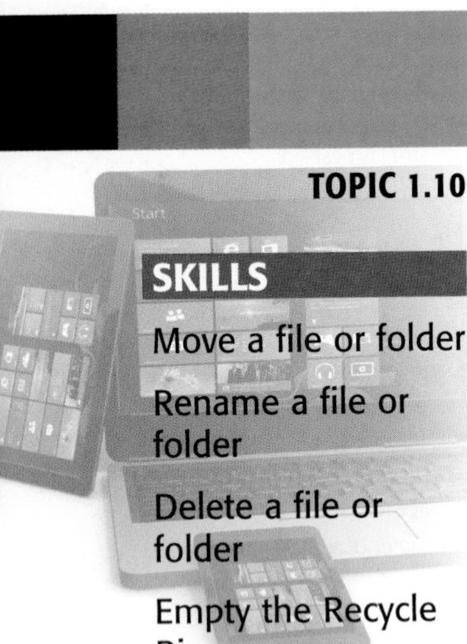

TOPIC 1.10

SKILLS

Move a file or folder

Rename a file or folder

Delete a file or folder

Empty the Recycle Bin

Eject a USB flash drive

Moving, Renaming, and Deleting Files and Folders, and Ejecting a USB Flash Drive

File Explorer is also used to move, rename, and delete files and folders. Sometimes you will copy a file or save a file in a folder and later decide you want to move it elsewhere. You may also assign a file name to a file or folder and later decide you want to change the name. Files or folders no longer needed can be deleted to clean up the disk. When you are finished using a USB flash drive, you should properly eject the drive to avoid problems that can occur when files are not properly closed.

Moving Files

Files are moved using a process similar to copying. Begin by selecting files and choosing **Cut** in the File Explorer ribbon. Navigate to the destination location and choose Paste. When files are cut they are removed from the source location.

1. At the Start Screen, launch the desktop and open File Explorer.
2. Tap or click Computer in the Navigation pane and double-tap or double-click the Removable Disk for your USB flash drive.
3. Double-tap or double-click *ComputerCourse* in the Content pane.
4. Double-tap or double-click *ChapterTopicsWork* in the Content pane.

Assume that you decide that the files copied from the Student_Data_Files Ch1 folder in the last topic should be stored inside a folder within ChapterTopicsWork.

5. Tap or click the New folder button in the ribbon, type **Ch1** and tap or press Enter.
6. Swipe your finger up over the file names starting at **Winter** and ending at **Lighthouse**; or single-click ***Lighthouse***, hold down the Shift key, and single-click ***Winter***.
7. Tap or click the Cut button in the Clipboard group.
8. Double-tap or double-click the *Ch1* folder.
9. Tap or click the Paste button in the Clipboard group.

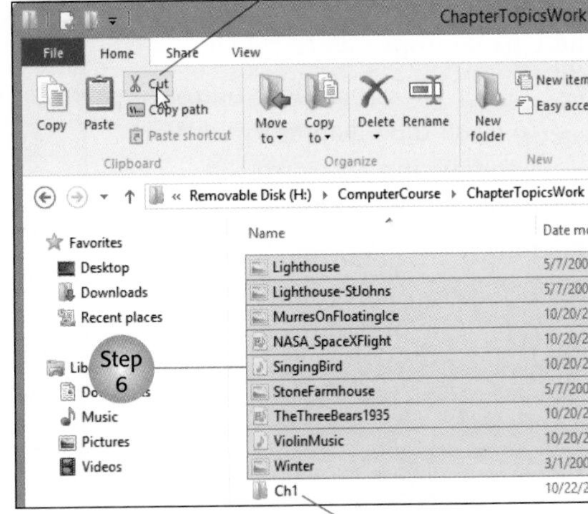

The files are removed from the ChapterTopicsWork folder and placed within the Ch1 folder.

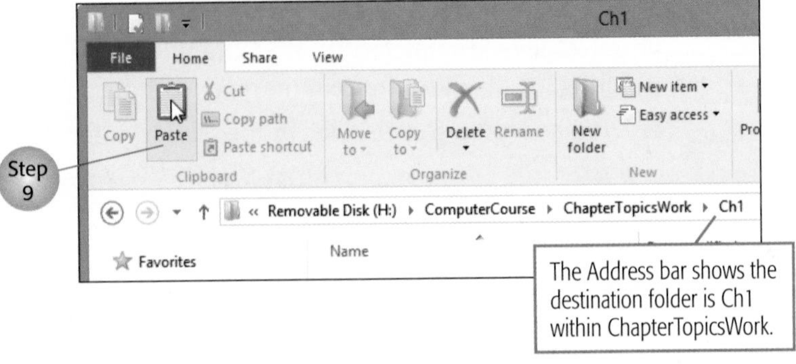

Ctrl + X is the universal keyboard shortcut to Cut.

10. Tap or click the Back button to return to the previous list.

Notice the files are no longer in the ChapterTopicsWork folder.

11. Tap or click the Forward button (right-pointing arrow next to Back button) to return to the Ch1 folder.

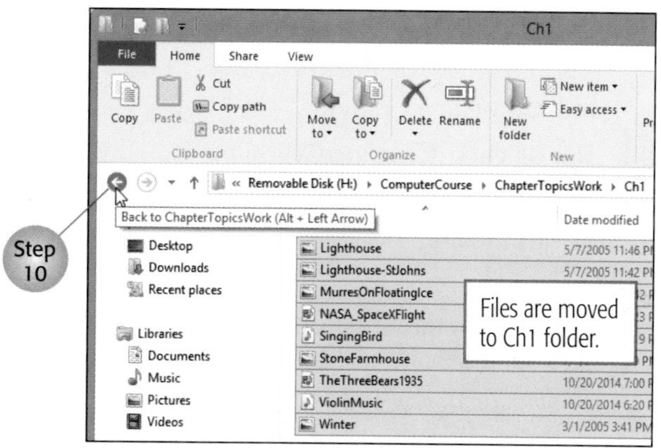

Renaming Files and Folders

At times you will receive a file from someone else and decide you want to rename the file to something more meaningful to you, or you may decide upon a new name for a file or folder after the file or folder was created. A **Rename** button is in the Organize group in the Home tab of the File Explorer ribbon.

12. Double-tap or double-click the file named ***Winter*** in the Content pane. The photograph opens in the Photos app or in Windows Photo Viewer, depending on the setup for the computer you are using.

Assume a friend sent you this picture of a weeping birch tree laden with snow in a winter scene. You decide to rename the picture.

13. Close Windows Photo Viewer or close the Photos app. If the picture opened in the Photos app, switch back to the desktop to return to File Explorer.

14. If necessary, tap once or single-click to select the file named ***Winter*** in the Content pane.

15. Tap or click the Rename button in the Organize group.

16. Type **TreeCoveredWithSnow** and tap or press Enter.

17. Tap once or single-click to select the file named ***ViolinMusic***.

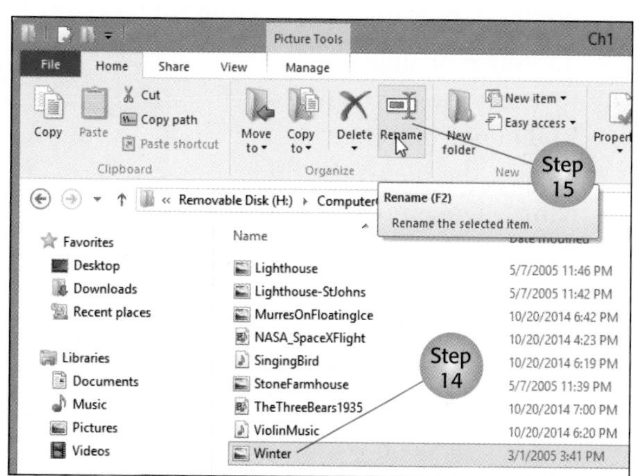

Assume this file is the song Donny Boy played on a violin and recorded by you as you heard the song at an outdoor event.

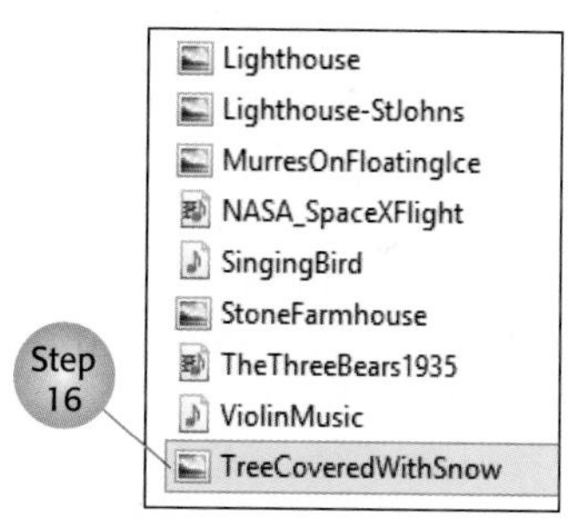

Move Files or Folders

1. Display desktop.
2. Tap or click File Explorer.
3. Navigate to source data storage medium and/or folder.
4. Select files or folder to be moved.
5. If necessary, tap or click Home tab.
6. Tap or click Cut button.
7. Navigate to destination storage medium and/or folder.
8. Tap or click Paste button.

Rename Files or Folders

1. Display desktop.
2. Tap or click File Explorer.
3. Navigate to data storage medium and/or folder.
4. Select file to be renamed.
5. If necessary, tap or click Home tab.
6. Tap or click Rename button.
7. Type new name and tap or press Enter.

oops!

Can't remember how to close an app and switch back? Drag from the top of the window to the bottom to close the Photos App and then swipe in from the left edge, or point to the top left corner and click to return to the desktop.

18 Tap or click the Rename button, type **DonnyBoyViolinMusic**, and tap or press Enter.

19 Tap or click *ComputerCourse* in the Address bar.

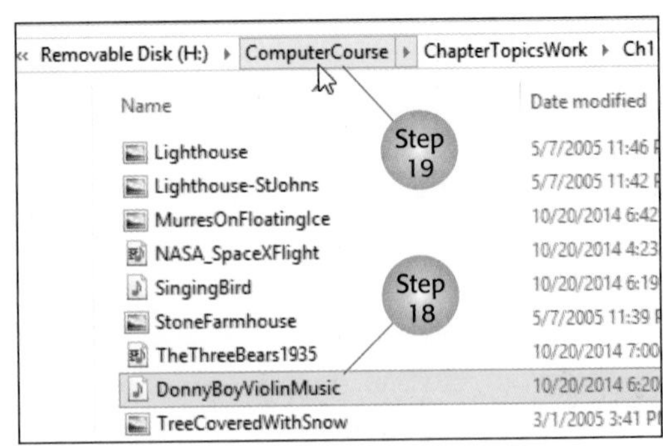

You can rename a folder as well as a file.

20 If necessary, tap once or single-click to select the folder named *ChapterTopicsWork*.

21 Tap or click the Rename button, type **CompletedTopicsByChapter**, and tap or press Enter.

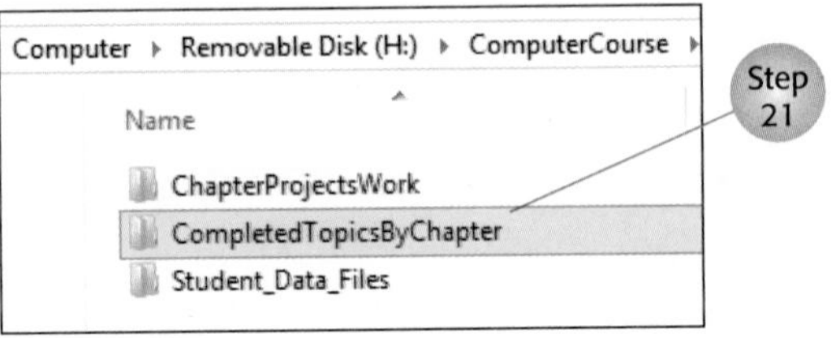

Deleting Files and Folders

Delete files or folders when you no longer need to keep them, or if you have copied files or folders to a removable storage medium for archive purposes and want to delete them from the local disk to free up space. Files and folders deleted from the local hard disk are moved to the Recycle Bin. While it is in the Recycle Bin, you can restore the file back to its original location if you deleted the file in error. Files deleted from a USB flash drive are not sent to the Recycle Bin; therefore, exercise caution when deleting a file from a USB flash drive.

By default, the Recycle Bin is set to hold a maximum of approximately 920 MB. Be aware that when the maximum is reached, some files will be permanently deleted to make room for new deleted files.

22 Double-tap or double-click the folder named *CompletedTopicsByChapter*, and double-tap or double-click the folder named *Ch1*.

23 Tap once or single-click to select the file named ***Lighthouse*** and then slide or drag the file to the folder named Documents in the Navigation pane.

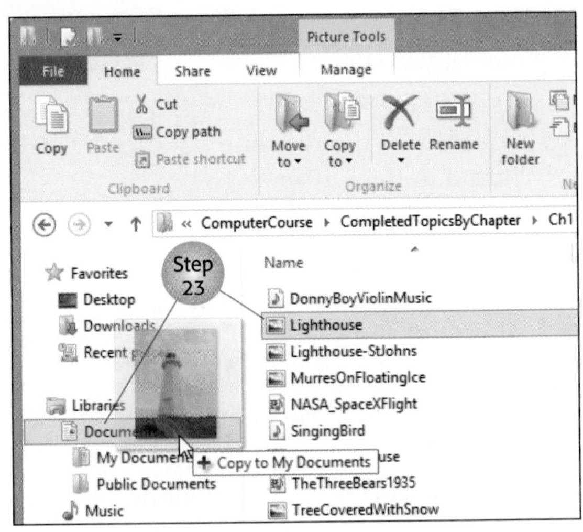

Sliding or dragging a file from a folder on one storage medium to a location on another storage medium copies the file. As you slide or drag, Windows shows a thumbnail of the picture and automatically expands the Documents folder name in the Navigation pane to show two folders: My Documents (your personal files and folders) and Public Documents (files and folders that you want to share with others). The Documents library is automatically configured to connect both My Documents and Public Documents to the Documents library.

Dragging a file or folder on the same storage medium moves the file. To be sure of the operation you want to perform, drag a file or folder to another location using the right-mouse button. When you release the mouse, a shortcut menu appears at which you can choose to Copy or Move.

24 Tap once or click Documents in the Navigation pane.

25 Tap once or click ***Lighthouse*** to select the file and tap or click the **Delete** button in the Organize group (tap or click the top of the button—not the down-pointing arrow).

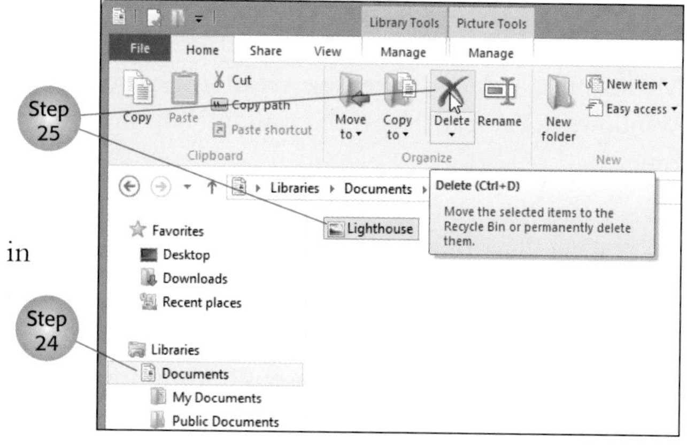

26 Tap or click Computer in the Navigation pane and double-tap or double-click the Removable Disk for your USB flash drive.

27 Double-tap or double-click *ComputerCourse*, *CompletedTopicsByChapter*, and *Ch1*.

28 Tap once or single-click to select ***SingingBird*** and tap or click the Delete button.

29 Tap or click Yes at the Delete File message box that appears.

30 Close the Ch1 File Explorer window.

31 Double-tap or double-click the Recycle Bin icon on the desktop.

32 Tap or click the Empty Recycle Bin button in the ribbon.

33 Tap or click Yes to permanently delete the file at the Delete File message box.

File deleted at Step 25 was moved here.

34 Close the Recycle Bin window.

35 Tap or click the Show hidden icons button (up-pointing arrow) in the Notification area of the Taskbar and tap or click the **Safely Remove Hardware and Eject Media** icon.

36 Tap or click *Eject Mass Storage* at the pop-up menu.

37 Remove your USB flash drive from the computer when the message appears that it is safe to do so.

38 Remove the student resources CD from the DVD drive and display the Start screen.

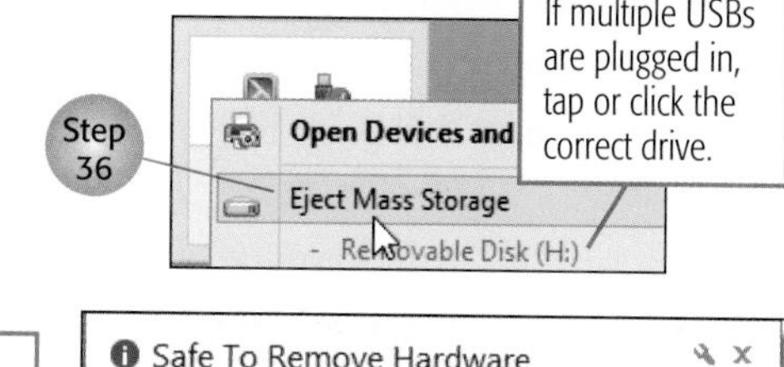

If multiple USBs are plugged in, tap or click the correct drive.

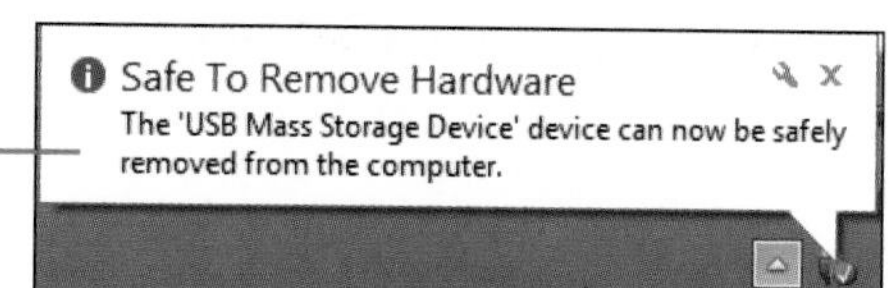

Safe To Remove Hardware
The 'USB Mass Storage Device' device can now be safely removed from the computer.

Message appears when USB can be safely removed.

Delete Files or Folders
1. Display desktop.
2. Tap or click File Explorer.
3. Navigate to data storage medium and/or folder.
4. Select files or folder to be deleted.
5. If necessary, tap or click Home tab.
6. Tap or click Delete button.
7. If prompted, tap or click Yes.

Empty the Recycle Bin
1. Display desktop.
2. Tap twice or double-click Recycle Bin.
3. Tap or click Empty Recycle Bin.
4. Tap or click Yes.

The confirmation message appears when you delete a file from a USB device because the files are permanently deleted, not sent to the Recycle Bin from which they could be restored.

oops!

Other files in your Recycle Bin? Other files may appear in your Recycle Bin from previous work. To be safe, select and delete only the **Lighthouse** file in this activity.

oops!

The Safely Remove Hardware and Eject Media icon is not always hidden; you may not have to reveal it with the Show hidden icons up-pointing arrow.

Always eject the USB flash drive using this process to avoid data corruption.

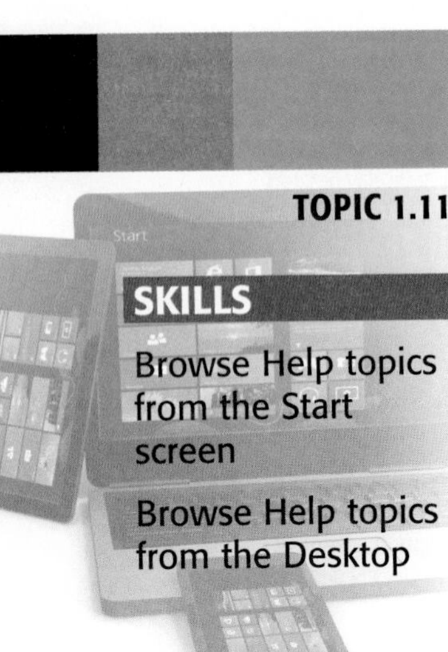

TOPIC 1.11
SKILLS
Browse Help topics from the Start screen
Browse Help topics from the Desktop

Finding Help in Windows

Microsoft includes an extensive set of online resources to assist you as you learn Windows 8. You can access the online Help from the Start screen or the Desktop app.

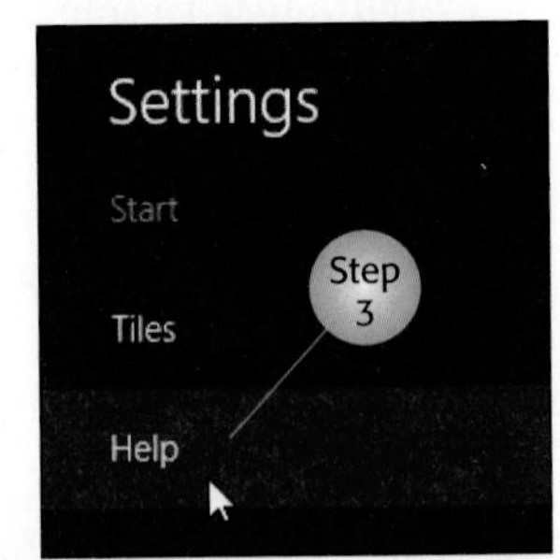

1. At the Start screen, reveal the Charms bar.
2. Tap or click the Settings charm.
3. Tap or click **Help** in the top section of the Settings pane.
4. Tap or click Adding apps, websites, and more to Start.

Windows launches the Internet Explorer app or other default browser and displays the web page with help information on how to pin apps, websites, and other programs to the Start screen.

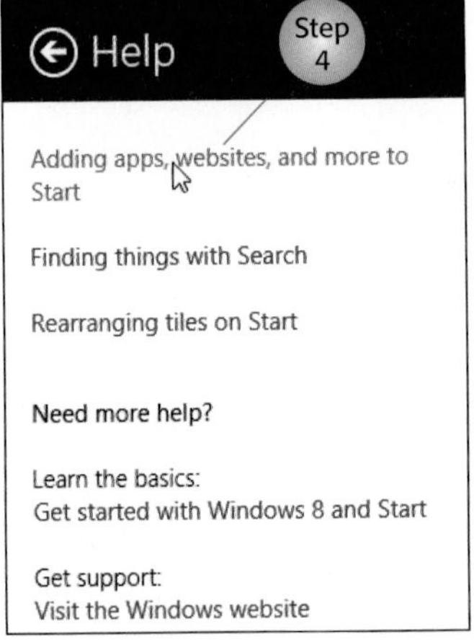

5. Slide or scroll down and read the information on how to pin various types of apps, websites, playlists, contacts, and files that you use frequently to the Start screen and then close the Internet Explorer app.
6. Display the desktop.
7. Reveal the Charms bar and tap or click Settings.
8. Tap or click Help in the top section of the Settings pane.

A Windows Help and Support window opens with three main gateways to help information: Get started, Internet & networking, and Security, privacy & accounts.

9. At the Windows Help and Support window, tap or click Get started.

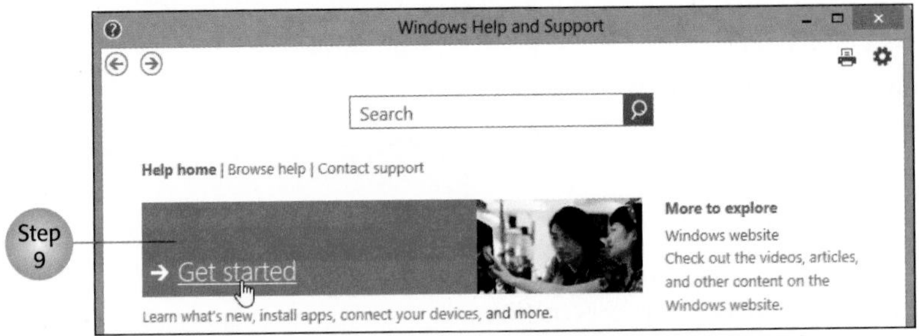

10. Tap or click Browse help near the top of the window.
11. Tap or click Performance and maintenance.
12. Tap or click the Back button twice.
13. Tap or click Touch: swipe, tap, and beyond.
14. Slide or scroll down and view the information provided in the Help window.

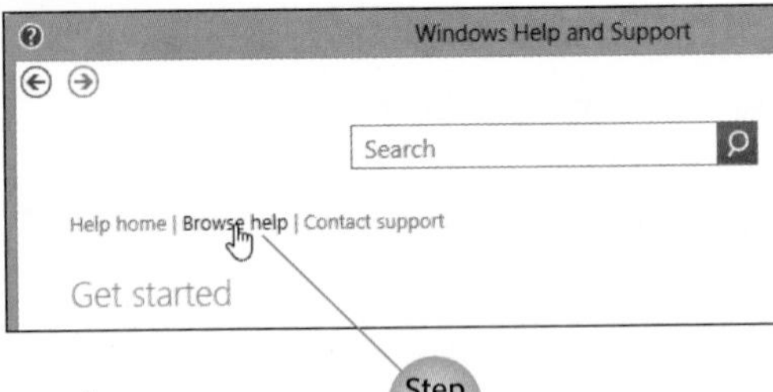

Did You Know?

Some companies and user communities have created web forums where you can get help with Windows by posting questions. Members respond in threads with answers or advice. One company in the United Kingdom has created more than 300 tutorials on how to use Windows 8 and posted them for anyone to read. Search **Windows 8 Forums** *in your favorite search engine.*

oops!

Links do not appear as instructed here? Online help is updated by Microsoft and subject to change. Links may move or change. If necessary, tap or click another appropriate link in place of the one in the instructions.

15 Tap or click the Back button.

16 Tap or click in the Search text box, type **sound**, and tap or press Enter, or tap or click the Search button.

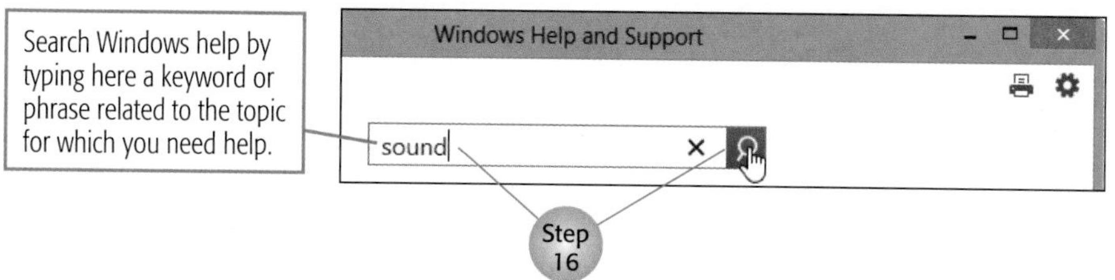

17 Tap or click Tips for fixing common sound problems.

18 Tap or click I can't hear any sound from my PC.

19 Read the expanded information in the Help window.

As you have experienced in this topic, you can navigate Windows Help by clicking links to article titles or by searching by keyword or phrase.

20 Close the Windows Help and Support window.

21 Display the Start screen.

Use Help from the Start Screen

1. Reveal Charms bar.
2. Tap or click Settings charm.
3. Tap or click Help.
4. Tap or click Help category.
5. Read Help information in Internet Explorer app.

Use Help from the Desktop

1. Display desktop.
2. Reveal Charms bar.
3. Tap or click Settings charm.
4. Tap or click Help.
5. Tap or click link to help category, Browse help OR type search keyword or phrase in Search text box and tap or click Search button.

Figure 1.12 The Windows page on Facebook. The page is frequently updated and may not appear exactly as shown here.

youtube.com/windows

Go to the Windows Youtube channel to browse videos on Windows 8. You can find how-to videos and Windows 8 Tips videos.

Windows Information at Social Media Websites

Windows help is also on Facebook. Go to facebook.com/windows and explore the links to resources Microsoft has put on its Facebook page, as shown in Figure 1.12. This page is frequently updated with new and modified links, photos, and posts. Microsoft publishes solutions to frequently reported problems and includes a search facility to search Windows support from within Facebook. You can also follow Windows on Twitter at twitter.com/windows.

Concepts Review

Topic	Key Concepts	Key Terms
Using Touch, Mouse, and Keyboard Input to Navigate Windows 8	The Windows 8 user interface is a Start screen with tiles that are used to start apps. Some tiles display notifications or status updates in real time. A gesture is an action or motion you perform with your finger, stylus, or mouse on a touch-enabled device. Touch gestures are tap, press and hold, slide or drag, swipe, pinch, and stretch. The touch keyboard appears onscreen when typed characters are expected, such as in text messages. The touch keyboard is also available in thumb mode and handwriting mode. A mouse, trackball, touchpad, or other pointing device is used to navigate Windows 8 on traditional laptops, notebooks, or desktop PCs. Mouse actions are point, click, double-click, right-click, drag, and scroll. Move the pointing device on a desk surface to move a white arrow pointer on the screen and use mouse buttons or scroll wheels to perform an action. Pressing the Windows logo key brings up the Start screen. Navigating Windows 8 with a keyboard command generally involves pressing the Windows logo key, Ctrl, Alt, or a function key with a letter.	Windows 8 User interface (UI) Start screen Tiles Applications Apps Gestures Touch keyboard Mouse Trackball Touchpad Pointer Keyboard commands
Starting Windows 8 and Exploring Apps	The Lock screen appears when you start Windows 8 or resume use from sleep mode. A user account is a user name and password used to sign in to Windows. Signing in to Windows using a hotmail.com or live.com email address is considered a Microsoft account and means that your settings are stored online and synced with other devices. Signing in with a local account means that your settings are not shared with other devices and you do not see live updates on some of the tiles in the Start screen. The Start screen appears once you have signed in to Windows. Several built-in apps are included with Windows 8 automatically run in full screen mode when launched. The Photos app shows pictures stored on the local PC and from SkyDrive, Facebook, and Flickr if the services have been connected to the sign-in account. The Calendar app is used to enter appointments or events and will show birthdays from Facebook if connected. Use the Store app to search for and download new apps. Switch between apps using touch gestures, the mouse, or by pressing Alt + Tab and cycling through the open apps.	Lock screen User account Microsoft account Local account Photos app Calendar app Store app

Topic	Key Concepts	Key Terms
Revealing Charms Bar, Searching for an App, and Closing Apps	Swipe from the right edge of the screen or point to the top right or bottom right corner to reveal the Charms bar. Charms are used to access system resources or commands. The Search charm is used to search for something in apps, settings, or files, or on the Web. As you type in the Search text box, Windows returns a list of programs that matches the characters in real time. Apps that are not used are eventually closed by Windows; however, you can close an app when you are done with it by swiping or dragging from the top of the screen down to the bottom.	Charms bar Charms
Locking the Screen, Signing Out, and Shutting Down Windows 8	Lock the screen if you need to leave your PC or mobile device for a short period of time by tapping or clicking your account name and choosing Lock. Locking leaves all documents and apps open but unavailable to anyone but yourself. Tap or click your account name and choose Sign out to close all apps and documents (also referred to as logging off). Perform a shut-down command if you want to turn off the power to the PC or mobile device. Shut down is accessed from the Power button in the Settings pane opened from the Settings charm.	Sign out Logging off Shut down
Customizing the Start Screen	You can customize the Start screen by adding or removing tiles, rearranging tiles, resizing a tile, and by turning off live updates. Select a tile by pulling the tile down until a check mark appears or by right-clicking the tile. Commands are revealed along the bottom of the screen when a tile is selected. Unpin from Start removes the selected tile, and Pin to Start adds the selected tile to the Start screen. Move tiles to a new location on the Start screen by sliding the tile using touch or dragging using the mouse. App tiles are either square or rectangular in shape and can be resized larger or smaller. Select a tile and choose the Turn live tile off command to stop a tile from displaying notifications or status updates.	Unpin from Start Pin to Start Turn live tile off
Personalizing the Start and Lock Screens	Tap or click Change PC settings from the Settings charm to personalize the lock and start screens. You can choose from five other pictures for the Lock screen or browse to a picture on your PC or mobile device. Tap or click the first plus symbol in the Lock screen apps section of the PC settings window to add an app that will provide notifications to the Lock screen. Choose from 20 different designs for the background of the Start screen and drag a color slider to change the color scheme used in Windows 8.	Change PC settings

continued....

Topic	Key Concepts	Key Terms
Using the Desktop	The Desktop tile launches the Windows 8 desktop, which is the same as the Windows 7 desktop but without a Start button. The desktop displays icons used to launch programs such as the Recycle Bin, Internet Explorer, File Explorer, and a Taskbar. Desktop apps such as Microsoft Word or Microsoft Excel contain standard features for moving, resizing, and closing windows. The Close button displays at the top right corner of a desktop app window and is used to close the app window. Some programs are pinned to the desktop Taskbar. A notification area at the right end displays the current date and time along with icons to access volume control, network status, and the Action Center.	Desktop Recycle Bin Taskbar File Explorer Notification area Close button
Browsing Files with File Explorer	A file is any document, spreadsheet, picture, or other text or image saved as digital data. When you create a file, you assign a unique file name that allows you to identify and retrieve the file. File Explorer is the utility in Windows used to browse contents of storage devices and perform file management tasks. A Libraries window opens when you launch File Explorer. A library is a name assigned to a group of related files. Windows creates four libraries by default: Documents, Music, Pictures, and Videos. A computer window displays all of the available storage devices. A folder is a name assigned to a placeholder or container that will store a group of related files. A subfolder is a folder created inside another folder. You browse content by tapping or clicking names in the Navigation pane or tapping twice or double-clicking names in the Content pane.	File File name Libraries window Library Computer window Folder Subfolder
Creating Folders and Copying Files and Folders	Creating folders in advance of creating files sets up the organizational structure for later use. In File Explorer, a ribbon provides buttons organized into tabs and groups that are used to carry out file management tasks. Tap or click the New folder button and type a folder name to create a new folder. Copying a file or folder makes an exact duplicate of a document, spreadsheet, presentation, picture, video, music file, or other object in another folder and/or storage medium. Make copies of important files as backups. Begin a copy task by first selecting the file or folder to be copied, then use the Copy and Paste commands.	New folder Ribbon Copy Paste

Topic	Key Concepts	Key Terms
Moving, Renaming, and Deleting Files and Folders, and Ejecting a USB Flash Drive	Files are moved by selecting the files or folders, choosing Cut, navigating to the new destination drive and/or folder, and choosing Paste. Use the Rename button to change the name of a file you have received from someone else, or that you have created and assigned a name that you later decide is not satisfactory. Select the file or folder to be renamed and tap or click the Rename button in the Organize group of the Home tab in File Explorer. Type a new name and press Enter. Files deleted from a hard disk drive are sent to the Recycle Bin and remain there until the Recycle Bin is emptied. Files deleted from a USB flash drive are not sent to the Recycle Bin. Select files or folders to be deleted and tap or click the Delete button in the Organize group of the Home tab. Open the Recycle Bin to view files deleted from the hard disk drive. Emptying the Recycle Bin permanently deletes the files or folders. Eject a USB flash drive using the Safely Remove Hardware and Eject Media icon in the Notification area of the Taskbar.	Cut Rename Delete Safely Remove Hardware and Eject Media
Finding Help in Windows	An extensive online help resource is available by revealing the Charms bar and choosing Settings. Help accessed from the Start screen displays as web pages in the Internet Explorer app. When Help is accessed from the desktop, a Windows Help and Support window opens in which you can browse help topics or search Help by typing a keyword or phrase in the Search text box. Help is also available on Facebook at facebook.com/windows.	Help

Multiple Choice

1. This term refers to an action or motion you perform with your finger or stylus on a touch-enabled device.
   a. Writing
   b. Gesture
   c. Navigate
   d. Interface
2. The white arrow on a Windows screen that appears when using a mouse is referred to as the ____________.
   a. I-beam
   b. trackball
   c. scroller
   d. pointer
3. Signing in with this type of account means you can see live updates from social media services.
   a. Local
   b. Microsoft
   c. Facebook
   d. Twitter
4. Built-in apps for Windows 8 automatically run in this mode.
   a. Desktop
   b. Start screen
   c. Full screen
   d. Live

5. This bar displays along the right edge of the screen when you swipe in, or point to the top right or bottom right corner.
   a. Apps bar
   b. Charms bar
   c. Settings bar
   d. Switch list
6. This charm is used to find an app.
   a. Search charm
   b. Find charm
   c. Settings charm
   d. Share charm
7. If you are leaving your computer for a short period of time, you should do this so that someone else cannot see your work.
   a. Turn off the computer.
   b. Freeze the Start screen.
   c. Lock the screen.
   d. Hide your computer.
8. Do this action when you are finished with a Windows session for the day.
   a. Sign out.
   b. Lock the screen.
   c. Restart.
   d. Freeze the Start screen.
9. A selected tile displays with this symbol.
   a. ×
   b. ✓
   c. !
   d. #
10. Select this option to stop headlines from displaying on a selected Finance tile.
    a. Pin to Start
    b. Uninstall
    c. Turn live tile off
    d. Turn notifications off
11. Choose this option from the Settings charm to change the Lock screen picture.
    a. Change PC settings
    b. Personalize
    c. Lock screen
    d. Browse
12. The background of the Start screen can be customized with a different design and/or ____________.
    a. pixel scheme
    b. tile scheme
    c. notification scheme
    d. color scheme
13. Launch this tile from the Start screen to find File Explorer.
    a. Computer
    b. Desktop
    c. Libraries
    d. Files
14. This is the name of the bar that displays along the bottom of the desktop.
    a. Taskbar
    b. Charms bar
    c. Notification bar
    d. System bar
15. The Libraries or Computer window contains the Navigation pane and the __________ pane.
    a. Files
    b. Content
    c. Organize
    d. Tools
16. Tap or click this option in the Navigation pane to view all of the available storage options.
    a. Libraries
    b. Desktop
    c. Favorites
    d. Computer
17. This is the name for the area within the File Explorer window that organizes buttons into tabs and groups.
    a. Ribbon
    b. Organize
    c. Tools
    d. Menu
18. A folder created within another folder is sometimes referred to as a ______________.
    a. folder path
    b. subfolder
    c. folder hierarchy
    d. structure
19. After choosing Copy and navigating to the destination folder, tap or click this button in the Clipboard group.
    a. Copy to
    b. Copy path
    c. Cut
    d. Paste
20. To move a file, use this button in the Clipboard group.
    a. Cut
    b. Move
    c. Delete
    d. Transfer

21. Use this button in File Explorer to change the name of a file or folder.
    a. New name
    b. Rename
    c. Change name
    d. Easy change
22. Deleted files from a hard disk drive are sent to this location.
    a. Taskbar
    b. Recycle Bin
    c. Trash
    d. USB flash drive
23. Use this charm to access Help from the Start screen.
    a. Share
    b. Devices
    c. Settings
    d. Find
24. Help information is displayed in this app when accessed from the Start screen.
    a. Desktop
    b. Internet Explorer
    c. Windows
    d. Microsoft

Crossword Puzzle

ACROSS

1 Button in Settings pane to access Shut Down command
3 Option to make square-shaped tile rectangular
4 Area at right end of Taskbar
8 Open to display Libraries
9 Used to access system resources and commands

DOWN

1 Category in PC Settings for Lock screen options
2 Mouse button used to select a tile
5 Name assigned to a place to store a group of related files
6 Button used to move a file
7 Account type where settings are not synced with other devices

Matching

Match the term with the statement or definition.

_______	1. Start screen	a.	Logging off
_______	2. Photos	b.	Personalize Start screen
_______	3. Search charm	c.	Cut or Copy
_______	4. Sign out	d.	Desktop app
_______	5. Unpin	e.	Safely Remove Hardware
_______	6. PC settings	f.	Displays Apps screen
_______	7. Recycle Bin	g.	User interface
_______	8. File Explorer	h.	Remove tile
_______	9. Eject Mass Storage	i.	Built-in app

Project 1 Exploring Windows 8 Apps

Individual

Deliverable: Screen capture of Start screen with Switch list

1. Start Windows 8 and sign in.
2. Reveal the Charms bar and choose the Search charm. From the Apps list, launch the Travel app. Browse the list of featured destinations and tap or click a destination of your choice. Slide or scroll the destination information, reading the Overview, browsing photos, panoramas, list of attractions, and so on.
3. Display the Start screen and launch the News app. Slide or scroll the top news stories and tap or click a story that interests you.
4. Display the Start screen and launch the Store app. Slide or scroll to the Education category and tap or click the tile to the Top free Education apps.
5. Display the Start screen and reveal the Switch list in the left pane.
6. Press the Print Screen key on the keyboard to capture an image of your screen with the Switch list displayed. The key may be labeled Prt Sc, PrtScrn, or PrtSc and is generally located in the top row of keys at the right near the last function key. On some PCs or devices you may need to press Shift + Print Screen or a function key with Print Screen. If you are using a tablet without a keyboard or if the Switch list does not remain on screen when you press Print Screen, check with your instructor for instructions on how to submit projects with screen capture deliverables.
7. Use the Search charm to search for and launch the Paint app. Paint is a desktop app and will open in the Windows 8 desktop.
8. Tap or click the Paste button in the Home tab of the Paint ribbon.
9. Tap or click the Save button on the Quick Access toolbar. At the Save As dialog box, navigate to your USB flash drive, select the current file name in the *File name* text box, type **C1-Project1-AppsSwitchList-Your Name**, and tap or click the Save button. (You will move this file to another location in Project 4.)
10. Close the Paint window and close the desktop app.
11. Switch to and close each of the three apps you launched in this project.
12. Submit the project to your instructor in the manner she or he has requested.

Project 2 Customizing the Start Screen

Individual

Deliverable: Screen capture with customized Start screen

Note: Skip steps in this project that ask you to customize a tile if the tile is already at the instructed setting.

1. At the Windows Start screen, select the Calendar tile and resize the tile smaller.
2. Select the News tile and resize the app smaller.
3. Select the Store tile and resize the app larger.
4. Select the People tile and turn the live tile off.
5. Select the Photos tile and turn the live tile off.
6. Rearrange the tiles that you have customized in this project within the first group of tiles in a manner that suits you.
7. Capture an image of your customized Start screen and paste it into a new Paint document. See Project 1, Steps 6 to 8 if you need help.
8. Save the image in Paint on your USB flash drive as **C1-Project2-CustomizedStartScreen-Your Name**.
9. Close the Paint window and close the desktop app.
10. Submit the project to your instructor in the manner she or he has requested.
11. Restore the Calendar, News, Store, People, and Photos tiles to their original settings and rearrange the tiles back to their original locations.

Project 3 Browsing Files with File Explorer

Individual

Deliverable: Screen capture with File Explorer window

1. Start File Explorer.
2. Insert your USB flash drive into an empty USB port. If a new Removable Disk window opens, close the window.
3. At the Libraries window, navigate to Computer and then display in the Content pane the Removable Disk for your USB flash drive.
4. Navigate the following folders: ComputerCourse, CompletedTopicsByChapter, Ch1.
5. With the Ch1 files displayed in the Content pane, change the View to Large Icons.
6. Capture an image of the desktop with the File Explorer window open and paste it into a Paint document.
7. Save the image in Paint on your USB flash drive as **C1-Project3-FileExplorerWindow-Your Name**.
8. Close the Paint window, close the File Explorer window, and close the desktop app.
9. Submit the project to your instructor in the manner she or he has requested.

Project 4 Performing File Management Tasks

Individual

Deliverable: Screen capture with File Explorer window

1. Start File Explorer and display in the Content pane the ChapterProjectsWork folder on your USB flash drive.
2. Create a new folder named *Ch1*.
3. Navigate to the Student_Data_Files folder within the ComputerCourse folder and copy the Ch1 folder to the ComputerCourse folder.
4. Display in the Content pane the Ch1 folder within the ComputerCourse folder.
5. Select all files within the folder and move them to the Ch1 folder within the ChapterProjectsWork folder.
6. With the Content pane displaying the files in the Ch1 folder within ChapterProjectsWork, do the following:
   a. Delete the files named **FireworksWithApplause**, **Winter**, and **TheThreeBears1935**.
   b. Rename the file **MurresOnFloatingIce** to ***BirdsOnIceFloe***.
   c. Rename the file **BMMF** to ***DrumsSolo***.
   d. Create a new folder named *NASA*.
   e. Select and move the following files to the NASA folder: **Apollo11_NYParade**, **Armstrong&Scott_Landing_March1966**, **Armstrong_OntheMoon_July20_1969**, **NASA_SpaceXFlight**.
   f. If necessary, change the View to List view.
7. Capture an image of the desktop with the File Explorer window showing the Content pane for the Ch1 folder within ChapterProjectsWork and paste it into a Paint document.
8. Save the image in Paint on your USB flash drive as **C1-Project4-Ch1FileExplorerWindow-Your Name**.
9. Close the Paint window.
10. Display in the Content pane the ComputerCourse folder and delete the folder named *Ch1*.
11. Create a new folder named *ScreenCaptures* within the Ch1 folder in ChapterProjectsWork and then move all of the Paint files created with screen captures to the new folder.
12. Close the File Explorer window.
13. Submit the project (from Step 8) to your instructor in the manner she or he has requested.
14. Eject the USB flash drive and close the desktop app.
15. Sign out of Windows.

Chapter 2

Navigating and Searching the Web

After succesfully completing this chapter, you will be able to:

- Describe the Internet, World Wide Web, web browser, web address, and hyperlink
- Navigate the Web using Internet Explorer
- View multiple websites within the same browser window
- Bookmark favorite websites
- Navigate the Web using Google Chrome
- Navigate the Web using Mozilla Firefox
- Use find and search tools to find information on the Web
- Print a web page
- Download content from web pages

For many people reading this textbook, the Internet is part of daily life, used to search for information, connect with friends and relatives, watch videos, listen to music, play games, or shop. Mobile devices such as tablets and smartphones allow people to browse the Web anywhere at any time. Being able to effectively navigate and search the Web is a requirement for all workers and consumers.

In this chapter you will learn definitions for Internet terminology and how to navigate the Web using the three most popular Web browsers. You will also learn to use search tools to find information quickly, print information from websites, view multiple websites in a browsing session, bookmark favorites, and copy information from websites to your local PC.

Notes: While the emphasis in this chapter is on using Internet Explorer 10, which is included with Windows 8, feel free to work through the topic activities and projects using Google Chrome or Firefox. In that case, be aware that for some topics, the steps provided may need to be altered to suit the Google Chrome or Firefox browser.

If you are using a computer with Windows 7 and an earlier version of Internet Explorer (such as version 9), the steps you complete and screens you see will vary from the ones shown in this chapter. If necessary, check with your instructor for alternate instructions.

No student data files are required to complete this chapter.

TOPIC 2.1

SKILLS

Define Internet

Define World Wide Web

Describe Web address

Introduction to the Internet and the World Wide Web

The **Internet (Net)** is a global network linking individuals, businesses, schools, governments, nonprofit organizations, research institutions, and others. The physical structure that connects thousands of other networks to make this worldwide network operational is known as the Internet. High speed communications and networking equipment is used on the Internet to transmit data from one computer to another. For example, a request sent from your computer to display a web page such as flight times from an airline's schedule would travel through several other networks such as telephone, cable, or satellite company networks to reach the airline's web server. This collection of networks that provides the pathway for data to travel is the Internet.

The World Wide Web

The collection of electronic documents circulated on the Internet in the form of **web pages** make up the **World Wide Web (Web** or **WWW)**. A web page is a document that contains text and multimedia content such as images, video, sound, and animation (Figure 2.1). Web pages also contain **hyperlinks** (referred to as **links**), which allow you to move from one page to another page. Web pages are stored in a format that is read and interpreted for display within a **web browser**, which is a software program used to view web pages. A website is a collection of related web pages for one organization or individual. For example, the collection of web pages linked to the main page for your school make up your school's website. All of the web pages and resources such as photos, videos, sounds, and animations that make the website work are stored on a computer called a web server. Web servers are connected to the Internet continuously.

You connect your PC or mobile device to the Internet by subscribing to Internet service through an **Internet Service Provider (ISP)**, a company that provides access to the Internet's infrastructure for a fee. The ISP will provide you with the equipment needed to connect to the ISP's network as well as instructions for installing and setting up the equipment to work with your computer or other mobile devices. Once your account and equipment are set up, you can start browsing the Web using a browser software program such as Internet Explorer, Google Chrome, or Firefox.

Many people connect wirelessly to the Internet from multiple mobile devices.

Web Addresses

Each web page has a unique text-based **web address** that allows you to navigate to the page. Web Addresses are also called **URLs (Uniform Resource Locators)**. One way to navigate the Web is to type a web address for an organization into the web browser's Address bar. For example, to view the main web page for the publisher of this textbook you would use the web address *http://www.emcp.com*. Since *http* and *www* are used in most web addresses, you can often navigate to a page by typing only the portion of the address after *www*. The parts of the web address (URL) http://www.nasa.gov/topics/universe/index.html shown in Figure 2.1 are explained in Table 2.1.

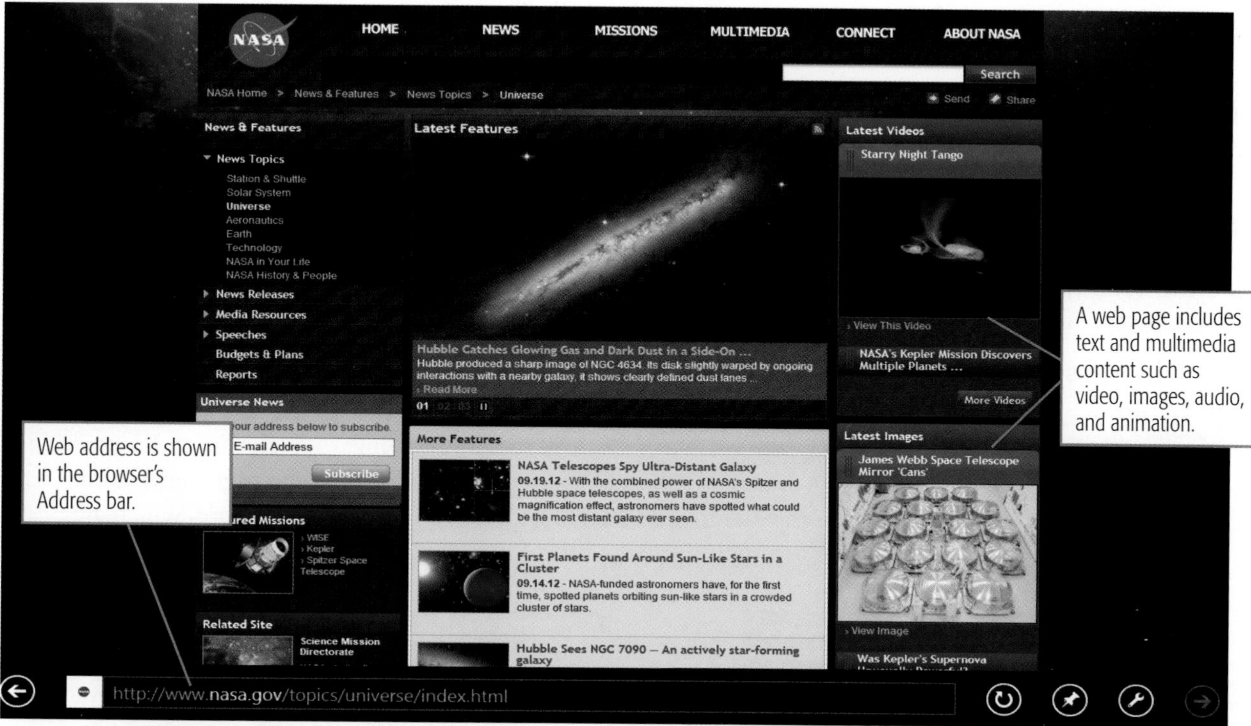

Figure 2.1 A web page such as this one from NASA includes text and multimedia content. Web pages are identified by a web address, which is typed into the browser's Address bar or shown in the Address bar when you navigate to the page from a search engine.

Table 2.1	**The Parts of the Web Address (URL) http://www.nasa.gov/topics/universe/index.html**	
Part of URL	**What It Means**	**Examples**
http://	Hypertext Transfer Protocol. A protocol is a set of rules that defines how data is sent over the Internet. Since http is used most of the time, you can omit this part of the web address. Other types of protocols are used to transfer files (ftp) or to send data securely (https).	http ftp https
www.nasa.gov	Domain name. A domain name is a text-based address that indicates the server on the Internet that stores the web page. The last three letters (gov) are called the extension and indicate the type of organization that owns the content. In the *Examples* column are popular extensions that you will recognize from your browsing experiences. Some domain names end with a two-character country code. For example: ebay.ca is the Canadian website for the popular online auction site ebay.	com (business) edu (education) gov (government) net (network providers) org (nonprofits)
/topics/universe/	Path to the web page. The forward slash (/) and text after the slash indicate the folder names on the web server in which the web page is stored. The number of folders and folder names indicate the organizational structure for the web pages that comprise a website.	path folder names will vary
index.html	Web page file name. The file name extension indicates the language used to create the web page. Html stands for *Hypertext Markup Language*, which uses tags to describe content and is widely used.	file names will vary

Many times when you open a web browser, you are looking for information and do not know the web addresses for the pages you want to view. In this case, you use search tools to find web pages that you want to view. You will learn to find web pages using search tools in Topic 2.5.

TOPIC 2.2

SKILLS

Navigate the Web using Internet Explorer

View multiple websites within the same window

Add a page to Favorites

Navigating the Web Using Internet Explorer 10

Internet Explorer (IE) is the web browser included with Microsoft Windows. In Windows 8, IE version 10 is used. You can open Internet Explorer from a tile in the Start screen or from the Internet Explorer icon in the Windows 8 Desktop Taskbar.

The browser app that you launch from the Internet Explorer Start screen tile is slightly different than the browser you launch from the Desktop Taskbar, as shown in Figure 2.2. The Start screen app provides the most page viewing area because the Address bar is located at the bottom of the window and disappears as you scroll down a web page, meaning the web page will fill the entire window. Right-click the mouse or swipe from the bottom or top edge to reveal the Address bar and tabs for multiple page viewing in the window.

Using the Desktop IE window will feel more familiar for users with IE experience in Windows 7 or earlier. The Address bar and tabs for multiple page viewing are located at the top along with the Home, Favorites, and Tools buttons, which are located at the top right just below the Minimize, Maximize, and Close buttons.

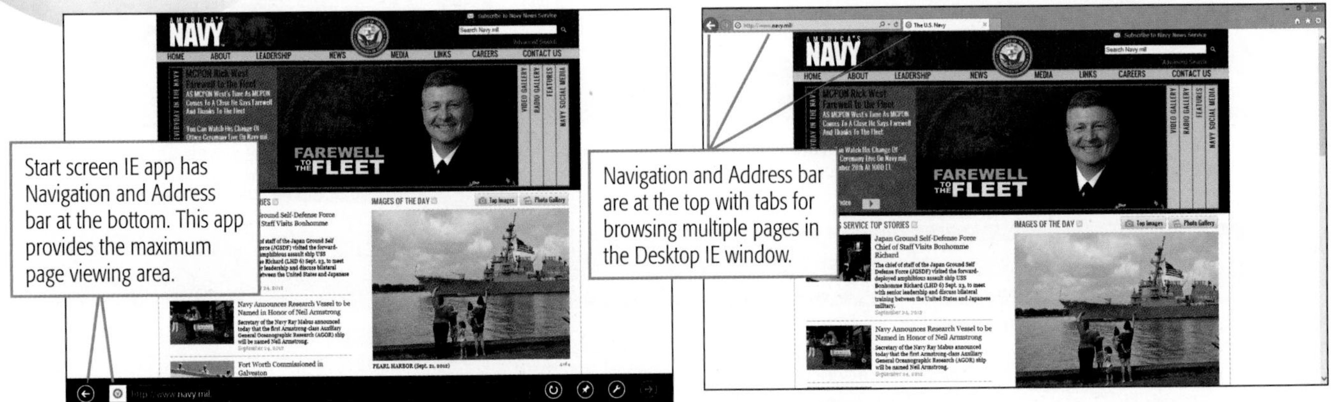

Figure 2.2 The Internet Explorer app from the Windows 8 Start screen (left) varies from the IE window launched from the Desktop (right).

Starting Internet Explorer and Displaying a Web Page

oops!

Internet Explorer tile starts in Desktop version? This occurs when the default browser has been set to a browser other than IE. Change back to IE to complete this chapter by opening the Control Panel from the desktop, then choosing this sequence: Programs, Default Programs, Set your default programs, Internet Explorer (in Programs list), Set this program as default, OK.

1. Tap or click the Internet Explorer tile from the Start screen and review the layout and tools in the IE window, as shown in Figure 2.3 on the next page.

The IE window fills the screen with the default home page that is set for the browser.

Figure 2.3 Internet Explorer 10 app launched from Start screen. The default page that displays in your window may vary from the one shown.

2. Drag to select the text in the **Address bar** or click to select the existing web address, type **www.loc.gov**, and then tap or press Enter (on the touch keyboard, the Enter key is labeled Go).

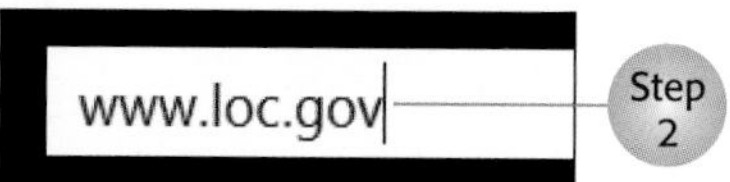

Touch keyboard not active? You may need to tap inside the selected text to bring up the touch keyboard.

3. Tap or click Digital Preservation in the *Resources & Programs* section at the right side of the Library of Congress page.
4. Tap or click the **Back** control or slide right to return to the Library of Congress home page (move back one web page).
5. Tap or click the **Forward** control or slide left to return to the Digital Preservation page (move forward one web page).
6. Tap or click View the tips in the *Preserving Your Digital Memories* section.

The Personal Archiving page at the Library of Congress contains links to articles with useful information on how to preserve your personal memories. Consider further exploring the links at this web page if you have an interest in preserving personal information.

Resources & Programs

American Folklife Center
Preserving & presenting traditional culture

Center for the Book
Promoting books, reading & literacy

Copyright Royalty Board
Determining statutory royalty rates & distributing royalties

Digital Preservation
A national partnership to preserve new media

Step 3

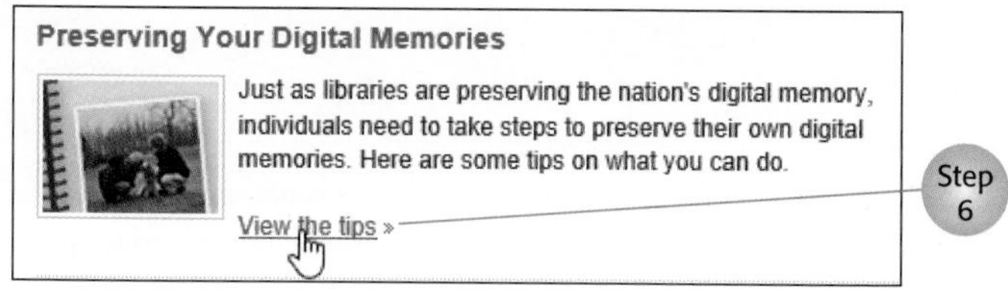

Preserving Your Digital Memories
Just as libraries are preserving the nation's digital memory, individuals need to take steps to preserve their own digital memories. Here are some tips on what you can do.
View the tips »
Step 6

As you begin typing a URL, IE displays matches above the Address bar that begin with similar text from the History list. Tap or click the page if it appears in the list.

You may be prompted to turn on the Flip Ahead feature. Flip Ahead looks for the next page in a website, such as page 2 of an article, and lets you move to the next page without having to locate the next page hyperlink.

oops!

Page Not Found error? This message occurs when you have made a typing mistake when entering the web address. Select the text in the Address bar and try again.

7. Drag to select the text in the Address bar or click to select the existing web address, type **www.nasa.gov/topics/universe/index.html**, and then tap or press Enter (Go on touch screen keyboard).

www.nasa.gov/topics/universe/index.html

Step 7

8. If necessary, slide or scroll down to the *Latest Images* section at the right side of the page and tap or click the View Archives button link.
9. Slide or scroll down the web page and notice that the page fills the screen as the navigation controls disappear.

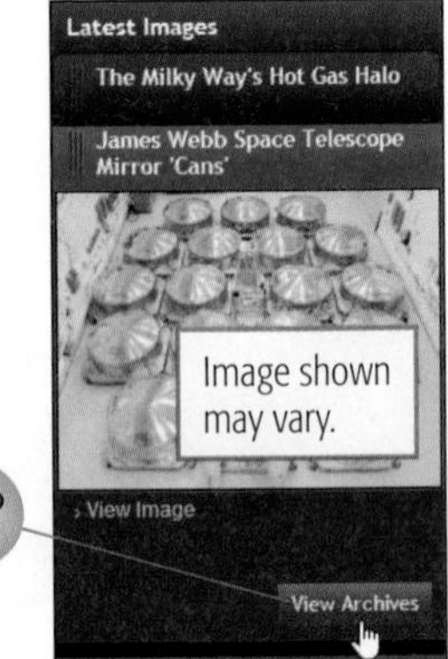

Displaying Multiple Web Pages and Pinning a Site

Open multiple web pages within the same IE window by displaying each page in its own tab. Switch between web pages by displaying the tabs and clicking the tab control for the page you want to view. This is called **tabbed browsing**. Web pages you visit frequently can be pinned to the **Favorites** list or the Start screen.

10. Swipe up from the bottom edge of the screen or right-click to reveal the navigation controls and browser tabs, as shown in Figure 2.4.
11. Tap or click the **New Tab** control at the top right of the IE window that displays as a plus symbol inside a circle to open a new blank page.

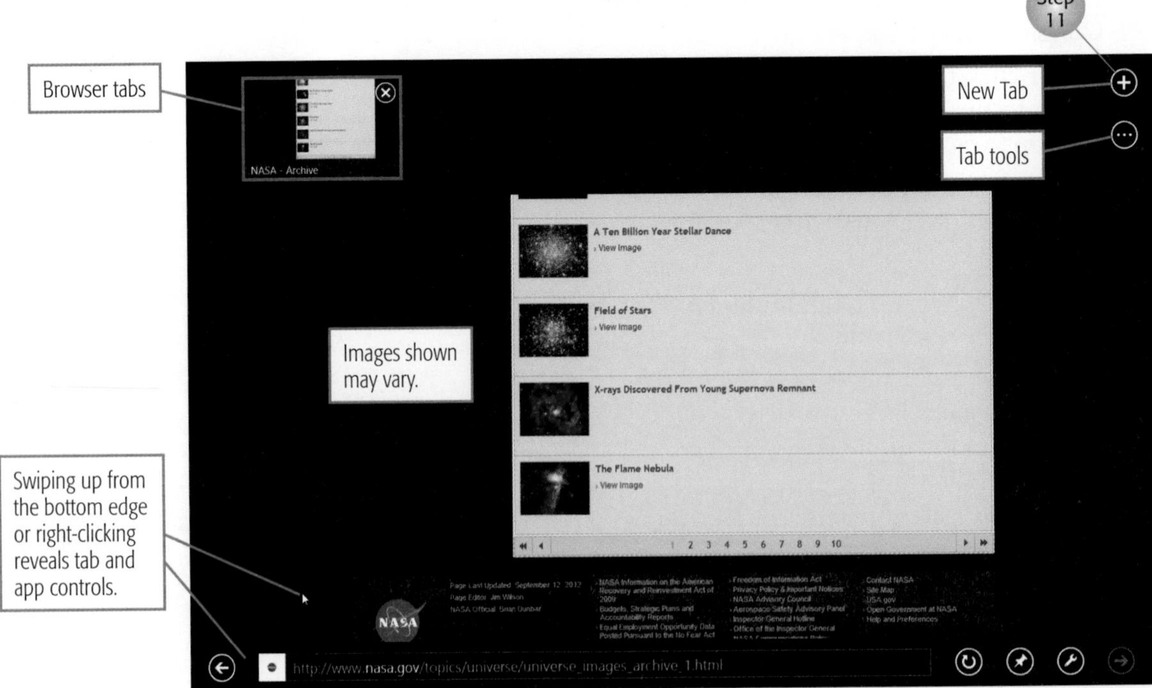

Figure 2.4 Browser tabs for displaying multiple web pages and navigation controls appear when you swipe up from the bottom edge or right-click a web page.

12 Type **www.flickr.com/commons** in the Address bar and then tap or press Enter.

The Commons at flickr contains collections of photos from the world's public photography archives. Images in the commons have no known copyright restrictions. The next time you need a picture or photo for a project, consider sourcing an image from this website.

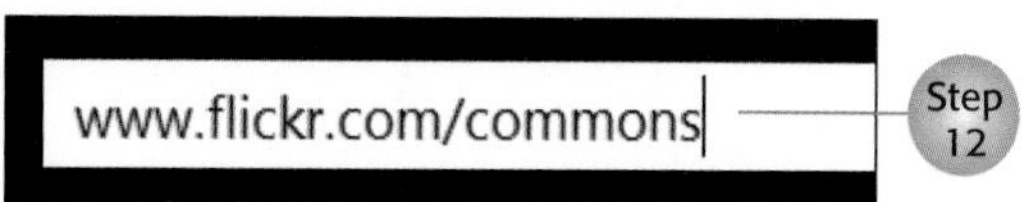

13 Swipe up from the bottom edge of the screen or right-click to reveal the tabs and then click the tab with the title NASA - Archive to switch pages.

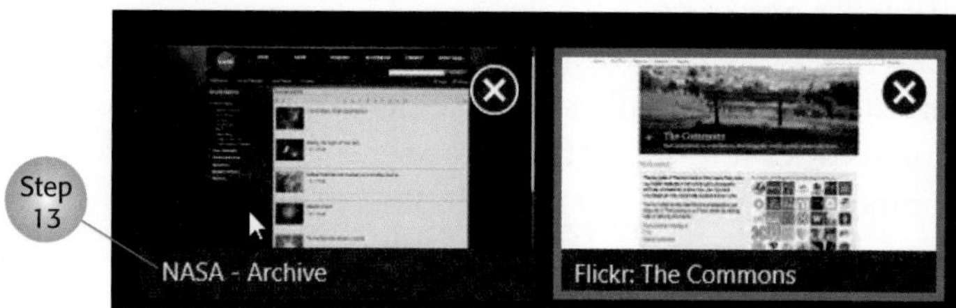

14 Reveal the tabs and tap or click the **Close Tab** control (displays with an × inside a circle) in the NASA - Archive tab.

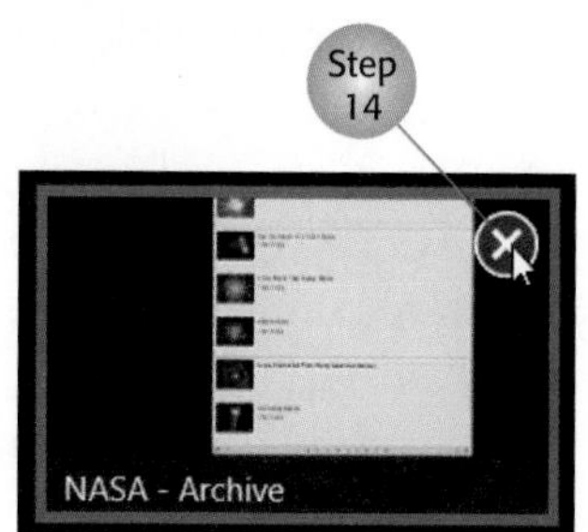

15 Tap or click in an unused space on the page to hide the tab controls.

16 Swipe up from the bottom edge or right-click, tap or click the **Pin site** control (displays as a push pin inside a circle), and then tap or click *Add to favorites*.

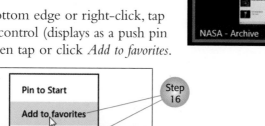

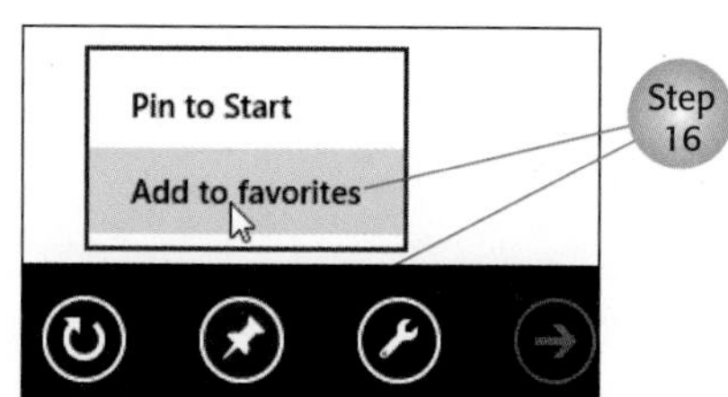

17 Tap or click in the Address bar to display the *Frequent* and *Favorites* lists above the Address bar.

Slide or scroll if necessary to view all Frequent and Favorites tiles.

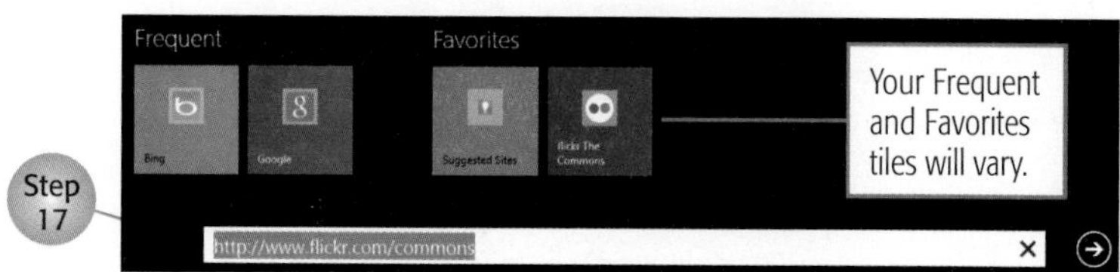

18 Tap or click any tile in the *Frequent* section to display the web page.

19 Close the IE app.

Start the IE App
Tap or click Internet Explorer tile from Start screen.

Display a Web Page
Tap or click in Address bar, type URL, and tap or press Enter.

Display Multiple Web Pages
1. Swipe up from bottom edge of screen or right-click.
2. Tap or click New Tab control.
3. Type URL for new web page.
4. Tap or press Enter.

Close a Tab
1. Swipe up from bottom edge of screen or right-click.
2. Tap or click Close Tab control.

Pin a Web Page to Favorites
1. Swipe up from bottom edge of screen or right-click.
2. Tap or click Pin site control.
3. Tap or click *Add to favorites*.

Select *Pin to Start* from the Pin site control pop-up list to add a web page as a tile on the Start screen.

Press and hold or right-click a tile and tap or click *Remove* to delete it from the Frequent or Favorites list.

TOPIC 2.3

SKILLS

Navigate the Web using Google Chrome

View multiple websites within the same window

Bookmark a page

Use the Find tool

Navigating the Web Using Google Chrome

Google Chrome is a free web browser for Windows-compatible PCs, Macs, or Linux PCs. The popularity of Google Chrome has been steadily increasing; the browser offers fast page loading and searching directly from the Address bar using Google. Complete the steps in this topic if you have the Google Chrome web browser installed on your device; otherwise, skip to the next topic.

Starting Google Chrome and Displaying a Web Page

1. Tap or click the Google Chrome tile from the Start screen and review the layout and tools in the Google Chrome window, as shown in Figure 2.5.

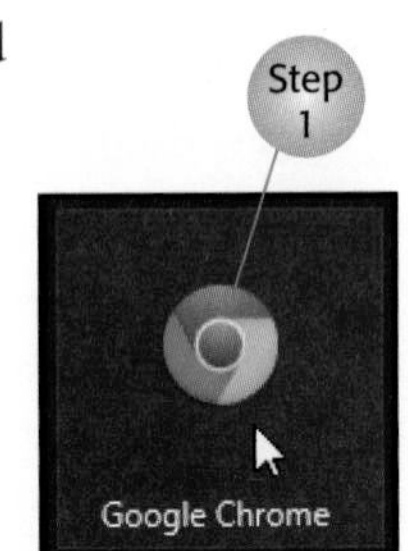

The Google Chrome window is launched in the Desktop app. If Google Chrome is not currently set as the default browser, you may be prompted to set it as the default browser in a message bar below the omnibox. Do not set Google Chrome as the default browser until after you have completed all of the topics in this chapter.

2. If a message displays asking you to sign in to Google Chrome, tap or click Skip for now.

3. If necessary, tap or click in the **omnibox**, type **www.pinterest.com**, and then tap or press Enter.

Pinterest is a social media website that is an online organizer for collecting your favorite pictures from the Web.

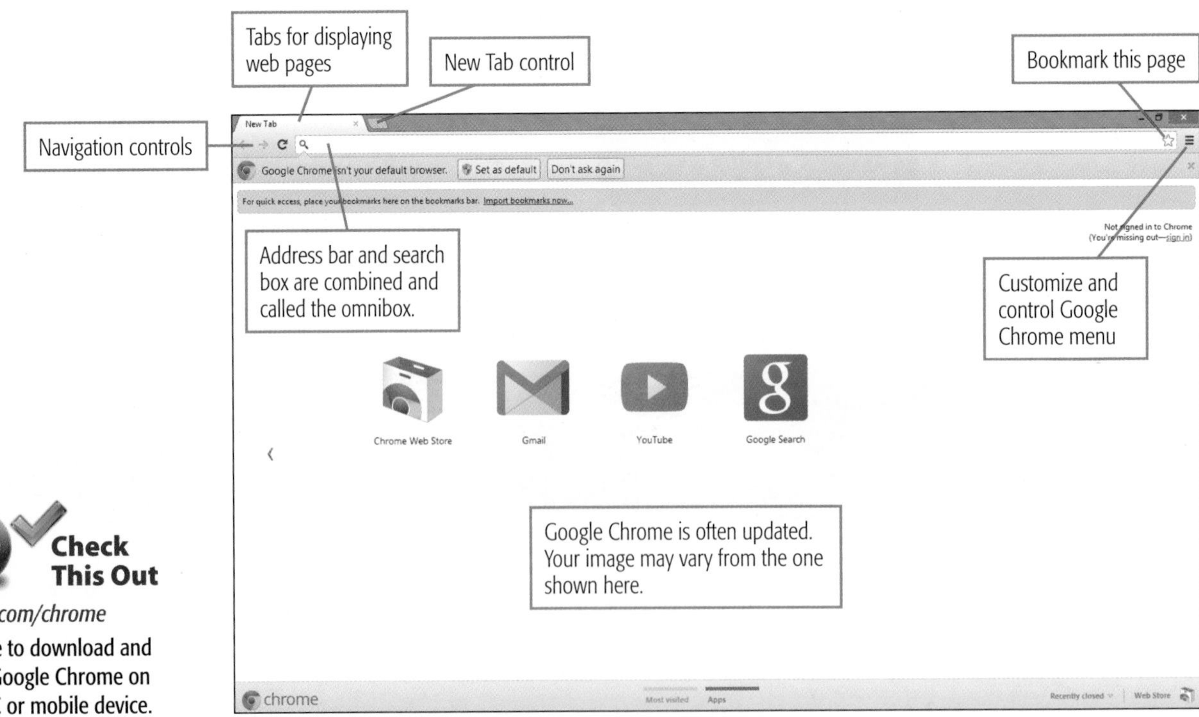

Figure 2.5 The Google Chrome window opens in the Desktop app.

Check This Out

google.com/chrome

Go here to download and install Google Chrome on your PC or mobile device.

4 Press and hold over Categories just below the Pinterest heading or point on Categories to see the drop-down list of headings by which images are grouped.

5 Tap or click a category heading that interests you. For example, tap or click the *Animals* category.

6 Slide or scroll down and view the pictures posted in the category you selected.

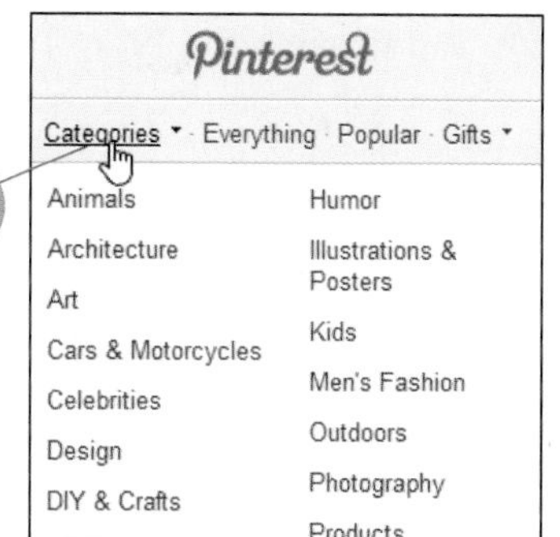

Displaying Multiple Web Pages and Bookmarking Pages

Similarly to IE, Google Chrome uses tabbed browsing to display more than one web page within the same browser window. Click a new tab and navigate to a web address to browse to a new site without closing the existing web page. Google Chrome displays a page name at the top of the tab along with a Close button. Web pages you visit frequently can be bookmarked by clicking the Bookmark this page icon (white star) at the right end of the omnibox.

If you sign in to Google Chrome using your Google account, your bookmarks and other browser preferences are saved and can be accessed on other PCs or mobile devices.

7 Tap or click the **Bookmark this page** icon (white star) at the right end of the omnibox.

The white star changes to a gold star, and the Bookmark dialog box appears.

8 Tap or click Done to close the Bookmark dialog box.

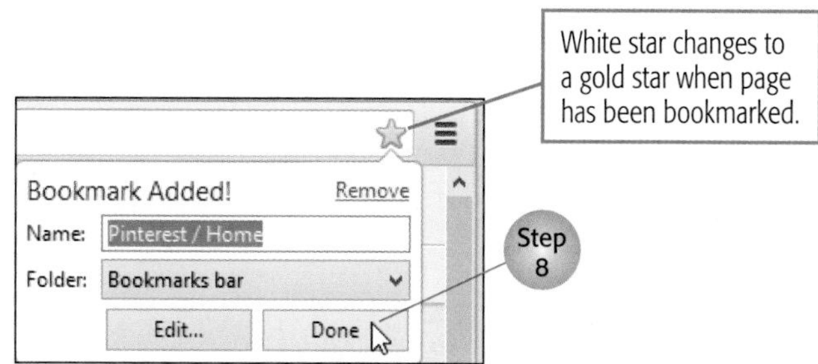

By default, bookmarks are added to the bookmarks bar, which is docked below the omnibox.

9 Tap or click the **Customize and control Google Chrome** button (displays with three short bars next to the star at the right end of the omnibox), tap or point to *Bookmarks* at the drop-down menu, and then tap or click *Show bookmarks bar.*

The **Bookmarks bar** appears below the omnibox.

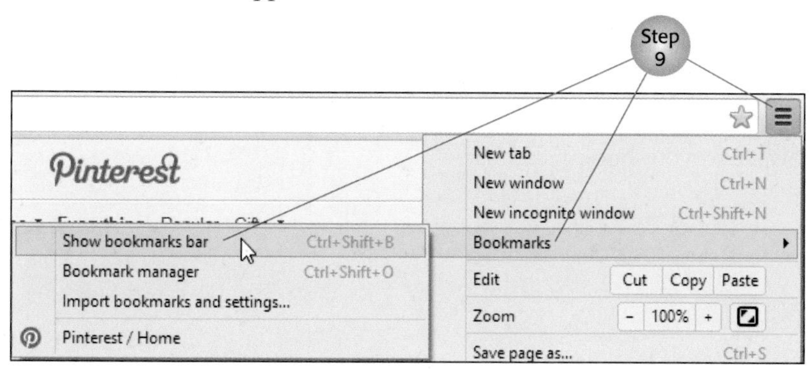

10 Tap or click the New Tab control next to the Pinterest / Home tab to open a new tab, type **www.youtube.com**, and then tap or press Enter.

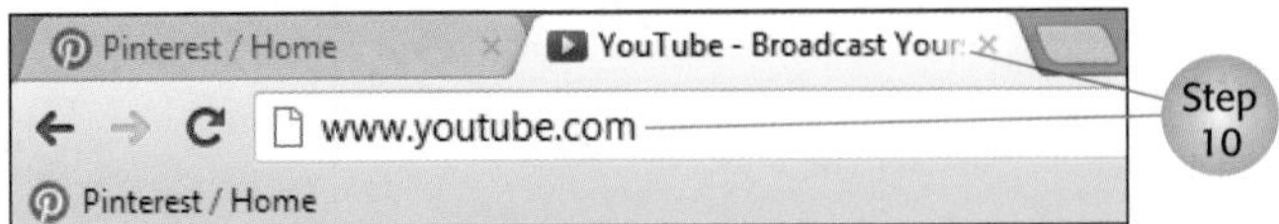

11 Tap or click the white star and then tap or click Done to add youtube.com to the Bookmarks bar.

Go to *Settings* from the Customize and control Google Chrome menu to change the default search engine.

Searching the Web from the Omnibox

Google Chrome allows you to type a search phrase directly in the omnibox, and search results from Google (or other default search engine) appear in the window.

12 Tap or click the New Tab control next to the YouTube tab, type **seven wonders of the world**, and then tap or press Enter.

Notice that as you type, searches that match your entry appear in a drop-down list below the omnibox. If one of the searches is what you are looking for, tap or click the item.

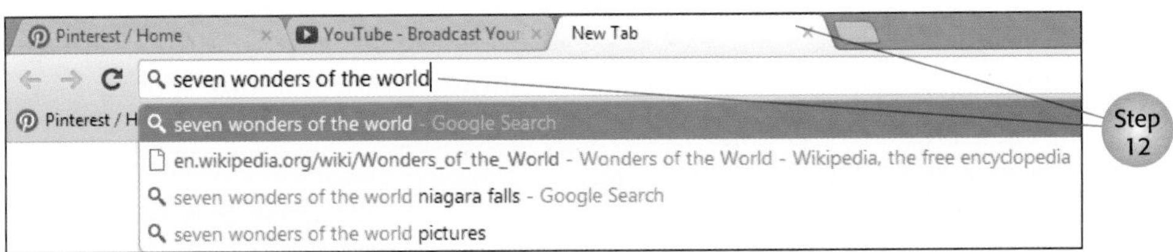

13 Tap or click Images for seven wonders of the world and slide or scroll down to view the pictures. Choose a different link if the specified link is not shown in your results list.

14 Tap or click in the omnibox to select the current entry, type **great wall of china**, and then tap or press Enter.

15 Tap or click Great Wall of China - Wikipedia, the free encyclopedia.

Finding Text on a Page

Use the Find command to locate a specific word or phrase on a web page. The Find command is accessed from the Customize and control Google Chrome menu.

16 Tap or click the Customize and control Google Chrome button and then tap or click *Find* at the drop-down menu.

This opens the **Find bar** at the right side of the window below the bookmarks bar.

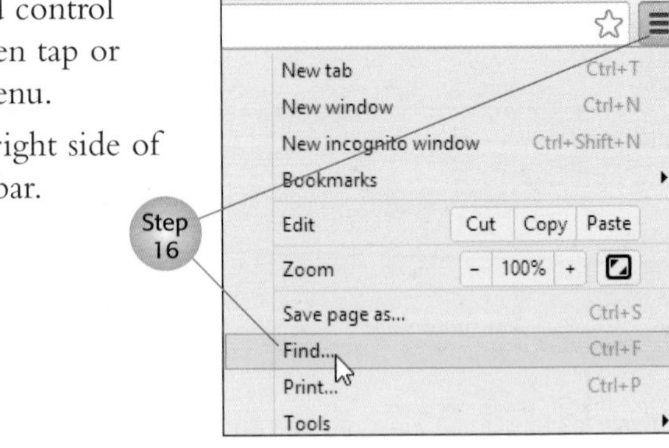

17 Type **ming dynasty** in the Find bar text box.

The currently selected match is shaded with an orange background, and the number of matches found on the web page displays in the Find bar next to the find text.

18 Tap or click Next in the Find bar to scroll the page to the next occurrence of *ming dynasty*.

19 Continue tapping or clicking Next until you have seen all occurrences.

20 Tap or click the Close button at the top right of the Google Chrome window to close Google Chrome.

21 Close the Desktop app.

Start the Google Chrome App
Tap or click Google Chrome tile from Start screen.

Display a Web Page
Tap or click in Address bar, type URL, and tap or press Enter.

Display Multiple Web Pages
1. Tap or click New Tab control.
2. Type URL for new web page.
3. Tap or press Enter.

Bookmark a Web Page
1. Display desired web page.
2. Tap or click white star.
3. Tap or click Done.

Display the Bookmarks Bar
1. Tap or click Customize and control Google Chrome button.
2. Tap or point to *Bookmarks*.
3. Tap or click *Show bookmarks bar*.

Find Text on a Web Page
1. Tap or click Customize and control Google Chrome button.
2. Tap or click *Find*.
3. Type text to find.
4. Tap or click Next for each occurrence.

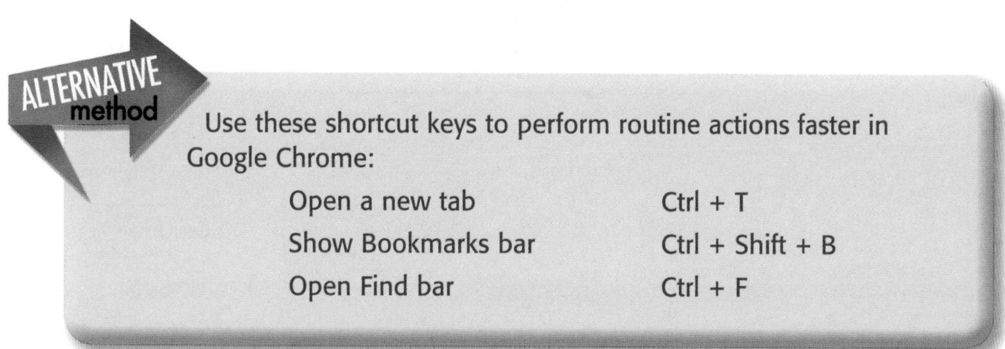

Use these shortcut keys to perform routine actions faster in Google Chrome:

Open a new tab	Ctrl + T
Show Bookmarks bar	Ctrl + Shift + B
Open Find bar	Ctrl + F

Google Chrome's Incognito Browsing

Tap or click the Customize and control Google Chrome button and tap or click *New incognito window* to open a new tab for **private browsing**. Web pages you visit while incognito will not appear in the browser history or search history, and any cookies that are created are automatically deleted after all incognito windows are closed.

TOPIC 2.4

SKILLS

Navigate the Web using Mozilla Firefox

View multiple websites within the same window

Bookmark a page

Use the Find tool

mozilla.org/firefox

Go here to download and install Mozilla's Firefox web browser on your PC or mobile device.

Navigating the Web Using Mozilla Firefox

Mozilla's Firefox is a free web browser that runs on Windows-compatible PCs, Macs, or Linux PCs. The software program is published by the nonprofit Mozilla Foundation. At the time of writing, Firefox was the third most popular web browser after IE and Google Chrome. Firefox fans use the browser for its speed in loading web pages. Complete the steps in this topic if you have the Firefox web browser installed on your device; otherwise, skip to the next topic.

Starting Firefox and Displaying a Web Page

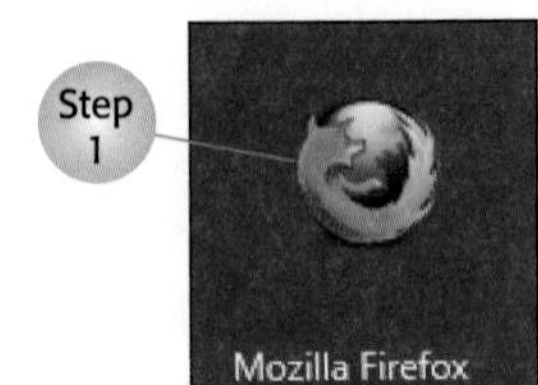

1. Tap or click the Mozilla Firefox tile from the Start screen and review the layout and tools in the Firefox window, as shown in Figure 2.6. Tap or click No if prompted to set Firefox as the default browser.

   The Firefox window is launched in the Desktop app.

2. Tap or click in the **Location bar** that displays Go to a Website, type **commons.wikimedia.org**, and then tap or press Enter.

   Wikimedia Commons is a media file repository maintained by volunteers. Go to this site to find images and sound and video clips that are free to use or copy by following the terms specified by the author, which often require only that you credit the source.

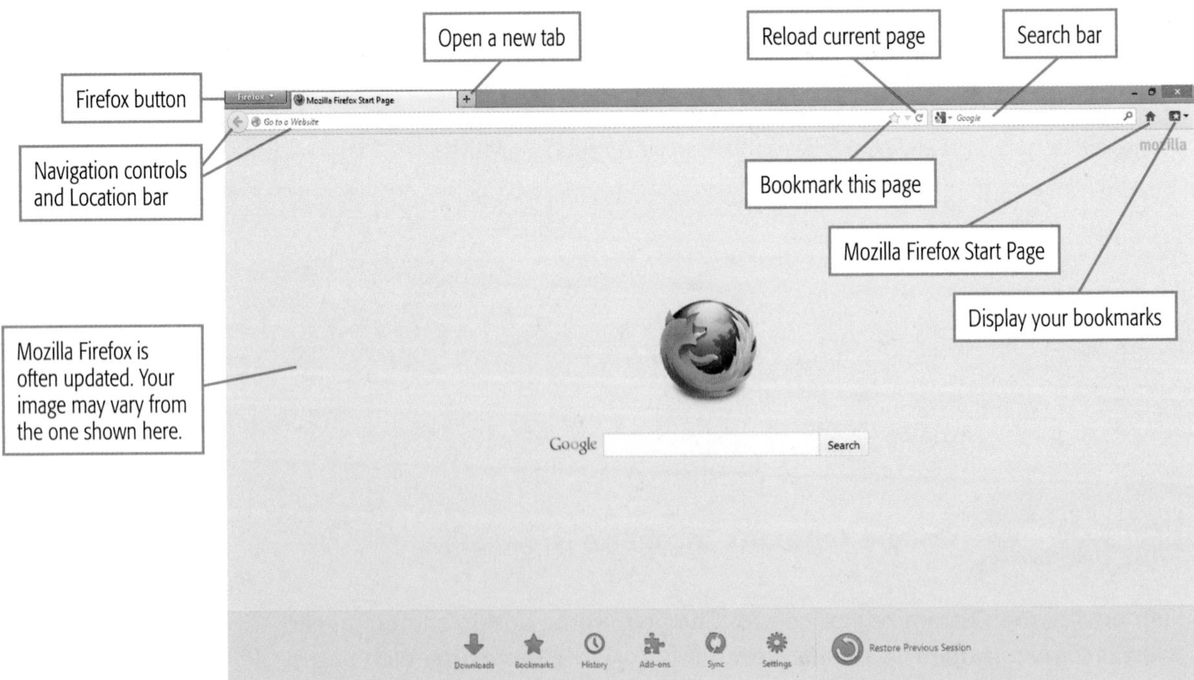

Figure 2.6 Mozilla Firefox is a free, open-source web browser that opens in the Desktop app.

3 Tap or click in the *Search Wikimedia Commons* text box near the top right of the Wikimedia Commons page that displays the word Search, type **clownfish**, and then tap or click the search icon (magnifying glass) or tap or press Enter.

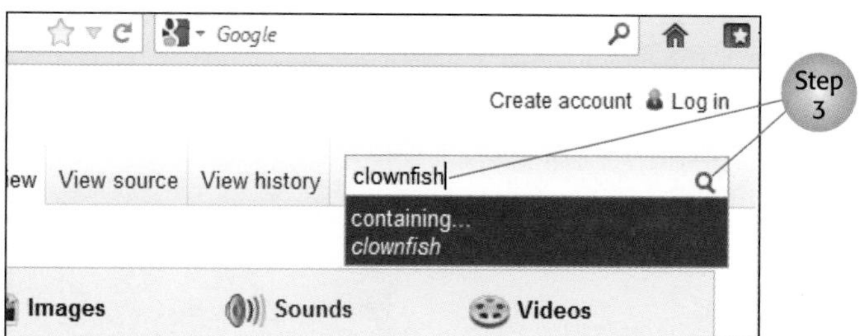

Did You Know?

At the time of writing, more than 14 million free-use images, sound clips, and other media files were available at Wikimedia Commons.

4 Slide or scroll down and view the pictures of clownfish.

Displaying Multiple Web Pages and Bookmarking Pages

Similarly to IE and Google Chrome, Firefox provides for tabbed browsing. Tap or click the **Open a new tab** control (displays with a plus symbol) and type a web address in the Location bar. Firefox displays a title for a page in the tab along with a Close button. Web pages you visit frequently can be bookmarked by clicking the Bookmark this page icon (white star) at the right end of the Location bar.

5 Tap or click the Bookmark this page icon (white star) at the right end of the Location bar.

The white star changes to gold for bookmarked pages.

Firefox includes a Bookmarks bar that displays below the Location bar. Turn on the Bookmarks bar from the Display your bookmarks menu. Add a web page to the Bookmarks bar by displaying the page and then dragging the page's icon from the Location bar onto the Bookmarks bar.

6 Tap or click the Open a new tab control (displays as a plus symbol) next to the Wikimedia tab.

7 Type **wikitravel.org** and then tap or press Enter.

Wikitravel is a worldwide travel guide written and updated by travelers.

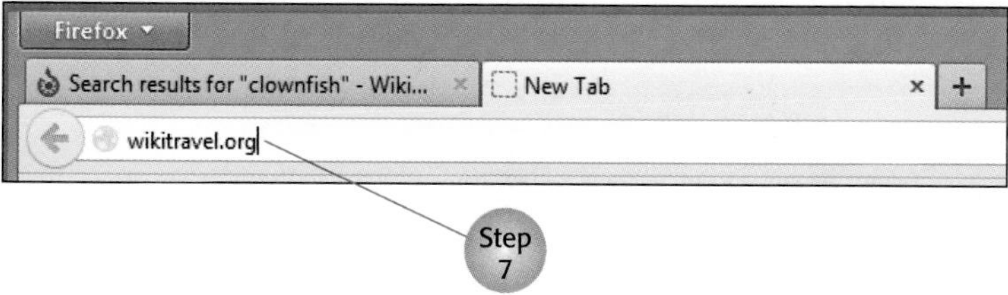

8 Tap or click the Bookmark this page icon (white star) to add the page to your bookmarks.

9 Tap or click the **Display your bookmarks** button at the right end of the Location bar (last button), tap or click *Recently Bookmarked*, and then tap or click *Search results for "clownfish" - Wikimedia Commons* at the side menu.

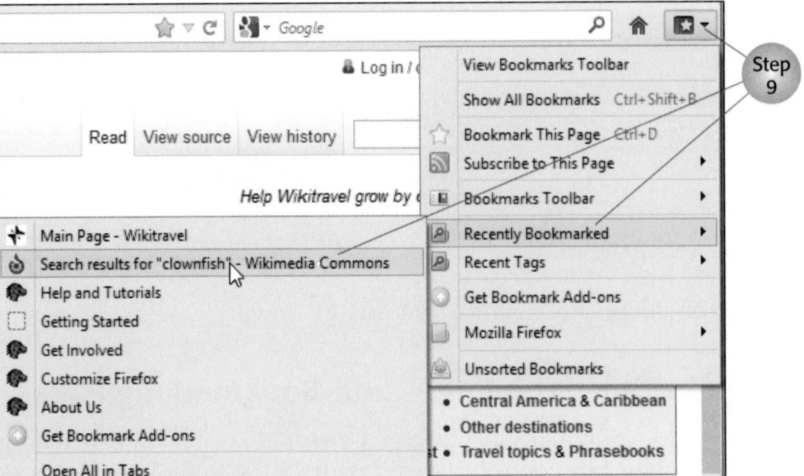

App Tip

To delete a bookmark, display the web page, tap or click the gold star in the Location bar, and tap or click Remove Bookmark in the Edit this Bookmark box.

10 Tap or click the Close Tab icon in the second tab titled Search results for "clownfish" - Wikimedia Commons to close the page.

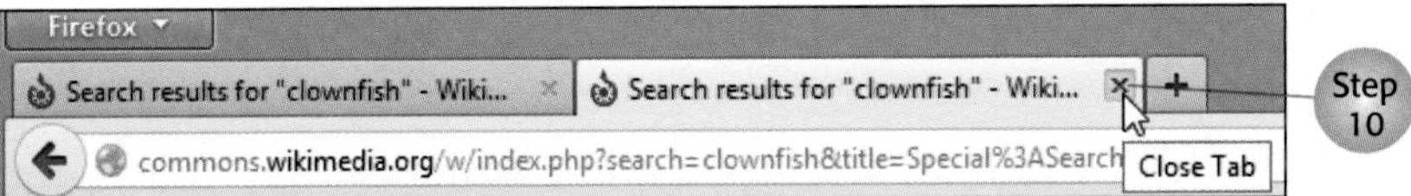

Finding Text on a Page

Open the Find bar in Firefox to search for all occurrences of a word or phrase on a web page. The Find bar is accessed from the Firefox button.

11 Tap or click the Firefox button at the top left of the window and then tap or click *Find* at the drop-down menu.

The Find bar opens at the bottom left of the Firefox window with an insertion point positioned in the Find text box. As you begin typing an entry in the text box, Firefox will immediately begin highlighting matches for the search text on the current web page. If no matches are found, Firefox sounds a chime and shades the Find box red.

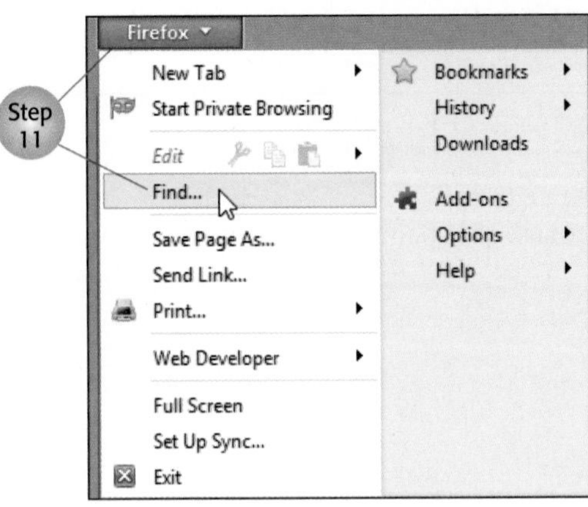

12 Type **ocellaris**.

The first matched occurrence of the search text is shaded green.

13 Tap or click Next to move to the next occurrence of *ocellaris* on the page.

14 Continue tapping or clicking Next until you return to the first occurrence near the top of the page.

15 Tap or click the Close Find bar button (displays with an ×) at the left end of the Find bar.

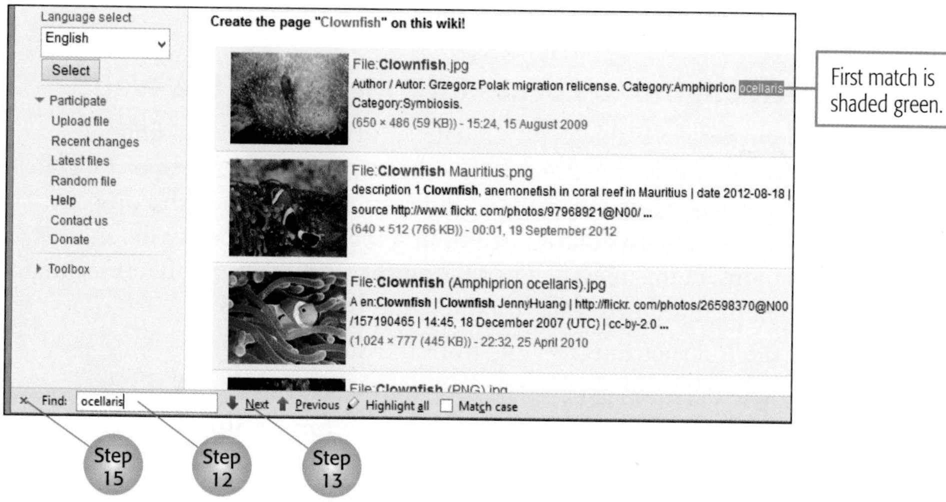

Start the Firefox App
Tap or click Mozilla Firefox tile from Start screen.

Display a Web Page
Tap or click in Location bar, type URL, and tap or press Enter.

Display Multiple Web Pages
1. Tap or click Open a new tab.
2. Type URL for new web page.
3. Tap or press Enter.

Bookmark a Web Page
1. Display desired web page.
2. Tap or click white star.

Display Bookmarks
1. Tap or click Display your bookmarks.
2. Tap or click *Recently Bookmarked*.
3. Tap or click desired bookmark.

Open the Find Bar
1. Tap or click Firefox button.
2. Tap or click *Find*.

Search Using the Search Bar
Type search phrase in Search bar and tap or press Enter.

Searching the Web Using the Search Bar

Search for information using a popular search engine such as Google or Bing by typing a search phrase in the **Search bar** near the top right of the Firefox window.

16 Tap or click in the Search bar near the top right of the window, type **tropical fish**, and then tap or press Enter, or tap or click the search button.

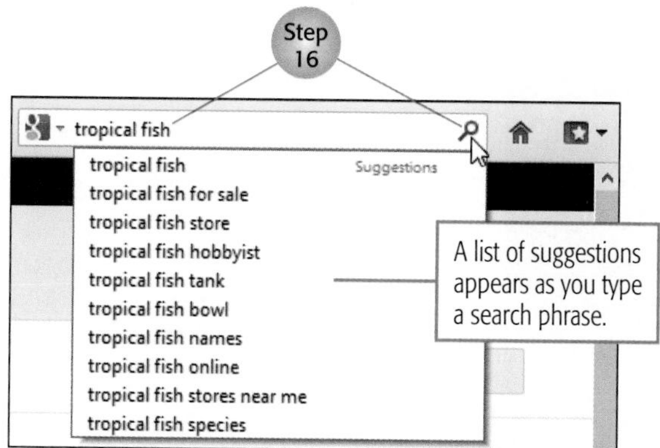

Choose a different search engine by tapping or clicking the search engine's icon in the Search bar and selecting a different search engine at the drop-down list.

17 Tap or click a link to a web page that interests you from the search results list.

18 Tap or click the Close button at the top right of the Firefox window to close Firefox.

19 Close the Desktop app.

TOPIC 2.5

SKILLS

Use search tools to find information on the Web

Narrow search results by applying advanced search options

Print a web page, including selected pages only

Searching for Information and Printing Web Pages

A **search engine** is a company that indexes web pages by keywords and provides a search tool with which you can search their indexes to find web pages. To create indexes, search engines use programs called **spiders** or **crawlers** that read web pages and other information supplied by the website owner.

Some search engines provide a list of topics or subjects by which you can navigate or search in addition to a search tool. Search engines also provide advanced tools, which you can use to narrow search results.

Using a Search Engine to Locate Information on the Web

Several search engines are available, with Google and Bing the two leading companies; however, consider searching using other search engines such as Dogpile, Ask, and Yahoo! as well because you will get different results from each company. Spider and crawler program capabilities and timing for indexing create differences in search results among companies. Depending on the information you are seeking, performing a search in more than one search engine is a good idea.

1 Tap or click the Internet Explorer tile from the Start screen.

2 If Bing is not the default page displayed, drag to select the text in the Address bar or click to select the existing web address, type **bing.com**, and then tap or press Enter.

3 With the insertion point positioned in the Search text box, type **cover letter examples** and then tap or press Enter (Enter key displays as *Search* on touch keyboard in Bing), or tap or click the Search button (magnifying glass).

Notice that Bing provides search suggestions that match the characters you type in a drop-down list below the Search text box as soon as you begin typing. Tap or click a search suggestion if you see a close match.

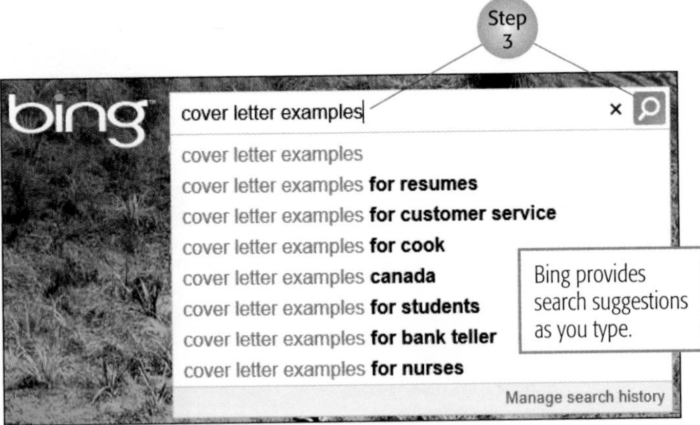

4 Slide or scroll down the search results page and tap or click a link to a page that interests you.

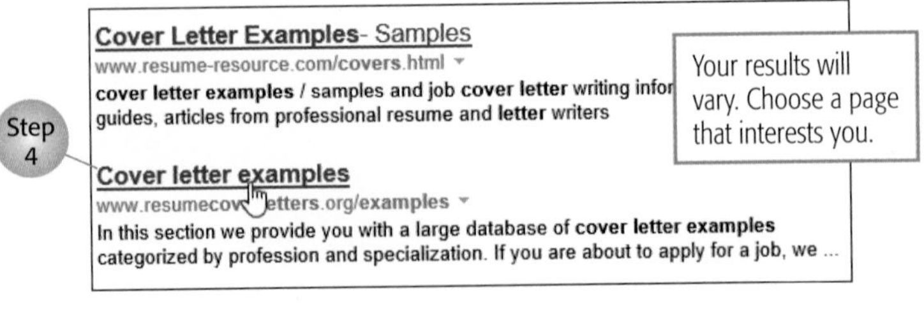

Check This Out

dogpile.com

Go here to perform a search using a metasearch search engine. Metasearch search engines send your search phrase to other search engines and show you one list of search results from the wider group.

5 Read a few paragraphs about cover letters at the page you selected.

6 Tap or click the Back button or slide right to return to the search results list.

7 Select the text in the Address bar, type **yahoo.com**, and then tap or press Enter.

8 With the insertion point positioned in the Search text box, type **cover letter examples** and then tap or press Enter, or tap or click the Search button next to the text box.

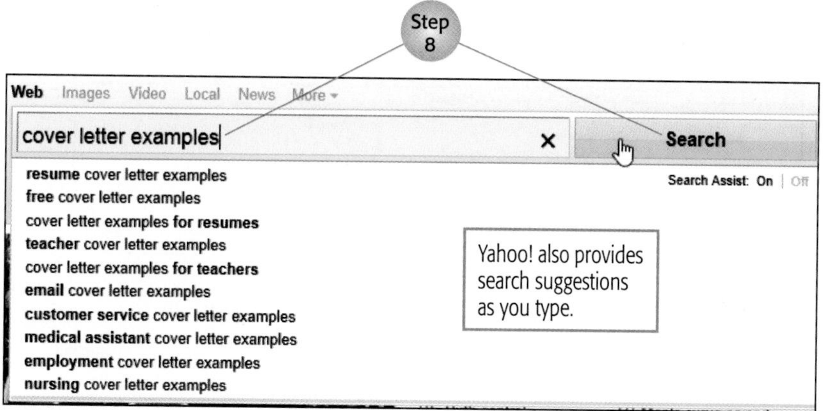

Tap or click a category above a search box or along the top of a search engine's web page to restrict search results to a specific type of content such as Images, Videos, Maps, or News.

9 Slide or scroll down the search results page. Notice that some links are to the same web pages that you saw in Bing's search results; however, the same page may be in a different order in the list or you may notice new links not shown by Bing.

Using Advanced Search Options

In both Bing and Yahoo!, the search results for the cover letter examples resulted in millions of links in the results page. Search engines provide tools to help you narrow the search results. Each search engine provides different tools. Explore the options at the search engine you prefer or look for a help link that provides information on how to use **advanced search tools**.

10 Slide or scroll to the top of the search results page and tap or click the Options link at the right of the Search button.

11 Tap or click Advanced Search at the drop-down list.

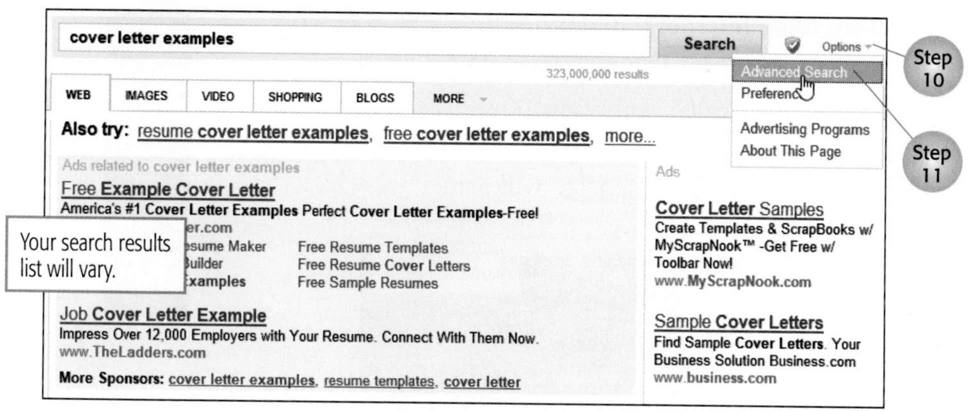

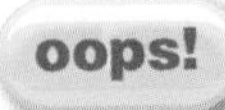

No *Only .edu domains* option? If you are browsing using Yahoo! Canada, choose *Only .org domains* instead.

Yahoo!'s advanced search tools include specifying phrases to include or exclude, and restricting searches to a specific file format, country, or language.

12 Tap or click the *Only .edu domains* option.

13 Tap or click the Yahoo! Search button at the top of the Advanced Web Search page.

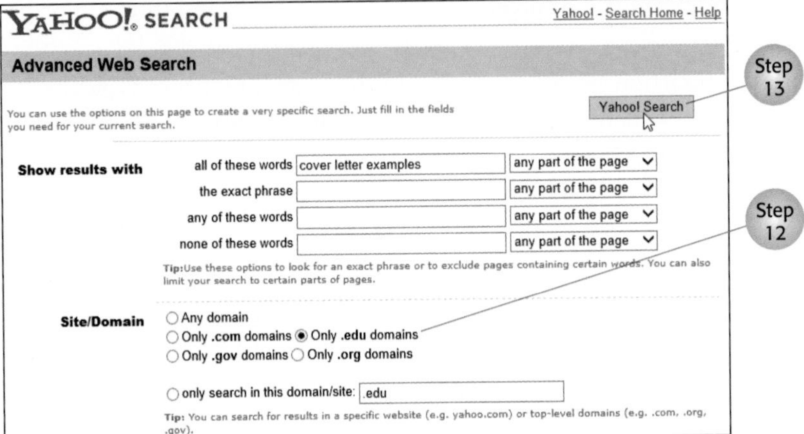

14 Tap or click *Past month* in the *FILTER BY TIME* section at the left side of the search results page.

Notice the search results list is now significantly reduced from the millions in the prior results list.

15 Slide or scroll down the search results page and tap or click a link to a page that interests you.

Printing a Web Page

Printing a web page can sometimes be frustrating because web pages are designed for optimal screen viewing (not printing). Many times you may print a web page only to discard a second or third page that you did not need, or the content printed did not fit the width of the paper and the printout was unusable.

Did You Know?

Some web pages provide a link to view the page in a printable format. Look for a View Printable *link, which reformats the content for a letter-size page that you can print.*

16 Select the text in the Address bar, type **studentaffairs.stanford.edu/cdc/resumes/cover-ltr-writing**, and then tap or press Enter.

This page contains several tips for writing effective cover letters. Assume you decide to print the page for later use when you are looking for a job.

17 Reveal the charms and tap or click Devices. Skip to Step 23 if you are using Internet Explorer in the Desktop version.

A list of installed printers appears in the Devices pane.

18 Tap or click the printer you want to use.

The page displays in a Printer pane with a preview window that allows you to view how the page will print.

oops!

No printer shown in the Devices list? Tap or click Microsoft XPS Document Writer, which prints to a file similar to Adobe's PDF.

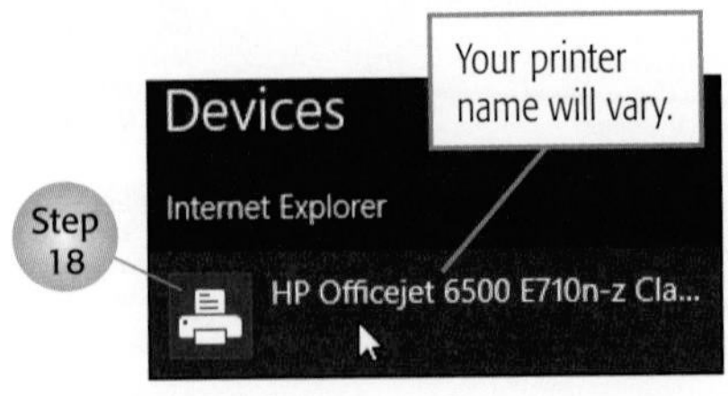

19 Slide left in the preview window or tap or click the Next Page arrow to view all of the pages that need to be printed.

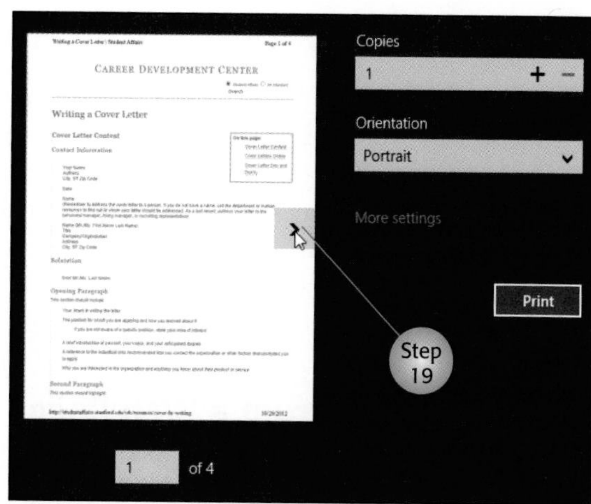

The web page needs four pages to print, with the last page being unnecessary. The More settings link provides more print options; however, an option to control individual pages to print is not available. In the next steps, you will load the page in the Desktop IE app, which provides a Print dialog box.

20 Tap or click in an unused space on the web page to remove the Printer pane.

21 If necessary, swipe up from the bottom edge of the screen or right-click to display the navigation and app controls.

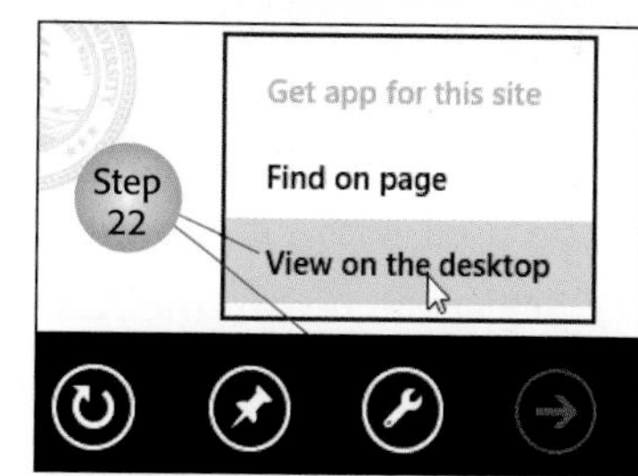

22 Tap or click the Page Tools control at the bottom right of the window (displays as a wrench) and then tap or click *View on the desktop*.

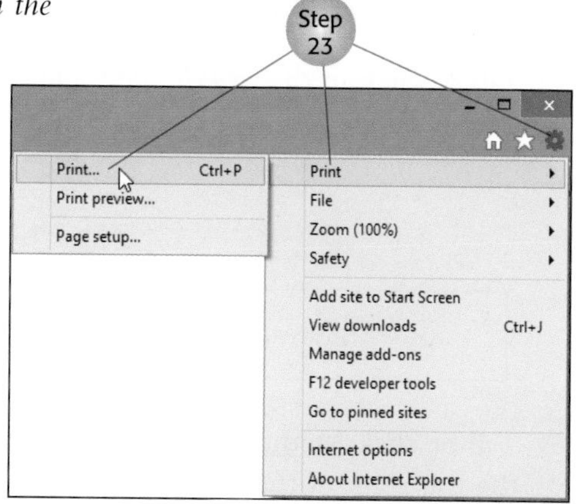

23 Tap or click the Tools widget at the top right of the IE window (just below the Close button), tap or click *Print*, and then tap or click *Print* at the Print menu.

24 Tap or click *Pages* in the *Page Range* section of the Print dialog box, type **1-3** in the *Pages* text box, and then tap or click the Print button.

Only pages 1, 2, and 3 of the web page print.

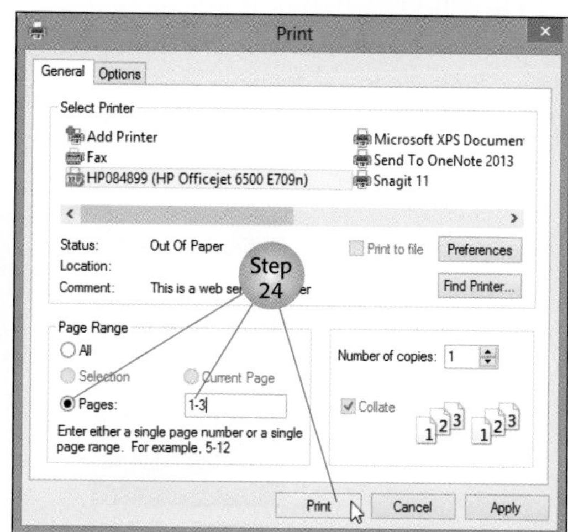

25 Close Internet Explorer.

26 Close the Desktop.

Use a Search Engine to Find Information
1. Start Internet Explorer.
2. Type URL for desired search engine and tap or press Enter.
3. Type search phrase in Search text box.
4. Tap or press Enter.

Use Yahoo!'s Advanced Web Search Options
1. Start Internet Explorer.
2. Type **yahoo.com** in Address bar and tap or press Enter.
3. Type search phrase in Search text box.
4. Tap or press Enter.
5. Tap or click Options link.
6. Tap or click Advanced Search.
7. Select desired advanced search options.
8. Tap or click Yahoo! Search.

Print a Web Page
1. Display desired web page.
2. Reveal charms.
3. Tap or click Devices.
4. Tap or click desired printer name.
5. Set print options as desired.
6. Tap or click Print.

Print Selected Web Pages
1. Display desired web page.
2. Tap or click Page tools control.
3. Tap or click *View on the desktop*.
4. Tap or click Tools widget.
5. Tap or click *Print*, tap or click *Print* again.
6. Tap or click *Pages*.
7. Type pages to print.
8. Tap or click Print.

Use *Page setup* from the Print drop-down menu to change print options such as page orientation and margins.

TOPIC 2.6

SKILLS

Download a picture from a web page

View the picture in the Pictures library

Downloading Content from a Web Page

Copying an image, audio clip, video clip, or music file (such as MP3) from a web page to your PC or mobile device is referred to as **downloading** content. Most content is protected by copyright law from being used by someone else without permission. Before you download content, check the website for restrictions against copying information. Look for a contact link and request permission from the website owner to use the content if no restrictions are shown. Always cite the original source of any content you copy from a web page.

Saving a Picture from a Web Page

Saving content generally involves selecting an object and displaying a context menu from which you can select to copy or save the object.

1. Tap or click the Internet Explorer tile from the Start screen.

Assume you want to find an image of the Grand Canyon for a project. You decide to use the flickr Commons page to find a picture in the public domain that can be used without copyright restrictions.

2. Select the text in the Address bar to reveal the Frequent and Favorites tiles.
3. Tap or click the Flickr: The Commons tile in the Favorites list (you added this tile to Favorites in Topic 2.2).

Step 3

Flickr: The Commons

4. If necessary, slide or scroll down to the section titled *A Commons Sampler.*
5. Tap or click in the *Search The Commons* text box, type **grand canyon**, and then tap or press Enter, or tap or click the SEARCH button.

oops!

Don't have flickr The Commons in your Favorites list? If necessary, type *flickr.com/commons* in the Address bar and tap or press Enter.

Step 5

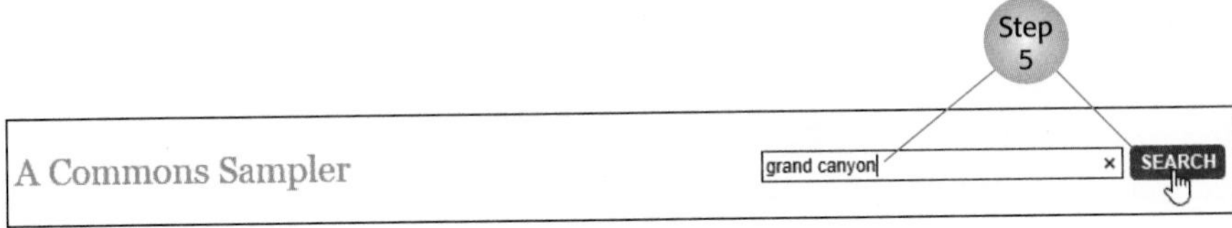

6. Tap or click Medium in the *View* section at the top right of the search results page if the current View setting is not Medium.
7. Slide or scroll down and view the images in the search results page.
8. Tap or click a picture that you like and want to save.

Step 6

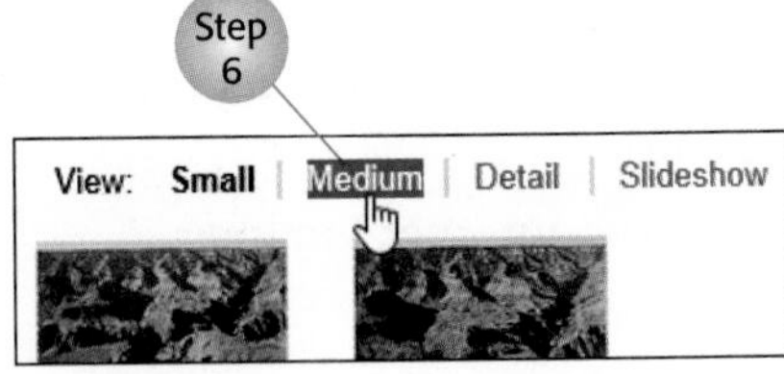

Step 8

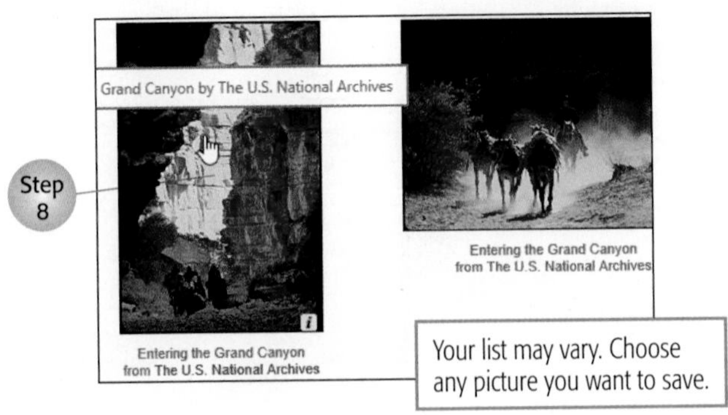

Your list may vary. Choose any picture you want to save.

9 At the next page, slide or scroll down if necessary and read the description below the photograph. Note the access and use restrictions, if any.

10 If necessary, slide or scroll back up the page and press and hold over the picture or right-click to reveal the context menu.

11 Tap or click Medium 500 at the View menu that appears over the picture.

12 At the Photo / All sizes page, press and hold or right-click the picture to display the shortcut menu and then tap or click *Save to picture library*.

Step 11

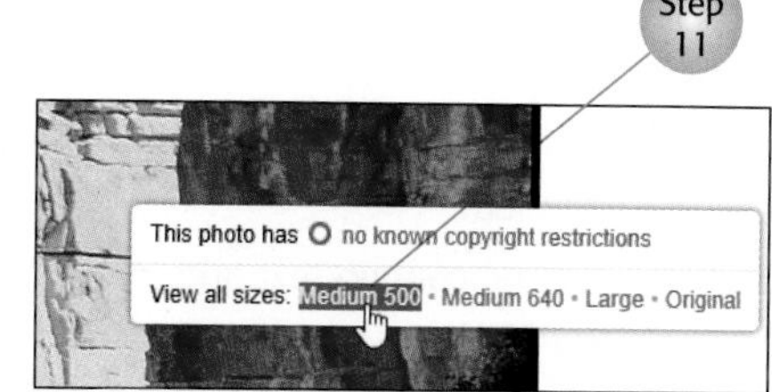

Save a Picture from a web page

1. Display desired web page.
2. Press and hold or right-click image.
3. Tap or click *Save to picture library*.

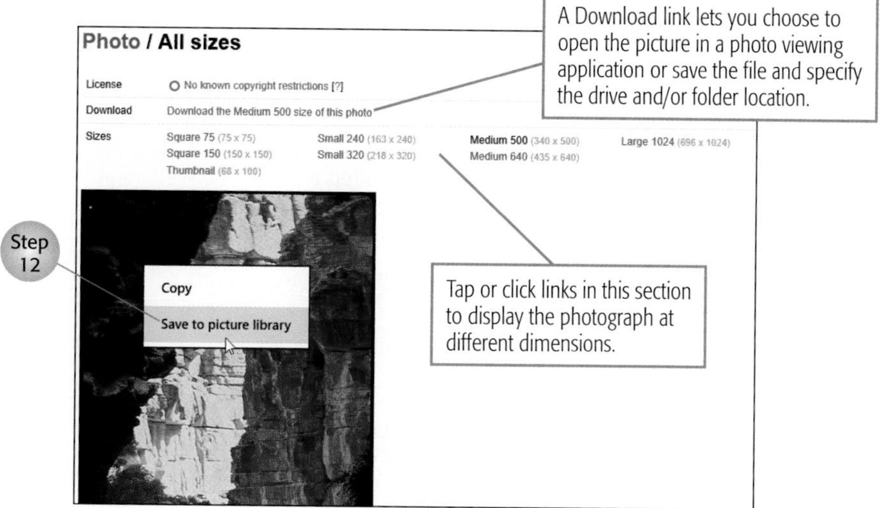

Step 12

oops!

Different context menu? In Google Chrome, Firefox, and IE 9 or earlier, right-clicking a picture shows a shortcut menu from which you select *Save image as* or *Save picture as* and choose a storage medium and/or folder in which to save the file.

13 Close the IE app.

14 Tap or click the Photos app from the Start screen.

15 If necessary, tap or click the Pictures library in the Photos app window.

16 The Grand Canyon photo downloaded from the flickr Commons page is shown in the Pictures library. If necessary, slide or scroll right to view the picture.

17 Close the Photos app.

Step 15

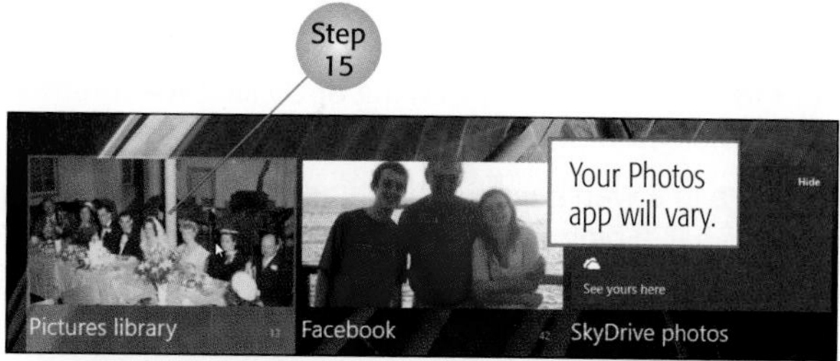

Step 16

A picture downloaded from a web page can be inserted into a document or presentation by opening an Insert Picture dialog box and specifying the drive, folder, and file name for the image.

Concepts Review

Topic	Key Concepts	Key Terms
Introduction to the Internet and the World Wide Web	The Internet is the physical structure that represents the global network that links together individuals and organizations. All of the web pages circulated on the Internet form the World Wide Web. Documents that contain text and multimedia elements are called web pages. A web page also contains hyperlinks, which are used to move from one page to another. A web browser is a software program used to view web pages such as Internet Explorer, Google Chrome, and Mozilla Firefox. An Internet Service Provider is a company that provides Internet service to individuals and businesses for a fee. A web address is a unique text-based address, also called a Uniform Resource Locator, that identifies each web page on the Internet. A web address is made up of parts that define the protocol, domain, folder, and file name for the web page. You use search tools to find a web page when you do not know the web address.	Internet (Net) Web pages World Wide Web (Web or WWW) Hyperlinks Links Web browser Internet Service Provider (ISP) Web address Uniform Resource Locator (URL)
Navigating the Web Using Internet Explorer	Internet Explorer (IE) is the web browser included with Microsoft Windows. In Windows 8, Internet Explorer version 10 is included. The IE app launched from the Start screen varies from the IE app launched from the Desktop in the placement of the navigation tools and Address bar, as well as the page viewing area. Start Internet Explorer by tapping or clicking the Internet Explorer tile from the Start screen. Navigate to a web page by selecting the current text in the Address bar, typing the URL for the web page, and tapping or clicking Enter. Tap or click hyperlinks on web pages to navigate to the linked page. Tap or click the Back control or slide right to move back one page. Tap or click the Forward control or slide left to move forward one page. Tabbed browsing means you have multiple web pages open in an IE window, with each web page in a separate tab. Swipe up from the bottom or right-click to reveal controls and tap or click the New Tab control to open a new tab in which to display a web page. Close a web page by revealing the tab controls and tapping or clicking the Close Tab control for the page. Display a web page, reveal controls, tap or click the Pin site control, and tap or click Add to favorites to add a web page to the Favorites tiles.	Internet Explorer (IE) Address bar Back Forward Tabbed browsing Favorites New Tab Close Tab Pin site

Topic	Key Concepts	Key Terms
Navigating the Web Using Google Chrome	Google Chrome is a free web browser for Windows-compatible PCs, Linux PCs, or Macs. Google Chrome is becoming more popular because of its loading speed for web pages and ability to search directly from the Address bar. Start Google Chrome by tapping or clicking the Google Chrome tile from the Start screen. Google Chrome launches in the Desktop. In Google Chrome, the Address bar and Search box are combined and referred to as the omnibox. Tap or click the Bookmark this page icon (white star) to add a web page to the Bookmarks bar. Use the Customize and control Google Chrome button to access the Bookmarks menu and turn on the display of the Bookmarks bar. Tap or click the New Tab control to open a new tab in which to display another web page. Open the Find bar from the Customize and control Google Chrome menu to locate all occurrences of a word or phrase in the current web page. Private browsing with Google Chrome's incognito browsing feature lets you browse web pages without tracking history or saving cookies from the web pages visited.	Google Chrome Omnibox Bookmark this page Customize and control Google Chrome Bookmarks bar Find bar Private browsing
Navigating the Web Using Mozilla Firefox	Mozilla Firefox is a free web browser for Windows-compatible PCs, Linux PCs, or Macs. Start Mozilla Firefox by tapping or clicking the Mozilla Firefox tile from the Start screen. Mozilla Firefox launches in the Desktop. Display a web page by typing the URL in the Location bar and tapping or pressing Enter. Tap or click the Open a new tab control to display a web page in another tab. Add a web page to the Bookmarks bar by tapping or clicking the Bookmark this page icon (white star). Tap or click the Display your bookmarks button to show a bookmarked page from the Recently Bookmarked list. Tap or click the Firefox button to open the Find bar to locate all occurrences of a word or phrase on the current web page. Type a search word or phrase in the Search bar to search for information using the default search engine.	Mozilla Firefox Location bar Open a new tab Display your bookmarks Search bar

continued....

Topic	Key Concepts	Key Terms
Searching for Information and Printing Web Pages	A company that indexes web pages by keywords using programs called spiders or crawlers and provides a search tool to find the pages is called a search engine. Google and Bing are two leading search engines; however, several other companies provide search tools, such as Yahoo!, Ask, and Dogpile. Use more than one search engine because you will get different results from each due to differences in spider and crawling programs and timing differentials. To find information using a search engine, launch a web browser, type the URL for the desired search engine, type a search word or phrase in the search text box, and tap or press Enter. Each search engine provides tools for advanced searching, which narrows the search results list. For example, at Yahoo!, the Advanced Web Search page provides options to include or exclude words in the search and restrict search results to types of domains, file formats, country, or language. Print a web page by selecting a printer from the Devices list, which is accessed by revealing charms. Printing selected pages from a web page requires that you display the page in the Desktop IE app and open the Print dialog box from the Tools widget.	Search engine Spiders Crawlers Advanced search tools
Downloading Content from a Web Page	Copying an image, audio clip, video clip, or music file from a web page to your PC or mobile device is called downloading. Most content is protected by copyright law. Check a website for restrictions on copied content and request permission to use before downloading. Saving content generally involves selecting an object and displaying a context menu at which you specify to copy to the clipboard or save the object as a file on your PC or mobile device. Pictures downloaded from a web page are automatically saved to the Pictures library and can be viewed from the Photos app.	Downloading

Multiple Choice

1. Web pages are stored in a format that is read and interpreted for display by this type of software program.
   a. Hypertext
   b. Internet Reader Program
   c. Internet Service Provider
   d. Web browser
2. A web address is also referred to as a(n) ______________.
   a. HTTP
   b. URL
   c. ISP
   d. WWW
3. Internet Explorer 10 can be launched from the Start screen or in this app.
   a. Desktop
   b. Photos
   c. People
   d. News
4. In Internet Explorer 10, use this control to display a second web page in the same window.
   a. New Tab
   b. Pin site
   c. Favorites
   d. Page tools

5. In Google Chrome you type the web address in this box.
   a. Find box
   b. Tab box
   c. Omnibox
   d. Bookmark box
6. Tap or click this icon in Google Chrome to add a web page to the bookmarks bar.
   a. Customize and control Google Chrome
   b. Refresh
   c. Start page
   d. White star
7. Firefox is published by this foundation.
   a. Wikimedia
   b. Open Source Alliance
   c. Mozilla
   d. Wikimedia Commons
8. Open the Find bar in Firefox by tapping or clicking this button.
   a. Search
   b. Firefox
   c. Bookmarks
   d. Reload
9. Search engines index web pages using this type of program.
   a. Spiders
   b. Browsers
   c. Trawlers
   d. Hypertext
10. Tap or click this charm in the IE app to select a printer to print a web page.
    a. Search
    b. Devices
    c. Printers
    d. Settings
11. Copying an image from a web page is referred to as ____________________.
    a. Uploading
    b. Freeloading
    c. Copyrighting
    d. Downloading

Crossword Puzzle

ACROSS

4 Address bar and search box combined in Google Chrome
7 Bookmark this page icon in Google Chrome
8 Company such as Google or Bing
10 Global network
11 Web address
12 Search text box in Firefox

DOWN

1 Library where downloaded pictures are saved
2 Add to favorites control in IE 10
3 Saving a picture from a web page
5 Type URL here in Firefox
6 Wrench control in IE 10
9 Plus symbol inside circle in IE 10

Matching

Match the term with the statement or definition.

_______ 1. Web address
_______ 2. Internet Explorer 10 Start screen app
_______ 3. Google's web browser
_______ 4. Mozilla's web browser
_______ 5. Saved links
_______ 6. Advanced search options
_______ 7. Tools widget in IE 10 Desktop app
_______ 8. Save to picture library

a. Only edu domains
b. Used to print selected pages
c. Bookmarks
d. URL
e. Chrome
f. Downloading
g. Firefox
h. Maximum page viewing

Project 1 Browsing Web Pages

Individual

Deliverable: Printed web pages, document with screen captures, or Microsoft XPS documents

1. Start Internet Explorer, Google Chrome, or Mozilla Firefox and navigate to **www.nga.gov**, which is the web page for the National Gallery of Art in Washington, D.C.
2. Navigate to the Exhibitions page and then tap or click the link to a current exhibition of your choosing.
3. Add the page to Favorites (IE) or bookmark the page (Google Chrome or Firefox).
4. Do ONE of the following tasks (check with your instructor for his or her preferred output method):
   a. Save a screen capture of the web page you visited in a file named **C2-Project1-WebBrowsing1-Your Name**.
   b. Select Microsoft XPS Document Writer from Devices and print the web page to an XPS document (.oxps). A file will be automatically saved in your Documents folder with a file name that is the title of the web page. Rename the file to **C2-Project1-WebBrowsing1-Your Name**. *This option is recommended if you are working on a tablet.*
5. Open a new tab and navigate to **www.navy.mil**, the web page for the U.S. Navy.
6. Add the page to Favorites (IE) or bookmark the page (Google Chrome or Firefox).
7. Navigate to one of the Navy News Service Top Stories.
8. Save a screen capture of the web page, or print the page to an XPS document. Use the same method you followed in Step 4 and name the new file **C2-Project1-WebBrowsing2-Your Name**.
9. Close the tab for the National Gallery of Art page.
10. Display the Favorites tiles (IE) or the bookmarks bar (Google Chrome or Firefox) and save a screen capture of the browser window in a file named **C2-Project1-WebFavorites-Your Name**.
11. Close Internet Explorer, Google Chrome, or Mozilla Firefox and any other apps you opened.
12. Submit the project to your instructor in the manner she or he has requested.

Project 2 Searching for Information on the Web

Individual

Deliverable: Document with search criteria and search results information

1. Start Internet Explorer, Google Chrome, or Mozilla Firefox.
2. Display the web page for your favorite search engine and search for information on resume writing tips.
3. Start a new WordPad (find using All Apps or Search charm) document and record the following information:
   a. The search engine you used and the search phrase you typed to find information.
   b. The number of pages returned in the search results list.

4. Next, return to the web browser and apply search options at the search engine website to help you narrow the search results. If necessary, use the Help feature for the search engine to learn how to specify advanced search options or use a different search engine that offers more options for narrowing a search.
5. Switch to the document window and type a description of the search options you applied and the number of pages returned in the new search results list.
6. Switch to the web browser, navigate to one of the links on the search results page, and read the information on resume writing tips. Select and copy the URL in the Address bar (IE), omnibox (Google Chrome), or Location bar (Firefox).
7. Switch to the document window, paste the URL of the page you visited below the search statistics, and add in your own words a brief summary of new information you learned by reading the web page.
8. Save the document as **C2-Project2-ResumeSearch-Your Name**.
9. Close the web browser and document apps.
10. Submit the project to your instructor in the manner she or he has requested.

Project 3 Downloading Content from a Web Page

Individual

Deliverable: Document with Downloaded Photograph of World War I Soldiers

1. Start Internet Explorer, Google Chrome, or Mozilla Firefox and navigate to The Commons page at flickr.
2. Search The Commons for pictures of soldiers from World War I.
3. Select and download a picture to the Pictures library.
4. Start a new WordPad document and paste the picture from the Pictures library into it. (Use the Picture button in the Home tab or the Insert tab, depending on the document app.)
5. Switch to the web browser, select and copy the URL for the photograph, and paste it below the picture in the document.
6. Save the document as **C2-Project3-WWIPicture-Your Name**.
7. Close the web browser and document apps.
8. Submit the document to your instructor in the manner she or he has requested.

Project 4 Exploring a New Search Engine

Individual or Pairs

Deliverable: Document with Comparison Information for two Search Engines

1. Start Internet Explorer, Google Chrome, or Mozilla Firefox, navigate to your favorite search engine web page, and search for information on job interview techniques.
2. Next, conduct a search using the phrase "top five popular search engines."
3. Read at least one article in the search results list. Choose a search engine from the article you read that you do not normally use. If you are doing this project in pairs, each person selects a different search engine.
4. Navigate to the web page for the new search engine that you selected and conduct a search on job interview techniques. Use the same search phrase at each search engine.
5. Compare the search results from each search engine. Was the number of pages in the search results close to the same number? On page one of search results at each search engine, how many web pages were repeated and how many web pages were different? Did one search engine seem to return more targeted results? Do you think you will use the new search engine in the future or will you revert back to the one you favored before?
6. Create a WordPad document with answers to the questions and, for the last question, provide your reasons. Include the two search engines and the search phrase you used to complete this project.
7. Save the document as **C2-Project4-SearchEngineComparison-Your Name**.
8. Close the web browser and document apps.
9. Submit the document to your instructor in the manner she or he has requested.

Chapter 3

Exploring Microsoft Office 2013 Essentials

After successfully completing this chapter, you will be able to:

- Identify various editions of Microsoft Office 2013 and the system requirements
- Start an Office program and identify common features
- Open, save, print, export, close, and start new documents in the Backstage view
- Customize the Quick Access toolbar (QAT)
- Perform commands using the ribbon, QAT, and Mini toolbar
- Select options in dialog boxes and task panes
- Copy text, an object, and formatting options using the Clipboard
- Use Microsoft Office Help
- Save and open files from SkyDrive
- Set your display options to match the illustrations used in the textbook

Microsoft Office 2013 is a suite of software programs that includes applications such as Word, Excel, PowerPoint, Access, Outlook, and OneNote. The suite is available in various editions that package the programs in collections geared toward a home, business, or student customer using the programs under a traditional desktop installation or a subscription-based installation called Office 365. The Professional edition includes all of the programs included in this textbook.

Word is a program used to create, edit, and format text. Use Excel when your focus is to enter, calculate, format, and analyze numerical data. PowerPoint is an application used to create slides for an oral or kiosk-style presentation that includes text, images, sound, video, or other multimedia. Access is a database program in which you organize, store, and manage related data, such as information about customers or products. In addition to these four pillar applications, Outlook is included as a program to manage personal information such as mail, calendar, contacts, and tasks, and OneNote is included for storing and sharing information in notebooks.

One reason the Microsoft Office suite is so popular is because several features or elements are common to all of the programs. Once you learn your way around one of the applications in the suite, another application looks and operates similarly, making the learning process faster and easier.

In this chapter you will learn how to navigate the Microsoft Office 2013 interface and perform file-related tasks or routines common to all of the applications. You will customize the Quick Access toolbar and learn about choosing options using various methods. You will also learn how to save and open files to and from SkyDrive as an alternative to using a USB flash drive.

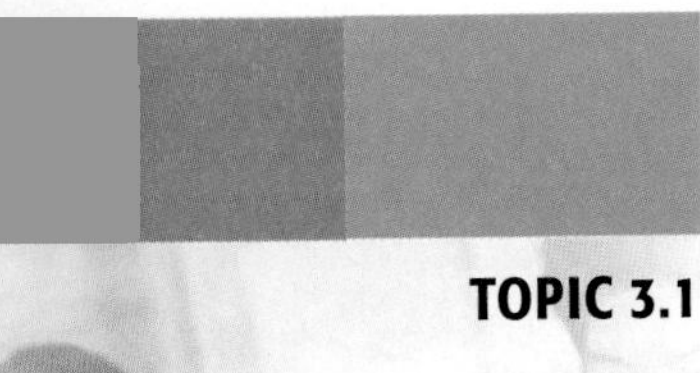

TOPIC 3.1

SKILLS

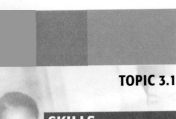

- Start an Office program
- Switch between programs
- Start a new presentation
- Explore the ribbon interface

Starting and Switching Programs, Starting a New Presentation, and Exploring the Ribbon Interface

All of the programs in the Microsoft Office suite start the same way and share some common features and elements. Microsoft Office applications are desktop apps, meaning they are launched from the Windows 8 desktop.

Microsoft Office 2013 Editions

The Microsoft Office 2013 suite is packaged in various collections of programs, as shown in Table 3.1. The suite is also available through a subscription as Office 365. **Office 365** adds email, shared calendars, office web apps, instant messaging, and other web services to the standard productivity applications. An advantage to an Office 365 subscription is that these extras are accessible on more than one device with which you have Internet access, and updates to the suite are automatically pushed to the installed devices. For example, Office 365 Home Premium can be run on up to five devices with one subscription.

Table 3.1	Microsoft Office 2013 Editions
Edition	**What It Includes**
Office Home and Student 2013	Word, Excel, PowerPoint, and OneNote
Office Home and Business 2013	Word, Excel, PowerPoint, OneNote, and Outlook
Office Professional 2013	Word, Excel, PowerPoint, Access, Publisher, OneNote, and Outlook

The editions listed in Table 3.1 do not represent all of the available suites. For example, Microsoft also packages a suite called Microsoft Office University that is available only to verified students and faculty of postsecondary institutions, and an Office RT version for installation with Windows RT that is designed to conserve energy use on mobile devices.

Microsoft Office 2013 System Requirements

Table 3.2 on the next page provides the standard system requirements for installing Microsoft Office 2013. Generally, if the PC or mobile device is successfully running Windows 7 or Windows 8, then Office 2013 will also work on the same hardware provided there is enough free disk space for the program files. Note that Office 2013 cannot be installed on a computer running Windows XP or Windows Vista.

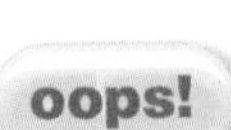

Do you have Microsoft Office 2013 with **Windows 7**?

In Windows 7, you start at the desktop. To start an Office application:

1. Click the Start button.
2. Point to or click *All Programs*.
3. Click *Microsoft Office*.
4. Click the name of the desired program.

Starting a Program in the Microsoft Office 2013 Suite

To start any of the programs in the Microsoft Office 2013 suite, tap or click the program's tile on the Start screen. The Windows 8 desktop launches first, and the program opens within a window in the desktop.

You can also reveal the Charms bar and tap or click the Search charm to locate the tile in the Apps list. Finally, type the first few characters of the program name at the Start screen or in the Search text box. For example, typing *ex* at the Start screen or in the Search Apps text box would show Excel 2013 in the Apps results list.

Table 3.2	Microsoft Office 2013 System Requirements
Hardware Component	**Requirement**
Processor	1 gigahertz (GHz) or faster processor
Memory	1 gigabyte (GB) of RAM for a 32-bit processor 2 gigabytes (GB) of RAM for a 64-bit processor
Disk space	3.0 gigabytes (GB) available free space
Operating system	Windows 7 or Windows 8
Internet browser	Internet Explorer (IE) version 8 or higher; Mozilla Firefox version 10 or higher; Google Chrome version 17 or higher; or Apple Safari version 5 or higher
Input devices	Touch-enabled input, mouse, or keyboard are all supported. Touch capability has been included in Office 2013 to work with touch gestures supported under Windows 8.

Launch an Office Application
Tap or click desired tile.

Switch between Applications
Tap button on Taskbar for desired application or, if multiple documents are open in application, point to button on Taskbar and tap or click thumbnail representing document.

1. At the Windows 8 Start screen, tap or click the tile for **Word 2013**.

   You may need to slide or scroll the Start screen to find the tile. If necessary, swipe up or right-click and then tap or click All Apps to find the Word 2013 tile in the Apps list.

2. Notice that the Desktop app launches first and then Microsoft Word opens inside a window within the desktop. If the Word screen does not fill the entire desktop above the Taskbar, tap or click the Maximize button near the top right corner of the window (second button from right).

   Your window is already maximized if you see this button near the top right corner of the window.

   Note: If asked to sign in, enter your Microsoft account email address and password.

3. Compare your screen with the **Word Start screen** shown in Figure 3.1.
4. Display the Start screen and tap or click the **Excel 2013** tile. If the Excel screen does not fill the desktop, tap or click the Maximize button.
5. Compare the Excel Start screen with the Word Start screen shown in Figure 3.1.

oops!

Windows 7 users at Steps 4, 6, and 8, start another program by clicking the Start button, pointing to or clicking *All Programs*, clicking *Microsoft Office*, and clicking the desired application.

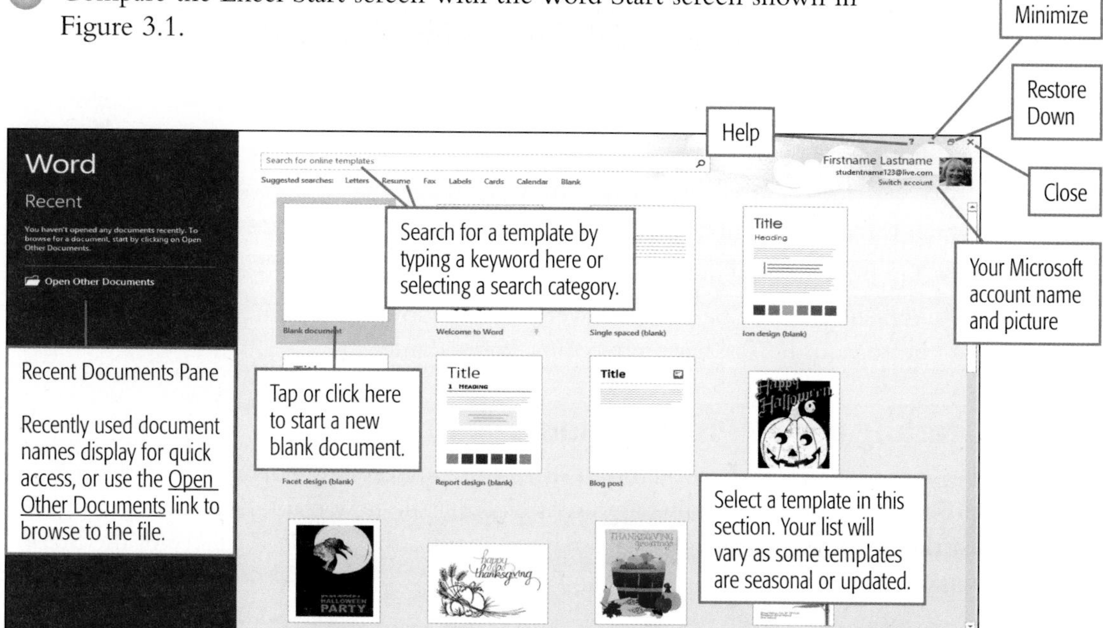

Figure 3.1 Word 2013 opens with the Word Start screen shown here. The Start screen for all Office apps shows the Recent list with the most recent documents opened next to the Templates gallery.

Tap or click the thumbnail for a template to view a larger picture of the template, a description, and the Create button.

Each Office application opens in a Start screen. The left pane shows recent files opened and a link to open other files not shown in the recent documents list. Next to the recent files list, thumbnails for templates are shown with the first thumbnail used to start a new blank document, workbook, presentation, or database. At the top right of the Start screen are the Help, Minimize, Restore Down, and Close buttons, with your Microsoft account name and picture below the buttons if you are signed in.

6 Display the Start screen and tap or click the **PowerPoint 2013** tile. If necessary, maximize the window.

7 Compare the PowerPoint Start screen window with the Word window shown in Figure 3.1 on the previous page.

8 Display the Start screen and tap or click the **Access 2013** tile. If necessary, maximize the window and then compare the Access window with the Word window in Figure 3.1.

Each Office program has its own color scheme. Notice that Word is blue, Excel is green, PowerPoint is orange, and Access is maroon.

Switching between Office Programs

Because programs within the Microsoft suite open in the desktop, the Taskbar displays along the bottom of the screen with a button for each Office program. Switch to another open program by tapping or clicking the program's Taskbar button.

Point to a button on the Taskbar to see a thumbnail appear above the button with a preview of the open document. If more than one document is open, the button will appear cascaded as if multiple buttons are layered on top of each other. Point to the layered button to see a separate thumbnail for each open document.

9 Point to the Taskbar button representing Excel and tap or click the button to switch to the Excel window.

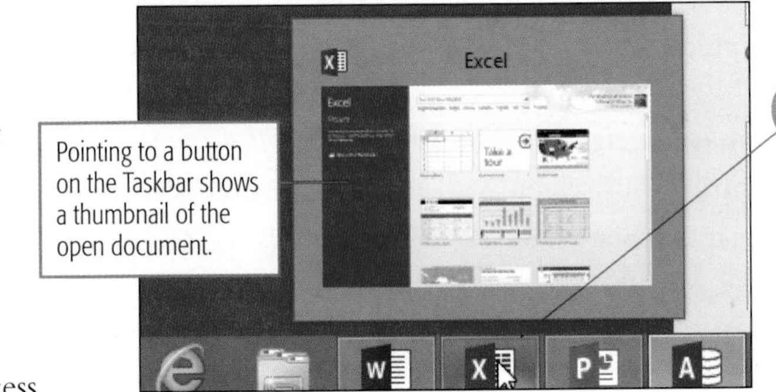
Excel
Pointing to a button on the Taskbar shows a thumbnail of the open document.
Step 9

10 Tap or click the Taskbar button representing Access to switch to the Access window.

11 Tap or click the Close button (× button) at the top right corner of the Access window.

Step 11
Close
Firstname Lastname
studentname123@live.com

Access closes and you are returned to Excel, which is the last program that you accessed.

12 Tap or click the Close button to close Excel.

13 You should now be in the PowerPoint window. If necessary, tap or click the button on the Taskbar representing PowerPoint.

Starting a New Presentation

For any program in the Microsoft Office suite, start a new document, workbook, presentation, or database by tapping or clicking the new blank document, workbook, presentation, or database thumbnail in the *Templates* gallery of the Start screen.

14 Tap or click *Blank Presentation* in the Templates and themes gallery of the PowerPoint window.

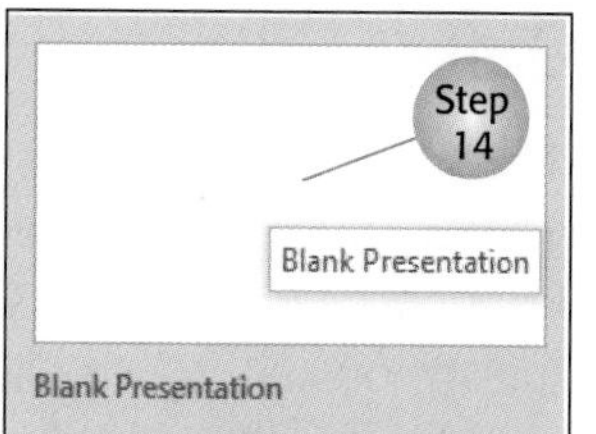

Start a new Office Document, Workbook, Presentation, or Database

Tap or click thumbnail for new blank document, blank workbook, blank presentation, or blank desktop database in Templates gallery.

Exploring the Ribbon Interface

The ribbon interface appears along the top of each Office application. Buttons within the ribbon are used to access commands and features within the program. The ribbon is split into individual tabs, with each tab divided into groups of related buttons, as shown in Figure 3.2. Word, Excel, PowerPoint, and Access all have the FILE and HOME tabs as the first two tabs in the ribbon. The FILE tab is used to perform document-level routines such as saving, printing, and exporting. This tab is explored in the next topic. The HOME tab always contains the most frequently used features in each application such as formatting and editing buttons.

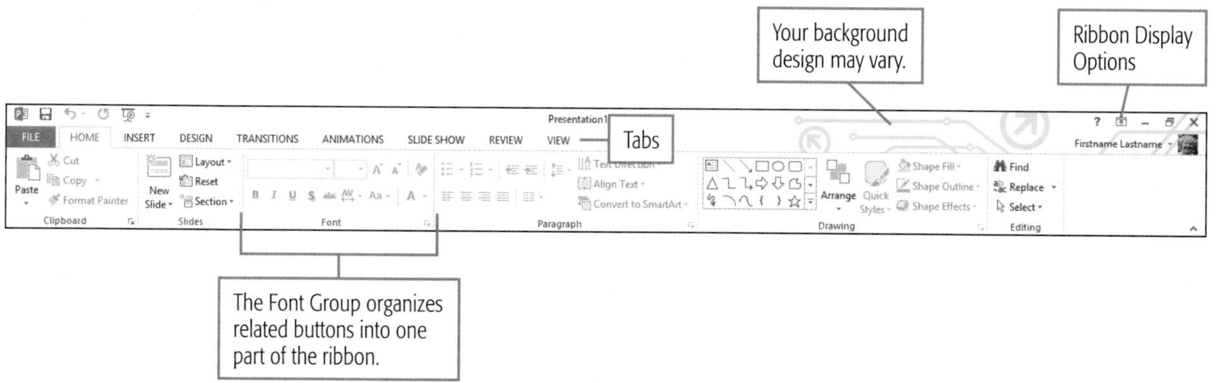

Figure 3.2 The ribbon in PowerPoint. The ribbon appears along the top of each Office application window and contains buttons to access features and commands.

The **Ribbon Display Options button** near the top right of the window is used to change the ribbon display from *Show Tabs and Commands* to *Show Tabs*, which hides the command buttons until you tap or click a tab, or *Auto-hide Ribbon*, which displays the ribbon only when you tap or click along the top of the window.

Ribbon is showing more or fewer buttons, or the buttons look different than shown here? The screen resolution for your PC or mobile device affects the ribbon display. In Topic 3.8 you will learn how to change the display. For now, the instructions will not ask you to tap or click anything you cannot see or identify by the button label or icon.

15 Tap or click the INSERT tab to view the groups and buttons in PowerPoint's INSERT ribbon.

16 Click the button on the Taskbar representing Word and tap or click Blank document to start a new Word document.

17 Tap or click the INSERT tab to view the groups and buttons in Word's INSERT ribbon.

18 Tap or click the DESIGN tab in Word and review the buttons in Word's DESIGN ribbon.

19 Switch to PowerPoint and tap or click the DESIGN tab in PowerPoint.

20 Spend a few moments exploring other tabs and then close PowerPoint.

21 Spend a few moments exploring other tabs in Word and then close Word.

22 Display the Start screen.

TOPIC 3.2

SKILLS

Open, Save As, Print, and Close a document

Export a document as a PDF file

Using the Backstage View to Manage Documents

The **FILE tab** is used in all Office applications to open the **Backstage view**. Backstage view is where you find file management commands such as Open, Save, Save As, Print, Share, Export, and Close. If you have been working on a document within an application and want a blank document or template, you use the Backstage view to start a new document. You also use the Backstage view to display information about a document, protect the document, and manage document properties and versions.

Each application in the Microsoft Office suite provides options that you can personalize at the Backstage view through the Options dialog box. You also can manage your Microsoft account and/or connected services and change the background or theme for all of the Office applications in the Account tab of the Backstage view.

Note: Plug your USB flash drive into an empty USB port before starting this topic.

1. Start Microsoft Word.
2. At the Word Start screen, tap or click Open Other Documents.

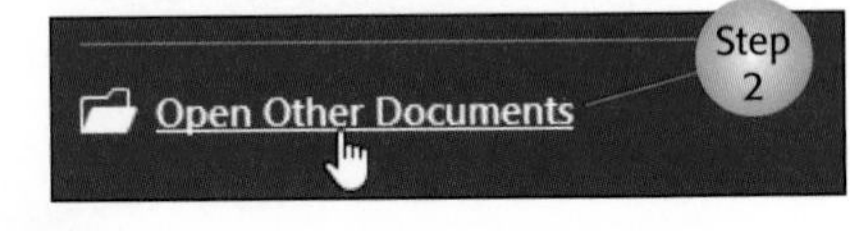

3. Tap or click *Computer* in the Open tab Backstage view.

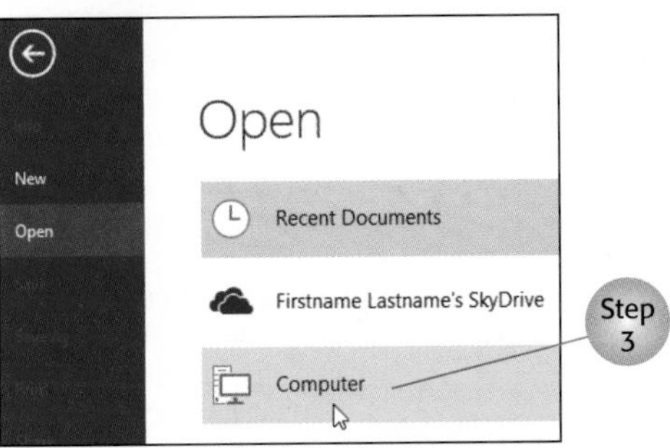

4. Tap or click the Browse button in the Computer pane.
5. Slide or scroll down and tap or click the Removable Disk for your USB flash drive in the Navigation pane of the Open dialog box.
6. Double-tap or double-click the *ComputerCourse* folder in the Content pane.

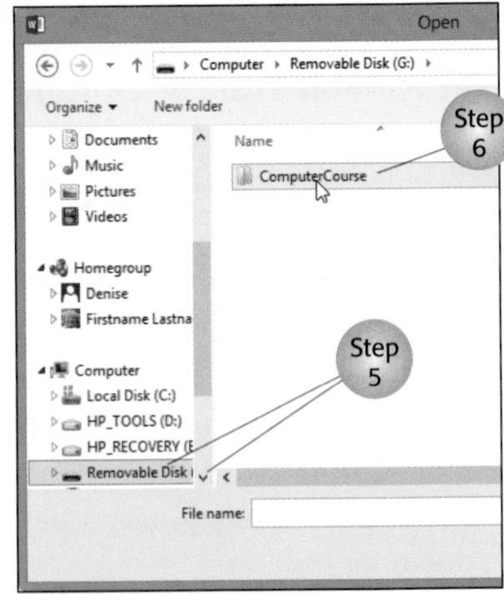

7. Double-tap or double-click the *Student_Data_Files* folder and then the *Ch3* folder.

The Word document **Cottage_rental_listing** within the Ch3 subfolder is displayed in the Content pane. Within an Office application, the Open dialog box by default shows only files created in the active application.

8. Double-tap or double-click the Word document named ***Cottage_rental_listing***.

In the next steps you will use the Save As command to save a copy of the document in another folder.

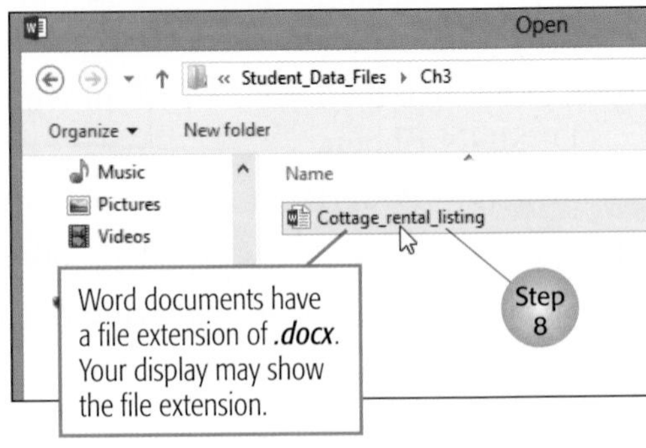

9. Tap or click the FILE tab to display the Backstage view.

When a document is open, Backstage view displays the Info tab with document properties for the active file and buttons to protect, inspect, and manage versions of the document.

The Save As command is used to save a copy of a document in another location or to save a copy of a file in the same location but with a different file name.

10 Tap or click Save As.

11 With *Computer* already selected in the Save As Backstage view, tap or click the *Ch3* folder in the *Current Folder* section or the Browse button in the Computer pane.

The Save As dialog box opens with the folder and drive selected from which the document was opened.

12 Tap or click the Up arrow button next to the Back and Forward buttons. Windows 7 users tap or click *Student_Data_Files* in the Address bar. (Windows 7 does not have an Up arrow button in the Open or Save As dialog boxes.)

The Up arrow button moves to the previous folder level.

13 Tap or click the Up arrow button a second time. Windows 7 users tap or click *ComputerCourse* in the Address bar.

14 Double-tap or double-click the *CompletedTopicsByChapter* folder.

15 Tap or click the New folder button in the Command bar, type **Ch3**, and tap or press Enter.

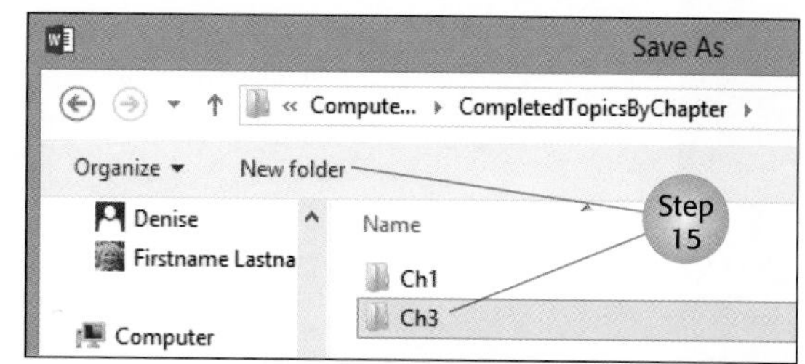

16 Double-tap or double-click the *Ch3* folder.

17 Tap or click in the *File name* text box or select the current file name, type **3.2-CottageListing-Your Name**, and tap or press Enter, or tap or click the Save button.

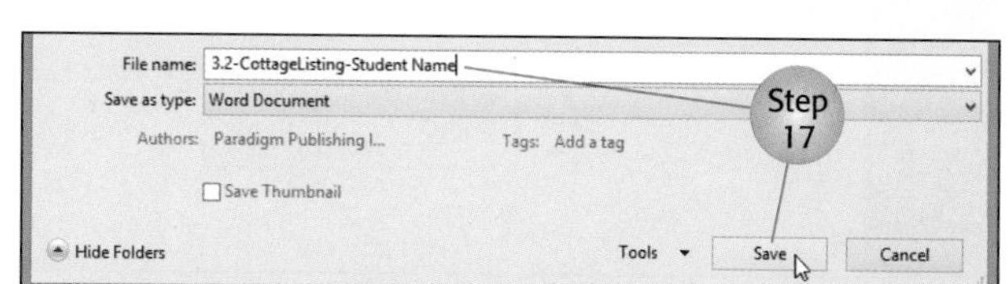

18 Tap or click in the document next to *List Date:* below the address *3587 Bluewater Road* (in the second column of the table) and type the current date.

19 Tap or click next to *Assigned Agent:* below the date (in the second column of the table) and type your name.

COTTAGE LISTING	
Owner:	Sandstone Cottage Rentals Inc.
	P. O. Box 364
	St. Paul, MN 55102
	info@sandstone.emcp.net
Cottage:	Cottage Number 13-598
Address:	3587 Bluewater Road
List Date:	October 25, 2014
Assigned Agent:	Student Name

Step 18 Step 19

Your date will vary.

Open a Document

1. At Word Start screen, tap or click Open Other Documents.
2. Tap or click Computer.
3. Tap or click Browse or folder in Recent Folders list.
4. Navigate to drive and/or folder, then double-tap or double-click file name.

Use Save As to Save a Copy of a Document

1. Tap or click File tab.
2. Tap or click Save As.
3. Tap or click Browse or folder name in folder list.
4. Navigate to desired drive and/or folder.
5. If necessary, change file name.
6. Tap or click Save.

oops!

Typing mistake? Press Backspace to delete what you have typed if you make an error and then retype the text. You can also drag across text and press Delete.

Printing a Document

Ctrl + P is the keyboard command to display the Print tab Backstage view.

Display the Print tab Backstage view when you want to preview and print a document. Before printing, review the document in the **Print Preview** pane of the Backstage view shown in Figure 3.3. The bottom of the Print Preview pane shows the number of pages needed to print the document, and navigation buttons are included to move to the next page and previous page in a multipage document.

Choose the printer on which to print the document in the *Printer* section and modify the print settings and page layout options in the *Settings* section. When you are ready to print, tap or click the Print button.

20 Tap or click the FILE tab to display the Backstage view and then tap or click Print.

21 Examine the document in the Print Preview pane, check the name of the default printer, and review the default options in the *Settings* section.

When print settings are changed, the options are stored with the document so you do not need to change them again the next time you want to print.

22 Tap or click the Print button to print the document.

The document is sent to the printer, and the Backstage view closes.

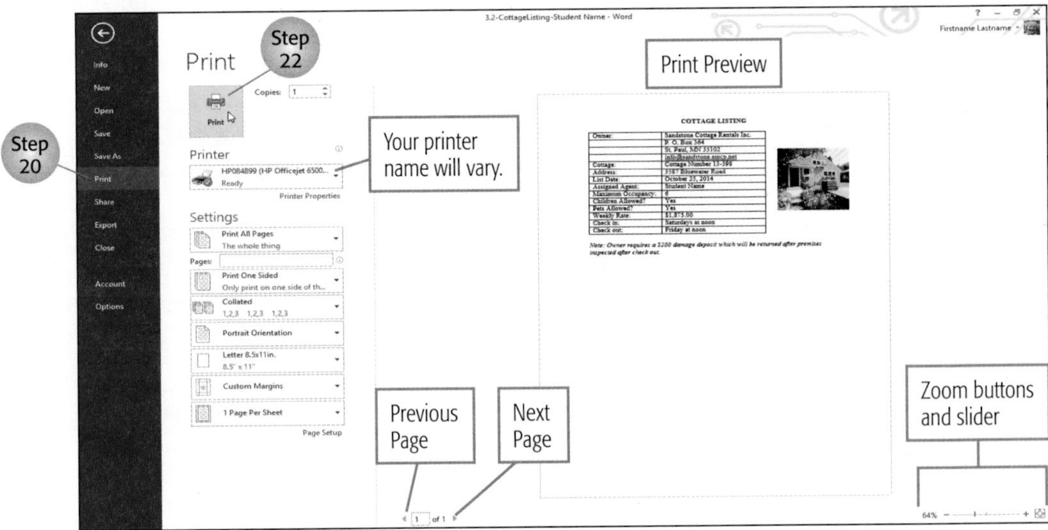

Figure 3.3 Print Tab Backstage View

Exporting a Document as a PDF File

New to Word 2013 is the ability to open and modify PDF documents.

Many people exchange documents in PDF format via email or websites. The advantage of a PDF file is that the document looks and prints as it would in the application in which it was created but without having to open or install the source program. A Word document can be sent to someone who does not have Word installed on his or her computer if the file is exported as a PDF.

A **PDF document** is a document saved in Portable Document Format, an open standard for exchanging electronic documents developed by Adobe systems. Anyone can view a PDF document with the free Adobe Reader application.

23 Tap or click the FILE tab and tap or click Export.

24 With *Create PDF/XPS Document* selected in the Export tab Backstage View, tap or click the Create PDF/XPS button.

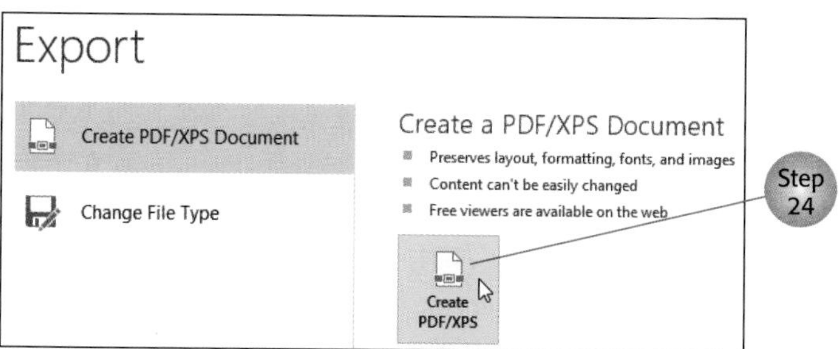

25 Tap or click the Publish button at the Publish as PDF or XPS dialog box.

By default, the PDF is created in the same drive and folder in which the Word document resides and with the same file name but with a file extension of *.pdf*. Because PDF files have a different file extension, the same name can be used for both the Word document and the PDF document.

Step 25

26 By default, the published PDF document opens in the Windows Reader app (or Adobe Reader in Windows 7).

27 Close the Reader app and return to Microsoft Word.

28 Tap or click the FILE tab and then tap or click Close.

29 Tap or click the Save button when prompted at the message box asking if you want to save your changes. Leave Microsoft Word open for the next topic.

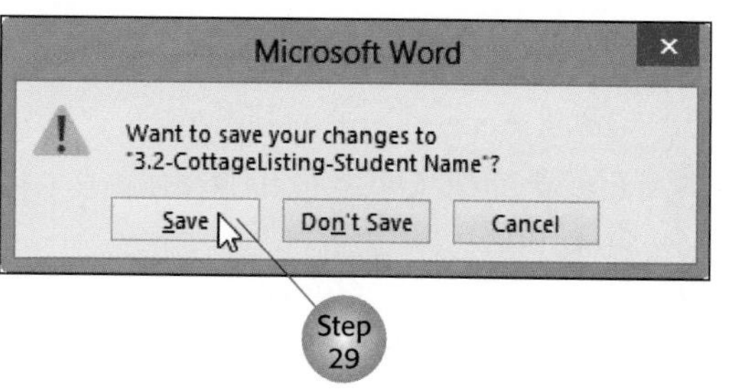

Step 29

Close a document when you are finished editing, saving, printing, and publishing. A blank window displays when no documents are open.

Print a Document

1. Tap or click FILE tab.
2. Tap or click Print.
3. Preview and/or change options as necessary.
4. Tap or click Print.

Export as PDF

1. Tap or click FILE tab.
2. Tap or click Export.
3. Tap or click Create PDF/XPS.
4. Tap or click Publish.

PDF does not open in Reader app? The default settings on your PC or mobile device may differ. Your PDF may open in another reader app or may not open at all. Close the app that opens and switch back to Microsoft Word or skip Step 27.

Pinning Documents and Folders to Recent lists

At the Open tab Backstage view, you can pin frequently used files to the *Recent Documents* list. Frequently used folders can be pinned to the Open or Save As tab Backstage views with *Computer* selected. Point to the file name or folder name and tap or click the push pin icon that displays at the right to pin the item to the list.

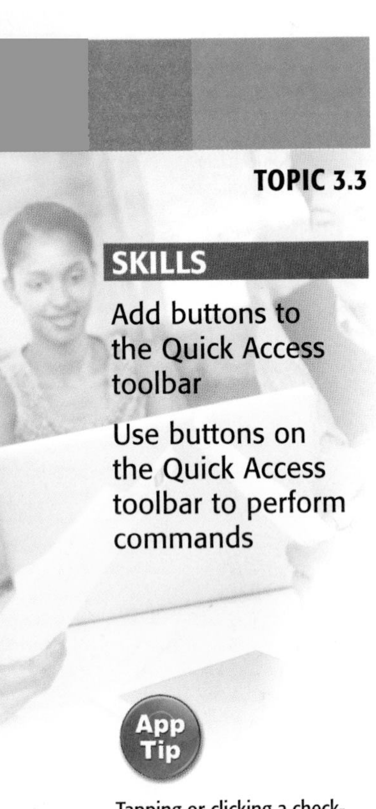

TOPIC 3.3
SKILLS
Add buttons to the Quick Access toolbar
Use buttons on the Quick Access toolbar to perform commands

App Tip

Tapping or clicking a check-marked option removes the button from the QAT.

Customizing and Using the Quick Access Toolbar

The **Quick Access toolbar** (QAT) is at the top left corner of each Office application window. With the default installation, the QAT has buttons to Save, Undo, and Repeat (which changes to Redo after Undo has been used). A touch-enabled tablet or other device includes a fourth button to optimize the spacing between commands for the mouse or for touch. Most people customize the QAT by adding more buttons that are used often.

To add a button to the QAT, tap or click the Customize Quick Access Toolbar button at the end of the QAT (displays as a down-pointing arrow with a bar above) and then tap or click the desired button at the drop-down list.

Note: Skip this topic if the QAT on the computer you are using already displays the New, Open, Quick Print, and Print Preview and Print buttons in Word, PowerPoint, and Excel. Skip any steps in which a drop-down list option already displays with a check mark, which means the button is already added to the QAT.

1. At a blank Word screen, tap or click the Customize Quick Access Toolbar button at the end of the QAT.

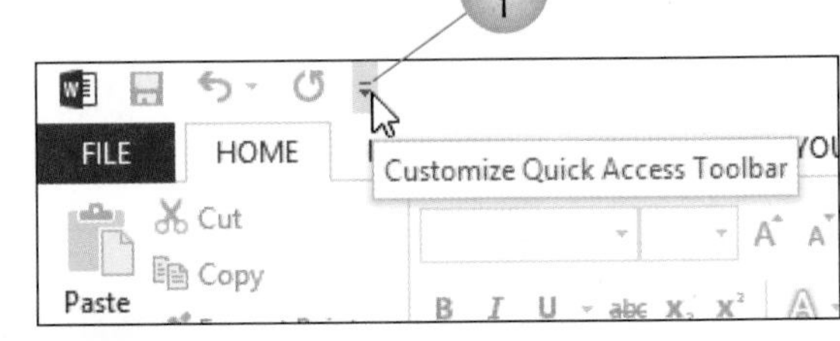

2. Tap or click *New* at the drop-down list.

   Options displayed with a check mark are already added to the QAT. Buttons added to the QAT are added at the end.

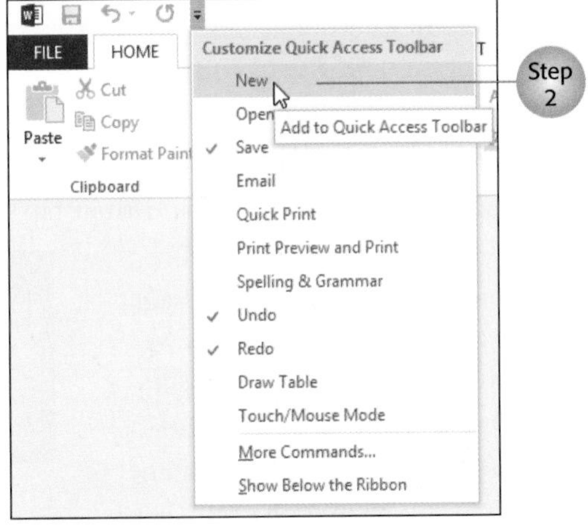

3. Tap or click the Customize Quick Access Toolbar button.
4. Tap or click *Open* at the drop-down list.
5. Tap or click the Customize Quick Access Toolbar button.
6. Tap or click *Quick Print* at the drop-down list.
7. Tap or click the Customize Quick Access Toolbar button.
8. Tap or click *Print Preview and Print* at the drop-down list.

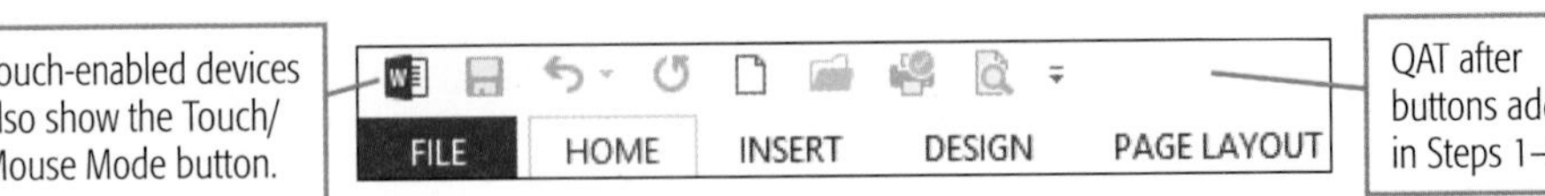

9. Tap or click the Open button on the QAT.

   The Open tab Backstage view opens with the *Recent Documents* list. On a PC with Windows 7, the Open button on the QAT displays the Open dialog box.

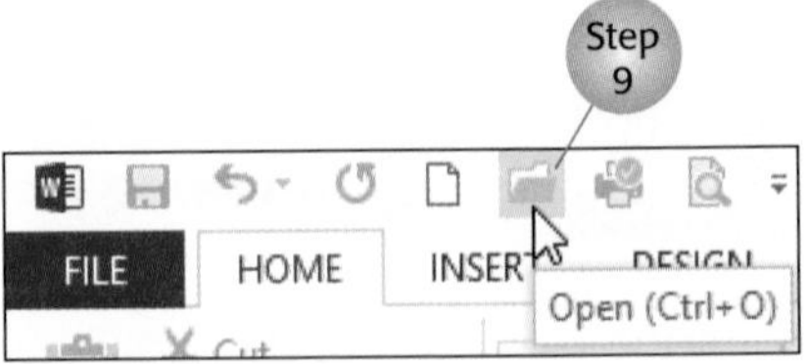

10 Tap or click the file named ***3.2-CottageListing-Student Name*** in the *Recent Documents* list, or double-tap or double-click the file in the Open dialog box for Windows 7 users.

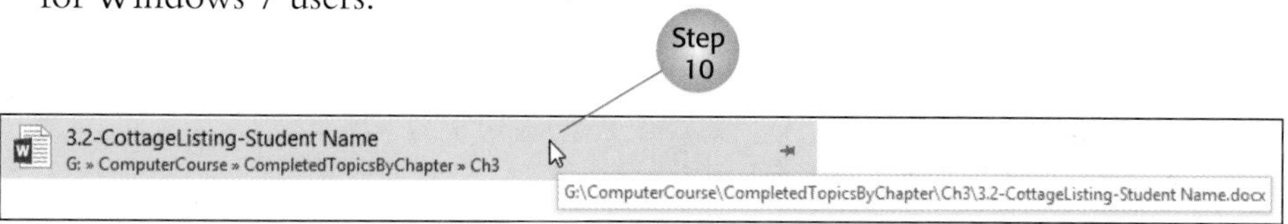

Add a Button to the QAT
1. Tap or click Customize Quick Access toolbar button.
2. Tap or click desired button at drop-down list.

11 Tap or click the Print Preview and Print button on the QAT.

The Print tab Backstage view opens.

The Quick Print button added to the QAT automatically sends the current document to the printer using the active printer and print settings.

12 Tap or click the Back button (left-pointing arrow inside circle) to return to the document without printing.

13 Display the Windows Start screen and start PowerPoint 2013.

14 Tap or click Blank Presentation at the PowerPoint Start screen.

Notice the customized QAT does not carry over to other Microsoft applications.

15 Customize the QAT in PowerPoint by adding the New, Open, Quick Print, and Print Preview and Print buttons.

16 Close PowerPoint.

17 Display the Windows Start screen, start Excel 2013, and tap or click Blank Workbook at the Excel Start screen.

18 Customize the Excel QAT to add the New, Open, Quick Print, and Print Preview and Print buttons.

19 Close Excel.

20 At the Word document, tap or click the FILE tab and then tap or click Close.

21 Tap or click the New button on the QAT.

A new blank document window opens. Leave this document open for the next topic.

For Office applications, the keyboard command Ctrl + F4 closes the current document and Alt + F4 closes the program.

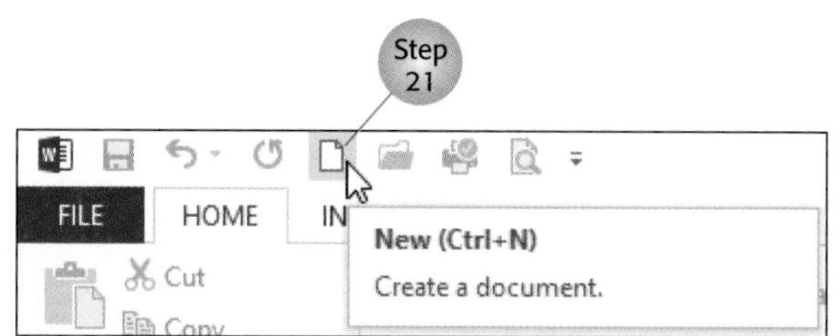

Selecting Text or Objects, Using the Ribbon and Mini Toolbar, and Selecting Options in Dialog Boxes

TOPIC 3.4

SKILLS

- Select text and objects
- Perform commands using the ribbon and Mini toolbar
- Display a task pane and dialog box
- Choose options in a dialog box

Creating a document, worksheet, presentation, or database involves working with the ribbon to select options or perform commands. Some options involve using a button, list box, or gallery, and some commands cause a task pane or dialog box to open in which you select options.

In many instances, before you choose an option from the ribbon, you first select text or an object as the target for the action. Select text by tapping or clicking within a word, paragraph, cell, or placeholder, or by dragging across the text you want to select. Select an object, such as a picture or other graphic, by tapping or clicking the object.

Selected objects display with a series of selection handles. A **selection handle** is a circle or square icon at the middle and/or corners of an object, or at the beginning and end of text on touch-enabled devices. Selection handles are used to manipulate the object or to define the selection area on touch-enabled devices. Table 3.3 provides instructions for selecting text using a mouse or touch and for selecting an object.

Table 3.3 Selecting Text and Objects Using the Mouse and Touch

Selecting Text Using a Mouse	Selecting Text Using Touch	Selecting Objects
Point at the beginning of the text or cell to be selected. The pointer displays as I, called an I-beam in Word and PowerPoint, or as ✣, called a cell pointer in Excel. Hold down the left mouse button, and drag to the end of the text or cells to be selected. Release the mouse button. Summer vacation destinations In some cases, a Mini toolbar displays when you release the mouse after selecting text. Summer vacation destinations Mini toolbar	Tap at the beginning of the text to be selected. A selection handle appears below the text (displays as an empty circle). Summer vacation destinations selection handle Touch the selection handle and slide your finger across the screen to the end of the text or cells to be selected. Summer vacation destinations A second selection handle appears at the end of the selected text when you remove your finger from the screen. Use the selection handles to redefine the area if necessary. To display the Mini toolbar, tap inside the selected text area. The toolbar displays already optimized for touch. Mini toolbar	Tap or click the object. Selection handles appear at the ends, corners, and middle (depending on width and height) of each side of the object. A LAYOUT OPTIONS button also appears next to a selected object with options for aligning and moving the object with surrounding text. LAYOUT OPTIONS button for selected object

1 At a blank Word screen, type **Summer vacation destinations** and tap or press Enter.

2 Type **Explore the beaches of Florida and experience the Florida sunset with friends or family.** and tap or press Enter.

3 Select the title *Summer vacation destinations* and display the **Mini toolbar**. If using a touch-enabled device, tap inside the selection area to display the Mini toolbar.

The Mini toolbar that appears next to selected text or with the shortcut menu contains frequently used formatting commands.

Select Text or an Object
Tap or click in word, paragraph, cell, or placeholder or tap or click the object OR tap or point at beginning of text and drag or slide selection handle to end of text.

Format Text Using the Mini Toolbar
1. Select text.
2. Click desired button on Mini toolbar OR tap inside selected text to display Mini toolbar and tap desired button.

If necessary, refer to the instructions in Table 3.3 for selecting text using the mouse or touch.

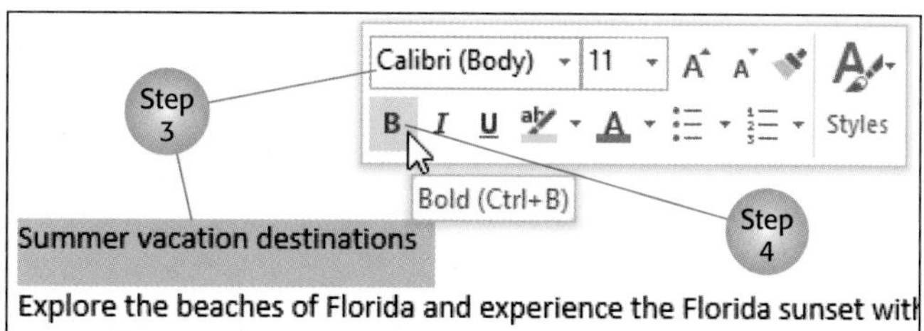

4 Tap or click the Bold button on the Mini toolbar.

All of the buttons available on the Mini toolbar are also available in the ribbon.

5 Tap or click in the blank line below the sentence that begins with *Explore* to deselect the title.

6 Tap or click the INSERT tab in the ribbon.

7 Tap or click the Pictures button in the Illustrations group.

This opens the Insert Picture dialog box.

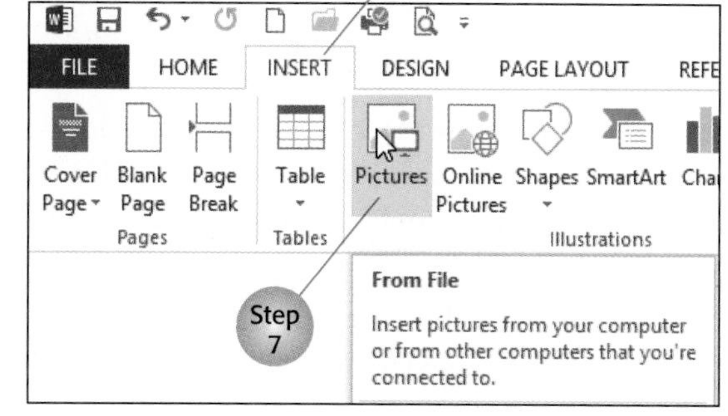

8 Slide or scroll down the Navigation pane and tap or click the Removable Disk for your USB flash drive.

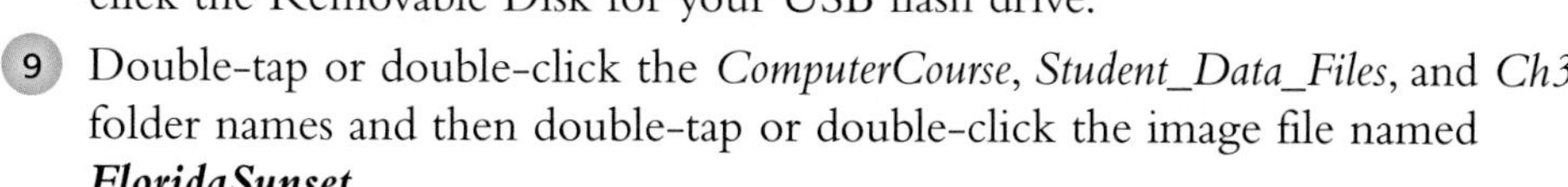

9 Double-tap or double-click the *ComputerCourse*, *Student_Data_Files*, and *Ch3* folder names and then double-tap or double-click the image file named ***FloridaSunset***.

The **FloridaSunset** image file is inserted in the document and is automatically selected.

10 Slide or drag the selection handle at the bottom right corner of the image until the picture is resized to the approximate height and width shown at the right.

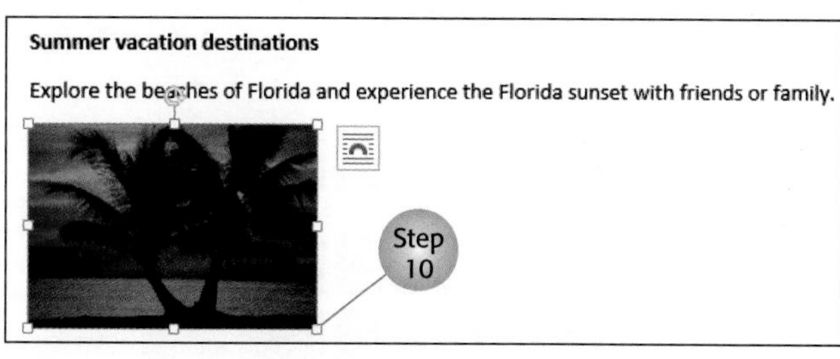

oops!

No selection handles? If you tap or click away from the object, the selection handles disappear. Tap or click the picture to redisplay the selection handles.

When using a mouse to resize, the pointer changes shape to a double-headed diagonal arrow (⤡) when you point at the bottom right corner of the image. Drag downward and to the right when you see this icon. The pointer changes shape to a crosshairs—a large, thin, black cross (+)—while you drag the mouse. When you release the mouse, the selection handles reappear.

The first time a document is saved, the Save As tab Backstage view appears.

11 Tap or click the Save button on the QAT.

12 Tap or click *Computer* and tap or click the *Ch3* folder within CompletedTopicsByChapter in the *Recent Folders* list.

13 Type **3.4-VacationDestinations-Your Name** and then tap or press Enter or tap or click the Save button.

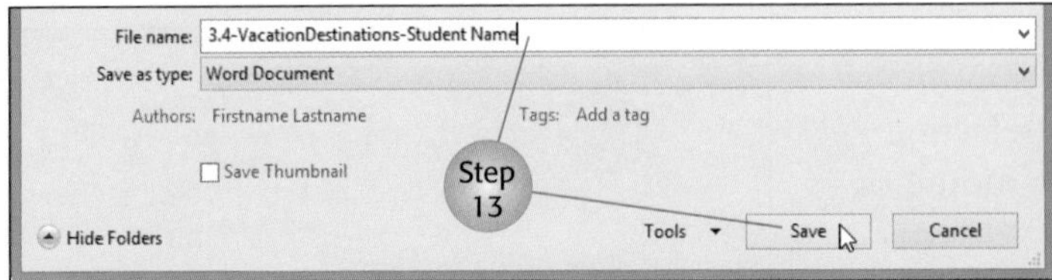

Live preview lets you see the effect of a change before applying the option. Watch the text or object change as you move the mouse over each option.

Working with Objects, Contextual Tabs, and Dialog Boxes

An **object** is a picture, shape, chart, or other item that can be manipulated separately from text or other objects around it. When an object is selected, a contextual ribbon tab appears. More than one contextual tab may appear. **Contextual tabs** contain commands or options related to the type of object that is currently selected.

Some buttons in the ribbon display a drop-down **gallery**. A gallery displays visual representations of options for the selected item in a drop-down list or grid. Pointing to an option in a gallery displays a **live preview** of the selected text or object if the option is applied.

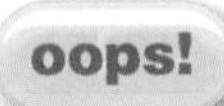

PICTURE TOOLS FORMAT tab not visible? This tab appears only when a picture is selected. Tap or click the picture to display the contextual tab.

14 Tap or click the Corrections button in the Adjust group of the PICTURE TOOLS FORMAT tab.

15 Point to the last option in the *Corrections* gallery.

Notice the picture brightens significantly when you point to the option.

16 Tap or click the last option in the *Corrections* gallery to apply the *Brightness +40% Contrast +40%* correction.

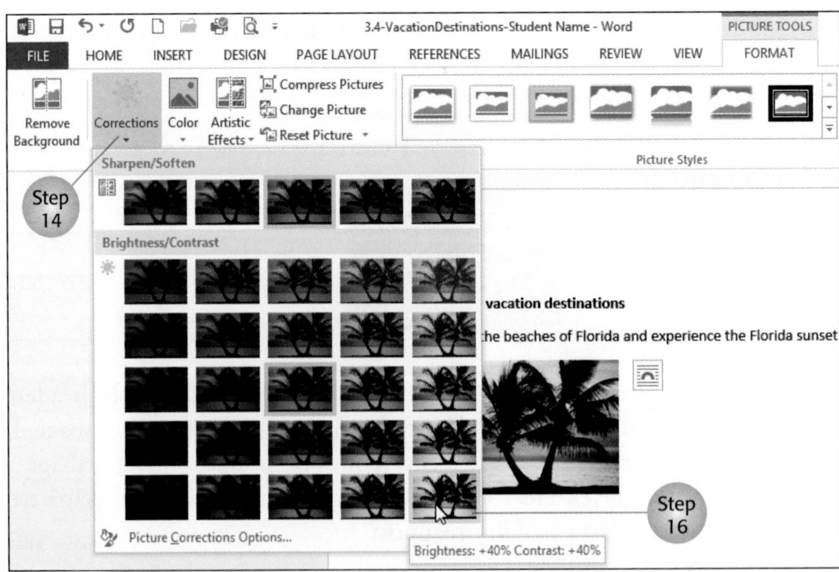

Some ribbon groups have a small button at the bottom right corner of the group that displays with a diagonal downward-pointing arrow (⬊). This button is called a **dialog box launcher**. Tapping or clicking this button causes a task pane or a dialog box to appear. A **task pane** appears at the left or right side of the window, whereas a **dialog box** opens in a separate window above (or, from the viewer's perspective, in front of) the document. Task panes and dialog boxes contain more options related to the ribbon group as buttons, lists, sliders, check boxes, text boxes, and option buttons.

Display the Contextual Tab
Tap or click object.

Display the Task Pane or Dialog Box
Tap or click dialog box launcher at bottom right of ribbon group.

17. Tap or click the dialog box launcher at the bottom right corner of the Picture Styles group.

The Format Picture task pane opens at the right. You will work in a task pane in the next topic.

18. Tap or click the Close button (×) at the top right corner of the Format Picture task pane.

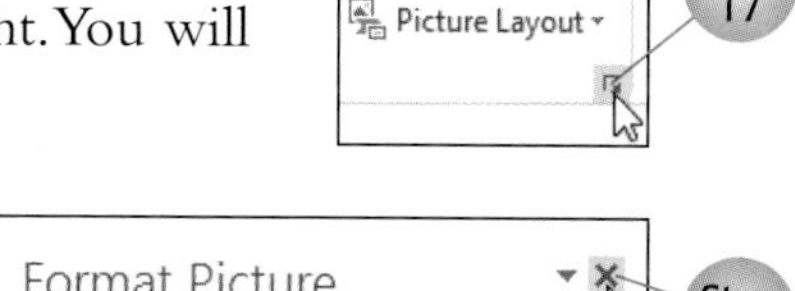

19. Tap or click the dialog box launcher at the bottom right corner of the Size group.
20. The Layout dialog box opens with the Size tab active.
21. Select the current value in the *Absolute* text box in the *Width* section and type 3.
22. Tap or click the Text Wrapping tab and tap or click the *Square* option.
23. Tap or click OK to close the Layout dialog box.
24. With the picture still selected, slide the picture up to the top of the document, or position the pointer on top of the picture and drag the picture up to the top of the document. Release the picture when the green horizontal and vertical **alignment guides** show that the picture is aligned at the top and left margins.

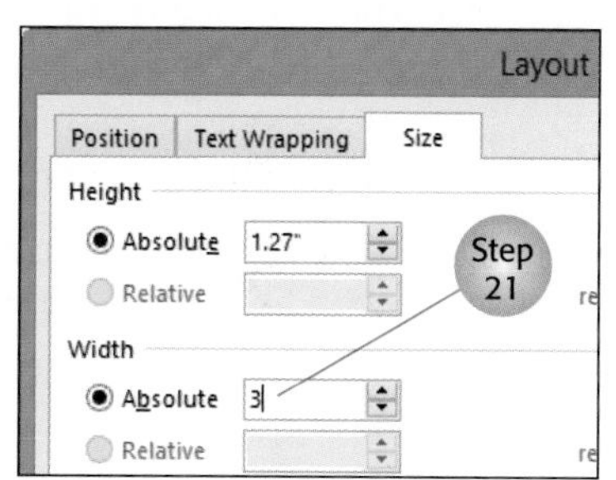

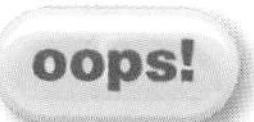

Measurement displays with cm (centimeters)? Change to inches at the Options dialog box from the FILE tab. Select Advanced pane and slide or scroll down to *Display* section.

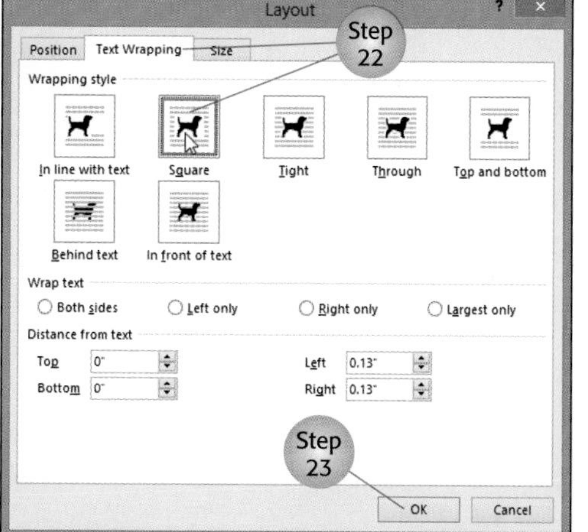

Vertical and horizontal lines called alignment guides are new in Office 2013. Guides help you place and align objects while the object is being manipulated.

Alignment guides show the picture is aligned at the top left margin.

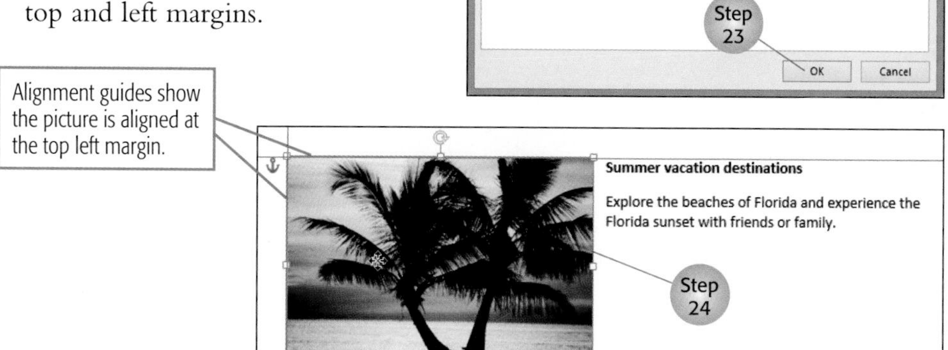

25. Tap or click the Save button on the QAT. Leave the document open for the next topic.

Because the document has already been saved once, the Save button saves the changes using the existing file name and location.

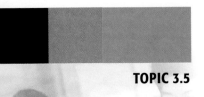

TOPIC 3.5

SKILLS

Copy and paste text and an object

Copy and paste formatting options using Format Painter

Use a task pane to format a selected object

Using the Office Clipboard

The Clipboard group is standardized across all Microsoft Office programs. The buttons in the Clipboard group are Cut, Copy, Paste, and Format Painter. You used Cut, Copy, and Paste in Chapter 1 when you learned how to move and copy files and folders. Cut, Copy, and Paste are also used to move or copy text or objects.

Format Painter is used to copy formatting options from selected text or an object to other text or another object.

1. With the **3.4-VacationDestinations-Your Name** document still open, display the Windows Start screen, start PowerPoint 2013, and tap or click Blank Presentation.
2. Tap or click *Click to add title* in the placeholder on the blank slide and type **Florida Sunset**.

3. Switch back to Word.
4. Select the sentence that begins with *Explore* below the title and tap or click the Copy button in the Clipboard group of the HOME tab.

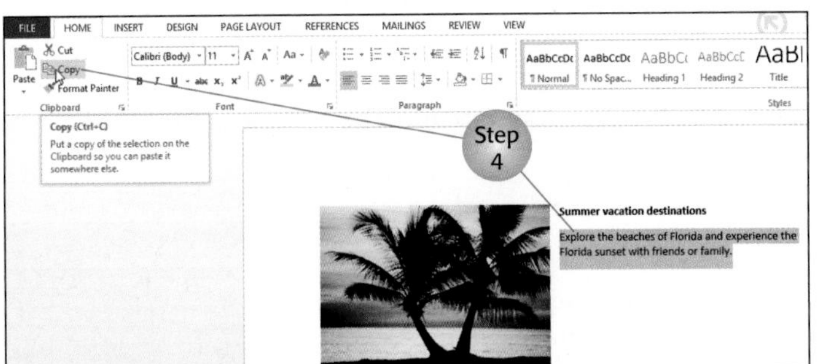

5. Switch to PowerPoint and tap or click *Click to add subtitle.*
6. Tap or click the top of the Paste button in the Clipboard group. (Do *not* tap or click the down-pointing arrow on the button.)

The selected text that was copied from Word is pasted into the slide in PowerPoint. Notice also the Paste Options button that appears below the pasted text.

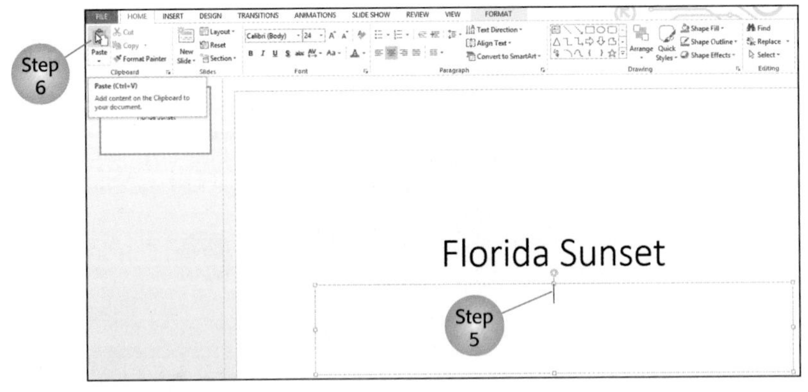

Some buttons in the ribbon have two parts. Tapping or clicking the top or left of the button causes the default action to occur. Tapping or clicking the bottom or right of the button (down-pointing arrow) displays a list of options to modify the action that occurs.

7 Tap or click the Paste Options button to display the *Paste Options* gallery.

Paste Options vary depending on the pasted text or object. Buttons in the gallery allow you to change the appearance or behavior of the pasted text or object in the destination location.

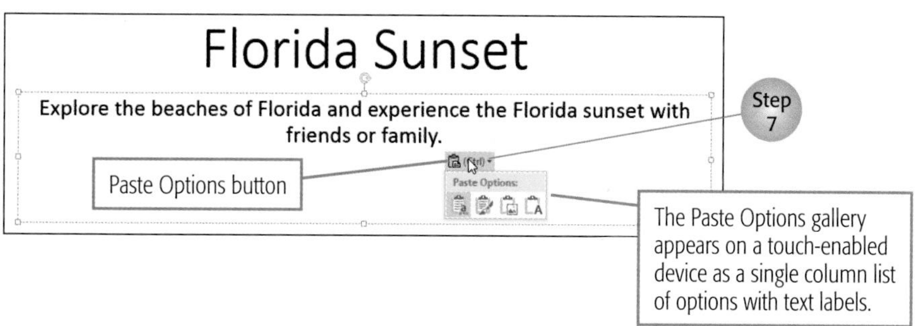
Florida Sunset
Explore the beaches of Florida and experience the Florida sunset with friends or family.
Paste Options button
Step 7
The Paste Options gallery appears on a touch-enabled device as a single column list of options with text labels.

8 Switch back to Word.

9 Tap or click to select the picture, tap or click the Copy button, switch to PowerPoint, and then tap or click the Paste button. (Remember not to tap or click the down-pointing arrow on the Paste button.)

The pasted picture is dropped onto the slide over the text.

10 Tap or click the Paste Options button that appears below the pasted picture.

Notice that the Paste Options for a picture are different than the Paste Options for text.

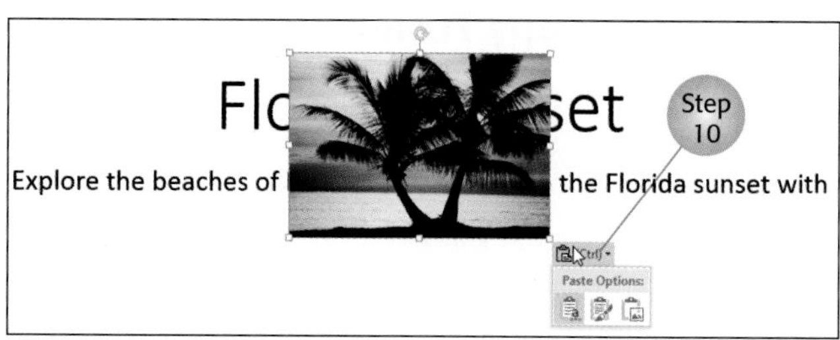
Step 10
Explore the beaches of
the Florida sunset with

11 Tap or click in the white space away from the picture to remove the *Paste Options* gallery.

12 If necessary, tap or click the picture to select the object.

13 Slide or drag the selected picture below the text. Release the picture when the orange guide shows the picture is aligned with the middle of the text placeholders.

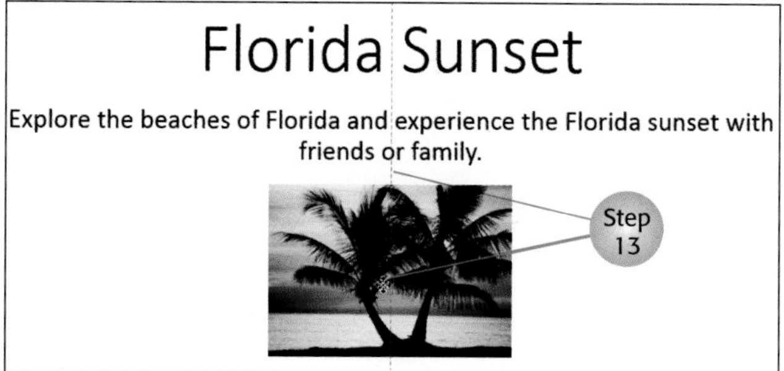
Florida Sunset
Explore the beaches of Florida and experience the Florida sunset with friends or family.
Step 13

14 Tap or click the Save button on the QAT.

Quick STEPS

Copy and Paste Text or an Object

1. Select text or object.
2. Tap or click Copy button.
3. Navigate to destination document or location within current document.
4. Tap or click Paste button.

App Tip

Paste Options are helpful if different formatting is in place in the source or destination documents and you want to control which formatting is applied to the pasted text or object.

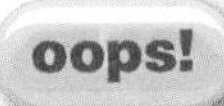

Don't remember how to navigate to your USB flash drive or to folders or subfolders? Refer to Topic 3.2 for help navigating drives and folders.

15 At the Save As tab Backstage view, tap or click *Computer* and tap or click Browse.

16 Navigate to the Ch3 subfolder in the CompletedTopicsByChapter folder on your USB flash drive.

17 Select the current text in the *File name* text box, type **3.5-FloridaSunset-Your Name**, and tap or press Enter, or tap or click Save.

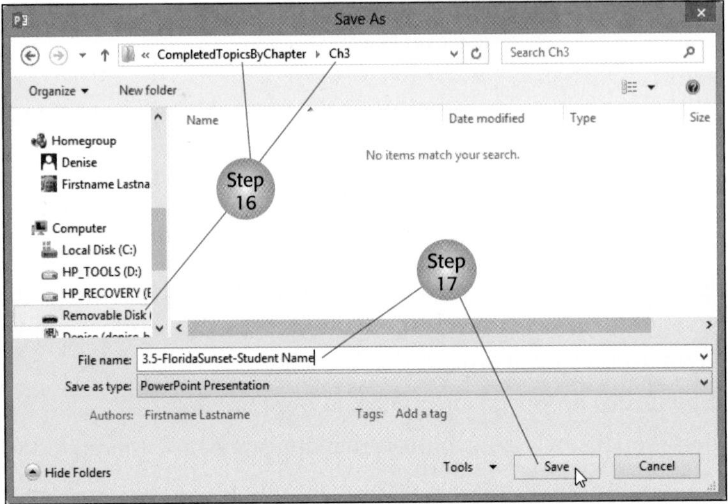

Using Format Painter to Copy Formatting Options

Sometimes instead of copying text or an object, you want to copy formatting options. Format Painter copies to the clipboard the formatting attributes for selected text or an object.

Tap once or single-click the Format Painter button to do a one-time copy of formatting options. Double-tap or double-click the Format Painter button if you want to paste the formatting options multiple times. Double-tapping or double-clicking the Format Painter button turns the feature on. The feature stays on until you tap or click the button again to turn the feature off. Buttons that operate as on or off are called **toggle buttons**.

18 Select the first occurrence of the word *Florida* in the subtitle on the slide.

19 Tap or click the Font button arrow (down-pointing arrow at right of Font Color button) in the Font group of the HOME tab.

20 Tap or click the *Purple* color square (last option in *Standard Colors* section).

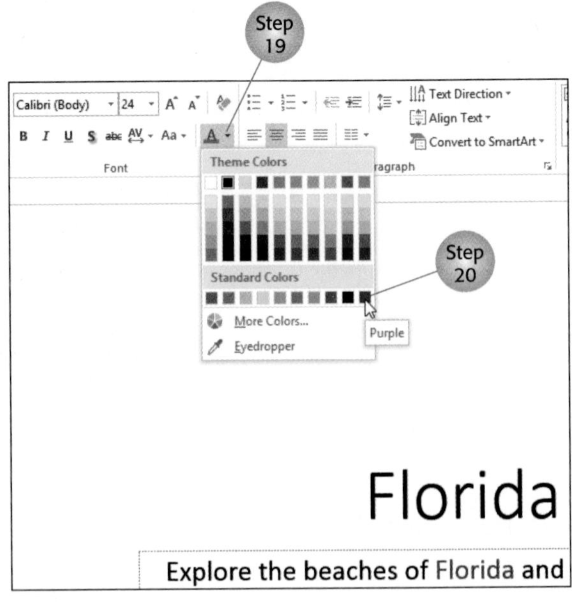

21 With the text still selected, tap or click the Italic button in the Font group.

22 With the text still selected, tap or click the Format Painter button (displays as a paint brush) in the Clipboard group.

23 Slide or drag across the second occurrence of the word *Florida* in the subtitle.

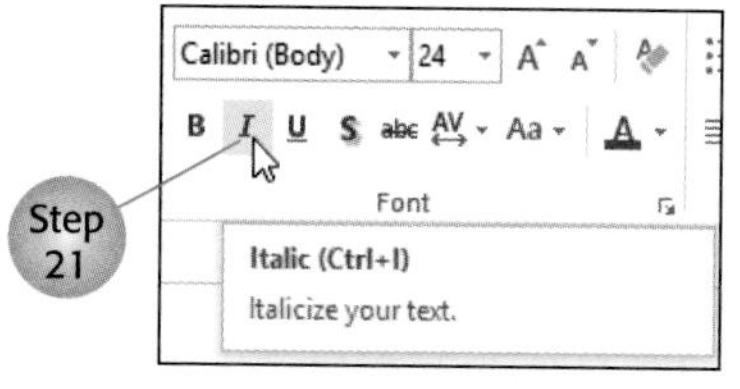

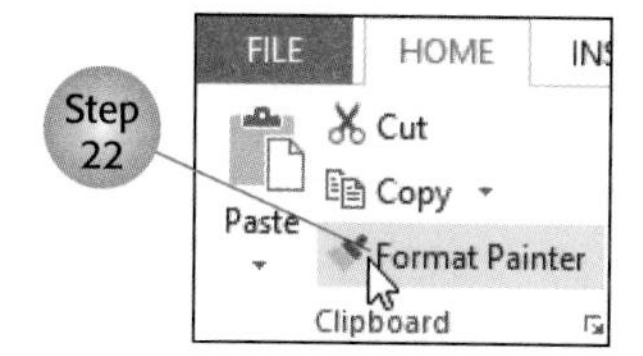

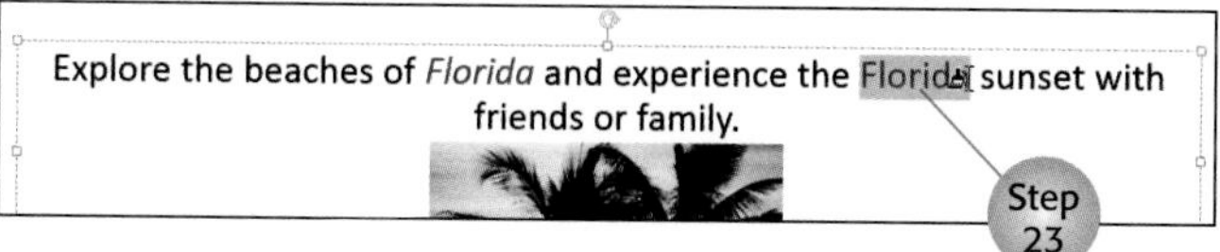

24 Tap or click in white space away from the selected text to deselect the text.

25 Tap or click the Save button on the QAT.

26 Tap or click to select the picture and display the contextual tab.

27 If necessary, tap or click the PICTURE TOOLS FORMAT tab.

28 Tap or click the *Drop Shadow Rectangle* option in the *Picture Styles* gallery (fourth picture style option).

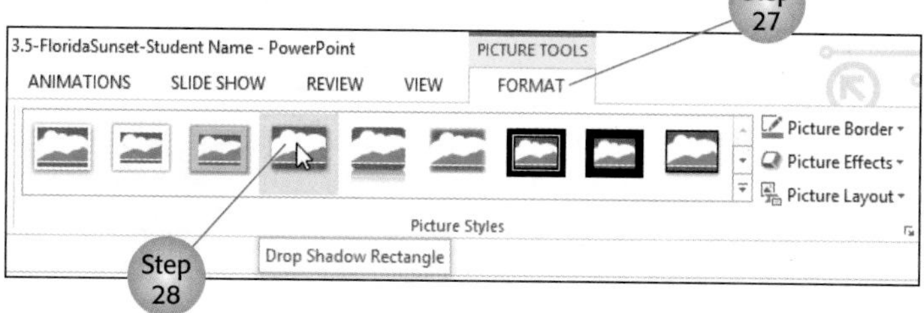

29 With the picture still selected, tap or click the HOME tab, tap or click the Format Painter button, and tap or click the title text *Florida Sunset* at the top of the slide.

30 With the Florida Sunset placeholder selected, tap or click the dialog box launcher in the Drawing group of the HOME tab.

31 Tap or click the Size & Properties button (last button) in the Format Shape task pane.

32 Tap or click TEXT BOX to expand the options in the task pane.

33 Tap or click the Vertical alignment button arrow (down-pointing arrow next to *Bottom*) and tap or click *Middle* at the drop-down list.

34 Close the Format Shape task pane.

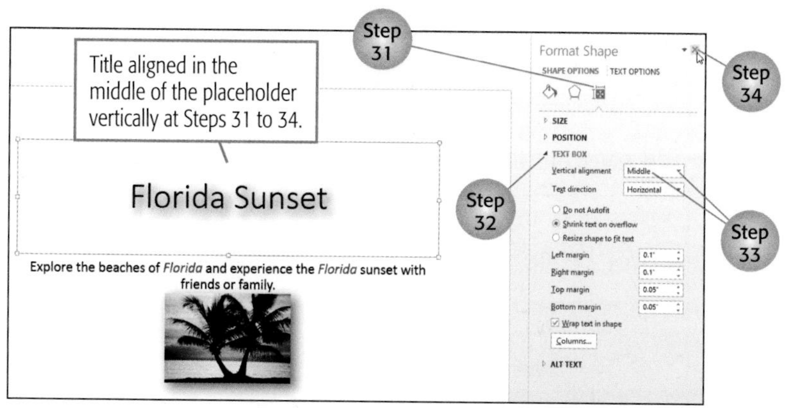

35 Save, then close PowerPoint. Leave the Word document open for the next topic.

Copy and Paste Formatting Options

1. Select text or object with desired formatting applied.
2. Tap or click Format Painter button.
3. Tap, click, or drag to select desired text or object to which formatting is to be copied.

When using a mouse, the pointer displays with a paint brush attached when Format Painter is active.

You can also align text in a PowerPoint placeholder using the Align Text button in the Paragraph group.

TOPIC 3.6

SKILLS

Use the Help feature to browse help topics and search for information on Office.com

oops!

Word Help window is mostly empty and displays Can't connect message? When the device is not connected to the Internet you are using offline help. Proceed to Step 6. Be aware your search results will differ and you will need to substitute a different link at Step 7. After Step 8, proceed to Step 12.

Finding Help in an Office Program

Microsoft provides an extensive set of online resources to assist you as you learn Office 2013. You can access Help within any Office application by tapping or clicking the Help button (displays as a question mark) near the top right corner of the application window.

1. With the **3.4-VacationDestinations-Your Name** document still open, tap or click the Microsoft Word Help button near the top right corner of the window (displays as a question mark ?).

A Word Help window opens inside the Word window.

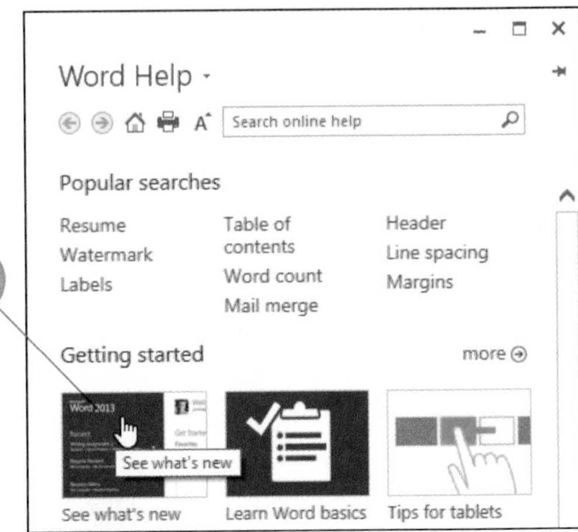

2. Tap or click See what's new in the *Getting Started* section.
3. Slide or scroll down and review the headings in the *What's new in Word 2013* article.
4. Read a paragraph below a heading about a new feature that interests you.
5. Tap or click the Back button to return to the main Word Help window.

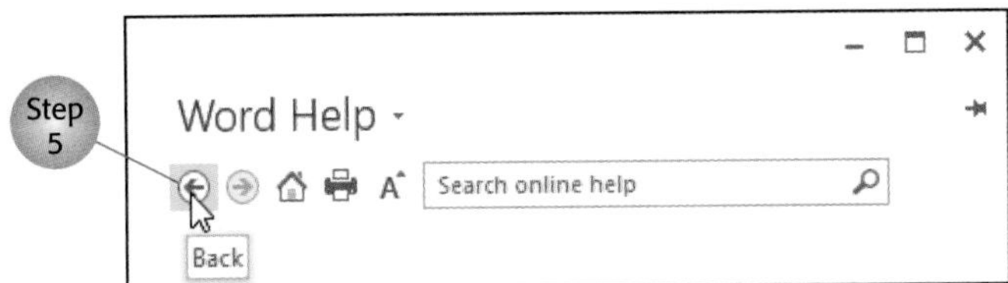

6. Tap or click in the *Search online help* text box, type **add page numbers**, and then tap or press Enter or tap or click the Search button (displays as a magnifying glass).

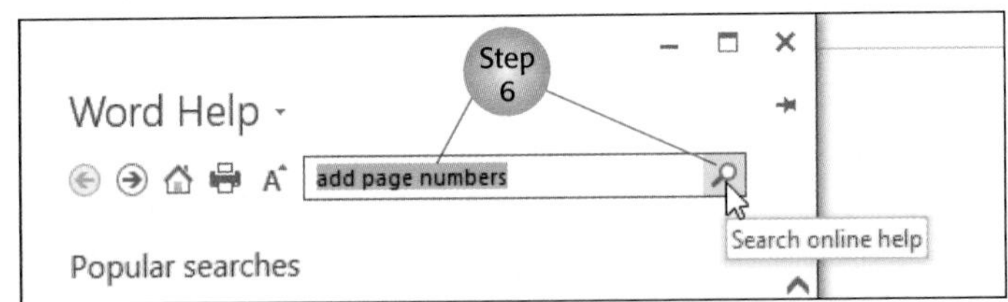

7. Tap or click Add page numbers.

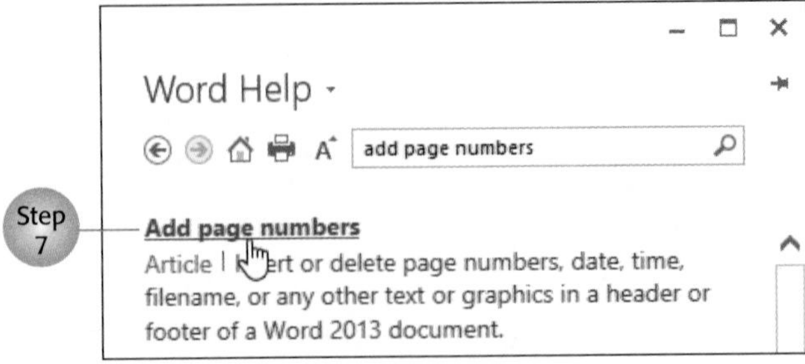

8. Slide or scroll down to review the Add page numbers article.

Check This Out

office.microsoft.com

Go here to find help by product. At the Support link, you can search for help articles or browse links to training videos and tutorials.

9. Tap or click the Home button near the top of the Word Help window to return to the main page.

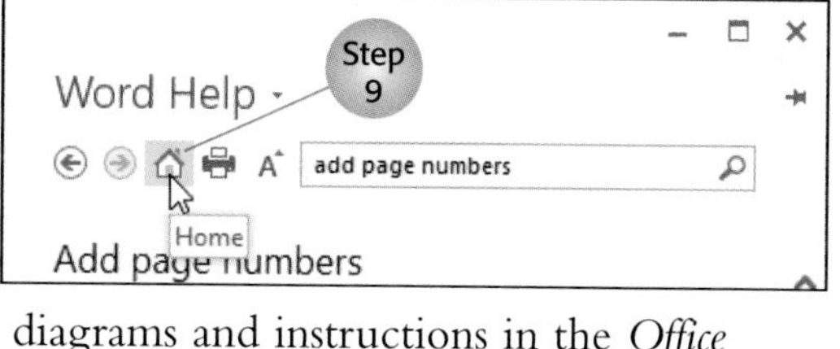

10. Tap or click Tips for tablets.

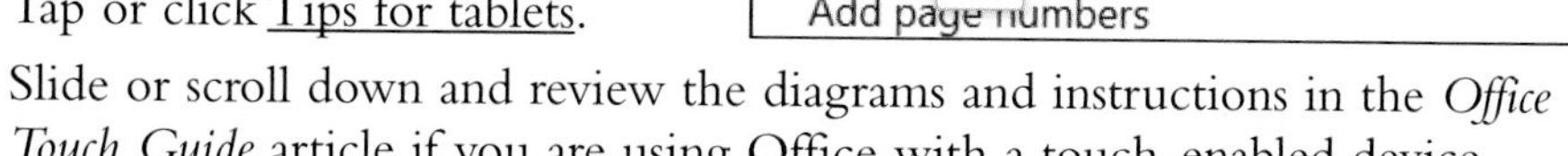

11. Slide or scroll down and review the diagrams and instructions in the *Office Touch Guide* article if you are using Office with a touch-enabled device.

This article contains information on how to use touch gestures to work with Office.

12. Tap or click the Back button to return to the main page.

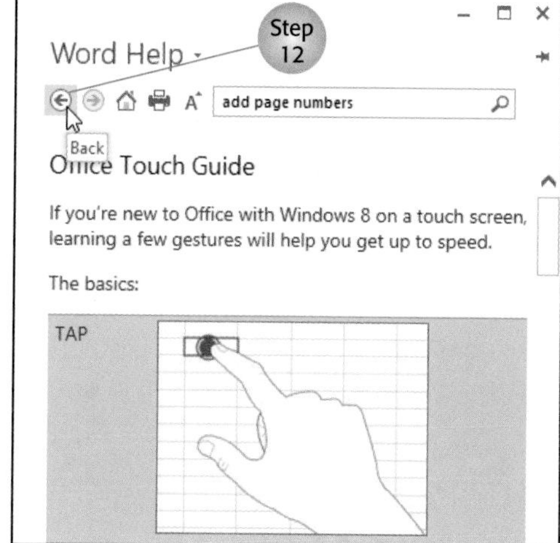

You can find help for an Office application by tapping or clicking a link in the *Popular searches* section, an article in the *Getting Started* section, or by typing a keyword or phrase in the *Search online help* text box. Microsoft also includes links to online training modules at Office.com.

13. Close the Word Help window.
14. Close the **3.4-VacationDestinations-Your Name** document. Tap or click the Save button if prompted to save changes to the document.
15. Close Microsoft Word. Tap or click the No button when prompted to keep the last item you copied.

Use Help

1. Tap or click Help button within Office application.
2. Tap or click link to popular search or other article OR type search keyword or phrase in *Search online help* text box and tap or click Search button.
3. Tap or click link in search results.

In Office 2013, ScreenTips have been enhanced to provide more information about the button's feature and use, and in some cases the ScreenTip even provides step-by-step instructions. Point to a button with the mouse to display a ScreenTip.

Figure 3.4 The Office page on Facebook. The page is frequently updated and may not appear exactly as shown here.

Microsoft Office Resources on Facebook

Microsoft has a Facebook page for Office (Figure 3.4). Go to facebook.com/office and check out the links to resources such as the Microsoft Community, where you can post questions, search answers, view videos, read blogs, and more.

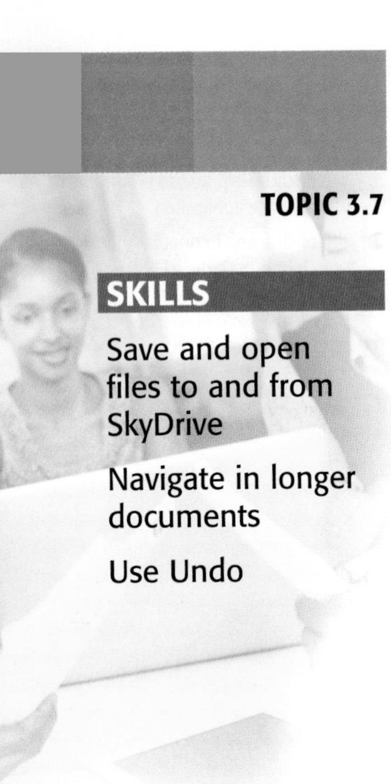

Using SkyDrive for Storage, Scrolling in Documents, and Using Undo

SkyDrive is secure online storage available to individuals signed in with a Microsoft account (often referred to as cloud storage). You can save files to and open files from SkyDrive, meaning you have access to the files from any device as long as you have an Internet connection. You may prefer to use SkyDrive as the place to store your completed work. SkyDrive can also be used if you forget your USB flash drive one day and need to save a file worked on at school or at home.

When working with longer documents, you will need to scroll the display or change the zoom settings to see more or less text within the window. The Zoom feature is explored in the next topic. Undo restores the document if you make a mistake.

Note: To complete this activity you need to be signed in with a Microsoft account. If you do not have a Microsoft account, skip the SkyDrive section in Steps 2 to 19 and proceed to Step 20 after opening the presentation.

1. Start PowerPoint 2013 and open the presentation named **SpeechTechniques** from the Student_Data_Files folder on your USB flash drive.
2. Tap or click the FILE tab and tap or click Save As.
3. Tap or click *Your Name's SkyDrive* (where *Your Name* is your first and last name) at the top left of the Save As tab Backstage view.
4. Tap or click the *Documents* folder name in the *Recent Folders* section of the *Your Name's SkyDrive* folder list, or tap or click the Browse button and then double-tap or double-click the *Documents* folder name.

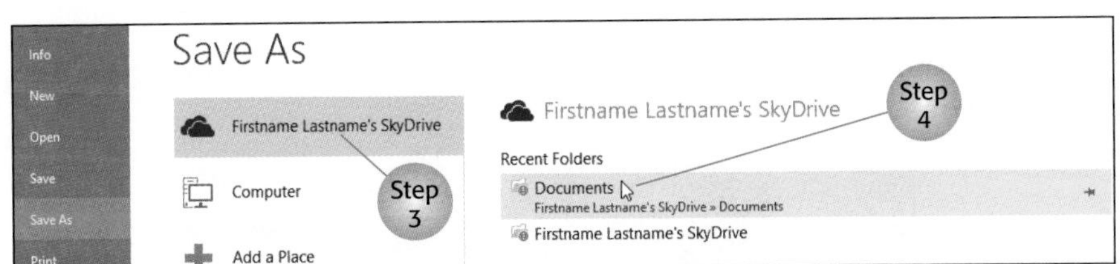

5. Type **3.7-SpeechTechniques-Your Name** in the *File name* text box at the Save As dialog box and then tap or press Enter or tap or click Save.

The file will be uploaded to your online storage space at SkyDrive.

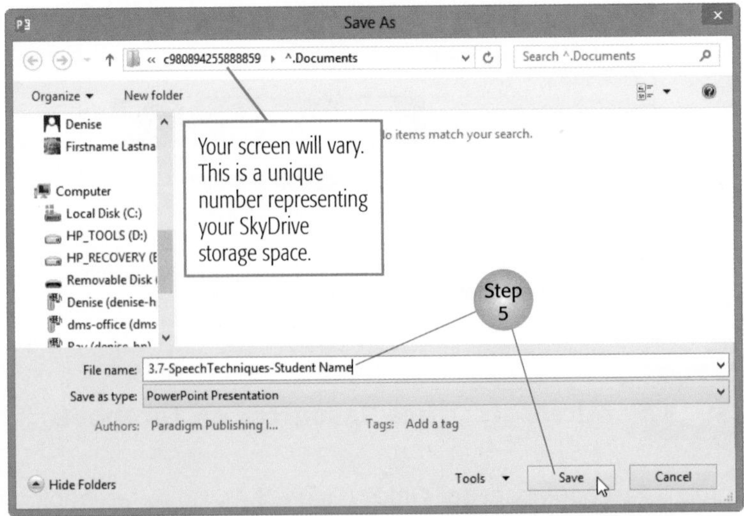

Nothing happening yet? A short delay as SkyDrive accesses your storage on Microsoft servers may occur.

You can access the file you will save to SkyDrive from any device even if the device does not have a local copy of PowerPoint. You will learn about the Office web apps in Chapter 15.

App Tip

The Save button on the QAT displays with an Internet Explorer icon when you are working with a document saved to SkyDrive.

A progress message displays in the Status bar as the file is uploaded.

Progress message displays as file is uploaded

Save a File to SkyDrive

1. Sign in with your Microsoft account.
2. Tap or click FILE tab.
3. Tap or click Save As.
4. Tap or click SkyDrive account name.
5. Tap or click Browse or choose folder in Recent folders list.
6. If necessary, navigate to desired folder.
7. If necessary, type name for file in *File name* text box.
8. Tap or click Save.

If you decided to use SkyDrive for all completed work, you should use folders on SkyDrive to keep each chapter's completed files together. In the next steps, you will save the presentation to SkyDrive a second time by creating a folder as you save the file.

6 Tap or click the FILE tab and tap or click Save As.

7 With your SkyDrive account already selected at the Save As tab Backstage view, tap or click the Browse button.

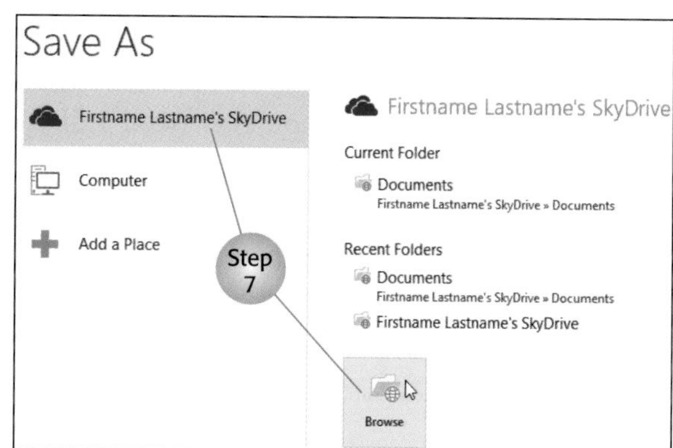

8 At the Save As dialog box, tap or click the New folder button in the Command bar.

Notice that the file saved at Step 5 appears in the Content pane.

9 Type **CompletedTopicsByChapter** and then tap or press Enter.

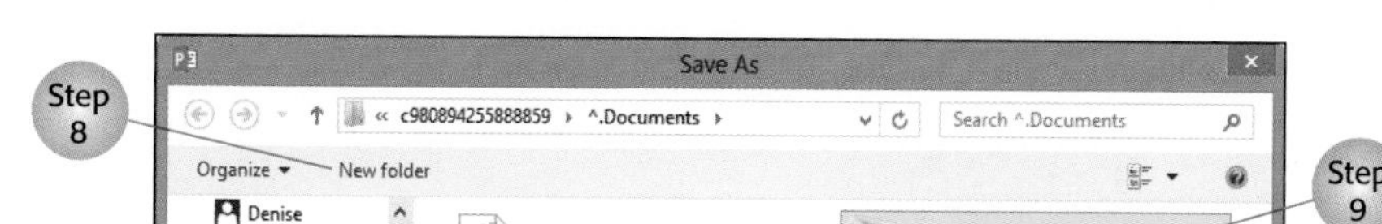

10 Double-tap or double-click the *CompletedTopicsByChapter* folder name to open the folder.

11 Tap or click the New folder button in the Command bar, type **Ch3**, and tap or press Enter.

12 Double-tap or double-click the *Ch3* folder name.

Save As « ^.Docum... › CompletedTopicsByChapter ›

Organize New folder

Denise Firstname Lastna Ch3 Folders

Step 11

13 Tap or click the Save button to save the presentation using the same name as before.

You now have two copies of the presentation saved on SkyDrive.

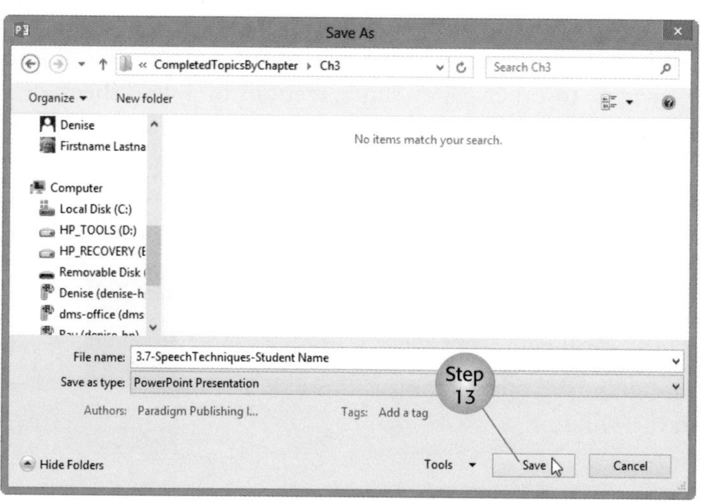

You may notice a one- or two-second delay when navigating folders in the Open or Save As dialog box when working on SkyDrive. If necessary, wait a few seconds for the screen to update.

14 Tap or click the FILE tab and then tap or click Close.

15 Tap or click the Open button on the QAT.

Because you just closed the **SpeechTechniques** presentation, you will notice the presentation appears twice in the *Recent Presentations* list. Notice that your SkyDrive account is associated with each of these entries. You could reopen the presentation from SkyDrive using the *Recent Presentations* list; however, in the next steps, you will use Browse to practice opening a file from SkyDrive in case a file you need is not in the *Recent* list for the Office application.

16 Tap or click *Your Name's SkyDrive* at the top left of the Open tab Backstage view.

You will notice the folder you need is in the *Recent Folders* list; however, you will practice navigating in case you ever need a file that has not been recently opened.

17 Tap or click the Browse button.

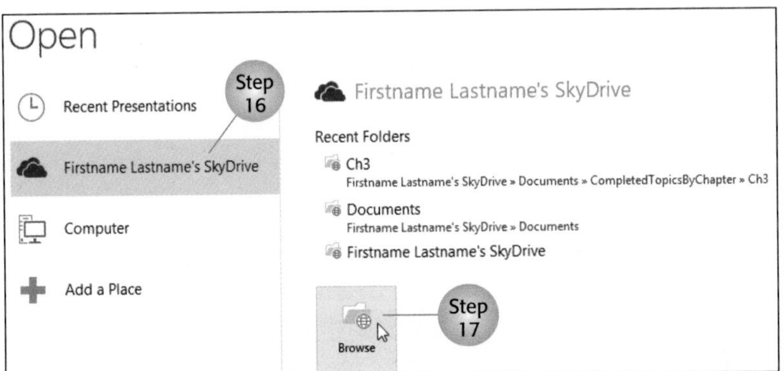

18 Double-tap or double-click the folder names *Documents*, *CompletedTopicsByChapter*, and *Ch3*.

19 Double-tap or double-click the ***3.7-SpeechTechniques-Your Name*** file name in the Content pane.

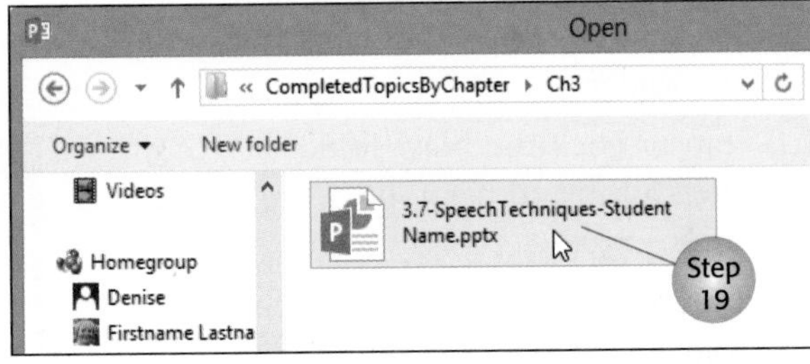

Navigating folders on SkyDrive is the same as navigating folders on your USB flash drive.

Horizontal and vertical scroll bars appear when the file exceeds the viewing area.

Using the Scroll Bars

Until now, the files you have used in this chapter were small and able to be seen in one window. Larger files display with a horizontal and/or vertical scroll bar that allows you to navigate to other pages, slides, sections of a worksheet, or part of an Access object. **Scroll bars** have arrow buttons at the top and bottom or left and right ends that are used to scroll up, down, left, or right. A **scroll box** in the scroll bar between the two arrow buttons is also used to scroll. PowerPoint and Word have two buttons at the bottom of the vertical scroll bar that are used to navigate to the next or previous slide or page.

20 Tap or click the Next Slide button at the bottom of the vertical scroll bar.

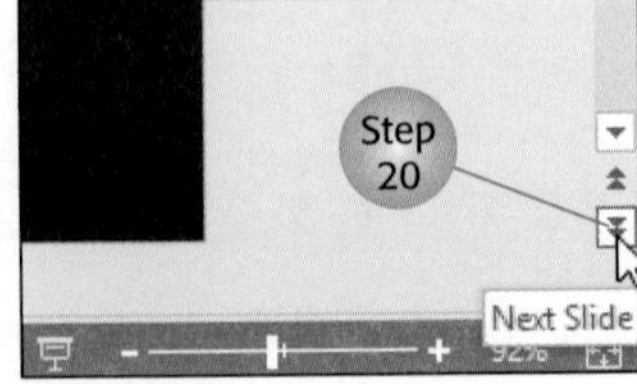

The second slide in the presentation is the slide now shown in the window.

21 Tap or click the Next Slide button two more times to move to Slide 4.

22 Tap or click the up arrow button at the top of the vertical scroll bar repeatedly until you are returned to the first slide.

23 Slide or drag the scroll box at the top of the vertical scroll bar downward until you reach the end of the slides.

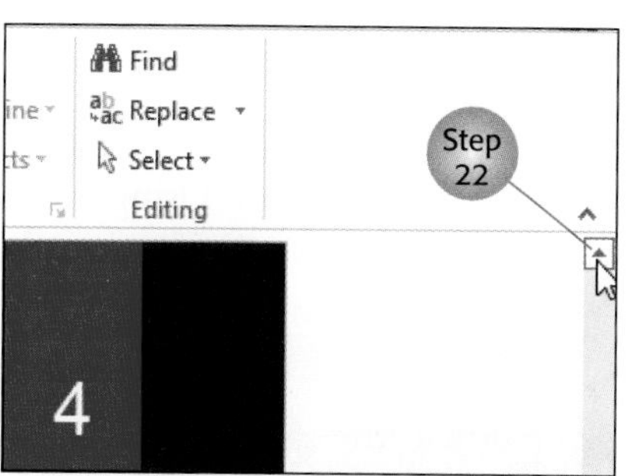

Notice that as you slide or drag the scroll box downward, a ScreenTip displays the slide numbers and titles for the slides so you know when to release your finger or the mouse.

24 Press the Ctrl + Home keys on your keyboard.

Ctrl + Home is the universal keyboard shortcut for returning to the beginning of a file.

25 Press the Ctrl + End keys on your keyboard.

Ctrl + End is the universal keyboard shortcut for navigating to the end of a file.

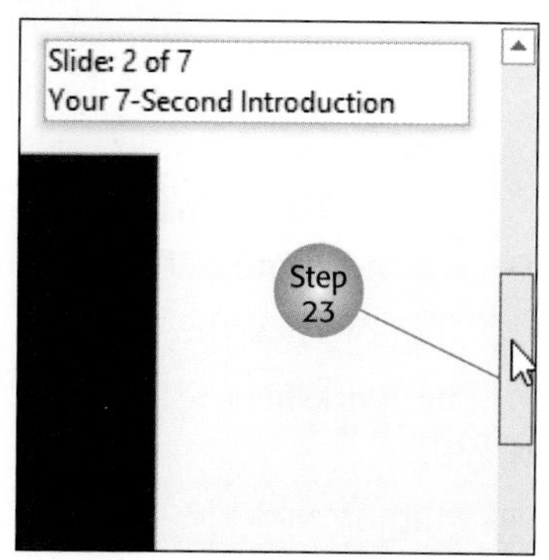

Scroll within a File
Tap or click arrow button for desired direction to scroll in horizontal or vertical scroll bar OR slide or drag scroll box in horizontal or vertical scroll bar.

Use Undo
Tap or click Undo button on QAT.

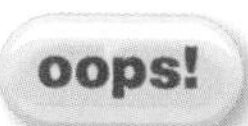

Using Touch Keyboard? Skip Steps 24 and 25 as the Touch Keyboard does not have Home and End keys.

Using Undo

The **Undo** command in all Office applications can be used to restore a document, presentation, worksheet, or Access object to its state before the last action that was performed. This can be a real life saver if you make a change to a file and do not like the results. Note that not all actions (such as Save) can be reversed with Undo.

26 Navigate to the first slide in the presentation.

27 Select the title text *Speech Techniques*.

28 Tap or click the Bold button on the Mini toolbar or in the Font group of the HOME tab.

29 With the text still selected, tap or click the Underline button on the Mini toolbar or in the Font group of the HOME tab.

30 Tap or click in any part of the slide away from the selected text to deselect the title text.

31 Tap or click the Undo button on the QAT. Do *not* tap or click the down-pointing arrow on the button.

The underline is removed from the title text and the text is selected.

32 Tap or click the Undo button a second time to remove the bold formatting.

33 Deselect the text and tap or click the Save button on the QAT.

34 Close the presentation and close PowerPoint.

Undo stores multiple actions. To undo an action that was not the last action performed, tap or click the Undo button arrow and then tap or click the desired action in the drop-down list.

Use the Redo button on the QAT if you change your mind after using Undo and want the action reapplied to the document.

TOPIC 3.8
SKILLS
Change the Zoom setting
Change the screen resolution to match textbook illustrations

Changing Display Options

Word, Excel, and PowerPoint display a **Zoom slider** bar near the bottom right corner of the window. Using the slider, you can zoom out or zoom in to view more or less of a document, worksheet, slide, or presentation.

1. Start Excel 2013 and open the workbook named **CutRateRentals** from the Ch3 folder in Student_Data_Files.
2. Look at the Zoom slider bar near the bottom right corner of the Excel window. Notice the percentage displayed is 100%. Tap or click the **Zoom In** button (displays as a plus symbol).

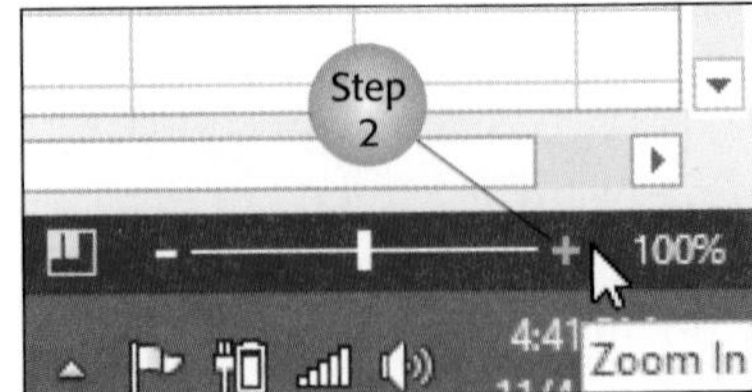

The worksheet magnification increases by 10%. Notice the zoom percentage is now 110%.

3. Tap or click the Zoom In button two more times.

The worksheet is now much larger in the display area and the zoom percentage is 130%.

4. Tap or click the **Zoom Out** button (displays as a minus symbol).

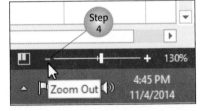

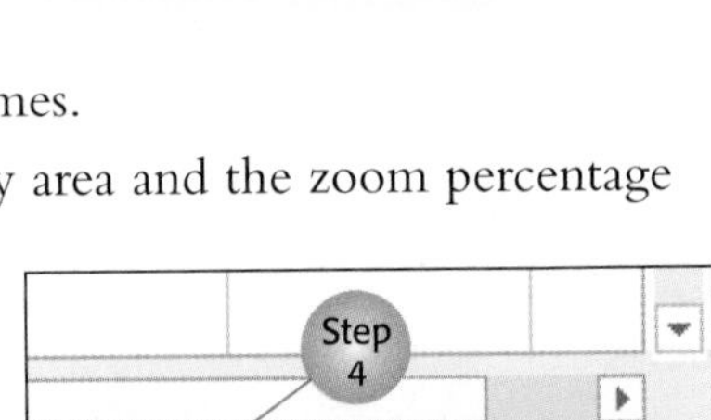

Zoom Out decreases the magnification by 10% each time the button is used.

5. Slide or drag the Zoom slider left or right and watch magnification of the worksheet decrease or increase as you move the slider.
6. Slide or drag the Zoom slider to the middle of the slider bar to return the zoom to 100%.

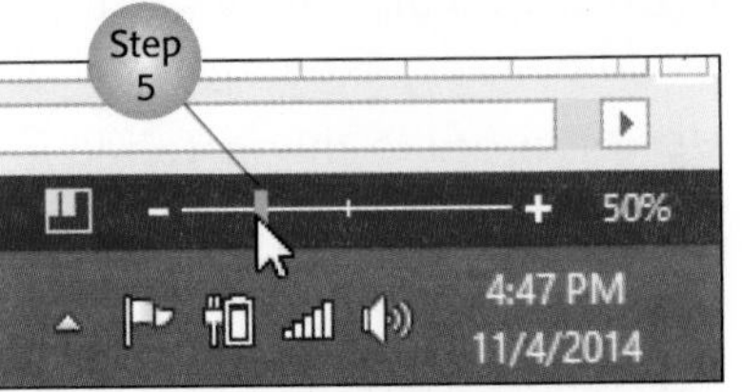

7. Tap or click *100%* at the right of the Zoom In button.

This opens the Zoom dialog box in which you can choose a predefined magnification, type a custom percentage value, or choose the *Fit selection* option to fit a group of selected cells to the window.

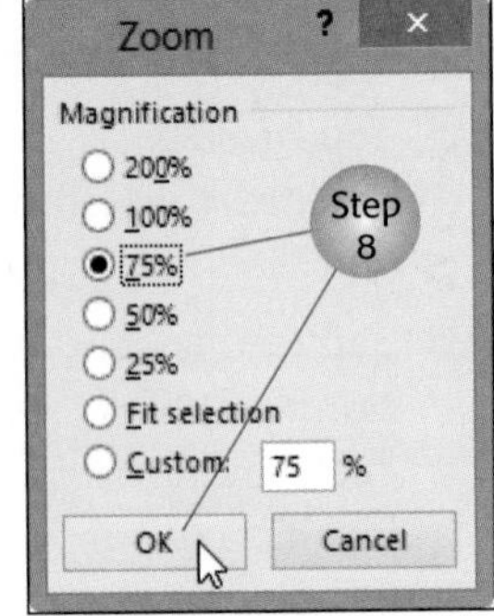

8. Tap or click *75%* and tap or click OK or press Enter.
9. Return the zoom magnification to 100% by dragging the Zoom slider to the middle of the slider bar.

Zoom In, Zoom Out, the Zoom slider, and the Zoom dialog box function the same in Word and PowerPoint.

Having trouble using the Zoom slider on a touch device? Tap the buttons or the percentage number to open the Zoom dialog box (steps 7 to 8), or use the Zoom buttons in the VIEW tab.

App Tip

The VIEW tab in Word, PowerPoint, and Excel contains a Zoom group with buttons to change zoom magnification. Access does not include the Zoom feature.

Viewing and Changing Screen Resolution

You may have noticed that your ribbon has fewer or more buttons than the ones shown in this textbook or that, in some cases, buttons show icons only (no labels). The appearance of the ribbon is affected by the screen resolution, as shown in Figure 3.5 on the next page.

Screen resolution refers to the number of picture elements, called pixels, that make up the image shown on the display. A pixel is a square with color values. Thousands of pixels are used to render the images you see on your display. Resolution is expressed as the number of horizontal pixels by the number of vertical pixels.

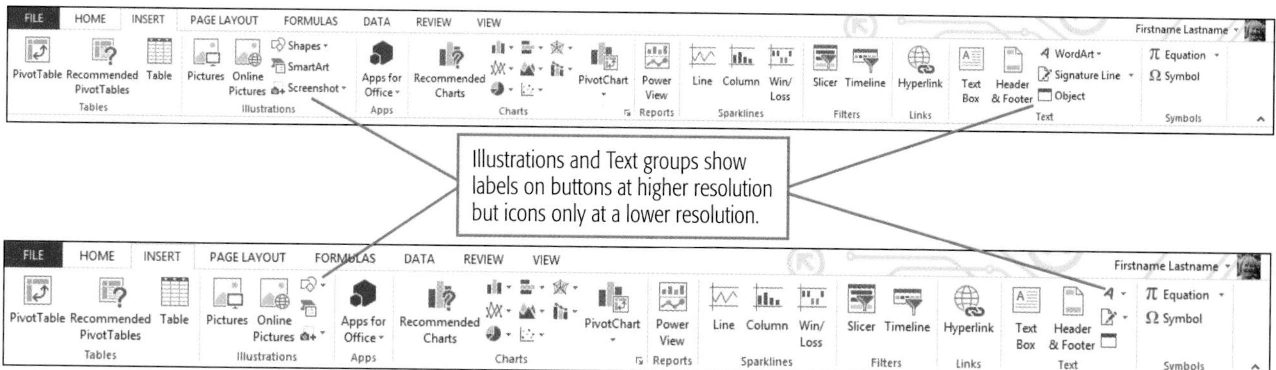

Figure 3.5 Excel's INSERT tab shown at 1440 x 900 (above) and at 1280 x 800 (below). The ribbon shows more or fewer buttons and/or displays buttons with or without labels at varying resolution settings. The lower resolution shown above is the setting from a tablet.

Note: Check with your instructor before proceeding. Some schools do not allow the display properties to be changed. If necessary, perform these steps on your personal PC or mobile device.

10 Minimize the Excel window to display the desktop.

11 Press and hold or right-click an unused area of the desktop to display the shortcut menu and then tap or click *Screen resolution*.

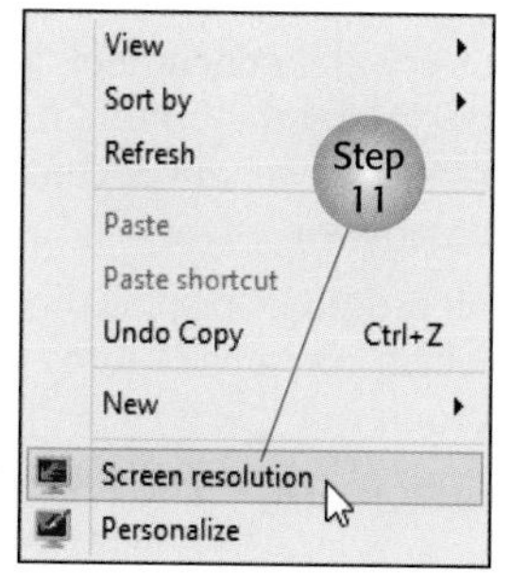

12 If the current setting for *Resolution* is *1440 x 900*, skip to Step 15; otherwise, tap or click the *Resolution* button and slide or drag the slider up or down as needed until the resolution is *1440 x 900*. (Use the highest setting possible if your device cannot display 1440 x 900.)

13 Tap or click the Apply button.

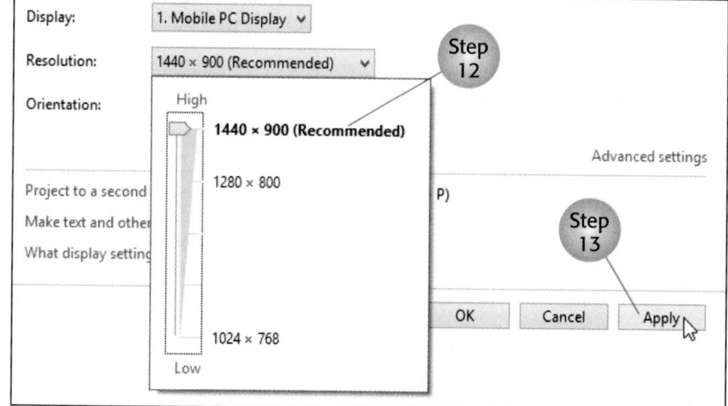

14 Tap or click the Keep changes button.

15 Tap or click OK to close the Screen Resolution window.

16 Tap or click the Excel button on the Taskbar to restore the Excel window.

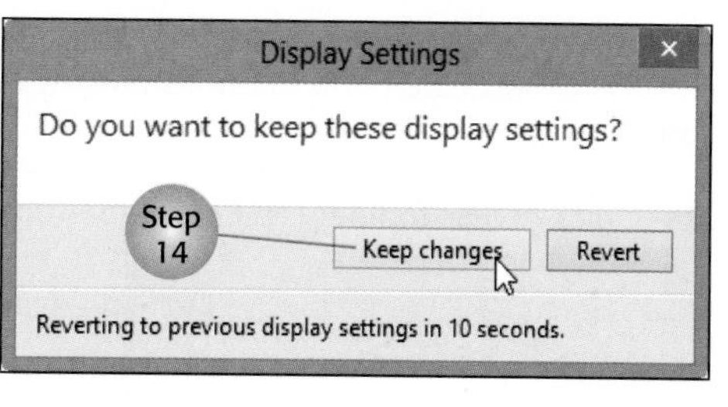

If you changed your screen resolution, examine the ribbon to see if there was a change in the quantity and/or display of the buttons (Figure 3.5).

17 Close the **CutRateRentals** worksheet and close Excel.

Change Zoom Magnification
Tap or click Zoom In or Zoom Out button or drag Zoom slider to desired setting OR

1. Tap or click zoom percentage.
2. Select desired zoom option.
3. Tap or click OK.

Screen resolution is an operating system setting. A higher resolution uses more pixels and means the image quality is sharper or clearer. It also means more content can be displayed in the viewing area.

Screen resolution won't go to 1440 x 900 or you cannot change the resolution? Choose a setting close to 1440 x 900 OR close the Screen Resolution dialog box. You do not need to change the screen resolution to successfully use this textbook. Just be aware that some illustrations won't match exactly what you see on your display.

Concepts Review

Topic	Key Concepts	Key Terms
Starting and Switching Programs, Starting a New Presentation, and Exploring the Ribbon Interface	All programs in the Microsoft Office suite are considered desktop apps, start the same way, and share common features. The Microsoft Office suite is sold in various editions including various subscription plans called Office 365. Generally, any PC or mobile device that is successfully running Windows 7 or Windows 8 with at least 3.0 GB of free space can run Microsoft Office 2013. To start a program in the Microsoft Office suite, tap or click the program's tile at the Start screen or search for the tile in the Apps list. An Office program starts with the application's Start screen, which shows a list of recently opened files and a Templates gallery. Switch between applications by tapping or clicking the desired program's button on the Taskbar in the desktop. Start a new document, workbook, or presentation by tapping or clicking the button in the Templates gallery of the Start screen for a new document, workbook, presentation, or database. All programs display the ribbon along the top of the window, which contains buttons for commands and features within the program. Buttons within the ribbon are divided into tabs and groups to organize related features together.	Office 365 Word 2013 Word Start screen Excel 2013 PowerPoint 2013 Access 2013 Ribbon Display Options button
Using the Backstage View to Manage Documents	The FILE tab is used in all Office applications to open the Backstage view. The Backstage view is where you perform document-level commands such as Open, Save, Save As, Print, Share, Export, and Close. Use the Open Other Documents link at the Word Start screen to navigate to a document not in the Recent Documents list. Use the Save As command to save a copy of a document in another location or in the same location with a different file name. At the Print tab Backstage view you can preview a document and change the printer and/or print settings before printing. A PDF document is an open standard created by Adobe systems for exchanging electronic documents. Use the Export command to publish a Word document in PDF format.	FILE tab Backstage view Print tab Backstage view Print Preview PDF document
Customizing the Quick Access Toolbar	The Quick Access toolbar (QAT) is at the top left of each Office application window. Add or remove buttons to/from the QAT by tapping or clicking the Customize Quick Access Toolbar button and tapping or clicking the desired option at the drop-down list. The QAT can be customized individually for each Office application.	Quick Access Toolbar

Topic	Key Concepts	Key Terms
Selecting Text or Objects, Using the Ribbon and Mini Toolbar, and Selecting Objects in Dialog Boxes	Before choosing an option from the ribbon, a task pane, or a dialog box, you often first select text or an object. Selected objects display with circle or square icons around the perimeter called selection handles, which are used to resize or otherwise manipulate the object. The Mini toolbar contains the same buttons as the ribbon and appears near selected text or with shortcut menus. Sliding or dragging a selection handle resizes a picture, shape, chart, or other item referred to as an object. Contextual tabs are tabs that appear with buttons related to the selected object. A gallery is a drop-down list or grid with visual representations of options that display a live preview of each option with the selected text or object. The dialog box launcher causes a task pane or dialog box to appear. Task panes and dialog boxes provide additional options for the related ribbon group as buttons, lists, sliders, check boxes, text boxes, and option buttons. Horizontal and vertical alignment guides appear when moving an object to help you place and align the object with text or margins.	Selection handle Mini toolbar Object Contextual tabs Gallery Live preview Dialog box launcher Task pane Dialog box Alignment guide
Using the Office Clipboard	The Clipboard group in the ribbon is standardized across all Office applications. Use Cut, Copy, and Paste buttons to move or copy text or objects. A Paste Options button appears when you paste text or an object with options for modifying the paste action. Use the Format Painter button to copy formatting options. A button that operates in an on or off state is called a toggle button.	Format Painter Toggle buttons
Finding Help in an Office Program	Access Help within any Office application by tapping or clicking the Help button that displays as a question mark near the top right corner of the window. Find help by following links to popular searches or articles, or by typing a search keyword or phrase. Go to facebook.com/office to find help at Microsoft Office's Facebook page.	
Using SkyDrive for Storage, Scrolling Documents, and Using Undo	SkyDrive is cloud storage where you can save files that can be accessed from any other device using your Microsoft account. Select your SkyDrive account at the Open and Save As tab Backstage view. Saving and navigating folders on SkyDrive is similar to saving and navigating folders on a USB flash drive. Horizontal and vertical scroll bars with arrow buttons and a scroll box are used to navigate larger documents. The Undo feature is used to reverse an action performed to restore a document to its previous state.	SkyDrive Scroll bars Scroll box Undo

continued....

Topic	Key Concepts	Key Terms
Changing Display Options	Use the Zoom In, Zoom Out, Zoom slider, and Zoom dialog box in Word, Excel, and PowerPoint to increase or decrease the magnification setting. Screen resolution refers to the number of horizontal and vertical pixels used to render an image on the display. The screen resolution setting for your PC or mobile device affects the display of the ribbon. Screen resolution is set at the desktop by opening the operating system's Screen Resolution window.	Zoom slider Zoom In Zoom Out Screen resolution

Multiple Choice

1. Which of the following is *not* an application within the Microsoft Office 2013 suite?
   a. Word
   b. Excel
   c. Internet Explorer
   d. Access
2. To switch to another open Office application, tap or click the button for the application in the ____________.
   a. Title bar
   b. Taskbar
   c. ribbon
   d. templates gallery
3. This tab opens the Backstage view.
   a. INSERT
   b. HOME
   c. VIEW
   d. FILE
4. Export a document in this file format that is a common standard used for exchanging documents electronically.
   a. PDF
   b. RDF
   c. DOC
   d. PUB
5. This toolbar is located at the top left corner of each Office application window.
   a. New
   b. Quick Print
   c. File
   d. Quick Access
6. If you customize the toolbar at the top left corner in Word, the revised toolbar also appears automatically updated in Excel and PowerPoint.
   a. True
   b. False
7. The circles or squares that appear around a selected object are called ________________.
   a. object handles
   b. zoom handles
   c. format handles
   d. selection handles
8. This term refers to a tab that appears with buttons related to a selected object.
   a. object tab
   b. contextual tab
   c. format tab
   d. quick access tab
9. A drop-down list that displays a live preview of options is called a ____________.
   a. task pane
   b. dialog box
   c. gallery
   d. guide
10. Tap or click this button to open a task pane or dialog box.
   a. dialog box launcher
   b. task pane launcher
   c. object launcher
   d. selection launcher

11. Cut, Copy, and Paste buttons are found in this group in the HOME tab.
    a. Alignment
    b. Clipboard
    c. Editing
    d. Insert
12. Use this button to copy formatting options.
    a. Format Painter
    b. Copy Formats
    c. Paste Formats
    d. Cut Formats
13. The Help button displays as this symbol.
    a. Exclamation mark (!)
    b. Plus symbol (+)
    c. Question mark (?)
    d. Hyphen (-)
14. SkyDrive is referred to as this type of storage.
    a. backup
    b. cloud
    c. extra
    d. redundant
15. This feature will reverse an action.
    a. Undo
    b. Redo
    c. Cut
    d. Restore
16. This slider is used to increase or decrease the magnification of the screen.
    a. Zoom
    b. Magnify
    c. Display
    d. Personalize

Crossword Puzzle

ACROSS

2 Guides that help you place objects when moving
5 Name for buttons that have an on and off state
6 Name of pane that opens at left or right side of window
8 Online file storage
9 Reverse last action
11 Tab that opens Backstage view
12 Name of toolbar at top left of Office apps
15 Tab in Backstage view used to create a PDF

DOWN

1 Opening window for all Office apps
3 Shows gallery option applied to selection in advance
4 Name of toolbar that appears with selected text
7 Navigational element in scroll bar between arrows
10 Picture, shape, or chart
13 Save a copy of a file in another location
14 Dialog box to change magnification setting

Matching

Match the term with the statement or definition.

_______ 1. Ribbon
_______ 2. Backstage view
_______ 3. Quick Access toolbar
_______ 4. Gallery
_______ 5. Format Painter
_______ 6. SkyDrive
_______ 7. Scroll bars
_______ 8. Zoom In

a. Frequently used buttons
b. Cloud storage
c. Copy formats
d. FILE tab
e. Navigate long documents
f. Interface to access commands
g. Increase magnification
h. Live preview

Project 1 Start a New Presentation and Copy Object to Slide from Excel

Individual

Deliverable: PowerPoint Presentation

1. Start Excel 2013 and open the student data file named **CutRateRentals**.
2. Start a new blank presentation in PowerPoint 2013.
3. Type **CutRate Car Rentals** as the slide title text.
4. Use the Layout button in the Slides group of the HOME tab to change the slide layout option to *Title Only*.
5. Select the title text, apply formatting options of your choice, and then deselect the text.
6. Switch to Excel, select and copy the pie chart, switch to PowerPoint, and then paste the chart on the slide.
7. Save the presentation as **C3-Project1-CutRateRentals-Your Name** in a new folder named Ch3 in the ChapterProjectsWork folder on your USB flash drive.
8. Close the presentation, close PowerPoint, and then close Excel.
9. Submit the presentation to your instructor in the manner she or he has requested.

Project 2 Modifying a Presentation and Copying to Word

Individual

Deliverable: Word Document and PDF Document

1. Start PowerPoint and open the **C3-Project1-CutRateRentals-Your Name** presentation.
2. Use Save As to save a copy of the file as **C3-Project2-CutRateRentals-Your Name**.
3. Select and resize the chart so that the chart fills most of the slide below the title.
4. With the chart still selected, move the chart as needed so that it is centered below the title.
5. With the chart still selected, use the Change Colors gallery in the Chart Styles group of the CHART TOOLS DESIGN tab to change the color scheme for the pie chart to another color of your choosing.
6. With the chart still selected, use the Shape Styles gallery in the CHART TOOLS FORMAT tab to apply a shape style option of your choosing. ***Hint: Tap or click the More button (bottom button that displays with a bar and down-pointing arrow below it at right end of gallery) to view more options in a drop-down grid.***
7. Select the title text and change the font color to a color of your choosing.
8. Save the revised presentation using the same name.
9. Start a new blank document in Word 2013.
10. Copy the slide title text from the PowerPoint presentation and paste the text into the Word document. After the text is pasted, use the Paste Options button to apply the *Keep Source Formatting* option if the text is not pasted with source formatting already applied.
11. If necessary, press Enter to create a new blank line after the title text.
12. Copy the chart from the PowerPoint presentation and paste it below the title in the Word document.
13. Save the Word document as **C3-Project2-CutRateRentals-Your Name** in the Ch3 folder in ChapterProjectsWork.
14. Export the Word document as a PDF with the same name and save in the same location.
15. Close the Reader app if necessary.
16. Close the document in Word, close Word, and close PowerPoint.

Project 3 Florida Vacation Flyer

Individual or Pairs
Deliverable: Flyer as document or PDF

1. Research a Florida destination that you would like to travel to during the next school break, including the approximate cost for one week. Include in the cost estimate travel, lodging, food, visitor attractions, and souvenirs.
2. Make a list of five to 10 points to include in the flyer based on the research you conducted. For example, provide a list of tourist attractions or events that make the destination inviting.
3. Create a flyer in Word named **C3-Project3-FloridaFlyer-Your Name** and saved in the Ch3 folder in ChapterProjectsWork similar to the one shown in Figure 3.6, substituting your information where noted. Use your best judgment to determine options to apply to the text. Apply the following options to the picture: +40% Brightness and Contrast correction, width of 2.5 inches, Top and Bottom Text Wrapping, and Reflected Rounded Rectangle Picture Style.
4. Export the flyer as a PDF with the same name and saved in the same location, and close Word.
5. Submit the flyer to your instructor in the manner she or he has requested.

Florida Vacation

Are you ready for a week of fun and adventure?

Read on to learn about a fantastic Florida vacation.

When: (insert next break week dates here)

Where: (insert Florida destination here)

Reasons not to miss this trip:

(list five to ten points here)

Estimated Cost: (insert approximate cost here)

Figure 3.6 Project 3 Florida Flyer Document

Chapter 4

Organizing and Managing Class Notes Using OneNote

After successfully completing this chapter, you will be able to:

- Open and close an existing notebook
- Add and edit content
- Add sections and pages to a notebook
- Link external content to a notebook
- Tag notes
- Search notes
- Create a new notebook
- Share a notebook

OneNote is a note-taking software application referred to as a digital notebook. Think of OneNote as the electronic equivalent of a binder with notes written on loose leaf paper organized by dividers. Note-taking software can store, organize, search, and share notes of any type, including typed notes, handwritten notes on a tablet, web pages, pictures, documents, presentations, worksheets, emails, appointments, contacts, and more. A OneNote notebook can collect everything you want to keep track of for a subject or topic in one place.

OneNote notebooks can be stored on SkyDrive so that you can access the notes from any device with an Internet connection. Another advantage to storing the notebook on SkyDrive is that you can share the notebook with others. More than one person can edit a page at the same time. For group projects, OneNote is a useful tool for collaborating and sharing ideas, research, and content.

In this chapter you will learn how to open an existing notebook; create a new OneNote notebook; add sections, pages, and content; tag and search notes; and share a notebook with others.

Opening a Notebook and Adding Notes, Sections, and Pages

Topic 4.1

SKILLS

- Open an existing notebook
- Create and move a note
- Apply color to note text
- Add a section and page

A **OneNote notebook** is organized into sections, which are accessed by tabs across the top of the notebook. Think of sections as the dividers you would use in a binder to organize notes by subject, topic, or category. Within each section you add pages. Notes or other content are added to a page. You can add as many sections and pages as you like to organize a notebook. Notes can be typed or content added anywhere on a page.

1 From the Windows Start screen, start **OneNote 2013**.

The first time OneNote is started, a Start screen appears with information on how to use OneNote (Figure 4.1). The default notebook called *My Notebook* opens. You can store everything in My Notebook or create separate notebooks for keeping notes organized. For example, you may want to create one notebook for school-related content and another for personal content.

Note: The Start screen shown in Figure 4.1 may not appear depending on the configuration for the computer you are using.

Figure 4.1 The OneNote Start screen opens with My Notebook and the Quick Notes tab active. You can learn about using OneNote from the Start screen by reading the content and following links to videos.

2 Tap or click My Notebook (or Notebooks) near the top left corner of the OneNote window (below the ribbon) and tap or click *Open Other Notebooks* at the drop-down list.

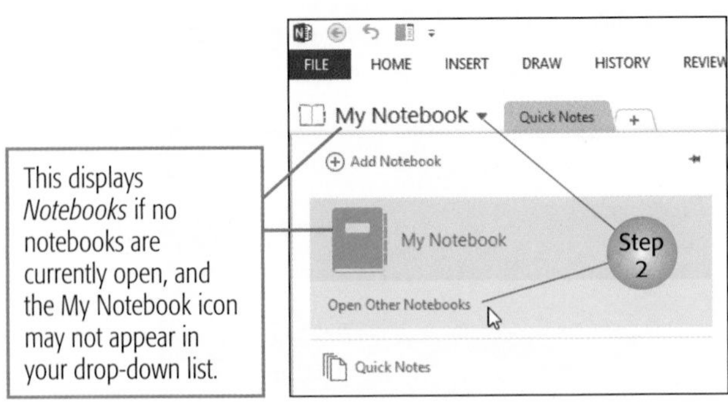

3 At the Open Notebook Backstage view, tap or click Computer in the *Open from other locations* section, and then tap or click the Browse button.

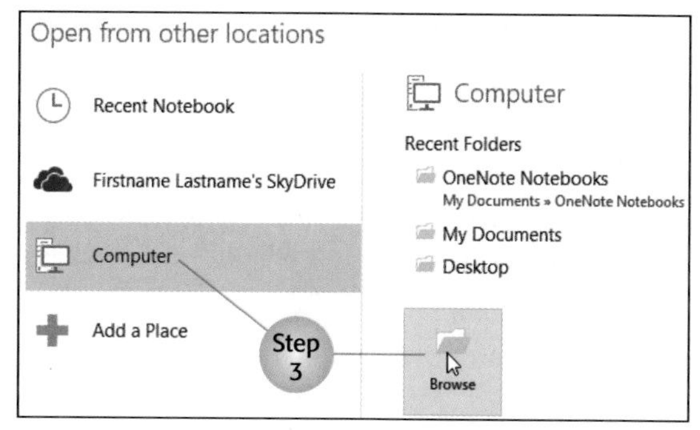

oops!

Can't see the Browse button? You may need to slide or scroll down the *Computer* pane to see the button.

4 Navigate to the Removable Disk for your USB flash drive in the Navigation pane, and double-tap or double-click the *ComputerCourse*, *Student_Data_Files*, and *Ch4* folder names in the Open Notebook dialog box.

5 Double-tap or double-click the *BusTechnologyCourse* folder name.

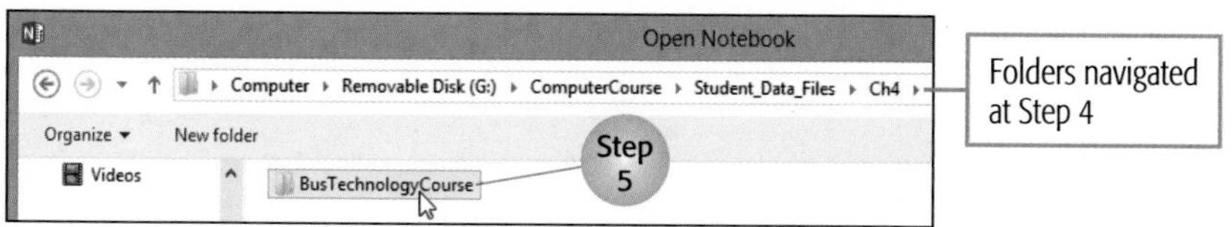

OneNote differs from other Office apps in that the name that appears as the notebook name is the name of a *folder* (not an individual file). Each OneNote section is a *separate file saved within the notebook folder*.

6 Double-tap or double-click the file named ***Open Notebook***.

Open Notebook
« ComputerCourse › Student_Data_Files › Ch4 › BusTechnologyCourse
Organize New folder
Videos
Open Notebook
Step 6

By default, OneNote creates a table of contents file named Open Notebook within a folder named for each notebook created. The table of contents file is similar to a table of contents for a book in that it stores the name of each section added to the notebook. OneNote saves each section in a separate file within the notebook folder.

7 Review the information on the Business Technology page in the *CourseInformation* section. If necessary, slide or scroll down to view all information.

8 Tap or click anywhere within the text *Prof. J. Wickham*.

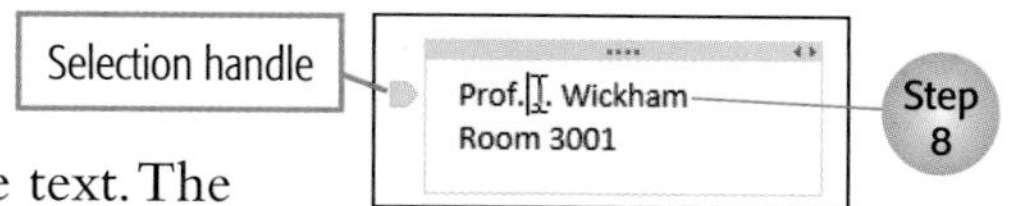

Notice that a box surrounds the note text. The box is referred to as a **note container**. Notice also that a selection handle appears at the left side of the note container.

9 Tap or click the selection handle at the left of the note container to select the text *Prof. J. Wickham*.

10 Tap or click the Bold button on the Mini toolbar.

Step 10
Calibri 11
B I U
Prof. J. Wickham
Room 3001
Step 9

Using touch? Remember to tap inside a selection to display the Mini toolbar.

11 Tap or click in the blank white space at the right of the Prof. J. Wickham note container and type **Office hours every Tuesday from 12:00 to 1:00**.

12 Slide or drag the gray bar at the top of the note container to move the note next to *Prof. J. Wickham* in the approximate location shown.

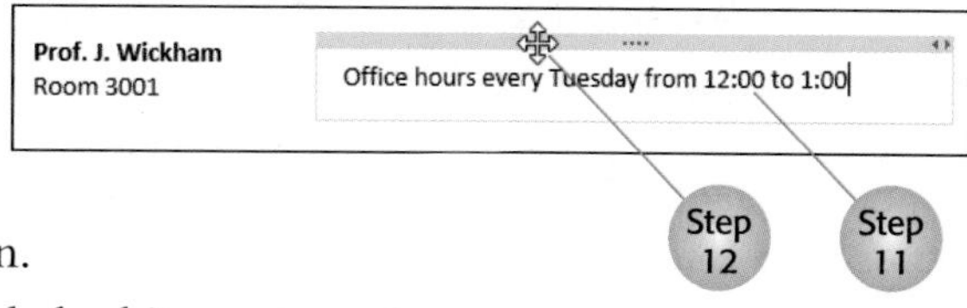

When using a mouse, a four-headed white arrow pointer appears when you point to the top gray bar on the note container. Drag the note container when you see this pointer.

To delete a note, select the note text using the selection handle or the gray bar at the top of the note container and press the Delete key on the keyboard or choose Cut in the HOME tab.

Using Color to Highlight Notes

OneNote includes a Text Highlight Color tool that is used to apply color highlighting to notes just as you would use a highlighter to highlight important points in a textbook. The Text Highlight Color tool is in the Basic Text group of the HOME tab and also in the Mini toolbar. Tap or click the button to apply the default yellow highlighting to the selected text or use the down-pointing arrow on the button to apply a different highlight color.

13 Select the text *Examine various social media and communications applications* in the *Performance Objectives* section and tap or click the Text Highlight Color button in the Mini toolbar to highlight text using the default color.

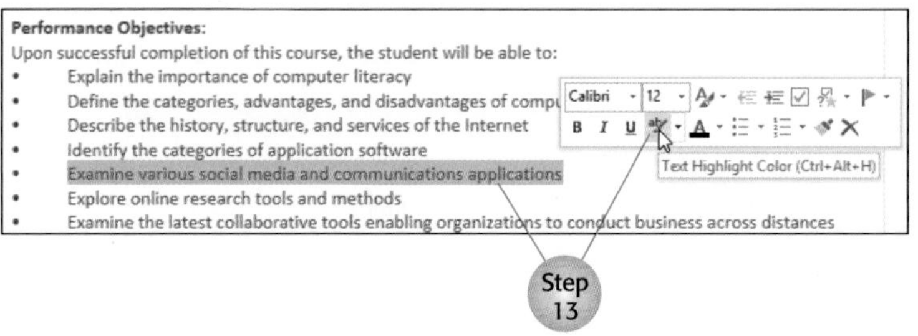

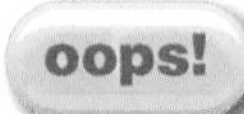

Ribbon is not pinned? Tap or click the HOME tab and tap or click the push pin icon at the bottom right corner of the ribbon to keep the buttons visible while you work.

14 Select the text *conducting work online and across distances via collaborative tools* in the *Course Description* section, tap or click the Text Highlight Color button arrow in the HOME tab, and then tap or click Green (second color option).

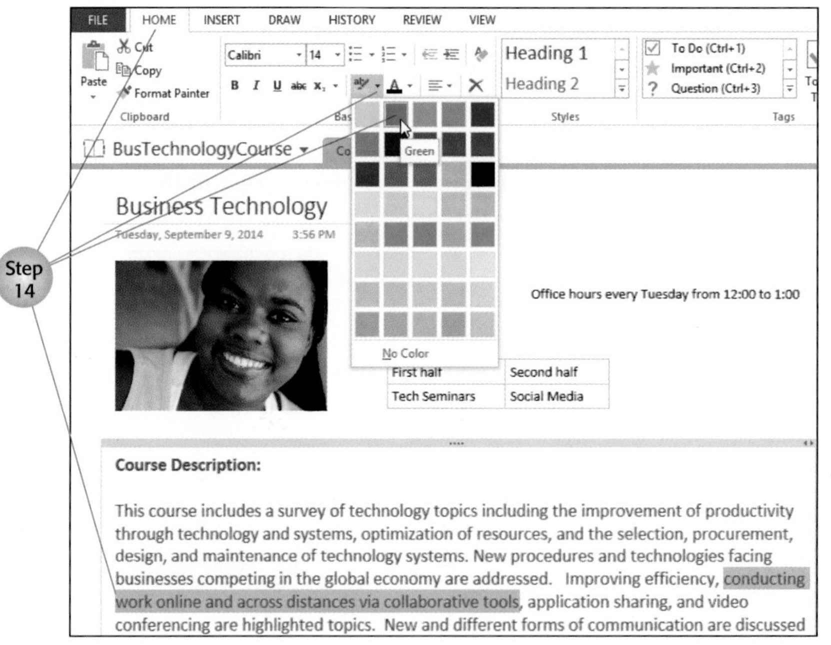

Adding Sections and Pages

A section is like a divider in a binder. Create sections to organize the notebook by category, topic, or subject. Each section can have multiple pages. To create a new section in a notebook, tap or click the **Create a New Section tab** (displays as a plus symbol) along the top of the notebook window, type a name for the section, and then tap or press Enter. A blank page displays in the new section with an insertion point in the page title section. Type a title for the page and tap or press Enter.

Tap or click the **Add Page icon** in the Pages pane to add another new page to the section. Type a title for the page and tap or press Enter.

15 Tap or click the Create a New Section tab (displays as a plus symbol) next to the CourseInformation tab.

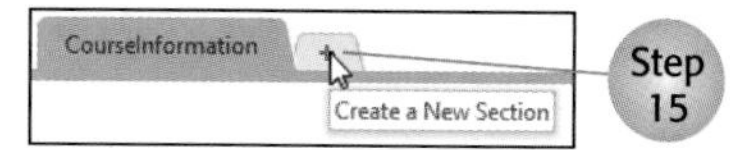

16 Type **WebPages** and tap or press Enter.

17 With the insertion point blinking in the page title placeholder, type **Technology Web Pages** and tap or press Enter.

18 Tap or click the Create a New Section tab, type **TechnologyImages**, and then tap or press Enter.

19 Type **Pictures for Technology Topics** as the page title and tap or press Enter.

20 Tap or click the WebPages tab to display the section.

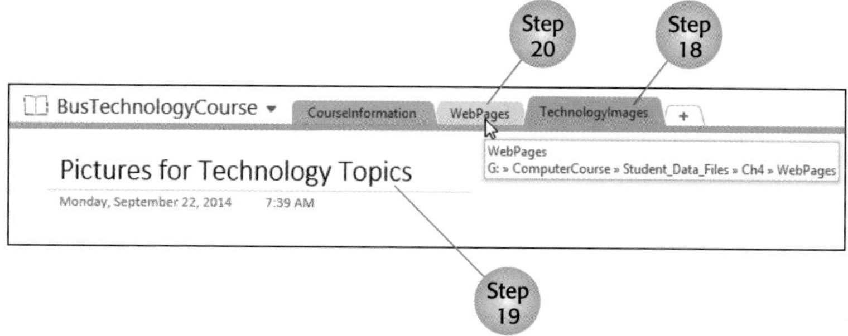

21 Tap or click the Add Page icon (displays as a plus symbol inside a circle) in the Pages pane.

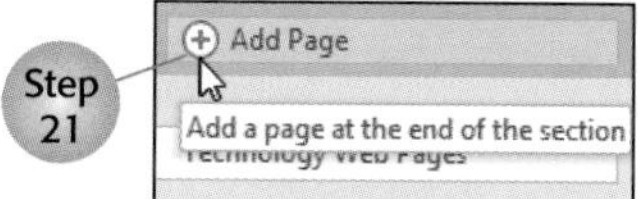

22 Type **Technology Web Links** as the page title and tap or press Enter. Leave OneNote open for the next topic.

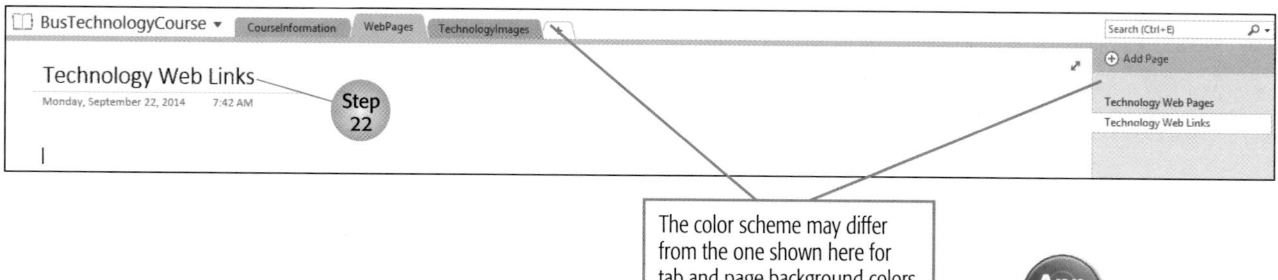

The color scheme may differ from the one shown here for tab and page background colors.

Quick STEPS

Open a Notebook

1. Tap or click My Notebook or Notebooks.
2. Tap or click *Open Other Notebooks*.
3. Navigate to drive and/or notebook folder name.
4. Double-tap or double-click *Open Notebook*.

Add a Note to a Page

1. Tap or click at desired location on page.
2. Type note text.
3. Tap or click in blank space outside note container.

Add a Section and Page to a Notebook

1. Tap or click Create a New Section tab.
2. Type section title.
3. Tap or press Enter.
4. Type page title.
5. Tap or press Enter.

Add a Page to a Section

1. Make active desired section tab.
2. Tap or click Add Page icon.
3. Type page title.
4. Tap or press Enter.

App Tip

Notice that a Save button is not provided in OneNote; changes are saved automatically.

Tips for Typing Notes

OneNote automatically formats text into a table when you type some text and then press the Tab key. Each time you press Tab, a new column is inserted into the table. Press Enter to add a new row. You can also perform a calculation in OneNote by typing an expression. When you press the spacebar after an equals sign, OneNote calculates the expression. For example, typing *15*12=* and then pressing the spacebar causes OneNote to calculate the result and show *15*12=180* in the note container.

Topic 4.2

SKILLS

Insert a link to a web page

Insert a copy of a web page

Insert a screen clipping

Inserting Web Content into a Notebook

Web content can be inserted into a notebook as a link, as a web page, or as a screen clipping. The method you use will vary depending on the content and the frequency of updates to the content. For example, you may want to use a link if a web page updates frequently. Embed a copy of the web page directly into OneNote if you are not concerned with updates occurring in the content you are capturing. A screen clipping is useful if you want to embed only a portion of a web page.

You can also use the standard copy and paste tools to copy text from a web page and paste it into a notebook. When you paste text copied from a web page, OneNote automatically includes the source URL with the pasted text.

1. With the BusTechnologyCourse notebook open and the *WebPages* section active, tap or click anywhere on the page, type **www.techmeme.com**, and then tap or press Enter.

OneNote automatically formats web addresses as hyperlinks.

2. Type **Techmeme provides daily summaries of leading technology stories on the web.** and tap or click in a blank area away from the note container.

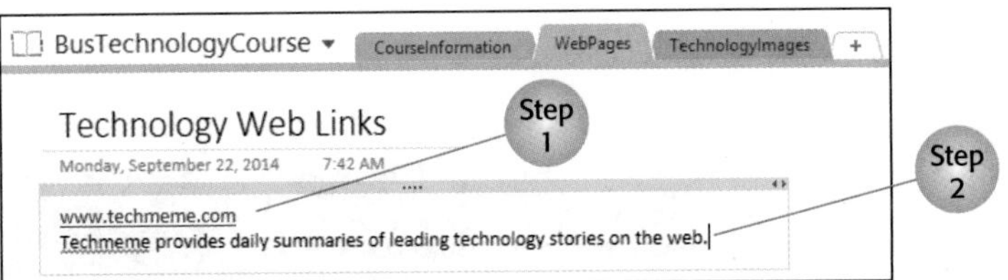

oops!

Web page not found? Check that you typed the web address as shown. As an alternative, find an article on Tim Berners-Lee that you can embed into OneNote.

3. Tap or click www.techmeme.com to view the web page in the Internet Explorer or other browser window.
4. Select the web address in the Internet Explorer Address bar, type **wikipedia.org/wiki/tim_berners-lee**, and then tap or press Enter.

To embed a copy of a web page into a OneNote notebook, use the **Send to OneNote button** (OneNote button with scissors) in the Windows Taskbar.

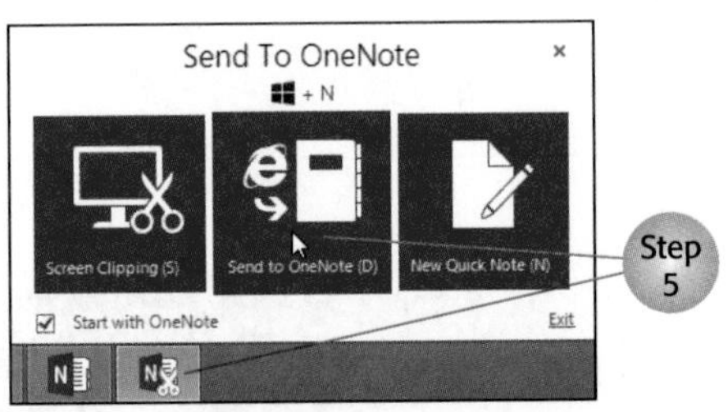

5. Tap or click the Send to OneNote button in the Taskbar and tap or click *Send to OneNote* at the pop-up menu.

oops!

Send to OneNote button not in Taskbar? Display the Search charm, type *Send to OneNote* in the *Search* box, and launch the app from the Search results.

6. At the Select Location in OneNote dialog box, tap or click *WebPages* in the *BusTechnologyCourse* section list and tap or click OK. ***Hint: You may need to tap or click the OneNote button in the Taskbar to display the Select Location in OneNote dialog box.***

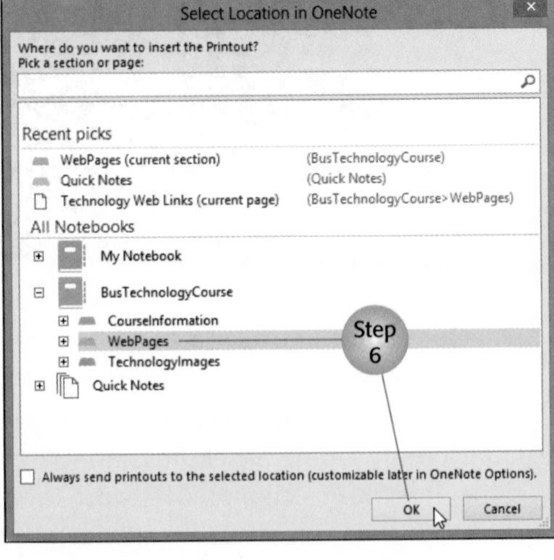

OneNote inserts the web page as it would appear if the page had been printed, with the first page of the web page as a new page in the selected section and a subpage below the web page for each additional printed page (Figure 4.2).

From Internet Explorer or any Office app, you can also send a copy of the current document to OneNote by printing the document using the Send to OneNote 2013 printer.

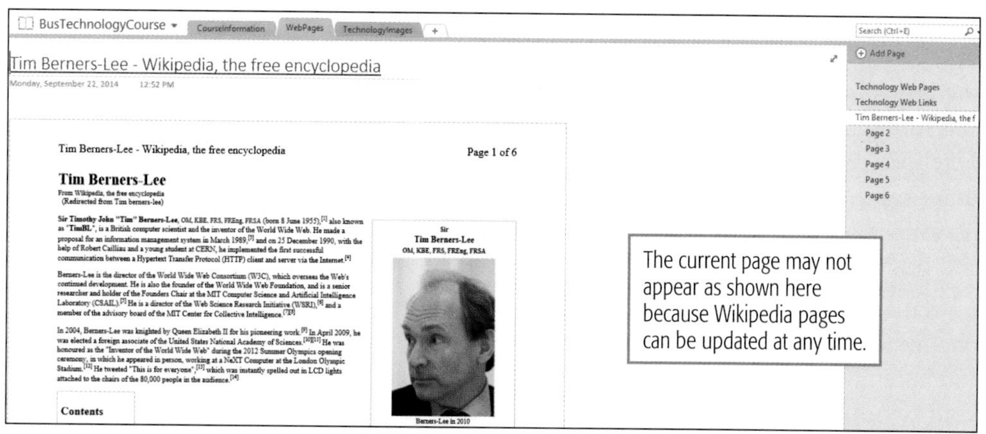

The current page may not appear as shown here because Wikipedia pages can be updated at any time.

Figure 4.2 A web page copied into OneNote. OneNote embeds the page as it would appear if printed. The page title is a hyperlink to the source URL.

7 Switch back to the browser window, select the web address in the Address bar, type **wikipedia.org/wiki/3d_printer**, and then tap or press Enter.

Assume you want to save the picture of the 3D printer shown in the Wikipedia article on 3D printing.

8 Tap or click the Send to OneNote button in the Taskbar and then tap or click *Screen Clipping* at the pop-up menu.

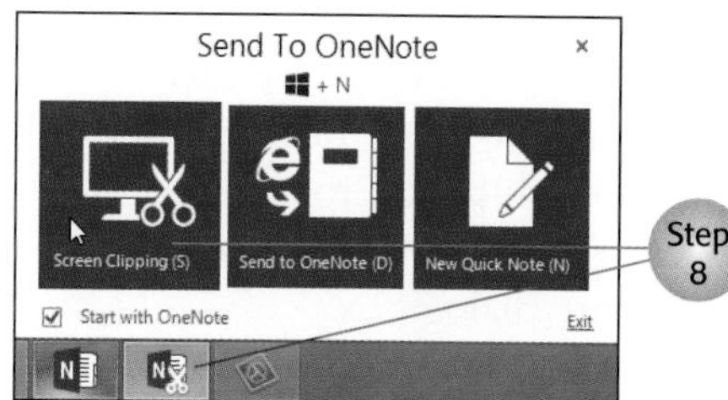

The screen dims and a crosshairs pointer (+) displays.

9 Slide or drag the crosshairs from the top left to the bottom right of the 3D printer image located at the right side of the Wikipedia page as shown.

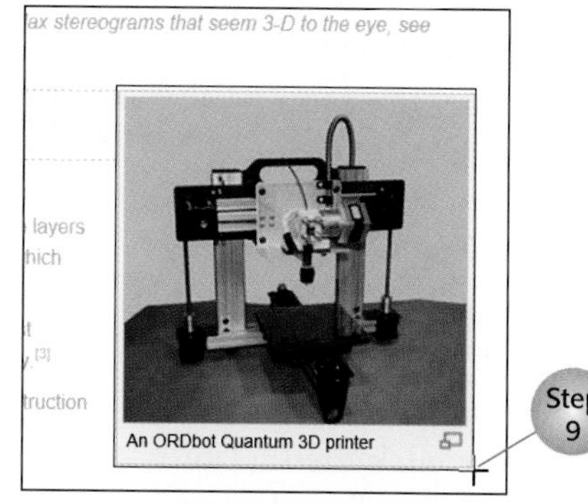

10 Tap or click the expand button (displays as a plus symbol) next to BusTechnologyCourse in the *All Notebooks* section of the Select Location in OneNote dialog box.

11 Tap or click *TechnologyImages* in the expanded list of sections and then tap or click the Send to Selected Location button.

12 Close the browser window.

13 If necessary, tap or click the TechnologyImages section tab and tap or click the 3D printing page in the Pages pane. Leave OneNote open for the next topic.

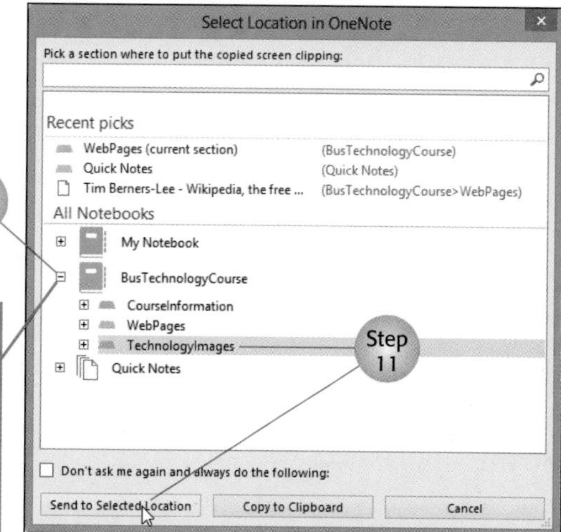

Add a Link to a Web Page
Tap or click anywhere on page and type web address.

Add a Copy of a Web Page
1. Open Internet Explorer.
2. Browse to web page.
3. Tap or click Send to OneNote button on Taskbar.
4. Tap or click *Send to OneNote*.
5. Select section in notebook.
6. Tap or click OK.

Capture a Portion of a Web Page as a Screen Clipping
1. Open Internet Explorer.
2. Browse to web page.
3. Tap or click Send to OneNote button on Taskbar.
4. Tap or click *Screen Clipping*.
5. Slide or drag to select area to capture.
6. Select section in notebook.
7. Tap or click Send to Selected Location.

Picture shown not on the web page? Capture an image of another picture from the page if the one shown is no longer available.

The Send to OneNote button also includes *New Quick Note*. Quick Notes are short reminders for things you might write on a sticky note. Each Quick Note is a page in the *Quick Notes* section, which can be viewed by selecting *Quick Notes* at the Notebooks drop-down list.

Topic 4.3

SKILLS

Insert a picture

Insert a document

Embed a copy of a presentation

You can also drag and drop a picture onto a OneNote page from a Libraries or Pictures window.

Inserting Files into a Notebook

Pictures, documents, presentations, workbooks, contacts, emails, appointment details, and more can be embedded into a OneNote notebook. Consider using a OneNote notebook as a repository to collect all of the data related to a course, subject, or other topic. The advantage to assembling all of the content in one place is that you no longer need to keep track of web links or web pages separately from documents and other notes for a subject.

Items are inserted into a OneNote page using buttons from the INSERT tab. A document can be inserted as an icon that links to the source file, or the contents can be embedded into the notebook. Once inserted, you can annotate the files with your own notes.

1. With the BusTechnologyCourse notebook open and the 3D printing page active in the *TechnologyImages* section, tap or click the *Pictures for Technology Topics* page.
2. Tap or click the INSERT tab and tap or click the Pictures button in the Images group.
3. Navigate to the Ch4 folder in Student_Data_Files on the Removable Disk for your USB flash drive at the Insert Picture dialog box.
4. Double-tap or double-click the image named ***AnalogCptr_1950s***.
5. With an insertion point positioned in the note container below the image, type **Analog computer from the 1950s** and then tap or click in a blank area outside the note container.
6. Tap or click the Create a New Section tab, type **Documents** as the section title, and then tap or press Enter.

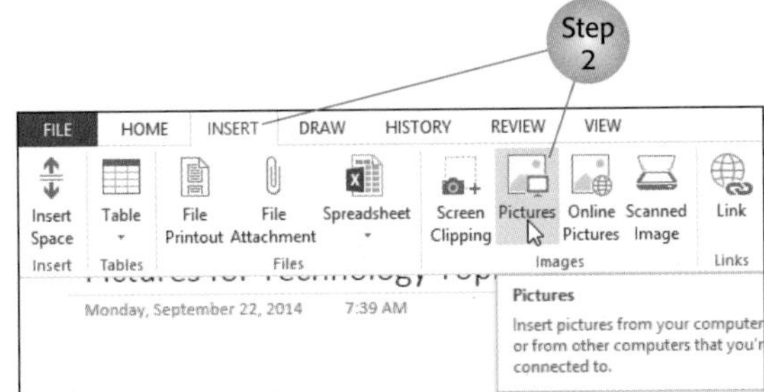

7. Type **Course Documents** as the page title and tap or press Enter.

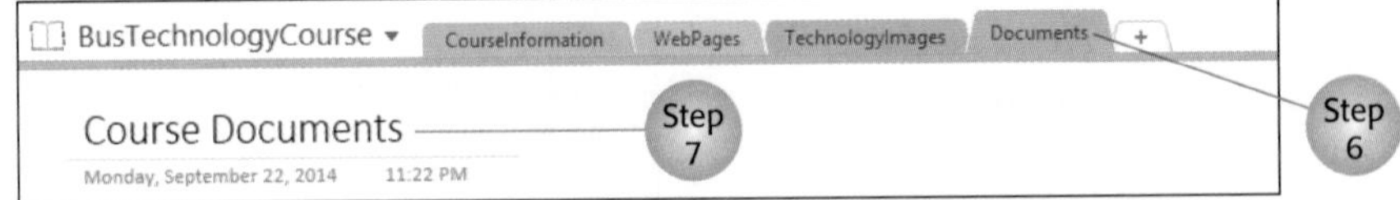

8. Tap or click the File Attachment button in the Files group of the INSERT tab.

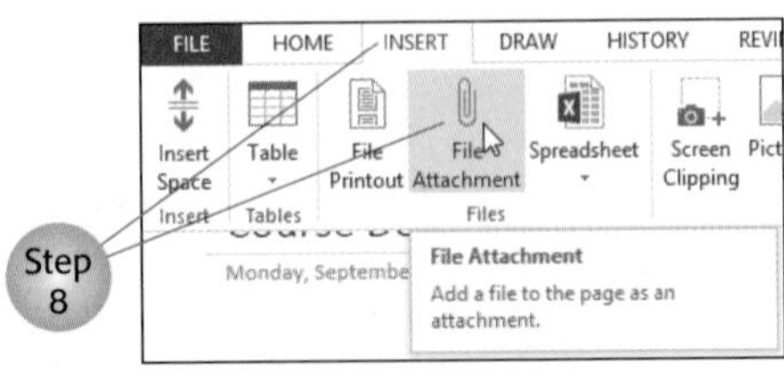

9 Navigate to the Ch4 folder in Student_Data_Files on your USB flash drive at the Choose a file or a set of files to insert dialog box.

10 Double-tap or double-click the Word document named ***Tech_Wk1_SocialMedia***.

11 Tap or click Attach File at the Insert File dialog box.

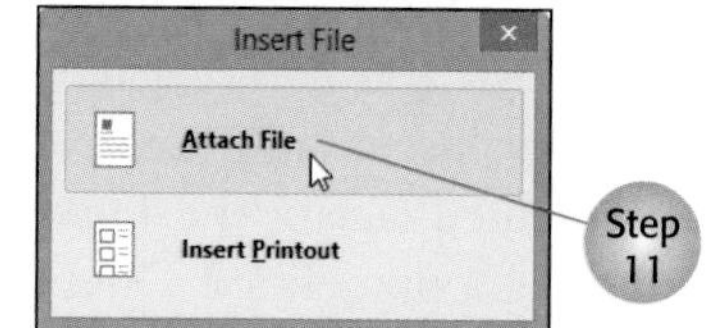

12 With an insertion point positioned in the note container below the Word document icon and file name, type **Week 1 Assignment** and then tap or click in a blank area outside the note container.

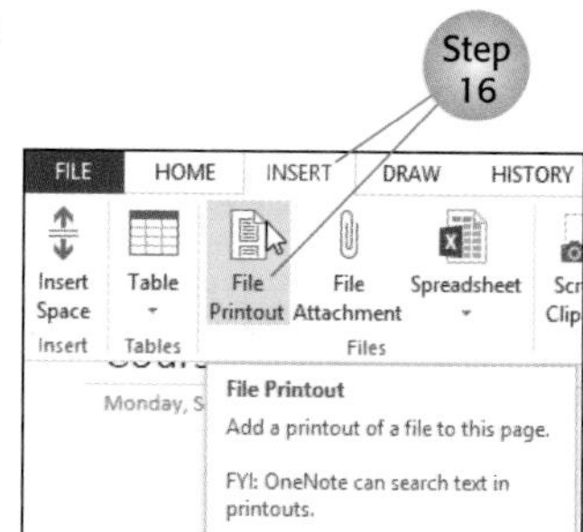

A document inserted as a file displays an icon above the file name. The file is linked to the source location and can be launched from OneNote.

13 Double-tap or double-click the Word document icon, tap Open if using touch, and then tap or click OK at the Warning message that opening attachments could harm your computer or data.

14 Slide or scroll down and view the Word document and then close Word.

15 Create a new section titled *Presentations* with a page title *Course Presentations*.

16 With the Course Presentations page active, tap or click the File Printout button in the Files group of the INSERT tab.

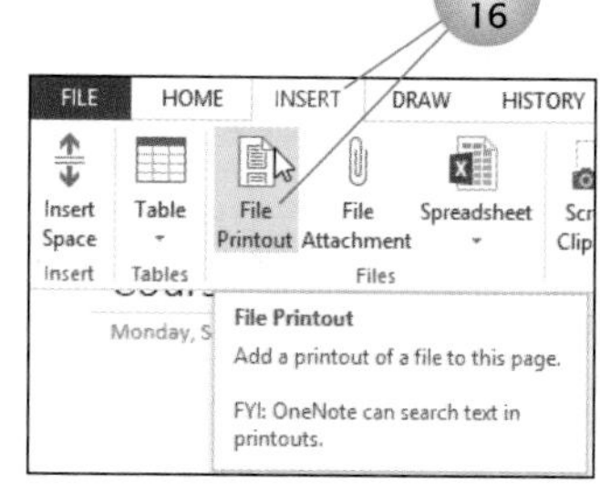

17 Double-tap or double-click the PowerPoint presentation named ***Tech_Wk1***.

18 Slide or scroll down and view the PowerPoint slides inserted into the OneNote page. Leave OneNote open for the next topic.

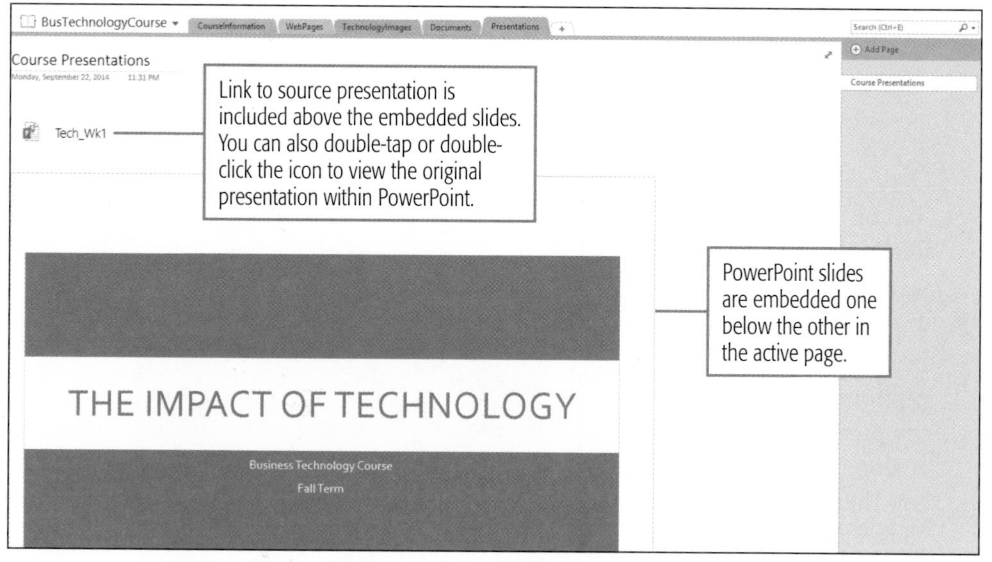

BusTechnologyCourse
Course Presentations
Tech_Wk1
Link to source presentation is included above the embedded slides. You can also double-tap or double-click the icon to view the original presentation within PowerPoint.
PowerPoint slides are embedded one below the other in the active page.
THE IMPACT OF TECHNOLOGY
Business Technology Course
Fall Term

Quick STEPS

Insert a Picture
1. Make desired page active.
2. Tap or click INSERT tab.
3. Tap or click Pictures button.
4. Navigate to drive and/or folder.
5. Double-tap or double-click image file name.
6. If necessary, type descriptive note.
7. Tap or click in blank area outside note container.

Insert a File as an Icon
1. Make desired page active.
2. Tap or click INSERT tab.
3. Tap or click File Attachment button.
4. Navigate to drive and/or folder.
5. Double-tap or double-click file name.
6. Tap or click Attach File.
7. If necessary, type descriptive note.
8. Tap or click in blank area outside note container.

Embed File Contents
1. Make desired page active.
2. Tap or click INSERT tab.
3. Tap or click File Printout button.
4. Navigate to drive and/or folder.
5. Double-tap or double-click file name.
6. If necessary, type descriptive note.
7. Tap or click in blank area outside note container.

Changes that occur in the file after the file has been inserted into OneNote as a printout are not updated. Be aware that the note container may not contain the most up-to-date content.

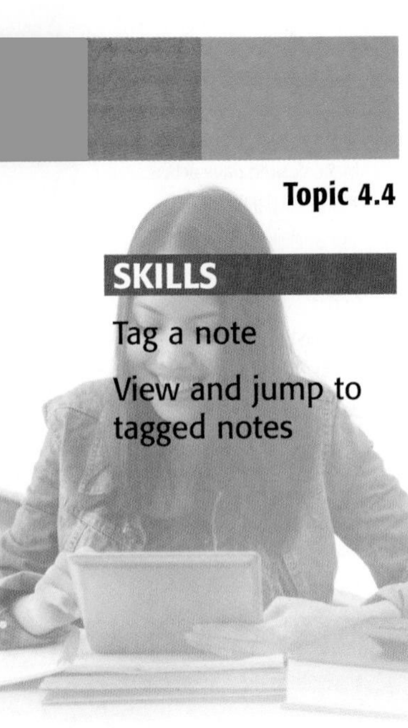

Topic 4.4

SKILLS

Tag a note

View and jump to tagged notes

Tagging Notes, Viewing Tags, and Jumping to a Tagged Note

A **tag** is a category assigned to a note that allows you to identify the note later as an item that you have flagged as important, as a question, as a definition, as an item for a to-do list, as an idea, or for some other purpose. OneNote includes a gallery of predefined tags in the Tags group of the HOME tab. You can customize tags by modifying a predefined OneNote tag or by creating a new tag of your own.

Once tags have been assigned to items in the notebook, you can display the **Tags Summary pane** and use the pane to navigate quickly to a tagged item.

1. With the BusTechnologyCourse notebook open and the Course Presentations page active in the *Presentations* section, tap or click the WebPages section tab.
2. Tap or click the Technology Web Links page.
3. Tap or click at the beginning of the note text *Techmeme provides daily summaries of leading technology stories on the web*, tap or click the HOME tab, and then tap or click *Important* in the Tags gallery.

OneNote inserts the tag icon for the Important tag (a gold star) next to the note text.

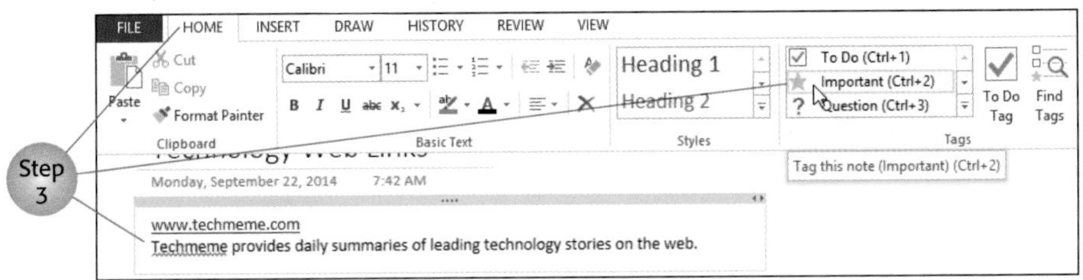

4. Tap or click the Tim Berners-Lee page.
5. Double-tap or double-click after the bolded title *Tim Berners-Lee* within the embedded web page to place an insertion point, and tap or click *Important* in the Tags gallery.

OneNote inserts the tag inside a new note container on the page.

6. Type **Use this information in Project 1**.

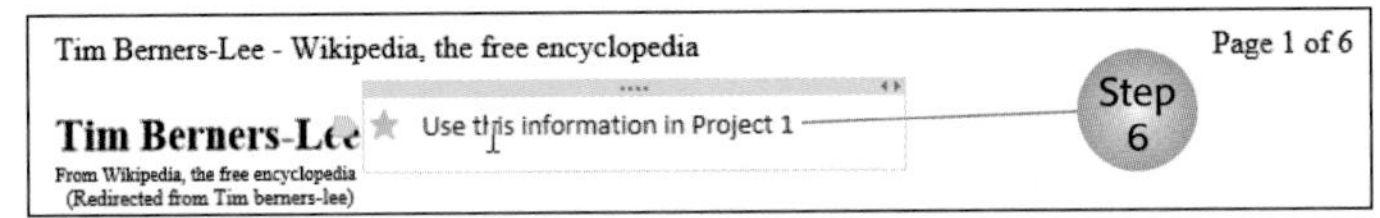

7. Tap or click the TechnologyImages section tab.
8. Tap or click at the beginning of the caption text below the picture of the analog computer, and then tap or click *? Question* in the Tags gallery.
9. Tap or click the Presentations section tab.

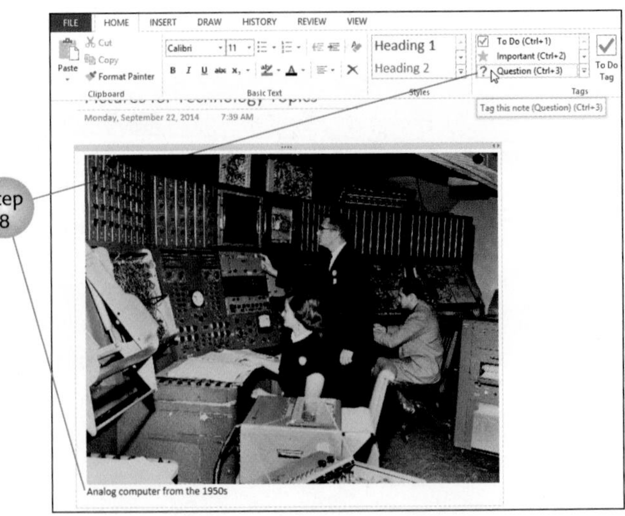

10 Slide or scroll down the page of embedded PowerPoint slides to the slide with the title *REFLECTION BLOG* and double-tap or double-click to place the insertion point at the right of the slide title.

11 Tap or click the More button (displays as a short bar with a down-pointing arrow below) at the bottom of the Tags gallery to display more predefined tag options.

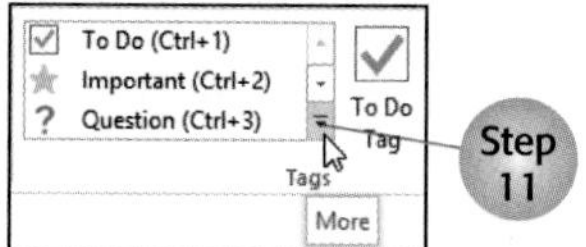

12 Tap or click *Remember for blog* in the drop-down gallery.

13 Type **Blog entry homework** in the note container next to the tag icon.

Once tags have been applied to notes, you can view all of the tagged notes and jump to a specific item that you need to review. Tap or click the Find Tags button in the Tags group of the HOME tab to display in a Tags Summary pane at the right side of the OneNote window a list of tagged items grouped by tag category.

14 Tap or click the Find Tags button in the Tags group.

The Tags Summary pane opens at the right side of the OneNote window.

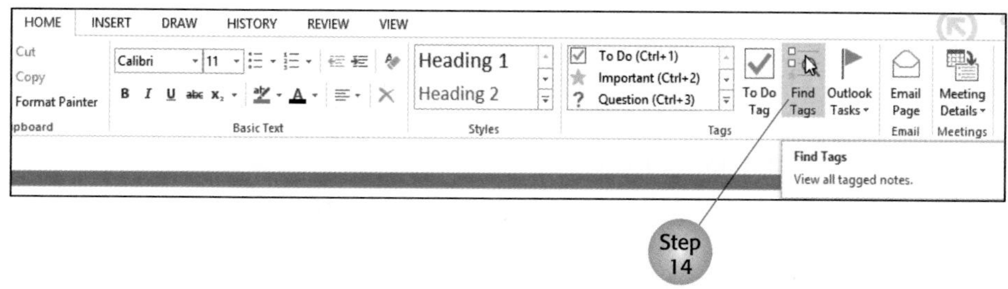

15 Tap or click Techmeme provides daily summa… in the Tags Summary pane.

OneNote jumps to the Technology Web Links page in the *WebPages* section of the notebook.

16 Tap or click each of the other tag links in the Tags Summary pane to jump to each tagged item in the notebook.

17 Tap or click the Close button at the top right of the Tags Summary pane. Leave OneNote open for the next topic.

Tag a Note
1. Position insertion point at beginning of note or item.
2. Tap or click HOME tab.
3. Tap or click desired tag in Tags gallery.

View All Tags
1. Tap or click HOME tab.
2. Tap or click Find Tags button.

Jump to a Tagged Item
Tap or click desired tagged note in Tags Summary pane.

Use the *Search* list box at the bottom of the Tags Summary pane to specify locations that should be searched for tags. For example, you can view tags from all open notebooks or from the active section only.

Using the To-Do Tag

You can use the Tags feature to create a to-do list by tagging items in your notebook with the To-Do tag. OneNote inserts a blank check box at the left of note text tagged with *To Do*. Tap or click the check box when a task has been completed to mark the item finished.

Topic 4.5

SKILLS

Search notes

Close a notebook

Searching Notes and Closing a Notebook

An advantage to using an electronic notebook instead of a paper-based notebook is the ability to search all of the pages in the notebook for a keyword or phrase and instantly locate each occurrence of the note text. The Search feature in OneNote searches all of the pages within all of the open notebooks. Type a search keyword or phrase in the *Search* text box located above the Pages pane at the right side of the OneNote window. OneNote begins listing pages with matches in a drop-down list and highlights matches on each page. Tap or click a page in the search results to view the matches.

When you close OneNote, the active notebook is left open so that you are returned to the place you left off when you start OneNote again. You may instead choose to close a notebook when you are finished working. One reason for closing a notebook is when you want to search for a keyword in another open notebook that you know also exists in the current notebook. Closing the current notebook will avoid pages showing up in search results that you are not interested in reviewing.

1. With the BusTechnologyCourse notebook open, tap or click the CourseInformation section tab.
2. Tap or click in the *Search* text box above the Pages pane that displays with the entry *Search (Ctrl + E)*, and type **Tim Berners-Lee**.

   OneNote begins displaying matches as soon as you start typing.
3. Tap or click *Page 3* in the search results list to navigate to the page and review the highlighted text entries on the page.

   OneNote is able to provide search results from content embedded from external sources.
4. Select *Tim Berners-Lee* in the *Search* text box and type **analog**.
5. Tap or click *Pictures for Technology Topics* in the search results list to navigate to the page with the picture of the analog computer.

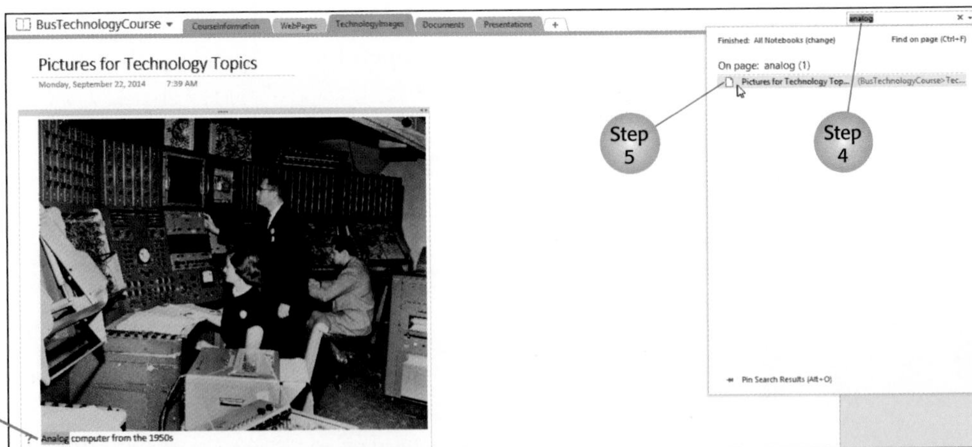

OneNote highlights matches to the search text on each page in the search results list.

6. Select *analog* in the *Search* text box and then type **blog**.
7. Tap or click each entry in the search results list to review each item.

8 Tap or click the Close button at the right of the *Search* text box to close the search results list.

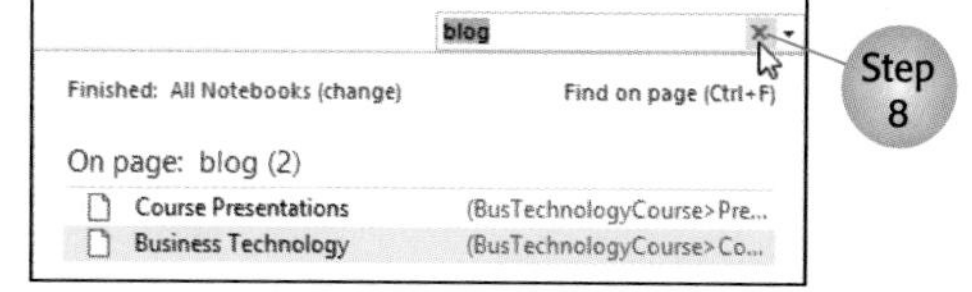

Because OneNote automatically saves changes to notebooks as you work, you can leave all of your notebooks open and be assured that changes are being updated. However, a notebook can be closed by selecting *Close* from the Settings drop-down list at the **Notebook Information Backstage view**.

9 Tap or click the FILE tab.

10 Tap or click the **Settings button** at the Notebook Information Backstage view.

11 Tap or click *Close* at the Settings drop-down list.

OneNote closes the BusTechnologyCourse notebook.

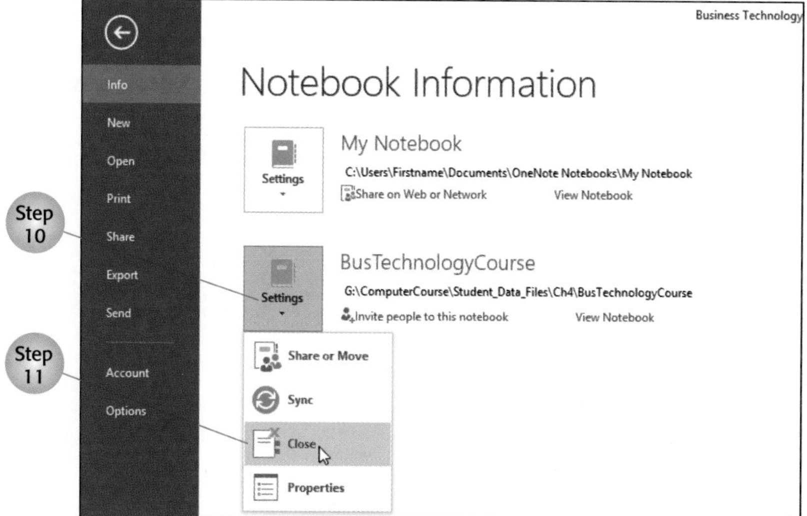

Search Notes
1. Tap or click in *Search* text box.
2. Type search keyword or phrase.
3. Tap or click pages in search results list.

Close a Notebook
1. Tap or click FILE tab.
2. Tap or click Settings button.
3. Tap or click *Close*.

To search for a keyword or phrase on the active page only, press Ctrl + F. OneNote displays *Find on page* in a yellow box next to the *Search* text box. Type the search keyword or phrase in the *Search* text box. OneNote displays an up and down arrow in the yellow box with the number of matches found. Tap or click the arrows to navigate to the matches on the current page.

Beyond Basics

Printing and Exporting Notebook Sections

Print a notebook section by making the desired section active, tapping or clicking the FILE tab, and then tapping or clicking Print. Use Print Preview at the Print tab Backstage view to view and modify print settings such as the print range, paper size, and page orientation. Consider exporting a page, section, or notebook as a PDF or XPS file instead of printing. Display the Export tab Backstage view, choose what you want to export and the export format, and then tap or click the Export button. OneNote displays the Save As dialog box in which you choose the drive, folder, and file name for the exported file.

Topic 4.6

SKILLS

Create a new notebook

Share a notebook using SkyDrive

Creating a New Notebook and Sharing a Notebook

Some people may choose to organize all of their notes for all purposes within one notebook (the default My Notebook file), using sections and pages to create an organizational structure. Others may choose to create separate notebooks in which to organize notes. For example, you may want to have a separate notebook for home, work, and school items.

Another reason to create a separate notebook may be when you want to share a notebook with other people. For example, if you are working with a group on a project you can create a notebook that all members of the group can use to post research, links, ideas, or other notes. A shared notebook is stored on SkyDrive.

Note: Check with your instructor for the name of the person with whom you will share the notebook created in this topic. At Step 13 you will need the Microsoft account email address for the classmate.

1 Tap or click the FILE tab. If necessary, tap or click New.

2 If necessary, tap or click your SkyDrive account name at the **New Notebook Backstage view**.

3 Tap or click in the *Notebook Name* text box and type **MyElectives-xx**. Substitute your first and last initials for *xx*.

4 Tap or click the Create Notebook button.

oops!

SkyDrive account name not shown? If you are signed in with a local account, your SkyDrive account name does not appear; however, a Sign In button is available so that you can switch to your Microsoft account from within OneNote.

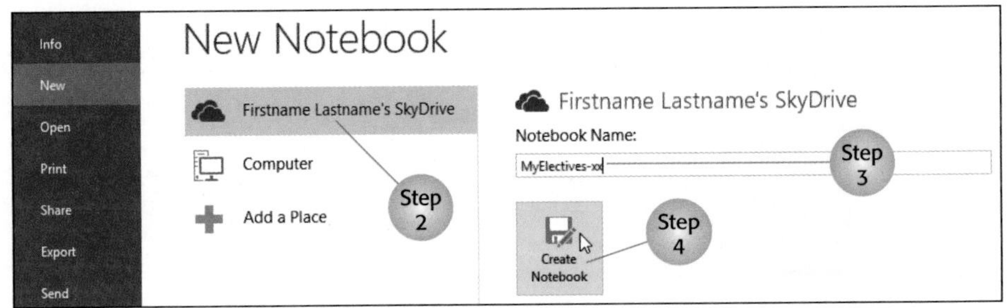

5 Tap or click Not now at the Microsoft OneNote message box asking if you would like to share the notebook with other people.

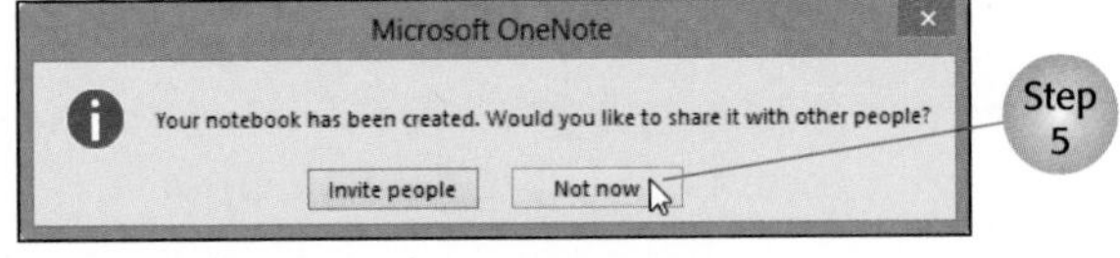

You will set up the sharing feature later in this topic. OneNote opens a new notebook with one section created titled *New Section 1*.

6 Press and hold or right-click the New Section 1 tab and tap or click *Rename* at the shortcut menu.

7 Type **ChildLit** and tap or press Enter.

8 Type **Children's Literature** as the page title and tap or press Enter.

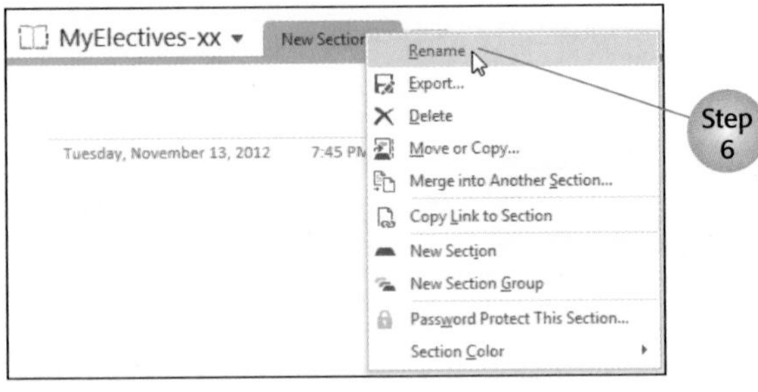

9 Embed a copy of the PowerPoint presentation file named ***ChildLitPres*** into the current page.

oops!

Don't remember how to embed files? Refer to Topic 4.3, Step 16.

10 Add a second section tab named *Film* with a page title of *Film Genres*, and embed a copy of the Word document named ***ApNowReflectionPaper***.

You decide to share the notebook with a classmate taking the same electives as you so that you can each add notes to the notebook.

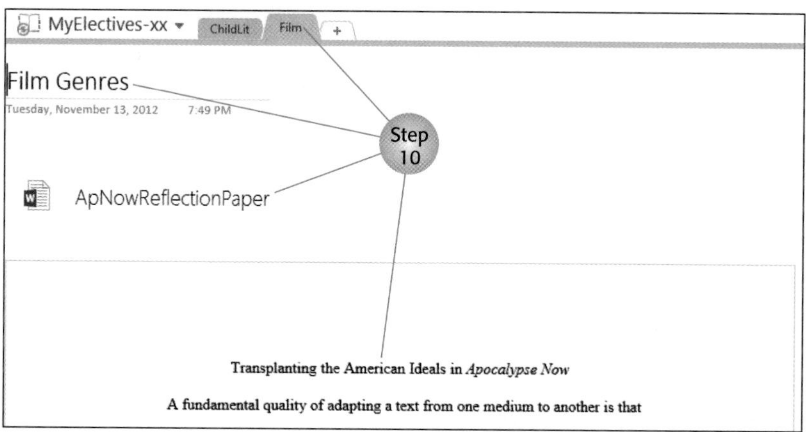

Create a New Notebook

1. Tap or click FILE tab.
2. Tap or click New.
3. If necessary, change notebook storage location.
4. Type name for new notebook.
5. Tap or click Create Notebook button.

Share a Notebook

1. Tap or click FILE tab.
2. Tap or click Settings button.
3. Tap or click *Share or Move*.
4. Type email address.
5. Type message text.
6. Tap or click Share button.
7. Tap or click Back button.

11 Tap or click the FILE tab.

12 Tap or click the Settings button and tap or click *Share or Move* at the drop-down list.

13 At the **Share Notebook Backstage view**, tap or click in the *Type names or e-mail addresses* text box and type the classmate's Microsoft account email address.

14 Tap or click in the message box and type **Here is a notebook I created that we can use to share notes for our electives.**

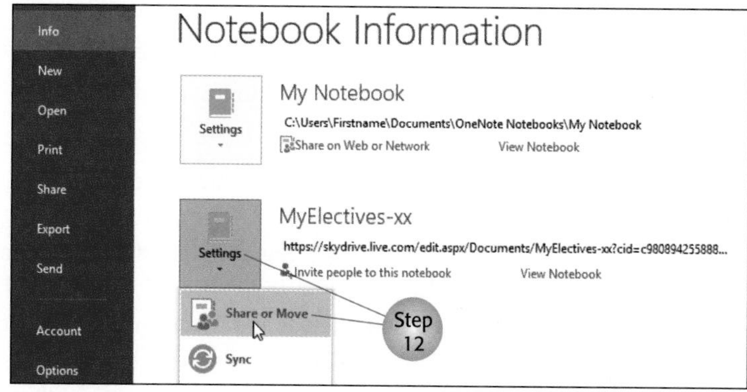

15 Tap or click the Share button.

When sharing is completed, the student's name is shown in the *Shared with* section of the Backstage view.

16 Tap or click the Back button.

17 Close the MyElectives-xx notebook and close OneNote.

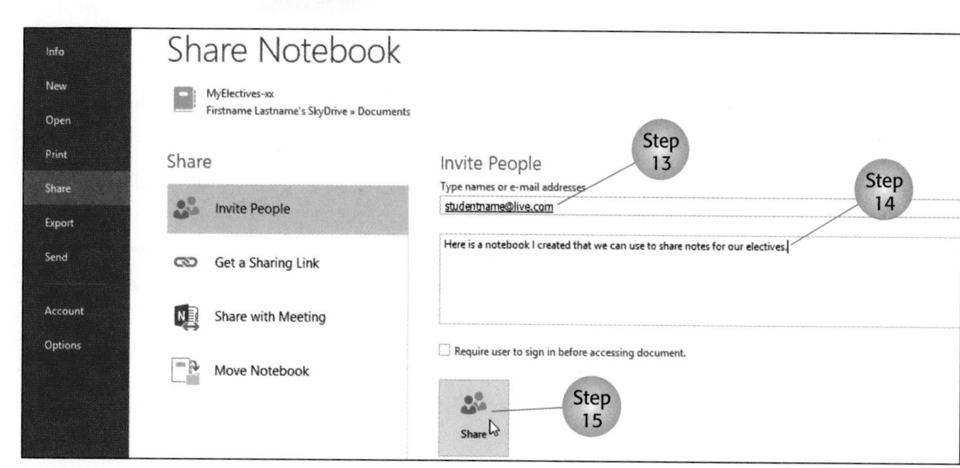

Optional

18 Log in to SkyDrive at skydrive.live.com.

19 Open the shared notebook from the Shared folder and add a note to one of the pages. (You determine the note text.)

20 Exit the OneNote Web app and then sign out and close SkyDrive.

Concepts Review

Topic	Key Concepts	Key Terms
Opening a Notebook and Adding Notes, Sections, and Pages	OneNote 2013 is a note-taking software application that is the electronic equivalent of a binder with loose leaf notes separated by dividers. A OneNote notebook is organized into sections, which are tabs across the top of the window. Each section can have multiple pages. Tap or click My Notebook to open another notebook and navigate to the file named Open Notebook stored within a folder named the same as the notebook name. Each note on a page is stored within a note container, which is a box that surrounds the note text. Slide or drag the gray bar along the top of the note container to move a note. Use the Text Highlight Color tool to add color to notes similarly to using a highlighter to emphasize text in a textbook. A section is used to organize notes by category, topic, or subject; new sections are created using the Create a New Section tab. Within a section, notes are added to pages. Pages can be added to a section using the Add Page icon in the Pages pane.	OneNote notebook OneNote 2013 Note container Create a New Section tab Add Page icon
Inserting Web Content into a Notebook	A web address is automatically converted to a hyperlink in a note container. A copy of a web page can be embedded into a notebook using the Send to OneNote button on the Taskbar. An embedded web page is inserted into a notebook as if the web page had been printed on a printer. The title of an embedded web page is a hyperlink to the source website. A portion of a web page can be captured and inserted into a notebook using the Screen Clipping tool on the Send to OneNote button.	Send to OneNote button
Inserting Files into a Notebook	A OneNote notebook can be used as a repository to collect all of the files related to a course, subject, or other topic. From the INSERT tab you can insert pictures, a file as an icon linked to the source document, or a file as a printout, which embeds a copy of the file's contents into the notebook.	
Tagging Notes, Viewing Tags, and Jumping to a Tagged Note	A tag is a category assigned to a note. Tags are useful to identify notes that you want to flag for later review or follow up. OneNote includes a gallery of predefined tags such as *Important* or *Definition*. You can modify the predefined tags or create a new tag of your own. The Find Tags button in the HOME tab causes the Tags Summary pane to display with links to each tagged note.	Tag Tags Summary pane

Topic	Key Concepts	Key Terms
Searching Notes and Closing a Notebook	OneNote can search all pages in all open notebooks for a keyword or phrase typed in the *Search* text box. OneNote begins highlighting matches to the search keyword or phrase and displaying pages in the search results list as soon as you begin typing. Close a notebook using the Settings button at the Notebook Information Backstage view.	Notebook Information Backstage view Settings button
Creating a New Notebook and Sharing a Notebook	A new notebook can be created on SkyDrive or in a drive connected to the PC or mobile device at the New Notebook Backstage view. Notebooks saved to SkyDrive can be shared with other people. More than one person can edit a page at the same time when a notebook is shared. Use the Settings button at the Notebook Information Backstage view to share a notebook by typing the email address and a short message for each invitee.	New Notebook Backstage view Share Notebook Backstage view

Multiple Choice

1. Notes or other content are added inside a box called a ________________.
   a. section
   b. page
   c. selection handle
   d. note container
2. The Create a New Section tab displays with this symbol.
   a. ×
   b. +
   c. -
   d. *
3. This option from the Send to OneNote button allows you to capture a portion of a web page to insert into a notebook.
   a. Screen Clipping
   b. Capture to OneNote
   c. Printout
   d. Embed to OneNote
4. A web address is automatically formatted by OneNote as a(n) ________________.
   a. hyperlink
   b. embedded web page
   c. screen clipping
   d. Internet icon
5. Pictures or other files are added to a notebook using buttons in this tab in the ribbon.
   a. FILE
   b. INSERT
   c. VIEW
   d. HOME
6. Use this button to add a Word document as an icon in a notebook.
   a. File Printout
   b. File Attachment
   c. File Icon
   d. File Picture
7. This is the icon that appears next to a note tagged as Important.
   a. Red exclamation mark
   b. Orange check mark
   c. Gray question mark
   d. Gold star
8. This pane at the right side of the OneNote window is used to navigate to a tagged item in the notebook.
   a. Tags Summary
   b. View All Tags
   c. Tagged Items
   d. Tag Navigation

9. By default, the search feature in OneNote searches for a keyword or phrase in ________________.
   a. the current notebook only
   b. the current page only
   c. the current section only
   d. all pages in all open notebooks

10. A notebook is closed using this button at the Notebook Information Backstage view.
   a. Close
   b. Settings
   c. File
   d. Info

11. Display this view to share a notebook with other people.
   a. Notebook Information Backstage view
   b. Share Notebook Backstage view
   c. Multiple Notebooks Backstage view
   d. Settings Notebook Backstage view

12. A list of the people with whom a notebook has been shared is displayed in this section of the Backstage view.
   a. Notebook Information
   b. Shared with
   c. Invitees
   d. Settings

Crossword Puzzle

ACROSS

2 Button used to close a notebook
7 Button on Taskbar for embedding web content
8 Location where a shared notebook is stored
9 Button in Images group to insert a photograph
10 Gold star icon tag

DOWN

1 Option for capturing a portion of a web page
2 Tabs in a notebook
3 Button to display Tags Summary pane
4 Tab to access New Notebook Backstage view
5 Button in Files group to embed a copy of a file
6 Default notebook
7 Text box used to find all occurrences of a word

Matching

Match the term with the statement or definition.

_______ 1. Tabs		a. File Attachment
_______ 2. Text Highlight Color		b. Important
_______ 3. Send to OneNote		c. View matches
_______ 4. File Icon		d. Yellow background
_______ 5. File Printout		e. SkyDrive
_______ 6. Tag		f. Embed web page
_______ 7. Search		g. Copy of document
_______ 8. Share notebook		h. Sections

Project 1 Start a New Notebook and Create Notebook Structure

Individual

Deliverable: OneNote Notebook (continued in Project 2)

1. Create a new folder named *Ch4* in the ChapterProjectsWork folder on your USB flash drive.
2. Start OneNote 2013 and display the New Notebook Backstage view. Create a new notebook as follows:
   a. Select Computer as the storage place.
   b. Type **C4-Project1-NB-Your Name** as the Notebook Name.
   c. Tap or click Create in a different folder, navigate to the Ch4 folder in the ChapterProjectsWork folder on your USB flash drive, and then tap or click Create.
3. Rename the New Section 1 tab *Computer Research* and add the page title *Images.*
4. Add a new section titled *Law Course* with a page titled *Current Topics in Law.*
5. Add a new section titled *Tourism Course* with a page titled *Presentations.*
6. Add a new section titled *Volunteer Work* with a page titled *Medical Clinic Association Conference.*
7. Leave the notebook open if you are continuing on to Project 2; otherwise, close the notebook and submit the notebook to your instructor in the manner she or he has requested.

Project 2 Adding Notes and External Content to a Notebook

Individual

Deliverable: OneNote Notebook (continued in Project 3)

1. If necessary, open the notebook created in Project 1.
2. Embed a copy of the Excel file **MedClinicsFees** on the Medical Clinic Association Conference page in the *Volunteer Work* section. (Do *not* use the Spreadsheet button in the INSERT tab; use the button you learned about in Topic 4.3.)
3. Embed a copy of the PowerPoint file **WaikikiPres** on the Presentations page in the *Tourism Course* section.
4. Insert the Word document **FamilyAndLawAssgnt** as an icon on the Current Topics in Law page in the *Law Course* section and type **Assignment 1 due in week 5** as note text below the icon.
5. Insert the image file **IBMCptr_1961** on the Images page in the *Computer Research* section and type **IBM computer from 1961** as note text below the photograph.
6. Add a new page to the *Computer Research* section with the page title *History of Computers* and add a hyperlink to the web address www.computerhistory.org/timeline. Type **The timeline from the Computer History Museum provides the history of computing starting in 1939 and continuing to 1994.**
7. Leave the notebook open if you are continuing on to Project 3; otherwise, close the notebook and submit the notebook to your instructor in the manner she or he has requested.

Project 3 Tagging Notes and Adding a Copy of a Web Page

Individual

Deliverable: OneNote Notebook or PDF of Exported Notebook

1. If necessary, open the notebook created in Projects 1 and 2.
2. Assign the To Do tag at the beginning of the note text below the Word document icon on the Current Topics in Law page in the *Law Course* section.
3. Type **This is included in test 1** in a new note at the top of the PowerPoint slides embedded on the Presentations page in the *Tourism Course* section and assign the Important tag to the note.
4. Open a browser window and search for a recent article about 3D printing technology. Use the Screen Clipping tool to capture and copy the title and the first few paragraphs of an article that you find to a new page in the *Computer Research* section. Type **Article for project 1** in a new note above the embedded content and assign the note the Important tag.
5. Tap or click the FILE tab and tap or click Export. Select *Notebook* in the Export Current section and *PDF (*.pdf)* in the Select Format section at the Export tab Backstage view and tap or click the Export button. Save the PDF in the Ch4 folder in ChapterProjectsWork on your USB flash drive.
6. Close the notebook.
7. Submit the OneNote notebook or PDF file to your instructor in the manner she or he has requested.

Project 4 Creating a Notebook Repository for Projects

Individual

Deliverable: Shared Notebook on SkyDrive

Note: Check with your instructor for his or her Microsoft account email address for Step 7, or for alternative instructions if he or she prefers that you create the MyProjects notebook on your USB flash drive and not share the notebook.

1. Create a new notebook stored in your SkyDrive account with the name **MyProjects-Your Name**. Tap or click Not now when asked if you want to invite people to share the notebook.
2. Create the following sections and pages:

Sections	Pages
Windows	Chapter 1
Internet	Chapter 2
Office	Chapter 3
OneNote	Chapter 4
Outlook	Chapter 5
Word	Chapters 6 and 7
Excel	Chapters 8 and 9
PowerPoint	Chapters 10 and 11
Access	Chapters 12 and 13
Integrating	Chapter 14
CloudTech	Chapter 15

3. Make the Chapter 1 page in the *Windows* section active and insert a copy of the first project file that you completed for Chapter 1. Insert a copy of each remaining project file for Chapter 1, adding a new page for each file. Label each page with the project number from which you insert the copy.
4. Make the Chapter 2 page in the *Internet* section active and repeat the process you completed at Step 3 to insert a copy of each project file that you completed for Chapter 2.

5. Make the Chapter 3 page in the *Office* section active and repeat the process you completed at Step 3 to insert a copy of each project file that you completed for Chapter 3. Note that you can insert a copy of more than one file one below the other on the same page.
6. Make the Chapter 4 page in the *OneNote* section active and insert a copy of the PDF created for Project 3.

Note: If you receive any error messages when OneNote attempts the File Printout command, open the file in the source application (such as Paint or the Reader app) and use the Send to OneNote button on the Taskbar or print from the source application using the Send to OneNote 2013 printer. If you experience other technical difficulties with the Send to OneNote button or printer command, perform the Send to OneNote steps in a computer lab at your school where you can ask for technical assistance.

7. Share the notebook with your instructor, typing an appropriate message after entering your instructor's Microsoft account email address.
8. Close the notebook and then close OneNote.

Note: Closing the notebook may take a few moments while the notebook's changes are synced to SkyDrive.

Chapter 5

Communicating and Scheduling Using Outlook

After successfully completing this chapter, you will be able to:

- Create, send, read, reply to, and forward email messages
- Attach a file to a message
- Delete a message and empty the Deleted Items folder
- Use file attachment tools to manage file attachments
- Schedule and edit appointments and an event
- Schedule and accept a meeting request
- Add and edit contacts
- Create, update, and delete tasks
- Search Outlook messages, appointments, contacts, or tasks

Microsoft Outlook is a software application often referred to as a **personal information management (PIM) program**. PIM programs organize items such as email messages, appointments or meetings, events, contacts, to-do lists, and notes. Reminders and flags help you remember and follow up on activities.

In the workplace Outlook is often used with an Exchange server, which allows employees within the organization to easily share calendars, schedule meetings, and assign tasks. Consider using Outlook on your home PC or mobile device to connect to your ISP's mail server and manage your messages. Outlook can also help you organize your time, activities, address book, and to-do list.

In this chapter you will learn how to use Outlook for email, scheduling, organizing contacts, and keeping a to-do list.

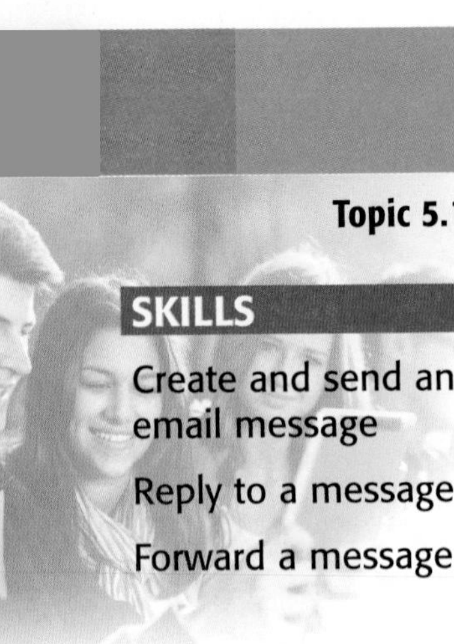

Topic 5.1

SKILLS

Create and send an email message

Reply to a message

Forward a message

Using Outlook to Send Email

Electronic mail (email) is communication between individuals by means of sending and receiving messages electronically. Email is the business standard for communication in today's workplaces. Individuals also use email to communicate with relatives and friends around the world. While text messaging is popular for brief messages between individuals, email is still used to send longer messages or file attachments.

Setting Up Outlook

The screen that you see when you start Outlook for the first time depends on whether a prior version of Outlook existed on the computer you are using. **Outlook 2013** can transfer information from an older version of Outlook to a new data file or, if no prior data file exists, will present a Welcome to Outlook 2013 screen at startup. Tap or click Next at the welcome screen and tap or click Next at the second screen to add a new account. At the Add Account dialog box shown in Figure 5.1, enter your name, email address, and email password and tap or click Next. Outlook automatically configures the email server settings displaying progress messages as each part is completed. Tap or click Finish when completed to start Outlook.

In instances where Outlook cannot automatically set up your email account, additional information will be required such as the incoming and outgoing mail server address. Contact your ISP if necessary for this information.

Note: The instructions in this chapter assume Outlook has already been set up and that you are connected to the Internet with an always-on connection (high-speed Internet service) at school or at home. If necessary, connect to the Internet and sign in to your email account before starting the topic activities. Check with your instructor for assistance if you are not sure how to proceed.

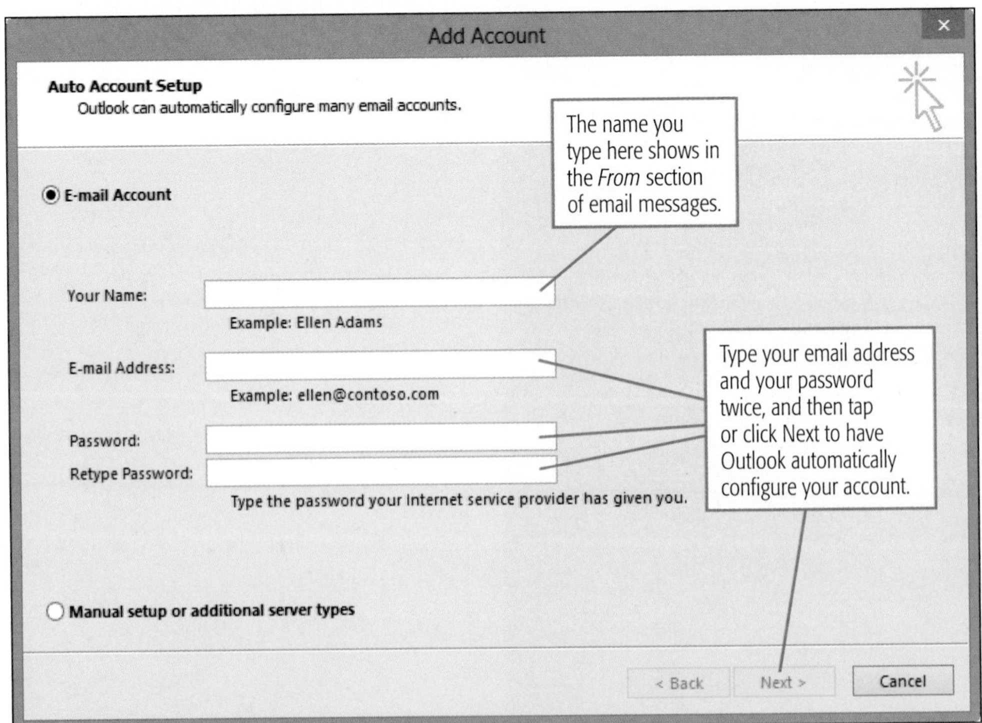

Figure 5.1 Outlook can automatically set up most email accounts with your name, email address, and password.

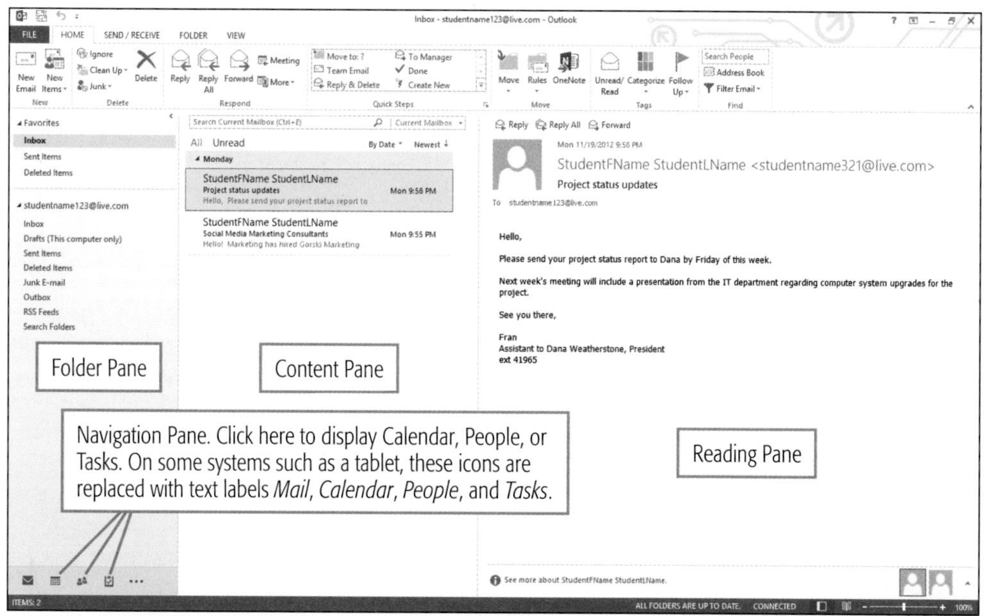

Figure 5.2 The Outlook window. By default, the Inbox folder is active and Outlook automatically connects to the mail server and checks for new messages when Outlook is started.

Once Outlook has been set up to send and receive email messages, the Outlook window appears similar to the one shown in Figure 5.2. By default, **Mail** is the active tool when Outlook is started with the **Inbox** folder shown. Messages in the Content pane are shown with the newest message received at the top of the message list. The left pane, called the Folder pane, is used to switch the display to another mail folder. At the bottom of the Folder pane is the Navigation pane, used to navigate to another Outlook item such as Calendar. The right pane, called the Reading pane, displays the contents of the selected message.

Outlook window looks different than the one shown here? Turn on the Folder pane by tapping or clicking VIEW, Folder Pane, *Normal*. Turn on the Reading pane by tapping or clicking VIEW, Reading Pane, *Right*.

Creating and Sending a Message

Tap or click the **New Email button** in the New group of the HOME tab to start a new email message. Type the recipient's email address in the *To* text box, type a brief description in the *Subject* text box, and then type your message text in the white message text box. Tap or click the Send button when finished.

Note: Check with your instructor for instructions on whom you should exchange messages and meeting requests with for this chapter. Your instructor may designate an email partner to each person or allow you to choose your email partner. If necessary, you can send messages to yourself.

1 From the Windows Start screen, start Outlook 2013.

2 Tap or click the New Email button in the New group of the HOME tab.

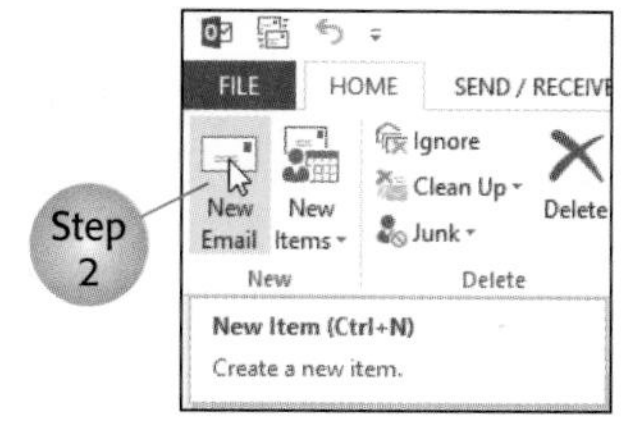

If you are sending a message to multiple people, type a comma (,) or semicolon (;) between email addresses in the *To* text box.

As a courtesy to the recipient, always include a *Subject* line that accurately describes the purpose of the message. People who receive many emails in a day use the subjects to prioritize their Inboxes.

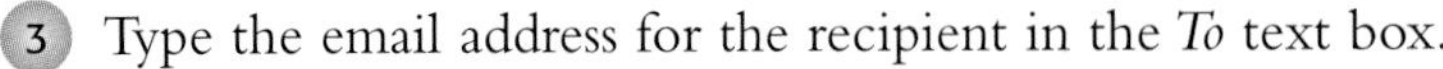

3 Type the email address for the recipient in the *To* text box.

4 Tap or press the Tab key twice, or tap or click in the *Subject* text box.

5 Type **Social Media Project**.

6 Tap or press Enter, or tap or click in the Message text window and type the following text:

Hi (type recipient's name), [tap or press Enter twice]

I think we should do our project on Pinterest.com. Pinterest is a virtual pinboard where people pin pictures of things they have seen on the Internet that they want to share with others. [tap or press Enter twice]

What do you think?

7 Tap or press Enter twice at the end of the message text and type your name as the sender.

8 Tap or click the Send button.

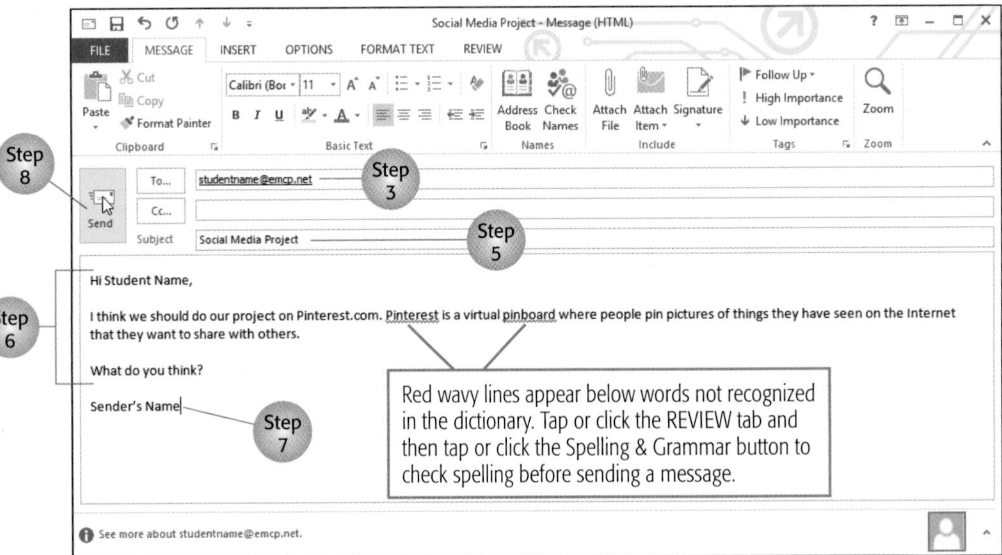

Create and Send an Email Message

1. Tap or click New Email button.
2. Type address in *To* text box.
3. Type brief description in *Subject* text box.
4. Type message text in message window.
5. Tap or click Send.

Reply to a Message

1. Tap or click Reply button in Reading pane.
2. Type reply message.
3. Tap or click Send.

Replying to a Message

New messages appear at the top of the message list in the Content pane with message headers that show the sender, subject, time, and first line of message. Tap or click to select a message header and reply directly from the Reading pane using the **Reply button**. Replying from the Reading pane is called an **inline reply**.

As an alternative, double-tap or double-click the message header in the Content pane to open the message in a Message window from which you can choose to Reply or Forward the message.

9 Tap or click the SEND / RECEIVE tab and then tap or click the Send/Receive All Folders button in the Send & Receive group to update the Content pane. (Skip this step if you can already see the message sent to you by a classmate or yourself from Step 8.)

10 If necessary, tap or click to select the message header and read the message text in the Reading pane.

If you are online when a new message is received, a chime sounds and a preview of the message appears in a desktop alert near the top right of your screen (or bottom right in Windows 7).

11 Tap or click the Reply button at the top of the message in the Reading pane.

12 Type the following reply message text and then tap or click the Send button.

(Type the name of the person from whom you received the message), [Enter twice]

I agree. I have a few pictures we can use to practice with if you want to set up a sample account at Pinterest.com. [Enter twice]

(Type your name)

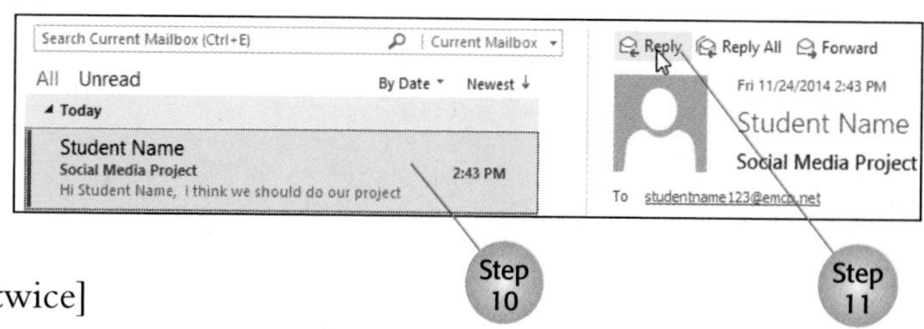

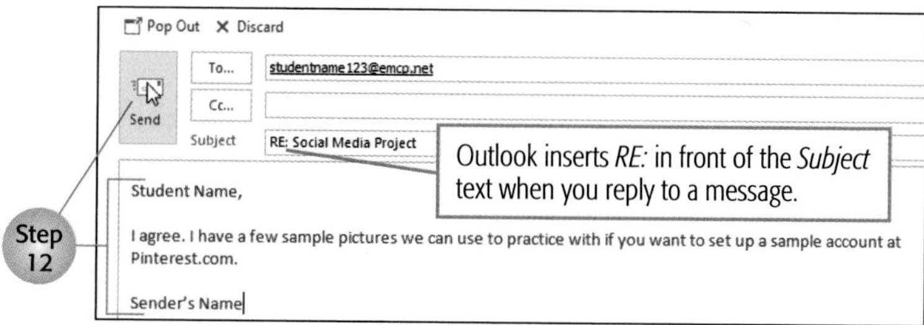

Outlook inserts *RE:* in front of the *Subject* text when you reply to a message.

Reading pane off? Turn on the Reading pane by tapping or clicking VIEW, Reading Pane, *Right*.

Use Reply All to send a reply in which more than one person was included in the initial message. Use good judgment with Reply All and be sure that all of the other recipients really need to see your response.

Forwarding a Message

Forward a message if you want someone else to receive a copy of a message you have received. Choose the **Forward button**, type the email address for the person to whom you want to forward the message, and type a brief explanation if desired before sending the message.

Think carefully before forwarding a message to be certain that the original sender would not object to another person reading the message without his or her permission. If in doubt, do not forward the message.

13 With the message header for the message selected at Step 10 still active, tap or click the Forward button in the Reading pane.

14 Type the email address for the recipient in the *To* text box.

15 Tap or click in the message window above the original message text and type the following text:

Hi (type recipient's name), [Enter twice]

Do you want to join our group for the social media project? See message below discussing Pinterest.com. [Enter twice]

(Type your name)

16 Tap or click the Send button.

Forward a Message

1. Tap or click Forward button in Reading pane.
2. Type address in *To* text box.
3. Type message.
4. Tap or click Send.

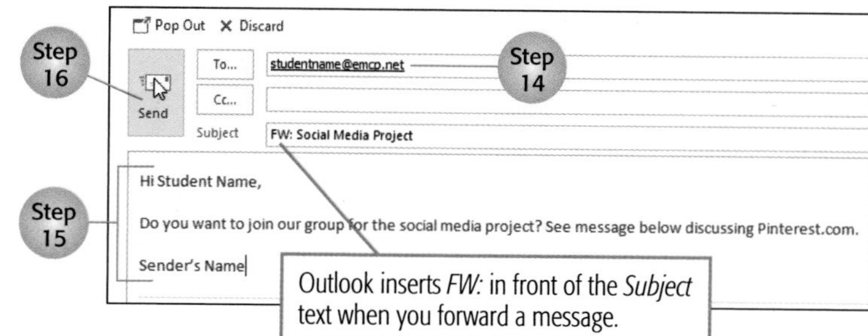

Outlook inserts *FW:* in front of the *Subject* text when you forward a message.

Email Signatures

A **signature** is a closing automatically inserted at the bottom of each sent message. Signatures usually include contact information for the sender such as name, title, department, company name, and contact telephone numbers.

To create a signature, open a message window, tap or click the Signature button in the MESSAGE tab, and tap or click *Signatures*.

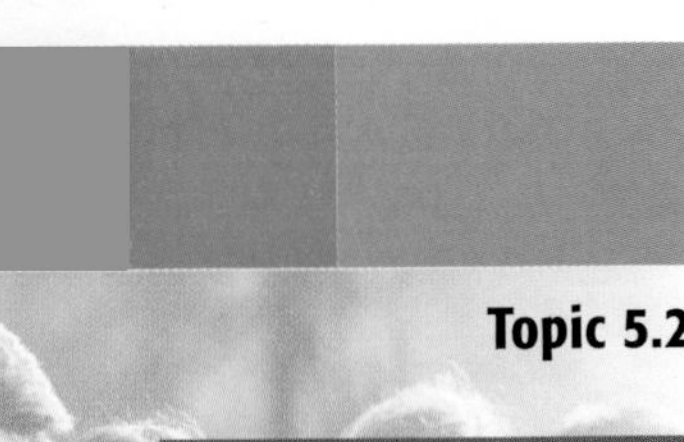

Topic 5.2

SKILLS

Attach a picture to a message

Delete a message

Empty Deleted Items folder

Attaching a File to a Message and Deleting Messages

Files are often exchanged between individuals via email. To attach a file to an email message, use the **Attach File** button in the Include group of the MESSAGE tab. The recipient of an email message with a file attachment can choose to open the file from the mail server or save it to a storage medium.

Messages that are no longer needed should be deleted to keep your mail folders to a manageable size. You can delete a message in the Inbox folder if you replied to the message because you can view the original text with your reply from Sent Items. Consider setting aside a time each week to clean up your Inbox by deleting messages.

1 With Outlook open and Inbox the active folder, tap or click the HOME tab if HOME is not the active tab.

2 Tap or click the New Email button in the New group.

3 Type the email address for the recipient in the *To* text box.

Notice that as you begin typing an email address, Outlook provides email addresses that match what you are typing in a drop-down list. This feature is referred to as **AutoComplete**. Rather than type the entire email address, you can tap or click the correct recipient in the AutoComplete list.

4 Tap or press the Tab key twice, or tap or click in the *Subject* text box.

5 Type **Picture for Pinterest**.

6 Tap or press Enter, or tap or click in the Message text window and type the following text:

Hi (type recipient's name), [Enter twice]

Attached is a picture we can put on Pinterest.

7 Tap or press Enter twice at the end of the message text and type your name as the sender.

8 Tap or click the Attach File button in the Include group of the MESSAGE tab in the message window.

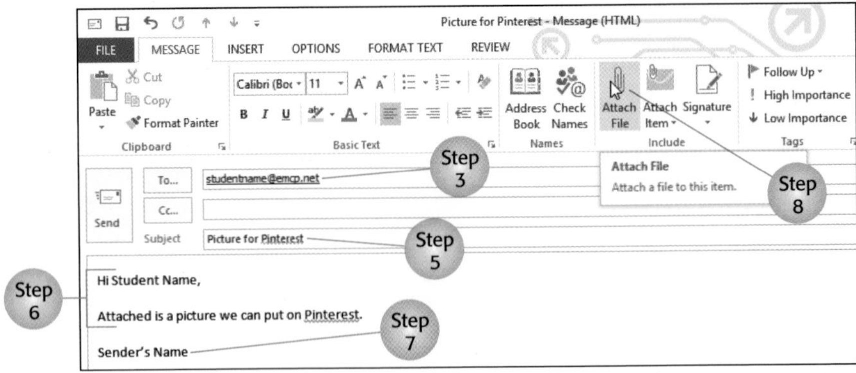

9 At the Insert File dialog box, navigate to the Student_Data_Files folder in the ComputerCourse folder on your USB flash drive.

10 Double-tap or double-click the *Ch5* folder name.

11 Double-tap or double-click the file named ***MurresOnFloatingIce***.

Outlook adds the file to an *Attached* field below the *Subject* text box.

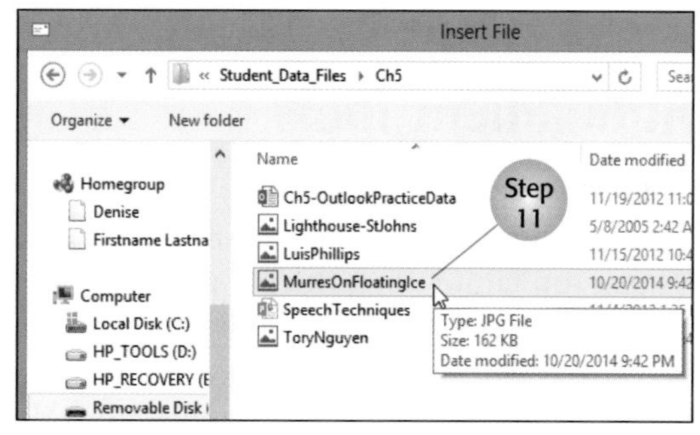

12 Tap or click the Send button.

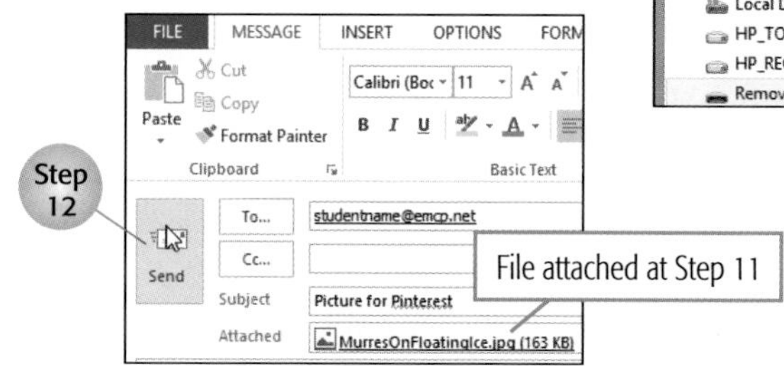

Over time your mail folders (Inbox and Sent Items) can become filled with messages that are no longer needed. To delete messages, select the message headers and tap or click the Delete button in the Delete group of the HOME tab. Deleted messages are moved to the **Deleted Items** folder. Periodically, empty the Deleted Items folder to permanently delete the messages.

13 Tap or click the Send/Receive All Folders button on the Quick Access toolbar (second button from left) to update your Inbox folder. (Skip this step if you can already see the message sent to you by a classmate or yourself from Step 12.)

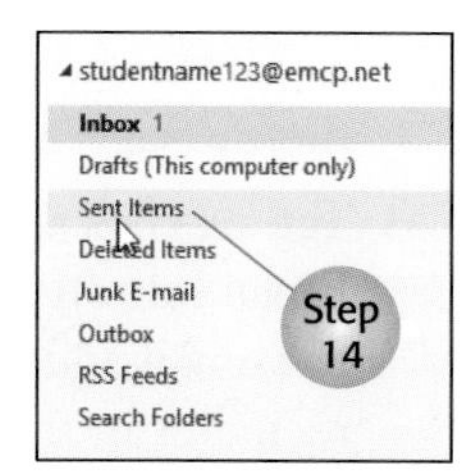

14 Tap or click *Sent Items* in the Folder pane.

15 If necessary, tap or click to select the message header for the message with the picture attached that you sent to a classmate or yourself in this topic.

16 Tap or click the Delete button in the Delete group of the HOME tab.

17 Tap or click *Deleted Items* in the Folder pane.

Notice the message you deleted appears in the Content pane.

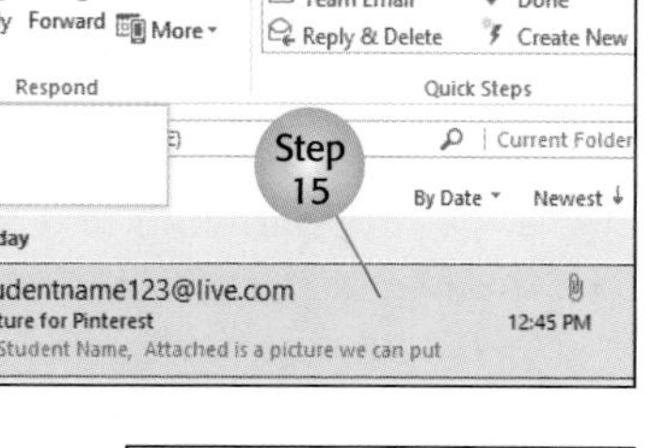

18 Press and hold or right-click *Deleted Items* in the Folder pane and then tap or click *Empty Folder*.

19 Tap or click Yes at the Microsoft Outlook message box asking if you want to continue to permanently delete everything in the Deleted Items folder.

20 Tap or click *Inbox* in the Folder pane.

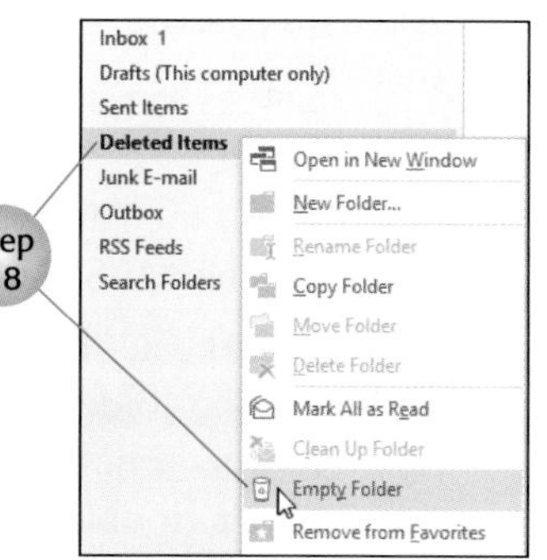

Attach a File to a Message

1. Open new message window.
2. Type address in *To* text box.
3. Type brief description in *Subject* text box.
4. Type message text in message window.
5. Tap or click Attach File button.
6. Navigate to desired drive and/or folder.
7. Double-tap or double-click file name.
8. Tap or click Send.

Delete a Message

1. Select message(s) in Content pane.
2. Tap or click Delete button.

Empty Deleted Items Folder

1. Press and hold or right-click *Deleted Items* in Folder pane.
2. Tap or click *Empty Folder*.
3. Tap or click Yes.

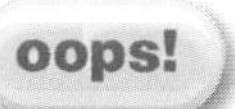

Folder pane off or minimized? Tap or click VIEW, Folder Pane, *Normal*.

Select multiple messages for deletion using the Windows standards: Shift + click to select adjacent message headers or Ctrl + click to select nonadjacent message headers.

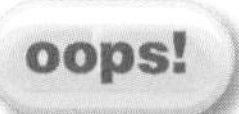

Lots of messages in *Deleted Items*? As a precaution, tap or click No at Step 19. At a later time, review all of the messages in Deleted Items to ensure it is safe to permanently delete them.

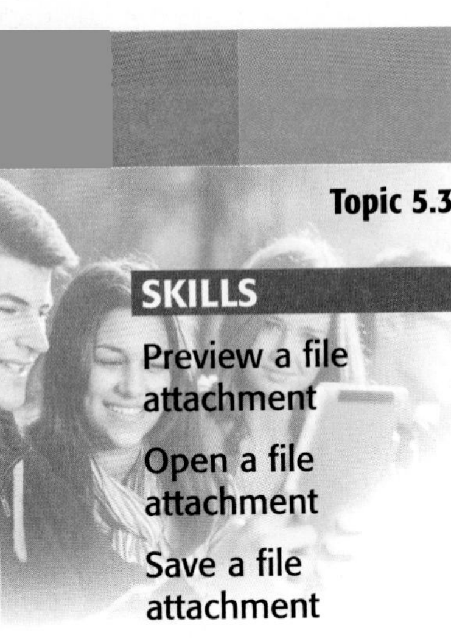

Topic 5.3

SKILLS

Preview a file attachment

Open a file attachment

Save a file attachment

Previewing File Attachments and Using File Attachment Tools

When you receive an email message with a file attached, you can preview, open, save, or print the file attachment from the Reading pane or from a message window. When you tap or click the file name in the Reading pane, the message text disappears and is replaced with the contents of the attached file. Some files cannot be viewed within the Reading pane. In those instances, double-tap or double-click the file name to open the file attached to the message.

When a file is selected in the Reading pane or in a message window, the ATTACHMENTS tab becomes active with buttons to open, print, save, remove, select, or copy the file.

1. With Outlook open and Inbox the active folder, tap or click the message header for the message received in the previous topic with the file attachment. (Skip this step if the message header is already selected.)

2. Tap or click the file name ***MurresOnFloatingIce.jpg*** in the Reading pane.

   Outlook removes the message text and displays in the Reading pane the picture attached to the message. Notice also the ATTACHMENT TOOLS ATTACHMENTS tab becomes active in the ribbon.

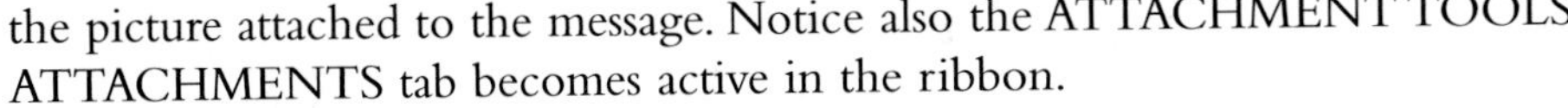

3. Tap or click the Message icon in the Reading pane to return the display to the message text.

4. Tap or click the New Email button and type the email address for the recipient in the *To* text box.

5. Tap or click in the *Subject* text box and type **Presentation for Business class.**

6. Type the following text in the Message text window:

   Hi (type recipient's name), [Enter twice]

   Attached is the PowerPoint presentation for our group project. [Enter twice]

   (Type your name)

7. Tap or click the Attach File button in the MESSAGE tab.

8. At the Insert File dialog box, with the Ch5 folder in the Student_Data_Files folder the active folder, double-tap or double-click the file named ***SpeechTechniques***.

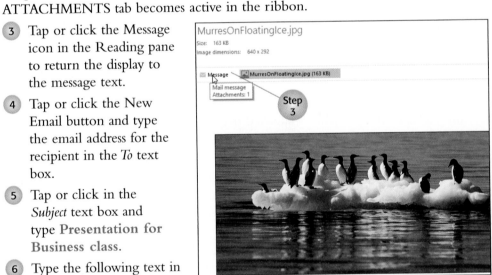

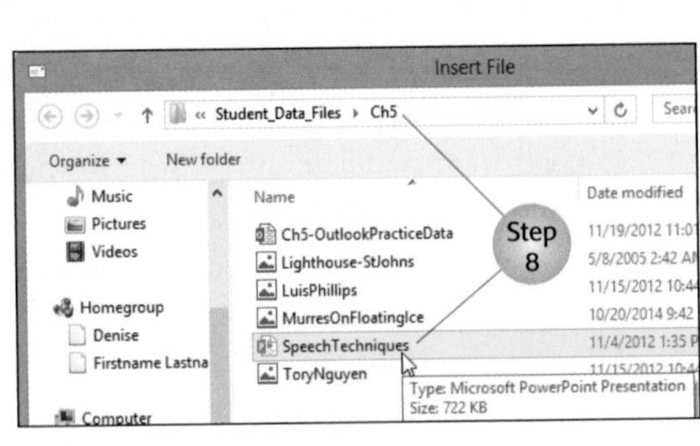

9 Tap or click the Send button.

10 Tap or click the Send/Receive All Folders button on the Quick Access toolbar to update your Inbox folder. (Skip this step if you can already see the message sent to you by a classmate or yourself from Step 9.)

11 Tap or click the message header for the message received with the subject *Presentation for Business Class.*

12 Tap or click the file name ***SpeechTechniques.pptx*** in the Reading pane.

13 Slide or scroll down the Reading pane to the last slide in the presentation.

14 Tap or click the Open button in the Actions group of the ATTACHMENT TOOLS ATTACHMENTS tab.

Microsoft PowerPoint starts with the **SpeechTechniques.pptx** file open. Notice the Title bar and Message bar displayed below the ribbon tabs indicate the presentation is open in **Protected view**. Protected view allows you to read the file's contents in the source application; however, editing the file is not permitted until you tap or click the Enable Editing button in the Message bar.

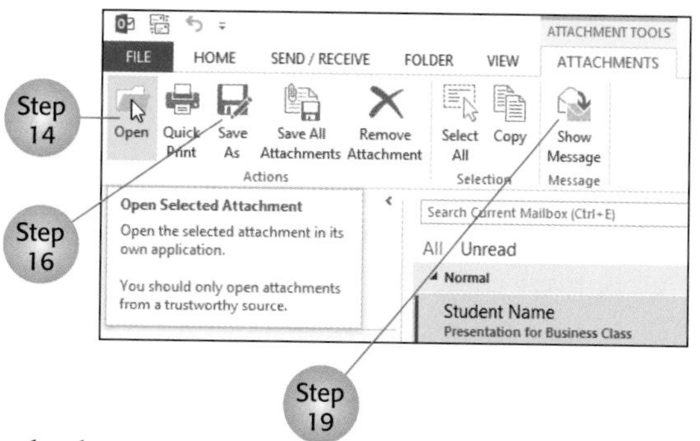

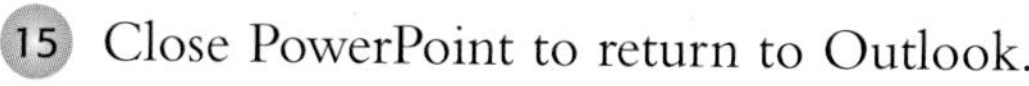

15 Close PowerPoint to return to Outlook.

16 Tap or click the Save As button in the ATTACHMENTS tab.

17 At the Save Attachment dialog box, navigate to the CompletedTopicsbyChapter folder on your USB flash drive, and create a new folder named *Ch5.*

18 Double-tap or double-click the *Ch5* folder and tap or click the Save button.

19 Tap or click the Show Message button in the Message group of the ATTACHMENTS tab.

Preview a File Attached to a Message

Tap or click file name in Reading pane.

Open a File Attached to a Message

1. Tap or click file name in Reading pane.
2. Tap or click Open button.

Save a File Attached to a Message

1. Tap or click file name in Reading pane.
2. Tap or click Save As button.
3. Navigate to drive and/or folder.
4. Tap or click Save.

Be Cautious Opening File Attachments!

Outlook blocks certain file types attached to messages that are known to be the target for viruses and are considered unsafe. However, even with Outlook's protection you should exercise caution when opening a file received in an email message. Only open files received from people you know and trust and always make sure you have real-time, up-to-date virus protection turned on. When in doubt, delete the file or message without opening it.

Scheduling Appointments and Events in Calendar

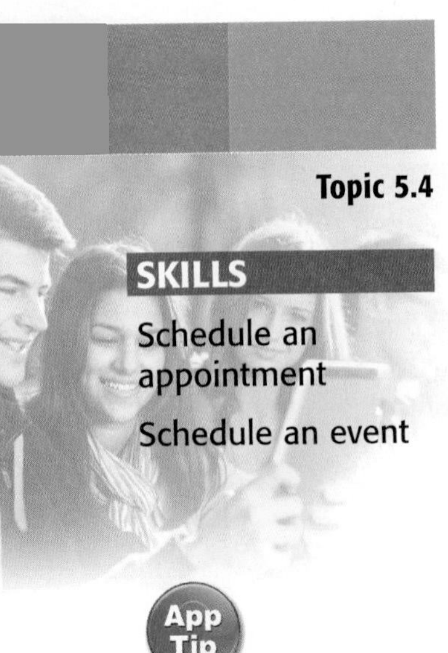

The **Calendar** tool in Outlook is used to schedule appointments and events such as meetings or conferences. An **appointment** is any activity where you want to track the day or time that the activity begins and ends in your schedule or that you want to be reminded to be somewhere. For example, an appointment can be a class, a meeting, a medical test, or a lunch date.

Note: In this topic and the next two topics, you will schedule appointments, an event, and a meeting in October 2015. Check with your instructor, if necessary, for alternate instructions that schedule these items in the current month or in October of the current year.

1. With Outlook open and Inbox the active folder, tap or click Calendar in the Navigation pane.

Step 1

Outlook displays the current date or month in the Content pane in Day or Month view. A **Date Navigator** displays above the Folder pane with the current month and directional arrow buttons to browse forward or back to upcoming or previous months.

App Tip

New to Outlook 2013 is the current weather displayed next to the current date or month.

2. If necessary, tap or click the Day button in the Arrange group of the HOME tab, and then tap or click the Go to Date launcher button (downward-pointing diagonal arrow) at the bottom right of the Go To group.

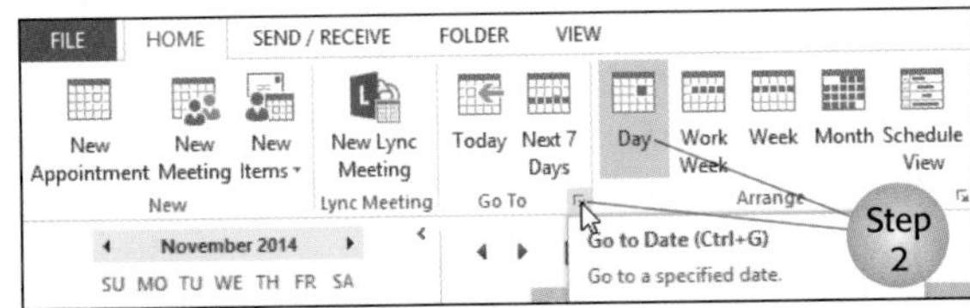

May 10 displayed instead of October 5? Change the Region Format in the Control Panel to English (United States) and try Step 3 again.

3. At the **Go To Date** dialog box, type **10/5/2015** and then tap or press Enter, or tap or click OK.

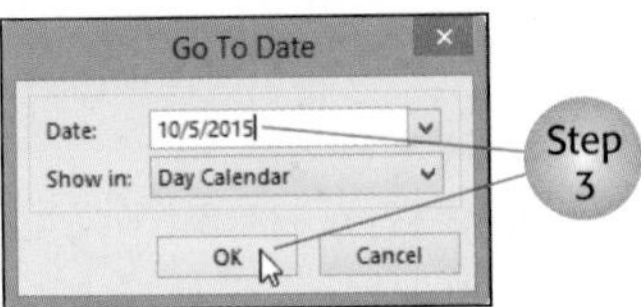

4. Tap or click next to 9:00 a.m. in the Appointment area, type **Meet with program adviser**, and tap or press Enter, or tap or click in another time slot outside the appointment box.

By default, Outlook schedules the appointment for a half hour.

5. Drag the bottom boundary of the appointment box to 10:00 a.m. if you are using a mouse; otherwise, double-tap to open the appointment, tap the *End time* list arrow, tap *10:00 AM (1 hour)*, and then tap Save & Close.

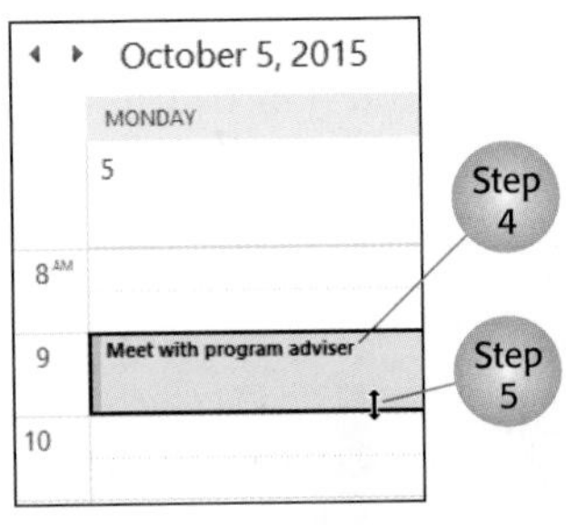

App Tip

A feature called *peek* works with a mouse. Point to Calendar, People, or Tasks in the Navigation pane to view current information in a pop-up. For example, peek at the day's appointments without leaving Mail by simply pointing to Calendar.

6. Tap or click next to 11:00 a.m. in the Appointment area.
7. Tap or click the **New Appointment button** in the New group of the HOME tab.

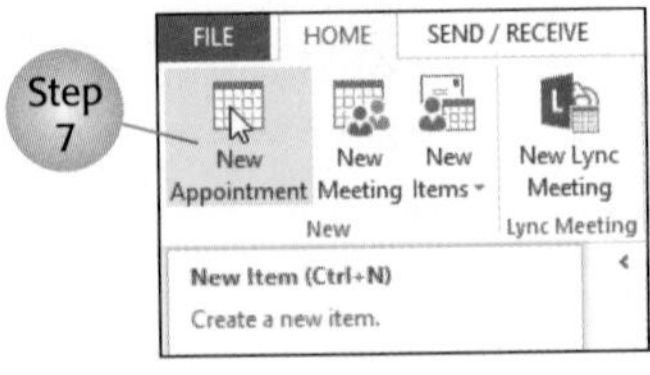

An Appointment window opens in which you can provide more details about the appointment.

8 Type **Intern Interview** in the *Subject* text box.

9 Tap or press Tab, or tap or click in the *Location* text box and type **Room 3001**.

10 Tap or click the *End time* list arrow and tap or click *12:00 PM (1 hour)* at the drop-down list.

11 Tap or click the Save & Close button in the Actions group of the APPOINTMENT tab in the Appointment window.

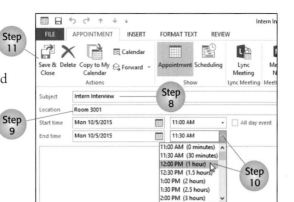

An **event** differs from an appointment in that it is an activity that lasts an entire day or longer. Examples of events include conferences, trade shows, or vacations. An event does not occupy a time slot in the Calendar. Event information appears in a banner along the top of the day in the Appointment area.

12 Double-tap or double-click in the white space with the date (*5*) at the top of the Appointment area below MONDAY and above the 8 a.m. time slot to open an Event window.

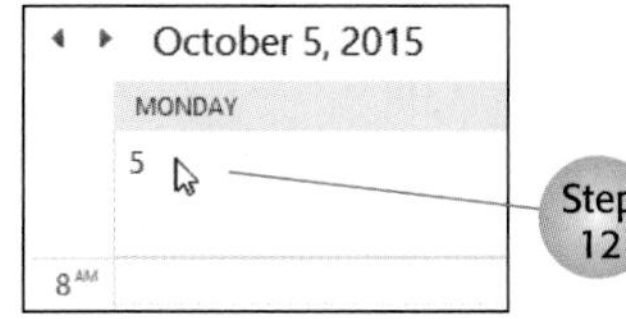

13 Type **Career Fair** in the *Subject* text box.

14 Tap or press Tab, or tap or click in the *Location* text box and type **Student Center**.

15 Tap or click the Save & Close button in the Actions group of the EVENT tab in the Event window.

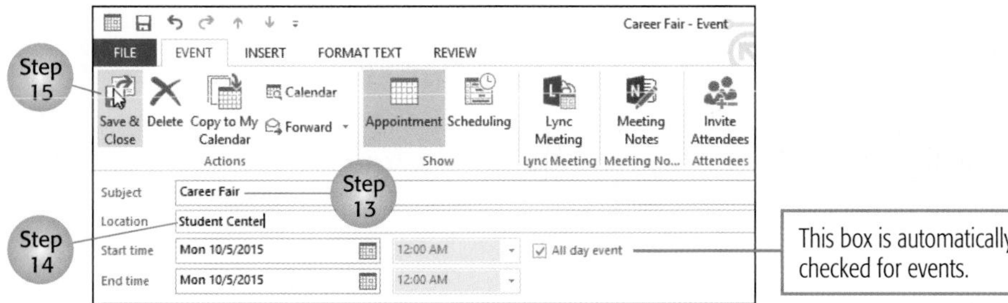

16 Tap or click next to a blank time slot in the Appointment area.

Schedule an Appointment

1. Display the Calendar.
2. Navigate to appointment date.
3. Tap or click next to appointment time.
4. Type appointment description.
5. Tap or press Enter.

OR

1. Display the Calendar.
2. Navigate to appointment date.
3. Tap or click next to appointment time.
4. Tap or click New Appointment button.
5. Enter appointment details in Appointment window.
6. Tap or click Save & Close.

Schedule an Event

1. Display the Calendar.
2. Navigate to event date.
3. Double-tap or double-click in white space next to date above Appointment area.
4. Enter event description.
5. Enter event location.
6. Tap or click Save & Close.

Change the End time date if the event lasts more than one day.

Appointment Reminders and Tags

By default, new appointments have a reminder set at 15 minutes. Turn off the reminder or change the reminder time by selecting an appointment in the Appointment area and using the *Reminder* list box in the Options group of the CALENDAR TOOLS APPOINTMENT tab.

You can also assign tags to a selected appointment using the buttons in the Tags group. For example, assign the Private tag to a personal appointment so that no one with shared access to your calendar can see the appointment details.

Scheduling a Recurring Appointment and Editing an Appointment

Topic 5.5

SKILLS

Schedule a recurring appointment

Edit an appointment

An appointment that occurs on a regular basis at fixed intervals need only be entered once in Outlook and set up as a recurring appointment. Open the **Recurrence** dialog box to enter the recurrence pattern for a repeating appointment.

1. With Outlook open and Calendar active with October 5, 2015 displayed in the Appointment area, tap or click the Forward button to display October 6, 2015 in the Appointment area.

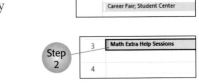

2. Tap or click next to 3:00 p.m. in the Appointment area, type **Math Extra Help Sessions**, and then tap or press Enter.

3. With the Math Extra Help Sessions appointment box selected in the Appointment area, tap or click the Recurrence button in the Options group of the CALENDAR TOOLS APPOINTMENT tab.

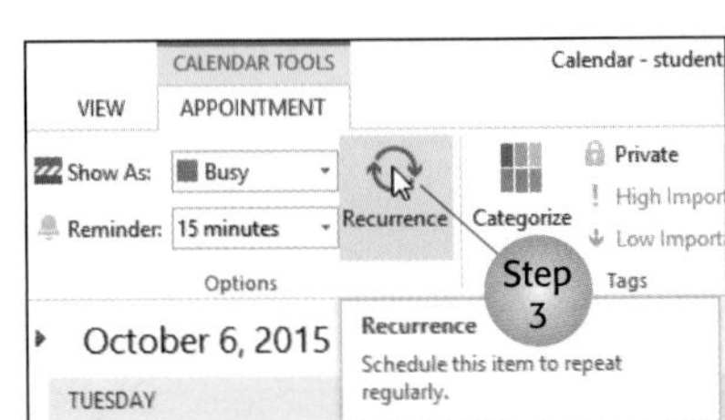

By default, Outlook sets the *Recurrence pattern* details for the appointment to recur *Weekly* at the same day and time as the appointment.

4. At the Appointment Recurrence dialog box, select *10* in the *End after* text box and type 5.

5. Tap or click OK.

A recurring icon displays at the right end of the appointment box in the Appointment area.

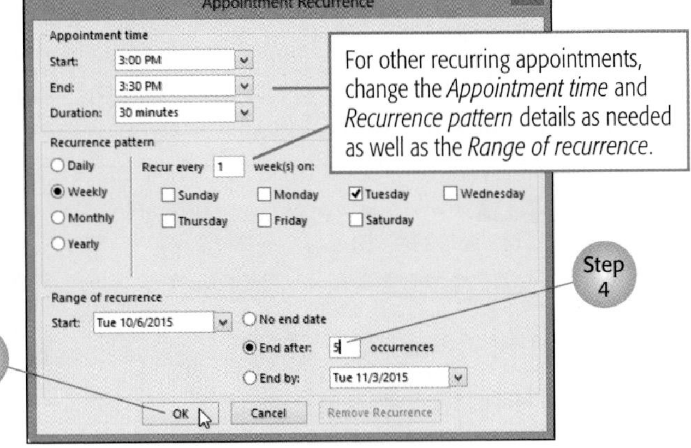

6. Tap or click *13* in the October 2015 calendar in the *Date Navigator* section of the Folder pane to move to the following Tuesday's appointments.

Notice the Math Extra Help Sessions appointment appears in the Appointment window.

7. Tap or click *20* in the October 2015 calendar in the Date Navigator.

Notice the Math Extra Help Sessions appointment appears in the Appointment window.

8. Tap or click the Go to Date launcher button in the Go To group, type **11/17/2015** in the Go To Date dialog box, and then tap or press Enter, or tap or click OK.

Notice the Math Extra Help Sessions appointment does not appear in the Appointment window because the range of recurrence has ended.

oops!

CALENDAR TOOLS APPOINTMENT tab not visible? Tap or click the appointment box to select the appointment and display the tab.

Consider entering your class schedule in the Outlook calendar for the current semester as recurring appointments.

Assign options or tags to an existing appointment by selecting the appointment and using the buttons in the CALENDAR TOOLS APPOINTMENT tab. Change the subject, location, day, or time of an appointment by opening the Appointment window.

9. Display October 5, 2015 in the Calendar.
10. Tap or click to select the appointment scheduled at 11:00 a.m.

A selected appointment box displays with a black outline. A pop-out opens at the left with the appointment details when you point at or tap an appointment.

11. Tap or click the Open button in the Actions group of the CALENDAR TOOLS APPOINTMENT tab.

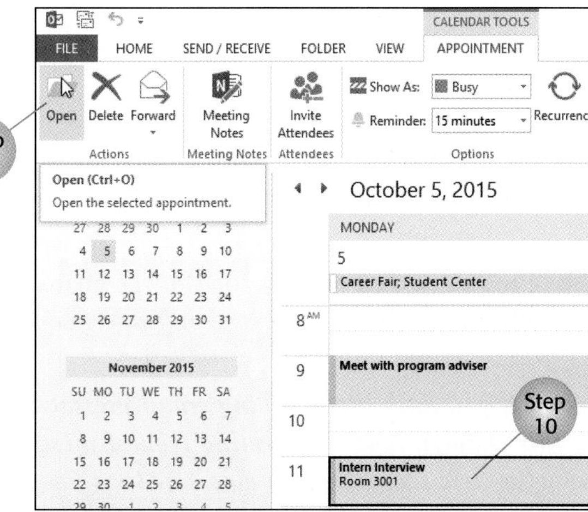

Assume the intern interview has been rescheduled to Tuesday.

12. Tap or click the calendar icon in the *Start time* text box.
13. Tap or click *6* in the drop-down calendar.
14. Tap or click Save & Close.
15. Display October 6, 2015 in the Appointment area.

Notice the Intern Interview appointment appears next to 11:00 a.m.

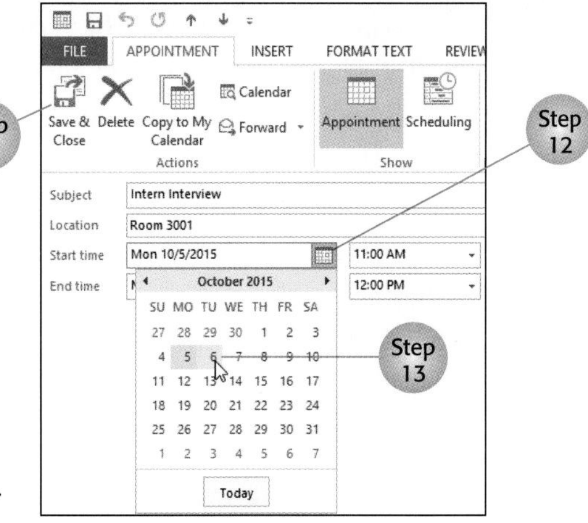

Schedule a Recurring Appointment

1. Display Calendar.
2. Navigate to appointment date.
3. Tap or click next to appointment time.
4. Type appointment description.
5. Tap or press Enter.
6. Tap or click Recurrence button.
7. Enter recurrence pattern and/or range details.
8. Tap or click OK.

Edit an Appointment

1. Select appointment.
2. Tap or click Open button.
3. Change appointment details as needed.
4. Tap or click Save & Close.

ALTERNATIVE method

Consider using the following keyboard shortcuts to work with appointments:

- Ctrl + N to open a new Appointment window
- Ctrl + O to open the Appointment window for the selected appointment
- Ctrl + G to open the Go To Date dialog box
- Ctrl + P to print the current day's appointments

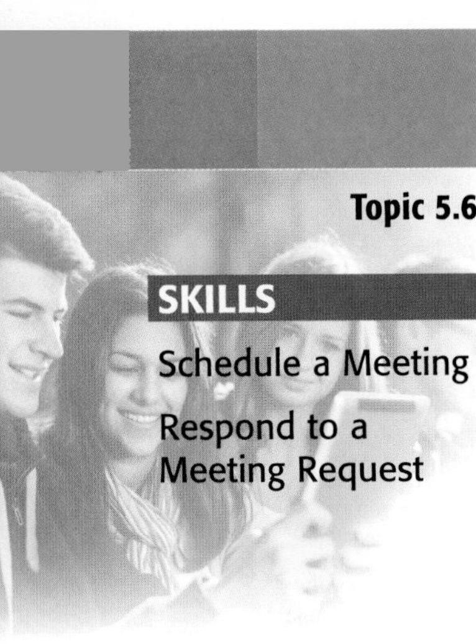

Topic 5.6

SKILLS

Schedule a Meeting

Respond to a Meeting Request

Scheduling a Meeting

Scheduling a **meeting** involves selecting the day and time and opening a Meeting window in which you enter the email addresses for the individuals you want to invite to the meeting, the meeting topic, location, and other details as needed. Meeting attendees receive a **meeting request** email message. Responses to the meeting request are sent back to the meeting organizer via buttons in the email message window or Reading pane.

1. With Outlook open and Calendar active with October 6, 2015 displayed in the Appointment area, tap or click next to 1:00 p.m. in the Appointment area.
2. Tap or click the **New Meeting button** in the New group.
3. Type the email address for the classmate with whom you have been exchanging emails in the *To* text box.

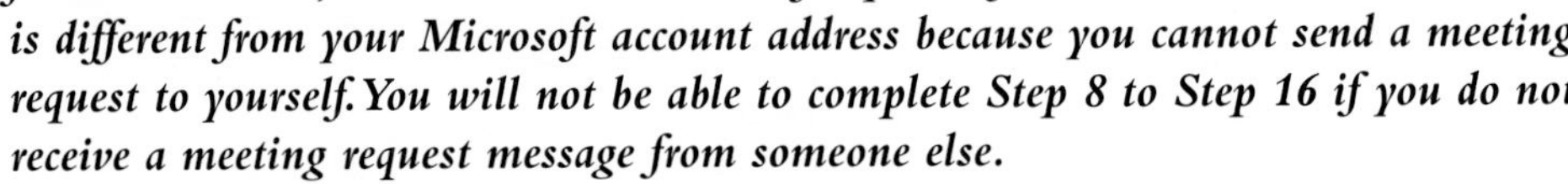

Note: If you have been sending email messages to yourself in this chapter, send the meeting request message to a friend or relative, or use an email address for yourself that is different from your Microsoft account address because you cannot send a meeting request to yourself. You will not be able to complete Step 8 to Step 16 if you do not receive a meeting request message from someone else.

4. Tap or press Tab, or tap or click in the *Subject* text box and type **Fundraising Planning Meeting**.
5. Tap or press Tab, or tap or click in the *Location* text box and type **Room 1010**.
6. Tap or click the *End time* list arrow and tap or click *2:30 PM (1.5 hours)* at the drop-down list.
7. Tap or click the Send button.

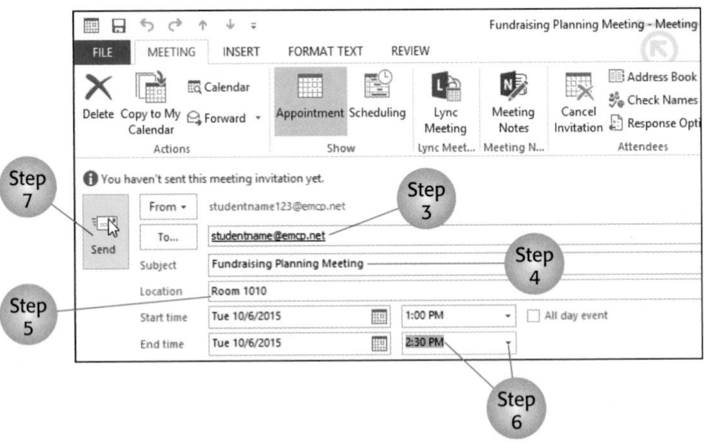

8. Tap or click Mail in the Navigation pane.

9. Tap or click the Send/Receive All Folders button on the Quick Access toolbar to update your Inbox folder. (Skip this step if you can already see the meeting request message sent to you by a classmate at Step 7.)

Consider using the space in the message window below *End time* to type a meeting agenda or other explanatory text to inform attendees about the purpose of the meeting.

10 Tap or click to select the message header for the meeting request to view the message details in the Reading pane.

The Accept, Tentative, Decline, Propose New Time, and Calendar buttons along the top of the Reading pane are used to respond to the meeting organizer. Outlook also displays your Calendar in the Reading pane so that you can see if you are available at the requested day and time.

11 Double-tap or double-click the message header to open the Meeting window.

12 Tap or click the **Accept button** in the Respond group of the MEETING tab.

13 Tap or click *Send the Response Now* at the drop-down list.

Notice that the meeting request email message is deleted from your Inbox once you have responded to the meeting invitation.

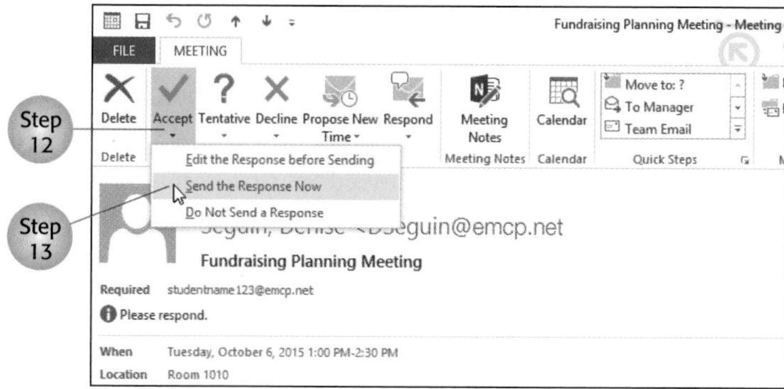

14 Tap or click *Sent Items* in the Folder pane.

15 Tap or click the message header for the message sent to the meeting organizer with your Accepted reply and read the message sent to the meeting organizer in the Reading pane.

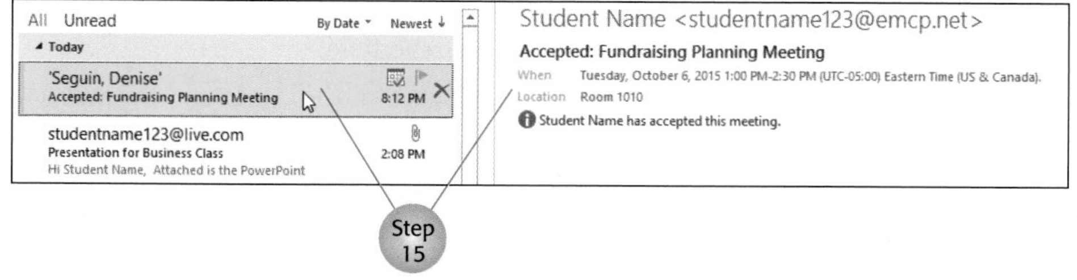

16 Tap or click *Inbox* in the Folder pane.

Schedule a Meeting
1. Display Calendar.
2. Navigate to meeting date.
3. Tap or click next to meeting time.
4. Tap or click New Meeting button.
5. Enter meeting details.
6. Tap or click Send.

Accept a Meeting Request
1. Display Inbox.
2. Select meeting request message header OR open Meeting window.
3. Tap or click Accept button.
4. Tap or click *Send the Response Now*.

Updating and Canceling a Meeting

If you need to reschedule a meeting, open the Meeting window, make the required changes to the day, time, or location, and tap or click the Send Update button. Outlook will send an email message to each attendee with the updated information. To delete a meeting, open the Meeting window and tap or click the Cancel Meeting button in the Actions group. Outlook sends an email message to each attendee informing each person that the meeting is canceled and removes the meeting from each person's calendar.

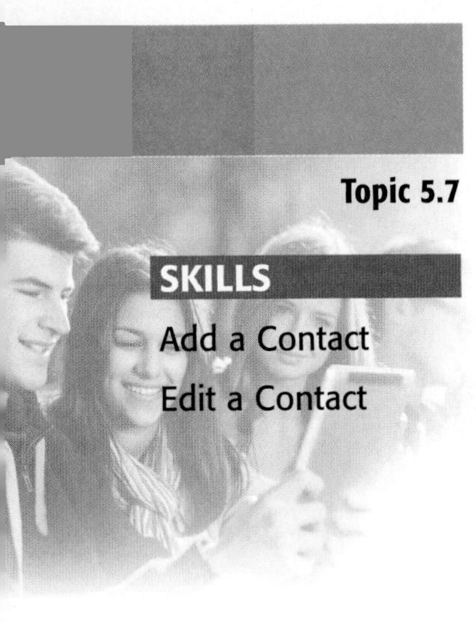

Topic 5.7

SKILLS

Add a Contact

Edit a Contact

Adding and Editing Contacts

The **People** tool in Outlook is used to store contact information such as email addresses, mailing addresses, telephone numbers, and other information about the people with whom you communicate. Think of People as an electronic address book. If you have a picture of an individual, you can display the person's picture with his or her contact information in the **People card**.

1. With Outlook open and Inbox the active folder, tap or click People in the Navigation pane.

2. Tap or click the **New Contact button** in the New group.

Step 2 — FILE | HOME | SEND / RECEIVE — New Contact | New Contact Group | New Items | Delete — New | Delete

3. At the Contact window, type **Tory Nguyen** in the *Full Name* text box.
4. Tap or press Tab, or tap or click in the *Company* text box.

   Notice the *File as* text box automatically updates when you move past the *Full Name* field with the person's last name followed by first name. The *File as* entry is used to organize the People list alphabetically by last names.

5. Type **NuWave Personnel** in the *Company* text box.
6. Tap or press Tab, or tap or click in the *Job title* text box and type **Recruitment Specialist**.
7. Tap or click in the *E-mail* text box and type **tory@emcp.net**.
8. Tap or click in the *Business* text box in the *Phone numbers* section and type **8885559840**.
9. Tap or click in the *Mobile* text box in the *Phone numbers* section and type **8885553256**.

   Notice that the phone numbers automatically format to show brackets around the area code and hyphens when you move past the field.

10. Tap or click the picture image control box between the name and business card sections of the Contact window (displays a person icon inside a gray-shaded box).

App Tip

You can also add a picture using the Picture button in the Options group of the CONTACT tab.

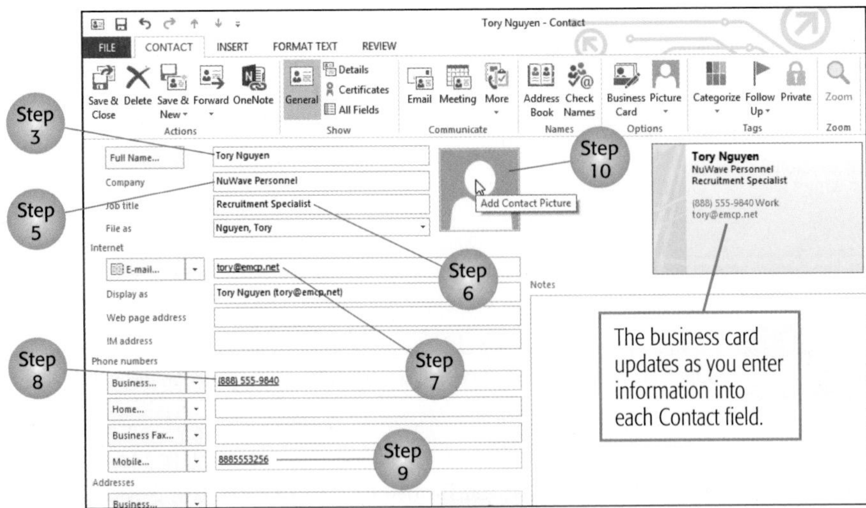

11. At the **Add Contact Picture** dialog box, navigate to the Ch5 folder in the Student_Data_Files folder and double-tap or double-click the file named ***ToryNguyen***.
12. Tap or click the Save & Close button in the Actions group of the CONTACT tab.

A selected person's information displays in the Reading pane in a People card with links to schedule a meeting or send an email to that person. Tap or click *Edit* to open the People card fields for editing in the Reading pane, or double-tap or double-click the name in the People list to add or modify information in a People card window.

13 Tap or click Edit near the top right of the Reading pane with Tory Nguyen's information displayed.

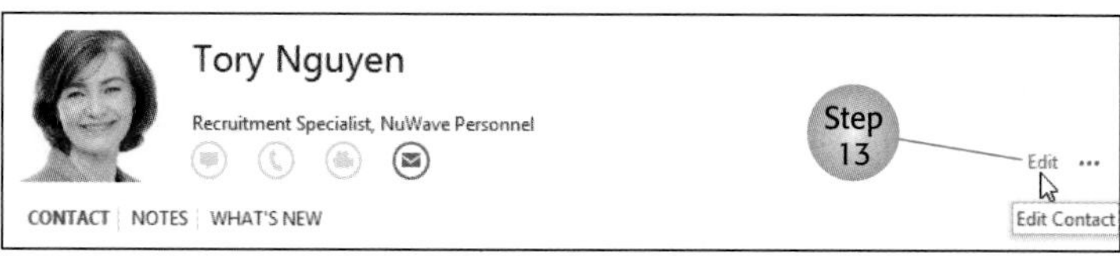

14 Tap or click at the end of the *Work* telephone number *(888) 555-9840*, tap or press the spacebar and type **extension 3115**.

15 Tap or click the Save button at the bottom right of the Reading pane.

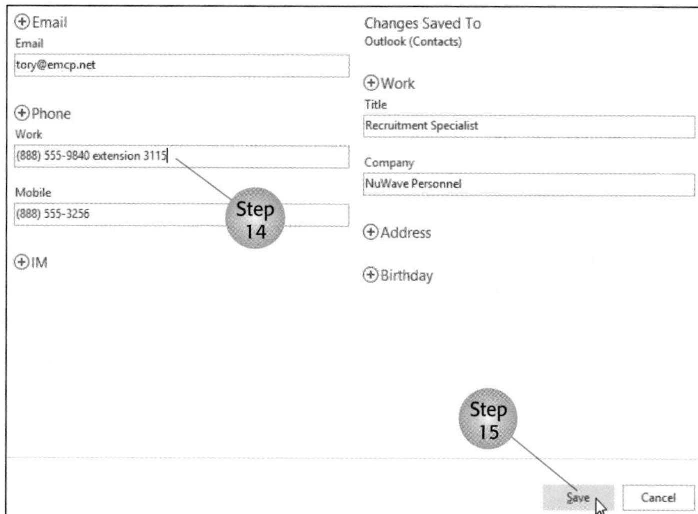

16 Double-tap or double-click in the white space at the bottom of the People list.

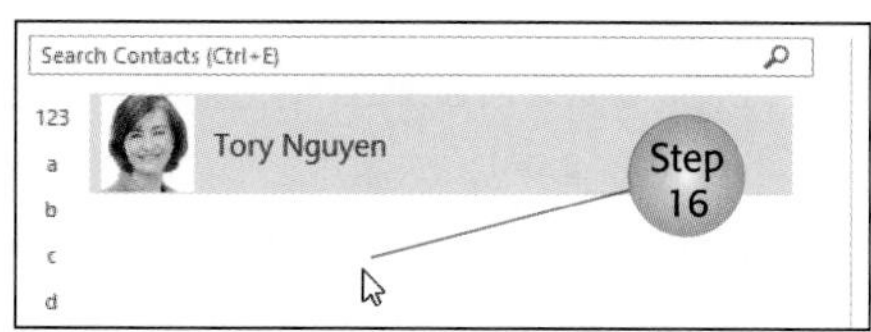

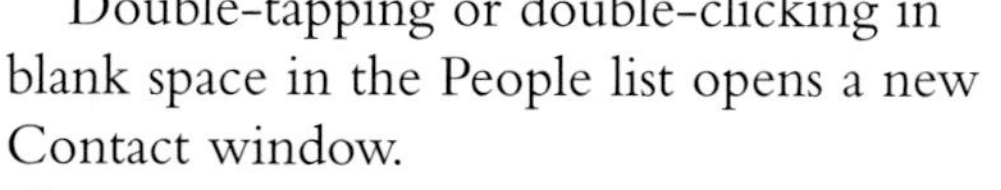

Double-tapping or double-clicking in blank space in the People list opens a new Contact window.

17 Enter your instructor's name, your school name, and your instructor's email address in the Contact window and tap or click Save & Close.

Add a Contact

1. Display People.
2. Tap or click New Contact button.
3. Enter contact information as required.
4. Tap or click Save & Close.

Edit a Contact

1. Select contact in People list.
2. Tap or click Edit in Reading pane.
3. Edit information as required.
4. Tap or click Save.

oops!

No Reading pane? Your Contact view may be set to Business Card or Card. Tap or click People in the Current View group of the HOME tab. If necessary, tap or click VIEW, Reading Pane, Right.

oops!

A Check Full Name dialog box may appear after you enter a name. This happens when Outlook cannot determine the first and last name. For example, typing errors or hyphenated names can cause the dialog box to open. Enter or edit the text as needed and tap or click OK.

ALTERNATIVE method

You can also edit a contact by opening the full Contact window. To do this, tap or click the Outlook (Contacts) link below *View Source* in the Reading pane for the selected person. This causes the same Contact window to open that you used to add the person. Use this method if you need to change a contact's picture or access the complete set of people fields or ribbon options.

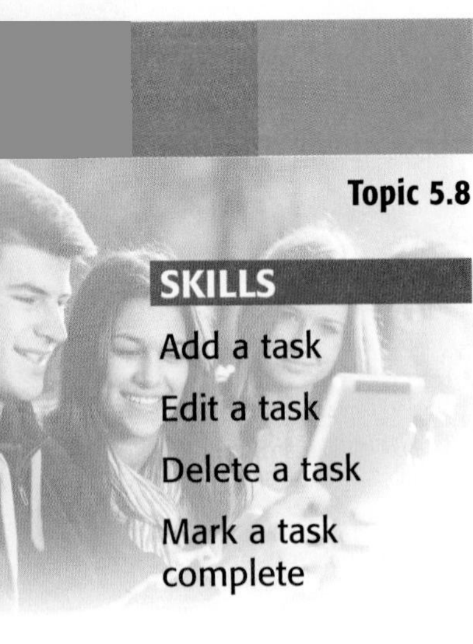

Topic 5.8

SKILLS

Add a task

Edit a task

Delete a task

Mark a task complete

oops!

Tasks icon not visible? Slide or drag the right boundary for the Folder pane to the right OR tap or click the button with the three dots and tap or click *Tasks* at the pop-up list.

Adding and Editing Tasks

Working with **Tasks** in Outlook is similar to maintaining a to-do list. Outlook provides the ability to track information about a task such as how much of the task is completed, how much time has been spent on the task, the priority for the task, and the task's due date.

1. With Outlook open and People active, tap or click Tasks in the Navigation pane and then tap or click To-Do List in the Current View group if To-Do List is not active.

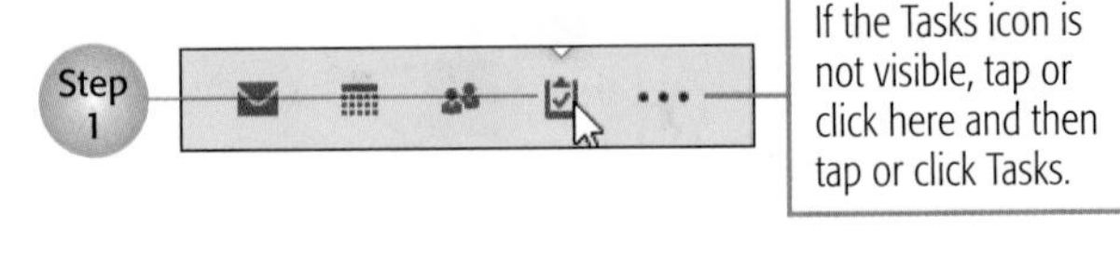

2. Tap or click in the text box at the top of the **To-Do List** that displays *Type a new task*, type **Do research on Pinterest**, and tap or press Enter.

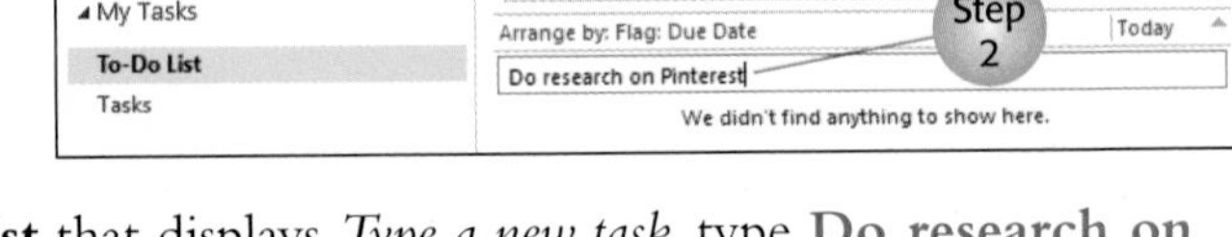

Outlook adds the task to the To-Do list under a flag with the heading *Today*.

3. Type **Gather pictures to create Pinterest pinboard** and tap or press Enter.

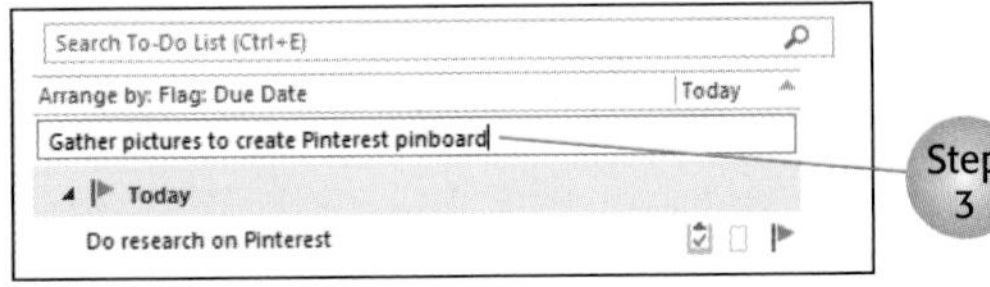

4. Type **Create resume for Career Fair** and tap or press Enter.

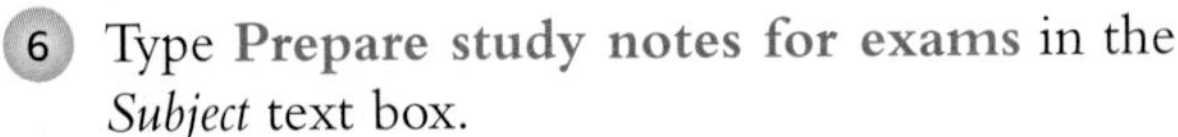

5. Tap or click the **New Task button** in the New group.

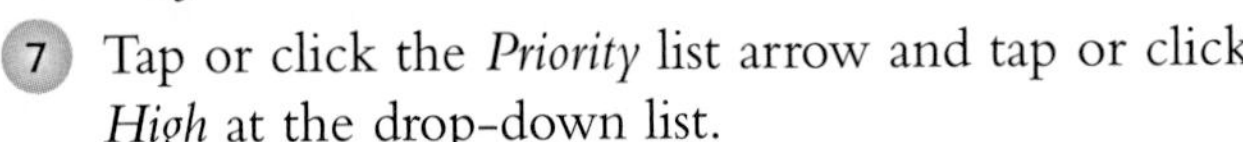

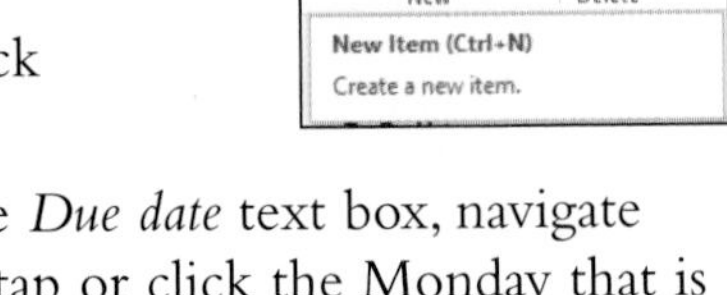

6. Type **Prepare study notes for exams** in the *Subject* text box.
7. Tap or click the *Priority* list arrow and tap or click *High* at the drop-down list.
8. Tap or click the calendar icon at the right of the *Due date* text box, navigate to the last month of your current semester, and tap or click the Monday that is one week before the last week of your semester.
9. Tap or click the Save & Close button in the Actions group of the TASK tab.

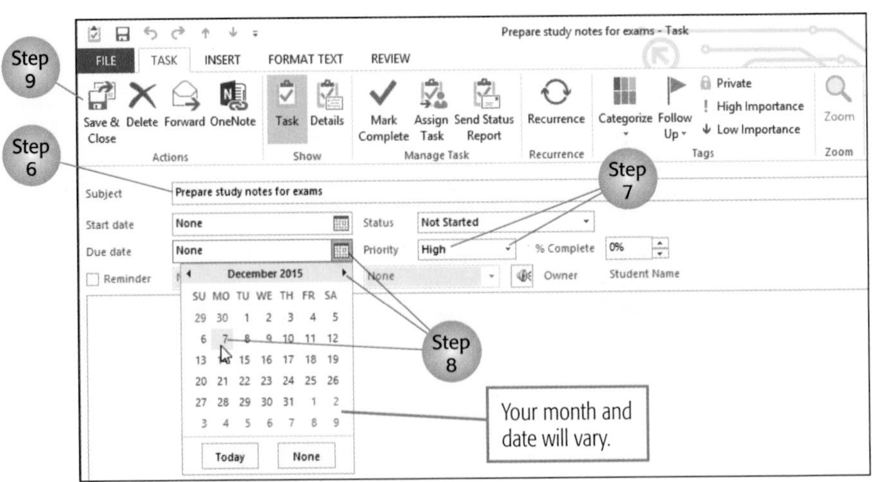

Editing or updating a task can include activities such as assigning or changing a due date, assigning a priority, entering the percentage of completion, or changing a task's status.

When a task is completed, use the Remove from List button in the Manage Task group or mark the task as complete in the Task window.

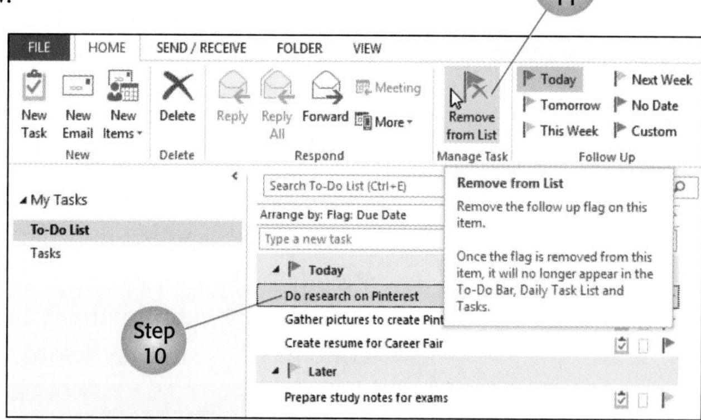

10 Tap or click the task entry *Do research on Pinterest.*

11 Tap or click the Remove from List button in the Manage Task group.

Notice the task is removed from the To-Do list. You can also use the Delete button in the Delete group of the HOME tab to remove a task.

12 Double-tap or double-click the task entry *Create resume for Career Fair* to open the Task window.

13 Tap or click the Mark Complete button in the Manage Task group of the TASK tab.

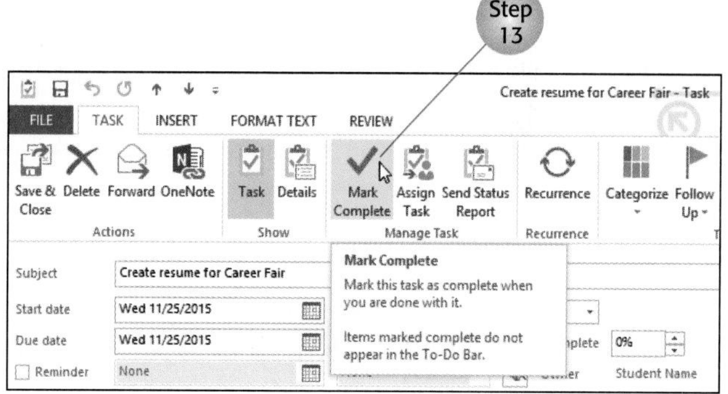

14 Double-tap or double-click the task entry *Gather pictures for Pinterest pinboard.*

15 Tap or click the *Status* list arrow and tap or click *Waiting on someone else* at the drop-down list.

16 Tap or click in the white space below the *Reminder* options and type **Waiting for Leslie to send me pictures from her renovation clients.**

17 Tap or click Save & Close.

Notice the updated task details appear in the Reading pane for the selected task.

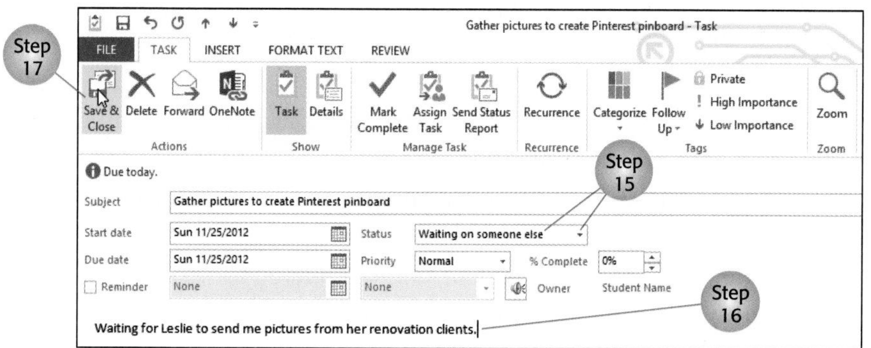

18 Display the Inbox.

Add a Task

1. Display Tasks.
2. Tap or click in *Type a new task* text box.
3. Type task description.
4. Tap or press Enter.

OR

1. Display Tasks.
2. Tap or click New Task button.
3. Enter task details.
4. Tap or click Save & Close.

Remove from List versus Mark Complete

Remove from List deletes the task while **Mark Complete** retains the task in the task list with a line drawn through the task and a gray check mark showing the task is finished. Mark Complete should be used if you need to retain task information for timekeeping or billing purposes. Display the complete Tasks list by tapping or clicking *Tasks* in the Folder pane.

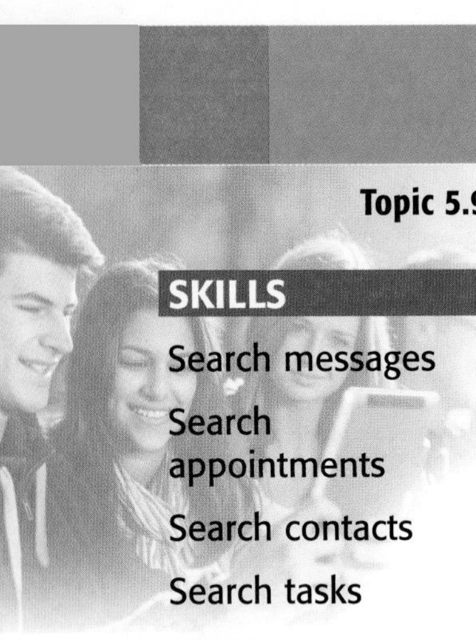

Topic 5.9
SKILLS
Search messages
Search appointments
Search contacts
Search tasks

The keyboard shortcut Ctrl + E opens the *Search* text box.

Searching Outlook Items

Outlook's Search feature is a powerful tool used to quickly find a message, appointment, contact, or task. A *Search* text box located between the ribbon and content is used to find items. Outlook begins a search as soon as you start typing in the *Search* text box. Matched items are highlighted in the search results. Once located, you can open an item to view or edit the information.

1. With Outlook open and Inbox active, tap or click in the *Search* text box at the top of the Content pane (displays *Search Current Mailbox*).
2. Type **pinterest**.

Outlook immediately begins matching messages in the Content pane with the characters as you type. Matched words are highlighted in both the Content pane and Reading pane. The list that remains is filtered to display all messages that contain the search keyword.

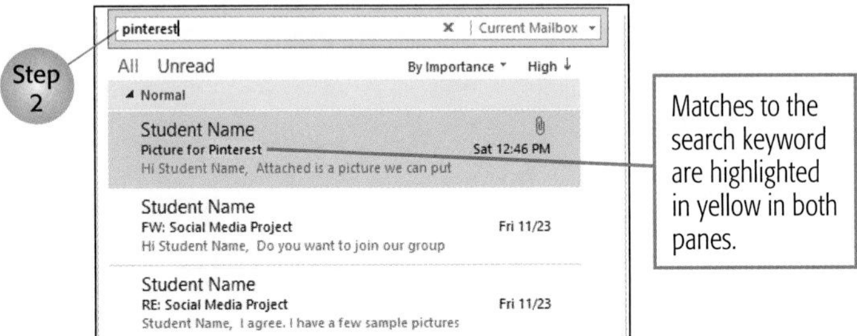

3. Tap or click each message in the search results list.

Notice for each message, Pinterest is highlighted in the Reading pane.

4. Tap or click the Close Search button in the *Search* text box to close the search results list and return to the Inbox.

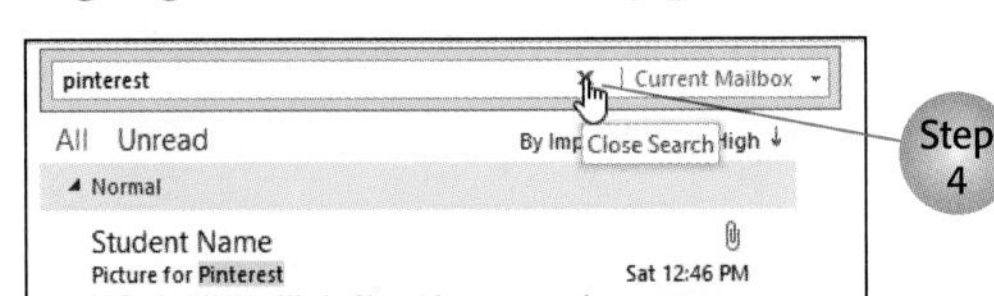

5. Display the Calendar.
6. Tap or click in the *Search* text box at the top right of the Appointment area (displays *Search Calendar*) and type **career fair**.

Outlook displays the appointment found with the search keywords in a filtered list.

7. Double-tap or double-click the entry in the filtered list to view the details in the Event window and then tap or click Save & Close.
8. Tap or click the Close Search button to restore the Calendar to the current day's appointments.

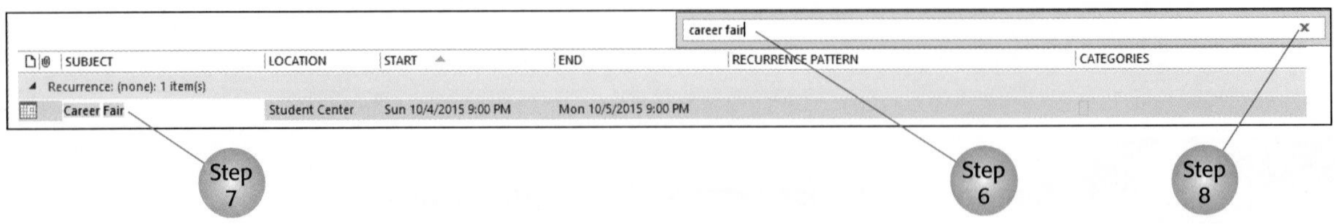

9 Display People.

10 Tap or click in the *Search* text box at the top of the People list (displays *Search Contacts*) and type **nuwave**.

Outlook displays the contact for Tory Nguyen who works at NuWave Personnel. You can use the Search feature to find any Outlook item by any field within the item. For example, you could find a contact by name, job title, company name, or even telephone number.

11 Tap or click the Close Search button to restore the People list.

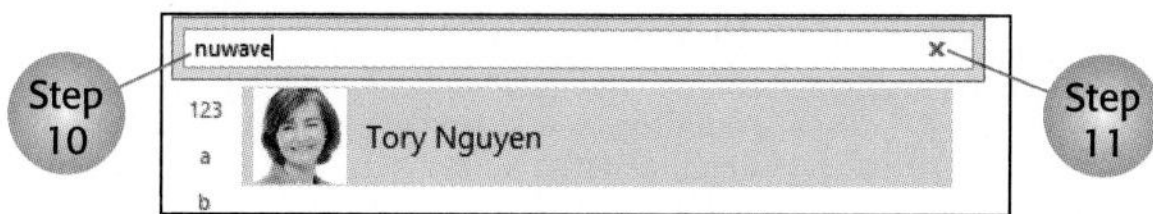

12 Display Tasks.

13 Tap or click in the *Search* text box at the top of the To-Do list (displays *Search To-Do List*) and type **ex**.

Outlook displays the task entry *Prepare study notes for exams*. Outlook can match items with only a partial entry for a word.

14 Tap or click the Close Search button to restore the To-Do list.

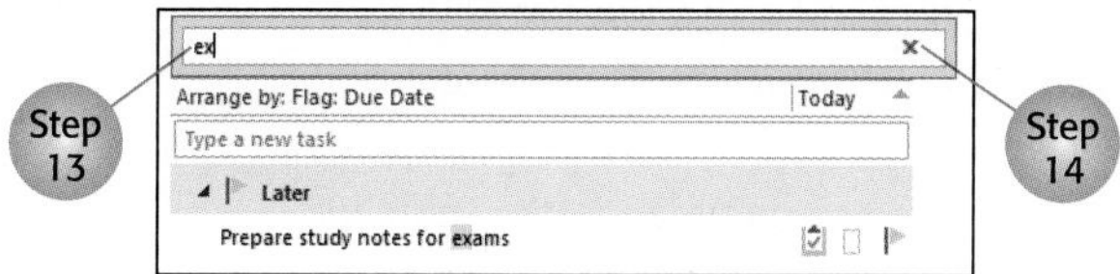

15 Display Mail with the Inbox folder.

16 Close Outlook.

Search for an Outlook Item

1. Display Mail, Calendar, People, or Tasks.
2. Tap or click in *Search* text box.
3. Type search keyword.

Other Search and Filter Techniques

The HOME tab in Mail, Calendar, People, and Tasks contains a *Search People* text box in the Find group. Use this text box to find a contact from any Outlook area. You can tap or click a person in the Search results list to view the contact information in a People card.

In Mail, the Find group also contains a Filter Email button. Use this button to filter the message list by categories such as *Unread, Has Attachments, Flagged,* or *Important*.

Concepts Review

Topic	Key Concepts	Key Terms
Using Outlook to Send Email	Microsoft Outlook 2013 is an application for organizing messages, appointments, contacts, and tasks and is referred to as a personal information management (PIM) program. Electronic mail (email) is the exchange of messages between individuals electronically. When you start Outlook for the first time, existing email account information is transferred to Outlook 2013 or you set up a new email account at the Add Account dialog box. When Outlook is started, Mail is the active application with the Inbox folder active. The Inbox displays email messages with the newest message received at the top of the Content pane. Create and send a new email message using the New Email button. Tap or click the message header for a new message received to read the message contents in the Reading pane. Reply directly to a message by tapping or clicking the Reply button in the Reading pane (referred to as an inline reply). Send a copy of a message you have received to someone else using the Forward button. A signature is a closing containing your name and other contact information that is inserted automatically at the end of each message.	Personal information management program (PIM) Electronic mail (email) Outlook 2013 Inbox New Email button Reply button Inline reply Forward button Signature
Attaching a File to a Message and Deleting Messages	Files are often exchanged between individuals via email messages. Attach a file to a message using the Attach File button in the Include group of the MESSAGE tab. As you type an email address in the *To* text box, the AutoComplete feature shows email addresses in a drop-down list that match what you are typing. Delete messages from mail folders that are no longer needed to keep folders to a manageable size. Deleted messages are moved to the Deleted Items folder. Empty the Deleted Items folder to permanently delete messages.	Attach File button AutoComplete Deleted Items

Topic	Key Concepts	Key Terms
Previewing File Attachments and Using File Attachment Tools	Preview a file attached to a message by tapping or clicking the file name in the Reading pane. While a file is being previewed, message text is temporarily removed from the Reading pane. Some files cannot be viewed in the Reading pane and must be viewed by double-tapping or double-clicking the file name. Open or Save a file using buttons in the Actions group of the ATTACHMENT TOOLS ATTACHMENTS tab. A file opened from an email message is opened in Protected view. Protected view allows you to read the contents, but you cannot edit the file until you tap or click the Enable Editing button in the Message bar. Certain types of files known to contain viruses are automatically blocked by Outlook.	Protected View
Scheduling Appointments and Events in Calendar	The Calendar is used to schedule appointments and events. An appointment is any activity for which you want to record the occurrence by day and time. A Date Navigator at the top of the Folder pane displays the current month with directional arrows to browse to the previous or next month. Use the Go To Date dialog box to display a specific date in the Appointment area of the Calendar. Tap or click next to the time in the Appointment area and type a description to enter a new appointment. A new appointment can also be entered in an Appointment window by tapping or clicking the New Appointment button. An event is an appointment that lasts an entire day or longer. Events appear in a banner along the top of the date in the Appointment area. Double-tap or double-click in the white space between the Appointment area and the date to enter a new event in an Event window.	Calendar Appointment Date Navigator Go To Date New Appointment button Event
Scheduling a Recurring Appointment and Editing an Appointment	An appointment that occurs at fixed intervals on a regular basis can be entered once, and Outlook schedules the remaining appointments automatically. Tap or click the Recurrence button to set the recurrence pattern and range of recurrence details for a recurring appointment. Select an appointment in the Appointment area to assign options or tags to the appointment in the CALENDAR TOOLS APPOINTMENT tab. Open the Appointment window to make changes to the subject, location, day, or time.	Recurrence

continued....

Topic	Key Concepts	Key Terms
Scheduling a Meeting	A meeting is an appointment in which you invite people that you want to attend the meeting. Information about a meeting is sent to people via a meeting request email message. Tap or click the New Meeting button to enter the email addresses for meeting attendees and the meeting particulars. A meeting attendee responds to a meeting request from the Reading pane or the message window by tapping or clicking respond buttons such as Accept. Meetings can be updated or canceled, and Outlook automatically informs all attendees via email messages.	Meeting Meeting request New Meeting button Accept button
Adding and Editing Contacts	Use the People tool to store and manage contact information for the people with whom you communicate in a People card. Tap or click the New Contact button or double-tap or double-click in a blank area of the People list to open a Contact window and add information to a People card. Tap or click the picture image control for a contact to select a picture of a contact in the Add Contact Picture dialog box. A contact's picture displays in the People card. The People card for a selected individual in the People list displays in the Reading pane. Tap or click *Edit* in the Reading pane or double-tap or double-click a person's name to edit the contact information in the People card.	People People Card New Contact button Add Contact Picture
Adding and Editing Tasks	Use Tasks in Outlook to maintain a To-Do list. Tap or click in the *Type a new task* text box to add a task to the To-Do list. Tap or click the New Task button to enter a new task in a Task window. Open a Task window to add a due date or to add other task information such as a priority or status. Select a task and use the Remove from List button when a task is completed. Open a task and use the Mark Complete button to indicate a task is completed; completed tasks are retained in the Task list but removed from the To-Do list.	Tasks To-Do List New Task button Remove from List Mark Complete
Searching Outlook Items	A *Search* text box appears at the top of Mail, Calendar, People, and Tasks in which you can quickly search for an item by typing a keyword or phrase. Outlook begins to match items as soon as you begin typing a search keyword. Matches to the search keyword are highlighted in the filtered lists. A *Search People* text box also appears in the Find group of the HOME tab in Mail, Calendar, People, and Tasks with which you can view the People card for an individual.	

Multiple Choice

1. This is the name of the default Mail folder that is active when Outlook is started.
   a. New Mail
   b. Inbox
   c. Sent Items
   d. Deleted Items
2. A reply typed directly from the Reading pane is referred to as a(n) ________ reply.
   a. direct
   b. instant
   c. inline
   d. quick
3. This button is used to send a copy of a presentation to someone via email.
   a. Attach PPT
   b. Attach Document
   c. Attachment
   d. Attach File
4. A deleted message is moved to this folder.
   a. Deleted Items
   b. Deleted Messages
   c. Deleted Mail
   d. Deletions
5. Preview a file sent by email in this pane.
   a. Folder pane
   b. Navigation pane
   c. Reading pane
   d. Content pane
6. Save a selected file received via email using the Save as button in this tab.
   a. ATTACHMENTS
   b. FILE
   c. VIEW
   d. MESSAGE
7. Open this dialog box to navigate to a specific date in the Calendar.
   a. Go To Date
   b. Go To Appointment
   c. Launch Date
   d. Date Navigator
8. An appointment that lasts an entire day is referred to as a(n) __________.
   a. event
   b. conference
   c. all-day appointment
   d. task
9. Use this button to set up an appointment that occurs on a regular basis at fixed intervals.
   a. Repeat
   b. Recurrence
   c. Manage Appointment
   d. Copy
10. Use buttons in this tab to add options or tags to a selected appointment.
    a. CALENDAR TOOLS OPTIONS
    b. CALENDAR TOOLS APPOINTMENT
    c. APPOINTMENT TOOLS OPTIONS
    d. APPOINTMENT TOOLS CALENDAR
11. An email message that invites you to an upcoming meeting is referred to as a(n) __________.
    a. attendance request
    b. meeting requirement
    c. meeting request
    d. meeting message
12. Tap or click this button to send a confirmation to the meeting organizer that you will attend a meeting.
    a. Tentative
    b. Accept
    c. Reply
    d. OK
13. Add a new contact to the People list using the New Contact button or by double-tapping or double-clicking in this pane.
    a. People list
    b. Reading pane
    c. Folder pane
    d. Navigation pane
14. Tap or click here to change a contact's telephone number in the Reading pane.
    a. Edit Source
    b. Edit
    c. Link Contacts
    d. What's New
15. A new task appears at the top of this list.
    a. Assignment list
    b. Job list
    c. Today list
    d. To-Do list
16. Use this button to indicate a task is completed but retain the task information in the Task list.
    a. Remove from List
    b. Mark Complete
    c. Delete
    d. Manage Task

17. This feature allows you to locate items in Outlook by typing a keyword.
    a. Find
    b. Search
    c. Filter
    d. Arrange

18. Tap or click this button to remove a filtered list after finding an item that matched your keyword.
    a. Close Arrange
    b. Close Filter
    c. Close Search
    d. Close Find

Crossword Puzzle

ACROSS

4 Button in Mail that starts source application to view attached file
5 Activity you want to track in Calendar
7 Button to set up a repeating activity in Calendar
9 Where deleted messages are moved
10 Tool to locate items in Outlook by keyword
13 Navigation pane option to maintain To-Do list
14 Button to respond to an email message
15 All-day activity entered in Calendar

DOWN

1 Attached files opened in the source application display in this view
2 Option to delete an item from the To-Do list
3 Send copy of email message to someone else
6 Button to schedule meeting
8 A file sent with an email message
11 Navigation pane option to view contacts
12 Where to find a meeting request

Matching

Match the term with the statement or definition.

_______ 1. Personal Information Management (PIM)
_______ 2. Signature
_______ 3. Empty Folder
_______ 4. Reading pane
_______ 5. Calendar
_______ 6. Meeting
_______ 7. People
_______ 8. Tasks

a. Option to permanently delete messages
b. Preview a file attachment
c. Appointment with email addresses
d. To-Do list
e. Contacts
f. Microsoft Outlook
g. Message closing text
h. Scheduling

Project 1 Open an Outlook Data File and Add and Edit Items

Individual

Deliverable: Updated Outlook Data File (continued in Project 2)

1. Create a new folder named *Ch5* in the ChapterProjectsWork folder on your USB flash drive.
2. Start Outlook 2013 and make sure the Folder pane and Reading pane are displayed.
3. Open an existing Outlook data file with Outlook items by completing the following steps:
   a. Tap or click FILE and then tap or click Open & Export.
   b. Tap or click Open Outlook Data File.
   c. At the Open Outlook Data File dialog box, navigate to the Ch5 folder in the Student_Data_Files folder on your USB flash drive and double-tap or double-click the file named ***Ch5-OutlookPracticeData***. (A new entry appears in the Folder pane below your current mail folders with the title *Ch5-OutlookPracticeData*.)
4. Tap or click the white right-pointing arrow next to **Ch5-OutlookPracticeData** in the Folder pane to expand the folder list, and tap or click the black diagonal downward-pointing arrow next to your email address (or your Outlook user name) in the Folder pane to collapse the folder list. (The Folder pane now should show only the mail folders in the new data file opened at Step 3.)

Note: For the remaining steps in this project and the next project, complete all tasks using the folders in the expanded folder list for Ch5-OutlookPracticeData.

5. Make Inbox active to view the two messages and forward each message to yourself (use your email address) with the message text *Here is a copy of the message from (enter sender's name in the original message)*.
6. Display all of the other folders in the data file by selecting the three dots in the Navigation pane and choosing *Folders* at the pop-up list. If necessary, collapse again the list of folders for your regular email account.
7. Tap or click Calendar in the Folder pane and display October 12, 2015 in the Appointment area. Make the following changes to appointments in the Calendar (respond Yes to any messages that appear about reminders):
   a. On Monday, October 12, add *Room A-109* as the appointment location.
   b. Change the lunch with Taylor Gorski from Tuesday, October 13 to Wednesday, October 14 at 1:00 p.m.
   c. Make the doctor appointment on Wednesday, October 14, 1.5 hours in duration.
   d. Make the Health and Safety Training on Thursday, October 15 a recurring appointment at the same day and time for three weeks.
8. Tap or click Contacts in the Folder pane, and make the following changes to the People list:
   a. Change the *Work* telephone number for Xavier Borman to *888-555-4523*.
   b. Change the *Title* for Taylor Gorski to *President & CEO*.
   c. Add a new person to the People list with the following contact information and add a picture using the file named ***LuisPhillips*** in the Ch5 folder in Student_Data_Files:
      Luis Phillips, NewAge Advertising, Sales Representative, luis@emcp.net
9. Tap or click Tasks in the Folder pane and make the following changes:
   a. Remove the task *Find volunteers to help at conference* from the To-Do list.
   b. Mark the task *Update project wiki pages* completed.
   c. Change the due date for the task *Research click marketing strategies* to October 22, 2015.
   d. Add the following new tasks:
      Compile report from volunteer survey
      Return equipment rented for conference
10. Leave Outlook open if you are continuing to Project 2; otherwise, press and hold or right-click ***Ch5-OutlookPracticeData*** and choose *Close "Ch5-OutlookPracticeData"* at the shortcut menu; then close Outlook and submit the project to your instructor in the manner she or he has instructed.

Project 2 Sending Outlook Items to a OneNote Notebook and Creating a PDF

Individual

Deliverable: Page in OneNote notebook and PDF with Outlook Items Completed in Project 1

Note: You must have completed Project 4 in Chapter 4 and Project 1 in this chapter before starting this project.

1. Start OneNote 2013 and open the MyProjects notebook created in Chapter 4, Project 4.
2. Switch to Outlook and make Calendar active. Display October 12, 2015 in the Appointment area and send the calendar to your OneNote notebook by completing the following steps:
   a. Tap or click the Month button in the Arrange group of the HOME tab.
   b. Display the Print tab Backstage view and change the Printer to *Send to OneNote 2013*.
   c. Tap or click the Print button.
   d. Switch to OneNote 2013 using the button on the Taskbar.
   e. At the Select Location in OneNote dialog box, tap or click the plus symbol next to *Outlook* in the section list for the MyProjects-YourName notebook and tap or click *Chapter 5*. Tap or click OK. (The Calendar will appear on the Chapter 5 page in OneNote.)
3. Switch to Outlook and display the Contacts folder. Send the People list to your OneNote notebook by completing steps similar to those in Steps 2b to 2e. Accept the default *Card Style* format for the print *Settings*.
4. Switch to Outlook and display the Tasks folder. Send the Task list to your OneNote notebook by completing steps similar to those in Steps 2b to 2e.
5. Switch to Outlook. Press and hold or right-click *Ch5-OutlookPracticeData* in the Folder pane and tap or click *Close "Ch5-OutlookPracticeData"*.
6. Tap or click the white right-pointing arrow next to your email address (or your Outlook user name) to expand the folder list.
7. Make Inbox active and tap or click Send/Receive All Folders if necessary to update the message list.
8. Open the first message window for the message you forwarded to yourself in Project 1, Step 5. Send a copy of the message to your OneNote notebook by completing steps similar to those in Steps 2b to 2e and then close the message window. Accept the default *Memo Style* format.
9. Switch to Outlook and repeat Step 8 for the second message you forwarded to yourself in Project 1, Step 5.
10. With OneNote open and the Chapter 5 page in the *Outlook* section active, display the Export tab Backstage view. With *Page* selected by default in the *Export Current* section, select *PDF (*.pdf)* in the *Select Format* section and choose *Export*. Navigate to the Ch5 folder in the ChapterProjectsWork folder on your USB flash drive. Type **C5-Project2-Your Name** in the *File name* text box and tap or click the Save button.
11. Leave OneNote open if you are continuing to Project 3; otherwise, close the notebook and close OneNote.
12. In Outlook, tap or click Mail in the Navigation pane to restore the Folder pane to the default folder list that displays mail folders only.
13. Leave Outlook open if you are continuing to Project 3; otherwise, close Outlook and submit the project to your instructor in the manner she or he has requested.

Project 3 Organizing Your School Activities in Outlook

Individual
Deliverable: Page in OneNote notebook and PDF with New Outlook Items

1. In OneNote, create a new page in the *Outlook* section with the title *Project 3*.
2. Switch to Outlook, make Calendar active, and make sure the current date is displayed. Create appointments for your class schedule for all of the courses you are currently taking as recurring appointments in the calendar for the remainder of the current semester.
3. Add other appointments to your Outlook calendar for any other school activities that you want to attend. For example, add an appointment or event for any extracurricular school activity.
4. Make People active and add your teacher's contact information to the People list.
5. Make Tasks active and create in the To-Do list a task entry for each upcoming project and assignment (including due dates) of which you are aware in each of the courses you are currently taking.
6. Send the calendar in Month view, the People list in Card Style, and the To-Do list to the Project 3 page in the *Outlook* section of your OneNote notebook.
7. Create a PDF of the Project 3 page in your OneNote notebook, saving the PDF in the Ch5 folder in the ChapterProjectsWork folder on your USB flash drive with the name **C5-Project3-Your Name**.
8. Close your MyProjects notebook in OneNote and close OneNote.
9. Close Outlook.
10. Submit the project to your instructor in the manner she or he has requested.

Chapter 6

Creating, Editing, and Formatting Documents Using Word

After successfully completing this chapter, you will be able to:

- Create and edit a new document
- Insert and delete text
- Insert symbols and special characters
- Check spelling and grammar
- Find and replace text
- Move text
- Insert bullets and numbering
- Format text using font options
- Change paragraph alignment, indent, and spacing
- Choose a Style Set and apply styles
- Create a new document from a template

Microsoft Word (referred to as Word) is a **word processing application** used to create documents that are composed mostly of text for personal, business, or school purposes. Word documents can also include pictures, charts, tables, or other visual elements to make the document more interesting and easier to understand. Examples of the types of documents you might create in Word are letters, essays, reports, invitations, recipes, agendas, contracts, and resumes. Any type of document that you need to create that is mostly text can easily be generated using Word.

Word automatically corrects some errors as you type and indicates other potential spelling and grammar errors for you to consider. Other features provide tools to format and enhance a document. In this chapter you will learn how to create, edit, and format documents. You will create new documents starting from a blank page and other documents by selecting from Word's template gallery.

Note: If you are using a tablet, consider completing this chapter using a USB or wireless keyboard because you will be typing longer passages of text.

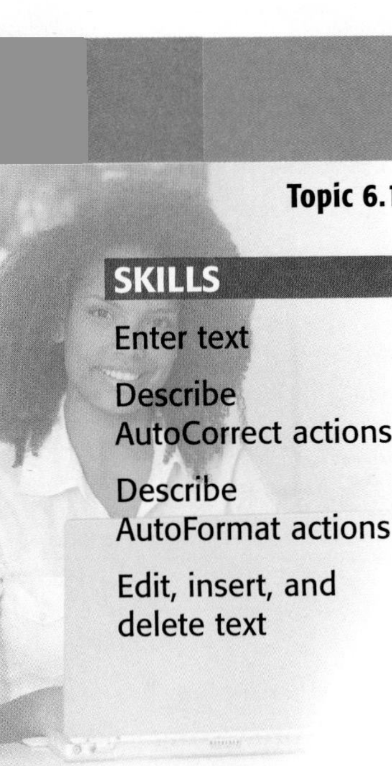

Topic 6.1

SKILLS

- Enter text
- Describe AutoCorrect actions
- Describe AutoFormat actions
- Edit, insert, and delete text

Creating and Editing a New Document

Recall from Chapter 3 that when Microsoft Word starts, you are presented with the Word Start screen from which you choose to open an existing document, create a new blank document, or search for and select a template to create a new document. Generally, creating a new blank document involves typing the document text, editing the text, and correcting errors. As you type, Word's AutoCorrect and AutoFormat features help you fix common typing errors and format common characters.

1. Start Word 2013.
2. At the Word Start screen, tap or click *Blank document* in the *Templates* gallery and compare your screen with the one shown in Figure 6.1.

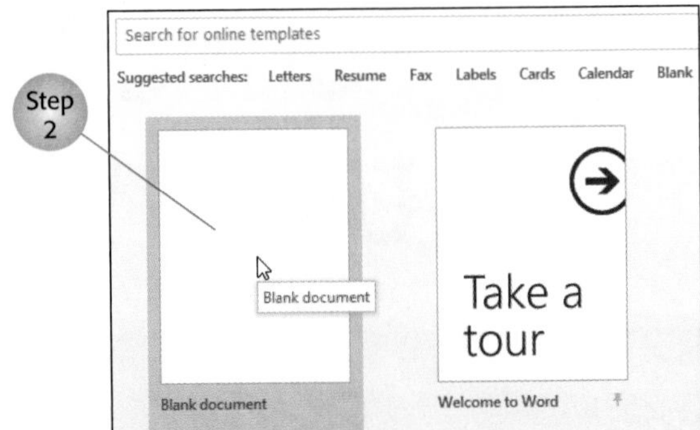

If necessary, review the ribbon interface and QAT described in Chapter 3. Table 6.1 describes the elements shown in Figure 6.1.

3. Type **Social Bookmarking** and tap or press Enter.

Notice that extra space is automatically added below the text before the next line.

4. Type the text on the next page allowing the lines to end automatically; tap or press Enter only where indicated.

Word will move text to a new line automatically when you reach the end of the current line. This feature is called **wordwrap**. Word will also put a red wavy line

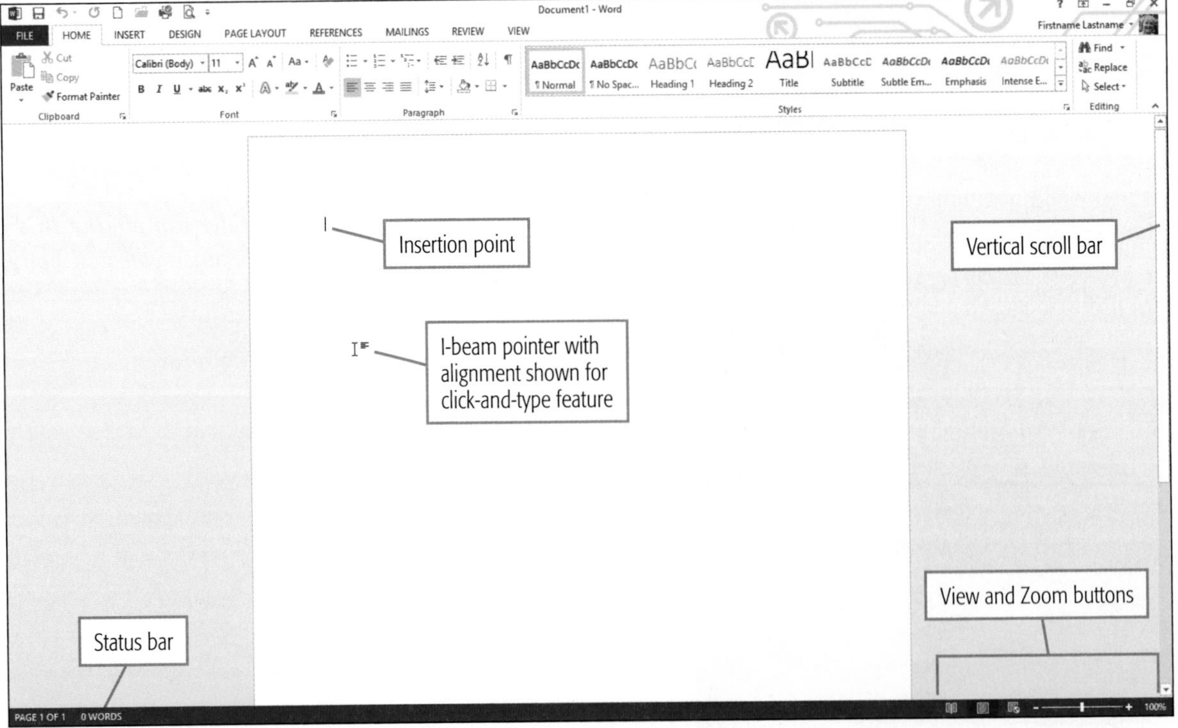

Figure 6.1 A new blank document screen. Word's default settings show a new document in Print Layout view and with rulers turned off; your display may vary if settings have been changed on the computer you are using. See Table 6.1 for a description of screen elements.

Table 6.1	Word Features
Feature	Description
Insertion point	Blinking vertical bar indicates where the next character typed will appear.
I-beam pointer	Pointer appearance for text entry or selection when you move the pointer using a mouse or trackpad. The I-beam pointer displays with a paragraph alignment option (left, center, or right) depending on the location of the I-beam within the current line. You can double-tap or double-click and type text anywhere on a page and the alignment option will be left-aligned, center-aligned, or right-aligned. This feature is called **click and type**.
Status bar	Displays page number with total number of pages and number of words in the current document. The right end of the Status bar has view and zoom options. The default view is Print Layout view, which shows how a page will look when printed with current print options.
Vertical scroll bar	Use the scroll bar to view parts of a document not shown in the current window.
View and Zoom buttons	By default, Word opens in Print Layout view. Other view buttons include Read Mode and Web Layout view. Read Mode is a new view in Word 2013 that maximizes reading space and removes editing tools, providing a more natural environment for reading. Zoom buttons, as you learned in Chapter 3, are used to enlarge or shrink the display.

below the word *bookmarklet*. Red wavy lines below words indicate words that are not found in Word's dictionary, indicating a possible spelling error. Correct typing mistakes as you go using the Backspace key to delete the character just typed and then retype the correct character. You will learn other editing methods later in this topic.

> **Social bookmarking websites are used to organize, save, and share web content. Links are called bookmarks and include tags, which are keywords you assign to the content when you create the bookmark.** [Tap or press Enter]
>
> **Many websites now include icons for popular social bookmarking sites that capture the page references for bookmarking. Another way to bookmark a page is to add the bookmarklet for the social bookmarking site you use to your browser's toolbar. Bookmarklets add a bookmark instantly when clicked.** [Tap or press Enter]

AutoCorrect also fixes common capitalization errors such as two initial capitals, no capital at the beginning of a sentence, and no capital in the name of a day. AutoCorrect also turns off the Caps Lock key and corrects text when a new sentence is started with the key left on. Use Undo if AutoCorrect changes text that you don't want changed.

5 Type **teh** and tap or press the spacebar. Notice that Word changes the text to *The*.

A feature called **AutoCorrect** changes commonly misspelled words as soon as you press the spacebar.

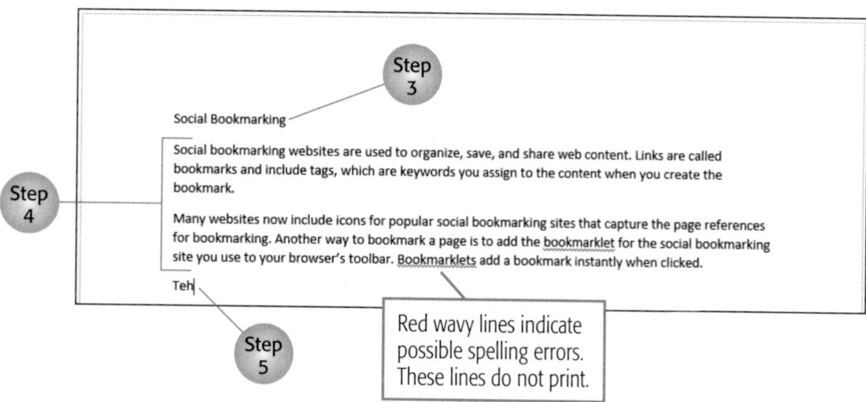

6. Type **popular social bookmarking site Pinterest.com is used to pin pictures found on the Web to virtual pinboards.** and tap or press Enter.
7. Type **a study by a marketing company found that 1/2 of frequent web surfers use a social bookmarking site, with Pinterest the 1st choice for most females.** and tap or press Enter.

Notice that Word automatically corrects the capitalization of the first word in the sentence, 1/2 is changed to a fraction character (½), and 1st is automatically formatted as an ordinal with the st shown as superscript text (superscript characters are smaller text placed at the top of the line). The **AutoFormat** feature automatically changes some fractions, ordinals, quotes, hyphens, and hyperlinks as you type. AutoFormat also converts straight apostrophes (') or quotation marks (") to smart quotes ('smart quotes'), also called curly quotes ("curly quotes").

App Tip

AutoFormat does not recognize all fractions. For example, typing 1/3 will not format to the one-third fraction character. You will learn about inserting symbols for these characters in the next topic.

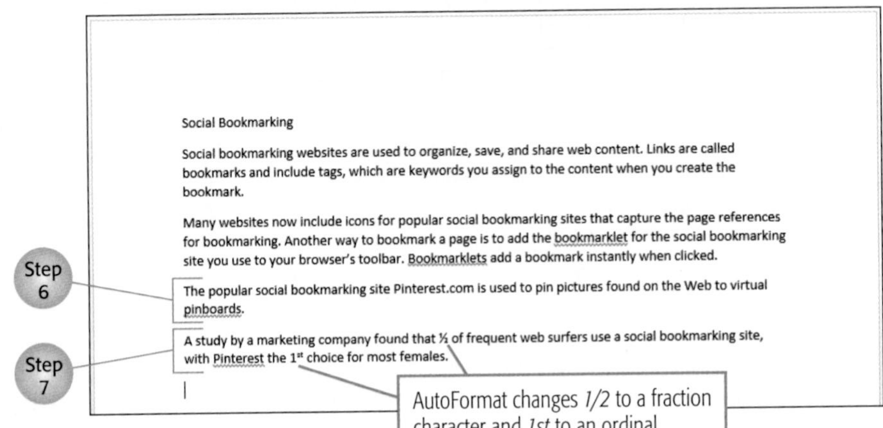

Social Bookmarking

Social bookmarking websites are used to organize, save, and share web content. Links are called bookmarks and include tags, which are keywords you assign to the content when you create the bookmark.

Many websites now include icons for popular social bookmarking sites that capture the page references for bookmarking. Another way to bookmark a page is to add the bookmarklet for the social bookmarking site you use to your browser's toolbar. Bookmarklets add a bookmark instantly when clicked.

The popular social bookmarking site Pinterest.com is used to pin pictures found on the Web to virtual pinboards.

A study by a marketing company found that ½ of frequent web surfers use a social bookmarking site, with Pinterest the 1st choice for most females.

Step 6
Step 7
AutoFormat changes *1/2* to a fraction character and *1st* to an ordinal.

8. Tap or click the Save button on the QAT.

Because this is the first time the document has been saved, the Save As Backstage view appears.

9. Tap or click *Computer* and tap or click the Browse button.
10. At the Save As dialog box, navigate to the CompletedTopicsByChapter folder on your USB flash drive and create a new folder named *Ch6*.
11. Double-tap or double-click the *Ch6* folder name.
12. Select the current text in the *File name* text box, type **6.1-SocialMediaProject-Your Name**, and tap or press Enter or tap or click the Save button.

Many times when you are creating a new document, you need to make changes to the text after the text has been typed. In some cases, you need to correct typing errors you did not notice as you typed, you want to change a word or phrase to some other text, you want to add new text, or you want to remove some text. A change made to a document after the document has been typed is called **editing**. The first step to edit text is to move the insertion point to the location where you want to make a change.

13. Tap or click to position the insertion point at the beginning of the last paragraph that begins with the text *A study by a marketing company* (insertion point will be blinking just left of *A*), type **Experian Hitwise**, and press the spacebar.

Step 13

Experian Hitwise A study by a marketing company found that ½ of frequent web surfers use a social bookmarking site, with Pinterest the 1st choice for most females.

Word automatically inserts the new text and moves existing text to the right.

14 With the insertion point still positioned at the left of *A* in *A study*, press the Delete key until you have removed *A study by*, type (, tap or click to position the insertion point just after the *y* in *company*, and then type) **conducted a survey of frequent web surfers and**.

15 Position the insertion point just left of ½, press the Delete key until you have removed *½ of frequent web surfers*, and then type **one-half**.

16 Position the insertion point at the left of *1st*, delete *1st*, and then type **first**.

17 Position the insertion point below the last paragraph and type your first and last name.

18 Check your text with the document shown in Figure 6.2. If necessary, make further corrections by moving the insertion point and inserting and deleting text as needed.

Social Bookmarking

Social bookmarking websites are used to organize, save, and share web content. Links are called bookmarks and include tags, which are keywords you assign to the content when you create the bookmark.

Many websites now include icons for popular social bookmarking sites that capture the page references for bookmarking. Another way to bookmark a page is to add the bookmarklet for the social bookmarking site you use to your browser's toolbar. Bookmarklets add a bookmark instantly when clicked.

The popular social bookmarking site Pinterest.com is used to pin pictures found on the Web to virtual pinboards.

Experian Hitwise (a marketing company) conducted a survey of frequent web surfers and found that one-half use a social bookmarking site, with Pinterest the first choice for most females.

Student Name

Figure 6.2 Document text for 6.1-SocialMediaProject-Student Name

19 Tap or click the Save button on the QAT. Leave the document open for the next topic.

Because the document has already been assigned a file name at Step 12, the Save button saves the document's changes using the same name.

You can also move the insertion point by pressing the Right arrow key on the keyboard. Use the Up, Down, Left, or Right arrow keys to move within a document. Hold down an arrow key to rapidly move the insertion point.

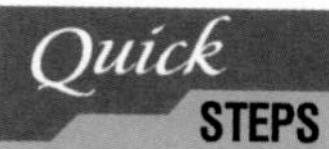

Create a New Document
1. Start Word 2013.
2. Tap or click *Blank document*.
3. Type text.

Save a New Document
1. Tap or click Save button on QAT.
2. Navigate to drive and/or folder.
3. Enter file name.
4. Tap or click Save.

Save a Document Using the Existing Name
Tap or click Save button on QAT.

Edit a Document
1. Position insertion point at location of change.
2. Type new text or delete text as needed.
3. Save changes.

Line Breaks versus New Paragraphs

As you have learned in this topic, you press Enter only at the end of a short line of text (such as the title) or at the end of a paragraph. Pressing Enter is referred to as inserting a **hard return** and in Word creates a new paragraph. By default, line spacing in Word 2013 is set to 1.08, and 8 points of space is added after each paragraph. A point is a measurement system in which 1 point is equal to about 1/72 of an inch in height. Think of 8 points as approximately .11 of an inch of space added after each hard return.

If you want to end a short line of text and do not want an extra 8-point space added after the line, use the **Line Break** command Shift + Enter (hold down the Shift key while pressing Enter). A line break moves to the next line without creating a new paragraph. For example, use Shift + Enter when typing an address in a letter.

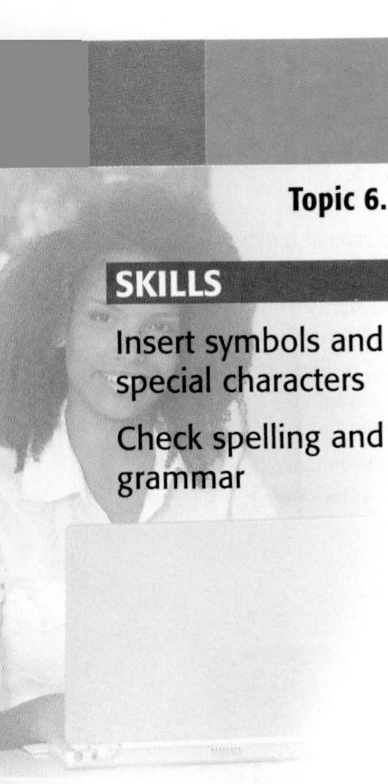

Topic 6.2

SKILLS

Insert symbols and special characters

Check spelling and grammar

Inserting Symbols and Completing a Spelling and Grammar Check

In some documents you need to insert a symbol or special character such as a copyright symbol (©), registered trademark (™), or a fraction character for a fraction that AutoCorrect does not recognize such as one-third (⅓). Symbols and special characters are inserted using the ***Symbol* gallery** or the Symbol dialog box.

The **Spelling & Grammar** button in the REVIEW tab starts Word's Spelling and Grammar feature, which is used to review a document and correct spelling and grammar errors.

1. With the **6.1-SocialMediaProject-Your Name** document open, position the insertion point after *n* in *Experian* in the last paragraph.

Experian is a registered trademark, so you will add the registered trademark symbol after the name.

2. Tap or click the INSERT tab.
3. Tap or click the Symbol button in the Symbols group.
4. Tap or click *Trade Mark Sign* at the *Symbol* gallery.

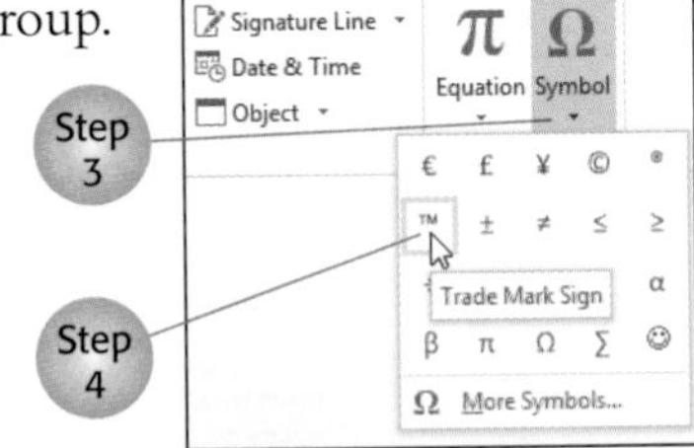

5. Position the insertion point after the period at the end of the paragraph that begins *Experian* and press the spacebar to insert a space.
6. Type **The survey sample size of 1,000 interviews provides a standard error at 95% confidence of** and press the spacebar.
7. Tap or click the Symbol button and tap or click *More Symbols* at the *Symbol* gallery.

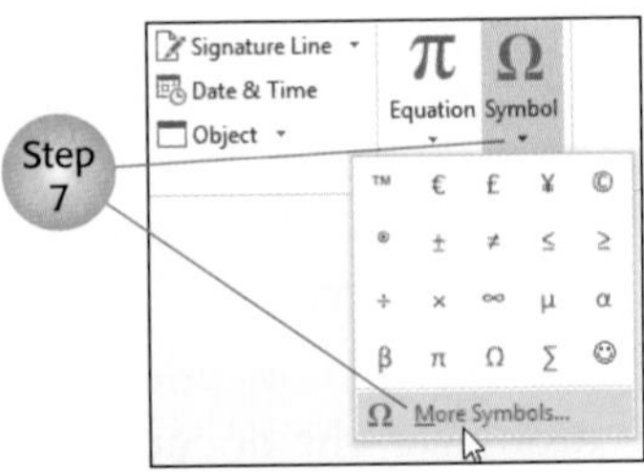

8. At the Symbol dialog box, with *Font* set to *(normal text)*, and *Subset* set to *Basic Latin*, scroll down the symbol list as needed, tap or click ±, and tap or click Insert.

oops!

Different font and/or subset? Use the *Font* or *Subset* list arrow to change the option to *(normal text)* and *Basic Latin* if the Symbol dialog box has different settings.

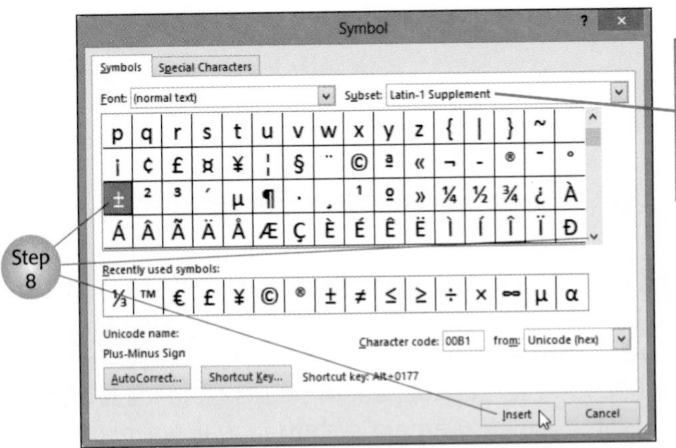

The *Subset* changes to *Latin-1 Supplement* when you select the plus-minus symbol in the symbol list.

9. Tap or click Close to return to the document and then type **3%.**.

You may have noticed the Plus-Minus Sign symbol is also available in the *Symbol* gallery. In Steps 7 to 9 you practiced using the Symbol dialog box so that you will know how to find a symbol that is not in the drop-down gallery.

The Spelling feature works by matching words in the document with words in a dictionary. Words that have no match are flagged as errors, and the Spelling task pane opens at the right side of the window with suggestions for the word not found and buttons to ignore, change, or add the word.

Word's Spelling feature also checks for duplicate words and presents the option to automatically remove the repeated word. Spelling and Grammar helps you correct many errors; however, you still need to proofread your documents. For example, the errors in the following sentence escaped detection: The plain fair was expensive!

10 Tap or click the REVIEW tab and then tap or click the Spelling & Grammar button in the Proofing group.

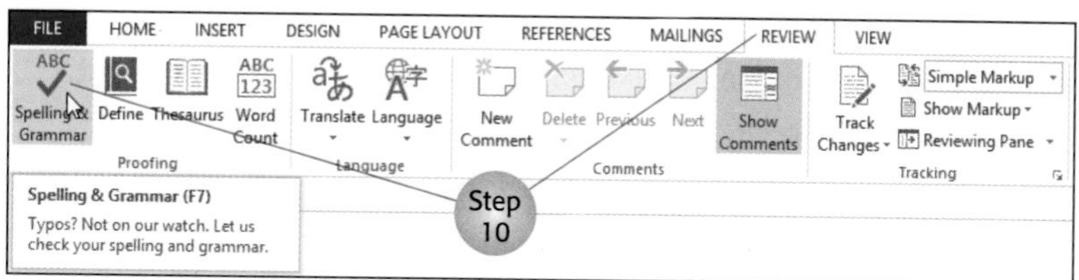

11 When the word *bookmarklet* is selected, tap or click the Ignore All button in the Spelling task pane.

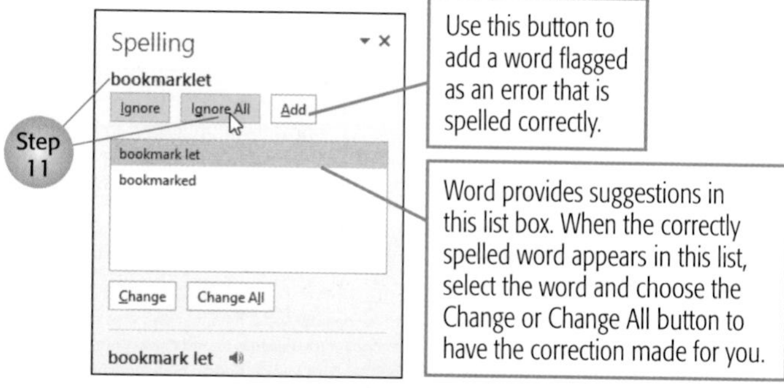

12 When the word *bookmarklets* is selected, tap or click the Ignore All button in the Spelling task pane.

13 Choose Ignore when *pinboards* is selected.

14 Choose Ignore when *Hitwise* is selected.

15 Choose Ignore when *Pinterest* is selected.

16 Tap or click OK at the message that the spelling and grammar check is complete.

17 Save the document using the same name. Leave the document open for the next topic.

ALTERNATIVE method

Consider using the following typing alternatives to insert a symbol:

Type *(c)* to have AutoCorrect insert the copyright symbol ©

Type *(r)* to have AutoCorrect insert the registered symbol ®

Type *(tm)* to have AutoCorrect insert the registered trademark symbol ™

To view the complete list of AutoCorrect entries, tap or click the FILE tab, then choose Options, *Proofing* (left pane of Word Options dialog box), and the AutoCorrect Options button.

Press and hold or right-click a word with a red wavy line to view suggested replacements in a shortcut menu. You can also instruct Word to *Ignore All* or *Add to Dictionary* at the shortcut menu.

Spell check stopped at a different word? Respond to other errors as needed to correct variations that have occurred when you typed the document text in the previous topic.

Quick STEPS

Insert Symbol from Symbol Dialog Box

1. Position insertion point.
2. Tap or click INSERT tab.
3. Tap or click Symbol button.
4. Tap or click *More Symbols*.
5. If necessary, change font or subset.
6. Scroll down to locate symbol.
7. Tap or click symbol.
8. Tap or click Insert button.
9. Tap or click Close button.

Perform a Spelling and Grammar Check

1. Tap or click REVIEW tab.
2. Tap or click Spelling & Grammar button.
3. Ignore, Ignore All, Add, Change, or Change All as needed.
4. Tap or click OK.

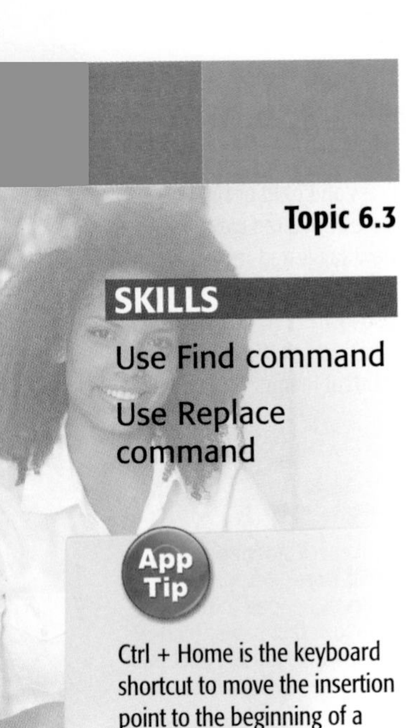

Topic 6.3

SKILLS

Use Find command

Use Replace command

App Tip

Ctrl + Home is the keyboard shortcut to move the insertion point to the beginning of a document.

Finding and Replacing Text

The Find and Replace features move the insertion point to each occurrence of a word or phrase (**Find**), or automatically change each occurrence of a word or phrase to something else (**Replace**). Find is helpful if, for example, you think you have overused a particular term. Replace makes short work of editing a document if a word or phrase needs to be changed throughout.

1. With the **6.1-SocialMediaProject-Your Name** document open, position the insertion point at the beginning of the document.
2. Tap or click the HOME tab.
3. Tap or click the Find button in the Editing group.

This opens the Navigation pane at the left side of the Word document window.

Step 3: Find (Ctrl+F) Find text or other content in the document.

4. Type **social bookmarking** in the *Search* box.

When you finish typing, Word highlights in the document all of the occurrences of the search word or phrase and displays the search results below the *Search* box. The total number of occurrences appears at the top of the RESULTS list. Each entry in the search results list is a link that moves to the search word location in the document when tapped or clicked (Figure 6.3).

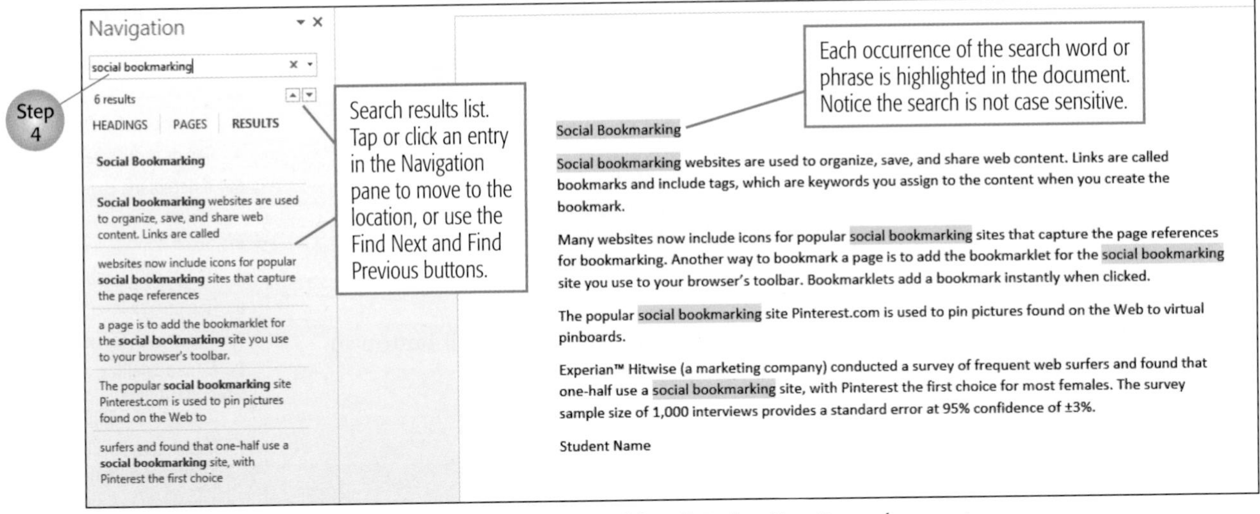

Figure 6.3 Search results for *social bookmarking* in 6.1-SocialMediaProject-Your Name document

App Tip

You can find text using a partial word search. For example, entering *exp* would find *Experian*, *expert*, and *experience*. Use partial word searches if you are not sure of correct spelling.

5. Tap or click each entry one at a time in the RESULTS list in the Navigation pane.

Notice that each occurrence of the search word is selected as you move to the phrase location.

6. Tap or click the Close button at the top right of the Navigation pane to close the pane.

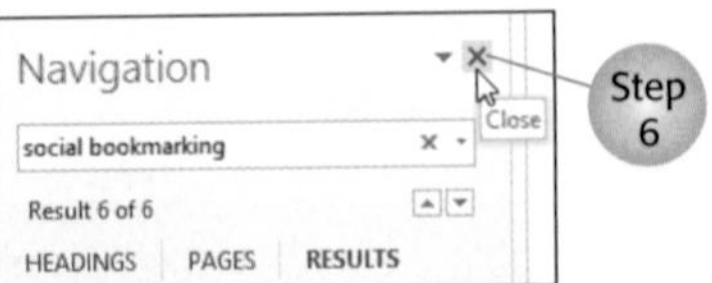

7 Position the insertion point at the beginning of the document.

8 Tap or click the Replace button in the Editing group of the HOME tab.

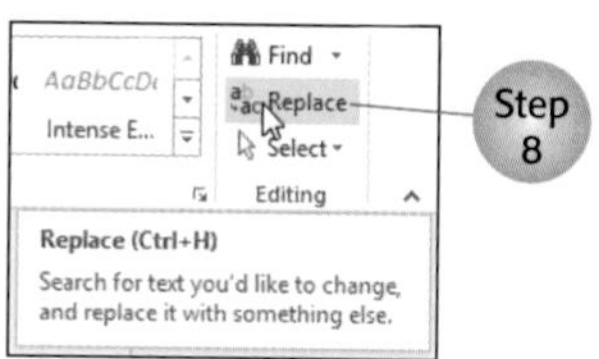

Find and Replace searches start from the location of the insertion point.

9 At the Find and Replace dialog box, with *social bookmarking* selected in the *Find what* text box, type **bookmarklet**.

10 Tap or press Tab, or tap or click in the *Replace with* text box and type **bookmark button**.

11 Tap or click the Replace All button.

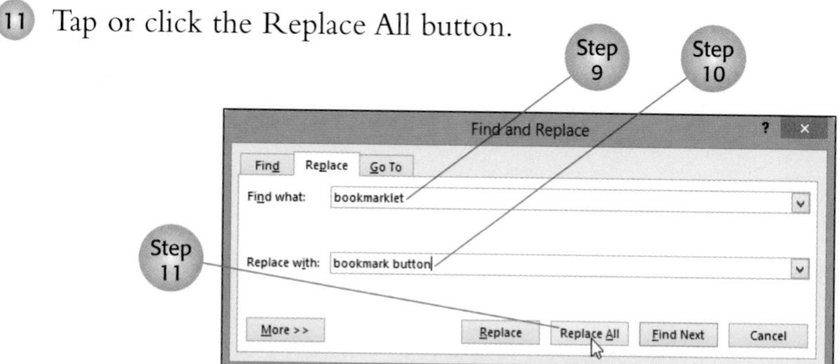

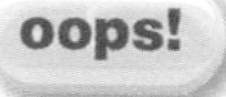

No replacements made? Tap or click OK and check your spelling in the *Find what* text box. Correct the text and try Replace All again. Still have 0 replacements? Cancel the Replace command and check the spelling of *bookmarklet* within your document. Correct the text in the document and repeat Steps 8 to 12.

12 Tap or click OK at the message that 2 replacements were made.

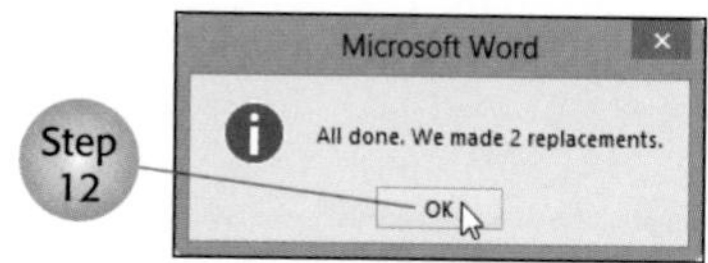

Find Text
1. Position insertion point at beginning of document.
2. Tap or click Find button.
3. Type search text.

Replace Text
1. Position insertion point at beginning of document.
2. Tap or click Replace button.
3. Type *Find what* text.
4. Tap or press Tab, or tap or click in *Replace with* text box.
5. Type replacement text.
6. Tap or click Replace All.
7. Tap or click OK.
8. Tap or click Close button.

13 Tap or click the Close button to close the Find and Replace dialog box.

Notice that Word matches the correct case of a word when the word is replaced at the beginning of a sentence, as seen in the last sentence of the paragraph that begins with *Many websites now include*.

14 Save the document using the same name. Leave the document open for the next topic.

Using the Thesaurus to Replace a Word

Sometimes when you find yourself overusing a word, you are stuck for an alternative word to use in its place in one or two occurrences. Consider using the **Thesaurus** to help you find a word with a similar meaning. Thesaurus is located in the Proofing group of the REVIEW tab. Position the insertion point anywhere within a word you want to change and start the Thesaurus. Point to a word in the results list in the Thesaurus task pane and use the down-pointing arrow that appears at the end of a highlighted word to choose *Insert*.

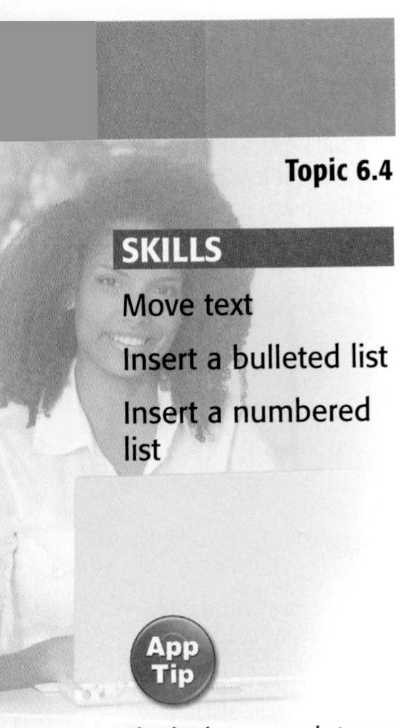

Topic 6.4

SKILLS

- Move text
- Insert a bulleted list
- Insert a numbered list

App Tip

The dot that appears between words with hidden formatting symbols displayed indicates you pressed the spacebar.

oops!

Forgot how to select text? Refer to Topic 3.4 in Chapter 3 for help with selecting text and objects.

Moving Text and Inserting Bullets and Numbering

In Chapter 3 you learned how to use the Copy, Paste, and Format Painter buttons in the Clipboard group of the HOME tab. In this topic you will use the Cut button to move a selection. Bulleted and numbered lists are used to set apart information that is structured in short phrases or sentences. Bullets set apart a list of items that are entered in no particular sequence. A numbered list is used for a sequential list of tasks, items, or other text.

1. With the **6.1-SocialMediaProject-Your Name** document open, position the insertion point at the beginning of the paragraph that begins with *The popular social bookmarking site.*

2. Tap or click the Show/Hide button in the Paragraph group of the HOME tab.

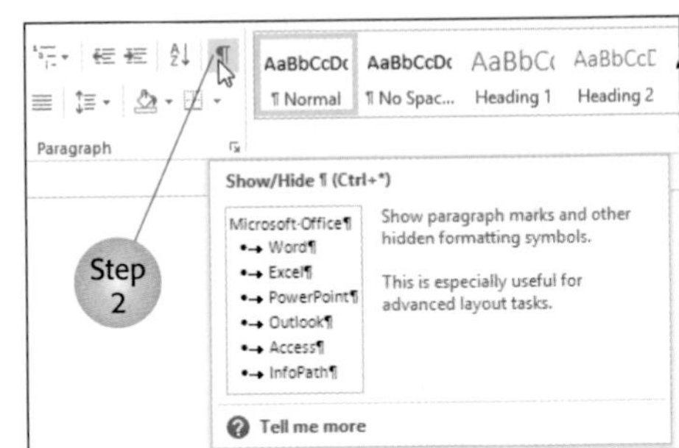

Show/Hide turns on the display of hidden formatting symbols. For example, each time you tap or press Enter, a paragraph symbol (¶) is inserted in the document. Revealing these symbols is helpful when you are preparing to move or copy text because you often want to make sure you move or copy the paragraph symbol with the paragraph.

3. Select the paragraph *The popular social bookmarking site Pinterest.com is used to pin pictures found on the Web to virtual pinboards.* Make sure to include the paragraph formatting symbol at the end of the text in the selection.

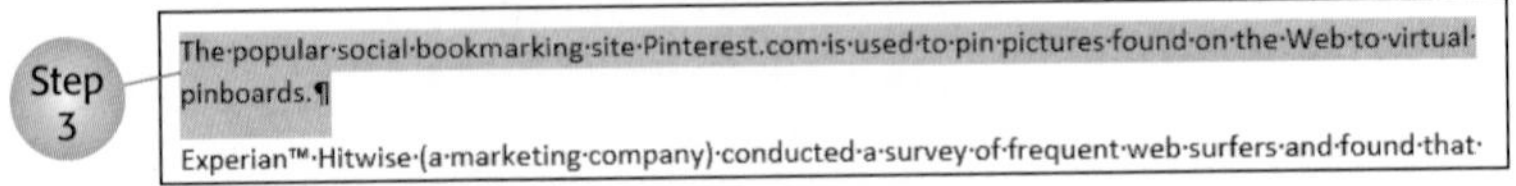

4. Tap or click the Cut button in the Clipboard group of the HOME tab.

The text is removed from the current location and placed in the Clipboard.

5. Position the insertion point at the beginning of the paragraph that begins with *Many websites now include.*

Step 6 · Step 4 — FILE | HOME | INSERT | DESIGN · Cut · Copy · Paste · Format Painter · Clipboard · Calibri (Body) · Cut (Ctrl+X) · Remove the selection and put it on the Clipboard so you can paste it somewhere else.

6. Tap or click the top of the Paste button in the Clipboard group (do *not* tap or click the down-pointing arrow on the button).

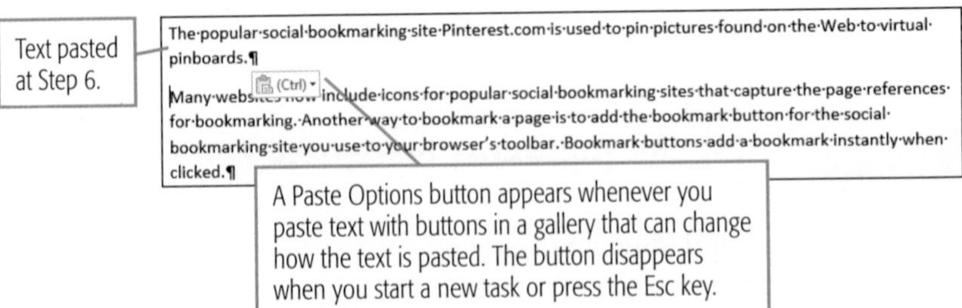

7. Tap or click the Show/Hide button to turn off the display of hidden formatting symbols.

8 Position the insertion point after the period that ends the sentence *The popular social networking site Pinterest.com is used to pin pictures found on the Web to virtual pinboards*, press the spacebar, type **Other social bookmarking sites include:**, and then tap or press Enter.

9 Tap or click the left part of the **Bullets button** in the Paragraph group of the HOME tab (do *not* tap or click the down-pointing arrow on the button).

Step 9

Paragraph

Bullets

Create a bulleted list.

Click the arrow to change the look of the bullet.

This indents and inserts the default bullet character, which is a solid round bullet.

10 Type **StumbleUpon.com** and tap or press Enter.

11 Type **Delicious.com** and tap or press Enter.

12 Type **Digg.com** and tap or press Enter.

13 Type **Reddit.com**.

Steps 10-13

The popular social bookmarking site Pinterest.com is used pinboards. Other social bookmarking sites include:

- StumbleUpon.com
- Delicious.com
- Digg.com
- Reddit.com

Many websites now include icons for popular social bookm

14 Position the insertion point after the period that ends the sentence *Bookmark buttons add a bookmark instantly when clicked*, press the spacebar, type **To add a bookmark button:**, and then tap or press Enter.

15 Tap or click the left part of the **Numbering button** in the Paragraph group of the HOME tab (do *not* tap or click the down-pointing arrow on the button).

This indents and inserts 1.

16 Type **Display the browser's Favorites toolbar.** and then tap or press Enter.

17 Type **Right-click the bookmark button and choose Add to favorites.** and then tap or press Enter.

18 Type **Choose Add button at dialog box that appears.**

Many websites now include icons for popular social bookmarking sites that capture the page references for bookmarking. Another way to bookmark a page is to add the bookmark button for the social bookmarking site you use to your browser's toolbar. Bookmark buttons add a bookmark instantly when clicked. To add a bookmark button:

1. Display the browser's Favorites toolbar.
2. Right-click the bookmark button and choose Add to favorites.
3. Choose Add button at dialog box that appears.

19 Save the document using the same name. Leave the document open for the next topic.

ALTERNATIVE method

The **AutoFormat as You Type** feature creates automatic bulleted and numbered lists when you do the following:

Type *****, **>**, or **–**, press the spacebar, type text, and then tap or press Enter (bulleted list)

Type **1.**, press the spacebar, type text, and tap or press Enter (numbered list)

Immediately use Undo if an automatic list appears and you do not want to create a list. An AutoCorrect Options button will appear with which you can turn off automatic lists.

The Bullets button arrow is used to choose a different bullet character from the Bullet Library.

Similarly to the Bullets button, the Numbering button arrow is used to choose a different number format from the Numbering Library.

Move Text
1. Select text.
2. Tap or click Cut button.
3. Position insertion point.
4. Tap or click Paste button.

Create a Bulleted List
1. Tap or click Bullets button.
2. Type first list item.
3. Tap or press Enter.
4. Type second list item.
5. Tap or press Enter.
6. Continue typing until finished.

Create a Numbered List
1. Tap or click Numbering button.
2. Type first numbered item.
3. Tap or press Enter.
4. Type second numbered item.
5. Tap or press Enter.
6. Continue typing until finished.

Topic 6.5

SKILLS

Change font and font options

Change paragraph alignment

Formatting Text with Font and Paragraph Alignment Options

Generally, you enter and edit text in a new document and then turn your attention to the document's appearance. The process of changing the appearance of the text is referred to as **formatting**. Changing the appearance of characters is called **character formatting**. Changing the appearance of a paragraph is called **paragraph formatting**. In some cases, the first step in formatting is to select the characters or paragraphs to be changed.

Some people prefer to format as they type. In that case, you can change the character or paragraph options before typing.

Applying Font Formatting

The Font group in the HOME tab contains the buttons used to change character formatting. A **font** is also referred to as a typeface and includes the design and shape of the letters, numbers, and special characters. A large collection of fonts is available from simple to artistic to suit a variety of documents. The font size is set in points. As you learned in Topic 6.1, one point is approximately 1/72 of an inch in height. The default font and font size in a new document is 11-point Calibri.

The Font group also includes buttons to increase or decrease the font size, change the case, change the font style (bold, italic, or underline) or font color, highlight text, and add font effects (outline, shadow, glow, reflection, and accents).

oops!

Mini toolbar disappeared? The Mini toolbar disappears if you move away from it after selecting text. Use the Font button arrow in the Font group of the HOME tab instead.

1. With the **6.1-SocialMediaProject-Your Name** document open, select the title text at the top of the document *Social Bookmarking*.
2. Tap or click the Font button arrow in the Mini toolbar.
3. Slide or scroll down and tap or click *Century Gothic* in the *Font* gallery.
4. With the title text still selected, tap twice or click twice the Increase Font Size button in the Mini toolbar or in the Font group of the HOME tab.

Make several font changes at once in the Font dialog box. Tap or click the Dialog Box Launcher button at the bottom right of the Font group.

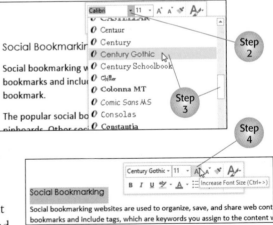

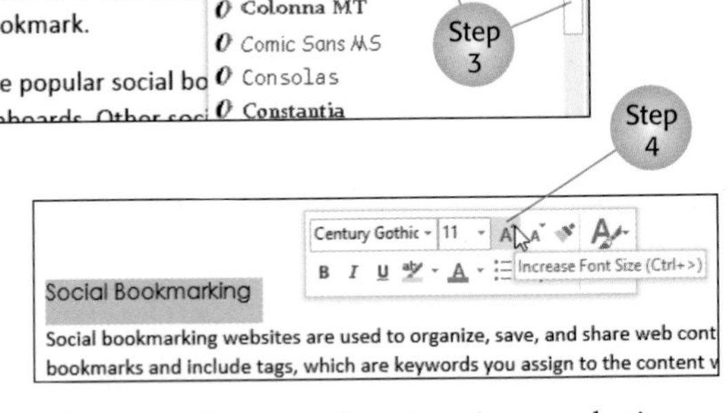

The first time you increase the font size, the size changes to 12. The second time, the size changes to 14 points and continues to increase 2 point sizes each time until you reach 28. After 28 points, the size changes to 36, 48, and then 72.

5. With the title text still selected, tap or click the Bold button in the Mini toolbar or in the Font group of the HOME tab.
6. With the title text still selected, tap or click the Font Color button (do *not* tap or click the Font Color button arrow) in the Mini toolbar or in the Font group of the HOME tab.

Use the Font Color button arrow to choose a color other than red. Once the color is changed, the new color can be applied to the next selection without using the button arrow. The color on the button resets to red after Word is closed.

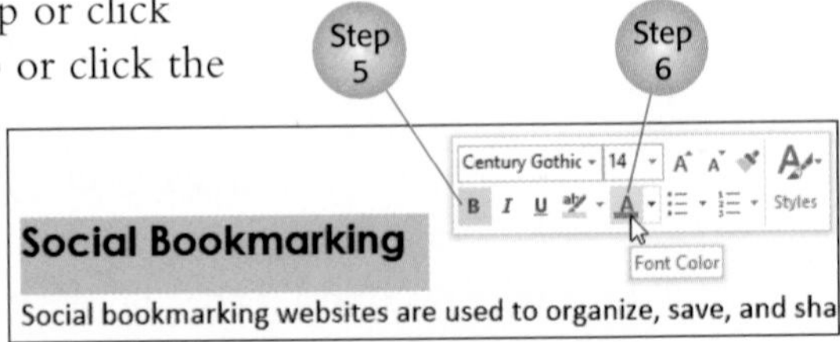

The default Font Color is Red.

7. Tap or click in the document away from the selected title to deselect the text.

Applying Paragraph Formatting

The Paragraph group in the HOME tab contains the buttons used to change paragraph formatting. You have already used the Bullets and Numbering buttons in this group. The bottom row of buttons in the group contains the buttons for changing the alignment of paragraphs from the default **Align Left** to **Center**, **Align Right**, or **Justify**. Justified text adds space within a line so that the text is distributed evenly between the left and right margins. You will explore other buttons in this group in the next topic.

8 Tap or click the insertion point anywhere within the title text *Social Bookmarking*.

To format a single paragraph, you do not need to select the paragraph text because paragraph formatting applies to all text within the paragraph to the point where a hard return was inserted.

9 Tap or click the Center button in the Paragraph group of the HOME tab.

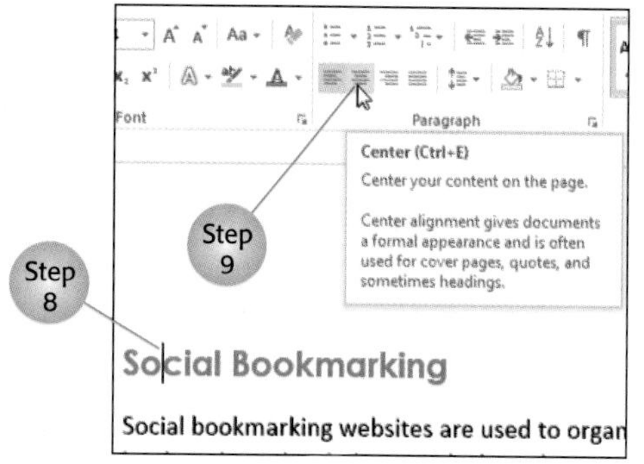

10 Tap or click the insertion point anywhere within the first paragraph of text and tap or click the Justify button in the Paragraph group of the HOME tab.

Justified text spreads the lines out so that the text ends evenly at the right margin.

11 With the insertion point still positioned in the first paragraph, tap or click the Align Left button in the Paragraph group of the HOME tab.

12 Save the document using the same name. Leave the document open for the next topic.

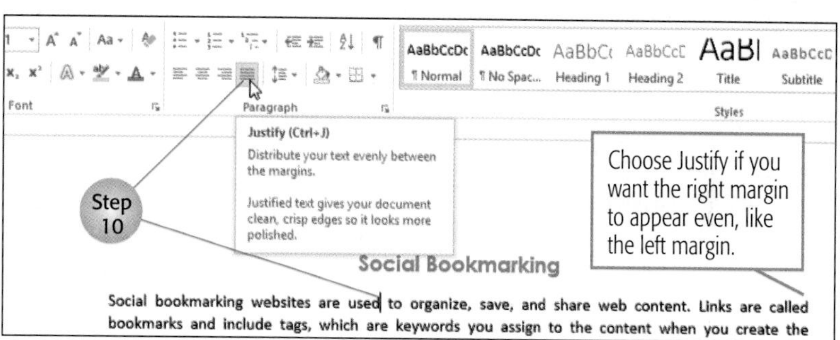

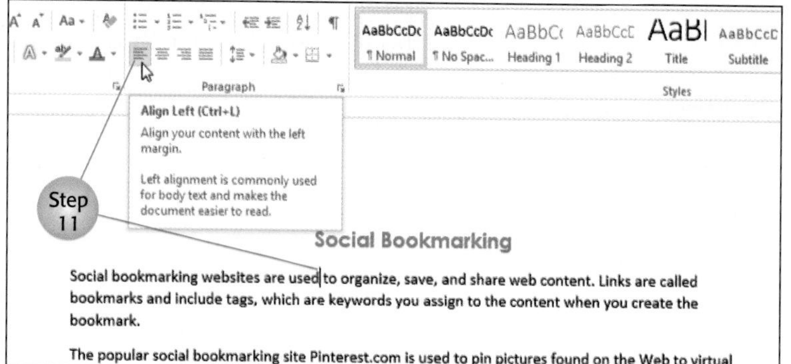

The following keyboard shortcuts change paragraph alignment:

Ctrl + L	Align Left	Ctrl + R	Align Right
Ctrl + E	Center	Ctrl + J	Justify

Change Font
1. Select text.
2. Tap or click Font button arrow.
3. Slide or scroll down to desired font.
4. Tap or click font.

Increase Font Size
1. Select text.
2. Tap or click Increase Font Size button.

Change Font Color to Red
1. Select text.
2. Tap or click Font Color button.

Change Paragraph Alignment
1. Tap or click in paragraph.
2. Tap or click Align Left, Center, Align Right, or Justify button.

Select more than one paragraph first if you want to apply the same alignment option to multiple paragraphs.

Use the Clear All Formatting button in the Font group to remove all formatting from selected text.

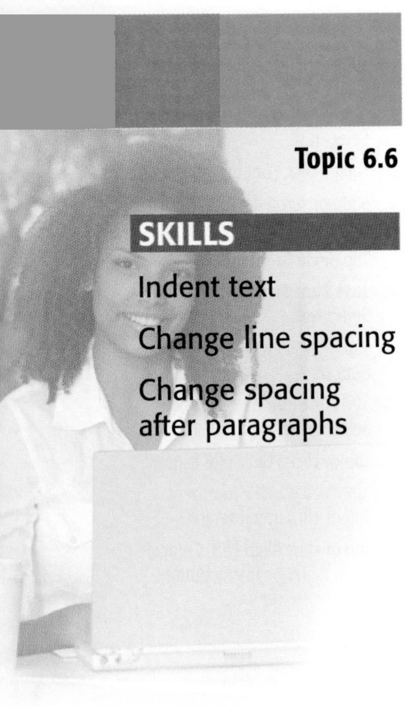

Topic 6.6

SKILLS

Indent text

Change line spacing

Change spacing after paragraphs

Indenting Text and Changing Line and Paragraph Spacing

Paragraphs are indented to set the paragraph apart from the rest of the document. In reports, essays, or research papers, long quotes are indented. A paragraph can be indented for the first line only, or for all lines in the paragraph. Paragraphs can also be indented from the right margin. A paragraph where the first line remains at the left margin but subsequent lines are indented is called a **hanging indent**. Hanging indents are used in bulleted lists, numbered lists, bibliographies, and works cited pages.

Use the **Line and Paragraph Spacing button** in the Paragraph group to change the spacing between lines of text within a paragraph and to change the spacing before and after paragraphs.

1. With the **6.1-SocialMediaProject-Your Name** document open, position the insertion point at the left margin of the first paragraph (begins with the text *Social bookmarking websites*).
2. Tap or press the Tab key.

Pressing the Tab key indents the first line only 0.5 inch. The AutoCorrect Options button also appears. Use the button if you want to change the first line indent back to a Tab, stop setting indents when you press Tab, or change other AutoFormat options.

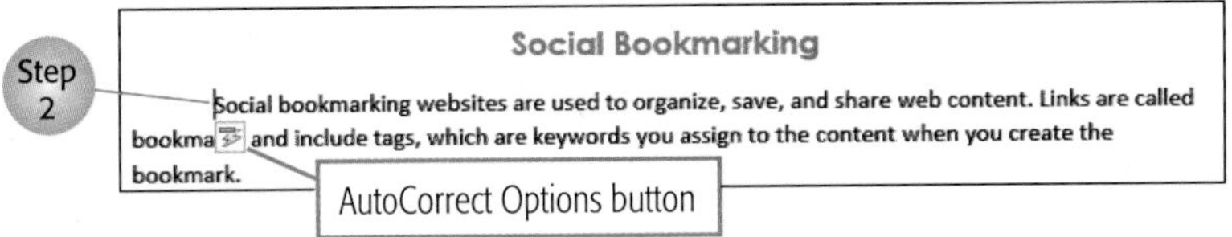

Each time you tap or click the Increase Indent button, the paragraph indents 0.5 inch. Tap or click the button as many times as needed to indent to the desired position.

3. Position the insertion point anywhere within the second paragraph (begins with the text *The popular*).
4. Tap or click the **Increase Indent button** in the Paragraph group of the HOME tab.

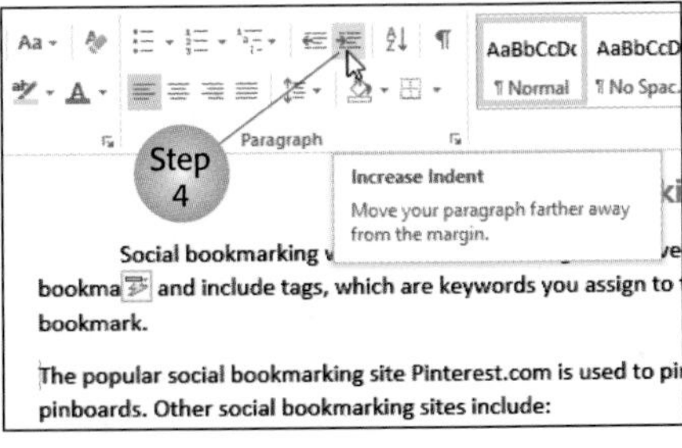

5. With the insertion point still positioned in the second paragraph, tap or click the **Decrease Indent button** in the Paragraph group of the HOME tab.

Decrease Indent moves the paragraph back to the left margin.

When a paragraph has been indented more than one position, decrease indent moves the paragraph left toward the margin one position (0.5 inch) each time the button is tapped or clicked.

6. Position the insertion point anywhere within the third paragraph (begins with the text *Many websites now include*).

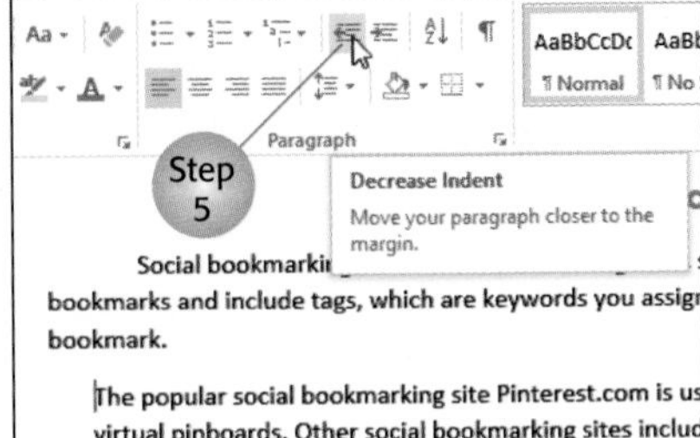

7 Tap or click the Line and Paragraph Spacing button in the Paragraph group of the HOME tab and then tap or click *Line Spacing Options* at the drop-down list.

8 Select the current entry in the *Left* text box and type 0.5.

9 Select the current entry in the *Right* text box and type 0.5.

10 Tap or click OK.

The paragraph is indented from both margins by 0.5 inch.

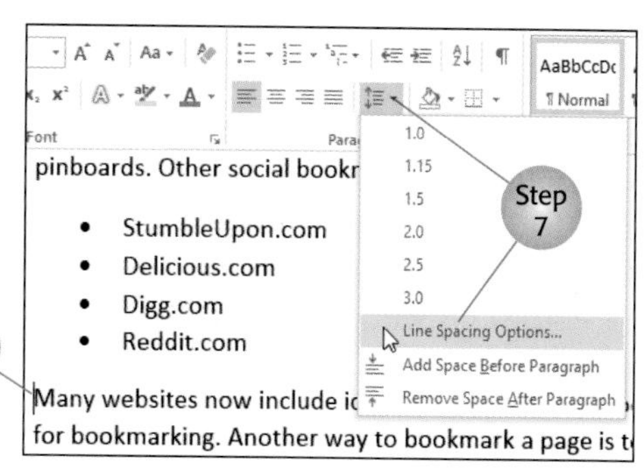

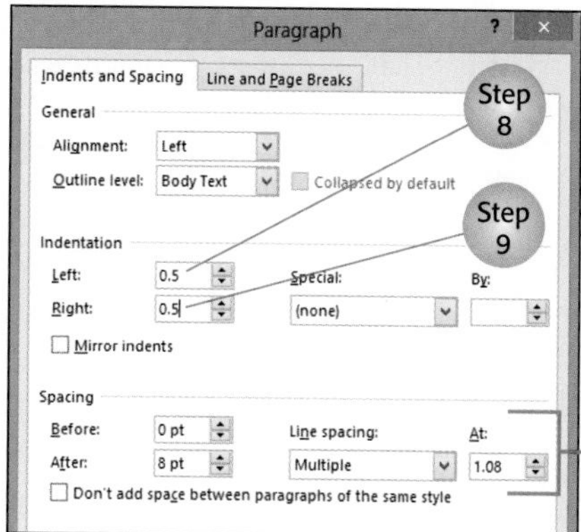

You can also adjust the spacing before or after paragraphs or change line spacing in this section of the dialog box.

11 With the insertion point still positioned in the paragraph that begins with the text *Many websites*, tap or click the Line and Paragraph Spacing button and then tap or click *Line Spacing Options*.

12 Change the entry in the *Left* and *Right* text boxes to *0*.

13 Tap or click the *Special* list arrow and tap or click *First line*.

14 Tap or click OK.

15 Format the second paragraph that begins with the text *The popular* and the last paragraph that begins with the text *Experian* with a first line indent.

16 Tap or click the Select button in the Editing group of the HOME tab and tap or click *Select All* at the drop-down list.

17 Tap or click the Line and Paragraph Spacing button and tap or click *1.5* at the drop-down gallery.

The line spacing is changed to 1.5 lines for the entire document. Notice the other line spacing options are *1.0*, *1.15*, *2.0*, *2.5*, and *3.0*.

18 With the entire document still selected, tap or click the Line and Paragraph Spacing button and then tap or click *Remove Space After Paragraph* at the drop-down gallery.

19 Tap or click in any section of the document to deselect the text.

20 Save the document using the same name. Leave the document open for the next topic.

Indent a Paragraph from Both Margins

1. Position insertion point in paragraph.
2. Tap or click Line and Paragraph Spacing button.
3. Tap or click *Line Spacing Options*.
4. Change *Left* value.
5. Change *Right* value.
6. Tap or click OK.

Change Spacing Before and After Paragraphs

1. Position insertion point or select paragraphs.
2. Tap or click Line and Paragraph Spacing button.
3. Tap or click *Add Space Before Paragraph* or *Remove Space After Paragraph*.

Ctrl + A is the keyboard shortcut to Select All.

ALTERNATIVE method

The PAGE LAYOUT tab also contains a Paragraph group with the same Indent and Spacing options you used in this topic. Use the *Left* and *Right* text boxes to indent paragraphs or the *Before* and *After* text boxes to change the spacing inserted before and after paragraphs.

In the DESIGN tab, use the Paragraph Spacing button in the Document Formatting group to set line and paragraph spacing options for the entire document, including new paragraphs.

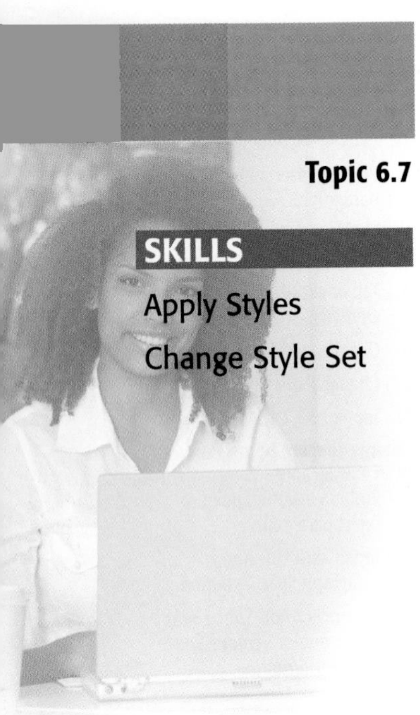

Topic 6.7

SKILLS

Apply Styles

Change Style Set

Formatting Using Styles

A **style** is a set of predefined formatting options that can be applied to selected text or paragraphs with one step. The Styles group in the HOME tab shows the styles that have been supplied with Word. You can also create your own styles. Two rows of Style buttons are available in the *Styles* gallery. Use the More button at the bottom of the scroll bar at the right of the *Styles* gallery to show the second row of Style options and the *Create a Style*, *Clear Formatting*, and *Apply Styles* options.

Once Styles have been applied, buttons in the Document Formatting group of the DESIGN tab change the **Style Set**, which changes the look of a document. Each Style Set has different formatting options associated with each style.

1. With the **6.1-SocialMediaProject-Your Name** document open, tap or click the FILE tab and tap or click Save As.
2. With *Computer* already selected in the Save As Backstage view, tap or click the folder name that appears below *Current Folder* in the right pane.

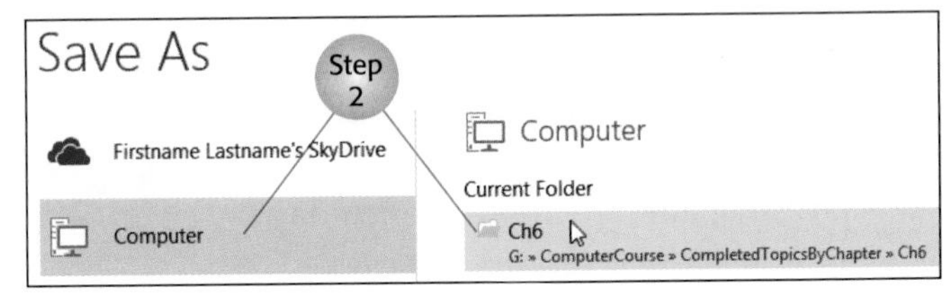

3. At the Save As dialog box, with the text in the *File name* text box already selected, tap or click at the beginning of the file name or press the Home key on the keyboard.
4. Change *6.1* at the beginning of the file name to *6.7* by moving the insertion point and inserting and deleting text.
5. Tap or press Enter, or tap or click the Save button.
6. Position the insertion point anywhere within the title text *Social Bookmarking*.
7. Tap or click the *Title* style in the *Styles* gallery in the HOME tab.

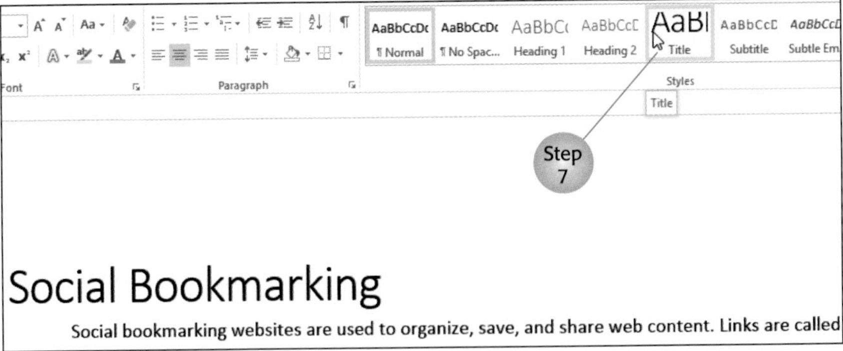

8. Position the insertion point anywhere within the first paragraph of text below the title.
9. Tap or click the More button in the *Styles* gallery. The button displays with a bar above a down-pointing arrow.
10. Tap or click the *Quote* style in the second row of the *Styles* gallery.

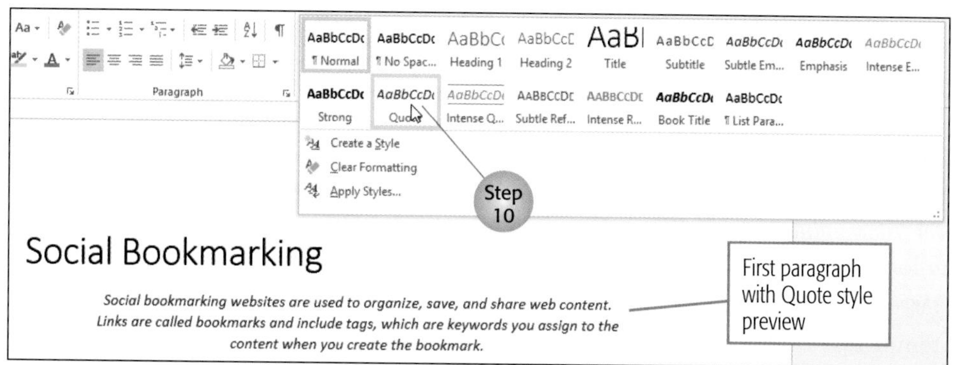

Format Using Styles
1. Select text or position insertion point.
2. Tap or click desired Styles button.

Change Style Set
1. Tap or click DESIGN tab.
2. Tap or click desired Style Set.

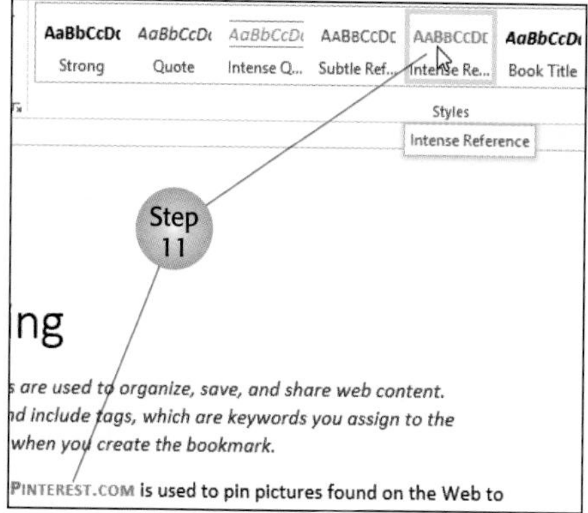

11 Select *Pinterest.com* in the second paragraph and tap or click the *Intense Reference* style in the *Styles* gallery.

12 Deselect *Pinterest.com*.

Once styles have been applied to text, you can experiment with various Style Sets in the Document Formatting group of the DESIGN tab. Changing the Style Set changes font and paragraph formatting options. Two rows of Style Sets are in the *Document Formatting* gallery.

13 Tap or click the DESIGN tab.

14 Tap or click the *Basic (Stylish)* Style Set in the *Document Formatting* gallery (fourth option from left).

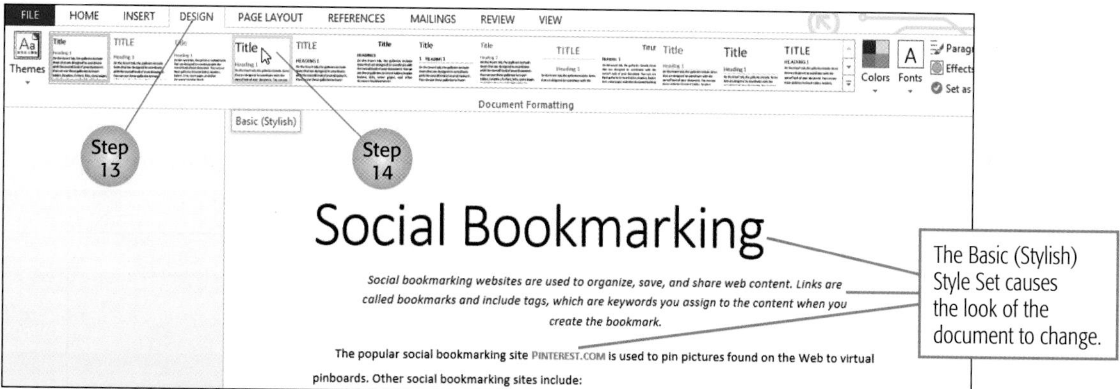

15 Position the insertion point anywhere within the title text *Social Bookmarking*.

16 Tap or click the HOME tab and tap or click *Heading 1* in the Styles group.

The title text formats to the options stored in the Heading 1 style in the new Style Set. The formatting is also affected by the document **Theme** (set of colors and fonts).

Change the theme at the DESIGN tab.

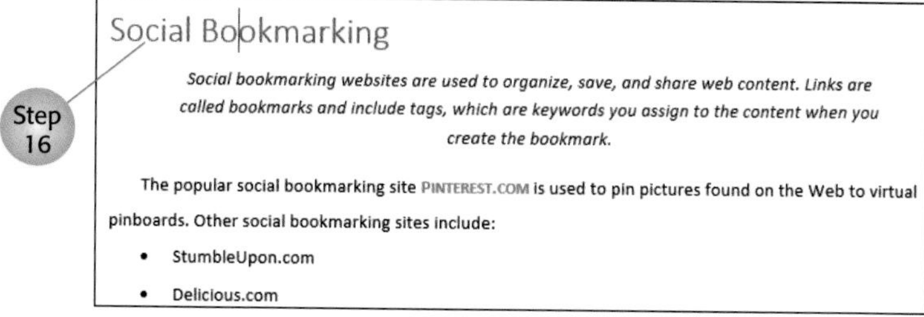

17 Save the document using the same name (**6.7-SocialMediaProject-Your Name**).

18 Close the document. Leave Word open for the next topic.

Topic 6.8

SKILLS

Create a new document from a template

Creating a New Document from a Template

A **template** is a document that has been created with formatting options applied. Several professional-quality templates for various types of documents are available that you can use rather than creating a new document from scratch. At the Word Start screen you can browse and preview available templates by category, or in the *Search for online template* search box, type in a keyword for the type of document you are looking for and browse through search results.

When Word is already opened, the New tab Backstage view is used to browse for a template.

1. Tap or click the FILE tab and then tap or click New.
2. At the New tab Backstage view, tap or click Letters in the *Suggested searches* section.

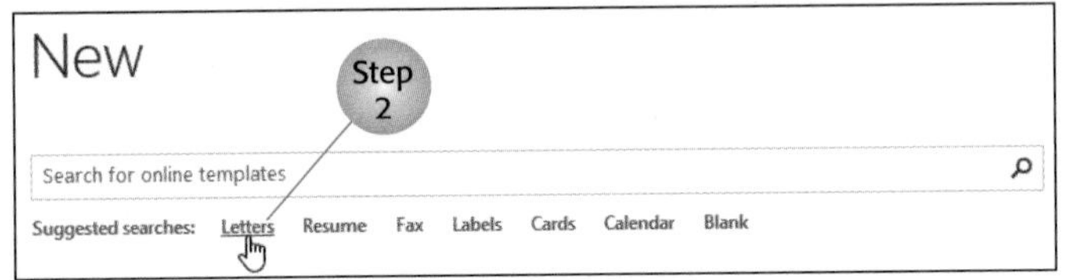

3. Slide or scroll down and review the various types of letter templates available, then tap or click Home at the top of the New tab Backstage view.

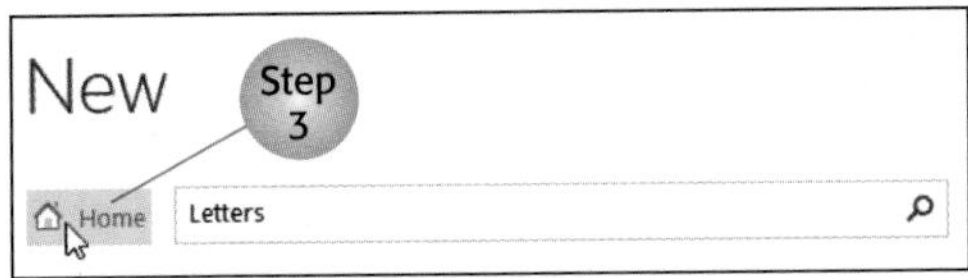

4. Tap or click in the *Search for online templates* search box, type **time sheet**, and tap or press Enter, or tap or click the Start searching button (displays as a magnifying glass at end of the search box).

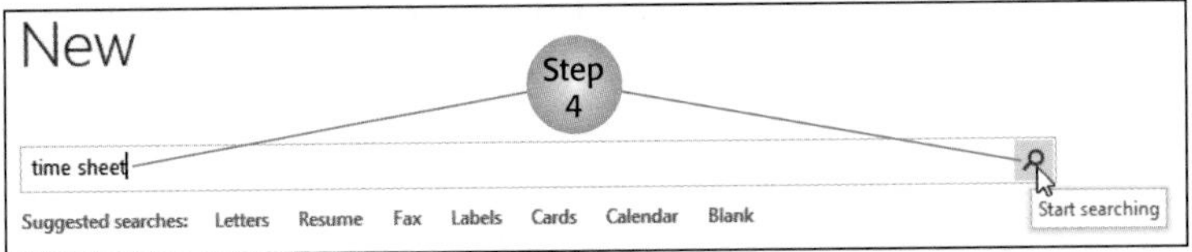

oops!

Your Time Sheet template looks different? Available templates are changed often. If the first template looks different, close the preview and look for one that is closest to the one shown. If necessary, adjust the remaining instructions to suit the available templates.

5. Tap or click the first *Time Sheet* template in the *Templates* gallery.

A preview of the template opens with a description that provides information on the template design.

6. Tap or click the Create button.

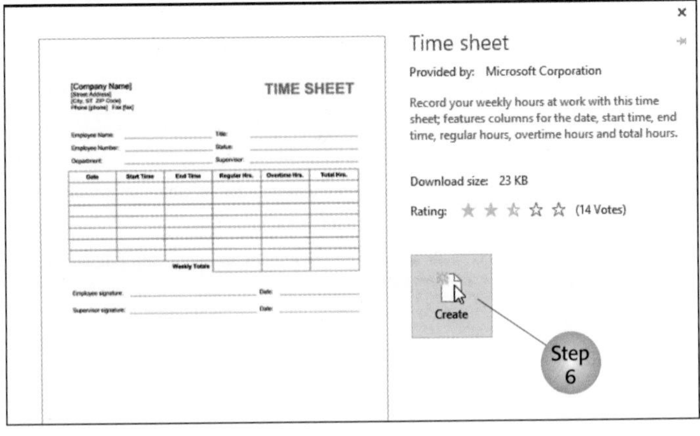

7. Tap or click *[Company Name]* and type **A+ Tutoring Advantage**.
8. Tap or click *[Street Address]* and type **1015 Montreal Way**.
9. Tap or click *[City, ST ZIP Code]* and type **St. Paul, MN 55102**.
10. Tap or click *[phone]* and type **888-555-3125**.
11. Tap or click *[fax]* and type **888-555-3445**.

A+ Tutoring Advantage
1015 Montreal Way
St. Paul, MN 55102
Phone 888-555-3125 Fax 888-555-3445

TIME SHEET

12. Tap or click next to *Employee Name* and type your name.
13. Complete the remainder of the time sheet document using the text shown in Figure 6.4 by completing steps similar to Step 12.

A+ Tutoring Advantage
1015 Montreal Way
St. Paul, MN 55102
Phone 888-555-3125 Fax 888-555-3445

TIME SHEET

Step 12

Employee Name: Student Name   Title: Computer Tutor
Employee Number: 101   Status: Part-time
Department: Computers   Supervisor: Dayna Summerton

Date	Start Time	End Time	Regular Hrs.	Overtime Hrs.	Total Hrs.
Oct. 13	9:00 am	12:00 pm	3.0		3.0
Oct. 14	1:00 pm	4:30 pm	3.5		3.5
Oct. 15	7:00 pm	9:30 pm	2.5		2.5
Oct. 16	10:00 am	1:00 pm	3.0		3.0
		Weekly Totals	12.0		12.0

Employee signature: ______________________ Date: __________

Supervisor signature: ______________________ Date: __________

Figure 6.4 Completed time sheet for 6.8-Oct13to16Timesheet-Your Name.

14. Save the completed time sheet in the Ch6 folder in the CompletedTopicsByChapter folder on your USB flash drive as **6.8-Oct13to16TimeSheet-Your Name**. Choose OK when a message displays that the document will be upgraded to the newest file format.
15. Close the document.

[Company Name] is referred to as a text placeholder. Look for these placeholders in a template to indicate where to personalize the document. Other templates include descriptive text within the template that describes how to use the template.

Create New Document from a Template

1. Tap or click FILE tab.
2. Tap or click New.
3. Search for template design.
4. Tap or click desired template.
5. Tap or click Create button.
6. Complete document as required.

Template Designs

Templates are available for any type of document. The next time you need to type a letter, memo, report, invitation, announcement, flyer, or labels, look for a template design.

Concepts Review

Topic	Key Concepts	Key Terms
Creating and Editing a New Document	A word processing application is software used to create documents that are composed mostly of text. Start a new blank document from the Word Start screen. Creating a new document generally involves typing text, editing text, and correcting errors. Double-tapping or double-clicking on the page in blank space and typing is referred to as click and type. Text is automatically aligned left, center, or right depending on the location in the line at which click and type occurs. Wordwrap is the term that describes Word moving text to the next line automatically when you reach the right margin. As you type new text, AutoCorrect fixes common misspellings, and AutoFormat automatically converts some text to fractions, ordinals, quotes, hyphens, and hyperlinks. Pressing the Enter key creates a new paragraph and is called a hard return. A change made to text that has already been typed is referred to as editing and involves inserting, deleting, and replacing characters. The first step in editing is to position the insertion point at the location of the change. Press Shift + Enter to insert a Line Break command, which moves to the next line without adding extra spacing.	Word processing application Click and type Wordwrap AutoCorrect AutoFormat Editing Hard return Line Break
Inserting Symbols and Completing a Spelling and Grammar Check	Symbols or special characters such as a copyright symbol or registered trademark are entered using the *Symbol* gallery or Symbol dialog box. AutoCorrect recognizes some special characters and symbols and converts them automatically. The Spelling & Grammar button is used to match words in the document with words in the dictionary; words not found are flagged as potential errors. During a spell check, a word not found in the dictionary is highlighted and suggestions for replacement appear in the Spelling task pane. Ignore, Ignore All, Add, Change, or Change All are buttons in the Spelling task pane used to respond to each potential error.	*Symbol* gallery Spelling & Grammar
Finding and Replacing Text	The Find feature highlights all occurrences of a keyword or phrase and provides in the Navigation pane a link to each location in the document. Use Replace if you want Word to automatically change each occurrence of a keyword or phrase with another word or phrase. Find a word with a similar meaning in the Thesaurus.	Find Replace Thesaurus

Topic	Key Concepts	Key Terms
Moving Text and Inserting Bullets and Numbering	Turn on the display of hidden formatting symbols using the Show/Hide button in the Paragraph group. Hidden formatting symbols such as the paragraph symbol are inserted in a document whenever the Enter key is pressed. Displaying formatting symbols is helpful when moving text to make sure the paragraph symbol is selected before cutting the text. Bullets are items in a list that are entered in no particular sequence. The default bullet symbol is a solid round bullet. Additional bullet options are available using the Bullets button arrow. A numbered list is a sequential series of tasks or other items that are each preceded by a number. AutoFormat as You Type creates a bulleted list when you start a new line with *, >, or – and then press the spacebar. AutoFormat as You Type creates a numbered list when you start a new line by typing 1. and then press the spacebar.	Bullets button Numbering button AutoFormat as You Type
Formatting Text with Font and Paragraph Alignment Options	Changing the appearance of text is called formatting. Character formatting involves applying changes to the appearance of characters, whereas paragraph formatting changes the appearance of an entire paragraph. Use buttons in the Font group of the HOME tab to change character formatting. A font is also called a typeface and refers to the design and shape of letters, numbers, and special characters. Change a font, font size, case, font style, font color; highlight text; and add font effects to change character formats. Change a paragraph's alignment from the default Align Left to Center, Align Right, or Justify using the buttons in the bottom row of the Paragraph group in the HOME tab. Justified text has extra space within a line so that the left and right margins are even.	Formatting Character formatting Paragraph formatting Font Align Left Center Align Right Justify

continued....

Topic	Key Concepts	Key Terms
Indenting Text and Changing Line and Paragraph Spacing	Indent a paragraph such as a long quote to set the paragraph apart from others in the document. Press Tab at the beginning of a paragraph to indent only the first line or change *Special* to *First line* at the Paragraph dialog box. A paragraph in which all lines are indented except the first line is called a hanging indent. Indent all lines of a paragraph using the Increase Indent button or change the *Left* text box entry at the Paragraph dialog box. A paragraph indents 0.5 inch each time the Increase Indent button is tapped or clicked. Use the Decrease Indent button to move a paragraph closer to the left margin; the paragraph moves left 0.5 inch each time the button is tapped or clicked. Indent a paragraph from both margins using the *Left* and *Right* text boxes in the Paragraph dialog box. Change line spacing by selecting the desired spacing option from the Line and Paragraph Spacing button. Extra space can be added or removed before or after paragraphs using options from the Line and Paragraph Spacing button or the Paragraph dialog box. Indents and paragraph spacing can also be set using text boxes in the Paragraph group of the PAGE LAYOUT tab.	Hanging indent Line and Paragraph Spacing button Increase Indent button Decrease Indent button
Formatting Using Styles	Format text by applying a style, which is a set of predefined formatting options. Two rows of styles are available in the *Styles* gallery of the HOME tab. Change the Style Set using buttons in the Document Formatting group of the DESIGN tab. Each Style Set applies a different set of formatting options for the styles in the HOME tab, meaning you can change a document's appearance by changing the Style Set. A Theme is a set of colors, fonts, and font effects that alter the appearance of a document.	Style Style Set Theme
Creating a New Document from a Template	A template is a document that is already set up with text and/or formatting options. Browse available templates in the template gallery at the Word Start screen or at the New tab Backstage view. Find a template by browsing the gallery by a category or by typing a keyword in the *Search for online templates* search box. Tap or click a template design to preview the template and create a new document based upon the template. Within a template, text placeholders or instructional text is included to help you personalize the document.	Template

Multiple Choice

1. This feature fixes common misspellings as you type.
   a. AutoFormat
   b. AutoCorrect
   c. AutoSpell
   d. Click and Type
2. This feature automatically converts text such as 1/2 to a fraction character.
   a. AutoFormat
   b. AutoCorrect
   c. AutoSpell
   d. Click and Type
3. Insert a trademark sign using this gallery.
   a. Styles
   b. Document Formatting
   c. Spelling
   d. Symbol
4. In this task pane you can instruct Word to ignore a word that is spelled correctly but that Word has highlighted as a potential error.
   a. Spelling
   b. Styles
   c. Navigation
   d. Replace
5. Use this feature to locate all occurrences of a word in the current document.
   a. Replace
   b. Navigate
   c. Find
   d. Search
6. A word or phrase can be automatically changed to another word or phrase throughout the entire document using this feature.
   a. Replace
   b. Navigate
   c. Find
   d. Search
7. This button in the Clipboard group is used to remove selected text from its current location and paste it at another location.
   a. Move
   b. Cut
   c. Copy
   d. Select All
8. Set apart a list of items that is in no particular sequence with this button in the Paragraph group of the HOME tab.
   a. Numbering
   b. Decrease Indent
   c. Bullets
   d. Justify
9. Changing the appearance of text is referred to as ________________.
   a. formatting
   b. editing
   c. justifying
   d. organizing
10. Apply a different font to selected text using this toolbar.
    a. Formatting
    b. Editing
    c. Mini
    d. Styles
11. Pressing the Tab key at the beginning of a paragraph creates this type of indent.
    a. Hanging
    b. First line
    c. Left
    d. Special
12. Open this dialog box to indent a paragraph from both margins.
    a. Indent
    b. Paragraph
    c. Alignment
    d. Format
13. This button in the Paragraph group moves text closer to the left margin.
    a. Increase Indent
    b. Align Left
    c. Decrease Indent
    d. Align Right
14. Buttons in this gallery allow you to apply a set of predefined formatting options in one step.
    a. Styles
    b. Font
    c. AutoFormat
    d. AutoCorrect Options
15. Browse available templates at the Word Start screen or this Backstage view.
    a. Info
    b. New
    c. Open
    d. Options

Crossword Puzzle

ACROSS

1 Button to use when flagged error is not a misspelling
3 Use to create a document from one already formatted
5 A set of colors, fonts, and font effects
10 Move all lines of a paragraph left 0.5 inch
11 Feature that causes Navigation pane to open
12 Dialog box to insert a special character
14 Move all lines of a paragraph right 0.5 inch

DOWN

2 Button to format a sequential list of steps
3 Feature that shows words with a similar meaning
4 Fixes spelling of *teh* after you press spacebar
6 Document Formatting buttons change this
7 Do this with Cut and Paste
8 Option that makes left and right margins appear even
9 Feature that converts *1st* to an ordinal
13 Group for character formatting options

Matching

Match the term with the statement or definition.

_______ 1. Word
_______ 2. Symbol
_______ 3. Thesaurus
_______ 4. Move text
_______ 5. AutoFormat as You Type
_______ 6. Character formatting
_______ 7. Hanging
_______ 8. Style
_______ 9. Template

a. Clipboard group
b. Indent used in lists
c. Font group
d. Synonyms
e. Title
f. Word processing
g. New tab Backstage view
h. Plus-Minus sign
i. Automatic lists

Project 1 Creating and Editing a New Document

Individual

Deliverable: Word document (continued in Project 2)

1. At a new blank document, type the following text, pressing Enter only where indicated.
   Social Media Popularity, Profitability, and Privacy [Tap or press Enter]
   Ninety-six percent of Americans and Canadians between the ages of 16 and 24 are Internet users. For most people, a majority of time spent on the Internet involves the use of social communication websites such as Facebook. All ages prefer the convenience and accessibility of social media websites to connect with family, friends, and acquaintances. [Tap or press Enter]
   Social media websites such as Facebook make money using a traditional model of selling advertisements such as banner and pop-up ads. Facebook games such as Farmville also provide a source of income for Facebook. In 2012 Facebook launched a service called Facebook Gifts, which lets Facebook users send presents to one another. [Tap or press Enter]
   Users of social media websites such as Facebook need to be wary of privacy issues and security threats. The risk of identity theft, clickjacking, and phishing scams is rising due to the popularity of social media. Review privacy options and keep personal information that could identify you to a stranger to a minimum at each social network. Consider asking your family and friends not to tag you in pictures without your knowledge. [Tap or press Enter]
   Your Name [Tap or press Enter]
2. Save the document as **C6-Project1-SocialMedia-Your Name** in a new folder named *Ch6* within the ChapterProjectsWork folder on your USB flash drive.
3. Edit the document as follows:
   a. In the first sentence change *16 and 24 are Internet users* to *10 and 34 are social media users.*
   b. In the second sentence change *social communication websites* to *social networking websites.*
   c. Add the following sentence to the end of the second paragraph.
      Also in 2012, Facebook reported over $150 million from mobile ads, which represent their fastest growing revenue source.
   d. Delete the last sentence in the first paragraph that begins with *All ages prefer.*
   e. Delete the second sentence in the second paragraph that begins with *Facebook games.*
   f. Move the last sentence that begins with *Consider asking* to the beginning of the last paragraph (before the sentence that begins *Users of social media websites*).
   g. Type the following new paragraph after the third paragraph and before your name.
      When posting content at a social media website, be mindful not to violate copyright by copying pictures that belong to someone else. Look for a copyright symbol © or refer to terms of use before downloading content. Be careful also not to misrepresent or misuse a registered trademark of a company. Look for the ® or ™ symbol to identify a company's trademark.
   h. Replace all occurrences of *social media* with *social networking.* When finished, change *networking* in the title to *Networking.*
4. Complete a spelling and grammar check of the document.
5. Proofread the document carefully to make sure the document is error-free.
6. Save the revised document using the same name (**C6-Project1-SocialMedia-Your Name**).
7. Leave the document open if you are continuing to Project 2; otherwise, close the document and submit the project to your instructor in the manner she or he has requested.

Project 2 Editing and Formatting a Document

Individual

Deliverable: Word document

Note: You must have completed Project 1 before starting this project.

1. If necessary, open **C6-Project1-SocialMedia-Your Name**.
2. Use Save As to change the file name to **C6-Project2-SocialMediaFormatted-Your Name**, saving in the same folder.
3. Type the following new paragraph and bulleted list between the second and third paragraphs.
   Facebook's $1 billion revenue from last year is segmented as follows:
   - **85 percent from ads (including mobile ads)**
   - **14 percent from games (such as Farmville)**
   - **1 percent from other sources (such as Facebook Gifts)**
4. Format the document as follows:
   a. Change the title to 12-point Verdana bold red font and center-aligned.
   b. Indent the first line of each paragraph.
   c. Justify the first two and the last two paragraphs.
   d. Select the entire document, change the line spacing to 1.5, and remove the space after paragraphs.
5. Depending on the method used to format a paragraph with a first line indent, the indent position for the last three paragraphs may be at 0.25 inch instead of the 0.5 inch in the first two paragraphs. This occurs because the bullet list formatting carries over to the paragraphs before and after. If necessary, change the first line indent position to 0.5 inch for the last three paragraphs by positioning the insertion point within the paragraph and opening the Paragraph dialog box.
6. Save the revised document using the same name (**C6-Project2-SocialMediaFormatted-Your Name**).
7. Submit the project to your instructor in the manner she or he has requested.
8. Close the document.

Project 3 Formatting with Styles

Individual

Deliverable: Word document

Note: You must have completed Project 1 before starting this project.

1. Open **C6-Project1-SocialMedia-Your Name**.
2. Use Save As to change the file name to **C6-Project3-SocialMediaStyles-Your Name**, saving in the same folder.
3. Apply the Heading 1 style to the document title.
4. Select all of the text below the title except for your name at the bottom of the document and apply the Emphasis style.
5. Select your name at the bottom of the document and apply the Intense Reference style.
6. Change the Style Set to *Black & White (Classic)*.
7. Save the revised document using the same name (**C6-Project3-SocialMediaStyles-Your Name**).
8. Submit the project to your instructor in the manner she or he has requested.
9. Close the document.

Project 4 Creating an Invoice from a Template

Individual

Deliverable: Invoice document from template

1. Search for and select a service invoice template of your choosing to create a new document.
2. Personalize the template by adding your name as the company name and your school's address, city, state, ZIP Code, and phone as the company information. Fill in other company information with fictitious information if necessary.
3. Using today's date, create invoice 136 to:

   Leslie Taylor
   HBC Enterprises
   1240 7th Street West
   St. Paul, MN 55102
   888-555-6954
   Customer ID: CA6-3312

   a. Type the body of the invoice as follows:

Qty	*Description*	*Unit Price*	*Total*
5 hours	**Social media consulting**	**65.00**	**325.00**

   b. Add appropriate sales tax for your area. Check with your instructor if necessary for sales tax rates in your state or province.

   c. Make sure the total at the bottom of the invoice is 325.00 plus tax.

   d. Add or delete other information as needed so that the invoice is of mailable quality.
4. Save the document in the Ch6 folder within the ChapterProjectsWork folder on your USB flash drive as **C6-Project4-InvoiceTemplate-Your Name**.
5. Submit the project to your instructor in the manner she or he has requested.
6. Close the document.

Project 5 Campus Flyer from Template

Individual

Deliverable: Campus Flyer

1. Create a flyer for your school campus similar to the one shown in Figure 6.5. Use a current date and a location suitable for concerts on or near your campus. Add current popular band names to the *FEATURING* section. Enter a fictitious web address and sponsor information. Make any other changes you think are necessary.

Note: Search for the template shown using the keywords* student flyer *at the New tab Backstage view.

2. Save the flyer in the Ch6 folder within the ChapterProjectsWork folder on your USB flash drive as **C6-Project5-CampusBandBattleFlyer-Your Name**.
3. Submit the project to your instructor in the manner she or he has requested.
4. Close the document.

CAMPUS
BAND
BATTLE

WHEN
June 8th, 2012
8pm – 12pm

WHERE
Student Union
Auditorium
1234 Academic Circle, Berkeley, CA

FEATURING · Your Band Name · Your Band Name · Your Band Name · Your Band Name · Your Band Name · Your Band Name

WEB ADDRESS

ALL AGES
EVENT

ADVANCE
TICKETS
$18 General
$36 VIP
Group rates
available on site

AT THE DOOR
$20 General
$40 VIP
Group rates
available on site

SPONSORS
Adventure Works
Alpine Ski House
Contoso, Ltd.
Fourth Coffee
Margie's Travel
School of Fine Art
The Phone Company
Wingtip Toys

BENEFITING
The School of Music
and the University
Arts and
Entertainment
Council

Figure 6.5 Project 5 Campus Flyer

Project 6 Internet Research and Composing a New Document

Individual or Pairs

Deliverable: Word document

1. Listen to the audio file named ***Project6_Instructions***. The file is located in the Ch6 folder in the Student_Data_Files folder on your USB flash drive.
2. Complete the research and compose the document as instructed.
3. Save the document in the Ch6 folder within the ChapterProjectsWork folder on your USB flash drive as **C6-Project6-SocialMediaResearch-Your Name**.
4. Submit the project to your instructor in the manner she or he has requested.
5. Close the document.

Project 7 Sending Project Work to OneNote Notebook

Individual

Deliverable: New Page in Shared OneNote notebook

1. Start OneNote and open the MyProjects notebook created in Chapter 4, Project 4.
2. Make Word the active section and add a new page titled *Chapter 6 Projects*.
3. Switch to Word. For each project that you completed, open the document, send the project to OneNote 2013 selecting the Chapter 6 Projects page in the Word section in the MyProjects notebook, and then close the document.
4. Close your MyProjects notebook in OneNote and close OneNote.
5. Close Word.
6. Submit the project to your instructor in the manner she or he has requested.

Chapter 7

Enhancing a Document with Special Features

After successfully completing this chapter, you will be able to:

- Insert images into a document
- Add borders and shading to text
- Insert a text box into a document
- Create and format a table
- Change page layout options
- Format a research paper with a header and page numbers
- Insert citations and a works cited page
- Display a document in different views in Word
- Insert comments
- Create a resume and cover letter

Several features in Word allow you to add visual appeal, organize information, or format a document for a special purpose such as a research paper. Word provides different views in which to work and navigate a document and includes collaborative tools such as comments for working on a document with other people. Several resume and cover letter templates are available in Word to help you build these important job search documents.

In this chapter, you will enhance documents already typed and finalize an academic research paper by adding formatting, citations, and a works cited page. Lastly, you will create a resume and cover letter using templates.

Inserting, Editing, and Labeling Images in a Document

Topic 7.1

SKILLS

- Insert clip art
- Insert a picture
- Edit a picture
- Insert a caption

Graphic elements such as pictures, clip art, shapes, SmartArt, charts, or other types of images help a reader understand content or add visual appeal to a document. Office.com provides a large selection of royalty-free photos and illustrations. If you have a picture stored at an online service such as Flickr, Facebook, or SkyDrive, you can insert the image directly from the Web. Pictures saved to your PC or mobile device can also be inserted into a document. Once inserted, images can be edited and labeled with a caption.

Inserting Pictures from Online Sources

You can search for a suitable image for a document in the Microsoft Office **clip art gallery** or on the Web using Bing without leaving the Word document. You can also choose to insert a photo you have saved at an online service without leaving the Word document.

1. Start Word 2013 and open the document **InsulaSummary_AddictionsCourse**.

   This document is located in the Ch7 folder in the Student_Data_Files folder on your USB flash drive.

2. Using Save As, navigate to the CompletedTopicsByChapter folder on your USB flash drive, create a new folder named *Ch7*, and save a copy of the document within the Ch7 folder as **7.1-InsulaSummary-Your Name**.
3. Position the insertion point at the beginning of the first paragraph of text.
4. Tap or click the INSERT tab and then tap or click the **Online Pictures button** in the Illustrations group.

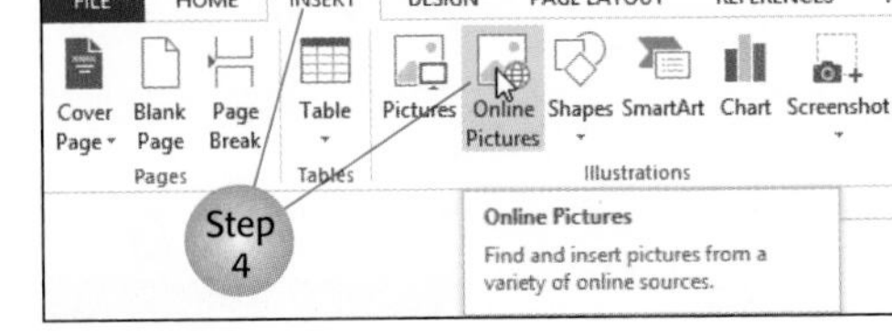

5. At the Insert Pictures dialog box with the insertion point positioned in the *Office.com Clip Art* search text box, type **scientist** and then tap or press Enter, or tap or click the Search button (displays as a magnifying glass).

App Tip

New to Word 2013 is the ability to choose photos directly from an online service such as Flickr or Facebook. Another new feature is the Online Video button in the Media group used to add and play videos within a Word document.

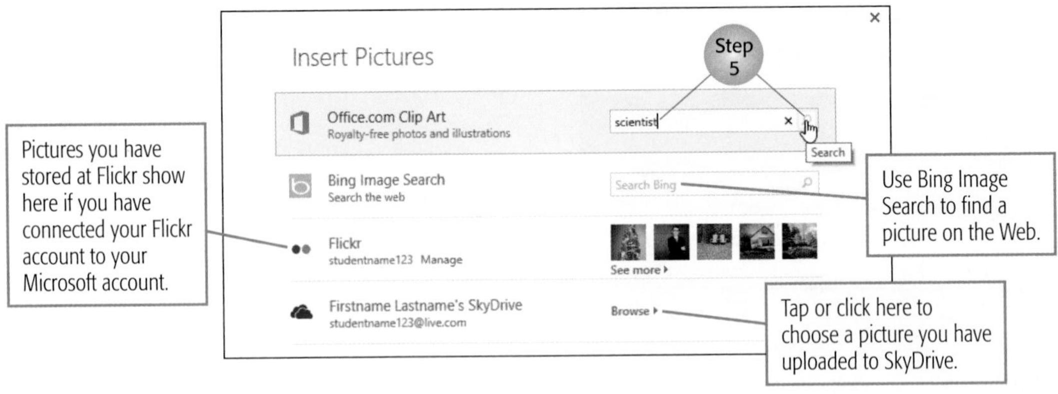

6 Slide or scroll down the search results list to the image shown at the right, tap or click to select the image, and then tap or click the Insert button.

7 Tap or click the **Layout Options button** that appears to the right of the inserted image.

8 Tap or click *Square*, the first option in the *With Text Wrapping* section of the *LAYOUT OPTIONS* palette, and then tap or click the Close button.

The *LAYOUT OPTIONS* gallery provides choices to control how text wraps around the picture object and whether the picture should remain fixed at its current position or move with the text. Notice also that the PICTURE TOOLS FORMAT tab becomes active when a picture is selected. You will work with buttons in this tab later in this topic.

9 Slide or drag the picture right until the right edge of the picture is aligned at the right margin.

As you move the picture, green alignment guides help you position the image at the top of the paragraph and at the right margin.

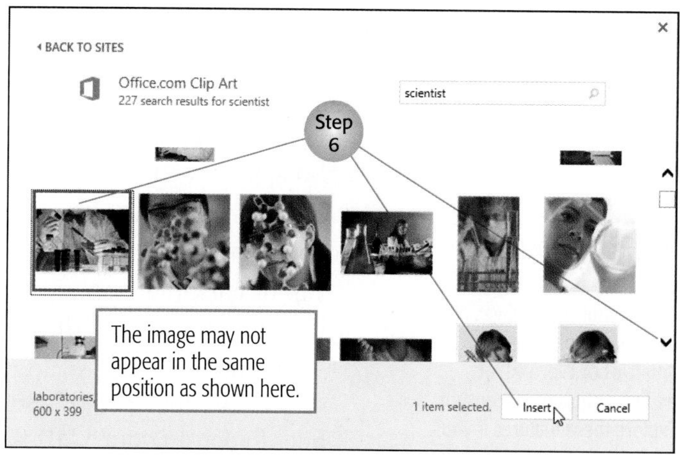

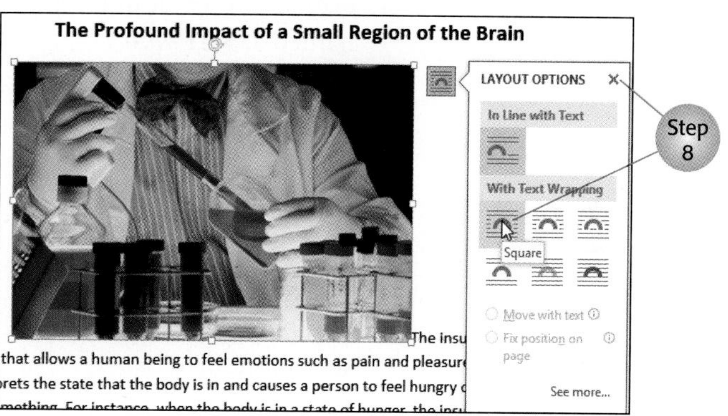

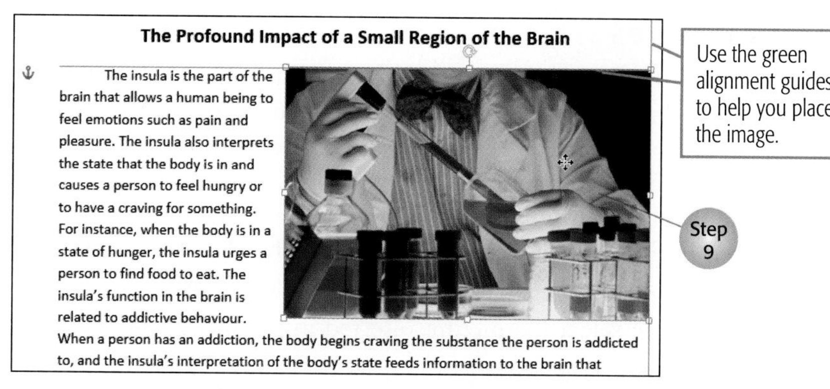

Image shown not in search results? Choose another suitable image if the one shown is not available.

Live layout and alignment guides (also called smart guides) are new to Word 2013.

10 Slide or drag the selection handle at the bottom left of the image up and toward the right until the picture is resized to the approximate size shown.

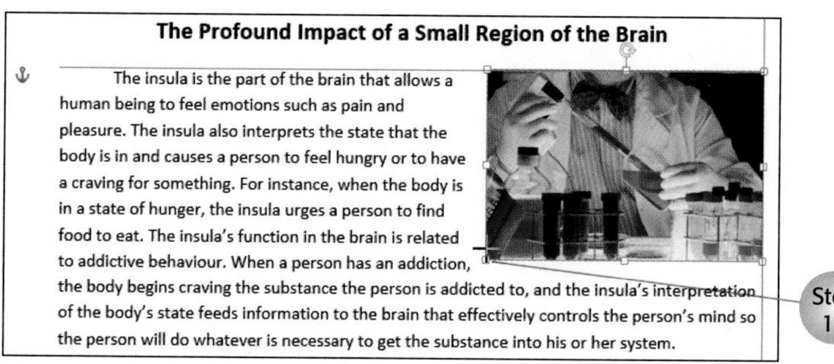

11 Save the revised document using the same name (**7.1-InsulaSummary-Your Name**).

Inserting Pictures from Your Computer

Images you have scanned or imported from your digital camera to your PC or mobile device can be inserted into the document using the **Pictures button** in the Illustrations group. The Layout Options button and PICTURE TOOLS FORMAT tab also appear for a picture that has been inserted from your PC.

App Tip

Create your own images by drawing Shapes, creating SmartArt or WordArt, or adding a chart or screenshot. Explore these features if you want to add a graphic but do not have a picture available.

12 Position the insertion point at the beginning of the second paragraph in the document.

13 Tap or click the Pictures button in the Illustrations group of the INSERT tab.

14 At the Insert Picture dialog box, navigate to the Ch7 folder in the Student_Data_Files folder on your USB flash drive and double-tap or double-click the image named ***USCPhoto***.

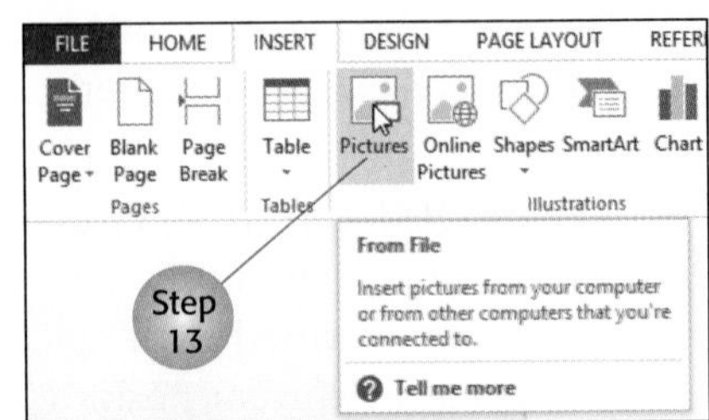

15 Tap or click the Layout Options button, tap or click *Square*, and then close the *LAYOUT OPTIONS* palette.

16 Resize the picture to the approximate size shown in the image at right and position the photo at the left margin.

Step 16

the person will do whatever is necessary to get the substance into his or her system.

If scientists could alter how the insula works in living people, the insula could be used to treat or cure drug addictive behaviour by focusing on regions that are involved in one's decision making. If the insula could be altered to focus on decision making in areas that involve habits, addiction could be controlled. Scientists could weaken some social functions in the insula that give a person the temptation toward a habit such as drugs or alcohol.

Editing Pictures

Buttons in the PICTURE TOOLS FORMAT tab are used to edit an image inserted into a document. Use options in the Adjust group to modify a picture's appearance such as the sharpness, contrast, or color tone, or to apply an artistic effect. Add a border or picture effect with options in the Picture Styles group. Change the picture's position, text wrapping option, order, alignment, or rotation with buttons in the Arrange group. Crop or specify exact measurements for the picture's height and width with buttons in the Size group.

17 Tap or click to select the picture inserted in the first paragraph.

18 Tap or click *Soft Edge Rectangle* (sixth option) in the Picture Styles group of the PICTURE TOOLS FORMAT tab.

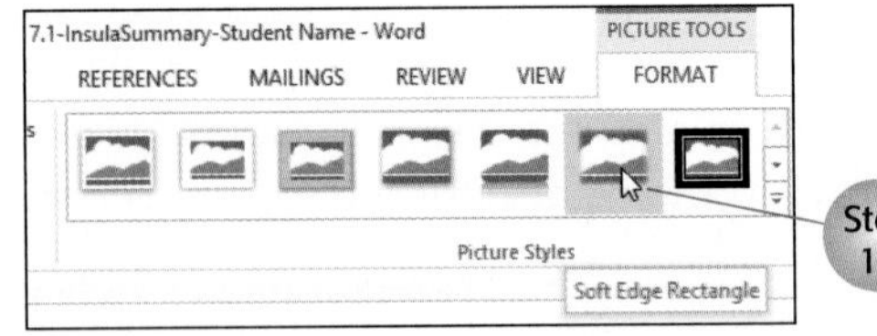

19 Tap or click to select the picture inserted in the second paragraph.

20 Tap or click the Color button in the Adjust group and tap or click *Saturation: 400%* (last option) in the *Color Saturation* section of the drop-down gallery.

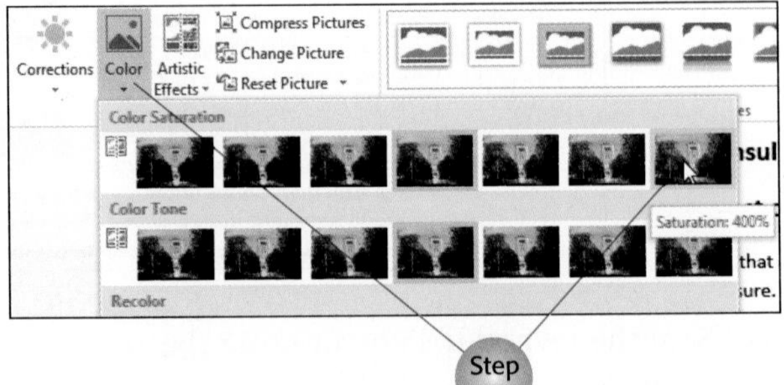

You will notice the picture appears brighter than it did before. Saturation refers to the purity of colors in a photo. Some digital cameras use a low saturation level, making pictures' color seem dull; increasing the saturation level brightens a picture.

Inserting a Caption with a Picture

Adding a caption below a photograph can help a reader understand the picture's context, or you can use captions to number figures in a report. With the **Insert Caption** feature, Word will automatically number pictures, inserting the number after the label Figure.

21 With the picture in the second paragraph still selected, tap or click the REFERENCES tab.

22 Tap or click the Insert Caption button in the Captions group.

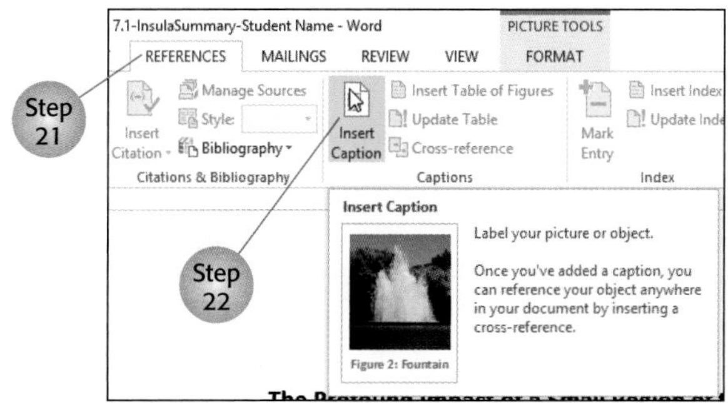

23 At the Caption dialog box, with the insertion point positioned in the *Caption* text box, press the spacebar and type **Insula research is being done at the University of Southern California.**

24 Tap or press Enter or tap or click OK.

25 Tap or click in the document outside the caption box to deselect the caption.

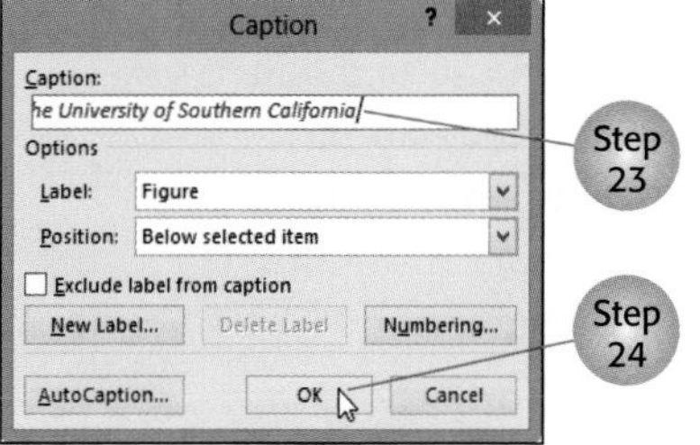

26 Save the revised document using the same name (**7.1-InsulaSummary-Your Name**). Leave the document open for the next topic.

For advanced documents, such as a research report, Word can automatically generate a Table of Figures from captions.

Insert Clip Art or Online Photo
1. Position insertion point.
2. Tap or click INSERT tab.
3. Tap or click Online Pictures button.
4. Type search word or phrase.
5. Select desired image.
6. Tap or click Insert.

Insert an Image from the Computer
1. Position insertion point.
2. Tap or click INSERT tab.
3. Tap or click Pictures button.
4. Navigate to drive and/or folder.
5. Double-tap or double-click desired image.

Edit a Picture
1. Select image.
2. Change layout options, resize, move, or otherwise edit picture as needed.

Insert a Caption
1. Select image.
2. Tap or click REFERENCES tab.
3. Tap or click Insert Caption button.
4. Type caption text.
5. Tap or click OK.

Cropping and Removing a Picture's Background

You can remove unwanted portions of a picture with the Crop tool in the Size group of the PICTURE TOOLS FORMAT tab. Tap or click the Crop button and then use the crop handles to modify the picture. The portion of the image that will remain appears normal, while the cropped area becomes dark gray. Tap or click outside the image to complete the crop action.

The Remove Background button in the PICTURE TOOLS FORMAT tab is another tool you can use to remove portions of a photo. With this button, you can focus on an object in the foreground of a picture and remove the background. For example, with a photo of an airplane in the sky, you can select the airplane and have Word remove the sky in the background.

Adding Borders and Shading and Inserting a Text Box

Topic 7.2

SKILLS

Add a paragraph border

Add shading within a paragraph

Add a border to a page

Insert a text box

Use *Borders and Shading* from the *Borders* gallery to create a custom border in the Borders and Shading dialog box in which you change the border style, color, and width.

oops!

Orange, Accent 6, Lighter 80% not in color gallery? Choose a color similar to light orange, or pick another color of your choice.

Add a border and/or add color behind text (called **shading**) to make text stand out from the rest of a document. You can add borders and shading to a single paragraph, to a group of selected paragraphs, or choose to add a page border to the entire page. You can also add a line that spans the entire page width by choosing *Horizontal Line* at the ***Borders* gallery**.

A text box is used to set a short passage of text apart from the rest of a document. Word includes several built-in text box styles that can be used for this purpose.

1. With the **7.1-InsulaSummary-Your Name** document open, select the first two lines of the document that are the title and subtitle text.
2. Tap or click the HOME tab and then tap or click the Borders button arrow in the Paragraph group.

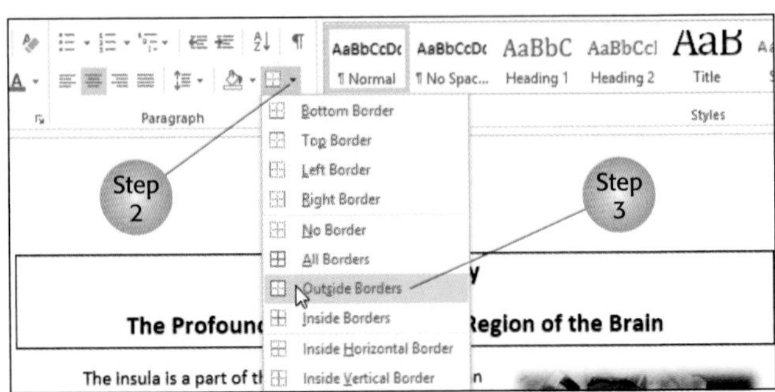

3. Tap or click *Outside Borders* at the *Borders* gallery.
4. With the text still selected, tap or click the Shading button arrow in the Paragraph group.

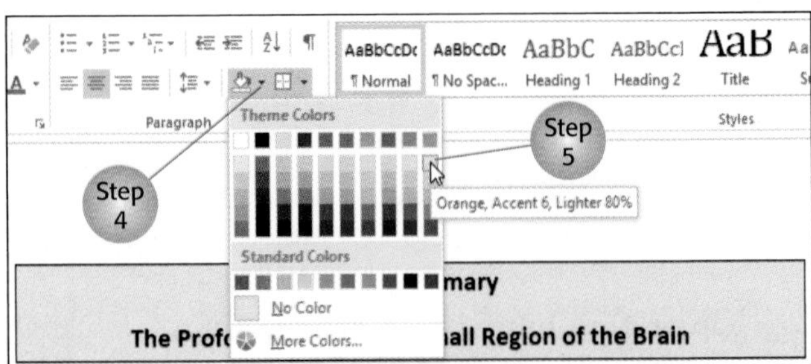

5. Tap or click *Orange, Accent 6, Lighter 80%* at the *Shading* color gallery (last color in second row of *Theme Colors* section).
6. Tap or click in any paragraph to deselect the text.
7. Tap or click the DESIGN tab.
8. Tap or click the **Page Borders button** in the Page Background group.

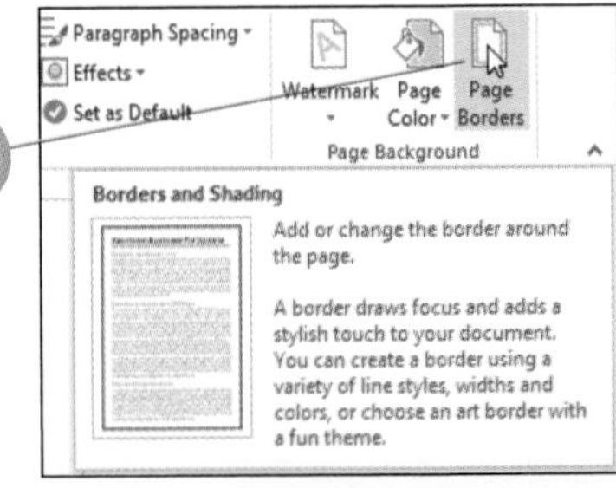

9. At the Borders and Shading dialog box with the Page Border tab selected, tap or click *Shadow* in the *Setting* section.
10. Tap or click the *Width* list arrow and then tap or click *1 ½ pt* at the drop-down list.
11. Tap or click OK.

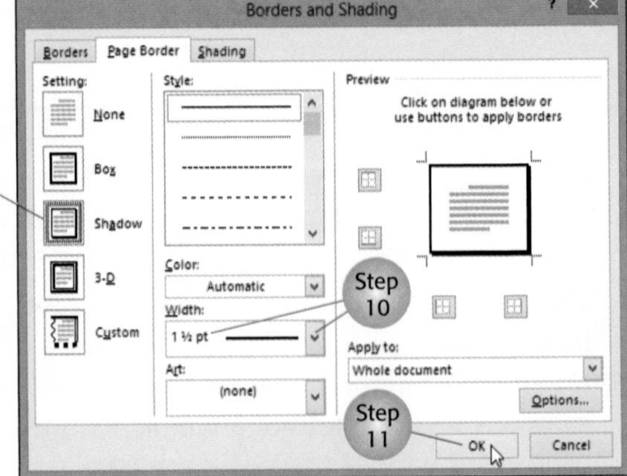

Inserting text inside a box is a way to draw the reader's attention to an important quote or point in a document. A quote inside a text box is called a **pull quote**.

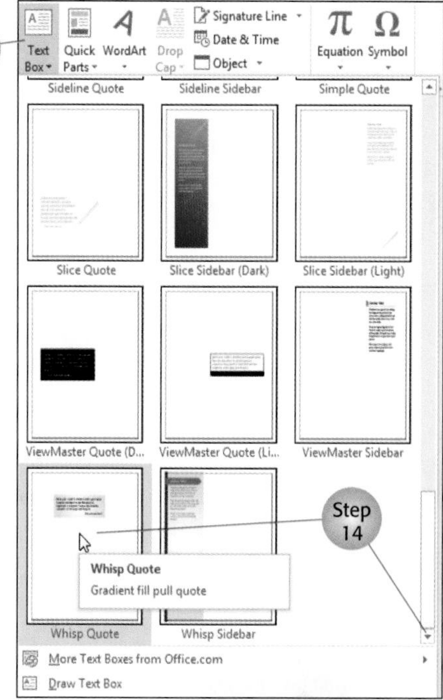

12 Position the insertion point at the end of the document and tap or click the INSERT tab.

13 Tap or click the **Text Box button** in the Text group.

14 Slide or scroll down and then tap or click *Whisp Quote* at the drop-down list.

Word adds the text box with default text already selected inside the text box.

15 Type **Some people with damage to the insula were able to quit smoking instantly!**

16 Press and hold or right-click *[Cite your source here]* and choose *Remove Content Control* at the shortcut menu.

17 Slide or drag the text box (point to the border of the box if using a mouse) to the bottom of the page to the approximate location shown.

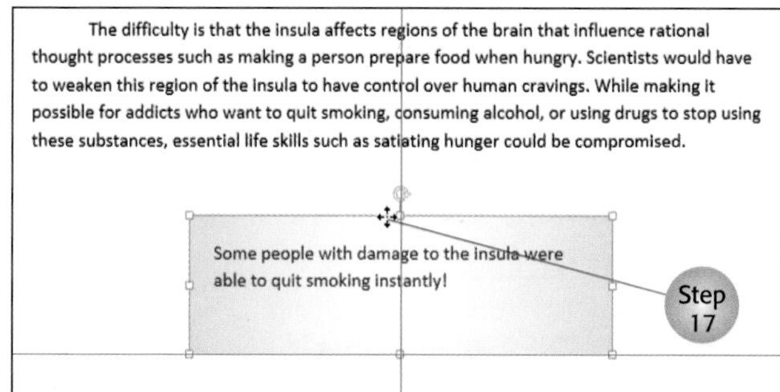

18 Slide or drag the bottom middle selection handle up to reduce the height of the text box as shown.

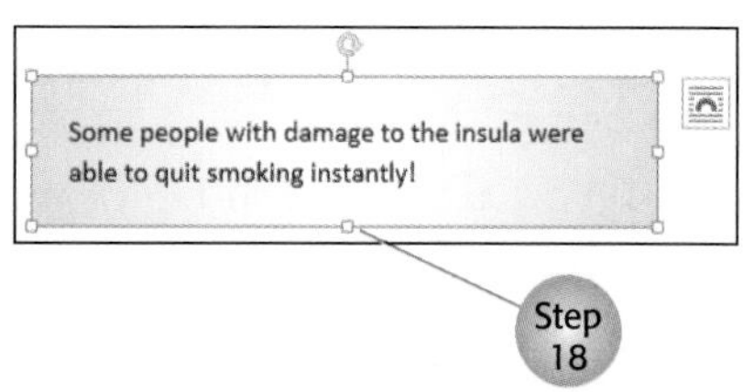

19 Tap or click in any paragraph to deselect the text box and save the revised document using the same name (**7.1-InsulaSummary-Your Name**).

20 Close the document.

Add a Paragraph Border
1. Select paragraph(s).
2. Tap or click Borders button arrow.
3. Tap or click desired border style.

Add Shading to a Paragraph
1. Select paragraph(s).
2. Tap or click Shading button arrow.
3. Tap or click desired color.

Add a Page Border
1. Tap or click DESIGN tab.
2. Tap or click Page Borders button.
3. Select desired *Setting* and *Style*, *Color*, *Width*, or *Art* options.
4. Tap or click OK.

Insert a Text Box
1. Tap or click INSERT tab.
2. Tap or click Text Box button.
3. Tap or click desired text box style.
4. Type text.
5. Move and/or resize box as needed.

Formatting Tools to Edit a Text Box

Use buttons in the DRAWING TOOLS FORMAT tab to edit a text box. You can change the text box shape style, fill, or outline and add shape effects. Edit the appearance of the text inside the box by applying a WordArt style, changing the text fill or outline, adding text effects, or changing the alignment or direction of the text.

Topic 7.3

SKILLS

Insert a table

Type data in a new table grid

Use the *Recent Folders* list at the Open tab Backstage view with *Computer* selected to return to the Student_Data_Files folder with just one tap or click.

Inserting a Table

A **table** is used to organize and present data in columns and rows. Text is typed within a **table cell**, which is a rectangular box that is the intersection of a column and a row. When you create a table, you specify the number of columns and rows the table will hold and Word creates a blank grid within which you type the table data.

You can also create a new table using **Quick Tables**, which are predefined tables with sample data that you can replace with your own text. Text that you want to place side-by-side, or in rows, is ideal for a table. For example, a price list or a catalog with items and descriptions is ideal for a table.

1. Open the document **RezMealPlans** from the Ch7 folder in Student_Data_Files.
2. Save the document as **7.3-RezMealPlans-Your Name** in the Ch7 folder in CompletedTopicsByChapter.
3. Position the insertion point at the left margin in the blank line below the subheading *Meal Plans with Descriptions*.
4. Tap or click the INSERT tab and then tap or click the Table button in the Tables group.
5. Tap or click the box in the drop-down grid that is three columns to the right and two rows down (*3x2 Table* displays above grid).
6. With the insertion point positioned in the first table cell, type **Meal Plan Name** and then tap or press Tab, or tap or click in the next cell.

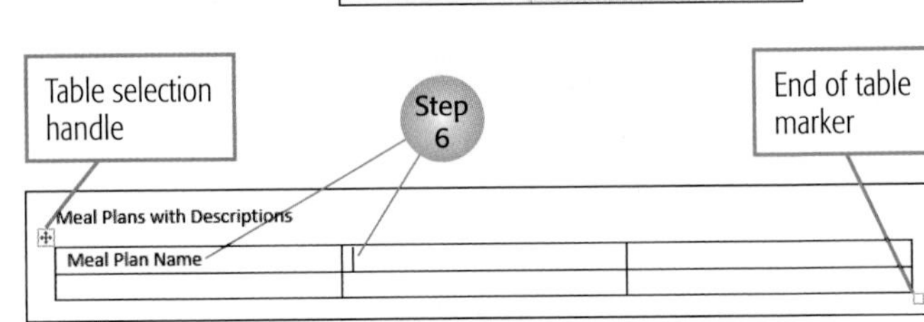

7. Type **Cost** and then tap or press Tab, or tap or click in the next cell.
8. Type **Description** and then tap or press Tab, or tap or click in the first cell in the second row.
9. Type the second row of data as follows. When you finish typing the text in the last column, tap or press Tab to add a new row to the table automatically.

Minimum	**$1,900**	**Suitable for students with small appetites who plan to be away from residence most weekends.**

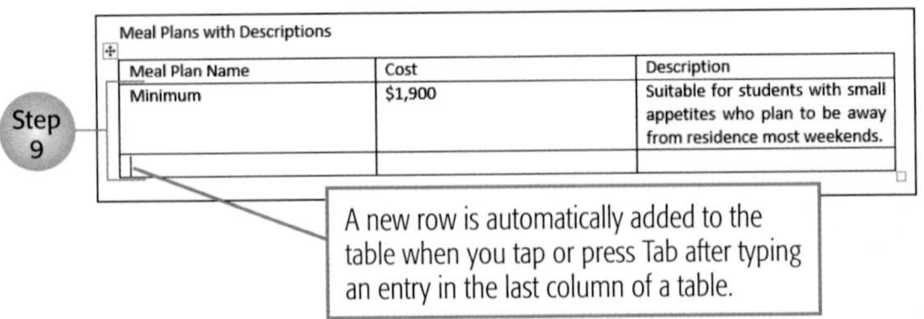

10. Type the remainder of the table as shown in Figure 7.1 by completing steps similar to those in Steps 6 to 9, except do not tap or press Tab after typing the last table cell entry.

The advantage to using a table versus typing information in tabbed columns is that information can wrap around within a table cell.

oops!

Added a new row by mistake? Tap or click the Undo button to remove the extra row.

Meal Plans with Descriptions

Meal Plan Name	Cost	Description
Minimum	$1,900	Suitable for students with small appetites who plan to be away from residence most weekends.
Light	$2,100	Best plan for students with a lighter appetite who spend occasional weekends on campus.
Full	$2,200	Full is the most popular plan. This plan is for students with an average appetite who will stay on campus most weekends.
Plus	$2,300	Students with a hearty appetite who will stay on campus most weekends choose the Plus plan.

The column alignment is Justified because of the document's style set. Generally, cells are aligned left in new tables.

Figure 7.1 Table data for first table in Topic 7.3 with the default design and layout options shown

11 Position the insertion point at the left margin in the blank line below the subheading *Meal Plan Fund Allocations*.

12 Tap or click the Table button in the INSERT tab and then tap or click *Insert Table* at the drop-down list.

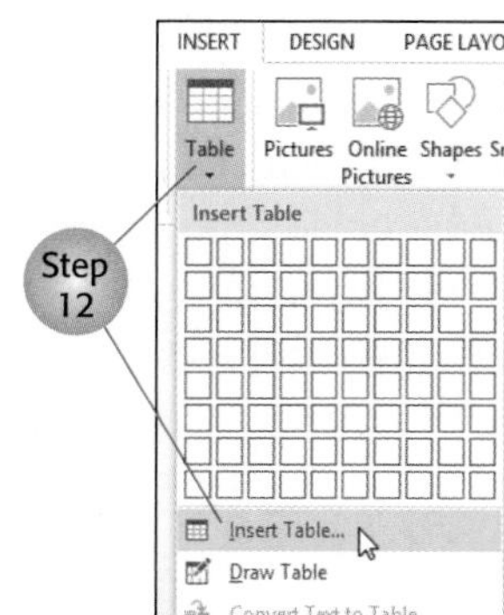

You can also insert a new table using a dialog box in which you specify the number of columns and rows.

13 At the Insert Table dialog box, with the value in the *Number of columns* text box already selected, type 5 and then tap or press Tab, or select the value in the *Number of rows* text box.

14 Type 5 and then tap or press Enter, or tap or click OK.

15 Type the data in the new table as shown in Figure 7.2. Tap or click in the paragraph below the table after typing the text in the last table cell.

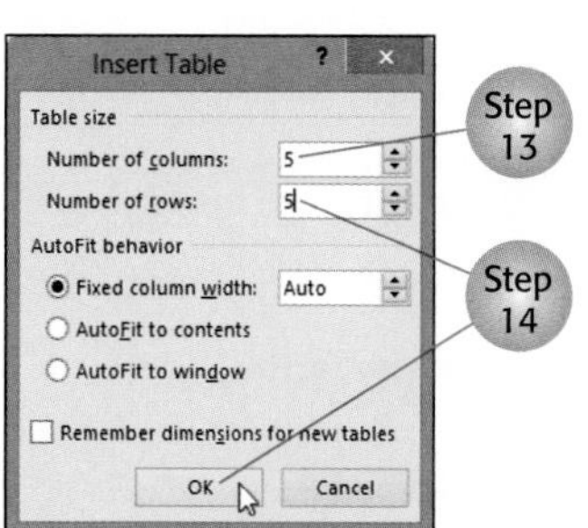

Insert a Table

1. Tap or click INSERT tab.
2. Tap or click Table button.
3. Tap or click box in drop-down grid for desired columns and rows.
4. Type table text.

OR

1. Tap or click INSERT tab.
2. Tap or click Table button.
3. Tap or click *Insert Table*.
4. Type number of columns.
5. Change *Number of rows* to desired value.
6. Tap or click OK.
7. Type table text.

Meal Plan Fund Allocations

Meal Plan Name	Total Cost	Operating Fund	Basic Fund	Flex Fund
Minimum	$1,900	$100	$1,575	$225
Light	$2,100	$100	$1,725	$275
Full	$2,200	$100	$1,775	$325
Plus	$2,300	$100	$1,850	$350

Note that the Basic fund is tax exempt and is designed for use at all on-campus restaurants. Flex fund purchases are taxable.

Tap or click outside the table grid after typing the last table cell entry to avoid adding a new row to the table.

Figure 7.2 Table data for second table in Topic 7.3

16 Save the document using the same name (**7.3-RezMealPlans-Your Name**). Leave the document open for the next topic.

Topic 7.4

SKILLS

Apply and customize a table style

Insert and delete rows and columns

Change column width

Change cell alignment

Merge cells

Formatting and Modifying a Table

Once a table has been inserted into the document, use buttons in the TABLE TOOLS DESIGN and LAYOUT tabs to format the table's appearance and add or delete rows and columns. Choose a predesigned collection of formatting options that add borders, shading, and color to a table from the ***Table Styles*** gallery.

1. With the **7.3-RezMealPlans-Your Name** document open, position the insertion point in any table cell within the first table.
2. Tap or click the TABLE TOOLS DESIGN tab.
3. Tap or click the More button (displays with a bar and down-pointing arrow) in the *Table Styles* gallery.
4. Tap or click *Grid Table 4 – Accent 2* (third option in fourth row in *Grid Tables* section).

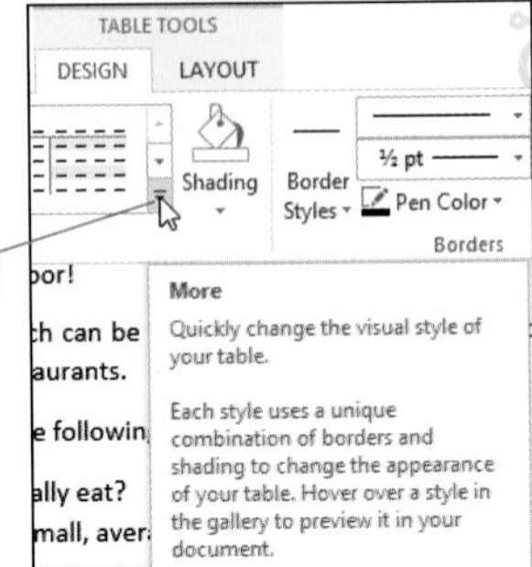

Notice the formatting applied to the column headings and text in the first column. Shading applied to every other row makes the table data easier to read (referred to as **banded rows**) and the border around each cell is now colored. The check boxes in the Table Style Options group, the Shading button in the Table Styles group, and the buttons in the Borders group are used to further modify the table formatting.

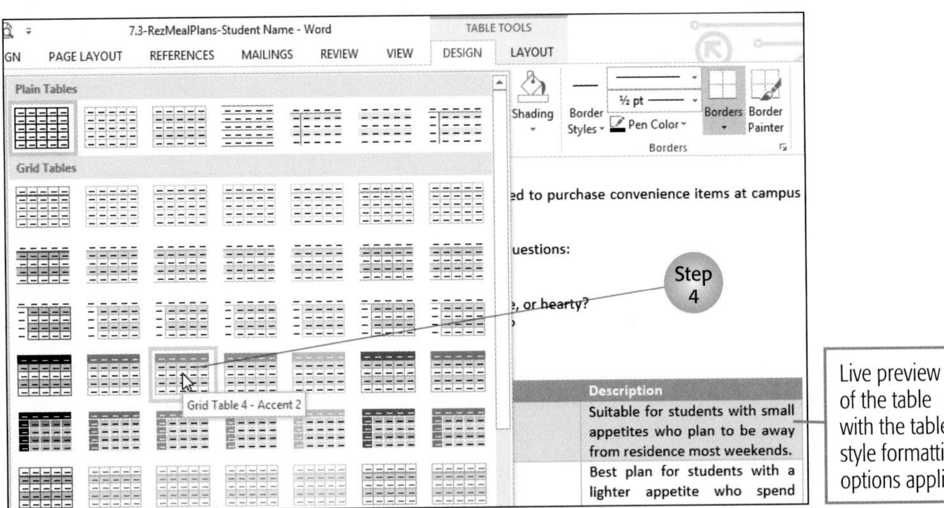

Live preview of the table with the table style formatting options applied

5. Tap or click the *First Column* check box in the Table Style Options group to remove the check mark.

Notice the bold formatting is removed from the text in the first column.

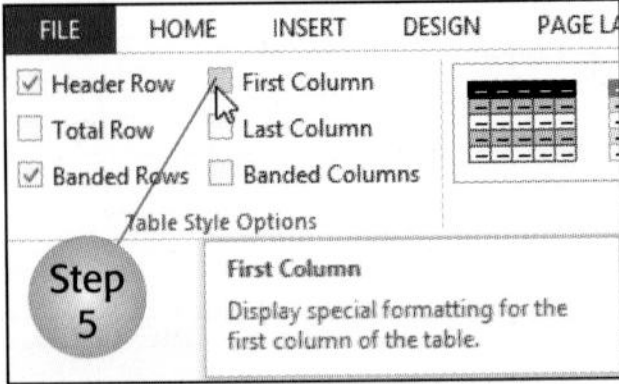

6 Select the column headings in the first row of the table, tap or click the Shading button arrow in the Mini toolbar or in the Table Styles group of the TABLE TOOLS DESIGN tab, and then tap or click *Orange, Accent 2, Darker 50%* (sixth option in last row of *Theme Colors* section).

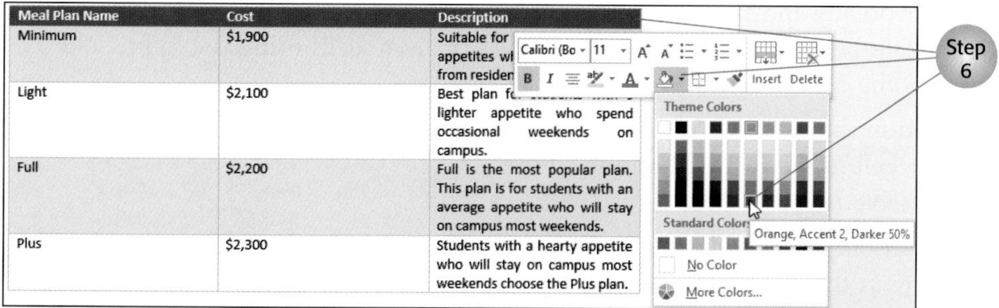

Inserting and Deleting Columns and Rows

Buttons in the Rows & Columns group of the TABLE TOOLS LAYOUT tab are used to insert or delete columns or rows. Position the insertion point within a table row and tap or click the Insert Above or Insert Below button to add a new row to the table. The Insert Left and Insert Right buttons are used to add a new column to the table.

Position the insertion point within a table cell, select multiple rows or columns or select the entire table, and then tap or click the Delete button to delete cells, a column, a row, or the table.

7 Position the insertion point within any table cell in the third row of the first table (begins with *Light*).

8 Tap or click the TABLE TOOLS LAYOUT tab.

9 Tap or click the Delete button in the Rows & Columns group.

10 Tap or click *Delete Rows* at the drop-down list.

11 Position the insertion point within any table cell in the third row of the second table (begins with *Light*), tap or click the Delete button, and tap or click *Delete Rows.*

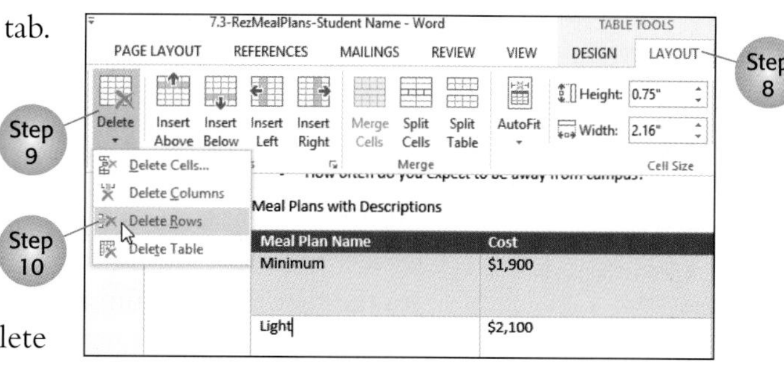

12 Position the insertion point within any table cell in the last column of the first table.

13 Tap or click the Insert Left button in the Rows & Columns group.

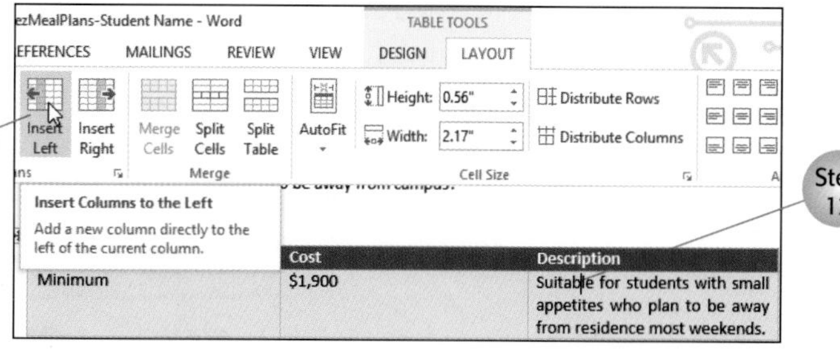

A new column is created between the *Cost* and *Description* columns. Notice that Word adjusts each column to be the same width. New rows are inserted by following a similar process.

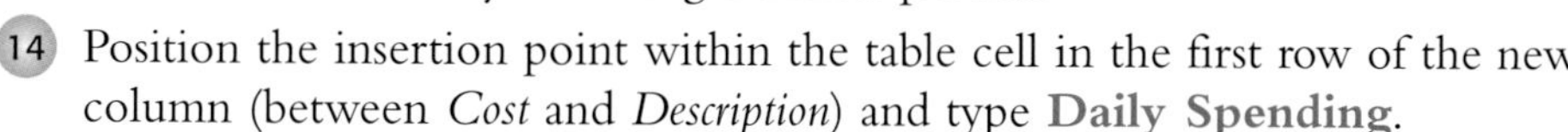

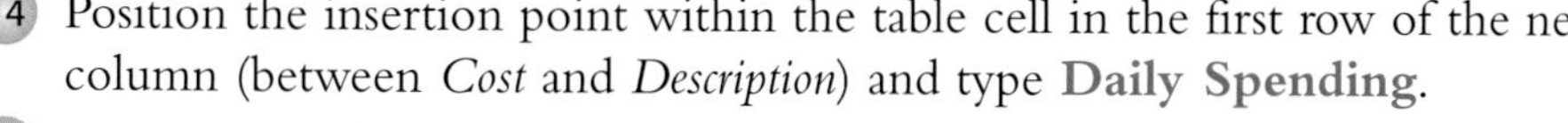

14 Position the insertion point within the table cell in the first row of the new column (between *Cost* and *Description*) and type **Daily Spending**.

15 Type the values below the column heading in rows 2, 3, and 4 as follows:

$17.38

$20.23

$21.12

Format a Table
1. Position insertion point within table cell.
2. If necessary, tap or click TABLE TOOLS DESIGN tab.
3. Select desired Table Styles option.
4. Customize Table Style Options, Shading, or Borders as needed.

Insert Columns or Rows
1. Position insertion point in desired table cell.
2. If necessary, tap or click TABLE TOOLS LAYOUT tab.
3. Tap or click Insert Above, Insert Below, Insert Left, or Insert Right button.

Delete Columns or Rows
1. Position insertion point in desired table cell.
2. If necessary, tap or click TABLE TOOLS LAYOUT tab.
3. Tap or click Delete button.
4. Tap or click desired option at drop-down list.

Modify Column Width
1. Position insertion point within table cell in desired column.
2. If necessary, tap or click TABLE TOOLS LAYOUT tab.
3. Change *Width* measurement value to desired width.

Modify Cell Alignment
1. Select column, row, or table cells.
2. If necessary, tap or click TABLE TOOLS LAYOUT tab.
3. Tap or click desired button in Alignment group.

Merge or Split Cells
1. Select column, row, or table cells.
2. If necessary, tap or click TABLE TOOLS LAYOUT tab.
3. Tap or click Merge Cells or Split Cells button.

Modifying Column Width and Alignment and Merging Cells

Adjust the width of a column by dragging the border line between columns left or right. You can also enter precise width measurements in the *Width* text box in the Cell Size group. Use the buttons in the Alignment group to align text within cells horizontally and vertically. Combine two or more cells into one cell using the Merge Cells button or divide a cell into two or more cells using the Split Cells button in the Merge group.

16 Position the insertion point within any table cell in the second column of the first table (column heading is *Cost*).

17 Tap or click the *Width* down-pointing arrow in the Cell Size group until the value is *1"*.

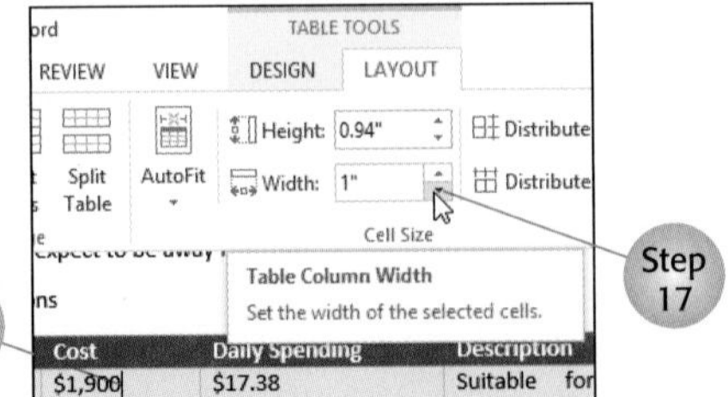

Step 16

You can also drag the right column border left or right to resize a column width or select the value in the text box and type a measurement value.

18 Position the insertion point within any table cell in the last column of the first table (column heading is *Description*) and tap or click the *Width* up-pointing arrow until the value is 2.3".

19 With the insertion point still positioned within the last column of the first table, tap or click the Select button in the Table group and then tap or click *Select Column* at the drop-down list.

Step 18

20 Tap or click the Align Top Left button in the Alignment group (first button).

21 Select the first column in the first table (column heading is *Meal Plan Name*) and tap or click the Align Center button in the Alignment group (second button in second row).

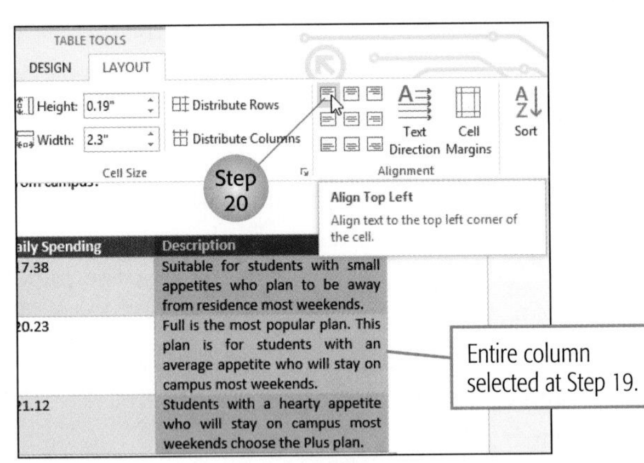

22 Repeat step 21 to Align Center the second and third columns in the first table.

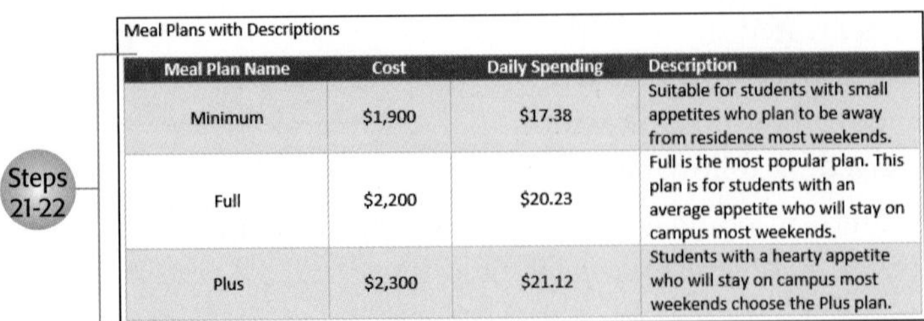

Meal Plans with Descriptions

Meal Plan Name	Cost	Daily Spending	Description
Minimum	$1,900	$17.38	Suitable for students with small appetites who plan to be away from residence most weekends.
Full	$2,200	$20.23	Full is the most popular plan. This plan is for students with an average appetite who will stay on campus most weekends.
Plus	$2,300	$21.12	Students with a hearty appetite who will stay on campus most weekends choose the Plus plan.

Steps 21-22

23 Position the insertion point within any table cell in the first row of the second table and tap or click the Insert Above button in the Rows & Columns group.

24 With the new row already selected, tap or click the Merge Cells button in the Merge group.

25 With the new row still selected, type **Breakdown of Meal Plan Cost by Fund** and then tap or click the Align Top Center button in the Alignment group (second button in first row).

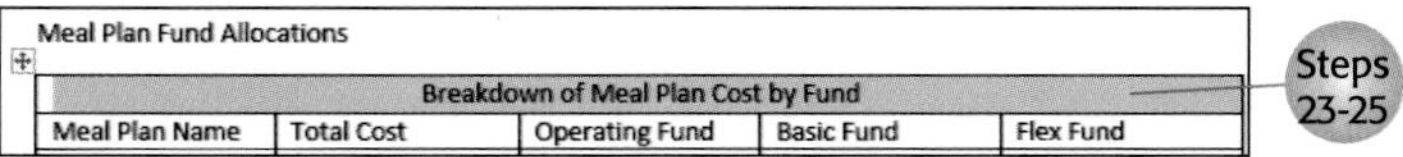

Meal Plan Fund Allocations
Breakdown of Meal Plan Cost by Fund
Meal Plan Name
Total Cost
Operating Fund
Basic Fund
Flex Fund

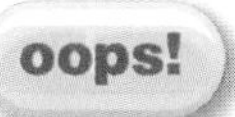

Merged row selected too? Select the cells by sliding or dragging with a mouse—do not use the Select button because *Select Column* will include the merged cell.

26 Select the column headings and all of the values in columns 2, 3, 4, and 5 in the second table and then tap or click the Align Center button.

27 With the insertion point positioned within any table cell in the second table, tap or click the Select button and then tap or click *Select Table*.

28 Tap or click the TABLE TOOLS DESIGN tab.

29 Tap or click the Borders button in the Borders group and then tap or click *No Border* at the drop-down list.

App Tip

You can also select the table with a mouse by clicking the Table selection handle at the top left corner of the table.

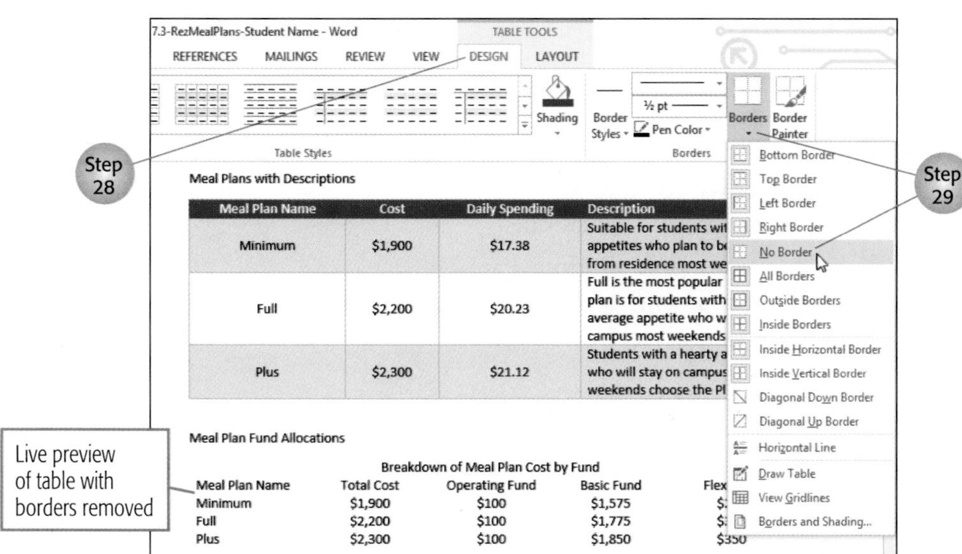

Create a table for any type of columnar text instead of setting tabs—tables are simpler to create and have more formatting options.

30 Tap or click in the paragraph below the table to deselect the table.

31 Apply the Heading 2 style to the text *Meal Plans with Descriptions* and *Meal Plan Fund Allocations* above the first and second tables.

32 Save the document using the same name (**7.3-RezMealPlans-Your Name**) and then close the document.

ALTERNATIVE method

In this topic you used buttons in the TABLE TOOLS DESIGN and LAYOUT tabs to format and modify tables. Press and hold or right-click within a table cell or with table cells selected to display a context-sensitive shortcut menu and Mini toolbar. Use options from the shortcut menu or Mini toolbar to insert or delete cells, columns, or rows, merge or split cells, change a border style, or modify table properties.

Topic 7.5

SKILLS

Change page orientation

Change margins

Insert a page break

App Tip

Use the Size button in the Page Setup group to change the paper size to legal (8.5 x 14), envelope, or several other predefined photo or index card sizes.

The Columns button in the Page Setup group formats a document into two or more newspaper-style columns of text.

Changing Page Layout Options

By default, new documents in Word are set up for a letter-sized page (8.5 x 11 inches) in portrait orientation with one-inch margins at the left, right, top, and bottom. **Portrait** orientation means that the text on the page is vertically oriented with a 6.5-inch line length (8.5 inches minus two inches for the left and right margins). This is the orientation commonly used for most documents and books. You can change to **landscape** orientation, where the text is rotated to the wider side of the page with a 9-inch line length.

1. Open the document **ChildLitBookRpt** from the Ch7 folder in Student_Data_Files.
2. Save the document as **7.5-ChildLitBookRpt-Your Name** in the Ch7 folder in CompletedTopicsByChapter.
3. Tap or click the PAGE LAYOUT tab.
4. Tap or click the Orientation button in the Page Setup group and then tap or click *Landscape*.

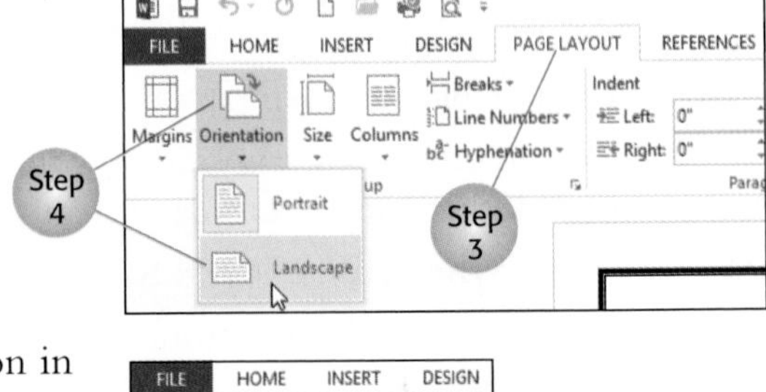

Notice the width of the page is extended, and the page is now wider than it is tall.

5. Slide or scroll down to view the document in landscape orientation.
6. With the insertion point positioned at the top of the document, tap or click the Margins button in the Page Setup group.
7. Tap or click *Custom Margins* at the drop-down list.

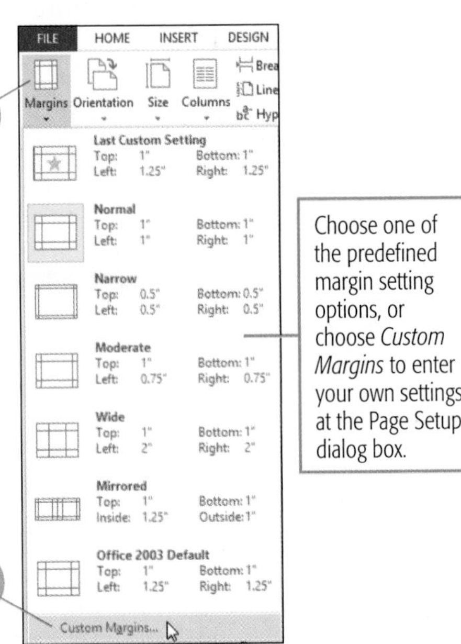

Choose one of the predefined margin setting options, or choose *Custom Margins* to enter your own settings at the Page Setup dialog box.

8. With the insertion point positioned in the *Top* text box in the *Margins* section of the Page Setup dialog box, tap or press Tab twice, or select the current value in the *Left* text box and type 1.2.
9. Tap or press Tab, or select the current value in the *Right* text box, type 1.2, and tap or press Enter, or tap or click OK.
10. Slide or scroll down to view the document with the new left and right margin settings.

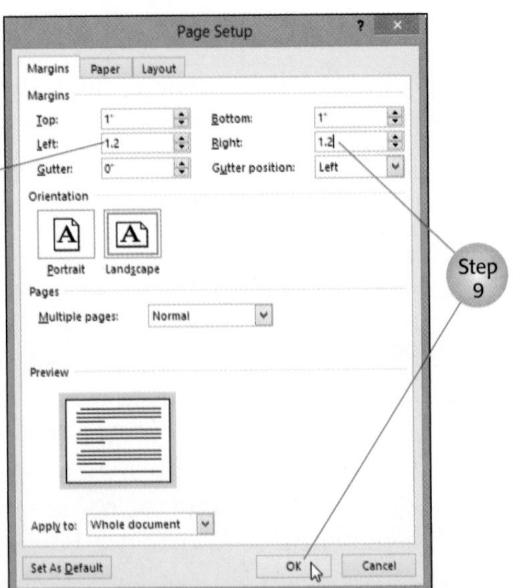

Sometimes you want to end a page before the point at which Word ends a page automatically and starts a new page (referred to as a **soft page break**). Soft page breaks occur when the maximum number of lines that can fit within the current page size and margins has been reached. A page break that you insert at a different location is called a **hard page break**.

11 Position the insertion point at the left margin next to the subtitle *The Allegories* near the bottom of page 1.

12 Tap or click the INSERT tab.

13 Tap or click the Page Break button in the Pages group.

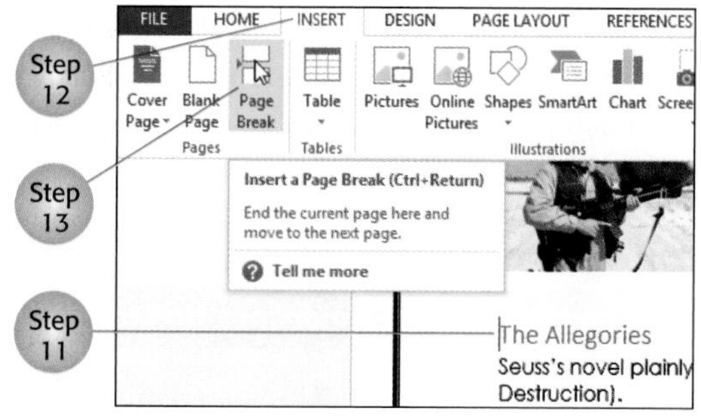

Notice that all of the text from the insertion point onward is moved to page 2.

14 Slide or scroll up and down to view the book report with the new page break.

15 Save the document using the same name (**7.5-ChildLitBookRpt-Your Name**) and then close the document.

ALTERNATIVE method

You can also insert a Page Break using the Breaks button in the Page Setup group of the PAGE LAYOUT tab or by using the keyboard command Ctrl + Enter.

Insert hard page breaks as your last step in preparing a document because hard page breaks do not adjust if you add or delete text.

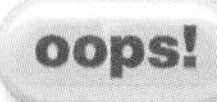

Page break at wrong location? Press Backspace until the page break is deleted or use Undo to remove the page break. Position the insertion point at the correct location and try Step 13 again.

Change to Landscape Orientation
1. Tap or click PAGE LAYOUT tab.
2. Tap or click Orientation button.
3. Tap or click *Landscape*.

Change Margins
1. Tap or click PAGE LAYOUT tab.
2. Tap or click Margins button.
3. Tap or click predefined margin option.

OR
1. Tap or click PAGE LAYOUT tab.
2. Tap or click Margins button.
3. Tap or click *Custom Margins*.
4. Set custom measurements.
5. Tap or click OK.

Insert a Hard Page Break
1. Position insertion point.
2. Tap or click INSERT tab.
3. Tap or click Page Break button.

Beyond Basics

Changing Page Layout for a Section of a Document

By default, changes such as margins or orientation affect the entire document. A **section break** is inserted to change page layout options for a portion of a document. The Breaks button in the Page Setup group of the PAGE LAYOUT tab is used to insert a section break. Choose *Next Page* to insert a section break that also starts a new page or choose *Continuous* to have the section break start at the insertion point position without starting a new page. For example, use section breaks if you want one page in a document to be landscape while the other pages are portrait. To do this, insert a section break where you want a landscape page, change the orientation to landscape, then insert another section break after the landscape page and return the orientation to portrait.

Formatting a Research Paper with a Header and Page Numbers

Topic 7.6

SKILLS

Insert a header

Insert page numbers

Chances are you will have to submit a research paper or essay during the course of your education that is formatted for a specific **style guide** (a set of rules for paper formatting and referencing). Style guides are used in academic and professional writing; MLA (Modern Language Association) and APA (American Psychological Association) are the two most popular guides. See Table 7.1 for general MLA and APA guidelines.

Table 7.1 Formatting and Page Layout Guidelines for MLA and APA

Item	MLA	APA
Paper size and margins	8.5 x 11 with one-inch margins	8.5 x 11 with one-inch margins
Font size	12-point; typeface is not specified other than that it should be easily readable	12-point, with Times New Roman the preferred typeface
Line and paragraph spacing	2.0 with no spacing between paragraphs	2.0 with no spacing between paragraphs
Paragraph indent	Indent first line one-half inch	Indent first line one-half inch
Page numbering	Top right of each page one space after your last name	Top right of each page with paper's title all uppercase at the left margin on the same line
Title page	No (unless specifically requested by your instructor)	Yes Running Head: title of the paper at left margin all uppercase with page number at right margin one-inch from the top. In the upper half of the page centered horizontally include: Title of the paper Your name School name
First page	Top left corner (double-spaced): Your name Instructor's name Course title Date A double-space below the above headings center the title (title case) and then begin the paper.	Center the word *Abstract* at the top of the page. Type a brief summary of the paper in a single paragraph in block format (no indents). Limit yourself to approximately 150 words. Start paper on a new page after the Abstract with the paper's title centered (title case) at the top of the page.
Bibliography	Create separate Works Cited page at end of document organized alphabetically by author.	Create separate References page at end of document organized alphabetically by author.

owl.english.purdue.edu/owl/resource/747/01

Go here for a comprehensive MLA guide.

A **header** is text that appears at the top of each page and a **footer** is text that appears at the bottom of each page. Word provides several predefined headers and footers or you can create your own. Page numbers are added to a document within a header or footer.

1. Open the document **CohabitationEssay** from the Ch7 folder in Student_Data_Files.
2. Save the document as **7.6-CohabitationEssay-Your Name** in the Ch7 folder in CompletedTopicsByChapter.

3 Slide or scroll down and review the formatting in the essay. Notice the paper size, font, margins, line and paragraph spacing, and first line indents are already formatted.

4 Position the insertion point at the beginning of the document and replace the text *Toni McBride* with your first and last name.

The first four lines of this report are set up in MLA format for a first page; however, you need to add the page numbering for an MLA report.

5 Tap or click the INSERT tab and tap or click the Header button in the Header & Footer group.

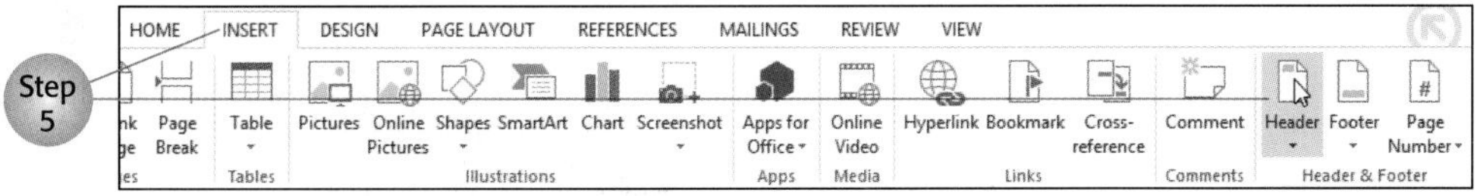

6 Tap or click *Edit Header* at the drop-down list.

7 Tap or press Tab twice to move the insertion point to the right margin, type your last name, and then press the spacebar.

8 Tap or click the **Page Number button** in the Header & Footer group of the HEADER & FOOTER TOOLS DESIGN tab.

9 Tap or point to *Current Position* and then tap or click *Plain Number.*

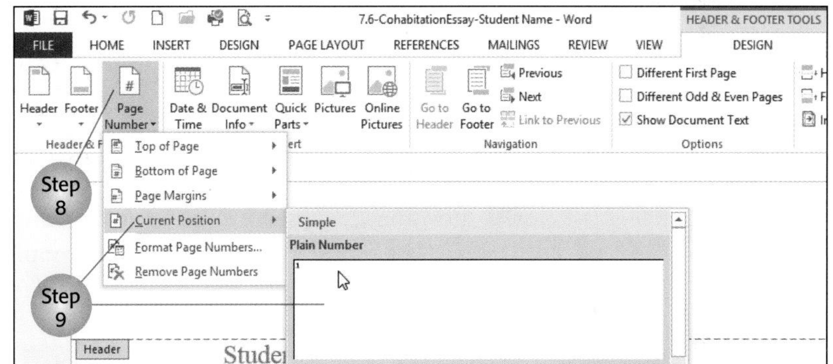

10 Select your last name and the page number in the Header pane.

11 Tap or click the Font button arrow in the Mini toolbar, slide or scroll down the font list, and then tap or click *Times New Roman.*

12 Tap or click the Font Size button arrow in the Mini toolbar and then tap or click *12.*

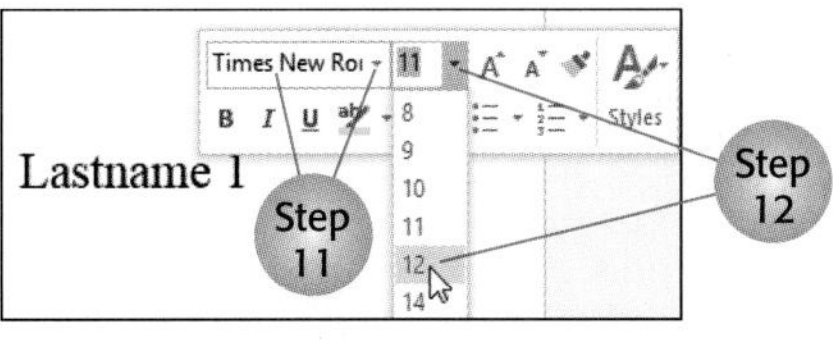

13 Tap or click within the Header pane to deselect the text.

14 Tap or click the Close Header and Footer button in the Close group of the HEADER & FOOTER TOOLS DESIGN tab.

15 Slide or scroll down through the document to view your last name and the page number at the top of each page.

16 Save the document using the same name (**7.6-CohabitationEssay-Your Name**). Leave the document open for the next topic.

Insert a Header or Footer

1. Tap or click INSERT tab.
2. Tap or click Header or Footer button.
3. Tap or click built-in option or choose *Edit Header* or *Edit Footer*.
4. Type text and/or add options as needed.
5. Tap or click Close Header and Footer button.

Insert Page Numbering

1. Within Header or Footer pane, tap or click Page Number button.
2. Tap or point to *Current Position*.
3. Tap or click page number option.
4. Tap or click Close Header and Footer button.

Mini toolbar not visible? Tap or click the HOME tab and change the font and font size using the buttons in the Font group. Tap or click the HEADER & FOOTER TOOLS DESIGN tab at Step 13.

owl.english.purdue.edu/owl/resource/560/01

Go here for a comprehensive APA guide.

Removing Page Number from First Page

In many reports or books, a header and/or page number is suppressed on the first page. Tap or click the *Different First Page* check box in the HEADER & FOOTER TOOLS DESIGN tab to create a First Page header that you can leave blank.

Topic 7.7

SKILLS

Edit a citation

Insert a citation

Inserting and Editing Citations

Direct quotations copied from sources or material you have written in an academic paper that is paraphrased from a source needs to be referenced in a **citation** (source of the information used). Word provides tools to manage sources, insert citations, and edit citations.

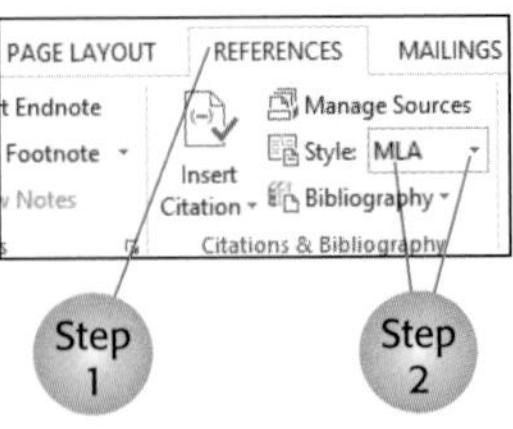

1. With the **7.6-CohabitationEssay-Your Name** document open, tap or click the REFERENCES tab.
2. Look at the *Style* option in the Citations & Bibliography group. If the *Style* is not *MLA*, tap or click the *Style* arrow and then tap or click *MLA* at the drop-down list. (You may need to slide or scroll down the list.)

You will begin by editing an existing citation.

3. Position the insertion point within the *(Jay par. 12)* citation at the end of the indented quotation after the first paragraph (begins with *Cohabitation in the. . .*) to display the citation placeholder.

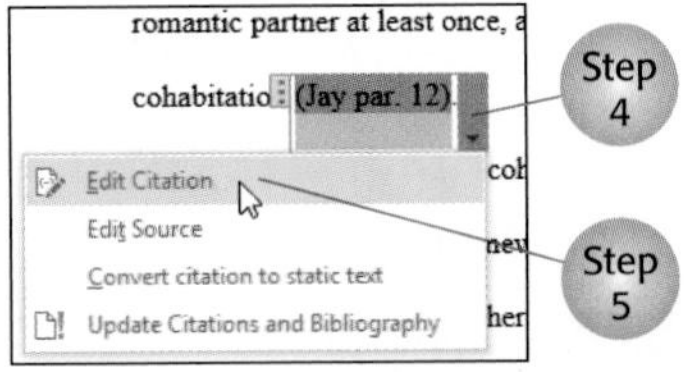

4. Tap or click the Citation Options arrow that appears.
5. Tap or click *Edit Citation*.
6. Type **par. 9** at the Edit Citation dialog box in the *Pages* text box and then tap or press Enter, or tap or click OK.
7. Position the insertion point left of the period that ends the last sentence in the third paragraph that begins *According to a research study done at Ohio . . ,* and press the spacebar.
8. Tap or click the Insert Citation button in the Citations & Bibliography group.
9. Tap or click *Add New Source* at the drop-down list.

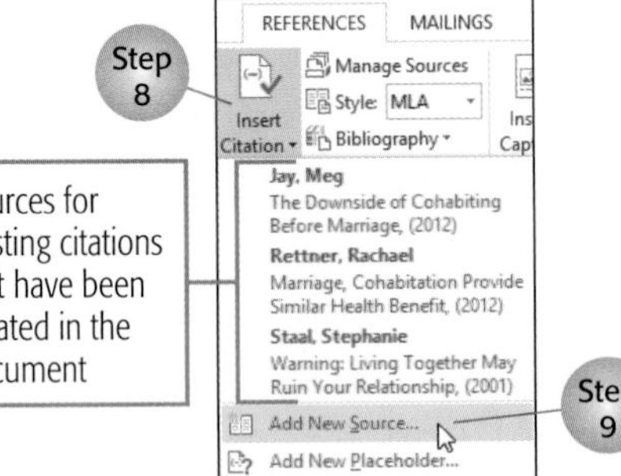

10. At the Create Source dialog box, tap or click the *Type of Source* list arrow and then tap or click *Document From Web site* at the drop-down list. (You may need to slide or scroll down the list.)
11. Tap or click in the *Author* text box and type **Grabmeier, J.**.
12. Tap or click in the *Name of Web Page* text box and type **Couples Live Together for Convenience, Not to Test Marriage**.
13. Tap or press Tab, or tap or click in the *Name of Web Site* text box and type **Ohio State University**.
14. Continue tapping or pressing Tab, or tapping or clicking in the designated text boxes and typing the information as shown below:

Year	**2004**	*Month Accessed*	**November**
Month	**July**	*Day Accessed*	**15**
Day	**28**	*Medium*	**Web**
Year Accessed	**2015**		

Did You Know?

In the seventh edition of the MLA handbook, URLs are no longer required. MLA advises writers to include URLs only if a reader is unlikely to find the source without the web address.

15 Tap or click OK.

16 Tap or click in the *(Grabmeier)* citation, tap or click the Citation Options arrow, and then tap or click *Edit Citation.*

17 Type **2-3** in the *Pages* text box at the Edit Citation dialog box and then tap or click OK.

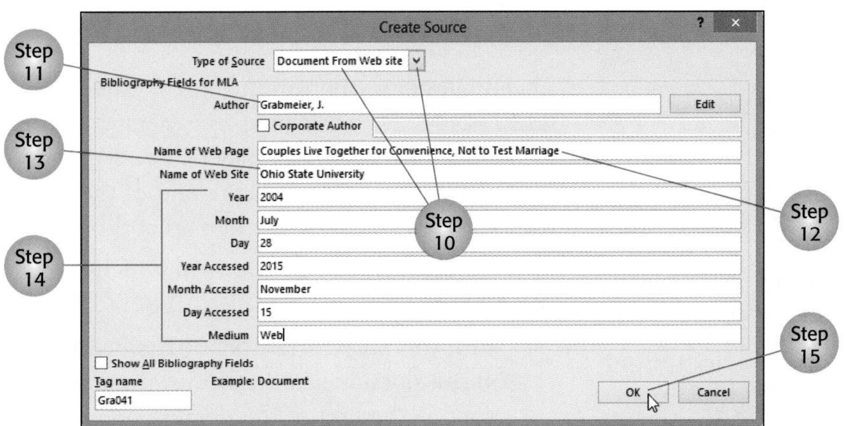

18 Position the insertion point left of the period at the end of the indented quotation on page 2 (third paragraph that begins *In the past 25 years. . .*), press the spacebar, tap or click the Insert Citation button, and then tap or click *Add New Source.*

19 Change the *Type of Source* to *Journal Article* and then tap or click to insert a check mark in the *Show All Bibliography Fields* check box near the bottom left of the dialog box.

20 Enter the information in the designated text boxes as follows. (You will have to slide or scroll down to find the *Volume* and *Issue* text boxes):

Author	**Popenoe, D.**
Title	**Cohabitation, Marriage, and Child Wellbeing: A Cross-National Perspective**
Journal Name	**Society**
Year	**2009**
Month	**July**
Day	**9**
Pages	**429-486**
Volume	**46**
Issue	**5**
Medium	**Print**

21 Edit the citation to add *432* as the page number by completing steps similar to Steps 16 to 17.

22 Position the insertion point left of the period at the end of the quotation in the third paragraph on page 3 that reads *"More than 40% of . . . convert to marriage"* and press the spacebar.

23 Tap or click the Insert Citation button and tap or click *Popenoe, D.* at the drop-down list.

24 Edit the citation to add *480* as the page number.

25 Save the document using the same name (**7.6-CohabitationEssay-Your Name**). Leave the document open for the next topic.

Insert a Citation with a New Source
1. Position insertion point.
2. Tap or click REFERENCES tab.
3. Tap or click Insert Citation button.
4. Tap or click *Add New Source.*
5. If necessary, change *Type of Source.*
6. Enter information as needed.
7. Tap or click OK.

Insert a Citation with an Existing Source
1. Position insertion point.
2. Tap or click REFERENCES tab.
3. Tap or click Insert Citation button.
4. Tap or click source.

Edit a Citation
1. Position insertion point in citation.
2. Tap or click Citation Options button.
3. Tap or click *Edit Citation.*
4. Type page reference.
5. Tap or click OK.

MLA recommends the abbreviations n. pag. *for a source without page numbers,* n.d. *for a source without a date, and* N.p. *for a source without a publisher.*

Editing a Source

To change the source information for a citation, position the insertion point within the citation, tap or click the Citation Options arrow, and then tap or click *Edit Source*. This opens the Edit Source dialog box where you can make changes to the bibliography fields for the reference.

Topic 7.8

SKILLS

Create a Works Cited page

Browse a document in different views

Creating a Works Cited Page and Using Word Views

The Bibliography button in the Citations & Bibliography group of the REFERENCES tab is used to generate a **Works Cited** page for MLA papers or a References page for APA papers. The MLA style guide requires a Works Cited page to be on a separate page at the end of the document organized alphabetically by author's name, or by title when an author's name is absent.

Word provides various views in which to review a document, including a new Read Mode view that provides maximum screen space for reading longer documents.

1. With the **7.6-CohabitationEssay-Your Name** document open, move the insertion point to the end of the document and tap or press Enter to move to a new blank line.
2. Tap or click the INSERT tab and then tap or click the Page Break button to start a new page.
3. Tap or click the REFERENCES tab.
4. Tap or click the **Bibliography button** in the Citations & Bibliography group.
5. Tap or click *Works Cited* in the drop-down list.

Word automatically generates the Works Cited page. In the next steps you will format the text to match the font, size, and spacing of the rest of the document.

6. Select all of the text in the Works Cited page.

Word surrounds the entire text on the page with a border and displays a Bibliographies button and an Update Citations and Bibliography button along the top of the placeholder.

7. Tap or click the HOME tab and make the following changes to the selected text:
   a. Change the font to 12-point Times New Roman.
   b. Change the line spacing to 2.0 and remove space after paragraphs.
8. Select the title text *Works Cited*, change the font color to Automatic (black), and center the title.

Do not change formatting until you are sure your Works Cited page is complete because the page will revert to predefined formats if you make changes to sources and update the Works Cited page.

Did You Know?

The seventh edition of the MLA guide now requires all entries in a reference list to include the medium in which the reference has been published; for example: Film, Print, or Web.

Bibliographies button used to change to a different bibliography style or to convert the Works Cited page to static text that can be edited.

Regenerate the Works Cited page using this button if you make a change to any of the source information.

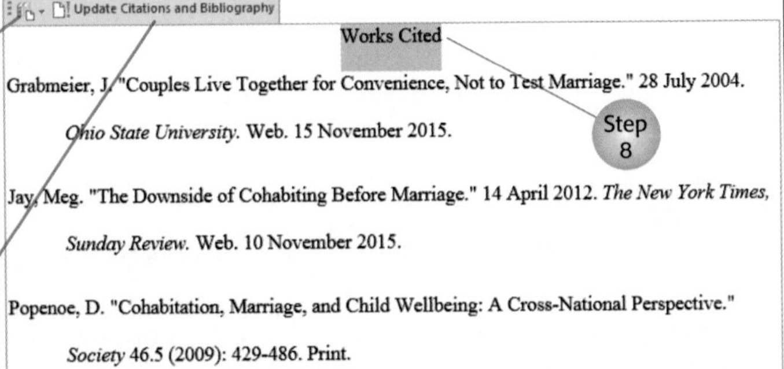

The default view for new documents is **Print Layout view**, which displays the document as it will appear when printed. **Read Mode view** displays a document full screen in columns, allowing you to read longer documents more easily without screen elements such as the QAT and ribbon. **Draft view** hides print elements such as headers and footers. **Web Layout view** displays a document as it would appear as a web page, and **Outline view** displays content as bulleted points.

9 Position the insertion point at the beginning of the document.

10 Tap or click the VIEW tab and then tap or click the Read Mode button in the Views group.

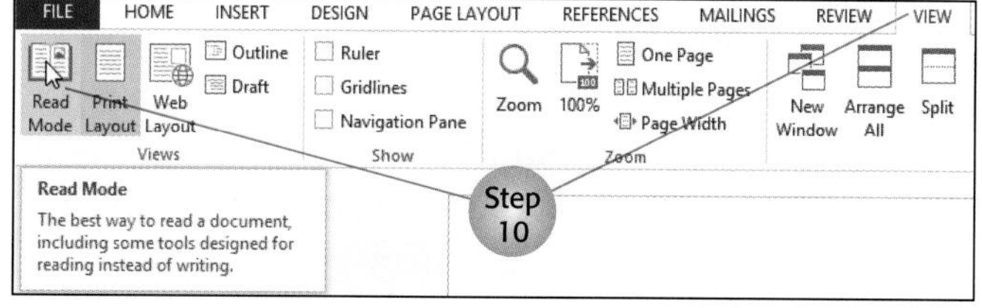

Use Read Mode to view a document without editing.

11 Tap or click the Next Screen button (right-pointing arrow inside circle at the middle right side of the screen) to move to the next screen until you have reached the end of the document.

12 Tap or click the VIEW tab, tap or point to *Layout*, and then tap or click *Paper Layout* at the drop-down list to display the document as single pages instead of screens in columns.

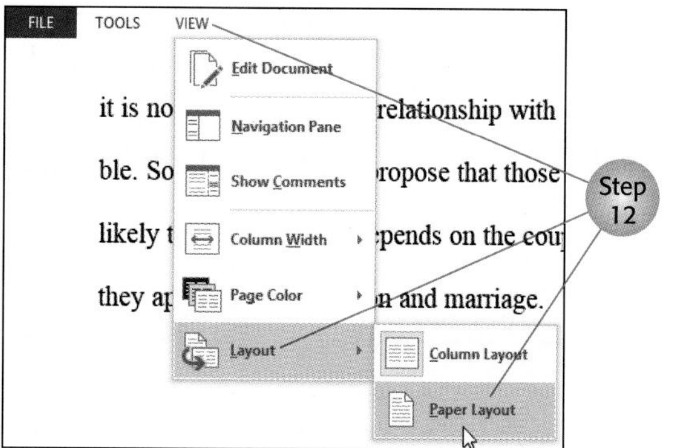

13 Browse the document.

14 Tap or click the VIEW tab and then tap or click *Edit Document* to return to Print Layout view.

15 Tap or click the Draft button in the Views group of the VIEW tab to view just the text in the document and then browse the document.

16 Tap or click the Print Layout view button near the right end of the Status bar.

17 Save the document using the same name (**7.6-CohabitationEssay-Your Name**). Leave the document open for the next topic.

New to Word 2013 is the *Welcome back!* balloon that appears near the lower right corner of the screen when you reopen a document. Tap or click the balloon to scroll to where you left the document when you closed it.

Turn on the Navigation pane (VIEW tab, Navigation Pane) and tap or click PAGES to move through a document by tapping or clicking miniature page thumbnails.

Quick STEPS

Generate a Works Cited Page
1. Position insertion point at end of document.
2. Insert page break.
3. Tap or click REFERENCES tab.
4. Tap or click Bibliography button.
5. Tap or click *Works Cited*.
6. Format as required.

Change Document View
1. Tap or click VIEW tab.
2. Tap or click desired view button.

Footnotes and Endnotes

In some academic papers, you need to insert footnotes or endnotes. **Footnotes** are explanatory comments or source information placed at the bottom of a page. **Endnotes** are explanatory comments or source information that appear at the end of a section or document. Position the insertion point and use the Insert Footnote or Insert Endnote button in the REFERENCES tab to add these elements.

Inserting and Replying to Comments

Topic 7.9

SKILLS

- Insert comments
- Change the Markup view
- Reply to a comment
- Mark a comment done

If necessary, open the Word Options dialog box from the FILE tab to change the user name to another name.

Comments is a collaborative tool in Word that is useful when working on a document with another person or team. A **comment** is a short note associated with text that provides explanatory information to a reader. A comment can also be used to pose a question to document reviewers. New to Word 2013 is the ability to reply to a comment and mark a comment as done.

When working in teams or on group projects, consider using comments in documents to explain portions of your text, ask questions of your teammates, or add general feedback.

1. With the **7.6-CohabitationEssay-Your Name** document open, position the insertion point at the beginning of the document.
2. Select the word *Canada* at the end of the first paragraph in the document.
3. Tap or click the REVIEW tab.
4. Tap or click the New Comment button in the Comments group.

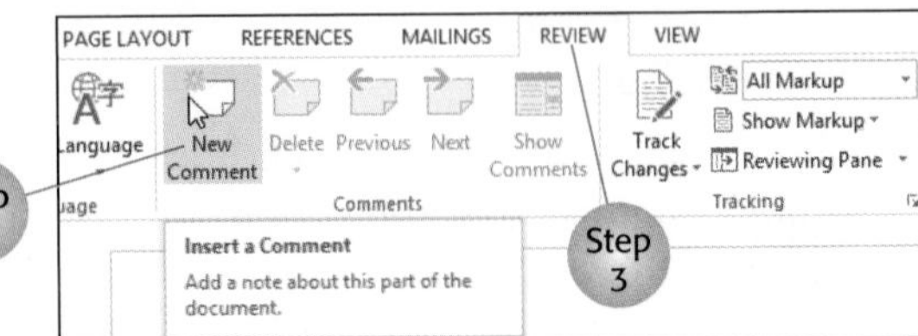

Word opens a new comment box (referred to as a comment balloon) in the **Markup Area** at the right side of the screen.

5. Type **Consider looking for research specific to Europe?** and then tap or click in the document outside the comment box.

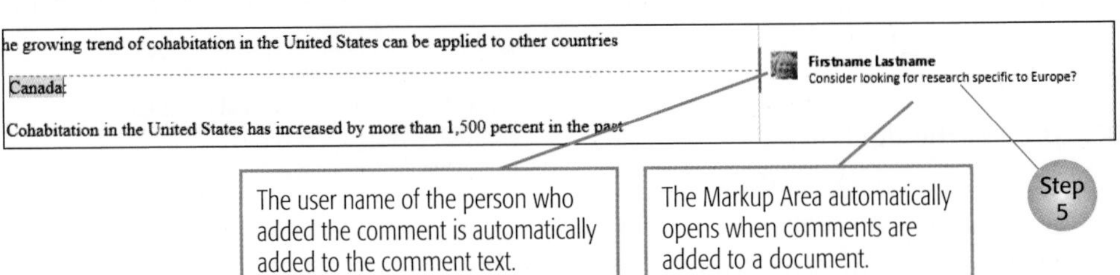

6. Select *In the 1960s* in the second sentence of the third paragraph.
7. Tap or click the New Comment button.
8. Type **Change the final copy to: Until the 1990s** and then tap or click in the document.

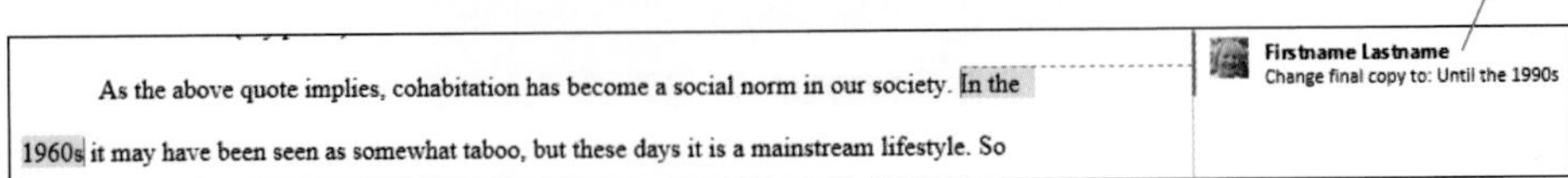

9. Position the insertion point at the beginning of the subheading *Advantages of Cohabitation* near the bottom of the first page and insert a page break.
10. Position the insertion point at the beginning of the subheading *Disadvantages of Cohabitation* near the bottom of the second page and insert a page break.
11. Position the insertion point at the beginning of the document.
12. If necessary, tap or click the REVIEW tab.

13 Tap or click the Display for Review button arrow in the Tracking group (currently displays *All Markup* or *Simple Markup*), and tap or click *No Markup* at the drop-down list.

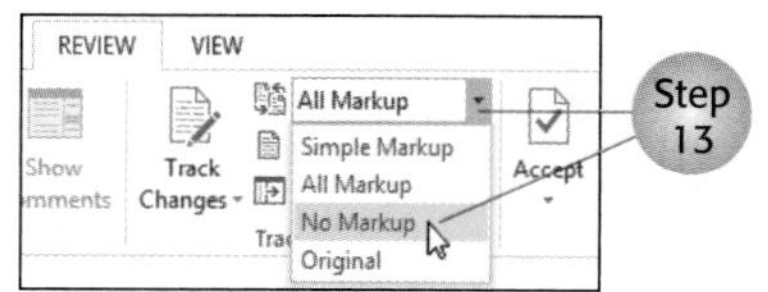

Notice the two comments on page 1 are removed from the document display.

14 Tap or click the Display for Review button arrow and tap or click *Simple Markup* at the drop-down list.

15 Tap or point to the first comment box on page 1.

Notice Word shows a callout line pointing to the text with which the comment is associated. The comment box also displays a Reply button.

16 Tap or click the Reply button (displays as a small white page with a left-pointing arrow) in the first comment box.

17 Type **Asked Prof Williamson and she said it was not necessary** and then tap or click in the document.

Notice the reply comment text is indented below the original comment in a conversation-style dialogue.

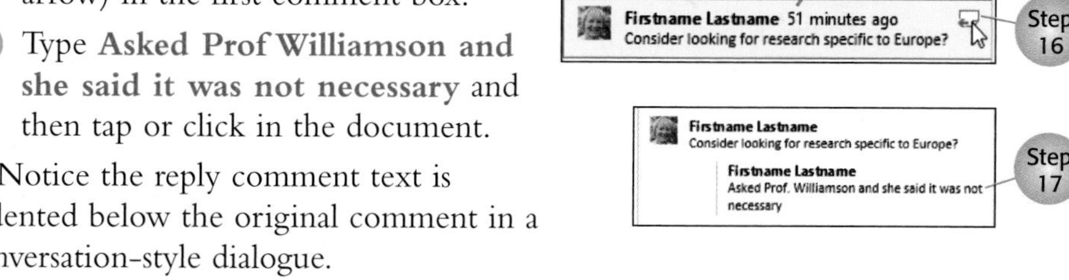

18 Edit the second sentence in the third paragraph from *In the 1960s* to *Until the 1990s* by tapping or clicking after *In* (and *60*), using Backspace to remove text, and then typing the new text. (You are editing using this method so that the comment is not deleted.)

19 Press and hold or right-click the second comment box on page 1 and then tap or click *Mark Comment Done* at the shortcut menu.

20 Tap or click in the document outside the comment box.

Notice the comment text is dimmed for the comment marked as done.

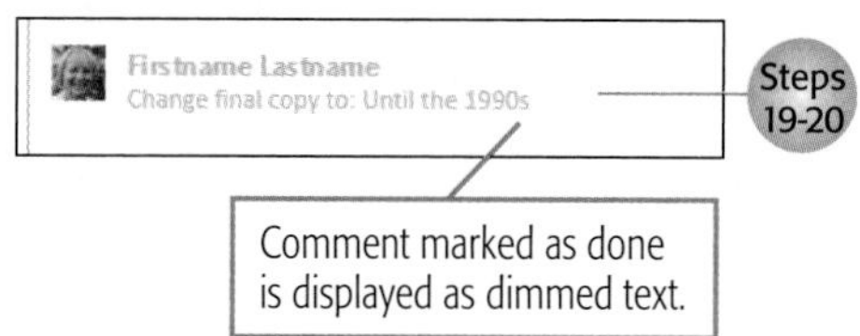

21 Save the document using the same name (**7.6-CohabitationEssay-Your Name**) and then close the document.

Simple Markup revision view is a new view for Word 2013 that sports a less cluttered look at a document's changes and comments.

You can also delete a comment instead of marking the comment done.

Insert a Comment
1. Position insertion point or select text.
2. Tap or click REVIEW tab.
3. Tap or click New Comment button.
4. Type comment text.
5. Tap or click in document.

Reply to a Comment
1. Tap or point to comment box.
2. Tap or click Reply button.
3. Type reply text.
4. Tap or click in document.

Mark a Comment Done
1. Press and hold or right-click comment.
2. Tap or click *Mark Comment Done*.

Change Display for Review
1. Tap or click REVIEW tab.
2. Tap or click Display for Review button arrow.
3. Tap or click desired markup view.

Tracking Changes made to a Document

In situations in which a document will be circulated to multiple readers for revisions, turning on track changes is a good idea. Track changes (REVIEW tab) logs each person's insertions, deletions, and formatting changes. Changes can be reviewed, accepted, and rejected in the Revisions pane.

Topic 7.10

SKILLS

Create a resume

Create a cover letter

Did You Know?

Most recruiters advise job seekers to begin a job search with a reverse chronological resume style which lists your work experience from most to least recent.

Creating a Resume and Cover Letter from Templates

Word provides more than 40 professionally designed and formatted resume and cover letter templates that take the work out of designing and formatting these two crucial documents, letting you focus your efforts on writing documents that will win you a job interview!

1. Tap or click the FILE tab and then tap or click New.
2. At the New tab Backstage view, tap or click Resume below the *Search for online templates* search box.

Step 2

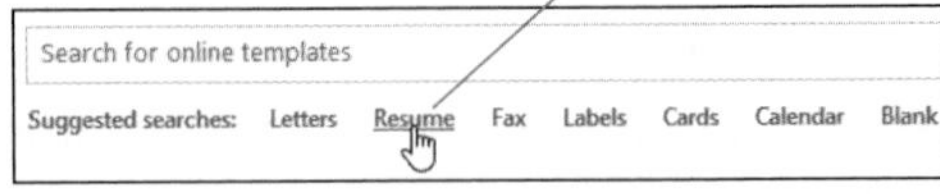

3. Tap or click *Entry Level* in the *Category* list.
4. Tap or click *Resume for recent college graduate* in the *Templates* gallery.
5. Tap or click the Create button.
6. Select your name in the *Author* placeholder and type **Dana Jelic**.
7. Select and delete the *Street Address* and *City, ST ZIP Code* placeholders.
8. Select the *Phone Number* placeholder and type **800-555-4577**.
9. Select the *E-mail Address* placeholder and type **jelic@domain.net**.

This is the number of available templates in the gallery for the category and will vary as templates are frequently updated.

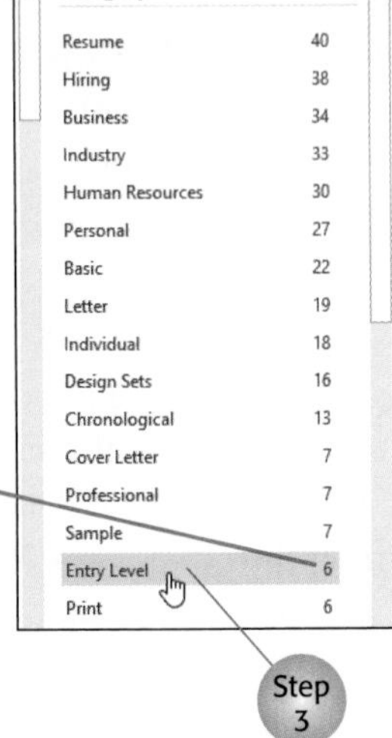

Step 3

Step 8

Step 6

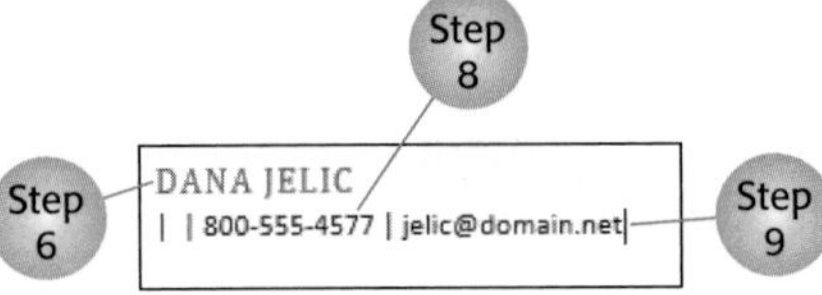

Step 9

App Tip

Print multiple copies of a resume by changing the *Copies* value at the Print tab Backstage view.

10. Type the remainder of the resume as shown in Figure 7.3 by selecting and editing text in placeholders, or by deleting placeholders or text.

OBJECTIVE

Creative and team-oriented liberal arts graduate seeking an entry-level position as a Conference Coordinator in order to leverage planning and communication skills to organize and ensure seamless operation of conferences in a topnotch facility.

EDUCATION

Bachelor of Arts degree June 2015

Williams College, MA

- Major: English
- Minor: Sociology
- Overall GPA 3.91; Honors in each semester
- Completed a semester in Helsingor, Denmark, January 2014

SKILLS & ABILITIES

Organization and Communication

- Campus Editor at *The Williams Record*, independent student newspaper for Williams College. Wrote and edited columns for regular features and assisted Editor-in-chief with other newspaper organization tasks.
- Community and Diversity Rep for College Council, 2013 to 2015

EXPERIENCE

Library Assistant 2013 to Present

Sawyer Library, Williams College

- Check in and out library materials at circulation desk
- Sort and shelve books

English Peer Tutor 2013 to 2014

Williams College

- Tutored English students
- Organized English peer study group

Figure 7.3 Resume text for Topic 7.10

career-advice.monster.com

Go here for articles and examples on how to write effective resumes and cover letters.

11. Save the document as **7.10-JelicResume-Your Name** in the Ch7 folder in CompletedTopicsByChapter. Tap or click OK if a message appears about upgrading to the newest file format.
12. Close the resume document and display the New tab Backstage view.
13. Tap or click <u>Letters</u> below the *Search for online templates* search box and then tap or click *Cover Letter* in the *Category* list.
14. Tap or click the *Sample resume cover letter in response to a technical position advertisement* and then tap or click the Create button.
15. Create the letter as shown in Figure 7.4 by selecting and editing text in placeholders, or by deleting placeholders or text.

Dana Jelic
880 Main Street
Williamstown, MA 01267

May 12, 2015

Ms. Patel
Conference Manager
Williams College
39 Chapin Hall Drive
Williamstown, MA 01267

Dear Ms. Patel:

I am writing in response to your advertisement in The Williams Record for a Conference Coordinator. After reading your job description, I am confident that my planning and organizational skills and my passion for representing Williams College are a perfect match for this position. As a graduate of Williams College I am very familiar with the college venues and local area attractions.

I would bring to Williams College a broad range of skills, including:

- Excellent time management skills
- Ability to organize complex tasks
- Experienced communicator

I would welcome the opportunity to further discuss this position with you. If you have questions or would like to schedule an interview, please contact me by phone at 800-555-4577 or by email at jelic@domain.net. I have enclosed my resume for your review, and I look forward to hearing from you.

Figure 7.4 Cover letter text for Topic 7.10

16. Tap or click the PAGE LAYOUT tab and then tap or click the Page Setup dialog box launcher.
17. If necessary, tap or click the Layout tab in the Page Setup dialog box.
18. Tap or click the *Vertical alignment* list arrow, tap or click *Center* at the drop-down list, and then tap or click OK.
19. Save the document as **7.10-JelicCoverLetter-Your Name** in the Ch7 folder in CompletedTopicsByChapter and then close the document.

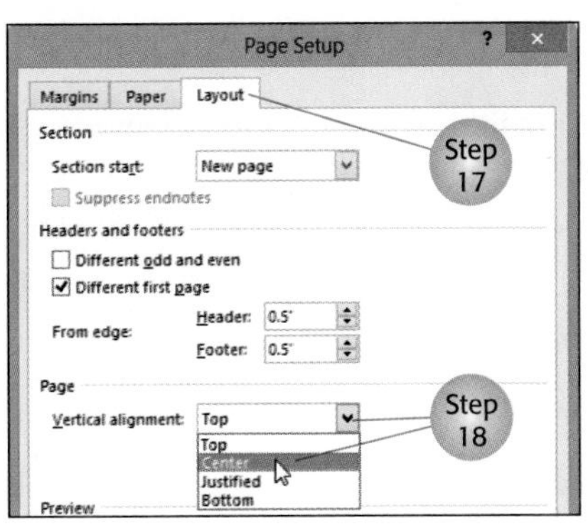

Use the Envelopes or Labels button in the Create group of the MAILINGS tab to generate an envelope or label for a letter.

Create a Resume

1. Tap or click FILE tab.
2. Tap or click New.
3. Tap or click <u>Resume</u>.
4. Tap or click category if desired.
5. Tap or click desired template.
6. Tap or click Create button.
7. Edit as required.

Create a Cover Letter

1. Tap or click FILE tab.
2. Tap or click New.
3. Tap or click <u>Letters</u>.
4. Tap or click *Cover Letter* category.
5. Tap or click desired template.
6. Tap or click Create button.
7. Edit as required.

Vertically center a letter to make sure the letter has a professional appearance. For short letters, add extra space between letter elements to balance the content on the page.

Concepts Review

Topic	Key Concepts	Key Terms
Inserting, Editing, and Labeling Images in a Document	Graphic elements assist with comprehension and/or add visual appeal to documents. Insert a picture from the clip art gallery, the Web, or an online service such as Flickr using the Online Pictures button in the Illustrations group of the INSERT tab. Buttons in the *Layout Options* palette are used to control how text wraps around the picture and the picture's position on the page. The Pictures button in the INSERT tab is used to insert pictures stored on your computer. Edit an image's appearance and/or add special effects using buttons in the PICTURE TOOLS FORMAT tab. A caption is explanatory text above or below a picture that is added using the Insert Caption button in the REFERENCES tab. Word automatically numbers pictures as Figures.	Clip art gallery Online Pictures button Layout Options button Pictures button Insert Caption
Adding Borders and Shading, and Inserting a Text Box	Add a border or shading to paragraphs to make text stand out on a page. Shading is color applied to the page behind the text. Apply a border to selected text using the *Borders* gallery from the Borders button arrow in the Paragraph group of the HOME tab. Add shading using the Shading button arrow in the Paragraph group of the HOME tab. A page border surrounds the entire page and is added from the Page Borders button in the Page Background group of the DESIGN tab. A pull quote is a quote inside a text box. Insert text inside a box using the Text Box button in the Text group of the INSERT tab.	Shading Borders gallery Page Borders button Pull quote Text Box button
Inserting a Table	A table is a grid of columns and rows in which you type text and is used when you want to arrange text side-by-side or in rows. A table cell is a rectangular-shaped box in the table grid that is the intersection of a column and a row into which you type text. Create a table by tapping or clicking a box in a drop-down grid or by entering the number of columns and rows in the Insert Table dialog box. Tapping or pressing Tab in the last table cell automatically adds a new row to the table. Quick Tables are predesigned tables with sample data such as calendars and tabular lists.	Table Table cell Quick Tables

Topic	Key Concepts	Key Terms
Formatting and Modifying a Table	Apply a predesigned collection of borders, shading, and color to a table using an option from the *Table Styles* gallery. Shading or other formatting applied to every other row to make the table data easier to read is called banded rows. Check boxes in the Table Style Options group are used to customize the formatting applied from a Table Styles option. Apply shading or borders using buttons in the Table Styles and Borders group of the TABLE TOOLS DESIGN tab. New rows and columns are inserted above, below, left, or right of the active table cell using buttons in the Rows & Columns group of the TABLE TOOLS LAYOUT tab. Remove selected table cells, rows, columns, or the entire table using options from the Delete button in the Rows & Columns group. Adjust the width of a column by changing the *Width* text box value in the Cell Size group of the TABLE TOOLS LAYOUT tab or by dragging the column border. Buttons to change alignment options for selected table cells are found in the Alignment group of the TABLE TOOLS LAYOUT tab. Cells in a table can be merged or split using buttons in the Merge group of the TABLE TOOLS LAYOUT tab.	Table Styles Banded rows
Changing Page Layout Options	New Word documents are automatically formatted for a letter-sized page with one-inch margins in portrait orientation. Portrait orientation means the text on the page is oriented to the taller side (8.5-inch width) while landscape orientation rotates the text to the wider side of the page (11-inch measurement becomes the page width). Change the margins by choosing one of the predefined margin options or by entering measurements for the top, bottom, left, and right margins at the Page Setup dialog box. A soft page break is a page break that Word inserts automatically when the maximum number of lines that can fit on a page has been reached. A hard page break is a page break inserted by you in a different location than the soft page break occurred. A section break is inserted from the Breaks button in the Page Setup group of the PAGE LAYOUT tab and is used to format a portion of a document with different page layout options.	Portrait Landscape Soft page break Hard page break Section break
Formatting a Research Paper with a Header and Page Numbers	A style guide is a set of rules for formatting and referencing academic papers. MLA and APA are the two most popular style guides used for academic writing. A header is text that appears at the top of each page, while a footer is text that appears at the bottom of each page. Tap or click the INSERT tab and choose the Header or Footer button to create a header or footer in the Header or Footer pane. Page numbers are added to a document at the top or bottom of a page within a Header or Footer pane using the Page Number button in the HEADER & FOOTER TOOLS DESIGN tab.	Style guide Header Footer Page Number button

continued....

Topic	Key Concepts	Key Terms
Inserting and Editing Citations	A citation provides a reader with the reference for information that is quoted or paraphrased within an academic paper. Position the insertion point where a citation is needed and use the Insert Citation button in the REFERENCES tab to create a reference. Select an existing source for a citation or choose *Add New Source* to create a new reference. At the Create Source dialog box, begin by choosing the *Type of Source* for the reference, and then fill in the bibliography fields as needed. Edit a citation to add a page number or paragraph number to the reference.	Citation
Creating a Works Cited Page and Using Word Views	The MLA style guide requires a Works Cited page as a separate page at the end of the document with the references used for the paper. Use the Bibliography button in the Citations & Bibliography group of the REFERENCES tab to generate a Works Cited page formatted for the MLA style guide. Print Layout view displays the document as it will appear when printed. Read Mode view displays a document full screen in columns or pages without editing tools. Draft view hides print elements such as headers, footers, and page numbering. Web Layout view displays the document as a web page. Outline view displays content as bullet points. Footnotes are sources or explanatory comments placed at the bottom of a page in an academic paper. Endnotes are sources or explanatory comments placed at the end of a section or document in an academic paper.	Works Cited Bibliography button Print Layout view Read Mode view Draft view Web Layout view Outline view Footnotes Endnotes
Inserting and Replying to Comments	A comment is a short note associated with text that provides explanatory information or poses a question to a reader. Select text that you want to associate with a comment and type the comment text inside a comment box by tapping or clicking the New Comment button in the REVIEW tab. Comments display in the Markup Area, which is a pane that opens at the right side of the document when comments are added. A document with comments can be shown with *No Markup*, *Simple Markup*, or *All Markup*, which refers to the way in which comment boxes are displayed. Tap or point inside a comment box and use the Reply button to enter reply text that responds to a comment. Mark a comment as done to retain the comment text but display the comment dimmed in the Markup Area.	Comment Markup Area
Creating a Resume and Cover Letter from Templates	More than 40 professionally designed resume and cover letter templates are available in Word. At the New tab Backstage view, select the Resume hyperlink to browse templates for resumes in various styles, themes, and purposes by category. At the New tab Backstage view, select the Letters hyperlink and the *Cover Letter* category to locate a cover letter template.	

Multiple Choice

1. Search for images in the Clip Art gallery from this button in the INSERT tab.
   a. Pictures
   b. Online Pictures
   c. Shapes
   d. SmartArt
2. Label a picture using this Insert option.
   a. Text box
   b. SmartArt
   c. Caption
   d. Citation
3. Color added to the background of a paragraph is applied using this button in the Paragraph group.
   a. Borders
   b. Text Highlight Color
   c. Page Background
   d. Shading
4. A short passage of text inside a box is created with this button in the INSERT tab.
   a. Pictures
   b. Text Box
   c. Quick Parts
   d. WordArt
5. Tables are used to type text arranged in columns and rows within rectangular-shaped boxes called __________.
   a. table cells
   b. spreadsheets
   c. text boxes
   d. headers
6. Use this option from the *Table* drop-down list to create a table by typing a value for the number of columns and rows.
   a. Insert Table
   b. Create Table
   c. Draw Table
   d. Make Table
7. New rows and columns are added to an existing table using buttons in the Rows & Columns group of the TABLE TOOLS _________ tab.
   a. DESIGN
   b. LAYOUT
   c. FORMAT
   d. DRAWING
8. Adjust the width of a column in a table by changing the *Width* value in this group of buttons.
   a. Cell Layout
   b. Cell Design
   c. Cell Alignment
   d. Cell Size
9. A document's orientation can be changed to landscape using the Orientation button in this tab.
   a. HOME
   b. PAGE LAYOUT
   c. DESIGN
   d. INSERT
10. A page break inserted automatically by Word is called a ______ page break.
    a. hard
    b. soft
    c. manual
    d. section
11. Text that appears at the top of each page is called a ____________.
    a. header
    b. footer
    c. quick part
    d. section
12. Page numbers are added to the top of each page inside this pane.
    a. Header
    b. Footer
    c. Quick Part
    d. Section
13. Add a page number reference to an existing citation by selecting this option from the Citation Options arrow list.
    a. New source
    b. Edit source
    c. New citation
    d. Edit citation
14. When creating a new source for a citation, this option is usually changed first at the Create Source dialog box.
    a. Type of Source
    b. Author
    c. Name of Web Page
    d. Medium
15. Use this button in the REFERENCES tab to create a Works Cited page.
    a. Bibliography
    b. Insert Citation
    c. Manage Sources
    d. Style
16. This Word view displays documents full screen without editing tools.
    a. Draft
    b. Print Layout
    c. Outline
    d. Read Mode

17. Comments are displayed in this area.
    a. Markup
    b. Revisions
    c. Print Layout
    d. Review
18. A comment displayed as dimmed text has had this option applied.
    a. Mark Comment Complete
    b. Mark Comment Finished
    c. Mark Comment Replied
    d. Mark Comment Done
19. Browse for a resume or cover letter template in this Backstage view.
    a. Info tab
    b. New tab
    c. Open tab
    d. Share tab
20. Vertically center a letter on the page in this dialog box.
    a. Page Layout
    b. Page Alignment
    c. Page Setup
    d. Page Options

Crossword Puzzle

1 2 3 4 5 6 7 8 9 10 11 12 13 14 15 16

ACROSS

1 Default view for Word documents
5 Text that appears at the bottom of each page
7 Display option to remove display of comments
12 Button to insert photo stored on computer
13 Predesigned resumes or cover letters
14 Option to type your own margin measurements
15 Text orientated to the wider side of the page
16 Rules for formatting and referencing academic papers

DOWN

1 Quote inside a text box
2 Button to change text wrapping option for a picture
3 References page for MLA papers
4 Combine two or more cells into one
6 Button to draw a border around the entire page
8 Collection of predesigned table formatting options
9 Short note associated with text
10 Reference in academic paper that credits source
11 Predesigned table with sample data

Matching

Match the term with the statement or definition.

_______ 1. Adds border or effect to photo
_______ 2. Graphic with short passage of text
_______ 3. Ideal for typing a price list
_______ 4. Every other row is shaded
_______ 5. Start a new page
_______ 6. Style guide
_______ 7. Add source of information
_______ 8. New view in Word 2013
_______ 9. Respond to a comment
_______ 10. Document to send with resume

a. Banded rows
b. MLA or APA
c. Read Mode
d. Text Box
e. Cover letter
f. Picture Styles
g. Reply button
h. Page Break
i. Table
j. Insert Citation

Project 1 Enhancing a Document with Visual Elements

Individual

Deliverable: National Park Trip Planner document (continued in Project 2)

1. Open **GrandCanyonHikingPlanner**.
2. Save the document as **C7-Project1-GrandCanyonTripPlanner-Your Name** in a new folder named *Ch7* within the ChapterProjectsWork folder on your USB flash drive.
3. Insert, label, and edit pictures as follows:
   a. Insert the picture named ***ScorpionRidge*** at the right margin aligned with the first line of text in the first paragraph and with the *Square* text wrapping option. You determine an appropriate size for the picture with the paragraph.
   b. Insert the picture named ***BrightAngelPoint*** at the left margin aligned with the first line of text in the last paragraph and with the *Square* text wrapping option. Do not resize the picture.
   c. Add a caption below the picture inserted at Step 3a with the label text *Scorpion Ridge, North Rim.* Accept all default caption options.
   d. Add a caption below the picture inserted at Step 3b with the label text *Bright Angel Point, North Rim.* Accept all default caption options.
   e. Apply a Picture Style of your choosing to both pictures.
   f. Apply Color Saturation at 200% to both pictures.
4. Add borders, shading, and a text box as follows:
   a. Select the sentence in the second paragraph below the subtitle *Park Entrance Fees* (begins *Admission to the park. . .*), center the text, and add an outside border.
   b. Add *Blue, Accent 1, Lighter 80%* shading to the same sentence selected in Step 4a.
   c. Add a *Blue, Accent 1*, 1 ½ point, Shadow page border to the document.
   d. Insert an *Austin Quote* text box and type the following text inside the box:
   Grand Canyon National Park is a World Heritage Site
   e. Move the text box inserted at Step 4d so that the bottom of the text box aligns at the center of the page and bottom margin.
5. Save the revised document using the same name (**C7-Project1-GrandCanyonTripPlanner-Your Name**).
6. Leave the document open if you are continuing to Project 2; otherwise, close the document and submit the project to your instructor in the manner she or he has requested.

Project 2 Inserting, Formatting, and Modifying a Table into a Document

Individual

Deliverable: National Park Trip Planner document

Note: You must have completed Project 1 before starting this project.

1. If necessary, open **C7-Project1-GrandCanyonTripPlanner-Your Name**.
2. Use Save As to change the file name to **C7-Project2-GrandCanyonTripPlanner-Your Name**, saving in the same folder.
3. Position the insertion point at the end of the document text and tap or press Enter until you create a new blank line at the left margin below the picture of Bright Angel Point.

4. Insert a 5 x 5 table and type the following text in the table grid at the default table cell options:

Rim	Trail Name	Round Trip Distance	Round Trip Estimated Time	Elevation Change
South	Rim Trail	13 miles (21 km)	All day depending on desired distance	200 feet (60 m)
South	Bright Angel Trail	3 miles (4.8 km) to 9.2 miles (14.8 km)	From 2 to 9 hours depending on desired distance	2,112 feet (644 m) to 3,060 feet (933 m)
North	Bright Angel Point	0.5 miles (0.8 km)	30 minutes	200 feet (60 m)
North	Widforss Trail	10 miles (16 km)	6 hours	200 feet (60 m)

5. Format the table as follows:
   a. Apply a table style of your choosing.
   b. Deselect the *First Column* table style option if it is selected.
   c. Change the font size to 10 for all of the text in the table cells.
6. Modify the layout of the table as follows:
   a. Set the width of the first column to 0.6 inches, and the third, fourth, and fifth columns to 1.5 inches.
   b. Align all table cells at the center horizontally and vertically.
   c. Insert a new row above row 4 and type the following text in the new table cells:

South	Kaibab Trail	1.8 miles (2.9 km) to 6 miles (9.7 km)	From 1 to 6 hours depending on desired distance	600 feet (180 m) to 2,040 feet (622 m)

   d. Insert a new row at the bottom of the table and type the following text in the table cells:

North	Kaibab Trail	1.4 miles (2.3 km) to 4 miles (6.4 km)	From 1 to 4 hours depending on desired distance	800 feet (245 m) to 1,450 feet (445 m)

7. If necessary, delete extra space above or below the table to make sure the text box remains at the bottom center of the page.
8. Save the revised document using the same name (**C7-Project2-GrandCanyonHikingPlanner-Your Name**).
9. Submit the project to your instructor in the manner she or he has requested.
10. Close the document.

Project 3 Completing a Research Report with Formatting, Citations, and Works Cited

Individual

Deliverable: Academic Paper in MLA Format

1. Open **EtanerceptEssay**.
2. Use Save As to change the file name to **C7-Project3-EtanerceptEssay-Your Name**, saving in the Ch7 folder within ChapterProjectsWork.
3. Select the entire document and change the font, line and paragraph spacing, and paragraph indents to conform to MLA guidelines (see Table 7.1 in Topic 7.6). ***Hint: Turn on the display of nonprinting symbols to determine where paragraphs end to correctly complete the first line indent formatting.***
4. Insert your name, your instructor's name, the title of your course, and the current date at the top of the first page as per MLA guidelines (see Table 7.1 in Topic 7.6).
5. Add page numbering one space after your last name at the right margin in a header and format the header text to the same font and font size as the rest of the document.

6. Edit existing citations in the document as follows:
   a. Edit the source for Bradley and Desmeules in the first paragraph to change the second author's first name from *Marie* to *Mary*, and the page from *215* to *225*.
   b. Change the page from *61* to *65* for the Hashkes and Laxer citation at the end of the indented quotation on page 2.
7. Position the insertion point at the end of the quotation that reads "*The Etanercept injection is used to reduce signs and symptoms of active arthritis . . . This medicine may also slow the progression of damage to the body from active arthritis or rheumatoid arthritis*" and insert a new citation referencing *par. 14* from the following new source:

Type of Source	Document from Web site		
Author	**Jarvis, B.; Faulds, D.**		
Name of Web Page	**Etanercept: a review of its use in rheumatoid arthritis**		
Name of Web Site	**PubMed, US National Library of Medicine**		
Year	**1999**	*Month Accessed*	**March**
Month	**June**	*Day Accessed*	**15**
Year Accessed	**2015**	*Medium*	**Web**

8. Position the insertion point at the end of the quotation that reads "*When Etanercept is administered alone or in combination with methotrexate in patients with refractory rheumatoid arthritis, significant reductions in disease activity occur within two weeks and are sustained for at least 6 months*" and cite *par. 20* from the Jarvis and Faulds source.
9. Position the insertion point at the end of the sentence that reads *Missed doses will mean that the TNF protein is no longer being effectively controlled and inflammation, pain, and disease progression will quickly return within a month from stopping treatment* and insert a new citation referencing *par. 12* from the following new source:

Type of Source	Document from Web site		
Author	(leave blank)		
Name of Web Page	**Medication Guide: Enbrel (Etanercept)**		
Name of Web Site	**Immunex Corporation**		
Year	**2011**	*Month Accessed*	**March**
Month	**December**	*Day Accessed*	**25**
Year Accessed	**2015**	*Medium*	**Web**

10. Create and format a Works Cited page on a separate page at the end of the document.
11. Save the revised document using the same name (**C7-Project3-EtanerceptEssay-Your Name**).
12. Submit the project to your instructor in the manner she or he has requested and then close the document.

Project 4 Resume and Cover Letter with Comments

Individual

Deliverable: Personal Resume and Cover Letter Targeted to a Specific Job Ad

1. Find a recent job ad for a position in your field of study.
2. Choose a resume template that you like and create a new resume for yourself that could be used as an application for the job ad.
3. Insert at least two comments in the resume. Each comment should be associated with an entry in your resume and pose a specific question to your instructor asking him or her for tips on how to improve the entry, or provide additional explanation as to the writing style or tone that you used.
4. Choose a cover letter template that you like and write a cover letter to enclose with the resume written specifically for the requirements in the job ad.
5. Add the URL or other source for the job ad that you used for this project in a comment associated with the current date text in the cover letter.
6. Save the resume as **C7-Project4-Resume-Your Name** and save the cover letter as **C7-Project4-CoverLetter-Your Name**.
7. Submit the resume and cover letter to your instructor in the manner she or he has requested.

Project 5 Enhance and Format a Tourist Information Document

Individual

Deliverable: Travel Information Flyer

1. Open **HangzhouTravelInfo**.
2. Format the document as shown in Figure 7.5 using the following information:
   a. The font used is 11-point Book Antiqua for the body of the document and 16-point Antiqua for the title and subtitle.
   b. The subheadings are 14-point with the Subtitle style and *Dark Blue* font color applied.
   c. Substitute your name in the footer in place of *Student Name*.
   d. The image is a picture named ***Hangzhou*** with the *Simple Frame, Black* picture style; locate the clip art shown or a similar clip art image by searching using the keyword *pagoda*; the text box is the *Grid Quote* with the font formatting changed to 12-point Book Antiqua and the case changed.
   e. Use your best judgment to match other formatting shown.
3. Save the revised document as **C7-Project5-HangzhouTravelInfo-Your Name** in the Ch7 folder within ChapterProjectsWork.
4. Submit the project to your instructor in the manner she or he has requested.
5. Close the document.

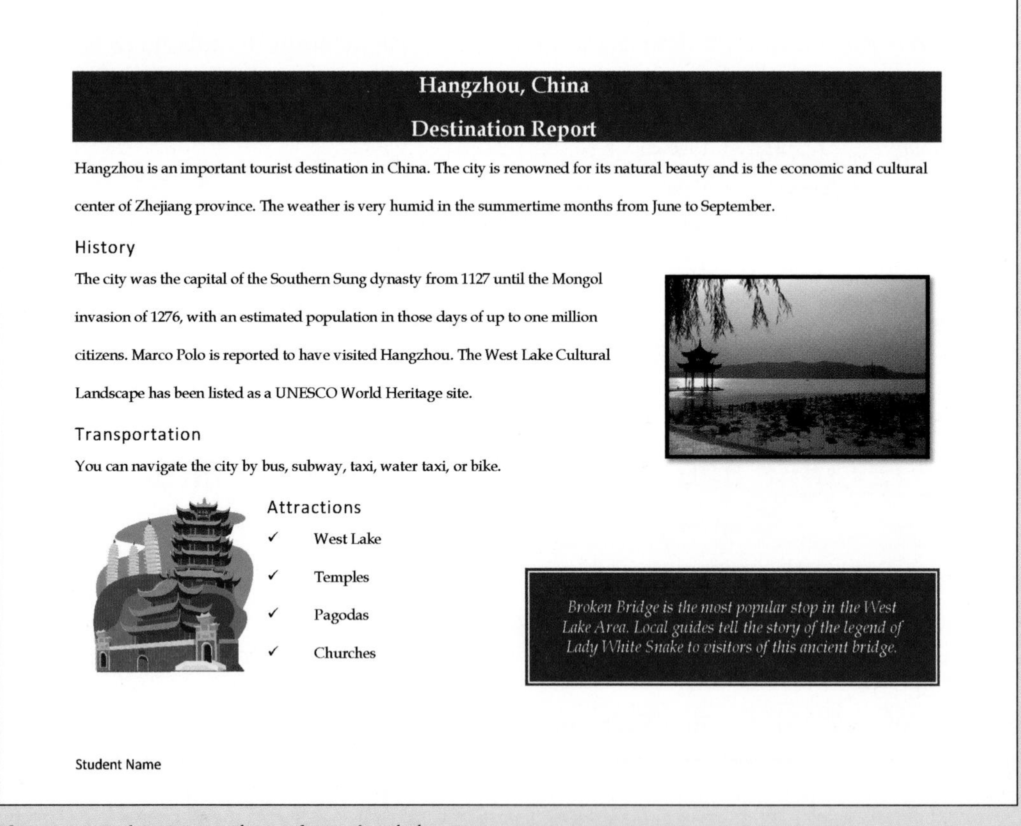

Hangzhou, China

Destination Report

Hangzhou is an important tourist destination in China. The city is renowned for its natural beauty and is the economic and cultural center of Zhejiang province. The weather is very humid in the summertime months from June to September.

History

The city was the capital of the Southern Sung dynasty from 1127 until the Mongol invasion of 1276, with an estimated population in those days of up to one million citizens. Marco Polo is reported to have visited Hangzhou. The West Lake Cultural Landscape has been listed as a UNESCO World Heritage site.

Transportation

You can navigate the city by bus, subway, taxi, water taxi, or bike.

Attractions

- ✓ West Lake
- ✓ Temples
- ✓ Pagodas
- ✓ Churches

Broken Bridge is the most popular stop in the West Lake Area. Local guides tell the story of the legend of Lady White Snake to visitors of this ancient bridge.

Student Name

Figure 7.5 Project 5 Hangzhou Informational Flyer

Project 6 Composing a New Flyer

Individual or Pairs

Deliverable: Food Drive Flyer

1. Listen to the audio file named ***Project6_Instructions***. The file is located in the Ch7 folder in the Student_Data_Files folder on your USB flash drive.
2. Create the flyer as instructed.
3. Save the flyer in the Ch7 folder within the ChapterProjectsWork folder on your USB flash drive as **C7-Project6-FoodDriveFlyer-Your Name**.
4. Submit the project to your instructor in the manner she or he has requested.
5. Close the document.

Project 7 Sending Project Work to OneNote Notebook

Individual

Deliverable: New Page in Shared OneNote notebook

1. Start OneNote and open the MyProjects notebook created in Chapter 4, Project 4.
2. Make Word the active section and add a new page titled *Chapter 7 Projects*.
3. Switch to Word. For each project that you completed, open the document, send the project to OneNote 2013 selecting the Chapter 7 Projects page in the Word section in the MyProjects notebook, and then close the document.
4. Close your MyProjects notebook in OneNote and close OneNote.
5. Close Word.
6. Submit the project to your instructor in the manner she or he has requested.

Chapter 8

Creating, Editing, and Formatting Worksheets Using Excel

After successfully completing this chapter, you will be able to:

- Create and edit a worksheet
- Format cells with font, alignment, number, and style options
- Adjust column widths and row heights
- Use the Fill feature to enter data
- Add a column or row of values with AutoSum
- Insert and delete columns and rows
- Sort data
- Change print options
- Display formulas in cells
- Insert and rename worksheets
- Copy cells between worksheets
- Use Go To and Freeze Panes

Microsoft Excel (referred to as Excel) is a **spreadsheet application** used to create, analyze, and present information that is organized into a grid of columns and rows. Data is calculated, analyzed, and can be graphed in a chart. The ability to do "what-if" analysis during which one or more values are changed to view the effect on other values is a popular feature of Excel. Examples of the type of data for which Excel is used include budgets, income, expenses, investments, loans, schedules, grade books, attendance, inventory, and research data. Any information that can be set up in a grid-like structure is suited to Excel.

Files that you save in Excel are called **workbooks**. A workbook contains a collection of **worksheets**; a worksheet is the structure into which you enter, edit, and manipulate data. Think of a workbook as a binder and a worksheet as a page within the binder. Initially, a workbook has only one worksheet (page), but you can add more as needed.

Many of the features that you learned about in Word operate the same or similarly in Excel, which will make learning Excel faster and easier. You will begin by creating new worksheets in a blank workbook and then open other worksheets in which to practice navigating, editing, sorting, and formatting tasks.

Note: If you are using a tablet, consider using a USB or wireless keyboard because parts of this chapter involve a fair amount of typing.

Topic 8.1

SKILLS

Enter text and values

Create formulas

Edit cells

Creating and Editing a New Worksheet

When you start a new blank workbook, you begin at a worksheet that is divided into columns and rows. The intersection of a column and a row is called a **cell** into which you type text, a value, or a formula. The cell with the green border around its edges is called the **active cell**. Each cell is identified with the letter of the column and the number of the row that intersect to form the cell. For example, A1 refers to the cell in column A, row 1.

A new workbook starts with one worksheet labeled *Sheet1* that has columns labeled A to Z, AA to AZ, BA to BZ, and so on to the last column, which is labeled XFD. Rows are numbered 1, 2, 3, up to 1,048,576.

Method for Creating a New Worksheet

Generally you begin a new worksheet by entering titles and column and row headings to give the worksheet an organizational layout and provide context for the reader. Next, you enter values in the columns and rows. Complete the worksheet by inserting formulas that perform calculations or otherwise summarize data.

1. Start Excel 2013.
2. At the Excel Start screen, tap or click *Blank workbook* in the *Templates* gallery and compare your screen with the one shown in Figure 8.1.

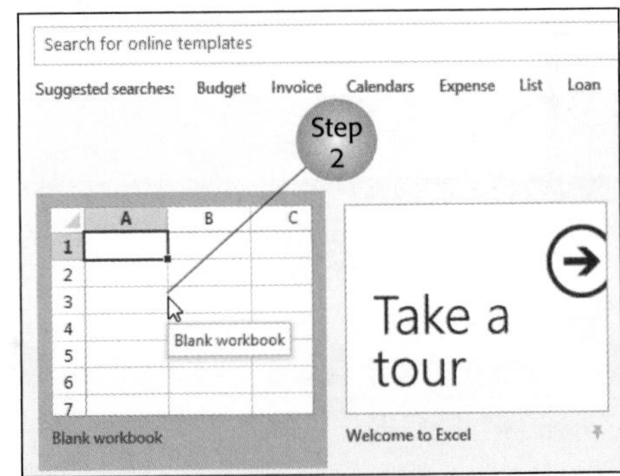

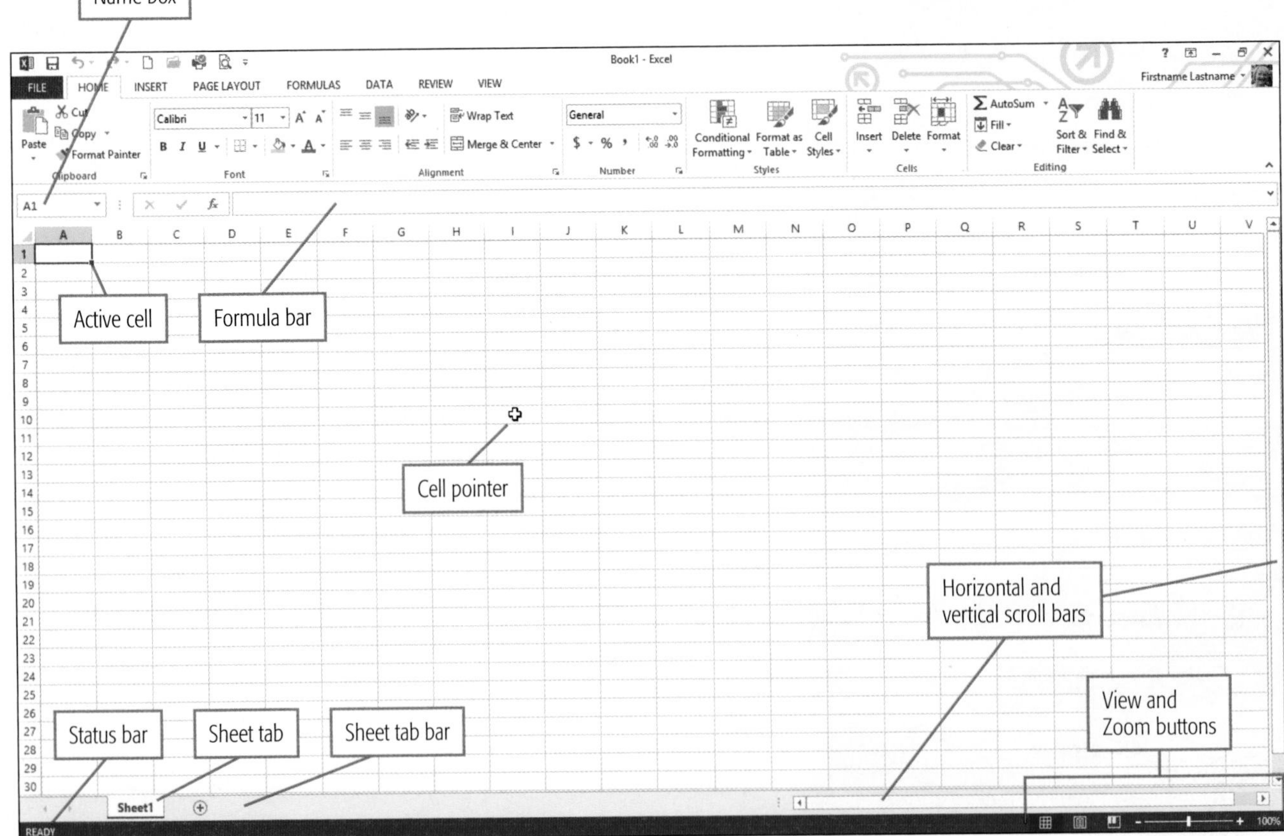

Figure 8.1 A new blank worksheet in Excel. The worksheet area below the ribbon is divided into columns and rows, which creates cells in which data is typed. See Table 8.1 for a description of screen elements.

Table 8.1	Excel Features
Feature	**Description**
Active cell	Location in the worksheet in which the next typed data will be stored or that will be affected by a command. Move the active cell position by tapping or clicking in another cell or by using the Arrow keys.
Cell pointer	Icon that displays when you are able to select cells with the mouse by clicking or dragging. On touch devices with no mouse attached, tap a cell to display selection handles (round circles) at the top left and bottom right corners.
Formula bar	Displays contents stored in the active cell and is also used to create formulas.
Horizontal and vertical scroll bars	Use the scroll bars to view parts of a worksheet not shown in the current viewing area.
Name box	Displays active cell address or name assigned to active cell.
Sheet tab	Displays the name of the active worksheet. By default, new sheets are named *Sheet#* where # is the number of the sheet in the workbook.
Sheet tab bar	Area with sheet tabs used to navigate between worksheets and New sheet button used to insert a new worksheet.
Status bar	Displays messages indicating the current mode of operation; READY indicates the worksheet is ready to accept new data.
View and Zoom buttons	Excel opens by default in Normal view. Other view buttons include Page Layout and Page Break Preview. Zoom buttons are used to enlarge or shrink the display.

When you start a new worksheet, the active cell is positioned in A1 at the top left corner of the worksheet area. Entries are created by moving the active cell and typing text, a value, or a formula.

3. With A1 the active cell, type **Car Purchase Cost** and then tap or press Enter, or tap or click in A2 to make A2 the active cell.

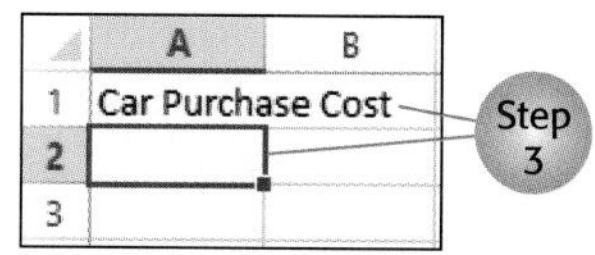

4. Type **Pre-owned Ford Focus Sedan** and then tap or press Enter twice, or tap or click in A4.
5. Type **Total Purchase Price** and then tap or click in A6.
6. Type **Loan Details:** and then tap or click in B7.
7. Type the remaining row headings by moving the active cell and typing the text shown in the image at right.

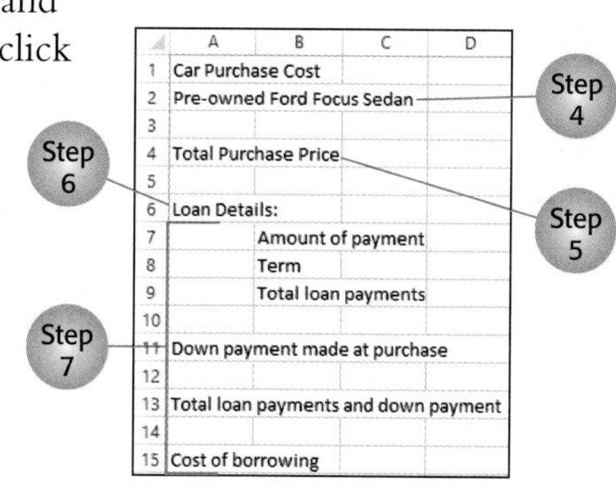

8. Tap or click in F4, type **16700.00**, and then tap or click in E7.

Notice Excel does not display the decimal place values that you typed. By default, zeros to the right of a decimal are not stored or shown. You will learn how to format the display of values in the next topic.

You can use Arrow keys to move the active cell up, down, left, or right.

Excel's AutoComplete matches an entry in the same column with the first few characters that you type. Accept an AutoComplete entry with Tab, Enter, or an Arrow key, or continue typing to ignore the suggestion.

By default, text entries align at the left edge of a cell while numeric entries are right-aligned.

9 Type the remaining values by moving the active cell and typing the numbers shown below.

	A	B	C	D	E	F
1	Car Purchase Cost					
2	Pre-owned Ford Focus Sedan					
3						
4	Total Purchase Price					16700
5						
6	Loan Details:					
7		Amount of payment			470.05	
8		Term			36	
9		Total loan payments				
10						
11	Down payment made at purchase				1700	

Step 9

Creating Formulas to Perform Calculations

A **formula** is used to perform mathematical operations on values. A formula entry begins with the equals sign (=) to indicate to Excel the entry that follows is a calculation. Following the equals sign, type the first cell address that contains a value you want to use, type a mathematical operator such as a +, and then type the second cell address. Continue typing cell addresses with mathematical operators between each address until finished.

The mathematical operators are + (addition), - (subtraction), * (multiplication), / (division), and ^ (exponentiation).

10 Tap or click to make E9 the active cell and then type **=e7*e8**.

11 Tap or click the Enter button in the Formula bar.

Excel calculates the result and displays the value in E9. Notice that the worksheet area displays the formula results while the entry in the Formula bar displays the formula used to calculate the result. Notice also that Excel capitalizes column letters in cell addresses within formulas.

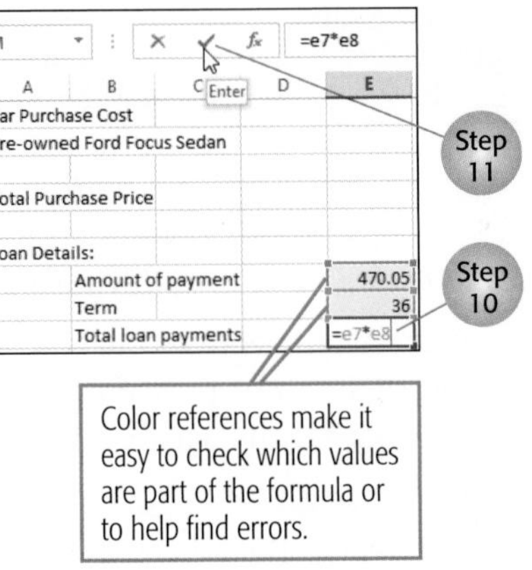

12 Make F13 the active cell and type =.

Another way to enter a formula is to use the pointing method in which you tap or click the desired cells instead of typing their cell addresses.

13 Tap or click E9.

A moving dashed border surrounds E9, the cell is color coded, and the address *E9* is inserted in the formula cell.

oops!

Tapped or clicked the wrong cell? Simply tap or click the correct cell—the cell reference is not fixed in the formula until you type an operator. You can also press the Esc key to start over.

14 Type +.

15 Tap or click E11 and then tap or click the Enter button in the Formula bar, or tap or press Enter.

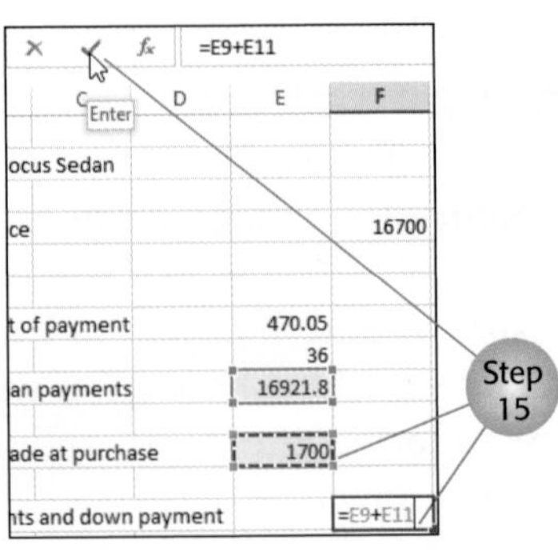

16 Make F15 the active cell and type the formula **=f13-f4**, or enter the formula using the pointing method.

The result, *1921.8*, displays in the cell.

Editing Cells

A cell can be changed by making the cell active and typing a new entry to replace the existing contents. Double-tap or double-click to open a cell for editing in the worksheet area. You can also edit the active cell's contents by inserting or deleting text or values in the Formula bar.

Press the Delete key to delete the contents in the active cell, or tap or click the **Clear button** in the Editing group of the HOME tab and then tap or click *Clear All* at the drop-down list.

17 Make E7 the active cell, type **480.95**, and then tap or press Enter.

Notice the new payment amount caused the values in E9, F13, and F15 to update.

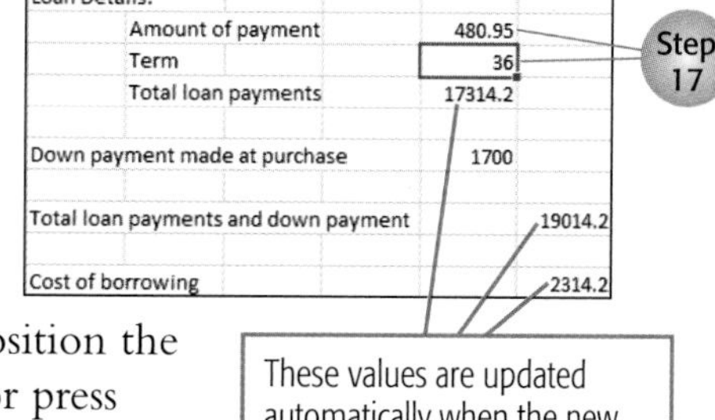

These values are updated automatically when the new loan payment is entered in E7.

18 Double-tap or double-click cell F4, position the insertion point between *6* and *7*, tap or press Backspace to remove *6*, type **5**, and then tap or click any other cell.

4 Total Purchase Price 15700

Step 18

19 Make E11 the active cell, tap or click in the Formula bar, position the insertion point between *1* and *7*, press Backspace to remove *1*, and then tap or click any other cell.

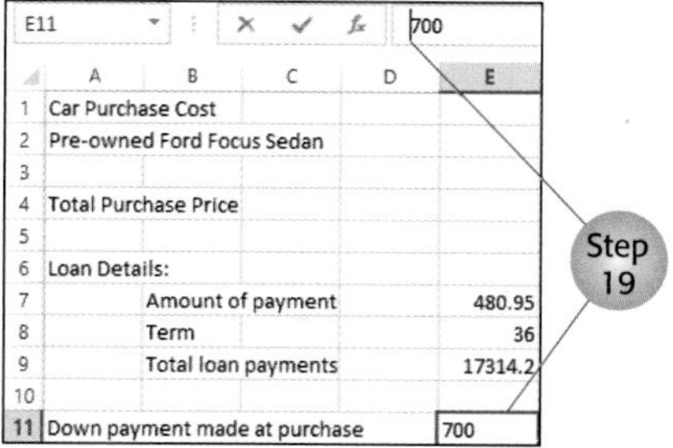

20 Save the new workbook as **8.1-CarCost-Your Name** in a new folder named *Ch8* in the CompletedTopicsByChapter folder on your USB flash drive. Leave the workbook open for the next topic.

Enter a Formula
1. Activate formula cell.
2. Type =.
3. Type first cell address.
4. Type operator symbol.
5. Type second cell address.
6. Continue Steps 3–5 until finished.
7. Tap or press Enter.

Edit a Cell
1. Double-tap or double-click cell.
2. Position insertion point.
3. Insert or delete text as needed.
4. Tap or press Enter.

F2 is the keyboard command to edit a cell.

AutoCorrect operates in Excel; however, red wavy lines do *not* appear below misspelled words. Consider using the Spelling feature in the Proofing group of the REVIEW tab to spell check all worksheets.

Order of Operations in Formulas

Excel gives precedence to exponentiation, multiplication, and division before addition and subtraction when calculating a formula. Use parentheses around a part of the formula you want calculated first such as addition before multiplication or division. For example, in the formula *=(A1+A2)*A3*, Excel adds the values in A1 and A2 first and then multiplies the result by the value in A3.

Topic 8.2

SKILLS

Change the font
Apply bold
Format values
Add borders
Merge cells

Formatting Cells

Similarly to Word, the HOME tab in Excel contains the formatting options for changing the appearance of text, values, or formula results. The Font group contains buttons to change the font, font size, and font color, and to apply bold, italic, underline, borders, and shading. The alignment group contains buttons to align text or values within the cell's edges.

Selecting Cells Using the Mouse

Select cells with a mouse by positioning the cell pointer (large white cross icon ✚) in the starting cell and dragging in the required direction until all cells have been included in a shaded selection rectangle. Select nonadjacent cells by holding down the Ctrl key while you click the mouse in each desired cell. New to Excel 2013 is the Quick Analysis button that displays when a group of cells has been selected. You will learn about the options available from this button in Chapter 9.

Selecting Cells Using Touch

Selecting cells on a touch device in Excel is similar to selecting text in Word with the exception that two selection handles display in the active cell, as shown in Figure 8.2. As in Word, tap inside the selection area to display the Mini toolbar.

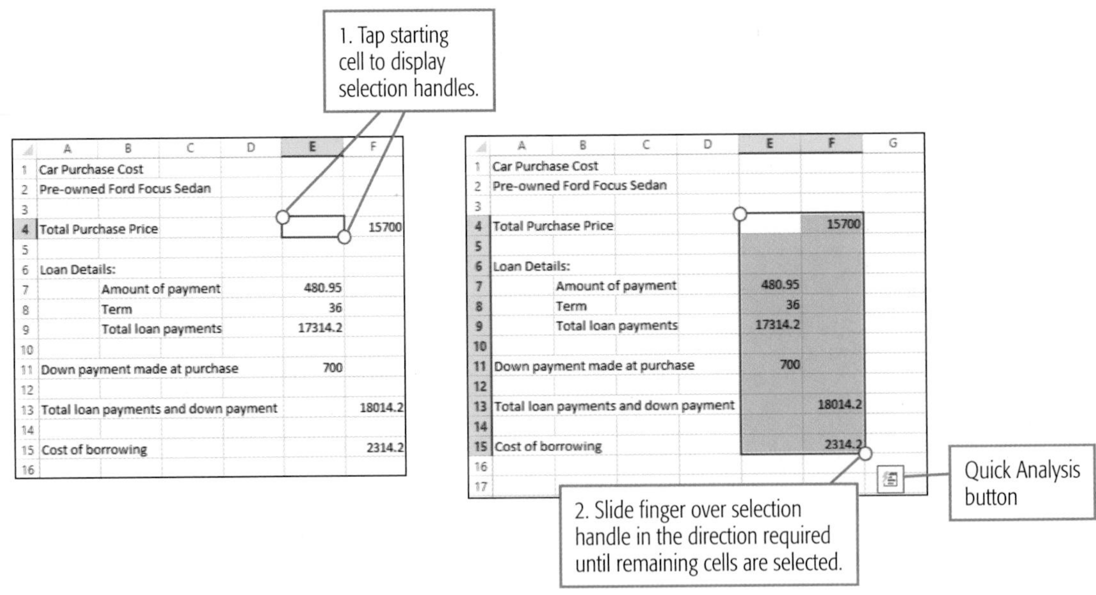

Figure 8.2 Selecting cells using a touch device

App Tip

Select cells using the keyboard by holding down the Shift key while you press an arrow key (Up, Down, Left, or Right).

1 With the **8.1-CarCost-Your Name** workbook open, starting at cell A1, select all of the cells down and right to F15.

A rectangular-shaped group of cells is referred to as a **range**. A range is referenced with the address of the cell at the top left corner, a colon (:), and the address of the cell at the bottom right corner. For example, the reference for the range selected in Step 1 is *A1:F15*.

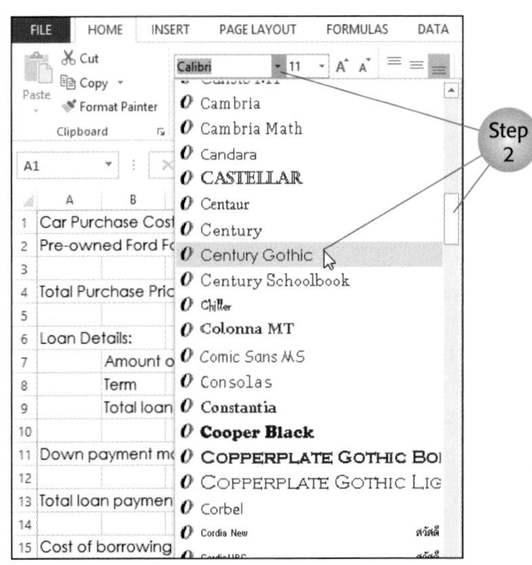

2 Tap or click the Font button arrow in the HOME tab, slide or scroll down the font gallery, and then tap or click *Century Gothic*.

3 Tap or click in any cell to deselect the range.

4 Select A1:A2 and then tap or click the Bold button in the Font group.

Notice the entire text in A1 and A2 is bold, including the characters that spill over the edge of column A into columns B, C, and D. This is because the entire text entry is stored in the cell that was active when the text was typed. Overflow text in adjacent columns is not problematic when the adjacent columns are empty. You will learn how to widen a column in the next topic.

5 Select cell F15 and then tap or click the Bold button.

Formatting Values

By default, cells in a new worksheet are all in the General format, which has no specific appearance options. Buttons in the Number group of the HOME tab are used to format the appearance of numeric entries in a worksheet. Add a dollar symbol, a comma in the thousands, and/or adjust the number of decimal places to improve the appearance of values. Use the Percent Style format to convert decimal values to percentages and include the percent symbol.

Use the Number Format list arrow (next to *General*) to choose other formats for dates, times, fractions, or scientific values, or to open the Format Cells dialog box from the *More Number Formats* option.

6 Select E4:F15.

7 Tap or click the Comma Style button in the Number group.

Comma Style formats values with a comma in thousands and two decimal places.

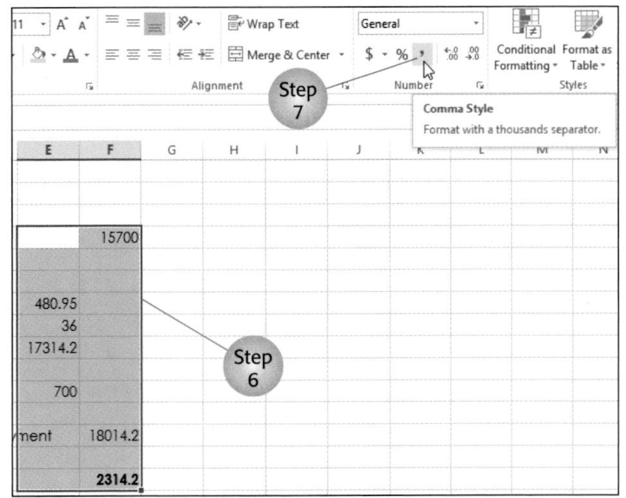

Excel automatically widens columns as needed when you apply a format that adds more characters to a column such as Comma Style.

8 Select F4 and tap or click the Accounting Number Format button in the Number group. (Do not tap or click the down-pointing arrow on the button.)

Accounting Number Format adds a currency symbol ($ for United States and Canada), comma in thousands, and two decimal places. Use the Accounting Number Format button arrow to choose a currency symbol other than the dollar symbol (such as € for Euros).

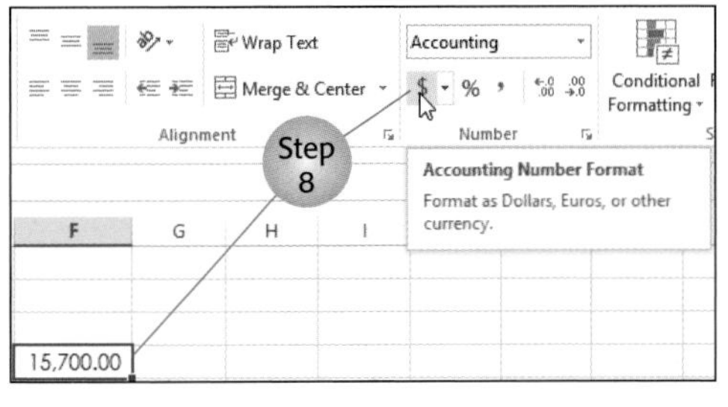

Accounting Number Format aligns the currency symbol at the left edge of the cell. The Currency option (Number Format list) places the currency symbol immediately left of the value. Use Accounting Number Format if you want all dollar symbols to align at the same position.

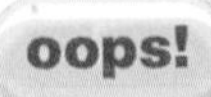

Apply the wrong format or select the wrong cell? Use the Undo command or simply apply the correct format to the cell or range.

9 Select E7 and apply the Accounting Number Format.

10 Select F13:F15 and apply the Accounting Number Format.

11 Select E8 and tap twice or click twice the Decrease Decimal button.

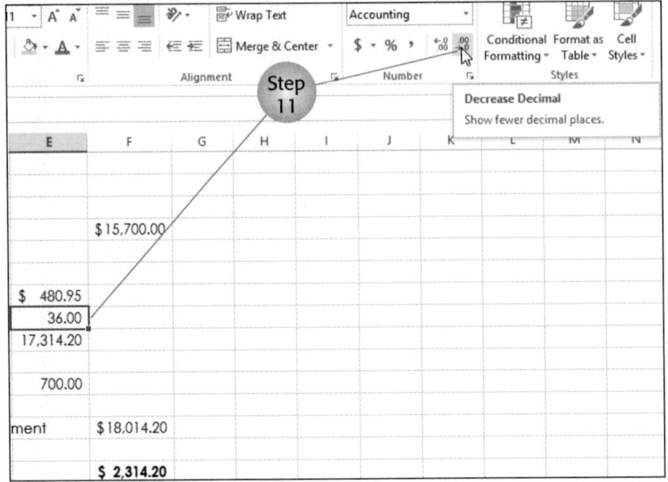

One decimal place is removed from the active cell or range each time you tap or click the **Decrease Decimal button**. Tap or click the **Increase Decimal button** to add one decimal place.

Adding Borders

Borders in various styles and colors can be added to the top, left, bottom, or right edge of a cell. Borders are used to underscore column headings or totals or to otherwise emphasize cells.

12 Select F13.

13 Tap or click the Bottom Border button arrow in the Font group.

14 Tap or click *Top and Bottom Border* at the drop-down list.

15 Select F15.

16 Tap or click the Top and Bottom Border button arrow and tap or click *Bottom Double Border* at the drop-down list.

17 Tap or click in any other cell to view the border style applied to F15.

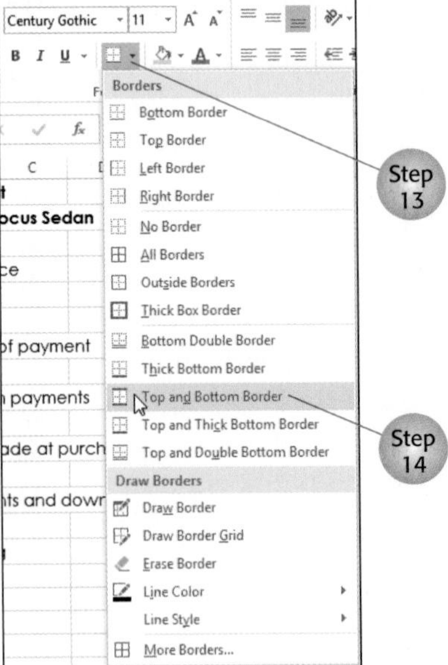

The Borders button updates to the most recently selected border style so that you can apply the same border to another cell or range by simply tapping or clicking the button (not the arrow).

Merging Cells

A worksheet title is often centered across the columns used in the worksheet. The **Merge & Center button** in the Alignment group is used to combine a group of cells into one large cell and center its contents. Use the Merge & Center button arrow to choose to merge without centering or to unmerge a merged cell.

18 Select A1:F1.

19 Tap or click the Merge & Center button in the Alignment group.

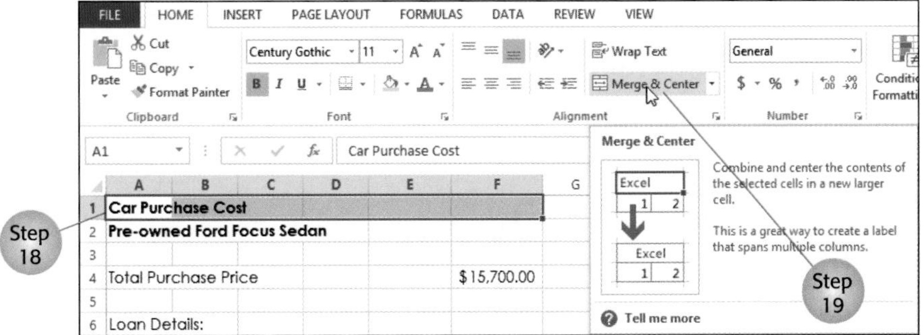

20 Select A2:F2 and tap or click the Merge & Center button.

21 Save the workbook using the same name (**8.1-CarCost-Your Name**). Leave the workbook open for the next topic.

Change a Font
1. Select cell(s).
2. Tap or click Font button arrow.
3. Tap or click desired font.

Change Numeric Format
1. Select cell(s).
2. Tap or click style button in Number group.

Adjust Decimal Places
1. Select cell(s).
2. Tap or click Increase Decimal or Decrease Decimal button.

Add Borders
1. Select cell(s).
2. Tap or click Borders button arrow.
3. Tap or click border style.

Merge Cells
1. Select cells.
2. Tap or click Merge & Center button.

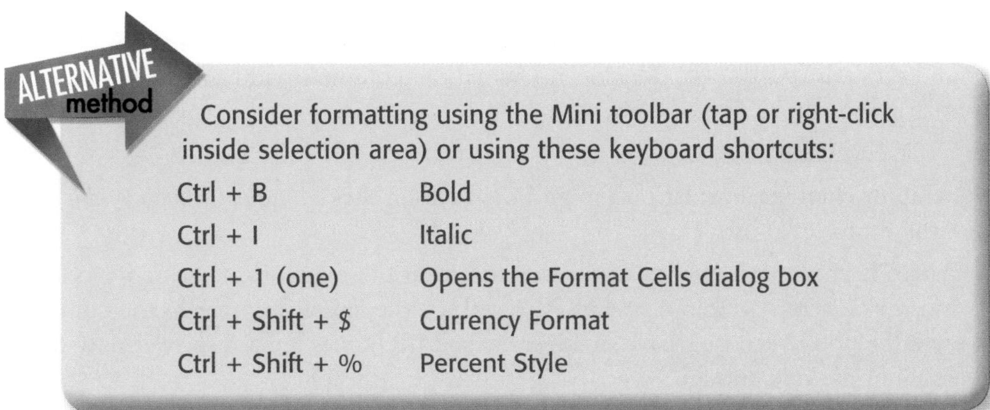

Consider formatting using the Mini toolbar (tap or right-click inside selection area) or using these keyboard shortcuts:

Ctrl + B	Bold
Ctrl + I	Italic
Ctrl + 1 (one)	Opens the Format Cells dialog box
Ctrl + Shift + $	Currency Format
Ctrl + Shift + %	Percent Style

Format Cells Dialog Box

Tapping or clicking the dialog box launcher button at the bottom right of the Font, Alignment, or Number group opens the Format Cells dialog box. Use the dialog box to apply multiple formats in one operation, to further customize format options, or to apply font effect options such as strikethrough, superscript, or subscript.

Adjusting Column Width and Row Height, and Changing Alignment

Topic 8.3

SKILLS

- Adjust column width
- Adjust row height
- Change cell alignment

In a new worksheet, each column width is 8.43 and each row height is 15. You can make cells larger by widening a column's width or increasing a row's height. In many instances, Excel automatically makes columns wider and rows taller to accommodate the cell entry, formula result, or format that you apply. Manually changing the column width or the row height is a technique used to add more space between cells to improve readability or emphasize a section of the worksheet.

1. With the **8.1-CarCost-Your Name** workbook open, make active any cell in column E.

2. Tap or click the Format button in the Cells group in the HOME tab and then tap or click *Column Width* at the drop-down list.

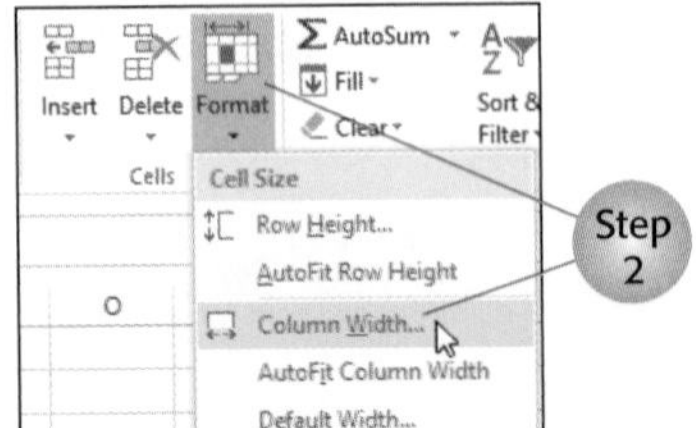

3. Type **15** in the *Column width* text box at the Column Width dialog box and then tap or press Enter, or tap or click OK.

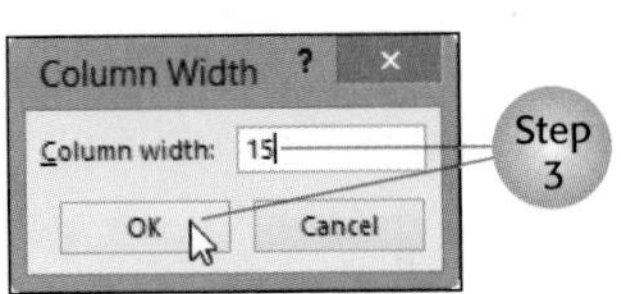

4. Make active any cell in column F, tap or click the Format button, and then tap or click *Column Width* at the drop-down list.

5. Type **10** at the Column Width dialog box and then tap or press Enter, or tap or click OK.

Notice the cells with values in column F have been replaced with a series of pound symbols (######). This occurs when the column's width has been made too narrow to show all of the characters.

6. Make active F4.

7. Tap or click the Format button and then tap or click *AutoFit Column Width* at the drop-down list.

AutoFit changes the width of the column to fit the contents of the active cell. F4 was made active at Step 6 because this cell has the largest number in the column. Notice the pound symbols have disappeared and the values are redisplayed now that the column is wide enough.

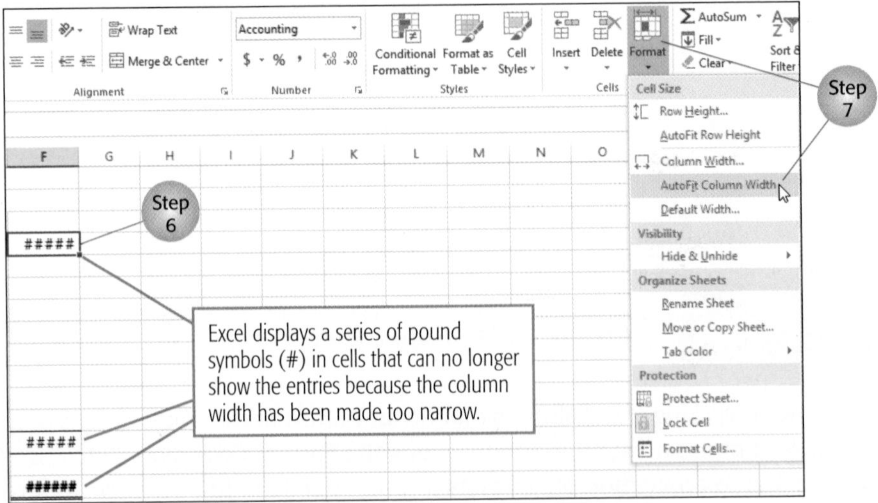

8. Select A1:A2.

Select cells in multiple rows or columns to change the height or width of more than one row or column at the same time.

9. Tap or click the Format button and then tap or click *Row Height* at the drop-down list.

10. Type **26** in the *Row height* text box at the Row Height dialog box and then tap or press Enter, or tap or click OK.

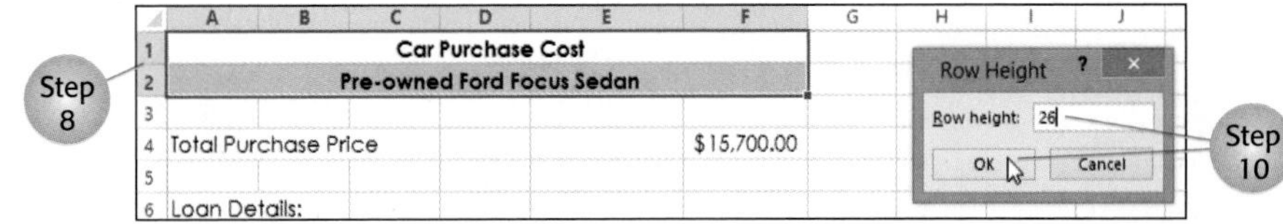

The Alignment group of the HOME tab contains buttons to align the entry of a cell horizontally and/or vertically. You can align at the left, center, or right horizontally, or at the top, middle, or bottom vertically.

11. With A1:A2 still selected, tap or click the **Middle Align button** in the Alignment group.

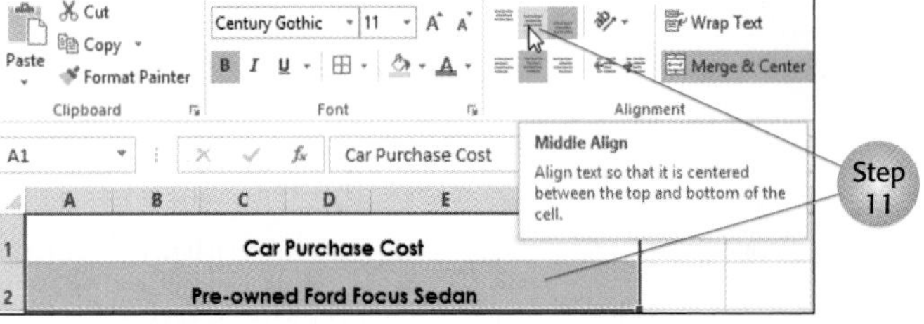

Middle Align centers text vertically within a cell.

12. Make active any cell in row 15.

13. Tap or click the Format button, tap or click *Row Height*, type **26**, and then tap or press Enter, or tap or click OK.

14. Select A15:F15 and then tap or click the Middle Align button.

15. Tap or click in any cell to deselect the range.

16. Save the workbook using the same name (**8.1-CarCost-Your Name**) and then close the workbook.

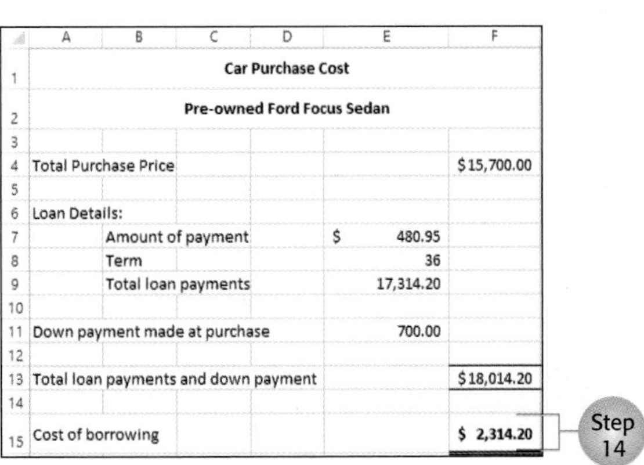

	A	B	C	D	E	F
1	Car Purchase Cost					
2	Pre-owned Ford Focus Sedan					
3						
4	Total Purchase Price					$15,700.00
5						
6	Loan Details:					
7		Amount of payment		$	480.95	
8		Term			36	
9		Total loan payments			17,314.20	
10						
11	Down payment made at purchase				700.00	
12						
13	Total loan payments and down payment					$18,014.20
14						
15	Cost of borrowing					$ 2,314.20

Step 14

Change Column Width
1. Activate cell within column.
2. Tap or click Format button.
3. Tap or click *Column Width*.
4. Type width.
5. Tap or click OK.

Change Row Height
1. Activate cell within row.
2. Tap or click Format button.
3. Tap or click *Row Height*.
4. Type height.
5. Tap or click OK.

AutoFit Column Width or Row Height
1. Activate cell.
2. Tap or click Format button.
3. Tap or click *AutoFit Row Height* or *AutoFit Column Width*.

ALTERNATIVE method

Change column widths using a mouse by dragging the column boundary at the right of the column letter to the right to increase the width or left to decrease the width. Change row height using a mouse by dragging the row boundary below the row number up to decrease the height or down to increase the height. Double-click the right column boundary or the bottom row boundary to AutoFit the column width or row height.

Entering or Copying Data with the Fill Command and Using AutoSum

Topic 8.4

SKILLS

- Use Auto Fill to enter a series
- Use Fill Right to copy a value
- Use the fill handle to enter data
- Add a column with AutoSum

The **Auto Fill** feature in Excel is used to enter data automatically based on a pattern or series that exists in an adjacent cell or range. For example, if *Monday* is entered into cell A1, Auto Fill can enter *Tuesday*, *Wednesday*, and so on automatically in the cells immediately right or below A1. Excel fills many common text or number series and also detects patterns for other data when you select the first few entries in a list. When no pattern or series applies, the fill feature can be used to copy an entry or formula across or down to other cells.

New to Excel 2013 is the **Flash Fill** feature that works to automatically fill data as soon as a pattern is recognized. When Flash Fill presents a suggested list in dimmed text, tap or press Enter to accept the suggestions, or ignore the suggestions and continue typing. A Flash Fill Options button appears when a list is presented with options to undo Flash Fill, accept the suggestions, or select changed cells.

1. Tap or click the New button in the QAT, or tap or click the FILE tab, tap or click New, and then tap or click *Blank workbook*.
2. Type the text entries in A2:A13 as shown in the image at right.
3. Change the width of column A to 18.
4. Make B1 the active cell, type **Sep**, and then tap or click the Enter button in the Formula bar.
5. Select B1:I1.
6. Tap or click the **Fill button** in the Editing group and then tap or click *Series* at the drop-down list.

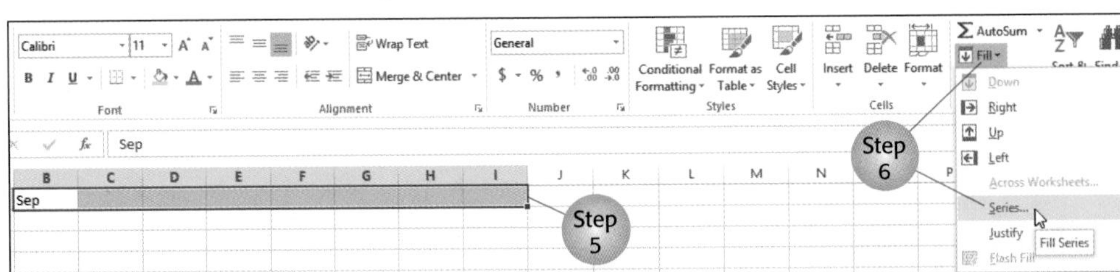

7. Tap or click *AutoFill* in the *Type* section of the Series dialog box and then tap or click OK.

   AutoFill enters the column headings *Oct* through *Apr* in the selected range.

8. Make B3 the active cell, type **875**, and then tap or click the Enter button.
9. Select B3:I3, tap or click the Fill button, and then tap or click *Right* at the drop-down list.

   Fill Right copies the entry in the first cell to the other cells within the selected range.

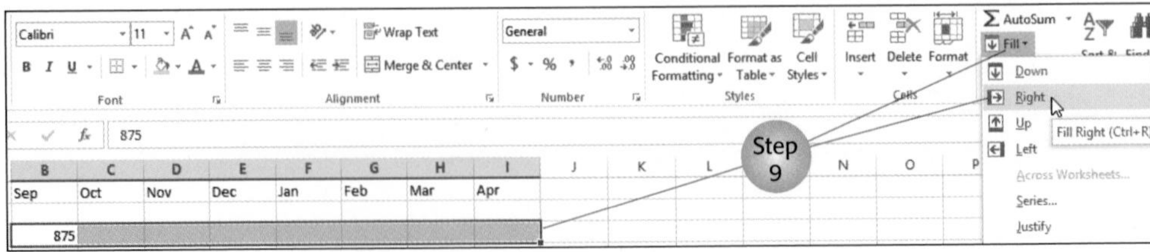

10 Enter the remaining values as shown in the image at right. In rows 5, 6, and 7, use Fill Right to enter the data by completing steps similar to those in Steps 8 and 9.

	A	B	C	D	E	F	G	H	I
1		Sep	Oct	Nov	Dec	Jan	Feb	Mar	Apr
2	Expenses								
3	Housing	875	875	875	875	875	875	875	875
4	Food	260	340	310	295	320	280	300	345
5	Transportation	88	88	88	88	88	88	88	88
6	Cell phone	48	48	48	48	48	48	48	48
7	Internet	42	42	42	42	42	42	42	42
8	Entertainment	150	110	95	175	100	85	95	120
9	Total Expenses								

Step 10

Using the Fill Handle to Copy Cells

A small, green square at the bottom right corner of the active cell (or selected range) is called the **fill handle**. When you point at the square with a mouse, the cell pointer changes appearance from the large white cross to the fill handle (+). Drag right or down when you see the fill handle icon to copy data or a formula, or extend a series from the active cell or range to adjacent cells.

Using the Fill Handle on a Touch Device

Tapping a cell on a touch device displays the active cell with two selection handles instead of the fill handle. See Figure 8.3 for instructions on how to use the fill handle on a touch device.

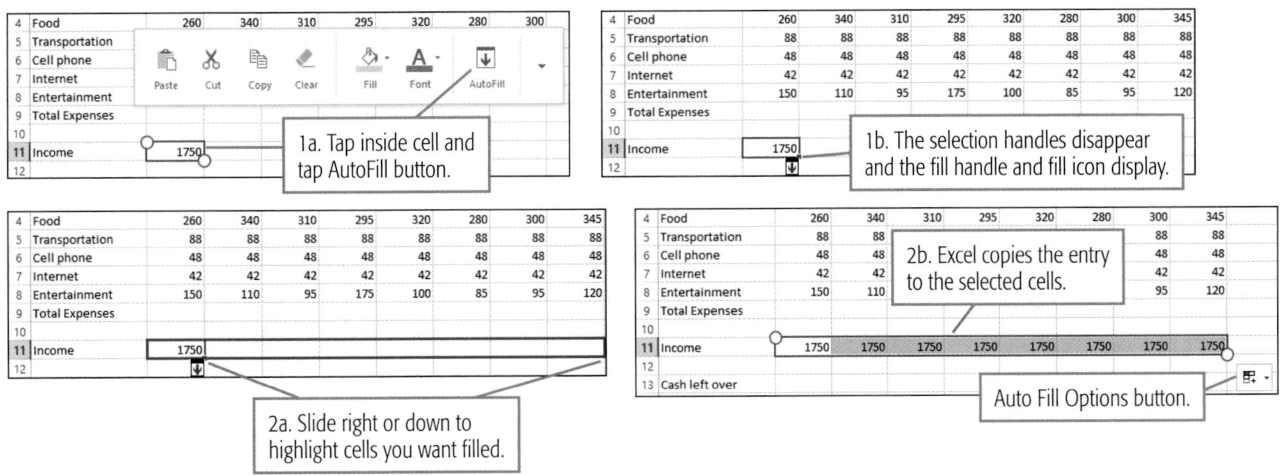

Figure 8.3 Using the fill handle on a touch device

11 Make B11 the active cell, type **1750**, and then tap or click the Enter button.

12 Slide or drag the fill handle right to I11.

The value *1750* is copied to the cells in the selected range. See Beyond Basics at the end of this topic for more information about using the versatile fill handle.

oops!

Don't see fill handle? The fill handle may have been turned off. Open the Excel Options dialog box with Advanced tab (FILE, Options, *Advanced*) and then tap or click *Enable fill handle and cell drag-and-drop* to insert a check mark.

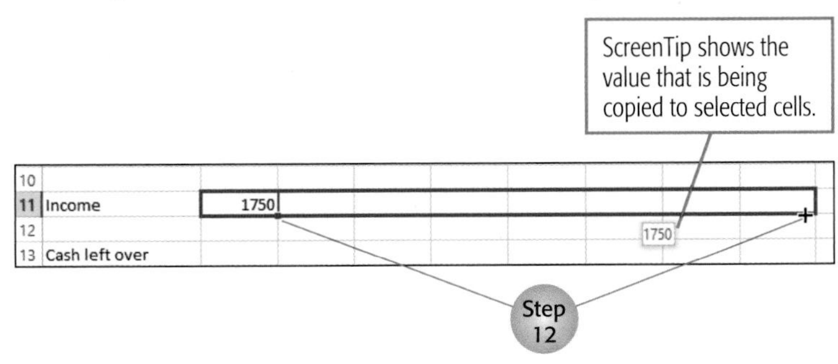

Using the SUM function

To add the expenses in B9, you could type the formula *=b3+b4+b5+b6+b7+b8*; however, Excel includes a built-in preprogrammed function called SUM that can be used to add a column or row of numbers. The SUM function is faster and easier to use. To add the expenses in B9 using SUM, you would type the formula *=SUM(b3:b8)*. Notice you need to provide only the range of cells to add within parentheses after *=SUM* rather than each individual cell reference. Because the SUM function is used frequently, an **AutoSum button** is included in the HOME tab that automatically detects the range to be added.

In most cases the suggested range is correct; however, always check to make sure the included cells are the correct cells to be added. If necessary, drag to select a different range before completing the formula.

13. Make B9 the active cell.
14. Tap or click the AutoSum button in the Editing group of the HOME tab. (Do not tap or click the down-pointing arrow at the right of AutoSum.)

   Excel inserts the formula *=SUM(B3:B8)* in B9 with the suggested range *B3:B8* selected.

15. Tap or click the Enter button, or tap or press Ctrl + Enter to complete the formula (Ctrl + Enter completes the entry and keeps the active cell in B9.)

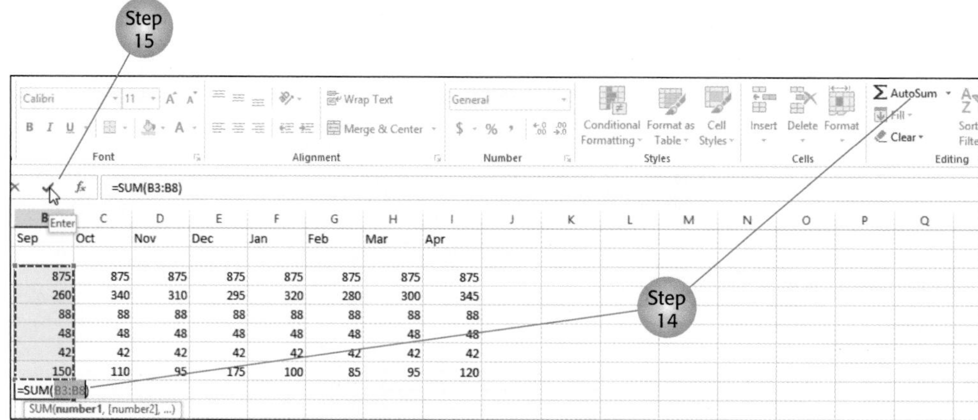

16. With B9 still the active cell, slide or drag the fill handle right to I9.

   In this instance, using the fill handle copies the formula in B9 to the selected cells.

17. Make B13 the active cell, type **=b11-b9**, and then tap or click the Enter button or tap or press Ctrl + Enter.
18. With B13 the active cell, slide or drag the fill handle right to I13.

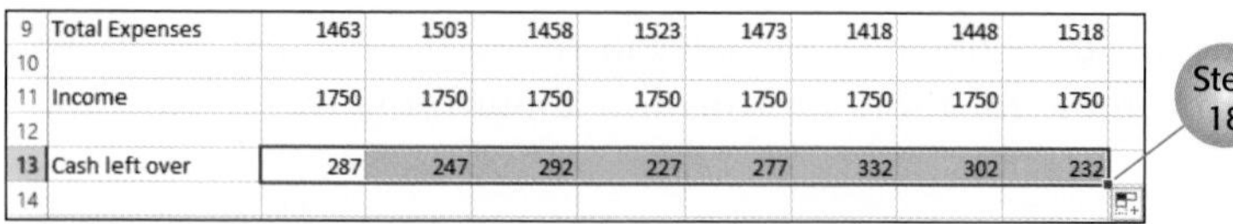

9	Total Expenses	1463	1503	1458	1523	1473	1418	1448	1518
10									
11	Income	1750	1750	1750	1750	1750	1750	1750	1750
12									
13	Cash left over	287	247	292	227	277	332	302	232
14									

19. Make J1 the active cell, type **Total**, and then tap or press Enter.

20 Make J3 the active cell and tap or click the AutoSum button.

In this instance, Excel suggests the range B3:I3 in the SUM function. Excel looks for values immediately above or left of the active cell. Because no value exists above J3, Excel correctly suggests adding the values to the left in the same row.

21 Tap or click the Enter button to accept the formula.

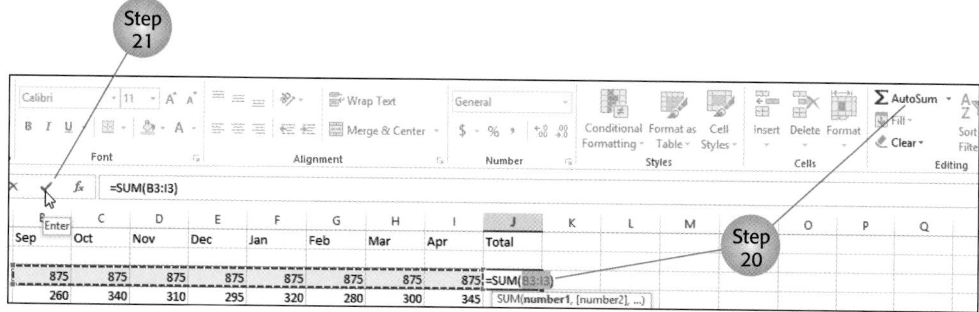

22 With J3 the active cell, slide or drag the fill handle down to J13.

23 Make J10 the active cell and press the Delete key, or tap or click the Clear button in the Editing group and then tap or click *Clear All* at the drop-down list.

24 Make J12 the active cell and repeat the instruction in Step 23.

	A	B	C	D	E	F	G	H	I	J
1		Sep	Oct	Nov	Dec	Jan	Feb	Mar	Apr	Total
2	Expenses									
3	Housing	875	875	875	875	875	875	875	875	7000
4	Food	260	340	310	295	320	280	300	345	2450
5	Transportation	88	88	88	88	88	88	88	88	704
6	Cell phone	48	48	48	48	48	48	48	48	384
7	Internet	42	42	42	42	42	42	42	42	336
8	Entertainment	150	110	95	175	100	85	95	120	930
9	Total Expenses	1463	1503	1458	1523	1473	1418	1448	1518	11804
10										
11	Income	1750	1750	1750	1750	1750	1750	1750	1750	14000
12										
13	Cash left over	287	247	292	227	277	332	302	232	2196

Step 24

25 Save the new workbook as **8.4-SchoolBudget-Your Name** in the Ch8 folder in CompletedTopicsByChapter on your USB flash drive. Leave the workbook open for the next topic.

With options from the Clear button drop-down list, you can clear only contents and leave formatting intact or vice versa.

AutoFill Series

1. Select range.
2. Tap or click Fill button.
3. Tap or click *Series*.
4. Tap or click *AutoFill*.
5. Tap or click OK.

Fill Right

1. Select range.
2. Tap or click Fill button.
3. Tap or click *Right*.

Copy Using Fill Handle

1. Make cell active.
2. Slide or drag fill handle in required direction.

Add with the SUM Function

1. Activate formula cell.
2. Tap or click AutoSum button.
3. Tap or click Enter button OR select correct range and tap or click Enter button.

More Examples of Using the Fill Command

Excel's Fill command can detect patterns in values, dates, times, months, days, years, or other data. The pattern is detected based on the cells selected before dragging the fill handle. Following are some examples of series the fill handle can extend. In each example, you would select both cells in column A and column B and then drag the fill handle right to extend the data.

Column A	Column B	Extends this data when fill handle is dragged right
10	20	30, 40, 50, and so on
9:00	10:00	11:00, 12:00, 1:00 and so on
2014	2015	2016, 2017, 2018 and so on
Year 1	Year 2	Year 3, Year 4, Year 5 and so on

Topic 8.5

SKILLS

Insert a new row

Insert a new column

Delete a row

oops!

Only one cell inserted instead of an entire row? Tapping or clicking the top part of the Insert button inserts a cell instead of an entire new row. Use Undo and then try again, making sure to tap or click the arrow on the bottom part of the Insert button to access the drop-down list.

Inserting and Deleting Rows and Columns

New rows or columns are inserted or deleted using the Insert or Delete buttons in the Cells group of the HOME tab. New rows are inserted above the row in which the active cell is positioned, and new columns are inserted to the left.

Cell references within formulas and formula results are automatically updated when new rows or columns with data are added to or removed from a worksheet.

1. With the **8.4-SchoolBudget-Your Name** workbook open, make active any cell in row 4.
2. Tap or click the **Insert button** arrow in the Cells group of the HOME tab.
3. Tap or click *Insert Sheet Rows* at the drop-down list.

A new blank row is inserted between *Housing* and *Food*.

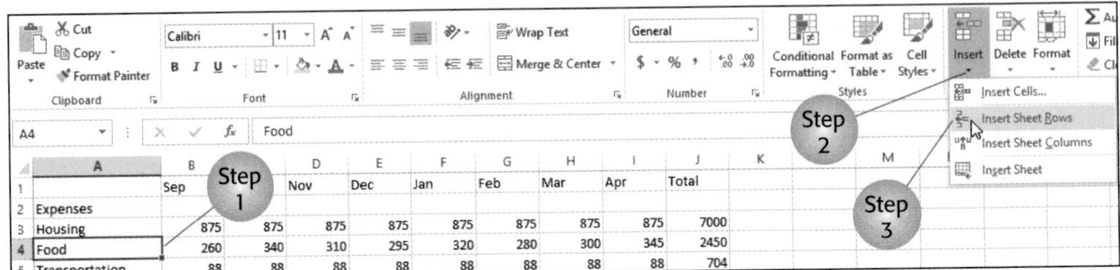

	A	B	C	D	E	F	G	H	I	J
1		Sep		Nov	Dec	Jan	Feb	Mar	Apr	Total
2	Expenses									
3	Housing	875	875	875	875	875	875	875	875	7000
4	Food	260	340	310	295	320	280	300	345	2450
5	Transportation	88	88	88	88	88	88	88	88	704

4. Type the following entries in the cells indicated:

A4	Utilities	F4	128
B4	110	G4	106
C4	115	H4	118
D4	132	I4	112
E4	147		

5. Make J3 the active cell and slide or drag the fill handle down to J4 to copy the SUM formula to the new row.

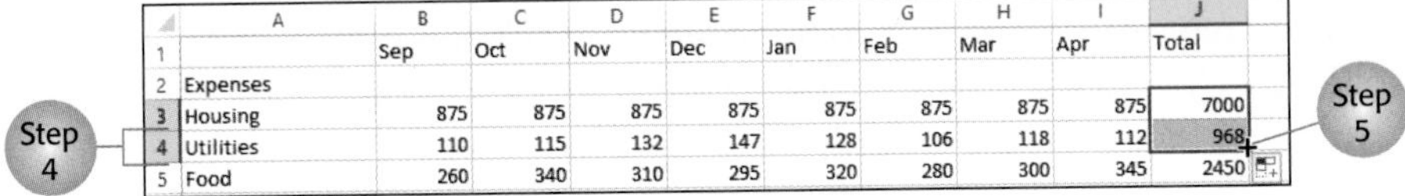

	A	B	C	D	E	F	G	H	I	J
1		Sep	Oct	Nov	Dec	Jan	Feb	Mar	Apr	Total
2	Expenses									
3	Housing	875	875	875	875	875	875	875	875	7000
4	Utilities	110	115	132	147	128	106	118	112	968
5	Food	260	340	310	295	320	280	300	345	2450

App Tip

With a mouse you can also insert multiple rows by selecting the row numbers along the left edge of the worksheet area, right-clicking, and then choosing *Insert*.

6. Select A1:A2, tap or click the Insert button arrow, and then tap or click *Insert Sheet Rows*.

Two rows are inserted above the worksheet.

7. Make A1 the active cell and type **Proposed School Budget**.
8. Make A2 the active cell and type **First Year of Program**.
9. Merge & Center A1 in columns A to J.
10. Merge & Center A2 in columns A to J.

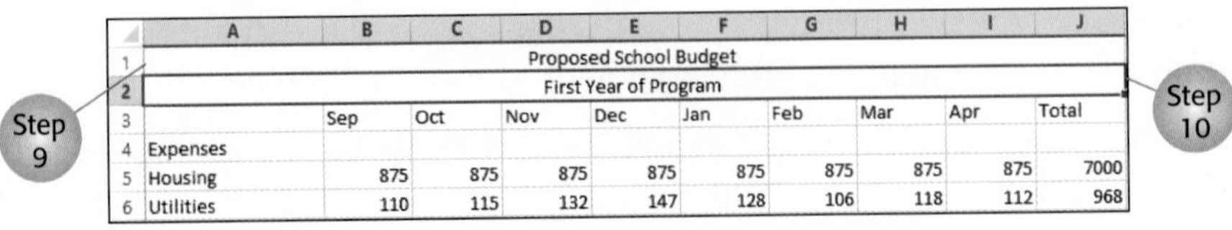

	A	B	C	D	E	F	G	H	I	J
1	Proposed School Budget									
2	First Year of Program									
3		Sep	Oct	Nov	Dec	Jan	Feb	Mar	Apr	Total
4	Expenses									
5	Housing	875	875	875	875	875	875	875	875	7000
6	Utilities	110	115	132	147	128	106	118	112	968

11 Make any cell in column J active.

12 Tap or click the Insert button arrow and then tap or click *Insert Sheet Columns* at the drop-down list.

A new column is inserted between *Apr* and *Total*. Notice also an **Insert Options button** appears. Options from this button are used to format the new column with the same format options as those in the column at the left or the column at the right of the new column.

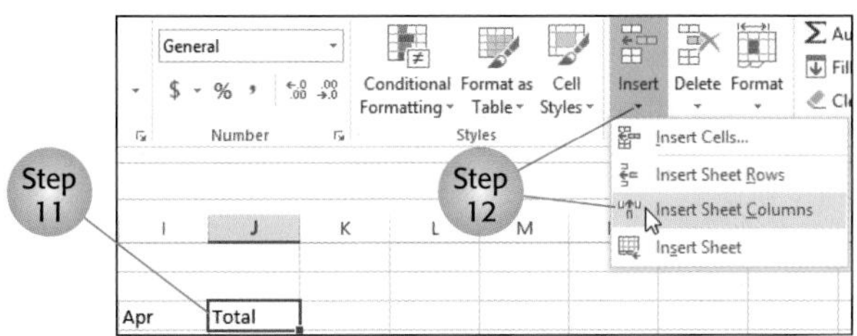

To delete a single row or column, position the active cell in any cell within the row or column to be removed and choose *Delete Sheet Rows* or *Delete Sheet Columns* from the **Delete button** arrow drop-down list. Remove multiple rows or columns from the worksheet by first selecting the range of rows or columns to be deleted.

13 Make any cell in row 10 active.

14 Tap or click the Delete button arrow and then tap or click *Delete Sheet Rows* at the drop-down list.

Row 10 is removed from the worksheet, and existing rows below are shifted up to fill in the space.

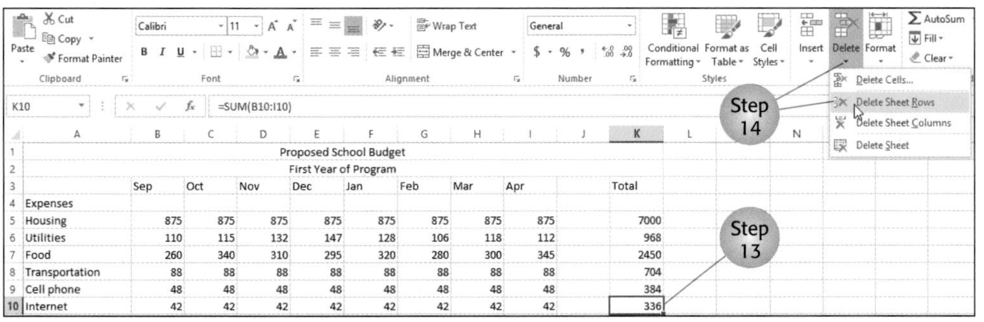

15 Save the workbook using the same name (**8.4-SchoolBudget-Your Name**). Leave the workbook open for the next topic.

Insert Rows or Columns

1. Activate cell or select range.
2. Tap or click Insert button arrow.
3. Tap or click *Insert Sheet Rows* or *Insert Sheet Columns*.

Delete Rows or Columns

1. Activate cell or select range.
2. Tap or click Delete button arrow.
3. Tap or click *Delete Sheet Rows* or *Delete Sheet Columns*.

Delete a column by performing similar steps except choose *Delete Sheet Columns* at the Delete button drop-down list.

Inserting and Deleting Cells

The Insert and Delete buttons are also used to insert or delete cells within a worksheet. Select the range of cells you need to add and choose *Insert Cells* from the Insert button drop-down list. At the Insert dialog box, choose whether you want to shift existing cells right or down.

Select the range of cells to delete, choose *Delete Cells* at the Delete button drop-down list, and then select whether to shift existing cells left or up to fill the space.

Topic 8.6

SKILLS

Sort rows of data

Apply cell styles

Sorting and Applying Cell Styles

A range in Excel can be rearranged by sorting in either ascending or descending order on one or more columns. For example, you can sort a list of names and cities first by the city and then by the last name. To sort by more than one column, select the range and open the Sort dialog box from the Sort & Filter button drop-down list.

1. With the **8.4-SchoolBudget-Your Name** workbook open, select A5:K10.

   Notice you do not include the heading in A4 or the total row in the sort range.

2. Tap or click the **Sort & Filter button** in the Editing group of the HOME tab.

3. Tap or click *Sort A to Z* at the drop-down list.

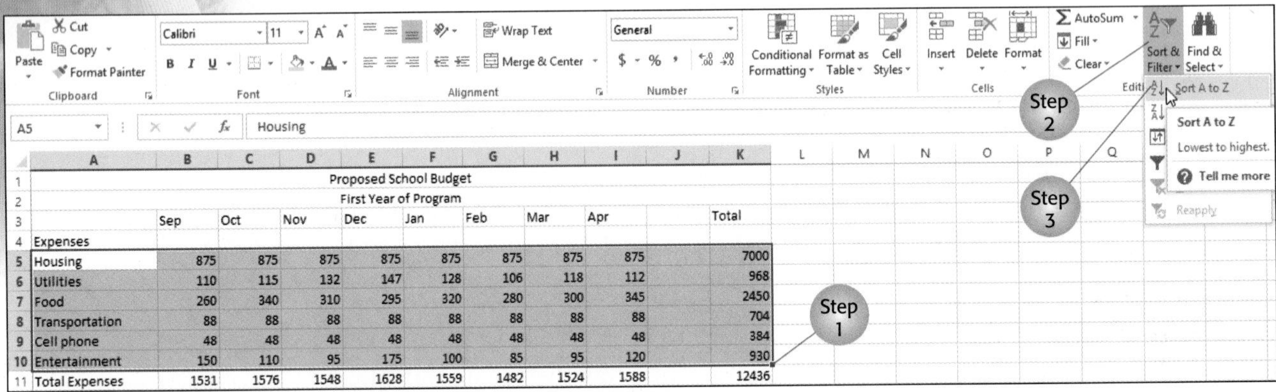

	A	B	C	D	E	F	G	H	I	J	K
1					Proposed School Budget						
2					First Year of Program						
3		Sep	Oct	Nov	Dec	Jan	Feb	Mar	Apr		Total
4	Expenses										
5	Housing	875	875	875	875	875	875	875	875		7000
6	Utilities	110	115	132	147	128	106	118	112		968
7	Food	260	340	310	295	320	280	300	345		2450
8	Transportation	88	88	88	88	88	88	88	88		704
9	Cell phone	48	48	48	48	48	48	48	48		384
10	Entertainment	150	110	95	175	100	85	95	120		930
11	Total Expenses	1531	1576	1548	1628	1559	1482	1524	1588		12436

4. Tap or click in any cell to deselect the range and review the new order of the expenses.

5. Select A5:K10.

6. Tap or click the Sort & Filter button and then tap or click *Custom Sort* at the drop-down list.

7. At the Sort dialog box, tap or click the *Sort by* list arrow in the *Column* section and then tap or click *Column K*.

8. Tap or click the *Order* list arrow (currently displays *Smallest to Largest*) and then tap or click *Largest to Smallest*.

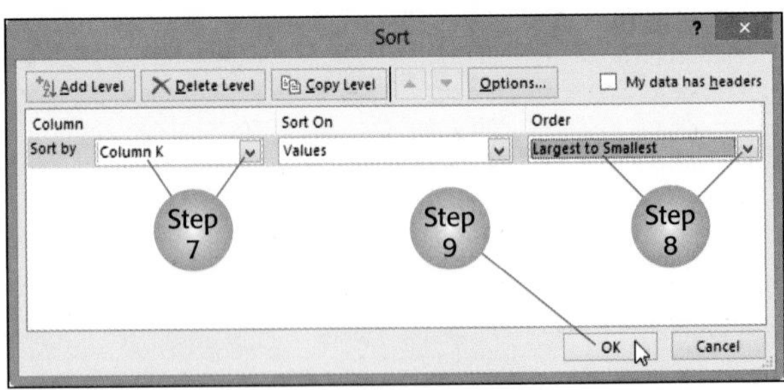

9. Tap or click OK.

   The range is rearranged in descending order from highest expense total to lowest.

10. Tap or click in any cell to deselect the range and review the new order of expenses.

Similar to Word's Styles feature, **Cell Styles** in Excel are a set of predefined formatting options that can be applied to a single cell or a range. Using Cell Styles to format a worksheet is faster and promotes consistency in worksheets. The *Cell Styles* gallery groups styles by the sections *Good, Bad and Neutral, Data and Model, Titles and Headings, Themed Cell Styles*, and *Number format.*

11 Make A1 the active cell and then tap or click the **Cell Styles button** in the Styles group of the HOME tab.

12 Tap or click *Heading 1* in the *Titles and Headings* section of the *Cell Styles* gallery.

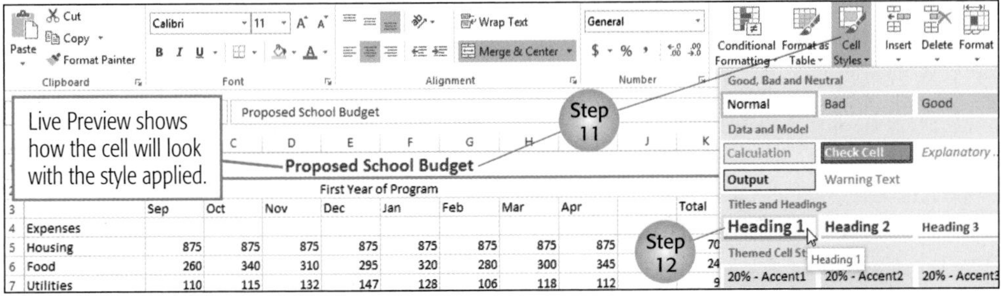

13 Make A2 the active cell, tap or click the Cell Styles button, and then tap or click *Heading 4* in the *Titles and Headings* section of the *Cell Styles* gallery.

14 Apply the Heading 4 Cell Style to A4, A13, and A15.

15 Select B3:K3, apply the *Accent1* style in the *Themed Cell Styles* section of the *Cell Styles* gallery, and then Center the cells.

16 Select B5:K15 and apply the *Comma [0]* style in the *Number Format* section of the Cell Styles gallery.

17 Select B15:K15 and apply the *Total* style in the *Titles and Headings* section of the Cell Styles gallery.

18 Tap or click in any cell to deselect the range, and compare your worksheet with the one shown in Figure 8.4.

	A	B	C	D	E	F	G	H	I	J	K
1	Proposed School Budget										
2	First Year of Program										
3		Sep	Oct	Nov	Dec	Jan	Feb	Mar	Apr		Total
4	Expenses										
5	Housing	875	875	875	875	875	875	875	875		7,000
6	Food	260	340	310	295	320	280	300	345		2,450
7	Utilities	110	115	132	147	128	106	118	112		968
8	Entertainment	150	110	95	175	100	85	95	120		930
9	Transportation	88	88	88	88	88	88	88	88		704
10	Cell phone	48	48	48	48	48	48	48	48		384
11	Total Expenses	1,531	1,576	1,548	1,628	1,559	1,482	1,524	1,588		12,436
12											
13	Income	1,750	1,750	1,750	1,750	1,750	1,750	1,750	1,750		14,000
14											
15	Cash left over	**219**	**174**	**202**	**122**	**191**	**268**	**226**	**162**		**1,564**

Figure 8.4 Sorted worksheet with cell styles applied

19 Save the workbook using the same name (**8.4-SchoolBudget-Your Name**). Leave the workbook open for the next topic.

No Cell Styles button? On larger displays the Cell Styles gallery displays in place of the Cell Styles button. Tap or click the More button to view the Cell Styles gallery.

If you are using a mouse, hold down the Ctrl key and click A4, A13, and A15 to format all three cells in one operation.

Sort a Range by the First Column
1. Select range.
2. Tap or click Sort & Filter button.
3. Tap or click *Sort A to Z* or *Sort Z to A*.

Custom Sort
1. Select range.
2. Tap or click Sort & Filter button.
3. Tap or click *Custom Sort*.
4. Change options and/or add levels as needed.
5. Tap or click OK.

Apply Cell Styles
1. Select cell or range.
2. Tap or click Cell Styles button.
3. Tap or click desired cell style.

Workbook Themes

Options in the *Titles and Headings* and *Themed Cell Styles* sections change depending on the active theme (set of colors, fonts, and effects). Change the theme for a workbook using the *Themes* gallery in the PAGE LAYOUT tab.

Changing Orientation and Scaling and Displaying Cell Formulas

Topic 8.7

SKILLS

Preview a worksheet

Change orientation

Display cell formulas

Change scaling

By default, new Excel workbooks have print options set to print the active worksheet on a letter-sized page (8.5 x 11 inches), in portrait orientation, and with 0.75-inch top and bottom margins and 0.7-inch left and right margins. Preview a new worksheet before printing to make sure these print options are appropriate.

Workbooks are often distributed as PDF files and circulated electronically. Always preview the worksheet and change print options as needed before exporting as PDF because PDF files are essentially the electronic view of the printed worksheet.

1. With the **8.4-SchoolBudget-Your Name** workbook open, display the Print tab Backstage view and compare your screen with the one shown in Figure 8.5.

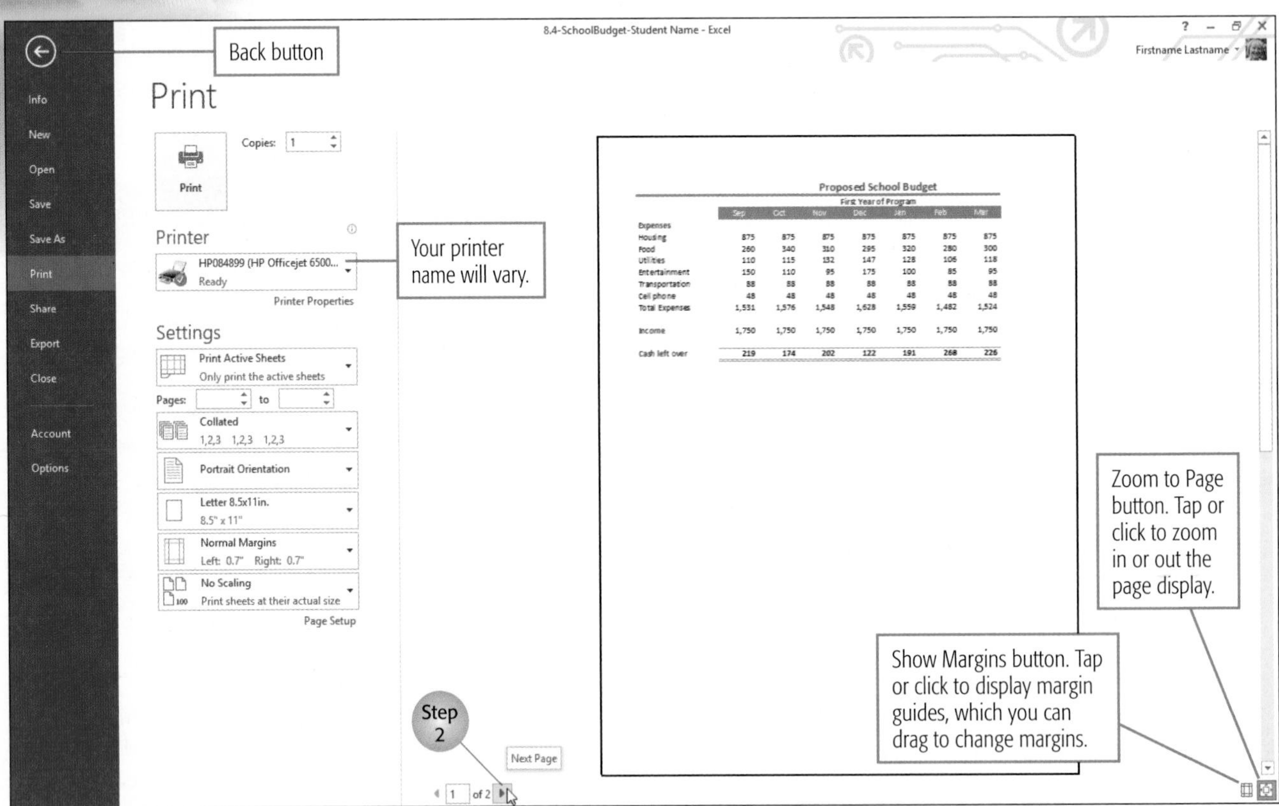

Figure 8.5 Print tab Backstage view with first page displayed for the **8.4-SchoolBudget-Student Name** worksheet

2. Tap or click the Next Page button at the bottom of the preview area to view the second page of the worksheet.
3. Tap or click the Orientation button (displays *Portrait Orientation*) and then tap or click *Landscape Orientation* at the drop-down list.

Notice the worksheet now fits on one page. Landscape is a common layout used for wide worksheets.

4. Tap or click the Back button to return to the worksheet and then save the revised workbook using the same name (**8.4-SchoolBudget-Your Name**).

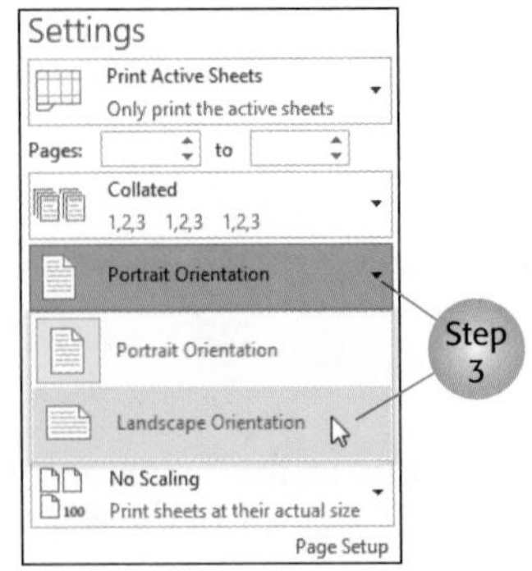

Change the Orientation

1. Display Print tab Backstage view.
2. Tap or click Orientation button.
3. Tap or click *Landscape Orientation*.

Formula results display in the worksheet area with the formula used to generate the result visible in the Formula bar when a cell is active. On a printed copy of the worksheet only the formula result is printed. You may want to print a second copy of the worksheet with the formulas displayed in the cell as a backup or documentation strategy for a complex or otherwise important worksheet.

Ctrl + ` (called grave accent usually located above the Tab key) is the keyboard command to turn on or off the display of formulas.

5. Tap or click the FILE tab and then tap or click Options.
6. Tap or click *Advanced* in the left pane of the Excel Options dialog box.
7. Slide or scroll down the Advanced options for working with Excel until you reach the section titled *Display options for this worksheet.*
8. Tap or click to insert a check mark in the *Show formulas in cells instead of their calculated results* check box.
9. Tap or click OK.
10. Slide or scroll right if necessary to review the worksheet with formulas displayed.

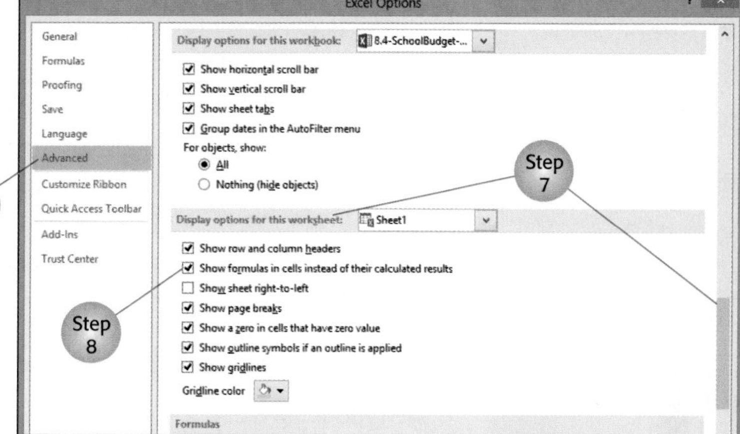

11. Display the Print tab Backstage view.
12. Tap or click the Scaling button (displays *No Scaling*) and then tap or click *Fit Sheet on One Page*.

Fit Sheet on One Page shrinks the size of text on the printout to fit all columns and rows on one page.

13. Tap or click the Back button to return to the worksheet.
14. Use Save As to save a copy of the worksheet with the formulas displayed in the Ch8 folder in CompletedTopicsByChapter as **8.4-SchoolBudgetWithFormulasDisplayed-Your Name**.
15. Close the workbook.

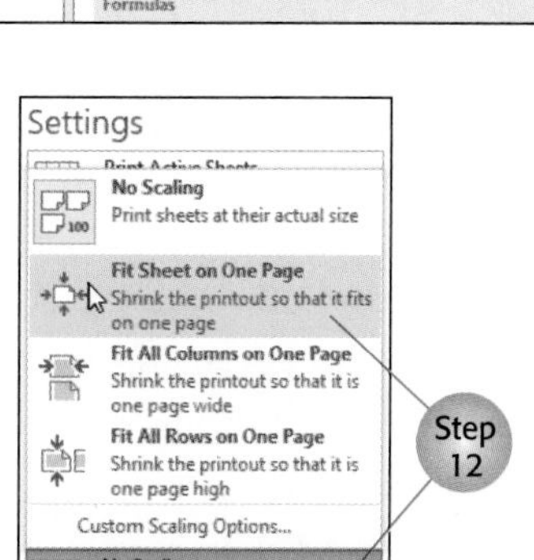

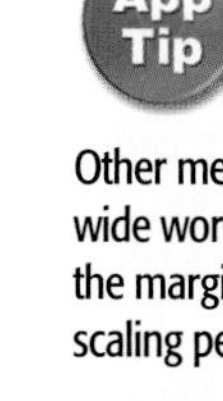

Other methods used to print wide worksheets are decreasing the margins and changing the scaling percentage.

ALTERNATIVE method

Tap or click PAGE LAYOUT and use the Margins and Orientation buttons in the Page Setup group, the *Width* and *Height* lists, and the *Scale* text box options in the Scale to Fit group to change print options.

Display Cell Formulas

1. Tap or click FILE tab.
2. Tap or click Options.
3. Tap or click *Advanced.*
4. Slide or scroll down dialog box.
5. Tap or click *Show formulas in cells instead of their calculated results.*
6. Tap or click OK.

Scale a Worksheet

1. Display Print tab Backstage view.
2. Tap or click Scaling button.
3. Tap or click scaling option.

More Scaling Options

The scaling option **Fit All Columns on One Page** shrinks the size of text until all of the columns fit the page width; more than one page may print if there are many rows. **Fit All Rows on One Page** shrinks the size of text until all of the rows fit the page height; more than one page may print if there are many columns.

Inserting and Renaming a Worksheet, Copying Cells, and Indenting Cells

Topic 8.8

SKILLS

Insert a new worksheet

Rename worksheets

Copy cells

Indent cells

Other options on the sheet tab shortcut menu are used to delete, move, copy, hide, or protect entire sheets, and to change the color of the background in the sheet tab.

oops!

Pasted to the wrong starting cell? Slide or drag the border of the selected range to the correct starting point or use Cut and Paste to move cells.

A workbook can contain more than one worksheet. Use multiple worksheets as a method to organize or group data into manageable units. For example, a homeowner might have one household finance workbook in which he or she keeps track of bills and loans in one worksheet, savings and investments in a second worksheet, and a household budget in a third worksheet. Insert, rename, and navigate between worksheets using the sheet tabs in the **Sheet tab bar** near the bottom of the window.

1. Open the **8.4-SchoolBudget-Your Name** workbook.
2. Tap or click the **New sheet button** (plus symbol inside circle) next to the Sheet1 tab in the Sheet tab bar.

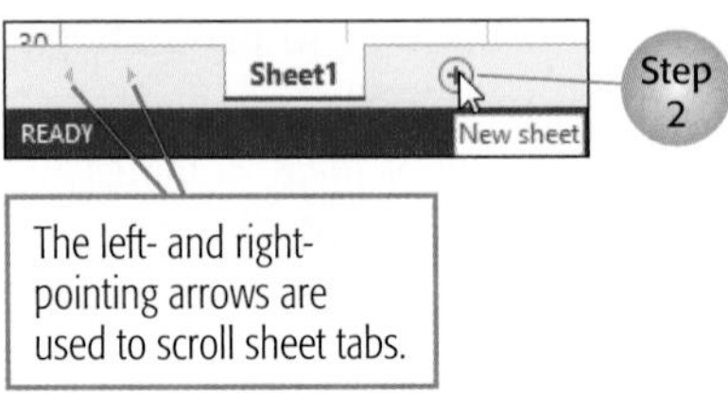

The left- and right-pointing arrows are used to scroll sheet tabs.

3. Tap or click the Sheet1 tab to make Sheet1 the active worksheet.
4. Press and hold or right-click the Sheet1 tab and tap or click *Rename* at the shortcut menu.

5. Type **First Year** and tap or press Enter.
6. Press and hold or right-click the Sheet2 tab, tap or click *Rename*, type **Second Year**, and then tap or press Enter.
7. Tap or click the First Year tab to make First Year the active worksheet.
8. Select A4:A15 and tap or click the Copy button in the Clipboard group of the HOME tab.

9. Make Second Year the active worksheet, make A4 the active cell, and then tap or click the top portion of the Paste button (not the down-pointing arrow) in the Clipboard group.
10. Tap or click the Paste Options button and then tap or click *Keep Source Column Widths*.
11. Make First Year the active worksheet, select A1:K3, and then tap or click the Copy button.
12. Make Second Year the active worksheet, make A1 the active cell, and then tap or click the Paste button.
13. Edit A2 in the Second Year worksheet to change *First* to *Second*.

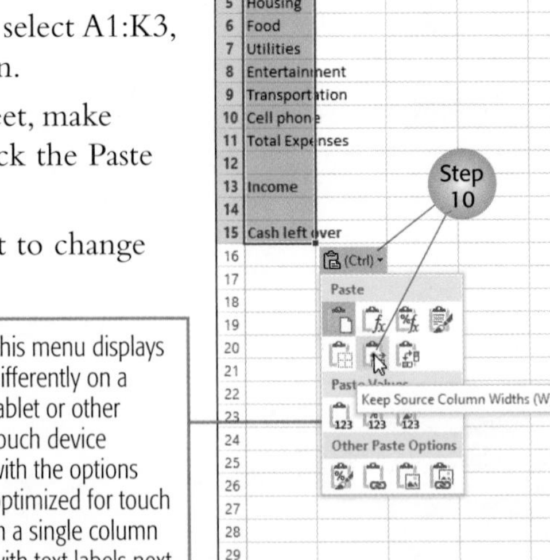
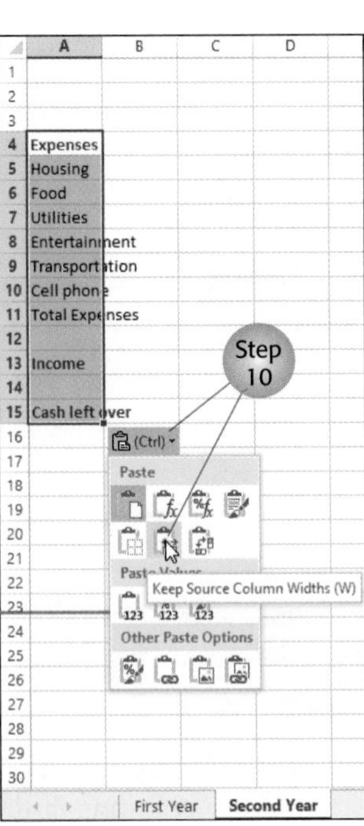

This menu displays differently on a tablet or other touch device with the options optimized for touch in a single column with text labels next to each button.

14 Enter the data, complete the formulas, and format the cells in the Second Year worksheet, as shown in Figure 8.6.

	A	B	C	D	E	F	G	H	I	J	K
1	Proposed School Budget										
2	Second Year of Program										
3		Sep	Oct	Nov	Dec	Jan	Feb	Mar	Apr		Total
4	Expenses										
5	Housing	910	910	910	910	910	910	910	910		7,280
6	Food	245	330	298	285	308	275	295	355		2,391
7	Utilities	112	118	140	151	131	118	122	124		1,016
8	Entertainment	160	95	100	185	110	95	90	125		960
9	Transportation	90	90	90	90	90	90	90	90		720
10	Cell phone	50	50	50	50	50	50	50	50		400
11	Total Expenses	1,567	1,593	1,588	1,671	1,599	1,538	1,557	1,654		12,767
12											
13	Income	1,800	1,800	1,800	1,800	1,800	1,800	1,800	1,800		14,400
14											
15	Cash left over	**233**	**207**	**212**	**129**	**201**	**262**	**243**	**146**		**1,633**

Figure 8.6 Completed Second Year worksheet

Use the fill handle, copy formulas from the First Year sheet to the Second Year sheet, and/or use the Format Painter feature to copy data, formulas, and formatting whenever possible.

Insert a Worksheet
Tap or click New sheet button.

Rename a Worksheet
1. Press and hold or right-click sheet tab.
2. Tap or click *Rename*.
3. Type new name.
4. Tap or press Enter.

Indent Cells
1. Activate cell or select range.
2. Tap or click Increase Indent button.

The Increase Indent button in the Alignment group of the HOME tab moves an entry approximately one character width inward from the left edge of a cell each time the button is tapped or clicked. Use this feature to indent entries in a list below a subheading. The Decrease Indent button moves an entry approximately one character width closer to the left edge of the cell each time the button is tapped or clicked.

15 With Second Year still the active worksheet, select A5:A10 and then tap or click the Increase Indent button in the Alignment group of the HOME tab.

16 Make A11 the active cell and tap twice or click twice the Increase Indent button.

17 Change the orientation to landscape for the Second Year worksheet.

18 Make First Year the active worksheet, indent once A5:A10, and indent twice A11.

19 Save the workbook using the same name (**8.4-SchoolBudget-Your Name**) and then close the workbook.

Step 15

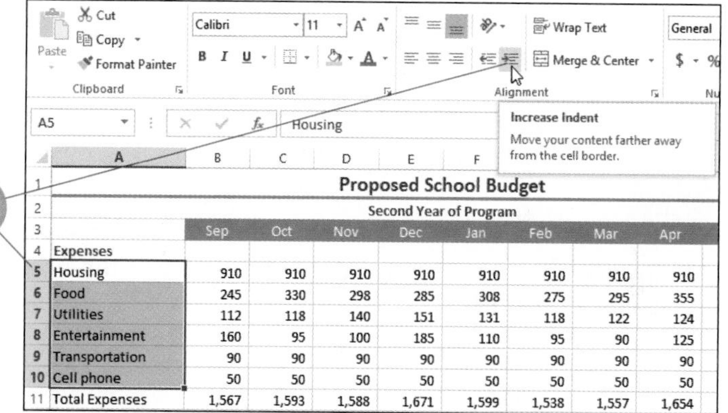

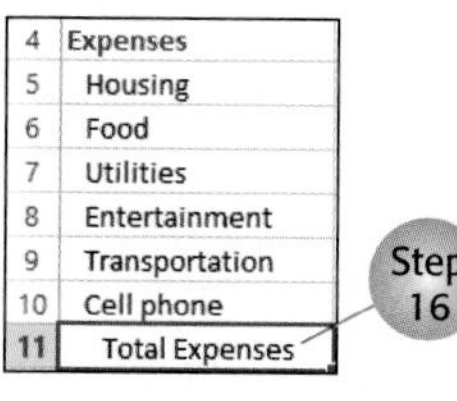

App Tip

Each worksheet has its own page layout/print options.

Another way to rename a worksheet is to double-tap or double-click the sheet tab, type a new name, and then tap or press Enter.

Scrolling Sheet Tabs in the Sheet tab bar

Use the left- and right-pointing arrows to the left of the first sheet tab to scroll to sheet tabs not currently visible, or press and hold or right-click an arrow to open the Activate dialog box, tap or click the sheet to make active, and then tap or click OK.

Using Go To, Freezing Panes, and Shading, Wrapping, and Rotating Cell Entries

Topic 8.9

SKILLS

- Use Go To
- Freeze panes
- Add fill color
- Wrap text
- Rotate text

Ctrl + G is the keyboard command for Go To.

In large worksheets where you cannot see all cells at once, use the **Go To** and **Go To Special** commands to move the active cell to a specific location in a worksheet. Column or row headings are not visible when you scroll right or down beyond the viewing area, making it difficult to relate text or values. The **Freeze Panes** option fixes column and/or row headings in place for scrolling large worksheets.

1. Open the **NSCSuppliesInventory** workbook from the Ch8 folder in Student_Data_Files.
2. Save the workbook as **8.9-NSCSuppliesInventory-Your Name** in the Ch8 folder in CompletedTopicsByChapter.
3. Slide or scroll down the worksheet area until the titles and column headings are no longer visible.
4. Tap or click the **Find & Select button** in the Editing group of the HOME tab and then tap or click *Go To* at the drop-down list.

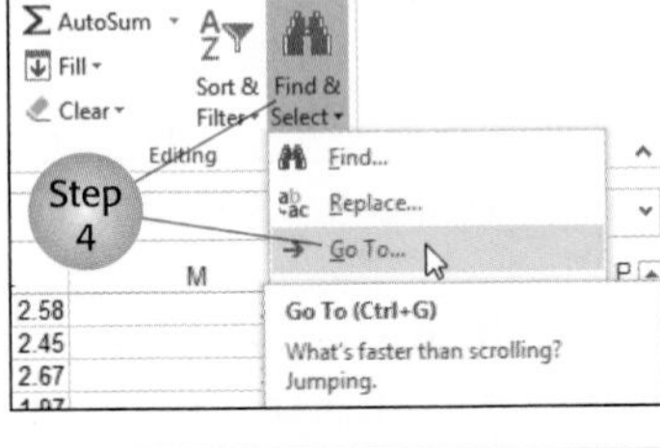

5. At the Go To dialog box, type a4 in the *Reference* text box, and then tap or press Enter, or tap or click OK.

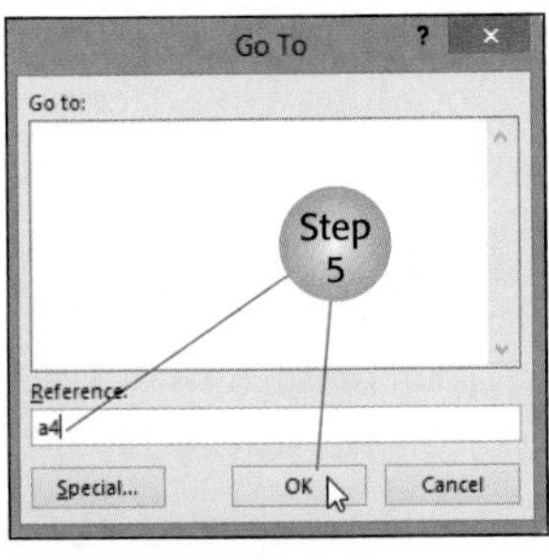

6. Tap or click the Find & Select button and then tap or click *Go To Special*.
7. Tap or click *Last cell* in the Go To Special dialog box and tap or click OK.

Use the Last cell option in the Go To Special dialog box in a large worksheet to move the active cell to the bottom right of the worksheet.

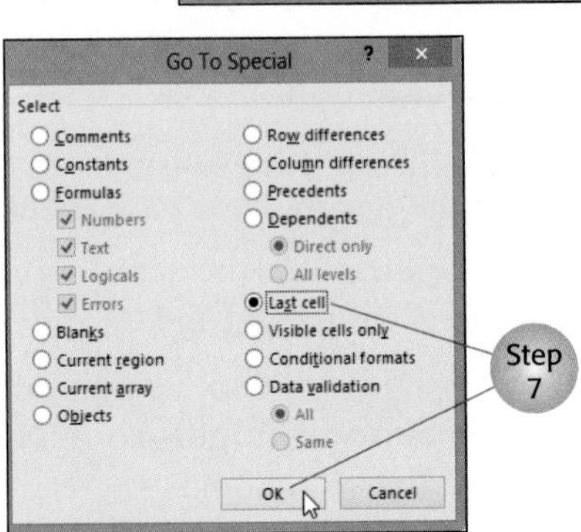

The active cell position determines which rows and columns are fixed—all rows above and all columns left of the active cell are frozen.

8. Use Go To to move the active cell back to A4.
9. If necessary, slide or scroll up until you can see the first three rows of titles and column headings.
10. With A4 the active cell, tap or click the VIEW tab and then tap or click the Freeze Panes button in the Window group.
11. Tap or click *Freeze Panes* at the drop-down list.
12. Slide or scroll down past all data. Notice that rows 1 to 3 do not scroll out of the viewing area.

Once cells have been frozen, *Freeze Panes* from the Freeze Panes button changes to *Unfreeze Panes*.

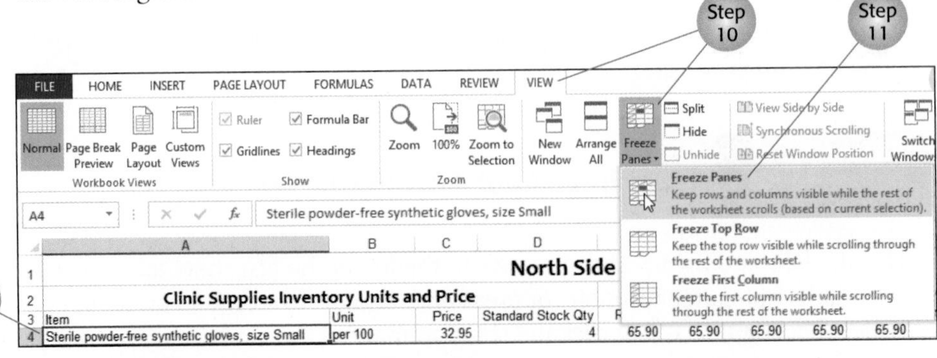

Column headings can be formatted to stand out from the rest of the worksheet by shading the background of the cell or rotating the cell entries. Cells with long entries can still be housed in narrower columns by formatting the text to automatically wrap within the width of the cell.

13 Slide or scroll to the top of the worksheet and select A1.

14 Tap or click the HOME tab, tap or click the **Fill Color button** arrow in the Font group, and then tap or click *Orange, Accent 6* (last color in first row of *Theme Colors* section) at the drop-down gallery.

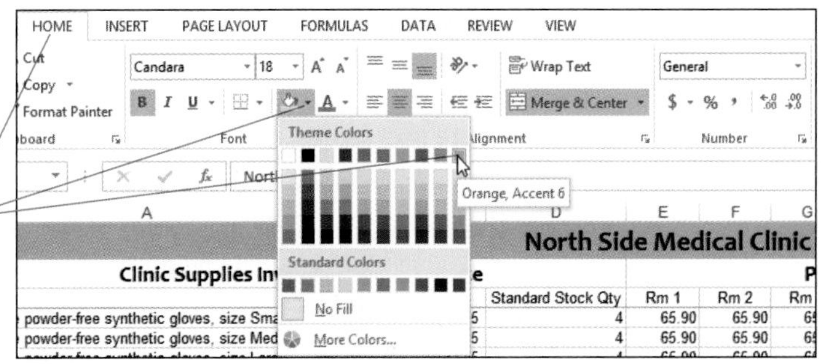

15 Select A2:M2 and apply *Orange, Accent 6, Lighter 60%* fill color (last option in third row of *Theme Colors* section).

16 Select A3:M3 and apply *Orange, Accent 6, Lighter 80%* fill color (last option in second row of *Theme Colors* section).

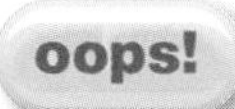

Forgot how to change row height and column width? Refer to Topic 8.3.

17 Make M3 the active cell, change the row height to 30, and change the column width to 10.

18 With M3 still the active cell, tap or click the **Wrap Text button** in the Alignment group.

Notice the entire column heading is visible again with the text wrapping within the cell.

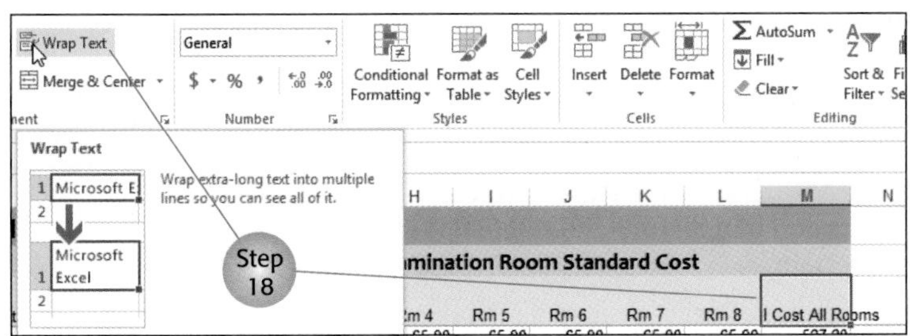

Freeze Panes
1. Activate cell below and right of cells to freeze.
2. Tap or click VIEW tab.
3. Tap or click Freeze Panes button.
4. Tap or click *Freeze Panes*.

Shade Cell Background
1. Select cell or range.
2. Tap or click Fill Color button arrow.
3. Tap or click desired color.

Rotate Cells
1. Select cell or range.
2. Tap or click Orientation button in Alignment group.
3. Tap or click rotate option.

19 Make D3 the active cell, change the column width to 9, and then tap or click the Wrap Text button.

20 Select E3:L3, tap or click the Orientation button in the Alignment group, and then tap or click *Angle Counterclockwise* at the drop-down list.

Angle Counterclockwise rotates the text within the cell boundaries 45 degrees.

21 Tap or click any cell to deselect the range and then display the Print tab Backstage view.

22 Change settings to *Landscape Orientation* and *Fit All Columns on One Page* and then go back to the worksheet display.

23 Save the workbook using the same name (**8.9-NSCSuppliesInventory-Your Name**) and then close the workbook.

Rotate column headings diagonally or vertically in narrow columns.

Concepts Review

Topic	Key Concepts	Key Terms
Creating and Editing a New Worksheet	A spreadsheet is an application in which data is created, analyzed, and presented in a grid-like structure of columns and rows. A workbook is an Excel file that consists of a collection of individual worksheets. A new workbook opens with a blank worksheet into which you create text, values, and formulas. The intersection of a column and a row is called a cell. The active cell is indicated with a green border and is the location into which the next data typed will be stored. Create a worksheet by making a cell active and typing text, a value, or a formula. A formula is used to perform mathematical operations on values. Formula entries begin with an equals sign and are followed by cell references with operators between the references. Edit a cell by typing new data to overwrite existing data, by double-tapping or double-clicking to open the cell for editing, or by inserting or deleting characters in the Formula bar. Press Delete or use the Clear button to delete the contents in the active cell.	Spreadsheet application Workbooks Worksheets Cell Active cell Formula Clear button
Formatting Cells	The Font group in the HOME tab contains buttons to change the font, font size, font color, and font style and to apply borders and shading. Select cells with the mouse by positioning the cell pointer over the starting cell and dragging in the required direction. Select cells using touch by tapping the starting cell and then sliding your finger over a selection handle until the remaining cells are inside the selection rectangle. A rectangular-shaped group of cells is called a range and is referenced with the starting cell address, a colon, and the ending cell address (e.g., A1:F15). By default, cells in a new worksheet have the General format, which has no specific formatting options. Comma Style adds a comma in thousands and two decimal places. Accounting Number Format adds a dollar symbol, comma in thousands, and two decimal places. The Decrease Decimal button and Increase Decimal button remove or add one decimal place each time the button is tapped or clicked. Borders in various styles and colors can be added to the edges of a cell. The Merge & Center button in the Alignment group is often used to center a worksheet title over multiple columns.	Range Comma Style Accounting Number Format Decrease Decimal button Increase Decimal button Merge & Center button

Topic	Key Concepts	Key Terms
Adjusting Column Width and Row Height, and Changing Alignment	A technique to add more space between cells to improve readability or emphasize a section is to widen a column or increase the height of a row. Open the Column Width dialog box to enter a new value for the width of the column in which the active cell is positioned. Excel displays a series of pound symbols when a column width has been made too narrow to display all of the cell contents. AutoFit changes the width of a column to fit the contents of the active cell. Open the Row Height dialog box to enter a new value for the height of the row in which the active cell is positioned. Align a cell at the left, center, or right horizontally, or top, middle, or bottom vertically using buttons in the Alignment group. The Middle Align button centers a cell's contents vertically.	AutoFit Middle Align button
Entering or Copying Data with the Fill Command and Using AutoSum	Auto Fill can be used to automatically enter data in a series or pattern based upon an entry in an adjacent cell. A new feature in Excel 2013 is Flash Fill, which automatically suggests entries when a pattern is detected. Select a range and use the Fill button to open the Series dialog box or copy an entry down, right, up, or left. The small, green square at the bottom right of an active cell is the fill handle and can be used to copy data and formulas or to enter a series. Excel includes the AutoSum button in the HOME tab that is used to enter a SUM function to add a column or row of numbers.	Auto Fill Flash Fill Fill button Fill handle AutoSum button
Inserting and Deleting Columns and Rows	A new row is inserted above the active cell or selected range. A new column is inserted left of the active cell or selected range. Use the Insert button in the Cells group to insert new rows or columns. Options for formatting new rows or columns are available from the Insert Options button that appears when rows or columns are inserted. Delete rows or columns from the Delete button in the Cells group. The Insert and Delete buttons can also be used to insert or delete cells within the worksheet.	Insert button Insert Options button Delete button
Sorting and Applying Cell Styles	A range can be sorted in ascending or descending order by one or more columns. Select a range and choose the sort order option from the Sort & Filter button in the Editing group to arrange the rows by the entries in the first column. Open the Sort dialog box to sort by more than one column or to choose a different column in the range by which to sort. Cell Styles are a set of predefined formatting options. Use Cell Styles to format faster and/or promote consistency among worksheets. Select cells and use the Cell Styles button to choose a set of formatting options.	Sort & Filter button Cell Styles Cell Styles button

continued....

Topic	Key Concepts	Key Terms
Changing Orientation and Scaling, and Displaying Cell Formulas	New workbooks print on a letter-size page, in portrait orientation, with top and bottom margins of 0.75-inch and left and right margins of 0.7-inch. Change print options even if you are only exporting the workbook as a PDF because PDFs are generated using the print settings. Change to landscape orientation using the Orientation button at the Print tab Backstage view or in the Page Setup group of the PAGE LAYOUT tab. Landscape is a common layout used for wide worksheets. Open the Excel Options dialog box with the *Advanced* pane active to turn on or turn off the display of formulas in cells. Fit Sheet on One Page scales text on a printout so that all columns and rows print on one page. Fit All Columns on One Page is a scaling option that shrinks text to fit all columns in one page width. Fit All Rows on One Page is a scaling option that shrinks text to fit all rows in one page height.	Fit Sheet on One Page Fit All Columns on One Page Fit All Rows on One Page
Inserting and Renaming a Worksheet, Copying Cells, and Indenting Cells	The Sheet tab bar near the bottom left of the window is used to insert, rename, and navigate among sheets in a workbook. Tap or click the New sheet button in the Sheet tab bar to insert a new worksheet. Press and hold or right-click a sheet tab and choose *Rename* to type a new name for a worksheet. Copy and paste cells between worksheets using the Copy and Paste buttons in the Clipboard group. *Keep Source Column Widths* from the Paste Options button lets you paste new cells with the same column width as the source cell.	Sheet tab bar New sheet button
Using Go To, Freezing Panes, and Shading, Wrapping, and Rotating Cell Entries	Go To and Go To Special are options from the Find & Select button used to move to a specific cell in a large worksheet. Freeze Panes fixes rows and/or columns in place for scrolling in large worksheets so that column and row headings do not scroll out of the viewing area. All rows above and all columns left of the active cell are frozen when Freeze Panes is turned on. Cells are shaded with color using the Fill Color button in the Font group. Long text entries in cells can be displayed in narrow columns by wrapping text within the cell's column width using the Wrap Text button in the Alignment group. Angle Counterclockwise is an option from the Orientation button in the Alignment group that rotates text within a cell 45 degrees.	Go To Go To Special Freeze Panes Find & Select button Fill Color button Wrap Text button Angle Counterclockwise

Multiple Choice

1. Which of the following is *not* a valid cell or range reference?
   a. Z1
   b. 3Z
   c. Z1:Z100
   d. AA1
2. Which of the following is *not* a valid operator for a formula?
   a. *
   b. +
   c. -
   d. @
3. By default, cells in a new worksheet have this format.
   a. General
   b. Comma Style
   c. Accounting Number Format
   d. Number
4. This feature is often used to center titles in a worksheet.
   a. Orientation
   b. Wrap Text
   c. Merge & Center
   d. Merge Columns
5. This symbol displays across a cell in a column in which the width is too narrow.
   a. @
   b. $
   c. *
   d. #
6. This option from the Format button sets the width of the column to fit the contents of the active cell.
   a. AutoFit
   b. AutoWidth
   c. AutoAlign
   d. AutoSize
7. This feature is used to enter data automatically into a range based upon a pattern or series.
   a. Auto Fit
   b. Auto Enter
   c. Auto Complete
   d. Auto Fill
8. The button creates a SUM function in the active cell.
   a. AutoSum
   b. AutoAdd
   c. AutoFunction
   d. AutoFormula
9. The Insert button to add a new row or column is found in this group in the HOME tab.
   a. Cells
   b. Alignment
   c. Styles
   d. Editing
10. This button appears when a new column has been inserted with options to apply formatting to the new column from the column at the left or the column at the right.
    a. Insert Options
    b. Column Options
    c. Auto Options
    d. Fill Options
11. Choose this option from the Sort & Filter button drop-down list to sort a range by a column other than the first column.
    a. Sort
    b. Custom Sort
    c. Sort Columns
    d. Sort Order
12. Buttons in this gallery are used to apply a predefined collection of formatting options to the selected cell or range.
    a. Cell Formats
    b. Cell Styles
    c. Cell Formatting
    d. Format Painter
13. Open this dialog box to turn on the display of cell formulas.
    a. Formula Options
    b. Format Cells
    c. Excel Options
    d. Sheet Options
14. This setting at the Print tab Backstage view will fit a two-page worksheet on one page.
    a. Shrink to Fit
    b Scale to Fit
    c. Fit All Text on One Page
    d. Fit Sheet on One Page
15. Use this area to navigate to a different worksheet in the workbook.
    a. Sheets bar
    b. Sheet tab bar
    c. Navigation bar
    d. Scroll bar

16. This button will move text within the active cell approximately one character width away from the left edge of the cell.
    a. Left Indent
    b. Increase Indent
    c. Indent
    d. Decrease Indent
17. This option fixes in place for scrolling purposes all rows above the active cell.
    a. Fix Rows
    b. Freeze Rows
    c. Freeze Top Row
    d. Freeze Panes
18. This option is used to rotate text within the cell 45 degrees.
    a. Angle Counterclockwise
    b. Rotate 45
    c. Rotate Up
    d. Angle Right

Crossword Puzzle

ACROSS

3 Button to vertically center a cell
4 Dialog box to move active cell to specific address
5 Layout often used for wide worksheets
7 Format that displays 1000.5 as 1,000.50
10 =E7*E8
15 Rectangular block of cells
16 Predefined set of formats for a cell
17 Button that creates SUM function

DOWN

1 Button to insert a new worksheet
2 Excel file
6 Small square at bottom right of active cell
8 Cell with green border
9 Button to display a long cell entry in a narrow column
11 Button to open Column Width dialog box
12 Option from shortcut menu to type new name for worksheet
13 Button to shrink text for printing large worksheet
14 Rearrange order of rows in range

Matching

Match the term with the statement or definition.

_______ 1. Intersection of a column and a row
_______ 2. Displays contents stored in active cell
_______ 3. Group of cells
_______ 4. Adds dollar symbol to values
_______ 5. Copies first cell to remaining cells in range
_______ 6. Heading 1
_______ 7. Wide worksheet setting
_______ 8. Plus symbol inside circle button
_______ 9. Move to last cell
_______ 10. Applies color to background of cell

a. Accounting Number Format
b. Cell Styles
c. Landscape Orientation
d. Fill Color
e. New sheet
f. Cell
g. Go To Special
h. Range
i. Formula bar
j. Fill

Project 1 Creating and Editing a New Workbook

Individual

Deliverable: Excel worksheet with Auction Fee Calculations (continued in Project 2)

1. Start a new blank workbook and enter the text and values in the worksheet as shown in Figure 8.7.

	A	B	C	D	E	F	G	H	I	J
1	Fees Paid for Video Game Online Auctions									
2	Auctions ended in January									
3										
4	AuctionID	Game			Platform	Sale Price	Fee	Shipping	Fee	Total Fee
5	25687	Ghost Recon Future Soldier			Xbox 360	40.99		4.99		
6	31452	Far Cry 3			Xbox 360	39.99		4.99		
7	98563	Call of Duty Black Ops II			Xbox 360	37.99		4.99		
8	17586	Halo 4			Xbox 360	35.99		4.99		
9	32586	Call of Duty Black Ops II			PS 3	33		7.99		
10	45862	Legends of Troy			PS 3	50		6.5		
11	13485	Skyrim			Windows	37		5		
12	65985	Grand Theft Auto V			Windows	58.99		5		

Figure 8.7 Project 1 worksheet

2. Save the workbook as **C8-Project1-AuctionFees-Your Name** in a new folder named *Ch8* within the ChapterProjectsWork folder on your USB flash drive.
3. Enter the following formulas by typing the formula in the active cell or by using the pointing method:
   G5 =F5*.10　　J5 =G5+I5
   I5 =H5*.10
4. Use the fill handle to copy each formula to the remaining rows in columns G, I, and J.
5. Type **Total Fees Paid for January Auctions** in B13.
6. Use the AutoSum button to calculate the totals in G13 and I13.

Note: Flash Fill should automatically calculate the total in J13; however, if no total appears in J13, calculate the total yourself.

7. Edit the worksheet as follows:
   a. Change the sale price of Halo 4 from *35.99* to *43.99*.
   b. Change the platform for Skyrim from *Windows* to *PS 3*.
   c. Change the shipping for Skyrim from *5.00* to *6.50*.
   d. Type the current year one space after January in A2 so that the entry reads *Auctions ended in January 2015*. (Your year will vary.)
8. Proofread carefully to make sure the worksheet is error-free.
9. Change the scaling option to fit all columns on one page.
10. Save the revised workbook using the same name (**C8-Project1-AuctionFees-Your Name**).
11. Leave the workbook open if you are continuing to Project 2; otherwise, close the workbook and submit the project to your instructor in the manner she or he has requested.

Project 2 Editing and Formatting a Worksheet

Individual

Deliverable: Excel worksheet with Auction Fee Calculations

Note: You must have completed Project 1 before starting this project.

1. If necessary, open **C8-Project1-AuctionFees-Your Name**.
2. Use Save As to change the file name to **C8-Project2-AuctionFeesFormatted-Your Name**, saving in the same folder.
3. Insert a new row above row 12 and type the following auction item information in the appropriate cells:
   57834 **Angry Birds Trilogy** **PS 3** **29.99** (sale price) **6.50** (shipping)

Note: The formulas in fees cells should be automatically created; however, if no fees are calculated, enter the required formulas yourself.

4. Insert a blank column between columns I and J so that the *Total Fee* column is set apart from the rest of the data.
5. Change the width of column B to *25* and then delete columns C and D.
6. Change the height of row 4 to *25* and middle-align the column headings.
7. Format the worksheet as follows:
   a. Merge and center the titles in row 1 and row 2 over columns A through I.
   b. Left-align A5:A13 and center-align E4 and G4.
   c. Apply Comma Style to D5:I14.
   d. Add a *Thick Bottom Border* to A4:I4 and a *Top and Double Bottom Border* to E14, G14, and I14.
   e. Select A1:A2 and change the font to *Cambria*, the font size to *16*, the font color to *Dark Blue*, and apply bold.
   f. Select A4:I4, apply bold, and add *Gold, Accent 4* shading.
   g. Bold B14, E14, G14, and I14.
8. Select A5:I13 and sort the range by the *Game* column in ascending order.
9. Change the worksheet to landscape orientation.
10. Save the revised workbook using the same name (**C8-Project2-AuctionFeesFormatted-Your Name**).
11. Turn on the display of cell formulas.
12. Use Save As to save a copy of the worksheet with the formulas displayed as **C8-Project2-AuctionFeesWithCellFormulas-Your Name**.
13. Submit the project to your instructor in the manner she or he has requested.
14. Close the workbook.

Project 3 Formatting with Styles and Inserting a New Worksheet

Individual

Deliverable: Excel workbook with Cancer Patient Statistics in two worksheets

1. Open **CancerStatsReport**.
2. Use Save As to change the file name to **C8-Project3-CancerStatsReport-Your Name**, saving in the Ch8 folder in ChapterProjectsWork.
3. Merge and center the titles in row 1 and row 2 over columns A through G.
4. Wrap the text in A3:G3.
5. Change column widths as follows:
   Column B to *10* Column E to *10*
   Column C to *9* Column F to *20*
6. Apply cell styles of your choosing to A1, A2, and A3:G3 to improve the appearance of the worksheet.
7. Insert a new worksheet in the workbook and change the name to **Quarter 2**.
8. Rename the ReportData worksheet to **Quarter 1**.
9. Copy A1:G3 from the Quarter 1 sheet and paste it to A1 in the Quarter 2 sheet, keeping the source column widths.

10. Copy A4:G30 from the Quarter 1 sheet and paste it to A4 in the Quarter 2 sheet.
11. In the Quarter 2 sheet, clear the contents of A4:A30 and G4:G30.
12. Set the print settings for each worksheet to *Fit All Columns on One Page*.
13. Freeze the first three rows in each worksheet.
14. Save the revised workbook using the same name (**C8-Project3-CancerStatsReport-Your Name**).
15. Submit the project to your instructor in the manner she or he has requested.
16. Close the workbook.

Project 4 Creating a Weekly Schedule from a Template

Individual

Deliverable: Worksheet with a schedule for the current week

1. You learned about creating new documents from templates in Word in Chapter 6. Excel also has many templates available for creating new workbooks that are grouped into the categories *Budget*, *Invoice*, *Calendars*, *Expense*, *List*, *Loan*, and *Schedule*. Search for and select a template of your choosing to create a weekly schedule using the *Schedule* category.
2. Enter your schedule for the current week into the new worksheet. Make sure the schedule is complete with all of your classes and other activities.
3. Save the workbook in the Ch8 folder within ChapterProjectsWork as **C8-Project4-WeeklySchedule-Your Name**.
4. Submit the project to your instructor in the manner she or he has requested.
5. Close the workbook.

Project 5 Creating a Party Expense Worksheet

Individual

Deliverable: 25th Anniversary Party Expense Worksheet

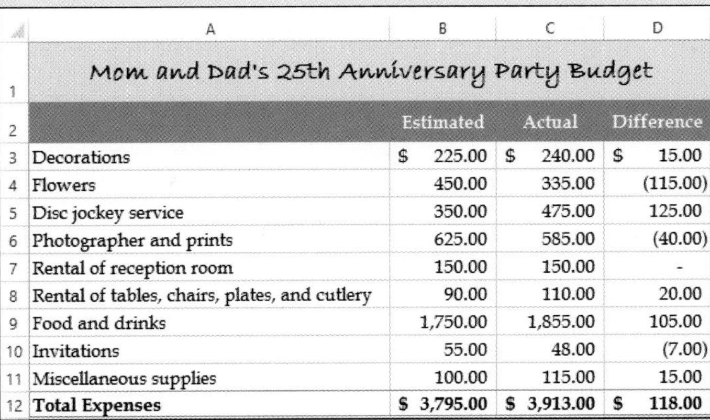

	A	B	C	D
1	Mom and Dad's 25th Anniversary Party Budget			
2		Estimated	Actual	Difference
3	Decorations	$ 225.00	$ 240.00	$ 15.00
4	Flowers	450.00	335.00	(115.00)
5	Disc jockey service	350.00	475.00	125.00
6	Photographer and prints	625.00	585.00	(40.00)
7	Rental of reception room	150.00	150.00	-
8	Rental of tables, chairs, plates, and cutlery	90.00	110.00	20.00
9	Food and drinks	1,750.00	1,855.00	105.00
10	Invitations	55.00	48.00	(7.00)
11	Miscellaneous supplies	100.00	115.00	15.00
12	**Total Expenses**	**$ 3,795.00**	**$ 3,913.00**	**$ 118.00**

Figure 8.8 Project 5 worksheet

1. Create a worksheet similar to Figure 8.8 with the following information:
   a. The amounts in the *Difference* column are formulas that calculate the actual expenses minus the estimated expenses, and the values shown in row 12 are formulas.
   b. The width of column A is 42, and columns B, C, and D is 12. The height of row 1 is 36 and row 2 is 24.
   c. The font and size used in A1 is 16-point Bradley Hand ITC. The font for the rest of the cells in the worksheet is Book Antiqua.
   d. A2:D2 have the Accent6 cell style applied and A12:D12 have the Total cell style applied.
   e. Use your best judgment for any other format options such as shading.
2. Save the worksheet in the Ch8 folder within the ChapterProjectsWork folder as **C8-Project5-PartyExpenses-Your Name**.
3. Submit the project to your instructor in the manner she or he has requested.
4. Close the workbook.

Project 6 Internet Research and Composing a New Workbook

Individual or Pairs

Deliverable: Excel workbook with costs for a spring break trip

1. Listen to the audio file named ***Project6_Instructions***. The file is located in the Ch8 folder in the Student_Data_Files folder.
2. Complete the research and compose the worksheet as instructed.
3. Save the workbook in the Ch8 folder within ChapterProjectsWork as **C8-Project6-SpringBreakContest-Your Name**.
4. Submit the project to your instructor in the manner she or he has requested.
5. Close the workbook.

Project 7 Sending Project Work to OneNote Notebook

Individual

Deliverable: New Page in Shared OneNote notebook

1. Start OneNote and open the MyProjects notebook created in Chapter 4, Project 4.
2. Make Excel the active section and add a new page titled *Chapter 8 Projects*.
3. Switch to Excel. For each project that you completed, open the document, send the project to OneNote 2013 selecting the Chapter 8 Projects page in the Excel section in the MyProjects notebook, and then close the workbook. Make sure to include all worksheets in workbooks with more than one sheet tab.
4. Close your MyProjects notebook in OneNote and close OneNote.
5. Close Excel.
6. Submit the project to your instructor in the manner she or he has requested.

Chapter 9

Working with Functions, Charts, Tables, and Page Layout Options in Excel

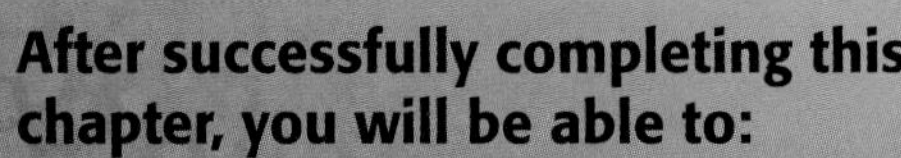

After successfully completing this chapter, you will be able to:

- Create formulas with absolute addresses and range names
- Create statistical and date functions
- Perform decision making using the logical IF function
- Use the PMT function to calculate a loan payment
- Insert and modify charts and Sparklines
- Use Page Layout view
- Change margins, add a header, and center a worksheet
- Insert comments
- Format cells as a table
- Sort and filter data in a table

Excel's function library is updated and expanded with each new release of the software. Several hundred preprogrammed formulas grouped by category in the function library are used to perform data analysis, decision making, or data modeling. Charts are widely used to present data or results of analysis in a visual snapshot. Excel provides Page Layout view for previewing page layout and print options. Collaborative tools such as Comments allow individuals to add notes or other feedback into a worksheet. Data organized in a list format is best suited for the Table feature, which allows you to easily format, sort, and filter large blocks of data.

In this chapter, you continue working with formulas by learning about the various types of references used in formulas and how to use functions to perform basic statistical, date, financial, and logical analysis. Next, you explore strategies for presenting data with the inclusion of charts, comments, and tables as well as formatting a worksheet with page layout options and print options.

Topic 9.1

SKILLS

Create a formula with an absolute address

Create a range name

Create a formula with a range name

Using Absolute Addressing and Range Names in Formulas

The formulas in the previous chapter used cell references considered **relative addresses**, where column letters and row numbers change relative to the destination when a formula is copied. For example, the formula *=SUM(A4:A10)* becomes *=SUM(B4:B10)* when copied from a cell in column A to a cell in column B. Relative addressing is the most common addressing method.

Sometimes you need a formula in which one or more addresses should not change when the formula is copied. In these formulas, use cell references that are **absolute addresses**. A dollar symbol precedes a column letter and/or row number in an absolute address, for example, *=$A$10*. Some formulas have both a relative and an absolute reference; these are referred to as **mixed addresses**. See Table 9.1 for formula addressing examples.

Table 9.1 Cell Addressing and Copying Examples

Formula	Type of Reference	Action If Formula Is Copied
=B4*B2	Relative	Both addresses will update.
=$B$4*$B$2	Absolute	Neither address will update.
=B4*$B$2	Mixed	The address B4 will update; the address $B$2 will not update.
=B4*$B2	Mixed	The address B4 will update; the row number in the second address will update but the column letter will not.
=B4*B$2	Mixed	The address B4 will update; the column letter in the second address will update but the row number will not.

1. Start Excel 2013 and open the workbook named ***FinancialPlanner*** from the Ch9 folder in Student_Data_Files.
2. Use Save As to save a copy of the workbook as **9.1-FinancialPlanner-Your Name** in a new folder named *Ch9* in the CompletedTopicsByChapter folder.
3. Review the worksheet noticing the three rates in row 2; these rates will be used to calculate gross pay, payroll deductions, and savings amounts.
4. Make C4 the active cell, type **=b4*b2**, and then tap or click the Enter button in the Formula bar or tap or press Ctrl + Enter.

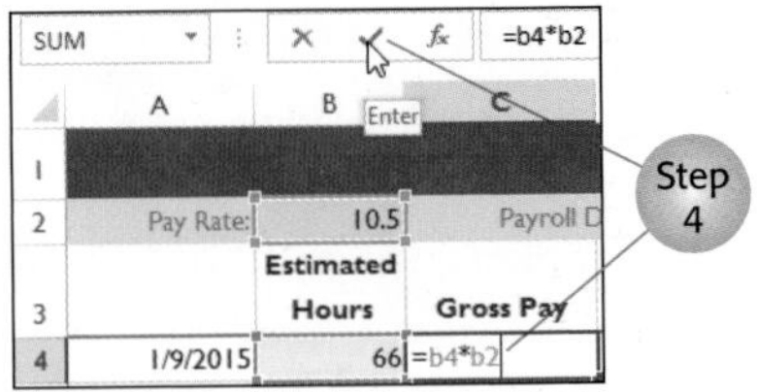
SUM
=b4*b2
Enter
Pay Rate:
10.5
Payroll D
Estimated
Hours
Gross Pay
1/9/2015
66
=b4*b2
Step 4

5. Use the fill handle in C4 to copy the formula to C5:C30.
6. Make C5 the active cell and look at the formula in the Formula bar.

The #VALUE! error occurs because B3 is a label and has no mathematical value.

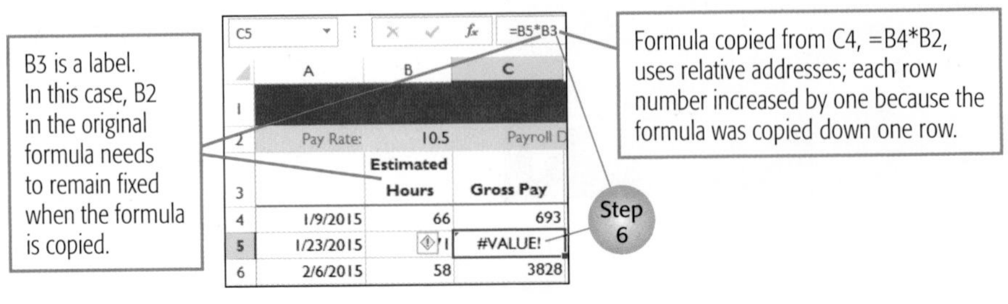
B3 is a label. In this case, B2 in the original formula needs to remain fixed when the formula is copied.
C5
=B5*B3
Pay Rate:
10.5
Payroll D
Estimated
Hours
Gross Pay
1/9/2015
66
693
1/23/2015
#VALUE!
2/6/2015
58
3828
Step 6
Formula copied from C4, =B4*B2, uses relative addresses; each row number increased by one because the formula was copied down one row.

7 Select C5:C30 and press the Delete key, or tap or click the Clear button in the Editing group and then tap or click *Clear All*.

8 Make C4 the active cell and edit the formula so that it reads *=B4*\$B\$2*.

9 Use the fill handle in C4 to copy the formula to C5:C30.

10 Make D4 the active cell and enter the formula **=c4*\$e\$2**.

SUM | =B4*$B$2
Pay Rate: 10.5 Payroll De
Estimated Hours | Gross Pay
1/9/2015 | 66 | =B4*$B$2
Step 8

11 Make E4 the active cell and enter the formula **=c4-d4**.

12 Select D4:E4 and use the fill handle to copy the formulas to D5:E30.

A cell or a range can be referenced by a descriptive label, which makes a formula easier to understand. For example, the formula *=Hours*PayRate* is readily understood. Names are also used when a formula needs an absolute reference because a cell or range name is automatically absolute. Cell or range names are assigned using the *Name* box at the left end of the Formula bar. Use the Name Manager button in the FORMULAS tab to manage cell names after they are created.

13 Make G2 the active cell, tap or click in the *Name* text box at the left end of the Formula bar, type **SaveRate**, and then tap or press Enter.

A range name can use letters, numbers, and some symbols. Spaces are not valid in a range name, and the first character in a name must be a letter, an underscore, or a backward slash (\).

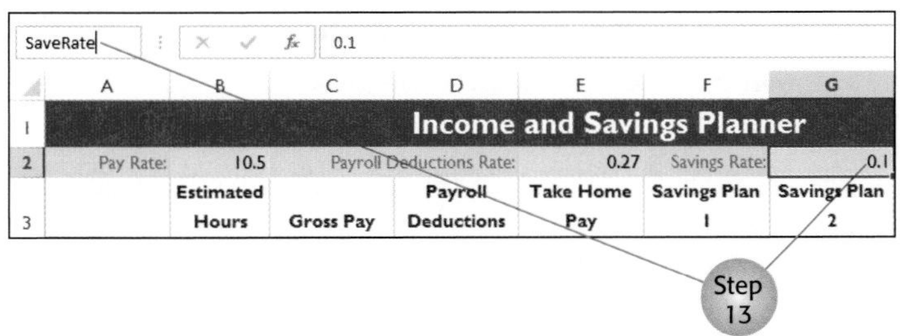

14 Make F4 the active cell, type **=e4*SaveRate**, and then tap or press Ctrl + Enter or tap or click the Enter button.

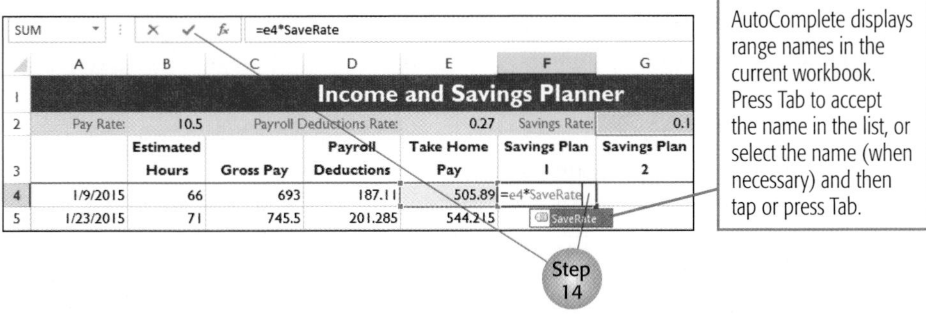

AutoComplete displays range names in the current workbook. Press Tab to accept the name in the list, or select the name (when necessary) and then tap or press Tab.

15 Use the fill handle in F4 to copy the formula to F5:F30.

16 Save the revised workbook using the same name (**9.1-FinancialPlanner-Your Name**). Leave the workbook open for the next topic.

Press function key F4 to make an address absolute. F4 cycles though variations of absolute and mixed addresses for the reference in which the insertion point is positioned.

Make Cell Reference Absolute
Type dollar symbol before column letter and/or row number OR press F4 to cycle through variations of addressing.

Name a Cell or Range
1. Select cell or range.
2. Type name in *Name* text box.
3. Tap or press Enter.

A range name can also be used in the Go To dialog box to move the active cell.

Upper and lowercase letters separate words in a range name; however, range names are not case sensitive—*SaveRate* and *saverate* are considered the same name.

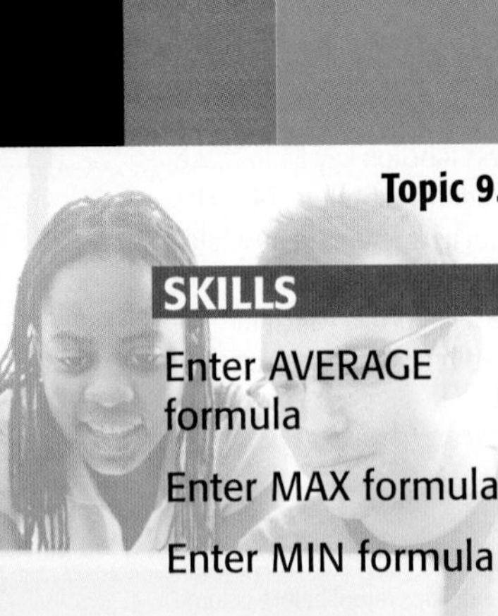

Topic 9.2

SKILLS

Enter AVERAGE formula

Enter MAX formula

Enter MIN formula

Entering Formulas Using Statistical Functions

Excel's function library contains more than 400 preprogrammed formulas grouped into 13 categories. All formulas that are based on functions begin with the name of the function followed by the function's parameters within parentheses. The parameters for a function (referred to as an **argument**) will vary depending on the formula chosen and can include a value, a cell reference, a range, multiple ranges, or a combination of values with references.

1. With the **9.1-FinancialPlanner-Your Name** workbook open, make I4 the active cell.

2. Tap or click the AutoSum button arrow in the Editing group of the HOME tab and then tap or click *Average* at the drop-down list.

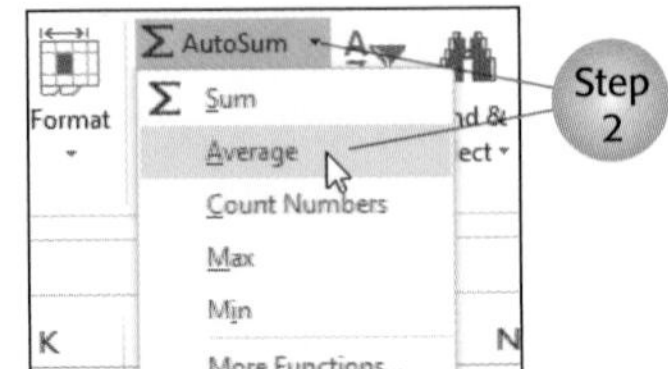

Excel enters *=AVERAGE(B4:H4)* in the formula cell with the range *B4:H4* selected. In this instance, Excel suggests the wrong range.

3. With the range B4:H4 highlighted in the formula cell, select B4:B30 and then tap or click the Enter button or tap or press Enter.

Excel returns the result *68.962963* in the formula cell, which is the arithmetic mean of the hours in column B. If empty cells or cells containing text are included in the formula's argument, they are ignored.

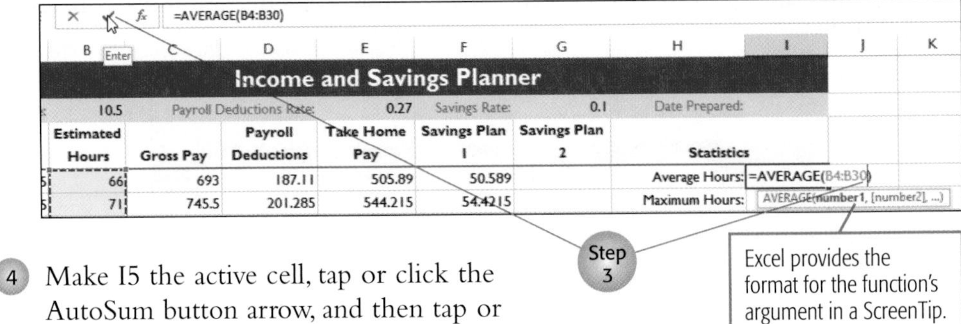

4. Make I5 the active cell, tap or click the AutoSum button arrow, and then tap or click *Max* at the drop-down list.

5. Type **b4:b30** and then tap or press Enter or tap or click the Enter button.

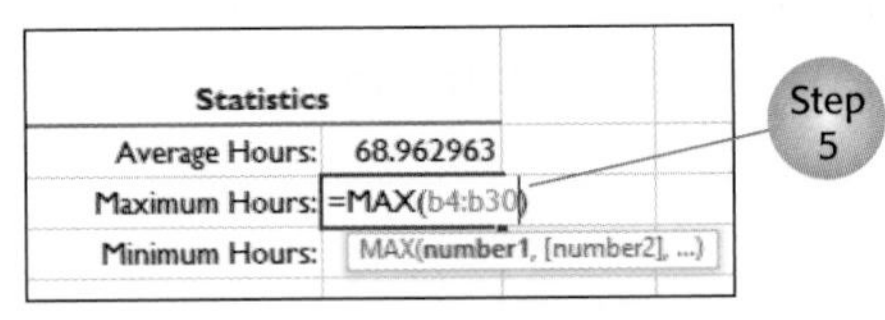

Excel returns the value *80* in the formula cell. MAX returns the largest value found in the range included in the argument.

6. Make I6 the active cell, type **=min(b4:b30)**, and then tap or press Enter or tap or click the Enter button.

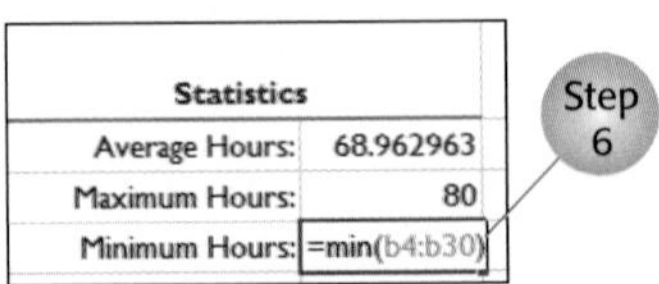

The result *48* is shown in I6. MIN returns the smallest value within the range included as the argument.

Excel's Insert Function dialog box assists with finding and entering functions and their arguments into a formula cell. A variety of methods can be used to open the Insert Function dialog box, including tapping or clicking the Insert Function button in the Formula bar.

7. Make I8 the active cell and then tap or click the Insert Function button in the Formula bar (button right of Enter button).
8. Tap or click the *Or select a category* list arrow and then tap or click *Statistical* at the drop-down list.
9. Tap or click *AVERAGE* in the *Select a function* list box and then tap or click OK.

B	C	D	E	F	G	H	I
Income and Savings Planner							
10.5	Payroll Deductions Rate:		0.27	Savings Rate:	0.1	Date Prepared:	
Estimated Hours	Gross Pay	Payroll Deductions	Take Home Pay	Savings Plan 1	Savings Plan 2	Statistics	
66	693	187.11	505.89	50.589		Average Hours:	68.962963
71	745.5	201.285	544.215	54.4215		Maximum Hours:	80
58	609	164.43	444.57	44.457		Minimum Hours:	48
65	682.5	184.275	498.225	49.8225			
66	693	187.11	505.89	50.589		Average Savings:	

Step 7

10. Type **f4:f30** in the *Number1* text box at the Function Arguments dialog box and then tap or press Enter or tap or click OK.

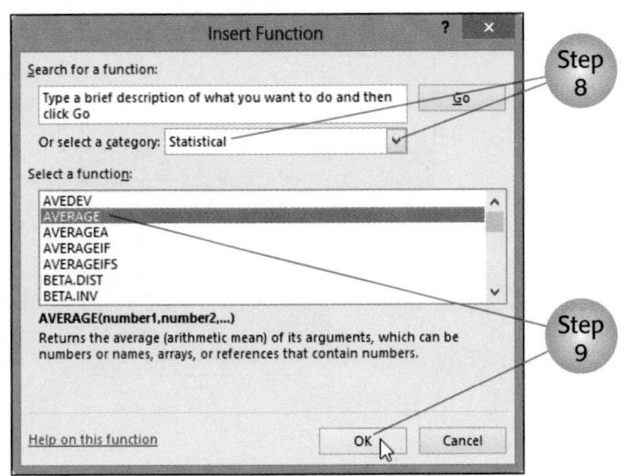

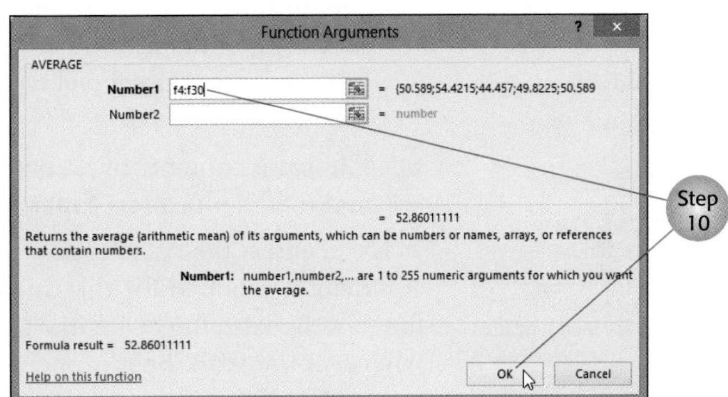

11. Make I9 the active cell, tap or click the AutoSum button arrow, and then tap or click *More Functions* at the drop-down list.
12. With the text already selected in the *Search for a function* text box, type **max** and then tap or press Enter or tap or click the Go button.
13. With MAX selected in the *Select a function* list box, tap or click OK.
14. Type **f4:f30** in the *Number1* text box at the Function Arguments dialog box and then tap or press Enter or tap or click OK.

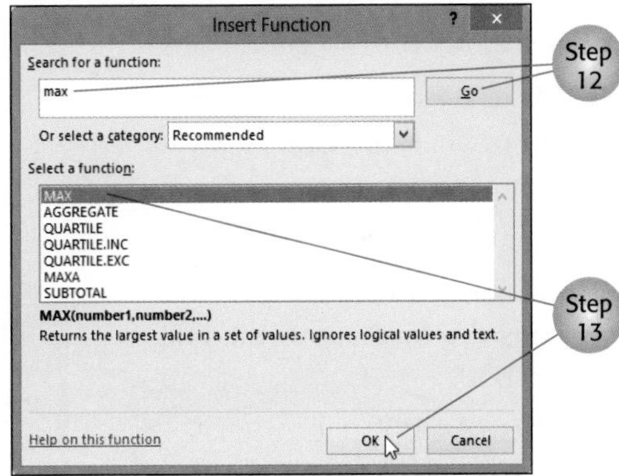

15. Make I10 the active cell, tap or click the AutoSum button arrow, and then tap or click *Min* at the drop-down list.
16. Type **f4:f30** and then tap or press Enter or tap or click the Enter button.
17. Save the revised workbook using the same name (**9.1-FinancialPlanner-Your Name**). Leave the workbook open for the next topic.

AVERAGE, MAX, or MIN Functions

1. Activate formula cell.
2. Tap or click AutoSum button arrow.
3. Tap or click required function.
4. Type or select argument range.
5. Tap or press Enter.

COUNT Function

The *Count Numbers* option from the AutoSum button arrow inserts the COUNT function, which returns the number of cells from the range included in the argument that have values. Use the function COUNTA if you want to count all of the non-empty cells within a range.

Entering, Formatting, and Calculating Dates

Topic 9.3

SKILLS

Enter a valid date

Enter the current date using a function

Create a formula using a date

Format dates

oops!

General instead of *Date* appears? Excel did not recognize your entry as a valid date. Generally, this is because of a typing error. Try Step 2 again. Still *General*? You may need to check the Region in the Control Panel.

The function *=NOW()* returns the current date and time in the active cell.

A date typed into a cell in normal date format such as *May 1, 2015* or *5/1/2015* is stored as a numerical value. Times are stored as decimal values representing fractions of a day. Because dates and times are stored as values, calculations can be performed using the cells, and various date and time formats can be applied to the results.

Consider using Excel to calculate elapsed time for scheduling, payroll, membership, or other purposes that involve analysis of date or time.

1. With the **9.1-FinancialPlanner-Your Name** workbook open, make I2 the active cell.
2. Type **12/20/2014** and then tap or press Enter.
3. Make I2 the active cell and notice that *Date* appears in the *Number Format* list box. See Table 9.2 on the next page for examples of cell entries that Excel will recognize as a valid date.

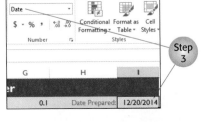

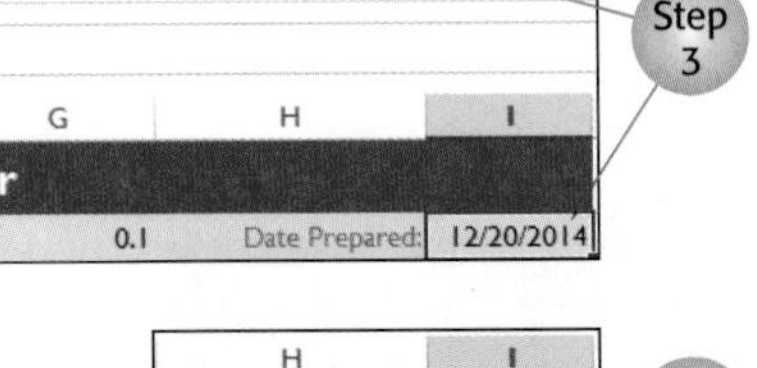

4. Clear the contents of I2, type **=today()**, and then tap or press Enter.

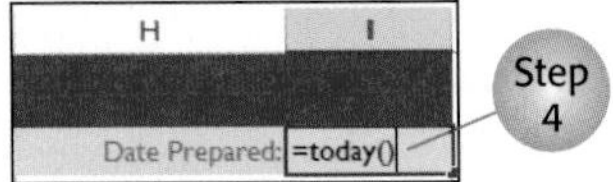

Excel enters the current date into the cell. No argument is required for this function. The TODAY function updates the cell entry to the current date whenever the worksheet is opened or printed. Do not use *=TODAY()* if you want the date to stay the same.

5. Make B3 the active cell and insert a new column.
6. Type **Pay Date** in B3 and then tap or click A3.
7. Type **End Date** in A3 and then tap or click the Enter button.
8. Select A3:B3 and center-align the cells.
9. Make B4 the active cell, type **=a4+7**, and then tap or click the Enter button.

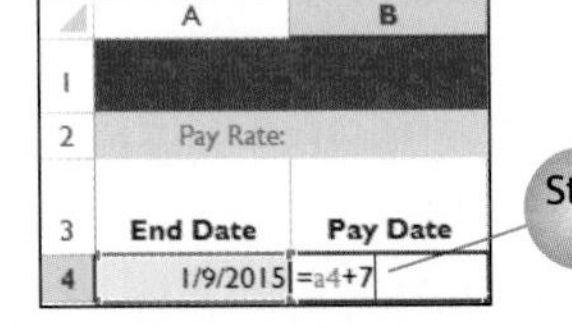

Excel returns *1/16/2015* in B4, which is 7 days from January 9, 2015.

10. Use the fill handle in B4 to copy the formula to the range B5:B30.
11. Select A4:B30, tap or click the *Number Format* list arrow (down-pointing arrow next to *Date*), and then tap or click *More Number Formats* at the drop-down list.
12. At the Format Cells dialog box with *Date* selected in the *Category* list box, tap or click *14-Mar-12* in the *Type* list box and then tap or click OK.

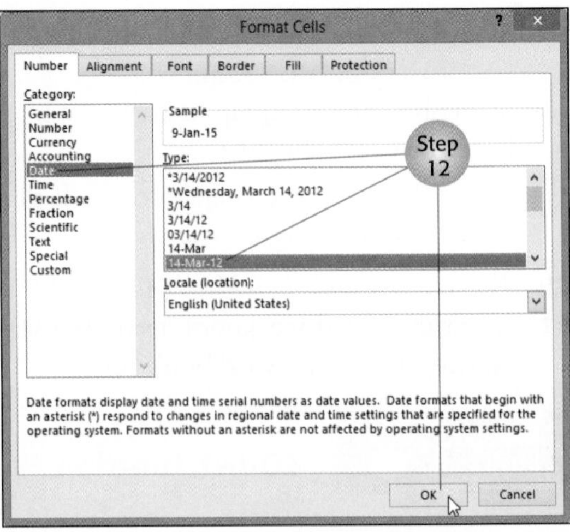

13. Tap or click any cell to deselect the range.
14. Save the revised workbook using the same name (**9.1-FinancialPlanner-Your Name**). Leave the workbook open for the next topic.

	A	B
3	**End Date**	**Pay Date**
4	9-Jan-15	16-Jan-15
5	23-Jan-15	30-Jan-15
6	6-Feb-15	13-Feb-15
7	20-Feb-15	27-Feb-15
8	6-Mar-15	13-Mar-15
9	20-Mar-15	27-Mar-15
10	3-Apr-15	10-Apr-15
11	17-Apr-15	24-Apr-15
12	1-May-15	8-May-15
13	15-May-15	22-May-15
14	29-May-15	5-Jun-15
15	5-Jun-15	12-Jun-15
16	19-Jun-15	26-Jun-15
17	3-Jul-15	10-Jul-15
18	17-Jul-15	24-Jul-15
19	31-Jul-15	7-Aug-15
20	7-Aug-15	14-Aug-15
21	21-Aug-15	28-Aug-15
22	4-Sep-15	11-Sep-15
23	18-Sep-15	25-Sep-15
24	2-Oct-15	9-Oct-15
25	16-Oct-15	23-Oct-15
26	30-Oct-15	6-Nov-15
27	6-Nov-15	13-Nov-15
28	20-Nov-15	27-Nov-15
29	4-Dec-15	11-Dec-15
30	18-Dec-15	25-Dec-15

Formatted dates in A4:B30

TODAY Function

1. Activate formula cell.
2. Type **=today()**.
3. Tap or press Enter.

Did You Know?

Many businesses that operate globally have adopted the International Standards Organization (ISO) date format YYYY-MM-DD to avoid confusion with a date written as 02/04/03 which could mean February 4, 2003 (US) or April 2, 2003 (UK). Another strategy is to format a date with the month spelled out like the format used at Step 12.

Table 9.2	Entries Excel Recognizes as Valid Dates or Times
Dates	**Times**
12/20/15; 12-20-15	4:45 (stored as 4:45:00 AM)
Dec 20, 2015	4:45 PM (stored as 4:45:00 PM)
20-Dec-15 or 20 Dec 15 or 20/Dec/15	16:45 (stored as 4:45:00 PM)
Note that the year can be entered as two digits or four digits and the month as three characters or spelled in full. Times are generally entered as hh:mm, but in situations that require a higher level of accuracy, they are entered as hh:mm:ss.	

You can also enter dates into cells as DATE functions. A DATE function is typed as *=DATE(Year,Month,Day)*. For example *=DATE(2014,12,20)*.

Beyond Basics

Region Setting and Dates

The Region setting in the Control Panel affects the format that Excel 2013 will recognize as a valid date. Following are examples of date format by region:

English (United States)	*m/d/yy*
English (Canada)	*yy/m/d* (Windows 8) or *d/m/yy* (Windows 7)
English (United Kingdom)	*d/m/yy*

To change the Region, open the Control Panel from the Desktop and select the Region icon or the Clock, Language, and Region category.

Using the IF Function

Logical functions are used when you need a formula to perform a calculation based upon a condition or comparison of a cell with a value or the contents of another cell. For example, in column G of the Income and Savings Planner worksheet, you calculated a savings value based on the take-home pay amounts in column F. Suppose you decide that you cannot afford to contribute to your savings plan unless your take home pay is more than $500. The formula in column G does not accommodate this scenario; however, an IF formula can analyze the take-home pay and calculate the savings for those values that are over your minimum.

1. With the **9.1-FinancialPlanner-Your Name** workbook open, make H4 the active cell.
2. Tap or click the FORMULAS tab.

   The category drop-down lists in the Function Library group are another way that you can find an Excel function to insert into a cell.

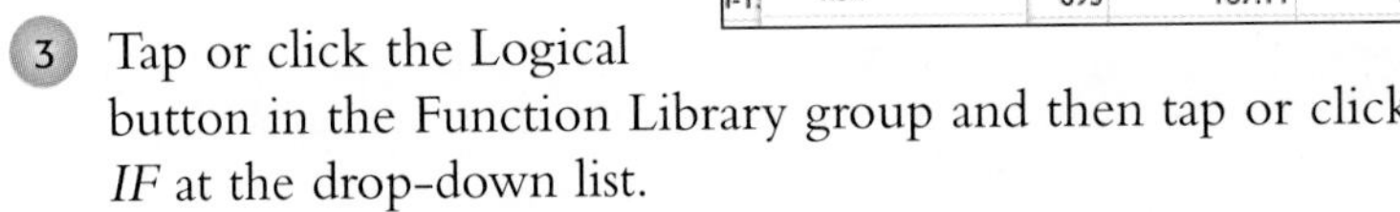
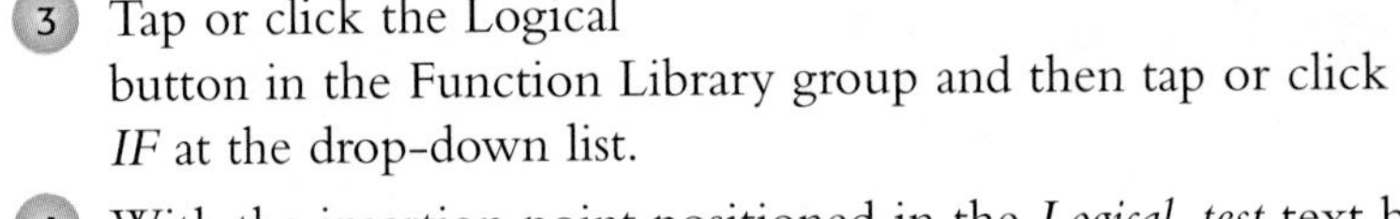

3. Tap or click the Logical button in the Function Library group and then tap or click *IF* at the drop-down list.
4. With the insertion point positioned in the *Logical_test* text box at the Function Arguments dialog box, type **f4>500** and tap or press Tab, or tap or click in the *Value_if_true* text box.

   A logical test is a statement to evaluate a comparison so that one of two actions can be performed. In this case, the statement *f4>500* tells Excel to determine if the value that resides in F4 is greater than 500. All logical tests result in either a true or a false response—either the value is greater than 500 (true) or the value is not greater than 500 (false). See Table 9.3 on the next page for more examples of logical tests.

5. Type **f4*SaveRate** and then tap or press Tab or tap or click in the *Value_if_false* text box.

   The statement in the *Value_if_true* text box is the formula you want Excel to calculate when the logical test proves true. In other words, if the value in F4 is greater than 500, you want Excel to multiply the value in F4 times the value in the cell named SaveRate (.10).

6. Type **0** and then tap or click OK.

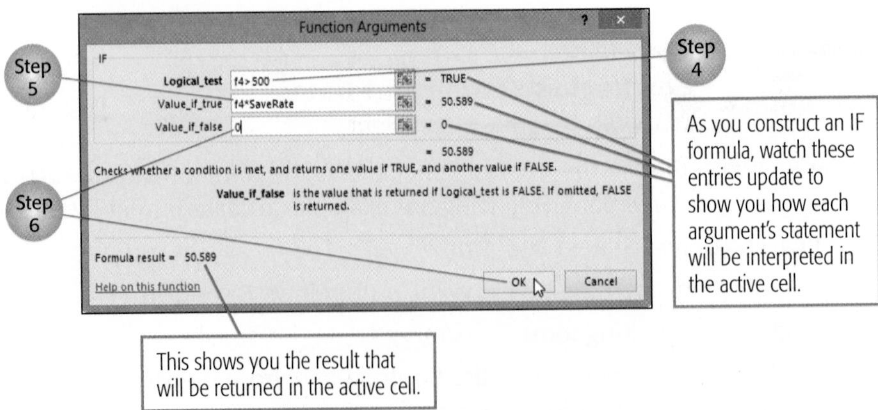

Cannot locate > on touch keyboard? With the &123 keyboard active, tap the button with the right-pointing arrow inside a circle above &123 to display the next symbol palette where > is located.

App Tip

Formulas, values, or text are all valid entries for the *Value_if_true* and *Value_if_false* text boxes.

The *Value_if_false* statement is the formula you want Excel to calculate when the logical test proves false. In other words, if the value in F4 is 500 or less, you want zero placed in the cell because you have decided that you cannot afford to contribute to your savings plan.

7 Look in the Formula bar at the IF statement entered into the active cell *=IF(F4>500,F4*SaveRate,0)*.

Using the Function Arguments dialog box to build an IF statement is a good idea because the commas and parentheses are inserted automatically in the correct positions within the formula.

8 Use the fill handle in H4 to copy the formula to the range H5:H30.

9 Review the results in H5:H30. Notice the cells that have 0 appear in a row where the take-home pay value in column F is 500 or less.

10 Select C4:H30, tap or click the Quick Analysis button that appears below the selection, tap or click TOTALS, and then tap or click the Sum button in the *TOTALS* gallery (first button).

Excel creates SUM functions in each column in the range in row 31.

11 Select D4:H31, tap or click the HOME tab, and then tap or click the Comma Style button.

12 Apply the Comma Style format to C2 and J4:J10.

13 Apply the Percent Style format to F2 and H2.

	A	B	C	D	E	F	G	H	I	J
1	Income and Savings Planner									
2	Pay Rate:		10.50	Payroll Deductions Rate:		27%	Savings Rate:	10%	Date Prepared:	1/23/2013
3	End Date	Pay Date	Estimated Hours	Gross Pay	Payroll Deductions	Take Home Pay	Savings Plan 1	Savings Plan 2	Statistics	
4	9-Jan-15	16-Jan-15	66	693.00	187.11	505.89	50.59	50.59	Average Hours:	68.96
5	23-Jan-15	30-Jan-15	71	745.50	201.29	544.22	54.42	54.42	Maximum Hours:	80.00
6	6-Feb-15	13-Feb-15	58	609.00	164.43	444.57	44.46	-	Minimum Hours:	48.00
7	20-Feb-15	27-Feb-15	65	682.50	184.28	498.23	49.82	-		
8	6-Mar-15	13-Mar-15	66	693.00	187.11	505.89	50.59	50.59	Average Savings:	52.86
9	20-Mar-15	27-Mar-15	60	630.00	170.10	459.90	45.99	-	Maximum Savings:	61.32
10	3-Apr-15	10-Apr-15	63	661.50	178.61	482.90	48.29	-	Minimum Savings:	36.79

First 10 rows showing formatting applied at Steps 11 to 13

14 Select C31:H31 and add a Top and Double Bottom Border.

15 Save the revised workbook using the same name (**9.1-FinancialPlanner-Your Name**). Leave the workbook open for the next topic.

Table 9.3 IF Statement Logical Test Examples

Logical Test	Condition Evaluated	IF Statement Example
F4>=500	Is the value in F4 greater than or equal to 500?	=IF(F4>=500,F4*SaveRate,0)
F4<500	Is the value in F4 less than 500?	=IF(F4<500,0,F4*SaveRate)
F4<=500	Is the value in F4 less than or equal to 500?	=IF(F4<=500,0,F4*SaveRate)
F4=$K$2	Is the value in F4 equal to the value in K2? Assume value in K2 is the take-home pay value for which you will set aside savings.	=IF(F4=$K$2,F4*SaveRate,0)
Hours<>0	Is the value in the cell named Hours not equal to 0?	=IF(Hours<>0,Hours*PayRate,0) Calculates Gross Pay when hours have been logged

Quick STEPS

IF Function

1. Activate formula cell.
2. Tap or click FORMULAS tab.
3. Tap or click Logical button.
4. Tap or click *IF*.
5. Type *Logical_test* statement.
6. Type value or formula in *Value_if_true* text box.
7. Type value or formula in *Value_if_false* text box.
8. Tap or click OK.

Percent Style multiplies the value in the cell by 100 and adds a percent symbol (%) to the cell.

Using the PMT Function

Financial functions in Excel can be used for a variety of tasks that involve saving or borrowing money, such as calculating the future value of an investment, the present value of an investment, or borrowing criteria such as interest rates, terms, or payments. If you are considering a loan or mortgage, use Excel's PMT function to determine an estimated loan payment. The PMT function uses a specified interest rate, number of payments, and loan amount to calculate a regular payment. Once a payment is shown, you can manipulate the interest rate, term, or loan amount to find a payment with which you are comfortable.

1. With the **9.1-FinancialPlanner-Your Name** workbook open, tap or click the LoanPlanner sheet tab.

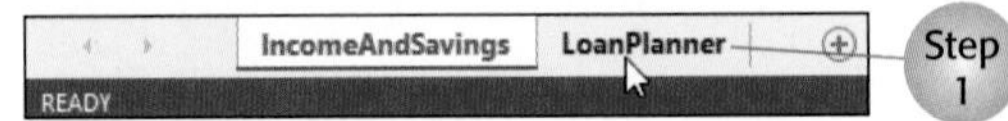

2. Make B7 the active cell.
3. Tap or click the FORMULAS tab, tap or click the Financial button, slide or scroll down the drop-down list, and then tap or click *PMT*.

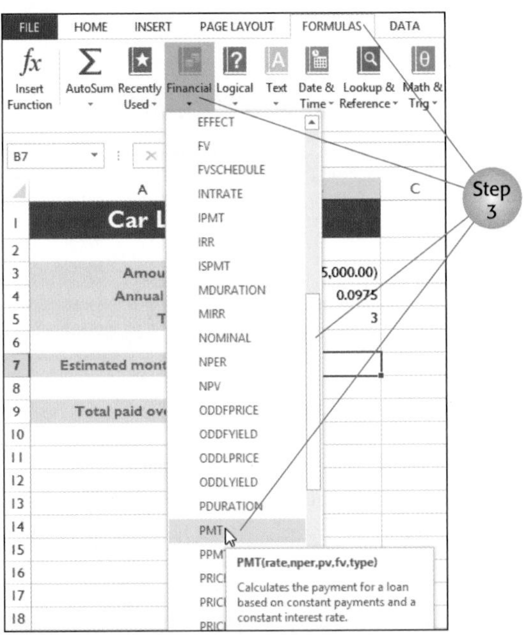

oops!

Can't see B4? Slide or drag the Function Arguments title bar right until the dialog box is no longer obscuring your view of columns A and B.

4. With the insertion point positioned in the *Rate* text box at the Function Arguments dialog box, tap or click B4 and then type **/12**.

The interest rate in B4 is expressed as the interest rate per year. Typing /12 after B4 causes Excel to divide the interest rate in B4 by 12 to calculate the monthly interest rate. To use the PMT function correctly, you need to ensure that the time periods are all the same. In other words, if you want to find a monthly payment, you need to make sure the rate and terms are also in monthly units. Most lending institutions express interest with the annual rate (not monthly) but compound the interest monthly.

5. Tap or click in the *Nper* text box, tap or click B5, and then type ***12**.

The value in B5 is the number of years you will take to pay back the loan. Multiplying the value times 12 will convert the value to the number of months to repay the loan. Most lending institutions express the repayment term in years (not months).

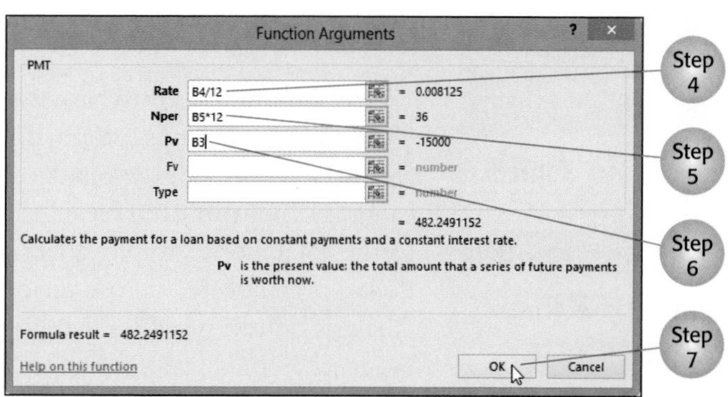

6 Tap or click in the *Pv* text box and then tap or click B3.

Pv stands for present value and represents the amount you want to borrow (referred to as the principal). Notice the amount borrowed is entered as a negative value in this worksheet. By default, Excel considers payments as negative values because money is subtracted from your bank balance when you make a loan payment. By entering a negative number for the amount borrowed, the PMT formula will return a positive value for the calculated loan payment. Whether you prefer to show a negative value for the amount borrowed or for the estimated monthly loan payment is a matter of personal preference; both options are acceptable.

7 Tap or click OK.

Excel returns the payment *$482.25* in B7.

8 Look in the Formula bar at the PMT statement entered into the active cell *=PMT(B4/12,B5*12,B3).*

9 Make B9 the active cell and enter the formula **=b7*b5*12**.

Excel calculates the total cost for the loan to be $17,360.97.

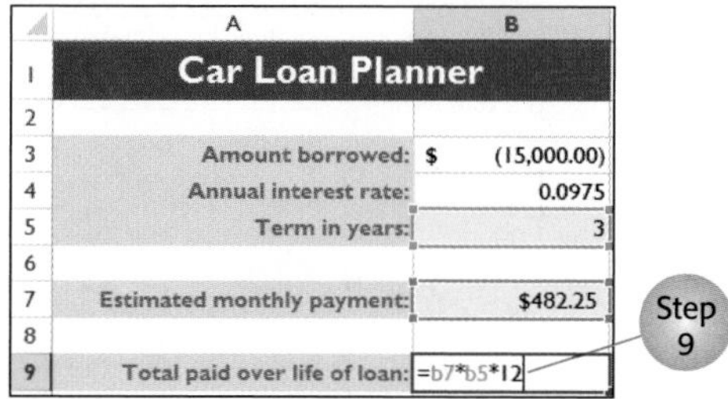

10 Change the value in B5 from *3* to *4*.

Notice that increasing the term one more year reduces your monthly payment; however, the total cost of the loan increases because you are making more payments.

11 Save the revised workbook using the same name (**9.1-FinancialPlanner-Your Name**) and close the workbook.

PMT Function

1. Activate formula cell.
2. Tap or click FORMULAS tab.
3. Tap or click Financial button.
4. Slide or scroll down list.
5. Tap or click *PMT*.
6. Enter *Rate* particulars.
7. Enter *Nper* particulars.
8. Enter *Pv* value or reference.
9. Tap or click OK.

PMT assumes a constant payment and a constant interest rate; this function cannot be used to estimate loan payments where the payment or interest rate is variable.

Type a negative symbol in front of PMT if the amount borrowed is a positive value and you want the payment to be a positive value. For example, *=-PMT(B4/12,B5*12,B3)*.

Using FV to Calculate the Future Value of an Investment

Another useful financial function is FV, which is used to calculate the future value of a series of regular payments that earn a constant interest rate. For example, if you deposit $100 each month for 10 years into an investment account that earns 9.75% per year (compounded monthly), the FV function *=FV(9.75%/12,10*12,100)* calculates the value of the account after the 10-year period to be $20,193.76.

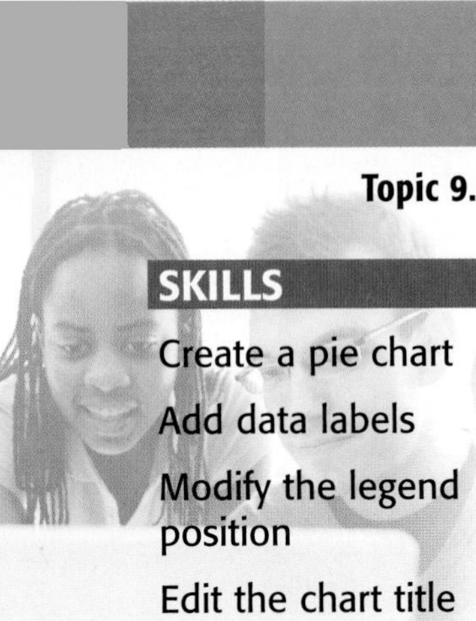

Topic 9.6

SKILLS

Create a pie chart

Add data labels

Modify the legend position

Edit the chart title

Roll the mouse over the chart options to see a live preview of the data graphed in the chart above the gallery.

Creating and Modifying a Pie Chart

Charts are often used to provide a visual snapshot of data. Many readers find that charts illustrate trends, proportions, and comparisons more distinctly than numbers alone. Excel provides 10 categories of charts with multiple styles within each category. In a **pie chart**, each data point (pie slice) is sized to show its proportion to the total. For example, governments often use a pie chart to illustrate how tax dollars are allocated across various programs and services. Excel 2013's new Quick Analysis button provides live previews of popular chart styles with selected data.

1. Open the workbook named ***SocialMediaStats***.
2. Use Save As to save a copy of the workbook as **9.6-SocialMediaStats-Your Name** in the Ch9 folder in CompletedTopicsByChapter.
3. Select A5:B10.

Before you can insert a chart you first need to select the data that you want Excel to represent in a chart.

4. Tap or click the Quick Analysis button that appears below the selection area and then tap or click the CHARTS tab.
5. Tap or click *Pie* at the *Charts* gallery.

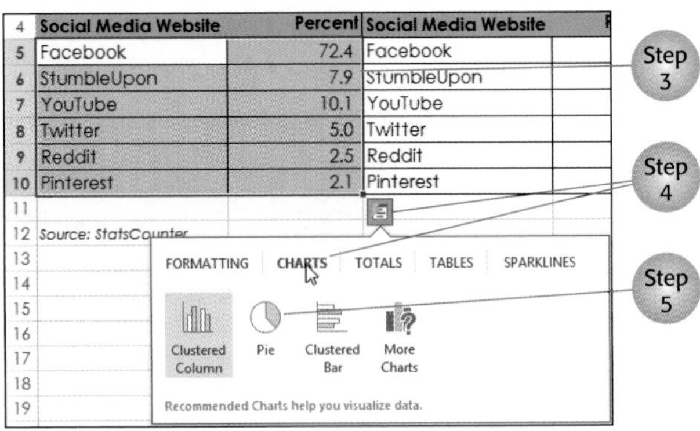

Excel graphs the data in a pie chart and places the chart overlapping the worksheet's cells within a chart object window. Notice also that the chart object is selected with selection handles, three chart editing buttons, and the CHART TOOLS DESIGN and FORMAT tabs in the ribbon.

6. With the chart selected, slide or drag the chart with your finger or mouse over any white unused area inside the chart's borders to the approximate location shown below.

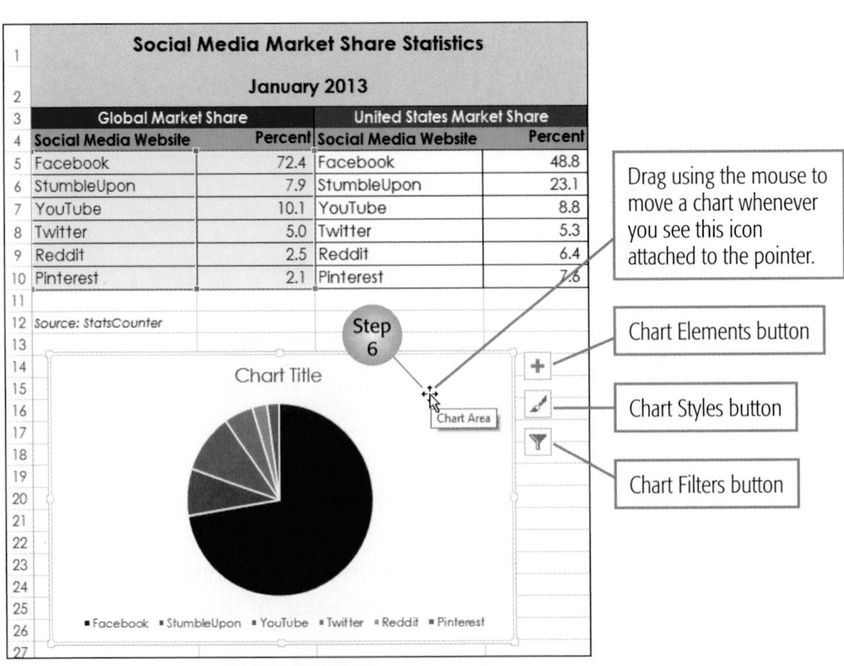

Social Media Website	Percent	Social Media Website	Percent
Facebook	72.4	Facebook	48.8
StumbleUpon	7.9	StumbleUpon	23.1
YouTube	10.1	YouTube	8.8
Twitter	5.0	Twitter	5.3
Reddit	2.5	Reddit	6.4
Pinterest	2.1	Pinterest	7.6

Source: StatsCounter

7 Tap or click the Chart Elements button (displays as a plus symbol next to the chart).

8 Tap or click the *Data Labels* check box to insert a check mark, tap or point at the right end of the *Data Labels* option when the right-pointing arrow appears, and then tap or click *Outside End.*

Although pie charts show proportions well, adding data labels allows a reader to include context with the size of each pie slice.

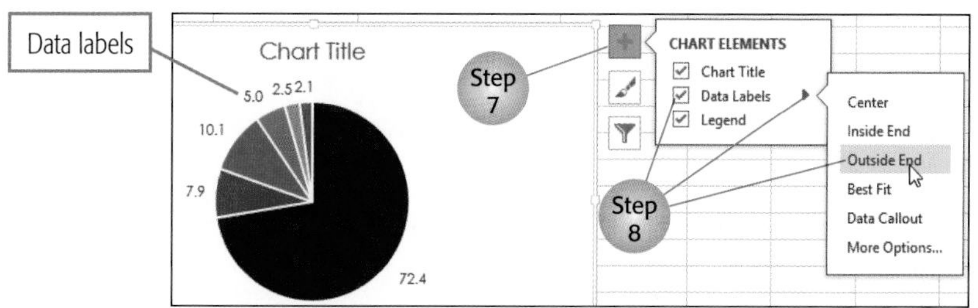

Create a Pie Chart

1. Select range.
2. Tap or click Quick Analysis button.
3. Tap or click CHARTS.
4. Tap or click *Pie*.
5. Move and/or modify chart elements as required.

9 With CHART ELEMENTS still displayed, tap or click at the right end of *Legend* when the right-pointing arrow appears and then tap or click *Right.*

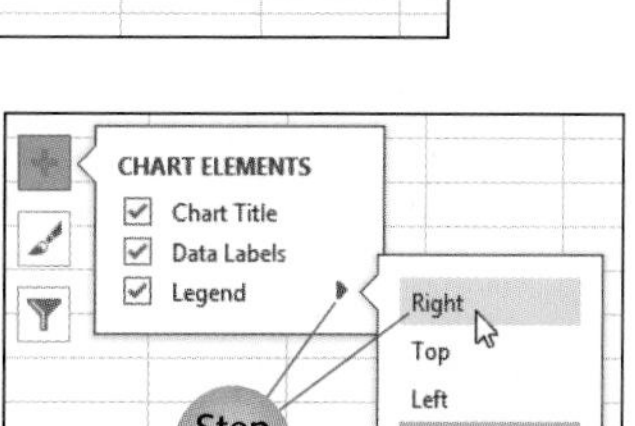

10 Tap or click to select the *Chart Title* object inside the chart window, slide or drag to select *Chart Title*, type **Global Market Share**, and then tap or click in any white unused area within the chart to deselect the title.

Selecting with touch? Tap *Chart Title* to display selection handles, tap inside the selected object, and then tap the Edit Text button in the Mini toolbar.

11 Select C5:D10 and insert a pie chart, as shown in Figure 9.1, by completing steps similar to those in Steps 4 to 10.

12 Save the revised workbook using the same name (**9.6-SocialMediaStats-Your Name**). Leave the workbook open for the next topic.

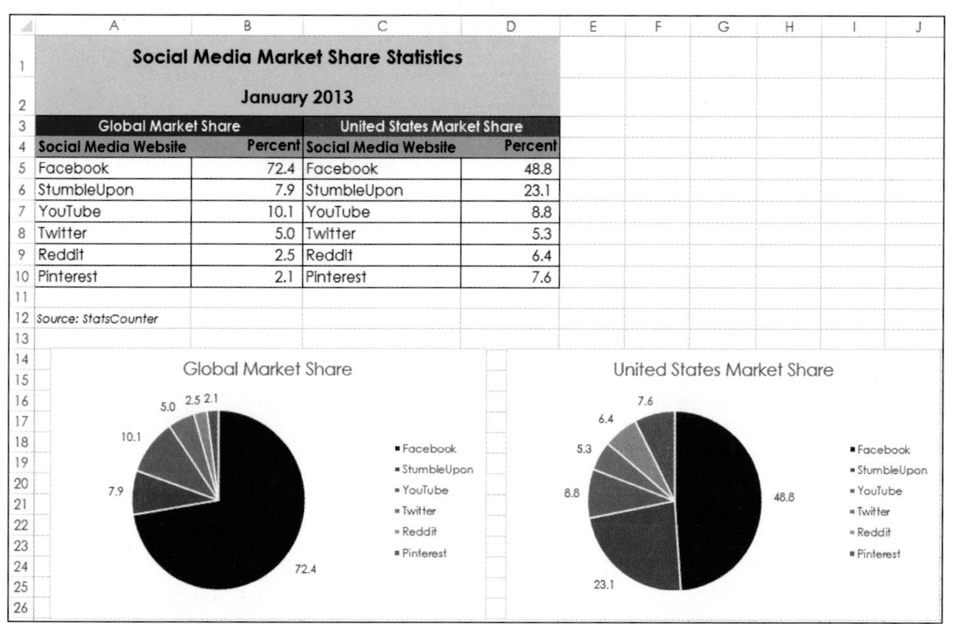

Social Media Market Share Statistics			
January 2013			
Global Market Share		United States Market Share	
Social Media Website	Percent	Social Media Website	Percent
Facebook	72.4	Facebook	48.8
StumbleUpon	7.9	StumbleUpon	23.1
YouTube	10.1	YouTube	8.8
Twitter	5.0	Twitter	5.3
Reddit	2.5	Reddit	6.4
Pinterest	2.1	Pinterest	7.6

Source: StatsCounter

Figure 9.1 Side-by-side pie charts

A popular technique to emphasize a pie slice is to move the slice away from the rest of the pie (called a *point explosion*). To do this, tap or click to select the pie slices, then tap or click to isolate the individual slice and slide or drag it away from the pie.

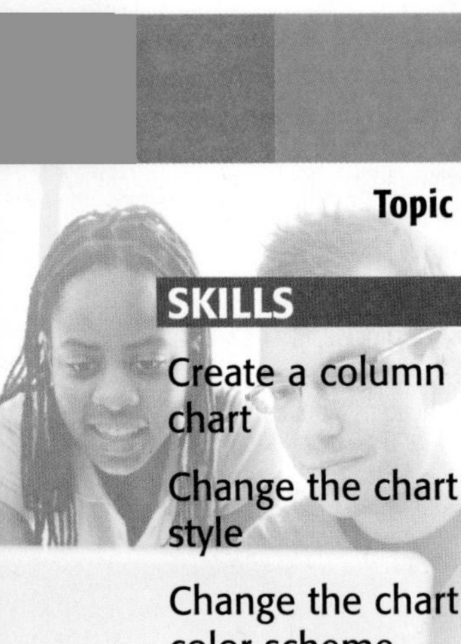

Topic 9.7

SKILLS

- Create a column chart
- Change the chart style
- Change the chart color scheme
- Add axis titles

Creating and Modifying a Column Chart

In a **column chart**, each data point is a colored bar that extends up from the **category axis** (horizontal axis, also called x-axis) with the bar height representing the data point's value on the **value axis** (vertical axis, also called y- or z-axis). Use a column chart to compare one or more series of data side by side. Column charts are often used to identify trends or illustrate comparisons over time or categories.

1. With the **9.6-SocialMediaStats-Your Name** workbook open, tap or click the Facebook sheet tab.
2. Select A7:B14.
3. Tap or click the Quick Analysis button, tap or click CHARTS, and then tap or click *Clustered Column*.
4. Slide or drag the chart until the top left corner is positioned in row 1 under column letter C (see Figure 9.2 on the next page).
5. Slide or drag the bottom right selection handle down and right to resize the chart until the bottom right corner is at approximately the bottom right border of J16 (see Figure 9.2 on the next page).
6. With the chart selected, tap or click the Chart Styles button (displays as a paintbrush next to the chart).
7. Slide or scroll down to the bottom of the STYLE list and then tap or click the last option in the gallery (*Style 16*).

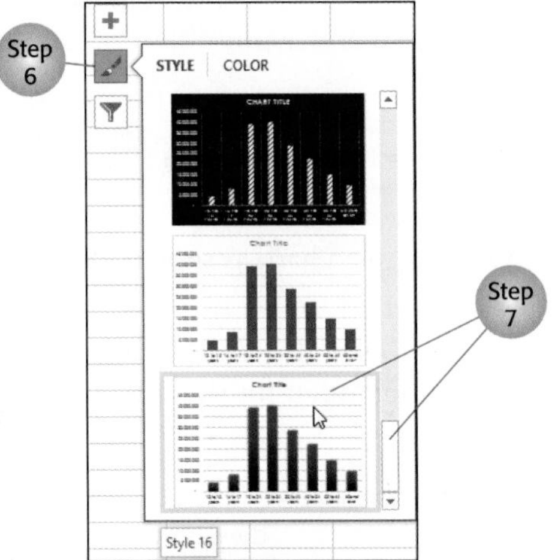

8. With the *Chart Styles* gallery still open, tap or click COLOR and then tap or click the third row in the *Colorful* section of the color gallery (*Color 3*).

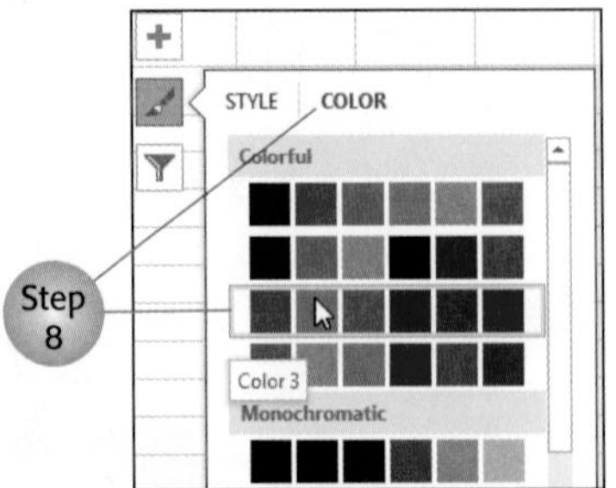

9. Tap or click the Chart Elements button.

Additional chart elements options are available for column charts that are not possible with a pie chart.

10 Tap or click the *Axis Titles* check box to insert a check mark.

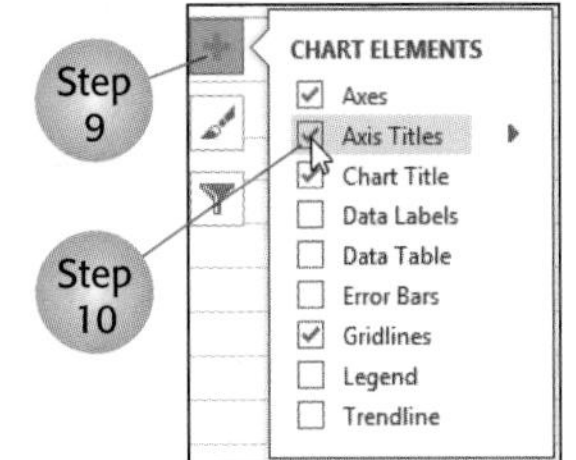

Excel adds an Axis Title object to the vertical axis and to the horizontal axis.

11 With the *Axis Title* object along the vertical axis already selected, select the title text and type **Millions**.

12 Tap or click to select the *Axis Title* object along the horizontal axis and tap or press Delete to remove the object.

13 Edit the *Chart Title* to **Facebook Audience by Age Group**.

14 Compare your chart to the one shown in Figure 9.2. If necessary, redo an action in Steps 4 to 13.

15 Save the revised workbook using the same name (**9.6-SocialMediaStats-Your Name**). Leave the workbook open for the next topic.

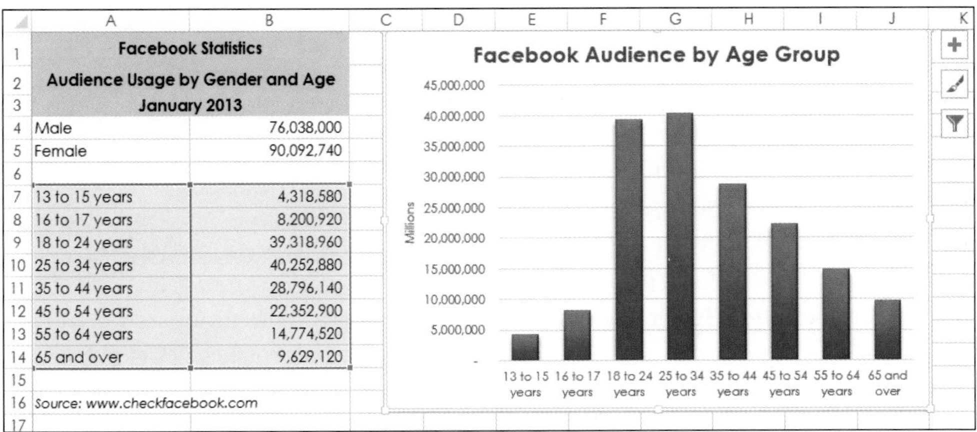

Figure 9.2 Column chart

Create a Column Chart

1. Select range.
2. Tap or click Quick Analysis button.
3. Tap or click CHARTS.
4. Tap or click *Clustered Column*.
5. Move and/or modify chart elements as required.

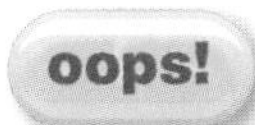

Using touch? Tap inside the selected *Axis Title* object to display the Mini toolbar and then tap the Delete button.

ALTERNATIVE method

Charts can also be created using the buttons in the Charts group of the INSERT tab. Select the data range, tap or click the INSERT tab, and then tap or click the button for the desired chart type in the Charts group.

Once a chart has been inserted, the CHART TOOLS DESIGN and FORMAT tabs contain the same options to modify the chart as those found in the *Chart Elements* and *Chart Styles* galleries.

Recommended Charts

Not sure which chart type best represents your data? New to Excel 2013 is the **Recommended Charts** feature. Select the data you want to graph, and Excel will show a series of customized charts that best suit the selection. Use the *More Charts* option from the Quick Analysis button or tap or click the INSERT tab and then tap or click the Recommended Charts button in the Charts group.

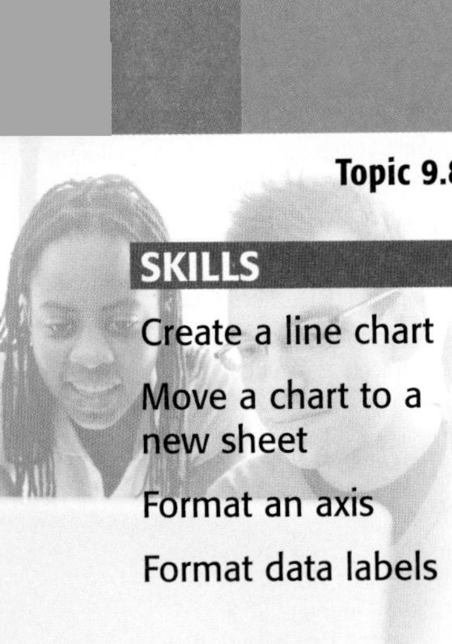

Topic 9.8
SKILLS
Create a line chart
Move a chart to a new sheet
Format an axis
Format data labels

Creating and Modifying a Line Chart

Line charts are best suited for data where you want to illustrate trends and changes in values over a period of time. With a **line chart**, a reader can easily spot a trend, or identify growth spurts, dips, or unusual points in the series. Line charts are also often used to help predict future values based on the direction of the line.

1. With the **9.6-SocialMediaStats-Your Name** workbook open, tap or click the FacebookUserTimeline sheet tab.
2. Select A4:B12.
3. Tap or click the Quick Analysis button, tap or click CHARTS, and then tap or click *Line*.
4. With the chart selected, tap or click the **Move Chart button** in the Location group of the CHART TOOLS DESIGN tab.

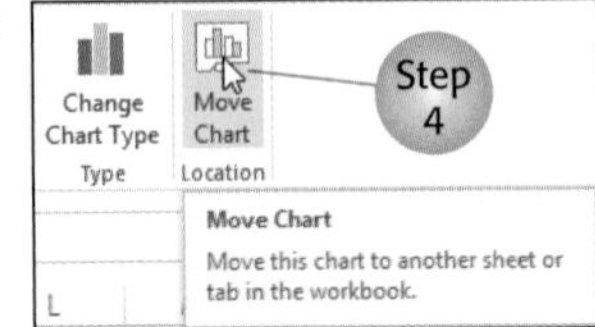

5. Tap or click *New sheet*, type **FBUserTimelineChart**, and then tap or press Enter or tap or click OK.

Moving a chart to its own chart sheet automatically scales the chart to fit a letter-sized page in landscape orientation.

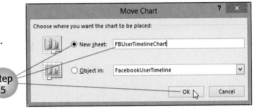

6. With the CHART TOOLS DESIGN tab active, tap or click the second option in the *Chart Styles* gallery (*Style 2*).
7. Tap or click the Change Colors button in the Chart Styles group and then tap or click the third row in the *Colorful* section of the color gallery (*Color 3*).

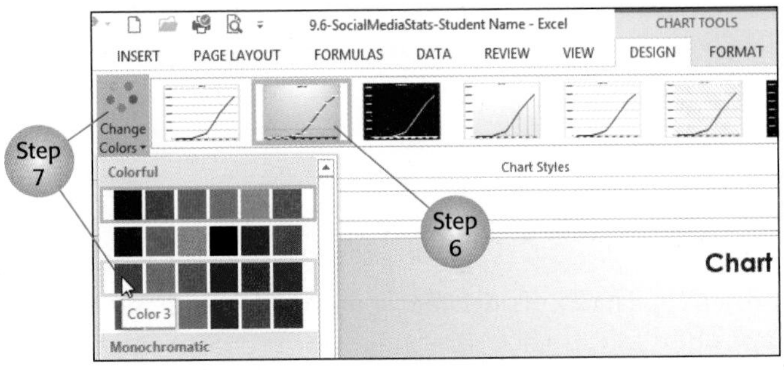

8. Edit the *Chart Title* to **Facebook User Timeline**.

In the next step you will correct the axis labels. Excel incorrectly converted the dates that were in column A, changing *Dec* to *Jan*.

9. Tap or click to select the dates in the category axis along the bottom of the chart. Make sure you see a border and selection handles around the axis labels.
10. Double-tap or double-click inside the selected axis labels to open the Format Axis task pane at the right side of the window.
11. Tap or click *Text axis* in the *AXIS OPTIONS* section of the task pane.

Notice the axis labels change to show the December dates as they appeared in the worksheet.

12. Close the Format Axis task pane.

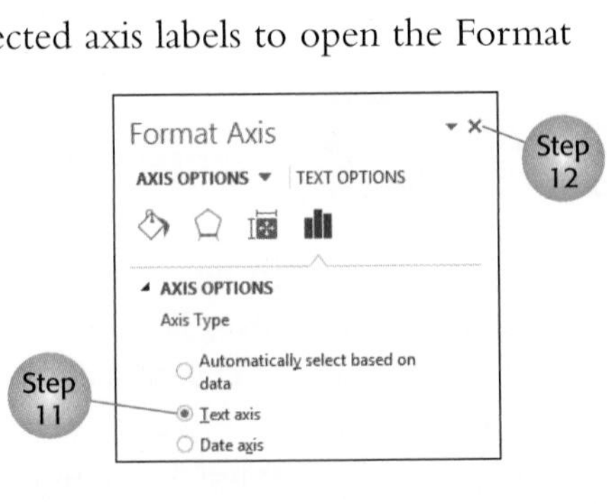

oops!

No border around dates? Tap or click the axis labels a second time. Sometimes the chart is selected the first time you tap or click.

13 Tap or click any data value on a data point in the line chart to select the entire series of data labels.

14 Tap or click the CHART TOOLS FORMAT tab and then tap or click the Format Selection button in the Current Selection group.

This opens the Format Data Labels task pane.

15 Tap or click *Above* in the *Label Position* section of the Format Data Labels task pane with the LABEL OPTIONS tab active.

16 Tap or click TEXT OPTIONS, and then tap or click *TEXT FILL* to expand the options list.

17 Tap or click the Color button and then tap or click *Black, Text 1* (second color in first row).

18 Close the Format Data Labels task pane and then tap or click in the window outside the chart to deselect the data labels.

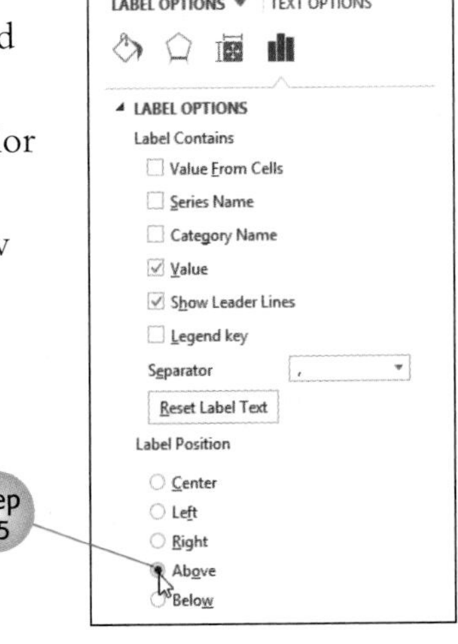

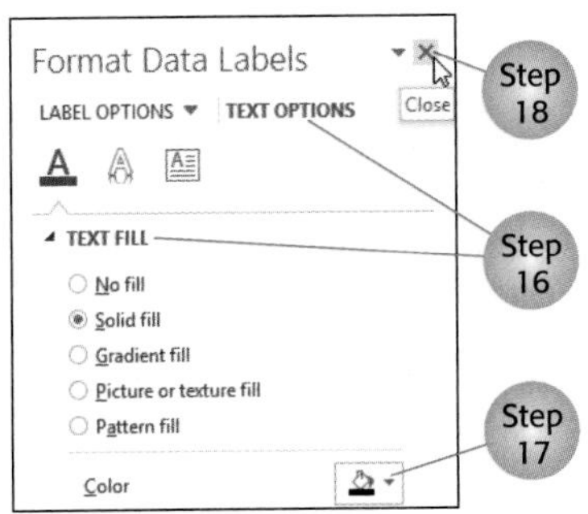

Step 18

Step 16

Step 17

Step 15

19 Compare your chart with the chart shown in Figure 9.3 and make corrections if necessary.

20 Save the revised workbook using the same name (**9.6-SocialMediaStats-Your Name**). Leave the workbook open for the next topic.

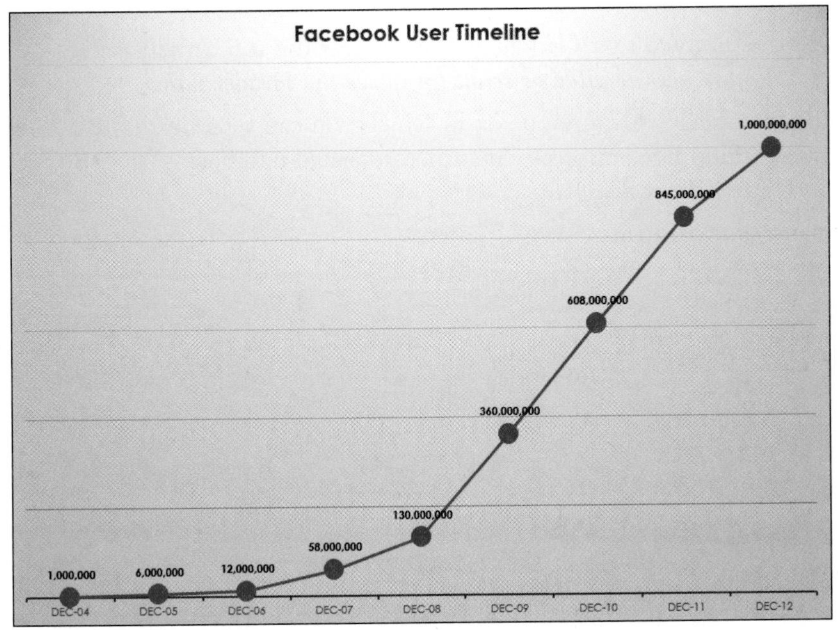

Figure 9.3 Line chart created in new chart sheet

Create a Line Chart

1. Select range.
2. Tap or click Quick Analysis button.
3. Tap or click CHARTS.
4. Tap or click *Line*.
5. Move and/or modify chart elements as required.

Using Page Layout View, Adding a Header, and Changing Margins

Topic 9.9

SKILLS

Work in Page Layout view

Add a header

Change margins

Center worksheet horizontally and vertically

View buttons are also at the right end of the Status bar next to the Zoom buttons. Page Layout view is the middle of the three view buttons.

oops!

Can't see the full width of the page? If you're using a tablet or device with a small screen, decrease the Zoom to less than 100% until you can view the page width.

Tap or click the Go to Footer button in the Navigation group of the HEADER & FOOTER TOOLS DESIGN tab to move to the Footer sections.

In **Page Layout view** you can preview page layout options similarly to Print Preview; however, you also have the advantage of being able to edit the worksheet. The worksheet is divided into pages with white space around the edges of each page showing the size of the margins and a ruler along the top and left of the column letters and row numbers. Pages and cells outside the active worksheet are grayed out; however, you can click any page or cell and add new data.

1. With the **9.6-SocialMediaStats-Your Name** workbook open, tap or click the SocialMediaWebsites sheet tab, and then tap or click E1.
2. Tap or click the VIEW tab and then tap or click the Page Layout button in the Workbook Views group.

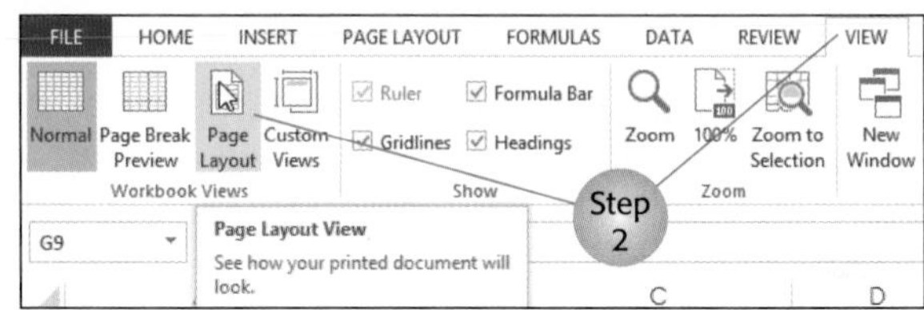

Notice in Page Layout view you can see that the right pie chart is split over two pages.

3. Tap or click the PAGE LAYOUT tab, tap or click the Orientation button in the Page Setup group, and then tap or click *Landscape* at the drop-down list.
4. Tap or click the *Width* list arrow in the Scale to Fit group (displays *Automatic*) and then tap or click *1 page* at the drop-down list.

Inserting a Header or Footer

As with Word, a header prints at the top of each page and a footer prints at the bottom of each page. Headers and footers are divided into three sections with the left section left-aligned, the center section centered, and the right section right-aligned by default.

5. Tap or click the dimmed text *Click to add header* near the top center of the page. ***Hint: You may need to slide or scroll up to see the Header pane.***

The Header pane opens with three boxes in which you can type header text and/or add header and footer options such as pictures, page numbering, the current date or time, and file or sheet names.

6. Type your first and last names.

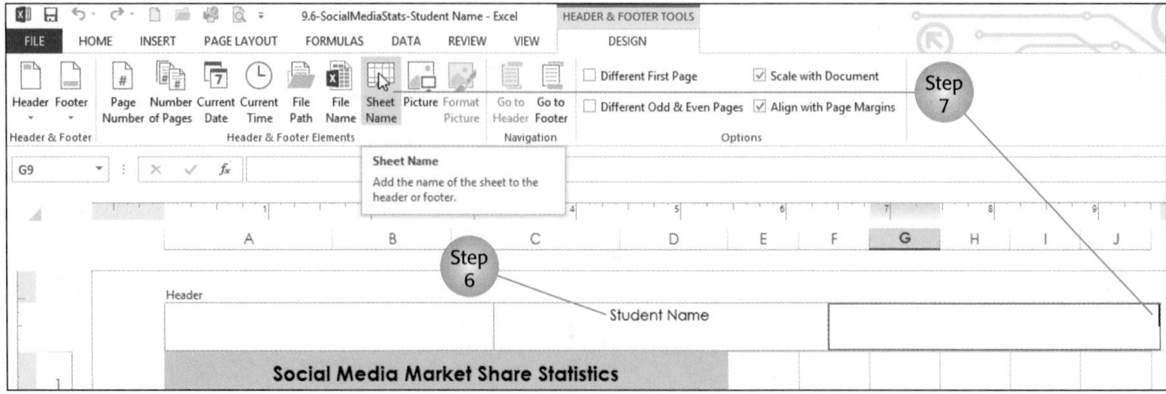

7 Tap or click at the right of the center section text box in the Header pane to open the right section text box and then tap or click the Sheet Name button in the Header & Footer Elements group of the HEADER & FOOTER TOOLS DESIGN tab.

Excel inserts the code *&[Tab]*, which is replaced with the sheet tab name when you tap or click outside the Header section.

8 Tap or click at the left of the Header pane to open the left section text box and then tap or click the File Name button in the Header & Footer Elements group.

Excel inserts the code *&[File]*, which is replaced with the file name when you tap or click in the worksheet area.

9 Tap or click in any cell in the worksheet area.

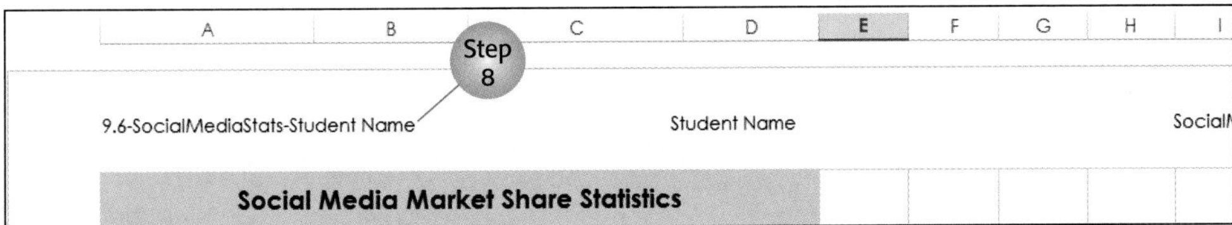

Changing Margins

Worksheet margins are 0.75 inch top and bottom and 0.7 inch left and right with the header or footer printing 0.3 inch from the top or bottom of the page. Adjust margins to add more space around the edges of a page or between the header and footer text and the worksheet. Center a smaller worksheet horizontally and/or vertically to improve the page's appearance.

10 Tap or click the PAGE LAYOUT tab, tap or click the Margins button in the Page Setup group, and tap or click *Wide*.

The *Wide* preset margin option changes the top, bottom, left, and right margins to 1 inch and the header and footer margins to 0.5 inch.

11 Tap or click the Margins button and tap or click *Custom Margins*.

12 Tap or click the *Horizontally* and the *Vertically* check boxes in the *Center on page* section to insert a check mark in each box and then tap or click OK.

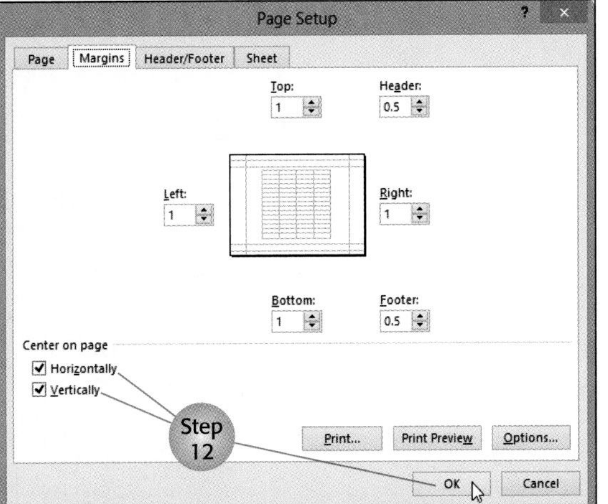

13 Tap or click the Facebook sheet tab, tap or click A6, change to Page Layout view, and modify print options by completing steps similar to those in Steps 3 to 12 to improve the appearance of the printed worksheet.

14 Save the revised workbook using the same name (**9.6-SocialMediaStats-Your Name**) and then close the workbook.

Add a Header
1. Switch to Page Layout view.
2. Tap or click *Click to add header*.
3. Type header text in center section or tap or click left or right section.
4. Add header elements as required.
5. Tap or click in worksheet area.

Change Margins
1. Tap or click PAGE LAYOUT tab.
2. Tap or click Margins button.
3. Tap or click preset option OR tap or click *Custom Margins* and change margins at Page Setup dialog box.

Center the Worksheet
1. Tap or click PAGE LAYOUT tab.
2. Tap or click Margins button.
3. Tap or click *Custom Margins*.
4. Tap or click *Horizontally* and/or *Vertically* check boxes.
5. Tap or click OK.

Page Layout view is not available for chart sheets; however, you can add a header or change margins in Print Preview by using the Margins button or Page Setup link.

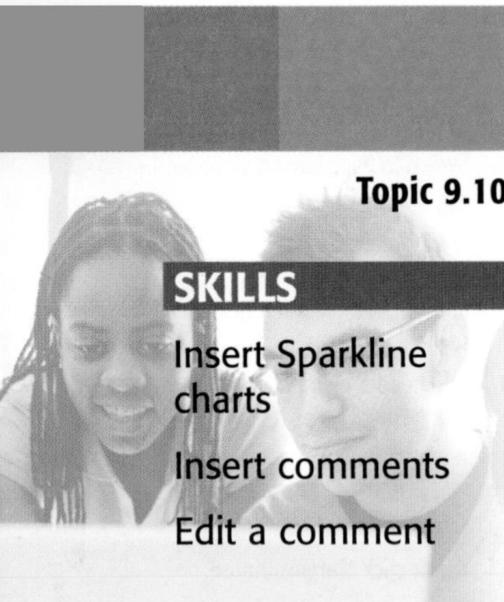

Topic 9.10

SKILLS

Insert Sparkline charts

Insert comments

Edit a comment

Creating and Modifying Sparklines and Inserting Comments

Sparklines are miniature charts inserted into individual cells within a range in the worksheet. Sparklines are used to draw attention to trends or variations in data on a smaller scale than a column or line chart. Excel offers three types of Sparkline charts: Line, Column, or Win/Loss.

A comment attached to a cell pops up when the reader points or clicks the cell. Comments are used to add explanatory information, pose questions, or provide other feedback to readers when a workbook is shared.

1. Open the workbook named ***SchoolBudget***.
2. Use Save As to save a copy of the workbook as **9.10-SchoolBudget-Your Name** in the Ch9 folder in CompletedTopicsByChapter.
3. Make K3 the active cell.
4. Tap or click the INSERT tab and then tap or click the Column button in the Sparklines group.

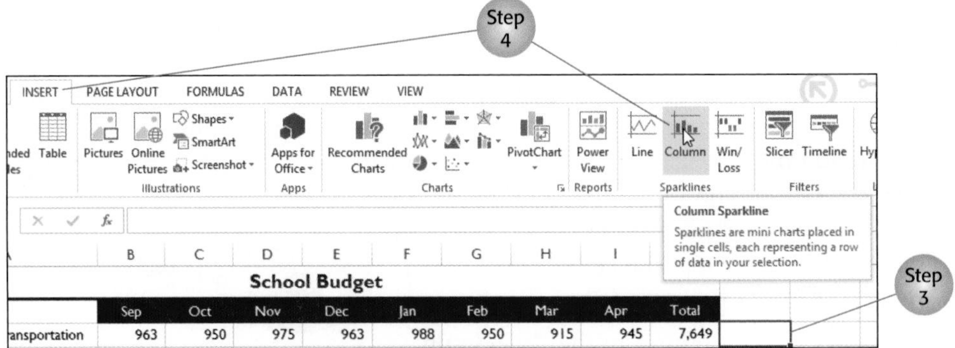

5. Type **b3:i3** in the *Data Range* text box at the Create Sparklines dialog box and then tap or press Enter or tap or click OK.

Excel embeds a column chart within the cell.

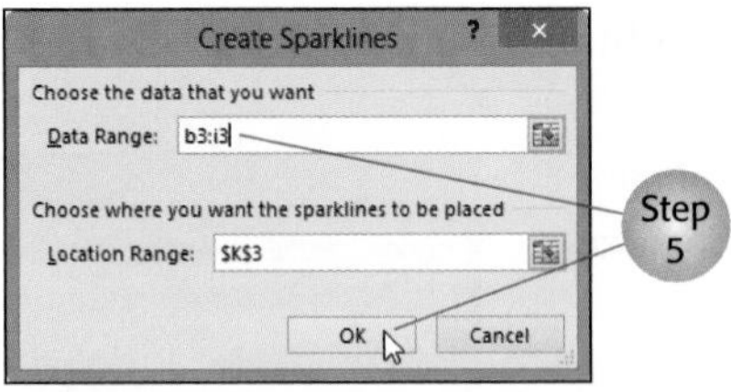

App Tip

Increase the row height and/or column width to enlarge Sparkline charts.

6. Use the fill handle to copy the Sparklines column chart from K3 to K4:K11.

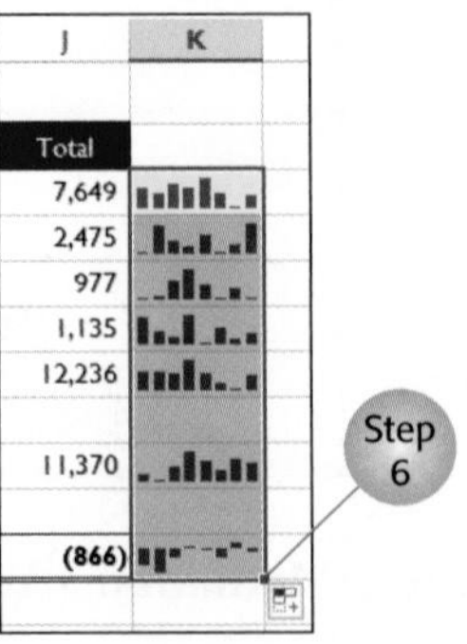

7 Tap or click the *High Point* check box in the Show group of the SPARKLINE TOOLS DESIGN tab to insert a check mark.

Excel colors red the bar in the column chart with the highest value. Other options in the tab are used to change the type or style, emphasize other points, show markers, or edit the data source.

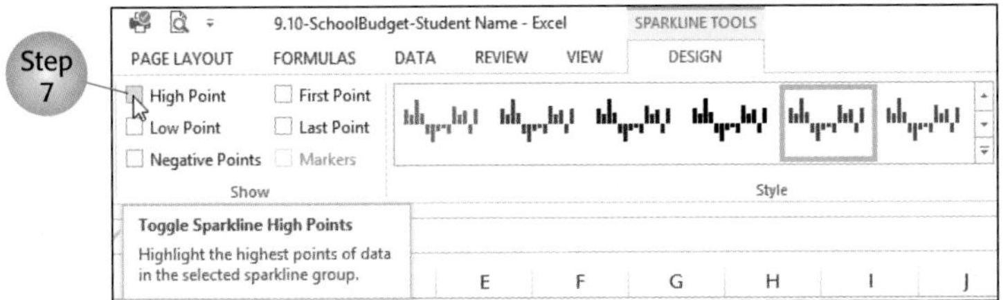

8 Make K2 the active cell, type **Trend**, and then tap or click E9.

9 Tap or click the REVIEW tab and then tap or click the New Comment button in the Comments group.

10 Type **Assuming extra hours during Christmas break.** and tap or click I3.

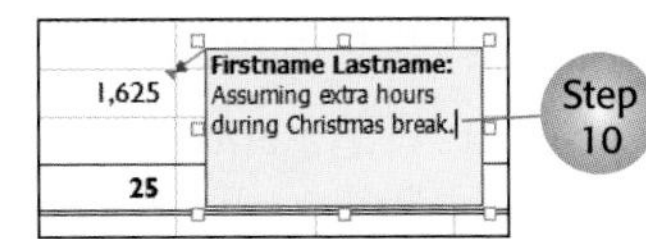

Excel inserts a diagonal red triangle in the upper right corner of a cell to indicate a comment exists for the cell.

11 Tap or click the New Comment button, type **May be able to use last month's rent.**, and tap or click any cell.

12 Tap I3 and tap the Show/Hide Comment button in the Comments group, or point to I3 with the mouse to display the comment in a pop-up box.

13 If necessary, tap or click I3 to activate the cell.

14 Tap or click the Edit Comment button in the Comments group and edit the comment text to *May be able to use last month's rent, which lowers this value to 55.*

15 Tap or click any cell to finish editing the Comment box

16 Tap or click the Show All Comments button in the Comments group to display both comment boxes in the worksheet.

17 Tap or click the Show All Comments button to turn off the display of comment boxes.

18 Save the revised workbook using the same name (**9.10-SchoolBudget-Your Name**) and close the workbook.

Insert Sparklines

1. Activate cell.
2. Tap or click INSERT tab.
3. Tap or click required Sparklines chart button.
4. Type source data range.
5. Tap or click OK.

Insert a Comment

1. Activate cell.
2. Tap or click REVIEW tab.
3. Tap or click New Comment button.
4. Type comment text.
5. Tap or click any cell.

Printing Comments

By default, comments do not print with a worksheet. You can choose to print a list of comments on a separate page after the worksheet prints, or you can turn on the display of the comment boxes and print the worksheet with the comments as shown in the worksheet. Use the *Comments* option in the *Print* section of the Page Setup dialog box with the Sheet tab active to specify the print option.

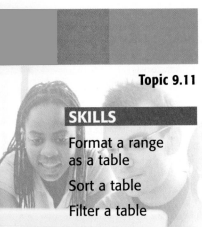

Topic 9.11

SKILLS

- Format a range as a table
- Sort a table
- Filter a table

Working with Tables

Format a range of cells as a table to analyze, sort, and filter data as an independent unit. A worksheet can have more than one table, which means you can isolate and analyze data in groups. A table also allows you to choose from a variety of preformatted table styles, which is faster than manually formatting a range. Use tables for any block of data organized in a list format.

A **filter** temporarily hides any data that does not meet a criterion. Use filters to look at subsets of data without deleting rows in the table.

1. Open the workbook named ***CalorieActivityTable***.
2. Use Save As to save a copy of the workbook as **9.11-CalorieActivityTable-Your Name** in the Ch9 folder in CompletedTopicsByChapter.
3. Select A3:D23.
4. Tap or click the Quick Analysis button, tap or click the TABLES tab, and then tap or click the Table button.
5. Select A1:A2 and apply *White, Background 1, Darker 5%* fill color (first color in second row).
6. Make A4 the active cell.
7. Tap or click the TABLE TOOLS DESIGN tab and then tap or click the *Table Style Medium 1* option in the *Table Styles* gallery (option to the left of the active style).

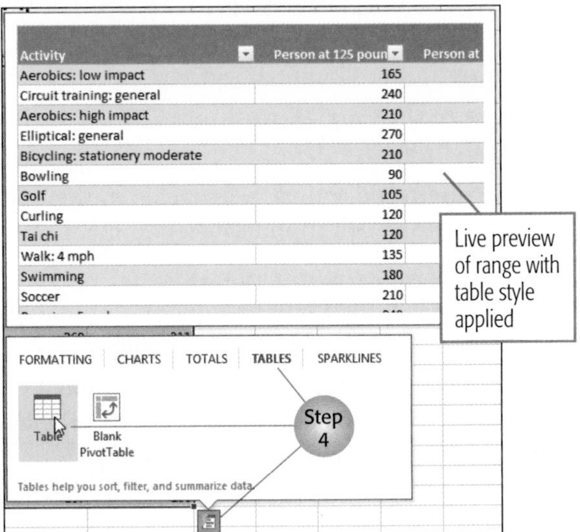

Recall from Chapter 7 that different formatting applied to every other row is referred to as *banded rows* and is used to improve readability. The fill color, border style, and other options vary by table style.

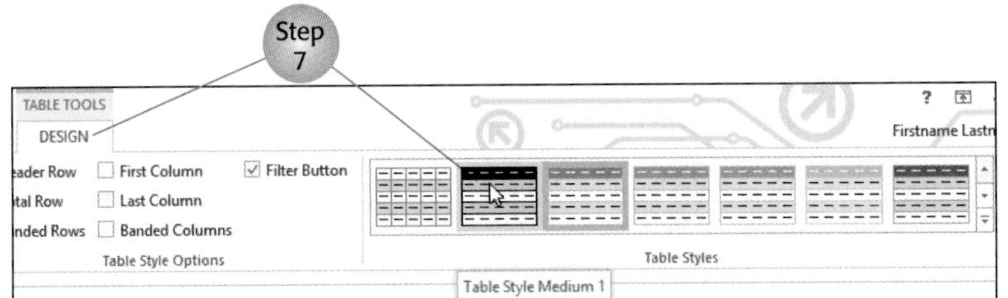

8. Tap or click the Filter button at the top of the *Activity* column in the table (displays as down-pointing arrow).
9. Tap or click *Sort A to Z* at the drop-down list.

The table rows are sorted in ascending order by the activity descriptions.

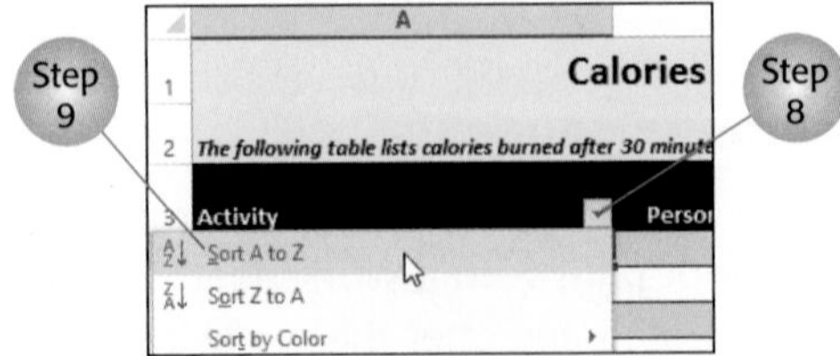

10 Tap or click the Filter button at the top of the *Person at 155 pounds* column.

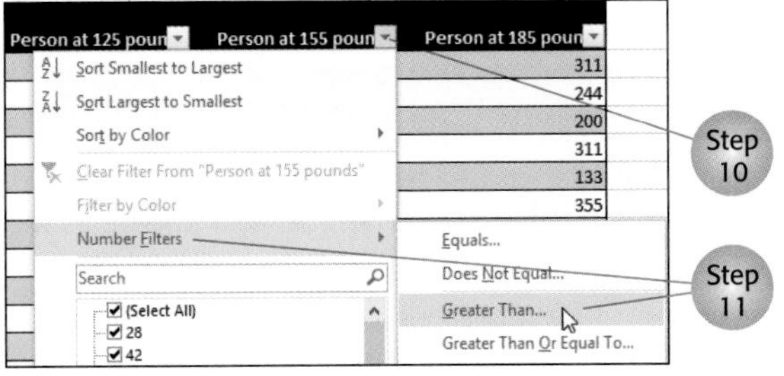

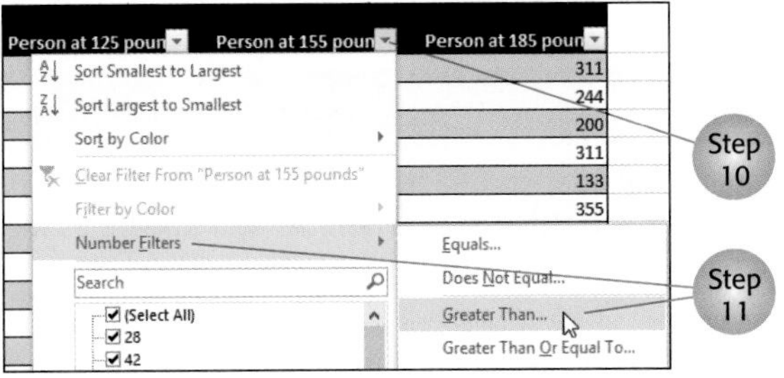

A check box is included for each unique value within the column. Filter a table by clearing check boxes for values or items you do not want to see in the filtered list, or use the *Filter by Color* and *Number Filters* options to specify a filter condition.

11 Tap or point to *Number Filters* and then tap or click *Greater Than.*

12 Type **200** at the Custom AutoFilter dialog box with the insertion point positioned in the text box at the right of *is greater than* and then tap or click OK.

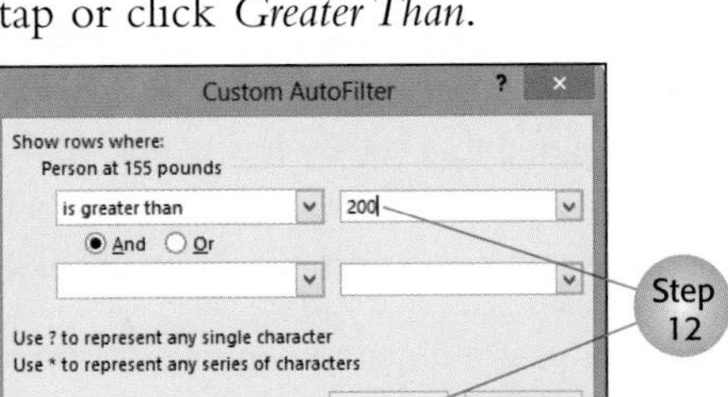

Excel filters the table and displays only those activities in which the calories burned are more than 200 for a person at 155 pounds.

13 Tap or click the Filter button at the top of the *Person at 155 pounds* column and tap or click *Clear Filter from "Person at 155 pounds".*

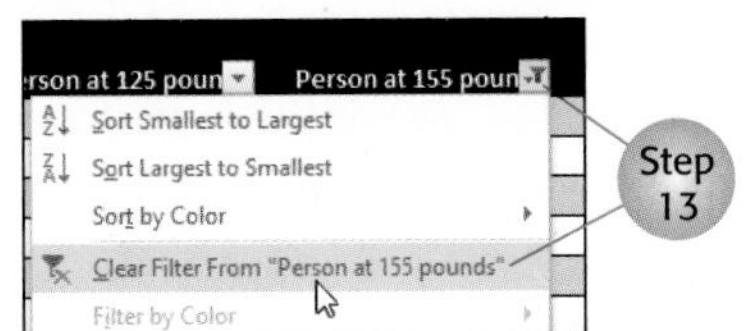

Clearing a filter redisplays the entire table.

14 Change the orientation to landscape and center the worksheet horizontally.

15 Save the revised workbook using the same name (**9.11-CalorieActivityTable-Your Name**) and close the workbook.

Format a Table
1. Select range.
2. Tap or click Quick Analysis button.
3. Tap or click TABLES.
4. Tap or click Table button.

Sort a Table
1. Tap or click Filter button at top of column by which to sort.
2. Tap or click *Sort A to Z* or *Sort Z to A*.

Filter a Table
1. Tap or click Filter button at top of column by which to filter.
2. Clear check boxes for items you want to hide OR tap or point to *Text Filters* or *Number Filters* and specify criterion.

A funnel icon appears in the Filter button in the column being used to filter a table, and the row numbers display in blue.

You can filter a table by one column and then filter again by another column to further drill down to the data you want to analyze.

New to Excel 2013 is the ability to add Filter Slicer panes to filter a table. A Slicer pane contains all of the unique values for a column within the table. Tap or click a value within the pane to filter the table. Use the Insert Slicer button in the Tools group of the TABLE TOOLS DESIGN tab and insert a check mark for each column heading for which a Slicer pane is needed.

Beyond Basics

Conditional Formatting

Another tool that is used to highlight or review cells is **conditional formatting**. Conditional formatting applies formatting options only to cells that meet a specified criterion. Select a range, tap or click the Quick Analysis button, and then tap or click the desired conditional formatting button in the FORMATTING tab. More conditional formatting options are available from the Conditional Formatting button in the Styles group of the HOME tab.

Concepts Review

Topic	Key Concepts	Key Terms
Using Absolute Addresses and Range Names in Formulas	By default, a cell address in a formula is a relative address, which means the column letter or row number will update as the formula is copied. A dollar symbol in front of a column letter or row number makes an address absolute and means the reference will not update when the formula is copied. A formula that has both relative and absolute addresses is referred to as a mixed address. A descriptive label can be assigned to a cell or range and used in a formula. A name is assigned to a cell by typing the label in the *Name* text box. A cell or range name is automatically an absolute address.	Relative addresses Absolute addresses Mixed addresses
Entering Formulas Using Statistical Functions	A formula that uses a function begins with the function name followed by the parameters for the formula (called the argument) within parentheses. The AVERAGE function returns the arithmetic mean from the range used in the formula. The MAX function returns the largest value from the range. The MIN function returns the smallest value from the range. The Insert Function dialog box accessed from the Insert Function button provides tools to find and enter a function and argument. The Count numbers option from the AutoSum drop-down list returns the number of cells with values in the range.	Argument
Entering, Formatting, and Calculating Dates	A valid date or time entered into a cell is stored as a numerical value and can be used in formulas. The TODAY function enters the current date into the cell and updates the date whenever the worksheet is opened or printed. Date and time cells can be formatted to a variety of month, day, and year combinations at the Format Cells dialog box with the *Date* category selected. The format in which Excel expects a date to be entered is dependent on the Region setting in the Control Panel. In the United States, the date is expected to be in the format m/d/y.	
Using the IF Function	The IF function performs a comparison of a cell with a value of another cell and performs one of two calculations depending on whether the comparison proves true or false. Use the Insert Function dialog box to assist with entering an IF statement's arguments. The *logical_test* argument is the statement you want Excel to evaluate to determine which calculation to perform. The *value_if_true* argument is the value or formula if the logical test proves true. The *value_if_false* argument is the value or formula if the logical test proves false.	

Topic	Key Concepts	Key Terms
Using the PMT Function	Financial functions can be used for a variety of financial calculations that involve saving or borrowing money. The PMT function calculates a regular loan payment from a specified interest rate, term, and amount borrowed. Make sure the interest rate and terms are in the same units as the payment you want calculated. For example, divide the interest rate by 12 and/or multiply the term times 12 to calculate a monthly payment from an annual rate or terms. In the PMT argument, *Rate* means the interest rate, *Nper* means the term, and *Pv* means the amount borrowed. The FV function calculates the future value of a regular series of payments that earn a constant interest rate.	
Creating and Modifying a Pie Chart	Charts are often used to portray a visual snapshot of data. A pie chart shows each data point as a pie slice. The size of each pie slice in the chart represents the value of the data point in proportion to the total of all of the values. Use the CHARTS tab in the *Quick Analysis* gallery to create a pie chart from a selected range. The Chart Elements button is used to add or modify a chart title, data labels, or legend.	Pie chart
Creating and Modifying a Column Chart	A column chart shows one bar for each data point extending upward from a horizontal axis with the height of the bar representing its value. The horizontal axis in a column chart is the category axis, also called the x-axis, and shows the labels for each bar. The vertical axis in a column chart is called the value axis, also known as the y- or z-axis, and is scaled to the values of the bars graphed. A column chart is used to show trends or comparisons over time. The Chart Styles button is used to choose a style for a column chart or change the color scheme. The *Axis Titles* option from the Chart Elements button is used to add titles to each axis in a column chart. The Recommended Charts feature is new to Excel 2013 and provides a set of customized charts recommended for the data you have selected.	Column chart Category axis Value axis Recommended Charts
Creating and Modifying a Line Chart	A line chart helps a reader identify trends, growth spurts, dips, or unusual points in a data series. Use the Move Chart button in the Location group of the CHART TOOLS DESIGN tab to move a chart from the worksheet into a chart sheet. A chart in a chart sheet is automatically scaled to fill a letter-sized page in landscape orientation. Change axis options in the Format Axis task pane or data label options in the Format Data Labels task pane.	Line chart Move Chart button

continued....

Topic	Key Concepts	Key Terms
Using Page Layout View, Adding a Header, and Changing Margins	In Page Layout view the worksheet is divided into pages with white space depicting the size of the margins and a ruler along the top and left edges. You can see page layout and print options in Page Layout view while viewing and editing the worksheet. Add a header in Page Layout view by tapping or clicking the dimmed text *Click to add header*. Use buttons in the HEADER & FOOTER TOOLS DESIGN tab to add options to a header or footer such as a picture, page numbering, date or time, or file or sheet names. Change to a preset set of margins from the Margins button in the PAGE LAYOUT tab, or choose *Custom Margins* to enter your own margin settings. Open the Page Setup dialog box with the Margins tab to center a worksheet horizontally and/or vertically.	Page Layout view
Creating and Modifying Sparklines and Inserting Comments	Miniature charts embedded into a cell are called Sparklines. Sparkline charts emphasize trends or variations in data on a smaller scale. Activate a cell and choose a Sparkline chart type from the INSERT tab. Once created, add or modify Sparkline options using buttons in the SPARKLINE TOOLS DESIGN tab. Comments appear in pop-up boxes when you point or click a cell with an attached comment. Excel displays a diagonal red triangle in a cell with a comment. Use the New Comment button in the REVIEW tab to add a comment.	Sparklines
Working with Tables	A block of data set up in list format can be formatted as a table for formatting, analyzing, sorting, or filtering purposes. A filter temporarily hides data that does not meet a criterion. Use a filter to review subsets of data without deleting rows. Use the Filter button at the top of a column to sort or filter a table. Conditional formatting applies formatting options to cells within a range that meet a criterion.	Filter Conditional formatting

Multiple Choice

1. This symbol in an address makes the reference absolute.
   a. #
   b. !
   c. :
   d. $
2. A range name automatically uses this type of referencing.
   a. Relative
   b. Absolute
   c. Mixed
   d. Auto
3. This statistical function returns the arithmetic mean from the range.
   a. MEDIAN
   b. COUNT
   c. AVERAGE
   d. MAX
4. This is the term for a function's parameters within parentheses.
   a. Arguments
   b. Criteria
   c. Range
   d. Logical test

5. This function enters the current date into the cell and updates the entry each time the worksheet is opened.
   a. =DATE()
   b. =TODAY()
   c. =TODAY(now)
   d. =NOW(today)
6. This setting in the Control Panel affects the format that Excel recognizes as valid for a date.
   a. Date and Time
   b. Region
   c. PC Settings
   d. System
7. The IF function is located in this category button in the Function Library group.
   a. Logical
   b. Statistical
   c. Financial
   d. Text
8. Enter the formula to evaluate a condition or comparison for an IF statement in this text box in the Function Arguments dialog box.
   a. Value_if_true
   b. Value_if_false
   c. Logical test
   d. Formula result
9. This is the financial function that calculates a regular payment for a loan.
   a. PYT
   b. PMT
   c. FV
   d. RATE
10. This is the financial function that calculates the value of an investment at the end of a series of regular payments that earned a constant interest rate.
    a. PMT
    b. FV
    c. PYT
    d. RATE
11. In this type of chart, each data point is sized to show its value as a proportion to the total.
    a. Column
    b. Line
    c. Sparklines
    d. Pie
12. This button is *not* one of the three buttons that appear next to a chart used for modifying the chart.
    a. Chart Elements
    b. Chart Styles
    c. Chart Filters
    d. Chart Analysis
13. This feature presents a series of customized charts that is best suited to portray the data in the selected range.
    a. Sparklines
    b. Recommended Charts
    c. Chart Series
    d. PivotCharts
14. In a column chart, each data point is a colored bar that extends upward from this axis.
    a. Value axis
    b. Category axis
    c. Z-axis
    d. Legend axis
15. Use this button to have a chart object placed in its own chart sheet.
    a. Move Chart
    b. Graph Chart
    c. Chart Sheet
    d. Chart Styles
16. Open this task pane to make changes to the way Excel has generated the axis labels in a chart.
    a. Format Labels
    b. Format Axis
    c. Format Chart
    d. Format Title
17. This view allows you to add a header to a worksheet by tapping or clicking in the Header pane.
    a. Print Preview
    b. Page Break Preview
    c. Normal view
    d. Page Layout
18. Use this option from the Margins drop-down list to open a dialog box in which you can center a worksheet horizontally or vertically on the printed page.
    a. Custom Margins
    b. Preset Margins
    c. Page Layout
    d. Wide
19. This type of chart is embedded within a single cell.
    a. Pie
    b. Line
    c. Column
    d. Sparklines
20. This indicator in a cell appears when a comment is attached to the cell.
    a. Diagonal green triangle
    b. Diagonal red triangle
    c. Green bullet
    d. Red bullet

21. This feature temporarily hides rows in a table that do not meet a specified criterion.
    a. Quick Analysis
    b. Table Styles
    c. Filter
    d. Sort

22. Tap or click this button to restore the full table after viewing a subset of data.
    a. Sort
    b. Quick Analysis
    c. Table Styles
    d. Filter

Crossword Puzzle

ACROSS

5 Function that uses an interest rate, term, and amount borrowed
6 Address with both relative and absolute reference
9 Function that finds the smallest number in the range
10 Format for a large block of data that can be sorted independently
11 Function that finds the largest number in the range
12 Type of chart often used to predict future values
13 View in which you can adjust print options and still edit worksheet
14 Function that can evaluate two alternatives
16 Miniature charts in cells
17 Format for a cell entry such as 12/20/2016

DOWN

1 Text that appears in a pop-up box when cell is activated
2 Preset margin option that changes top, bottom, left, and right margins to 1 inch
3 Name for horizontal axis in a column chart
4 Button that appears below selected range used to create a chart
7 Term for chart element added to a pie slice to show its value
8 Name for vertical axis in a column chart
15 Box where you type a label to assign to a cell

Matching

Match the term with the statement or definition.

_______	1. Default type of cell addressing	a. Argument
_______	2. Fixed address not updated during copy	b. Logical test
_______	3. Function parameters	c. Pie
_______	4. A date is stored as this	d. Header
_______	5. *F4>500* is an example of this	e. Table
_______	6. One of the arguments in PMT	f. Relative
_______	7. Chart that shows proportions to whole	g. Sparklines
_______	8. Chart for identifying a trend	h. Nper
_______	9. Print sheet name at top of each page	i. Absolute
_______	10. Miniature charts	j. Value
_______	11. Filter buttons appear at top of columns	k. Column

Project 1 Adding Statistical, Date, Financial, and Logical Functions to a Workbook

Individual

Deliverable: Worksheet with Auction Fee Financial Analysis and Mortgage Options

1. Open **AuctionFeesandMortgagePlanner**.
2. Use Save As to change the file name to **C9-Project1-AuctionFeesandMortgagePlanner-Your Name** in a new folder named *Ch9* within the ChapterProjectsWork folder on your USB flash drive.
3. In J2 enter a formula that will insert the current date and update the date each time the workbook is opened or printed.
4. Assign the following names to the cells indicated:
   C2 AuctionFee G2 PaymentFee
5. Complete the formulas required in the worksheet using the following information:
   a. In column B, calculate the payment due dates as 5 days following the auction end date.
   b. In column D, calculate the auction fees as the sale price times the auction fee percentage. Use the range name created in Step 4 in the formula.
   c. In column E, calculate the payment processing fees as the sale price times the payment fee percentage. Use the range name created in Step 4 in the formula.
   d. In column F, calculate the net auction earnings as the sale price minus the auction fee and payment processing fee.
   e. In column G, calculate the amount to transfer to the checking account as the value that resides in net auction earnings for those instances in which the net auction earnings are less than or equal to $20.00; otherwise, calculate the amount as 50 percent of the net auction earnings.
   f. In column H, calculate the amount to transfer to the investment account as 50 percent of the net auction earnings for those instances in which the net auction earnings are more than $20.00; otherwise, show zero in the cell.
   g. In column J, calculate the three sets of required statistics. Use the labels to help you determine the functions and arguments required.
   h. In row 27, calculate totals for columns C through H.
6. Format C2 and G2 to Percent Style, format the dates in columns A and B to the style *14-Mar*, and format all other values to Comma Style.
7. Make MortgageAnalysis the active worksheet and complete the formulas required in the worksheet using the following information:
   a. In B7 and D7, calculate the estimated monthly payments.
   b. In B9 and D9, calculate the total paid over the life of each mortgage.
8. For each worksheet, change page layout options as necessary to make sure the worksheet will fit on one page centered horizontally and with your name centered in a header, the file name at the left margin in a footer, and the sheet name at the right margin in a footer.
9. Save the revised workbook using the same name (**C9-Project1-AuctionFeesandMortgagePlanner-Your Name**).
10. Submit the project to your instructor in the manner she or he has requested.
11. Close the workbook.

Project 2 Creating and Modifying Charts

Individual

Deliverable: Worksheet with Charts Illustrating Vacation Destination Statistics

1. Open **VacDestinations**.
2. Use Save As to change the file name to **C9-Project2-VacDestinations-Your Name**, saving in the Ch9 folder within ChapterProjectsWork.
3. With the TopVacDestinations sheet active, create a pie chart at the bottom left of the worksheet area that graphs the Worldwide destinations and percentages. Create a second pie chart at the bottom right of the worksheet area that graphs the United States and Canada destinations and percentages. Add and/or modify chart elements you think are appropriate to make sure the charts are easy to read and understand.
4. With the NationalParks worksheet active, create a clustered column chart that graphs the national parks and visitors. Position the chart where you think the chart looks good and add and/or modify chart elements you think are appropriate to make sure the chart is easy to read and understand.
5. With the InternationalTravel worksheet active, select A3:D15 and create a line chart in a chart sheet named *InternationalTravelChart*. Add and/or modify chart elements you think are appropriate to make sure the chart is easy to read and understand.
6. For the three worksheets with charts, change page layout options as necessary to make sure the worksheet will fit on one page centered vertically and with your name centered in a header, the file name at the left margin in a footer, and the sheet name at the right margin in a footer. ***Hint: Add the header and footer in the InternationalTravelChart sheet using the Page Setup link in Print Preview.***
7. Save the revised workbook using the same name (**C9-Project2-VacDestinations-Your Name**).
8. Submit the project to your instructor in the manner she or he has requested.
9. Close the workbook.

Project 3 Adding Sparklines and Comments

Individual

Deliverable: Worksheet with Comments and Sparklines Illustrating School Newspaper Budget Values

1. Open **SchoolPaperBudget**.
2. Use Save As to change the file name to **C9-Project3-SchoolPaperBudget-Your Name**, saving in the Ch9 folder within ChapterProjectsWork.
3. Create line Sparklines in column K that graph the budget values for September through April. Show the high and low points. Add and/or modify any other Sparkline elements you think are appropriate.
4. Add the following comments to the cells indicated:
   E9 Christmas ads expected to increase 10% this year.
   I5 New ISP contract takes effect in April.
   I9 Consider end-of-year special pricing to raise ad revenue.
5. Display the worksheet in Print Preview and use the Page Setup link to open the Page Setup dialog box. Change the *Comments* option to *At end of sheet* in the Sheet tab.
6. Save the revised workbook using the same name (**C9-Project3-SchoolPaperBudget-Your Name**).
7. Submit the project to your instructor in the manner she or he has requested.
8. Close the workbook.

Project 4 Working with Tables

Individual

Deliverable: Worksheet with Model Home Pricing Table

1. Open **ModelHomes**.
2. Use Save As to change the file name to **C9-Project4-ModelHomes-Your Name**, saving in the Ch9 folder within ChapterProjectsWork.

3. Format A5:E20 as a table.
4. Change to a table style of your choosing.
5. Sort in ascending order by the *Description* column.
6. Add totals below each model home that sum the total cost of the upgrades.
7. In A23 enter the text **TOTAL MODEL HOME PRICE WITH UPGRADES**.
8. Create formulas in B23:E23 that show the total price of each model home with the base price and total upgrade costs.
9. Change the worksheet to landscape orientation, centered vertically, and with your name centered in a header and the file name centered in a footer.
10. Save the revised workbook using the same name (**C9-Project4-ModelHomes-Your Name**).
11. Submit the project to your instructor in the manner she or he has requested.
12. Close the workbook.

Project 5 Creating a Worksheet and Charts to Show Food Drive Results

Individual

Deliverable: Worksheet with Food Drive Results and Charts

1. Create a worksheet similar to the one shown in Figure 9.4 with the following additional information:
   a. The workbook theme is *Frame*.
   b. The charts are clustered bar charts using *Style 13*.
   c. Set the height for row 1 to *28.50* and row 2 to *21.00*. Set the width of column A to *16.50*.
   d. The font size for row 1 is 18 points and row 2 is 12 points.
   e. Use your best judgment for any other format options such as shading.
2. Save the worksheet in the Ch9 folder within the ChapterProjectsWork folder as **C9-Project5-FoodDrive-Your Name**.

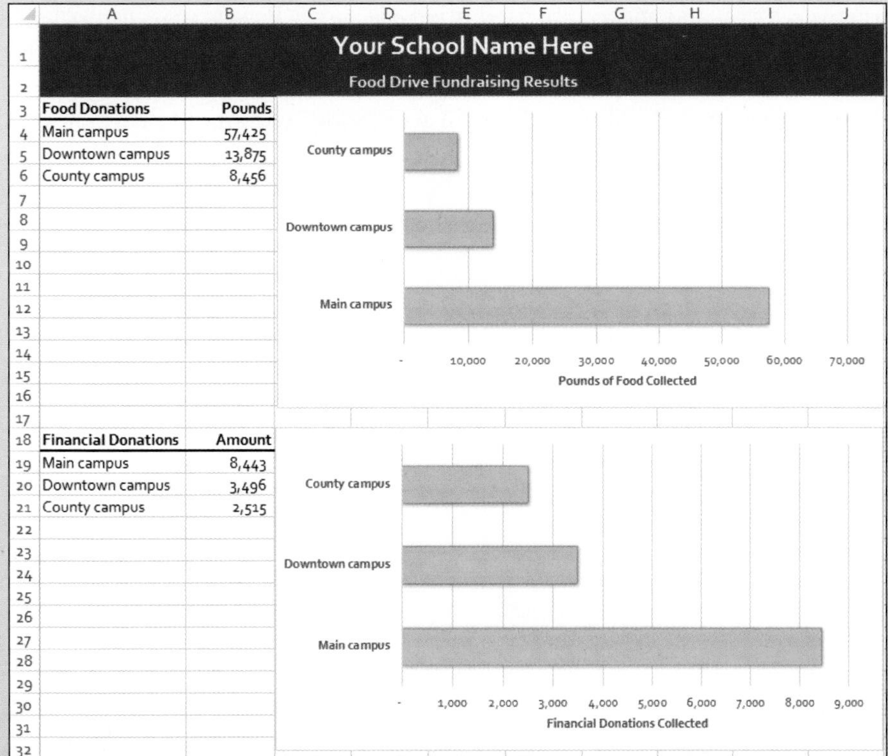

Figure 9.4 Project 5 Food Drive Worksheet and Charts

3. Change the top margin to 1.5 inches. Make sure the worksheet will fit on one page in portrait orientation with your name centered in a header and the file name centered in a footer.
4. Save the workbook again using the same name (**C9-Project4-FoodDrive-Your Name**).
5. Submit the project to your instructor in the manner she or he has requested.
6. Close the workbook.

Project 6 Internet Research and Composing a New Workbook

Individual or Pairs

Deliverable: Worksheet with Membership Statistical Data and Line Chart

1. Listen to the audio file named ***Project6_Instructions***. The file is located in the Ch9 folder in the Student_Data_Files folder.
2. Complete the research and compose the worksheet and chart as instructed.
3. Save the workbook in the Ch9 folder within ChapterProjectsWork as **C9-Project6-Instagram-Your Name**.
4. Submit the project to your instructor in the manner she or he has requested.
5. Close the document.

Project 7 Sending Project Work to OneNote Notebook

Individual

Deliverable: New Page in Shared OneNote notebook

1. Start OneNote and open the MyProjects notebook created in Chapter 4, Project 4.
2. Make Excel the active section and add a new page titled *Chapter 9 Projects*.
3. Switch to Excel. For each project that you completed, open the workbook, send the project to OneNote 2013 selecting the Chapter 9 Projects page in the Excel section in the MyProjects notebook, then close the workbook. Make sure to include all worksheets in workbooks with more than one sheet tab.
4. Close your MyProjects notebook in OneNote and close OneNote.
5. Close Excel.
6. Submit the project to your instructor in the manner she or he has requested.

Chapter 10

Creating, Editing, and Formatting a Presentation Using PowerPoint

After successfully completing this chapter, you will be able to:

- Create a new presentation based on a theme
- Insert slides and add content
- Change the design theme and variants to the theme
- Insert a table on a slide
- Format slides using font and paragraph options
- Select, resize, align, and move slide placeholders
- Use Slide Sorter view
- Duplicate, move, and delete slides
- Modify the slide master
- Add notes and comments
- Run a presentation in Slide Show view and Presenter view
- Prepare slides for audience handouts or speaker notes

Presentations occur in a variety of meetings, seminars, classrooms, or other events for a variety of purposes. Some presentations are informational, while others are designed to deliver news or persuade you to buy a product or service. Some people use presentations at events such as weddings, anniversaries, or family reunions to entertain an audience. Often, a collection of slides that includes text and multimedia is displayed on a large screen to support a speaker's presentation. Other types of presentations are used to provide information to an individual at a self-running kiosk. You may have used a presentation as a study guide to prepare for an exam.

Microsoft PowerPoint is the **presentation application** in the Microsoft Office suite. The program is widely used to create a set of slides that incorporates text and multimedia. In this chapter you will learn how to create, edit, and format a presentation. You will create a presentation with a variety of text-based slide layouts; edit content and placeholders; move, duplicate, and delete slides; format slides using a variety of techniques; add notes and comments; and preview the presentation as a slide show. Lastly, you will preview options for audience and speaker handouts.

Note: If you are using a tablet, consider using a USB or wireless keyboard because you will be typing text in several slides for new presentations in this chapter.

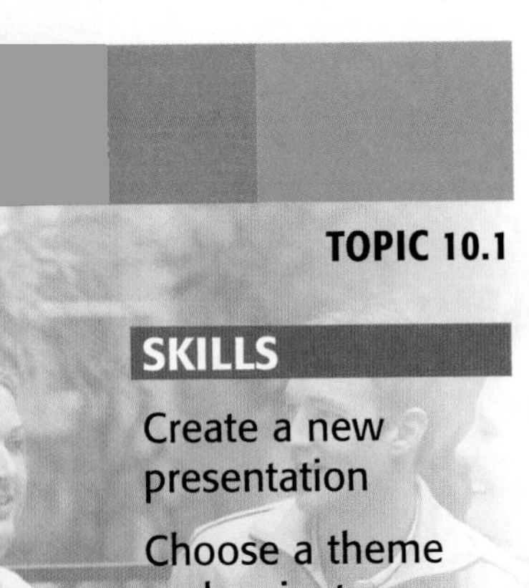

TOPIC 10.1

SKILLS

- Create a new presentation
- Choose a theme and variant
- Insert slides
- Edit text on slides

App Tip

Double-tap or double-click a theme to start a new presentation using the theme's default style and color scheme.

Creating a New Presentation and Inserting Slides

A new presentation can be created at the PowerPoint Start screen by choosing a template, a theme and variant on a theme, or by starting with a blank presentation. The first slide in a presentation is a **title slide** with a text **placeholder** for a title and a subtitle. A placeholder is a rectangular container on a slide that can hold text or other content. Each placeholder on a slide can be manipulated independently.

PowerPoint starts a new presentation with a title slide displayed in Normal view. In Normal view, the current slide displays in widescreen format in the **slide pane**. Numbered slide thumbnails display in the **Slide Thumbnail pane** at the left of the current slide. A Notes pane at the bottom and a Comments pane at the right can be opened as needed.

1. Start PowerPoint 2013.
2. At the PowerPoint Start screen, tap or click the *Ion* theme.

PowerPoint 2013 starts with a gallery of newly designed themes. Tap or click to preview a theme along with the theme's variants. **Variants** are a collection of different style and color schemes included in the theme family.

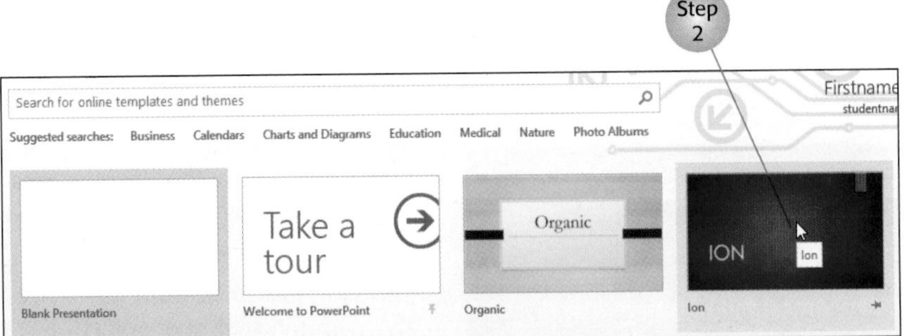

3. Tap or click the last variant (orange color scheme) and then tap or click the right-pointing arrow below the preview slide next to *More Images*.

When previewing variants, browse through the *More Images* slides to view the color scheme with a variety of content. This allows you to get a better perspective of the theme's or variant's style and colors before making your selection.

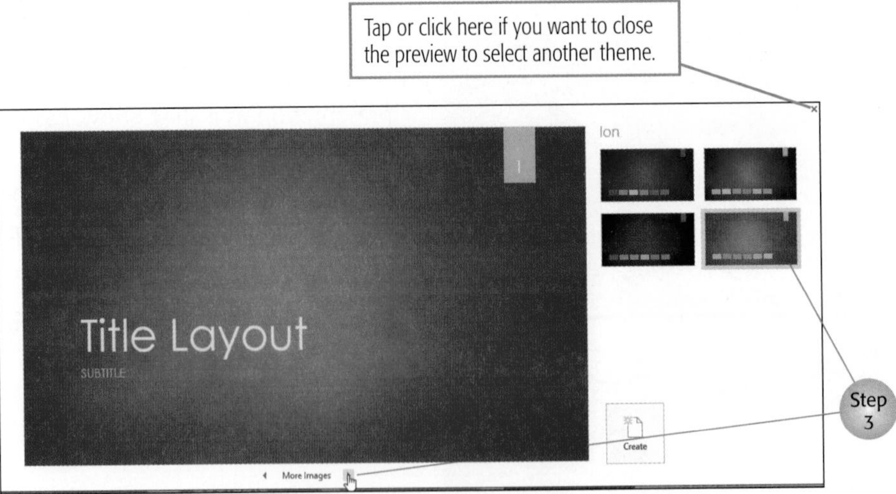

4. Tap or click the second variant (blue color scheme) and then tap or click the right-pointing arrow below the preview slide to view the blue color scheme with a Title and Content layout depicting a chart.

5 Tap or click the right-pointing arrow below the preview slide two more times to view other types of content with the blue color scheme.

6 With the Photo Layout in the preview, tap or click the Create button.

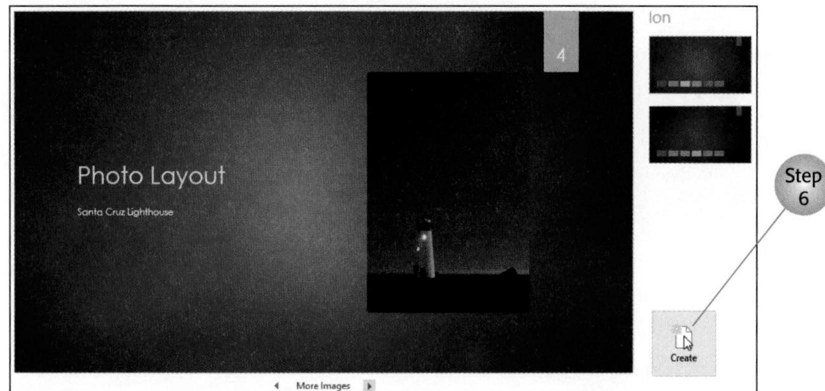

7 Compare your screen with the one shown in Figure 10.1.

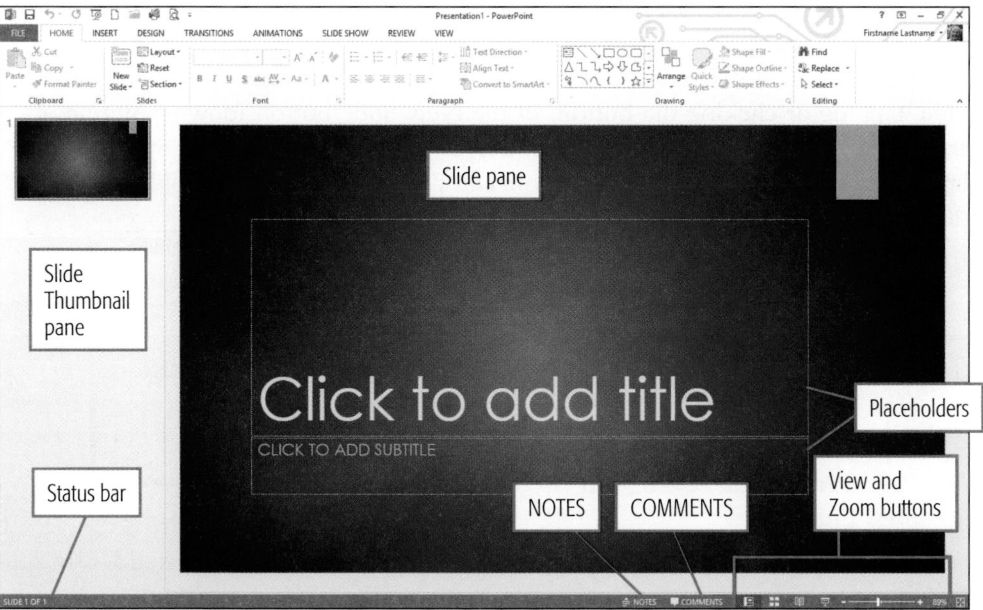

Figure 10.1 A new PowerPoint presentation with Ion theme and color variant in the default Normal view. See Table 10.1 for a description of screen elements.

Start a New Presentation
1. Start PowerPoint 2013.
2. Tap or click theme.
3. Tap or click variant.
4. Tap or click Create button.

Insert a Slide
Tap or click New Slide button in Slides group.

OR

1. Tap or click down-pointing arrow on New Slide button.
2. Tap or click required slide layout.

Edit Text
1. Activate slide.
2. Select text or tap or click in placeholder.
3. Type new text or change text as required.

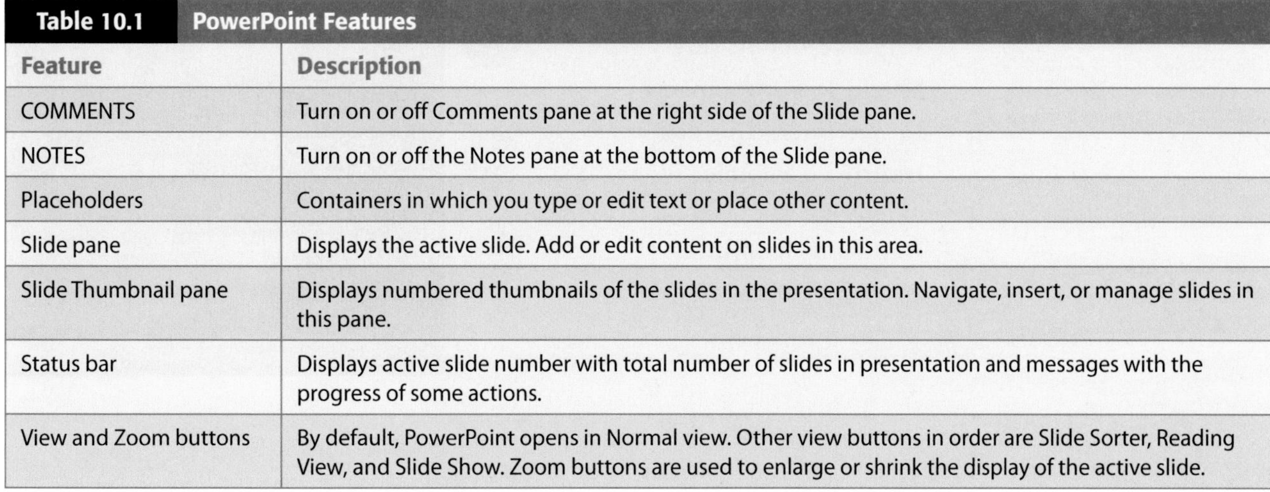

Table 10.1 PowerPoint Features

Feature	Description
COMMENTS	Turn on or off Comments pane at the right side of the Slide pane.
NOTES	Turn on or off the Notes pane at the bottom of the Slide pane.
Placeholders	Containers in which you type or edit text or place other content.
Slide pane	Displays the active slide. Add or edit content on slides in this area.
Slide Thumbnail pane	Displays numbered thumbnails of the slides in the presentation. Navigate, insert, or manage slides in this pane.
Status bar	Displays active slide number with total number of slides in presentation and messages with the progress of some actions.
View and Zoom buttons	By default, PowerPoint opens in Normal view. Other view buttons in order are Slide Sorter, Reading View, and Slide Show. Zoom buttons are used to enlarge or shrink the display of the active slide.

In PowerPoint 2013, slide size is *Widescreen (16:9)* by default. If necessary, change to *Standard (4:3)* using the Slide Size button in the Customize group of the DESIGN tab.

8 Tap or click *Click to add title* and type **Car Maintenance**.

9 Tap or click *CLICK TO ADD SUBTITLE* and type **Tips for all seasons**.

The subtitle text displays in all capital letters regardless of how you type the text because the Ion theme uses the All Caps font effect.

10 Tap or click in an unused area of the slide to close the placeholder.

Inserting New Slides

Change the layout for a slide after a slide has been inserted using the Layout button in the Slides group.

The **New Slide button** in the Slides group of the HOME tab is used to insert a new slide after the active slide. The button has two parts. Tapping or clicking the top part of the button adds a new slide with the Title and Content layout, which is the layout used most frequently. The content placeholder in this layout provides options to add text or a table, chart, SmartArt graphic, or picture or video to the slide. Tapping or clicking the bottom of the New Slide button (down-pointing arrow) provides a drop-down list of slide layouts and other new slide options. **Slide layouts** determine the number, position, and type of content placeholders for a slide.

11 Tap or click the top part of the New Slide button in the Slides group of the HOME tab.

12 Tap or click *Click to add title* and type **Why maintain a car?**.

13 Tap or click *Click to add text*, type **Preserve vehicle value**, and tap or press Enter.

Typing text in the content placeholder automatically creates a bulleted list. In the Ion theme, the bullet character is a green, right-pointing arrow.

14 Type the remaining bulleted list items, tapping or pressing Enter after each item except the last.

Prolong vehicle life
Improve driver safety
Spend less for repairs
Lower operating costs
Improved vehicle appearance
Reduced likelihood of breakdowns

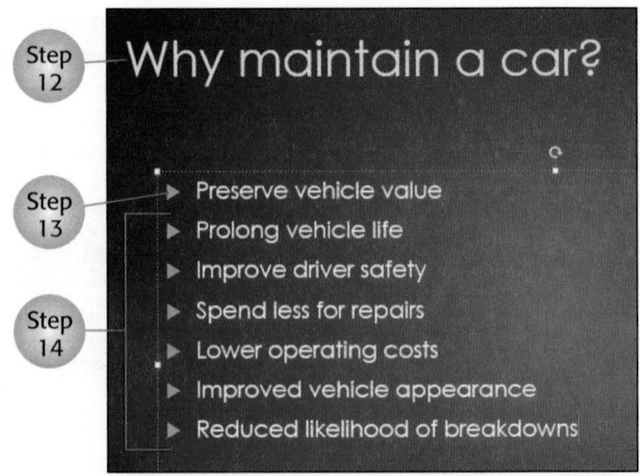

15 Tap or click the top part of the New Slide button in the Slides group.

16 Type the text in the third slide as shown in the image below.

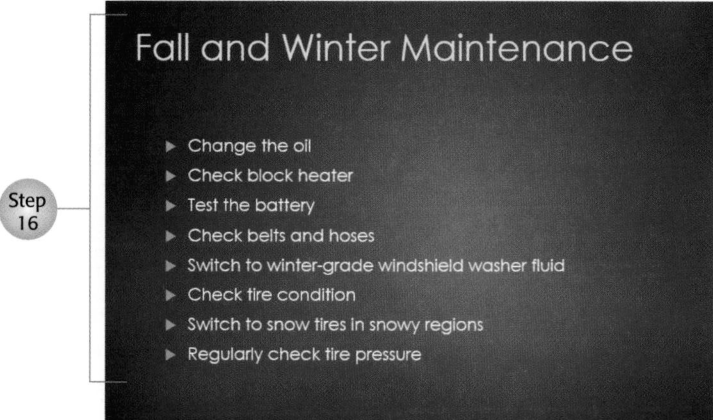

Tap or press Ctrl + Enter to move to the next placeholder on a slide or create a new slide when pressed in the last placeholder.

Editing Text on Slides

Activate the slide you want to edit by tapping or clicking the slide in the Slide Thumbnail pane. Select the text you want to change or delete, or tap or click in the placeholder to place an insertion point at the location where you want to edit text, and then type new text, change text, or delete text as needed.

17 Tap or click to select Slide 1 in the Slide Thumbnail pane.

18 Select ALL SEASONS in the subtitle text placeholder and type **car owners** so that the subtitle text now reads TIPS FOR CAR OWNERS.

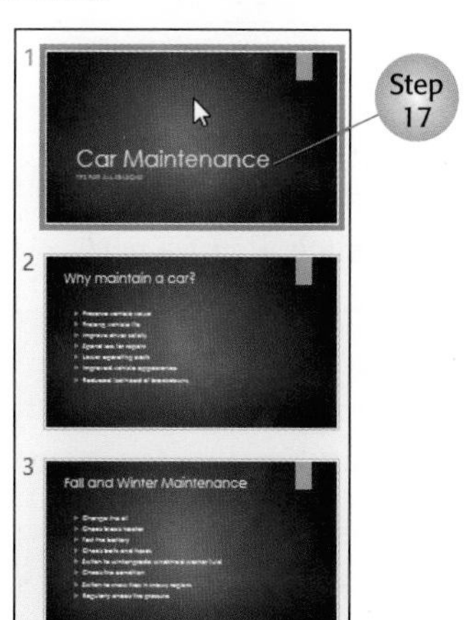

Always carefully spell check and proofread each slide in your presentation. Use the Spelling button in the Proofing group of the REVIEW tab as a starting point.

19 Select Slide 2 in the Slide Thumbnail pane.

20 Tap or click at the beginning of the text in the third bulleted list item, delete *Improve*, and type **Sustain**.

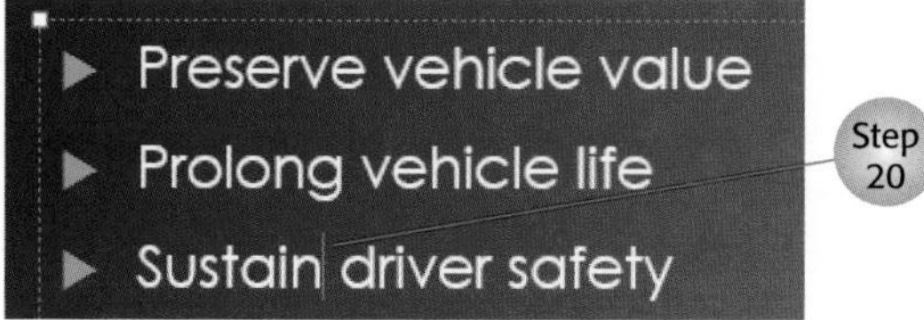

21 Tap or click to place an insertion point within the title placeholder and edit the title so that *m* in *maintain* and *c* in *car* are capital letters. The title should now read *Why Maintain a Car?*

22 Tap or click in an unused area of the slide to deactivate the placeholder.

23 Save the presentation as **10.1-CarMaintenance-Your Name** in a new folder named *Ch10* in the CompletedTopicsByChapter folder on your USB flash drive. Leave the presentation open for the next topic.

TOPIC 10.2

SKILLS

- Change theme
- Change variant
- Insert a table on a slide
- Modify table layout

Changing the Theme and Inserting and Modifying a Table

The presentation's theme and/or variant can be changed after a presentation has been created. To do this, tap or click the DESIGN tab and browse the themes and theme families in the *Themes* and *Variants* galleries.

1. With the **10.1-CarMaintenance-Your Name** presentation open, tap or click Slide 1 in the Slide Thumbnail pane.
2. Tap or click the DESIGN tab.
3. Tap or click the *Facet* theme in the *Themes* gallery (third option).

If you are using a mouse you can roll the mouse over the various theme options to view the active slide with a live preview of the theme.

4. Tap or click the More button at the bottom right of the *Variants* gallery.

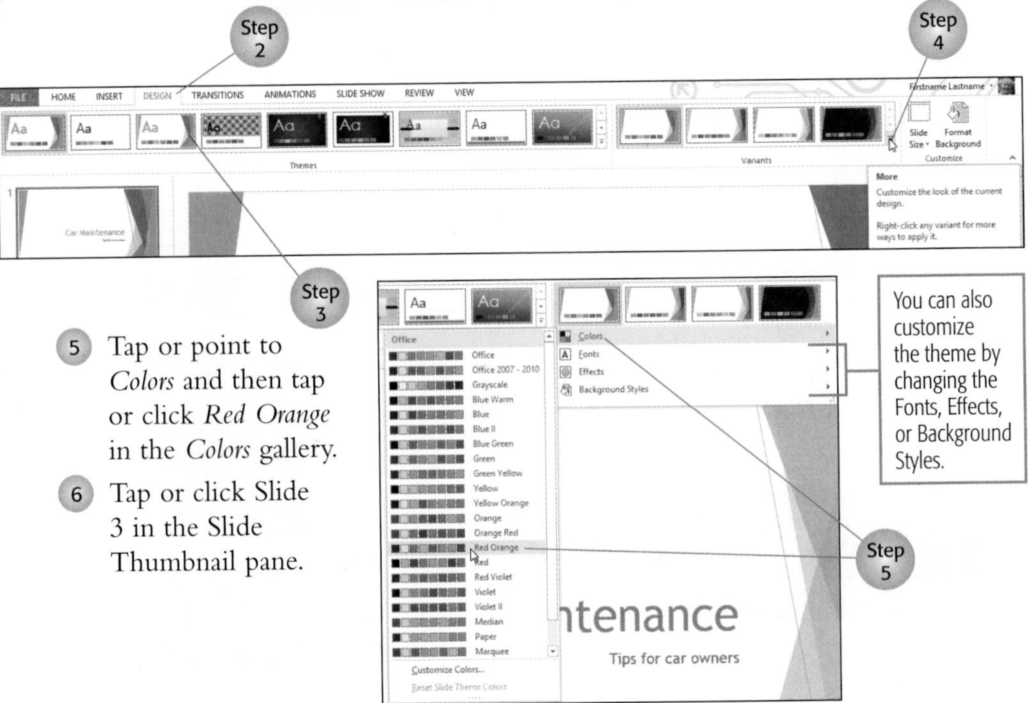

5. Tap or point to *Colors* and then tap or click *Red Orange* in the *Colors* gallery.
6. Tap or click Slide 3 in the Slide Thumbnail pane.

Inserting a Table on a Slide

PowerPoint includes a Table feature for organizing text on a slide in columns and rows similar to the Table feature in Word. To insert a table on a slide, tap or click the Insert Table button in the Content Placeholder.

7. Tap or click the HOME tab and then tap or click the top part of the New Slide button to insert a new slide with the Title and Content layout.
8. Tap or click *Click to add title* and type **Typical Annual Maintenance Costs.**
9. Tap or click the Insert Table button in the content placeholder.
10. Select *5* in the *Number of columns* text box and type 2.

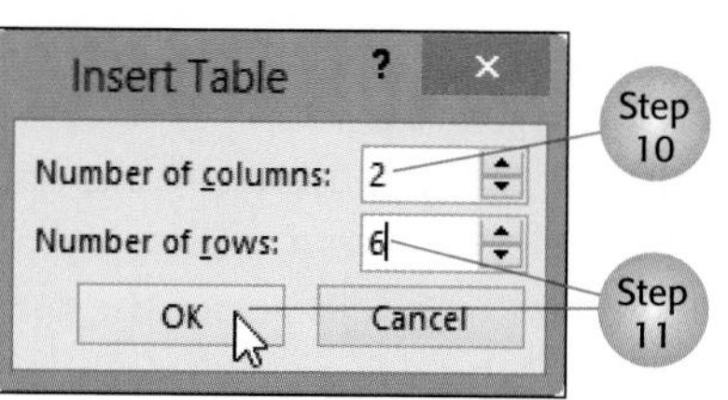

11 Select *2* in the *Number of rows* text box, type 6, and then tap or click OK.

PowerPoint inserts a table in the slide with the colors in the theme family.

12 With the insertion point positioned in the first cell in the table, type **Type of Car** and then tap or press Tab or tap or click in the second cell.

13 Type **Cost**.

14 Type the remaining entries in the table as follows:

Small size	**$600**
Medium size	**$675**
Large family sedan	**$750**
Minivan	**$775**
SUV	**$825**

Change Theme
1. Tap or click DESIGN tab.
2. Tap or click option in *Themes* gallery.
3. If desired, tap or click variant option.

Insert a Table on a Slide
1. Insert new slide.
2. Tap or click Insert Table button in content placeholder.
3. Enter number of columns.
4. Enter number of rows.
5. Tap or click OK.

Modifying a Table

The TABLE TOOLS DESIGN and LAYOUT tabs provide options for modifying and customizing a table with the same tools you learned about in Word. Use the sizing handles to enlarge or shrink the table size. Slide or drag the border of a table to move the table's position on the slide.

15 Slide or drag the right middle sizing handle left until the right border of the table ends below the first *e* in *Maintenance* in the title text.

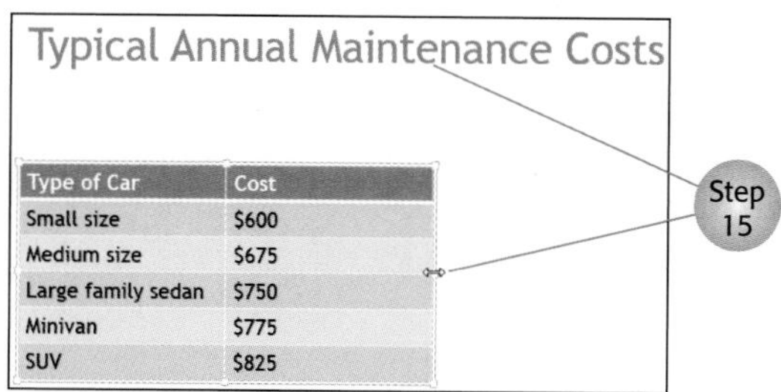

16 Tap or click in any cell in the second column.

17 Tap or click the TABLE TOOLS LAYOUT tab, tap or click the Select button in the Table group, and then tap or click *Select Column* at the drop-down list.

18 Tap or click the Center button in the Alignment group.

19 Tap or click in any cell in the first column, select the current entry in the *Width* text box in the Cell Size group of the TABLE TOOLS LAYOUT tab, type **3.5**, and then tap or press Enter.

oops!

Table appears too small with first column wrapping text? You probably changed the width using the *Width* text box in the Table Size group instead of the Cell Size group. Use Undo and try Step 19 again.

20 Slide or drag the top border of the table to move the table until it is positioned at the approximate location shown in the image at right.

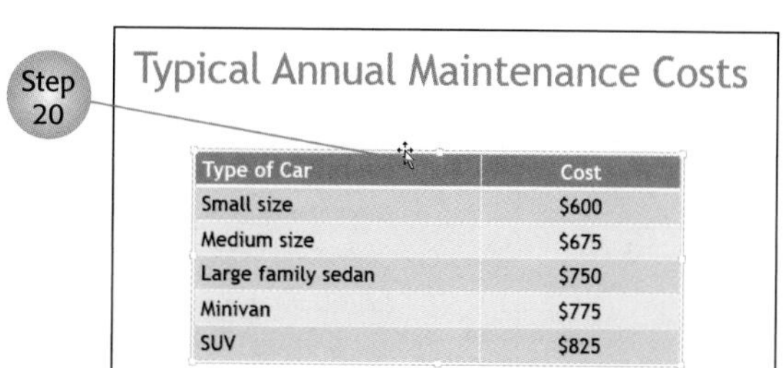

21 Save the revised presentation using the same name (**10.1-CarMaintenance-Your Name**). Leave the presentation open for the next topic.

App Tip

A bulleted list can have up to eight levels.

Formatting Text with Font and Paragraph Options

Font and paragraph formatting options in PowerPoint are the same as those in Word and Excel. Select text within a placeholder and apply formatting changes to the selected text only, or select the placeholder and apply a formatting option to the entire placeholder.

1. With the **10.1-CarMaintenance-Your Name** presentation open, tap or click Slide 3 in the Slide Thumbnail pane.
2. Insert a new slide with the Title and Content layout.

New slides are inserted after the active slide. The new slide should be positioned between the Fall and Winter Maintenance slide and the Typical Annual Maintenance Costs slide.

3. Type **Spring and Summer Maintenance** as the slide title.
4. Type **Thoroughly clean vehicle** as the first bulleted list item in the content placeholder and then tap or press Enter.
5. With the insertion point positioned at the beginning of the second bulleted list item, tap or click the **Increase List Level button** in the Paragraph group of the HOME tab.

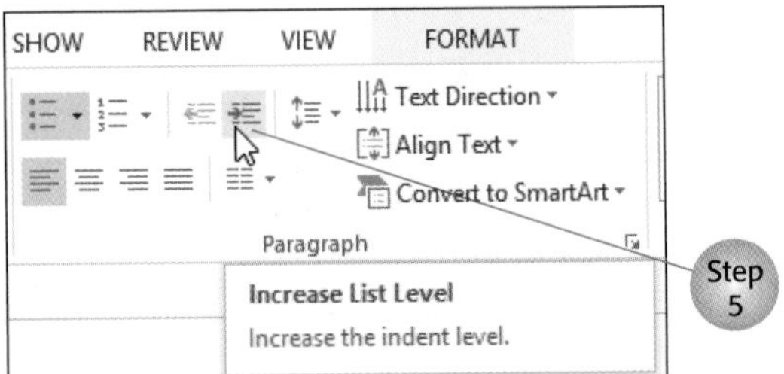

6. Type **Prevents rust by removing sand and salt accumulated from winter driving** and then tap or press Enter.
7. Tap or click the **Decrease List Level button** in the Paragraph group to move the bullet for the new item back to the previous level in the slide, type **Check cooling system**, and then tap or press Enter.

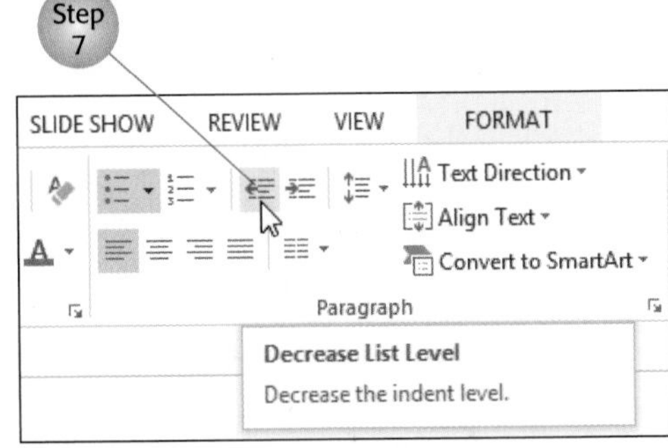

8. Type the remaining text on the slide as shown in the image below using the Increase List Level and Decrease List Level buttons as needed.

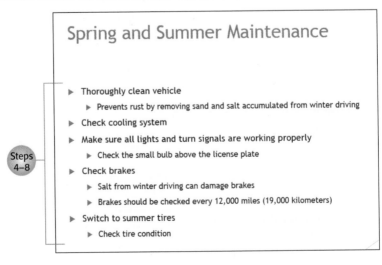

App Tip

You can also press Tab to increase the list level and Shift + Tab to decrease the list level.

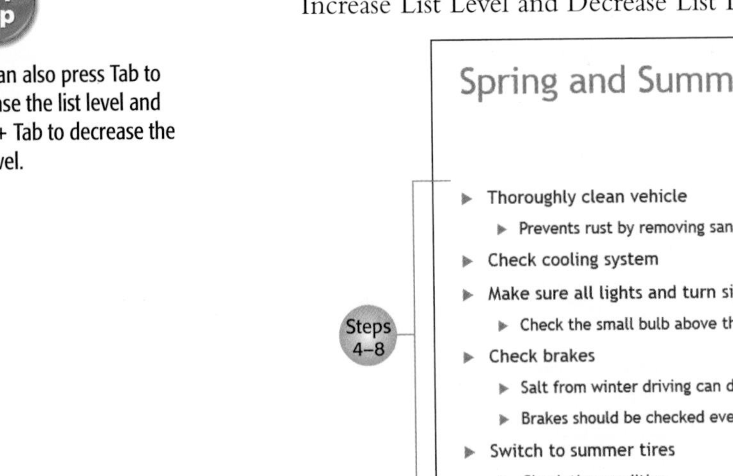

9 Select *12,000* in the content placeholder, tap or click the Font Color button arrow in the Mini toolbar or in the Font group of the HOME tab, and then tap or click *Red, Accent 1* (fifth option in first row of *Theme Colors* section).

10 Tap or click the Bold button in the Font group.

11 Tap or click in the title text to activate the title placeholder.

12 Tap or click the Center button in the Paragraph group.

13 Tap or click the Align Left button in the Paragraph group to return the title placeholder to the default paragraph alignment.

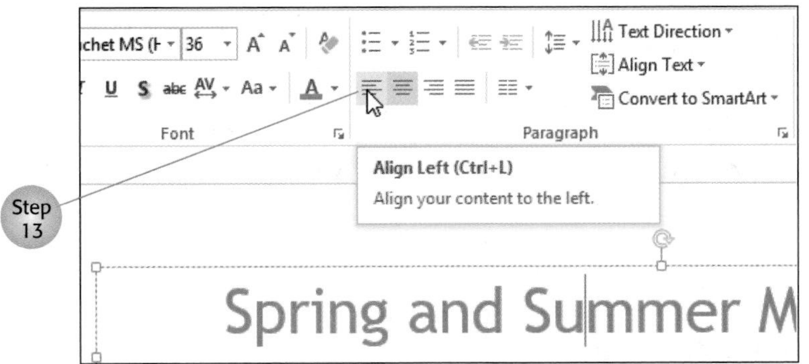

14 Save the revised presentation using the same name (**10.1-CarMaintenance-Your Name**). Leave the presentation open for the next topic.

Change Font Options

1. Select text.
2. Tap or click font option in Mini toolbar or Font group of HOME tab.

Change Paragraph Options

1. Activate placeholder or select text.
2. Tap or click paragraph option in Mini toolbar or Paragraph group of HOME tab.

The default paragraph spacing is single line spacing with 10 points of space before and 0 points of space after each paragraph. Use the Line Spacing button or open the Paragraph dialog box to make changes to these settings.

Changing the Bullet Symbol

The bullet symbols vary with each theme; however, you can change the bullet character to another symbol from the Bullets button arrow for an individual list item or a selected list. Tap or click *Bullets and Numbering* at the Bullets drop-down list to open the Bullets and Numbering dialog box. Choose the Picture button to select a bullet image, or the Customize button to select a bullet character from the Symbol dialog box. You can also change the size and color of the bullet character in the dialog box.

TOPIC 10.4

SKILLS

Insert a slide with comparison layout

Change bulleted list to numbered list

Resize a placeholder

Align placeholders

Move a placeholder

Selecting, Resizing, Aligning, and Moving Placeholders

The active placeholder displays with a border and selection handles, which are used to resize or move the placeholder. Paragraph or font options apply to the text in which the insertion point is positioned or to selected text. To apply a font or paragraph change to all of the text in a placeholder, tap or click the placeholder's border to remove the insertion point or deselect text.

1. With the **10.1-CarMaintenance-Your Name** presentation open, tap or click Slide 5 in the Slide Thumbnail pane.
2. Tap or click the down-pointing arrow on the New Slide button and tap or click *Comparison* at the drop-down list.

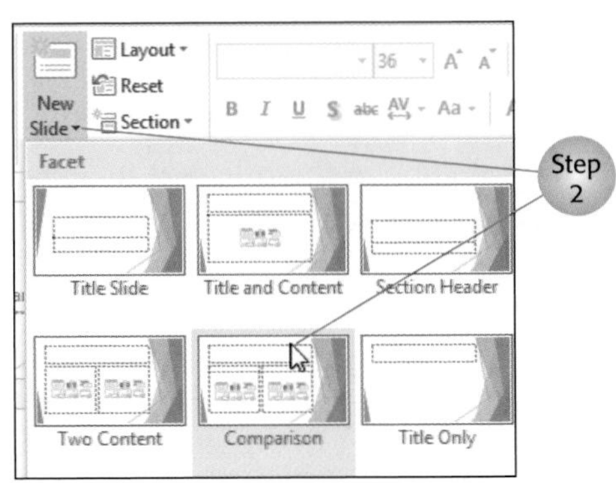

3. Type **Top 5 Cars Rated by Maintenance Costs** as the slide title.
4. Type the title and bulleted list text in the left and right content placeholders as shown in the image below.

Least Expensive	Most Expensive
▶ Honda Fit	▶ Nissan GT-R
▶ Toyota Corolla	▶ Chevrolet Corvette
▶ Toyota Yaris	▶ Mercedes-Benz SL-Class
▶ Chevrolet Aveo	▶ BMW Z4
▶ Ford Focus	▶ Chevrolet Camaro

Step 4

5. Tap or click anywhere within the bulleted list below the heading *Least Expensive* to activate the placeholder.
6. Tap or click anywhere along the border of the active placeholder to remove the insertion point from within the bulleted list text, selecting the entire placeholder.

The next action will affect all of the text within the placeholder. You can change font options or paragraph options for the entire bulleted list.

7. Tap or click the Numbering button in the Paragraph group to change the bulleted list to a numbered list. (Do *not* tap or click the down-pointing arrow on the button.)

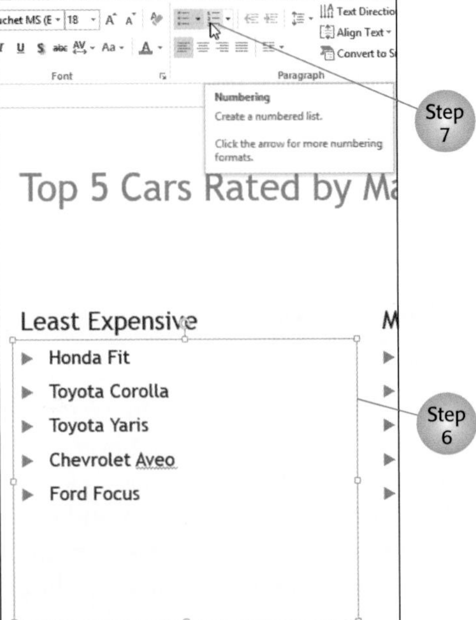

oops!

Only one bullet changed to a number? This occurs if you have an insertion point within the placeholder; only the item in the list at which the insertion point was positioned is changed. Go back to Step 6 and try again.

8 Tap or click anywhere in the bulleted list below *Most Expensive*, tap or click along the border of the placeholder to select the entire placeholder text, and then tap or click the Numbering button.

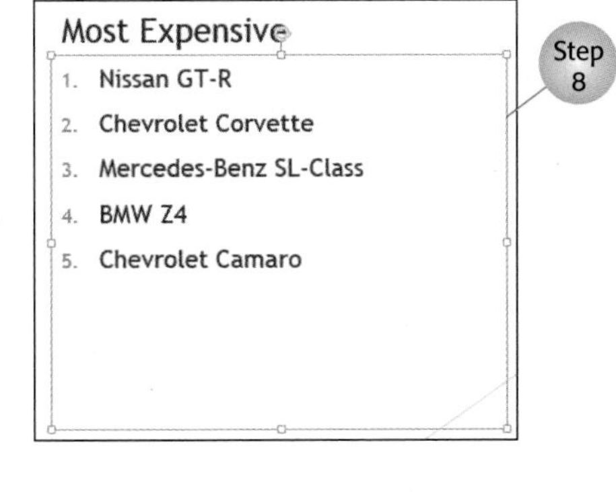

9 Select the numbered list placeholder below the title *Least Expensive*.

10 Slide or drag the right middle sizing handle left until the right border of the placeholder is at the approximate location shown in the image below.

11 Select the *Least Expensive* title placeholder and slide or drag the right middle sizing handle left to resize the placeholder until the smart guide appears, indicating the title placeholder is the same width as the content placeholder below it.

Smart guides, also called alignment guides, appear automatically to help you align, space, or size placeholders or objects evenly.

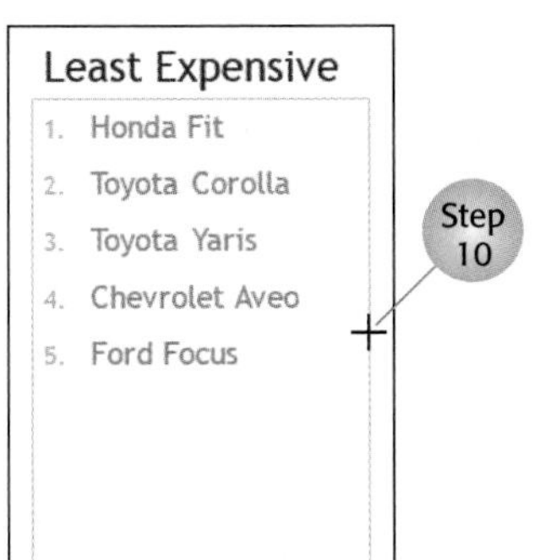

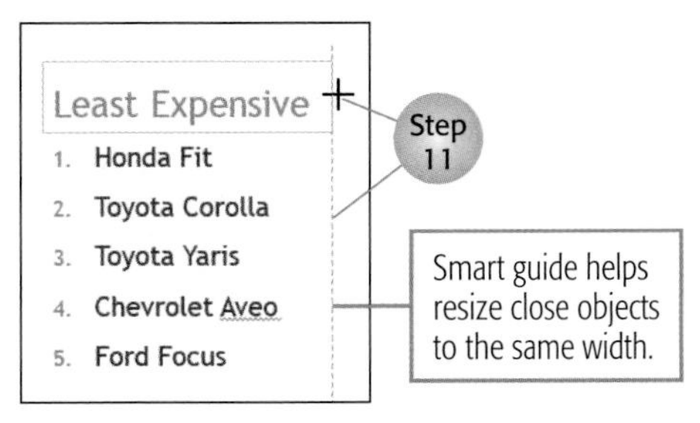

12 With the *Least Expensive* placeholder still selected, slide or drag the border of the placeholder right to move the placeholder until the smart guides appear as shown in the image at right.

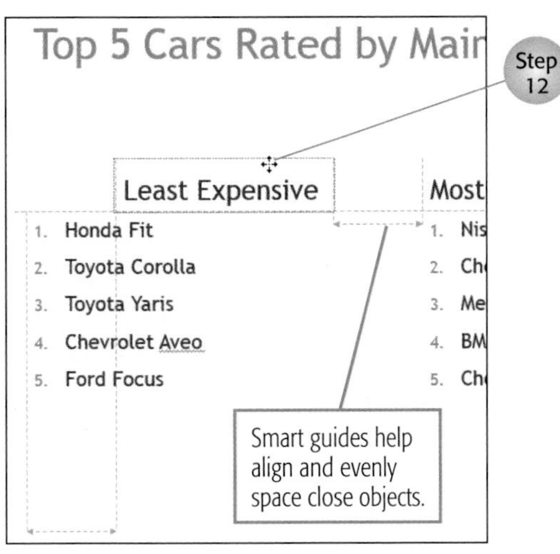

13 Select the numbered list placeholder below *Least Expensive* and slide or drag right until left, right, top, and bottom smart guides appear, indicating the placeholder is aligned evenly with the placeholders above and right.

14 Save the revised presentation using the same name (**10.1-CarMaintenance-Your Name**). Leave the presentation open for the next topic.

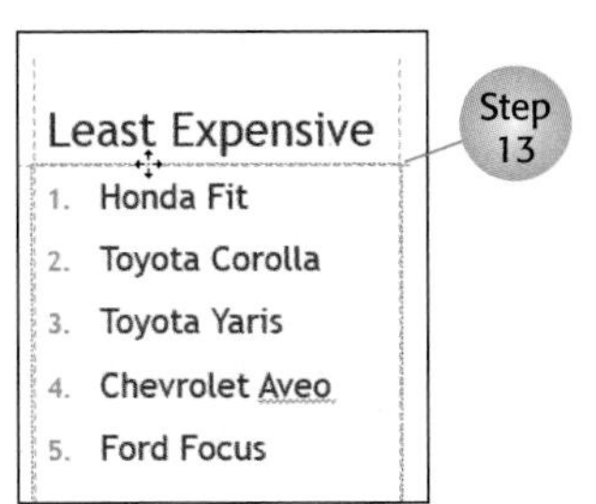

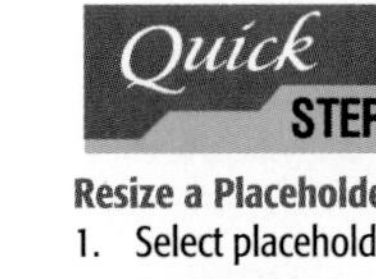

Resize a Placeholder
1. Select placeholder.
2. Slide or drag sizing handle as needed.

Move a Placeholder
1. Select placeholder.
2. Slide or drag placeholder border as needed.

The AutoFit feature , which is on by default, automatically scales the font size and adjusts spacing between points to fit text within a placeholder.

oops!

No right middle sizing handle? On a smaller-screened tablet, the right middle sizing handle may not appear. Slide the top right or bottom right sizing handle instead. Remove your finger when you see two smart guides—one at the bottom and one at the right.

Using Slide Sorter View and Moving, Duplicating, and Deleting Slides

TOPIC 10.5
SKILLS
Use Slide Sorter view
Move a slide
Duplicate a slide
Delete a slide

Slide Sorter view displays all of the slides in a presentation as slide thumbnails. In this view, you can easily rearrange the order of the slides by sliding or dragging a slide thumbnail to a new location. Select a slide in Slide Sorter view or Normal view to duplicate or delete the slide.

1. With the **10.1-CarMaintenance-Your Name** presentation open, tap or click the VIEW tab and tap or click the Slide Sorter button in the Presentation Views group.

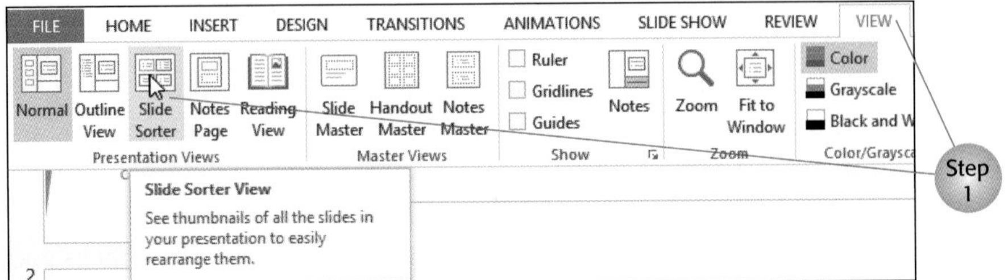

2. Tap or click Slide 5 to select the slide.
3. Slide or drag Slide 5 to the top row, placing it to the right of Slide 2.

As you slide or drag to move a slide in Slide Sorter view, the existing slides rearrange around the slide.

oops!

Using Touch? Slide right first and then upward to move the slide to the first row.

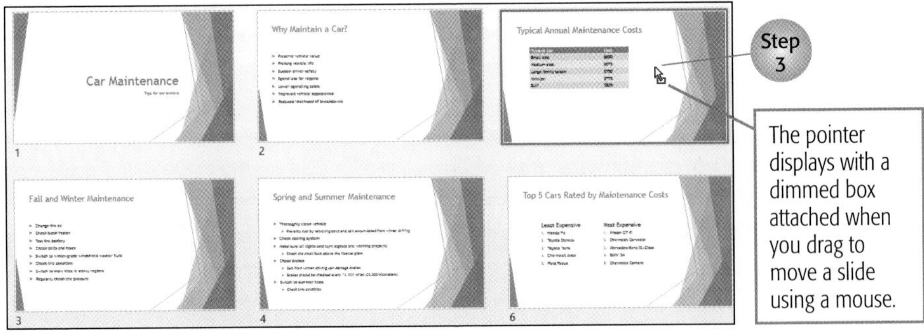

Duplicating a Slide

When you need to create a new slide with the same layout as an existing slide and with the placeholders sized, aligned, and positioned the same, make a duplicate copy of the existing slide. Once the slide is duplicated, all you have to do is change the text inside the placeholders. A duplicated slide is inserted in the presentation immediately after the slide selected to duplicate.

4. Tap or click to select Slide 6.
5. Press and hold to display the Mini toolbar, or right-click to display the shortcut menu.
6. Tap or click the Duplicate button on the touch Mini toolbar or the *Duplicate Slide* option at the shortcut menu.
7. Double-tap or double-click Slide 7 to return to Normal view.

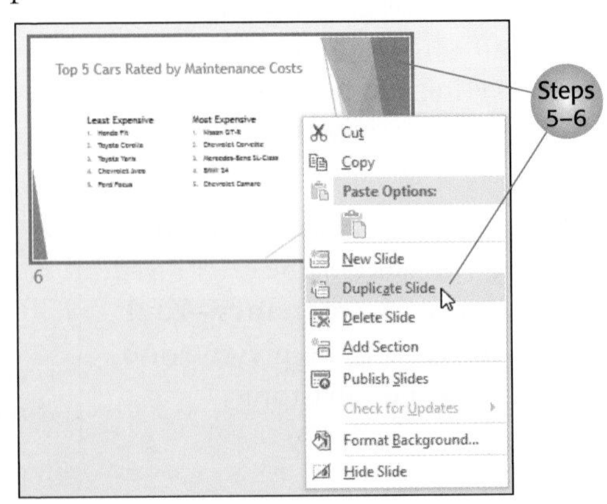

Deleting a Slide

Slides can be deleted in Slide Sorter view or Normal view by selecting the slide and displaying the Mini toolbar on touch devices or the shortcut menu on devices operated with a mouse.

8. Press and hold or right-click Slide 7 in the Slide Thumbnail pane to display the Mini toolbar or shortcut menu.
9. Tap or click the Delete button on the Mini toolbar or *Delete Slide* at the shortcut menu.
10. Save the revised presentation using the same name (**10.1-CarMaintenance-Your Name**). Leave the presentation open for the next topic.

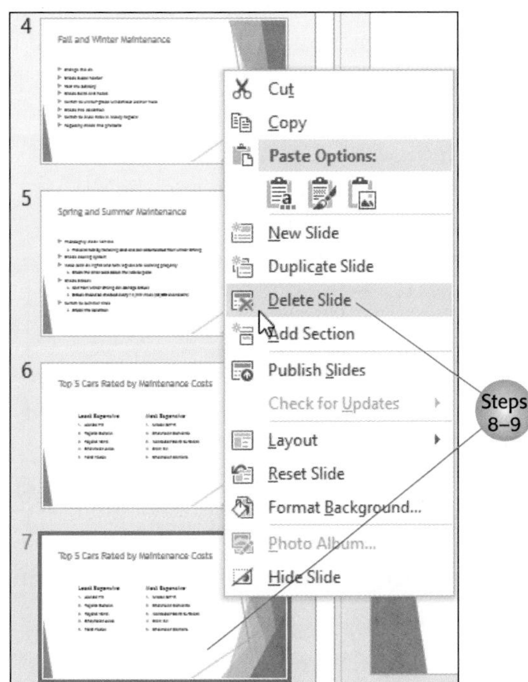

Select more than one slide to delete by holding down the Ctrl key while you click other slides, then right-click any selected slide and choose *Delete Slide*.

Slide Sorter View
Tap or click Slide Sorter button in Status bar.
OR
1. Tap or click VIEW tab.
2. Tap or click Slide Sorter button.

Move a Slide
Slide or drag slide in Slide Sorter view to required location.

Duplicate a Slide
1. Select slide.
2. Display Mini toolbar or shortcut menu.
3. Tap Duplicate button or click *Duplicate Slide*.

Delete a Slide
1. Select slide.
2. Display Mini toolbar or shortcut menu.
3. Tap Delete button or click *Delete Slide*.

ALTERNATIVE method

Consider using these alternative methods for moving and duplicating slides:

Move slide	In Normal view, slide or drag slide up or down in Slide Thumbnail pane.
Duplicate slide	Select slide, tap or click down-pointing arrow on New Slide button, and then tap or click *Duplicate Selected Slides*.

Hiding a Slide

You may have a slide in a presentation that you want to hide during a particular slide show because the slide does not apply to the current audience or provides more detail than you have time to explain. In Slide Sorter view or Normal view, press and hold or right-click the slide to be hidden and choose the Hide button on the Mini toolbar (touch devices) or *Hide Slide* (shortcut menu).

TOPIC 10.6

SKILLS

Display slide master

Format placeholders on slide master

App Tip

A slide master is also available for formatting handouts and notes.

Modifying the Slide Master

Each presentation that you create includes a slide master. A **slide master** determines the default formatting and paragraph options for placeholders when you insert new slides. If you want to make a change to a font or paragraph option for the entire presentation, making the change in the slide master will apply the change automatically to all slides in the presentation. For example, if you want a different font color for all of the slide titles, change the color on the slide master.

1. With the **10.1-CarMaintenance-Your Name** presentation open and the VIEW tab active, tap or click the Slide Master button in the Master Views group.

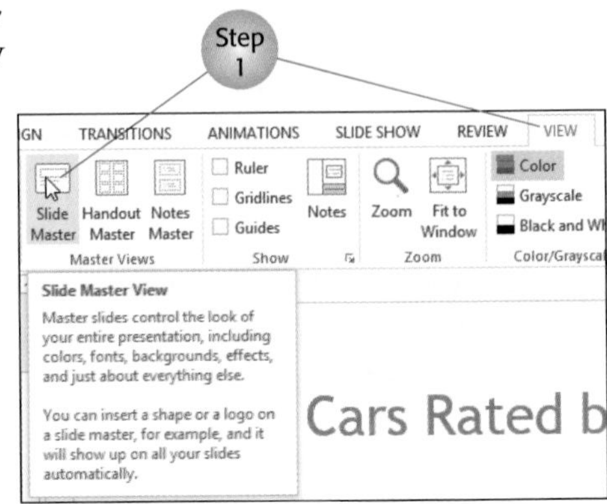

In **Slide Master view**, a slide master at the top of the hierarchy in the Slide Thumbnail pane controls the font, colors, paragraph options, and background for the entire presentation. Below the slide master is a variety of layouts for the presentation. Changes made to the slide master at the top of the hierarchy affect all of the slide layouts below it except the title slide.

2. Slide or scroll up the Slide Thumbnail pane to the first slide.
3. Tap or click to select Slide 1.
4. Tap or click the border of the title text placeholder on the slide master to select the placeholder.

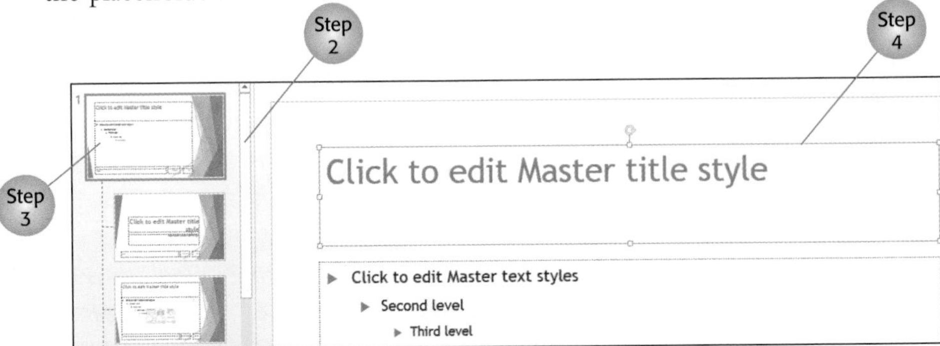

App Tip

Formatting changes made on individual slides override the slide master. Presentations should have a consistent look; therefore, limit individual slide formatting changes to only when necessary such as to indicate a change in topic or speaker.

5. Tap or click the HOME tab, tap or click the Font Color button arrow, and then tap or click *Dark Red, Accent 6* (last color in first row of *Theme Colors* section).

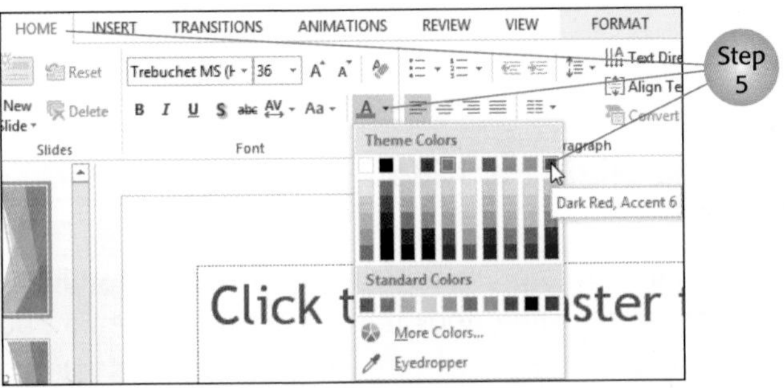

6. Tap or click the border of the content placeholder to select the placeholder and then tap or click the Bullets button arrow in the Paragraph group.

7 Tap or click *Bullets and Numbering* at the drop-down list.

8 Tap or click the Color button in the Bullets and Numbering dialog box and then tap or click *Dark Red, Accent 6*.

9 Tap or click the *Hollow Square Bullets* option (first option in second row).

10 Tap or click OK.

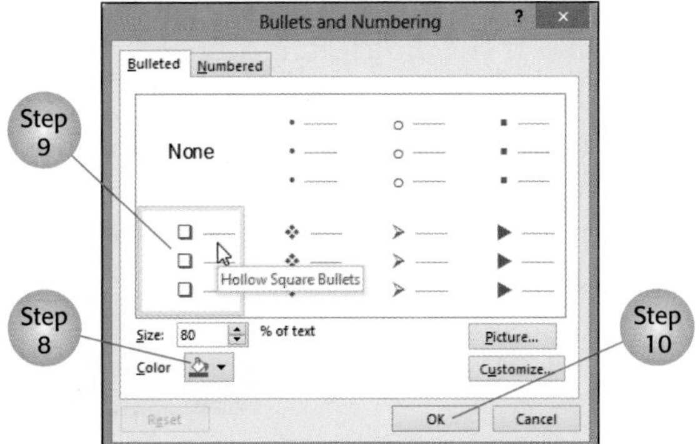

Slide Master View

1. Tap or click VIEW tab.
2. Tap or click Slide Master button.

11 Tap or click the SLIDE MASTER tab.

12 Tap or click the Close Master View button in the Close group.

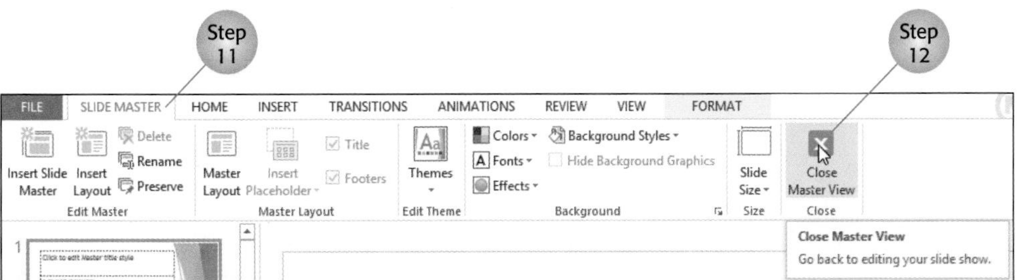

13 Tap or click the Previous Slide or Next Slide buttons at the bottom of the vertical scroll bar or tap or click each slide in the Slide Thumbnail pane to scroll through and view each slide in the presentation.

Notice that the font color for the title text and the bullet character are changed on each slide *after* the title slide. A title slide has its own slide master and is the first layout below slide 1 in the slide master hierarchy.

14 Save the revised presentation using the same name (**10.1-CarMaintenance-Your Name**). Leave the presentation open for the next topic.

Page Up and Page Down also display the previous or next slide in the presentation.

Adding Text to the Bottom of Each Slide

Add text to the bottom of each slide in a footer placeholder by selecting the *Footer* check box and typing footer text at the Header and Footer dialog box with the Slides tab active (INSERT tab, Header & Footer button). Use the Slide Master to format the footer text to a different font, font size, or color as required. For example, many speakers use the Footer placeholder to add a company name or presentation title at the bottom of each slide.

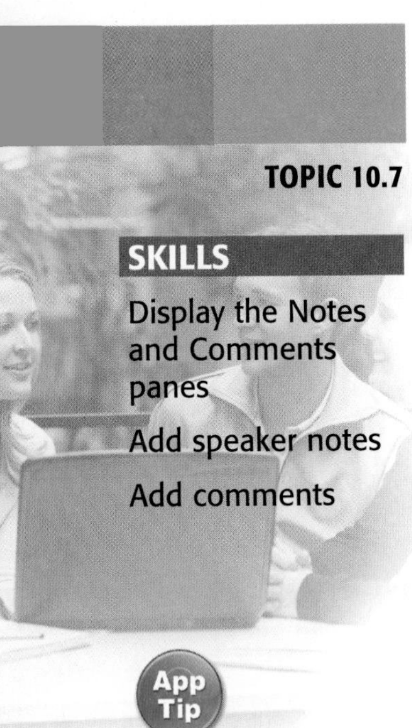

TOPIC 10.7

SKILLS

Display the Notes and Comments panes

Add speaker notes

Add comments

App Tip

Text in the Notes pane is visible to the presenter but not the audience during a slide show.

Adding Notes and Comments

Notes, generally referred to as speaker notes, are text typed in the **Notes pane** below the Slide pane in Normal view. Use notes to type reminders for the presenter, or use this pane to add more details about the slide content for the person giving the presentation.

Comments can be added to slides and will appear in the **Comments pane** at the right of the Slide pane. If you are creating a presentation with a group of people, use comments to provide feedback or pose questions to others in the group.

1. With the **10.1-CarMaintenance-Your Name** presentation open, display Slide 1 in the Slide pane.
2. Tap or click the NOTES button in the Status bar to turn on the display of the Notes pane at the bottom of the Slide pane. Skip this step if the Notes pane is already visible.

Step 2

NOTES COMMENTS

Notes

3. Tap or click *Click to add notes* in the Notes pane and then type **Begin this slide with the statistic that approximately 5.2% of motor vehicle accidents are caused by vehicle neglect.**.

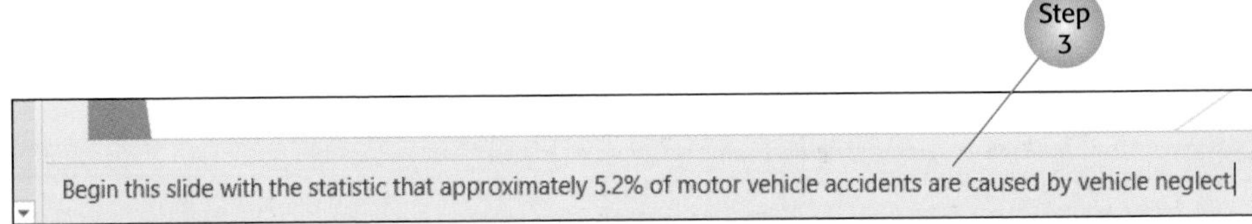

4. Display Slide 3 in the Slide pane.
5. Slide or drag the top border of the Notes pane upward to increase the height of the pane by approximately one-half inch.

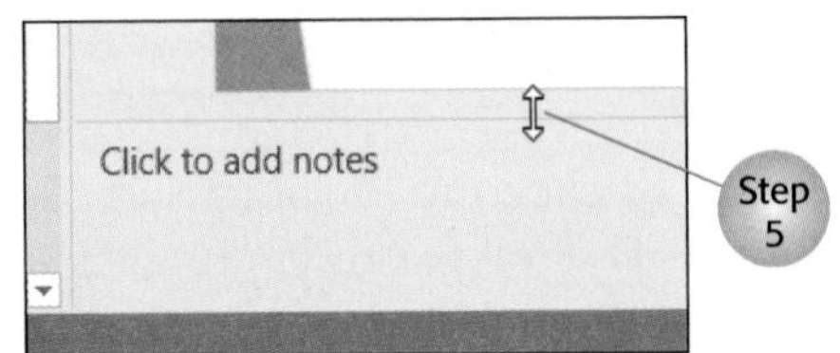

6. Tap or click in the Notes pane and type **Mention that these costs are estimated for a driving distance of 12,000 miles (19,000 kilometers) per year.**.
7. Tap or press Enter twice and type **Ask the audience if anyone wants to share the total amount paid each year to maintain his or her vehicle.**.

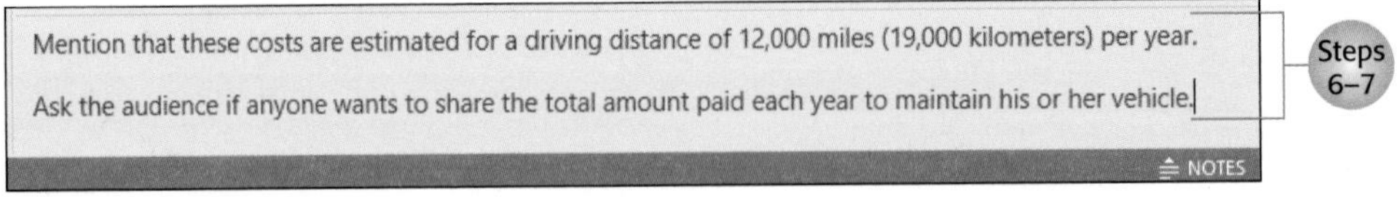

8. Tap or click the NOTES button to turn off the Notes pane.
9. Tap or click the COMMENTS button in the Status bar to turn on the Comments pane.
10. Tap or click the New button near the top of the Comments pane.

PowerPoint opens a comment box in the Comments pane with your account name associated with the comment.

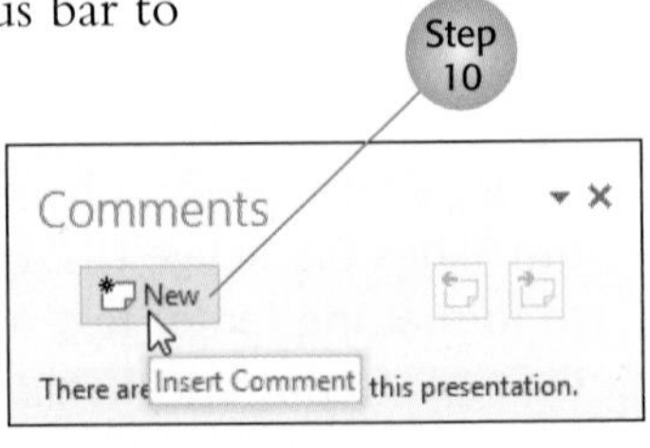

11 Type **Consider adding the source of these statistics to the slide.**.

12 Tap or click Slide 4 in the Slide Thumbnail pane, tap or click the New button in the Comments pane, and then type **Add more information for any of these points?**.

13 Tap or click in the Comments pane outside the Comment box to close the comment.

14 Close the Comments pane.

A comment balloon appears in the top left corner of a slide for which a comment has been added.

Previous and Next buttons used to navigate to all of the comments in a presentation

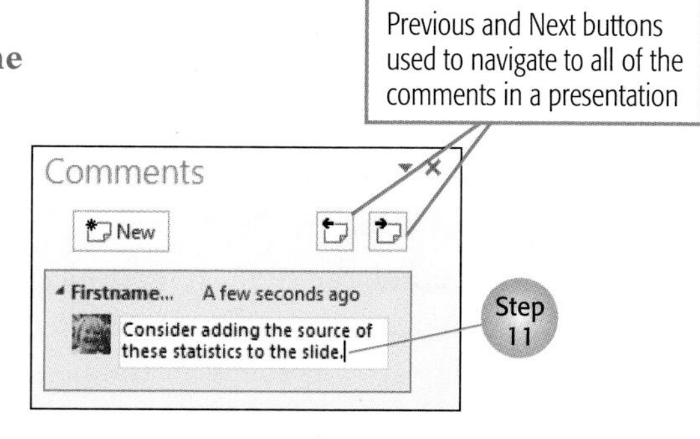

Step 11

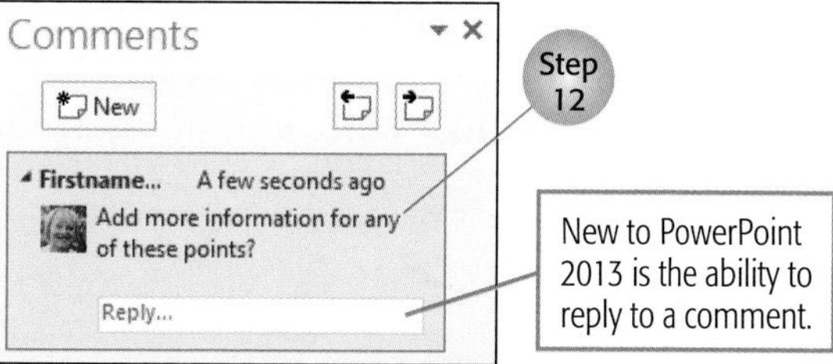

Step 12

New to PowerPoint 2013 is the ability to reply to a comment.

Comment balloon displays on slides with comments. Tap or click the balloon to open the Comments pane and view the comments and replies.

Fall and Winter Maintenance

15 Save the revised presentation using the same name (**10.1-CarMaintenance-Your Name**). Leave the presentation open for the next topic.

Add Notes

1. Activate required slide.
2. Tap or click NOTES button.
3. Type note text in Notes pane.

Add Comments

1. Activate required slide.
2. Tap or click COMMENTS button.
3. Tap or click New button.
4. Type comment text.

A prompt appears in the Status bar when you open a presentation that has comments, informing you of their existence in the file.

ALTERNATIVE method

A comment can also be added to selected text on a slide. The comment balloon displays at the end of the selected text. To do this, select the text and reveal the Comments pane, or tap or click the New Comment button in the REVIEW tab.

Deleting or Hiding Comments

Tapping a comment or pointing to a comment with the mouse in the Comments pane displays a Delete icon (black X) at the top right of the comment, which you can tap or click to delete the comment. Hide comment balloons with the Show Comments button in the Comments group of the REVIEW tab by removing the check mark next to *Show Markup* at the drop-down list.

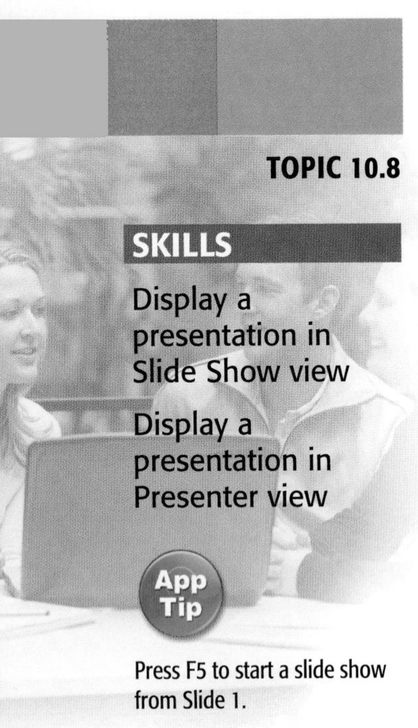

Press F5 to start a slide show from Slide 1.

Displaying a Slide Show

Display the presentation in **Slide Show view** to preview the slides as they will appear to an audience. In Slide Show view, each slide fills the screen with the ribbon and other PowerPoint elements removed; however, tools to navigate and annotate slides are available.

In **Presenter view**, the slide show displays full screen on one monitor (the monitor the audience will see), and in Presenter view on a second monitor. Presenter view displays a preview of the next slide, notes from the Notes pane, a timer, and a slide show toolbar along with other options.

1. With the **10.1-CarMaintenance-Your Name** presentation open, tap or click the SLIDE SHOW tab and then tap or click the **From Beginning button** in the Start Slide Show group.

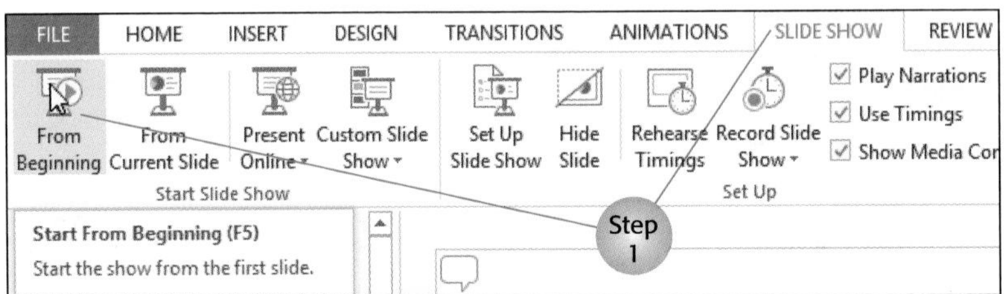

2. Tap or click the right-pointing arrow that appears in the Slide Show toolbar near the bottom left corner of the screen to move to Slide 2 (see Figure 10.2).

If you are using a mouse or keyboard, you can also click anywhere on a slide or press the Page Down key to move to the next slide.

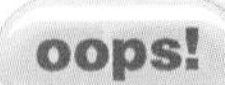

Using Touch? Tap the slide to display the Slide Show toolbar.

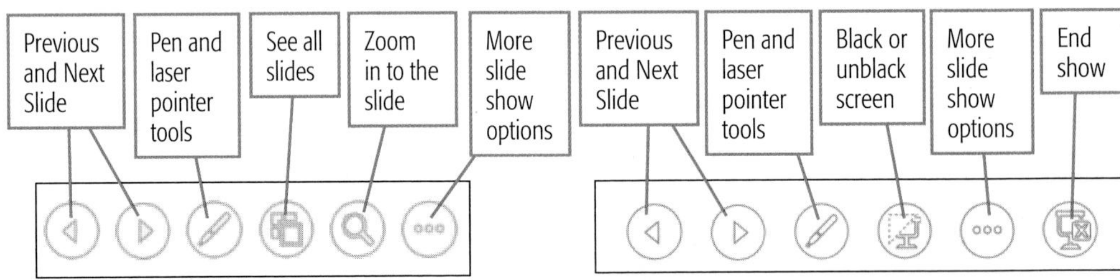

Figure 10.2 The Slide Show toolbar for a mouse-enabled device (left) and for a touch-enabled device (right). See Table 10.2 for a description of each button.

Table 10.2 Slide Show Toolbar Buttons

Button	Description
Previous Slide and Next Slide	Display the previous or next slide in the presentation.
Pen and laser pointer tools	Point, write on the slides, or highlight text during a presentation.
See all slides	View all slides in the presentation similarly to Slide Sorter view. Use this to jump to a slide out of sequence during a presentation.
Zoom in to the slide	Use this button to slide or click on a portion of a slide that you want to enlarge to temporarily fill the screen for a closer look. Tap or click the button again or right-click to restore the slide.
More slide show options	Displays a pop-up menu with more options. On mouse-enabled devices, use this button to end the show or black/unblack the screen during a presentation.
Black or Unblack screen	On a touch-enabled device, this button blacks the screen or unblacks the screen.
End show	On a touch-enabled device, use this button to end the show.

3 Continue tapping or clicking the Next Slide arrow to navigate through the remaining slides in the presentation until the black screen appears.

After the last slide is viewed, a black screen is shown with the message *End of slide show, click to exit*. Many presenters leave the screen black when their presentation is ended until the audience has left because tapping or clicking to exit displays the presentation in Normal view on the screen.

4 At the black screen that appears, tap the screen and then tap the End show button (see Figure 10.2 on the previous page), or click anywhere on the screen to return to Normal view.

5 Display Slide 1 in the Slide pane and then tap or click the **Slide Show button** in the Status bar.

The Slide Show button in the Status bar starts the slide show at the active slide.

6 Tap or click the More slide show options button (button with three dots) in the Slide Show toolbar and then tap or click *Show Presenter View* at the pop-up list.

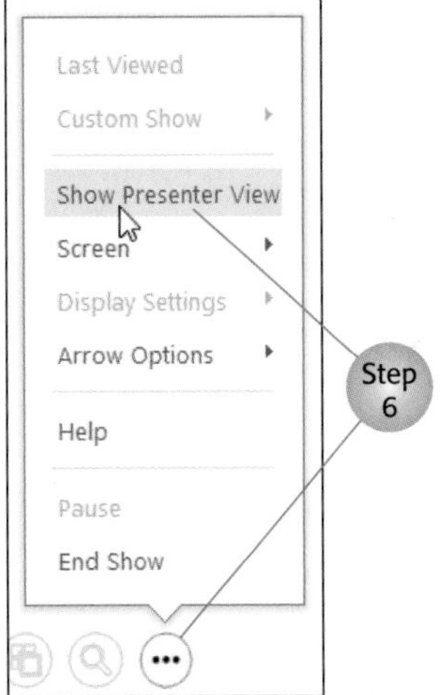

You can use Presenter view on a system with only one monitor to preview or rehearse a presentation. At a presentation venue, PowerPoint automatically detects the computer setup and chooses the correct monitor on which to show Presenter view.

7 Tap or click the Next Slide button in the slide navigator near the bottom of Presenter view until you have navigated to Slide 3 (see Figure 10.3).

8 Compare your screen with the one shown in Figure 10.3.

9 Continue tapping or clicking the Next Slide button until you reach Slide 6 and then tap or click End Slide Show at the top of the screen.

10 Leave the presentation open for the next topic.

Figure 10.3 Slide 3 in Presenter View

Display a Slide Show
1. Tap or click SLIDE SHOW tab.
2. Tap or click From Beginning button.

OR
1. Display Slide 1.
2. Tap or click Slide Show button in Status bar.

Display Presenter View
1. Display presentation as Slide Show.
2. Tap or click More slide show options button.
3. Tap or click *Show Presenter View*.

Did You Know?

Many speakers include a closing slide as the last slide in a presentation that is left on the screen until the audience has left. The closing slide contains the speaker's contact information, a favorite or memorable quote related to the topic, or a thank-you message.

You can also preview a slide show in Reading view where each slide fills the screen. A Title bar, Status bar, and Taskbar remain visible with buttons to navigate slides in the Status bar.

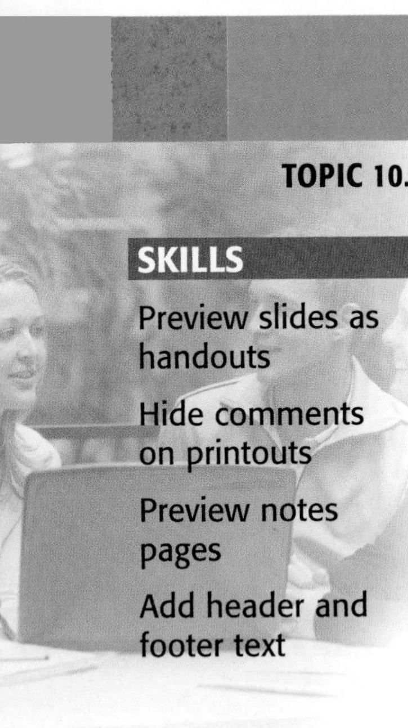

Preparing Audience Handouts and Speaker Notes

Some speakers provide audience members with a printout of their slides in a format that allows an individual to add his or her own handwritten notes during the presentation. PowerPoint provides several options for printing slides as handouts. Speakers who do not use Presenter view during a presentation may also print a copy of the slides with the notes included.

1. With the **10.1-CarMaintenance-Your Name** presentation open, tap or click the FILE tab and then tap or click Print.
2. At the Print tab Backstage view, tap or click the Full Page Slides list arrow in the *Settings* section.
3. Tap or click *3 Slides* in the *Handouts* section of the drop-down or pop-up list.

The option to print three slides per page provides horizontal lines next to each slide for writing notes.

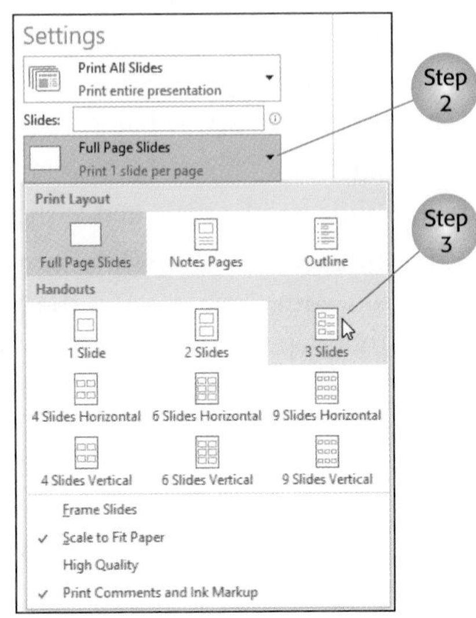

4. Tap or click the 3 Slides list arrow and tap or click *6 Slides Horizontal* at the drop-down or pop-up list.

Notice that the printout requires two pages even though only six slides are in the presentation. By default, comments print with the presentation; the second page is for printing the comments.

Preview various handout options before making a selection to make sure printouts will be legible for most people when slides have a lot of detailed content.

5. Tap or click the 6 Slides Horizontal list arrow and tap or click *Print Comments and Ink Markup* to remove the check mark. The printout is now only one page.
6. Tap or click the 6 Slides Horizontal list arrow and tap or click *Notes Pages* in the *Print Layout* section of the drop-down or pop-up list.

Notes Pages prints one slide per page with the slide at the top half of the page and notes or blank space in the bottom half.

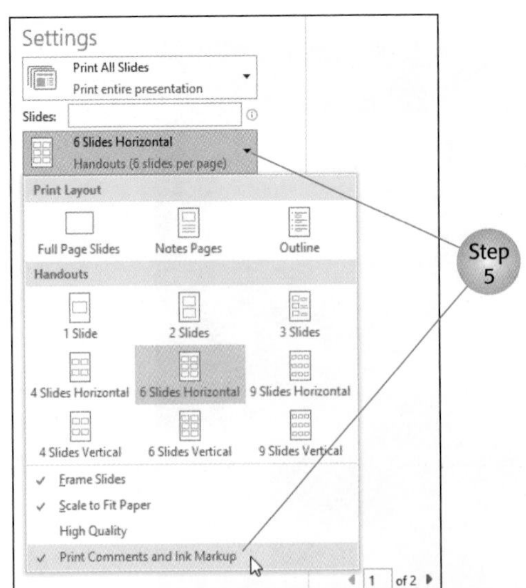

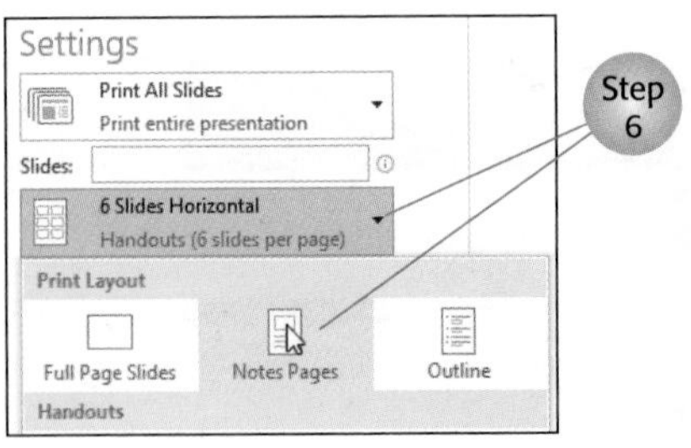

7 Tap or click the Next Page button to display Slide 2 in the *Preview* section.

8 Tap or click the Next Page button to display Slide 3.

Notice the notes text is displayed below the slide.

9 Tap or click the Edit Header & Footer link at the bottom of the *Settings* section.

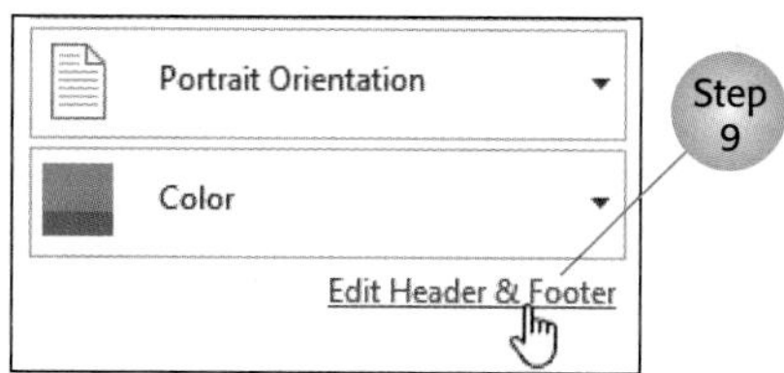

10 At the Header and Footer dialog box with the Notes and Handouts tab active, tap or click the *Header* check box to insert a check mark, tap or click in the *Header* text box, and then type your first and last names.

11 Tap or click the *Footer* check box to insert a check mark, tap or click in the *Footer* text box, and then type your school name.

12 Tap or click the Apply to All button.

13 Preview the header and footer text by scrolling through the remaining slides.

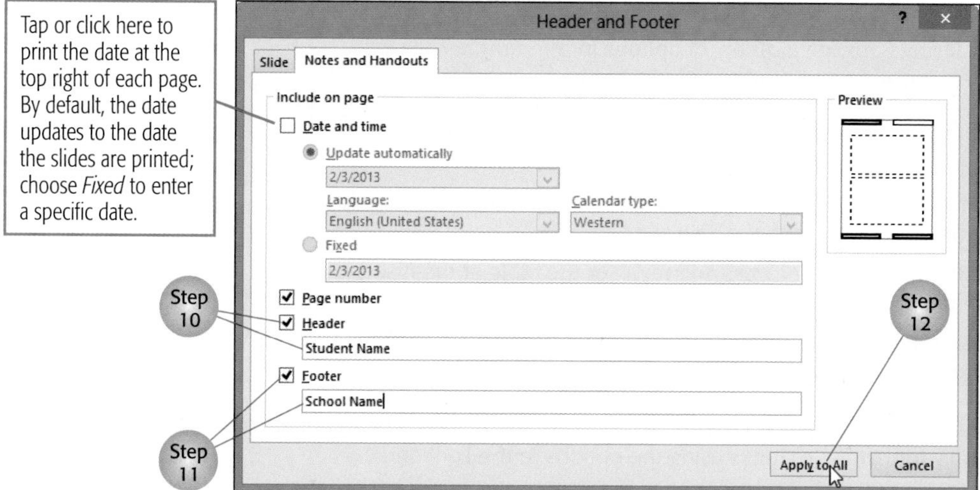

14 Tap or click the Back button to exit the Print tab Backstage view.

15 Save the revised presentation using the same name (**10.1-CarMaintenance-Your Name**) and then close the presentation.

Preview Slides as Handouts or Notes Pages

1. Tap or click FILE tab.
2. Tap or click Print.
3. Tap or click Full Page Slides list arrow.
4. Tap or click *Notes Pages* or *Handouts* option.

Add Header or Footer Text

1. Tap or click FILE tab.
2. Tap or click Print.
3. Tap or click Edit Header & Footer.
4. Type header or footer text as required.
5. Tap or click Apply to All button.

To conserve paper and ink some presenters publish their presentations to a web service such as slideshare.net instead of printing handouts.

Slide Size and Orientation for Printing

By default, slides print in landscape orientation when printed as slides or in portrait orientation when printed as notes or handouts. Change the orientation with the orientation list arrow in the *Settings* section of the Print tab Backstage view or at the *Custom Slide Size* option from the Slide Size button in the Customize group of the DESIGN tab.

Concepts Review

Topic	Key Concepts	Key Terms
Creating a New Presentation and Inserting Slides	A new presentation is created from the Start screen by choosing a template, a theme, or a blank presentation. A placeholder is a rectangular container in which you type text or insert other content. PowerPoint starts a new presentation with the title slide in widescreen format in Normal view. Normal view includes the Slide pane, which displays the active slide, and the Slide Thumbnail pane, which displays numbered thumbnails of all of the slides in a presentation. Variants of a theme family are based upon the same theme but with different colors, styles, and effects. Add or edit text on a slide by tapping or clicking inside the placeholder and typing or editing text. Use the New Slide button to add slides to the presentation using a slide layout. Slide layouts provide a variety of options for the number, placement, and types of placeholders on the slide.	Presentation application Title slide Placeholder Slide pane Slide Thumbnail pane Variants New Slide button Slide layouts
Changing the Theme and Inserting and Modifying a Table	Change the theme and/or variant for a presentation after the presentation has been started using the DESIGN tab. Insert a table on a slide using the Insert Table button located within the content placeholder of a new slide. Type the number of columns and rows for the table at the Insert Table dialog box and then tap or click OK. Tables in PowerPoint use the same methods and tools for entering text and modifying layout as those learned in Word.	
Formatting Text with Font and Paragraph Options	Select text within a placeholder or select the entire placeholder to apply formatting changes using the options in the Font and Paragraph groups of the HOME tab. Create a multilevel bulleted list using the Increase List Level and Decrease List Level buttons in the Paragraph group. Bullet symbols vary for each theme. You can change the bullet symbol character using the Bullets button arrow.	Increase List Level button Decrease List Level button
Selecting, Resizing, Aligning, and Moving Placeholders	The active placeholder displays with sizing handles and a border with which you can resize or move the placeholder. Smart guides are colored lines that appear on the slide as you resize or move placeholders to assist in aligning the placeholders or evenly spacing placeholders with other close objects.	Smart guides

Topic	Key Concepts	Key Terms
Using Slide Sorter View and Moving, Duplicating, and Deleting Slides	Slide Sorter view displays all slides as slide thumbnails and is used to rearrange the order of slides. Slide or drag a slide in Slide Sorter view to move the slide to a new location in the presentation. Duplicating a slide makes a copy of an existing slide with the placeholders sized, aligned, and positioned the same as the original slide. Delete a slide you no longer need in a presentation by selecting the slide or slides and using the Delete option from the Mini toolbar (touch) or shortcut menu (mouse). A slide can be hidden in the presentation if you do not want the slide to display in a slide show.	Slide Sorter view
Using Slide Master View	Each presentation has a slide master that determines the formatting and paragraph options for placeholders in new slides. Display the slide master to make formatting changes that you want to apply to all slides in the presentation automatically. Change to Slide Master view from the VIEW tab to modify the slide master. In Slide Master view, the Slide Thumbnail pane displays the slide master at the top of the hierarchy. Below the slide master, individual slide layouts are included for formatting. Add text to the bottom of each slide in a footer placeholder by typing footer text in the Header and Footer dialog box (INSERT tab, Header & Footer button). Use the footer placeholder on the slide master to apply formatting options to the footer text.	Slide Master Slide Master view
Adding Notes and Comments	The Notes pane appears below the Slide pane and is used to type speaker notes, reminders for the presenter, or more detailed information about the slide content for a reader. Reveal the Notes pane with the NOTES button in the Status bar. A comment is added to the active slide by displaying the Comments pane, tapping or clicking the New button, and then typing the comment text. Reveal the Comments pane with the COMMENTS button in the Status bar. Delete a comment using the Delete icon that appears when you tap or point to the comment text in the Comments pane. Hide comments by removing the check mark next to *Show Markup* at the Show Comments drop-down list (REVIEW tab)	Notes Pane Comments Pane

continued....

Topic	Key Concepts	Key Terms
Displaying a Slide Show	Slide Show view previews each slide as the audience will see the slide with a full screen. Display a slide show starting at Slide 1 by tapping or clicking the From Beginning button in the SLIDE SHOW tab. The Slide Show toolbar provides buttons to navigate slides, annotate slides, zoom into a slide, or black/unblack the screen during the presentation. After the last slide is shown, a black screen displays indicating the end of the slide show. The Slide Show button in the Status bar starts the slide show from the active slide in the Slide pane. Display a slide show and tap or click the More slide show options button to switch the view to Presenter view. Presenter view works with two monitors, where one monitor displays the slide show as the audience will see it and the second monitor displays the slide show in Presenter view. Presenter view can also be seen on a computer with only one monitor so that you can rehearse a presentation. In Presenter view, the speaker's monitor displays a timer and timer controls, a preview of the next slide, notes, and a slide show toolbar along with other options.	Slide Show view Presenter view From Beginning button Slide Show button
Preparing Audience Handouts and Speaker Notes	Preview slides formatted as handouts at the Print tab Backstage view. The *3 Slides* option provides lines next to each slide for writing notes. Various other horizontal or vertical options are available for printing slide thumbnails. By default, comments print on a separate page after the slides; to prevent comments from printing, remove the check mark next to *Print Comments and Ink Markup* from the slides option list. Choose the *Notes Pages* option to print one slide per page with the notes from the Notes pane. Add header and/or footer text to a printout using the Edit Header & Footer link at the bottom of the *Settings* section. By default, slides printed as slides print in landscape orientation, while slides printed as handouts or notes pages print in portrait orientation.	Notes Pages

Multiple Choice

1. This is the first slide that is created in a new presentation.
   a. Bulleted list
   b. Title slide
   c. Presenter slide
   d. Title and Content slide
2. This is the view that is active when a new presentation is created.
   a. Notes view
   b. Slide Sorter view
   c. Normal view
   d. Reading view
3. Use this tab in the ribbon to change the theme after the presentation has been created.
   a. SLIDE SHOW
   b. INSERT
   c. VIEW
   d. DESIGN
4. Use this button in the content placeholder to type text in a grid of columns and rows.
   a. Insert Table
   b. Create Table
   c. Draw Table
   d. Make Table
5. Use this button to move to the next level (right) in a bulleted list.
   a. Next Level
   b. Increase Indent
   c. Next Bullet
   d. Increase List Level
6. A new slide is inserted ________________.
   a. before the active slide
   b. after the active slide
   c. at the beginning of slides
   d. at the end of slides
7. Move a placeholder by sliding or dragging this part of the placeholder.
   a. any sizing handle
   b. guide line
   c. border
   d. move handle
8. These appear to help you align placeholders evenly as you resize or move a placeholder.
   a. smart lines
   b. smart tags
   c. smart tips
   d. smart guides
9. In this view, all of the slides in the presentation display as thumbnails so that you can easily rearrange the slide order.
   a. Slide view
   b. Slide Show view
   c. Slide Sorter view
   d. Slide Thumbnail view
10. Use this option to make an exact copy of the selected slide.
    a. Copy Slide
    b. Duplicate Slide
    c. Twin Slide
    d. Replica Slide
11. The formatting on this slide determines the default font and paragraph options for all new slides except title slides.
    a. Slide header
    b. Slide master
    c. Slide duplicate
    d. Slide control
12. This placeholder holds text that appears at the bottom of each slide.
    a. Footer
    b. Header
    c. Title
    d. Author
13. Type additional information about the content on the slide in this pane.
    a. Properties
    b. Notes
    c. Subject
    d. Text
14. This balloon appears on a slide when someone has typed feedback or posed a question about a slide.
    a. Comment
    b. Question
    c. Review
    d. Share
15. This view for a slide show shows a timer and a preview of the next slide.
    a. Slide Show view
    b. Slide Sorter view
    c. Set Up Show view
    d. Presenter view

16. This screen appears after the last slide in the presentation has been viewed.
    a. blue screen
    b. white screen
    c. black screen
    d. gray screen
17. Choose this handout option to have lines printed next to each slide.
    a. 6 Slides
    b. 6 Slides Vertical
    c. 9 Slides Vertical
    d. 3 Slides
18. Choose this Print Layout option to print one slide per page with each slide in the top half of the page.
    a. Outline
    b. Notes Pages
    c. Full Page Slides
    d. 1 Slide

Crossword Puzzle

ACROSS

1 Pane in which feedback for a slide is provided
5 Lines that help you align objects on a slide
7 View that displays all slides as thumbnails
8 Collections of color schemes for a theme
9 Container for text or other content

DOWN

2 View that displays when slide show is ended
3 Pane in which speaker reminders are typed
4 Option to print slides with speaker notes
5 View to preview slides as audience will see them
6 View to make global formatting changes

Matching

Match the term with the statement or definition.

_______ 1. Choose theme
_______ 2. Active slide
_______ 3. Default new slide layout
_______ 4. Change theme
_______ 5. Add subpoint below bullet text
_______ 6. Active placeholder
_______ 7. Remove slide
_______ 8. Change all slides
_______ 9. Status bar button
_______ 10. Display slide show
_______ 11. Handouts option

a. Title and Content
b. 3 Slides
c. Delete
d. Slide master
e. Start screen
f. NOTES
g. Presenter view
h. Slide pane
i. DESIGN tab
j. Selection handles
k. Increase List Level

Project 1 Creating and Editing a New Presentation

Individual

Deliverable: Presentation about world and U.S. landmarks (continued in Projects 2 and 3)

1. Start a new presentation, choosing a theme and variant that you like.
2. Save the presentation as **C10-Project1-Landmarks-Your Name** in a new folder named *Ch10* within the ChapterProjectsWork folder on your USB flash drive.
3. Create slides including multilevel lists, a table, and a comparison slide with the following information:

Slide 1	Title	Famous Landmarks	
	Subtitle	Your Name	
Slide 2	Title	World and National Landmarks	
	List	Top 5 World Landmarks	
		Top 5 U.S. Landmarks	
		Survey Results	
		Honorable Mentions	
Slide 3	Title	Top 5 World Landmarks	
	Multilevel List	The Pyramid of Khufu	
		Located in Giza, Egypt	
		Largest pyramid ever built	
		The Great Wall of China	
		Completed during the Ming dynasty (1368 to 1644)	
		Acropolis	
		UNESCO World Heritage Site	
		Parthenon Greek temple	
		Eiffel Tower	
		18,000 metallic parts joined by 2,500,000 rivets	
		Taj Mahal	
		Agra, India	
Slide 4	Title	Top 5 U.S. Landmarks	
	List	Statue of Liberty, New York	
		Grand Canyon, Arizona	
		Mount Rushmore, South Dakota	
		Independence Hall, Philadelphia	
		The National Mall, Washington, D.C.	
Slide 5	Title	Survey Results	
	Table	Social Media Website	Votes Cast
		Facebook	345,985
		Twitter	420,870
		Tumblr	155,329
Slide 6	Title	Honorable Mentions	
	Comparison	World Landmarks	U.S. Landmarks
	Slide Layout	Stonehenge, U.K.	Freedom Trail, Boston
		Edinburgh Castle, Scotland	Fort Sumter, Charleston
		Buckingham Palace, U.K.	The Alamo, San Antonio
		Machu Picchu, Peru	Gateway Arch, St. Louis

4. Perform a spelling check and carefully proofread each slide, making corrections as needed.
5. Edit Slide 3 as follows:
   a. Delete the entry *Largest pyramid ever built.*
   b. Delete the entry *UNESCO World Heritage Site.*

   c. Insert the text *Tower located in Paris has* before the entry that begins *18,000 metallic parts.*
   d. Insert the text *Marble mausoleum located in* before *Agra, India.*
6. Edit Slide 5, changing the votes cast by Facebook from *345,985* to *543,589.*
7. Save the revised presentation using the same name (**C10-Project1-Landmarks-Your Name**).
8. Leave the presentation open if you are continuing to Project 2; otherwise close the presentation and submit the project to your instructor in the manner she or he has requested.

Project 2 Editing and Formatting a Presentation

Individual

Deliverable: Presentation about world and U.S. landmarks (continued in Project 3)

Note: You must have completed Project 1 before starting this project.

1. If necessary, open **C10-Project1-Landmarks-Your Name**.
2. Use Save As to change the file name to **C10-Project2-Landmarks-Your Name**, saving in the same folder.
3. Change the theme and variant to another design of your choosing. Check each slide after you change the theme for corrections that may be needed. For example, a theme that uses the All Caps font in a title or subtitle may cause changes in capitalization when the theme is changed to one that does not use the All Caps font.
4. Display the slide master and make the following changes to the top slide in the hierarchy:
   a. Change the font color for all of the titles to another color of your choosing.
   b. Change the bullet character to a different symbol and color than the one used in the theme.
5. Display Slide 5 and modify the table layout and design as follows:
   a. Change the width of the first column to 3.5 inches.
   b. Change the width of the second column to 1.75 inches.
   c. Center-align the entries in the second column.
   d. Change the table style to another style of your choosing.
   e. Move the table so that the table is positioned at the approximate center of the slide below the title.
6. Display Slide 6 and make the following changes:
   a. Change the bullet character to a different symbol for the two lists than the symbol that was used on the slide master.
   b. Resize the left list placeholder so that the placeholder's right border ends just after the longest entry in the list. Resize the left title placeholder to the same width as the list.
   c. Move the left title and list placeholders closer to the right title and list. Align the two titles and lists at the approximate center below the slide title.
7. Save the revised presentation using the same name (**C10-Project2-Landmarks-Your Name**).
8. Leave the presentation open if you are continuing to Project 3; otherwise, close the presentation and submit the project to your instructor in the manner she or he has requested.

Project Rearranging Slides and Adding Notes and Comments

SNAP Grade It

Individual

Deliverable: Presentation about world and U.S. landmarks

Note: You must have completed Projects 1 and 2 before starting this project.

1. If necessary, open **C10-Project2-Landmarks-Your Name**.
2. Use Save As to change the file name to **C10-Project3-Landmarks-Your Name**, saving in the same folder.
3. Move the *Survey Results* slide so that it becomes the third slide in the presentation.
4. Move the *Honorable Mentions* slide after the *Survey Results* slide.
5. Display Slide 2 and edit the bulleted list to reposition the bottom two bulleted list items so they become the top two bulleted list items.

6. Display the *Survey Results* slide and type the following text in the Notes pane:
   Our first survey using social media for reader voting was a phenomenal success. Plans for next year's survey are to expand voting to include other social media sites. Ask the audience for suggestions.
7. Display the *Honorable Mentions* slide and type the following text in the Notes pane:
   All honorable mentions had at least 20,000 votes.
8. Display the *Top 5 World Landmarks* slide, select the bulleted list text below *Eiffel Tower*, and type the following comment:
   Should I remove the number of parts and rivets?
9. Display the Top 5 U.S. Landmarks and type the following comment for the entire slide:
   Should I add the number of votes for each landmark?
10. Save the revised presentation using the same name (**C10-Project3-Landmarks-Your Name**).
11. Submit the project to your instructor in the manner she or he has requested.
12. Close the presentation.

Project 4 Internet Research and Creating a Presentation from a Template

Individual or Pairs

Deliverable: Presentation about inventions

1. Start a new presentation, browsing the *Education* category of templates and choosing a template that you like.
2. Create slides for a presentation about the inventions listed below. For each invention, research four to five interesting facts about the invention and add the information in a bulleted list on the slide.
   Slide 1 (You determine an appropriate title and subtitle.)
   Slide 2 (You determine an appropriate introductory slide for the presentation.)
   Slide 3 The Telephone
   Slide 4 The Television
   Slide 5 The Automobile
   Slide 6 The Light Bulb
3. Delete slides that were downloaded as part of the template that are not needed for this presentation.
4. Save the presentation in the Ch10 folder within ChapterProjectsWork as **C10-Project4-Inventions-Your Name**.
5. Submit the project to your instructor in the manner she or he has requested.
6. Close the presentation.

Project 5 Creating a Graduation Party Planning Presentation

Individual

Deliverable: Presentation on college graduation party planning

1. Create a presentation similar to the one shown in Figure 10.4 on the next page with the following additional information:
   a. The theme is *Integral* with one of the variants selected.
   b. On the slide master the first-level bullet character is removed and the second- and third-level bullet characters are changed.
   c. On the slide master, the font color for the title is changed from the default color. Use your best judgment to choose a similar color.
   d. Use your best judgment to determine other formatting, placeholder size, and alignment.
2. Save the presentation in the Ch10 folder within the ChapterProjectsWork folder as **C10-Project5-GradParty-Your Name**.
3. Submit the project to your instructor in the manner she or he has requested.
4. Close the presentation.

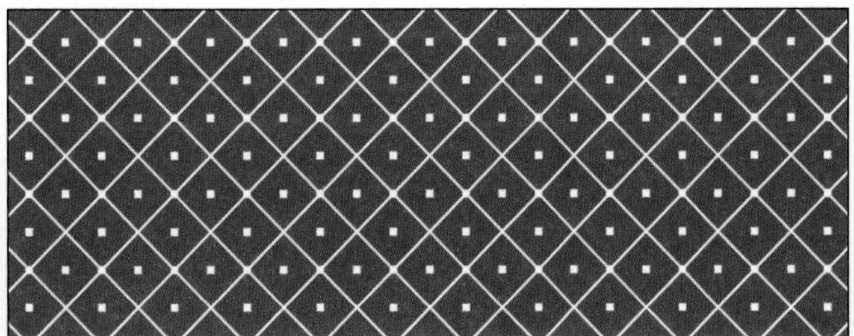

GRADUATION PARTY PLANNING | Student name

GRADUATION PARTY CHECKLIST

Date and venue

Budget

Invitations

Plan food, decorations, and entertainment

CHOOSE THE DATE AND VENUE

Survey close friends and family before setting the date

- ❑Find a date that conflicts the least with other events

Visit possible venues

- ❑Indoors
  - Restaurants, banquet or community halls
- ❑Outdoors
  - Local park, recreation area, or estate

BUDGET

Expense	Typical Budget
Location, Food, and Drinks	\$500 to \$750
Invitations	\$100 to \$150
Decorations	\$100 to \$150
Incidental Expenses	\$100

INVITATIONS

Finalize the guest list

Send out invitations four to six weeks in advance

Set the RSVP date three weeks before party

FOOD, DECORATIONS & ENTERTAINMENT

Choose caterer

- ❑Ask for recommendations from friends or family

Decorate around a theme

- ❑Choose a theme related to your program

Entertainment

- ❑Assemble your favorite music playlists
- ❑Plan to tell a few humorous stories from school

Figure 10.4 Project 5 Graduation Party Planning Presentation

Project 6 Internet Research and Composing a New Presentation

Individual or Pairs

Deliverable: Presentation about favorite U.S. or Canadian historical figure

1. Listen to the audio file named ***Project6_Instructions***. The file is located in the Ch10 folder in the Student_Data_Files folder.
2. Complete the research and compose the presentation as instructed.
3. Save the presentation in the Ch10 folder within ChapterProjectsWork as **C10-Project6-HistoricalFigure-Your Name**.
4. Submit the project to your instructor in the manner she or he has requested.
5. Close the presentation.

Project 7 Sending Project Work to OneNote Notebook

Individual

Deliverable: New page in shared OneNote notebook

1. Start OneNote and open the MyProjects notebook created in Chapter 4, Project 4.
2. Make PowerPoint the active section and add a new page titled *Chapter 10 Projects*.
3. Switch to PowerPoint. For each project that you completed, open the presentation, send the slides formatted as handouts with six slides horizontal per page and with your name in a header to OneNote 2013, selecting the *Chapter 10 Projects page* in the *PowerPoint* section in the MyProjects notebook, then close the presentation.
4. Close your MyProjects notebook in OneNote and close OneNote.
5. Close PowerPoint.
6. Submit the project to your instructor in the manner she or he has requested.

Chapter 11

Enhancing a Presentation with Pictures, Sound, Video, and Animation Effects

After successfully completing this chapter, you will be able to:

- Insert and resize pictures and clip art
- Insert and modify a SmartArt object
- Insert and modify WordArt
- Insert and modify a chart
- Draw and modify shapes and text boxes
- Add video and sound
- Add transition and animation effects
- Set up a self-running presentation

A presentation is more interesting when multimedia is used to reinforce and help a speaker communicate his or her main points. Incorporating various types of graphics, sound, and video into a presentation can help an audience understand the content and remain engaged.

In this chapter you will learn how to add graphics to slides using clip art, pictures, SmartArt, WordArt, charts, and drawn shapes; add text in a text box; add sound and video; and complete the presentation by adding transitions and animation effects. Lastly, you will learn how to set up a slide show that advances through the slides automatically.

Topic 11.1

SKILLS

Add an image from your PC

Add an image from clip art

Inserting Graphics from Clip Art and Picture Collections

The addition of a picture, illustration, diagram, or chart on a slide is used to emphasize content, add visual interest to slides, and help an audience understand and make connections with the information more easily than with text alone. As you learned in Chapter 7, pictures can be inserted that are stored on your PC or at an online service such as Flickr, Facebook, or SkyDrive. Microsoft's Office.com clip art collection contains thousands of clip art images, photos, and illustrations.

Inserting Pictures from Your Computer

Use the Pictures button in the Images group of the INSERT tab to add a picture that is stored as a file on your computer or a computer to which you are connected. Once inserted, move, resize, and/or modify the picture using buttons in the PICTURE TOOLS FORMAT tab. On a new slide, use the Pictures icon in the Content placeholder to add a picture to a slide.

1. Start PowerPoint and open the presentation named ***PaintedBunting***.
2. Use Save As to save a copy of the presentation as **11.1-PaintedBunting-Your Name** in a new folder named *Ch11* in the CompletedTopicsByChapter folder.
3. Browse through the presentation and read the slides.
4. Make Slide 2 the active slide.
5. Tap or click the INSERT tab and then tap or click the Pictures button in the Images group.
6. At the Insert Picture dialog box, navigate to the Ch11 folder within Student_Data_Files and double-tap or double-click ***PaintedBunting_NPS***.
7. Using one of the four corner selection handles, resize the image smaller to the approximate size shown in the image below.
8. Slide or drag the image to move the picture to the right side of the slide and align it with the horizontal and vertical smart guides that appear when the picture is even with the top of the text and the right margin on the slide.

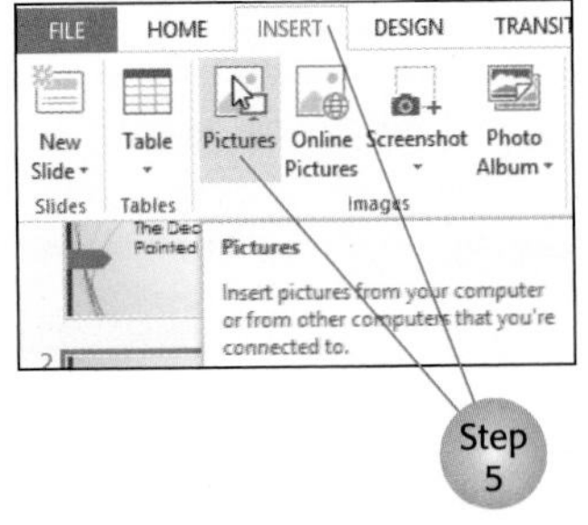

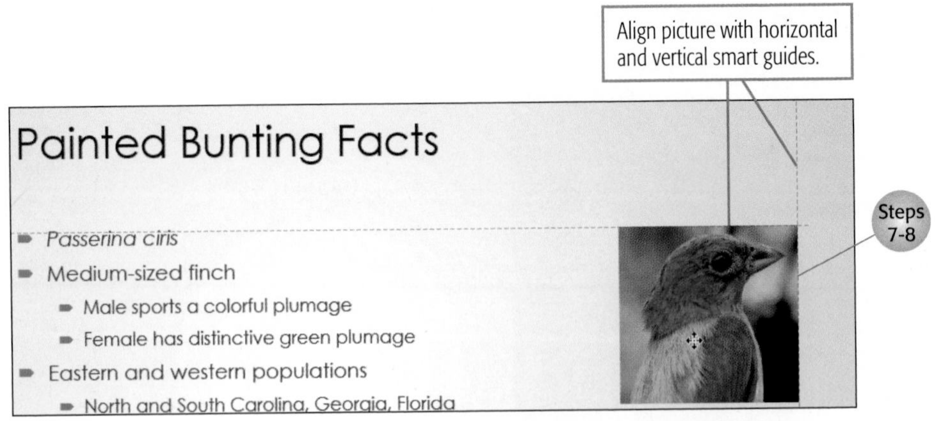

9. Insert the picture named ***PaintedBunting_Female*** near the bottom right of the slide as shown on the next page by completing steps similar to Steps 5 to 8.

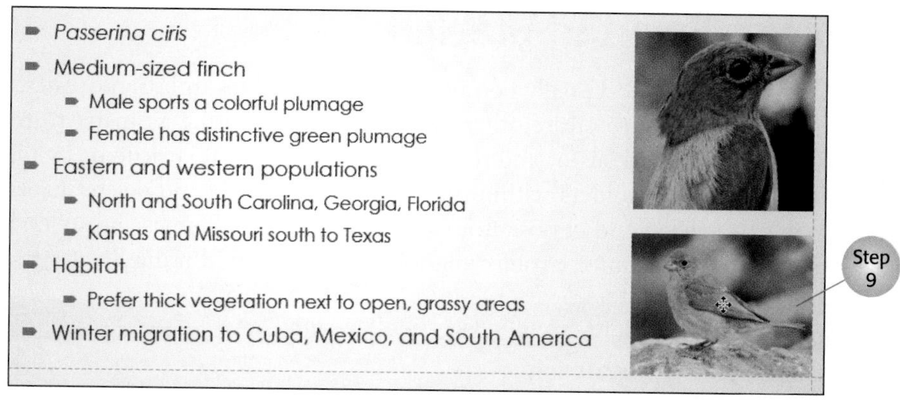
Passerina ciris
Medium-sized finch
Male sports a colorful plumage
Female has distinctive green plumage
Eastern and western populations
North and South Carolina, Georgia, Florida
Kansas and Missouri south to Texas
Habitat
Prefer thick vegetation next to open, grassy areas
Winter migration to Cuba, Mexico, and South America
Step 9

Quick STEPS

Insert an Image from the Computer

1. Activate slide.
2. Tap or click INSERT tab.
3. Tap or click Pictures button.
4. Navigate to drive and/or folder.
5. Double-tap or double-click desired image.
6. Resize and/or move as required.

Insert Clip Art or Online Photo

1. Activate slide.
2. Tap or click INSERT tab.
3. Tap or click Online Pictures button.
4. Type search key word.
5. Tap or press Enter.
6. Double-tap or double-click desired image.
7. Resize and/or move as required.

Inserting Pictures from Office.com

The Online Pictures button is in the Images group of the INSERT tab or in a content placeholder. Use the Online Pictures button to find suitable images in the clip art collection at Office.com, by completing a web search, or from pictures you have stored at your Flickr, Facebook, or SkyDrive account.

10 Make Slide 6 the active slide.

11 Tap or click the INSERT tab and then tap or click the Online Pictures button in the Images group.

12 With the insertion point positioned in the *Office.com Clip Art* search text box, type **bird watching** and then tap or press Enter, or tap or click the Search button (displays as a magnifying glass).

13 Double-tap or double-click the picture shown in the image below.

14 Resize and move the picture to the left side of the bulleted list and align it with the horizontal smart guide that appears when the center of the image is evenly positioned with the bulleted list.

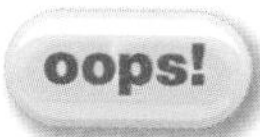
oops!

Image shown not in search results? Choose another suitable image if the one shown is not available.

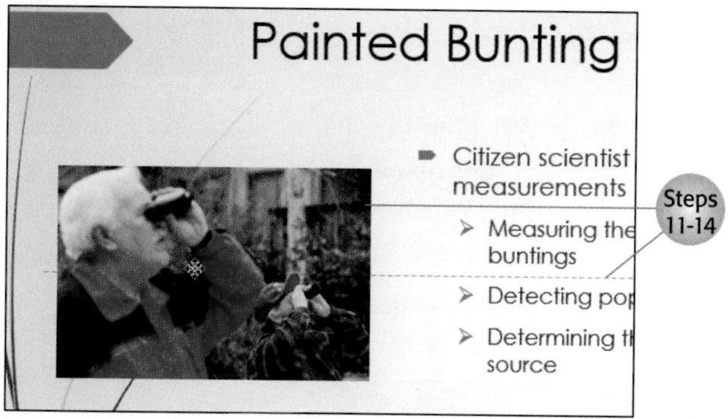
Painted Bunting
Citizen scientist measurements
Measuring the buntings
Detecting po
Determining t source
Steps 11-14

15 Save the revised presentation using the same name (**11.1-PaintedBunting-Your Name**). Leave the presentation open for the next topic.

Beyond Basics

Editing Images

Edit an image with buttons in the PICTURE TOOLS FORMAT tab using techniques similar to those you learned in Chapter 7. For example, you can apply a picture style or artistic effect; adjust the brightness, contrast, or sharpness; or change the color properties. Use buttons in the Arrange and Size group to layer the image with other objects, specify the position of the image on the slide, crop unwanted portions of the picture, or specify measurements for height and width.

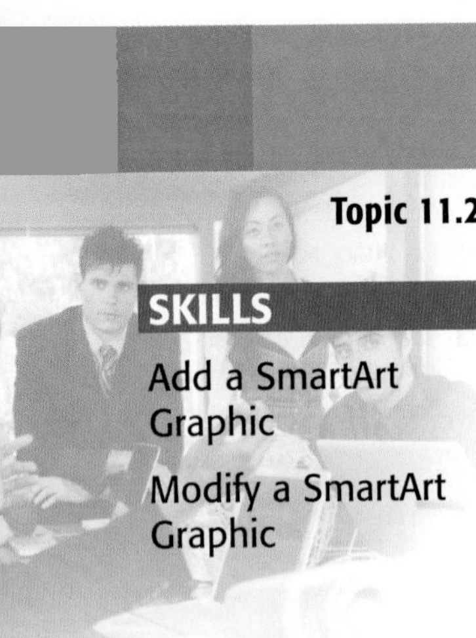

Topic 11.2

SKILLS

Add a SmartArt Graphic

Modify a SmartArt Graphic

Inserting a SmartArt Graphic

SmartArt uses graphics to visually communicate relationships in lists, processes, cycles, and hierarchies, or to create other diagrams. Begin creating a SmartArt graphic by choosing a predesigned layout and then adding text in the Text pane or by typing directly in the Text placeholders within the shapes. You can add and delete shapes to the graphic as needed and choose from a variety of color schemes and styles. See Table 11.1 for a description of layout category diagrams created using SmartArt.

Table 11.1	**SmartArt Graphic Layout Categories**
Layout Category	**Description**
List	Non-sequential tasks, processes, or other list items
Process	Illustrate a sequential series of steps to complete a process or task
Cycle	Show a sequence of steps or tasks in a circular or looped process
Hierarchy	Show an organizational chart or decision tree
Relationship	Show how parts or elements are related to each other
Matrix	Depict how individual parts or ideas relate to a whole or central idea
Pyramid	Show proportional or hierarchical relationships that build upward

1. With the **11.1-PaintedBunting-Your Name** presentation open and Slide 6 the active slide, tap or click the INSERT tab if necessary.

2. Tap or click the SmartArt button in the Illustrations group.

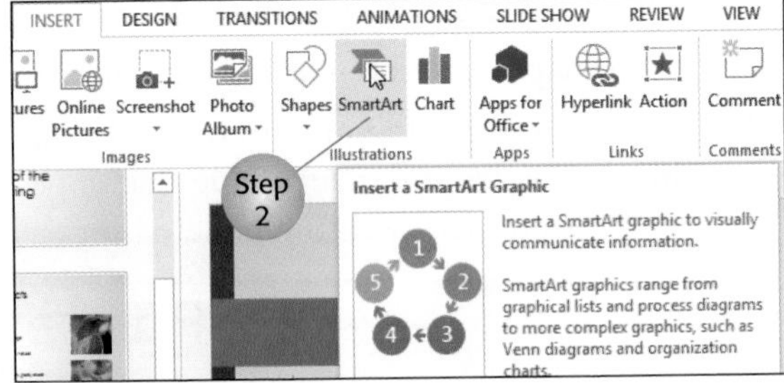

On a new slide with no other content, use the Insert a SmartArt Graphic icon in the Content placeholder to create a SmartArt object on a slide.

3. At the Choose a SmartArt Graphic dialog box, tap or click *Process* in the Category pane at the left, tap or click *Basic Chevron Process* in the layout pane in the center (second option in fifth row), and then tap or click OK.

PowerPoint places the SmartArt graphic in the center of the slide. Three shapes are automatically included in the *Basic Chevron Process* layout.

Select a layout in the center pane to preview the layout and read a description with suggestions for the layout's usage in the right pane.

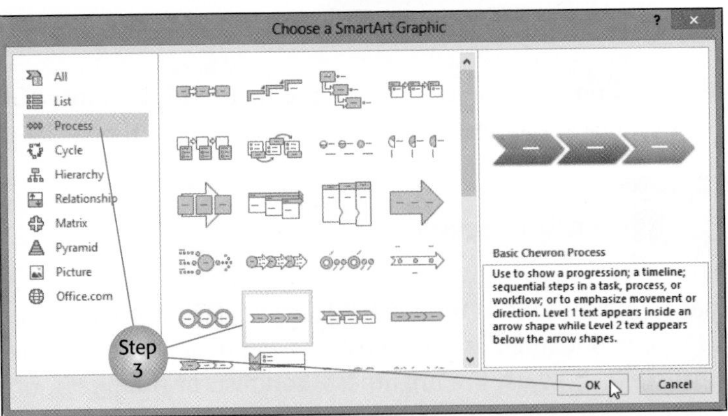

4 Tap or click the left-pointing arrow along the left border of the graphic if the Text pane is not visible; if the Text pane is already visible, proceed to Step 5.

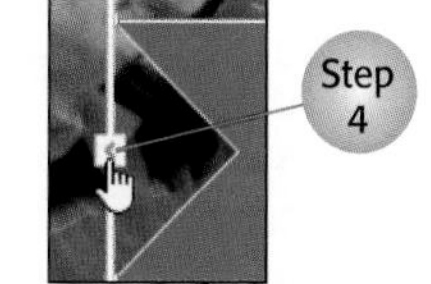

5 With the insertion point in the Text pane next to the first bullet, type **Band**; tap or click next to the second bullet and type **Observe**; and then tap or click next to the third bullet and type **Analyze**.

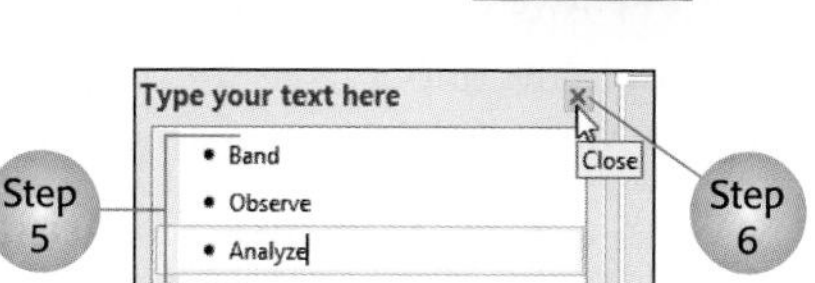

The SmartArt graphic updates as each word is typed in the Text pane to show the text in the shape. You can also add text to the shapes by typing text directly within the text placeholders inside each shape.

6 Tap or click the Close button to close the Text pane.

7 If necessary, tap or click the SMARTART TOOLS DESIGN tab.

8 Tap or click the More button at the bottom right of the *SmartArt Styles* gallery.

9 Tap or click *Polished* at the drop-down gallery (first option in *3-D* section).

10 Tap or click the Change Colors button in the SmartArt Styles group and then tap or click *Colorful – Accent Colors* at the drop-down gallery (first option in the *Colorful* section).

11 Slide or drag the border of the SmartArt graphic until the diagram is positioned near the bottom center of the slide, as shown in Figure 11.1.

12 Tap or click in an unused area of the slide to deselect the graphic.

13 Save the revised presentation using the same name (**11.1-PaintedBunting-Your Name**). Leave the presentation open for the next topic.

Press the Down Arrow key to move to the next bullet in the Text pane.

Quick STEPS

Insert a SmartArt Graphic

1. Activate slide.
2. Tap or click INSERT tab.
3. Tap or click SmartArt button.
4. Select category in left pane.
5. Select layout in center pane.
6. Tap or click OK.
7. Add text in Text pane or shapes.
8. Format and/or move as required.

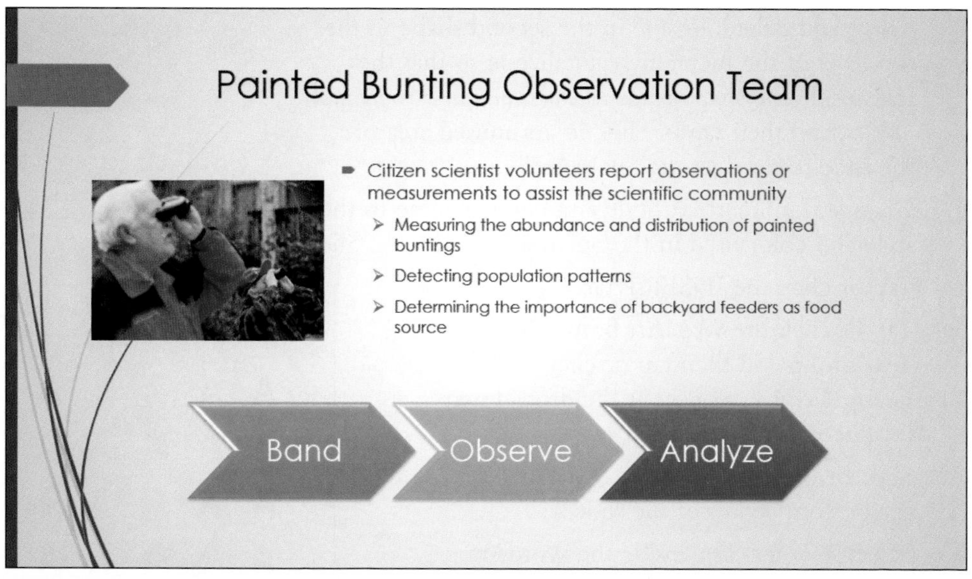

Figure 11.1 Completed Slide 6 with SmartArt graphic

Modifying a SmartArt Graphic

Use buttons in the Create Graphic group of the SMARTART TOOLS DESIGN tab to add shapes, change the direction of the layout (switch between *Right to Left* and *Left to Right*), and move shapes up or down the layout. Each shape in the layout can also be selected and moved or resized individually.

Topic 11.3

SKILLS

Convert text to a SmartArt Graphic

Insert and modify WordArt

Converting Text to SmartArt and Inserting WordArt

An existing bulleted list on a slide can be converted to a SmartArt graphic using the **Convert to SmartArt button** in the Paragraph group of the HOME tab. **WordArt** is text that is created and formatted as a graphic object. With WordArt you can create decorative text on a slide with a variety of WordArt Styles and text effects. A WordArt object can also have the text formed around a variety of shapes.

1. With the **11.1-PaintedBunting-Your Name** presentation open, make Slide 5 the active slide.
2. Tap or click in the bulleted list to activate the placeholder.
3. Tap or click the Convert to SmartArt button in the Paragraph group of the HOME tab.
4. Tap or click *Hierarchy List* at the drop-down gallery (second option in second row).

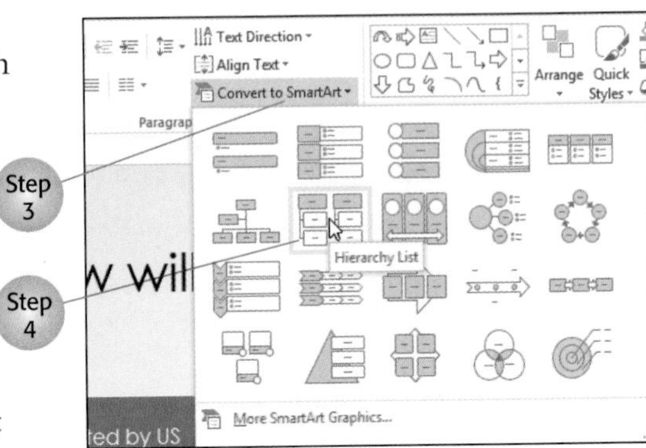

Step 3

Step 4

PowerPoint converts the text in the bulleted list into the selected SmartArt layout. Level 1 text from the bulleted list is placed inside shapes at the top level in the hierarchy diagram, with level 2 text in shapes below the corresponding level 1 box.

5. Close the Text pane if the Text pane is open.
6. Select and delete *Need to* in the second shape in the top level of the hierarchy, capitalize *m* so that the text inside the shape reads *Manage and preserve natural habitat*, and then tap or click in an unused area of the slide to deselect the SmartArt object.

Step 6

Manage and preserve natural habitat

Restore and conserve freshwater wetlands

7. Change the SmartArt Style and color scheme to the same style and color used in the SmartArt graphic on Slide 6.
8. Tap or click the INSERT tab.
9. Tap or click the WordArt button in the Text group and then tap or click *Fill – Green, Accent 1, Shadow* at the drop-down list (second option in first row).

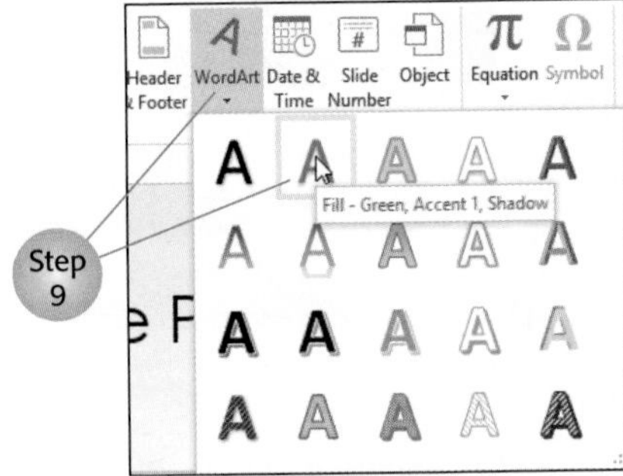

Step 9

10. Slide or drag the WordArt text box to the bottom center of the slide.
11. Select *Your text here* inside the WordArt text box and type **Help Save the Painted Bunting!**

Help Save the Painted Bunting!

Step 11

oops!

Other text is displayed inside the WordArt text box? This occurs if an insertion point is active inside another object with text when WordArt is created. Proceed to select whatever text is inside the box.

12 Tap or click the border of the WordArt text box to remove the insertion point and select the entire placeholder.

13 Tap or click the Text Effects button in the WordArt Styles group of the DRAWING TOOLS FORMAT tab, tap or point to *Glow*, and then tap or click *Lime, 5 pt glow, Accent color 3* (third option in first row of *Glow Variations* section).

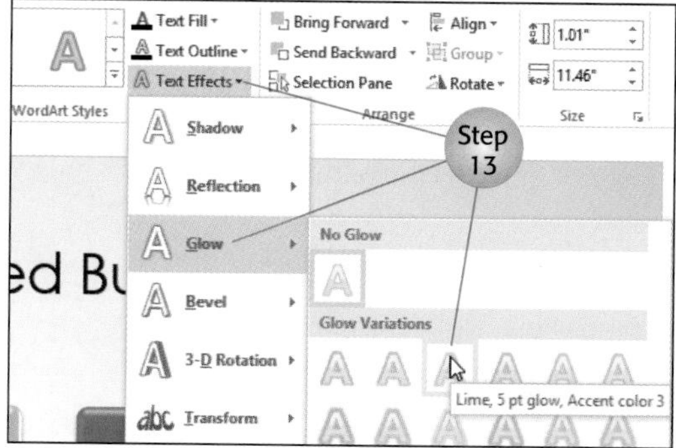

14 Slide or drag the border of the WordArt text box until the smart guide appears, indicating the object is aligned with the center of the object above, as shown in Figure 11.2.

15 Save the revised presentation using the same name (**11.1-PaintedBunting-Your Name**). Leave the presentation open for the next topic.

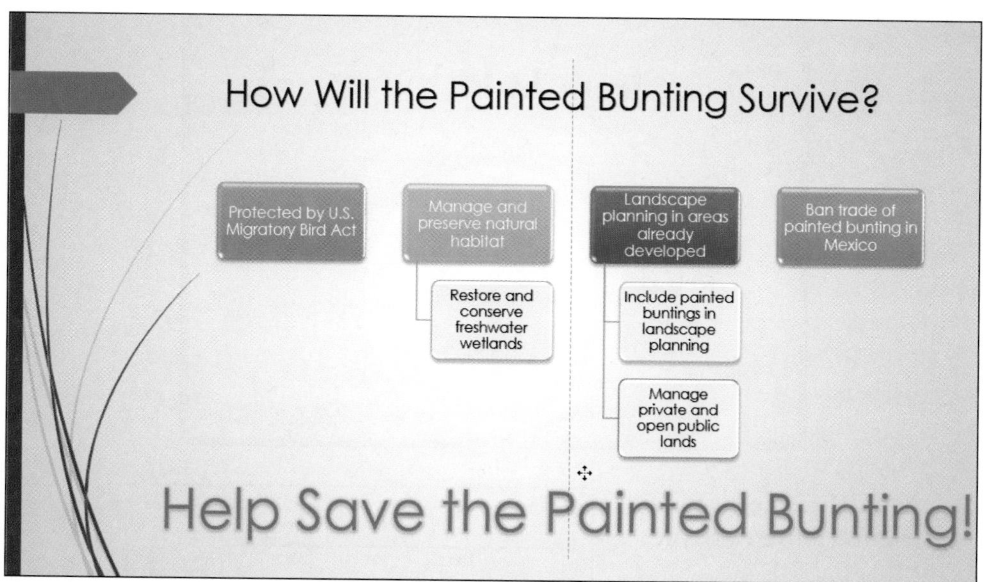

Figure 11.2 WordArt object aligned with center of SmartArt object

Insert WordArt

1. Activate slide.
2. Tap or click INSERT tab.
3. Tap or click WordArt button.
4. Select WordArt Style.
5. Move text box as required.
6. Select *Your text here*.
7. Type text.
8. Format as required.

You can apply more than one text effect to the same object.

Select text in a WordArt object and change the font size as you would any other text. Resize the text box using the selection handles if you make the text larger or smaller in size.

Transforming WordArt Text and Shape Styles

Use the *Transform* option from the Text Effects drop-down list to choose a shape around which WordArt text is formed. Text can be shaped to follow a circular or semi-circular path, slanted, or otherwise altered to create a distinctive effect. Experiment with options in the *Shape Styles* gallery to add a rectangular box around the WordArt.

Topic 11.4

SKILLS

Create a chart

Modify the chart style and color

Creating a Chart on a Slide

Charts similar to the ones you learned to create in Chapter 9 with Excel can be added to a slide in PowerPoint. Add a chart using the Insert Chart icon in a content placeholder or with the Chart button in the Illustrations group of the INSERT tab. Charts are commonly used in presentations to show an audience dollar figures, targets, budgets, comparisons, patterns, trends, or variations in numerical data.

1. With the **11.1-PaintedBunting-Your Name** presentation open, make Slide 3 the active slide.
2. Tap or click the Insert Chart icon in the content placeholder.
3. At the Insert Chart dialog box with *Column* selected in the category list and *Clustered Column* selected as the chart type, tap or click OK.

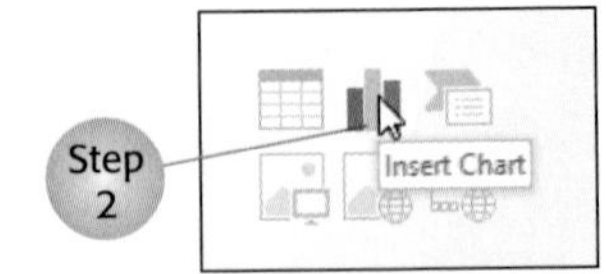

PowerPoint creates a sample chart on the slide and opens a chart data grid into which the data to be graphed is typed. As you enter labels and values into the chart data grid, the chart on the slide updates.

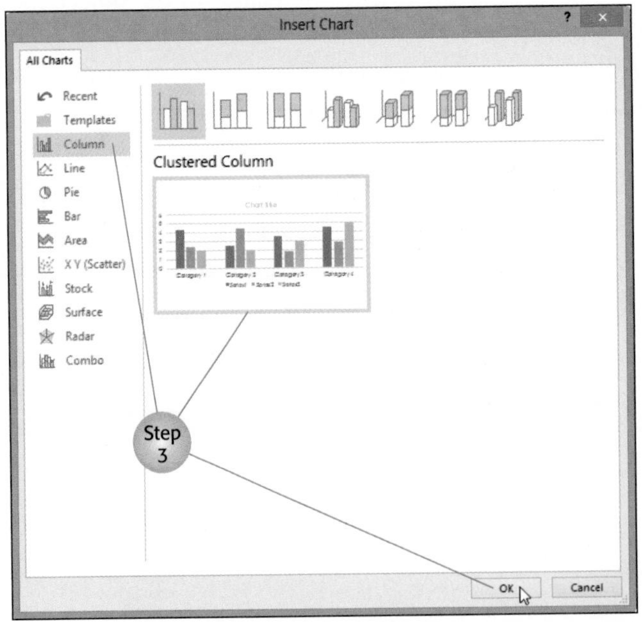

4. With B1 in the chart data grid the active cell, type 2011.
5. Tap or click in C1 and type 2012.
6. Type the remaining data in the cells in the chart data grid as shown in the image at right.
7. Select A5:D5, display the Mini toolbar (touch) or right-click, tap or click *Delete*, and then tap or click *Table Rows*.

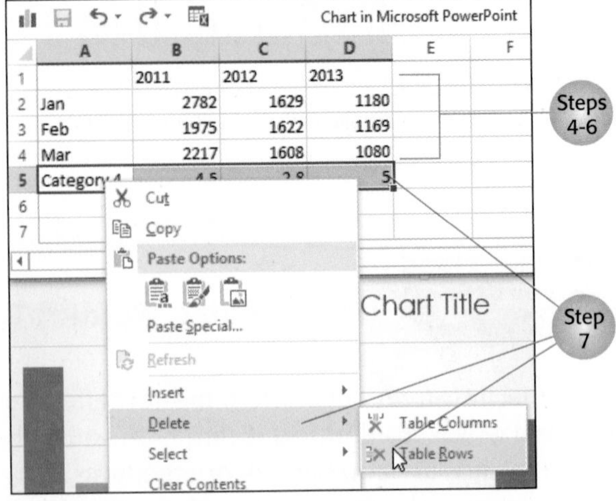

	A	B	C	D
1		2011	2012	2013
2	Jan	2782	1629	1180
3	Feb	1975	1622	1169
4	Mar	2217	1608	1080
5	Category 4			5

oops!

Using Touch? Tap the down-pointing arrow on the Mini toolbar to find *Delete* at the context menu.

8. Close the chart data grid.
9. Select *Chart Title* and type **Monthly Sightings in First Quarter**.
10. Select the chart so that the selection handles around the chart are displayed.
11. Change the Chart Style to *Style 4* (fourth option).
12. Change the chart colors to *Color 2* (second row in *Colorful* section).
13. Tap or click outside the chart to deselect the object and compare your slide with the one shown in Figure 11.3.
14. Save the revised presentation using the same name (**11.1-PaintedBunting-Your Name**). Leave the presentation open for the next topic.

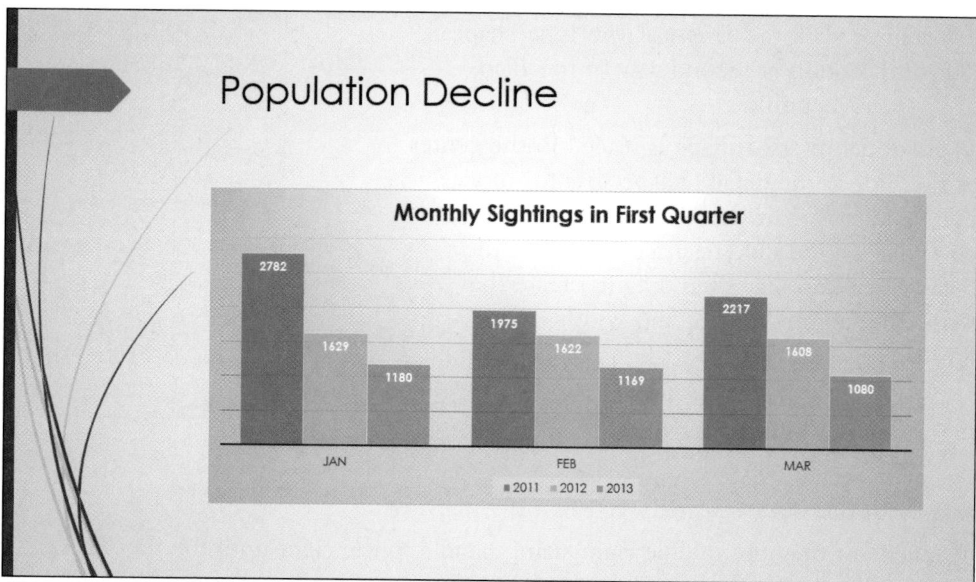

Figure 11.3 Completed Slide 3 with Clustered Column Chart

Don't remember how to change the chart style or color? Refer to Topic 9.7 on page 270 and review Steps 7 and 8.

Quick STEPS

Insert a Chart

1. Activate slide.
2. Tap or click Insert Chart icon in content placeholder.
3. Choose category and chart type.
4. Tap or click OK.
5. Add data in chart data grid.
6. Format as required.

ALTERNATIVE method

Sometimes the data needed to create a chart resides in an Excel worksheet. Rather than duplicate the data in PowerPoint, create the chart in Excel and paste a copy of the chart onto the PowerPoint slide. You will practice this method in Chapter 14.

Formatting Charts and Editing Data

Use the same tools you learned in Excel to modify and format charts in PowerPoint, such as the Chart Elements and Chart Styles button at the top right of the chart or with buttons in the CHART TOOLS DESIGN and CHART TOOLS FORMAT tabs.

To make a change to the source data for the chart, redisplay the chart data grid by tapping or clicking the top part of the Edit Data button in the Data group of the CHART TOOLS DESIGN tab.

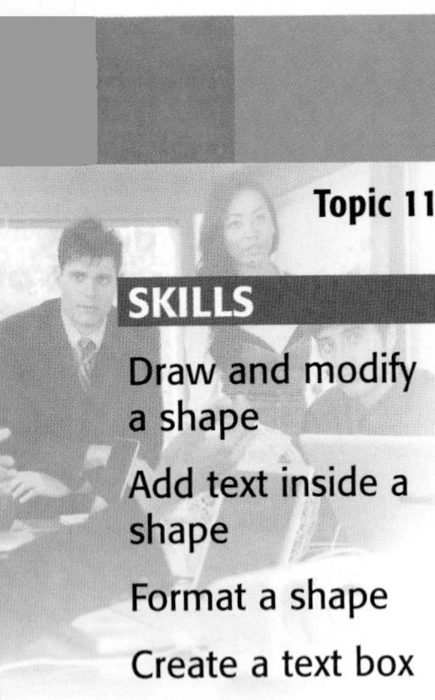

SKILLS

- Draw and modify a shape
- Add text inside a shape
- Format a shape
- Create a text box

Drawing Shapes and Adding Text Boxes

A graphic can be created by drawing a shape such as a line, rectangle, circle, arrow, star, banner, or other item. Once the shape is drawn, text can be added inside the shape and the shape can be formatted by changing the outline color or fill color or by adding an effect. A text box is text inside a rectangular object that can be manipulated independently from other objects on a slide.

1. With the **11.1-PaintedBunting-Your Name** presentation open and with Slide 3 the active slide, tap or click the INSERT tab if necessary.
2. Tap or click the **Shapes button** in the Illustrations group.
3. Tap or click the *Striped Right Arrow* shape (fifth option in second row of the *Block Arrows* section).

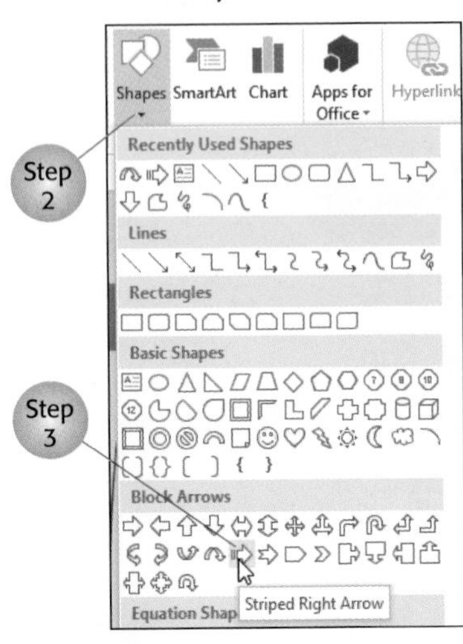

For touch users, a shape is placed in the center of the slide at the default shape size; for mouse users, the cross-hair pointer displays with which you click on the slide to place a shape at the default size. You may then drag to create the shape the required height and width.

4. If you are using a mouse, click on the slide inside the chart near the JAN bar for 2012 (with the value *1629*); if you are using touch, proceed to Step 5.
5. With the shape selected, type **A 41% decline!**
6. Slide or drag the middle right sizing handle to the right until the text fits on one line inside the arrow shape.

When drawing other shapes, hold down the Shift key while dragging the mouse to create a perfect square, circle, or straight line.

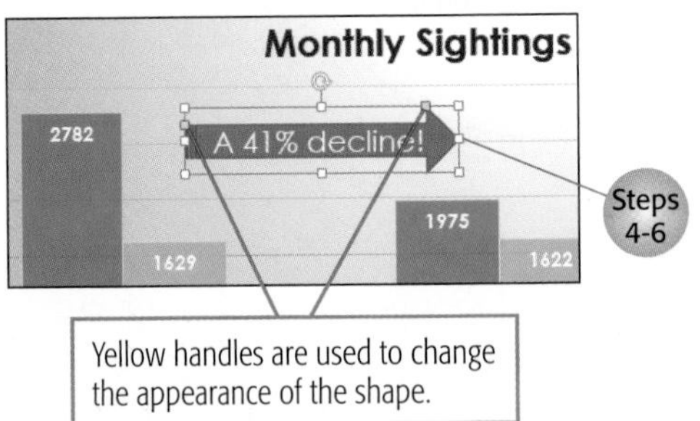

Yellow handles are used to change the appearance of the shape.

7. Slide or drag the rotation handle (circled arrow above top center sizing handle) in an upward diagonal direction toward the left until the shape is at the approximate angle shown in the image below.

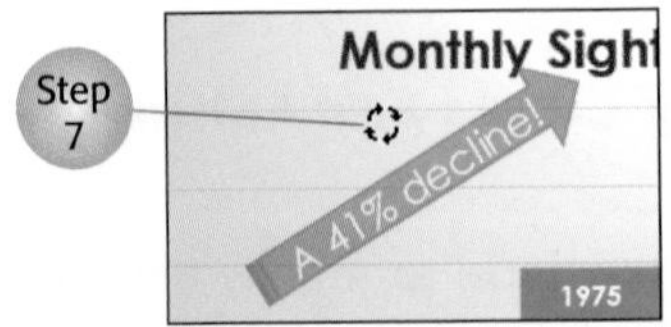

8. Slide or drag the arrow to the bottom left of the chart so that it points to the 2012 January bar, as shown in the image at right.

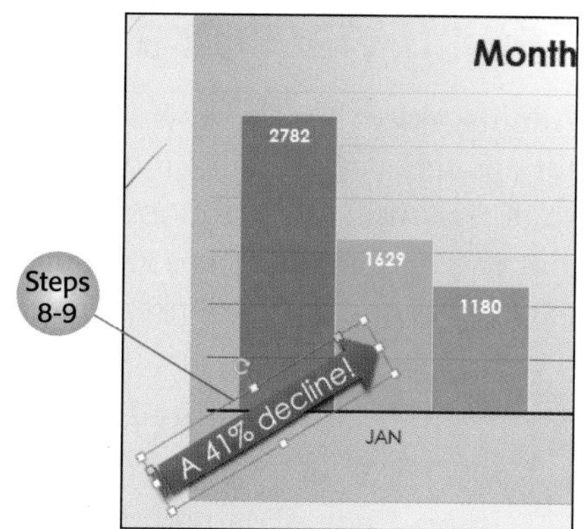

9. With the arrow shape still selected and the DRAWING TOOLS FORMAT tab active, tap or click the More button at the bottom right of the *Shape Styles* gallery and then tap or click *Intense Effect – Turquoise, Accent 6* (last option in gallery).

10. Tap or click the Text Box button in the Insert Shapes group of the DRAWING TOOLS FORMAT tab.

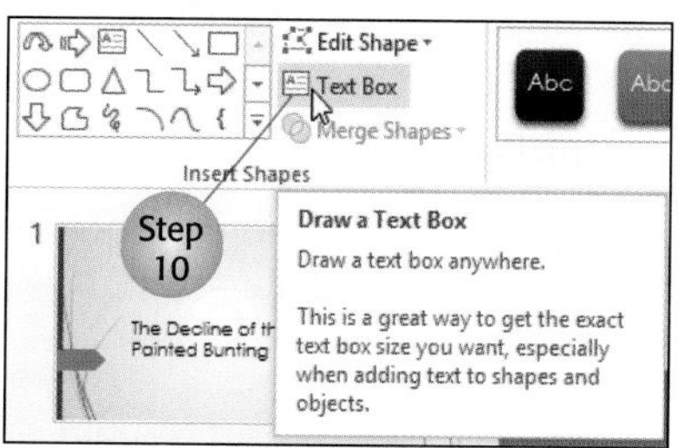

11. If you are using a mouse, click anywhere at the left side of the slide outside the chart to insert a text box with an insertion point; if you are using touch, proceed to Step 12.

12. Type **Source: Painted Bunting Observer Team, University of North Carolina Wilmington**.

13. Tap or click the border of the text box to remove the insertion point and select the entire placeholder, tap or click the HOME tab, and then tap or click the Italic button in the Font group.

14. Move and/or resize the text box, aligning the text box with the bottom of the chart as shown in the image below.

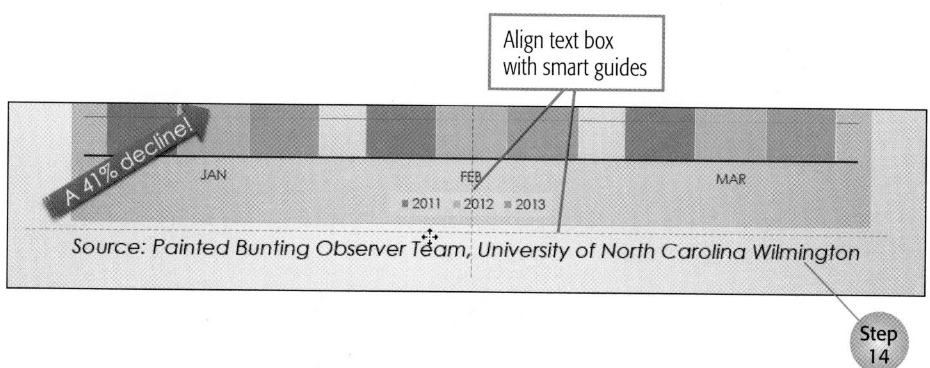

15. Save the revised presentation using the same name (**11.1-PaintedBunting-Your Name**). Leave the presentation open for the next topic.

Draw a Shape

1. Tap or click INSERT tab.
2. Tap or click Shapes button.
3. Tap or click required shape.
4. Mouse user: click to insert default shape.
5. Type text if required.
6. Resize, format, and move as required.

Create a Text Box

1. Tap or click INSERT tab.
2. Tap or click Text Box button.
3. Mouse user: click on slide.
4. Type text.
5. Resize, format, and move as required.

Action Buttons

A category of shapes called *Action Buttons* contains a series of buttons with actions assigned that are used to create a navigation interface or launch other items during a slide show. For example, draw the *Action Button: Home* button on a slide to move to the first slide when the button is clicked during a slide show.

Adding Video to a Presentation

Adding video to a presentation provides a more interesting multimedia experience for an audience. A high-quality video can show a process or task that is difficult to portray using descriptions or pictures. Video is widely used for instructional and entertainment purposes. Appropriately used, video provides a more enjoyable experience for the audience. You can play a video from a file stored on your PC or link to a video at YouTube or another online source.

1. With the **11.1-PaintedBunting-Your Name** presentation open, make Slide 6 the active slide.
2. Insert a new slide with the Title and Content layout and type **A Beautiful Bird** as the slide title.
3. Tap or click the Insert Video icon in the content placeholder.

4. At the Insert Video dialog box, tap or click the Browse From a file link in the *From a file* section.

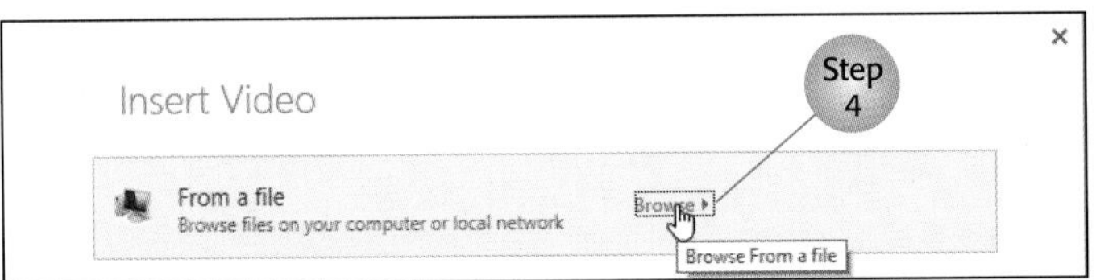

5. Navigate to the Ch11 folder in Student_Data_Files and double-tap or double-click the file named ***PaintedBuntingVideo***.
6. Tap or click the Play/Pause button below the video to preview the video clip.

The video plays for approximately 52 seconds.

7. Tap or click the VIDEO TOOLS PLAYBACK tab.
8. Tap or click the **Trim Video button** in the Editing group.

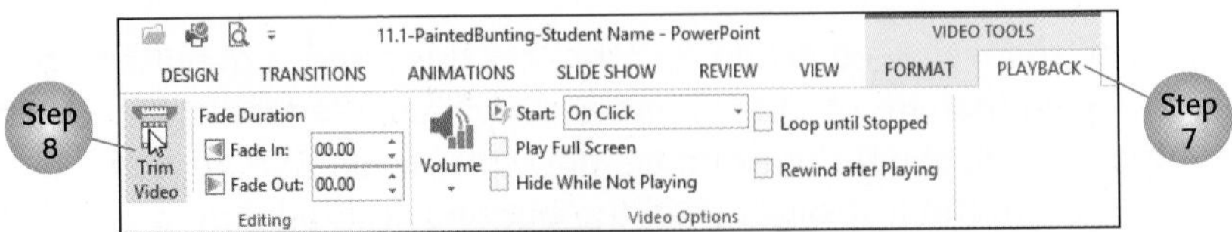

App Tip

PowerPoint recognizes most video file formats such as QuickTime movies, MP4 videos, MPEG movie files, Windows Media Video (wmv) files, and Adobe Flash Media.

Trimming a video allows you to show only a portion of a video file if the video is too long or if you do not wish to show parts at the beginning or end. Slide or drag the green or red slider to start playing at a later starting point and/or end before the video is finished, or enter the start and end times.

9 At the Trim Video dialog box, select the current entry in the *Start Time* text box and type **00:10**.

10 Select the current entry in the *End Time* text box and type **00:30**.

11 Tap or click the Play button to preview the shorter video clip.

12 Tap or click OK.

13 Tap or click the *Start* list arrow (displays *On Click*) in the Video Options group and then tap or click *Automatically*.

This option means the video will begin playing as soon as the slide is displayed in the slide show.

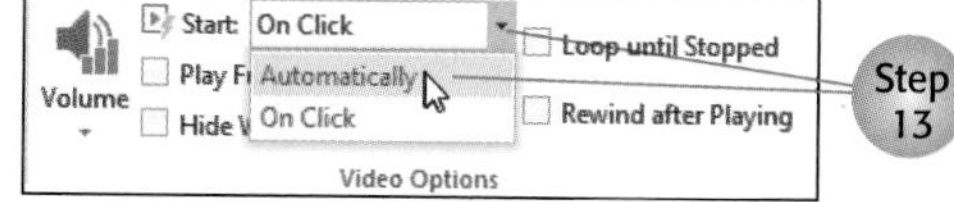

14 Slide or drag the video object left until the smart guide appears at the left, indicating the object is aligned with the slide title.

15 Tap or click the VIDEO TOOLS FORMAT tab and tap or click the *Soft Edge Rectangle* in the Video Styles group (third option).

16 Save the revised image using the same name (**11.1-PaintedBunting-Your Name**). Leave the presentation open for the next topic.

ALTERNATIVE method

Add video to an existing slide by tapping or clicking the INSERT tab, tapping or clicking the Video button in the Media group, and then choosing *Online Video* or *Video on my PC* at the drop-down list.

Link to a video at YouTube by typing the name of the video in the *Search YouTube* text box at the Insert Video dialog box. Select the video in the search results list and choose Insert.

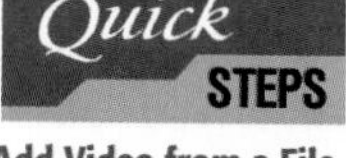

Add Video from a File on a PC

1. Tap or click Insert Video icon in placeholder.
2. Tap or click Browse From a file.
3. Navigate to drive and/or folder.
4. Double-tap or double-click video file.
5. Edit and/or format as required.

Other Video Playback Options

The video can be set to display full screen, to loop continuously so that the video repeats until the slide show has ended, and to fade in or out. Configure these settings in the Editing and Video Options group of the VIDEO TOOLS PLAYBACK tab.

Adding Sound to a Presentation

Adding music or other sound during a slide show is another method to add interest, communicate, or entertain an audience. For example, a speaker may choose to have music playing while the title slide is displayed, with the end of the music cueing the audience that the presentation is about to begin. Music can also be timed to play during a segment of a presentation during which a series of images is running.

Note: You will need headphones or earbuds if you are completing this topic in a computer lab at school where sound through the speakers is disabled.

1. With the **11.1-PaintedBunting-Your Name** presentation open, make Slide 1 the active slide and then tap or click the INSERT tab if necessary.

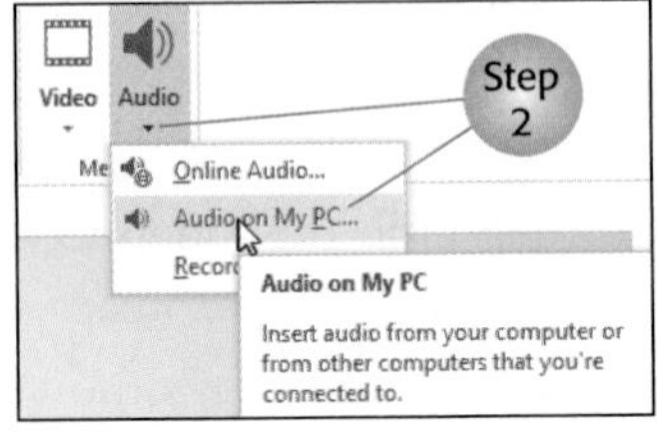

2. Tap or click the **Audio button** in the Media group and then tap or click *Audio on My PC* at the drop-down list.
3. Navigate to the Ch11 folder in Student_Data_Files and double-tap or double-click the file named ***Allemande***.
4. Slide or drag the sound icon to the bottom right of the slide.

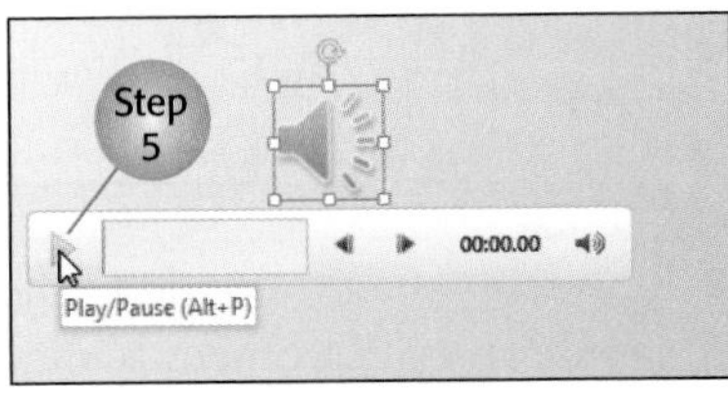

5. Tap or click the Play/Pause button and listen to the recording for a few seconds.

   The entire music clip plays for approximately two and a half minutes.

6. With the AUDIO TOOLS PLAYBACK tab active, tap or click the *Hide During Show* check box in the Audio Options group to insert a check mark.

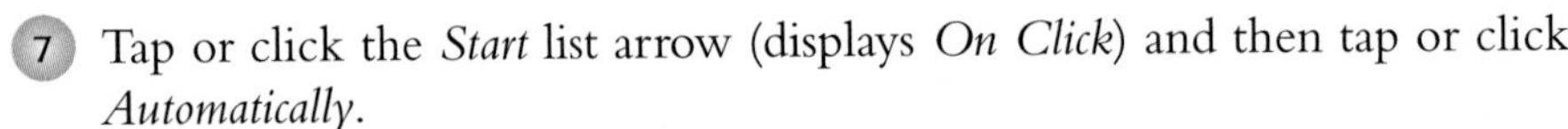

7. Tap or click the *Start* list arrow (displays *On Click*) and then tap or click *Automatically*.

   This option will start the music as soon as the slide is displayed in the slide show.
8. Tap or click the *Loop until Stopped* check box to insert a check mark.

   This option will cause the music to replay continuously until the slide is advanced during the slide show.

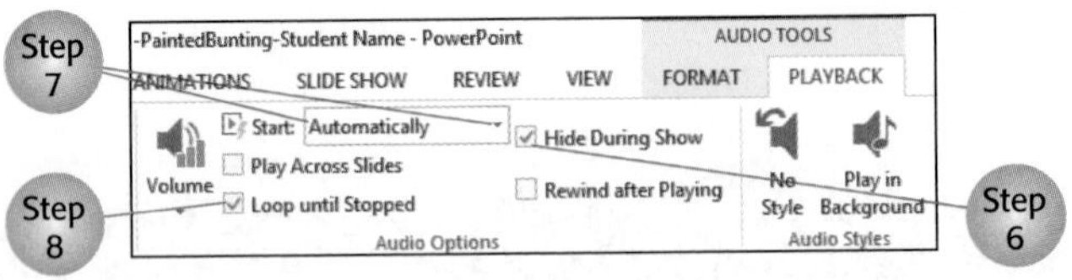

9. Make Slide 7 the active slide.

Choose *Online Audio* to search for royalty-free sound clips at Office.com, or choose *Record Audio* to record a new sound clip.

PowerPoint recognizes most audio file formats including MIDI files, MP3 and MP4 audio files, Windows audio files (.wav), and Window Media Audio files (.wma).

10 Insert the audio file named ***PaintedBunting_Song*** in the slide by completing steps similar to those in Steps 2 to 8.

The audio recording of the Painted Bunting bird song is slightly less than two seconds in length.

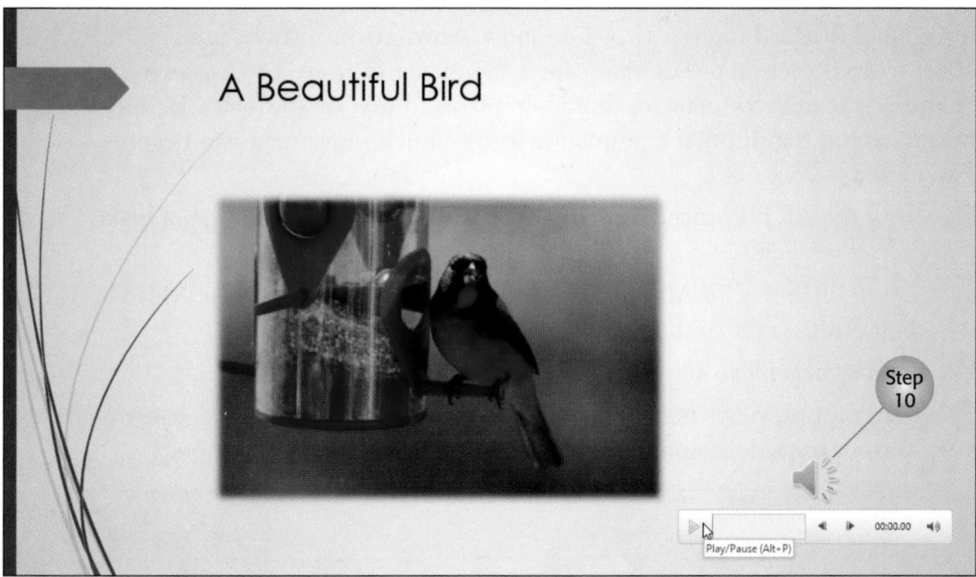

Add Audio from a File
1. Tap or click INSERT tab.
2. Tap or click Audio button.
3. Tap or click *Audio on My PC*.
4. Navigate to drive and/or folder.
5. Double-tap or double-click video file.
6. Edit playback options as required.

11 Insert a new slide after Slide 7 with the Title and Content layout and type **Photo, Video, and Audio Credits** as the slide title.

12 Insert a table, type the information shown in Figure 11.4, and then adjust the layout using your best judgment for column widths and position on the slide.

Always credit the source of images, audio, and video used in a presentation if you did not create the multimedia yourself. In this instance, the music from Slide 1 is not credited because the recording is in the public domain, and the picture on Slide 6 is not credited because you found the image using Office.com royalty-free clip art.

13 Save the revised presentation using the same name (**11.1-PaintedBunting-Your Name**). Leave the presentation open for the next topic.

Did You Know?

Many websites offer copyright-free or public domain multimedia. Include the keywords copyright free *or* public domain *in a search for a picture, audio, or video file. Check the terms of use at each site to be sure you credit sources appropriately because copyright-free allows free usage but requires attribution to the creator.*

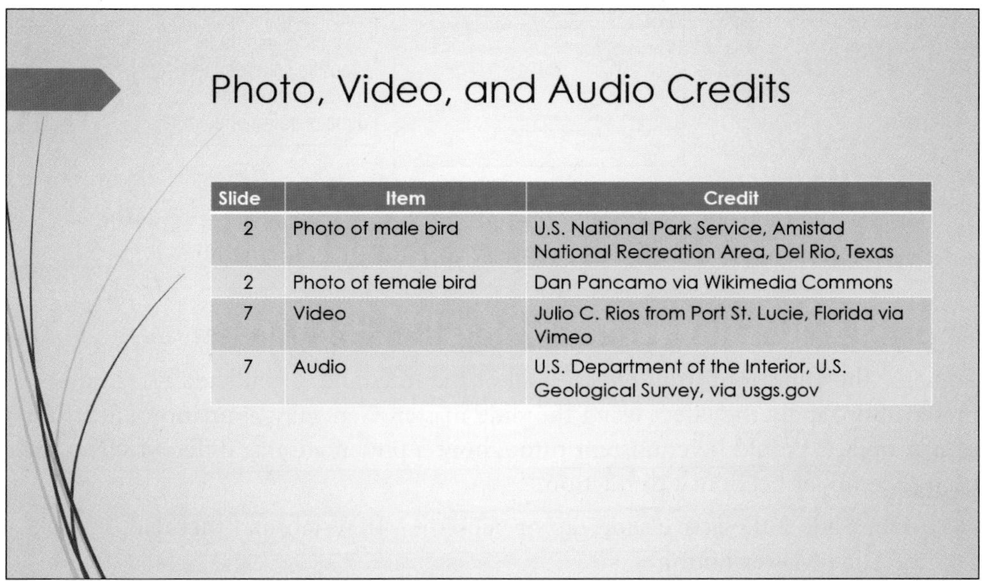

Slide	Item	Credit
2	Photo of male bird	U.S. National Park Service, Amistad National Recreation Area, Del Rio, Texas
2	Photo of female bird	Dan Pancamo via Wikimedia Commons
7	Video	Julio C. Rios from Port St. Lucie, Florida via Vimeo
7	Audio	U.S. Department of the Interior, U.S. Geological Survey, via usgs.gov

Figure 11.4 Table for Slide 8 with Multimedia Credits

Topic 11.8

SKILLS

Add transitions

Add animation on slide master

Add animation to individual objects

oops!

Trouble finding *Blinds*? On smaller-screened devices such as tablets, the *Transitions* gallery displays fewer buttons per row. Look for *Blinds* further right or down.

Adding Transitions and Animation Effects to a Slide Show

A **transition** is a special effect that appears as one slide is removed from the screen and the next slide appears. Text and objects can be revealed using a variety of techniques that add interest to a slide show. **Animation** involves adding a special effect to an object on a slide that causes the object to move or change in some way. Animation is used to focus on or add emphasis to text or an object. Be mindful not to overdo transition and animation as too much movement can become a distraction.

1. With the **11.1-PaintedBunting-Your Name** presentation open, make Slide 1 the active slide.
2. Tap or click the TRANSITIONS tab and then tap or click the More button at the bottom right of the *Transition to This Slide* gallery.
3. Tap or click *Blinds* in the *Exciting* section of the gallery.

PowerPoint previews the effect with the current slide so that you can experiment with various transitions and effects before making your final selection.

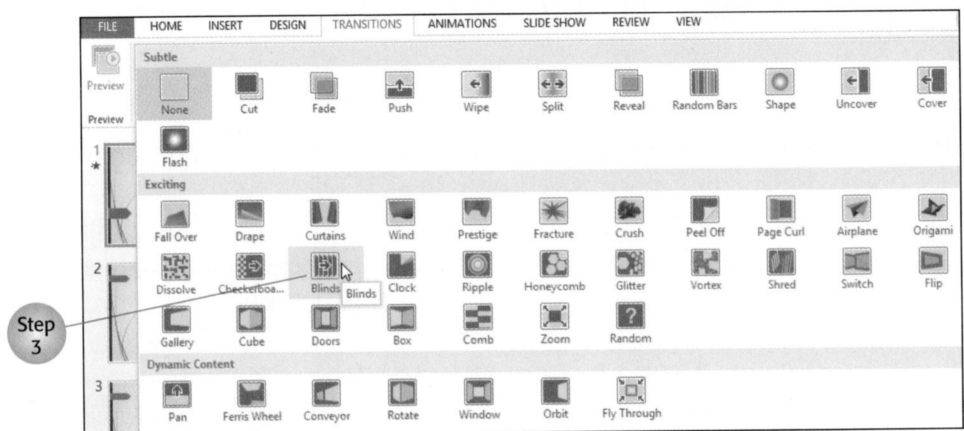

4. Tap or click the Apply To All button in the Timing group.

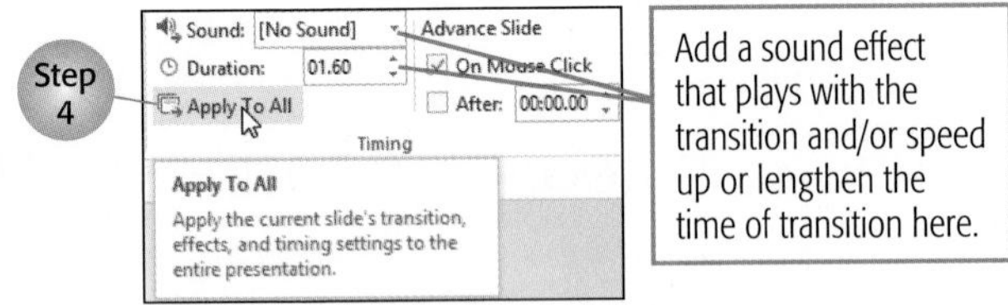

5. Display the slide show, advance through the first three slides to view the transition effect, and then end the show to return to Normal view.

Use the Effect Options button in the Transition to This Slide group to choose a variation for the selected transition (such as the direction the blinds move).

Applying Animation Effects Using the Slide Master

To apply the same animation effect to all of the titles and/or bulleted lists in a presentation, apply the effect using the slide master. Generally, animation effects for similar objects should be consistent throughout a presentation; a different effect on each slide might become a distraction.

6. Make Slide 2 the active slide, tap or click the VIEW tab, and then tap or click the Slide Master button.
7. Tap or click to select the border of the title placeholder on the slide master.

8 Tap or click the ANIMATIONS tab.

9 Tap or click *Split* in the *Animation* gallery.

See Table 11.2 for a description of Animation categories.

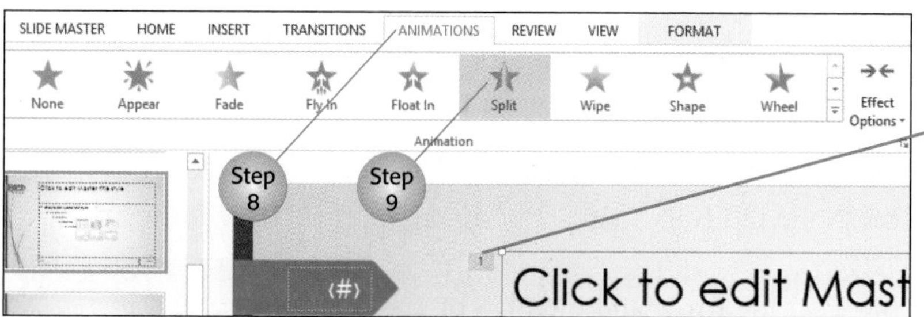

This icon displays the animation's sequence; the slide title will animate first.

The *Animation* gallery provides the most popular effects. View more effects by category using the options at the bottom of the gallery. For example, *More Entrance Effects* shows all 40 options.

10 Tap or click to select the border of the content placeholder and then tap or click the More button in the *Animation* gallery.

11 Tap or click *Zoom* in the *Entrance* section.

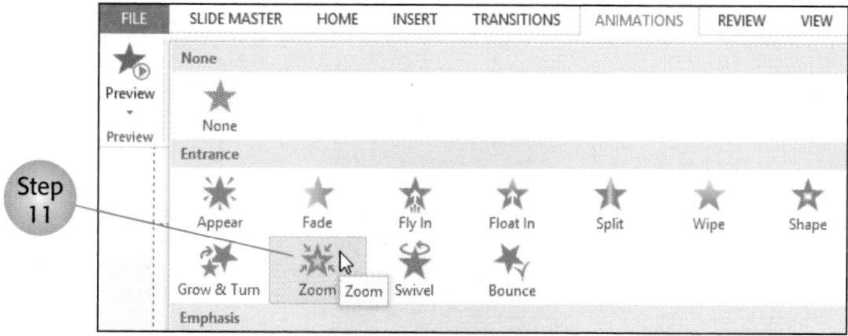

12 Tap or click the *Start* list arrow (displays *On Click*) in the Timing group and then tap or click *After Previous*.

13 Select the current entry in the *Duration* text box and type **1.5**.

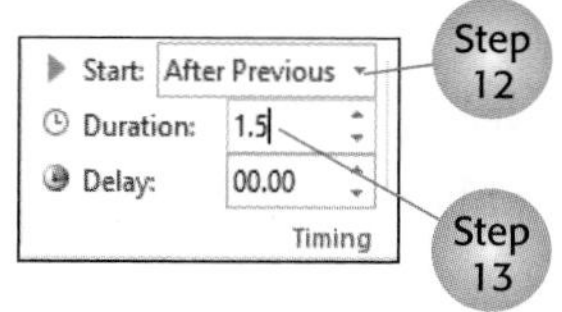

14 Tap or click the SLIDE MASTER tab and then tap or click the Close Master View button.

15 Make Slide 1 the active slide, run through the presentation in a slide show to view the transition and animation effects, and then return to Normal view.

Table 11.2	Animation Categories
Category	**Description**
Entrance	Most common animation effect in which the object animates as it appears on the slide
Emphasis	Animates text or object already in place by causing the object to move or to change in appearance; includes effects such as darkening, changing color, bolding, or underlining, to name a few
Exit	Animates the text or object after it has been revealed, such as by fading or flying off the slide
Motion Paths	An object moves along a linear path, an arc, or some other shape

Applying Animation Effects to Individual Objects

As you previewed the slide show, you probably noticed that images and other objects such as shapes or text boxes appeared on the slide before the title. You may want these items to remain hidden until the title and text have been revealed. To apply animation to an individual object, display the slide, select the object to be animated, and then apply the desired animation.

16 Make Slide 2 the active slide.

17 Select the male bird picture at the top right of the slide.

18 Tap or click the ANIMATIONS tab and then tap or click *Wipe* in the *Animation* gallery.

19 Tap or click the *Start* list arrow and then tap or click *After Previous*.

20 Tap or click to select the male bird picture and then tap or click the **Animation Painter button** in the Advanced Animation group.

Similar to the Format Painter button, the Animation Painter button is used to copy animation effects from one object to another.

21 Tap or click the female bird picture at the bottom right of the slide.

Animation Painter copies animation effects and options from one object to another.
Step 21

22 Make Slide 3 the active slide.

23 Select the arrow shape, apply the *Fly In* animation, and change the *Start* option to *After Previous*.

24 Copy the arrow shape's animation options to the text box object below the chart by completing steps similar to those in Steps 20 and 21.

25 Make Slide 5 the active slide.

26 Select the WordArt object at the bottom of the slide, apply the *Float In* animation, and change the *Start* option to *After Previous*.

27 Make Slide 6 the active slide.

28 Select the picture at the left side of the slide, apply the *Shape* animation, and change the *Start* option to *After Previous*.

29 Select the SmartArt graphic at the bottom of the slide. Make sure the entire graphic is selected and not an individual shape within the graphic.

30 Apply the *Fly-in* animation and change the *Start* option to *After Previous*.

31 Tap or click the Effect Options button and then tap or click *One by One* in the *Sequence* section of the drop-down list.

This option will cause each chevron in the graphic to animate on the slide one at a time, starting with the leftmost shape first.

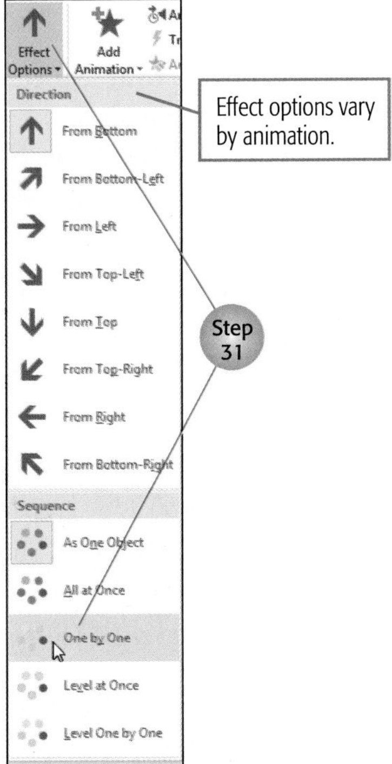

32 Run through the presentation in a slide show from the beginning to view the revised animation effects and then return to Normal view.

33 Save the revised presentation using the same name (**11.1-PaintedBunting-Your Name**). Leave the presentation open for the next topic.

Add a Transition
1. Tap or click TRANSITIONS tab.
2. Add transition effect.
3. Change effect options or timing options as required.
4. Tap or click Apply to All button.

Apply Animation to All Slides
1. Display slide master.
2. Tap or click ANIMATIONS tab.
3. Select placeholder.
4. Add animation effect.
5. Change effect options or timing options as required.
6. Close Slide Master view.

Apply Animation to an Individual Object
1. Activate slide.
2. Tap or click ANIMATIONS tab.
3. Select object.
4. Add animation effect.
5. Change effect options or timing options as required.

Did You Know?

You can deliver a presentation online using the free Office Presentation Service if you are signed in with a Microsoft account. Participants are able to view slides in a web browser. Access the service at the Share tab Backstage view.

Changing the Animation Sequence

To adjust the order in which objects are animated, display the required slide and open the Animation pane at the right side of the window. To do this, tap or click the Animation Pane button in the Advanced Animation group of the ANIMATIONS tab. Select the object that you want to move in the Animation pane and then use the Move Earlier or Move Later buttons in the Reorder Animation group.

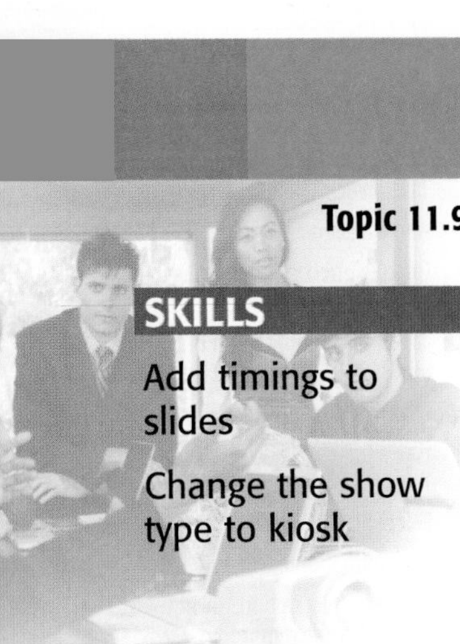

Topic 11.9
SKILLS
Add timings to slides
Change the show type to kiosk

Set Up a Self-Running Presentation

Some presentations are designed to be self-running, meaning that the slides are intended to be shown continuously at a kiosk or viewed at a PC by an individual. To create a presentation that advances through slides automatically, you need to set up a time for each slide to display and ensure that each slide's animation is set to start automatically for each object.

1. With the **11.1-PaintedBunting-Your Name** presentation open, use Save As to save a copy of the presentation in the current folder naming it **11.9-PaintingBuntingSelfRunning-Your Name**.
2. Make Slide 2 the active slide and display the slide master.
3. Select the border of the title placeholder.
4. Tap or click the ANIMATIONS tab and change the *Start* option in the *Timing* section to *After Previous*.
5. Close Slide Master view.
6. Make Slide 1 the active slide and select the sound icon.
7. Tap or click the AUDIO TOOLS PLAYBACK tab and then tap or click the *Play Across Slides* check box in the Audio Options group to insert a check mark.

This option will cause the music that starts at Slide 1 to continue playing through the remaining slides.

8. Tap or click the Volume button and then tap or click *Low* at the drop-down list.

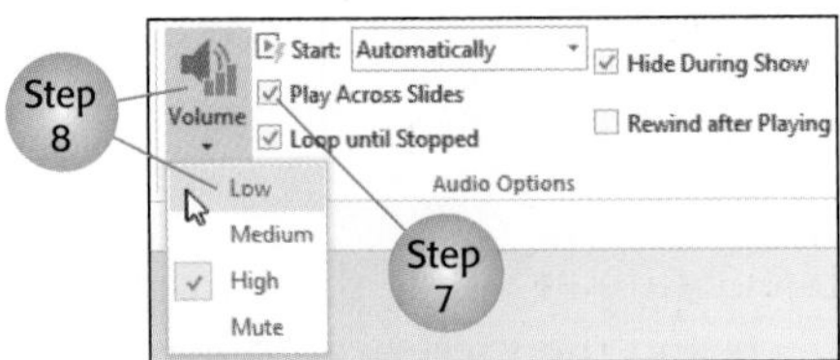

9. Make Slide 7 the active slide and then select and delete the sound icon to remove the audio.
10. Make Slide 8 the active slide and then select and delete the last row in the table.
11. Tap or click the TRANSITIONS tab.
12. Tap or click the *After* check box in the *Timing* section to insert a check mark, select the current entry in the *After* text box, and then type **0:25**.
13. Tap or click the Apply To All button.

All of the slides will be advanced automatically after the same 25-second duration. To set individual times for slides, activate a slide and enter a different time in the *After* text box.

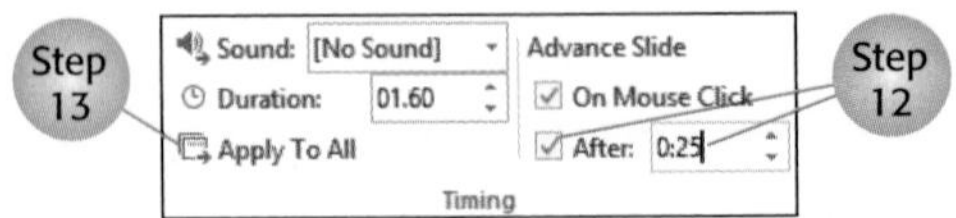

14. Make Slide 3 the active slide, select the entry in the *After* text box, and then type **0:10**.
15. Change the *After* time for Slide 5 and Slide 6 to **0:15** and for Slide 8 to **0:10**.

16 Tap or click the SLIDE SHOW tab and then tap or click the **Set Up Slide Show button** in the Set Up group.

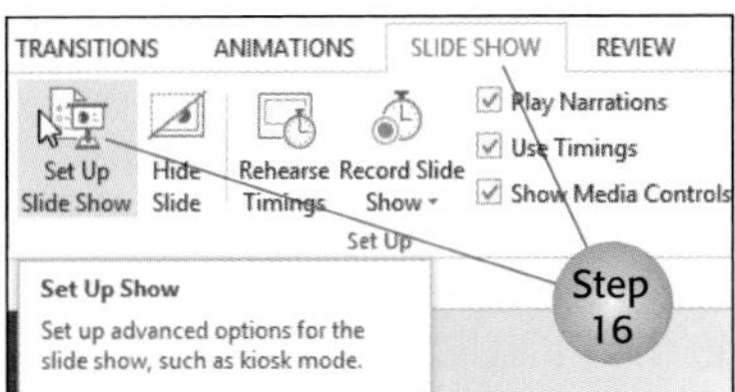

17 At the Set Up Show dialog box, tap or click the *Browsed at a kiosk (full screen)* option in the *Show type* section.

18 Tap or click OK.

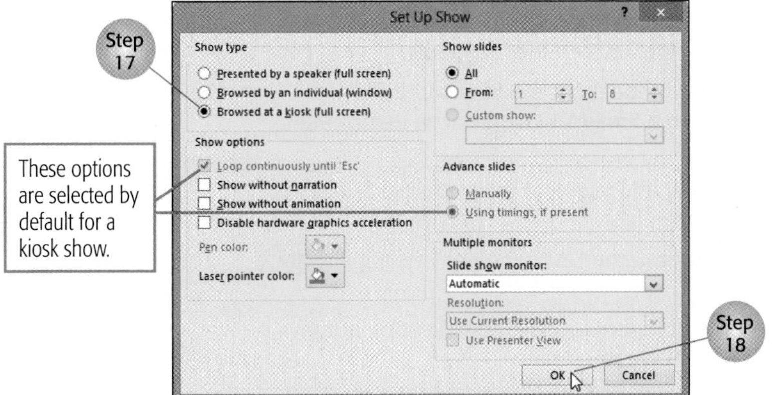

19 Start the slide show from the beginning and watch the presentation as it advances through all of the slides automatically. End the show when the presentation starts at Slide 1 again by pressing and holding to display the slide show toolbar and tapping the End Show button, or by pressing the ESC key.

20 Save the revised presentation using the same name (**11.9-PaintedBuntingSelf Running-Your Name**) and then close the presentation by pressing and holding to display the slide show toolbar and tapping the End Show button, or by pressing the ESC key.

Add Timing for a Slide
1. Tap or click TRANSITIONS tab.
2. Tap or click *After* check box.
3. Enter time in *After* text box.

Set Up a Kiosk Show
1. Tap or click SLIDE SHOW tab.
2. Tap or click Set Up Slide Show button.
3. Tap or click *Browsed at a kiosk (full screen)*.
4. Tap or click OK.

You can create an MPEG 4 (MP4) movie file that you can burn to a disc or upload to a website using *Create a Video* at the Export tab Backstage view.

Using Rehearse Timings

The **Rehearse Timings** feature (SLIDE SHOW tab) lets you assign a time to each slide as you run through a slide show with a timer active and a Recording toolbar. Use the Next button on the Recording toolbar to advance each slide, and PowerPoint will enter the times for each slide transition. This method lets you time each slide for a typical audience member after a suitable time has elapsed in the slide show.

Concepts Review

Topic	Key Concepts	Key Terms
Inserting Graphics from Clip Art and Picture Collections	A picture from your PC can be added to a slide using the Pictures button in the Images group of the INSERT tab or with the Pictures icon in the content placeholder on a new slide. Resize, move, or edit a picture by selecting the image and using the selection handles and/or buttons in the PICTURE TOOLS FORMAT tab. Find a picture or other image from the Office.com clip art collection, the Web, or collections stored at your Flickr, Facebook, or SkyDrive account using the Online Pictures button in the Images group of the INSERT tab.	
Inserting a SmartArt Graphic	SmartArt graphics use shapes with text to illustrate information in lists, processes, cycles, hierarchies, or other diagrams. Add a SmartArt graphic to a slide using the SmartArt button in the INSERT tab or the Insert a SmartArt Graphic icon in a content placeholder. Choose a SmartArt category and layout at the Choose a SmartArt Graphic dialog box. Text can be added to shapes in the Text pane or by typing directly inside a shape. Modify SmartArt styles or colors or edit the graphic using buttons in the SMARTART TOOLS DESIGN tab.	SmartArt
Converting Text to SmartArt and Inserting WordArt	A bulleted list can be converted into a SmartArt graphic using the Convert to SmartArt button in the Paragraph group of the HOME tab. WordArt is decorative text inside an independent object on a slide. Create WordArt using the WordArt button in the Text group of the INSERT tab. Type the WordArt text inside the text box and then add text effects, move, and or otherwise edit the object using buttons in the DRAWING TOOLS FORMAT tab.	Convert to SmartArt button WordArt
Creating a Chart on a Slide	Charts similar to those learned in Excel can be added to a slide. Insert a chart using the Insert Chart icon in the content placeholder or the Chart button in the Illustrations group of the INSERT tab. Choose the chart category and chart type at the Insert Chart dialog box. Type the data to be graphed in the chart data grid, which is a small Excel worksheet. Modify the chart using the buttons in the CHART TOOLS DESIGN and CHART TOOLS FORMAT tabs.	
Drawing Shapes and Adding Text Boxes	Draw your own graphics on a slide using the Shapes button in the INSERT tab. Type text inside a selected shape and then resize, move, or otherwise modify the shape using buttons in the DRAWING TOOLS FORMAT tab. A text box is a rectangular object in which you can type text and that can be moved, resized, or formatted independently. Create a text box using the Text Box button in the INSERT tab or the DRAWING TOOLS FORMAT tab.	Shapes button

Topic	Key Concepts	Key Terms
Adding Video to a Presentation	Add video to a slide using the Insert Video icon in a content placeholder or with the Video button in the Media group of the INSERT tab. You can select a video clip from a file on your PC or by finding a video clip at YouTube or another website. Use buttons in the VIDEO TOOLS PLAYBACK tab to edit a video or change the video options. Use the Trim Video button to change the starting and/or ending position of the video if you do not want to play the entire clip. Change the *Start* option if you want the video to start automatically when the slide is displayed in a slide show. Options in the VIDEO TOOLS FORMAT tab are used to format the video object.	Trim Video button
Adding Sound to a Presentation	Add audio to a slide using the Audio button in the Media group of the INSERT tab. Use buttons in the Audio Options group of the AUDIO TOOLS PLAYBACK tab to hide the sound icon during a slide show, start the audio automatically, play the sound in the background across all slides, or loop the audio continuously until the slide is advanced. Always credit the sources of all multimedia used in a presentation that you did not create yourself unless the media was obtained from a public domain resource or Office.com royalty-free collection.	Audio button
Adding Transitions and Animation Effects to a Slide Show	A transition is a special effect that appears as one slide is removed from the screen and another is revealed during a slide show. Animation causes an object to move or transform in some way. Select a transition at the *Transition to This Slide* gallery in the TRANSITIONS tab. The Apply to All button in the Timing group of the TRANSITIONS tab sets the same transition effect to all slides. Add an animation effect to a placeholder on the slide master to apply the effect to all slides in the presentation. Animation effects are selected in the *Animation* gallery of the ANIMATIONS tab. Specify how the animation will start and the animation's duration using options in the Timing group. Animate an individual object on a slide by selecting the object and then adding an animation effect from the *Animation* gallery. The Animation Painter button copies the animation effect and effect options from one object to another. Animation effects are grouped into four categories: Entrance, Emphasis, Exit, and Motion Paths. To change the sequence in which objects are animated, display the Animation pane, select the object to be reordered, and then use the Move Earlier or Move Later buttons in the Reorder Animation group.	Transition Animation Animation Painter button

continued....

Topic	Key Concepts	Key Terms
Set Up a Self-Running Presentation	A self-running presentation is set up to run a slide show continuously. To create a self-running presentation, each slide needs to have a time entered in the *After* text box in the Timing group of the TRANSITIONS tab, and each animated object needs to be set to start automatically. Open the Set Up Show dialog box (SLIDE SHOW tab) and choose *Browsed at a kiosk (full screen)* to instruct PowerPoint to play the slide show continuously until stopped. Use the Rehearse Timings feature (SLIDE SHOW tab) to set a time for each slide to display while watching a slide show with a timer and Recording toolbar active.	Set Up Slide Show button Rehearse Timings

Multiple Choice

1. Use this button in the Images group to search for an image in the Office.com clip art collection.
   a. Pictures
   b. Online Pictures
   c. Clip Art
   d. Media
2. Use this button in the Images group to add an image to a slide from a file on your PC.
   a. Pictures
   b. Online Pictures
   c. Computer
   d. Images
3. Add text inside a SmartArt shape by typing directly within the shape or here.
   a. text box
   b. text placeholder
   c. Text pane
   d. text container
4. This SmartArt layout category is best suited for creating an organization chart.
   a. List
   b. Process
   c. Relationship
   d. Hierarchy
5. Use this button to change a bulleted list into a SmartArt graphic.
   a. SmartArt Graphic
   b. Convert to SmartArt
   c. Transform to SmartArt
   d. Switch to SmartArt
6. Text that is created and formatted as a graphic object is referred to as ____________.
   a. SmartText
   b. WordArt
   c. TextArt
   d. TextPic
7. Use this icon in a content placeholder to add a clustered column chart to a slide.
   a. Insert Column Chart
   b. Insert Chart
   c. Insert Graph
   d. Insert Data
8. Data to be graphed in a chart is typed in this grid.
   a. table data
   b. bar data
   c. chart data
   d. graph data
9. Draw an arrow on a slide using this button from the INSERT tab.
   a. Block Arrows
   b. Shapes
   c. Illustration
   d. Draw
10. Type text inside this type of box to create an object that can be formatted independently of other objects.
    a. text box
    b. transition box
    c. graphic box
    d. animation box
11. Change the *Start* option to this setting to have video begin playing as soon as the slide is displayed in a slide show.
    a. After previous
    b. Before previous
    c. Automatically
    d. On start

12. Use this button in the Editing group of VIDEO TOOLS PLAYBACK to change the starting point at which a clip begins playing.
    a. On Start
    b. Edit Video
    c. Set Up Video
    d. Trim Video
13. Use this option from the Audio button to choose a sound clip stored on your computer.
    a. Audio on My PC
    b. Computer
    c. Local Disk
    d. PC Audio
14. This option in the AUDIO TOOLS PLAYBACK ribbon causes a sound clip to keep repeating until the slide is advanced in the slide show.
    a. Replay until Stopped
    b. AutoStart until Stopped
    c. Continuous until Stopped
    d. Loop until Stopped
15. This term refers to a special effect that occurs as the next slide in the slide show is revealed.
    a. animation
    b. transition
    c. conversion
    d. effect option
16. This term refers to a special effect added to an object on a slide that causes the object to move or change in some way.
    a. animation
    b. conversion
    c. transition
    d. effect option
17. The time that a slide should remain on screen during a self-running presentation is added in the *After* text box in this tab.
    a. ANIMATIONS
    b. SLIDE SHOW
    c. TRANSITIONS
    d. INSERT
18. Open this dialog box to specify that the show type is *Browsed at a kiosk (full screen)*.
    a. Show Type
    b. Set Up Show
    c. Animation Effects
    d. Slide Show

Crossword Puzzle

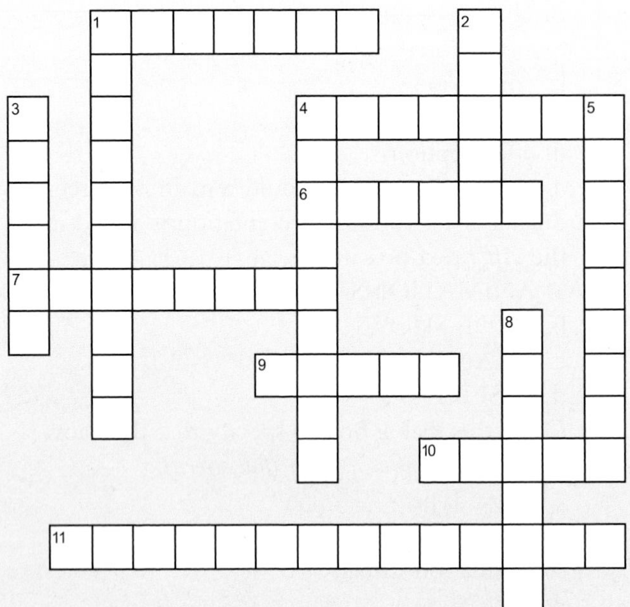

ACROSS

1 Object used to add text inside a rectangle
4 Graphic used to visually present a process
6 Ribbon tab for adding graphic elements to slides
7 Most common animation effect category
9 Graphic used to compare numbers
10 Media group button used to add sound
11 Button to access clip art

DOWN

1 Special effect as a new slide appears
2 Text box in which you type the time for a slide to display in a slide show
3 Button used to draw an arrow
4 Ribbon tab to find Set Up Slide Show button
5 Dialog box to edit ending point of video
8 Decorative text created as a graphic

Matching

Match the term with the statement or definition.

_______ 1. INSERT tab group for pictures
_______ 2. Basic Chevron Process layout
_______ 3. Add Glow special effect to WordArt
_______ 4. Present numerical data
_______ 5. Draw an arrow
_______ 6. Continuously play video clip
_______ 7. Hide sound icon
_______ 8. Transition option
_______ 9. Animation option
_______ 10. Copy animation
_______ 11. Self-running presentation

a. Video Options
b. Chart
c. Blinds
d. Animation Painter
e. Text Effects
f. Browsed at a kiosk (full screen)
g. Images
h. Shapes
i. Fly In
j. SmartArt
k. Audio Options

Project 1 Adding Graphics to a Presentation

Individual

Deliverable: Presentation about World War I (continued in Projects 2 and 3)

1. Open **WorldWar1Pres**.
2. Use Save As to change the file name to **C11-Project1-WorldWarIPres-Your Name** in a new folder named *Ch11* within the ChapterProjectsWork folder on your USB flash drive.
3. Make Slide 2 the active slide and insert the picture named ***MilitaryGroupWWI*** near the bottom right of the slide, resizing the image as needed.
4. Make Slide 6 the active slide and insert the picture named ***WeaponWWI*** at the right side of the slide next to the bulleted list, resizing the image as needed.
5. Make Slide 3 the active slide and convert the bulleted list to a SmartArt graphic. You determine an appropriate SmartArt layout. Apply a SmartArt Style of your choosing. Resize and/or make other formatting changes you think are appropriate.
6. Make Slide 4 the active slide and convert the bulleted list to the same SmartArt layout you used on Slide 3. Apply the same design and formatting changes so that Slide 3 and Slide 4 are consistent.
7. Make Slide 5 the active slide and insert a chart using the following information:
   a. Choose the *Bar* category and the *Clustered Bar* chart type.
   b. Enter the following data in the chart data grid. Delete columns and rows with sample data that are not needed for the chart.
      A2 Allied Forces B2 12.6
      A3 Central Forces B3 8.4
   c. Delete the *Series 1* legend that appears below the chart.
   d. Edit the *Series 1* title that appears above the chart to read *Millions of Soldiers*.
   e. Apply a chart style of your choosing.
8. Draw a shape positioned near the top right of the chart on Slide 5 using the *Explosion 1* option in the *Stars and Banners* category with the following text inside: *Allies bear 4.2 million more injuries!* Resize the shape, allowing the shape to flow outside the chart's border if necessary. Apply a shape style of your choosing.
9. Draw a text box positioned below the picture on Slide 6 with the following text inside the box: *Canadian artillery loading a field gun*. Change the font size to 14 points and italicize the text.
10. Draw a text box positioned below the chart on Slide 5 and aligned at the left edge with the following text inside the box: *Source: Military Research, UK*. Italicize the text.
11. Insert a new slide after Slide 7 with a Title Only layout and type the following text as the slide title: **100 Year Anniversary**. Create a WordArt object with the following text: *2014 to 2018*. Change the font size to 72 points and format the text with WordArt styles and text effects of your choosing.
12. Save the revised presentation using the same name (**C11-Project1-WorldWarIPres-Your Name**).
13. Leave the presentation open if you are continuing to Project 2; otherwise, close the presentation and submit the project to your instructor in the manner she or he has requested.

Project 2 Adding Sound and Video

Individual

Deliverable: Presentation about World War I (continued in Project 3)

Note: You must have completed Project 1 before starting this project.

1. If necessary, open **C11-Project1-WorldWarIPres-Your Name**.
2. Use Save As to change the file name to **C11-Project2-WorldWarIPres-Your Name**, saving in the same folder.
3. Make Slide 7 with the title *American Forces in France* the active slide.

4. Insert the video clip named ***AmericaGoesToWar*** from the Ch11 folder in Student_Data_Files on the slide. Edit the video as follows:
   a. Change the *Start* option to *Automatically*.
   b. Trim the video to start at *0:48* and end at *2:35*.
   c. Apply a video style of your choosing to the video object.
5. Add the audio clip named ***BulletsandBayonets*** from the Ch11 folder in Student_Data_Files on Slide 1 with the following audio options:
   a. Change the *Start* option to *Automatically*.
   b. Change the volume to *Low*.
   c. Set the audio to play across all slides.
   d. Hide the sound icon during a slide show.
6. Type the following photo, video, and audio credits in a table on the last slide. You determine the table style, column widths, and other format options.

Slide	Item	Credit
1	Music	United States marine band at George Mason University
2	Photo	City of Toronto archives via Wikimedia Commons
6	Photo	Canadian Department of National Defence via Wikimedia Commons
7	Video	America Goes Over (Part I), U.S. Army, Signal Corps via Internet Archive

7. Save the revised presentation using the same name (**C11-Project2-WorldWarIPres-Your Name**).
8. Leave the presentation open if you are continuing to Project 3; otherwise, close the presentation and submit the project to your instructor in the manner she or he has requested.

Project 3 Adding Transition and Animation Effects and Setting Up a Slide Show

Individual

Deliverable: Self-Running Presentation about World War I

Note: You must have completed Projects 1 and 2 before starting this project.

1. If necessary, open **C11-Project2-WorldWarIPres-Your Name**.
2. Use Save As to change the file name to **C11-Project3-WorldWarIPres-Your Name**, saving in the same folder.
3. Apply a transition of your choosing to all slides.
4. With Slide 2 the active slide, display the slide master and add an animation effect of your choosing to the title placeholder and the content placeholder. For each animation, change the *Start* option to *After Previous*. Return to Normal view when finished.
5. Apply an animation effect of your choosing to the following objects with the *Start* option changed to *After Previous* for each object:
   Photo on Slide 2
   Explosion shape and text box on Slide 5
   Photo and text box on Slide 6
   WordArt on Slide 8
6. Set the time for all slides to remain on the screen during a slide show to *0:15* (15 seconds).
7. Change the times for three slides as follows: Slide 1 to *0:05*; Slide 5 to *0:08*; Slide 8 to *0:05*.
8. Change the *Show type* to *Browsed by an individual (window)* at the Set Up Show dialog box.
9. Preview the slide show.
10. Save the revised presentation using the same name (**C11-Project3-WorldWarIPres-Your Name**) and then close the presentation.
11. Submit the project to your instructor in the manner she or he has requested.

Project 4 Creating a Self-Running Multimedia Presentation

Individual or Pairs

Deliverable: Presentation with Money-Saving Strategies for College Students

1. Create a presentation with six to eight slides with your best money-saving tips you can give to college students to help students survive on limited income while in school. Incorporate graphics, sound, and video into the presentation to make the presentation interesting and communicate your ideas.
2. Apply transition and animation effects of your choosing, setting up the slide show as a self-running presentation with appropriate times assigned for each slide.
3. Save the presentation in the Ch11 folder within the ChapterProjectsWork folder as **C11-Project4-MoneyTips-Your Name** and then close the presentation.
4. Submit the project to your instructor in the manner she or he has requested.

Project 5 Creating a Self-Running Multimedia Presentation

Individual

Deliverable: Presentation about Yellowstone National Park

1. Create a presentation similar to the one shown in Figure 11.5 on the next page with the following additional information:
   a. Theme is *Wood Type*.
   b. Picture and video files are as follows:
      Slide 2 **YellowstoneMap**
      Slide 3 **OldFaithfulGeyser_NPS**
      Slide 4 **GreatFountainGeyser**
      Slide 5 **InsideYellowstoneVideo**
   c. Use your best judgment to determine other formatting and alignment.
2. Apply transition and animation effects of your choosing, setting up the slide show as a self-running presentation. You determine appropriate times for each slide.
3. Save the presentation in the Ch11 folder within the ChapterProjectsWork folder as **C11-Project5-YellowstoneNP-Your Name**.
4. Submit the project to your instructor in the manner she or he has requested.
5. Close the presentation.

YELLOWSTONE NATIONAL PARK

The World's First National Park

A designated World Heritage Site and designated Biosphere Reserve

PARK FACTS

- Established in 1872
  - 3,472 square miles or 8,987 square km
- Park extends into three states
  - Wyoming, Montana, Idaho
- Home to the world's largest collection of geysers
- Also known for wildlife
  - Grizzly bears
  - Wolves
  - Herds of bison and elk

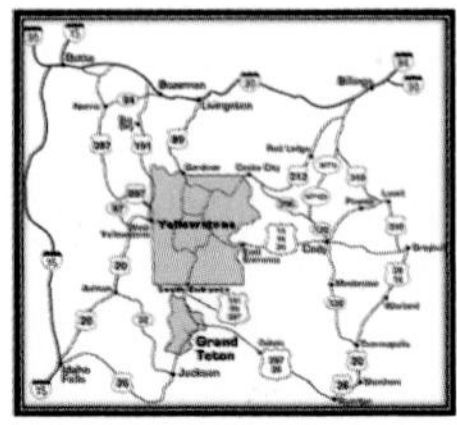

WHERE THE WORLD'S GEYSERS ARE PRESERVED

- Approximately one-half of the world's hydrothermal features
  - Park has more than 300 geysers
    - Old Faithful, most famous geyser
- Yellowstone is home to two-thirds of all geysers on earth!

Old Faithful and Beehive Geysers

WHAT IS A GEYSER?

Great Fountain Geyser

- Hot spring
- Near surface, constrictions prevent water from moving freely
- As water rises, steam forms
- Steam expands as it nears surface and erupts
- Eruptions can last 1 to 5 minutes
- Average height of eruption is 145 feet or 44 meters

PREDICTING GEYSER ACTIVITY

Inside Yellowstone

with

Park Ranger George Heinz

PHOTO AND VIDEO CREDITS

All photos and video courtesy of:

Yellowstone National Park, National Park Service, U.S. Department of the Interior

To view more multimedia from Yellowstone's Photo Collection, go to http://www.nps.gov/features/yell/slidefile/index.htm

Figure 11.5 Project 5 Yellowstone National Park Presentation

Project 6 Internet Research and Composing a New Multimedia Presentation

Individual or Pairs

Deliverable: Presentation about World War II

1. Listen to the audio file named ***Project6_Instructions***. The file is located in the Ch11 folder in the Student_Data_Files folder.
2. Complete the research, locate suitable images and video, and compose the presentation as instructed.
3. Save the presentation in the Ch11 folder within ChapterProjectsWork as **C11-Project6-WorldWarII-Your Name**.
4. Submit the project to your instructor in the manner she or he has requested.
5. Close the presentation.

Project 7 Sending Project Work to OneNote Notebook

Individual

Deliverable: New Page in Shared OneNote notebook

1. Start OneNote and open the MyProjects notebook created in Chapter 4, Project 4.
2. Make PowerPoint the active section and add a new page titled *Chapter 11 Projects*.
3. Switch to PowerPoint. For each project that you completed, open the presentation, send the slides formatted as handouts with six slides horizontal per page and with your name in a header to OneNote 2013, selecting the *Chapter 11 Projects* page in the *PowerPoint* section in the MyProjects notebook, then close the presentation.
4. Close your MyProjects notebook in OneNote and close OneNote.
5. Close PowerPoint.
6. Submit the project to your instructor in the manner she or he has requested.

Chapter 12

Using and Querying an Access Database

After successfully completing this chapter, you will be able to:

- Describe a database management system
- Define *field, field value*, and *record*
- Add, edit, and delete records using a datasheet
- Add, edit, and delete records using a form
- Find and replace data
- Sort and filter data
- Create queries
- Select records using criteria
- Perform calculations using a query
- Preview a database object

Organizations and individuals rely on data to complete transactions, make decisions, and otherwise store and track information. Data that is stored in an organized manner to provide information to suit a variety of purposes is called a **database**. Microsoft Access is a software program designed to organize, store, and maintain large amounts of data in an application referred to as a **database management system (DBMS)**. You interact with a DBMS several times a day as you complete your daily activities. Examples of the types of transactions that involve a DBMS include withdrawing cash from your bank account, completing purchases, looking up a telephone number, or programming your GPS.

In this chapter you will learn database terminology and how to navigate a DBMS, including how to open and close objects; add and maintain records using a datasheet and form; find and replace data; sort and filter data; and use queries to look up information and perform calculations.

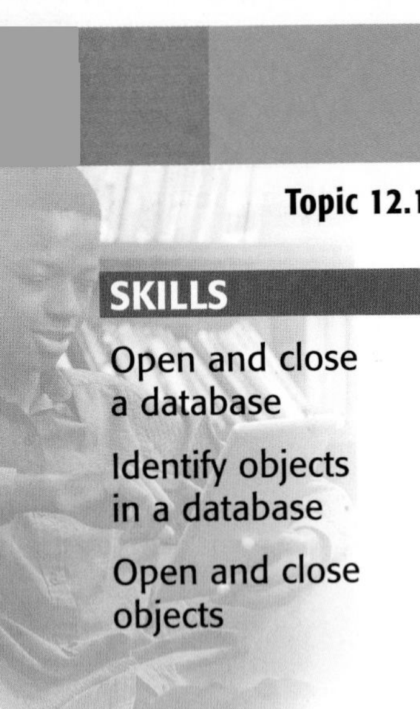

Topic 12.1

SKILLS

Open and close a database

Identify objects in a database

Open and close objects

Understanding Database Objects and Terminology

An Access database is structured and organized with a specific purpose to keep track of large amounts of similar data. For example, a library database is organized so that information for each book in the library such as the title, author, publisher, and price is entered and maintained. Making sure that the data is entered and updated in the same manner for each item is important so that information that is retrieved is complete and accurate. For this reason, a database is created with a structure that defines the data that will be collected for each item. Examining and practicing working with data in an existing database will help you understand the various terms that are used and the method with which data is organized before you create your own database.

Identifying a Database Object

An Access database is a collection of related objects in which you enter, edit, and view data. Access opens with a Navigation pane along the left side of the window in which you select the object that you want to view. Objects are grouped by type. Most databases include tables, queries, forms, and reports. See Table 12.1 for a description of each type.

Table 12.1	Access Objects
Object	**Description**
Table	Data is organized into a collection of tables, each of which opens in a datasheet that displays data in columns and rows similarly to a spreadsheet. A table stores data about one topic or subject only. For example, in the LibraryFines database, one table contains data about each student and another table contains data about each fine.
Query	A query is used to extract information from one or more tables in a single datasheet and can show all of the data or only a subset of data that meets a specific condition. For example, a query could show all library fines that have been assessed or only those fines that are unpaid.
Form	A form provides a user-friendly interface with which data is entered or updated. The layout of a form can be customized to suit a variety of needs.
Report	Reports are used for viewing or printing data from a table or query. Reports can include summary totals and a customized layout.

Opening a database displays the SECURITY WARNING message bar. Tap or click Enable Content only when you are sure the database has originated from a trusted source.

1. Start Access and open the database named ***LibraryFines*** from the Ch12 folder in Student_Data_Files.
2. Tap or click the Enable Content button in the SECURITY WARNING message bar that appears below the ribbon.

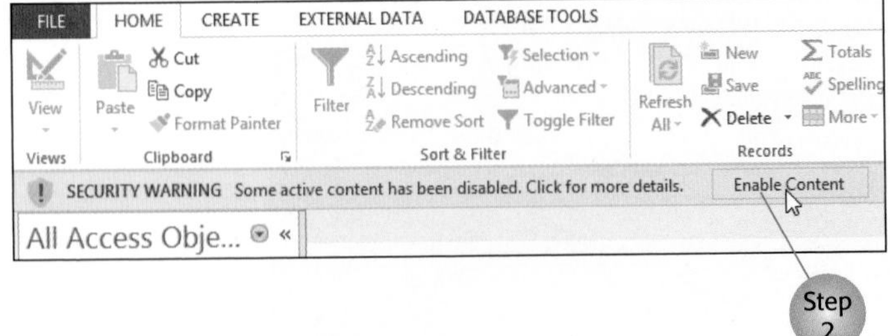

3. Compare your screen with the one shown in Figure 12.1.

4 If necessary, slide or drag right the gray border along the right side of the Navigation pane to expand the width of the pane until the title *All Access Objects* is entirely visible.

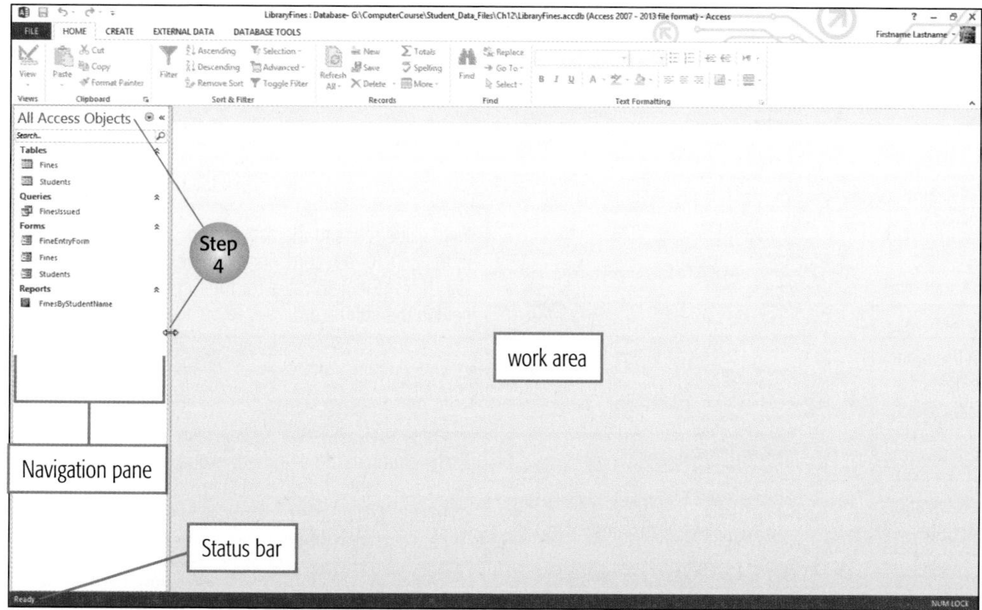

Figure 12.1 The LibraryFines Database opened in the Access window

Defining Database Terminology

Data in a database is organized by topic or subject about a person, place, event, item, or other category grouping in an object called a **table**. A database table is the first object that is created. The number of tables varies for each database depending on the information that needs to be stored. Tables are the building blocks for creating other objects such as a query, form, or report. In other words, you cannot create a query, form, or report without first creating a table.

5 Double-tap or double-click *Fines* in the Tables group in the Navigation pane.

The table opens in Datasheet view within a tab in the work area.

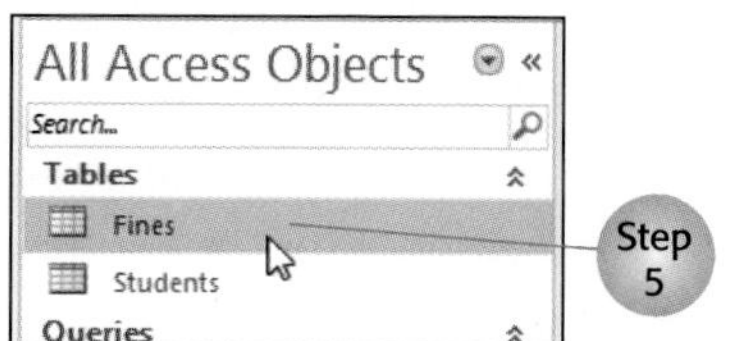

oops!

Trouble opening a table? Another way to open the table is to press and hold or right-click the object name and choose *Open*.

6 Double-tap or double-click *Students* in the Tables group in the Navigation pane and compare your screen with the one shown in Figure 12.2.

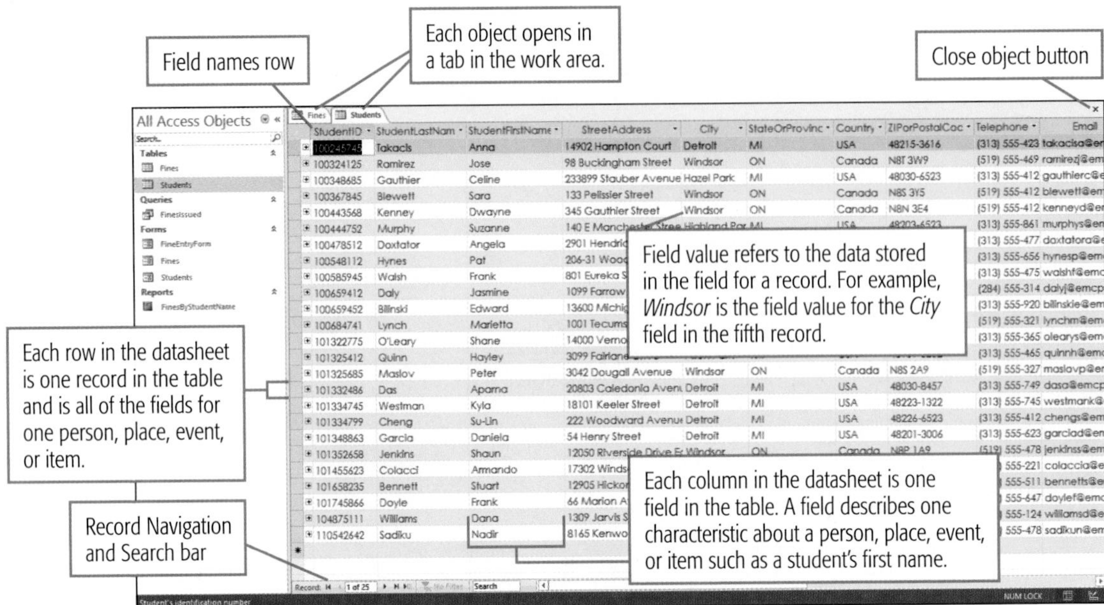

Figure 12.2 Datasheet View for Students Table in LibraryFines Database

A datasheet resembles a spreadsheet with the data organized in columns and rows. The information about the subject or topic of a table (such as students) is divided into columns, each of which is called a **field**. A field should store only one unit of information about a person, place, event, or item. For example, a mailing address is split into at least four fields so that the street address, city, state or province, and zip or postal code are separated. This allows the database to be sorted, filtered, or searched by any piece of information.

Each row in the datasheet shows all of the fields for one person, place, event, or item and is called a **record**. The data that is stored in one field within a record is called a **field value**.

7 Double-tap or double-click *FinesByStudentName* in the Reports group in the Navigation pane and review the report content and layout in the work area.

A **report** is designed to view or print data from one or more tables or queries in a customized layout and with summary totals. In this report, library fines are arranged and grouped by student name in alphabetical order.

8 Tap or click the Close button at the top right of the work area to close the report.

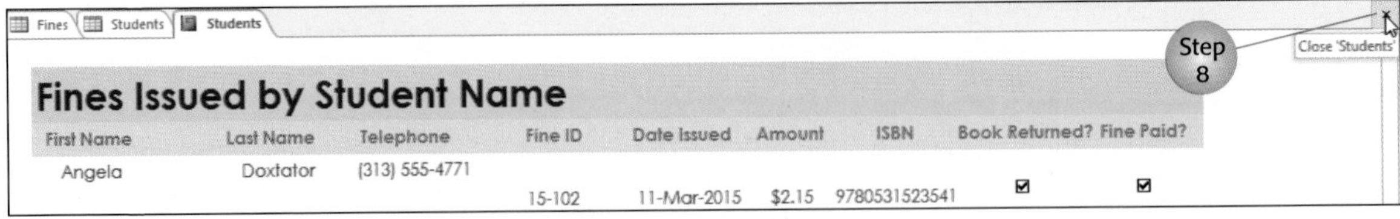

Forms can be created to resemble paper-based forms used within an organization.

9 Double-tap or double-click *FineEntryForm* in the Forms group in the Navigation pane.

A **form** is used to enter, update, or view one record at a time.

10 Tap or click the Next record button (right-pointing arrow) in the Record Navigation and Search bar located at the bottom of the form.

Buttons in the Record Navigation and Search bar are used to move to the first record, previous record, next record, or last record. Use the *Search* box to navigate to a record by typing a field value.

11 Tap or click the Previous record button (left-pointing arrow).

12 Tap or click the Last record button (right-pointing arrow with vertical bar) to move to the last record in the form.

13 Tap or click the First record button (left-pointing arrow with vertical bar) to move to the first record in the form.

14 Tap or click the Close button at the top right of the work area to close the form.

Overdue Book Fine Form

FineID 15-101
Student ID Look up 100548112
Date Fine Issued 10-Mar-2015
Amount $8.75
Overdue Book ISBN 9780763843011
Book Returned? ☑
Fine Paid? ☑
Date Paid 31-Mar-2015

Previous record
New (blank) record
First record
Last record
Search text box
Record: 1 of 17
Next record
Step 10

Open a Database Object

1. Open database file.
2. Double-tap or double-click object name in Navigation pane.

15 Double-tap or double-click *FinesIssued* in the Queries group in the Navigation pane.

A **query** opens in a datasheet similarly to a table. A query displays information from one or more tables and may show all of the records or only a subset of records that meet a specific condition.

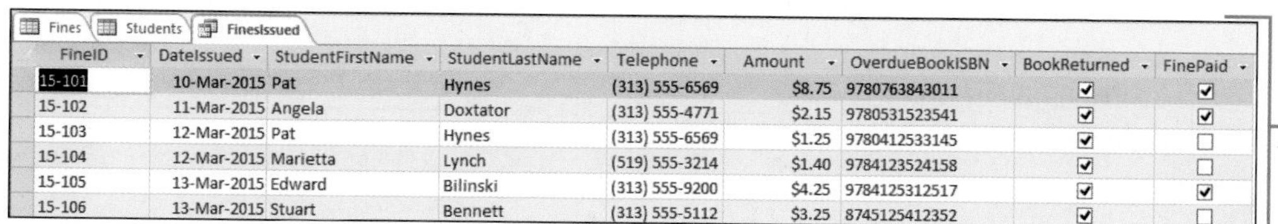

FineID	DateIssued	StudentFirstName	StudentLastName	Telephone	Amount	OverdueBookISBN	BookReturned	FinePaid
15-101	10-Mar-2015	Pat	Hynes	(313) 555-6569	$8.75	9780763843011	☑	☑
15-102	11-Mar-2015	Angela	Doxtator	(313) 555-4771	$2.15	9780531523541	☑	☑
15-103	12-Mar-2015	Pat	Hynes	(313) 555-6569	$1.25	9780412533145	☑	☐
15-104	12-Mar-2015	Marietta	Lynch	(519) 555-3214	$1.40	9784123524158	☑	☐
15-105	13-Mar-2015	Edward	Bilinski	(313) 555-9200	$4.25	9784125312517	☑	☑
15-106	13-Mar-2015	Stuart	Bennett	(313) 555-5112	$3.25	8745125412352	☑	☐

A query can show data from more than one table and display the fields in any order.

16 Close the query and the two tables.

17 Tap or click the FILE tab and then tap or click Close at the Info tab Backstage view.

Always close a database file using the FILE tab before exiting Access so that all temporary files used by Access while you are viewing and updating records are properly closed.

Close objects as soon as you are finished viewing or updating data. Some Access commands will not run if an object is open in the background.

One Database at a Time

Unlike Word, Excel, or PowerPoint, Access allows only one file to be open at a time in the current window. If you open a second database in the current window, Access automatically closes the existing database before opening the new one.

Topic 12.2

SKILLS

Add a new record in a datasheet

Adding Records Using a Datasheet

To add a new record to a table, open the table and tap or click the **New (blank) record button** in the Record Navigation and Search bar. Type the field values for the new record, using Tab or Enter to move to the next field in the datasheet. When you move past the last field in a new row in the datasheet, the record is automatically saved.

1. Reopen the database named ***LibraryFines***.
2. Use Save As to save a copy of the database as **12.2-LibraryFines-Your Name** in a new folder named *Ch12* in the CompletedTopicsbyChapter folder. At the Save As Backstage view, accept the default options *Save Database As* in the *File Types* section and *Access Database* in the *Save Database As* section.
3. Tap or click the Enable Content button in the SECURITY WARNING message bar.
4. Open the Fines table.
5. Tap or click the New (blank) record button in the Record Navigation and Search bar.
6. Type **15-118** in the *FineID* field and then tap or press Tab to move to the next field.

The next field, *StudentID*, has been set up to look up names and ID numbers in the Students table. In this field a drop-down list is used to select the field value.

7. Tap or click the down-pointing arrow in the *StudentID* field, tap or click *100478512 Angela Doxtator* in the pop-up list, and then tap or press Tab.

Pencil icon indicates the record is being edited. The pencil disappears when Access saves the changes.

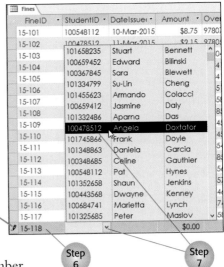

Access stores the student identification number as the field value once a selection is made in the list and the field value is connected to Angela Doxtator's record in the Students table.

8. Type **12apr2015** in the *DateIssued* field and tap or press Tab.

The date field has been set up to display underscores and dashes as soon as you begin typing to help you enter the date in the correct format *dd-mmm-yyyy*. This configuration also ensures that all dates are entered consistently in the database.

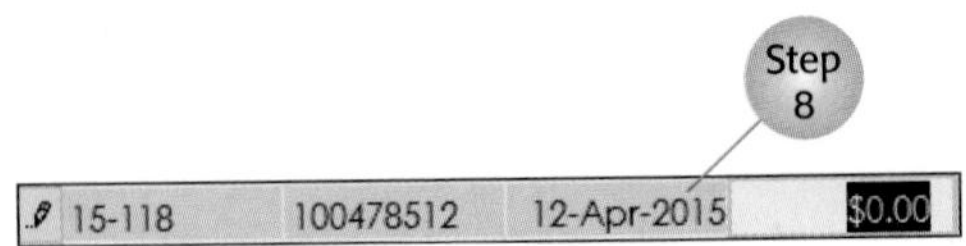

App Tip

You can also move to the next field by tapping or pressing the Enter key or by tapping or clicking in the next column.

oops!

Error message appears? This occurs when a date has not been typed in the pattern that has been set for the field. Tap or click OK, backspace to delete the date entry, and try Step 8 again.

9 Type **8.75** in the *Amount* field and then tap or press Tab.

10 Type **4348973098226** in the *OverdueBookISBN* field and then tap or press Tab.

11 Tap or press the spacebar to insert a check mark in the *BookReturned* field and then tap or press Tab.

BookReturned is a field that has been set up to store only one of two possible field values: *Yes* or *No*. Inserting a check mark stores *Yes*, while an empty check box stores *No*.

12 Tap or click the check box to insert a check mark in the *FinePaid* field and then tap or press Tab.

13 Type **15apr2015** in the *DatePaid* field and then tap or press Tab.

Moving to the next row in the datasheet automatically saves the record just typed and starts a new record.

Add New Record
1. Open table.
2. Tap or click New (blank) record button.
3. Type field values in new row in datasheet.
4. Close table.

Saving in a database is not left to chance! As soon as you complete a new record, Access saves the data to disk.

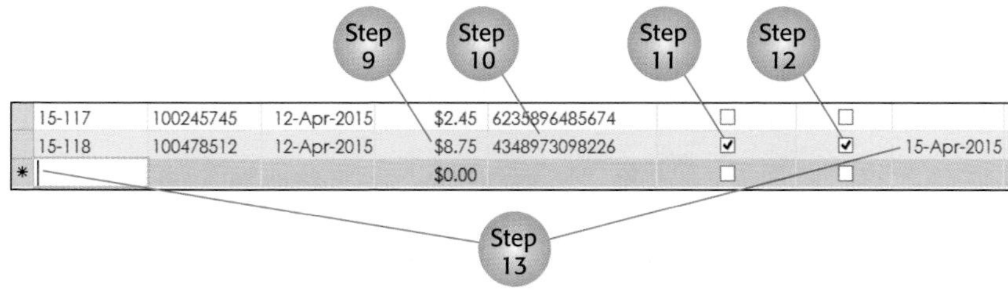

15-117	100245745	12-Apr-2015	$2.45	6235896485674	☐	☐	
15-118	100478512	12-Apr-2015	$8.75	4348973098226	☑	☑	15-Apr-2015
*			$0.00		☐	☐	

14 Add the following field values in the new row in the fields indicated:

FineID	**15-119**	*OverdueBookISBN*	**7349872345760**
StudentID	*101348863 Daniela Garcia*	*BookReturned*	Yes
DateIssued	**15apr2015**	*FinePaid*	No (leave blank)
Amount	**5.25**	*DatePaid*	(leave blank)

15-118	100478512	12-Apr-2015	$8.75	4348973098226	☑	☑	15-Apr-2015
15-119	101348863	15-Apr-2015	$5.25	7349872345760	☑	☐	
*			$0.00		☐	☐	

Step 14

15 With the insertion point positioned in the *FineID* field in a new row, close the Fines table. Leave the database open for the next topic.

ALTERNATIVE method

New records can also be added to the table using any of these other methods to start a new blank row at the bottom of the datasheet:

- New button in the Records group of the HOME tab
- Keyboard shortcut Ctrl + + (hold down Ctrl key and press plus symbol)
- Tap or click in the last cell in the table and tap or press Tab

Editing and Deleting Records in a Datasheet

Topic 12.3

SKILLS

Edit a record in a datasheet

Delete a record in a datasheet

As soon as you move to another record in the datasheet, the changes are automatically saved.

oops!

Using Touch? Tap at the end of murphy to place the insertion point in the field, tap Backspace to delete the text, and then type the new text.

Edit a field value in a datasheet by tapping or clicking in the table cell and inserting or deleting text as required. Select a record for deletion by tapping or clicking in the gray record selector bar along the left edge of the datasheet next to the record and then tap or click the Delete button in the Records group of the HOME tab. Access requires confirmation before deleting a record.

1. With the **12.2-LibraryFines-Your Name** database open, open the Students table.
2. Select the text *Murphy* in the *StudentLastName* column in the sixth row in the datasheet and type **Hall** as the new last name for Suzanne.

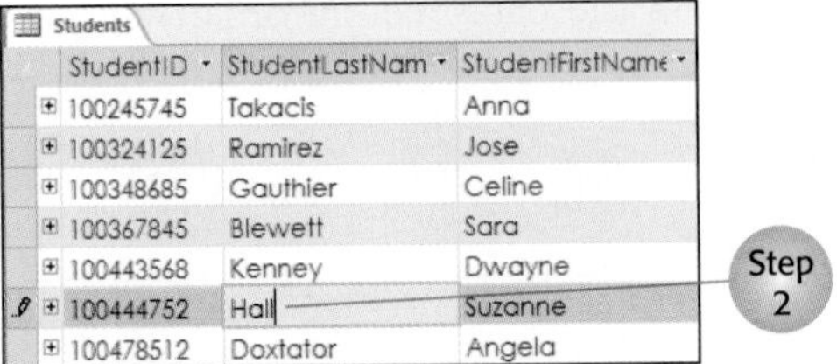

Students

StudentID	StudentLastNam	StudentFirstName
100245745	Takacis	Anna
100324125	Ramirez	Jose
100348685	Gauthier	Celine
100367845	Blewett	Sara
100443568	Kenney	Dwayne
100444752	Hall	Suzanne
100478512	Doxtator	Angela

3. Tap or press Tab eight times to move to the *Email* field.
4. Press F2 to open the field for editing, move the insertion point as needed, delete *murphy* at the beginning of the email address, and then type **hall** so that the email address becomes *halls@emcp.net*.

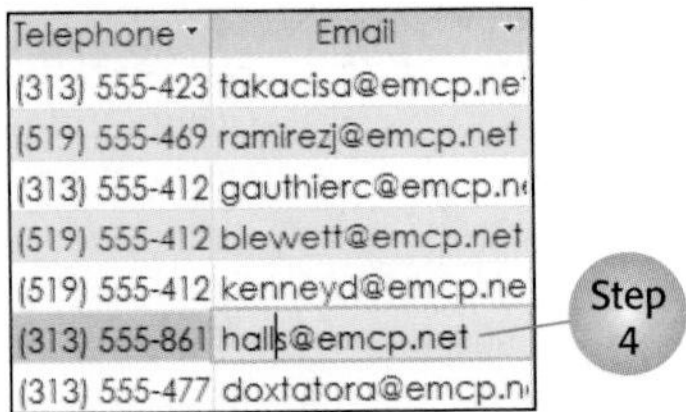

Telephone	Email
(313) 555-423	takacisa@emcp.ne
(519) 555-469	ramirezj@emcp.net
(313) 555-412	gauthierc@emcp.n
(519) 555-412	blewett@emcp.net
(519) 555-412	kenneyd@emcp.ne
(313) 555-861	halls@emcp.net
(313) 555-477	doxtatora@emcp.n

5. Tap or click at the end of *N8T 3W9* in the *ZIPorPostalCode* field in the second row in the datasheet to position the insertion point, tap or press Backspace to remove *3W9*, and then type **2E6**.

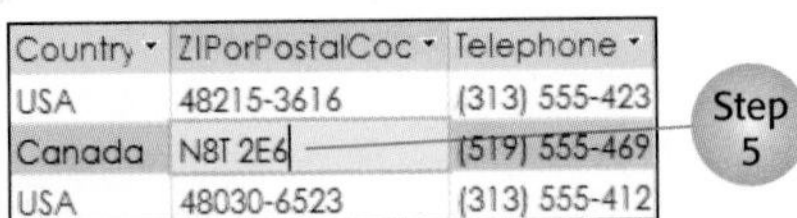

Country	ZIPorPostalCoc	Telephone
USA	48215-3616	(313) 555-423
Canada	N8T 2E6	(519) 555-469
USA	48030-6523	(313) 555-412

6. If necessary, slide left or scroll left until you can see the student names.

7 Tap or click in the record selector bar next to the record for the student *Das Aparna*.

The gray bar at the left edge of the datasheet is used to select a record. When using a mouse, the pointer displays as a black right-pointing arrow when positioned next to a record in the gray record selector bar.

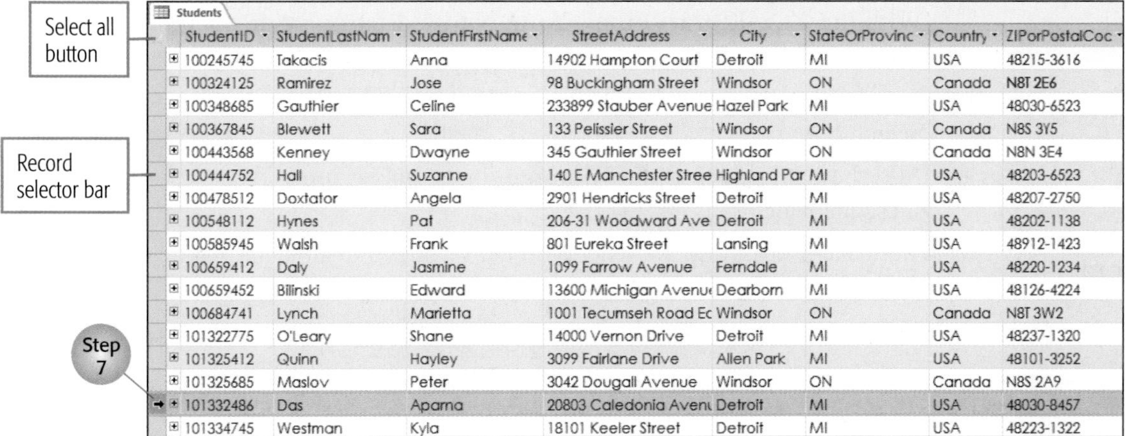

StudentID	StudentLastNam	StudentFirstName	StreetAddress	City	StateOrProvinc	Country	ZIPorPostalCoc
100245745	Takacis	Anna	14902 Hampton Court	Detroit	MI	USA	48215-3616
100324125	Ramirez	Jose	98 Buckingham Street	Windsor	ON	Canada	N8T 2E6
100348685	Gauthier	Celine	233899 Stauber Avenue	Hazel Park	MI	USA	48030-6523
100367845	Blewett	Sara	133 Pelissier Street	Windsor	ON	Canada	N8S 3Y5
100443568	Kenney	Dwayne	345 Gauthier Street	Windsor	ON	Canada	N8N 3E4
100444752	Hall	Suzanne	140 E Manchester Stree	Highland Par	MI	USA	48203-6523
100478512	Doxtator	Angela	2901 Hendricks Street	Detroit	MI	USA	48207-2750
100548112	Hynes	Pat	206-31 Woodward Ave	Detroit	MI	USA	48202-1138
100585945	Walsh	Frank	801 Eureka Street	Lansing	MI	USA	48912-1423
100659412	Daly	Jasmine	1099 Farrow Avenue	Ferndale	MI	USA	48220-1234
100659452	Bilinski	Edward	13600 Michigan Avenu	Dearborn	MI	USA	48126-4224
100684741	Lynch	Marietta	1001 Tecumseh Road Ec	Windsor	ON	Canada	N8T 3W2
101322775	O'Leary	Shane	14000 Vernon Drive	Detroit	MI	USA	48237-1320
101325412	Quinn	Hayley	3099 Fairlane Drive	Allen Park	MI	USA	48101-3252
101325685	Maslov	Peter	3042 Dougall Avenue	Windsor	ON	Canada	N8S 2A9
101332486	Das	Aparna	20803 Caledonia Avenu	Detroit	MI	USA	48030-8457
101334745	Westman	Kyla	18101 Keeler Street	Detroit	MI	USA	48223-1322

8 Tap or click the Delete button in the Records group of the HOME tab. Do *not* tap or click the down-pointing arrow on the button.

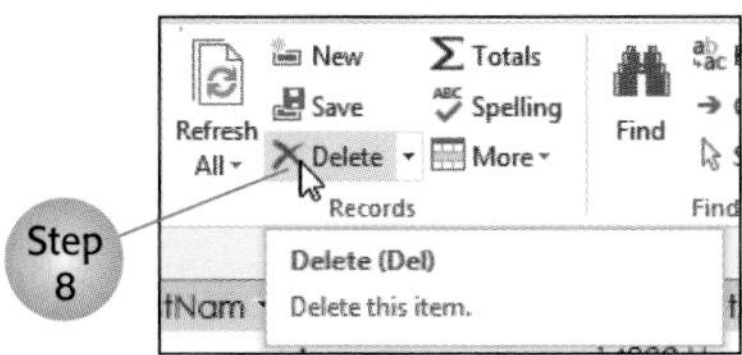

9 Tap or click Yes at the message box that appears asking if you are sure you want to delete the record.

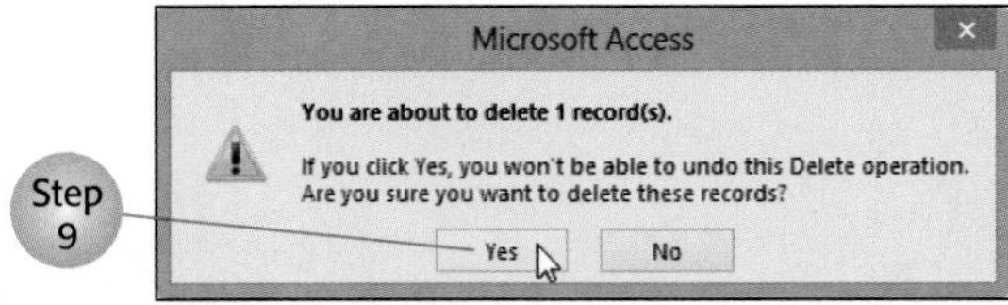

10 Close the Students table. Leave the database open for the next topic.

Edit a Record
1. Open table.
2. Tap or click in table cell.
3. Insert or delete text as required.

Delete a Record
1. Open table.
2. Select record.
3. Tap or click Delete button.
4. Tap or click Yes.

Be cautious with the Delete command because Undo does not work to restore a record. Consider making a backup copy of a database before deleting records.

Best Practices for Deleting Records

Depending on the purpose of the database, deleting records is generally not performed until the records to be deleted are copied to an archive database and/or a backup copy of the database has been made. In most cases, records should be retained for historical data purposes.

Topic 12.4

SKILLS

Add a record in a form

Edit a record in a form

Delete a record in a form

Adding, Editing, and Deleting Records in a Form

Recall from an earlier topic that a form is an interface that provides a different view for a table. Generally only one record is displayed at a time in a columnar layout. Forms are the preferred object for adding, editing, and deleting records.

1. With the **12.2-LibraryFines-Your Name** database open, open the form named *FineEntryForm*.
2. Tap or click the New (blank) record button in the Record Navigation and Search bar.
3. Add the field values as shown in the image below, using Tab to move to subsequent fields.

A new blank form displays when you tap or press Tab after the last field in a form.

4. Tap or click the First record button in the Record Navigation and Search bar to display the first record in the form.
5. Select *8.75* in the *Amount* field and type 7.25.

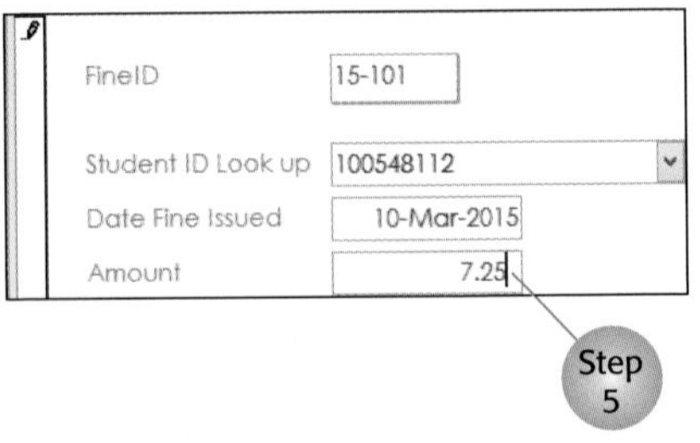

6 Tap or click the Next record button two times to display record 3 in the form.

7 Tap or click the Delete button arrow in the Records group of the HOME tab and then tap or click *Delete Record* at the drop-down list.

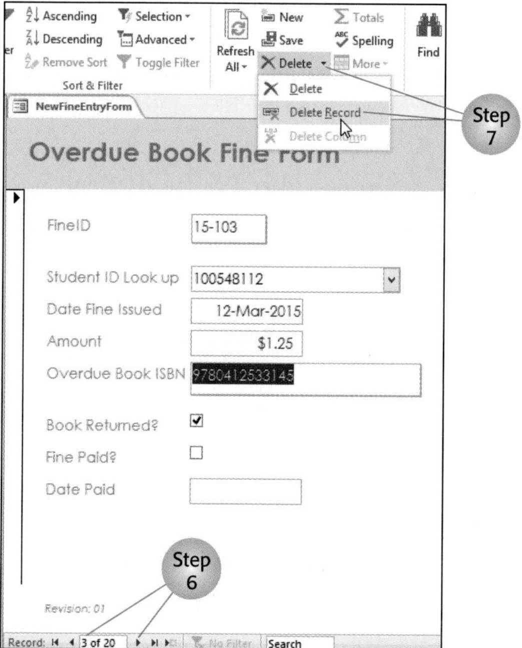

Delete a Record in a Form

1. Open form.
2. Display record.
3. Tap or click Delete button arrow.
4. Tap or click *Delete Record*.
5. Tap or click Yes.

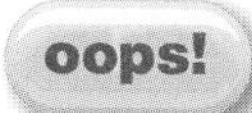

Only the current field value is deleted? This occurs when you do not use the arrow on the button to select the option to delete the entire record. Try Step 7 again, making sure to choose *Delete Record*.

8 Tap or click Yes at the message box that appears asking if you are sure you want to delete the record.

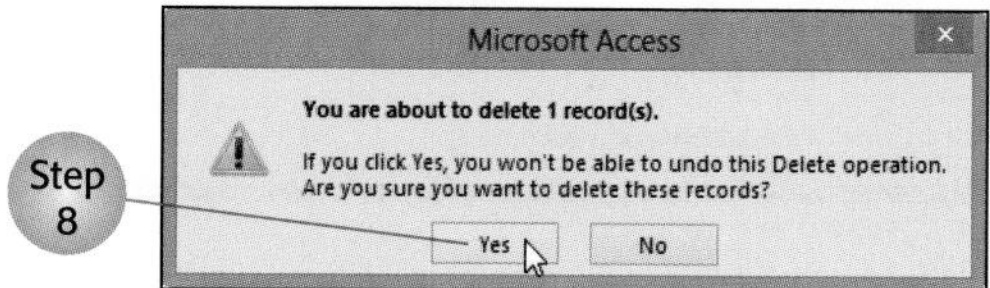

9 Close the form. Leave the database open for the next topic.

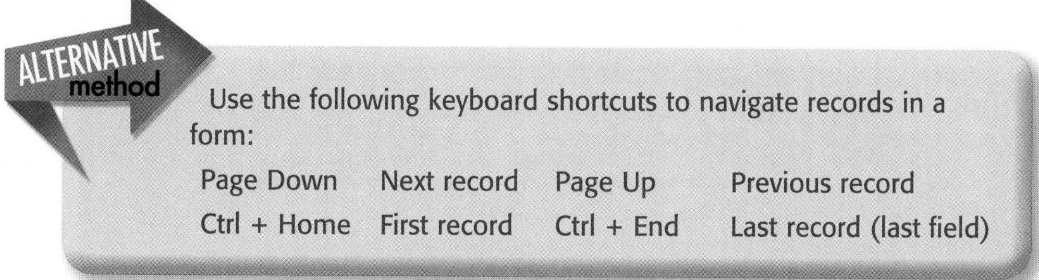

Use the following keyboard shortcuts to navigate records in a form:

Page Down	Next record	Page Up	Previous record
Ctrl + Home	First record	Ctrl + End	Last record (last field)

Using Find to Move to a Record

As databases expand to store hundreds or thousands of records, using the navigation buttons at the bottom of the form to locate a record that needs to be changed or deleted is not feasible. The Find feature locates a record instantly when you search by a name or ID number. You will use Find in the next topic.

Topic 12.5

SKILLS

Find and replace data

Adjust column widths

Finding and Replacing Data and Adjusting Column Widths

Similar to a word processor, the Find feature locates a field value in a datasheet or form. When a change needs to be made to all occurrences of a field value, use the Replace command to make the change automatically. Column widths in a datasheet can be made wider or narrower using techniques similar to those you learned in Excel.

1. With the **12.2-LibraryFines-Your Name** database open, open the Fines table.
2. Tap or click to place the insertion point within the *StudentID* field value in the first record.
3. Tap or click the Find button in the Find group of the HOME tab.

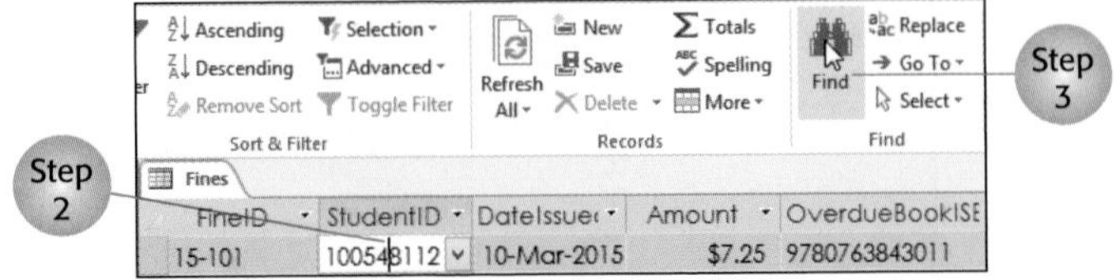

4. Type **101348863** in the *Find What* text box and then tap or click Find Next.

The first record (record 6) that matches the field value is made active.

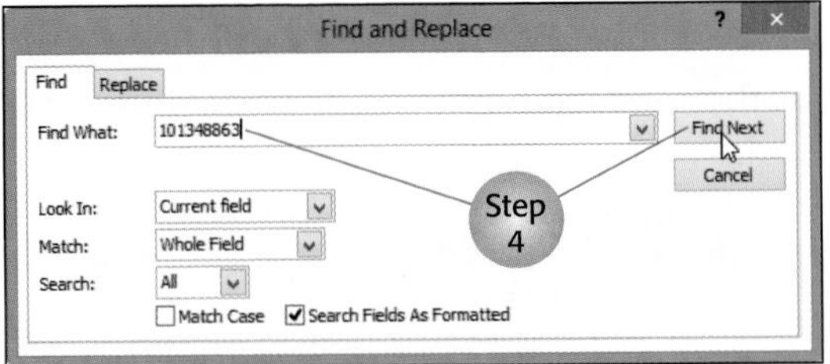

5. Continue tapping or clicking the Find Next button to review all occurrences of the matching field value.
6. Tap or click OK at the message that Microsoft Access has finished searching records.

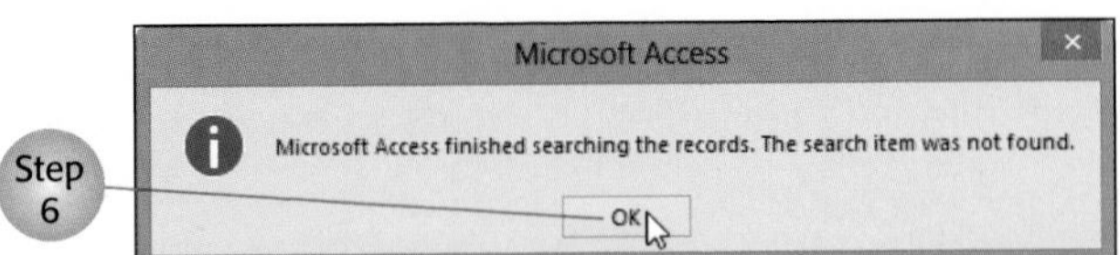

7. Tap or click Cancel to close the Find and Replace dialog box.
8. Tap or click to place the insertion point within the *FineID* field in the first record.
9. Tap or click the Replace button in the Find group.

oops!

No records found? Tap or click OK and then check that you typed the ID number without errors.

10 Type **15-** in the *Find What* text box and then tap or press Tab.

11 Type **2015-** in the *Replace With* text box.

12 Tap or click the *Match* list arrow and then tap or click *Any Part of Field* at the drop-down list.

13 Tap or click the Replace All button.

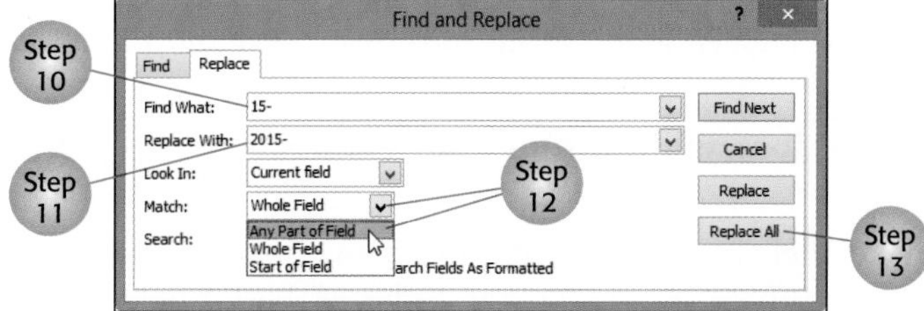

14 Tap or click Yes at the message asking if you want to continue and informing you that the Replace operation cannot be undone.

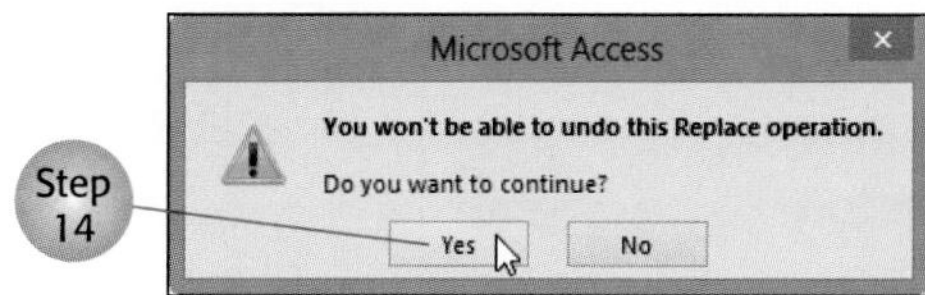

15 Close the Find and Replace dialog box.

16 Tap or click to place the insertion point in any record within the *DateIssued* field.

17 Tap or click the More button in the Records group of the HOME tab and then tap or click *Field Width* at the drop-down list.

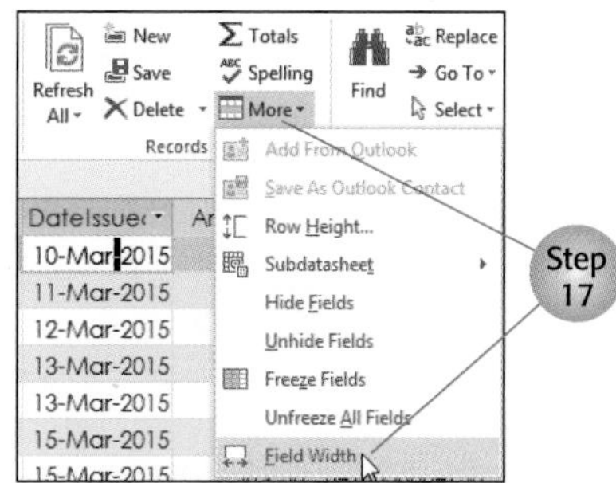

18 Tap or click Best Fit at the Column Width dialog box.

Best Fit is similar to AutoFit in Excel in that the column width is lengthened to accommodate the longest entry.

19 Close the Fines table. Tap or click Yes when prompted to save the changes to the layout of the table. Leave the database open for the next topic.

Saving changes to the layout of the table means that Access will retain the new column width for the *DateIssued* field when the table is reopened.

Find a Record

1. Open table or form.
2. Tap or click in field to be searched.
3. Tap or click Find button.
4. Type field value.
5. Tap or click Find Next until done.
6. Tap or click OK.
7. Close dialog box.

Replace a Field Value

1. Open table or form.
2. Tap or click in field to be searched.
3. Tap or click Replace button.
4. Type field value to find in *Find What* text box.
5. Type new text in *Replace With* text box.
6. Tap or click Replace All.
7. Tap or click Yes.
8. Close dialog box.

Adjust Column Width

1. Open table.
2. Tap or click in any record in column.
3. Tap or click More button.
4. Tap or click *Field Width*.
5. Type value or tap or click Best Fit.

ALTERNATIVE method

You can also adjust column widths using the following methods:

- Slide or drag the right column boundary in the field names row right or left.
- Double-tap or double-click the right column boundary to best fit the width.
- Type a value in the *Column Width* text box at the Column Width dialog box.

Topic 12.6

SKILLS

Sort records

Filter records

Sorting and Filtering Records

Records are initially arranged in the datasheet alphanumerically by the field in the table that has been defined as the primary key. A **primary key** is a field that contains the data that uniquely identifies each record in the table. Generally, the primary key is an identification number such as *StudentID* in the Students table. To change the order of the records, tap or click in the column by which to sort and use the Ascending or Descending buttons in the Sort & Filter group of the HOME tab.

1. With the **12.2-LibraryFines-Your Name** database open, open the Students table.

The primary key field in the Students table is the field named *StudentID*. Notice the records in the datasheet are arranged in order of the ID field values.

2. Tap or click to place the insertion point within any field value in the *StudentLastName* column.
3. Tap or click the Ascending button in the Sort & Filter group of the HOME tab.

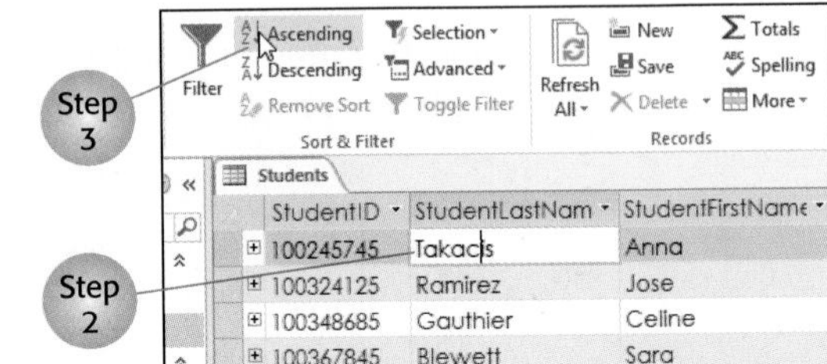

4. Close the Students table. Tap or click Yes when prompted to save the changes to the design of the table.

Selecting Yes to save changes to the design of the table means that the table will remain sorted by the *StudentLastName* field when you reopen the table.

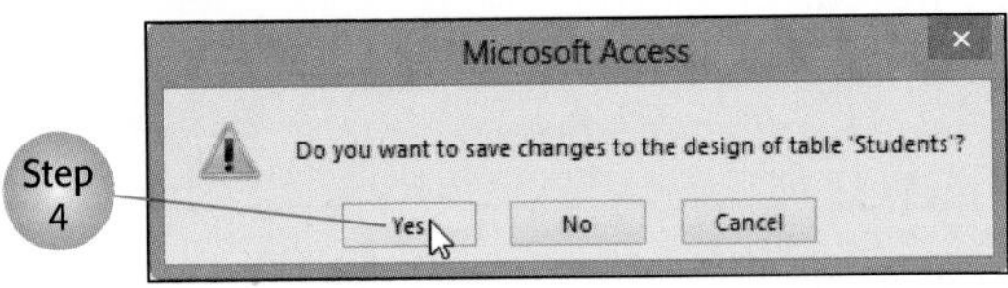

5. Open the Students form.
6. Tap or click the Next record button a few times to view the first few records. Notice the records are arranged by *StudentID*.
7. Tap or click the First record button to return the display to the first record.
8. Tap or click to place the insertion point in the *Student Last Name* field.
9. Tap or click the Ascending button in the Sort & Filter group.

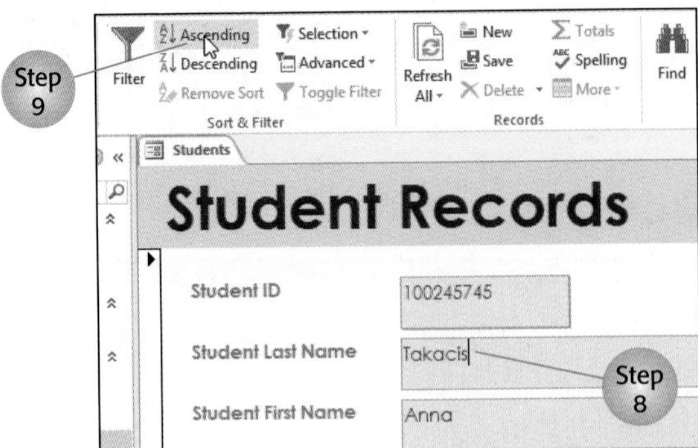

10. Scroll through the first 10 records in the form to view the sorted order and then close the form.

App Tip

When a datasheet is sorted by a field other than the primary key, an up-pointing arrow (ascending order) or down-pointing arrow (descending order) displays next to the name for the field used to sort.

11 Open the Students table. Notice the records are arranged alphabetically by the student last names.

You can filter a datasheet in Access using the same techniques you learned for filtering a table in Excel in Chapter 9. Recall that a filter temporarily hides the rows that you do not want to view.

12 Tap or click the filter arrow (down-pointing arrow) next to *Country*.

13 Tap or click the check box next to *USA* to clear the check mark from the box at the Sort & Filter list box and then tap or click OK.

The datasheet is filtered to show records for students who reside in Canada only.

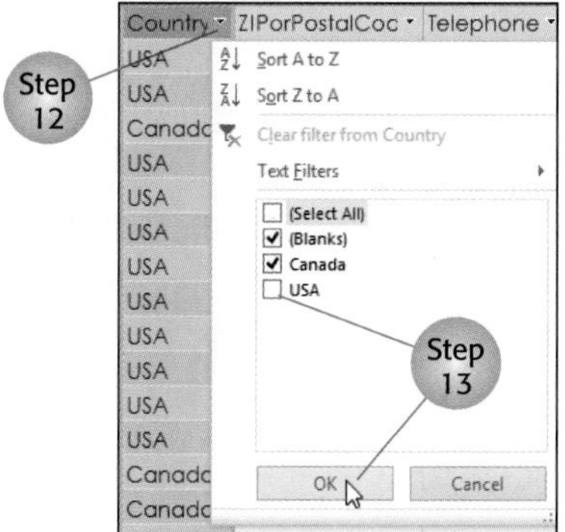

14 Tap or click the Toggle Filter button in the Sort & Filter group to clear the filter.

All records are now redisplayed.

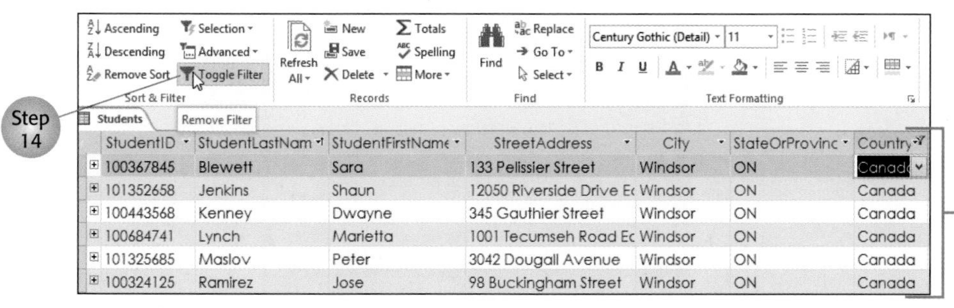

Filtered list of records after Step 13

15 Close the Students table. Tap or click No when prompted to save changes to the design of the table. Leave the database open for the next topic.

Sort a Datasheet or Form
1. Open table or form.
2. Tap or click in field by which to sort.
3. Tap or click Ascending or Descending button.

Filter a Datasheet
1. Open table.
2. Tap or click filter arrow next to field.
3. Clear check boxes as needed.
4. Tap or click OK.

Access displays a funnel icon next to a field used to filter a datasheet and displays *Filtered* highlighted in orange in the Record Navigation and Search bar.

oops!

Toggle Filter button not active? Tap or click the filter arrow button next to *Country* and tap or click *Clear Filter from Country* to redisplay all records.

Sorting by More Than One Field

Sort by more than one field in a datasheet by sliding or dragging the field names at the top of the datasheet to select the columns by which to sort and then choose Ascending or Descending order. Access sorts left to right. For example, if *StudentLastName* and *StudentFirstName* columns are selected, Access sorts first by last names and then by first names when two or more records have the same last name. Move a column to change the sort order if necessary. To move a field for sorting purposes, slide or drag the field name to the left.

Creating a Query Using the Simple Query Wizard

Queries are used to extract information from one or more tables in the database and display the results in a datasheet. Some queries are used to display fields from more than one table in the same datasheet. For example, in the LibraryFines database, the student names are in one table while the fines are in another table; a query can combine the names and fines in one datasheet. Other queries are designed to answer a question about the data; for example, *Which library fines are unpaid?*. The **Simple Query Wizard** assists with creating a query by making selections in a series of dialog boxes.

1. With the **12.2-LibraryFines-Your Name** database open, tap or click the CREATE tab.
2. Tap or click the Query Wizard button in the Queries group.

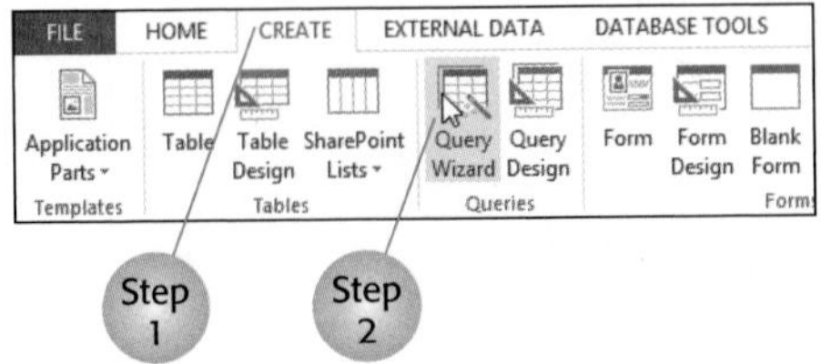

3. Tap or click OK at the New Query dialog box with *Simple Query Wizard* already selected.

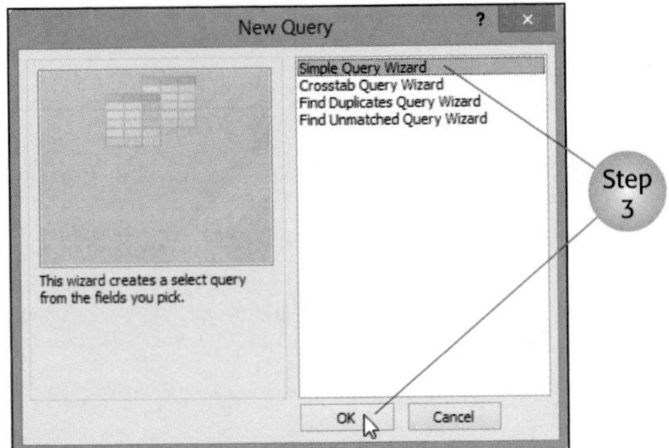

4. At the first Simple Query Wizard dialog box, tap or click the *Tables/Queries* list arrow and then tap or click *Table: Students* at the drop-down list. Skip this step if *Table: Students* is already displayed in the *Table/Queries* list box.

The first step in creating a query is to choose the tables or queries and the fields from each table or query that you want to display in a datasheet.

5. With *StudentID* already selected in the *Available Fields* list box, tap or click the Add Field button (displays as a right-pointing arrow) to move *StudentID* to the *Selected Fields* list box.

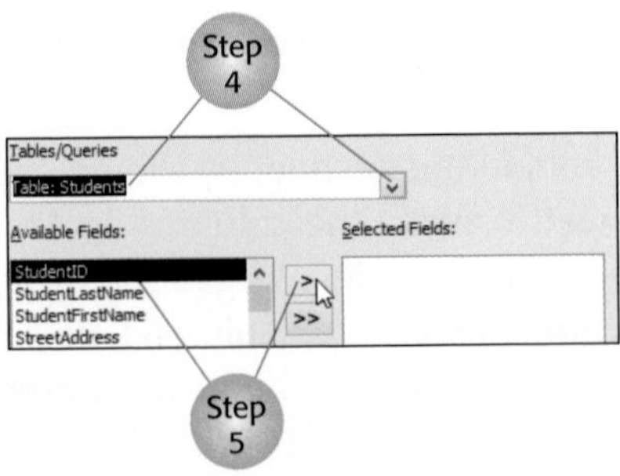

6 Double-tap or double-click *StudentFirstName* in the *Available Fields* list box to move the field to the *Selected Fields* list box.

Add fields to the *Selected Fields* list box in the order in which you want the fields displayed in the datasheet.

7 Double-tap or double-click the following fields in the *Available Fields* list box to move each field to the *Selected Fields* list box.

StudentLastName
Telephone
Email

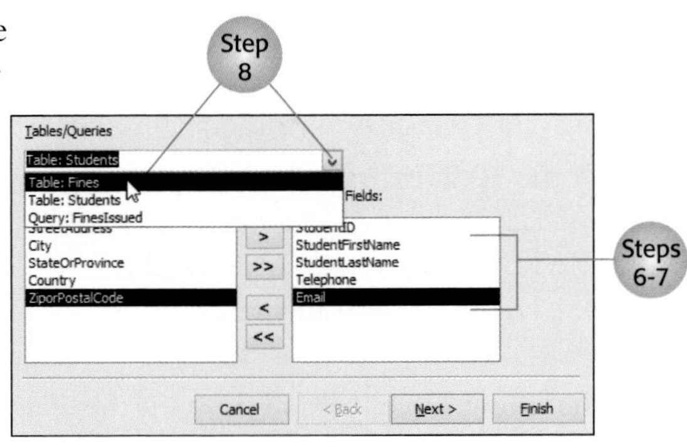

8 Tap or click the *Tables/Queries* list arrow and then tap or click *Table: Fines*.

9 Double-tap or double-click the following fields in the *Available Fields* list box to move each field to the *Selected Fields* list box.

DateIssued
Amount
FinePaid

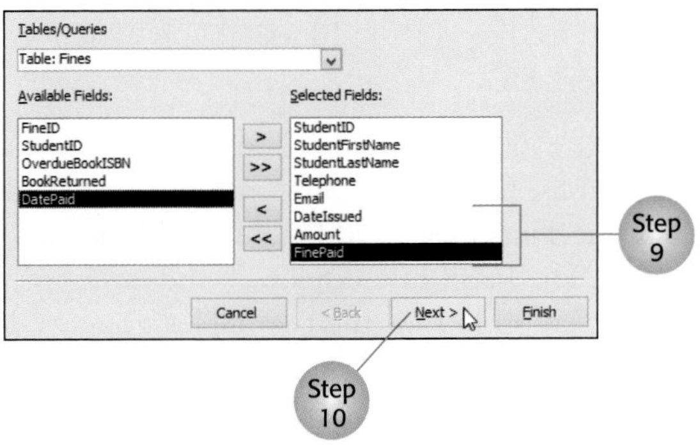

10 Tap or click Next.

11 Tap or click Next at the second Simple Query Wizard dialog to accept *Detail (shows every field of every record)* for the query results.

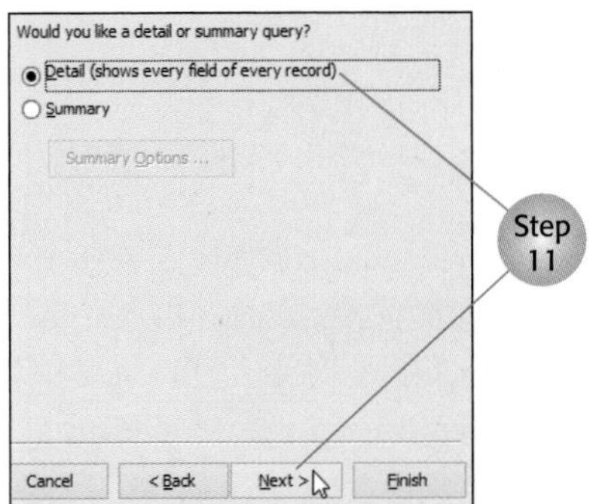

12 At the third Simple Query Wizard dialog box, select the current text in the *What title do you want for your query?* text box, type **StudentsWithFines**, and then tap or click Finish.

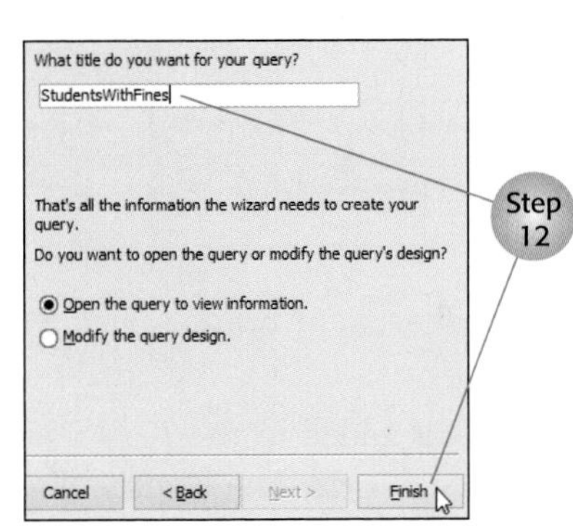

13 Review the query results datasheet. Notice the fields are displayed in the order selected at the first Simple Query Wizard dialog box.

14 Close the StudentsWithFines query. Leave the database open for the next topic.

Added the wrong field or the order is wrong? Move a field back to the *Available Fields* list box by selecting the field and using the Remove Field button (left-pointing arrow).

Create a Query Using Simple Query Wizard

1. Tap or click CREATE tab.
2. Tap or click Query Wizard button.
3. Tap or click OK.
4. Choose each table and/or query and fields in required order.
5. Tap or click Next.
6. Tap or click Next.
7. Type title for query.
8. Tap or click Finish.

Topic 12.8

SKILLS

Create a query using Design view

Creating a Query Using Design View

Every Access object has at least two views. In one view you browse the data in the table, query, form, or report. This is the view that is active when you open the object from the Navigation pane. Another view, called **Design view**, is used to set up or define the structure and/or layout of the table, query, form, or report. A query can be created in Design view, which displays a blank grid into which you add the fields you want to display in the query results.

1 With the **12.2-LibraryFines-Your Name** database open and with the CREATE tab active, tap or click the Query Design button in the Queries group.

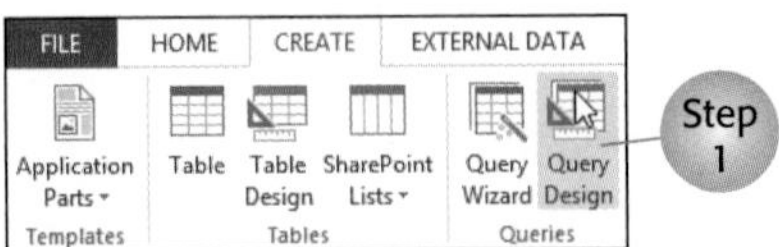

2 At the Show Table dialog box with the *Fines* table selected, tap or click the Add button.

A field list box for the Fines table is added to the top of the *Query1* design grid in the work area.

3 Double-tap or double-click *Students*.

A field list box for the Students table is added to the top of the design grid beside the *Fines* table field list box. A black join line connects the two tables together. The black line displays 1 and an infinity symbol (∞), which indicates the type of relationship for the two tables. You will learn about relationships in the next chapter.

4 Tap or click the Close button in the Show Table dialog box.

oops!

Closed the Show Table dialog box by mistake? Reopen the dialog box using the Show Table button in the Query Setup group of the QUERY TOOLS DESIGN tab.

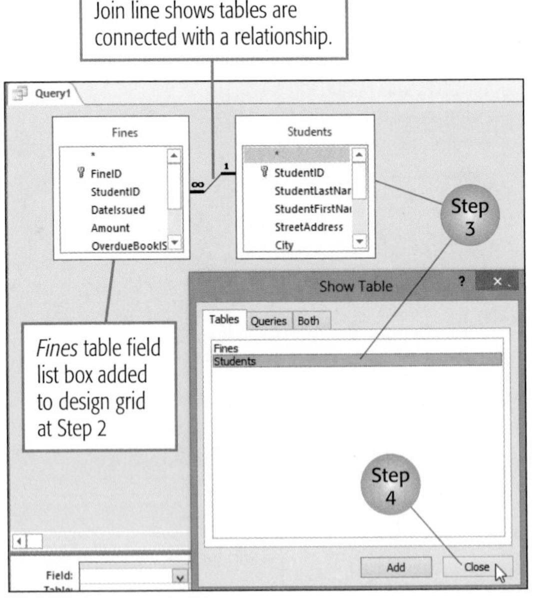

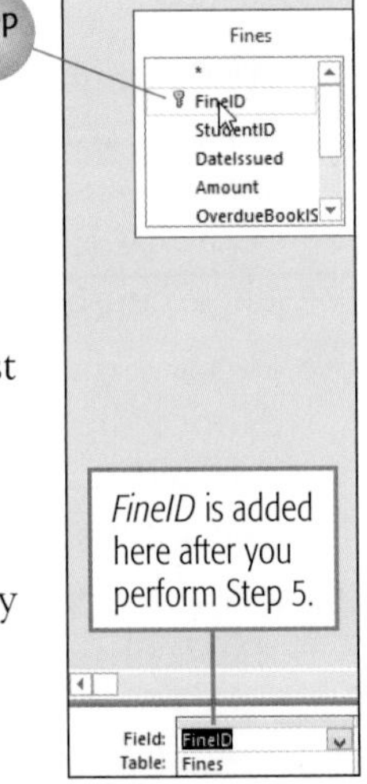

5 Double-tap or double-click *FineID* in the *Fines* table field list box.

FineID is added to the *Field* text box in the first column of the design grid. The blank columns in the bottom of the window represent the query results datasheet. You build the query by adding fields in the order you want them to appear in the datasheet by selecting fields from the table field list boxes in the top half of the window.

6 Double-tap or double-click the following fields in the *Fines* table field list box to add the fields to the query design grid.

DateIssued
Amount
BookReturned (slide or scroll down the table field list box to the field)

7 Double-tap or double-click the following fields in the *Students* table field list box to add the fields to the query design grid.

StudentFirstName
StudentLastName

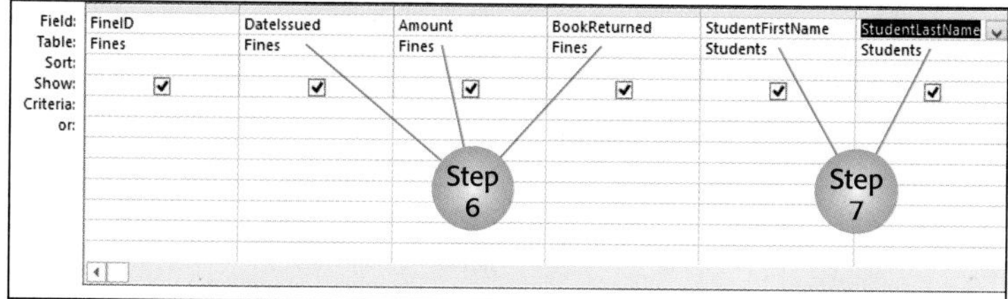

8 Tap or click the **Run button** in the Results group of the QUERY TOOLS DESIGN tab to view the query results datasheet.

A query is simply a set of instructions for which table names and field names display in a datasheet. The query results datasheet is not a duplicate copy of the data—each time a query is opened or run, the data is generated by extracting the field values from the tables.

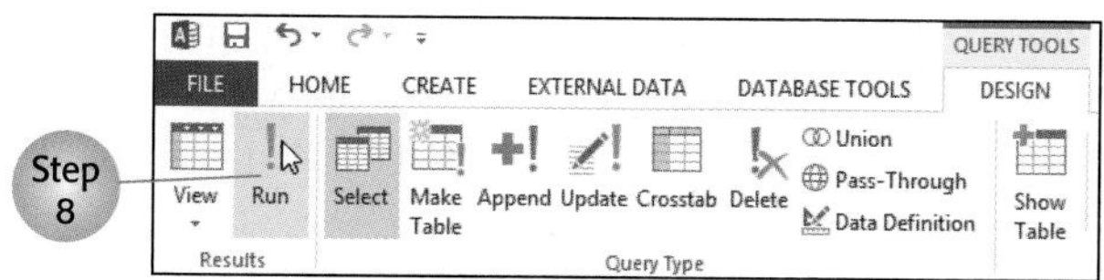

9 Tap or click the Save button in the Quick Access toolbar (QAT).

10 Type **BookReturnedList** at the Save As dialog box and tap or press Enter or tap or click OK.

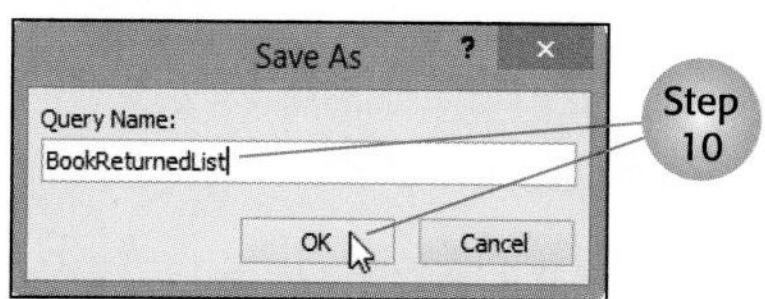

11 Close the BookReturnedList query. Leave the database open for the next topic.

Create a Query Using Design View

1. Tap or click CREATE tab.
2. Tap or click Query Design button.
3. Add tables to design grid.
4. Close Show Table dialog box.
5. Double-tap or double-click field names in table field list boxes.
6. Tap or click Run button.
7. Tap or click Save button.
8. Type query name.
9. Tap or click OK.

ALTERNATIVE method

Add fields to the design grid from the table field list boxes using these other methods:

- Slide or drag a field name from the table field list box to the Field text box in the desired column.
- Tap or click in a blank Field text box in the design grid, tap or click the down-pointing arrow that appears, and then tap or click the field name in the drop-down list.

Topic 12.9

SKILLS

Select records using criteria

Entering Criteria to Select Records in a Query

Both of the query results datasheets for the queries you created using the Simple Query Wizard and Design view displayed all records in the tables. Often, queries are created to select records from the tables that meet one or more conditions. For example, in this topic you will add a criterion to show only those records in which the fines are unpaid.

1. With the **12.2-LibraryFines-Your Name** database open, open the StudentsWithFines query.

2. Tap or click the View button in the Views group of the HOME tab. Do *not* tap or click the down-pointing arrow on the button.

The View button is used to switch between the query results datasheet and Design view.

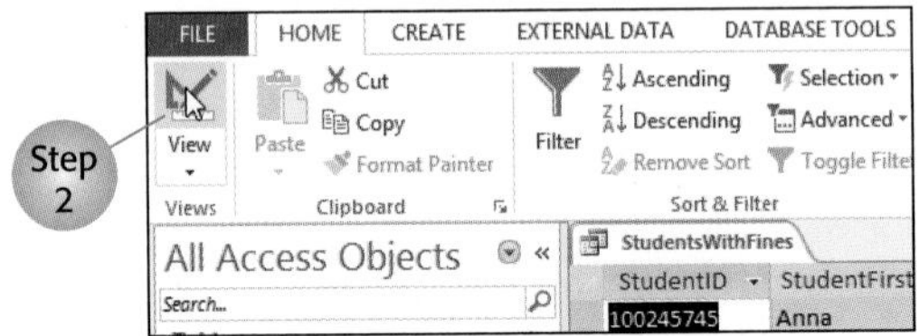

3. Tap or click in the *Criteria* box in the *FinePaid* column in the design grid, type No, tap or press the spacebar, and then tap or press Enter.

Access displays functions in a drop-down list as you type text that matches the letters in a function name. As you type *No*, the function wizard displays *Now* in a drop-down list. Typing a space after *No* causes the *Now* function to disappear. *FinePaid* is a field in which the field value is either *Yes* or *No*. By typing *No* in the *Criteria* box, you are instructing Access to select the records from the *Fines* table in which *No* is the field value for *FinePaid*.

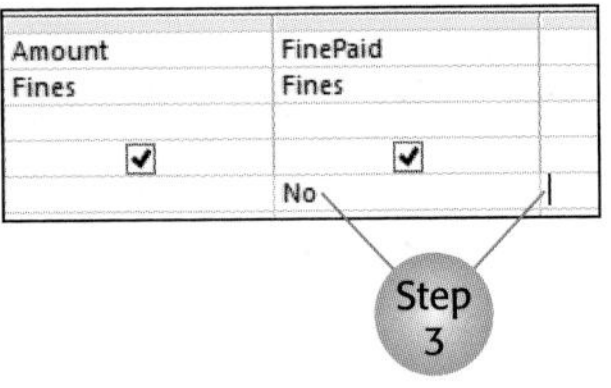

oops!

Empty datasheet? Use the View button to return to Design view and check that you typed *No* in the *FinePaid* column and/or that *No* is in the *Criteria* box of the column.

4. Tap or click the Run button.

Notice that 10 records are selected in the query results datasheet and that the check box in the *FinePaid* column for each record is empty.

StudentID	StudentFirstName	StudentLastName	Telephone	Email	DateIssued	Amount	FinePaid
100245745	Anna	Takacis	(313) 555-4235	takacisa@emcp.net	12-Apr-2015	$2.45	☐
100443568	Dwayne	Kenney	(519) 555-4125	kenneyd@emcp.net	15-Mar-2015	$12.50	☐
100443568	Dwayne	Kenney	(519) 555-4125	kenneyd@emcp.net	06-Apr-2015	$4.60	☐
100659412	Jasmine	Daly	(284) 555-3142	dalyj@emcp.net	30-Mar-2015	$2.40	☐
100684741	Marietta	Lynch	(519) 555-3214	lynchm@emcp.net	12-Mar-2015	$1.40	☐
101325685	Peter	Maslov	(519) 555-3276	maslovp@emcp.net	04-Apr-2015	$7.85	☐
101334799	Su-Lin	Cheng	(313) 555-4125	chengs@emcp.net	10-Apr-2015	$8.75	☐
101348863	Daniela	Garcia	(313) 555-6235	garciad@emcp.net	15-Mar-2015	$1.85	☐
101348863	Daniela	Garcia	(313) 555-6235	garciad@emcp.net	15-Apr-2015	$5.25	☐
101658235	Stuart	Bennett	(313) 555-5112	bennetts@emcp.net	13-Mar-2015	$3.25	☐
*							

Query results datasheet showing unpaid fines only

5 Tap or click the FILE tab and then tap or click Save As.

6 At the Save As Backstage view, tap or click *Save Object As* and then tap or click the Save As button.

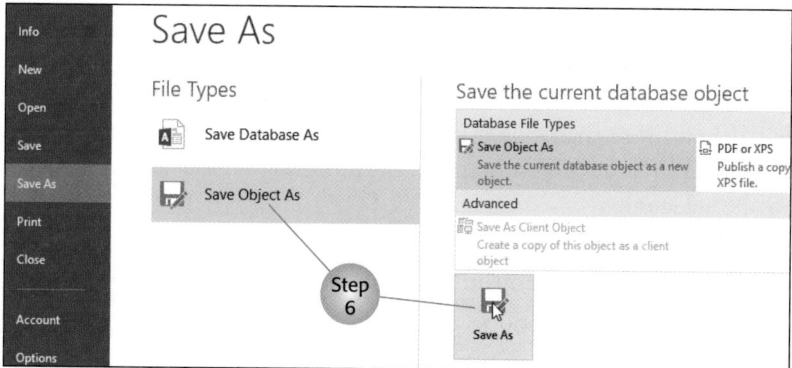

7 Type **UnpaidFines** in the *Save 'StudentsWithFines' to* text box at the Save As dialog box and then tap or press Enter or tap or click OK.

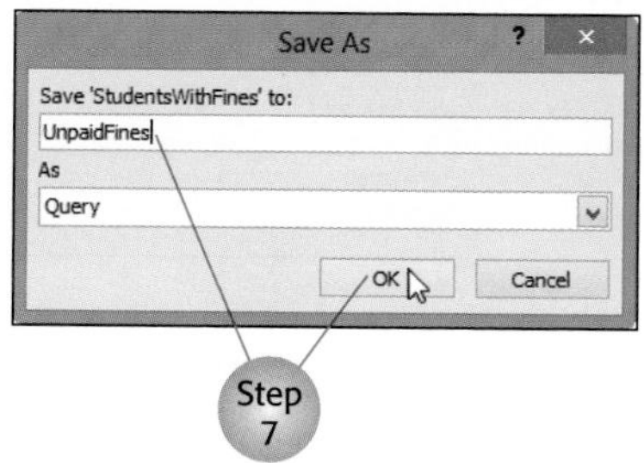

8 Close the UnpaidFines query. Leave the database open for the next topic.

See Table 12.2 for more criteria statement examples.

Table 12.2	Criteria Examples	
Field	**Entry Typed in Criteria Text Box**	**Records Selected**
Amount	<=5	Fines issued that were $5.00 or less
Amount	>5	Fines issued that were more than $5.00
DateIssued	March 15, 2015 (entry converts automatically to *#3/15/2015#)*	Fines issued on March 15, 2015
StudentLastName	Kenney (entry converts automatically to "Kenney")	Fines issued to student with the last name *Kenney*.

Select Records in a Query

1. Open query.
2. Tap or click View button.
3. Type criterion in *Criteria* box of field by which to select records.
4. Run query.
5. Save query or use Save As to save revised query using new name.

A query that extracts records is referred to as a select query.

Selecting Records using a Range of Dates

Table 12.2 provides the example that typing March 15, 2015 in the DateIssued field selects records of fines issued on March 15, 2015. What if one wanted to view a list of all of the fines issued in the month of March? To do this, type *Between March 1, 2015 and March 31, 2015* in the *Criteria* text box of the *DateIssued* column.

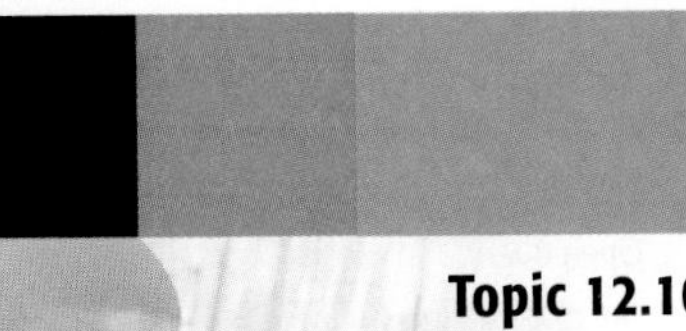

Entering Multiple Criteria to Select Records and Sorting a Query

Topic 12.10

SKILLS

- Select records using AND criteria
- Select records using OR criteria
- Sort query results

More than one criterion can be entered in the query design grid to select records. For example, you may want a list of all unpaid fines that are more than $5.00. When more than one criterion is on the same row in the query design grid, it is referred to as an *AND* statement, meaning that each criterion must be met for a record to be selected. When more than one criterion is on different rows in the query design grid, it is referred to as an *OR* statement, meaning that any criterion can be met for a record to be selected.

1. With the **12.2-LibraryFines-Your Name** database open, open the UnpaidFines query.
2. Tap or click the View button to switch to Design view.
3. Tap or click in the *Criteria* box in the *Amount* column, type **>5**, and then tap or press Enter.
4. Tap or click the Run button.

Amount	FinePaid
Fines	Fines
☑	☑
>5	No

Step 3

Multiple criteria typed in the same *Criteria* row means each condition must be met for a record to be selected.

StudentID	StudentFirstName	StudentLastName	Telephone	Email	DateIssued	Amount	FinePaid
100443568	Dwayne	Kenney	(519) 555-4125	kenneyd@emcp.net	15-Mar-2015	$12.50	☐
101325685	Peter	Maslov	(519) 555-3276	maslovp@emcp.net	04-Apr-2015	$7.85	☐
101334799	Su-Lin	Cheng	(313) 555-4125	chengs@emcp.net	10-Apr-2015	$8.75	☐
101348863	Daniela	Garcia	(313) 555-6235	garciad@emcp.net	15-Apr-2015	$5.25	☐

Query results datasheet showing unpaid fines over $5.00

5. Use *Save Object As* at the Save As Backstage view to save the revised query as *UnpaidFinesOver$5*.
6. Close the UnpaidFinesOver$5 query.
7. Tap or click the CREATE tab and then tap or click the Query Design button.
8. Double-tap or double-click *Students* in the Show Table dialog box and then tap or click the Close button.
9. Double-tap or double-click the following fields in the *Students* table field list box to add the fields to the query design grid.

   City
   StudentID
   StudentFirstName
   StudentLastName
   Telephone (slide or scroll down the table field list box to the field)

10. Tap or click in the *Criteria* box in the *City* column, type **Detroit**, tap or click in the row below *Detroit* next to *or*, type **Windsor**, and then tap or press Enter.

Access inserts double quotation marks at the beginning and end of a criterion for a field that contains text such as a city, name, or other field that is not used for calculating values.

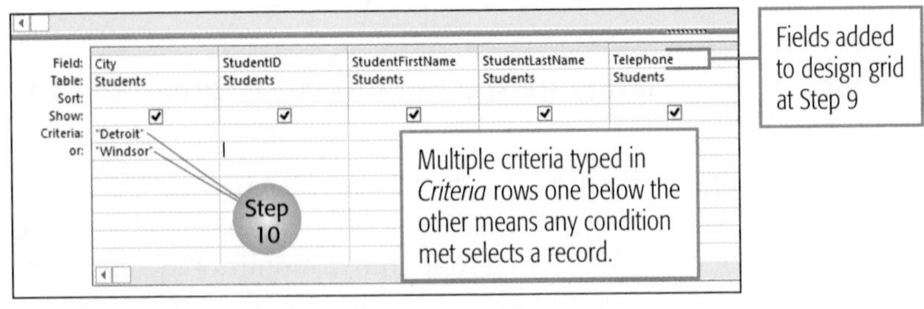
Field: City | StudentID | StudentFirstName | StudentLastName | Telephone
Table: Students | Students | Students | Students | Students
Sort:
Show:
Criteria: "Detroit"
or: "Windsor"
Step 10
Multiple criteria typed in Criteria rows one below the other means any condition met selects a record.
Fields added to design grid at Step 9

11 Tap or click the Run button.

Only students who reside in Detroit or Windsor are shown in the query results datasheet.

12 Tap or click the View button to return to Design view.

A query is sorted by choosing *Ascending* or *Descending* in the *Sort* list box of the column by which you want to sort. At Step 9 *City* was placed first in the design grid because Access sorts query results by column left to right. To arrange the records alphabetically by student last name grouped by cities, the *City* field needs to be positioned left of the *StudentLastName* field.

13 Tap or click in the *Sort* list box in the *City* column to place the insertion point and display the list arrow, tap or click the *Sort* list arrow, and then tap or click *Ascending*.

14 Tap or click in the *Sort* list box in the *StudentLastName* column, tap or click the list arrow that appears, and then tap or click *Ascending*.

Step 13

Field:	City	StudentID	StudentFirstName	StudentLastName
Table:	Students	Students	Students	Students
Sort:	Ascending			Ascending Descending (not sorted)
Show:	☑	☑	☑	
Criteria:	"Detroit"			
or:	"Windsor"			

Step 14

15 Tap or click the Run button.

The query results datasheet is sorted alphabetically by city and then by the student last name within each city.

DetroitAndWindsorStudents

City	StudentID	StudentFirstName	StudentLastNam	Telephone
Detroit	101658235	Stuart	Bennett	(313) 555-511
Detroit	101334799	Su-Lin	Cheng	(313) 555-412
Detroit	101455623	Armando	Colacci	(313) 555-221
Detroit	100478512	Angela	Doxtator	(313) 555-477
Detroit	101348863	Daniela	Garcia	(313) 555-623
Detroit	100548112	Pat	Hynes	(313) 555-656
Detroit	101322775	Shane	O'Leary	(313) 555-365
Detroit	110542642	Nadir	Sadiku	(313) 555-478
Detroit	100245745	Anna	Takacis	(313) 555-423
Detroit	101334745	Kyla	Westman	(313) 555-745
Detroit	104875111	Dana	Williams	(313) 555-124
Windsor	100367845	Sara	Blewett	(519) 555-412
Windsor	101352658	Shaun	Jenkins	(519) 555-478
Windsor	100443568	Dwayne	Kenney	(519) 555-412
Windsor	100684741	Marietta	Lynch	(519) 555-321
Windsor	101325685	Peter	Maslov	(519) 555-327
Windsor	100324125	Jose	Ramirez	(519) 555-469
*				

Sorted query results datasheet showing students who reside in either Detroit or Windsor

16 Save the query and name it **DetroitAndWindsorStudents**.

17 Close the DetroitAndWindsorStudents query. Leave the database open for the next topic.

Select Records Using AND
1. Open query in Design view.
2. Type criterion in *Criteria* box of first field by which to select.
3. Type criterion in *Criteria* box of second field by which to select.
4. Run query.

Select Records Using OR
1. Open query in Design view.
2. Type criterion in *Criteria* box of first field by which to select.
3. Type criterion in *or* box of second field by which to select.
4. Run query.

Sort a Query
1. Open query in Design view.
2. Tap or click in *Sort* box of column by which to sort.
3. Tap or click *Sort* list arrow.
4. Tap or click *Ascending* or *Descending*.

Selecting Using a Wildcard Character

A criterion can be entered that provides Access with a partial entry to match for selecting records. The asterisk is a wildcard character that can be inserted in a criterion in place of characters that you do not want to specify. For example, to select all students with the last name beginning with C, type *C** in the *Criteria* box in the *StudentLastName* column.

Creating a Calculated Field in a Query and Previewing a Datasheet

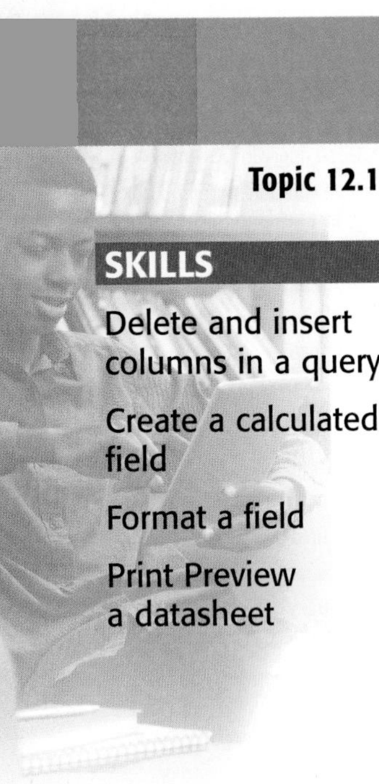

Topic 12.11

SKILLS

Delete and insert columns in a query

Create a calculated field

Format a field

Print Preview a datasheet

A calculated field can be created in a query that performs a mathematical operation on a numeric field. A database best practice is to avoid adding fields in a table with data that otherwise can be generated by performing calculations on other fields. For example, assume that in the LibraryFines database, each fine is also assessed a $2.50 administrative fee. Because the fee is a constant value, adding a field in the table to store the fee is not necessary. In this topic, you will use a query to calculate the total fine, including the administrative fee.

1 With the **12.2-LibraryFines-Your Name** database open, open the FinesIssued query.

2 Switch to Design view.

3 Tap or click in any cell in the *Telephone* column in the query design grid.

4 Tap or click the Delete Columns button in the Query Setup group of the QUERY TOOLS DESIGN tab.

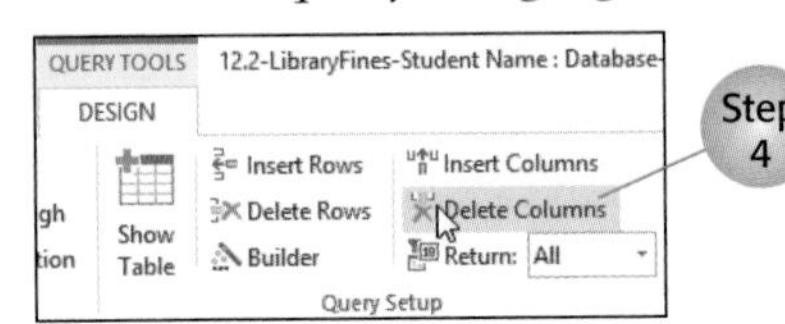

Use buttons in the Query Setup group to modify a query design by deleting columns or inserting new columns between existing fields.

5 Delete the *OverdueBookISBN* and *BookReturned* fields by completing steps similar to Steps 3 and 4.

oops!

Error message appears? Check your typing to make sure you typed a colon after *Fine with Admin Fee*, used square brackets, and that the entry has no other spelling errors.

6 With *FinePaid* the active field, tap or click the Insert Columns button in the Query Setup group.

7 With the insertion point positioned in the *Field* box in the new column between *Amount* and *FinePaid*, type **Fine with Admin Fee: [Amount]+2.50** and then tap or press Enter. Note that Access drops the zero at the end of the formula in the design grid.

8 Slide or drag the right column boundary line in the gray field selector bar at the top of the design grid to widen the column as shown in the image below.

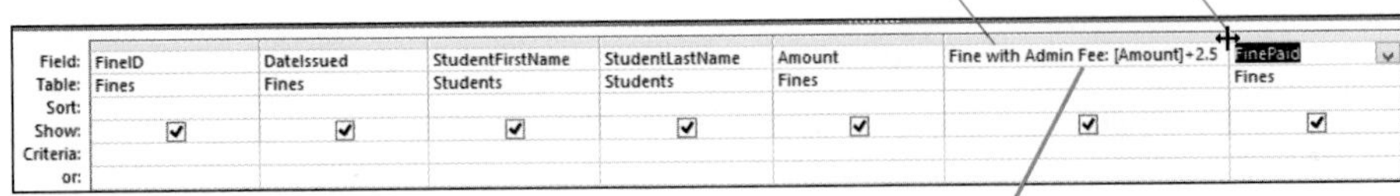

The text before the colon is the column heading for the calculated field *Fine with Admin Fee*. After the colon the mathematical expression *[Amount]+2.5* is typed. A field name to be used in a formula is typed within square brackets.

9 Tap or click the Run button.

Notice that the calculated field is not formatted the same as the *Amount* field, and the column needs to be widened to show the entire column heading.

10 Tap or click in any cell in the *Fine with Admin Fee* column, tap or click the More button in the Records group, tap or click *Field Width*, and then tap or click Best Fit.

11 Switch to Design view.

12 Tap or click in any cell in the calculated column in the query design grid and then tap or click the Property Sheet button in the Show/Hide group of the QUERY TOOLS DESIGN tab.

13 Tap or click in the *Format* box in the Property Sheet task pane, tap or click the list arrow that appears, and then tap or click *Currency* at the drop-down list.

14 Close the Property Sheet task pane.

15 Tap or click the Run button.

16 Use *Save Object As* at the Save As Backstage view to save the revised query as *FinesWithAdminFee*.

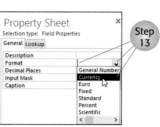

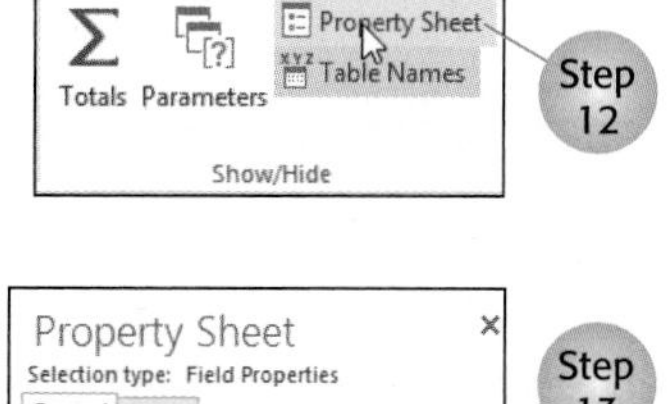

Create a Calculated Field in a Query

1. Open query in Design view.
2. Insert column if necessary.
3. Tap or click in *Field* box for calculated column.
4. Type formula.
5. Tap or press Enter.
6. Run query.
7. Save query.

A table datasheet or query results datasheet should be viewed in Print Preview before printing to make adjustments as necessary to the orientation and margins.

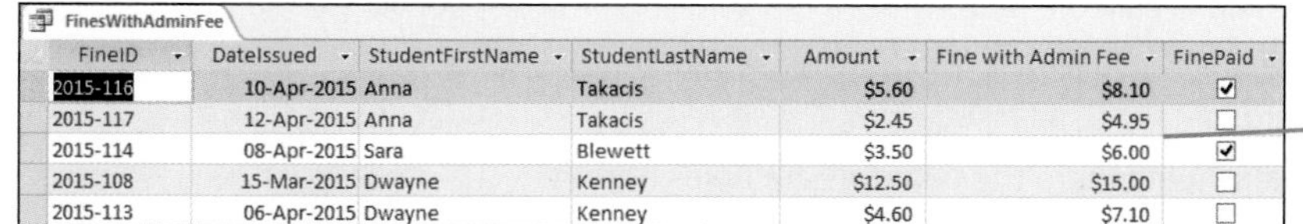

FinesWithAdminFee

FineID	DateIssued	StudentFirstName	StudentLastName	Amount	Fine with Admin Fee	FinePaid
2015-116	10-Apr-2015	Anna	Takacis	$5.60	$8.10	☑
2015-117	12-Apr-2015	Anna	Takacis	$2.45	$4.95	☐
2015-114	08-Apr-2015	Sara	Blewett	$3.50	$6.00	☑
2015-108	15-Mar-2015	Dwayne	Kenney	$12.50	$15.00	☐
2015-113	06-Apr-2015	Dwayne	Kenney	$4.60	$7.10	☐

First five records in FinesWithAdminFee query showing calculated *Fine with Admin Fee* column

17 Tap or click the FILE tab, tap or click Print, and tap or click *Print Preview* at the Print tab Backstage view.

18 Tap or click the Landscape button in the Page Layout group of the PRINT PREVIEW tab.

Notice that by default, Access prints the query name and the current date at the top of the page and the page number at the bottom of the page.

19 Tap or click the Close Print Preview button in the Close Preview group.

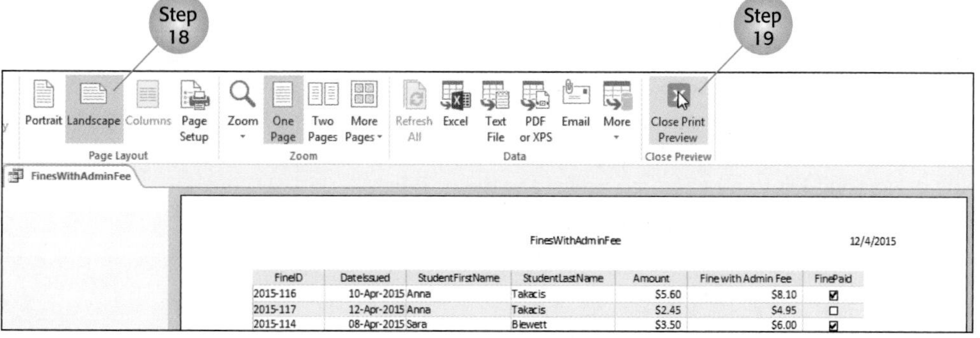

20 Close the FinesWithAdminFee query and then close the LibraryFines database.

Exporting Data from Access

Buttons in the Data group of the PRINT PREVIEW tab are used to export the active table, query, form, or report shown in the work area. For example, tap or click the PDF or XPS button to save a copy of the query results datasheet shown above in a PDF file.

Concepts Review

Topic	Key Concepts	Key Terms
Understanding Database Objects and Terminology	A database includes data stored in an organized manner to provide information for a variety of purposes. A database management system (DBMS) is a software program designed to organize, store, and maintain a database. An Access database is a collection of objects used to enter, maintain, and view data. Access opens with a Navigation pane along the left side of the window where you select the object in which you want to work. A table stores data about a single topic or subject such as people, places, events, items, or other category. Each characteristic about the subject or topic of a table is called a field. The data stored in a field is called a field value. A set of fields for one person, place, event, item, or other subject of a table is called a record. A table opens in a datasheet where the columns are fields and the rows are records. A report is an object in which you view or print data from the tables in a customized layout and with summary totals. A form is another interface with which you can view, enter, or edit data in a table that generally shows only one record at a time in a customized layout. Use buttons in the Record Navigation and Search bar to scroll records in a form. A query is used to combine fields from one or more tables in a single datasheet and may show all records or only some records that meet a condition.	Database Database management system (DBMS) Table Field Record Field value Report Form Query
Adding Records Using a Datasheet	New records are added to a table by opening the table datasheet and tapping or clicking the New (blank) record button in the Record Navigation and Search bar. Type field values in a new row at the bottom of the table datasheet, tapping or pressing Tab to move from one field to the next field. A field that displays with a down-pointing arrow means that you can enter the field value by selecting an entry from a drop-down list. Date fields can be set up to display underscores and hyphens to make sure dates are entered consistently in the correct format. A field that displays with a check box stores *Yes* if the box is checked and *No* if the box is left empty. Access automatically saves a new record as soon as you tap or press Tab to move past the last field.	New (blank) record button

Topic	Key Concepts	Key Terms
Editing and Deleting Records in a Datasheet	Edit a field value in a datasheet by tapping or clicking to place the insertion point within a field (cell) and inserting or deleting text as required. Function key F2 opens a field for editing. The gray bar along the left edge of a datasheet is used to select a record. Tap or click the Delete button in the Records group of the HOME tab to delete the selected record from the table. Access requires that you confirm a deletion before the record is removed. Generally, records are not deleted until data has been copied to an archive database and/or a backup copy of the database has been made.	
Adding, Editing, and Deleting Records in a Form	A form is the preferred object for adding, editing, and deleting records. A form displays one record at a time in a columnar layout. Add new records and edit field values in records using the same techniques as you used in a datasheet. To delete a record in a form, display the record, tap or click the Delete button arrow in the Records group of the HOME tab, and then tap or click *Delete Record* at the drop-down list. In a database with many records, navigating to a record using the Find feature is more efficient.	
Finding and Replacing Data and Adjusting Column Widths	Tap or click in the column in a datasheet that contains the field value you want to locate and use the Find command to move to all occurrences of the *Find What* text. Use the Replace command to find all occurrences of an entry and replace the field value with new text. Activate any cell in a column for which the width needs to be adjusted, tap or click the More button in the Records group, and then tap or click *Field Width*. The *Best Fit* button in the Column Width dialog box adjusts the width of the column to accommodate the longest entry.	Best Fit
Sorting and Filtering Records	Initially, a table is arranged alphanumerically by the primary key field values. A primary key is a field in the table that uniquely identifies each record such as *StudentID*. To sort by a field other than the primary key, tap or click in the field by which to sort and choose the Ascending or Descending button in the Sort & Filter group of the HOME tab. Filter a datasheet by clearing check boxes for items you do not want to view in the Sort & Filter list box accessed from the filter arrow next to the field name. Use the Toggle Filter button in the Sort & Filter group to redisplay all records. Sort by more than one field by selecting the columns before tapping or clicking the Ascending or Descending order button.	Primary key

continued....

Topic	Key Concepts	Key Terms
Creating a Query Using the Simple Query Wizard	Queries extract information from one or more tables in a single datasheet. The Simple Query Wizard helps you build a query by making selections in three dialog boxes. At the first Simple Query Wizard dialog box, choose each table or query and the fields in the order that you want them in the query results datasheet. At the second Simple Query Wizard dialog box, choose a detail or summary query. Assign a name to the query at the third Simple Query Wizard dialog box.	Simple Query Wizard
Creating a Query Using Design View	Every object in Access has at least two views. Opening an object from the Navigation pane opens the table, query, form, or report in Datasheet view. Design view is used to set up or define the structure or layout of an object. Design view for a query presents a blank grid of columns in which you add the fields in the order you want them in the query results datasheet. Add table field list boxes to the query design grid at the Show Table dialog box. Double-tap or double-click field names in the table field list boxes in the order you want the columns in the query results datasheet. The Run button is used after building a query in Design view to instruct Access to generate the query and show the query results datasheet.	Design view Run button
Entering Criteria to Select Records in a Query	Queries can be created that show only those records that meet one or more conditions. Use the View button in the Views group of the HOME tab to switch between Datasheet view and Design view in a query. Type the criterion by which you want records selected in the *Criteria* box of the column by which records are to be selected. In a field that displays check boxes, the criterion is either *Yes* or *No*.	
Entering Multiple Criteria to Select Records and Sorting a Query	More than one criterion entered in the same *Criteria* row in the query design grid is an AND statement, which means each criterion must be met for the record to be selected. More than one criterion entered in *Criteria* rows one below the other is an OR statement, which means that any condition can be met for the record to be selected. Choose *Ascending* or *Descending* in the *Sort* box for the column by which to sort query results in Design view. Access sorts a query by column left to right. If necessary, position the field to be sorted first to the left of another field that is to be sorted.	

Topic	Key Concepts	Key Terms
Creating a Calculated Field in a Query and Previewing a Datasheet	A calculated field can be created in a query that generates values using a mathematical expression. Use the Delete Columns and Insert Columns buttons in the Query Setup group of the QUERY TOOLS DESIGN tab to remove or add new columns in a query. A calculated column is created by typing in the *Field* box a column heading, a colon (:), and then the mathematical expression. Type a field name in a mathematical expression within square brackets. Open the Property Sheet task pane to format a calculated field. A table or query results datasheet should be previewed before printing to make adjustments to page orientation and/or margins.	

Multiple Choice

1. A single characteristic about a person, place, event, or item is referred to as a ____________.
   a. record
   b. field
   c. field value
   d. table
2. All of the data for a single topic or subject is stored in a ____________.
   a. field value
   b. record
   c. table
   d. field
3. A new record can be added in a datasheet or in this other object.
   a. report
   b. form
   c. database
   d. Print Preview
4. Tap or press _____ to move from field to field in a new record.
   a. Backspace
   b. F2
   c. Ctrl + Enter
   d. Tab
5. This icon in a datasheet or form indicates the record is being edited.
   a. asterisk
   b. funnel
   c. down-pointing arrow
   d. pencil
6. The Delete button is found in this group in the HOME tab.
   a. Records
   b. Sort & Filter
   c. Cells
   d. Find
7. Preferred object for adding and editing records.
   a. Print Preview
   b. query
   c. report
   d. form
8. This button moves to record 1 in a datasheet or form.
   a. First record
   b. Previous record
   c. Go to 1
   d. Home
9. Use this feature to move quickly to a specific record in a datasheet.
   a. Go to
   b. Find
   c. Next record
   d. Move
10. Use this option to change all occurrences of a field value automatically.
    a. Find
    b. Go to
    c. Find All
    d. Replace

11. Tap or click this arrow in a datasheet to hide records you do not want to view.
    a. Filter
    b. Remove
    c. Sort
    d. Delete
12. Tap or click this button to rearrange records alphabetically by the contents in the active field.
    a. First field
    b. Search
    c. Ascending
    d. Filter
13. Fields to be displayed in a query are added to this list box in the Simple Query Wizard.
    a. Available fields
    b. Selected fields
    c. Detail fields
    d. Summary fields
14. Results of a query display in a query results _______________.
    a. datasheet
    b. form
    c. report
    d. design grid
15. Add a field list box for a table to the query window at this dialog box.
    a. Add fields
    b. Selected fields
    c. Show fields
    d. Show table
16. Use this button after you define a new query to view the selected data.
    a. Show table
    b. Show records
    c. Run
    d. View query
17. Type text by which to select records in a query in this box.
    a. Field
    b. Sort
    c. Format
    d. Criteria
18. This button switches between Datasheet view and the query design grid.
    a. View
    b. Property Sheet
    c. Show Table
    d. Run
19. Multiple conditions all of which must be met to select records is this type of statement.
    a. OR
    b. AND
    c. Combo
    d. Wildcard
20. Multiple conditions any of which can be met to select records is this type of statement.
    a. Combo
    b. AND
    c. Wildcard
    d. OR
21. Which of the following entries is a valid formula for a calculated field?
    a. Fine with Admin Fee: (Amount)+2.50
    b. Fine with Admin Fee; [Amount]+2.50
    c. Fine with Admin Fee: [Amount]+2.50
    d. Fine with Admin Fee; (Amount)+2.50
22. Change to landscape orientation at this tab.
    a. PRINT PREVIEW
    b. PAGE SETUP
    c. PAGE LAYOUT
    d. CREATE

Crossword Puzzle

ACROSS

2 Datasheet with fields from more than one table
5 Displays fields in a columnar layout
6 All of the data for one person or item
9 View in which structure or layout of object is defined
10 Adjusts column width to longest entry
12 Statement where any condition can be met
13 All of the data about one topic or subject
14 Box in grid to enter condition to select records

DOWN

1 Field by which datasheet is initially sorted
3 Group with buttons to insert or delete columns in query
4 Item that indicates field values are either *Yes* or *No*
7 Statement in which all conditions must be met
8 Action in a datasheet or form that requires confirmation
11 Property to change a calculated field to Currency

Matching

Match the term with the statement or definition.

_______ 1. Datasheet
_______ 2. Last name
_______ 3. Add new record
_______ 4. Gray bar at left edge of datasheet
_______ 5. Scroll through records
_______ 6. Find any part of a field
_______ 7. Temporarily hide records
_______ 8. Assists with building a query
_______ 9. Create a query using a blank grid
_______ 10. Specify condition to select records
_______ 11. Multiple conditions in same row
_______ 12. Format a calculated field

a. New (blank) record
b. Property Sheet task pane
c. Design view
d. Filter
e. Simple Query Wizard
f. Criteria
g. Table
h. AND statement
i. Record selector
j. Match list arrow
k. Field
l. Record Navigation and Search bar

Project 1 Adding, Editing, and Deleting Records

Individual

Deliverable: Locker Rentals database (continued in all projects)

1. Open **LockerRentals** and tap or click Enable Content.
2. Use Save As to *Save Database As* and name the copy **C12-Projects-LockerRentals-Your Name** in a new folder named *Ch12* within the ChapterProjectsWork folder on your USB flash drive.
3. Enable content in the copy of the database.
4. Open the Students table. Add a new record using StudentID *999999999*. Type your first and last names in the appropriate fields and leave all of the other fields blank. Close the table.
5. Open the Rentals table. Add the following new record and then close the table when finished.

RentalNumber	Tab past this field as the number is assigned automatically by Access
LockerNumber	Select *A104* in the drop-down list
StudentID	Select *999999999 Your Name* in the drop-down list
DateRented	**15sep2015**
RentalPaid	*Yes*
DatePaid	**15sep2015**

6. Open the Lockers table and make the following changes to the data:
   a. Change all occurrences of *City Center* to *Downtown Campus*.
   b. Change the level number from *3* to *2* for locker numbers B108, B109, and B110.
   c. Change the locker type from *Box Size* to *Half Size* for locker numbers A101 and A102.
7. Delete the records for locker numbers A106 and C106.
8. Close the Lockers table.
9. Open the Rentals form and add the following new record:

RentalNumber	Tab past this field as the number is assigned automatically by Access
LockerNumber	Select *A102* in the drop-down list
StudentID	Select *101334799 Su-Lin Cheng* in the drop-down list
DateRented	**15sep2015**
RentalPaid	*Yes*
DatePaid	**15sep2015**

10. Use the Find feature to locate the record in the Locker Rentals form for locker number B100 and then delete the record.
11. Use the Find feature to locate the record in the Locker Rentals form for locker number B106 and then edit the record to show the rental paid on September 16, 2015.
12. Close the Rentals form.
13. Leave the database open if you are continuing to Project 2; otherwise, close the database and submit the project to your instructor in the manner she or he has requested.

Project 2 Sorting and Filtering Data

Individual

Deliverable: Locker Rentals database and PDF of filtered table (continued from Project 1)

1. If necessary, open **C12-Projects-LockerRentals-Your Name** and enable content.
2. Open the Rentals table and sort the table by *LockerNumber* in ascending order.
3. Close the Rentals table, saving the changes to the table design.
4. Open the Lockers table and filter the table to show only the Downtown Campus lockers.
5. ***Optional:*** With the filtered Lockers table active, create a PDF of the table by completing the following steps:
   a. Tap or click the EXTERNAL DATA tab.
   b. Tap or click the PDF or XPS button in the Export group.

c. At the Publish as PDF or XPS dialog box, navigate to the Ch12 folder within ChapterProjectsWork, select the current entry in the *File name* text box, type **C12-Project2-FilteredLockersTable-Your Name**, and then tap or click the Publish button.
d. If necessary, close the PDF window and return to Access.
e. Close the Export – PDF dialog box that asks if you want to save the export steps.
6. Close the Lockers table. Click No when prompted to save changes to the table design.
7. Leave the database open if you are continuing to Project 3; otherwise, close the database and submit the project to your instructor in the manner she or he has requested.

Project 3 Creating and Editing Queries

Individual

Deliverable: Locker Rentals database (continued from Project 2)

1. If necessary, open **C12-Projects-LockerRentals-Your Name** and enable content.
2. Create a query using the Simple Query Wizard using the following information:
   a. Choose the tables and fields in this order:
      Table: Lockers Add all fields
      Table: LockerTypesAndFees *RentalFee*
   b. Choose a detail query.
   c. Change the title to *LockerListWithFees*.
3. Switch to Design view for the LockerListWithFees query and sort the query by the *LockerNumber* field in ascending order.
4. Run the query.
5. Save and close the query.
6. Open the LockerListWithFees query and switch to Design view.
7. Enter criteria to select the lockers in the Allen Park campus building. Run the query. Use Save Object As to save the revised query as *AllenParkLockers* and then close the query.
8. Open the LockerListWithFees query and switch to Design view.
9. Enter criteria to select the lockers in the first level only of the Borden Avenue campus building. Run the query. Use Save Object As to save the revised query as *BordenAveL1Lockers* and then close the query.
10. Open the LockerRentals2015 query, switch to Design view, and delete the *DateRented* column.
11. Insert a new column to the left of the *RentalPaid* column and type the following formula in the *Field* box: **Rental Fee with Tax: [RentalFee]*1.05**
12. Format the *Rental Fee with Tax* column to Currency.
13. Run the query. Adjust the column width of the calculated column to Best Fit.
14. Save and close the query.
15. Open the LockerRentals2015 query. Switch to Design view. Enter criteria to select only those records where the rental fee has been paid. Run the query. Use Save Object As to save the revised query as *PaidLockerRentals2015* and then close the query.
16. Leave the database open if you are continuing to Project 4; otherwise, close the database and submit the project to your instructor in the manner she or he has requested.

Project 4 Previewing and Creating PDFs of Database Objects

Individual

Deliverable: PDFs of tables and queries in Locker Rentals database (continued from Project 3)

1. If necessary, open **C12-Projects-LockerRentals-Your Name** and enable content.
2. Open the Lockers table and display the table in the Print Preview window.
3. Tap or click the PDF or XPS button in the Data group of the PRINT PREVIEW tab. At the Publish as PDF or XPS dialog box, navigate to the Ch12 folder within ChapterProjectsWork and publish a PDF of the table, naming it **C12-Project4-LockersTable-Your Name**. If necessary, close the PDF window and return to Access. Close the Export – PDF dialog box.

4. Close the Print Preview window and then close the Lockers table.
5. Complete steps similar to Steps 2 to 4 to create a PDF for each of the following objects, changing the file names as noted.
   Note: Consider clearing the* Open file after publishing *check box in the Publish as PDF or XPS dialog box if the box is checked.

Object Name	*Name for PDF*
Rentals table	C12-Project4-RentalsTable-Your Name
AllenParkLockers	C12-Project4-AllenParkLockers-Your Name
BordenAveL1Lockers	C12-Project4-BordenAveL1Lockers-Your Name
LockerListWithFees	C12-Project4-LockerListWithFees-Your Name

6. Create a PDF for each of the following queries by completing steps similar to Steps 2 to 4, changing the page layout to landscape orientation and the margins to *Normal*.

Object Name	*Name for PDF*
LockerRentals2015	C12-Project4-LockerRentals2015-Your Name
PaidLockerRentals2015	C12-Project4-PaidLockerRentals2015-Your Name

7. Leave the database open if you are continuing to Project 5; otherwise, close the database and submit the project to your instructor in the manner she or he has requested.

Project 5 Modifying a Query to Add Criteria and a Calculation

Individual

Deliverable: PDF of query with calculated field (continued from Project 4)

1. If necessary, open **C12-Projects-LockerRentals-Your Name** and enable content.
2. Open the LockerListWithFees query and modify the query to create the query results datasheet shown in Figure 12.3. You determine the required calculated column *Field* expression as well as the criteria used to generate the query results datasheet. ***Hint: The rental fee is for eight months.***
3. Create a PDF of the query, naming it **C12-Project5-AllenParkAndBordenAveLockers-Your Name** and saving it in the Ch12 folder within ChapterProjectsWork. Make sure the datasheet fits on one page.
4. Use Save Object As to save the revised query as *AllenParkAndBordenAveLockers*, then close the query and close the LockerRentals database.
5. Submit the project to your instructor in the manner she or he has requested.

AllenParkAndBordenAveLockers

LockerNumber	LockerType	CampusBuilding	Level	RentalFee	Rental Fee Per Month
A101	Half size	Allen Park	1	$70.00	$8.75
A102	Half size	Allen Park	1	$70.00	$8.75
A103	Full Size Regular	Allen Park	1	$80.00	$10.00
A104	Full Size Regular	Allen Park	1	$80.00	$10.00
A105	Half size	Allen Park	1	$70.00	$8.75
A107	Full Size Regular	Allen Park	2	$80.00	$10.00
A108	Full Size Regular	Allen Park	2	$80.00	$10.00
A109	Full Size Wide	Allen Park	2	$95.00	$11.88
A110	Full Size Wide	Allen Park	2	$95.00	$11.88
A115	Full Size Regular	Allen Park	2	$80.00	$10.00
A120	Full Size Regular	Allen Park	2	$80.00	$10.00
B100	Full Size Regular	Borden Avenue	1	$80.00	$10.00
B101	Box Size	Borden Avenue	1	$65.00	$8.13
B102	Box Size	Borden Avenue	1	$65.00	$8.13
B103	Full Size Regular	Borden Avenue	1	$80.00	$10.00
B104	Full Size Wide	Borden Avenue	1	$95.00	$11.88
B105	Full Size Wide	Borden Avenue	1	$95.00	$11.88
B106	Full Size Regular	Borden Avenue	1	$80.00	$10.00
B107	Box Size	Borden Avenue	1	$65.00	$8.13
B108	Full Size Wide	Borden Avenue	2	$95.00	$11.88
B109	Full Size Wide	Borden Avenue	2	$95.00	$11.88
B110	Box Size	Borden Avenue	2	$65.00	$8.13
*					

Figure 12.3 Project 5 Query with Criteria and Calculated Column

Project 6 Sending Project Work to OneNote Notebook

Individual

Deliverable: New page in shared OneNote notebook

1. Start OneNote and open the MyProjects notebook created in Chapter 4, Project 4.
2. Make Access the active section and add a new page titled *Chapter 12 Projects*.
3. For each PDF you created in projects you completed in this chapter, send the PDF to OneNote 2013, selecting the Chapter 12 Projects page in the Access section in the MyProjects notebook.
4. Close your MyProjects notebook in OneNote and close OneNote.
5. Submit the project to your instructor in the manner she or he has requested.

Chapter 13

Creating a Table, Form, and Report in Access

After successfully completing this chapter, you will be able to:

- Create a new database
- List and describe guidelines for creating tables
- Create a new table
- Assign a primary key
- Add fields to a table
- Modify field properties
- Create a lookup list
- Identify relationship types
- Edit a relationship
- Create and edit a form
- Create and edit a report
- Compact and repair a database
- Back up a database

Creating a new database involves carefully planning the tables and other objects that will be needed by the individuals who will use the database. All of the data that need to be collected and stored are gathered and analyzed for the best possible way to define and group the elements into logical units. Tables are created first because they are the basis for all other objects. Tables that need to be connected for queries, forms, or reports are joined in a relationship. Objects such as queries, forms, and reports are created after the tables and relationships are defined.

In Chapter 12 you examined an existing database and added and edited data in a table and form. You also created queries to select records for a variety of purposes. Now that you have seen how Access data interacts with objects, you are ready to build a new database. In this chapter you will learn how to create a new database, create a new table, assign a primary key, modify field properties, edit relationships, create a form, create a report, compact and repair a database, and create a backup of a database.

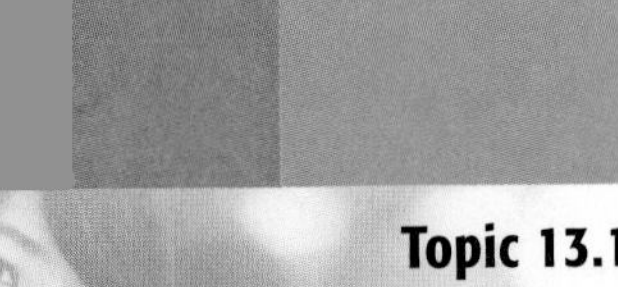

Creating a New Database File and Understanding Table Design Guidelines

Topic 13.1

SKILLS

Create a new database file

The first step in the process of creating a database is to assign a name and storage location for the new database file. Because Access saves records automatically as data is added to a table, the file name and storage location are required in advance. Once the file is created, Access displays a blank table. Before you create a new table, you must carefully plan the fields and field names and identify a primary key. Although the tables you will create in this chapter have already been planned, the guidelines in Table 13.1 provide you with an overview of the table design process.

Table 13.1	Guidelines for Planning a New Table
Guideline	**Description**
Divide data into the smallest possible units	A field should be segmented into the smallest units of information to facilitate sorting and filtering. For example, a person's name could be split into three fields: first name, middle name, and last name.
Assign each field a name	Up to 64 characters can be used in a field name with a combination of letters, numbers, spaces, and some symbols. Database programmers prefer short field names with no spaces. A field to store a person's last name could be assigned the name *LName*, *LastName*, or *Last_Name*. Access provides the ability to enter a longer descriptive title for column headings in datasheets, forms, and reports that is separate from the field name.
Assign each field a data type	Data type refers to the type of information that will be entered as field values. Look at examples of data to help you determine the data type. By assigning the most appropriate data type, Access can verify data as it is being entered for the correct format or type of characters. For example, a field defined as a Number field will cause Access to reject alphabetic letters typed into the field. The most common data types are Short text, Number, Currency, Date/Time, and Yes/No. Data types are described in Table 13.2 in the next topic.
Decide the field to be used as a primary key	Each table should have one field that uniquely identifies a record such as a student number, receipt number, or email address. Access creates an ID field automatically in a blank datasheet that can be used if the table data does not have a unique identifier. In some cases, a combination of two or more fields is used as a primary key.
Include a common identifier field in a table that will be joined to another table	Data should not be duplicated in a database. For example, a book title would not be stored in both the Books table and the Sales table. Instead, the book title is stored in the Books table only and a book ID field in the Sales table is used to join the two tables in a relationship. You will learn more about relationships in a later topic.

1. Start Access.
2. Tap or click *Blank desktop database* at the Access Start screen.

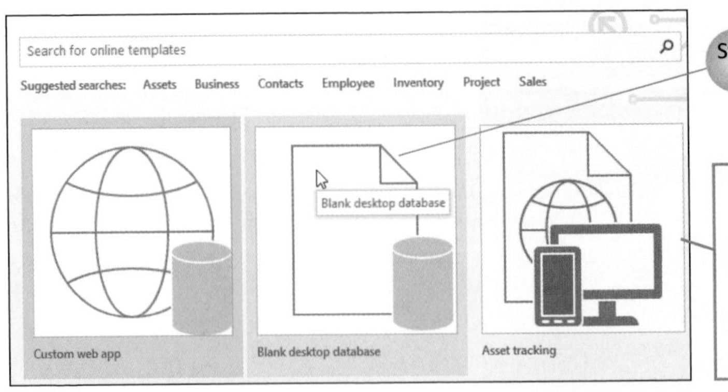

At the Access Start screen you can also choose to create a new database based on a template. Database templates have a set of predefined tables, queries, forms, and reports.

3 Type **13.1-UsedBooks-Your Name** in the *File Name* text box and then tap or click the Browse button (file folder icon).

4 At the File New Database dialog box, navigate to the CompletedTopicsByChapter folder on your USB flash drive, create a new folder named *Ch13*, double-tap or double-click to open the Ch13 folder, and then tap or click OK.

5 Tap or click the Create button.

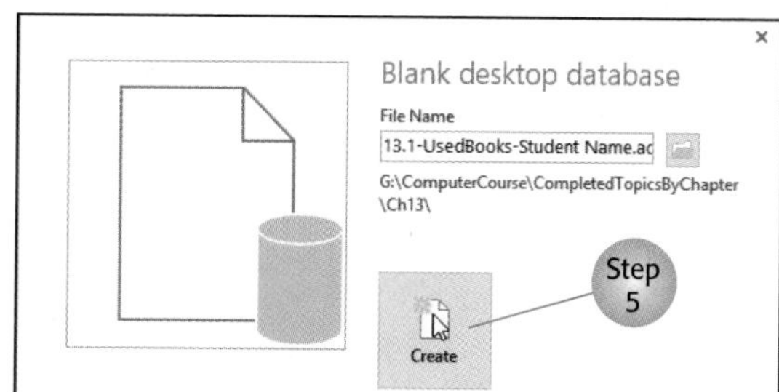

Access creates the database file and opens a new table datasheet named *Table1* in the work area, as shown in Figure 13.1. You can create a new table using the blank datasheet.

Create a New Database

1. Start Access.
2. Tap or click *Blank desktop database*.
3. Type file name.
4. Tap or click Browse button.
5. Navigate to drive and/or folder location.
6. Tap or click OK.
7. Tap or click Create.

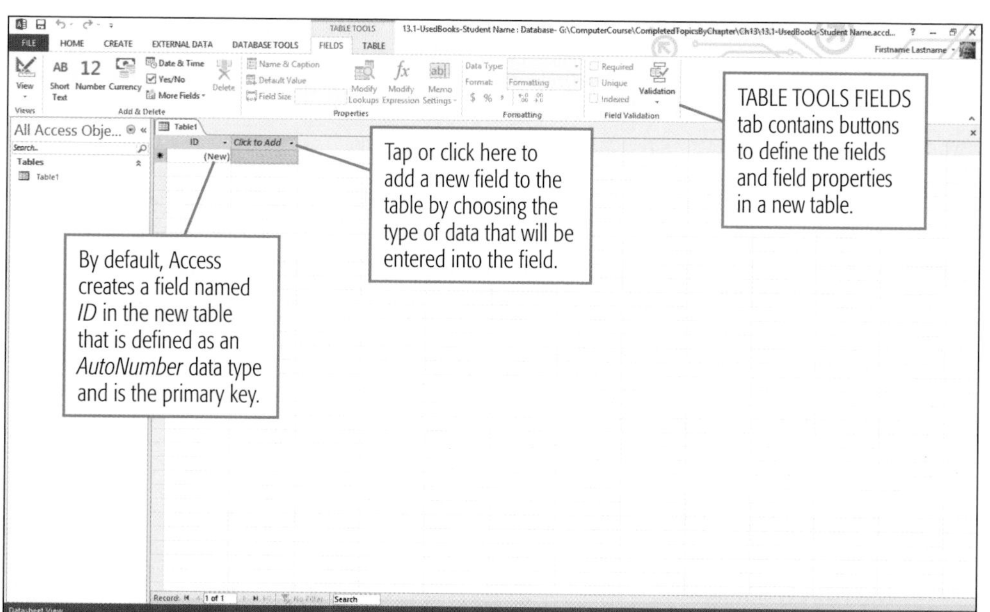

Figure 13.1 Blank table datasheet in new database file

6 Leave the blank table datasheet open for the next topic.

Each table in a database should contain information about one subject only. In this chapter you will create tables for a used textbook database that a student organization may use to keep track of students, textbooks, and sales. The three tables you will create in this chapter are described as follows:

Books: a table with the title, author, condition, and asking price for each book

Sales: a table that tracks each sale with the date, amount, and payment method

Students: a table with information about each student with textbooks for sale

A database designer may use data models by creating sample forms and reports before creating tables to make sure all data elements are included in the table design.

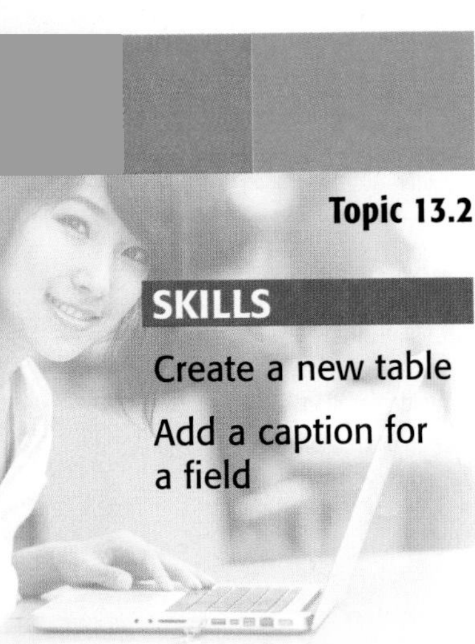

Topic 13.2

SKILLS

Create a new table

Add a caption for a field

Creating a New Table

A new table is created in a blank datasheet in Datasheet view by adding a column for each field. Begin by specifying the data type for a field and then typing the field name. Data types are described in Table 13.2. Once the fields have been defined, use the Save button on the QAT to assign the table a name.

Table 13.2	Field Data Types
Data Type	**Use for This Type of Field Value**
Short Text	Alphanumeric text up to 255 characters for names, identification numbers, telephone numbers, or other similar data
Number	Numeric data other than monetary values
Currency	Monetary values such as sales, costs, or wages
Date & Time or Date/Time	Dates or times that you want to verify, sort, select, or calculate
Yes/No	Data that can only be Yes or No or True or False
Lookup & Relationship or Lookup Wizard	A drop-down list with field values from another table or from a predefined list of items
Long Text or Rich Text	Alphanumeric text of more than 255 characters. Select Rich Text to enable formatting options such as font, font color, bold, and italic in the field values.
AutoNumber	A unique number generated by Access to be used as an identifier field
Hyperlink	Web addresses
Attachment	A file such as a picture attached to a field in a record
Calculated Field	A formula calculates the field value using data in other fields

1 With the **13.1-UsedBooks-Your Name** database open and with the blank datasheet for *Table1* open, tap or click the Date & Time button in the Add & Delete group of the TABLE TOOLS FIELDS tab.

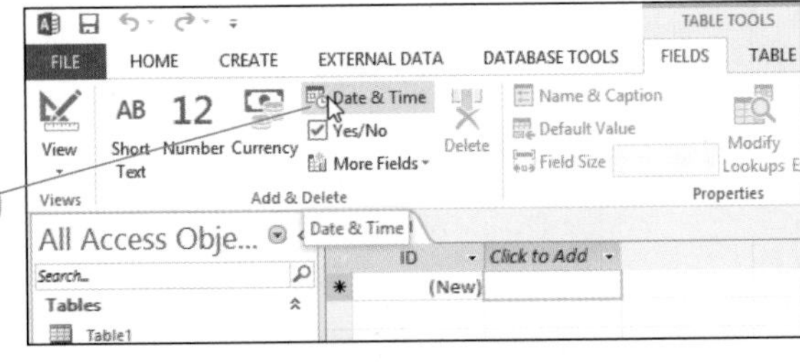

Choosing the most appropriate data type for a field is important for sorting, calculating, and verifying data. Access expects dates to be entered in the format m/d/y unless the region setting in the Control Panel is changed to another format.

App Tip

Access displays the field name as the column title in a datasheet unless an entry exists in the Caption property, in which case the caption text becomes the column title. (See Step 8.)

2 Type **SaleDate** and then tap or press Enter.

The *Click to Add* column opens the data type drop-down list for the next new field. Add a new field using either the *Click to Add* drop-down list or the buttons in the Add & Delete group of the TABLE TOOLS FIELDS tab.

3 Tap or click *Short Text* in the *Click to Add* drop-down list.

4 Type **BookID** and then tap or press Enter.

5 Tap or click *Currency*, type **Amount**, and then tap or press Enter.

6 Tap or click *Short Text*, type **PayMethod**, and then tap or press Enter.

7 Tap or click *SaleDate* to select the field.

8 Tap or click the Name & Caption button in the Properties group of the TABLE TOOLS FIELDS tab.

The **Caption property** is used to type a descriptive title for a field that includes spaces between words or the full text of an abbreviated field name.

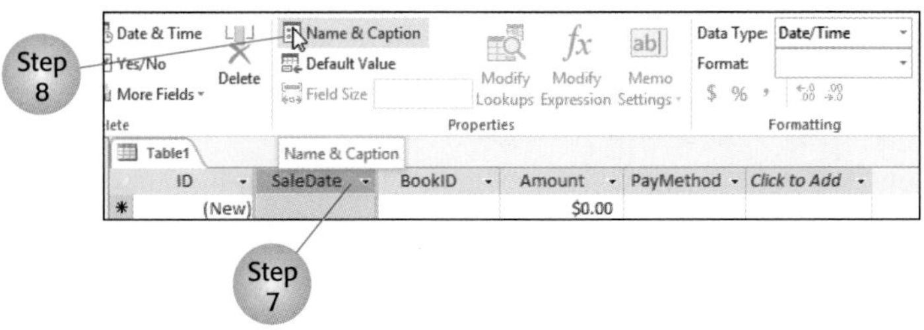

9 Tap or click in the *Caption* text box, type **Sale Date**, and then tap or click OK at the Enter Field Properties dialog box.

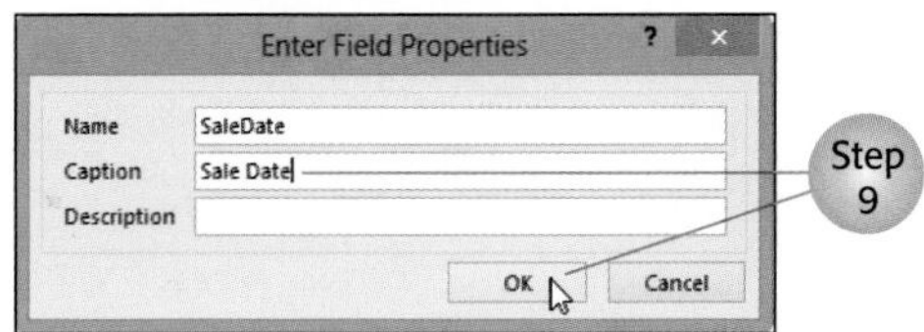

10 Tap or click to select the *Amount* field, tap or click the Name & Caption button, tap or click in the *Caption* text box, type **Sale Amount**, and then tap or click OK.

11 Slide or drag the right column boundary of the *Sale Amount* column until the entire column heading is visible.

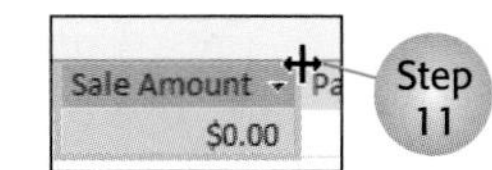

12 Tap or click to select the *PayMethod* field, tap or click the Name & Caption button, tap or click in the *Caption* text box, type **Payment Method**, and then tap or click OK.

13 Slide or drag the right column boundary of the *Payment Method* column until the entire column heading is visible.

14 Tap or click the Save button on the QAT.

15 Type **Sales** in the *Table Name* text box in the Save As dialog box and then tap or press Enter or tap or click OK.

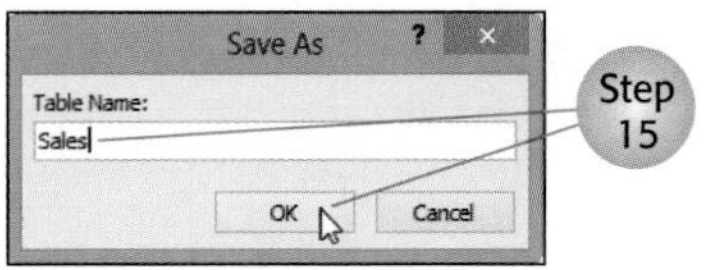

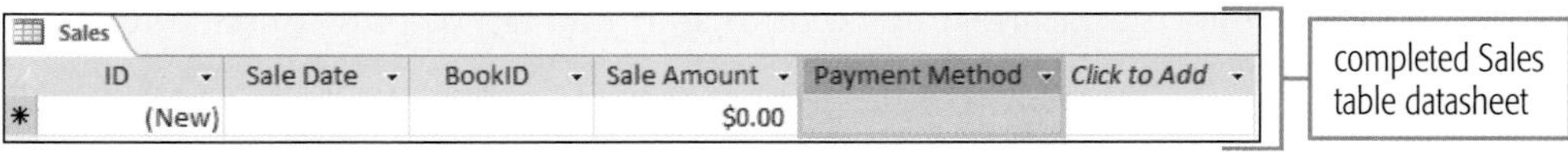

completed Sales table datasheet

16 Close the Sales table. Leave the database open for the next topic.

Create a Field in a New Table
1. With blank table datasheet open, tap or click data type button.
2. Type field name.
3. Tap or press Enter.

OR

1. With blank datasheet open, tap or click *Click to Add*.
2. Tap or click data type.
3. Type field name.
4. Tap or press Enter.

Add a Caption to a Field
1. Select field.
2. Tap or click Name & Caption button.
3. Tap or click in *Caption* text box.
4. Type caption text.
5. Tap or click OK.

Save a Table
1. Tap or click Save button.
2. Type table name.
3. Tap or click OK.

Double-tap or double-click the right column boundary to best fit the column width.

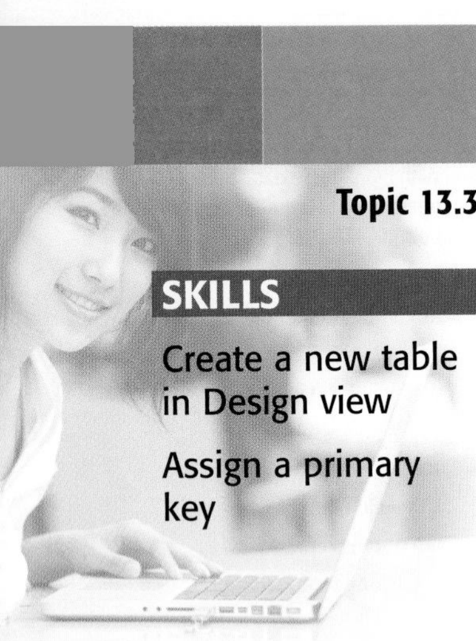

Topic 13.3
SKILLS
Create a new table in Design view
Assign a primary key

Creating a New Table in Design View and Assigning a Primary Key

A new table can be created in Design view in which fields are defined in rows in the top half of the work area. In the previous topic, the Sales table was created in Datasheet view, and Access automatically created the ID field and designated it as the primary key. In Design view, the *ID* field is not created for you. Recall that a primary key is a field that uniquely identifies each record in the table. Each new table should have a field assigned as the primary key. After creating the fields in the Design view window, assign the primary key and then save the table.

1. With the **13.1-UsedBooks-Your Name** database open, tap or click the CREATE tab.
2. Tap or click the Table Design button in the Tables group.

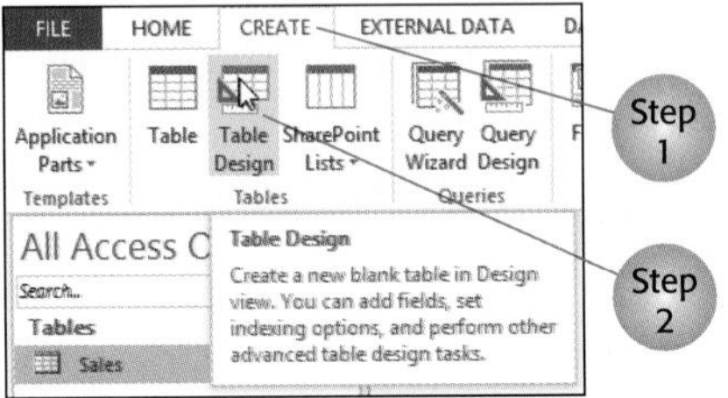

3. With the insertion point positioned in the first row of the *Field Name* column, type **StudentID** and then tap or press Enter.
4. With *Short Text* in the *Data Type* column, tap or press Enter to accept the default data type.
5. Tap or press Enter to move past the *Description* column and move down to the next row to start a new field.

Descriptions are optional entries. A description can be used to type additional information about a field or to enter instructions to end users who will see the description in the Status bar of a datasheet when the field is active.

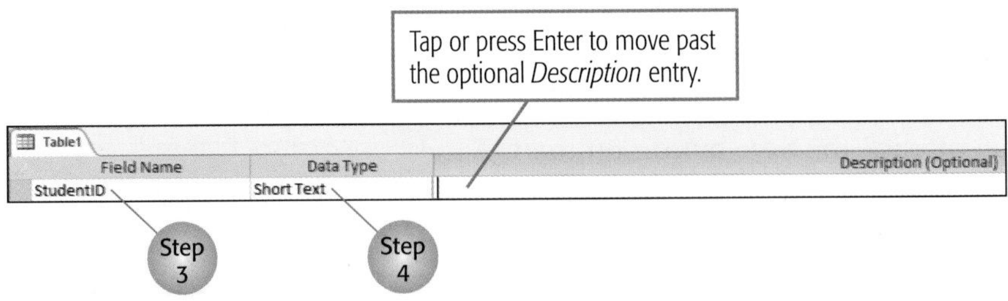

You can also use the Tab key to move to the next column in Design view.

6. Type **LName** in the *Field* Name column and then tap or press Enter three times to move to the next row.
7. Enter the remaining fields as shown in the image below by completing a step similar to Step 6.

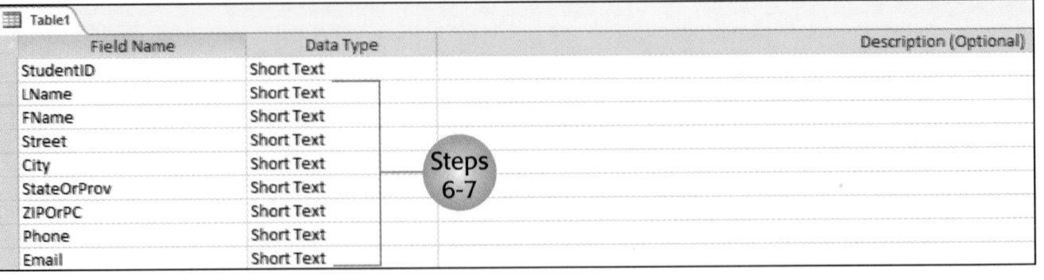

8 Tap or click to place the insertion point within the *StudentID* field name.

9 Tap or click the Primary Key button in the Tools group of the TABLE TOOLS DESIGN tab.

A key icon in the field selector bar (gray bar along left edge of *Field Name* column) indicates the field is designated as the primary key for the table.

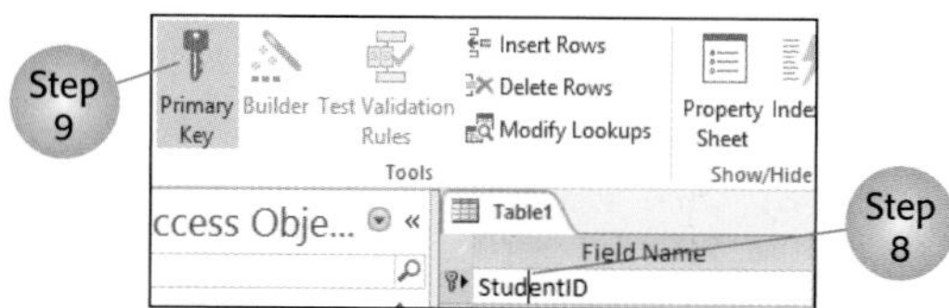

10 Tap or click the Save button on the QAT, type **Students**, and then tap or press Enter or tap or click OK.

11 Close the Students table.

12 Tap or click the CREATE tab and then tap or click the Table Design button.

13 Create the first five fields in the new table using the default Short Text data type as follows:

BookID
StudentID
Title
Author
Condition

14 Type **AskPrice** as the *Field Name* in the sixth row and then tap or press Enter.

15 Tap or click the *Data Type* list arrow and then tap or click *Currency* at the drop-down list.

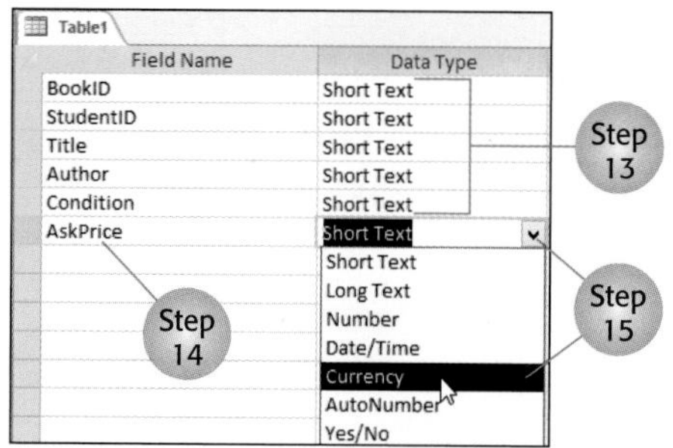

16 Tap or click to place an insertion point within the *BookID* field name and then tap or click the Primary Key button.

17 Tap or click the Save button on the QAT, type **Books**, and then tap or press Enter or tap or click OK.

18 Close the Books table. Leave the database open for the next topic.

Access will not allow field values to be duplicated in a primary key—always choose a primary key field that you are sure will never have field values that repeat.

Create a Table in Design View

1. Tap or click CREATE tab.
2. Tap or click Table Design button.
3. Type field name.
4. Tap or press Enter.
5. If necessary, change data type.
6. Tap or press Enter until new row is active.
7. Repeat Steps 3–6 until finished.
8. Assign primary key.
9. Save table.

Assign a Primary Key

1. If necessary, open table in Design view.
2. Tap or click in primary key field name.
3. Tap or click Primary Key button.
4. Save table.

Adding Fields to an Existing Table

Open a table in Datasheet view and use the *Click to Add* column to add a new field, or make active a field in the datasheet and use the buttons in the TABLE TOOLS FIELDS tab to add a new field after the active field.

1. With the **13.1-UsedBooks-Your Name** database open, open the Books table.
2. Tap or click the *Click to Add* column heading and then tap or click *Currency* at the drop-down list.

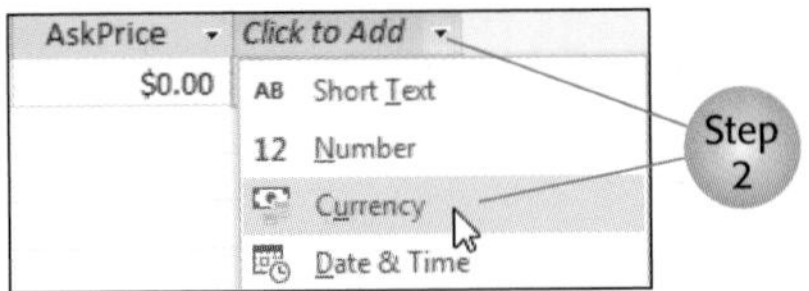

3. Type **StopPrice** and tap or press Enter.
4. Tap or click the top part of the View button in the Views group of the TABLE TOOLS FIELDS tab to switch to Design view.
5. Tap or click in the *Description* column in the *StopPrice* field row and type **Do not sell for lower than the student's stop price value**.

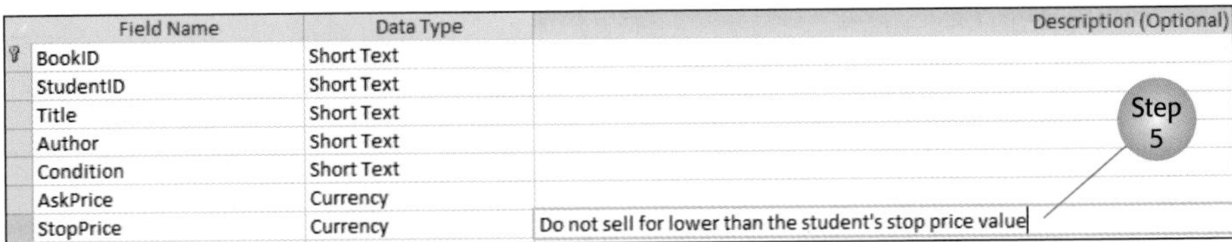

6. Save and close the Books table.
7. Open the Students table.
8. Tap or click to select the *Phone* field.
9. Tap or click the TABLE TOOLS FIELDS tab and then tap or click the Yes/No button in the Add & Delete group.

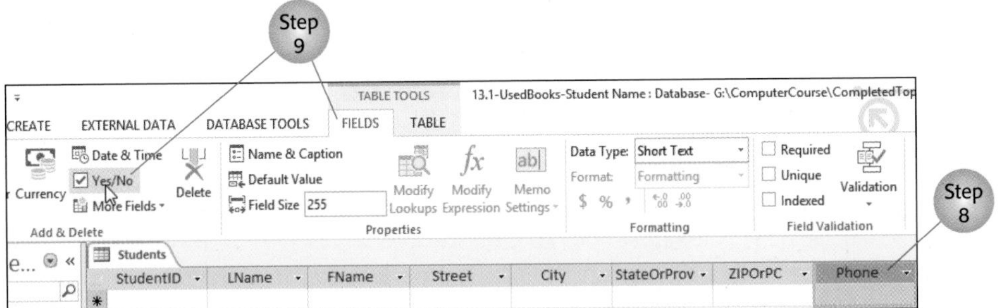

10. Type **DirectDeposit** and then tap or press Enter.
11. Slide or drag the right column boundary of the *DirectDeposit* field until the entire column heading is visible.

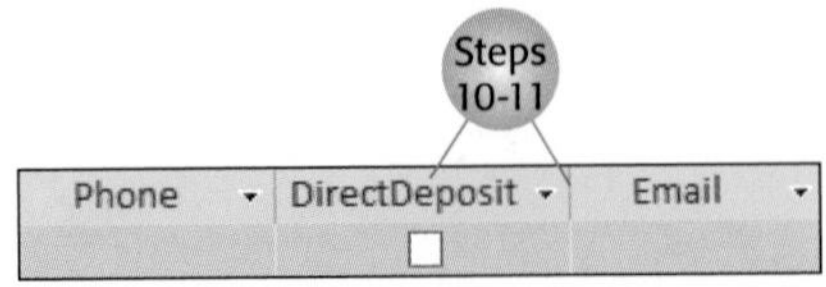

12 Save and close the Students table.

13 Open the Books table.

14 Tap or click to select the *StopPrice* field.

15 Look at the message that displays in the Status bar.

Notice that the text typed in the Description column for the field in Design view at Step 5 displays here. Description entries also display in the Status bar when a form is open that is based upon the same table.

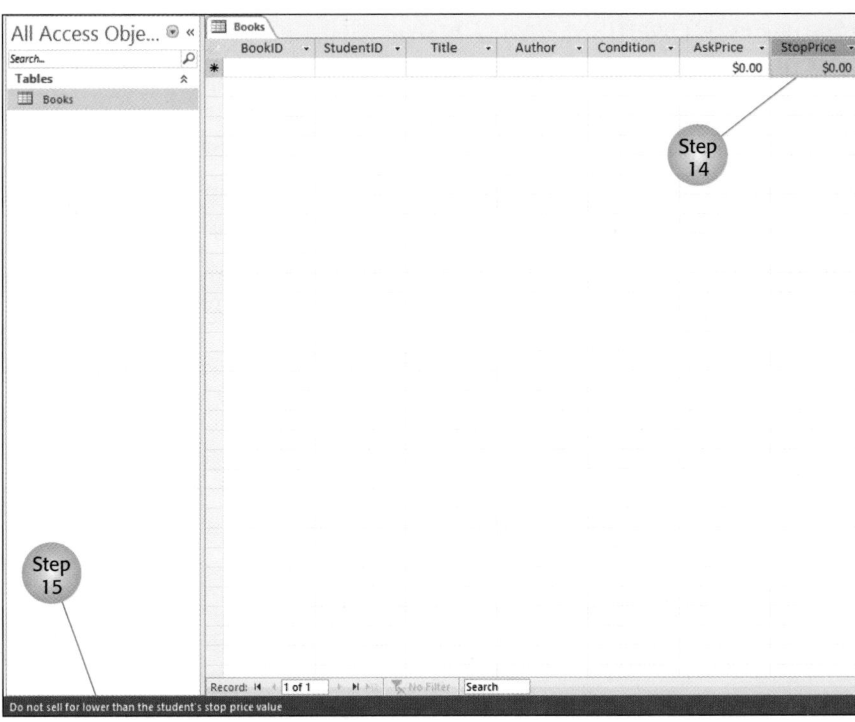

16 Close the Books table. Leave the database open for the next topic.

Add a Field

1. Open table.
2. Tap or click *Click to Add* column.
3. Tap or click data type.
4. Type field name.
5. Tap or press Enter.
6. Save table.

ALTERNATIVE method

Open a table in Design view and type a new field name in the next available row, or make a field active and use the Insert Rows button in the Tools group of the TABLE TOOLS DESIGN tab to add a new field above the active field.

Deleting Fields

Generally, a field that contains data should not be deleted because deleting a field causes all field values to be removed from the database. However, if a field added to a table is considered unnecessary, remove the field by opening the table in either Datasheet view or Design view. In Datasheet view, make the field active and use the Delete button in the Add & Delete group of the TABLE TOOLS FIELDS tab. In Design view, make the field active and use the Delete Rows button in the TABLE TOOLS DESIGN tab.

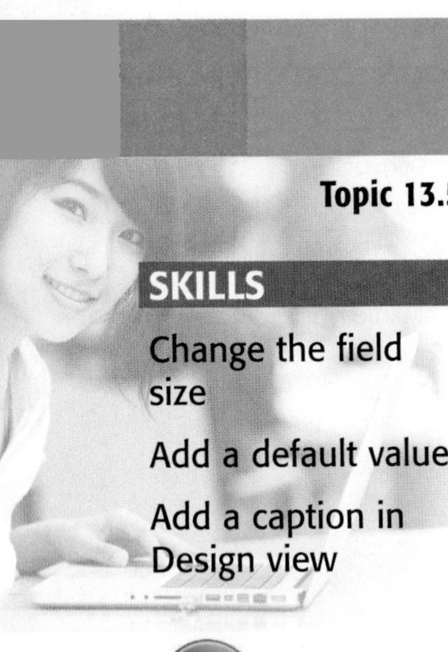

Topic 13.5

SKILLS

Change the field size

Add a default value

Add a caption in Design view

Options in the Field Properties pane vary by the field's data type. For example, a Date & Time field does not have the Field Size property.

Modifying Field Properties in Design View

Each field in a table has a set of field properties associated with the field. A **field property** is a single characteristic or attribute of a field. For example, the field name is a field property and the data type is another field property. Each field's properties can be modified to customize, format, or otherwise change the behavior of a field. The lower half of the work area of a table in Design view contains the **Field Properties pane** that is used to modify a field's properties other than the field name, data type, and description.

1. With the **13.1-UsedBooks-Your Name** database open, press and hold or right-click the Students table and then tap or click *Design view* at the shortcut menu.
2. Tap or click in the *StateOrProv* field name to select the field.
3. Double-tap, double-click, or slide or drag to select *255* in the *Field Size* property box in the Field Properties pane, type 2, and then tap or press Enter.

Setting a field size for a state or province field ensures that all new field values use the two-character abbreviation for addressing letters or creating labels from the database.

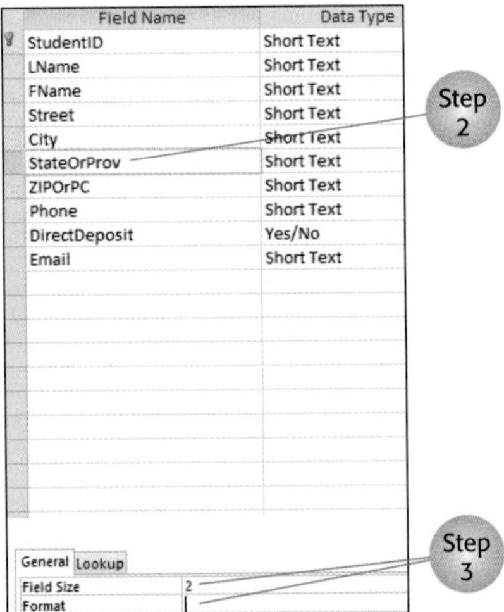

4. Tap or click in the *Default Value* property box, type **MI**, and then tap or press Enter.

Access automatically adds quotation marks to the text in a *Default Value* property box for a Short Text data type. Default value text is automatically entered in new records; the end user taps or presses Enter to accept the value, or types an alternative entry.

5. Tap or click in the *Caption* property box and then type **State or Province**.

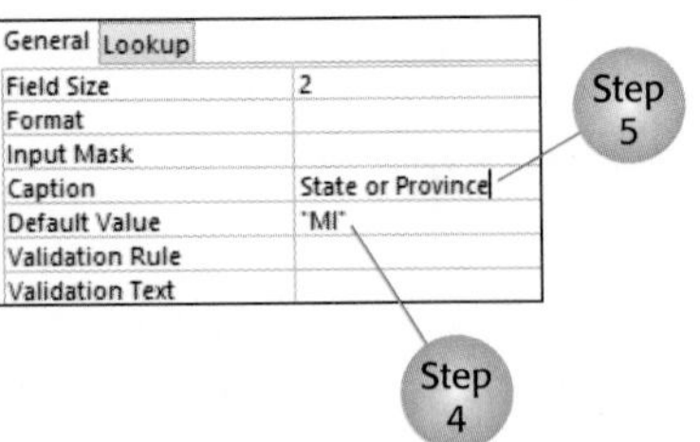

6. Tap or click in the *StudentID* field name to select the field, tap or click in the *Caption* property box, type **Student ID**, and then tap or press Enter.

7 Add the following caption properties by completing a step similar to Step 6.

Field Name	Caption
LName	**Last Name**
FName	**First Name**
Street	**Street Address**
ZIPOrPC	**ZIP or Postal Code**
Phone	**Telephone**
DirectDeposit	**Direct Deposit**
Email	**Email Address**

8 Save the table.

9 Tap or click the top part of the View button in the Views group to switch to Datasheet view.

10 Double-tap or double-click the right column boundary of column headings that are not entirely visible to best fit the column widths.

Notice that *MI* appears in the *State or Province* column by default.

11 Type your name and a fictitious student ID and address into a new record in the datasheet. If necessary, adjust column widths to show all data in all columns.

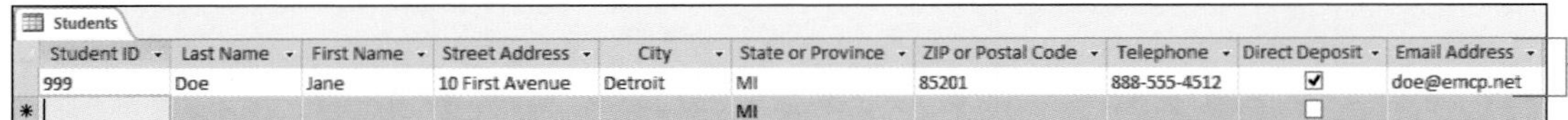
Students

Student ID	Last Name	First Name	Street Address	City	State or Province	ZIP or Postal Code	Telephone	Direct Deposit	Email Address
999	Doe	Jane	10 First Avenue	Detroit	MI	85201	888-555-4512	☑	doe@emcp.net
*					MI			☐	

Steps 10-11

12 Close the table, saving the changes to the table layout. Leave the database open for the next topic.

Modify a Field Property
1. Open table in Design view.
2. Tap or click in field name in top half of work area.
3. Tap, click, or select current value in field property box.
4. Type or select option from drop-down list.
5. Save table.

Field properties can also be changed for a table open in Datasheet view. Buttons in the Properties group of the TABLE TOOLS FIELDS tab can be used to enter a caption, default value, or field size. Modify or apply format, data validation, or required properties (see Beyond Basics) with buttons in the Formatting and Field Validation groups of the TABLE TOOLS FIELDS tab.

Beyond Basics

Formatting and Data Validation Field Properties

Other properties that are often changed for a field include:

- *Format.* Modifies the display of the field value. For example, a date can be formatted to display as a long date or medium date.
- *Validation*. Use a validation rule to enter an expression that is tested as each new field value is typed into a record. For example, the expression *>=5* in the *SaleAmount* field would ensure no amounts less than $5.00 are entered.
- *Required.* Select *Yes* to ensure that the field is not left blank in a new record. For example, a ZIP or Postal Code field should not be left blank.

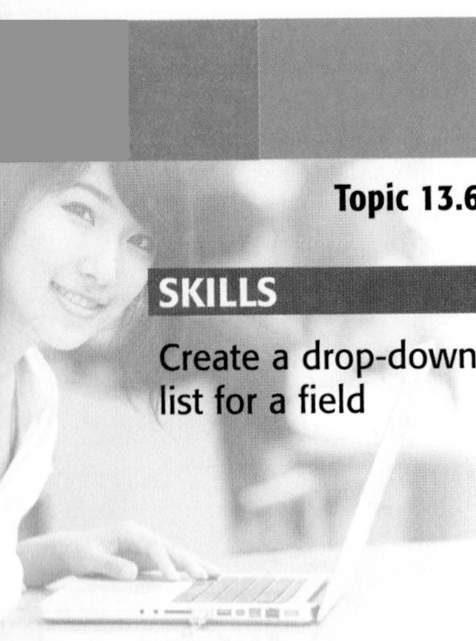

Topic 13.6
SKILLS
Create a drop-down list for a field

Creating a Lookup List

A **lookup list** is a drop-down list of field values that appears when a field is made active when new records are being added in a datasheet or form. The list entries can be a fixed list, or field values from another table can be shown in the list. A lookup list has many advantages, including consistency, accuracy, and efficiency when adding data in new records. Access provides the **Lookup Wizard** to assist with creating a lookup list's field properties.

1. With the **13.1-UsedBooks-Your Name** database open, press and hold or right-click the Books table and then tap or click *Design view* at the shortcut menu.
2. Tap or click in the *Condition* field name to select the field.
3. Tap or click the *Data Type* list arrow and then tap or click *Lookup Wizard* at the drop-down list.

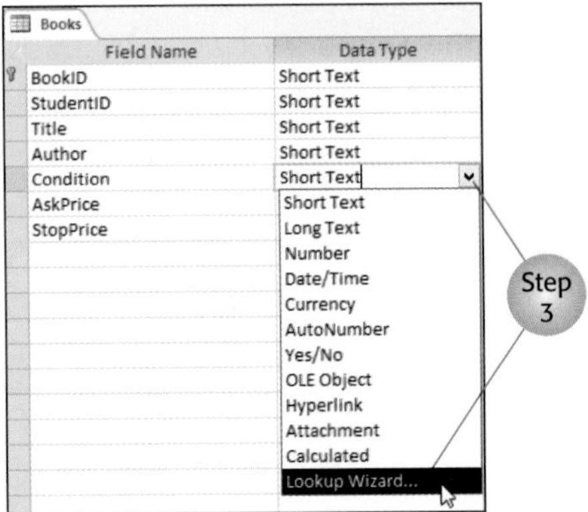

4. Tap or click *I will type in the values that I want* at the first Lookup Wizard dialog box and then tap or click Next.
5. Tap or click in the first blank row below *Col1* at the second Lookup Wizard dialog box and type **Excellent - Like new**.
6. Slide or drag the right column boundary approximately two inches to increase the column width.
7. Tap or click in the second row and type **Very Good - Minor wear to cover**.
8. Type the remaining entries in the list as shown in the image at right.
9. Tap or click Next.

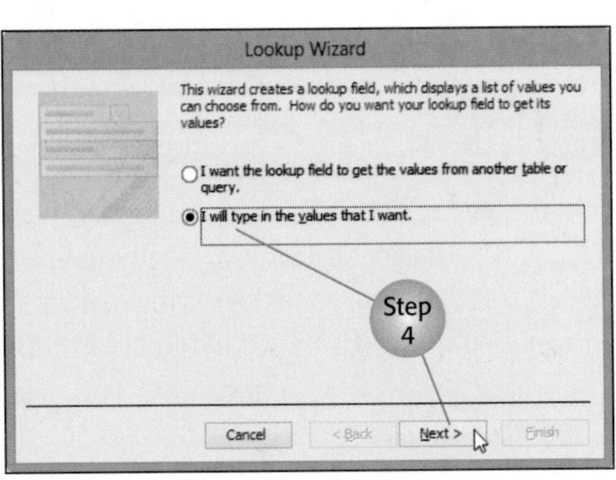

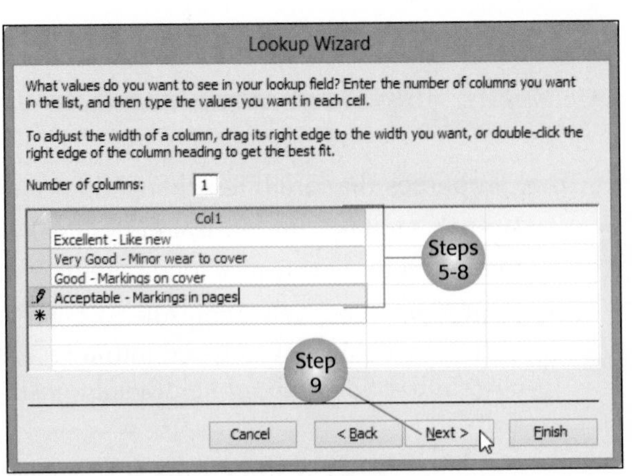

App Tip

You can also use the Tab or Down Arrow key to move to the next row in the column.

Tapped or pressed Enter by mistake? Tap or click the Back button to return to the list entries.

10 Tap or click Finish at the last Lookup Wizard dialog box.

11 Tap or click the Lookup tab in the Field Properties pane.

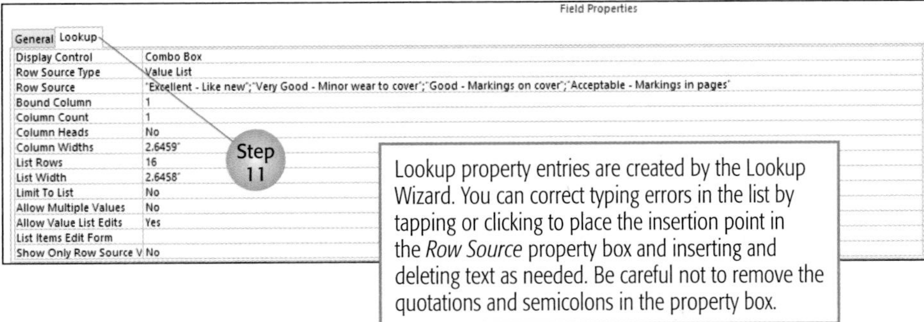

12 Save the table and then switch to Datasheet view.

13 Enter the following record as shown in the image below with the fictitious ID you created for yourself in the *StudentID* column. At the *Condition* field, tap or click the down-pointing arrow that appears and tap or click *Good - Markings on cover* in the drop-down list.

14 Adjust column widths as needed to show all data in each column.

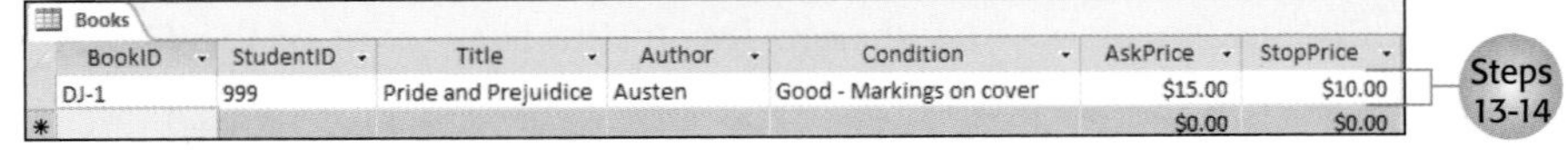

Books
BookID StudentID Title Author Condition AskPrice StopPrice
DJ-1 999 Pride and Prejuidice Austen Good - Markings on cover $15.00 $10.00
$0.00 $0.00
Steps 13-14

15 Close the table, saving the changes to the table layout.

16 Close the database.

You can limit field values to only those items in the list by changing the *Limit To List* property to *Yes*.

Create a Lookup List

1. Open table in Design view.
2. Tap or click *Data Type* list arrow for field.
3. Tap or click *Lookup Wizard*.
4. Tap or click *I will type in the values that I want*.
5. Tap or click Next.
6. Type list entries in *Col1* column.
7. Adjust column width.
8. Tap or click Next.
9. Tap or click Finish.
10. Save table.

Creating a Lookup List with Field Values in Another Table

To create a lookup list in which the entries are field values from a field in another table, proceed through the dialog boxes in the Lookup Wizard as follows:

1. Select *I want the lookup field to get the values from another table or query*.
2. Select the table or query name that contains the field values you want to use in the list.
3. Move the fields you want displayed in the drop-down list from the *Available Fields* list box to the *Selected Fields* list box.
4. Select a field to sort the list entries, or leave empty for an unsorted list.
5. Adjust column widths as needed and/or uncheck *Hide key column*.
6. Select the field that contains the field value you want to store if more than one field was chosen at Step 3.

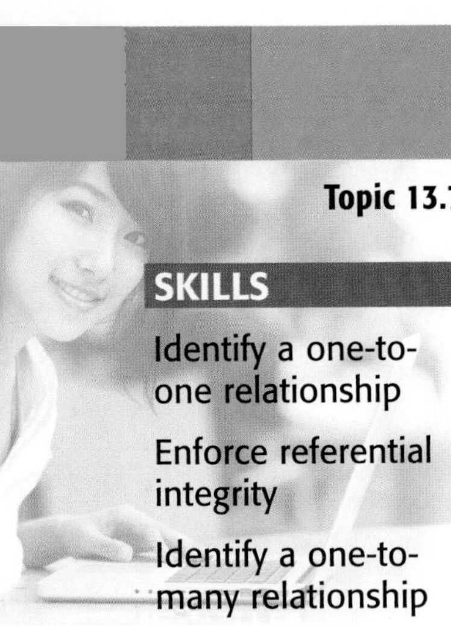

Topic 13.7

SKILLS

Identify a one-to-one relationship

Enforce referential integrity

Identify a one-to-many relationship

Displaying and Editing a Relationship

A relationship allows you to create queries, forms, or reports with fields from two tables. Relationships prevent duplication of data because an ID, name, or title of a book can be looked up in one table rather than repeating the field in other tables. When you create a lookup list that looks up field values in another table, Access automatically creates a relationship between the two tables.

1. Open the database named ***UsedBooks*** from the Ch13 folder in Student_Data_Files.
2. Use Save As to save a copy of the database as **13.7-UsedBooks-Your Name** in the Ch13 folder in CompletedTopicsbyChapter. Accept the default options *Save Database As* and *Access Database* at the Save As Backstage view.
3. Tap or click the Enable Content button in the SECURITY WARNING message bar.

This file is similar to the database you have been working on in this chapter but with the Books table modified, additional lookup lists, and with 10 records added to each table.

4. Open the Books table, review the datasheet, and then close the table.
5. Open the Sales table, review the datasheet, and then close the table.
6. Open the Students table and change *Doe* in the last record of the *Last Name* field to your last name.
7. Change *Jane* in the last record of the *First Name* field to your first name and then close the table.
8. Tap or click the DATABASE TOOLS tab and tap or click the Relationships button in the Relationships group.

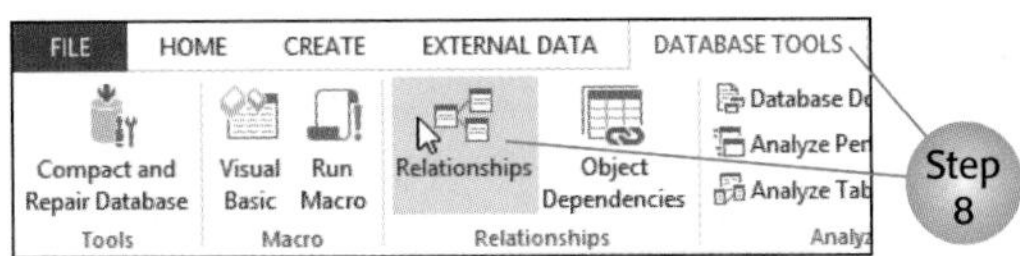

A field list box for each table is located in the Relationships window. A black join line connecting two table field list boxes indicates a relationship. Observe that each line connects a common field name.

9. Tap or click to select the black join line that connects the Books table field list box to the Sales table field list box, and then tap or click the Edit Relationships button in the Tools group of the RELATIONSHIP TOOLS DESIGN tab.

In the Edit Relationships dialog box that appears, *One-To-One* is shown in the *Relationship Type* section. A **one-to-one relationship** means that the two tables are joined on the primary key in each table. (*BookID* displays a key next to the field in each table field list box.) In this type of relationship, only one record can exist for the same *BookID* in each table.

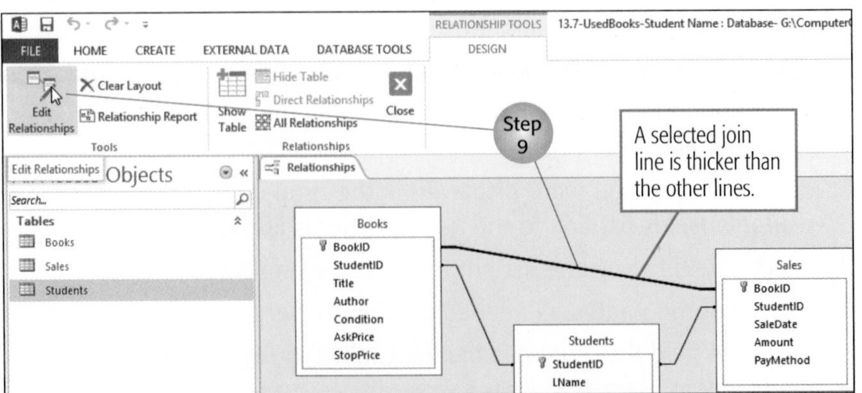

10 Tap or click to insert a check mark in the *Enforce Referential Integrity* check box and tap or click OK.

Turning on **Enforce Referential Integrity** means that a record in Books is entered first before a record with a matching *BookID* is entered in Sales. Books is the left table name below *Table/Query* and Sales is the right table name below *Related Table/Query*. The table below *Table/Query* is the one for which referential integrity is applied—the table in which new records are entered first. The table shown at the left is also referred to as the **primary table** (the table in which the joined field is the primary key and in which new records should be entered first).

11 Tap or click to select the black join line that connects the Books table field list box to the Students table field list box, and then tap or click the Edit Relationships button.

12 Tap or click to insert a check mark in the *Enforce Referential Integrity* check box and then tap or click OK.

A **one-to-many relationship** occurs when the common field used to join the two tables is the primary key in only one table (the primary table). *One* student can have *many* textbooks for sale. In this instance, a record must first be entered into Students (primary table) before a record with a matching student ID can be entered into Books (related table). A field added to a related table that is not a primary key and is included for the purpose of creating a relationship is called a **foreign key**.

13 Tap or click the Close button in the Relationships group. Leave the database open for the next topic.

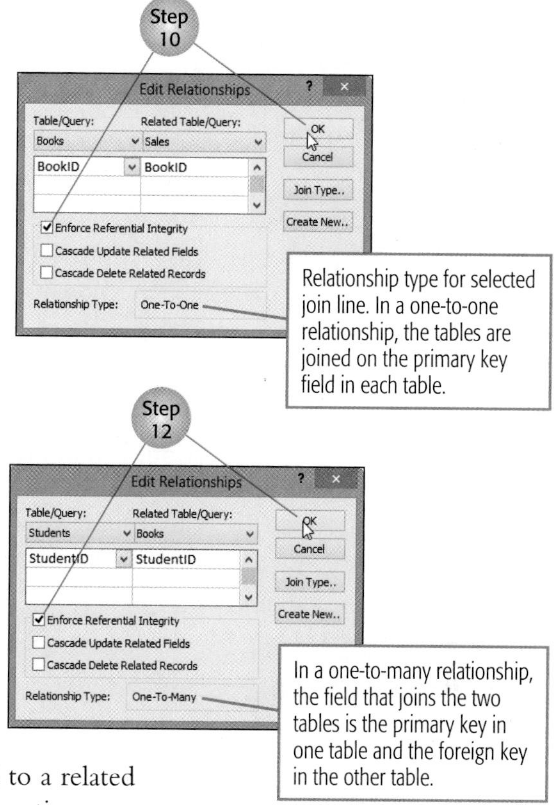

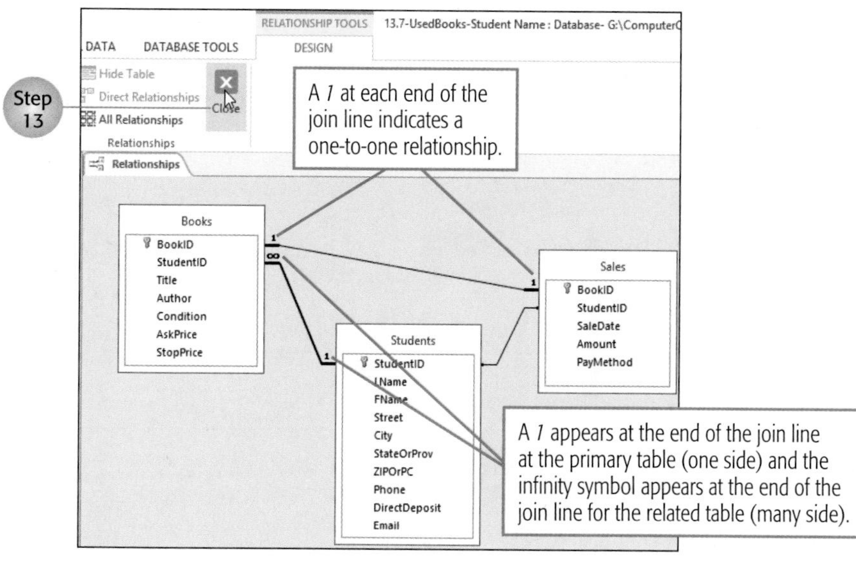

Display Relationships

1. Tap or click DATABASE TOOLS tab.
2. Tap or click Relationships button.

Enforce Referential Integrity

1. Display Relationships.
2. Tap or click to select black join line.
3. Tap or click Edit Relationships button.
4. Tap or click *Enforce Referential Integrity* check box.
5. Tap or click OK.

A one-to-many relationship is the most common type of relationship in databases.

Creating Relationships

To create a new relationship, slide or drag the common field name from the primary table field list box to the related table field list box. Always slide or drag starting from the primary table. If you need to add a table field list box to the window, use the Show Table button in the Relationships group.

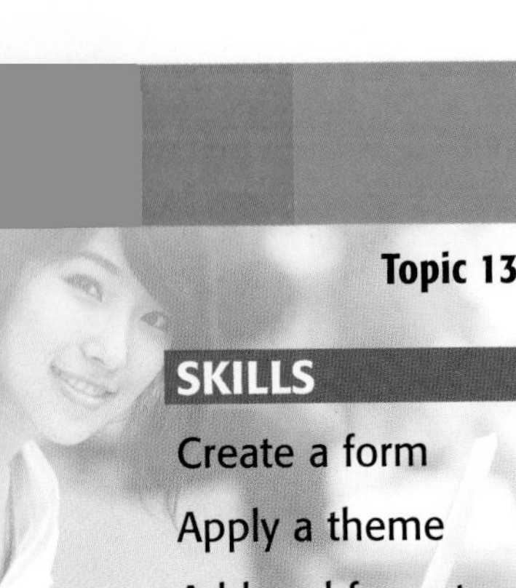

Topic 13.8

SKILLS

Create a form

Apply a theme

Add and format a picture

Format the form title

Buttons to switch between views are at the right end of the Status bar.

Creating and Editing a Form

The Forms group of the CREATE tab includes buttons to create forms ranging from a tool to create a simple form that adds all of the fields in the selected table, to tools for more complex forms that work with multiple tables. Once created, a form can be modified using buttons in the FORM LAYOUT TOOLS DESIGN, ARRANGE, and FORMAT tabs.

1. With the **13.7-UsedBooks-Your Name** database open, tap or click to select the Books table name in the Navigation pane if Books is not already selected.
2. Tap or click the CREATE tab.
3. Tap or click the Form button in the Forms group.

A form is created with all of the fields in the selected table arranged in a vertical layout and displayed in Layout view. **Layout view** is the view in which you edit a form's structure and appearance using buttons in the FORM LAYOUT TOOLS tabs. **Form view** is the view in which data is viewed, entered, and updated and is the view that is active when a form is opened from the Navigation pane.

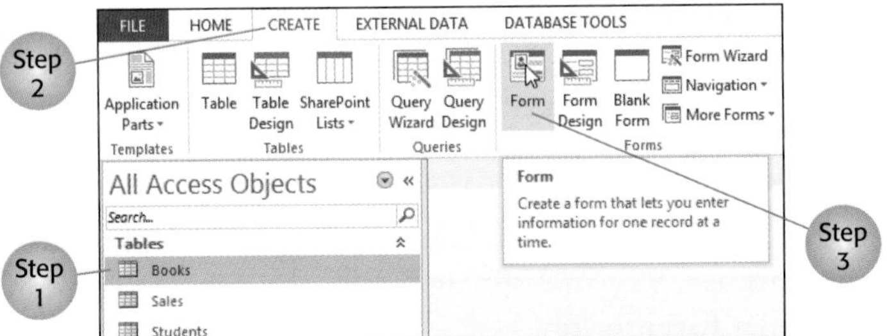

4. Tap or click the FORM LAYOUT TOOLS DESIGN tab if the tab is not already active, and then tap or click the Themes button in the Themes group.
5. Tap or click *Slice* (last option in second row of *Office* section).

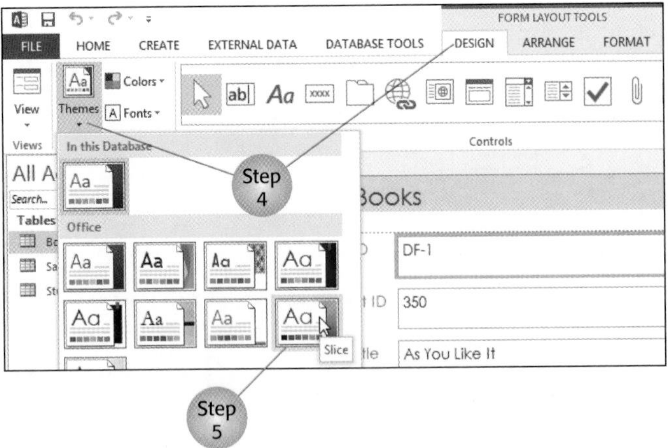

6. Tap or click the Logo button in the Header / Footer group.

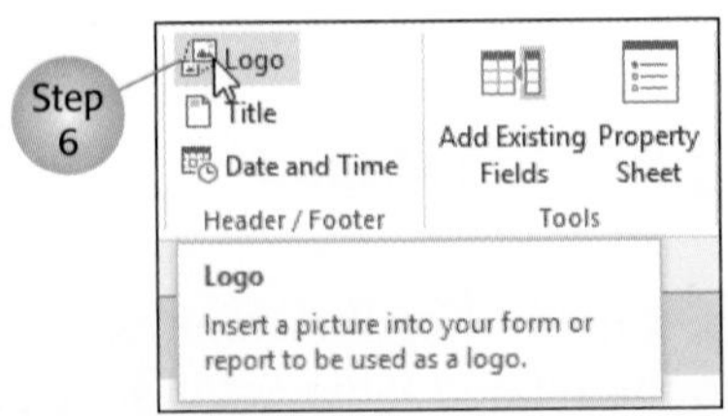

7 At the Insert Picture dialog box, navigate to the Ch13 folder in Student_Data_Files and double-tap or double-click the file named ***Textbooks***.

The picture is inserted into the selected logo **control object** near the top left of the form. A control object is a rectangular content placeholder in a form or report. Each control object can be selected and edited to modify the appearance of the content.

8 With the logo control object still selected, tap or click the Property Sheet button in the Tools group.

9 Tap or click in the *Size Mode* property box in the Property Sheet task pane with the Format tab active, tap or click the down-pointing arrow that appears, and then tap or click *Zoom*.

10 Select the current value in the *Width* property box and type 1.75.

11 Select the current value in the *Height* property box and type 1.25.

12 Close the Property Sheet task pane.

Property Sheet
Selection type: Image
Auto_Logo0
Format | Data | Event | Other | All

Visible	Yes
Picture Type	Embedded
Picture	Textbooks.jpg
Picture Tiling	No
Size Mode	Zoom
Picture Alignment	Center
Width	1.75"
Height	1.25"

Step 12 · Step 9 · Step 10 · Step 11

13 Tap or click the *Books* title to select the control object.

An orange border around the control object indicates the object is selected.

14 Tap or click the FORM LAYOUT TOOLS FORMAT tab.

15 Tap or click the Font Size button arrow and then tap or click *48* at the drop-down list.

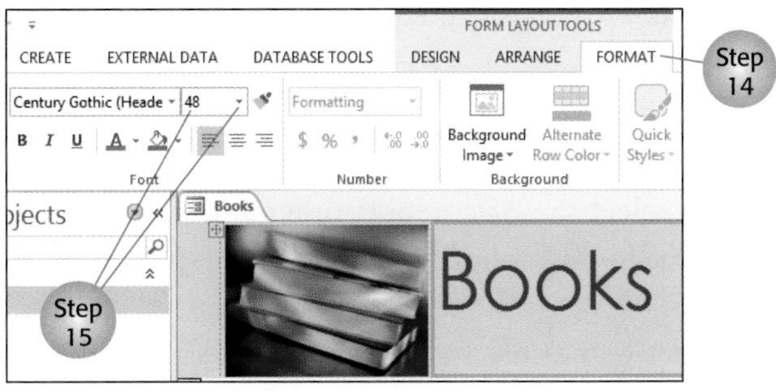

16 Tap or click the Save button in the QAT and then tap or click OK at the Save As dialog box to accept the default form name *Books*.

17 Close the Books form.

18 Double-tap or double-click the Books form in the Navigation pane to reopen the form, scroll through a few records, and then close the form. Leave the database open for the next topic.

Control objects are placeholders for pictures, text, field names, and field values.

The Zoom *Size/Mode* property fits the picture to the control object size maintaining proportions.

You can also slide or drag the orange border on a selected control object to resize the object.

Create a Form

1. Tap or click to select table or query in Navigation pane.
2. Tap or click CREATE tab.
3. Tap or click Form button.
4. Modify as required.
5. Tap or click Save button.
6. Type form name.
7. Tap or click OK.

Creating a Form Using the Form Wizard

Use the Form Wizard button in the Forms group of the CREATE tab to create a form in which you have control over the fields to include and over the form layout. Fields from related tables can be arranged in a columnar, tabular, datasheet, or justified layout.

Topic 13.9
SKILLS
Create a report
Resize control objects
App Tip

Reports use the same theme as forms so that all objects have a consistent look.

oops!

Textbooks image not shown? Access defaults to the last folder used at the Insert Picture dialog box. If necessary, navigate to the Ch13 folder in Student_Data_Files.

Creating, Editing, and Viewing a Report

A report is created using techniques similar to those used to create a form. The Reports group of the CREATE tab has a Report tool similar to the Form tool. Other buttons in the Reports group include options to design a report from a blank page, create a report using the Report Wizard, or generate mailing labels using the Label Wizard. Modify a report with buttons in the REPORT LAYOUT TOOLS tabs. Change the page layout options for printing purposes with buttons in the REPORT LAYOUT TOOLS PAGE SETUP tab.

1. With the **13.7-UsedBooks-Your Name** database open, tap or click to select the Sales table name in the Navigation pane.
2. Tap or click the CREATE tab and then tap or click the Report button in the Reports group.

A report is created with all of the fields in the Sales table arranged in a tabular layout. By default, Access includes the current date and time, page numbering, and totals for numeric fields.

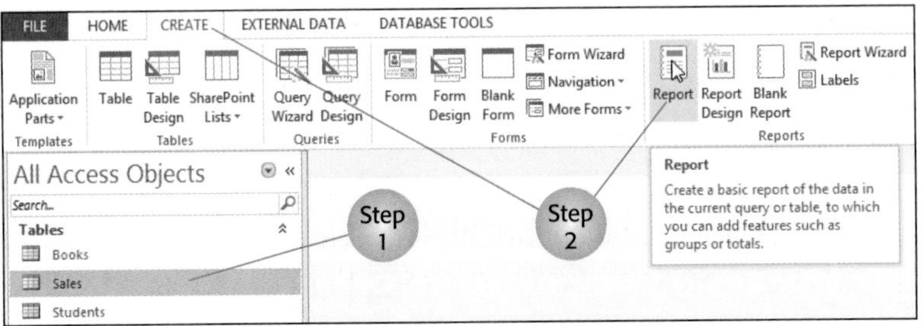

3. Tap or click the Logo button in the Header / Footer group and then double-tap or double-click the file named ***Textbooks***.
4. Open the Property Sheet, change the *Size/Mode*, *Width*, and *Height* properties to the same settings that you applied to the form's picture in the previous topic, and then close the Property Sheet task pane.
5. Tap or click to select the *Sales* report title control object, tap or click the REPORT LAYOUT TOOLS FORMAT tab, tap or click the Font Size button arrow, and then tap or click *48*.
6. Tap or click to select the current date control object near the top right of the report.
7. Slide or drag the right border of the control object left until the control ends just left of the vertical dashed line that extends the height of the report.

The vertical dashed line indicates a page break. Resize control objects so that all objects are to the left of the vertical dashed line to fit on one page.

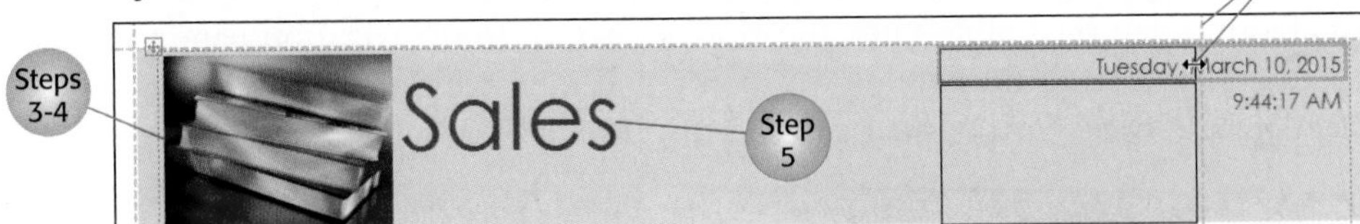

8. Tap or click to select the *Book ID* column heading control object.
9. Slide or drag the right border of the control object left approximately one-half inch to resize the object to the approximate width shown in the image at right.

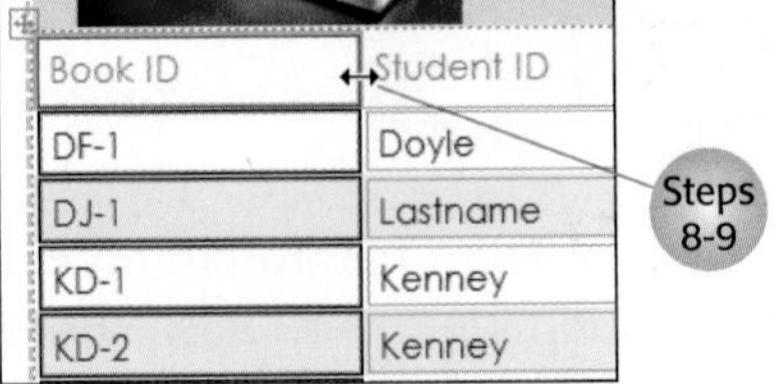

Notice that resizing a column heading control object resizes the entire column.

10 Select the *Page 1 of 1* control object and resize the control until the right border is just left of the vertical dashed line.

11 Select the control object with the total at the bottom of the *Sale Amount* column and slide or drag the bottom border of the control until the value is entirely visible within the object.

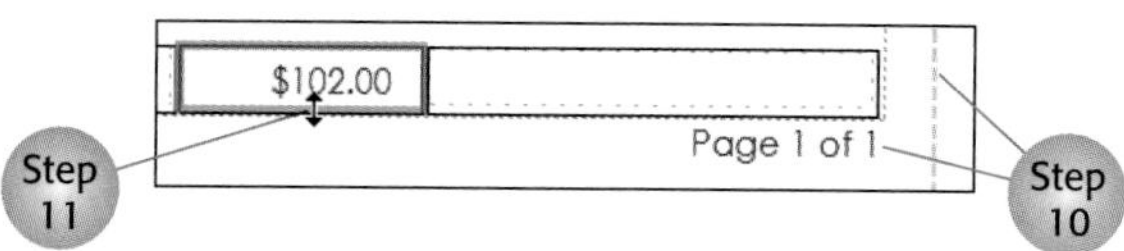

12 Tap or click the Print Preview button near the right end of the Status bar. Compare your report with the one shown in Figure 13.2. If necessary, switch to Layout view, resize control objects, and then switch back to Print Preview.

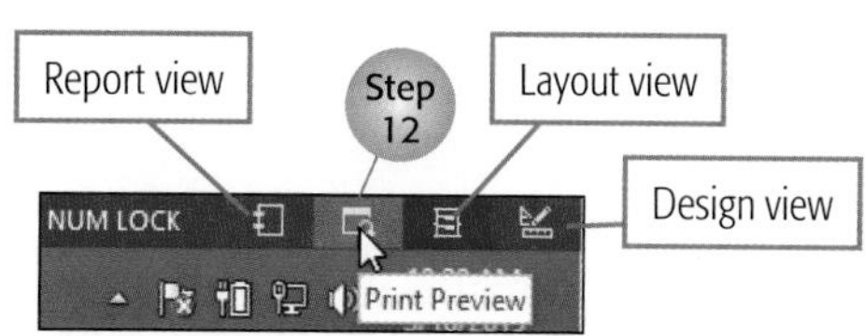

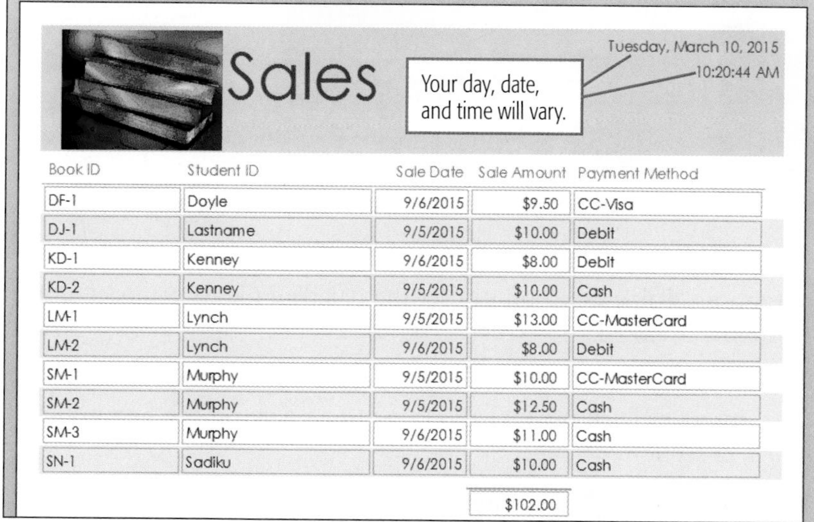

Book ID	Student ID	Sale Date	Sale Amount	Payment Method
DF-1	Doyle	9/6/2015	$9.50	CC-Visa
DJ-1	Lastname	9/5/2015	$10.00	Debit
KD-1	Kenney	9/6/2015	$8.00	Debit
KD-2	Kenney	9/5/2015	$10.00	Cash
LM-1	Lynch	9/5/2015	$13.00	CC-MasterCard
LM-2	Lynch	9/6/2015	$8.00	Debit
SM-1	Murphy	9/5/2015	$10.00	CC-MasterCard
SM-2	Murphy	9/5/2015	$12.50	Cash
SM-3	Murphy	9/6/2015	$11.00	Cash
SN-1	Sadiku	9/6/2015	$10.00	Cash
			$102.00	

Figure 13.2 Sales report for Topic 13.9

13 Tap or click the Close Print Preview button in the Close Preview group.

14 Tap or click the Report View button near the right end of the Status bar.

Report view is the view in which a report is opened from the Navigation pane. Report view is used for viewing data on the screen; the report cannot be edited in Report view.

15 Close the Sales report, saving changes to the report design and accepting the default report name of *Sales*. Leave the database open for the next topic.

Having difficulty resizing controls using touch? Open the Property Sheet for a selected control and change the *Width* and *Height* values. Use *.25* for the *Height* of the column total control.

Quick STEPS

Create a Report
1. Tap or click to select table or query in Navigation pane.
2. Tap or click CREATE tab.
3. Tap or click Report button.
4. Modify as required.
5. Tap or click Save button.
6. Type report name.
7. Tap or click OK.

Grouping and Sorting a Report

The Group & Sort button in the Grouping & Totals group of the REPORT LAYOUT TOOLS DESIGN tab toggles on and off the Group, Sort, and Total pane at the bottom of the work area. Turn on the pane and use the Add a group and Add a sort buttons to change the arrangement of records in the report.

Topic 13.10

SKILLS

Compact and repair a database

Create a backup copy of a database

App Tip

If a database is shared, make sure no one else is using the database before starting a compact and repair operation.

Compacting, Repairing, and Backing Up a Database

A database file becomes larger and fragmented over time as new records are added, edited, and deleted. The file size for the database may become larger than is necessary if the space previously used by records that have since been deleted is not compacted. The compacting process eliminates unused space in the file. Backing up a database file should be done regularly for historical record keeping and data loss prevention purposes.

1. With the **13.7-UsedBooks-Your Name** database open, tap or click the FILE tab.
2. At the Info tab Backstage view, tap or click the **Compact & Repair Database button**.

Access closes all objects and the Navigation pane during a compact and repair routine. The Navigation pane redisplays when the compacting and repairing is complete. For larger database files, compacting and repairing may take a few moments to process.

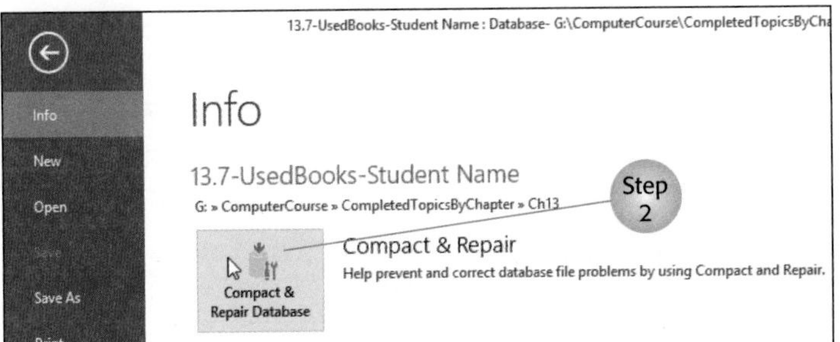

3. Tap or click the FILE tab and then tap or click Options.

At the Access Options dialog box, you can set the database file to compact and repair each time the file is closed.

4. Tap or click *Current Database* in the left pane of the Access Options dialog box.
5. Tap or click to insert a check mark in the *Compact on Close* check box in the *Application Options* section.

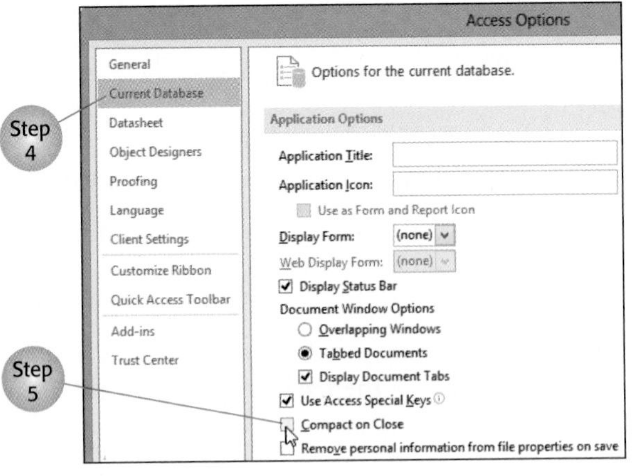

6 Tap or click OK to close the Access Options dialog box.

7 Tap or click OK at the message box that says the database must be closed and reopened for the option to take effect.

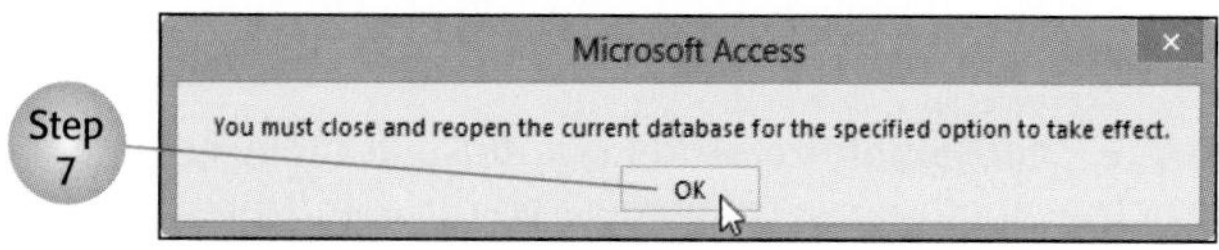

Microsoft Access
You must close and reopen the current database for the specified option to take effect.
OK
Step 7

8 Tap or click the FILE tab and tap or click Save As.

9 At the Save As Backstage view, tap or click *Back Up Database* in the *Advanced* section of the Save Database As pane.

10 Tap or click the Save As button.

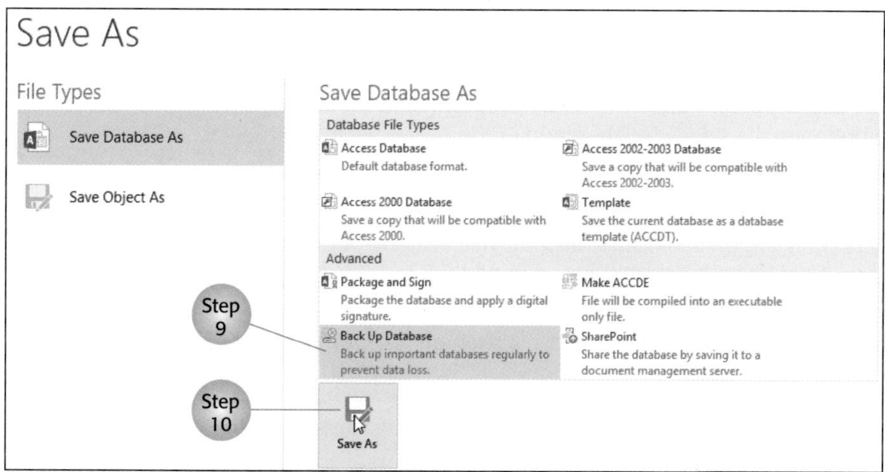

Access 2002-2003 Database
Save a copy that will be compatible with Access 2002-2003.
Access 2000 Database
Save a copy that will be compatible with Access 2000.

Package and Sign

Make ACCDE
File will be compiled into an executable only file.

Back up important databases regularly to prevent data loss.
SharePoint
Share the database by saving it to a document management server.

11 Tap or click the Save button at the Save As dialog box.

By default, the backup copy of the database is saved in the same folder as the current database and the file name is the same database file name with the current date added after an underscore at the end of the name, for example, 13.7-UsedBooks-Your Name_*currentdate*.

12 Close the database.

Compact and Repair a Database
1. Tap or click FILE tab.
2. Tap or click Compact & Repair Database button.

Turn on Compact on Close
1. Tap or click FILE tab.
2. Tap or click Options.
3. Tap or click *Current Database*.
4. Tap or click *Compact on Close*.
5. Tap or click OK twice.

Back Up a Database
1. Tap or click FILE tab.
2. Tap or click Save As.
3. Tap or click *Back Up Database*.
4. Tap or click Save As button.
5. Tap or click Save.

A backup should normally be saved on another storage medium. At the Save As dialog box, consider navigating to another drive or copy the backup file to another storage medium afterward.

Encrypting a Database with a Password

Assign a password to a database to prevent unauthorized access to confidential data stored in a database. A database has to be opened in exclusive mode to assign a password. To do this, close the current database and then display the Open dialog box. Navigate to the location of the database, select the database file, and then use the down-pointing arrow on the Open button to choose *Open Exclusive*. Enable content and then display the Info tab Backstage view. Tap or click the Encrypt with Password button and then type the password twice in the Set Database Password dialog box.

Concepts Review

Topic	Key Concepts	Key Terms
Creating a New Database File and Understanding Table Design Guidelines	Access database files require that you provide the name and file storage location before creating data. To create a new database file, choose *Blank desktop database* at the Access Start screen, type the file name, and browse to the desired drive and/or folder. Access displays a blank table datasheet in a new database. Planning a new table involves several steps, some of which include: dividing the data into fields, assigning each field a name, assigning each field a data type, deciding the field that will be the primary key, and including a common field to join a table to another table if necessary.	
Creating a New Table	In a blank table datasheet, begin a new field by first selecting the data type and then typing the field name. Choose the data type from the *Click to Add* drop-down list or by choosing a data type button in the Add & Delete group of the TABLE TOOLS FIELDS tab. An entry in the Caption property is used as a descriptive title that becomes the column heading for a field in a datasheet. Several data types are available such as Short Text, Number, Currency, and Date & Time. A data type is selected based upon the type of field value that will be entered into records. Save a table by tapping or clicking the Save button on the QAT and then entering a name for the table.	Caption property
Creating a New Table in Design View and Assigning a Primary Key	In Design view, a new table is created by defining fields in rows in the top half of the work area. Type a field name in the first row in the *Field Name* column and then specify the data type using the data type drop-down list. An optional description can be added for a field with additional information about the purpose of the field or with instructions on what to type into the field. Once the fields are defined, assign the primary key by placing an insertion point anywhere within the field name and then tapping or clicking the Primary Key button in the Tools group of the TABLE TOOLS DESIGN tab.	
Adding Fields to an Existing Table	Open a table and use the *Click to Add* column to add a new field to the end of an existing table datasheet. Select a column in a datasheet and use the buttons in the Add & Delete group of the TABLE TOOLS FIELDS tab to add a new field to the right of the selected field.	
Modifying Field Properties in Design View	Each field in a table has a set of associated field properties. A field property is a single characteristic or attribute of a field that customizes, formats, or changes the behavior of the field. The lower half of the Design view window is the Field Properties pane in which properties for a selected field are modified. The Field Size property is used to limit the number of characters that can be entered into a field. The Default Value property is used to specify a field value that is automatically entered in the field in new records. Other field properties that are often modified are the *Format*, *Validation*, and *Required* field properties.	Field property Field Properties pane

Topic	Key Concepts	Key Terms
Creating a Lookup List	A lookup list is a drop-down list of items that displays when a field is made active in a datasheet or form. Items in the lookup list can be predefined or extracted from one or more fields in another table. The Lookup Wizard presents a series of dialog boxes to help create the field properties for a lookup list field. Create a predefined list of entries by choosing *I will type in the values that I want* at the first Lookup Wizard dialog box. Type the list entries in the *Col1* column and adjust the column width as needed at the second Lookup Wizard dialog box.	Lookup list Lookup Wizard
Displaying and Editing a Relationship	A relationship is when two tables are joined together on a common field. Black join lines connecting a common field between two table field list boxes indicates a relationship has been created. A one-to-one relationship means that the two tables are joined on the primary key in each table. *Enforce Referential Integrity* causes Access to check that new records are entered into the primary table first before records with a matching field value can be entered into the related table. A primary table is the table in which the common field is the primary key and into which new records must first be entered. The primary table name is shown below *Table/Query* in the Edit Relationships dialog box. In a one-to-many relationship, the common field used to join the tables is the primary key in only one table (the primary table). A field added to a table that is not a primary key and is added for the purpose of creating a relationship is called a foreign key.	One-to-one relationship Enforce Referential Integrity Primary table One-to-many relationship Foreign key
Creating and Editing a Form	The Form button in the Forms group of the CREATE tab creates a new form with all fields in the selected table or query arranged in a columnar layout. Layout view is the view in which you modify the form's structure and appearance using buttons in the three FORM LAYOUT TOOLS tabs. Form view is the view in which a form is displayed when opened from the Navigation pane and is used to add, edit, and delete data. The Themes button is used to change the color scheme and fonts for a form. Use the Logo button to choose a picture to display in the Logo control object near the top left of the form. A control object is a rectangular placeholder for content. Each control object can be selected and modified to change the appearance of the control's content. Open the Property Sheet task pane to make changes to a selected picture's appearance. Change the *Size Mode* property of a picture to *Zoom* to fit the content to the object size and with the height and width proportions maintained. A control object can be resized by changing the values for the *Width* and *Height* in the Property Sheet task pane.	Layout view Form view Control object

continued....

Topic	Key Concepts	Key Terms
Creating, Editing, and Viewing a Report	The Report tool in the Reports group of the CREATE tab creates a report with all of the fields in the selected table or query in a tabular arrangement. Buttons in the REPORT LAYOUT TOOLS PAGE SETUP tab are used to change page layout options for printing purposes. Access creates a current date and time control, a page number control, and a total control for each numeric column in a new report. The vertical dashed line in a report indicates a page break. Resizing a column heading control object resizes the entire column. Report view is the view in which a report is displayed when opened from the Navigation pane and is the view that displays the data in the report.	Report view
Compacting, Repairing, and Backing Up a Database	The compact and repair process eliminates unused space in the database file. Use the Compact & Repair Database button at the Info tab Backstage view to perform a compact and repair operation. During the compact and repair routine, Access closes all objects and the Navigation pane. Turn on the *Compact on Close* option at the Access Options dialog box with *Current Database* selected. Display the Save As Backstage view and choose *Back Up Database* in the *Advanced* section to create a backup copy of the current database. Access adds the current date after an underscore character to the end of the current database file name when a backup is created.	Compact & Repair Database button

Multiple Choice

1. Choose this option from the Access Start screen to create a new database file.
   a. New database
   b. New blank database
   c. File New Database
   d. Blank desktop database
2. Which of the following is *not* a guideline for planning a new table?
   a. Divide data into the smallest unit
   b. Determine the number of records
   c. Assign each field a data type
   d. Decide the primary key
3. In a blank table datasheet, the data type can be selected from this drop-down list.
   a. Click to Add
   b. Data Type
   c. New Field
   d. Add & Delete
4. This property stores a descriptive title for a field that is used as the column heading in a datasheet.
   a. Long text
   b. Rich text
   c. Title
   d. Caption
5. An *ID* field that is assigned the primary key is *not* created automatically by Access when you create a table in this view.
   a. Datasheet view
   b. Design view
   c. Layout view
   d. New Table view
6. This icon appears in the field selector bar next to the field designated as the primary key.
   a. check mark
   b. asterisk
   c. key
   d. folder
7. New fields can be added to a table in this view.
   a. Datasheet view
   b. Layout view
   c. Report view
   d. New Table view
8. Assign a new field this data type to display a check box in the datasheet.
   a. Short Text
   b. Yes/No
   c. Rich Text
   d. Attachment

9. This field property is used to automatically insert a field value in new records.
   a. Format
   b. Field Size
   c. Required
   d. Default Value
10. Use this property to limit the number of characters in a field.
    a. Field Size
    b. Format
    c. Default Value
    d. Required
11. This is the name for a drop-down list that appears in a field in a datasheet or form.
    a. option list
    b. lookup list
    c. field list
    d. values list
12. This property contains the list entries and is used to correct typing errors after the list has been created.
    a. Row Source
    b. Bound Column
    c. Caption
    d. Display Control
13. In this relationship type, the common field that joins the tables is the primary key in each table.
    a. one-to-one relationship
    b. one-to-many relationship
    c. enforce referential integrity relationship
    d. foreign key relationship
14. In this type of relationship the common field that joins the tables is the primary key in only one of the two tables.
    a. foreign key relationship
    b. one-to-one relationship
    c. one-to-many relationship
    d. referential integrity relationship
15. This is the view in which a form is displayed after the form is generated with the Form button.
    a. Form view
    b. Datasheet view
    c. Layout view
    d. Design view
16. Use this button to insert a picture in the control object near the top left of a new form.
    a. Insert Picture
    b. Logo
    c. Insert Graphic
    d. Pictures
17. Which of the following is *not* a control object added to a report by Access for a report generated using the Report tool?
    a. Page numbering
    b. Current date and time
    c. Numeric column totals
    d. Table or query name
18. This is the view in which a report opens from the Navigation pane.
    a. Print Preview
    b. Design view
    c. Report view
    d. Layout view
19. Use this option to remove unused disk space from a database file.
    a. Back Up Database
    b. Compact & Repair Database
    c. Defragment Database
    d. Encrypt Database
20. This option at the Save As Backstage view saves a copy of the current database with the current date added to the end of the file name.
    a. Encrypt Database
    b. Defragment Database
    c. Back Up Database
    d. Compact & Repair Database

Crossword Puzzle

ACROSS

2 Rectangular placeholder for form or report content
3 Indicated by a black join line
4 Field property to limit *State* field to two characters
6 Field property for descriptive title for a field
12 Field property to add *MI* to *State* field in new records
13 Field that is not a primary key added to a table to create a relationship
14 REPORT LAYOUT TOOLS tab for changing page layout options

DOWN

1 Process that eliminates unused disk space
5 Property Sheet option to fit a picture to object size
7 Vertical dashed line in a report
8 Term for a drop-down list
9 Select data type for new field in this drop-down list
10 Button to assign the field that uniquely identifies each record
11 Backstage view to make a backup copy of file

Matching

Match the term with the statement or definition.

_______ 1. Create a new database file
_______ 2. Tab with data type buttons for new table
_______ 3. View in which fields are defined in rows
_______ 4. Column to tap or click to add a new field
_______ 5. Lower half of Design view
_______ 6. Single characteristic or attribute of a field
_______ 7. Assists with creating a drop-down list
_______ 8. Table in relationship in which records must be entered first
_______ 9. View in which data is entered and updated in a form
_______ 10. Button to add picture to a form or report
_______ 11. Removes unused disk space
_______ 12. Save copy of current database

a. Click to Add
b. Back Up Database
c. Primary table
d. Lookup Wizard
e. Logo
f. Form view
g. Blank desktop database
h. Field Properties pane
i. Compact on Close
j. TABLE TOOLS FIELDS tab
k. Field property
l. Design view

Project 1 Creating a New Database File and Creating Tables

Individual

Deliverable: Home listing database (continued in Project 2)

1. Create a new blank desktop database file named ***C13-Project1-Listings-Your Name*** in a new folder named *C13* in the ChapterProjectsWork folder on your USB flash drive.
2. Add the following fields in the blank *Table1* datasheet in addition to the default *ID* field:

Field Name	Data Type	Caption
SoldDate	Date & Time	Date Sold
SalePrice	Currency	Sale Price
Commission	Number	Commission Rate
SellingAgent	Short Text	Selling Agent

3. Adjust column widths so that all column headings are entirely visible.
4. Save the table as *Sales* and then close the table.
5. Create a new table in Design view using the following field names and data types:

Field Name	Data Type
ListingID	Short Text
AgentID	Short Text
StreetAdd	Short Text
ClientLName	Short Text
ClientFName	Short Text
ListDate	Date/Time
AskPrice	Currency
HomeType	Short Text

6. Assign *ListingID* as the primary key field.
7. Save the table naming it *Listings* and then close the table.
8. Create a third table in the database using the following field names. All of the fields are the Short Text data type. You decide the view in which to create the table.
   Field Name
   AgentID (assign this field as the primary key)
   LName
   FName
9. Save the table as *Agents* and then close the table.
10. Leave the database open if you are continuing to Project 2; otherwise, close the database and submit the project to your instructor in the manner she or he has requested.

Project 2 Adding Fields, Modifying Field Properties, and Creating a Lookup List

Individual

Deliverable: Home listing database and PDFs of tables (continued from Project 1)

1. If necessary, open **C13-Project1-Listings-Your Name** and enable content.
2. Open the Listings table, make *ClientFName* the active field, and add a new Short Text field named *ContactPhone*.

3. Switch to Design view and create a drop-down list for the *HomeType* field with the following list entries. Make *Single family home* the default value for the field.
   Single family home
   Condominium
   Townhouse
   Duplex
   Triplex
   Fourplex
   Other
4. Switch to Datasheet view, adjust the column widths as needed so that all column headings are entirely visible, and then close the table, savings changes to the layout.
5. Open the Sales table and then add a new Yes/No field named *SplitComm* to the end of the table. Add a caption to the field with the text *Split Commission?* and then adjust the column width to show the entire column heading.
6. Switch to Design view, make *Commission* the active field, and then change the following field properties:
   a. Type **.05** as the Default Value.
   b. Change the Field Size to *Double*.
   c. Change the Decimal Places to *2*.
   d. Change the Format to *Percent*.
7. Change the field name of the *ID* field to *ListingID* and then change the data type from *AutoNumber* to *Short Text*.
8. Save and close the Sales table.
9. Add the following captions to the fields in the Agents table and then adjust column widths in Datasheet view so that all column headings are entirely visible. Close the table, saving changes to the layout.

Field Name	Caption
AgentID	Agent ID
LName	Agent Last Name
FName	Agent First Name

10. Add a new record in the Agents table with your name and with *10* as the *AgentID*.
11. Add the following record in the Listings table:

ListingID	2015-1	*ContactPhone*	800-555-3225
AgentID	10	*ListDate*	03/15/2015
StreetAdd	98 First Street	*AskPrice*	87500
ClientLName	Jones	*HomeType*	Condominium
ClientFName	Marion		

12. Add the following new record to the Sales table:

ListingID	2015-1	*Commission Rate*	5.00%
Date Sold	03/22/2015	*SellingAgent*	10
Sale Price	82775	*Split Commission?*	Yes

13. Display each table datasheet in Print Preview and then create a PDF of the datasheet using the following file names and saving in the Ch13 folder in ChapterProjectsWork:

Table	Name for PDF
Agents	C13-Project2-Agents-Your Name
Listings (landscape; normal margins)	C13-Project2-Listings-Your Name
Sales (normal margins)	C13-Project2-Sales-Your Name

14. Close the **C13-Project1-Listings-Your Name** database.
15. Submit the project to your instructor in the manner she or he has requested.

Project 3 Editing Relationships, Creating a Form and a Report

Individual

Deliverable: Home listing database and PDFs of new objects (continued in Projects 4 and 5)

1. Open **HomeListings**.
2. Use Save As to *Save Database As*, naming the copy **C13-Project3-HomeListings-Your Name** in the Ch13 folder within ChapterProjectsWork.
3. Enable content in the copy of the database.
4. Display the relationships.
5. Edit each relationship to turn on *Enforce Referential Integrity*. With the relationships window active, tap or click the Relationship Report button in the Tools group. Create a PDF of the report, naming the PDF **C13-Project3-Relationships-Your Name** and saving in the Ch13 folder in ChapterProjectsWork. Close the report, saving the report using the default name, and then close the Relationships window.
6. Create a form using the Form tool for the Listings table and then modify the form as follows:
   a. Change to a theme of your choosing.
   b. Insert the picture named ***ForSale***. Change the Size Mode property to *Zoom*, the *Width* to 1.5 inches, and the *Height* to 1 inch.
   c. Change the font size for the title text to a size of your choosing.
   d. Make any other changes you think improve the appearance of the form.
   e. Save the form using the default form name.
7. Display the form in Print Preview. Change the margins to *Normal*. Open the Page Setup dialog box with the Columns tab active and then change the *Width* in the *Column Size* section to 7.5 inches. Create a PDF of the <u>first page only</u> of the form, naming the PDF **C13-Project3-Form-Your Name** and saving in the Ch13 folder in ChapterProjectsWork. ***Hint: Use the Options button in the Publish as PDF or XPS dialog box to choose* Page(s) 1 to 1.** Close the form, saving changes.
8. Create a report using the Report tool for the Sales table and then modify the report as follows:
   a. Insert the **ForSale** picture, applying the same changes as those applied to the picture in the form.
   b. Change the title text to a font size of your choosing.
   c. Resize controls as needed so that all objects fit on one page.
   d. Select and delete the total and the line above the total at the bottom of the *Sale Price* column.
   e. Make any other changes you think improve the appearance of the report.
   f. Save the report using the default report name.
9. Create a PDF of the report, naming the PDF **C13-Project3-Report-Your Name** and saving in the Ch13 folder in ChapterProjectsWork. Close the report.
10. Leave the database open if you are continuing to Project 4; otherwise, close the database and submit the project to your instructor in the manner she or he has requested.

Project 4 Compacting on Close and Backing Up a Database

Individual

Deliverable: Home listing database (continued in Project 5)

1. If necessary, open **C13-Project3-HomeListings-Your Name** and enable content.
2. Turn on the *Compact on Close* option.
3. Create a backup copy of the database, accepting the default file name and saving in the default folder.
4. Leave the database open if you are continuing to Project 5; otherwise, close the database and submit the project to your instructor in the manner she or he has requested.

Project 5 Creating a Query and Report

Individual

Deliverable: PDF of Report (continued from Project 4)

1. If necessary, open **C13-Project3-HomeListings-Your Name** and enable content.
2. Create a query using all of the fields in the Sales table. Insert a calculated column titled *Amount* between *Commission Rate* and *Selling Agent* as shown in Figure 13.3. You determine the field expression and format. Save the query, naming it **SalesCommissions.**
3. Create a report similar to the one shown in Figure 13.3 based on the SalesCommissions query. Use your best judgment to determine the formatting options. Save the report using the default name.

Sales Commissions

ListingID	Date Sold	Sale Price	Commission Rate	Amount	Selling Agent	Split Commission?
2015-1	3/22/2015	$82,775.00	5.00%	$4,138.75	Student last name	☑
2015-3	3/31/2015	$59,000.00	4.00%	$2,360.00	Davidson	☑
2015-4	3/30/2015	$72,000.00	5.00%	$3,600.00	Polaski	☑
2015-7	3/31/2015	$74,500.00	5.00%	$3,725.00	Ungar	☑
2015-9	3/25/2015	$64,500.00	5.00%	$3,225.00	Antoine	☑

Figure 13.3 Project 5 Sales Commissions report

4. Open the Page Setup dialog box with the Columns tab active and change the *Width* in the *Column Size* section to 8 inches. Create a PDF of the report, saving it as **C13-Project5-SalesCommissions-Your Name** in the Ch13 folder within ChapterProjectsWork.
5. Close the report and close the database.
6. Submit the project to your instructor in the manner she or he has requested.

Project 6 Sending Project Work to OneNote Notebook

Individual

Deliverable: New Page in Shared OneNote notebook

1. Start OneNote and open the MyProjects notebook created in Chapter 4, Project 4.
2. Make Access the active section and add a new page titled *Chapter 13 Projects*.
3. For each PDF you created in projects you completed in this chapter, send the PDF to OneNote 2013, selecting the Chapter 13 Projects page in the Access section in the MyProjects notebook.
4. Close your MyProjects notebook in OneNote and close OneNote.
5. Submit the project to your instructor in the manner she or he has requested.

Chapter 14

Integrating Word, Excel, PowerPoint, and Access Components

After successfully completing this chapter, you will be able to:

- Import Excel data into Access
- Export an Access query to Excel
- Embed an Excel chart in a document
- Embed Excel data in a presentation
- Edit an embedded object
- Link an Excel chart with a presentation
- Update links

The Microsoft Office suite is designed to easily share and integrate data among the programs. For some tasks you may have portions of a project distributed across more than one application. For example, you may have a chart in Excel and a list in Access that you want to add into a report in Word. The ability to integrate data means that you can use the program that best fits each task and/or the expertise of each person, and assemble the portions into a complete product without duplicating individual efforts.

In Chapter 3 you used the Copy and Paste buttons in the Clipboard group to copy text, a picture, and a chart between Word, Excel, and PowerPoint. Copy and paste is the method of choice for situations in which the data to be shared is not large and is not likely to need updating. In this chapter you will learn other methods for integrating data that include importing, exporting, embedding, and linking.

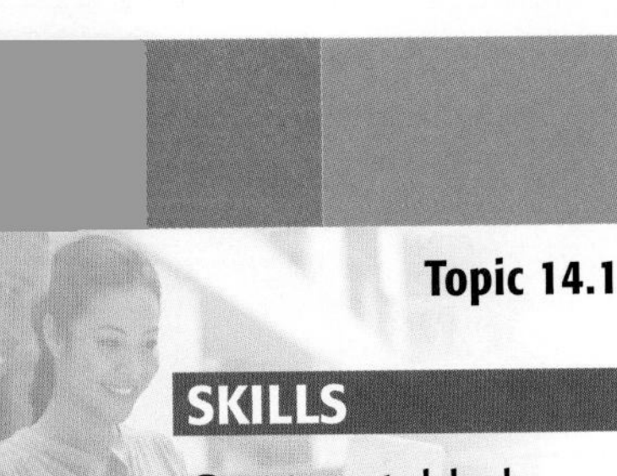

Topic 14.1

SKILLS

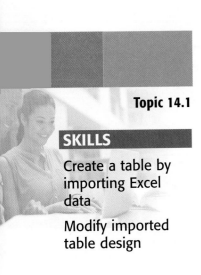

Create a table by importing Excel data

Modify imported table design

Importing Excel Worksheet Data into Access

A new Access table can be created from data in an Excel worksheet, or Excel data can be appended to the bottom of an existing Access table. Because an Excel worksheet and an Access datasheet use the same column and row structure, the two programs are often used to interchange data. To facilitate the import, the Excel worksheet should be set up like an Access datasheet with the field names in the first row and with no blank rows or columns within the data. The **Import Spreadsheet Wizard** is used to perform an import operation.

1. Start Access and open the **Parking** database from the Ch14 folder in Student_Data_Files.
2. Use Save As to save a copy of the database as **14.1-Parking-Your Name** in a new folder named *Ch14* within CompletedTopicsByChapter. Accept the default options *Save Database As* and *Access Database* at the Save As Backstage view.
3. Tap or click the Enable Content button in the SECURITY WARNING message bar.
4. Tap or click the EXTERNAL DATA tab.
5. Tap or click the Excel button in the Import & Link group.

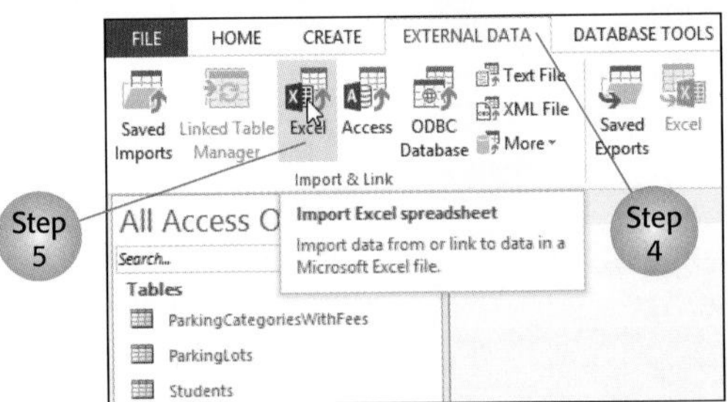

6. Tap or click the Browse button in the Get External Data – Excel Spreadsheet dialog box.
7. Navigate to the Ch14 folder in Student_Data_Files at the File Open dialog box and then double-tap or double-click ***ParkingRecords***.
8. Tap or click OK to accept the default option *Import the source data into a new table in the current database.*

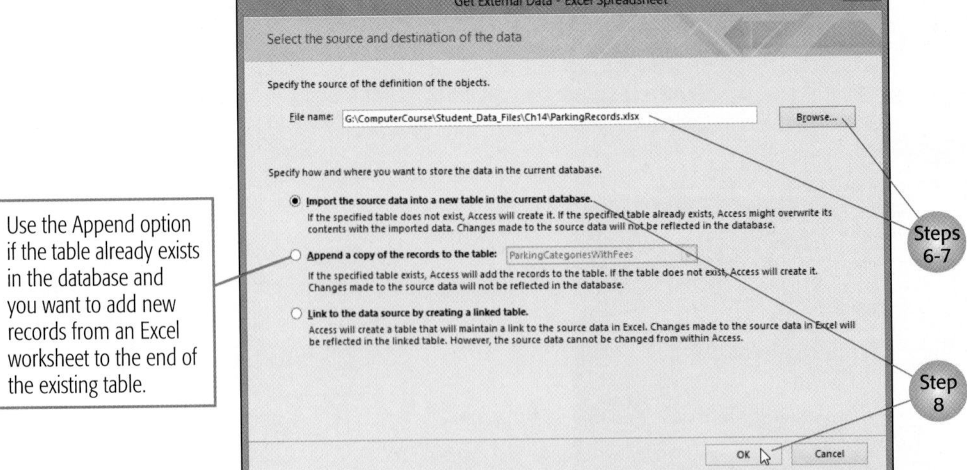

Use the Append option if the table already exists in the database and you want to add new records from an Excel worksheet to the end of the existing table.

9 At the first Import Spreadsheet Wizard dialog box, tap or click Next to accept the worksheet labeled *Student Parking Records*.

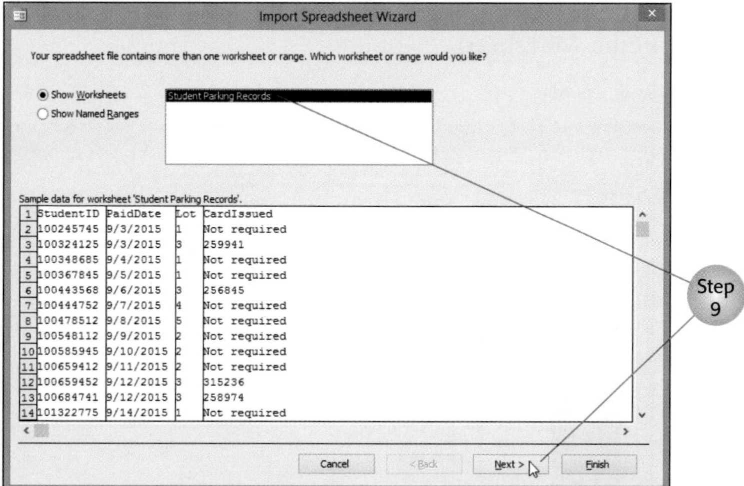

10 At the second Import Spreadsheet Wizard dialog box, tap or click Next with a check mark already inserted in the *First Row Contains Column Headings* check box.

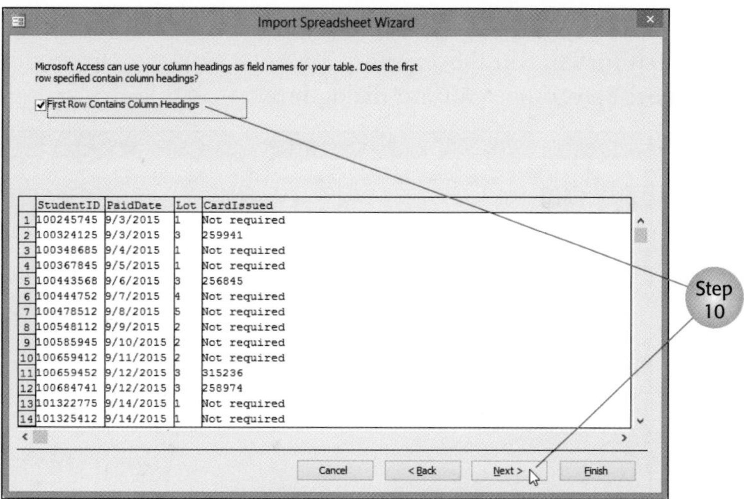

11 At the third Import Spreadsheet Wizard dialog box, tap or click the *PaidDate* column heading and look at the option selected in the *Data Type* list box.

Notice that Access has correctly identified the data as a Date field. At this dialog box, you can review each column and modify the options in the *Field Options* section as needed, or you can elect to make changes in Design view after the import is completed. If a column exists in the Excel worksheet that you do not wish to import into the table, select the column and insert a check mark in the *Do not import field (Skip)* check box.

12 Tap or click Next.

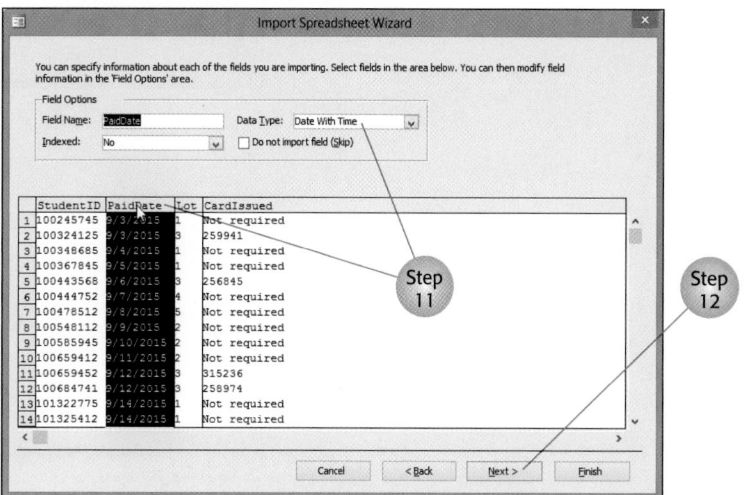

13 At the fourth Import Spreadsheet Wizard dialog box, tap or click *Choose my own primary key*.

Access inserts the *StudentID* field name in the list box next to the option (the first column in the worksheet).

14 Tap or click Next.

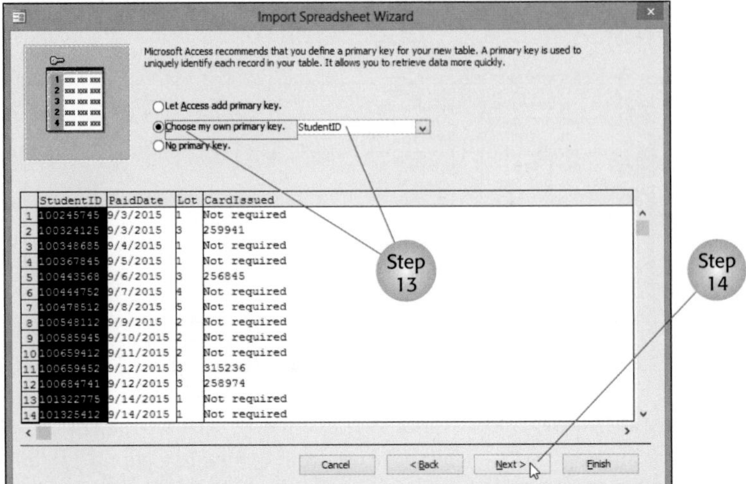

15 Type **ParkingSales** in the *Import to Table* text box and tap or click Finish at the last Import Spreadsheet Wizard dialog box.

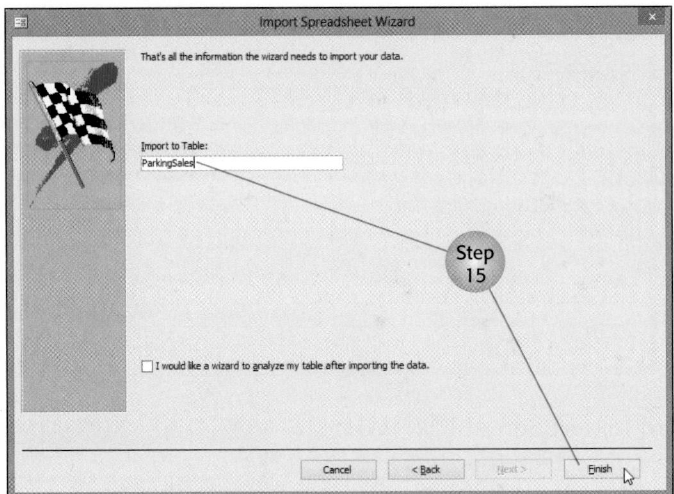

16 Tap or click Close to finish the import without saving the import steps at the Get External Data - Excel Spreadsheet dialog box.

For situations in which you frequently import from Excel to Access, you can save the import specifications so that you can repeat the import later using the same settings.

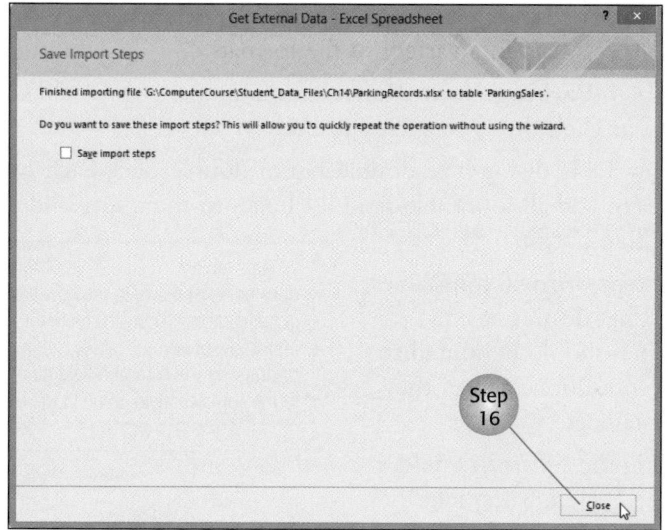

17 Open the ParkingSales table from the Navigation pane and review the datasheet.

18 Switch to Design view and review the field names and data types for the new table.

19 Tap or click the *Data Type* list arrow for the *Lot* field name and then tap or click *Short Text.*

In the Parking database, the Lot field should be defined as Short Text because lot numbers are not field values that you would add or subtract.

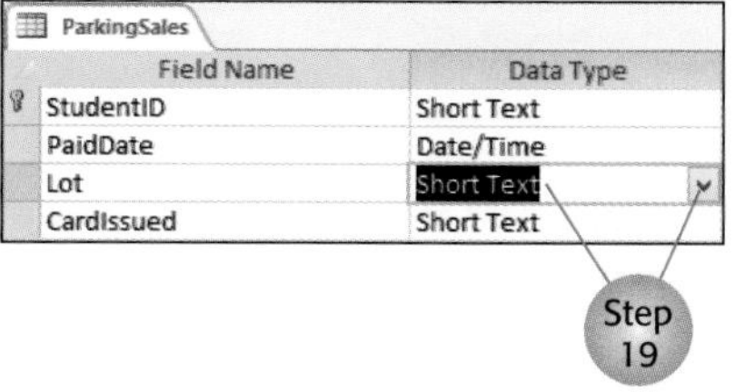

Field Name	Data Type
StudentID	Short Text
PaidDate	Date/Time
Lot	Short Text
CardIssued	Short Text

20 Save and then close the table. Leave the database open for the next topic.

Import Worksheet Data into Access

1. Open destination database.
2. Tap or click EXTERNAL DATA tab.
3. Tap or click Excel button in Import & Link group.
4. Tap or click Browse button.
5. Navigate to and double-tap or double-click Excel file.
6. Tap or click OK.
7. Tap or click Next with worksheet selected.
8. Tap or click Next with *First Row Contains Column Headings* selected.
9. Change *Field Options* for columns if desired and tap or click Next.
10. Choose primary key field and tap or click Next.
11. Type table name and tap or click Finish.
12. Tap or click Close.

Linking an Excel Worksheet to an Access Table

The option *Link to the data source by creating a linked table* at the Get External Data – Excel Spreadsheet dialog box is used when the data that is being imported is likely to be updated within Excel after the import is performed. Access will create a link between the source Excel worksheet and the Access table. Changes made to the Excel data will be automatically reflected in Access. Note that with this option the data cannot be changed from within Access.

Topic 14.2

SKILLS

Export an Access query to Excel

App Tip

Create relationships in the Relationships window if the tables to be joined will be used together in other objects such as a form or report.

Exporting an Access Query to Excel

Often, Access table data is exported to Excel to use the mathematical analysis tools available in a worksheet. Access creates a copy of the data within the selected table or query in an Excel worksheet file in the drive and/or folder that you specify. Buttons in the Export group of the EXTERNAL DATA tab provide options to send a copy of Access data in a variety of file formats.

1. With the **14.1-Parking-Your Name** database open, tap or click the CREATE tab and tap or click the Query Design button.
2. At the Show Table dialog box, double-tap or double-click each of the four table names to add all four table field list boxes to the query and then tap or click the Close button.

In the next steps you will join tables for those tables that do not have a relationship. Tables should be joined so that records are not duplicated in the query results datasheet.

3. Slide or drag the *StudentID* field name in the ParkingSales field list box to *StudentID* in the Students field list box.
4. Slide or drag the *Lot* field name in the ParkingSales field list box to *LotNo* in the ParkingLots field list box.

When a table is created by importing, a relationship does not exist between the new table and other tables in the database. You can create the relationships after importing, or join the tables within a query by sliding or dragging the common field name from one table to the common field name in the other table.

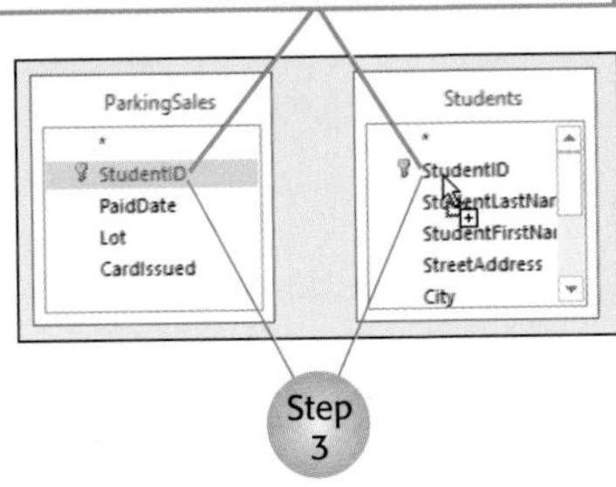

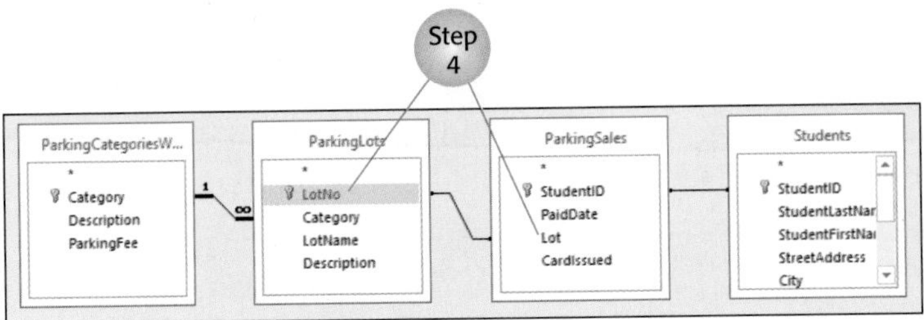

5. Double-tap or double-click the following fields to add the fields to the query design grid. (Note that you are selecting fields in the query from all four table field list boxes.)

Field Name	Table Name
StudentID	ParkingSales
StudentFirstName	Students
StudentLastName	Students
PaidDate	ParkingSales
Lot	Parking Sales
Description	ParkingLots
ParkingFee	ParkingCategoriesWithFees

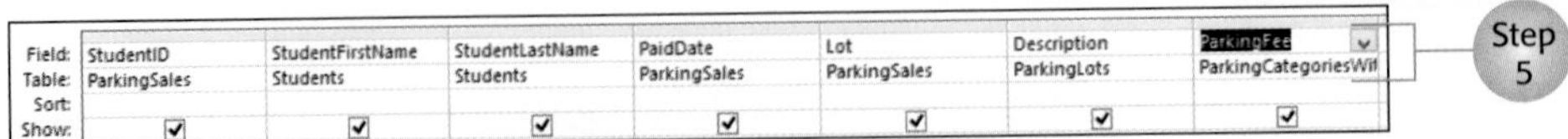

6. Tap or click the Run button in the Results group.
7. Save the query as **ParkingSales2015** and then close the query.

8 Tap or click to select the *ParkingSales2015* query name in the Navigation pane.

9 Tap or click the EXTERNAL DATA tab and tap or click the Excel button in the Export group.

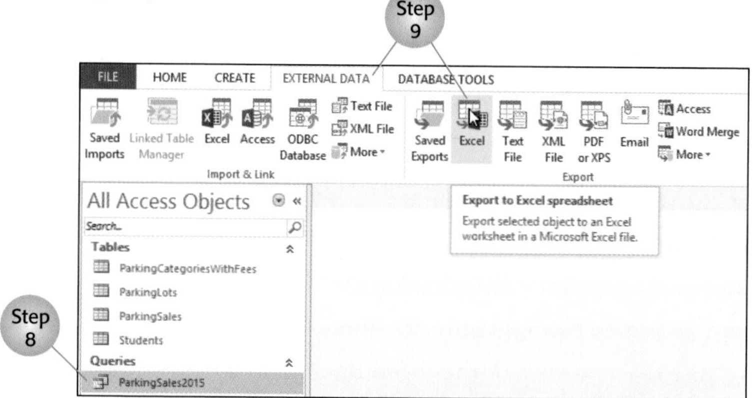

Export a Query to Excel

1. Open database.
2. Select query name.
3. Tap or click EXTERNAL DATA tab.
4. Tap or click Excel button in Export group.
5. Tap or click Browse button.
6. Type file name and navigate to destination folder.
7. Tap or click Save.
8. Specify export options.
9. Tap or click OK.
10. If Excel opened, review work-sheet and close Excel.
11. Tap or click Close.

10 At the Export – Excel Spreadsheet dialog box, tap or click the Browse button, type **14.2-ParkingSales-Your Name** in the *File name* text box, navigate to the Ch14 folder in CompletedTopicsByChapter, and then tap or click Save.

11 Tap or click to insert a check mark in the *Export data with formatting and layout.* check box.

12 Tap or click to insert a check mark in the *Open the destination file after the export operation is complete.* check box, and then tap or click OK.

Excel is started automatically with the data from the query results datasheet shown in a worksheet. Notice the first row contains the field names from the query and the worksheet tab is renamed to the query name.

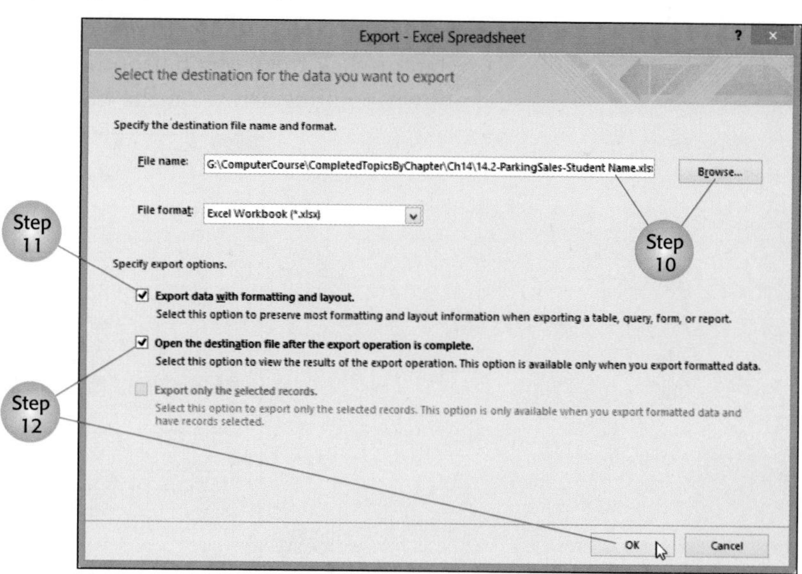

	A	B	C	D	E	F	G
1	StudentID	StudentFirstName	StudentLastName	PaidDate	Lot	Description	Parking Fee
2	100245745	Anna	Takacis	9/3/2015	1	Main campus north of Administration building	$250.00
3	100324125	Jose	Ramirez	9/3/2015	3	Main campus south of Technology wing	$200.00
4	100348685	Celine	Gauthier	9/4/2015	1	Main campus north of Administration building	$250.00
5	100367845	Sara	Blewett	9/5/2015	1	Main campus north of Administration building	$250.00
6	100443568	Dwayne	Kenney	9/6/2015	3	Main campus south of Technology wing	$200.00

First six rows in Excel after query is exported.

Green triangles are shown in the *StudentID* and *Lot* columns because the data is numeric but was exported from Access as text. Green triangles flag data that is a potential error. You can ignore the error flags here.

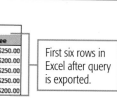

Go to the Export tab Backstage view in Word, Excel, and PowerPoint to find options for sending data outside the source program.

13 Close Excel to return to Access.

14 Tap or click Close at the Export - Excel Spreadsheet dialog box to finish the export without saving the export steps.

15 Close the database and then close Access.

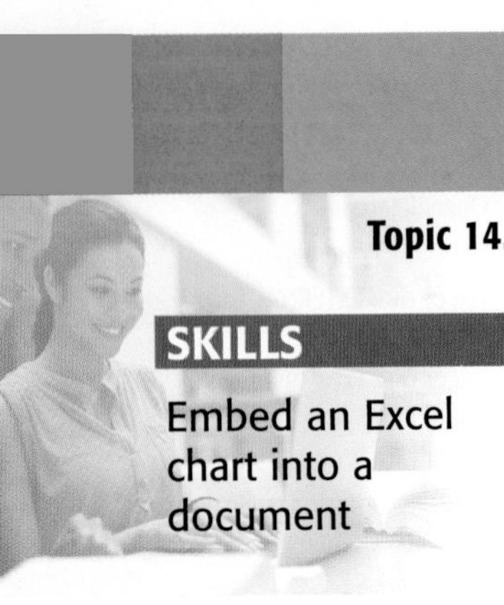

Topic 14.3

SKILLS

Embed an Excel chart into a document

Embedding an Excel Chart into a Word Document

In Chapter 3 you used Copy and Paste features to duplicate text and a chart between programs. You can also embed content as an object within a document, worksheet, or presentation. Embedding, like copying and pasting, inserts a duplicate of the selected text or object at the desired location. The program in which the data originally resides is called the **source program**, and the data that is copied is referred to as the **source data**. The program in which the data is embedded is referred to as the **destination program**, and the document, worksheet, or presentation into which the embedded object is placed is referred to as the **destination document**.

1. Start Excel and open **SocialMediaStats**.
2. Start Word and open **SocialMediaProject**.
3. Use Save As to save a copy of the Word document as **14.3-SocialMediaProject-Your Name** in the Ch14 folder within CompletedTopicsByChapter.
4. Switch to Excel and tap or click to select the pie chart with the title *Global Market Share.*
5. If necessary, tap or click the HOME tab.
6. Tap or click the Copy button in the Clipboard group. (Do *not* tap or click the down-pointing arrow on the button.)

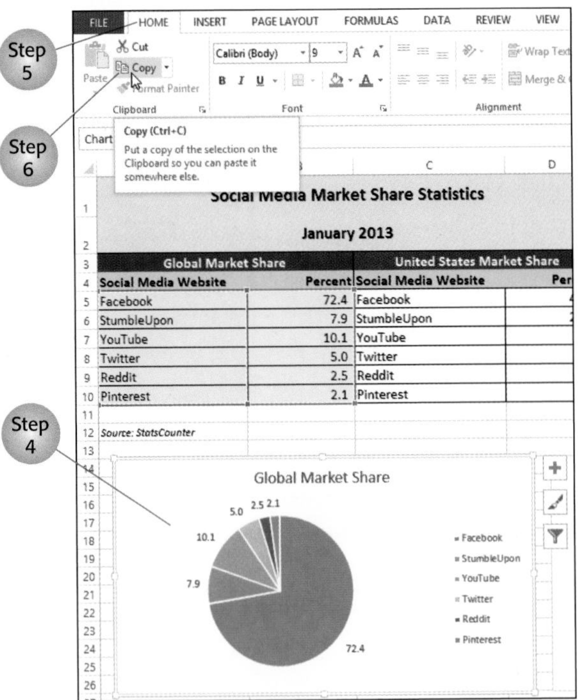

7. Switch to Word and tap or click to position the insertion point at the left margin on the blank line a double-space below the first table.

8 Tap or click the Paste button arrow and tap or click *Use Destination Theme & Embed Workbook* (first button in *Paste Options* section) at the drop-down list.

9 Tap or click to select the chart object and tap or click the Center button in the Paragraph group of the HOME tab.

Step 8

Use Destination Theme & Embed Workbook (H)

On touch-enabled devices, this drop-down list displays in a single column with text labels next to each button.

Social Media Website	Percent
Facebook	72.4
StumbleUpon	7.9
YouTube	10.1
Twitter	5.0
Reddit	2.5
Pinterest	2.1

Global Market Share

Live preview shows the chart with the active paste option.

The Chart feature is standardized in Word, Excel, and PowerPoint. A chart embedded within any of the three programs offers the CHART TOOLS tabs and three chart editing buttons with which the chart can be modified after being embedded.

10 Tap or click the CHART ELEMENTS button (button with plus symbol), tap or click at the right end of *Legend* (right-pointing arrow appears), and tap or click *Bottom*.

11 Switch to Excel and select and copy the pie chart with the title *United States Market Share*.

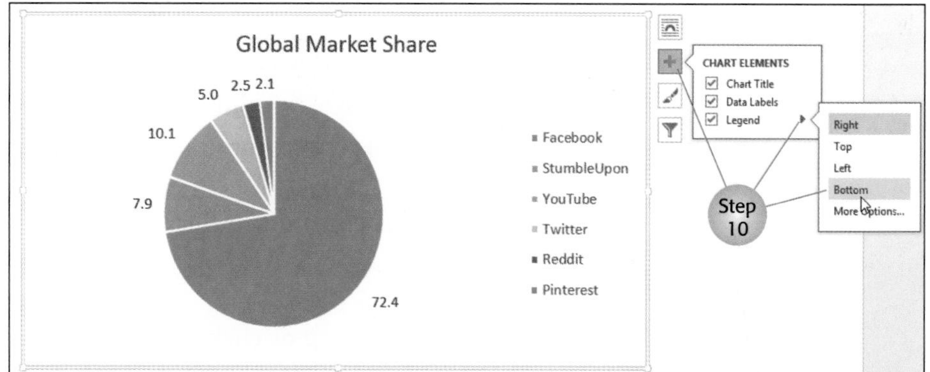

12 Switch to Word, position the insertion point at the bottom of the document, and then embed, center, and format the pie chart by completing steps similar to Steps 8 through 10.

13 Save the revised document using the same name (**14.3-SocialMediaProject-Your Name**) and then close Word. Leave Excel and the **SocialMediaStats** workbook open for the next topic.

Embed an Excel Chart into Word

1. Open worksheet in Excel.
2. Open document in Word.
3. Make Excel active, select and copy chart.
4. Switch to Word.
5. Position insertion point.
6. Tap or click Paste button arrow.
7. Tap or click *Use Destination Theme & Embed Workbook*.

ALTERNATIVE method

Another way to embed copied data is to select *Paste Special* at the Paste button arrow drop-down list in the destination document. This opens the Paste Special dialog box in which you select the source object in the *As* list box and then tap or click OK.

Topic 14.4

SKILLS

Embed Excel data into a presentation

Edit an embedded table

Embedding Excel Data into and Editing the Data in a PowerPoint Presentation

Embedding text or worksheet data uses the same process as for embedding a chart. Double-tap or double-click an embedded object to edit text or worksheet data in the destination location. Embedded text or cell data is edited using the tools from the source program. Tap or click outside the embedded object to end editing and restore the destination program's ribbon.

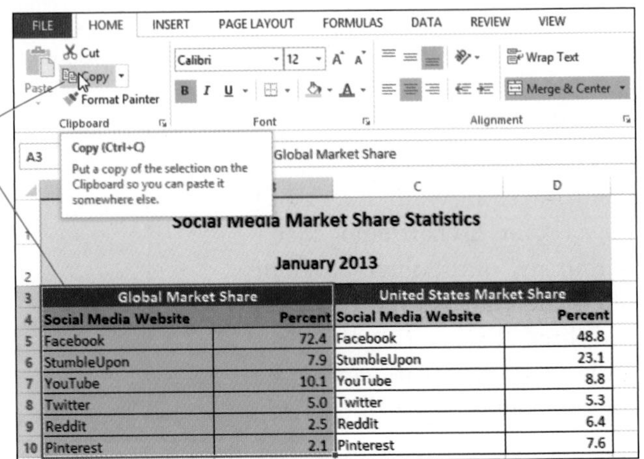

1. With Excel active and the **SocialMediaStats** workbook open, select and copy A3:B10.
2. Start PowerPoint and open **SocialMediaPres**.
3. Use Save As to save a copy of the presentation as **14.4-SocialMediaPres-Your Name** in the Ch14 folder within CompletedTopicsByChapter.
4. Make slide 3 the active slide.
5. Tap or click the Paste button arrow.
6. Tap or click *Embed* (third button in *Paste Options* section) at the drop-down list.
7. Tap or click the DRAWING TOOLS FORMAT tab, tap or click the Shape Fill button in the Shape Styles group, and then tap or click *White, Text 1* (second option in *Theme Colors* section).
8. Resize and position the embedded object to the approximate size and position shown in the image below.

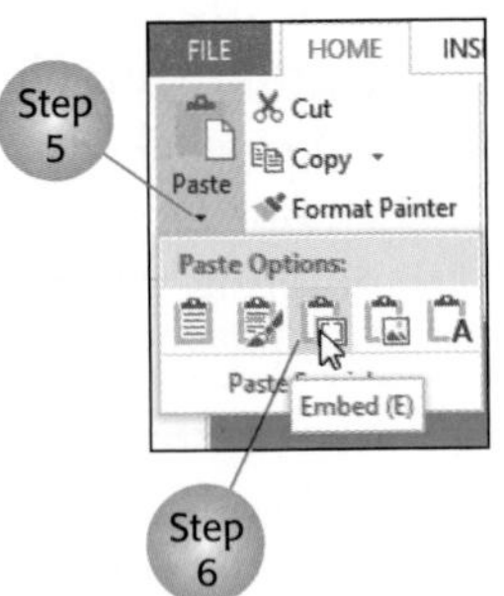

Step 8

Global Social Media Market Share in 2013

Global Market Share	
Social Media Website	Percent
Facebook	72.4
StumbleUpon	7.9
YouTube	10.1
Twitter	5.0
Reddit	2.5
Pinterest	2.1

9 Double-tap or double-click the inserted cells to open the embedded object for editing.

Notice the embedded cells open in an Excel worksheet and the ribbon changes to Excel's ribbon.

10 Select B5:B10 and tap or click the Decrease Decimal button in the Number group of the HOME tab.

11 Tap or click the slide outside the embedded object to end editing and restore PowerPoint's ribbon.

12 Switch to Excel and select and copy C3:D10.

13 Switch to PowerPoint, make slide 4 the active slide, and embed, format, resize, and position the copied cells by completing steps similar to those in Steps 5 through 11.

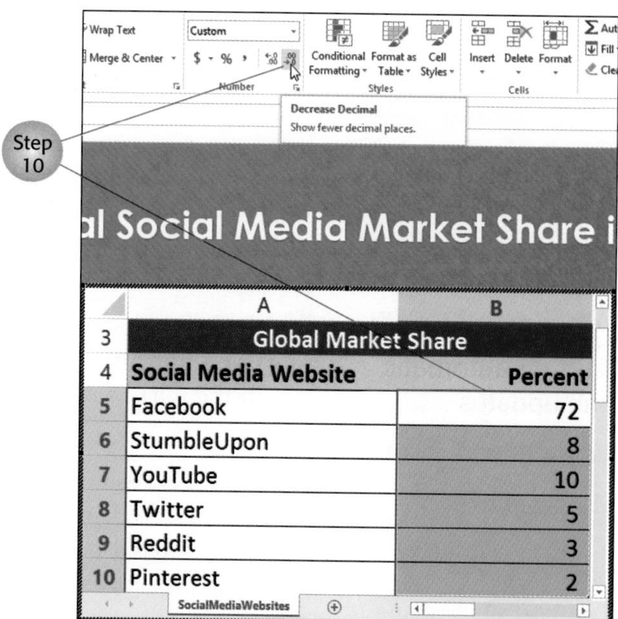

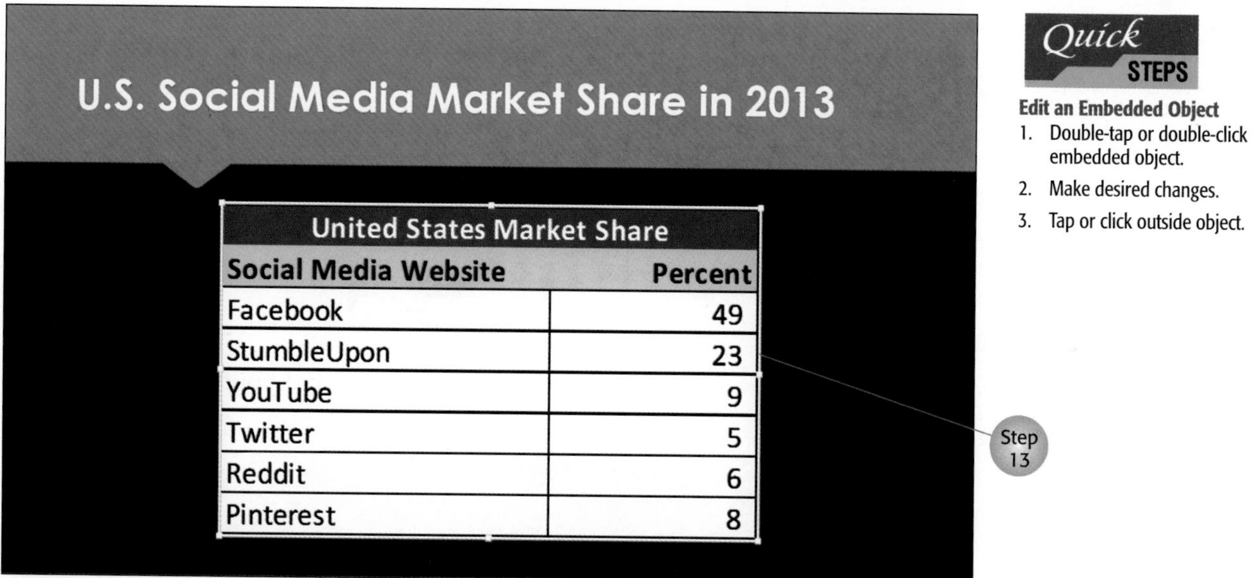

Quick STEPS

Edit an Embedded Object

1. Double-tap or double-click embedded object.
2. Make desired changes.
3. Tap or click outside object.

14 Save the revised presentation using the same name (**14.4-SocialMediaPres-Your Name**) and then close PowerPoint. Leave Excel and the **SocialMediaStats** workbook open for the next topic.

Embedding an Entire File

Embed an entire document or worksheet using the Object button in the INSERT tab. At the Object dialog box, tap or click the Create from File tab and use the Browse button to navigate to the file name. Note that this method embeds the entire file's contents at the insertion point, active cell, or active slide.

Linking an Excel Chart with a Presentation and Updating Links

Topic 14.5

SKILLS

Link an Excel chart with a presentation

Turn on automatic link updates

Edit a linked chart

Update links

Did You Know?

Linking is not just for integrating data between two different programs; you can link two documents in Word, two worksheets in Excel, or two tables in Access.

If the data that you want to integrate between two programs is continuously updated, copy and link the data instead of copying and pasting or copying and embedding. When copied data is linked, changes made to the source data can be automatically updated in any other document, worksheet, or presentation to which the data was linked.

1. With Excel active and the **SocialMediaStats** workbook open, use Save As to save a copy of the workbook as **14.5-LinkedSocialMediaStats-Your Name** in the Ch14 folder within CompletedTopicsByChapter.
2. Start PowerPoint and open **SocialMediaPres**.
3. Use Save As to save a copy of the presentation as **14.5-LinkedSocialMediaPres-Your Name** in the Ch14 folder within CompletedTopicsByChapter.
4. Switch to Excel and select and copy the *Global Market Share* pie chart.
5. Switch to PowerPoint and make slide 3 the active slide.
6. Tap or click the Paste button arrow.
7. Tap or click *Use Destination Theme & Link Data* (third button in *Paste Options* section).

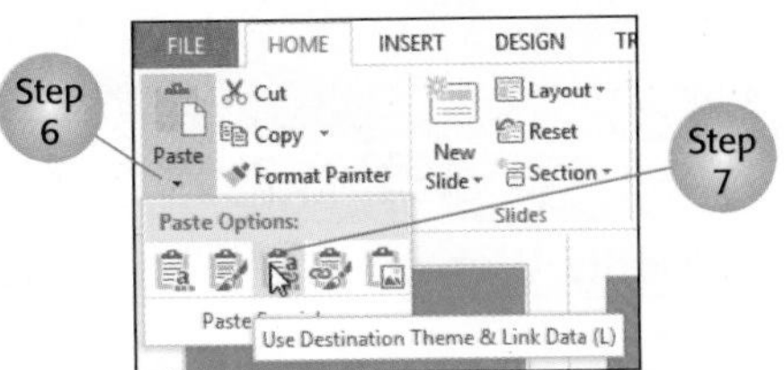

8. Resize and move the chart to the approximate size and position shown in the image below.

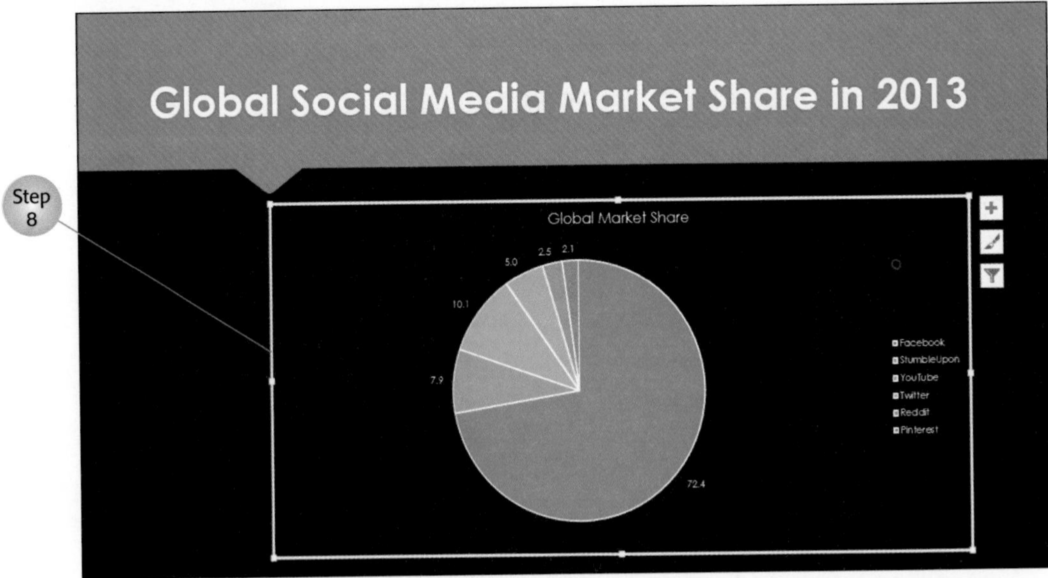

9. Switch to Excel and select and copy the *United States Market Share* pie chart.

10 Switch to PowerPoint, make slide 4 the active slide, and link, resize, and move the chart by completing steps similar to those in Steps 6 through 8.

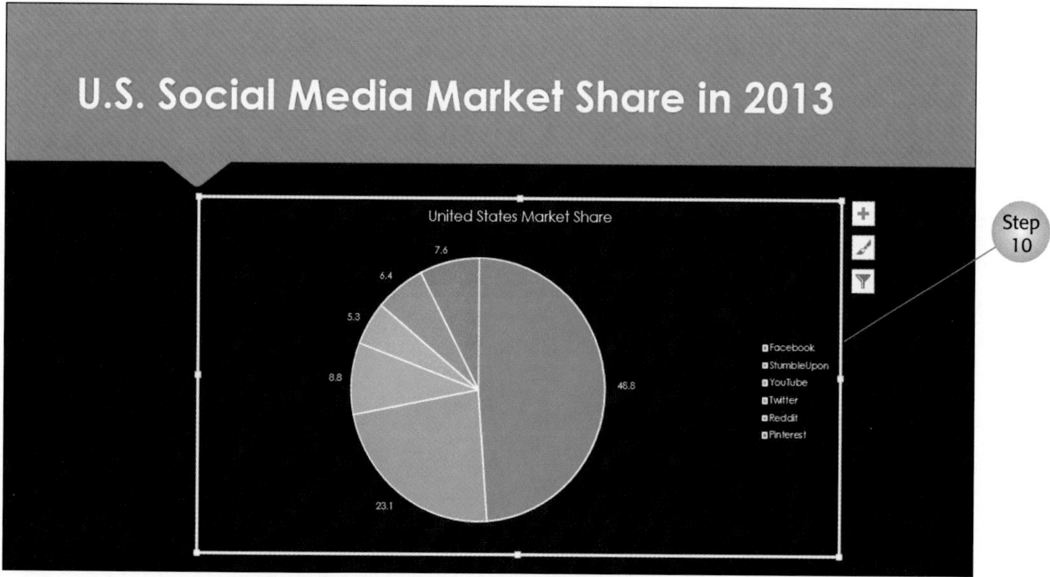

11 Tap or click the FILE tab and tap or click *Edit Links to Files* in the *Related Documents* section near the bottom right of the Info tab Backstage view.

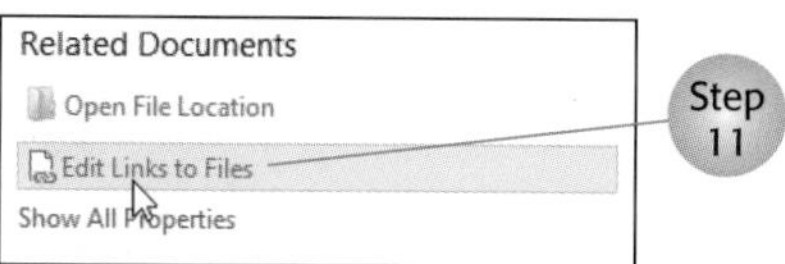

12 At the **Links dialog box**, tap or click to select the first link in the *Links* list box and then tap or click to insert a check mark in the *Automatic Update* check box.

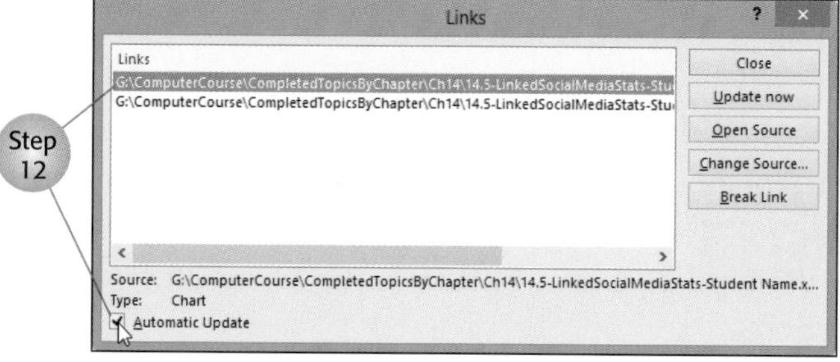

13 Tap or click to select the second link and then tap or click to insert a check mark in the *Automatic Update* check box.

14 Tap or click Close.

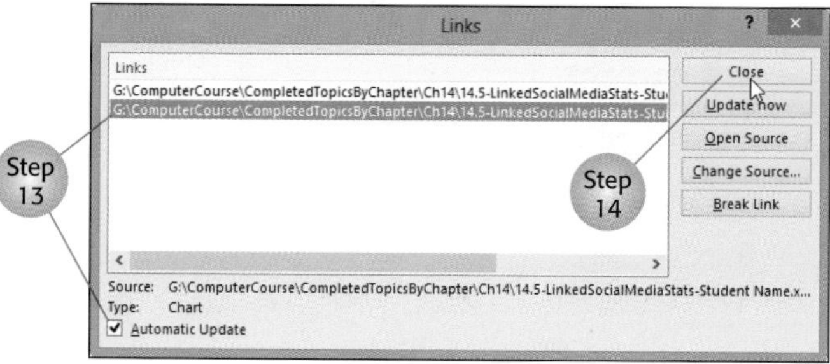

15 Tap or click the Back button at the Info tab Backstage view.

16 Save the revised presentation using the same name (**14.5-LinkedSocialMediaPres-Your Name**) and then close the presentation.

17 Switch to Excel.

18 Change the value in D6 from *23.1* to *5.1*.

19 Change the value in D7 from *8.8* to *18.8*.

20 Change the value in D10 from *7.6* to *15.6*.

Notice the pie chart updated after each change in value. The revised chart is noticeably different from the original pie chart.

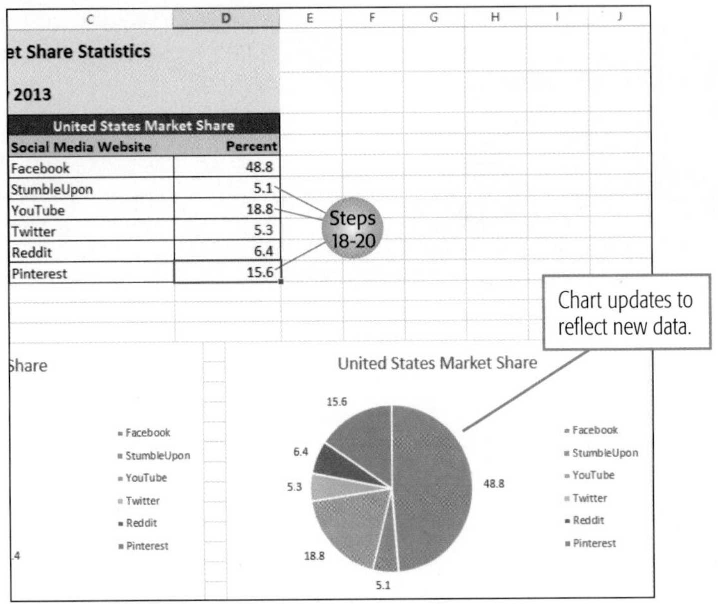

21 Save the revised worksheet using the same name (**14.5-LinkedSocialMediaStats-Your Name**) and then close Excel.

22 Switch to PowerPoint if PowerPoint is not already active and open **14.5-LinkedSocialMediaPres-Your Name**.

Because the presentation contains linked data that is set to automatically update, you are prompted to update links.

If the source and destination files are both open at the same time, changes made to the source reflect in the destination file immediately.

23 Tap or click the **Update Links button** at the Microsoft PowerPoint Security Notice dialog box.

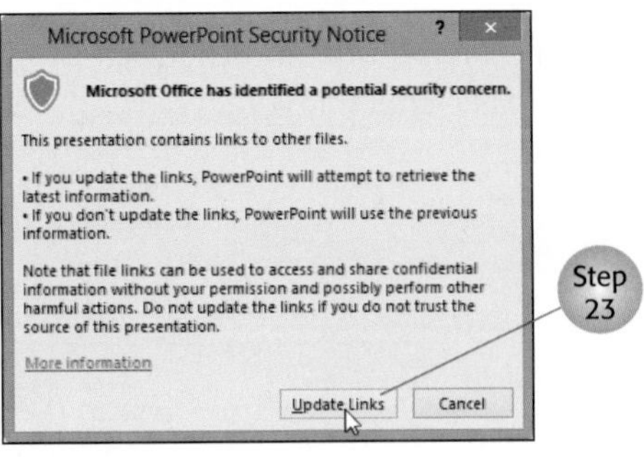

24 Make slide 4 the active slide. Notice that the chart is updated to reflect the same data as the revised Excel chart.

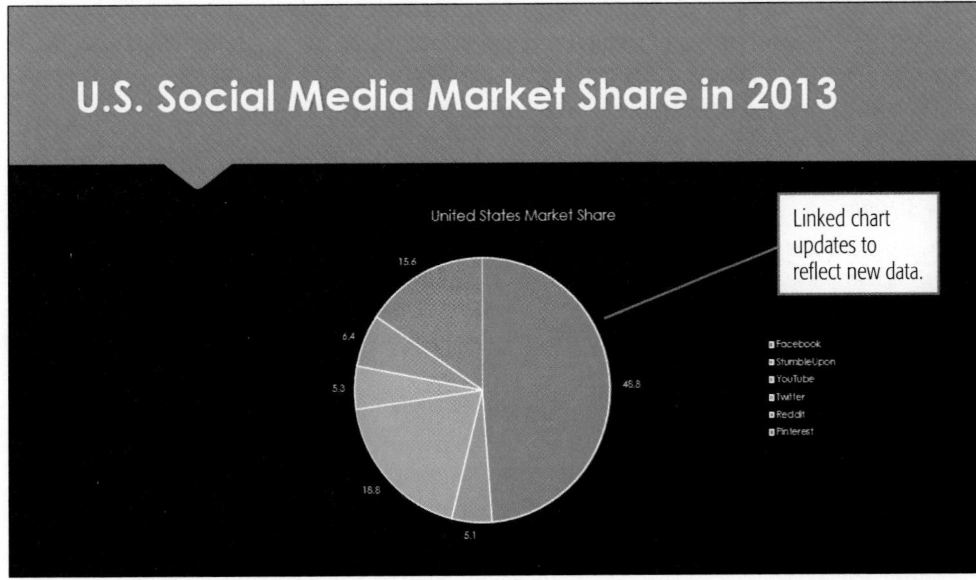

25 Make slide 3 the active slide and delete the title inside the chart above the pie.

26 Make slide 4 the active slide and delete the title inside the chart above the pie.

27 Save the revised presentation using the same name (**14.5-LinkedSocialMediaPres-Your Name**) and then close PowerPoint.

Link Data

1. Open source program and file.
2. Open destination program and file.
3. With source program active, select and copy data.
4. Switch to destination program.
5. Activate destination location.
6. Tap or click Paste button arrow.
7. Tap or click *Use Destination Theme & Link Data*.

Turn on Automatic Link Updates

1. Make destination file active.
2. Tap or click FILE tab.
3. Tap or click *Edit Links to Files*.
4. Select link.
5. Tap or click *Automatic Update* check box.
6. Tap or click Close.

ALTERNATIVE method

Another way to link copied data is to select *Paste Special* at the Paste button arrow drop-down list in the destination document. At the Paste Special dialog box, tap or click *Paste link*, make sure the correct source object is selected in the *As* list box, and then tap or click OK.

Managing Links

Open the Links dialog box (see Step 11) if the drive and/or folder for the source data in a linked file changes, or if you want to break a link to stop updating the destination data.

Concepts Review

Topic	Key Concepts	Key Terms
Importing Excel Worksheet Data into Access	The Import Spreadsheet Wizard starts when you tap or click the Excel button in the Import & Link group of the EXTERNAL DATA tab. Five dialog boxes in the Import Spreadsheet Wizard guide you through the steps to create a new table using data in an Excel worksheet. You can save the Excel import settings to repeat the import later using the same settings. Open an imported table in Design view to modify the table design after the import is complete.	Import Spreadsheet Wizard
Exporting an Access Query to Excel	Export table or query data to Excel using the Excel button in the Export group of the EXTERNAL DATA tab. Specify the file name, drive and/or folder, and export options at the Export – Excel Spreadsheet dialog box. You can elect to export the data with formatting and layout options in the datasheet and to automatically open Excel with the worksheet displayed when the export is complete. Export specifications can be saved to repeat the export later.	
Embedding an Excel Chart into a Word Document	Embedding inserts a copy of selected data as an object in a document, worksheet, or presentation. The program from which data is copied is called the source program. The data that is copied is referred to as the source data. The destination program is the program that receives the copied data. The destination document refers to the document, worksheet, or presentation into which copied data is pasted as an object. To embed copied data as an object, use the Paste button arrow in the destination document and choose the desired embed option from the drop-down list.	Source program Source data Destination program Destination document
Embedding Excel Data into and Editing the Data in a PowerPoint Presentation	Double-tap or double-click an embedded object to open the object data for editing using the source program's ribbon and tools. Tap or click outside the embedded object to end editing and restore the source program's ribbon. An entire document can be embedded using the Object button in the INSERT tab.	
Linking an Excel Chart with a Presentation and Updating Links	Link to source data that is continuously updated instead of copying and pasting or copying and embedding. To link copied data, use the Paste button arrow in the destination document and choose the desired link option from the drop-down list. Tap or click *Edit Links to Files* at the Info tab Backstage view to open the Links dialog box in which you manage links to source data. Select a link in the Links dialog box and insert a check mark in the *Automatic Update* check box to turn on automatic updates for the link. Tap or click the Update Links button in the Security Warning dialog box that appears when you open a file with a linked object to update data from the source.	Links dialog box Update Links button

Multiple Choice

1. This wizard is used to import Excel data into a new table.
   a. Import Excel Wizard
   b. Import Wizard
   c. Import Data Wizard
   d. Import Spreadsheet Wizard
2. Which of the following is *not* an option in the Get External Data – Excel Spreadsheet dialog box?
   a. Import source data into a new table
   b. Start Excel and open worksheet
   c. Append a copy of records to existing table
   d. Link to the data source
3. Do this action first before selecting the Excel button in the Export group to send a copy of Access data to an Excel worksheet.
   a. Select object to export in Navigation pane
   b. Start Excel
   c. Display the table in Design view
   d. Modify all data types to Short Text
4. Specify export options for Excel at this dialog box.
   a. File Open
   b. File Send to Excel
   c. Export – Excel Spreadsheet
   d. Save Export Options
5. This is the name of the program from which data is copied for embedding purposes.
   a. source
   b. destination
   c. embedded
   d. copied
6. This is the name of the program that receives the embedded data.
   a. copied
   b. destination
   c. embedded
   d. source
7. The ribbon from this program displays while an embedded object is being edited.
   a. source
   b. destination
   c. Windows Libraries
   d. embedded
8. Do this action to signal the end of editing an embedded object.
   a. Tap or click outside object
   b. Press Ctrl + Z
   c. Close the ribbon
   d. Tap or click inside object
9. Source data that is continuously updated should be inserted in a destination document using this integration method.
   a. Copy and paste
   b. Copy and embed
   c. Copy and link
   d. Copy and update
10. Open this dialog box to turn on automatic updates to source data.
    a. Embed
    b. Manage Links
    c. Paste Special
    d. Links

Crossword Puzzle

ACROSS

1 This program's ribbon is restored after editing embedded object

3 Ribbon tab to import and export in Access

5 Security warning button to use upon opening file with linked data

DOWN

2 Term for copied data for embedding or linking

3 Name for group of buttons for sending Access data to other programs

4 Dialog box to turn on automatic updates for linked data

Matching

Match the term with the statement or definition.

_______ 1. Create new Access table from worksheet

_______ 2. An option in Access dialog box to send copy of data to Excel

_______ 3. Button to use to embed copied data

_______ 4. Edit embedded object

_______ 5. Button that updates to most current source data

a. Paste button arrow

b. Double-tap or double-click object

c. Update Links

d. Export data with formatting and layout

e. Import & link group

Project 1 Importing and Exporting Data with Access and Excel

Individual

Deliverable: Database and worksheet with used books list

1. Start Access and open the **UsedBooks** database.
2. Use Save As to save a copy of the database as **C14-Project1-UsedBooks-Your Name** in a new folder named *Ch14* within ChapterProjectsWork.
3. Enable Content in the copy of the database.
4. Import the Excel workbook named ***BookList*** from the Ch14 folder in Student_Data_Files using the option *Append a copy of the records to the table* [Books] at the Get External Data – Excel Spreadsheet dialog box. Do not save the import steps.

Note: Only two dialog boxes are required in the Import Spreadsheet Wizard when you use the Append option.

5. Open the Books table when the import is complete, review the datasheet, and then close the table.
6. Create a query in Design view adding the Books table and the Students table to the query and with the following fields in order:

Field Name	Table Name
BookID	Books
FName	Students
LName	Students
Title	Books
Author	Books
Condition	Books
AskPrice	Books
StopPrice	Books

7. Save the query as **BookList** and then run the query.
8. Review the query results datasheet and then close the query.
9. Export the BookList query to Excel, saving the workbook as **C14-Project1-ExportedBookList-Your Name** in the Ch14 folder within ChapterProjectsWork. Select the options to export data with formatting and layout information and to open the destination when the export is complete. Do not save the export steps.
10. Make the following changes to the worksheet in Excel:
    a. Change each occurrence of *Jane Doe* to your first and last names in the *First Name* and *Last Name* columns.
    b. Change the orientation to *Landscape*.
    c. Make sure all columns will fit on one page.
    d. Create a header with the sheet tab name at the top center of the page and a footer with your name at the bottom center of the page.
11. Save the revised workbook using the same name (**C14-Project1-ExportedBookList-Your Name**) and then close Excel.
12. Close the database and then close Access.
13. Submit the project to your instructor in the manner she or he has requested.

Project 2 Embedding Data with Word and Excel

Individual

Deliverable: Document with embedded tables from Excel

1. Start Word and open **StatsCounterTables**.
2. Use Save As to change the file name to **C14-Project2-StatsCounterTables-Your Name**, saving in the Ch14 folder within ChapterProjectsWork.

3. Start Excel and open **SocialMediaStats**.
4. Select and copy A4:B10
5. Switch to Word and position the insertion point at the left margin a double-space below the first paragraph. Use *Paste Special* from the Paste button arrow to open the Paste Special dialog box. Select *Microsoft Excel Worksheet Object* in the *As* list box and choose OK to embed the worksheet data.
6. Center the embedded worksheet cells.
7. Embed C4:D10 from the Excel worksheet, inserting the object a double-space below the last paragraph in the document.
8. Center the embedded worksheet cells.
9. Edit both embedded objects to display two decimal places after each percent value. ***Hint: Before ending editing of each embedded object, make sure the cells displayed in the editing window are only the cells that were copied.***
10. Add your name in a footer in the document.
11. Save the revised document using the same name (**C14-Project2-StatsCounterTables-Your Name**) and then close Word.
12. Close Excel. Tap or click No if prompted to save changes to the worksheet when closing Excel.
13. Submit the project to your instructor in the manner she or he has requested.

Project 3 Linking Data between Word and Excel

Individual

Deliverable: Document with linked Excel charts

1. Start Word and open **StatsCounterCharts**.
2. Use Save As to change the file name to **C14-Project3-LinkedStatsCounterCharts-Your Name**, saving in the Ch14 folder within ChapterProjectsWork.
3. Start Excel and open **SocialMediaStats**.
4. Use Save As to change the file name to **C14-Project3-LinkedSocialMediaStats-Your Name**, saving in the Ch14 folder within ChapterProjectsWork.
5. Select, copy, and link the *Global Market Share* pie chart to the Word document a double-space below the first paragraph. Select the option to link using the destination theme. Center the chart in the document.
6. Select, copy, and link the *United States Market Share* pie chart to the Word document a double-space below the last paragraph. Select the option to link using the destination theme. Center the chart in the document.
7. Turn on the option for each linked object to automatically update.
8. Add your name in a footer in the document.
9. Save the revised document using the same name (**C14-Project3-LinkedStatsCounterCharts-Your Name**) and then close the document.
10. Make the following changes to the data in the Excel worksheet:

Cell Address	Current Entry	New Entry
B5	72.4	64.4
D5	48.8	41.8
A6	StumbleUpon	Instagram
B6	7.9	15.9
C6	StumbleUpon	Instagram
D6	23.1	30.1

11. Save the revised workbook using the same name (**C14-Project3-LinkedSocialMediaStats-Your Name**) and then close Excel.
12. With Word active, open **C14-Project3-LinkedStatsCounterCharts-Your Name**, and choose Yes when prompted to update links. Save and close the document after updating links and exit Word.
13. Submit the project to your instructor in the manner she or he has requested.

Project 4 Embedding Excel Data in PowerPoint

Individual

Deliverable: PowerPoint presentation with embedded Excel data

1. Start PowerPoint and open **TopVacDestinations**.
2. Modify the presentation to resemble the one shown in Figure 14.1 using the following information:
   a. The tables on slide 2 and slide 3 are embedded from the Excel worksheet named ***VacDestinations***.
   b. Edit the embedded objects to appear as shown in Figure 14.1.
   c. Add slide 4 as a new slide.
   d. Add the clip art image shown on the title slide. Substitute a suitable alternative image if the one shown is not available.
3. Save the revised presentation as **C14-Project4-TopVacDestinations-Your Name**.
4. Close PowerPoint and Excel.
5. Submit the project to your instructor in the manner she or he has requested.

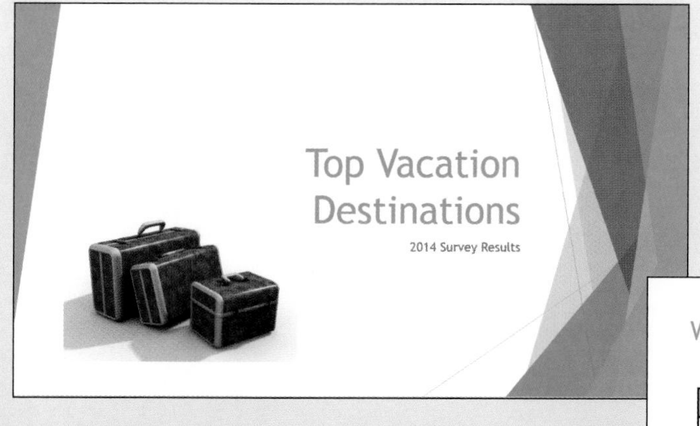

Worldwide Destinations

Destination	Percent
Barcelona	13
Beijing	11
Crete	10
Edinburgh	11
London	32
Paris	14
Zurich	10

United States and Canada Destinations

Destination	Percent
Las Vegas	16
Maui	18
Montreal	9
New York City	24
San Francisco	11
Toronto	14
Vancouver	9

2015 Survey

- Starts next month
- Results to be reported by the end of the year
- Expecting new destinations to appear from South America

Figure 14.1 Project 4 Vacation Destinations Survey Results presentation

Project 5 Sending Project Work to OneNote Notebook

Individual

Deliverable: New Page in Shared OneNote notebook

1. Start OneNote and open the MyProjects notebook created in Chapter 4, Project 4.
2. Make Integrating the active section and add a new page titled *Chapter 14 Projects*.
3. Send the following documents to OneNote selecting the Chapter 14 Projects page in the Integrating section in the MyProjects notebook. Skip any projects you were not assigned to complete.
   a. **C14-Project1-ExportedBookList-Your Name** from Excel.
   b. **C14-Project2-StatsCounterTables-Your Name** from Word.
   c. **C14-Project3-LinkedStatsCounterCharts-Your Name** from Word. Choose No when prompted to update links when you reopen this file.
   d. **C14-Project4-TopVacDestinations-Your Name** from PowerPoint. Send the slides formatted as handouts with four slides horizontal per page and with your name in a header. Save the changes when prompted when the file is closed.
4. Close your MyProjects notebook in OneNote and close OneNote.
5. Submit the project to your instructor in the manner she or he has requested.

Chapter 15

Using Windows Live SkyDrive and Other Cloud Computing Technologies

After successfully completing this chapter, you will be able to:

- Create a document in Microsoft Word Web App
- Create a worksheet in Microsoft Excel Web App
- Create a presentation in Microsoft PowerPoint Web App
- Edit a presentation in Microsoft PowerPoint Web App
- Upload and download files to and from SkyDrive
- Share documents in SkyDrive
- Create a document using Google Docs

Microsoft Office Web Apps are the web-based version of Word, Excel, PowerPoint, and OneNote that are accessed from SkyDrive. Web-based productivity software and storage technologies are called **cloud computing**. With cloud computing, all you need is a computer with a web browser to create and edit a document, worksheet, or presentation. With cloud computing technology such as Microsoft Office Web Apps, you do not need to install software on your PC or mobile device because all software and storage of documents is online. Google Docs is another popular web-based productivity suite. Both Microsoft and Google offer web-based productivity apps free to account holders.

In Chapter 3 you learned how to save a presentation to SkyDrive within PowerPoint. In this chapter you will learn to create and edit files using Microsoft Office Web Apps; upload, download, and share files in SkyDrive; and create a document using Google Docs from Google Drive.

Note: If you are using a tablet, consider completing this chapter using a USB or wireless keyboard because you will be typing longer passages of text. In this chapter, you will need to sign in with a Microsoft account and a Google account. If necessary, create a new account at each website. You may wish to check with your instructor before completing this chapter to confirm the required topics.

Creating a Document Using Microsoft Word Web App

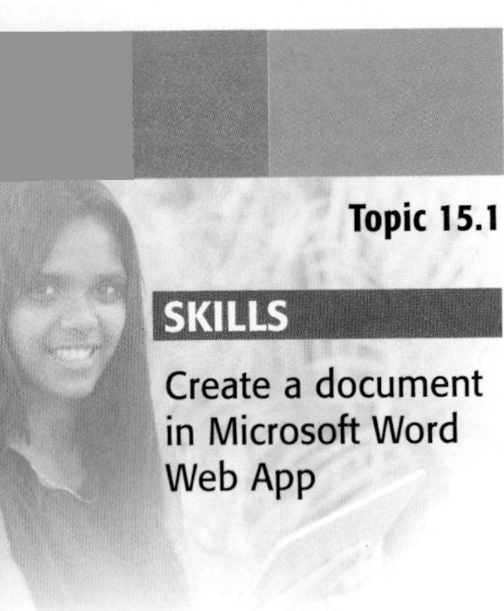

Topic 15.1
SKILLS
Create a document in Microsoft Word Web App

With Microsoft Office Web Apps, you create and edit documents within a web browser. **Microsoft Word Web App** is similar to the desktop version of Microsoft Word that you used in Chapters 6 and 7; however, Word Web App has fewer features than the desktop version. The program looks similar to the full-featured Microsoft Word, but you will notice that for some features, functionality within a browser environment is slightly different than the desktop version.

Note: Microsoft may update the Office Web Apps after publication of this textbook, in which case the information, steps, and/or screens shown here may vary.

1. Display the Desktop from the Windows 8 Start screen, or proceed to Step 2 if you are using Windows 7.
2. Tap or click the Internet Explorer icon in the Desktop taskbar.
3. Select the current text in the Address bar and then type **skydrive.com**.
4. If necessary, type your Microsoft account user name and password and then tap or click Sign in. Skip this step if you are already signed in to SkyDrive.

Once signed in, the SkyDrive window appears similar to the one shown in Figure 15.1.

oops!

Don't know your Microsoft account? If you have a hotmail.com or live.com email address, your email login is your Microsoft account; otherwise, tap or click the Sign up now link near the bottom right of the page and create a new account.

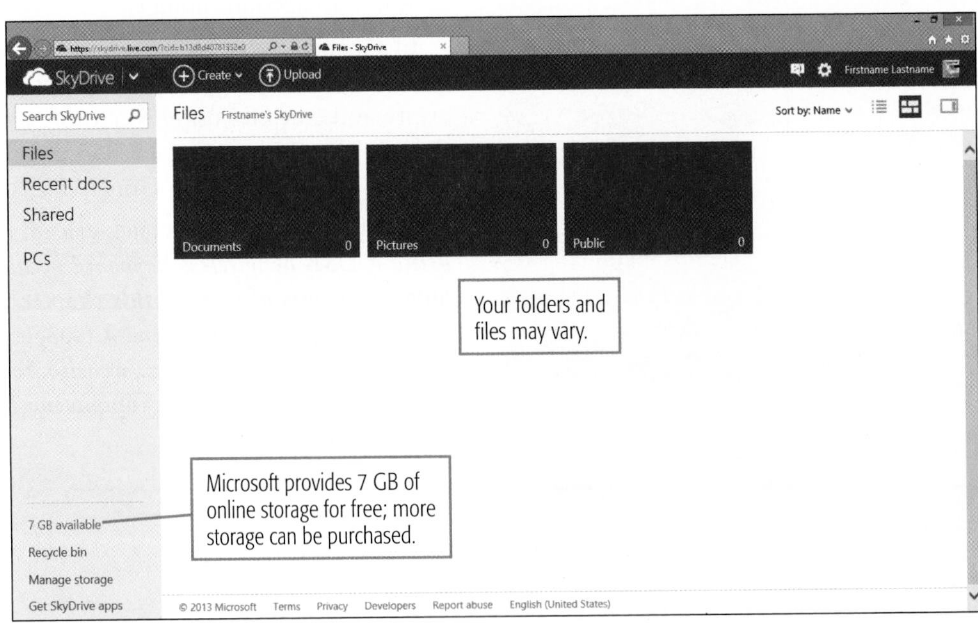

Figure 15.1 SkyDrive window for signed-in user

5 Tap or click Create next to SkyDrive near the top left of the window.

6 Tap or click Word document at the drop-down list.

7 Type **15.1-GreenComputing-Your Name** in the *New Microsoft Word document* text box and then tap or press Enter, or tap or click Create.

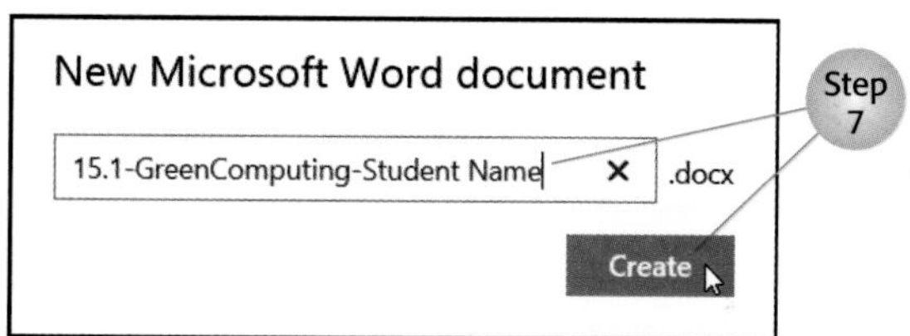

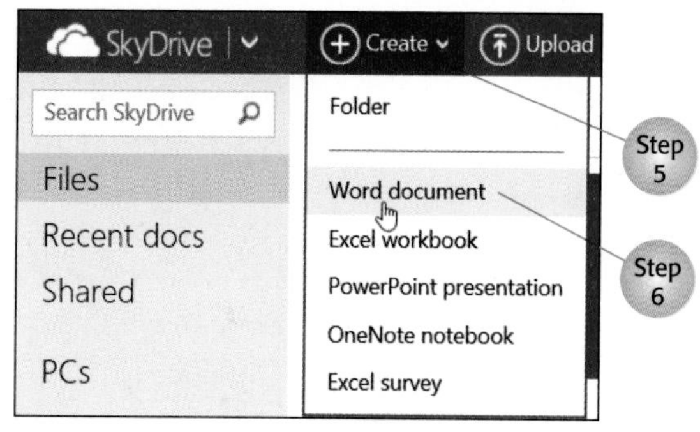

Word Web App documents are saved in the same file format as a desktop version of a Word document so that documents are transferable between editions.

Microsoft Word Web App launches, as shown in Figure 15.2.

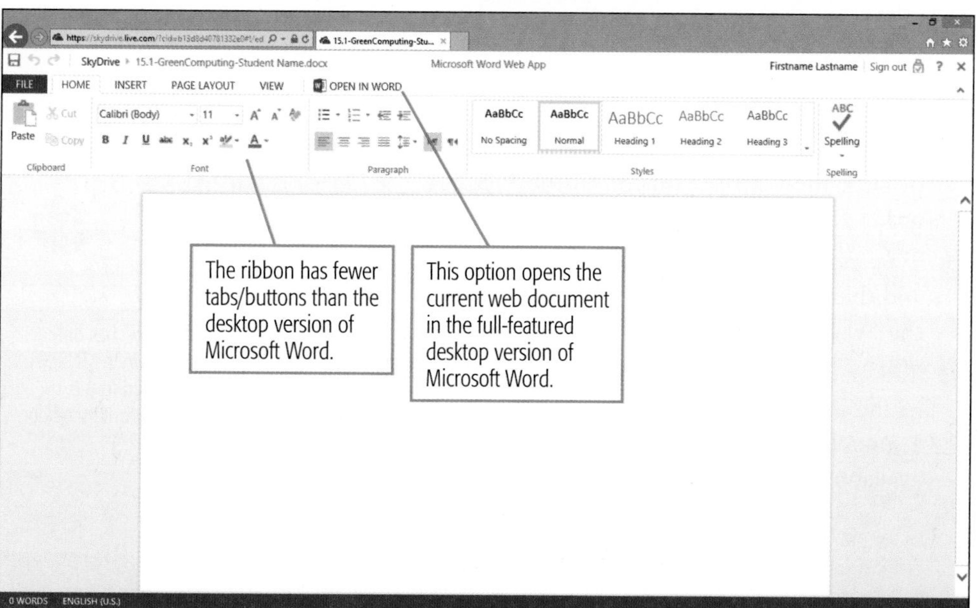

Figure 15.2 The Microsoft Word Web App window

8 Type the following text in the document window using all of the default settings:

What is Green Computing?

Green computing refers to the use of computers and other electronic devices in an environmentally responsible manner. Green computing can encompass new or modified computing practices, policies, and procedures. This trend is growing with more individuals and businesses adopting green computing strategies every year.

Strategies include the reduction of energy consumption of computers and other devices; reduction in use of paper, ink, and toner; and reuse, recycling, or proper disposal of electronic waste.

9 Proofread carefully and correct any typing errors that you find. If necessary, use the Spelling button in the Spelling group of the HOME tab to perform a spelling check of the document.

Use the same editing and formatting techniques in Word Web App as you learned in the desktop edition of Microsoft Word.

10 Center the title *What is Green Computing?*

11 Select all of the text in the document and change the font size to 12.

12 Select the two paragraphs of text and change the line spacing to 1.5.

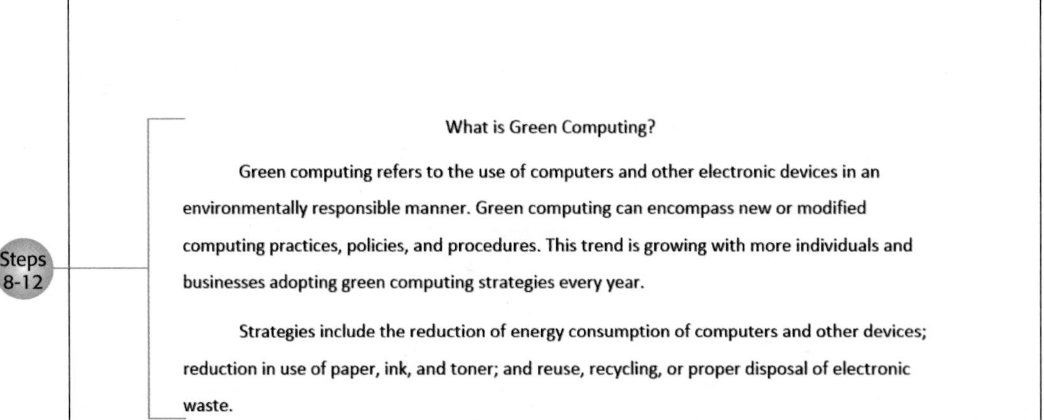

13 Position the insertion point at the end of the document on a new blank line.

14 Tap or click the INSERT tab and then tap or click the Clip Art button in the Pictures group.

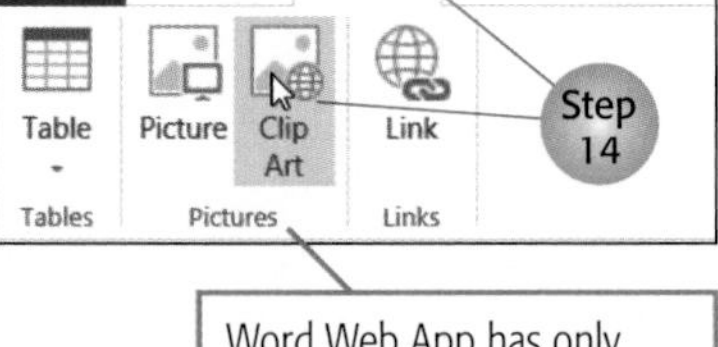

Word Web App has only three groups in the INSERT tab as opposed to the 10 found in the desktop edition of Word.

15 Type **recycling** in the *Insert Clip Art* text box and then tap or press Enter, or tap or click the Search button.

16 Tap or click the green recycling symbol picture shown in the image below and then tap or click Insert. Select a suitable alternative image if the one shown is not available.

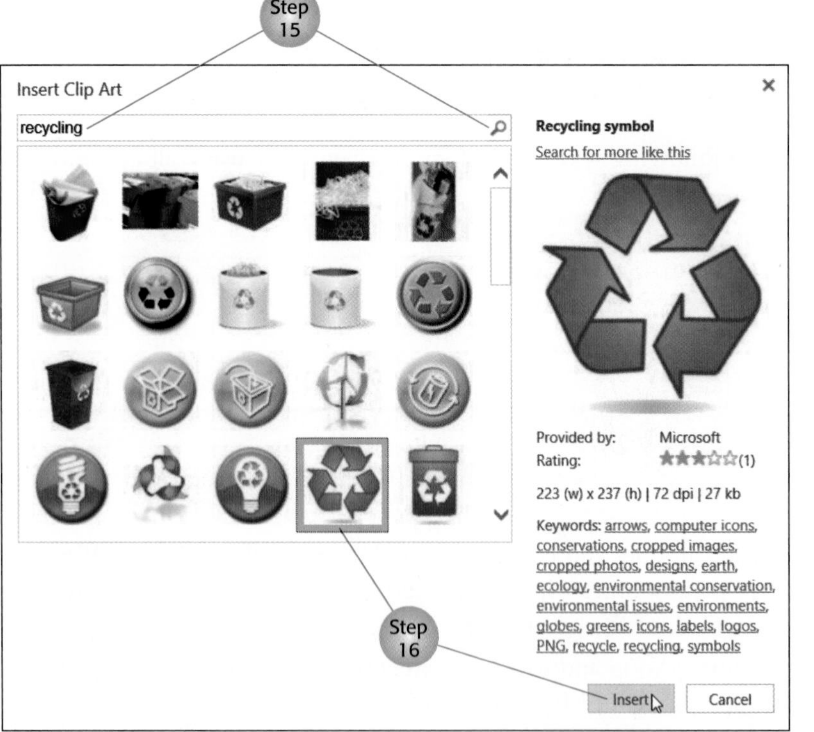

17 Tap or click the PICTURE TOOLS FORMAT tab.

18 Select the current value in the *Scale* text box, type **35**, and then tap or press Enter.

Notice that the clip art image does not have selection/resizing handles.

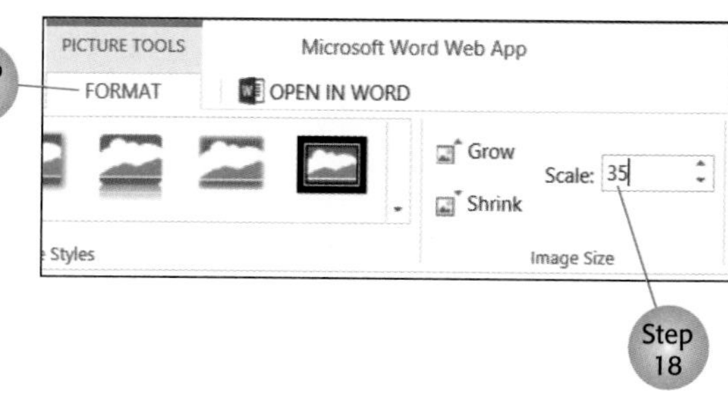

19 With the image still selected, tap or click the HOME tab and then tap or click the Center button in the Paragraph group.

20 Tap or click within the document text to deselect the image.

What is Green Computing?

Green computing refers to the use of computers and other electronic devices in an environmentally responsible manner. Green computing can encompass new or modified computing practices, policies, and procedures. This trend is growing with more individuals and businesses adopting green computing strategies every year.

Strategies include the reduction of energy consumption of computers and other devices; reduction in use of paper, ink, and toner; and reuse, recycling, or proper disposal of electronic waste.

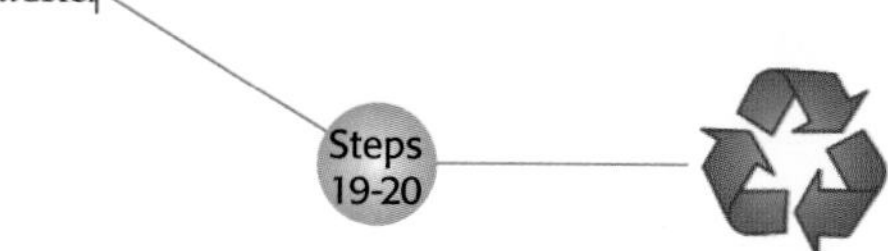

Switch to the desktop version of Word if you need access to the full set of picture formatting and editing tools.

21 Tap or click the FILE tab.

22 Tap or click Save at the Info tab Backstage view.

23 Tap or click the FILE tab and then tap or click Exit. Leave SkyDrive open for the next topic.

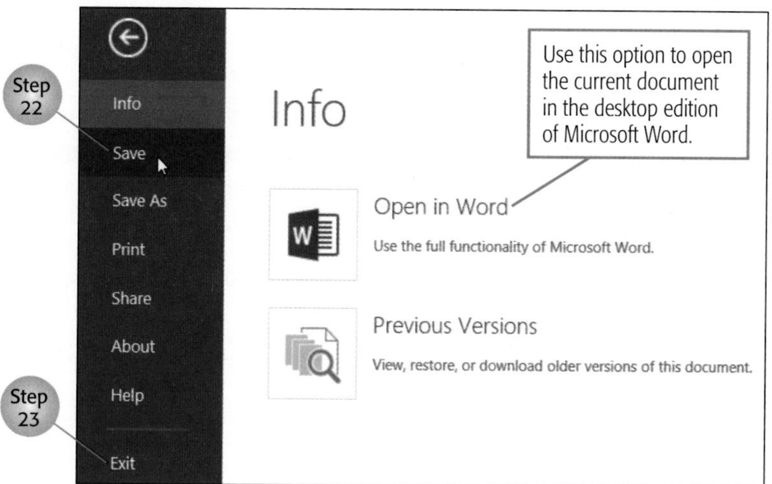

Create a printable PDF of the document at the Print tab Backstage view.

Create a Document in Word Web App

1. Open Internet Explorer.
2. Navigate to skydrive.com.
3. Sign in with Microsoft account.
4. Tap or click Create.
5. Tap or click Word document.
6. Type file name.
7. Tap or click Create.
8. Type, edit, and format document.
9. Save document.
10. Exit Word Web App.

A Word document tile is added to the *Files* list in SkyDrive. Additional options appear along the top of the SkyDrive window when a document tile is selected. You will use some of these options in later topics.

Document tile in SkyDrive *Files* list.

Topic 15.2

SKILLS

Create a worksheet in Microsoft Excel Web App

Creating a Worksheet Using Microsoft Excel Web App

Microsoft Excel Web App looks the same as the full-featured desktop edition of Excel; however, the ribbon contains fewer options, and functionality for some features will vary. You can create a basic worksheet in the web-based version of Excel, but for worksheets that need advanced formulas or editing, the desktop version of Excel is preferred.

1. With SkyDrive open, tap or click Create and then tap or click Excel workbook at the drop-down list.
2. Type **15.2-EnergySavings-Your Name** in the *New Microsoft Excel workbook* text box and then tap or press Enter, or tap or click Create.

Microsoft Excel Web App launches and opens a window similar to the window shown in Figure 15.3. Like Word, Excel Web App workbooks are saved in the same file format as the desktop version of Excel and are transferable between software editions.

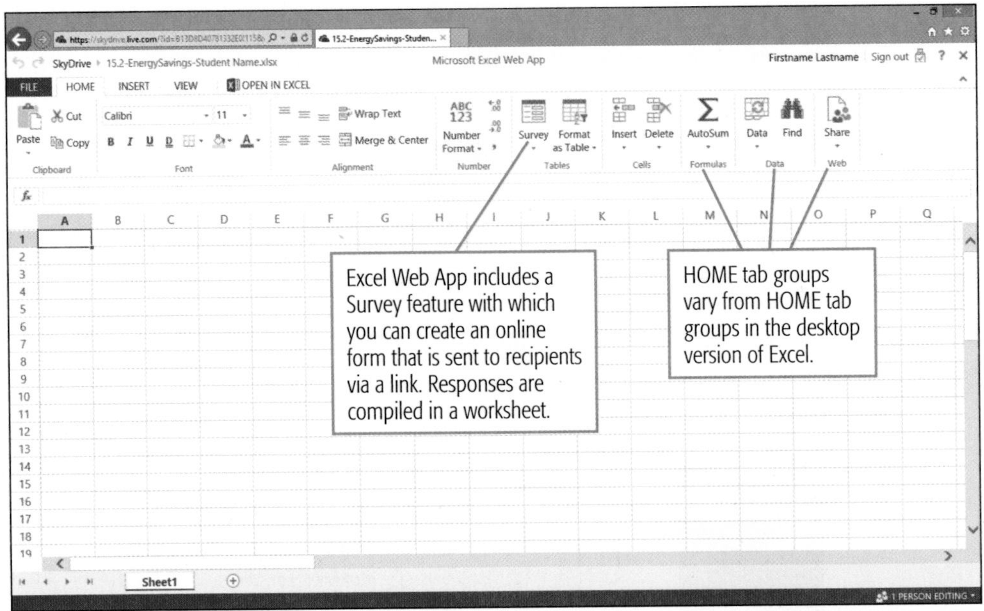

Figure 15.3 The Microsoft Excel Web App window. As with Word Web App, the Excel Web App ribbon has fewer tabs and buttons than the full-featured desktop version of Excel.

3. Type the labels and values in the cells as shown in the image below, substituting your first and last names for *Your Name* in A1.

	A	B	C	D	E	F	G	H	I	J	K
1	Your Name Energy Savings Calculator										
2											
3	Annual electricity cost to run computer continuously:										
4			Watts used		Kilowatts used		Cost per kilowatt hour (cents)			Total Cost	
5	Dell PC		200				10.9				
6											
7	Annual electricity cost to run computer only two hours per day (turned off or put in sleep mode when not in use):										
8											
9	Dell PC		200				10.9				
10											
11	Energy savings by turning off PC when not in use or using sleep mode:										

Step 3

4 Make E5 the active cell and type the formula **=(c5*24*365)/1000**.

The formula multiplies the watts used by a PC running continuously 24 hours per day, 365 days per year, and then divides the result by 1000 to convert watts to kilowatts.

5 Make J5 the active cell and type the formula **=e5*(g5/100)**.

The cost per kilowatt hour in G5 is divided by 100 to convert 10.9 to a decimal value representing cents.

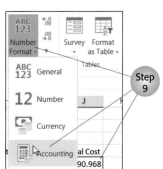

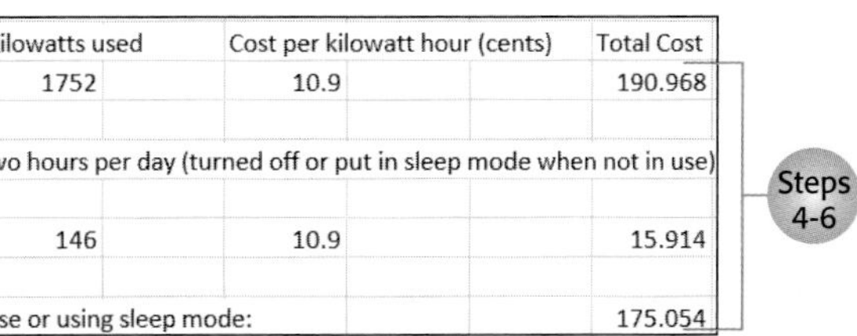

Kilowatts used	Cost per kilowatt hour (cents)	Total Cost
1752	10.9	190.968
two hours per day (turned off or put in sleep mode when not in use)		
146	10.9	15.914
use or using sleep mode:		175.054

Steps 4-6

6 Type the remaining formulas in the cells indicated:

E9 **=(c9*2*365)/1000**
J9 **=e9*(g9/100)**
J11 **=j5-j9**

7 Select A1:J1 and merge and center the worksheet title.

8 Bold the worksheet title and change the font size to 12.

9 Select J5, tap or click the Number Format button in the Number group of the HOME tab, and then tap or click *Accounting* at the drop-down list.

Step 9

10 Apply the Accounting Number format to J9 and J11.

11 With J11 the active cell, tap or click the Borders button in the Font group and then tap or click *Outside Borders* at the drop-down list.

Notice that fewer border options exist in Excel Web App.

12 With J11 still the active cell, apply bold and the *Dark Green* font color (sixth color in *Standard Colors* section).

	A	B	C	D	E	F	G	H	I	J
1	Your Name Energy Savings Calculator									
2										
3	Annual electricity cost to run computer continuously:									
4			Watts used		Kilowatts used		Cost per kilowatt hour (cents)			Total Cost
5	Dell PC		200		1752		10.9			$ 190.97
6										
7	Annual electricity cost to run computer only two hours per day (turned off or put in sleep mode when not in use):									
8										
9	Dell PC		200		146		10.9			$ 15.91
10										
11	Energy savings by turning off PC when not in use or using sleep mode:									$ 175.05

Formatted worksheet after Steps 7 to 12 completed.

13 Proofread carefully and correct any typing errors that you find.

14 Tap or click the FILE tab and tap or click Exit. Leave SkyDrive open for the next topic.

An Excel workbook tile is added to the *Files* list in SkyDrive.

Workbook tile in SkyDrive Files list.

Create a Workbook in Excel Web App

1. Open Internet Explorer.
2. Navigate to skydrive.com.
3. Sign in with Microsoft account.
4. Tap or click Create.
5. Tap or click Excel workbook.
6. Type file name.
7. Tap or click Create.
8. Type cell entries and format worksheet.
9. Exit Excel Web App.

Changes to the worksheet are saved automatically to the workbook in SkyDrive.

Display the worksheet in a printer-friendly format in a separate browser window from which you can print using the Print button at the Print tab Backstage view.

Topic 15.3

SKILLS

Create a presentation in Microsoft PowerPoint Web App

Creating a Presentation Using Microsoft PowerPoint Web App

A basic presentation that does not need to incorporate tables, charts, audio, or video can be created using **Microsoft PowerPoint Web App**. Other changes you will notice when working in the Web App is fewer animation and transition options, the inability to customize a slide show with timings or advanced animation options, and fewer views.

1. With SkyDrive open, tap or click Create and then tap or click PowerPoint presentation at the drop-down list.
2. Type **15.3-GreenComputingPres-Your Name** in the *New Microsoft PowerPoint presentation* text box and then tap or press Enter, or tap or click Create.

PowerPoint Web App launches and displays the Select Theme dialog box.

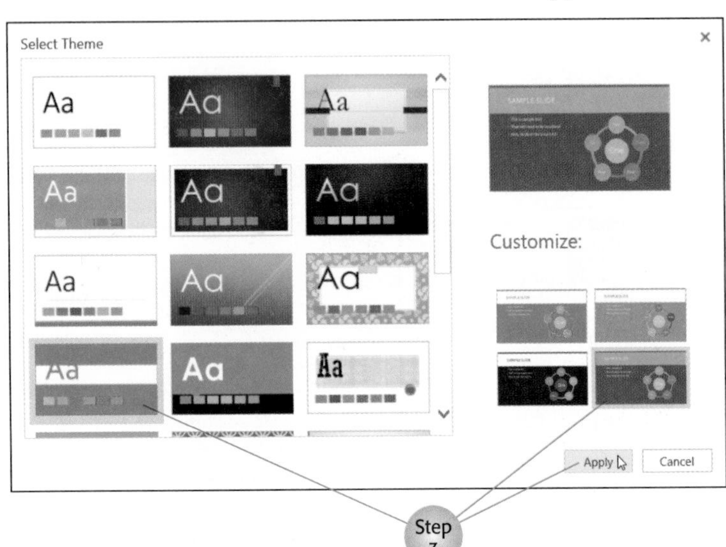

3. Tap or click *Banded* (first option in fourth row), tap or click *Variant 4* (last option), and then tap or click Apply.

A new presentation with the selected theme is started in the PowerPoint Web App window, as shown in Figure 15.4. As with Word and Excel, presentations are saved in the same file format and are transferable between PowerPoint Web App and the desktop version of PowerPoint.

Create a Presentation in PowerPoint Web App

1. Open Internet Explorer.
2. Navigate to skydrive.com.
3. Sign in with Microsoft account.
4. Tap or click Create.
5. Tap or click PowerPoint presentation.
6. Type file name.
7. Tap or click Create.
8. Enter and format slides.
9. Exit PowerPoint Web App.

PowerPoint Web App creates a printable PDF of full slides from the Print tab Backstage view.

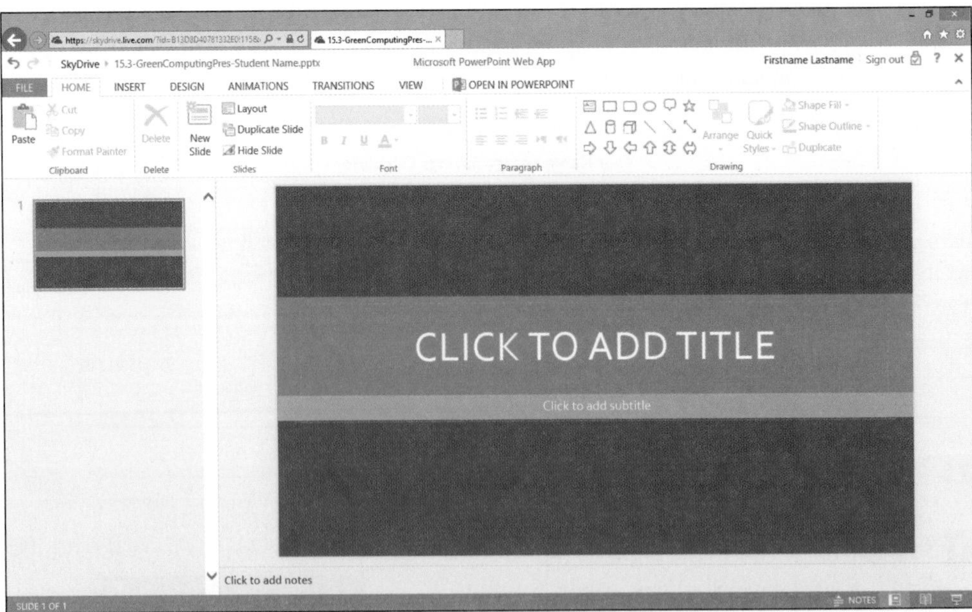

Figure 15.4 The Microsoft PowerPoint Web App window. PowerPoint Web App offers fewer options and does not have the SLIDESHOW and REVIEW tabs found in the desktop version of PowerPoint.

4 Type **Green Computing** as the slide title and your name as the subtitle.

Note that the font for this theme converts titles to all uppercase text.

5 Tap or click the New Slide button in the Slides group of the HOME tab.

6 At the New Slide dialog box, tap or click the *Title and Content* layout and then tap or click Add Slide.

Notice that content is limited to a SmartArt graphic, a picture, or clip art.

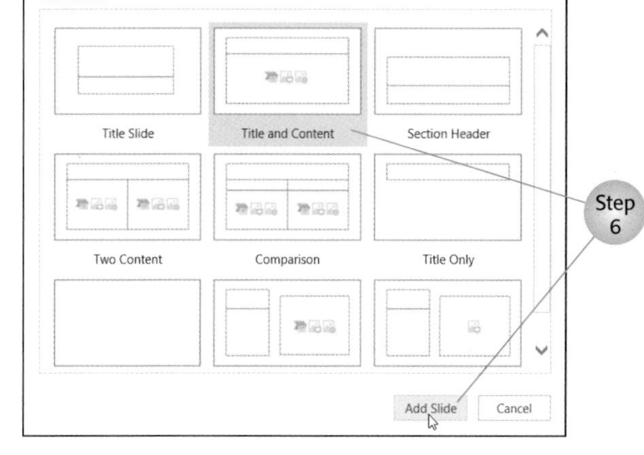

7 Type the text on Slide 2 as follows:

Slide title **What is Green Computing?**
Bulleted list **Use of computers and other electronic devices in an environmentally responsible manner including new or modified:**
computing practices
computing policies
computing procedures

8 Add another new slide with the *Title and Content* layout and type the text on Slide 3 as follows:

Slide title **Green Computing Strategies**
Bulleted list **Reduction in energy consumption**
Reduction in use of paper, ink, and toner
Reuse or recycling of devices
Proper disposal of e-waste

A slight delay may occur after typing or clicking outside a placeholder as the screen refreshes.

9 Make Slide 2 the active slide, tap or click the INSERT tab, and then tap or click the Clip Art button in the Images group.

10 Type **computers** in the *Clip Art* text box and tap or press Enter, or tap or click the Search button.

11 Slide or scroll down to the image shown at right, tap or click to select the image, and then tap or click Insert. (Select another image if the one shown is not available.)

12 Move the image to the approximate position as shown in the image at right.

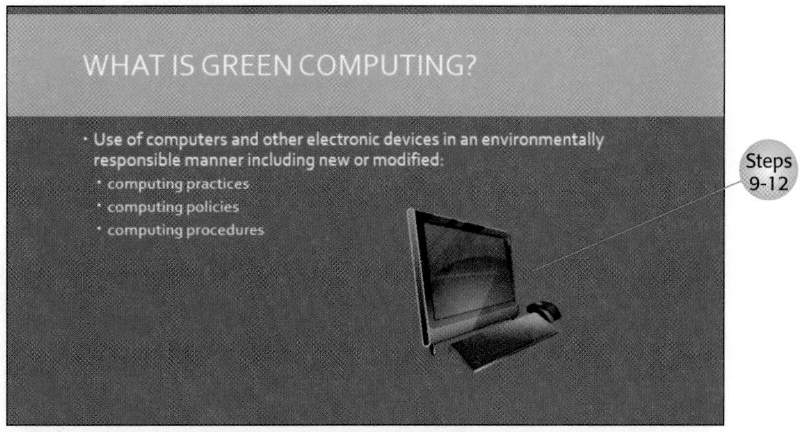

13 Make Slide 3 the active slide. Insert and position the clip art image at the approximate position as shown in the image at right. Search for the image by typing **recycling** in the *Clip Art* text box.

14 Tap or click the FILE tab and tap or click Exit. Leave SkyDrive open for the next topic.

A PowerPoint presentation tile is added to the *Files* list in SkyDrive.

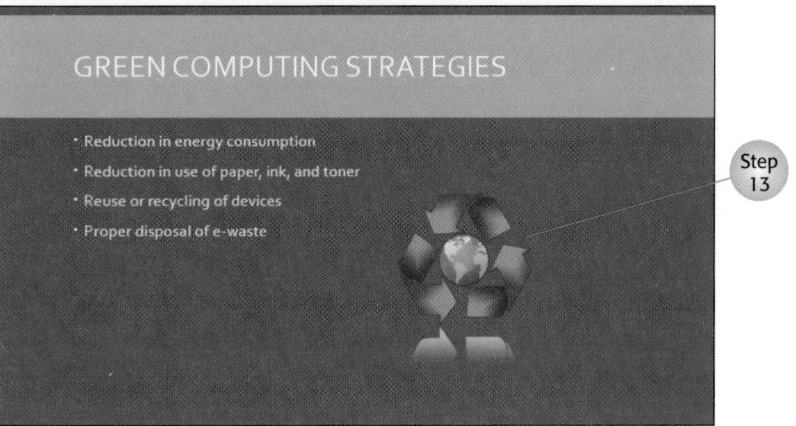

Topic 15.4

SKILLS

Edit a presentation in PowerPoint Web App

Editing a Presentation in Microsoft PowerPoint Web App

Open a presentation from SkyDrive to view the slides in Reading view. Switch to editing mode by choosing the full-featured version of PowerPoint or PowerPoint Web App from the EDIT PRESENTATION button near the top left of the Reading view window.

1. With SkyDrive open, tap or click to insert a check mark in the check box at the top right corner of the **15.3-GreenComputingPres-Your Name** tile, if the check box does not already have a check mark.

A check mark in the check box indicates the tile is selected. Additional options display along the top of the SkyDrive window when a tile is selected.

2. Tap or click Open. (Do *not* tap or click the down-pointing arrow next to *Open*.)

The presentation opens in Reading view, as shown in Figure 15.5.

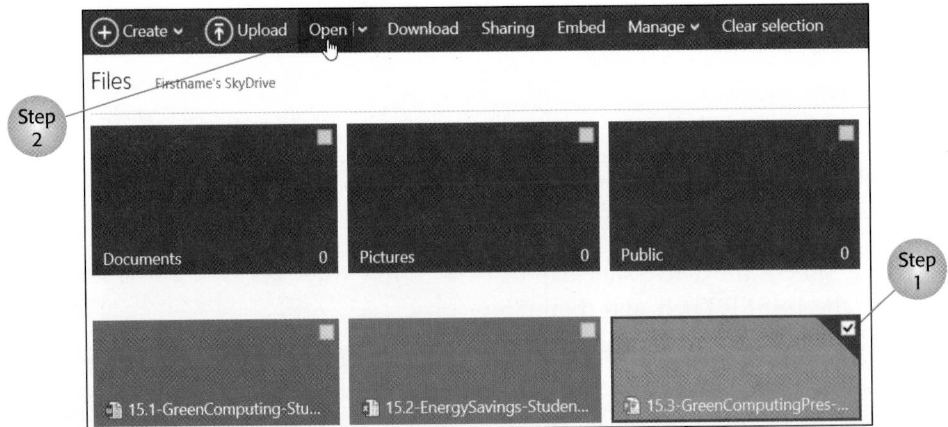

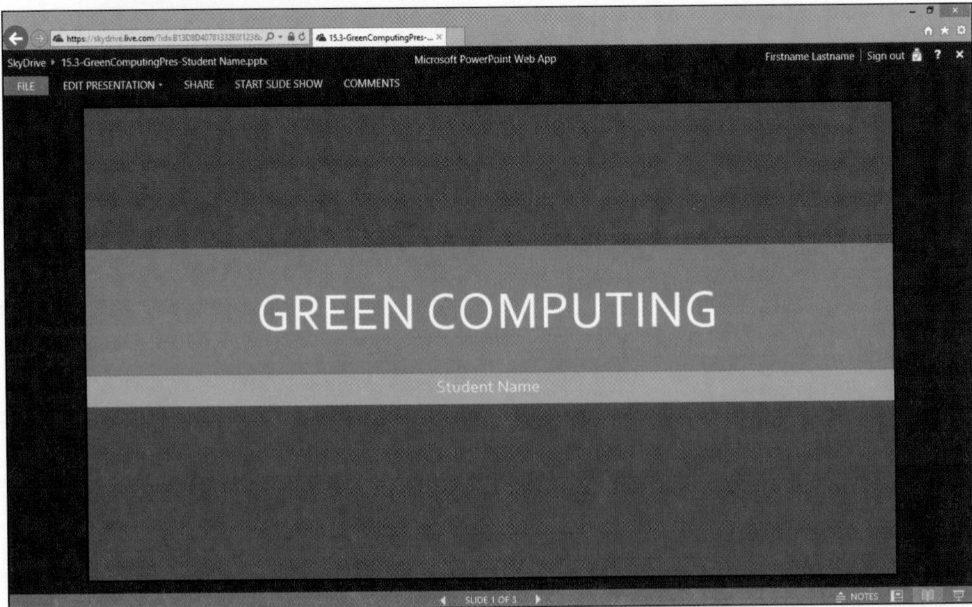

Figure 15.5 A presentation displays in Reading view in the PowerPoint Web App when opened from SkyDrive.

3 Tap or click the Next Slide button (displays as right-pointing arrow) in the Status bar to view Slide 2 in the window.

4 Tap or click the Next Slide button again to view Slide 3.

5 Tap or click *EDIT PRESENTATION* and then tap or click *Edit in PowerPoint Web App*.

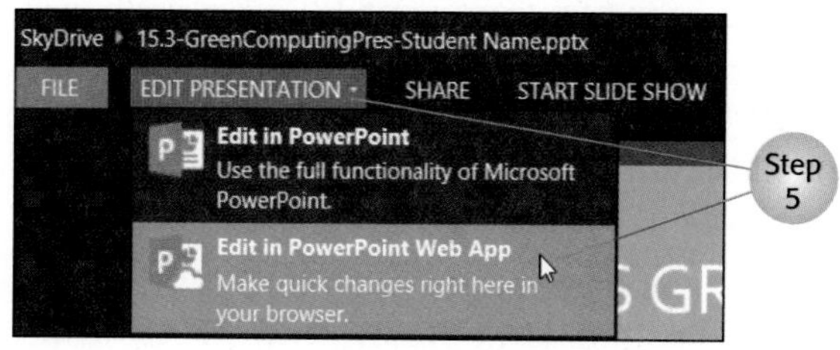

6 Make Slide 3 the active slide if necessary, and then type the following text on a new slide added to the end of the presentation using the *Title and Content* layout.

Slide title **Green Computing Example**

Bulleted list **A desktop PC can use up to 1700 kilowatt hours per year if left on continuously**

Turning off or putting the PC in sleep mode when not in use can save over 1600 kilowatt hours per year for average use of 2 hours per day

This strategy can save $175 per year for electricity cost at 10.9 cents per kilowatt hour

7 Search for the image shown below using the keyword *power strip*. Insert and move the clip art to the approximate position as shown. Substitute another image if the one shown in the image below is not available.

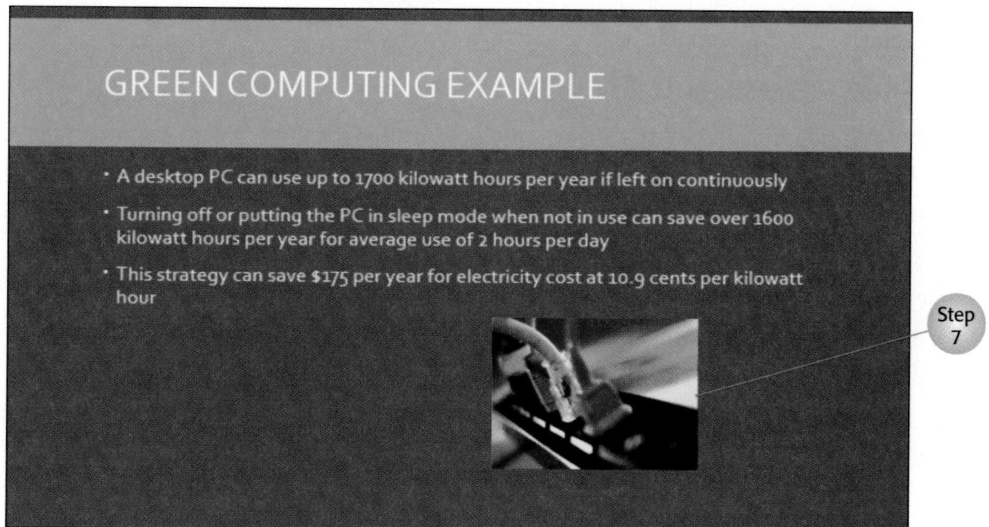

8 Tap or click the FILE tab and then tap or click Exit.

Edit a Presentation in PowerPoint Web App

1. Open Internet Explorer.
2. Navigate to skydrive.com.
3. Sign in with Microsoft account.
4. Select presentation tile.
5. Tap or click Open.
6. Tap or click EDIT PRESENTATION.
7. Tap or click *Edit in PowerPoint Web App*.
8. Edit as required.
9. Exit PowerPoint Web App.

ALTERNATIVE method

Open a document, workbook, or presentation by tapping or clicking the down-pointing arrow next to Open after selecting the tile and then choosing to open in the full-featured desktop version or the Web App version of Word, Excel, or PowerPoint.

Topic 15.5

SKILLS

Download files from SkyDrive

Upload files to SkyDrive

Move files to a folder on SkyDrive

oops!

No check box visible on tile? Move the mouse over the tile and a check box will appear.

Downloading and Uploading Files from and to SkyDrive

You can copy files from your PC or mobile device to SkyDrive for backup storage purposes; to access the files from another device instead of copying the files to a USB flash drive; or to share the files with other people. Conversely, you can download a file from SkyDrive to your local PC or mobile device to view or edit the file offline.

1. With SkyDrive open, tap or click to clear the check box for the **15.3-GreenComputingPres-Your Name** tile, and then tap or click to insert a check mark in the check box for the **15.1-GreenComputing-Your Name** Word document tile.
2. Tap or click Download at the top of the SkyDrive window.
3. Tap or click the down-pointing arrow on the Save button in the pop-up window at the bottom of Internet Explorer with the message asking if you want to open or save **15.1-GreenComputing-Your Name.docx** and then tap or click *Save as* at the pop-up list.

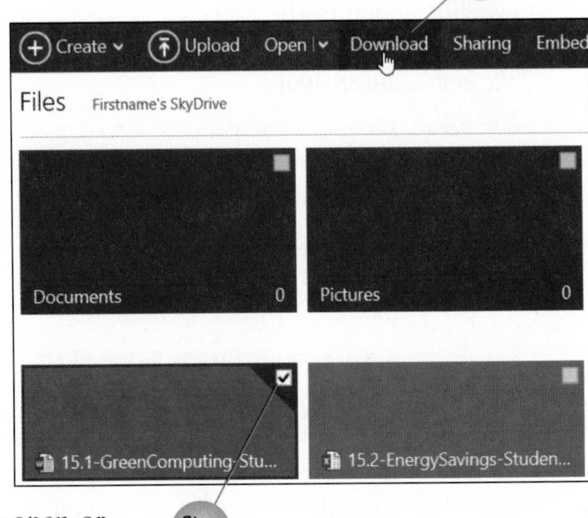

Do you want to open or save 15.1-GreenComputing-Student Name.docx (38.8 KB) from lncfqg.dm1.livefilestore.com? Open Save

Save
Save as
Save and open

Step 3

4. At the Save As dialog box, navigate to the CompletedTopicsByChapter folder on your USB flash drive, create a new folder named *Ch15*, double-tap or double-click the *Ch15* folder, and then tap or click Save.

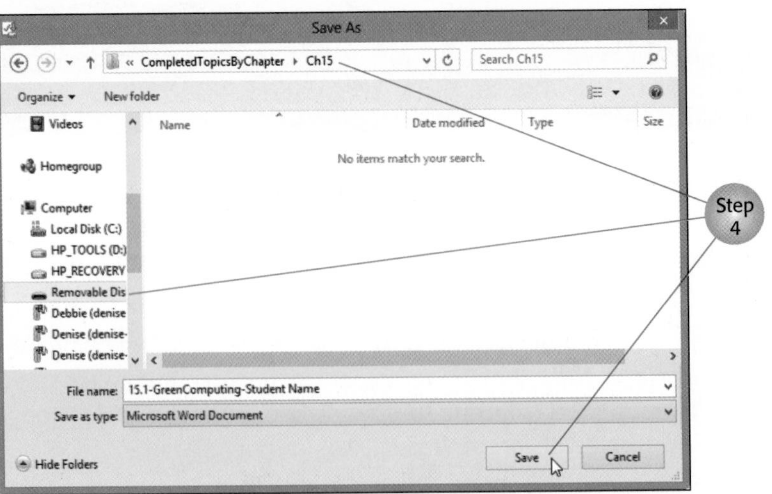

You can select and download multiple files in one operation. SkyDrive creates a zipped folder when more than one file is downloaded.

5 Close the pop-up window at the bottom of the Internet Explorer window.

6 Tap or click to clear the check mark in the check box for the **15.1-GreenComputing-Your Name** tile to deselect the tile.

7 Select and download the **15.2-EnergySavings-Your Name** workbook to the Ch15 folder by completing steps similar to those in Steps 1 through 6. Note that Ch15 will be the active folder at the Save As dialog box.

8 Select and download the **15.3-GreenComputingPres-Your Name** workbook to the Ch15 folder by completing steps similar to those in Steps 1 through 6. Note that Ch15 will be the active folder at the Save As dialog box.

In the next steps you will copy three pictures from your USB flash drive to your account storage at SkyDrive.

9 Tap or click Upload and then tap or click select them from your computer if you are using Windows 7; otherwise, proceed to Step 10.

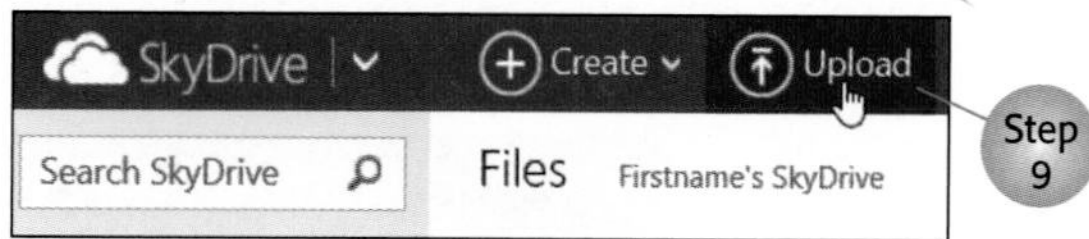

10 At the Choose File to Upload (Windows 8) or Open (Windows 7) dialog box, navigate to the Ch15 folder in Student_Data_Files, select the three files in the folder whose names begin with ***PaintedBunting***, and then tap or click Open.

The three files are uploaded to your account storage in SkyDrive. A progress message box appears at the bottom right of the window as the files are uploaded.

11 Select the three painted bunting picture tiles.

12 Tap or click Manage and then tap or click Move to at the drop-down list.

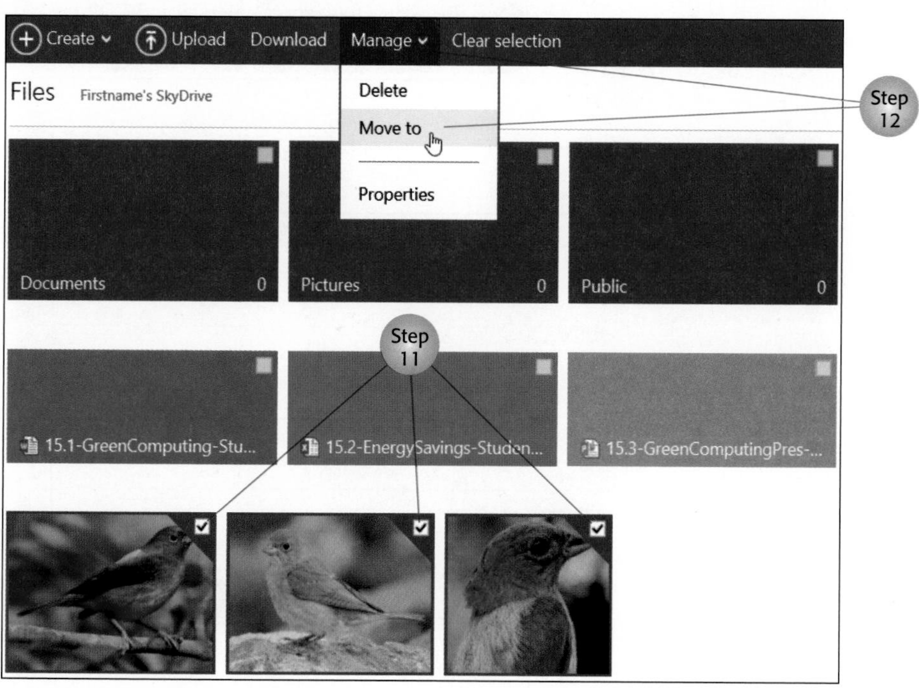

13 Tap or click *Pictures* in the folder list and then tap or click Move at the *The selected items will be moved to* dialog box. Leave SkyDrive open for the next topic.

Download a File from SkyDrive

1. Sign in to SkyDrive.
2. Select tile.
3. Tap or click Download.
4. Tap or click Save button arrow.
5. Tap or click *Save as*.
6. Navigate to drive and/or folder.
7. Tap or click Save.
8. Close pop-up window.

Upload a File to SkyDrive

1. Sign in to SkyDrive.
2. Tap or click Upload.
3. Navigate to drive and/or folder.
4. Select file(s) to upload.
5. Tap or click Open.
6. If necessary, move files to folder.

At the time of writing, Microsoft provides 7 GB of file storage for free at SkyDrive.

Files are uploaded to the active folder; consider displaying the Pictures folder and then uploading files instead of uploading first and then moving files.

Topic 15.6
SKILLS
Share a file on SkyDrive

Sharing a File on SkyDrive

SkyDrive is an excellent tool for collaborating on documents when working with a team. A team leader can create or upload documents to SkyDrive and then share the files with the team members who need them. An individual with shared access to a document receives an email with a link to the file. Changes to the file are made to the copy in SkyDrive so that only one document, worksheet, or presentation has to be managed. Sharing a file on SkyDrive is less cumbersome than sending a file as an email attachment and then trying to manage multiple versions of the same document.

Note: In this topic you will share a Word Web App document with a classmate. Check with your instructor for instructions on with whom you should share the Word document. If necessary, share the document with yourself by using an email address other than your Microsoft account.

1. With SkyDrive open, select the **15.1-GreenComputing-Your Name** document tile.
2. Tap or click Sharing.
3. Type the email address for a classmate in the *To* text box.

   More than one email address can be entered at the *To* text box. As with email messages, use a semicolon to separate email addresses.
4. Tap or click in the message box and then type **Please make your changes to the file accessed from this link.**.
5. Tap or click Share.

You can share files with anyone with a valid email address—the recipient does not have to have a Microsoft account.

oops!

Security check requested? Sometimes a security check is required before sharing a file. If necessary, tap or click the link to the security check, type the characters you see in the box, and tap or click Continue. If necessary, close the Hotmail tab in Internet Explorer to return to SkyDrive. You may need to re-enter the information in Steps 3 through 5 a second time including tapping or clicking Share again.

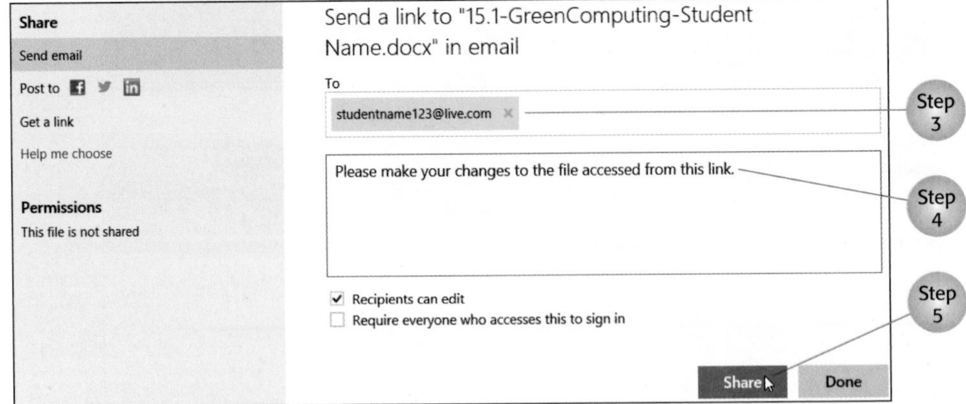

6 Tap or click Done when the classmate's name appears in the *Permissions* section.

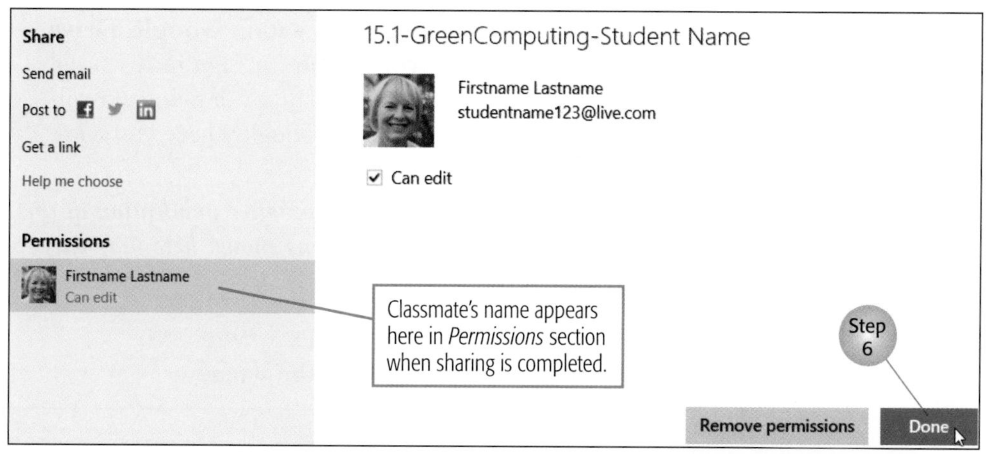

Share a File on SkyDrive

1. Sign in to SkyDrive.
2. Select tile.
3. Tap or click Sharing.
4. Type recipient's email address in *To* box.
5. Type message in message box.
6. Tap or click Share.
7. Tap or click Done.

7 Tap or click the down-pointing arrow next to SkyDrive.

8 Tap or click the Mail tile.

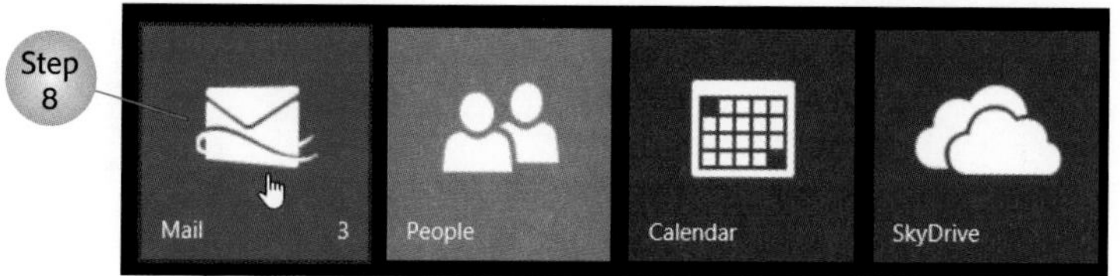

9 With *Inbox* the active mail folder, open the message received from a classmate with the subject *Student Name has shared a document with you.*

10 If a security warning appears at the top of the message window saying that links in the message have been blocked for your safety, tap or click the Show content link.

11 Tap or click the link to the file in the message window.

The file opens in Microsoft Word Web App.

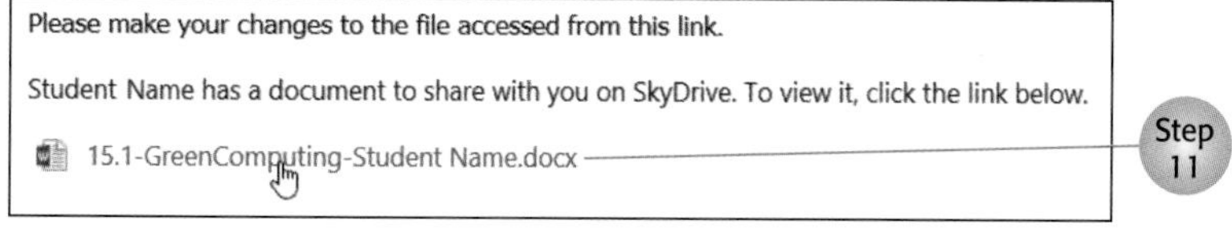

Please make your changes to the file accessed from this link.
Student Name has a document to share with you on SkyDrive. To view it, click the link below.
15.1-GreenComputing-Student Name.docx
Step 11

12 Tap or click FILE and then tap or click Exit to close the shared document.

13 Tap or click Shared in the left pane of SkyDrive to view the file details in the *Files shared with you* list.

14 Sign out of SkyDrive and close Internet Explorer.

oops!

No message? Check the email address that the classmate used to make sure the correct address was typed. If an address other than hotmail or live was used, you need to go to another mail program to find the message with the link. In that case, sign out of SkyDrive, launch your other mail program, and complete Steps 11 and 12. Note also that some mail programs may flag the message as Junk Mail. Check your Junk Mail folder if the message is not in your Inbox.

Topic 15.7
SKILLS
Create a document in Google Docs

Creating a Document Using Google Docs

Google Docs is the web-based productivity suite offered within **Google Drive** (Google's cloud storage service). With a Gmail account, you can sign in to Google Drive and create a document, presentation, spreadsheet, form, or drawing. Gmail accounts and web productivity apps are free to use. With Google Drive you can store up to 5 GB for free.

Note: Google may update Google Drive and/or Google Docs after publication of this textbook, in which case the information, steps, and/or screens shown here may vary.

oops!

Don't know your Google account? If you have a gmail.com email address, your email login is your Google account; otherwise, tap or click the Create an account for free link near the top left of the page to create a new account.

1. Start Internet Explorer from the Desktop.
2. Select the current text in the Address bar and then type **google.com**.
3. Tap or click the Sign in button near the top right of the window.
4. Type your Google account information and tap or click Sign in. Skip this step if you are automatically signed in when you go to the Google home page.
5. Tap or click Drive in the black bar at the top of the Google home page.

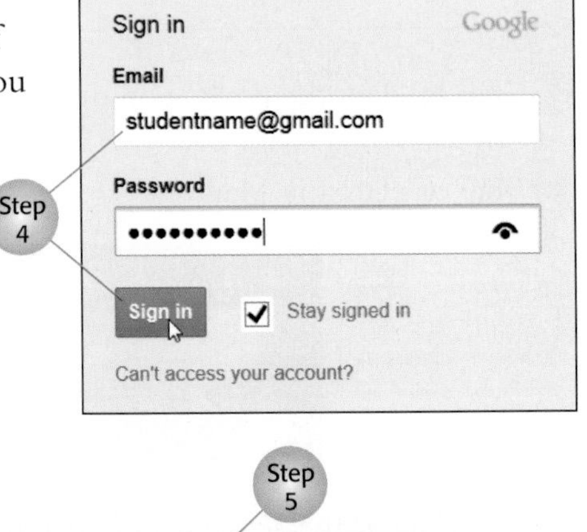

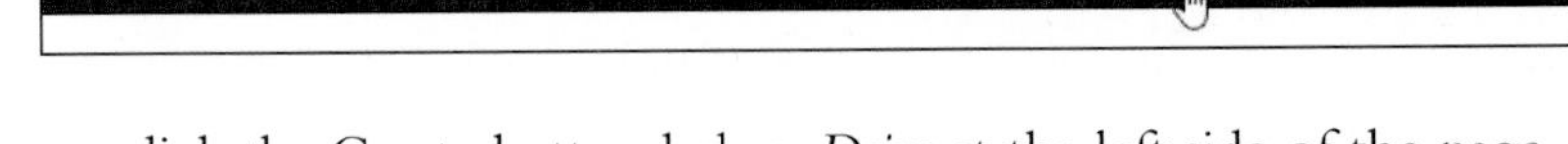

6. Tap or click the Create button below *Drive* at the left side of the page.
7. Tap or click Document at the drop-down list.

A document window opens similar to the one shown in Figure 15.6 on the next page.

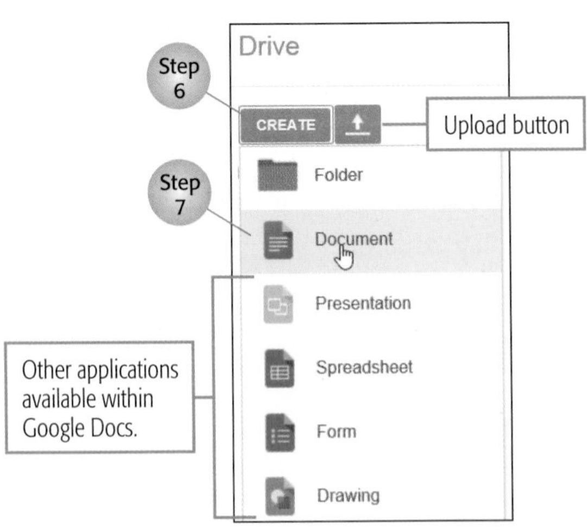

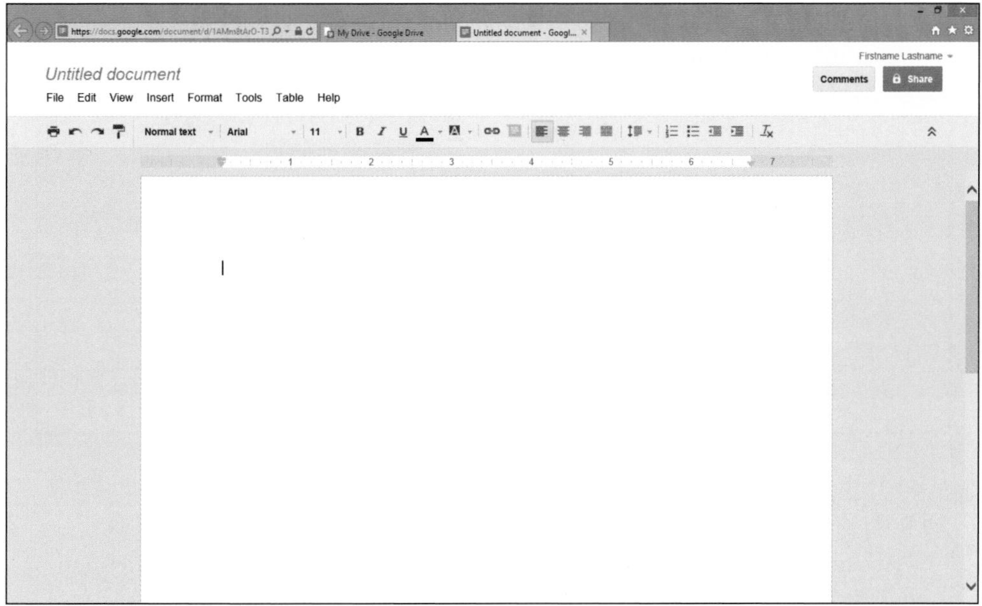

Figure 15.6 Google Docs document window. Google Docs automatically saves changes every few seconds to a document named *Untitled document.*

8 Type the following text in the document window using all of the default settings:

What is Cloud Computing?

Cloud computing refers to a delivery model of software and file management using web-based service providers where all resources are online. Consumers of cloud computing services access software and files via a web browser. Some cloud-based services are free, with fees charged to access more storage or software features. (Tap or press Enter twice after the period.)

You can upload and view a Word document in Google Docs.

9 Tap or click the File menu and then tap or click Rename at the drop-down list.

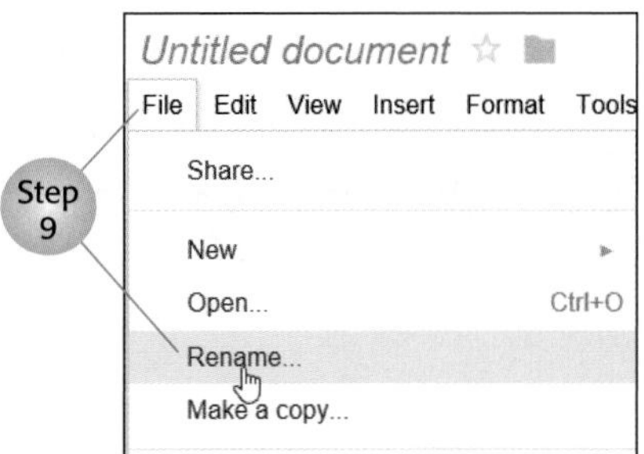

10 Type **15.7-CloudComputing-Your Name** in the *Enter a new document name* text box and then tap or click OK.

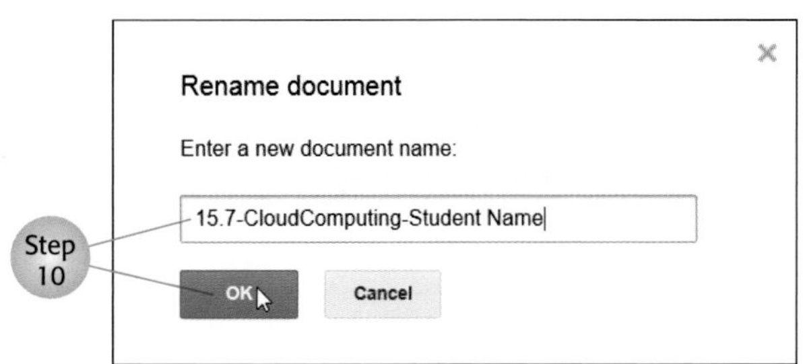

oops!

Using Touch? On the touch keyboard, hold down the Shift key while you use the right arrow key to select text, or use an external mouse. Touch selection gestures for Microsoft apps do not apply in Google Docs.

11 Select the title text *What is Cloud Computing?* and tap or click the Center align button in the toolbar.

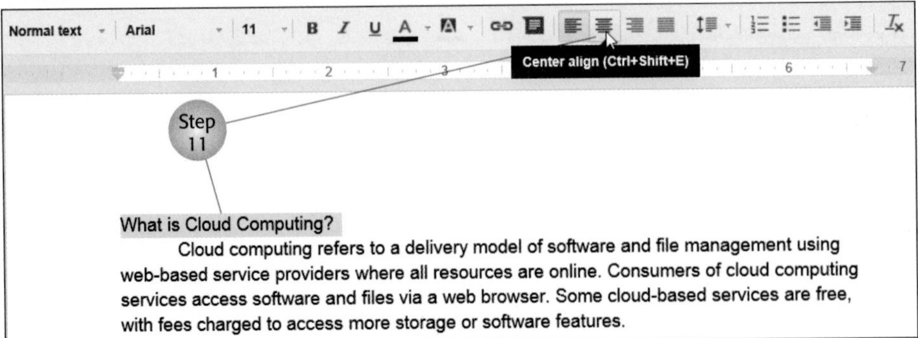

12 With the title text still selected, tap or click the Bold button, tap or click the Font Size button arrow, and then tap or click *14* at the drop-down list.

13 Select the paragraph text, tap or click the Line spacing button, and then tap or click *1.5* at the drop-down list.

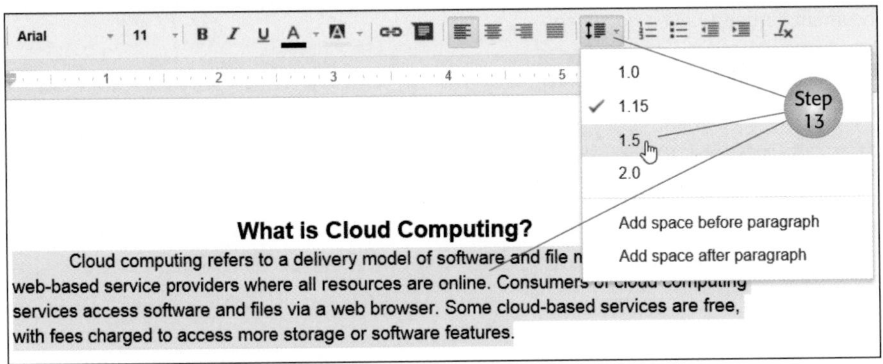

14 Deselect the text and position the insertion point on the blank line at the bottom of the document.

15 Tap or click the Insert menu and then tap or click Image at the drop-down list.

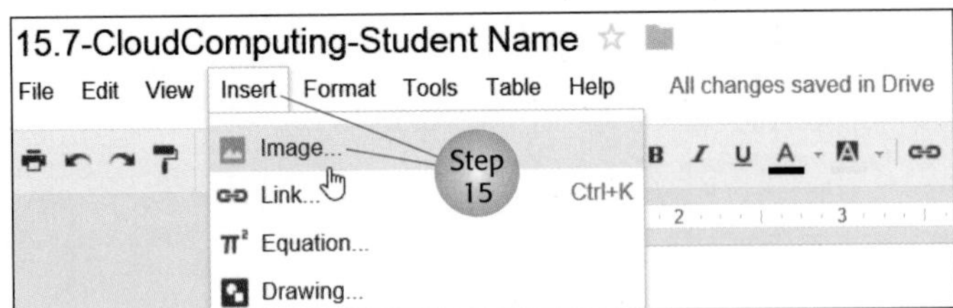

16 Tap or click the Choose an image to upload button in the middle of the Insert Image dialog box.

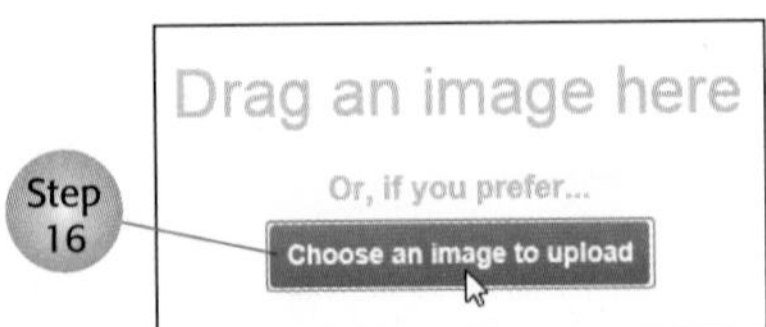

17 At the Choose File to Upload dialog box, navigate to the Ch15 folder in Student_Data_Files and then double-tap or double-click the file named ***Cloud-computing***.

18 Tap or click to select the image, resize the image using the resizing handles to approximately 2 inches wide by 1.5 inches tall, and then tap or click the Center align button.

19 With the image still selected, tap or click the Insert menu and tap or click Footnote at the drop-down list.

20 Type **Cloud computing image courtesy of Wikimedia Commons.** in the Footnote pane.

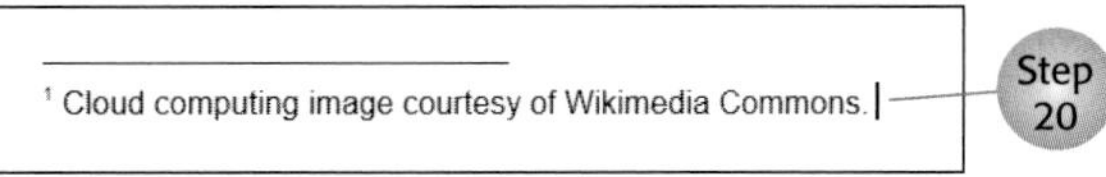

[1] Cloud computing image courtesy of Wikimedia Commons.
Step 20

21 Slide or scroll up to the top of the page.

22 If necessary, tap or click at the end of the paragraph to deselect the image.

23 Close the tabbed window for the document to return to Google Drive.

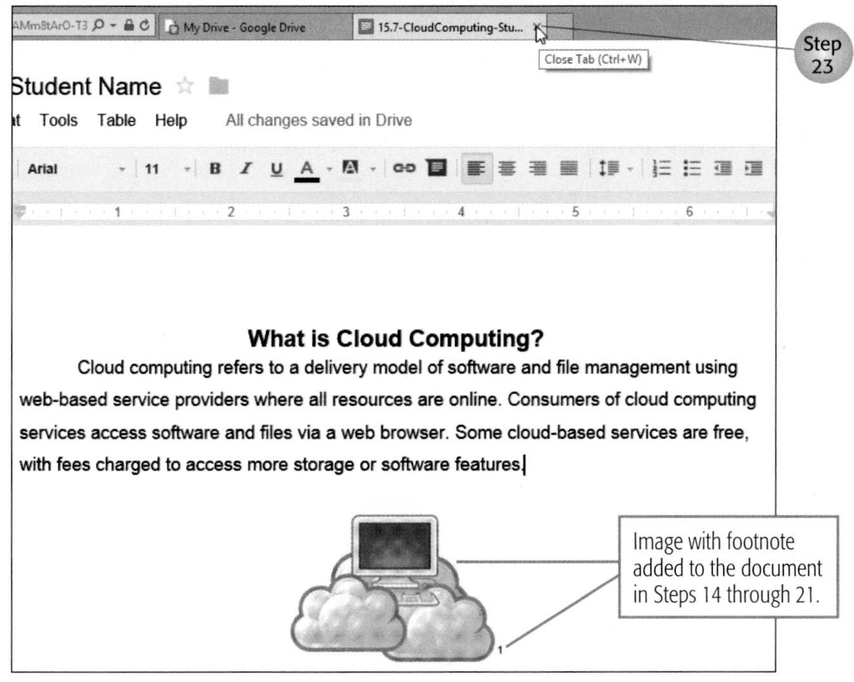

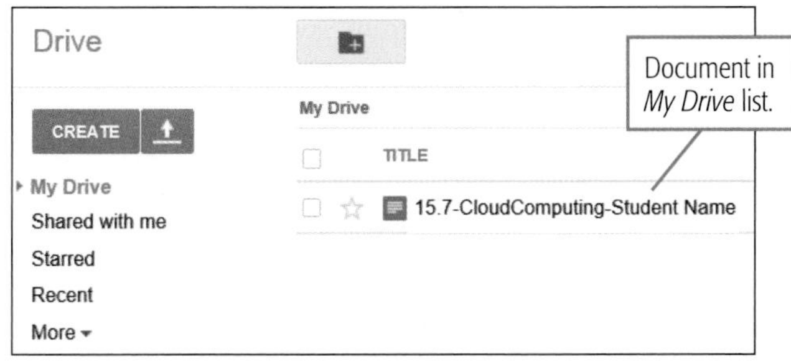

Image with footnote added to the document in Steps 14 through 21.

24 Tap or click your account icon or name near the top right of the window and then tap or click Sign out.

25 Close the Internet Explorer window.

ALTERNATIVE method

You can also navigate to Google Drive by typing the URL **drive.google.com** or **docs.google.com**.

oops!

Image won't move to Center? Make sure *Fixed position* below the image is displayed in blue text. If not, tap or click *In line with text* and then try the Center button again.

Quick STEPS

Create a Document in Google Drive

1. Open Internet Explorer.
2. Navigate to google.com.
3. Sign in with Google account.
4. Tap or click Create.
5. Tap or click Document.
6. Type, edit, and format document.
7. Tap or click File.
8. Tap or click Rename.
9. Type document name.
10. Tap or click OK.
11. Close window tab.

App Tip

Google Docs can be shared with others by selecting the file in the Google Drive list and using the Share button located above the file list.

Check This Out

zoho.com

Go here to check out another popular web-based productivity suite. Register for a free account at Zoho to access several web-based applications including Writer (word processor), Show (presentation), and Sheet (spreadsheet).

Concepts Review

Topic	Key Concepts	Key Terms
Creating a Document Using Microsoft Word Web App	Cloud computing is a service provided by companies in which all software and storage resources are provided online. Cloud computing applications and files are accessed from a web browser. Microsoft Word Web App is the web-based version of Word accessed from SkyDrive. Sign in to SkyDrive with a Microsoft account and use Create to start a new document in Microsoft Word Web App. Documents created in Word Web App are saved in the same file format as the desktop version of Word, meaning files can be transferred between editions. Word Web App has fewer ribbon tabs and options than the desktop version of Word, and some features' functions will vary slightly.	Cloud computing Microsoft Word Web App
Creating a Worksheet Using Microsoft Excel Web App	Microsoft Excel Web App is suited for basic worksheets; use the desktop version of Excel for worksheets that need advanced formulas or editing. Worksheets created in Excel Web App are saved in the same file format as the desktop version of Excel, meaning files can be transferred between editions. Like Word Web App, Excel Web App has fewer features than the desktop version and some functionality may vary.	Microsoft Excel Web App
Creating a Presentation Using Microsoft PowerPoint Web App	Use Microsoft PowerPoint Web App to create a presentation that does not need tables, charts, audio, video, or advanced animation or transition effects. Presentations created in PowerPoint Web App are saved in the same file format as the desktop version of PowerPoint, meaning files can be transferred between editions. When PowerPoint Web App is launched, you first select the presentation theme. Graphic content in slides is limited to SmartArt graphics, pictures, or clip art.	Microsoft PowerPoint Web App
Editing a Presentation in Microsoft PowerPoint Web App	To open a presentation, select a tile and use Open from SkyDrive. A presentation opens in Reading view from SkyDrive. Use the EDIT PRESENTATION button and choose to open the presentation in either the desktop version of PowerPoint or PowerPoint Web App.	
Downloading and Uploading Files from and to SkyDrive	Select tiles for files that you want to download or manage. Use Download to copy a file from SkyDrive to a folder on your local PC or mobile device. Use Upload to copy a file from your PC or device to your SkyDrive storage. Manage provides options to move or delete selected files.	
Sharing a File on SkyDrive	SkyDrive can be used to collaborate with team members by sharing one copy of a file among several users. Select a tile and choose Sharing to type the email address(es) for the individual(s) with whom you want to share a file. Individuals receive an email message with a link to the shared file on SkyDrive.	

Topic	Key Concepts	Key Terms
Creating a Document Using Google Docs	The web-based productivity suite offered by Google is called Google Docs. Sign in to Google with a Gmail account, tap or click Drive, and then tap or click the Create button to start a document, presentation, spreadsheet, form, or drawing. Google Drive is Google's online file storage service. Google Docs saves changes automatically every few seconds to an untitled document. Use the Rename option from the File menu to assign a name to the untitled document. Use options from the Menu bar drop-down lists and toolbar to add elements, edit, and format a document.	Google Docs Google Drive

Multiple Choice

1. Tap or click this option at SkyDrive to start a new document using Word Web App.
   a. Files
   b. Create
   c. Document
   d. New
2. The ribbon in Word Web App is exactly the same as the ribbon in the desktop version of Word.
   a. True
   b. False
3. Word and Excel Web App documents and spreadsheets are transferable to the desktop versions of Word and Excel.
   a. True
   b. False
4. Excel Web App is suited to a worksheet that needs advanced formulas and editing techniques.
   a. True
   b. False
5. Which of the following content can *not* be added to a slide using PowerPoint Web App?
   a. Audio
   b. SmartArt
   c. Pictures
   d. Clip Art
6. PowerPoint Web App contains the same set of transition options as the desktop version of PowerPoint.
   a. True
   b. False
7. Use this option in SkyDrive to view a selected presentation.
   a. Create
   b. Preview
   c. View
   d. Open
8. A presentation opens in this view from SkyDrive.
   a. Normal view
   b. Reading view
   c. Slide Show view
   d. Notes view
9. Use this option in SkyDrive to create a copy of a document created in Word Web App in a folder on your PC.
   a. Manage
   b. Upload
   c. Download
   d. New
10. Use this option to move a selected tile to a folder in SkyDrive.
    a. New
    b. Upload
    c. Download
    d. Manage
11. Use this option to send a link to someone else that lets him or her view a file you have stored on SkyDrive.
    a. Move to
    b. Manage
    c. Sharing
    d. Create

12. A link to a file created by someone else is sent to you via this option.
    a. Instant message
    b. Facebook message
    c. Twitter message
    d. Email message
13. Google Docs are accessed from this Google tool.
    a. Google Mail
    b. Google Presentations
    c. Google Images
    d. Google Drive
14. A Google account mostly likely ends with this domain.
    a. gmail.com
    b. hotmail.com
    c. live.com
    d. gmail.net

Crossword Puzzle

1 2 3 4 5 6 7 8 9

ACROSS

4 Create copy of file from SkyDrive to PC
5 Feature to let multiple people view or edit the same document
6 Selection you make at first dialog box in PowerPoint Web App
7 Create copy of file from PC to SkyDrive
8 Use this option to view slides in Reading view
9 Workbook tile displays in this SkyDrive list

DOWN

1 Sign in to this website to find Microsoft Office Web apps
2 Name for web-based version of Microsoft Word
3 Web-based productivity suite from Google

Matching

Match the term with the statement or definition.

_______ 1. Where to find Word Web App
_______ 2. Start new document, workbook, or presentation
_______ 3. Choose a theme
_______ 4. Check box at top right corner of tile
_______ 5. Store a copy of a file from your PC at SkyDrive
_______ 6. Collaboration tool
_______ 7. Gmail account

a. PowerPoint Web App
b. Upload
c. SkyDrive
d. Sharing
e. Create
f. Google Docs
g. Select tile

Project 1 Creating a Document with Word Web App

Individual

Deliverable: Document in SkyDrive

1. Start Internet Explorer and sign in to SkyDrive.
2. Create a new Word document in Microsoft Word Web App with the file name **C15-Project1-Office365-Your Name**, and then type the following text in a new document in Microsoft Word Web App using the default settings.

   What is Office 365?

   Office 365 is the subscription-based model for purchasing Office 2013. Office 365 Home Premium offers home users Office 2013 applications from the cloud for up to five PCs or Macs for $99 per year. At SkyDrive, registered users have access to Web Apps for Word, Excel, PowerPoint, and OneNote. According to Microsoft, the additional benefits included with an Office 365 subscription are:

   - **Web Apps for Outlook, Publisher, and Access**
   - **An extra 20 GB of storage at SkyDrive for a total of 27 GB when added to the free 7 GB offered to all users**
   - **60 Skype world minutes per month**

   Because Office 365 is hosted by Microsoft as a cloud computing technology, the software will always be up to date and accessible from any device with an Internet connection. Office 365 is ideal for consumers with multiple devices who want to view or edit documents from any location at any time.

   Purchasing an Office 365 subscription is a new option that home users may want to consider. Keep in mind that to continue using the software, the subscription fee must be paid annually. Whether the annual fee will be less expensive over the long run depends on the number of traditional software licenses you would buy and whether you upgrade immediately to new releases. Finally, consider if you need the additional options that the subscription is offering. For example, if you do not use Access, Publisher, or Skype, the additional benefits are not meaningful to you.
3. Perform a spelling check and carefully proofread the document.
4. Apply formatting options of your choosing to improve the appearance of the document.
5. Search for and insert a suitable clip art image at the bottom center of the document.
6. Save the revised document and then exit Microsoft Word Web App.
7. Submit the project to your instructor in the manner she or he has requested.

Project 2 Creating a Worksheet in Excel Web App

Individual

Deliverable: Workbook in SkyDrive

1. With SkyDrive open, create a new Excel workbook in Microsoft Excel Web App with the file name **C15-Project2-Office365CostComparison-Your Name**, and then set up the following information in a worksheet. You determine the worksheet layout.

Cost Comparison for Office 365 and Office 2013 Subscription fee versus standard software license for each PC			
Office 365 Home Premium		Office 2013 Desktop PC	
Annual subscription fee	99	Office 2013 Home and Student license fee	139.99
Estimated years to subscribe	4	Number of licenses to buy	3
TOTAL COST FOR OFFICE 365		TOTAL COST FOR OFFICE 2013	
Difference in cost Office 365 versus Office 2013 Desktop licensing			

2. Create formulas to calculate the total cost of Office 365, the total cost of Office 2013, and the difference between the two models.
3. Apply formatting options of your choosing to improve the appearance of the worksheet.
4. Exit Microsoft Excel Web App.
5. Submit the project to your instructor in the manner she or he has requested.

Project 3 Creating a Presentation in PowerPoint Web App

Individual

Deliverable: Presentation in SkyDrive

1. With SkyDrive open, create a new PowerPoint presentation in Microsoft PowerPoint Web App with the file name **C15-Project3-Office365Pres-Your Name**.
2. Select a theme and variant of your choosing.
3. On Slide 1 type **What is Office 365 Home Premium?** as the slide title and your name as the subtitle.
4. Add a minimum of two slides to the presentation with text that you compose that summarizes the main points from the text that you typed in Project 1. For example, in Slide 2 explain the cloud-based subscription model of purchasing Office 365, and in Slide 3 provide a list of what is included in Office 365 Home Premium.
5. Apply formatting options of your choosing to enhance the presentation.
6. Exit PowerPoint Web App.
7. Submit the project to your instructor in the manner she or he has requested.

Project 4 Download Project Files and File Management in SkyDrive

Individual

Deliverable: Downloaded project files on USB; Word document with screen images of file lists in SkyDrive

1. With SkyDrive open, select and download **C15-Project1-Office365-Your Name** to a new folder named *Ch15* within ChapterProjectsWork on your USB flash drive.
2. Select and download **C15-Project2-Office365CostComparison-Your Name** to the Ch15 folder in ChapterProjectsWork.
3. Select and download **C15-Project3-Office365Pres-Your Name** to the Ch15 folder in ChapterProjectsWork.
4. Use Create to create a new folder named *C15-Projects*.
5. Select and move the files created from Projects 1, 2, and 3 to the C15-Projects folder.
6. With Files the active list displayed in SkyDrive, create another new folder named *C15-Topics*.
7. Select and move the three files created from the topics in this chapter to the C15-Topics folder.
8. Capture an image of your desktop with *Files* active in your SkyDrive account. Start a new Word document using the desktop edition of Microsoft Word (not the Word Web App) and paste the image.
9. Switch back to SkyDrive, tap or click the C15-Projects folder tile and then capture an image of your desktop with the folder contents displayed. Paste the image into the Word document below the capture pasted at Step 8.
10. Switch back to SkyDrive, tap or click *Files* to return to the previous list, tap or click the C15-Topics folder tile, and then capture an image of your desktop with the folder contents displayed. Paste the image into the Word document below the capture pasted at Step 9.
11. Save the Word document as **C15-Project4-SkyDriveFiles-Your Name**.
12. Sign out of SkyDrive and close Word.
13. Submit the project to your instructor in the manner she or he has requested.

Project 5 Creating a Spreadsheet in Google Docs

Individual

Deliverable: PDF of Google Docs document and spreadsheet

1. Sign in to Google Drive and create the spreadsheet shown in Figure 15.7.
2. Rename the spreadsheet as **C15-Project5-CloudStorage-Your Name**.
3. Use your best judgment to determine font size and shading color for cells.
4. When the spreadsheet is completed, complete the following steps to download a PDF copy of the Google Docs spreadsheet.
   a. At Google Drive, insert a check mark in the check box for the Project 5 file.
   b. Tap or click the More button located near the top of the Google Drive window (below Google search text box) and then tap or click Download.
   c. At the Convert and Download dialog box, tap or click PDF and then tap or click Download.
   d. Choose Save As at the pop-up window and save the PDF file in the Ch15 folder within ChapterProjectsWork. Close the pop-up window when completed.
   e. Deselect the file for Project 5 and select the file for the document created in Topic 15.7. Download a copy of the document as a PDF to the Ch15 folder within CompletedTopicsByChapter.
5. Sign out of Google Drive and close Internet Explorer.
6. Submit the project to your instructor in the manner she or he has requested.

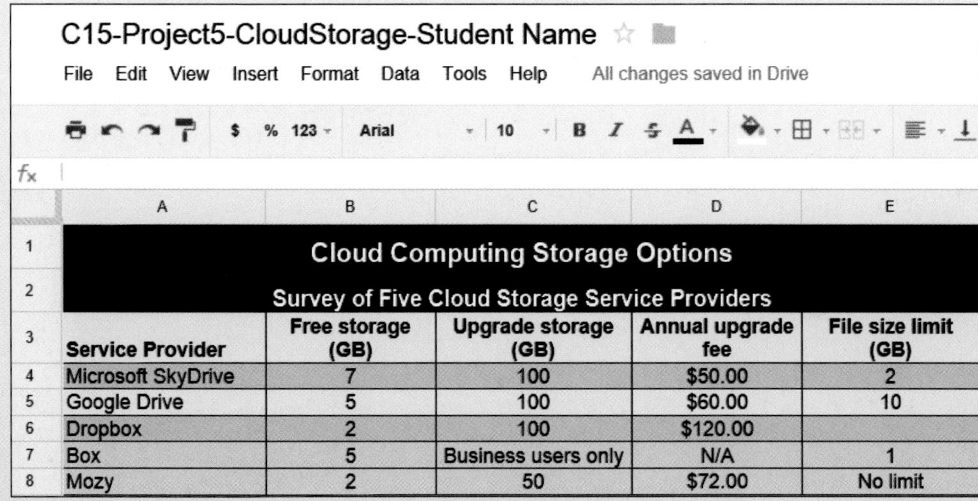

C15-Project5-CloudStorage-Student Name

File Edit View Insert Format Data Tools Help All changes saved in Drive

	A	B	C	D	E
1	Cloud Computing Storage Options				
2	Survey of Five Cloud Storage Service Providers				
3	Service Provider	Free storage (GB)	Upgrade storage (GB)	Annual upgrade fee	File size limit (GB)
4	Microsoft SkyDrive	7	100	$50.00	2
5	Google Drive	5	100	$60.00	10
6	Dropbox	2	100	$120.00	
7	Box	5	Business users only	N/A	1
8	Mozy	2	50	$72.00	No limit

Figure 15.7 Project 5 Cloud Computing Storage Options Google Docs spreadsheet

Project 6 Sending Project Work to OneNote Notebook

Individual

Deliverable: New Page in shared OneNote notebook

1. Start OneNote and open the MyProjects notebook created in Chapter 4, Project 4.
2. Make CloudTech the active section and add a new page titled *Chapter 15 Projects*.
3. Send the following project documents to OneNote, selecting the Chapter 15 Projects page in the CloudTech section in the MyProjects notebook. For each project, open the file downloaded from SkyDrive in the desktop version of the software to send the file to OneNote. Skip any projects you were not assigned to complete.
   a. **C15-Project1-Office365-Your Name** from Word.
   b. **C15-Project2-Office365CostComparison-Your Name** from Excel.
   c. **C15-Project3-Office365Pres-Your Name** from PowerPoint. Send the slides formatted as handouts with four slides horizontal per page and with your name in a header.
   d. **C15-Project4-SkyDriveFiles-Your Name** from Word.
   e. **C15-Project5-CloudStorage-Your Name** from Adobe Reader or Microsoft Reader.
4. Close your MyProjects notebook in OneNote and close OneNote.
5. Submit the project to your instructor in the manner she or he has requested.

Glossary

A

absolute addresses addresses with a dollar symbol before the column letter and/or row number so that the address will not change when the formula is copied to another column or row

Accept button button used to send a message to a meeting organizer indicating acceptance of meeting request

Access 2013 database management application in Microsoft Office suite used to organize, store, and manage related data such as customers, vendors, employees, or products

Accounting Number Format a number format in Excel that adds a currency symbol, comma in thousands, and two decimal places

active cell the cell with the green border around its edges and in which the next entry will be stored or that will be affected by a command

Add Contact Picture control used in a Contact window to add a picture of a contact to display in the People card

Add Page icon in OneNote, the icon is used to add a new page in a section; pages organize note content within a section

Address bar the area in a web browser in which the web address (also called a URL) for a web page is viewed or typed

advanced search tools options provided by search engines that are used to narrow search results

Align Left paragraph alignment in which lines of text are aligned at the left margin; left edge of page appears even

Align Right paragraph alignment in which text is aligned at the right margin; right edge of page appears even

alignment guides colored vertical and horizontal lines that appear to help you align and place objects; also called smart guides

Angle Counterclockwise option from Orientation button in Excel that rotates text within the cell boundaries by 45 degrees

animation involves adding a special effect to an object on a slide that causes the object to move or change in some way during a slide show

Animation Painter button button used to copy animation effects from one object to another object

applications (apps) programs used on a PC by individuals to do tasks; also called apps

appointment any activity in your schedule that you want to keep track of, or be reminded of, including the day and time the activity begins and ends, the subject, and the location

argument parameters for a function formula that appear in parentheses

Attach File button button used to attach a file (such as a photo) to an email message in Outlook

Audio button button in Media group of INSERT tab used to add a sound clip to a slide in a presentation

Auto Fill Excel feature that enters data automatically based on a pattern or series that exists in an adjacent cell or range

Auto Sum button button in Excel used to enter SUM formula or access other functions

AutoComplete feature in software programs in which entries that match the first few characters that you type are displayed in a list so that you can enter text by accepting a suggestion; suggested entries are derived from prior entries that have been typed

AutoCorrect software feature that automatically corrects commonly misspelled words when you press the spacebar

AutoFit column width setting that adjusts the width of the column to accommodate the length of the active cell or longest entry in the column

AutoFormat software feature that automatically formats text or replaces text with symbols or special characters

AutoFormat as You Type feature that creates automatic bulleted or numbered lists depending on the character typed at the beginning of a line

B

Back button in web browser or other software that moves backward one page or screen

Backstage view view accessed from FILE tab used to perform file management; start a new document; display file information; manage document properties; and customize application options

banded rows shading applied to every other row to make it easier to read data organized in a table

Best Fit column width dialog box option in Access that adjusts column width to accommodate the length of the longest entry

Bibliography button button used to generate a Works Cited or References page in an academic paper

Bookmark this page in Google Chrome, the white star at the right end of the omnibox used to bookmark a frequently used web page

Bookmarks bar in Google Chrome, the bar below the omnibox that displays buttons for bookmarked web pages

Borders gallery feature that adds a border to a paragraph or cell

Bullets button button used to format text as a list with a bullet symbol at the beginning of each line; bullets are used for a list of items that are in no particular order

C

Calendar tool in Microsoft Outlook used to schedule, manage, and store appointments, meetings, and events

Calendar app Windows 8 app used to view your appointments and reminders stored in your Microsoft account calendar

Caption property Access field property used to store a descriptive title for a field; caption text displays as the column heading or control label in a datasheet or form

category axis horizontal axis in a column chart with the names or other labels associated with each bar; also called the x-axis

cell the intersection of a column with a row into which you type text, a value, or a formula in Excel

Cell Styles set of predefined formatting options that can be applied to selected cells in a worksheet

Cell Styles button button in Styles group of HOME tab in Excel used to apply a cell style to the active cell or range

Center paragraph alignment in which text is aligned centered between the left and right margins

Change PC settings Windows 8 option to customize Start screen

character formatting changing the appearance of characters

charms icons used to access system resources and commands

Charms bar five icons (called charms) that display when you swipe from the right edge of the screen or move the pointer to the top right or bottom right corner and slide up or down

citation reference to the source used for a quotation or for paraphrased text in an academic paper

Clear button button used in Excel to clear contents, formats, or both contents and formats in a cell or range

click and type feature in Word in which you can double-tap or double-click anywhere on a page and start typing

clip art gallery collection of royalty-free photos and illustrations provided by Microsoft for insertion into documents, workbooks, or presentations

Close button the red button with white X that displays at the top right of a desktop application window

Close Tab a control in a web browser that when tapped or clicked closes the tab for a web page

cloud computing software and computing services accessed entirely on the Internet

column chart a chart in which each data point is represented by a colored bar extending upward from the category axis with the bar height extending to its corresponding value on the value axis

Comma Style a number format option in Excel that inserts a comma in thousands and with two decimal places

comment a short note associated with text that provides explanatory information, poses a question, or provides feedback

Comments pane pane at right side of Slide pane in Normal view in which comments are added to a presentation in PowerPoint

Compact & Repair Database button button at Info tab Backstage view used to perform a compact and repair routine for the current database

Computer window window used to view devices attached to PC or mobile device

conditional formatting applies formatting options to cells only if the cells meet a specified criterion

Contextual tabs tabs that appear when an object is selected that contain commands or options related to the type of object

control object a rectangular content placeholder in a form or report

Convert to SmartArt button button used to convert existing text into a SmartArt graphic object

Copy button or menu option used to make a duplicate copy of a file or selected text

crawlers programs that read web pages and other information to generate index entries; also called spiders

Create a New Section tab the control used to add a new section to a OneNote notebook; sections are used to organize notes by category, topic, or subject

Customize and control Google Chrome in Google Chrome, the button at the end of the omnibox used to access the menu system

Cut button or menu option used to move a file or selected text to another location

D

database data stored in an organized manner to provide information to suit a variety of purposes

database management systems (DBMS) software that organizes and keeps track of large amounts of data

Date Navigator the calendars displayed above the Folder pane with which you can change the day that is displayed in the Appointment area in the Calendar

Decrease Decimal button button used in Excel to remove one decimal place from each value each time the button is tapped or clicked

Decrease Indent button button that moves a paragraph closer to the left margin in a document or left edge of a cell in a worksheet each time the button is tapped or clicked

Decrease List Level button button used to move text left to the previous indent position within a bullet list placeholder

Delete button or menu option used to remove a file, folder, selected text, or other object from storage or a document

Delete button button in the Cells group in the HOME tab of the Excel ribbon used for deleting cells, rows, or columns

Deleted Items Mail folder in which messages that have been deleted are moved; messages are not permanently deleted until Deleted Items folder is emptied

Design view Access view for an object in which the structure and/or layout of a table, form, query, or report is defined

Desktop the display with icons that launch programs and a taskbar used to switch between open programs

destination document document, worksheet, or presentation into which copied data is pasted, embedded, or linked

destination program program into which copied data is pasted, embedded, or linked

dialog box a box that opens in a separate window with additional options or commands for the related ribbon group as buttons, lists, sliders, check boxes, text boxes, and option buttons

Dialog box launcher diagonal downward-pointing button located at bottom right of a group in the ribbon that opens a task pane or dialog box

Display your bookmarks in Mozilla Firefox, the button used to access the bookmarks menu system

downloading the practice of copying content from a web page to your PC or mobile device

Draft view displays a document in Word without print elements such as headers or footers

E

editing the practice of making changes to a document after the document has been typed

electronic mail (email) the sending and receiving of digital messages, sometimes with documents or photos attached

endnotes explanatory text or source information for noted text placed at the end of a paper or report

Enforce Referential Integrity Access relationship option that verifies as a new record is added to a related table that a record with the matching field value in the joined field already exists in the primary table in the relationship

event an activity in the Calendar that lasts an entire day or longer

Excel 2013 spreadsheet application in Microsoft Office suite used to calculate, format, and analyze primarily numerical data

F

Favorites web pages you visit frequently that have been pinned to a list

field one characteristic about a person, place, event, or item in an Access table; for example, *Birthdate* is a field in a table about students

Field Properties pane lower half of Design view window for an Access table that contains field properties for the active field

field property a characteristic or attribute for a field that defines the field's data, format, behavior, or other feature

field value data that is stored within one field in a record; for example, *Jane* is the field value for a *FirstName* field in a record for Jane Smith

file a document, spreadsheet, presentation, picture, or any text and/or image that is saved as digital data

File Explorer window used to browse files and folders and perform file management routines

file name a series of characters you assign to a document, spreadsheet, presentation, picture, or other text or image that allows you to identify and retrieve the file later

FILE tab ribbon tab that opens the Backstage view in which file management commands and application options are located

Fill button button in Editing group of HOME tab in Excel used to access fill options

Fill Color button button used in Excel to add shading to the background of a cell

fill handle small green square at bottom right corner of active cell or range used to extend the pattern or series in adjacent cells

filter temporarily hides data that does not meet a criterion

Find feature that moves insertion point or cell to each occurrence of a word or phrase

Find & Select button button in Editing group in Excel's HOME tab with Find, Replace, and Go To options

Find bar in Google Chrome, the area used to locate words or phrases on a web page

Fit All Columns on One Page Excel Scaling option in Print tab Backstage view that shrinks the size of text until all columns fit in the page width

Fit All Rows on One Page Excel Scaling option in Print tab Backstage view that shrinks the size of text until all rows fit in the page height

Fit Sheet on One Page Excel Scaling option in Print tab Backstage view that shrinks the size of text to fit all columns and rows on one page

Flash Fill Excel feature that automatically fills data in adjacent cells as soon as a pattern is recognized

folder a name assigned to a placeholder or container in which you store a group of related files

font a typeface that includes the design and shape of the letters, numbers, and special characters

footer text that appears at the bottom of each page

footnotes explanatory text or source information at the bottom of the page in which the source is noted

foreign key a field added to a related table that is not the primary key and is included for the purpose of creating a relationship

form Access object used to enter, update, or view records generally one record at a time

Form view access view in which data is viewed, entered, and updated and is the view that is active when a form is opened

Format Painter clipboard option used to copy formatting options from selected text or an object to other text or another object

formatting changing the appearance of text

formula cell entry beginning with an equals sign (=) and followed by a statement that is calculated to determine the value displayed in the cell

Forward button in web browser or other software that moves forward or to the next screen

Forward button button used to send a copy of an email message to someone else

Freeze Panes Excel option that fixes column and/or row headings in place so that headings do not scroll off the screen

From Beginning button button in PowerPoint SLIDE SHOW tab used to start a slide show from slide 1

G

gallery in a drop-down list or grid, visual representations of options that can be applied to a selection

gestures actions or motions you perform with your finger, thumb, stylus, or mouse

Go To feature to move active cell to a specific location in the worksheet

Go To Date the dialog box used to type a date to display in the Appointment area of the Calendar

Go To Special dialog box with options for moving the active cell by various cell attributes

Google Chrome free web browser from Google that runs on PCs or Macs

Google Docs web-based free productivity suite offered by Google

Google Drive Google's cloud file storage service

H

hanging indent a paragraph in which the first line remains at the left margin but subsequent lines are indented

hard page break a page break that you insert before the maximum number of lines that can fit on the page has been reached

hard return creating a new paragraph in a document by tapping or pressing the Enter key

header text that appears at the top of each page

Help reference system used to look up information on Windows or Microsoft Office application features

hyperlinks addresses that when clicked or tapped on a touchscreen take you to a related Web page

I

Import Spreadsheet Wizard Access wizard used to perform an import of Excel data into a new table in Access

Inbox Mail folder into which received email messages are placed

Increase Decimal button button used in Excel to add one decimal place to each value each time the button is tapped or clicked

Increase Indent button button that moves a paragraph away from the left margin in a document or left edge of a cell in a worksheet each time the button is tapped or clicked

Increase List Level button button used to move text right to the next indent position within a bullet list placeholder

inline reply composing a reply to the sender of an email message from the Reading pane in Outlook

Insert button button in Cells group in HOME tab of Excel ribbon used to insert new cells, rows, or columns

Insert Caption feature used to add text above or below an image to label the image or add other descriptive text

Insert Options button button that appears in worksheet area after a new row or column has been inserted with options for formatting the new row or column

Internet (Net) a global network that links together other networks such as government departments, businesses, nonprofit organizations, educational and research institutions, and individuals

Internet Explorer (IE) the web browser included with Microsoft Windows

Internet Service Provider (ISP) a company that provides access to the Internet's infrastructure for a fee

J

Justify paragraph alignment in which extra space is added between words so that the text is evenly distributed between the left and right margins; both sides of the page appear even with this alignment

K

keyboard commands a key or combination of keys (such as Ctrl plus a letter) that performs a command

L

landscape page layout orientation in which the text is rotated to the wider side of the page with a 9-inch line length at the default margin setting

Layout Options button Gallery that provides options to control how an image and surrounding text interact with each other

Layout view Access view in which you edit the structure and appearance of a form or report

Libraries window window that displays when you tap or click File Explorer button that is used to view and or manage files

library name for a collection of places where files are stored that allows you to view all documents in one window

Line and Paragraph Spacing button button in Word's Paragraph group used to change the spacing of lines between text within a paragraph and the spacing before and after a paragraph

Line Break tapping or pressing Shift + Enter creates a new line in a document without creating a new paragraph (avoids the extra space created when Enter is used)

line chart a chart in which the values are graphed in a continuous line that allows a reader to easily spot trends, growth spurts, or dips in values by the line's shape and trajectory

links addresses that when clicked or tapped on a touchscreen take you to a related web page

Links dialog box dialog box opened from Info tab Backstage view in which linked objects can be updated or otherwise managed

live preview displays a preview of text or an object if the active option from a gallery is applied

local account user name and password used to sign in to Windows 8 that is stored on the local PC or device (not a Hotmail or live.com email address)

Location bar in Mozilla Firefox, the area in which you type or view a web address

Lock screen the screen that displays when a Windows 8 computer is locked to prevent other people from seeing programs or documents you have open

logging off action that closes all apps and files and displays the lock screen; also called signing out

lookup list a drop-down list in an Access field in which the list entries are field values from a field in another table or a fixed list of items

Lookup Wizard Access wizard used to assist with creating a lookup list

M

Mail tool within Microsoft Outlook used to send, receive, organize, and store email messages

Mark Complete option to retain a completed task in the To-Do list with a line drawn through the task entry indicating the task has been finished

Markup Area area at the right side of the screen in which comments and other changes made to a document are shown

meeting an appointment in your Calendar to which people have been invited to attend via email messages

meeting request email message sent to an invitee of a meeting that you have scheduled in Calendar

Merge & Center button button used in Excel that combines a group of cells into one and centers the content within the combined cell

Microsoft account email address from Hotmail.com or live.com used to sign in to Windows 8

Microsoft Excel Web App web-based version of Microsoft Excel accessed from SkyDrive that is similar to the desktop version of Excel but has fewer features; some functionality within features may also vary from the desktop version

Microsoft PowerPoint Web App web-based version of Microsoft PowerPoint accessed from SkyDrive that is similar to the desktop version of PowerPoint but has fewer features; some functionality within features may also vary from the desktop version

Microsoft Word Web App web-based version of Microsoft Word accessed from SkyDrive that is similar to the desktop version of Word but has fewer features; some functionality within features may also vary from the desktop version

Middle Align button alignment button in Excel that centers text vertically between the top and bottom edges of the cell

Mini toolbar toolbar that appears next to selected text or with the shortcut menu that contains frequently used formatting commands

mixed addresses cell addresses in a formula that have a combination of relative and absolute referencing

mouse pointing device that is used for computer input

Move Chart button button used to move a selected chart to a new chart sheet in a workbook

Mozilla Firefox free web browser from Mozilla foundation that runs on PCs or Macs

N

New (blank) record button button located in Record Navigation and Search bar used to add a new record in a table or form

New Appointment button button used to add a new activity into the appointment area in the Calendar

New Contact button button used to add a new contact to the People list

New Email button button used to create a new email message in Outlook

New folder button used to create a new folder on a device

New Meeting button button used to schedule a meeting in Calendar for which others are invited to attend

New Notebook Backstage view view used in OneNote to create a new notebook

New sheet button button that displays as a plus symbol inside a circle used to add a new worksheet to an Excel workbook

New Slide button button used to insert a new slide after the active slide in a presentation

New Tab a control in a web browser that is tapped or clicked to open a new tab in which a web page can be displayed

New Task button button used to create a new task in Outlook using the Task window

note container a box on a OneNote page that contains note content

Notebook Information Backstage view view that displays when the FILE tab is tapped or clicked with a OneNote notebook open

Notes pages handout option for printing slides in which one slide is printed per page with the slide printed in the top half of the page and the speaker notes or blank space when no notes are present in the bottom half of the page

Notes pane pane below Slide pane in Normal view in which speaker notes are typed and edited

Notification area area at right end of taskbar with icons to view or change system settings or resources such as the date and time or speaker volume

Numbering button button used to format text as a list with sequential numbers or letters used at the beginning of each line

O

object a picture, shape, chart, or other item that can be manipulated separately from text or other objects around it

Office 365 subscription-based edition of Microsoft Office 2013

omnibox in Google Chrome, the combined address bar and search bar

OneNote 2013 note-taking software application included in the Microsoft Office 2013 suite

OneNote notebook electronic notebook created in OneNote organized into sections and pages in which you store, organize, search, and share notes of various types

one-to-many relationship an Access relationship in which the common field used to join two tables is the primary key in only one table

one-to-one relationship an Access relationship in which two tables are joined on the primary key field in each table

Online Pictures button button used to search for an image to insert into a document from the clip art gallery, the Web, Flickr, or SkyDrive

Open a new tab in Mozilla Firefox, the button that displays with a plus symbol used to open a new tab for displaying a web page

Outline view displays content as bullet points

Outlook 2013 personal information management (PIM) software application included in the Microsoft Office suite

P

Page Borders button button used to choose a border that is drawn around the perimeter of a page

Page Layout view Excel view in which you can add or modify print options while also viewing the worksheet

Page Number button button used to insert page numbering in a header or footer

paragraph formatting changing the appearance of paragraphs

Paste button or menu option used to insert the copied or cut text or file

PDF document a document saved in Portable Document Format that is an open standard for exchanging electronic documents developed by Adobe systems

People tool in Microsoft Outlook used to add, maintain, organize, and store contact information for people with whom you communicate

People card contact information for an individual displays in a People card in the Reading pane

personal information management (PIM) program software programs that help you organize messages, schedules, contacts, and tasks

Photos app Windows 8 app used to view pictures from a local device and connected online services

Pictures button button used to insert an image stored on your PC or mobile device into a document, workbook, or presentation

pie chart a chart in which each data point is sized to show its proportion to the total in a pie shape

Pin site control in Internet Explorer that displays as a push pin used to add a web page to the Favorites list

Pin to Start Windows 8 option to add selected title to the Start screen

placeholder rectangular container on a slide in which text or other content is added

pointer the white arrow or other icon that moves on the screen as you move a pointing device

portrait page layout orientation in which the text on the page is vertically oriented with a 6.5-inch line length at the default margin setting

PowerPoint 2013 presentation application in Microsoft Office suite used to create multimedia slides for an oral or kiosk-style presentation

presentation application software used to create slides for an electronic slideshow that may be projected on a screen

Presenter view PowerPoint view for a second monitor in a slide show that displays the slide show along with a preview of the next slide, speaker notes, timer, and slide show toolbar

primary key the field that contains the data that uniquely identifies each record in the table

primary table table in an Access relationship in which the joined field is the primary key and in which new records should be added first

Print Layout view default view in Word that shows the document as it will appear when printed

Print Preview right pane in Print tab Backstage view that shows how a document will look when printed

private browsing a browsing option in which web pages visited do not appear in history list and cookies are automatically deleted when the private browsing window is closed

Protected view view in which a file is opened when the file is opened as an attachment from an email message or otherwise downloaded from an Internet source; file contents can be read but editing is prevented until Enable Editing is performed

pull quote a quote placed inside a text box in a document

Q

query Access object used to display information from one or more tables

Quick Access toolbar toolbar with frequently used commands located at the top left corner of each Office application window

Quick Tables predefined tables with sample data

R

range a rectangular group of cells referenced with the top left cell address, a colon, and the bottom right cell address (e.g., A1:B9)

Read Mode view displays a document full screen in columns or pages without editing tools such as the QAT and ribbon

Recommended Charts Excel 2013 feature that will show a series of customized charts that best suit a data selection; access Recommended Charts from the More Charts Quick Analysis option or from the INSERT tab

record all of the fields for one person, place, event, or item within an Access table

Recurrence dialog box in which you set up particulars of an appointment that repeats at the same day and time each week for a set period of time

Recycle Bin Window used to view and/or restore deleted files

Rehearse Timings feature in PowerPoint used to assign times to slides by running through a slide show with a timer and Recording toolbar active

relative addresses default addressing method used in formulas in which column letters and row numbers update when a formula is copied relative to the destination

Remove from List option to delete a task from the To-Do list

Rename button or menu option used to change the name of a file, folder, or tab

Replace feature that automatically changes each occurrence of a word or phrase to something else

Reply button button used to compose a reply to the sender of an email message

report Access object used to display or print data from one or more tables or queries in a customized layout and with summary totals

Report view Access view that displays a report's data without editing tools and is the view that is active when the report is opened

ribbon interface that displays buttons for commands organized within groups and tabs

Ribbon Display Options button button used to change the ribbon display to show tabs only or auto-hide the ribbon

Run button button in QUERY TOOLS DESIGN tab used to instruct Access to perform the query instructions and display the query results datasheet

S

Safely Remove Hardware and Eject Media option used to eject a USB flash drive from a PC or mobile device

Screen resolution display setting that refers to the number of picture elements, called pixels, that make up the image shown on a display device

scroll bars horizontal and/or vertical bars for navigating a larger file when a document exceeds the viewing space within the current window

scroll box a box between the two arrow buttons in a scroll bar that is used to navigate a larger file that cannot fit within the viewing area

Search bar in Mozilla Firefox, the area used to type search phrases to find web pages

search engine a company that searches Web pages to index the pages by keyword or subject and provides search tools to find pages

section break used to change page layout options for a section of a document instead of the entire document

Selection handle circle or square icons that appear around a selected object or at the beginning and end of text on touch-enabled devices that are used to manipulate the object or define a text selection area

Send to OneNote button button that appears on Taskbar with which you can embed a copy of content from a web page or other resource, capture a screen clipping, or create a new quick note in a OneNote notebook

Set Up Slide Show button button used in PowerPoint to configure options for a slide show such as setting up a self-running presentation

Settings button button used in OneNote to close an open notebook

shading color added behind text

Shapes button button used to select the type of shape to be drawn on a slide, in a document, or in a worksheet

Share Notebook Backstage view view used in OneNote to share the current notebook with another individual by providing an email address

Sheet tab bar bar above Status bar at bottom left of Excel window where sheet tabs are displayed

shut down process to turn off the PC or mobile device to ensure all Windows files are properly closed

sign out action that closes all apps and files and displays the lock screen; also called logging off

signature the closing containing your name and other contact information that is inserted automatically at the end of each email message

Simple Query Wizard Access wizard that assists with creating a new query by making selections in a series of dialog boxes

SkyDrive secure online storage provided by Microsoft that is available to users signed in with a Microsoft account

slide layouts content placeholders that determine the number, position, and type of content for a slide

slide master a slide master in PowerPoint is included for each presentation and slide layout and determines the default formatting of placeholders on each new slide

Slide Master view view in which global changes to the formatting options for slides in a presentation are made

slide pane the pane that displays the current slide in Normal view

Slide Show button button in PowerPoint Status bar used to start a slide show from the active slide

Slide Show view PowerPoint view in which you preview slides full screen as they will appear to an audience

Slide Sorter view PowerPoint view in which all of the slides in the presentation are displayed as slide thumbnails; view is often used to rearrange the order of slides

Slide Thumbnail pane pane at left side of Normal view in which numbered thumbnails of the slides are displayed

smart guides colored vertical and horizontal lines that appear to help you align and place objects; also called alignment guides

SmartArt graphics used to visually communicate relationships in lists, processes, cycles, and hierarchies, or to create other object diagrams

soft page break a page break inserted automatically by Word when the maximum number of lines for the page has been reached with the current page size and margins

Sort & Filter button button in Editing group of HOME tab in Excel used to sort and filter a worksheet

source data data that is selected for copying to be integrated into another program

source program program in which data resides that is being copied for integration into another program

Sparklines miniature charts embedded into a cell in an Excel worksheet

Spelling & Grammar feature in software applications that flags potential errors, displays suggestions for correction, as well as other options for responding to the potential error

spiders programs that read web pages and other information to generate index entries; also known as crawlers

spreadsheet application software in which you work primarily with numbers that you organize, calculate, and chart

Start screen Windows 8 user interface that displays tiles used to launch apps or other programs

Store app Windows 8 app used to download or buy new apps for your device

style set of predefined formatting options that can be applied to selected text with one step

style guide set of rules (such as MLA or APA) for formatting academic essays or research papers

Style Set a set of formatting options for each style based upon the document's theme, which is changed with options in the Document Formatting group of the DESIGN tab

subfolder a folder within a folder

Symbol gallery gallery used to insert a special character or symbol such as a copyright symbol or fraction character

T

tabbed browsing a feature in web browsers that allows you to view multiple web pages within the same browser window by displaying each page in a separate tab

table text organized within a grid of columns and rows

table in an Access database, all of the data for one topic or subject; for example, Customers is one table in a database that tracks invoices

table cell a box that is the intersection of a column with a row in which you type text in a table

Table Styles collection of predefined table formatting options that include borders, shading, and color

tag a short category or other label attached to an item such as a note in a OneNote page that allows you to categorize or otherwise identify the item

Tags Summary pane in OneNote, the pane opened from the Find Tags button that is used to navigate to the location of a tagged item

task pane a pane that opens at the right or left side of an application window with additional options or commands for the related ribbon group as buttons, lists, sliders, check boxes, text boxes, and option buttons

Taskbar bar along the bottom of the desktop used to switch between open programs

Tasks tool in Microsoft Outlook used to maintain a to-do list

template a document with formatting options already applied

Text Box button button used to create a text box in a document, workbook, or presentation

theme a set of colors, fonts, and font effects that alter the appearance of a document, spreadsheet, or presentation

thesaurus feature for looking up a word to find alternative words with a similar meaning; the word looked up can be changed to one in the results list

tiles square or rectangular icons on Windows 8 Start screen used to launch apps or programs

title slide first slide in a presentation that generally contains a title and subtitle

To-Do List list of tasks to be done that is maintained in Outlook

toggle buttons buttons that operate as on or off

touch keyboard onscreen keyboard that displays for touch-enabled devices

touchpad a flat surface on a laptop or notebook operated with your finger(s) as a pointing device

trackball a mouse in which the user manipulates a ball to move the on-screen pointer

transition a special effect that plays during a slide show as one slide is removed from the screen and the next slide appears

Trim Video button button used to modify a video clip to show only a portion of the clip by changing the start and/or end times in the Trim Video dialog box

Turn live tile off Windows 8 option to stop displaying headlines or other notifications from online services within a tile on the Start screen

U

Undo command that restores a document to its state before the last action was performed

uniform resource locator (URL) a text-based address used to navigate to a website; also called a web address

Unpin from Start Windows 8 option to remove selected tile from the Start screen

Update Links button button to tap or click to cause linked objects to be updated with new data; button appears inside Security Notice dialog box when destination document with linked objects set to automatically update is opened

user account the user name and password that you type to gain access to a PC or mobile device

user interface (UI) the icons, menus, and other means with which a person interacts with the OS, software application, or hardware device

V

value axis vertical axis in a column chart scaled for the values that are being charted; also called the y- or z-axis

variants a collection of style and color schemes in the PowerPoint theme family

W

web address a text-based address to navigate to a website; also called uniform resource locator (URL)

web browser a software program used to view web pages

Web Layout view displays document in Word as a web page

web page a document that contains text and multimedia content such as images, video, sound, and animation

Windows 8 Microsoft's Operating System for PCs released in October 2012

Word 2013 Word processing application in Microsoft Office suite used to create, edit, and format text-based documents

word processing application software used to create documents containing mostly text

Word Start screen the opening screen that displays when you start Microsoft Word 2013

WordArt text that is created and formatted as a graphic object

wordwrap feature in word processing applications in which text is automatically moved to the next line when the end of the current line is reached

workbooks spreadsheet files saved in Excel

Works Cited page at the end of an MLA paper or report that provides the references for the sources used in the paper

worksheets the grid-like structure of columns and rows into which you enter and edit text, values, and formulas in Excel

World Wide Web the global collection of electronic documents circulated on the Internet in the form of web pages; also called Web or WWW

Wrap Text button alignment option in Excel that wraps text within the cell's column width

Z

Zoom In button that displays as a plus symbol at bottom right corner of application window that increases magnification by 10 percent each time button is tapped or clicked

Zoom Out button that displays as a minus symbol at bottom right corner of application window that decreases magnification by 10 percent each time button is tapped or clicked

Zoom slider slider bar located near bottom right corner of an application window that is used to change the magnification option

Index

* Boldface page numbers indicate figures and tables.

A

Absolute addresses in Excel, 258, 259

Access 2013, 71, 353–377, 389–409

- Best Fit in, 365
- color scheme in, 74
- column widths, adjusting, 364–365
- control objects in, 405
- database in
  - compacting, repairing and backing up, 408–409
  - encrypting, with password, 409
- data in
  - finding and replacing, 364–365
  - importing Excel worksheet into, 420–423
- datasheets in
  - adding records using, 358–359
  - editing and deleting records in, 360–361
  - previewing, 376–377
- data types in, **392**
- Design view in, 370
  - creating new tables in, 394–395
  - creating queries using, 370–371
  - modifying field properties in, 398–399
- Enforce Referential Integrity in, 403
- field properties in, 398
  - formatting and data validation, 399
  - modifying, in Design View, 398–399
- Field Properties pane in, 398
- fields in, 356
  - adding, to existing tables, 396–397
  - deleting, 397
  - sorting by more than one, 367
- field values in, 356
  - creating lookup list with, in another table, 400
- files in, creating new, **390,** 390–391
- finding and replacing data and adjusting column widths in, 364–365
- foreign key in, 403
- forms in, **354,** 356
  - adding, editing and deleting records in, 362–363
  - creating, using the Form Wizard, 405
  - creating and editing, 404–405
- Form view in, 404
- Form Wizard in, creating forms using, 405
- identifying database objects, **354,** 354–355
- Layout View in, 404
- lookup list in, 400
  - creating, 400–401
- Lookup Wizard in, 400
- opening, 74
- primary key in, 366
  - assigning, 394–395
- primary tables in, 403
- queries in, **354,** 357
  - calculated field in, 376–377
  - Design view in creating, 370–371
  - entering criteria to select records in, 372–373, **373**
  - entering multiple to sort, 374–375
  - exporting to Excel, 424–425
  - Simple Query Wizard in creating, 368–369
- records in, 356
  - adding, editing, and deleting in a form, 362–363
  - best practices for deleting, 361
  - datasheets in adding, 358–359
  - editing and deleting using datasheets, 360–361
  - entering criteria to select, in queries, 372–373, **373**
  - entering multiple criteria to select, 374–375
  - sorting and filtering, 366–367
  - using find to move to, 363
- relationships in
  - creating, 403
  - displaying and editing, 402–403
  - one-to-many, 403
  - one-to-one, 402
- reports in, **354,** 356
  - creating, editing, and viewing, 406–407
  - grouping and sorting, 407
- Simple Query Wizard in, creating queries using, 368–369
- tables in, **354,** 355
  - adding fields to existing, 396–397
  - creating lookup list with field values in, 400
  - creating new, 392
    - in Design View, 394–395
  - planning new, **390,** 390–391
  - primary, 403
- terminology in, 355–357
- wildcard characters in, 375

Accounting number format in Excel, 229–230

Action Buttons, 331

Action Center flag, 20

Add Account dialog box, 128

Add Contact Picture dialog box, 142

Adding

- in Access
  - records in forms, 362–363
- in Outlook
  - contacts in, 142–143

tasks in, 144–145
Address bar, 46, 47
Adobe Flash Media, 332
Adobe Reader, 78
Advanced search options, 59–60
Alignment guides, 85
Alignment in Excel, 232–233
Align Text button, 89
Animation in PowerPoint presentations, 336
adding, to slide show
applying to individual objects, 338–339
using slide master, **336,** 336–337
categories of, **337**
changing sequence of, 339
Animation Painter button, 338
APA (American Psychological Association), formatting and page layout guidelines, 202
Appointments in Outlook
editing, 138–139
reminders and tags for, 137
scheduling, 136–137
recurring, 138–139
Apps, 4
adding to the Lock screen, 19
closing, 13
launching, 3, **10,** 10–11
Microsoft Excel, 446
creating worksheet using, 446–447
Microsoft PowerPoint, 448
creating presentation using, 448–449
editing presentation in, 450–451
Microsoft Word, 442
creating document using, 442–445
need to close, 12
starting, 4
switching between, 11
Apps screen, 12
Arguments in Excel, 260
Arrow keys in Excel, 225, 228
Ask, 58
Attach File button, 132
Audience handouts in PowerPoint, 308–309
Audio file formats, PowerPoint recognition of, 334
AutoComplete, 132
in Excel, 225
AutoCorrect
in Excel, 227
in Word, 158, 159, **159**
AutoFill in Excel, 234, 237
AutoFit
in Excel, 232, 233
in PowerPoint, 299
AutoFormat in Word, 158, 160, 167
AutoSum in Excel, 236

B

Back button, 25, 47
Backspace in correcting typing errors, 77
Backspace key, 159
Backstage view, 76
Export tab, 117
in managing documents, 76–79
New Notebook, 118
Notebook Information, 117
Open tab, 79
Print tab, 77, 445
Save As tab, 79
Share Notebook, 119
Backup copy, 26
Balanced power plan, 15
Best Fit in Access, 365
Bing, 58, 59
Bookmark button, 167
Bookmarking pages, with Mozilla Firefox, 55–56
Bookmarks bar, 55
Borders
in Excel, 230, 231
in Word, 192–193
Browsing, tabbed, 48
Bullets
in PowerPoint, 296, 297, 326
in Word, 166–167

C

Calculator, 20
Calendar app, 10, 10–11, **11**
Calendar tool, 136
CALENDAR TOOLS APPOINTMENT tab, 138
Cell formulas, displaying in Excel, 242–243
Cells in Excel, 224
active, 224, 225
applying styles, 241
copying, 244–245
editing, 227
fill handle in copying, 235
formatting, 228–231
indenting, 244–245
inserting and deleting, 239
merging, 231
pointers for, 225
selecting
mouse in, 228
touch in, 228–229
shading, wrapping, and rotating, 246–247
sorting and applying styles in, 240–241
Character formatting in Word, 168
Charms, 11, 12
Charms bar, 12–13, 72
Charts
in Excel, 257
column, 270–271
embedding, into Word document, 426–427
line, 272–273
pie, 268–269
recommended, 271
in PowerPoint
creating, on slides, 328–329
formatting, 329
using data from Excel in creating, 329
Check Full Name dialog box, 143
Clip art
in Office.com, 322
in Word, 188
Close button, 20, **20**

Close Tab, 49
Cloud computing, 441
Cloud storage, 92
Color scheme
- in Access, 74
- in Excel, 74
- in PowerPoint, 74
- in Word, 74

Column charts in Excel
- category axis in, 270
- creating and modifying, 270–271
- value axis in, 270

Columns in Excel
- adjusting width, 232–233
- deleting, 238–239
- inserting, 238–239

Column widths, adjusting in Access, 364–365
Commas in email addresses, 130
Comma style format in Excel, 229
Comments
- in Excel, 257
  - inserting, 254–255
  - printing, 277
- in PowerPoint, 291
  - adding, 304–305
  - deleting or hiding, 305
- in Word, 208
  - inserting, 208–209
  - replying to, 208–209

Comments pane in PowerPoint, 290, 304
Computer. See Personal computer
Computer window, 22, **22**
Conditional formatting in Excel, 279
Contacts in Outlook, adding and editing, 142–143
Content, downloading, from web pages, 62–63
Content pane, 22, 129
Contextual tabs, 84
Control objects in Access, 405
Copy button, 26
Copyright-free multimedia, 335
COUNTA function in Excel, 261
COUNT function in Excel, 261
Cover letters in Word, creating from templates, 210–211
Crawlers, 58
Custom sort in Excel, 241

D

Data
- in Access, finding and replacing, 364–365
- in Excel
  - embedding and editing, into PowerPoint presentation, 428–429
  - entering or copying with Fill command, 234–237
  - importing, into Access, 420–423
- in PowerPoint, editing, 329

Database management system (DBMS), 353
Databases, 353
- in Access
  - compacting, repairing and backing up, 408–409
  - encrypting, with password, 409

Datasheets in Access
- adding records using, 358–359
- editing and deleting records in, 360–361
- previewing, 376–377

Data types in Access, 392
Date Navigator, 136
Dates in Excel, entering, formatting, and calculating, 262–263
Decimal places, adjusting, in Excel, 231
Delete button, 31
Deleted Items folder, 133
Delete key, 107
Deleting
- in Access
  - fields in, 397
  - records in datasheets in, 360–361
  - records in forms in, 362–363
- in Excel
  - cells in, 239
  - columns in, 238–239
  - rows in, 238–239
- notes, in OneNote, 107
- in PowerPoint
  - comments in, 305
  - slides in, 301
- tables in Word, 197

Design view in Access, 370
- creating new tables in, 394–395
- creating queries using, 370–371
- modifying field properties in, 398–399

Desktop
- getting help from, 33
- launching app, 21
- opening, 21
- showing, 21
- using the, 20–21

Desktop Taskbar, 46
Destination document, 426
Destination program, 426
Devices, 12
Dialog boxes, 85
Dialog box launchers, 85
Documents
- Backstage view in managing, 76–79
- creating
  - Google Docs in, 456–459
  - Microsoft Word Web App in, 442–445
- printing, 77
- scrolling in, 92–95
- sending, as PDF document, 78–79
- tracking changes made to, 209
- in Word
  - creating and editing new, 158–159, 161
  - creating from template, 174–175
  - cropping and removal picture background, 191
  - editing pictures for, 190–191
  - inserting captions with picture, 191
  - inserting pictures from computer, 190
  - inserting pictures from online sources, 188–189
  - saving new, 161

Dogpile, 58
Domain name, 45
Downloading, 62
- content, from a web page, 62–63

E

Editing
in Access
of records in datasheet, 360–361
of records in forms, 362–363
cells in Excel, 227
in Outlook
contacts in, 142–143
tasks in, 144–145
in PowerPoint
of Excel data in, 428–429
of images, 323
of text on slides, 291, 293
in Word, 161
of citations, 204–205
of documents, 158–161
of pictures, 190–191
of sources, 205
Effects Options button, 336
Email messages in Outlook
attaching files to, 132–133
creating, 129–130, **130**
deleting, 132–133
forwarding, 131
meeting request, 140
previewing attachments, 134–135
replying to, 130–131, **131**
sending, 129–130, **130**
signatures for, 131
Endnotes in Word, 207
Enforce Referential Integrity in Access, 403
Excel 2013, 223–247, 257–279
absolute addresses in, 258, 259
accounting number format in, 229–230
adding borders in, 230, 231
adjusting decimal places in, 231
alignment of text entries in, 225
arguments in, 260
Arrow keys in, 225, 228
AutoComplete in, 225
AutoCorrect in, 227
AutoFill in, 234, 237
AutoFit in, 232, 233
AutoSum in, 236
cells in, 224
active, 224, 225
copying, 244–245
displaying formulas, 242–243
editing, 227
formatting, 228–231
indenting, 244–245
inserting and deleting, 239
merging, 231
mouse in selecting, 228
pointers in, 225
shading, wrapping, and rotating, 246–247
sorting and applying styles in, 240–241
touch in selecting, 228–229
using fill handle to copy, 235
changing alignment in, 232–233
changing fonts in, 231
changing margins in, 275
changing numeric format in, 231
changing orientation in, 242
charts in, 257
column, 270–271
line, 272–273
pie, 268–269
recommended, 271
color scheme in, 74
columns in
adjusting width, 232–233
deleting, 238–239
inserting, 238–239
comma style format in, 229
comments in, 257
inserting, 254–255
printing, 277
conditional formatting in, 279
COUNTA function in, 261
COUNT function, 261
custom sort in, 241
data in
entering or copying with Fill command, 234–237
using, in creating PowerPoint chart, 329
dates in
entering, formatting, and calculating, 262–263
Region setting and, 263
Decrease Decimal button in, 230
editing of cells in, 227
embedding and editing data in PowerPoint presentation, 428–429
embedding charts into Word document, 426–427
exporting Access query to, 424–425
fill command in, 237
fill handle in, 235, 244
in copying cells, 235
on touch device, 235
filters in, 256
Filter Slicer panes in, 279
Find & Select button in, 246
Flash Fill in, 234
footers in, 274–275
format cells dialog box in, 231
formatting values in, 229–230
formula bar in, 225, 226
formulas in, 226
absolute addressing and range names in, 258–259
creating, to perform calculations, 226
equals sign in, 226
order of operations in, 227
statistical functions in entering, 260–261
Freeze Panes in, 246
function library in, 257
FV in calculating future value of investment in, 267
Go To command in, 246
headers in, 274–275
horizontal scroll bar in, 225
IF function in, 264–265
importing worksheet data into Access, 420–423
Increase Decimal button in, 230
linking charts with PowerPoint presentation and updating links, 430–433
linking worksheets to Access table, 423
mathematical operators in, 226
mixed addresses in, 258
name box in, 225

Page Layout view in, 274
Percent Style in, 265
PMT function in, 266–267
pound symbols in, 232
quick analysis in, 228
range in, 228, 240
names for, 259
sorting, 241
relative addresses in, 258
rows in
adjusting height, 232–233
deleting, 238–239
inserting, 238–239
scaling in
changing, 242
options in, 243
sheet tab bar in, 225
sheet tab in, 225
Slicer pane in, 279
sparklines in, 276
creating and modifying, 276–277
status bar in, 225
SUM function in, 236
adding with, 237
tables in, 278–279
vertical scroll bar in, 225
view button in, 225
VIEW tab in, 96
workbooks in, 223
themes of, 241
worksheets in, 223, **224**
centering, 275
creating new, 224–226
inserting and renaming, 244–245
renaming, 245
zoom button in, 225

Exchange server, use of Outlook with, 127
Exporting notebook sections, 117
Export tab Backstage view, 117

F

Facebook, Help for Windows on, 33, **33**
Favorites list, 48
Field properties in Access, 398
formatting and data validation, 399
modifying, in Design View, 398–399
Field Properties pane in Access, 398
Fields in Access, 356
adding, to existing tables, 396–397
deleting, 397
sorting by more than one, 367
Field values in Access, 356
creating lookup list with, in another table, 400
File attachments
cautiousness in opening, 135
for Email messages, 132–133
previewing, 134–135
File Explorer, 20, 28
browsing files with, 22–23
Files, 22
attaching to email messages, 132–133
browsing, with File Explorer, 22–23
copying, 26–27
creating new, in Access, **390,** 390–391
deleting, 30–31
downloading and uploading from and to SkyDrive, 452–453
inserting, into notebook, 112–113
moving, 28–29
name of, 22, 23
renaming, 29–30
sharing, on SkyDrive, 454–455
FILE tab, 75, 76
Fill command in Excel, 237
Fill handle in Excel, 235, 244
in copying cells, 235
on touch device, 235
Filter Email button, 147
Filtering of records, in Access, 366–367
Filters in Excel, 256
Filter Slicer panes in Excel, 279
Find & Select button in Excel, 246
Firefox. See Mozilla Firefox
Flash Fill in Excel, 234
Flickr, 188, 322, 323
Flickr Commons, 62
Flip Ahead, 47
Folder pane, 129
Folders, 23, 25
avoiding spaces in names of, 24
copying, 26–27
creating, 24–25
deleting, 30–31
renaming, 29–30
Font color button, 168
Font dialog box, 168
Fonts
in Excel, 231
in Word, 168, 169
Footers
in Excel, 274–275
in PowerPoint, 309
in Word, 202
Footnotes in Word, 207
Foreign key in Access, 403
Format Painter, 86
in copying formatting options, 88–89
Formatting options, Format Painter in copying, 88–89
Forms in Access, 354, 356
adding, editing and deleting records in, 362–363
creating and editing, 404–405
Form Wizard in creating, 405
Formula bar in Excel, 225, 226
Formulas in Excel, 226
absolute addressing and range names in, 258–259
creating, to perform calculations, 226
equals sign in, 226
order of operations in, 227
statistical functions in entering, 260–261
Form view in Access, 404
Form Wizard in Access, creating forms using, 405
Forward button, 47, 131
Forwarding Email messages, 131
Fractions, recognition of, in AutoFormat, 160
Freeze Panes in Excel, 246
Function library in Excel, 257

G

Gallery, 84
Gestures, 4, **4**
- pinch, **5**
- press and hold, **5**
- slide, **5**
- stretch, **5**
- swipe, **5**
- tap, **5**

Google account, 456
Google Chrome, 43, 44, 50
- navigating Web using, 50–53
  - bookmarking pages in, **51,** 51–52
  - customizing and controlling, 51–52
  - displaying web pages with, **50,** 50–51
    - multiple, **51,** 51–52
  - finding text on web page, **52,** 52–53
  - incognito browsing, 53
  - searching Web from the omnibox, 52, **52**
  - starting, 50

Google Docs, 456
- creating document using, 456–459
- sharing, 459

Go To command in Excel, 246
Go to Date dialog box, 136
Grammar check in Word, 162–163

H

Hanging indent in Word, 170
Hard page break, 201
Hard return, 161
Headers
- in Excel, 274–275
- in PowerPoint, 309
- in Word, 202

Help
- in an Office program, 90–91
- on Facebook, 33, **33**
- in Windows 8, 32–33

Hidden formatting in Word, 166
Home page, changing default, 46
HOME tab, 75
- Cut in, 107

Horizontal scroll bar in Excel, 225
Hyperlinks, 44
Hypertext Transfer Protocol, 45

I

I-beam pointer in Word, 159
IF function in Excel, 264–265
Images, editing, in PowerPoint presentation, 323
Import Spreadsheet Wizard, 420
Inbox folder, 129
Incline reply, 130
Incognito browsing, 53
Information, using search engine, to locate on the Web, 58–59
Inserting
- in Excel, 239
  - columns, 238–239
  - commands, 254–255
  - rows in, 238–239
  - worksheets, 245
- in PowerPoint
  - pictures, 322, **322, 323**
  - slides, 292–293
  - SmartArt graphics, **324**, 324–325
  - tables in, 294–295
  - WordArt in, 326–327
- in Word
  - caption with picture in documents, 191
  - citations in research paper formatting, 204–205
  - columns and rows in tables, 197
  - pictures from computer in documents, 190
  - pictures from online sources, 188–189

Insertion point in Word, 159, 161
Insert Picture dialog box, 63
International Standards Organization (ISO) date format, 263
Internet, 44
Internet Explorer (IE), 44, 46
Internet Explorer 10, 43
- navigating Web using
  - displaying web pages, **46,** 46–48, **47**
    - multiple, **48,** 48–49, **49**
  - pinning site in, 49
  - starting, 46

Internet Service Provider (ISP), 44
Investment, using FV to calculate future value of, 267
Items, searching for, in Outlook, 146–147

K

Keyboard. See also Touch keyboard
- commands, 6, **7,** 13
- full touch, **4**
- navigating Windows 8 with, **6,** 6–7

Keyboard shortcuts, 6, **7**
- for appointments, 139

Kiosk show, setting up, in PowerPoint presentation, 341

L

Landscape orientation, 200, 242
LAYOUT OPTIONS button, 82
Layout View in Access, 404
Libraries window, 22, **22**
Library, 22
Line breaks, 161
- versus new paragraphs in Word, 161

Line charts, 272
- creating and modifying, 272–273

Line spacing in Word, 170–171
Linking, 430
- of Excel chart with PowerPoint presentation, 430

Links, 44
- managing, 433

Links dialog box, 431
List view, 25
Live preview, 84
Live updates, turning off, 17, **17**
Local account, signing in with, 8–9
Lock screen, 8, **8,** 9
- adding app to the, 19
- changing background, 19
- personalizing, **18,** 18–19

Logging off, 14

Lookup list in Access, 400

creating, 400–401

with field values in another table, 400

Lookup Wizard in Access, 400

M

Maps app, 13, **13**

Margins in Excel, changing, 275

Mark Complete, Remove from List versus, 145

Mathematical operators in Excel, 226

Meetings in Outlook

requesting in email message, 140

scheduling, 140–141

updating, 141

Menu button, 7

Metasearch search engines, 58

Microsoft account, 442

signing in with, 8

Microsoft Excel Web App, 446

creating worksheet using, 446–447

Microsoft Office suite, 419

Microsoft Office University, 72

Microsoft PowerPoint Web App, 448

creating presentation using, 448–449

editing presentation in, 450–451

Microsoft Word Web App, 442

creating document using, 442–445

MIDI files, 334

Mini toolbar, 83, 168

Mixed addresses in Excel, 258

MLA (Modern Language Association), formatting and page layout guidelines, 202, 204, 206

Mobile devices, 43

shutting down, 15

Mouse

movements and actions, **7**

navigating Windows 8 with, 6, **6**

operating, 6

peek and, 136

selecting text and objects using, **82**

Mozilla Firefox, 43, 44, 54

Bookmarks bar in, 55

navigating Web using, 54–57

bookmarking pages, 55–56

displaying web pages, **54,** 54–55, **55**

multiple, 55–56

finding text on a page, 56–57

searching Web using Search bar, 57

starting Firefox, 54

MP3 audio files, 334

MP4 audio files, 334

MP4 videos, 332

MPEG 4 (MP4) movie file, creating, 341

MPEG movie files, 332

N

Name box in Excel, 225

Navigation pane, 22

New Appointment button, 136

New Contact button, 142

New Email button, 129

New folder button, 24

New Meeting button, 140

New Notebook Backstage view, 118

New Tab control, 48

Normal view in PowerPoint, 290

Notebook Information Backstage view, 117

Notebooks in OneNote

opening, 106–109

printing and exporting sections, 117

sharing, 118–119

Note containers, 107

Notepad, 20

Notes

in OneNote

deleting, 107

highlighting, with color, 108

jumping to tagged, 114–115

searching, 116–117

tagging, 114–115

typing, 109

in PowerPoint, 291

adding, 304–305

Notes Pages in PowerPoint, 308

Notes pane in PowerPoint, 290, 304

Note-taking software, 105

Notification area, 20

Numbered list, creation of, in Word, 167

Numbering in Word, 166–167

Numeric format in Excel, 231

O

Objects, 84

applying animation effects to individual, 338–339

selecting, using mouse and touch, **82**

Office 365, 71, 72

advantage to, 72

Office 2013, 71–97

alignment guides in, 85

Backstage view to manage documents in, 76–79

exporting document as PDF files, 78–79

printing documents, 78

changing display options, 96–97

screen resolution, 96–97

color schemes in, 74

customizing and using Quick Access toolbar, 80–81

exploring ribbon interface, 75

finding help in an Office program, 90–91

Office clipboard in, 86–89

using format painter to copy formatting options, 88–89

popularity of, 71, 72

Screen Tips in, 91

selecting text or objects, using the ribbon and mini toolbar, and selecting options in dialog boxes

contextual tabs, 84

dialog boxes, 85

objects, 84

task panes, 85

SkyDrive for storage, scrolling in documents, and using Undo in, 92–95

scroll bars in, 94–95

Undo command in, 95
starting new presentation in, 74–75
starting program in, 72–74
switching between programs in, 74
system requirements for, 72, **73**
Office Clipboard, using the, 86–89
Office.com
clip art in, 322
inserting pictures from, 323, **323**
Office Presentation Service, in delivering presentation online, 339
Office program, finding help in, 90–91
Office RT, 72
Omnibox, 50
searching Web from, 52, **52**
OneNote 2013, 71, 105–119
notebooks in
adding sections and pages to, 108–109
closing, 116–117
creating new, 118–119
inserting files in, 112–113
inserting Web content into, 110–111
opening, **106,** 106–109
printing and exporting sections, 117
sharing, 118–119
notes in
deleting, 107
highlighting, with color, 108
searching, 116–117
tagging, 114–115
typing, 109
pages in, 108–109
adding, 108–109
search features in, 116–117
sections in, 108
adding, 108–109
tagged notes in
jumping to, 114–115
tags in, 114
viewing, 114–115
Open tab Backstage view, 79
Operating systems. See also Google Chrome; Mozilla Firefox; Windows 8
purposes of, 3
Orientation
in Excel, 242
in PowerPoint, 309
in Word, 201
Outlook 2013, 71, 127–147
appearance of window, 129
appointments in
editing, 138–139
scheduling, 136–137
scheduling recurring, 138–139
Calendar tool in, 136
contacts in, adding and editing, 142–143
email messages in
attaching files to, 132–133
creating and sending, 129–130, **130**
deleting, 133
forwarding, 131
previewing attachments, 134–135
replying to, 130–131, **131**
signatures for, 131
meetings in
scheduling, 140–141
updating, 141
People tool in, 142
Remove from List versus Mark Complete, 145
scheduling events in, 136–137
setting up, **128,** 128–129, **129**
tasks, adding and editing, 144–145

P

Page breaks in Word
hard, 201
soft, 201
Page layout
in Excel, 274
in Word, 200–201
Page Not Found error, 48
Pages, adding in OneNote, 108–109
Paragraphs in Word
alignment of, 169
formatting, 168, 169
line breaks versus new in, 161
spacing of, 170–171
Password text box, 14
Paste button, 26
Paste Options, 87
Path to the web page, 45
PDF files, 78
creating printable at Print tab Backstage view, 445
exporting documents as, 78–79
exporting notebook sections as, 117
opening, 79
Peek, 136
Pen and Touch dialog box, 4
People card, 142
People tool in Outlook, 142
Percent Style in Excel, 265
Personal computer
adding video from file on, 333
inserting pictures from, into PowerPoint presentation, 322, **322**, **323**
shutting down, 15
Personal information management (PIM) program, 127
Personalizing Start and Stop screens, 18, 18–19
Photos app, 10, **10**
Pictures
adding for contacts, 142–143
inserting, into OneNote page, 112
inserting, into PowerPoint presentation
from computer, 322, **322**, **323**
from Office.com, 323, **323**
saving, from web pages, 62–63
in Word 2013
cropping and removing background, 191
editing, 190–191
inserting, from computer, 190
inserting, from online sources, 188–189
inserting caption with, 191
Pictures library, 22
PICTURE TOOLS FORMAT tab, 84, 323

Pie charts, creating and modifying, 268–269

Pinning sites with Internet Explorer 10, 48, 48–49, **49**

Pin site, 49

Pixels, 96

Placeholders in PowerPoint, 290, 291

selecting, resizing, aligning, and moving, 298–299

PMT function in Excel, 266–267

Point, 161

Pointer, 6

Point explosion, 269

Portrait orientation, 200, 242

Pound symbols in Excel, 232

PowerPoint 2013, 71, 289–309

audience handouts in, 308–309

AutoFit in, 299

bullets/bulleted list on, 296, 297, 326

changing symbol, 297

changing themes in, 294–295

color scheme in, 74

comments in, 291

adding, 304–305

deleting or hiding, 305

Comments pane in, 290, 304

editing of text on slides, 291, 293

embedding and editing Excel data into presentation in, 428–429

embedding entire file in, 429

linking Excel chart with, and updating links, 430–433

Normal view in, 290

notes in, 291

adding, 304–305

Notes Pages in, 308

Notes pane in, 290, 304

opening, 74

placeholders in, 290, 291

selecting, resizing, aligning, and moving, 298–299

presentations in, 321–341

adding sound to, 334–335

adding timing for, 341

adding video to, **332**, 332–333, **333**

animation in, 336

applying, to individual objects, 338–339

applying, using the slide master, **336,** 336–339

categories of, **337**

changing sequence of, 339

charts in

creating, on slides, 328–329

formatting, 329

creating new, 290–292

editing data in, 329

editing images in, 323

pictures in

inserting, from your computer in, 322, **322**, **323**

inserting from Office.com, 323, **323**

publishing, to a web service, 308

rehearse timings in, 341

setting up a self-running, 340–341

setting up kiosk show in, 341

shapes in

drawing, 330–331

transforming, 327

SmartArt graphics

converting text to, 326–327

inserting, **324**, 324–325

modifying, 325

text boxes in

adding, 330–331

transitions, 336

adding, to slide show, **336**, 336–339

WordArt in

inserting, 326–327

transforming, 327

Presenter view in, 306

recognition of audio file formats, 334

recognition of video file formats, 332

slide layouts in, 292

slide master in, 302

modifying, 302–303

Slide Master view in, 302

slide pane in, 290, 291

slide show in

displaying, 306–307

toolbar buttons for, 306

slides in

adding text to bottom of, 303

closing, 307

deleting, 301

duplicating, 300

editing text on, 293

footers on, 309

headers on, 309

hiding, 301

inserting, 292–293

inserting table on, 294–295

orientation of, 309

previewing, 309

size of, 309

slide size in, 292

Slide Sorter view in, 300

Slide Thumbnail pane in, 290, 291

Smart guides in, 299

speaker notes in, 308–309

status bar in, 291

tables in

inserting, on slides, 294–295

modifying, 295

text in

editing, 291

formatting, with font and paragraph options, 296–297

title slides in, 290

variants in, 290

view button in, 291

VIEW tab in, 96

zoom button in, 291

Power status indicator, 20

Presenter view in PowerPoint, 306

Previewing file attachments, 134–135

Primary key in Access, 366

assigning, 394–395

Primary tables in Access, 403

Printing

documents, 77

notebook sections, 117

web pages, 60–61

Print Preview pane, 77

Print tab Backstage view, 77
- creating printable PDF of document at, 445

Private browsing, 53
Protected view, 135
Public domain multimedia, 335
Pull quote in Word, 193

Q

Queries in Access, 354, 357
- calculated field in creating, 376–377
- criteria to select records in, 372–373, **373**
- Design view in creating, 370–371
- entering multiple to sort, 374–375
- exporting to Excel, 424–425
- Simple Query Wizard in creating, 368–369

Quick Access toolbar (QAT), 80
- customizing and using, 80–81
- Redo button on, 95
- Save button on, 92
- Undo button on, 95

Quick analysis in Excel, 228
Quick Notes, 111
Quick Print button, 81
QuickTime movies, 332

R

Range in Excel, 228, 240
- names for, 259
- sorting, 241

Reading pane, 131
Real time, 4
Records in Access, 356
- adding, editing, and deleting in a form, 362–363
- adding, using datasheets, 358–359
- best practices for deleting, 361
- editing and deleting using datasheets, 360–361
- entering criteria to select, in queries, 372–373, **373**
- entering multiple criteria to select, 374–375
- sorting and filtering, 366–367
- using find to move to, 363

Recurrence dialog box, 138
Recycle Bin, 20
- size of, 30
- window for, **21**

Redo button, 95
Red wavy lines, 158–159
Region setting, Excel and, 263
Rehearse timings in PowerPoint presentations, 341
Relationships in Access
- creating, 403
- displaying and editing, 402–403
- one-to-many, 403
- one-to-one, 402

Relative addresses in Excel, 258
Remove from List, versus Mark Complete, 145
Rename button, 29
Reply All, 131
Reply button, 130
Replying to email messages, 130–131
Reports in Access, 354, 356
- creating, editing, and viewing, 406–407
- grouping and sorting, 407

Research paper formatting in Word, 202–203
- citations, inserting and editing, 204–205
- editing sources, 205
- footnotes and endnotes in, 207
- removing page numbers from first page, 203
- word views in, 206–207
- Works Cited page, creating, 206–207

Restart, 15
Resume creation from templates in Word, 210–211
Ribbon, 24
- buttons in, 86

Ribbon Display Options button, 75
Ribbon interface, exploring, 75
Rows in Excel
- adjusting height, 232–233
- deleting, 238–239
- inserting, 238–239

S

Safely Remove Hardware and Eject Media icon, 31
Save As command, 76
Save As dialog box, 117
Save As tab Backstage view, 79
Scaling in Excel, 242, 243
Screen
- locking the, 14
- resolution of, 96, 97
  - viewing and changing, 96–97

Screen Resolution dialog box, 97
Scroll bars, 94–95
Scroll box, 94
Scroll wheel, 6
Search bar, searching Web using, in Mozilla Firefox, 57
Search charm, 12, **12,** 72
Search engines, 58
- metasearch, 58
- using, to locate information on the Web, 58–59

Search options, using advanced, 59–60
Search People text box, 147
Search text box, 116
Section break in Word, 201
Sections, adding in OneNote, 108–109
- adding, 108–109

Security check, sharing files on SkyDrive and, 454
Selection handles, 82, 83
Self-running presentation, setting up a, 340–341
Semicolons in email addresses, 130
Send to OneNote button, 111
Settings charm, 12, 21
Shading in Word, 192–193
Shapes
- drawing, in Word, 190
- in PowerPoint presentation
  - drawing, 330–331
  - transforming, 327

Share charm, 12
Share Notebook Backstage view, 119
Sheet tab bar in Excel, 225

Sheet tab in Excel, 225
Signature in email, 131
Signing in, 15
with local account, 8–9
with Microsoft account, 8
Sign out, 14
Simple Query Wizard in Access, creating queries using, 368–369
Sites, pinning, with Internet Explorer 10, 48, 48–49, **49**
SkyDrive, 92, 322, 323
account name, 118
downloading and uploading files from and to, 452–453
saving file to, 93
sharing files on, 454–455
storage of OneNote notebooks on, 105
using, for storage, scrolling in documents, and using Undo, 92–95
Sleep option, 15
Slicer pane in Excel, 279
Slide layouts in PowerPoint, 292
Slide master in PowerPoint, 302
applying animation effects using, 336–337, **337**
modifying, 302–303
Slide Master view in PowerPoint, 302
Slide pane in PowerPoint, 290, 291
Slideshare.net, 308
Slide show in PowerPoint
displaying, 306–307
toolbar buttons for, 306
Slides in PowerPoint
adding text to bottom of, 303
adding video to existing, 333
closing, 307
creating charts on, 328–329
deleting, 301
duplicating, 300
editing text on, 293
footers on, 309
headers on, 309
hiding, 301
inserting, 292–293
inserting table on, 294–295
orientation of, 309
previewing, 309
size of, 292, 309
Slide Sorter view in PowerPoint, 300
Slide Thumbnail pane in PowerPoint, 290, 291
SmartArt
in PowerPoint
converting text to, 326–327
inserting, 324–325
layout categories of, 324
modifying, 325
in Word, 190
Smart guides
in PowerPoint, 299
in Word, 189
Smartphones, 43
Soft page break, 201
Software, note-taking, 105
Sorting in Access
of queries, 374–375
of records, 366–367
Sound, adding, to PowerPoint presentation, 334–335
Source data, 426
Source program, 426
Sparklines in Excel, 276
creating and modifying, 276–277
Speaker notes in PowerPoint, 308–309
Spell Check in Word, 162–163
Spiders, 58
Spreadsheets, 223
Start screen, 4, **9,** 9–10, 14, 15
adding tile to, 17
changing design or color scheme, 19
customizing, **16,** 16–17
personalizing, **18,** 18–19
pinning and unpinning tiles to and from, **16,** 16–17
removing tile from, 17
using help from, 33
Status bar
in Excel, 225
in PowerPoint, 291
in Word, 159
Store app, 11
Styles in Word, 172
formatting using, 172–173
Stylus, 4
Subfolders, 23, 25
SUM function in Excel, 236
adding with, 237
Symbol insertion in Word, 162–163

T

Tabbed browsing, 48
Table cells in Word, 194
merging, 198–199
Tables
in Access, **354,** 355
adding fields to existing, 396–397
creating lookup list with field values in, 400
creating new, 392
in Design View, 394–395
linking Excel worksheet to, 423
planning new, **390,** 390–391
primary, 403
in Excel, 278–279
in PowerPoint
inserting, on slides, 294–295
modifying, 295
in Word, 194–195
banded rows in, 196
inserting and deleting columns and rows, 197
modifying column width and alignment and merging cells, 198–199
Tablets, 43
touch-enabled, 80
Tabs in OneNote 2013
viewing, 114–115
Tagged notes in One Note
jumping to, 114–115
Tags
appointment, in Outlook, 137
in OneNote, 114
To-Do, 115
viewing, 114, 115
Tags Summary pane, 114

Taskbar, 20

Task panes, 85

Tasks in Outlook

adding and editing, 144–145

Remove from List versus Mark Complete, 145

Templates in Word, 175

creating cover letters from, 210–211

creating new document from, 174–175

Text

finding on web page

using Google Chrome, **52,** 52–53

using Mozilla Firefox, 56–57

in PowerPoint

editing, 291

formatting, with font and paragraph options, 296–297

selecting, using mouse and touch, **82**

in Word

finding and replacing, 164–165

formatting, with font and paragraph alignment options, 168–169

indenting, 170–171

moving, 166–167

Text boxes

in PowerPoint presentations

adding, 330–331

resizing, 326

in Word

editing, 193

inserting, 192–193

Text entries in Excel

alignment of, 225

Text Highlight Color tool, 108

Themes in PowerPoint, changing, 294–295

Thesaurus in Word, 165

Thumbing in, 11

Tiles, 4, 9–10

adding, to Start screen, 17

pinning and unpinning, to and from the Start screen, **16,** 16–17

rearranging, 17

removing, from Start screen, 17

resizing, 17, **17**

selecting, 16, **16,** 17

Timing, adding, for slide, 341

Title slides in PowerPoint, 290

To-Do tag, 115

Toggle buttons, 88

Touch

in navigating Windows 8, 4, **4, 5**

selecting text and objects using, **82**

Touch device, using Zoom slider on, 96

Touch-enabled devices, 11

Touch keyboard, 4, **4,** 95, 458

in handwriting mode, **6**

in thumb mode, **6**

Touchpad, 6

Trackball, 6

U

Undo command, 95, 194

URLs (Uniform Resource Locators), 44–45

typing, 47

User account, 8

User interface (UI), 4

V

Values in Excel, formatting, 229–230

Variants in PowerPoint, 290

Vertical scroll bar

in Excel, 225

in Word, 159

Video

adding, to existing PowerPoint slides, 333

adding, to PowerPoint presentations, 332, 332–333, 333

linking to YouTube, 333

Video file formats, PowerPoint recognition of, 332

Video playback, options for, 333

VIDEO TOOLS PLAYBACK tab, 333

View buttons

in Excel, 225

in PowerPoint, 291

in Word, 159

View Printable link, 60

VIEW tab, 23, 96

in Excel, 96

in PowerPoint, 96

in Word, 96

W

Web

navigating, using Google Chrome, 50–53

bookmarking pages in, **51,** 51–52

customizing and controlling, 51–52

displaying web pages with, **50,** 50–51

multiple, **51,** 51–52

finding text on web page, **52,** 52–53

incognito browsing, 53

searching Web from the omnibox, 52, **52**

starting, 50

navigating, using Internet Explorer 10, 46–49

displaying web pages, **46,** 46–48, **47**

multiple, **48,** 48–49, **49**

pinning site in, 49

starting, 46

navigating, using Mozilla Firefox, 54–57

bookmarking pages, 55–56

displaying web pages, **54,** 54–55, **55**

multiple, 55–56

finding text on a page, 56–57

searching Web using Search bar, 57

starting Firefox, 54

searching using Search bar in Mozilla Firefox, 57

using search engine to locate information on the, 58–59

advanced options in, 59–60

metasearch, 58

Web addresses, 44–45

parts of, **45**

Web browsers, 44, 45. See also specific by name
Web content, inserting, into notebook, 110–111
Web forums, 32
Web pages, 44
- displaying
  - with Google Chrome, **50,** 50–51
    - multiple, **51,** 51–52
  - with Internet Explorer 10, **46,** 46–48, **47**
    - multiple, **48,** 48–49, **49**
  - with Mozilla Firefox, **54,** 54–55, **55**
    - multiple, 55–56
- downloading content from, 62–63
- file name for, **45**
- finding text on
  - with Google Chrome, **52,** 52–53
  - with Mozilla Firefox, 56–57
- path to, **45**
- printing, 60–61
- saving pictures from, 62–63

Web servers, 44
Web service, publishing presentations to, 308
Websites, 44
- copyright-free or public domain multimedia on, 335

What-if analysis, 223
Wikimedia Commons, 54, 55
Wildcard characters in Access, 375
Windows 7, 43, 72
- starting Microsoft Office in, 72, 73

Windows 8, 3, 4, 43
- finding help in, 32–33
- navigating
  - with keyboard, **6,** 6–7
  - with mouse, 6
  - with touch, 4, **4, 5**
- starting, 8–10
- user accounts at, 8
- user interface of, 4

Windows audio files (.wav), 334
Windows Help and Support window, 32
WindowsLive ID, 8
Windows lock screen, 14, 15
Windows logo key, 6–7, 14
Windows Media Audio (.wma) files, 334
Windows Media Video (.wmv) files, 332
Windows RT, 72
Windows session, signing out of, 14–15
Word 2013, 71, 157–175, 187–211
- AutoCorrect in, 158, 159, **159**
- AutoFormat in, 158, 160, 167
- borders in, 192–193
- bullet insertion in, 166–167
- changing page layout options, 200–201
- character formatting in, 168
- clip art gallery in, 188
- color scheme in, 74
- comments in, 208
  - inserting, 208–209
  - replying to, 208–209
- cover letter creation from templates, 210–211
- DESIGN tab in, 171
- documents in
  - creating and editing new, 158–159, 161
  - creating from template, 174–175
  - cropping and removal picture background, 191
  - editing pictures for, 190–191
  - inserting caption with picture, 191
  - inserting pictures from computer, 190
  - inserting pictures from online sources, 188–189
  - saving new, 161
  - sending, as PDF document, 78
  - tracking changes made to, 209
- editing in, 161
  - of citations, 204–205
  - documents, 158–161
  - pictures, 190–191
  - of sources, 205
- embedding Excel chart into document, 426–427
- endnotes in, 207
- fonts in, 169
  - changing, 169
- footnotes in, 207
- formatting using styles in, 172–173
- hanging indent in, 170
- hidden formatting in, 166
- I-beam pointer in, 159
- insertion point in, 159, 161
- landscape orientation in, 201
- line and paragraph spacing in, 170–171
- numbering in, 166–167
- opening, **73**
- page breaks in, 201
- page layout in, 200–201
- paragraph alignment in, 169
- paragraph formatting in, 168, 169
- pictures in
  - cropping and removing background, 191
  - editing, 190–191
  - inserting, from computer, 190
  - inserting, from online sources, 188–189
  - inserting caption with, 191
- portrait orientation in, 201
- pull quote in, 193
- research paper formatting, 202–203
  - citations, inserting and editing, 204–205
  - editing sources, 205
  - footnotes and endnotes in, 207
  - removing page numbers from first page, 203
  - word views in, 206–207
  - Works Cited page, creating, 206–207
- resume creation from templates in, 210–211
- section break in, 201
- shading in, 192–193
- shapes, drawing, 190
- SmartArt in, 190
- smart guides in, 189
- spelling and grammar check in, 162–163
- status bar in, 159
- symbol insertion in, 162–163
- tables in, 194–195

banded rows in, 196
inserting and deleting columns and rows, 197
modifying column width and alignment and merging cells, 198–199
templates in, 175
text box insertion in, 192–193
editing, 193
text in
finding and replacing, 164–165
formatting, with font and paragraph alignment options, 168–169
indenting, 170–171
moving, 166–167
thesaurus in word replacement in, 165
vertical scroll bar in, 159
View buttons in, 159
VIEW tab in, 96
Welcome back! balloon in, 207
WordArt in, 190
word search in, 164
wordwrap in, 158–159
Zoom buttons in, 159
WordArt
in PowerPoint
changing font size, 326
inserting, 326–327
transforming, 327
in Word, 190
Word processing, 157. See also Word 2013
Word search in Word, 164
Wordwrap in Word, 158–159
Workbooks in Excel, 223
themes of, 241
Worksheets in Excel, 223, **224**
centering, 275
creating, using Microsoft Web App, 446–447
creating new, 224–226
importing data into Access, 420–423
inserting and renaming, 244–245
linking to Access table, 423
World Wide Web (WWW), 44

X

XPS files, exporting notebook sections as, 117

Y

Yahoo!, 58, 59
advanced search tools in, 60
YouTube, linking video to, 333

Z

Zoho, 459
Zoom buttons
in PowerPoint, 291
in Word, 159
Zoom dialog box, 96
Zoom In button, 96
Zoom Magnification, changing, 97
Zoom Out button, 96
Zoom slider bar, 96

Photo Credits: *Page 3*: ©istockphoto.com/cogal. *4*: middle, right ©istockphoto.com/Mihai Simonia. *6*: middle, right top ©istockphoto.com/AlexGul; middle, right center ©istockphoto.com/Peng Wu; middle, right bottom ©istockphoto.com/Malgorzata Beldowska; bottom, left ©istockphoto.com/Kamil Krawczyk. *43*: ©istockphoto.com/dosrayitas. *44*: right ©istockphoto.com/Maksym Yemelynov. *71*: ©istockphoto.com/Joshua Hodge Photography. *105*: ©istockphoto.com/Alejandro Rivera. *127*: ©istockphoto.com/Damir Cudic. *157*: ©istockphoto.com/claudiobaba. *185*: top, right ©istockphoto.com/Soyhan Erim. *187*: ©istockphoto.com/Odine Corewijn. *223*: ©istockphoto.com/Jose Wilson Araujo. *257*: ©istockphoto.com/Leontura. *289*: ©istockphoto.com/RelaxFoto.de. *321*: ©istockphoto.com/Blend_Images. *353*: ©istockphoto.com/Machine Headz. *389*: ©istockphoto.com/zhangbo. *419*: ©istockphoto.com/Clerkenwell_Images. *441*: ©istockphoto.com/davidf.